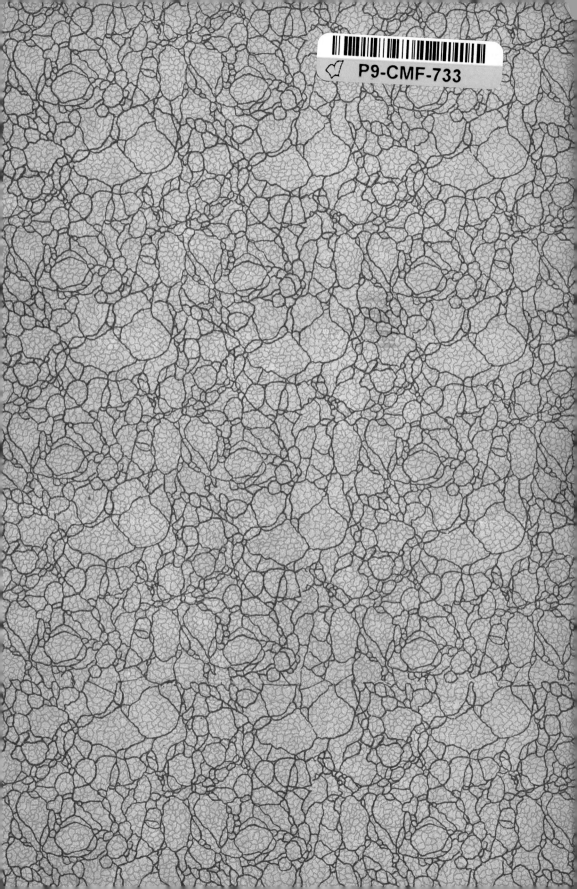

HARPER'S

NEW MONTHLY MAGAZINE.

VOLUME LXXIII.

JUNE TO NOVEMBER, 1886.

NEW YORK:

HARPER & BROTHERS, PUBLISHERS,

327 to 335 PEARL STREET,

FRANKLIN SQUARE.

1886.

CONTENTS OF VOLUME LXXIII.

JUNE TO NOVEMBER, 1886.

CONTENTS.

CONTENTS.

MONTHLY RECORD OF CURRENT EVENTS.

UNITED STATES.—Congress: Bills passed: Electoral Count, 157; Hancock Pension, 157; Lincoln Monument, 157; Labor Arbitration, 157; Congressional Library Building, 157; Mexican War Pension, 157; River and Harbor, 319, 806; Inter-State Commerce, 319, 806; Shipping, 480, 806; Pensions, 480, 806; Arthur Kill Bridge, 480; Chinese Indemnity, 480; Taxing Oleomargarine, 480, 806; Modifying Homestead Law, 480; Subsidy Bill, 644; Changing Presidential and Congressional Terms, 644; Naval Appropriation, 644; Relief of General Fitz-John Porter, 644; Surplus, 806; Fortifications, 806; Alien Landlord, 806; Total Appropriations, 805; The Cutting-Mexican Case: Correspondence, 806; Cutting released, 967. United States Army Bill rejected, 157; Free Coinage Bill defeated, 157; Mail Subsidy defeated, 480; Tariff Bill voted down, 480; Vance Bill to repeal Civil Service Law indefinitely postponed, 644. President Cleveland's Message on Labor Commission, 319. Extradition Treaty with Japan and Boundary Survey Treaty with Mexico ratified by Senate, 644. Adjournment of First Session, Forty-ninth Congress, 805; Number of Bills of Session, 805. George Hearst appointed United States Senator from California, 157; W. C. Whitthorne appointed United States Senator from Tennessee, 319; Nelson Aldrich reëlected United States Senator from Rhode Island, 480; A. P. Williams elected United States Senator from California, 806. Resignation of Governor Murray, of Utah, and Appointment of Caleb W. West, 157. Marriage of President Grover Cleveland, 480. State Elections: Rhode Island, 157; Oregon, 480; Alabama, 806; Arkansas, 967; Vermont, 967; Maine, 967. State Conventions, 480, 644. Geronimo's Surrender to General Miles, 967. Public Debt reduced, 319. Race between Mayflower and Galatea for America's Cup, 967. Anarchists' Riots, Chicago, 319; Anarchists' Conviction, 967. Adjournment of New York State Legislature, 480.

EUROPE, ASIA, SOUTH AMERICA, CENTRAL AMERICA, AND CANADA.—Great Britain: Gladstone's Home Rule Bill, 157; Home Rule Bill defeated, 480; Parnell's Land Bill, first reading, 967; Irish Land Purchase Bill, 319; Poor Law Guardians Bill, 480; Arms Bill, 480; Deceased Wife's Sister Bill, 480; Resignation of Messrs. Chamberlain and Trevelyan from the Cabinet, 157; Parliament prorogued, 644; Notice of Dissolution, 644; New Parliament, 644, 806; Mr. Gladstone's Retirement and Lord Salisbury's Appointment as Prime Minister, 806; The new Ministry, 806; Riots in Belfast, 806. Canada: Seizure of American fishing Schooners in Canadian Waters, 319; Cost and Casualties of Half-breed Rebellion, 480. France: Bill to expel the Princes, 481, 644;

the Banishment, 644; Sur-tax on Cereals, 644; Titles of Nobility Bill, 644; General Elections, 806. Bulgaria and Roumelia: Alexander to be recognized as Governor, 158; Alexander forced to abdicate, 967. Chinese Christians massacred, 967. Central and South America: Soto President of Costa Rica, 158; Caceres President of Peru, 158, 480, 644. Italy: Resignation of Depretis Ministry, 158. Greece: Ordered to disarm, 320; New Cabinet formed, 320, 480. Germany: Spirit Monopoly Bill rejected, 158; Anti-socialist Law prolonged, 158; Land of Poles in Posen expropriated, 158; Brandy Tax Bill, 644; Copyright with England, 644; Prussia and the Vatican, 967. Bavaria: Suicide of King Ludwig II. of Bavaria, 481; Burial of Ludwig II., 644; Otto King and Luitpold Regent, 644. Holland: Elections, 644; Rioting in Amsterdam, 806. Spain: Senatorial Elections, 320; Spain and Cuban Autonomy, 644; Freedom of Slaves in Cuba, 806.

DISASTERS: 158, 320, 481, 644, 806, 967.—Steamer Beda foundered, 158; Steam-ship Rapidan given up for lost, 158; Explosion on Steamer Colombia, 158; Railroad Accident near Greenfield, Massachusetts, 158; Tornado in Minnesota, 158; Town of Stry, Galicia, burned, 320; Break of Reservoir Dam near East Lee, Massachusetts, 320; Tornado in Kansas City, 320; Hurricane in Spain, 320; Storm in Ohio and Indiana, 320; Austrian Steamer Miroslav given up for lost, 481; Loss of Steamer Lyeemoon, 481; Akita, Japan, destroyed by fire, 481; Colliery Explosion in France, 644; Dynamite Explosion in the Atlantic Company's Works (New Jersey), 644; Loss of French Torpedo-boats, 644; Volcanic Eruption in New Zealand, 644; Theatre in British India burned, 806; Schooner Sarah Craig capsized, 806; Colliery Explosion in England, 806; Hurricane on Texas Coast, 967; Steamer Vera burned, 967; City of Mandalay flooded, 967; Earthquake in Greece, 967; Steamer Daniel Drew burned, 967; Colliery Explosion in Pennsylvania, 967; Railway Accident near Vienna, 967; Earthquake in United States, 967; Panic in a Church, Transylvania, 967; Railroad Collision near Buffalo, 967.

OBITUARY: 158, 320, 481, 644, 806, 967.—General Lloyd Aspinwall, 967; John Russell Bartlett, 481; "Ned Buntline," 806; Countess of Chambord, 158; General B. F. Cheatham, 967; Robert Barry Coffin, 481; Hon. David Davis, 644; John Dougall, 967; Moses A. Dow, 644; Maximilian W. Duncker, 806; Thaddeus Fairbanks, 158; Lord Farnborough, 481; Sir Samuel Ferguson, Q.C., LL.D., 806; Right Hon. William E. Forster, 158; Dolores Fosta, 967; Major-General George H. Gordon, 967; Right Rev. Joseph Hippolyte Guibert, 644; Dr. Frank H. Hamilton, 806; Hon. Samuel Hand, 481; Paul H.

CONTENTS.

CONTENTS.

POETRY.

"WHAT THEY MAY DO AT LITTLE HAMPTON IS BEYOND MY KNOWLEDGE."
From a drawing by Frederick Barnard.—[See page 33.]

HARPER'S
NEW MONTHLY MAGAZINE.

Vol. LXXIII.   JUNE, 1886.   No. CCCCXXXIII.

THE UNITED STATES NAVY.

IN TRANSITION.

BY REAR-ADMIRAL EDWARD SIMPSON, U.S.N.

THE condition of the navy of the United States is not such as any citizen of the country would desire. Pride in its navy was one of the earliest sentiments that inspired the hearts of the people when the United States took their place as a nation, and the memory of its deeds has not faded during the subsequent years of the country's aggrandizement. Time was when that section of the country most remote from the sea-coast was indifferent to it, owing to the more immediate demand on its attention for the development of internal resources; but the rapid settlement of our Western lands and the annihilation of distance produced by rapid communication have tended to preserve the unity of interests of the separate sections, and the happy system that obtains through which officers are appointed to the navy keeps it an object of personal concern to all the States of the Union.

The present condition of the navy is not such as to satisfy the desire of the people that it should be sustained on a footing commensurate with the position of the nation and in keeping with its ancient reputation. For many years circumstances have intervened to prevent a judicious rehabilitation of the navy, notwithstanding that its needs have been faithfully presented to Congress year after year. The country has been wonderfully favored with peace at home and abroad, and no urgent call to arms has roused the nation to prepare for war. The rapidity with which a large fleet of cruising ships for blockading purposes was extemporized during our civil war has left a hurtful impression on the public mind that in an emergency a similar effort might prove equally efficacious—disregarding altogether the difference in circumstances of contending with an enemy possessed of a naval force and with one possessed of none. The economists have suggested that as all that relates to ships, guns, and motive forces was being rapidly developed by others, it would be a saving of the people's money to await results, and to benefit by the experience of others; and, again, party rivalry and contentions have assisted to postpone action.

It has never been the intention that the navy should die from neglect and be obliterated. Yearly appropriations have been faithfully passed for the support of the *personnel*, and for such repairs as were found to be indispensable for the old ships that have been kept in commission; but it is now seen that this system of temporizing has been the poorest kind of economy. This money has been invested necessarily in perishable material, the amounts have been insufficient to compass new constructions, whether in ships or guns, and the only use that could be made of them was to repair wooden ships and convert cast-iron guns, whereas the work needed was to construct steel ships and to fabricate steel guns.

In referring to the navy of the past it is impossible to avoid recalling the feeling of pride with which an American seaman —officer or man—walked the deck of his ship. This feeling was common to the naval and commercial marine. Our wooden ships that sailed the ocean from 1840 to 1860 were the finest in the world. The old frigate *Congress* in 1842 was the noblest specimen of the frigates of the day, and the sloop of war *Portsmouth* was unsurpassed as a corvette. The clipper ships of that period need no eulogy beyond their own record. These ships were

U. S. SIDE-WHEEL STEAMER "POWHATAN."

the models for the imitation of all maritime nations, and among the constructors of the period can be recalled, without detriment to many others omitted, the names of Lenthall, Steers, Pook, and Delano. The poetry of sailing reached its zenith during this period.

But there is no sentiment in progress; its demands are practical and imperative, and the great motive power, steam, was being crowded to the front even during this the greatest development in the era of sails. Advanced ideas could not be resisted, and steam was admitted as an auxiliary; but our development in naval construction still stood us in good stead, and enabled us to supply ships with auxiliary steam-power, which continued to be prominent for many years as standards to which others found it to their advantage to conform.

Before the final abandonment in the navy of sailing ships, pure and simple, an effort at a compromise was made by limiting steam to side-wheel vessels, and a number of fine ships were built in the forties, which did good service, and were a credit to the country, answering as they did the demands of the time. The *Mississippi*, *Missouri*, *Susquehanna*, *Saranac*, and *Powhatan* carried the flag

to all parts of the world for many years, some of them enduring to bear their share in the late war, while the *Powhatan* is even now borne on the list of vessels of the navy.

This vessel was built at Norfolk, Virginia, in the year 1850. Her length is 250 feet; beam, 45 feet; draught of water, 19.6 feet. She has a displacement of 3980 tons, and attains a speed of 10.6 knots per hour with an indicated horse-power of 1172. The capacity of her coal-bunkers is 630 tons. Her battery consists of 16 ix-inch smooth-bore guns. She was built of seasoned live-oak, and though frequently under repairs, has retained so much of the strength of her original construction that she has escaped the sentence of condemnation to the present time. She is regarded as a venerable remnant of antiquity, but is found useful for the transportation of relief crews for ships at Aspinwall and Panama, and her powerful engine is put to good use for towing purposes.

The *Princeton*, of great fame, and the *San Jacinto*, were the only ships with screw-propellers that appeared in the period under consideration, the use of the screw being considered of doubtful propriety, to be tested by tentative experiments. These ships have long since disappeared, but the screw remains, and side wheels are relegated to boats for inland waters.

Confidence being established in the screw-propeller, construction on the principle of auxiliary steam-power was decided on, and ships of different classes were added to the navy in such numbers as the varied duties required.

There were those at that time who, wise beyond their generation, recognized the full meaning of the advent of steam, and saw that it must supplant sails altogether as the motive power for ships. These advocated that new constructions should be provided with full steam-power, with sails as an auxiliary; but the old pride in the sailing ship, with her taunt and graceful spars, could not be made to yield at once to the innovation; old traditions pointing to the necessity of full sail-power could not be dispelled; it was considered a sufficient concession to admit steam on any terms, and thus the conservative and temporizing course was adopted of retaining full sail-power, and utilizing steam as an auxiliary.

The United States government was not alone in this policy. It was the course pursued by all other maritime nations, and for some years the United States retained the lead in producing the most perfect types in this new phase of naval construction.

In 1854, Congress passed an act authorizing the construction of the *Merrimac* class of frigates. The ships that were immediately built under this act were the *Merrimac*, the *Wabash*, the *Minnesota*, the *Roanoke*, and the *Colorado*. All of these vessels got to sea during 1856 and 1857; they were followed, at an interval of a few years, by the *Franklin*, which was a larger ship, and an improvement on the original type.

The *Franklin* was built at Kittery, Maine. Her length is 266 feet; beam, 54 feet; draught of water, 24 feet. She has a displacement of 5170 tons, and attains a speed of 10 knots per hour with an indicated horse-power of 2065. The capacity of her coal-bunkers is 860 tons. Her frames are of seasoned live-oak, and she is in use as a receiving-ship.

The *Merrimac* was the first vessel of this type which got to sea. She was sent to European waters, and on her arrival in England, early in 1856, she became at once the object of the closest scrutiny, resulting in the unqualified approval of foreign naval architects. The English Admiralty proceeded to imitate the type, and many keels were soon laid in order to reproduce it. The ships built after this model were the crack ships of the time in the English navy, and carried the flags of the commanders-in-chief of fleets. It was a squadron of vessels of this type with which Admiral Lyons essayed to engage the Russian forts at Sebastopol.

In 1858, 1859, and 1860, the *Hartford* class of large corvettes appeared. These

U. S. FRIGATE "FRANKLIN," OF THE "MERRIMAC" CLASS.

are full-rigged ships. The class comprises the *Hartford*, the *Brooklyn*, the *Pensacola*, the *Richmond*, and the *Lancaster*.

The *Hartford* was built at Boston in 1858. Her length is 225 feet; beam, 44 feet; draught of water, 18.3 feet. She has a displacement of 2900 tons, and attains a

act of Congress prohibiting repairs on wooden ships when the expense shall exceed 20 per cent. of the cost of a new vessel, these ships must soon disappear from the navy list. When that time shall arrive, and steel cruisers shall be substituted, the name of the *Hartford*

U. S. SLOOP OF WAR "HARTFORD."

speed of 10 knots per hour with an indicated horse-power of 940. The capacity of her coal-bunkers is 241 tons. Her battery consists of 1 VIII-inch muzzle-loading rifle (converted) and 12 IX-inch smooth-bores. These ships were built of live-oak, and endure to the present day. They were reproduced by England and France when they made their appearance on the ocean. These are now the only ships in service which can accommodate a commander-in-chief of a squadron. They are kept constantly employed showing the flag abroad, but it is with difficulty that they are retained in suitable repair for service.

This class of ships has good speed under sail, with the wind free, but their light draught prevents them from being weatherly on a wind. Much of their cruising is done under sail, which tends to lengthen their existence. Under the late

should be preserved as closely associated with the glory that Farragut shed upon the navy.

In 1859 a new type of sloop of war was introduced, of which the *Kearsarge* will serve as an example. This ship was built at Kittery, Maine. Her length is 199 feet; beam, 33 feet; draught of water, 15.9 feet. She has a displacement of 1550 tons, and attains a speed of 11 knots per hour with an indicated horse-power of 842. The capacity of her coal-bunkers is 165 tons. Her battery consists of 2 VIII-inch muzzle-loading rifles (converted), 4 IX-inch smooth-bores, and 1 60-pounder. This has proved a very handy class of vessel, and for the year in which they were built they were considered as having very fair speed under steam, the proportion of space occupied by boilers and engines being more than had been assigned in previous constructions. Several ships of this class

U. S. SLOOP OF WAR "BROOKLYN."

were launched and put in commission before the war, which gave a new impetus to construction.

The types of vessels that were built during the war were selected for special purposes. The effort was made to multiply ships as rapidly as possible to blockade the coast and to enter shoal harbors; the "ninety-day gun-boats" and the "double-enders" were added to the navy list, and merchant steamers were purchased, and were armed with such batteries as their scantling would bear. All of these vessels have disappeared, with the exception of the *Tallapoosa*. The *Juniata* and *Ossipee*, of the *Kearsarge* type, but of greater displacement, were launched in 1862, and they are still in commission; and several vessels of large displacement and great speed were launched at about the close of the war, which were never taken into service, have been disposed of since, and form no part of our present navy.

The *New Ironsides* and the *Monitor* represented the two features of construction which, produced in this period of emergency, have continued to impress naval architecture.

As a sea-going iron-clad the *New Iron-*

U. S. SLOOP OF WAR "KEARSARGE."

U. S. IRON-CLAD "NEW IRONSIDES."

sides was, for the time and service required, a success. She was built at the yard of Mr. Cramp, in Philadelphia, in 1862. Her length was 230 feet; beam, 56 feet; draught of water, 15 feet. She had a displacement of 4015 tons, and attained a speed of 6 knots per hour with an indicated horse-power of 700. The capacity of the coal-bunkers was 350 tons. Her battery consisted of 20 xi-inch smooth-bore guns. She was built of wood, and was covered with armor four inches in thickness, which, with the inclination given to her sides, made her impervious to the artillery that was used against her during the war. In one engagement with the batteries on Sullivan's Island, Charleston Harbor, lasting three hours, she was struck seventy times, but at the end of the action, except some damage to a port shutter or two, she withdrew in as perfect fighting condition as when the action commenced. This ship does not appear on the navy list; she was destroyed by fire off the navy-yard at League Island, Pennsylvania.

The *Monitor* was, without doubt, the most remarkable production of the constructive art that appeared during the war. The original *Monitor* was lost at sea, but our illustration presents the *Passaic* class of Monitors, which quickly followed the original of this type.

The *Passaic* was built of iron, and was launched in 1862. Her length is 200 feet; beam, 46 feet; draught of water, 11.6 feet. She has a displacement of 1875 tons, and attains a speed of 7 knots per hour with an indicated horse-power of 377. The capacity of her coal-bunkers is 140 tons. Her battery consists of 1 xv-inch smooth-bore, and 1 xi-inch smooth-bore. Her sides are protected by five inches of laminated iron, and her turret by eleven inches of the same. This vessel and eleven others of her class constitute the entire armored fleet of the United States. Too much credit cannot be awarded to Captain Ericsson for his brilliant conception of this floating battery, and the navy must be ever grateful to him for preserving it from dire disaster, which was averted by the appearance of the original *Monitor* at the moment of a great crisis. These vessels bore themselves well through the storms of elements and battle during the war, proving capable of making sea-voyages, and of resisting the effects of the ar-

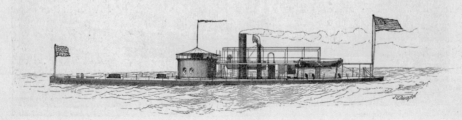

U. S. MONITOR "PASSAIC."

U. S. DOUBLE-TURRETED MONITOR "TERROR."

U. S. FRIGATE "TENNESSEE."

tillery that was in use during the period of their usefulness; but an interval of more than twenty years has produced such a change in artillery as to make the protection afforded by a few laminated plates of one-inch iron but a poor defence against it, which results in robbing this fleet of its once formidable character. Although many of the features of the original design may be retained in new constructions, most of the details will be changed, notably in the turret, in consequence of the greater weight resulting from the increased thickness of armor. The central spindle around which the Ericsson turret revolves must disappear, and the turret must turn on rollers under the base.

The effect produced abroad by the success of Ericsson's *Monitor* is so familiar to all that it hardly needs more than a passing allusion here. There is no doubt that the *Monitor* was the progenitor of all the turreted vessels in the fleets of the world; the essential principle of the vessel, however, was never viewed with favor. This principle consists in the low freeboard, which, besides reducing the size of the target, was intended to contribute to the steadiness of the hull as a gun platform by offering no resistance to the waves, which were expected to wash freely over the vessel's deck: the horizontal overhang of the *Passaic* class was intended to contribute

to resisting a rolling motion. The vessel was designed to be as a raft on the water, constantly submerged by the passing waves, hermetically sealed to prevent the admission of water, and artificially ventilated by means of blowers drawing air down through the turret. This was the most startling feature about the construction. The protection afforded to the battery by a circular turret having the form best suited to deflect projectiles, the employment of machinery to point the guns by the rotation of the turret, the protection to motive power, to anchoring apparatus, etc., all presented admirable points of advantage, but the almost perfect immersion of the hull, and the absence of motion due to the *great stability*, was the essential feature in the construction.

The double-turreted Monitors, of which the *Terror* indicates the class, were built with a sponsing, and it would have been better for the navy if this had been the only deviation made from the original design of Captain Ericsson. But it was not; the great mistake was made of building this class of Monitors of wood—a style of construction which had been already condemned abroad, in consequence of the impossibility of repairing an armored vessel so constructed, it being necessary to remove the armor for that purpose.

The *Miantonomoh, Monadnock,* and

Terror were completed and put in commission. The *Miantonomoh* made a cruise to European waters, spreading the fame of Ericsson, and proving the ability of a vessel of this type to navigate the high seas; the *Monadnock* made the voyage to the Pacific, passing through the Strait of Magellan; and the *Terror* was for a time on service on our eastern coast; but their lifetime was of short duration, and they are now being rebuilt, or rather new vessels, three of which bear their names, are now under construction, of iron, which will serve to make them efficient and durable.

It will hardly be a digression at this point to call attention more particularly to these double-turreted Monitors now under construction. They bear the following names, viz., *Puritan*, *Terror*, *Amphitrite*, *Miantonomoh*, and *Monad-*

nock. There has been much contention about the completion of these vessels, and imaginary defects have been ventilated in the newspapers. It may be that these attacks and erroneous statements have prejudiced the public mind, and that the idea may be entertained by some whose opinion is valued that there may be grounds for the doubts that have been expressed of their sea-worthiness. The practical effect of these statements has been to prevent Congress from appropriating money for the completion of the vessels, and this course on the part of Congress may have confirmed some in their doubts. Several boards of officers, most competent experts, have reported on them, recommending their completion, the last report being made by the Advisory Board, which may be regarded as the final decision, and should be accepted

U. S. SLOOP OF WAR "ADAMS."

U. S. SLOOP OF WAR "MARION."

without question.   The Advisory Board reports as follows:

"It is our opinion that it would be wise and expedient to finish these vessels at once, and for the following reasons, viz.:

"1. The hulls, as they are at present, are of excellent workmanship, fully up to the present standard condition of iron ship construction, whilst the flotation of the *Puritan* and the behavior of the *Miantonomoh* at sea confirm the correctness of the calculations of the designs.

"2. It is easily possible to complete the vessels by taking advantage of the recent developments in armor, guns, and machinery, without making any radical changes in the designs, so that their speed, endurance, battery power, protection, and sea-going qualities shall be fully equal to those of any foreign

U. S. SLOOP OF WAR "ALERT" (IRON).

iron-clad of similar dimensions designed previous to 1879.

"3. The vessels may be finished so as to develop all the above-mentioned advantages without making their total cost, when completed, in any way exorbitant, compared with the results obtained; again, the interests of our sea-coast defence require a force at least equal to that which would be represented by these vessels.

These vessels, with the exception of the *Monadnock*, have their machinery in place; the *Miantonomoh* has her side armor on; the others are finished as to their hulls, except the interior fittings, side armor, and turrets. The estimated cost to complete them is about four millions of dollars. When we consider the very slight defence that the country

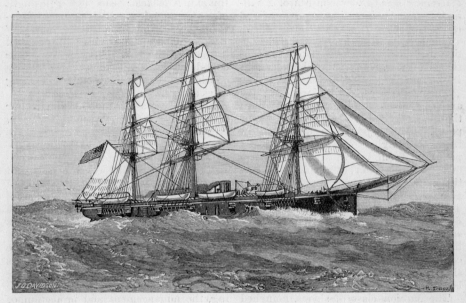

U. S. SLOOP OF WAR "TRENTON."

"We take the liberty of calling your attention to a certain erroneous impression which now exists with regard to these vessels. In one of the reports of these hulls a doubt was thrown on the correctness of the calculations of the *Puritan*. This doubt has spread in the public mind until it includes all the ships. The actual flotation of the *Puritan* and the *Miantonomoh* proves beyond question not only the reliability of the calculations, but also that the hulls of these vessels are lighter in proportion to the total displacement than those of any iron-clad low freeboard hulls afloat, with two exceptions.

"It has been the unfortunate custom, in arguments as to the value of the results to be obtained, to compare these vessels with such foreign ships as the *Inflexible* and the *Duilio*, to the evident disadvantage of the Monitors, no account whatever being taken of the fact that these vessels are double the size of the Monitors. If these hulls be compared with foreign ones of similar dimensions, no such disparity will appear."

now possesses in the single-turreted Monitors before alluded to, it would seem imperative to complete with all despatch these vessels, which would represent a force of real power.

These vessels are of iron as to the hulls, but they will be armored with steel or compound armor, and will be armed with the most powerful modern artillery that can be accommodated in their turrets. Their names appear in the navy list as "building." They were launched in 1883.

But to resume our notice of the present available ships of the navy.

The double-decked ship *Tennessee* is the only frigate, or "first-rate," that is borne on the list of vessels of the navy as available for sea-service. The ship has been for many years in commission as the flagship of the North Atlantic Station, but is now rapidly approaching that condition when the 20 per cent. law will consign her to "ordinary," from which she will probably be ultimately removed under the operation of the hammer of the auctioneer. She was launched in 1865. Her length is 335 feet; beam, 45 feet; draught of water, 21.8 feet. She has a displacement of 4840 tons, and attains a speed of 11 knots with an indicated horse-power of 1900. The capacity of her coal-bunkers is 381 tons. Her battery consists of 2 VIII-inch muzzle-loading rifles (converted), 16 IX-inch smooth-bores, and 4 80-pounders.

The vessels next in order of construction are those of the *Adams* class, small sloops of war, which were launched in 1874.

These vessels were built of wood. They are convenient and handy, and perform the duty required of a cruiser in time of peace. Engine-power is developed in them to a higher degree than in those preceding them, but in all else they are merely a repetition of earlier constructions. The *Adams* was launched in 1874. Her length is 185 feet; beam, 35 feet; draught of water, 14.3 feet. She has a displacement of 1375 tons, and attains a speed of 11.3 knots with an indicated horse-power of 715. The capacity of her coal-bunkers is 140 tons. Her battery consists of 1 XI-inch and 4 IX-inch smooth-bores and 1 60-pounder.

The *Marion* class of sloops, launched about the same period, are of an increased displacement and speed, but built of wood. The length of the *Marion* is 216 feet; beam, 37 feet; draught of water, 16.6 feet. She has a displacement of 1900 tons, and attains a speed of 12.9 knots per hour with an indicated horse-power of 966. The capacity of her coal-bunkers is 135 tons. Her battery consists of 1 VIII-inch muzzle-loading rifle (converted), 6 IX-inch smooth-bores, and 1 60-pounder.

The *Alert* is one of three vessels that were built of iron in 1874, the exceptional and spasmodic indication of an effort to change the material for construction, much induced by pressure from the iron interests of the country. This effort was made in a very mild and tentative manner, and was limited to this small class of diminutive vessels. The length of the *Alert* is 175 feet; beam, 32 feet; draught of water, 12.9 feet. She has a displacement of 1020 tons, and attains a speed of 10 knots per hour with an indicated horse-power of 655. The capacity of her coal-

bunkers is 133 tons. Her battery consists of 1 XI-inch and 4 IX-inch smooth-bores, and 1 60-pounder.

The shock attending the first step toward a change in the material for construction was so great as to cause a suspension of the effort, and in 1876 was launched the *Trenton*, built of wood, which represents the latest type on the list of the present navy. The length of this ship is 253 feet; beam, 48 feet; draught of water, 20.6 feet. She has a displacement of 3900 tons, and attains a speed of 12.8 knots per hour with an indicated horse-power of 2813. The capacity of her coal-bunkers is 350 tons. Her battery consists of 10 VIII-inch muzzle-loading rifles (converted).

The above is a fair presentation of our present navy. Of such vessels we have, larger and smaller, thirty-two which are fit for service as cruisers, exclusive of the old single-turreted Monitors. These cruisers are built of wood, have low speed, and are armed with smooth-bore guns, with a sprinkling of rifled cannon, converted on the Palliser system from smooth-bore cast-iron guns. Of what service is this force, this relic of a past age?

The duties of a navy, apart from the consideration of war, are manifold. As stated by the first Advisory Board, it is required for "surveying, deep-sea sounding, the advancement and protection of American commerce, exploration, the protection of American life and property endangered by wars between foreign countries, and service in support of American policy in matters where foreign governments are concerned."

With such a force as we possess it must be evident that it is impossible to discharge in an efficient manner all the duties of a navy. Our work in foreign surveys is limited to that of one small vessel on the west coast of North America; our deep-sea soundings are few and far between, dotted along the tracks pursued by our ships while going to and returning from distant stations; our commerce is protected; but we are unable to support any positive policy that the government might decide to declare in reference to, for example, the Monroe doctrine. To say nothing of European naval armaments, it is only necessary to point to some of the smaller powers in our own hemisphere that possess ships of war with which we have nothing fit to cope.

U. S. FRIGATE "CHICAGO" (STEEL).

Our people cannot desire to assume a position in the society of naval powers without supporting the position with dignity; they cannot wish their navy to be cited as a standard of inefficiency; they cannot wish to force their representatives (the officers of the navy) into a position of humiliation and mortification such as is imposed by being called on to deprecate criticism by labored explanations. Better abolish the navy and lower our pretensions.

But the fact seems to be that the rapidity of naval development has not been properly appreciated, and it is after a long interval of indifference that, attention being at last centred on the subject, it is seen how rapid its strides have been, and how utterly we are distanced in the race. There is evidently now in the country a growing desire to repair the effects of the past oversight, and we see Congress moving in the matter. As all political parties now unite in the necessity of effort in this direction, the hope is inspired that the subject is to be separated from those of a partisan character, and that the rehabilitation of the navy will be put on its proper level, and accepted as a national question in which all are alike interested.

Possessed as we are now of a navy such as has been indicated, the change that is about to be instituted involves a most violent transition. In reviewing our work of construction for the past thirty years we see no new type of cruiser. The only types of ships that we have are those that date before the war; since which we have but reproduced the same in classes of differing dimensions. From the sailing ship with auxiliary steam-power we have passed to the steamer with auxiliary sail-power; but we have no full-powered steamers, with or without sails. As long as it is considered necessary to spread as much canvas as is now used, the space assigned to boilers and engines is limited, and we fail to achieve full power; a reduction to the minimum of sail-power must be accepted before we can present a type of a full-powered steamer.

With the exception of two vessels of the *Alert* class built of iron, we have nothing but wooden hulls. We have continued to build in perishable material, requiring large sums to be spent in repairs, and ignoring the manufactures of the country which could have been aided in their development by the contrary course. We

have permitted the age of steel to reach its zenith without indicating that we were aware of its presence.

With the exception of a few Palliser converted rifles of VIII-inch calibre, our armaments consist of smooth-bore cast-iron guns which have composed our batteries for thirty years. These are now to be discarded, and their places to be filled with modern steel cannon.

Torpedoes, movable torpedoes, of which we know nothing practically, are to be brought to the front, and are to form part of our equipment. Torpedo-boats are to be brought into use, and details innumerable are now to be studied and worked out.

Conceive, then, a high-powered steamer with a minimum of canvas, built of steel, armed with modern steel artillery, and secondary battery of Hotchkiss guns, fitted for launching movable torpedoes, with protective deck over boilers and engines, divided into many water-tight compartments, giving protection to buoyancy, and compare such a ship with the type of the United States cruiser which we now possess, and an idea may be formed of the violence of the transition through which we are to pass. And there is nothing intermediate to break the suddenness of this change; there is no connecting link. The structure of to-day is placed in direct contrast with that of twenty-five years ago. This is the position in which we stand, and we can but accept the situation, from which there is no escape.

From all appearances, the navy is now to be given an opportunity of asserting itself, and the steps already taken to remedy the existing state of things can be stated in few words.

The origin of the effort dates from June, 1881, when the first Advisory Board was appointed to consider and to report on the need of appropriate vessels for the navy. This board, in its report of November 7, 1881, decided that the United States navy should consist of 70 unarmored cruisers of steel; it reported that there were 32 vessels in the navy fit for service as cruisers, and it indicated the character of the new vessels to be built. This board confined itself to the consideration of unarmored vessels, as it did not consider that the orders under which it acted required that it should discuss the subject of armored ships, though it expressed the opinion that such vessels were indispensable in time of war.

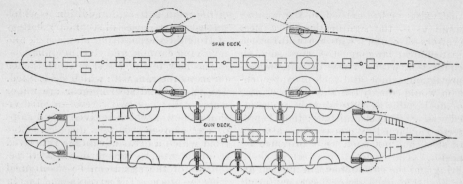

DECK PLANS OF THE U. S. FRIGATE "CHICAGO," SHOWING BATTERY.

Some time elapsed before any practical results followed from the action of this board, but in an act of Congress approved March 3, 1883, the construction of three steam-cruisers and a despatch-boat was authorized. These vessels are the *Chicago, Boston, Atlanta*, and *Dolphin*, and they are approaching completion, the *Dolphin* being already in commission.

In an act of Congress approved March 3, 1885, four additional vessels were authorized by Congress, for which preliminary plans and calculations have been made, which are now in the bureaus of the Navy Department, where designs are being prepared, on which bids can be made if proposals are issued for their construction by contract.

required it had to be imported at great cost to the builder. Those who contemplated bidding on the proposals issued by the government for the first four vessels had to consider this matter. Mr. John Roach, of New York and Chester, Pennsylvania, undertook the manufacture of this material, and finding that success attended his experiment, he was able to direct the steel-works at Thurlow, Pennsylvania, extensively to this line of business, and when the bids were opened it was found that this new industry, introduced

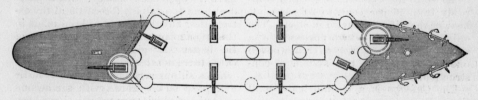

DECK PLAN OF THE U. S. SLOOP OF WAR "ATLANTA," SHOWING BATTERY.

This is the first step toward our new navy. We can count on an addition of seven steel cruisers and one despatch-boat as a nucleus. The present year will see four of these vessels completed, and it is possible that during the year following the four additional vessels can be launched.

Up to the time of the inception of these cruisers no steel for ship plates had been rolled in the United States. Construction in American iron plates had been extensively carried on, but if steel plating was

through his enterprise, enabled him to underbid all competitors. After receiving the contracts for the ships, Mr. Roach contracted with the Phœnix Iron Company, of Phœnixville, with Messrs. Park Brothers, of Pittsburgh, and the Norway Iron and Steel Works, of South Boston, for supplies of similar material; thus the first step in this effort to rehabilitate the navy resulted in introducing a new industry into the country. The still more extensive development of industries that will attend the work of rehabilitation as it advances will be treated farther on.

Before presenting the types of cruisers which are now to be introduced into the navy it may be well to refer to an error that exists, or has existed, in the popular mind as to the signification of a steel cruiser. To many who are uninformed in technical language the word steel, in connection with a vessel of war, implies protection, armor, and such misapprehension would convey the idea that a cruiser of steel is able to contend with an armored vessel. This is a mistake; there is protection obtained by constructing a vessel of steel, but not such as is provided by armor. The destructive effect of shellfiring and the development in modern artillery have made armor necessary for all vessels which can carry it, and has also made it necessary to provide all other protection possible to vessels that cannot carry armor. Although this protection cannot be given absolutely to the hull of such ships and to the *personnel*, it is provided to the *buoyancy* by the introduction of water-tight compartments and protective decks, which limit the destructive effect of the fire of the enemy and localize the water that may enter through shot holes. With a wooden hull it would not be possible to combine this precaution, for the reason of the difficulty in making water-tight joints between wood and metal, and in consequence of the weight that would be added to the wooden hull, which is already from 16 per cent. to 20 per cent. heavier than if constructed of steel. The only defensive advantage possessed by a steel unarmored cruiser over a wooden one is derived from this system of construction.

The *Chicago* is a steam-frigate, built throughout of steel of domestic manufacture, the outside plating being $\frac{9}{16}$ inch thick. Her length is 325 feet; beam, 48.2 feet; draught of water, 19 feet. She has a displacement of 4500 tons, and will attain a speed of 14 knots per hour with an indicated horse-power of 5000. The capacity of her coal-bunkers is 940 tons, and she carries a battery of 4 VIII-inch steel breech-loading guns in half-turrets, and 8 VI-inch and 2 V-inch steel breech-loaders on the gun-deck. This ship has nine athwart-ships bulkheads, dividing the hull into ten main water-tight compartments, and the machinery and boilers are covered by a protective deck one and a half inches in thickness. When the bunkers are full of coal she has a coal protection nine feet thick from the water-line to eight feet above it.

The deck plans show the arrangement of the main battery, in addition to which she carries a powerful secondary battery of Hotchkiss rapid-firing single-shot, and revolving cannon, and Gatling-guns.

The bow of the vessel is strengthened for using the ram with which she is fitted. The rudder and steering-gear are under water. She has two screws—a subdivision of power which is given to all ships of war of over 3000 tons displacement—from which a great advantage is derived if one engine be broken down, as three-fourths of the speed can be maintained with the other. The advantage of this in a naval action is obvious.

The *Atlanta*, of which the *Boston* is a counterpart, presents another type of a steel unarmored cruiser. She is a steam-corvette, or sloop of war, a single-decked ship. Her length is 276 feet; beam, 42 feet; draught of water, 16 feet 10 inches. She has a displacement of 3000 tons, and will attain a speed of 13 knots per hour with an indicated horse-power of 3500. The capacity of her coal-bunkers is 580 tons, and her battery consists of 2 VIII-inch steel breech-loading guns and 6 VI-inch, besides a secondary battery of Hotchkiss and Gatling guns.

In vessels of this class it is usual to have an open-deck battery, with a poop-deck and top-gallant forecastle at the extremities, but the effort has been made in this type to increase the effectiveness of the battery by giving the guns a more extended lateral train than is possible when a ship is arranged with a forecastle and poop-deck. These, with the accommodations which they provide, have been removed from the ends of the ship, and a superstructure has been erected amidships. This arrangement gives a clear sweep forward and aft for the powerful VIII-inch guns, enabling the forward gun to cover an all-around fire of from 40° abaft the beam on the port side to 30° abaft the beam on the starboard side, the after VIII-inch gun having a corresponding lateral sweep aft. Within the superstructure are mounted the 6 VI-inch guns, two on each side on the broadside, with a train of 60° before and abaft the beam, the other two being mounted at diagonally opposite corners in such a way as to admit of their use either on the broadside or for fire ahead or astern. This object is achieved by mounting the 2 VIII-inch guns *en échelon*, the forward gun being on the port side of the centre line of the ship,

U. S. SLOOP OF WAR "ATLANTA" (STEEL).

and the after VIII-inch gun on the starboard side of the same line. This is shown on the deck plan.

It does not require the discrimination of a professional eye to see the increased power given to the battery by this arrangement. It is an innovation that was very startling to the conservative mind, but the more familiar the idea becomes, the more favorable opinion grows to the change, and the more apparent becomes the increased offensive power of the ship. The extremities of this type of ship will not, of course, be so dry in heavy weather as if they had a forecastle and poop, but it must be remembered that every part of the spar-deck is from nine to ten feet above the water. The rig of the *Atlanta* will be that of a brig, but without head booms; the fire ahead of the forward guns is thus unobstructed, and the ram with which she is fitted is always clear for use. The division of the hull into water-tight compartments by athwart-ship bulkheads, and a protective deck over engines and boilers, form a part of the construction.

The *Dolphin*, though not regarded as a vessel for fighting purposes, is the type of a class that is needed in all navies for duty as a despatch-boat, or for the temporary accommodation of a commander-in-chief of a squadron who may desire to communicate rapidly with his ships at distant points. She is well fitted for the service, and is now in commission, demonstrating her ability to perform the work required of her. She could also be of service as a commerce destroyer, for which service she is equipped with one gun of long range. Her length is 240 feet; beam, 32 feet; draught of water, 14.25 feet. She has a displacement of 1485 tons, and attains a speed of 15 knots per hour.

Her advent into the navy marks an epoch—the inauguration of the successful manufacture in the United States of American rolled steel ship plating, equal to the best in the world, as shown by the most rigid government tests. The *Dolphin* is the first vessel, whether for naval or commercial purposes, that is built entirely of steel of domestic manufacture, and is the pioneer representative of other similar industries which will be developed as the rehabilitation of the navy proceeds. She has proved herself eminently successful, and is the fastest sea steamer of her displacement built in the United States, with

perhaps the exception of the steam-yacht *Atalanta*. She is a stanch vessel of great structural strength, and does credit to the ship-building profession of the country.

Of the additional cruisers authorized by the act of March 3, 1885, two are to be not less than 3000 tons nor more than 5000 tons displacement, one is to be a heavy armed gun-boat of 1600 tons displacement, and the other a light gun-boat of 800 tons displacement.

It is proposed in one of the larger vessels to reproduce the type of the *Atlanta* on a larger scale, while the other vessel of the same class will be provided with a poop and top-gallant forecastle, and will carry her forward and after guns on sponsings, by which means fire ahead and astern will be secured. This will make it necessary to limit the power of the battery of the second vessel to VI-inch guns, as the VIII-inch gun cannot conveniently be carried on sponsings in a vessel of this displacement, which will be about 4000 tons.

The heavy gun-boat will carry 6 VI-inch guns, the forward and after ones on sponsings; and the light gun-boat will carry 4 of the same guns.

In the construction of these additional vessels advantage will be taken of all our experience in our initial effort, and of whatever developments may have been made by others since our earlier vessels were designed. The designs of these will be completed and the specifications prepared before the publication of this paper.*

That the departure from the old standards is absolute is apparent in material, in armament, in speed, and in rig.

The causes that have led to this change in material may be found, first, in the change that has taken place in ordnance. The introduction of the rifled cannon, and its subsequent development, have increased very much the weight of this part of the equipment of a vessel of war, and the necessity of accommodating the stowage of charges of powder much increased in size, and of ammunition for the second-

---

* Readers who desire to inform themselves on the technical details of the construction of the new cruisers are referred to a paper submitted to the United States Naval Institute by Assistant Naval Constructor Francis T. Bowles, United States Navy, published in the Proceedings of the Institute, Vol. IX., No. 4.

U. S. DESPATCH-BOAT "DOLPHIN."

ary batteries, which must be most liberally supplied, makes an absolute demand on
an increased portion of space. Again, the
increased speed now considered indispensable makes a similar demand for space,
and carries with it as well an increased
proportion of the total displacement. In
a wooden hull it would be impossible to
reconcile these demands, in consequence
of the weight of the hull itself.

The hull and hull fittings of an unarmored cruiser built of wood will weigh
from 49 per cent. to 52 per cent. of the total
displacement. With high-powered engines it is doubtful if sufficient strength
can be obtained with even 52 per cent. of
the displacement for the hull, and this
must suppose the absence of all protection
to buoyancy, as water-tight compartments.

The hull and fittings of a steel cruiser,
exclusive of protective decks, will weigh
from 39 per cent. to 44 per cent. of the
total displacement.

Suppose a 4500-ton ship built of wood
weighing 50 per cent. of the total displacement, and the same ship built of
steel weighing 40 per cent. of the total displacement, the respective weights of the
hulls will be 2250 tons and 1800 tons, a
difference of 450 tons, the steel hull being
one-fifth or 20 per cent. lighter than the
wooden one. This will allow for in-

creased weight of ordnance, protective
deck, or increased coal endurance, as may
be decided when considering the service
on which the ship is to be employed.

But notwithstanding the saving thus
obtained, the question of weights is still
full of difficulties and embarrassments,
and it is found impossible in the same
structure to accommodate all demands
from the different departments concerned
in the equipment of a vessel of war. The
sail-power has been reduced, so as to save
weight of spars and sails, which have become of secondary importance, but this
will not satisfy all the requirements of
the problem. As articles appertaining
to the old method of equipment are removed, those belonging to what are considered necessary under the new order of
things are brought forward. Space is
still to be found for movable torpedoes,
for torpedo-boats, and for engines and appurtenances for electrical apparatus for
lighting the ship, for search light, and
other ordnance purposes. It is evident
that much study is needed to reduce
weights in all the essential parts, so as
to be able to accommodate all the devices
which the progress of ideas continues to
present. Much is yet to be done by the
substitution of steel for iron in many parts
of our engines, and experiments abroad
lead to the hope that the weights of boil-

ers may be much reduced, but as the question stands to-day it is impossible to provide any single ship with all the appliances that are considered necessary for a perfectly equipped vessel of war. Every ship, therefore, must present a compromise.

Another reason for the transition from wood to steel hulls is the durability of steel as compared with wood. Referring to the large sums of money that have been appropriated under the head of construction and repairs; for which there is now so little to show (and disregarding the question of administration, which of course is vital, but which has no place in this article), the main reason for the deficiency in the results is that all this money has been expended in perishable material. Every ship that has been built of wood since the war has been a mistake. The most serious error was committed when the wooden double-turreted Monitors of the *Miantonomoh* class were built, which, it is believed, was done against the protest of Captain Ericsson. The result was the early decay of these vessels, and the present defenceless condition of our sea-coast. The lifetime of a wooden ship is of short duration. It requires constant repairs, which amount in the long-run to rebuilding, and it is in this manner that so many of our old ships are still retained in service; but in the case of a wooden armored vessel these repairs are impossible without removing the armor. This was the condition of affairs with regard to these Monitors, and the consequence is that the country has to incur the expense of entirely new constructions. These are in durable material, and will give good account of themselves when called on.

The steel hulls that it is now the intention shall compose the fleet will, if well cared for, endure in perfect condition for thirty years. In fact, the lifetime of an iron or steel hull is not defined to any limit, and if a perfect anti-corrosive and anti-fouling composition can be produced, the limit may be regarded as indefinite.

The foregoing remarks on our new navy apply to unarmored cruisers. This is the only class of ship on which Congress has as yet taken any action. Unarmored cruisers supply a need in time of peace, but they cannot fulfil the purposes of war. At such a time the armored ship is recognized as indispensable, and there is every reason why the construction of armored vessels should proceed simultaneously with that of the unarmored cruisers. These are a more intricate problem for study, require much more time to build, and are required, while at peace, as a school of instruction in which to prepare for war. Our selection of armor has been much assisted by the investigations of others, and we are in a favorable condition to make a decision on this point; and the type of vessel best suited for a cruiser seems to be settled, by the uniform practice of foreign nations, in favor of the barbette.

But it must be remembered that at the present time we are not in a condition to proceed with the construction of armored vessels, depending on our own resources. We must go abroad to purchase armor, unless we set ourselves to the task of establishing works where it can be manufactured. The establishment of these plants is the first thing needful, and until this is done it is impossible to make ourselves independent in this matter. The construction of our first unarmored cruisers has introduced into the country the industry of rolling steel ship plates; the construction of our new ordnance and armored ships must introduce the new industries of casting and forging large masses of war material.

This subject, so far as it relates to ordnance, was referred to a mixed board of army and navy officers, known as the Gun Foundry Board, which, with the aid of the counsel of some of the ablest and leading steel manufacturers in the United States, submitted to Congress a report which presents a solution of the problem, and demonstrates on what terms the steel manufacturers of the country can be induced to work in accord with the government. This board had under consideration only the subject of foundries and factories for gun construction, but the casting and forging facilities required for guns would be applicable to armor; thus in providing means for the manufacture of one, the other purpose is equally subserved.

Senator Cameron, of Pennsylvania, has introduced a bill in the Senate founded on the recommendations of the Gun Foundry Board, but it has not yet been acted on; Congress, however, has supplemented the work of that board by the labors of committees from both Houses which have gone over the ground. The Senate committee, of which Senator Haw-

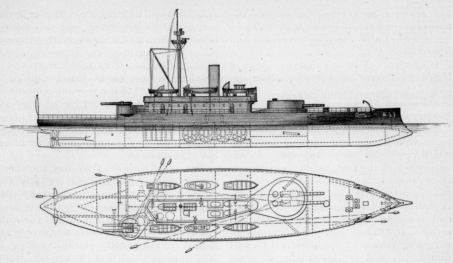

LIGHT-DRAUGHT COAST-DEFENCE VESSEL, WITH DECK PLAN.

ley was the chairman, has presented its report, accompanied by a valuable and exhaustive presentation of literature bearing on the matter. The report endorses the conclusions of the Gun Foundry Board, and urges the adoption of its recommendations. It is believed that the House committee will report much in the same line with that marked out by the Gun Foundry Board, and that Congress will be advised to expend large sums of money in this direction.

With material of domestic manufacture at hand, it would be the duty of the government to provide the navy with a fleet of ten armored cruisers of the most approved type. These vessels would form the outer line of defence of the coast during war, and should be of such force as to be able to contend with any second-class armored vessel of other nations. Some of them should be always in commission during times of peace, if only for instruction and practice purposes, and one should be assigned to each squadron abroad to carry the flag of the rear-admiral in command, to assert our position in the society of naval powers, able to give substantial "support to American policy in matters where foreign governments are concerned."

The ability to contend with armored vessels of the first class must be reserved for another type of ships, which are styled "coast-defence vessels," and without which our new navy will not be thoroughly equipped for contributing its full share in defence at home. In considering armored vessels, what was said before as to the character of compromise that obtains in vessels of war must be borne in mind. All desirable features cannot be concentrated in any one ship; the special duty for which the vessel is to be used controls the selection. The sea-going armored cruiser is expected to keep the sea for a lengthened period: she must have large coal endurance. She may be called on to sustain more than one engagement: her supply of ammunition must be large. Her speed must equal that of the fastest sea-going vessels of similar type to enable her to pursue an equal or avoid a superior force: hence much space and displacement must be assigned to engines and boilers. Thus the amount of her armor and the weight of her battery are affected by these other demands, which are the more imperative.

In the case of coast-defence vessels the conditions are changed, enabling in them the full development of both offensive and defensive properties. These vessels are assigned to duty on the coast: they must be as fit to keep the sea as are the armored cruisers, and they must be able to fight their guns in all weathers that the armored cruiser can fight, but they do not require the coal endurance nor the speed of the ship that is to keep the sea for lengthened periods, and the weight saved in coal and machinery can be utilized in battery and armor. Such vessels constitute the main line of naval defence, as they can be made almost absolutely invulnerable and irresistible.

Under an act of the last Congress a board on "fortifications and other defences" has been occupied in considering the defences of the coast, and there are recommended by this board two classes of "floating batteries" (so called), coast-defence vessels, and one class of low free-board vessels for harbor defence. An examination of the designs of these vessels shows them to be replete with merit, presenting some novel and valuable features. A justifiable limitation is put on the coal endurance and speed, though fair speed is secured, and it has been possible to design sea-going vessels of comparatively small dimensions and light draught, of great handiness and manœuvring power, to carry the heaviest guns, and capable of con-

sels for coast defence, the old war Monitors of the *Passaic* class; but the contrast between them and the vessels recommended by the Fortifications Board is about equal in degree with that between our wooden fleet and the new steel cruisers.

It is intended that a movable automatic torpedo shall be utilized by all armored vessels, either by means of a torpedo-boat to be carried by armored cruisers, or by the vessel itself in the case of coast and harbor defence ships.

The only torpedo that has succeeded thus far in recommending itself to the naval powers is that invented by Mr. Whitehead. Numerous efforts have been made by others in this field, but the difficulties that surround it are made very apparent by the paucity of the results. It will be understood that the torpedo, when launched, is left entirely to automatic control; hence, apart from the motive

THE HOWELL TORPEDO.

B, Fly-wheel. *C, C*, Screw Propellers. *D*, Diving Rudder. *E, E*, Steering Rudders. *F*, Water Chamber, containing Automatic Apparatus. *G*, Firing Pin. *H*, Position of Gun-cotton Magazine.

tending on equal terms with the heaviest European battle ships. The cut on page 23 represents the smaller of the type of coast-defence vessels.

The largest class will be armed with 2 107-ton guns in a turret, and 2 26-ton guns in a barbette. The thickness of armor will vary from 18 inches to 16 inches.

The second class will be armed with 2 75-ton guns in a turret, and 2 26-ton guns in a barbette. The thickness of armor will be from 16 to 11 inches.

The smallest vessels, for harbor defence, modified Monitors, will be armed with 2 44-ton guns in a turret, and 2 26-ton guns in a barbette. The thickness of armor will be from 13 to 10 inches.

A fleet composed of such vessels as are represented in the largest type would be able to engage an enemy at some distance from the coast—an important object in these days when the range of heavy rifled cannon makes it possible to shell towns from a great distance, from points remote from shore batteries.

Nominally we have now a fleet of ves-

power, it is necessary that it shall possess directive power, vertically to control immersion, and horizontally to control direction in the horizontal plane. In the Whitehead torpedo the immersion is well regulated, and if no deflecting influences are encountered, the direction is also preserved; but it fails where deflecting influences intervene. During the Turko-Russian war valuable experience was gained, and instances are known where the torpedo failed to operate from want of directive power. An instance is cited where a torpedo was deflected by striking the chain of a vessel at anchor, causing it to pass harmlessly to one side. Another instance is cited where the torpedo was deflected from the side of a ship owing to the angle at which it struck. It is evident that perfection cannot be associated with a weapon of this class that has not a strong directive force inherent in it.

The torpedo invented by Captain J. A. Howell, of the United States navy, possesses this property to an eminent degree, and it is regarded by most competent ex-

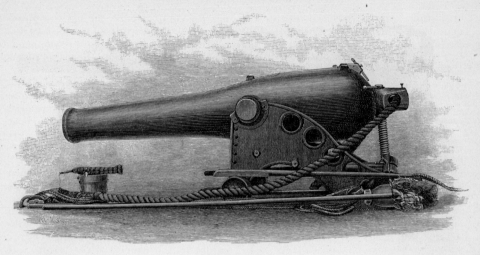

IX-INCH SMOOTH-BORE GUN.

perts as the successful rival of the White-head. In the Howell torpedo the power is stored in a fly-wheel revolving with great rapidity in a longitudinal vertical plane, and its gyroscopic tendency makes it impossible for the torpedo to deviate from its original course in a horizontal plane; the principle is the same as insures the accuracy of the rifle bullet, enabling it to resist deflecting influences. The latest experiments of Captain Howell in controlling the immersion of his torpedo are very successful, and it is probable that the auto-mobile torpedo for our new navy will be an American invention. Liberality in experiments is indispensable in perfecting a device of this kind; it is to be hoped that such may be extended to the Howell torpedo. It may be estimated that millions of dollars have been spent by European naval powers in experiments with the Whitehead torpedo; the United States government may have spent twenty-five hundred on the Howell.

The general reader is probably not aware of the effect on naval warfare produced by the introduction of the auto-mobile torpedo, affecting the constituents of the fleet itself. Formerly a fleet consisted of battle ships alone, or with store-ships to provide consumable articles; to these were later added despatch-boats for the service indicated by their title; but since the introduction of the torpedo an additional fleet of torpedo-boats is considered necessary for the protection of the battle ships. All armored ships are expected to carry at least one torpedo-boat, which is designed for operating against the enemy during an action at sea, and the universal adoption of this practice has led to the introduction into fleets of a new type of vessel, called torpedo-boat catchers, whose primary duty it is to destroy the torpedo-boats of the enemy. For this purpose these vessels have phenomenal speed, and besides their equipment of auto-mobile torpedoes, are provided with powerful batteries of single-shot and revolving Hotchkiss guns capable of penetrating all parts of a torpedo-boat. This type of vessel is now being constructed by the English and French governments, and will form one of the constituents of their fleets.

The torpedo-boat is undoubtedly one of the features that should be introduced into our new navy, not only for their possible use on the high seas, but for the purpose of supplementing the harbor-defence vessels, while the type of vessel known as the torpedo-boat catcher would be a powerful auxiliary to the armored cruisers on the first line, or the more powerful vessels forming the second line of the coast defence.

The transition in the artillery of the navy is as violent as is that in ships. We give an illustration of the IX-inch smooth-bore gun, the type of the guns which form the batteries of our ships of war. This gun, with the XI-inch of similar form but increased calibre and weight, had no peer at the time of its introduction into the navy, nor was it surpassed, if equalled, by other nations

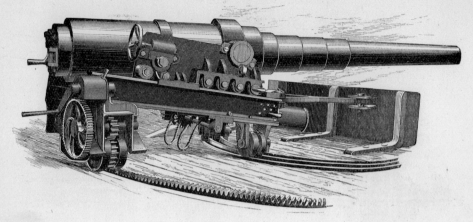

NEW VI-INCH STEEL BREECH-LOADING RIFLE.

during the period when armaments were confined to smooth bores. These guns contributed much to the high standing of the navy in the past—as much so as did the work of our naval constructors—and it

IX-inch smooth-bore as its substitute in the broadside batteries.

An inspection of the following table will show the comparative power of our present armaments and the proposed ones.

Gun.	Weight of Charge.	Weight of Projectile.	Muzzle Velocity.	Muzzle Energy.	Penetration in Wrought Iron.	Muzzle Energy per Ton of Gun.	Weight of Gun.	Weight of Carriage.
	Pounds.	Pounds.	Feet.	Foot Tons.	Inches.	Foot Tons.	Pounds.	Pounds.
IX-inch smooth-bore....................	10	73.5	1320	1117	*Nil*	279	9,000	1,250
XI-inch smooth-bore....................	15	136	1240	1450	...	203	16,000	7,500
VIII-inch converted muzzle-loading rifle	35	180	1450	2623	10.0	358	17,000	7,500
V-inch steel breech-loading rifle......	30	60	1915	1525	10.7	552	6,187	4,200
VI-inch steel breech-loading rifle.....	50	100	1915	2542	13.2	521	11,000	6,400
VIII-inch steel breech-loading rifle....	125	250	2050	7285	18.2	560	28,000	14,000
X-inch steel breech-loading rifle......	250	500	2100	15285	23.7	588	58,240	32,482
XII-inch steel breech-loading rifle.....	425	850	2100	25985	27.6	591	44 tons	....
XIV-inch steel breech-loading rifle.....	675	1350	2100	41270	32.2	550	75 tons	....
XVI-inch steel breech-loading rifle.....	1000	2000	2100	61114	36.8	571	107 tons	....

is with a feeling of regret that the necessity of abandoning them is recognized; they have performed an important part in the achievements of the navy, and occupy a page in its history which will always be referred to with pride and satisfaction; but their time is past; the rifled cannon has asserted itself, and the old weapon must be laid aside with what sentiment we may. Progress demands a change; it requires a development of energy in a projectile which cannot be communicated in a smooth-bore gun, and so we pass at one leap to the high-powered steel breech-loading rifle, from a gun whose penetrating power in wrought iron is zero to one which sends its projectile through a thickness of 13 inches.

A comparison of the cuts shows the contrast between the old and the new; the VI-inch rifle will take the place of the

The necessity of a change in our artillery has been known for many years, but it has been impossible to obtain steel of domestic manufacture for the purpose, and thus our ships have been forced to make their cruises abroad with antiquated and effete batteries, in painful contrast with those carried by ships of all other nationalities. A few converted rifle guns have been made, converted on the Palliser system by inserting in a cast-iron smooth-bore a tube of wrought iron rifled; but these are mere makeshifts, of doubtful advantage at best, and the practice has been abandoned altogether by the present Chief of the Bureau of Naval Ordnance, who has imported steel forgings from abroad for the guns on the new steel cruisers, there being no other means of securing modern batteries for the modern ships.

SPRINGHAVEN.

BY R. D. BLACKMORE.

CHAPTER XI.

NO PROMOTION.

"DO it again now, Captain Scuddy; do it again; you know you must."

"You touched the rim with your shoe, last time. You are bound to do it clean, once more."

"No, he didn't. You are a liar; it was only the ribbon of his shoe."

"I'll punch your head if you say that again. It was his heel, and here's the mark."

"Oh, Scuddy dear, don't notice them. You can do it fifty times running, if you like. Nobody can run or jump like you. Do it just once more to please me."

Kitty Fanshawe, a boy with large blue eyes and a purely gentle face, looked up at Blyth Scudamore so faithfully that to resist him was impossible.

"Very well, then; once more for Kitty," said the sweetest-tempered of mankind, as he vaulted back into the tub. "But you know that I always leave off at a dozen. Thirteen—thirteen I could never stop at. I shall have to do fourteen at least; and it is too bad, just after dinner. Now all of you watch whether I touch it anywhere."

A barrel almost five feet in height, and less than a yard in breadth, stood under a clump of trees in the play-ground; and Blyth Scudamore had made a clean leap one day, for his own satisfaction, out of it. Sharp eyes saw him, and sharp wits were pleased, and a strong demand had arisen that he should perform this feat perpetually. Good nerve, as well as strong spring, and compactness of power are needed for it; and even in this athletic age there are few who find it easy.

"Come, now," he said, as he landed lightly, with both heels together; "one of you big fellows come and do it. You are three inches taller than I am. And you have only got to make up your minds."

But all the big fellows hung back, or began to stimulate one another, and to prove to each other how easy it was, by every proof but practice. "Well, then, I must do it once more," said Blyth, "for I dare not leave off at thirteen, for fear of some great calamity, such as I never could jump out of."

But before he could get into the tub again, to prepare for the clear spring out of it, he beheld a man with silver buttons coming across the playing-field. His heart fell into his heels, and no more agility remained in him. He had made up his mind that Admiral Darling would forget all about him by Saturday; and though the fair image of Dolly would abide in that quiet mind for a long while, the balance of his wishes (cast by shyness) was heavily against this visit. And the boys, who understood his nature, with a poignant love—like that of our friends in this world—began to probe his tender places.

"One more jump, Captain Scuddy! You must; to show the flunky what you can do."

"Oh, don't I wish I was going? He'll have turtle soup, and venison, and two men behind his chair."

"And the beautiful young ladies looking at him every time he takes a mouthful."

"But he dare not go courting after thirteen jumps. And he has vowed that he will have another. Come, Captain Scuddy, no time to lose."

But Scudamore set off to face his doom, with his old hat hanging on the back of his head—as it generally did—and his ruddy face and mild blue eyes full of humorous diffidence and perplexity.

"If you please, sir, his honour the Hadmiral have sent me to fetch 'e and your things; and hoss be baiting along of the Blue Dragon."

"I am sorry to say that I forgot all about it, or, at least, I thought that he would. How long before we ought to start?"

"My name is Gregory, sir—Coachman Gregory—accustomed always to a pair, but doesn't mind a single hoss, to oblige the Hadmiral, once in a way. About half an hour, sir, will suit me, unless they comes down to the skittle-alley, as ought to be always on a Saturday afternoon; but not a soul there when I looked in."

Any man in Scudamore's position, except himself, would have grieved and groaned. For the evening dress of that time, though less gorgeous than of the age before, was still an expensive and elaborate affair; and the young man, in this ebb of fortune, was poorly stocked with raiment. But he passed this trouble with his usual calmness and disregard of trifles. "If I wear the best I have got," he thought, "I cannot be charged with disrespect. The Admiral knows what a sailor is; and, after all, who will look at me?" Accordingly he went just as he was, for he never wore an overcoat, but taking a little canvas kit, with pumps and silk stockings for evening wear, and all the best that he could muster of his Volunteer equipment.

The Admiral came to the door of the Hall, and met him with such hearty warmth, and a glance of such kind approval at his open throat and glowing cheeks, that the young man felt a bound of love and tender veneration towards him, which endured for lifetime.

"Your father was my dearest friend, and the very best man I ever knew. I must call you 'Blyth,'" said the Admiral, "for if I call you 'Scudamore,' I shall think perpetually of my loss."

At dinner that day there was no other guest, and nothing to disturb the present one, except a young lady's quick glances, of which he endeavored to have no knowledge. Faith Darling, a gentle and beautiful young woman, had taken a natural liking to him, because of his troubles, and simplicity, and devotion to his widowed mother. But to the younger, Dolly Darling, he was only a visitor, dull and stupid, requiring, without at all repaying, the trouble of some attention. He was not tall, nor handsome, nor of striking appearance in any way; and although he was clearly a gentleman, to her judgment he was not an accomplished, or even a clever one. His inborn modesty and shyness placed him at great disadvantage, until well known; and the simple truth of his nature forbade any of the large talk and bold utterance which pleased her as yet among young officers.

"What a plague he will be all day tomorrow!" she said to her sister in the drawing-room. "Father was obliged, I suppose, to invite him; but what can we do with him all the day? Sundays are dull enough, I am sure, already, without our having to amuse a gentleman who has scarcely got two ideas of his own, and is afraid to say 'bo' to a goose, I do believe. Did you hear what he said when I asked him whether he was fond of riding?"

"Yes; and I thought it so good of him, to answer so straightforwardly. He said that he used to be very fond of it, but was afraid that he should fall off now."

"I should like to see him. I tell you what we'll do. We will make him ride back on Monday morning, and put him on 'Blue Bangles,' who won't have seen daylight since Friday. Won't he jump about a bit! What a shame it is, not to let us ride on Sundays!"

Ignorant of these kind intentions, Scudamore was enjoying himself in his quiet, observant way. Mr. Twemlow, the rector of the parish, had chanced—as he often chanced on a Saturday, after buckling up a brace of sermons—to issue his mind (with his body outside it) for a little relief of neighbourhood. And these little airings of his chastening love—for he loved everybody, when he had done his sermon —came, whenever there was a fair chance of it, to a glass of the fine old port which is the true haven for an ancient Admiral.

"Just in time, Rector," cried Admiral Darling, who had added by many a hardship to his inborn hospitality. "This is my young friend Blyth Scudamore, the son of one of my oldest friends. You have heard of Sir Edmond Scudamore?"

"And seen him and felt him. And to him I owe, under a merciful Providence, the power of drinking in this fine port the health of his son, which I do with deep pleasure, for the excellence both of end and means."

The old man bowed at the praise of his wine, and the young one at that of his father. Then, after the usual pinch of snuff from the Rector's long gold box, the host returned to the subject he had been full of before this interruption.

"The question we have in hand is this. What is to be done with our friend Blyth? He was getting on famously, till this vile peace came. Twemlow, you called it that yourself, so that argument about words is useless. Blyth's lieutenancy was on the books, and the way they carry things on now, and shoot poor fellows' heads off, he might have been a post-captain in a twelvemonth. And now there seems nothing on earth before him better than Holy-Orders."

"Admiral Darling is kind enough to think," said Scudamore, in his mild, hesitative way, blushing outwardly, but smiling inwardly, "that I am too good to be a clergyman."

"And so you are, and Heaven knows it, Blyth, unless there was a chance of getting on by goodness, which there is in the Navy, but not in the Church. Twemlow, what is your opinion?"

"It would not be modest in me," said the Rector, "to stand up too much for my own order. We do our duty, and we don't get on."

"Exactly. You could not have put it better. You get no vacancies by shot and shell, and being fit for another world, you keep out of it. Have you ever heard me tell the story about Gunner MacCrab, of the *Bellerophon*?"

"Fifty times, and more than that," replied the sturdy parson, who liked to make a little cut at the Church sometimes, but would not allow any other hand to do it. "But now about our young friend here. Surely, with all that we know by this time of the character of that Bony, we can see that this peace is a mere trick of his to bamboozle us while he gets ready. In six months we shall be at war again, hammer and tongs, as sure as my name is Twemlow."

"So be it!" cried the Admiral, with a stamp on his oak floor, while Scudamore's gentle eyes flashed and fell; "if it is the will of God, so be it. But if it once begins again, God alone knows where France will be before you and I are in our graves. They have drained all our patience, and our pockets very nearly; but they have scarcely put a tap into our energy and endurance. But what are they? A gang of slaves, rammed into the cannon by a Despot."

"They seem to like it, and the question is for them. But the struggle will be desperate, mountains of carnage, oceans of blood, universal mourning, lamentation, and woe. And I have had enough trouble with my tithes already."

"Tithes are dependent on the will of the Almighty," said the Admiral, who paid more than he altogether liked; "but a war goes by reason and good management. It encourages the best men of the day, and it brings out the difference between right and wrong, which are quite smothered up in peace time. It keeps out a quantity of foreign rubbish and stuff only made to be looked at, and it makes people trust one another, and know what country they belong to, and feel how much they have left to be thankful for. And what is the use of a noble fleet, unless it can get some fighting? Blyth, what say you? You know something about that."

"No, sir, I have never been at close quarters yet. And I doubt—or at least I am certain that I should not like it. I am afraid that I should want to run down below."

Mr. Twemlow, having never smelled hostile powder, gazed at him rather loftily, while the young man blushed at his own truth, yet looked up bravely to confirm it.

"Of all I have ever known or met," said Admiral Darling, quietly, "there are but three—Nelson and two others, and one of those two was half-witted—who could fetch up muzzle to muzzle without a feeling of that sort. The true courage lies in resisting the impulse, more than being free from it. I know that I was in a precious fright the first time I was shot

at, even at a decent distance; and I don't
pretend to like it even now. But I am
pretty safe now from any further chance,
I fear. When we cut our wisdom-teeth,
they shelf us. Twemlow, how much
wiser you are in the Church! The older a man gets, the higher they promote
him."

"Then let them begin with me," the
Rector answered, smiling; "I am old
enough now for almost anything, and the
only promotion I get is stiff joints, and
teeth that crave peace from an olive. *Pla-
citam paci*, Mr. Scudamore knows the
rest, being fresh from the learned Stonnington. But, Squire, you know that I
am content. I love Springhaven, Springhaven loves me, and we chasten one another."

"A man who knows all the Latin you
know, Rector—for I own that you beat me
to the spelling-book—should be at least an
Archdeacon in the Church, which is equal
to the rank of Rear-Admiral. But you
never have pushed as you should do; and
you let it all off in quotations. Those are
very comforting to the mind, but I never
knew a man do good with them, unless
they come out of the Bible. When Gunner Matthew of the *Erigdoupos* was waiting to have his leg off, with no prospect
before him—except a better world—you
know what our Chaplain said to him; and
the effect upon his mind was such, that I
have got him to this day upon my land."

"Of course you have—the biggest old
poacher in the county. He shoots half
your pheasants with his wooden leg by
moonlight. What your Chaplain said to
him was entirely profane in the turn of a
text of Holy-Writ; and it shows how our
cloth is spoiled by contact with yours"—
for the Admiral was laughing to himself
at this old tale, which he would not produce before young Scudamore, but loved
to have out with the Rector—"and I hope
it will be a good warning to you, Squire, to
settle no more old gunners on your property. You must understand, Mr. Scudamore, that the Admiral makes a sort of
Naval Hospital, for all his old salts, on his
own estates."

"I am sure it is wonderfully kind in
him," the young man answered, bravely,
"for the poor old fellows are thrown to
the dogs by the country, when it has disabled them. I have not seen much of the
service, but quite enough to know that,
Mr. Twemlow."

"I have seen a great deal, and I say
that it is so. And my good friend knows
it as well as I do, and is one of the first
to lend a helping hand. In all such cases
he does more than I do, whenever they
come within his knowledge. But let us
return to the matter in hand. Here is a
young man, a first-rate sailor, who would
have been under my guardianship, I know,
but for—but for sad circumstances. Is he
to be grinding at Virgil and Ovid till all
his spirit goes out of him, because we have
patched up a very shabby peace? It can
never last long. Every Englishman hates
it, although it may seem to save his pocket. Twemlow, I am no politician. You
read the papers more than I do. How
much longer will this wretched compact
hold? You have predicted the course of
things before."

"And so I will again," replied the
Rector. "Atheism, mockery, cynicism,
blasphemy, lust, and blood-thirstyness cannot rage and raven within a few leagues
of a godly and just nation without stinking in their nostrils. Sir, it is our mission from the Lord to quench Bony, and
to conquer the bullies of Europe. We
don't look like doing it now, I confess.
But do it we shall, in the end, as sure as
the name of our country is England."

"I have no doubt of it," said the Admiral, simply; "but there will be a deal
of fighting betwixt this and then. Blyth,
will you leave me to see what I can do,
whenever we get to work again?"

"I should think that I would, sir, and
never forget it. I am not fond of fighting; but how I have longed to feel myself afloat again!"

CHAPTER XII.
AT THE YEW-TREE.

ALL the common-sense of England,
more abundant in those days than now,
felt that the war had not been fought out,
and the way to the lap of peace could
only be won by vigorous use of the arms.
Some few there were even then, as now
there is a cackling multitude, besotted
enough to believe that facts can be undone by blinking them. But our forefathers on the whole were wise, and knew
that nothing is trampled more basely
than right that will not right itself.
Therefore they set their faces hard, and

THE BIG YEW-TREE.

toughened their hearts like knotted oak, against all that man could do to them. There were no magnificent proclamations, no big vaunts of victory at the buckling on of armour, but the quiet strength of steadfast wills, and the stern resolve to strike when stricken, and try to last the longest. And so their mother-land became the mother of men and freedom.

In November, 1802, the speech from the throne apprised the world that England was preparing. The widest, longest, and deadliest war, since the date of gunpowder, was lowering; and the hearts of all who loved their kin were heavy, but found no help for it.

The sermon which Mr. Twemlow preached in Springhaven church was magnificent. Some parishioners, keeping memory more alert than conscience, declared that they had received it all nine, or it might be ten, years since, when the fighting first was called for. If so, that proved it none the worse, but themselves, for again requiring it. Their Rector told them that they thought too much of their own flesh-pots and fish-kettles, and their country might go to the bottom of the sea, if it left them their own fishing-grounds. And he said that they would wake up some day and find themselves turned into Frenchmen, for all things were possible with the Lord; and then they might smite their breasts, but must confess that they had deserved it. Neither would years of prayer and fasting fetch them back into decent Englishmen; the abomination of desolation would be set up over their doorways, and the scarlet woman of Babylon would revel in their sanctuaries.

"Now don't let none of us be in no hurry," Captain Tugwell said, after dwelling and sleeping upon this form of doctrine; "a man knoweth his own trade the best, the very same way as the parson doth. And I never knew no good to come of any hurry. Our lives are given us by the Lord. And He never would 'a made 'em threescore and ten, or for men of any strength fourscore, if His will had been to jerk us over them. Never did I see no Frenchman as could be turned to an Englishman, not if he was to fast and pray all day, and cut himself with knives at the going down of the sun. My opinion is that Parson Twemlow were touched up by his own conscience for having a nephew more French than English;

and 'Caryl Carne' is the name thereof, with more French than English sound to it."

"Why, he have been gone for years and years," said the landlord of the *Darling Arms*, where the village was holding council; "he have never been seen in these parts since the death of the last Squire Carne, to my knowledge."

"And what did the old Squire die of, John Prater? Not that he were to be called old—younger, I dare say, than I be now. What did he die of, but marrying with a long outlandish 'ooman? A femmel as couldn't speak a word of English, to be anyhow sure of her meaning! Ah, them was bad times at Carne Castle; and as nice a place as need be, until they dipped the property. Six grey horses they were used to go with to London Parliament every year, before the last Squire come of age, as I have heered my father say scores of times, and no lie ever come from his mouth, no more than it could from mine, almost. Then they dropped to four, and then to two, and pretended that the roads were easier."

"When I was down the coast, last week, so far as Littlehampton," said a stout young man in the corner, "a very coorous thing happened me, leastways by my own opinion, and glad shall I be to have the judgment of Cappen Zeb consarning it. There come in there a queer-rigged craft of some sixty ton from Halvers, desiring to set up trade again, or to do some smoogling, or spying perhaps. Her name was the *Doctor Humm*, which seem a great favorite with they Crappos, and her skipper had a queer name too, as if he was two men in one, for he called himself 'Jacks'; a fellow about forty year old, as I hauled out of the sea with a boat-hook one night on the Varners. Well, he seemed to think a good deal of that, though contrary to their nature, and nothing would do but I must go to be fated with him everywhere, if the folk would change his money. He had picked up a decent bit of talk from shipping in the oyster line before the war; and I put his lingo into order for him, for which he was very thankful."

"And so he was bound to be. But you had no call to do it, Charley Bowles." Captain Tugwell spoke severely, and the young man felt that he was wrong, for the elders shook their heads at him, as a traitor to the English language.

"Well, main likely, I went amiss. But

he seemed to take it so uncommon kind of me hitching him with a boat-hook, that we got on together wonderful, and he called me 'Friar Sharley,' and he tried to take up with our manners and customs; but his head was outlandish for English grog. One night he was three sheets in the wind, at a snug little crib by the river, and he took to the brag as is born with them. 'All dis contray in one year now,' says he, nodding over his glass at me, 'shall be of the grand nashong, and I will make a great man of you, Friar Sharley. Do you know what prawns are, my good friend?' Well, I said I had caught a good many in my time; but he laughed and said, 'Prawns will catch you this time. One tousand prawns, all with two hundred men inside him, and the leetle prawns will come to land at your house, Sharley. Bootiful place, quiet sea, no bad rocks. You look out in the morning, and the white coast is made black with them.' Now what do you say to that, Cappen Tugwell?"

"I've a-heered that style of talk many times afore," Master Tugwell answered, solidly; "and all I can say is that I should have punched his head. And you deserve the same thing, Charley Bowles, unless you've got more than that to tell us."

"So I might, Cappen, and I won't deny you there. But the discourse were consarning Squire Carne now just, and the troubles he fell into, before I was come to my judgment yet. Why, an uncle of mine served footman there — Jeremiah Bowles, known to every one, until he was no more heard of."

Nods of assent to the fame of Jeremiah encouraged the stout young man in his tale, and a wedge of tobacco rekindled him.

"Yes, it were a coorous thing indeed, and coorous for me to hear of it, out of all mast-head of Springhaven. Says Moosoo Jacks to me, that night when I boused him up unpretending: 'You keep your feather eye open, my tear,' for such was his way of pronouncing it, 'and you shall arrive to laglore, laglore — and what is still nobler, de monnay. In one two tree month, you shall see a young captain returned to his contray dominion, and then you will go to his side and say Jacks, and he will make present to you a sack of silver.' Well, I hailed the chance of this pretty smart, you may suppose, and I ask-ed him what the sailor's name would be, and surprised I was when he answered *Carne*, or *Carny*, for he gave it in two syllables. Next morning's tide, the *Doctor Humm* cleared out, and I had no other chance of discourse with Moosoo Jacks. But I want to know what you think, Cappen Zeb."

"So you shall," said the captain of Springhaven, sternly. "I think you had better call your Moosoo Jacks 'Master Jackass,' or 'Master Jackanapes,' and put your own name on the back of him. You been with a Frenchman hob and nobbing, and you don't even know how they pronounce themselves, unchristian as it is to do so. 'Jarks' were his name, the very same as Navy beef, and a common one in that country. But to speak of any Carne coming nigh us with French plottings, and of prawns landing here at Springhaven—'tis as likely as I should drop French money into the till of this baccy-box. And you can see that I be not going to play such a trick as that, John Prater."

"Why to my mind there never was bigger stuff talked," the landlord spoke out, without fear of offence, for there was no other sign-board within three miles, "than to carry on in that way, Charley. What they may do at Littlehampton is beyond my knowledge, never having kept a snug crib there, as you was pleased to call it. But at Springhaven 'twould be the wrong place for hatching of French treacheries. We all know one another a deal too well for that, I hope."

"Prater, you are right," exclaimed Mr. Cheeseman, owner of the main shop in the village, and universally respected. "Bowles, you must have an imagination the same as your uncle Jerry had. And to speak of the Carnes in a light way of talking, after all their misfortunes, is terrible. Why, I passed the old castle one night last week, with the moon to one side of it, and only me in my one-horse shay to the other, and none but a man with a first-rate conscience would have had the stomach to do so. However, I seed no ghosts that time, though I did hear some noises as made me use the whip; and the swing of the ivy was black as a hearse. A little drop more of my own rum, John: it gives me quite a chill to think of it."

"I don't take much account of what people say," Harry Shanks, who had a deep clear voice, observed, "without it is

"AFTER THAT THERE IS NOTHING MORE TO BE SAID."—[SEE PAGE 42.]

in my own family.   But my own cousin Bob was coming home one night from a bit of sweethearting at Pebbleridge, when, to save the risk of rabbit-holes in the dark, for he put out his knee-cap one time, what does he do but take the path inland through the wood below Carne Castle— the opposite side to where you was, Mas-ter Cheeseman, and the same side as the moon would be, only she wasn't up that night.   Well, he had some misgivings, as anybody must; still he pushed along, whistling and swinging his stick, and say-ing to himself that there was no such thing as cowardice in our family; till just at the corner where the big yew-tree is, that we sometimes starboard helm by when the tide is making with a nor'west wind; there Bob seed a sight as made his hair crawl. But I won't say another word about it now, and have to go home in the dark by myself arter'ards."

"Come, now, Harry!" "Oh, we can't stand that!" "We'll see you to your door, lad, if you out with it, fair and for-cible."

Of these and other exhortations Harry took no notice, but folded his arms across his breast, and gazed at something which his mind presented.

"Harry Shanks, you will have the man-ners"—Captain Tugwell spoke impressive-ly, not for his own sake, for he knew the tale, and had been consulted about it, but from sense of public dignity—"to finish the story which you began. To begin a yarn of your own accord, and then drop it all of a heap, is not respectful to present company. Springhaven never did allow such tricks, and will not put up with them from any young fellow. If your mean-ing was to drop it, you should never have begun."

Glasses and even pipes rang sharply upon the old oak table in applause of this British sentiment, and the young man, with a sheepish look, submitted to the voice of the public.

"Well, then, all of you know where the big yew-tree stands, at the break of the hill about half a mile inland, and how black it looms among the other stuff. But Bob, with his sweetheart in his head, no doubt, was that full of courage that he forgot all about the old tree, and the mur-der done inside it a hundred and twenty years ago, they say, until there it was, over his head a'most, with the gaps in it staring like ribs at him. 'Bout ship was the word, pretty sharp, you may be sure, when he come to his wits consarning it, and the purse of his lips, as was whistling a jig, went as dry as a bag with the bot-tom out. Through the grey of the night there was sounds coming to him, such as had no right to be in the air, and a sort of a shiver laid hold of his heart, like a cold hand flung over his shoulder. As hard as he could lay foot to the ground, away he went down hill, forgetting of his knee-cap, for such was the condition of his mind and body.

"You must understand, mates, that he hadn't seen nothing to skeer him, but only heard sounds, which come into his ears to make his hair rise; and his mind might have put into them more than there was, for the want of intarpreting. Perhaps this come across him, as soon as he felt at a better distance with his wind short; any-how, he brought up again' a piece of rock-stuff in a hollow of the ground, and be-gun to look skeerily backward. For a bit of a while there was nothing to distemper him, only the dark of the hill and the trees, and the grey light a-coming from the sea in front. But just as he were be-ginning for to call himself a fool, and to pick himself onto his legs for trudging home, he seed a thing as skeered him worse than ever, and fetched him flat upon his lower end.

"From the black of the yew-tree there burst a big light, brighter than a light-house or a blue thunder-bolt, and flying with a long streak down the hollow, just as if all the world was a-blazing. Three times it come, with three different colours, first blue, and then white, and then red as new blood; and poor Bob was in a condi-tion of mind must be seen before saying more of it. If he had been brought up to follow the sea, instead of the shoemaking, maybe his wits would have been more about him, and the narves of his symp-tom more ship-shape. But it never was borne into his mind whatever, to keep a lookout upon the offing, nor even to lie snug in the ferns and watch the yew-tree. All he was up for was to make all sail, the moment his sticks would carry it; and he feared to go nigh his sweetheart any more, till she took up with another fel-low."

"And sarve him quite right," was the judgment of the room, in high fettle with hot rum and water; "to be skeered of his life by a smuggler's signal! Eh, Cappen Zebedee, you know that were it?"

But the captain of Springhaven shook his head.

CHAPTER XIII.
WHENCE, AND WHEREFORE?

AT the rectory, too, ere the end of that week, there was no little shaking of heads almost as wise as Zebedee Tugwell's. Mrs. Twemlow, though nearly sixty years of age, and acquainted with many a sorrow, was as lively and busy and notable as ever, and even more determined to be the mis-tress of the house. For by this time her daughter Eliza, beginning to be twenty-five years old—a job which takes some years in finishing—began at the same time to approve her birth by a vigorous aim at the mastery. For, as everybody said, Miss Eliza was a Carne in blood and breed and fibre. There was little of the Twemlow stock about her—for the Twemlows were mild and humorous—but plenty of the strength and dash and wildness and contemptuous spirit of the ancient Carnes.

Carne *a carne*, as Mr. Twemlow said, when his wife was inclined to be masterful—a derivation confirmed by the family motto, " *Carne non caret carne.*" In the case, however, of Mrs. Twemlow, age, affliction, experience, affection, and perhaps above all her good husband's larger benevolence and placidity, had wrought a great change for the better, and made a nice old lady of her. She was tall and straight and slender still, and knew how to make the most, by grave attire and graceful attitude, of the bodily excellence entailed for ages on the lineage of Carne. Of moral goodness there had not been an equally strict settlement, at least in male heredity. So that Mrs. Twemlow's thoughts about her kith and kindred were rather sad than proud, unless some ignorance was shown about them.

"Poor as I am," said Mr. Twemlow, now consulting with her, " and poor as every beneficed clergyman must be, if this war returns, I would rather have lost a hundred pounds than have heard what you tell me, Maria."

" My dear, I cannot quite see that," his wife made thoughtful answer; "if he only had money to keep up the place, and clear off those nasty incumbrances, I should rejoice at his coming back to live where we have been for centuries."

"My dear, you are too poetical, though the feeling is a fine one. Within the old walls there can scarcely be a room that has a sound floor to it. And as for the roof, when that thunder-storm was, and I took shelter with my pony—well, you know the state I came home in, and all my best clothes on for the Visitation. Luckily there seems to be no rheumatism in your family, Maria; and perhaps he is too young as yet to pay out for it till he gets older. But if he comes for business, and to see to the relics of his property, surely he might have a bedroom here, and come and go at his liking. After all

his foreign fanglements, a course of quiet English life and the tone of English principles might be of the greatest use to him. He would never wish to see the Continent again."

"It is not to be thought of," said Mrs. Twemlow. "I would not have him to live in this house for fifty thousand pounds a year. You are a great deal wiser than I am, Joshua; but of his nature you know nothing, whereas I know it from his childhood. And Eliza is so strong-willed and stubborn—you dislike, of course, to hear me say it, but it is the fact—it is, my dear. And I would rather stand by our daughter's grave than see her fall in love with Caryl Carne. You know what a handsome young man he must be now, and full of French style and frippery. I am sure it is most kind of you to desire to help my poor family; but you would rue the day, my dear, that brought him beneath our quiet roof. I have lost my only son, as it seems, by the will of the Lord, who afflicts us. But I will not lose my only daughter, by any such folly of my own."

Tears rolled down Mrs. Twemlow's cheeks as she spoke of her mysterious affliction; and her husband, who knew that she was not weak-minded, consoled her by sharing her sorrow.

"It shall be exactly as you like," he said, after a quiet interval. " You say that no answer is needed; and there is no address to send one to. We shall hear of it, of course, when he takes possession, if, indeed, he is allowed to do so."

"Who is to prevent him from coming, if he chooses, to live in the home of his ancestors ? The estates are all mortgaged, and the park is gone, turned into a pound for Scotch cattle-breeding. But the poor old castle belongs to us still, because no one would take the expense of it."

"And because of the stories concerning it, Maria. Your nephew Caryl is a brave young fellow if he means to live there all alone, and I fear he can afford himself no company. You understand him so much better: what do you suppose his motive is ?"

"I make no pretence to understand him, dear, any more than his poor father could. My dear brother was of head-strong order, and it did him no good to contradict him, and indeed it was dangerous to do so; but his nature was as simple as a child's almost, to any one accustomed to him. If he had not married that grand French lady, who revelled in every extravagance, though she knew how we all were impoverished, he might have been living and in high position now, though a good many years my senior. And the worst of it was that he did it at a time when he ought to have known so much better. However, he paid for it bitterly enough, and his only child was set against him."

"A very sad case altogether," said the rector. "I remember, as if it were yesterday, how angry poor Montagu was with me. You remember what words he used, and his threat of attacking me with his horsewhip. But he begged my pardon, most humbly, as soon as he saw how thoroughly right I was. You are like him in some things, as I often notice, but not quite so generous in confessing you were wrong."

"Because I don't do it as he did, Joshua. You would never understand me if I did. But of course for a man you can make allowance. My rule is to do it both for men and women, quite as fairly as if one was the other."

"Certainly, Maria — certainly. And therefore you can do it, and have always done it, even for poor Josephine. No doubt there is much to be pleaded, by a candid and gentle mind, on her behalf."

"What! that dreadful creature who ruined my poor brother, and called herself the *Countess de Lune*, or some such nonsense! No, Joshua, no! I have not so entirely lost all English principle as to quite do that. Instead of being largeness, that would be mere looseness."

"There are many things, however, that we never understood, and perhaps never shall in this world," Mr. Twemlow continued, as if talking to himself, for reason on that subject would be misaddressed to her; "and nothing is more natural than that young Caryl should side with his mother, who so petted him, against his poor father, who was violent and harsh, especially when he had to pay such bills. But perhaps our good nephew has amassed some cash, though there seems to be but little on the Continent, after all this devastation. Is there anything, Maria, in his letter to enable us to hope that he is coming home with money?"

"Not a word, I am afraid," Mrs. Twemlow answered, sadly. "But take it, my dear, and read it to me slowly. You make

things so plain, because of practice every Sunday. Oh, Joshua, I never can be sure which you are greatest in—the Lessons or the Sermon. But before you begin I will shoot the bolt a little, as if it had caught by accident. Eliza does rush in upon us sometimes in the most unbecoming, unladylike way. And I never can get you to reprove her."

"It would be as much as my place is worth, as the maids say when imagined to have stolen sugar. And I must not read this letter so loud as the Lessons, unless you wish Lizzie to hear every word, for she has all her mother's quick senses. There is not much of it, and the scrawl seems hasty. We might have had more for three and fourpence. But I am not the one to grumble about bad measure—as the boy said about old Busby. Now, Maria, listen, but say nothing; if feminine capacity may compass it. Why, bless my heart, every word of it is French!" The rector threw down his spectacles, and gazed at his wife reproachfully. But she smiled with superior innocence.

"What else could you expect, after all his years abroad? I cannot make out the whole of it, for certain. But surely it is not beyond the compass of masculine capacity."

"Yes, it is, Maria; and you know it well enough. No honest Englishman can endure a word of French. Latin, or Greek, or even Hebrew—though I took to that rather late in life. But French is only fit for women, and very few of them can manage it. Let us hear what this Frenchman says."

"He is not a Frenchman, Joshua. He is an Englishman, and probably a very fine one. I won't be sure about all of his letter, because it is so long since I was at school; and French books are generally unfit to read. But the general meaning is something like this:

'MY BELOVED AND HIGHLY VALUED AUNT,—Since I heard from you there are many years now, but I hope you have held me in memory. I have the intention of returning to the country of England, even in this bad time of winter, when the climate is most funereal. I shall do my best to call back, if possible, the scattered ruins of the property, and to institute again the name which my father made displeasing. In this good work you will, I have faith, afford me your

best assistance, and the influence of your
high connection in the neighbourhood.
Accept, dear aunt, the assurance of my
highest consideration, of the most sincere
and the most devoted, and allow me the
honour of writing myself your most loving and respectful nephew,
                              'CARYL CARNE.'

Now, Joshua, what do you think of that?"

"Fine words and no substance; like all
French stuff. And he never even mentions me, who gave him a top, when he
should have had the whip. I will not
pretend to understand him, for he always
was beyond me. Dark and excitable,
moody and capricious, haughty and sarcastic, and devoid of love for animals.
You remember his pony, and what he did
to it, and the little dog that crawled upon
her stomach towards him. For your sake
I would have put up with him, my dear,
and striven to improve his nature, which
is sure to be much worse at six-and-twen-
ty, after so many years abroad. But I
confess it is a great relief to me that you
wisely prefer not to have him in this
house, any more at least than we can
help it. But who comes here? What a
hurry we are in! Lizzie, my darling, be
patient."

"Here's this plague of a door barred
and bolted again! Am I not to have an
atom of breakfast, because I just happened to oversleep myself? The mornings
get darker and darker; it is almost impossible to see to dress oneself."

"There is plenty of tinder in the
house, Eliza, and plenty of good tallow
candles," Mrs. Twemlow replied, having
put away the letter, while her husband
let the complainant in. "For the third
time this week we have had prayers without you, and the example is shocking for
the servants. We shall have to establish
the rule you suggest—too late to pray for
food, too late to get it. But I have kept
your help of bacon hot, quite hot, by the
fire. And the teapot is under the cozy."

"Thank you, dear mother," the young
lady answered, careless of words, if deeds
were in her favour, and too clever to argue
the question. "I suppose there is no kind
of news this morning to reward one for
getting up so early."

"Nothing whatever for you, Miss Lizzie," said her father, as soon as he had
kissed her. "But the paper is full of the
prospects of war, and the extent of the

preparations. If we are driven to fight
again, we shall do it in earnest, and not
spare ourselves."

"Nor our enemies either, I do hope
with all my heart. How long are we to
be afraid of them? We have always invaded the French till now. And for them
to talk of invading us! There is not a bit
of spirit left in this island, except in the
heart of Lord Nelson."

"What a hot little patriot this child
is!" said the father, with a quiet smile at
her. "What would she say to an Englishman, who was more French than English, and would only write French letters?
And yet it might be possible to find such
people."

"If such a wretch existed," cried Miss
Twemlow, "I should like to crunch him
as I crunch this toast. For a Frenchman I can make all fair allowance, because he cannot help his birth. But for
an Englishman to turn Frenchman—"

"However reluctant we may be to allow it," the candid rector argued, "they
are the foremost nation in the world, just
now, for energy, valour, decision, discipline, and I fear I must add patriotism.
The most wonderful man who has appeared in the world for centuries is their leader, and by land his success has been almost unbroken. If we must have war
again, as I fear we must, and very speedily, our chief hope must be that the Lord
will support His cause against the scoffer
and the infidel, the libertine and the assassin."

"You see how beautifully your father
puts it, Eliza; but he never abuses people.
That is a habit in which, I am sorry to
say, you indulge too freely. You show
no good feeling to anybody who differs
from you in opinion, and you talk as if
Frenchmen had no religion, no principles, and no humanity. And what do
you know about them, pray? Have you
ever spoken to a Frenchman? Have you
ever even seen one? Would you know
one if you even set eyes upon him?"

"Well, I am not at all sure that I
should," the young lady replied, being
thoroughly truthful; "and I have no wish
for the opportunity. But I have seen a
French woman, mother; and that is quite
enough for me. If they are so, what must
the men be?"

"There is a name for this process of
feminine reasoning, this cumulative and
syncopetic process of the mind, entirely

feminine (but regarded by itself as rational), a name which I used to know well in the days when I had the ten Fallacies at my fingers' ends, more tenaciously perhaps than the Decalogue. Strange to say, the name is gone from my memory; but —but—"

"But then you had better go after it, my dear," his wife suggested with authority. "If your only impulse when you hear reason is to search after hard names for it, you are safer outside of its sphere altogether."

"I am struck with the truth of that remark," observed the rector; "and the more so because I descry a male member of our race approaching, with a hat—at once the emblem and the crown of sound reason. Away with all fallacies; it is Church-warden Cheeseman!"

CHAPTER XIV.

A HORRIBLE SUGGESTION.

"CAN you guess what has brought me down here in this hurry?" Lord Nelson asked Admiral Darling, having jumped like a boy from his yellow post-chaise, and shaken his old friend's broad right hand with his slender but strenuous left one, even as a big bell is swung by a thin rope. "I have no time to spare—not a day, not an hour; but I made up my mind to see you before I start. I cannot expect to come home alive, and, except for one reason, I should not wish it."

"Nonsense!" said the Admiral, who was sauntering near his upper gate, and enjoying the world this fine spring morning; "you are always in such a confounded hurry! When you come to my time of life, you will know better. What is it this time? The Channel fleet again?"

"No, no; Billy Blue keeps that, thank God! I hate looking after a school of herring-boats. The Mediterranean for me, my friend. I received the order yesterday, and shall be at sea by the twentieth."

"I am very glad to hear it, for your sake. If ever there was a restless fellow —in the good old times we were not like that. Come up to the house and talk about it; at least they must take the horses out. They are not like you; they can't work forever."

"And they don't get knocked about like me; though one of them has lost his star-board eye, and he sails and steers all the better for it. Let them go up to the stable, Darling, while you come down to the beach with me. I want to show you something."

"What crotchet is in his too active brain now?" the elder and stronger man asked himself, as he found himself hooked by the right arm, and led down a track through the trees scarcely known to himself, and quite out of sight from the village. "Why, this is not the way to the beach! However, it is never any good to oppose him. He gets his own way so because of his fame. Or perhaps that's the way he got his fame. But to show me about over my own land! But let him go on, let him go on."

"You are wondering, I dare say, what I am about," cried Nelson, stopping suddenly, and fixing his sound eye—which was wonderfully keen, though he was always in a fright about it—upon the large and peaceful blinkers of his ancient commander; "but now I shall be able to convince you, though I am not a land-surveyor, nor even a general of land-forces. If God Almighty prolongs my life—which is not very likely—it will be that I may meet that scoundrel, Napoleon Bonaparte, on dry land. I hear that he is eager to encounter me on the waves, himself commanding a line-of-battle ship. I should send him to the devil in a quarter of an hour. And ashore I could astonish him, I think, a little, if I had a good army to back me up. Remember what I did at Bastia, in the land that produced this monster, and where I was called the Brigadier; and again, upon the coast of Italy, I showed that I understood all their dry-ground business. Tush! I can beat him, ashore and afloat; and I shall, if I live long enough. But this time the villain is in earnest, I believe, with his trumpery invasion; and as soon as he hears that I am gone, he will make sure of having his own way. We know, of course, there are fifty men as good as myself to stop him, including you, my dear Darling; but everything goes by reputation—the noise of the people—praise-puff. That's all I get; while the luckier fellows, like Cathcart, get the prize-money. But I don't want to grumble. Now what do you see?"

"Well, I see you, for one thing," the Admiral answered, at his leisure, being quite inured to his friend's quick fire, "and wearing a coat that would be a disgrace to any other man in the navy. And further on I see some land that I never shall get my rent for; and beyond that nothing but the sea, with a few fishing-craft inshore, and in the offing a sail, an outward-bound East Indiaman—some fool who wouldn't wait for convoy, with war as good as proclaimed again."

"Nothing but the sea, indeed ? The sweep of the land, and the shelter of the bay, the shoaling of the shore without a rock to break it, the headland that shuts out both wind and waves; and outside the headland, off Pebbleridge, deep water for a fleet of line-of-battle ships to anchor and command the land approaches—more-over, a stream of the purest water from deep and never-failing springs—Darling, the place of all places in England for the French to land is opposite to your front door."

"I am truly obliged to you for predict-ing, and to them for doing it, if ever they attempt such impudence. If they find out that you are away, they can also find out that I am here, as commander of the sea defences, from Dungeness to Selsey-Bill."

"That will make it all the more de-lightful to land at your front door, my friend; and all the easier to do it. My own plan is to strike with all force at the head-quarters of the enemy, because the most likely to be unprepared. About a year ago, when I was down here, a little before my dear father's death, without your commission I took command of your fishing-craft coming home for their Sun-day, and showed them how to take the beach, partly to confirm my own suspi-cions. There is no other landing on all the south coast, this side of Hayling Isl-and, fit to be compared with it for the use of flat-bottomed craft, such as most of Boney's are. And remember the set of the tide, which makes the fortunes of your fishermen. To be sure, he knows no-thing of that himself; but he has sharp rogues about him. If they once made good their landing here, it would be diffi-cult to dislodge them. It must all be done from the land side then, for even a 42-gun frigate could scarcely come near enough to pepper them. They love shoal water, the skulks—and that has en-abled them to baffle me so often. Not that they would conquer the country—all brag—but still it would be a nasty predica-ment, and scare the poor cockneys like the very devil."

"But remember the distance from Bou-logne, Hurry. If they cannot cross twen-ty-five miles of channel in the teeth of our ships, what chance would they have when the distance is nearer eighty ?"

"A much better chance, if they knew how to do it. All our cruisers would be to the eastward. One afternoon perhaps, when a haze is on, they make a feint with light craft toward the Scheldt—every Brit-ish ship crowds sail after them. Then, at dusk, the main body of the expedition slips with the first of the ebb to the westward; they meet the flood tide in mid-channel, and using their long sweeps are in Spring-haven, or at any rate the lightest of them, by the top of that tide, just when you are shaving. You laugh at such a thought of mine. I tell you, my dear friend, that with skill and good luck it is easy; and do it they should, if they were under my command."

If anybody else had even talked of such a plan as within the bounds of like-lihood, Admiral Darling would have been almost enraged. But now he looked doubtfully, first at the sea (as if it might be thick with prames already), and then at the land—which was his own—as if the rent might go into a Frenchman's pocket, and then at his old and admired friend, who had ruined his sleep for the summer.

"Happily they are not under your com-mand, and they have no man to compare with you;" he spoke rather nervously; while Nelson smiled, for he loved the praise which he had so well earned; "and if it were possible for you to talk non-sense, I should say that you had done it now. But two things surely you have overlooked. In the first place, the French can have no idea of the special opportu-nities this place affords. And again, if they had, they could do nothing, with-out a pilot well acquainted with the spot. Though the landing is so easy, there are shoals outside, very intricate and danger-ous, and known to none except the na-tives of the place, who are jealous to the last degree about their knowledge."

"That is true enough; and even I should want a pilot here, though I know every spit of sand eastward. But away fly both your difficulties if there should happen to be a local traitor."

"A traitor at Springhaven! Such a thing is quite impossible. You would laugh at yourself, if you only knew the character of our people. There never has been, and there never will be, a Springhaven man capable of treachery."

"That is good news, ay, and strange news too," the visitor answered, with his left hand on his sword, for he was now in full though rather shabby uniform. "There are not many traitors in England, I believe; but they are as likely to be found in one place as another, according to my experience. Well, well, I am very glad you have no such scoundrels here. I won't say a single word against your people, who are as fine a lot as any in the south of England, and as obstinate as any I could wish to see. Of an obstinate man I can always make good; with a limp one I can do nothing. But bear in mind every word you have heard me say, because I came down on purpose about it; and I generally penetrate the devices of the enemy, though they lead me on a wild-goose-chase sometimes, but only when our own folk back them up, either by lies or stupidity. Now look once more, for you are slower as well as a great deal wiser than I am. You see how this land-locked bight of Springhaven seems made by the Almighty for flat-bottomed craft, if once they can find their way into it; while the trend of the coast towards Pebbleridge is equally suited for the covering fleet, unless a gale from southwest comes on, in which case they must run for it. And you see that the landed force, by crowning the hill above your house and across the valley, might defy our noble Volunteers, and all that could be brought against them, till a hundred thousand cutthroats were established here. And Boney would make his head-quarters at the Hall, with a French cook in your kitchen, and a German butler in your cellar, and my pretty godchild to wait upon him, for the rogue loves pretty maidens."

"That will do. That is quite enough. No wonder you have written poems, Nelson, as you told us the last time you were here. If my son had only got your imagination—but perhaps you know something more than you have told me. Perhaps you have been told—"

"Never mind about that," the great sea-captain answered, turning away as if on springs; "it is high time for me to be off again, and my chaise has springs on her cables."

"Not she. I have ordered her to be docked. Dine with us you shall this day, if we have to dine two hours earlier, and though Mother Cloam rage furiously. How much longer do you suppose you can carry on at this pace ? Look at me. I have double your bodily substance; but if I went on as you do—you remember the twenty-four-pounder old Hotcoppers put into the launch, and fired it, in spite of all I could say to him ? Well, you are just the same. You have not got the scantling for the metal you carry and are always working. You will either blow up, or else scuttle yourself. Look here, how your seams are opening!" Here Admiral Darling thrust his thumb through the ravelled seam of his old friend's coat, which made him jump back, for he loved his old coat. "Yes, and you will go in the very same way. I wonder how any coat lasts so much as a month, with you inside it."

"This coat," said Nelson, who was most sweet-tempered with any one he loved, though hot as pepper when stirred up by strangers—"this coat is the one I wore at Copenhagen, and a sounder and kinder coat never came on a man's back. Charles Darling, you have made a bad hit this time. If I am no more worn out than this coat is, I am fit to go to sea for a number of years yet. And I hope to show it to a good many Frenchmen, and take as many ships, every time they show fight, as there are buttons on it."

"Then you will double all your captures at the Nile;" such a series of buttons had this coat, though mostly loose upon their moorings, for his guardian angel was not "domestic"; "but you may be trusted not to let them drift so. You have given me a lesson in coast-defence, and now you shall be boarded by the ladies. You possess some gifts of the tongue, my friend, as well as great gifts of hand and eye; but I will back my daughters to beat you there. Come up to the house. No turning of tail."

"I spoke very well in the House of Lords," said Nelson, in his simple way, "in reply to the speech of his Majesty, and again about the Commissioner's Bill; or at least everybody tells me so. But in the House of Ladies I hold my tongue, because there is abundance without it."

This, however, he failed to do when the matter came to the issue; for his godchild Horatia, more commonly called Dolly, happened to be in the mood for taking outrageous liberties with him. She possessed very little of that gift—most precious among women—the sense of veneration; and to her a hero was only a man heroic in acts of utility. "He shall do it," she said to Faith, when she heard that he was come again; "if I have to kiss him, he shall do it; and I don't like kissing those old men."

"Hush!" said her elder sister. "Dolly, you do say things so recklessly. One would think that you liked to kiss younger men! But I am sure that is not your meaning. I would rather kiss Lord Nelson than all the young men in the kingdom."

"Well done, Faith! All the young men in the kingdom! How recklessly you do say things! And you can't kiss him—he is *my* godfather. But just see how I get round him, if you have wits enough to understand it."

So these two joined in their kind endeavour to make the visitor useful, the object being so good that doubtful means might be excused for it. In different ways and for divers reasons, each of these young ladies now had taken to like Blyth Scudamore. Faith, by power of pity first, and of grief for her own misfortunes, and of admiration for his goodness to his widowed mother—which made his best breeches shine hard at the knees; and Dolly, because of his shy adoration, and dauntless defence of her against a cow (whose calf was on the road to terminate in veal), as well as his special skill with his pocketknife in cutting out figures that could dance, and almost sing; also his great

gifts, when the tide was out, of making rare creatures run after him. What avails to explore female reason precisely?—their minds were made up that he must be a captain, if Nelson had to build the ship with his one hand for him.

"After that, there is nothing more to be said," confessed the vanquished warrior; "but the daughters of an Admiral should know that no man can be posted until he has served his time as lieutenant; and this young hero of yours has never even held the King's commission yet. But as he has seen some service, and is beyond the age of a middy, in the present rush he might get appointed as junior lieutenant, if he had any stout seconders. Your father is the man, he is always at hand, and can watch his opportunity. He knows more big-wigs than I do, and he has not given offence where I have. Get your father, my dears, to attend to it."

But the ladies were not to be so put off, for they understood the difference of character. Lord Nelson was as sure to do a thing as Admiral Darling was to drop it if it grew too heavy. Hence it came to pass that Blyth Scudamore, though failing of the *Victory* and *Amphion*—which he would have chosen, if the choice were his—received with that cheerful philosophy (which had made him so dear to the school-boys, and was largely required among them) his appointment as junior lieutenant to the 38-gun frigate *Leda*, attached to the Channel fleet under Cornwallis, whose business it was to deal with the French flotilla of invasion.

THE HOME ACRE.

BY E. P. ROE.

IV.—THE VINEYARD AND ORCHARD.

HE who proposes to plant grape-vines will scarcely fail to take the sensible course of inspecting the varieties already producing fruit in his locality. From causes often too obscure to be learned with certainty, excellent kinds will prove to be well adapted to one locality and fail in others. If, therefore, when calling on a neighbor during August, September, or October, we are shown a vine producing fruit abundantly that is suited to our taste, a vine also which manifests unmistakable vigor, we may be reasonably sure

that it belongs to a variety which we should have, especially if it be growing in a soil and exposure somewhat similar to our garden plot. A neighbor worthy of the name will be glad to give us a few cuttings from his vine at the time of its annual pruning, and with very little trouble we also can soon possess the desired variety. When the vine is trimmed, either make yourself or have your friend make a few cuttings of sound wood from that season's growth. About eight inches is a good length for these vine slips, and they should contain at least two buds. Let each slip be cut off smoothly just under the lowest bud, and extend an inch or two above the uppermost bud. If these cuttings are obtained in November or December, they can be put into a little box with some of the moist soil of the garden, and buried in the ground below the usual frost line, say a foot or eighteen inches in our latitude. The simple object is to keep them in a cool, even temperature, but not a frosty one. Early in April dig up the box, open a trench in a moist but not wet part of the garden, and insert the cuttings perpendicularly in the soil so that the upper bud is covered barely one inch. In filling up the trench, press the soil carefully yet firmly about the cuttings, and spread over the surface just about them a little fine manure. The cuttings should be a foot apart from each other in the row. Do not let the ground become dry about them at any time during the summer. By fall these cuttings will probably have thrown out an abundance of roots, and have made from two to three feet of vine. In this case they can be taken up and set out where they are to fruit. Possibly but one or two of them have started vigorously. The backward ones would better be left to grow another year in the cutting bed. Probably we will not wish to cultivate more than one or two vines of the variety, but it is just as easy to start several cuttings as one, and by this course we guard against failure, and are able to select the most vigorous plant for our garden. By taking good care of the others we soon derive one of the best pleasures which our acre can afford—that of giving to a friend something which will enhance the productiveness of his acre, and add to his enjoyment for years to come.

Not only on our neighbor's grounds, but also on our own, we shall discover that some varieties are unusually vigorous, productive, and well adapted to our locality, and we may very naturally wish to have more vines of the same sort, especially if the fruit is to our taste. We can either increase this kind by cuttings, as has been described, or we can layer part of the vine that has won our approval by well-doing. I shall take the latter course with several delicious varieties in my vineyard. Some kinds of grapes do not root readily as cuttings, but there is little chance of failure in layering. This process is simply the laying down of a branch of a vine in early spring, and covering it lightly with soil so that some buds will be beneath the surface and others just at or a little above the surface. Those beneath will form roots, the others shoots, which by fall should be good vines for planting. Every bud that can reach the air and light will start upward, and thus there may be a thick growth of incipient vines that will crowd and enfeeble each other. The probabilities are that only two or three new vines are wanted; therefore all the others should be rubbed off at the start, so that the strength of the parent plant and the new roots that are forming may go into those few shoots designed to become eventually a part of our vineyard. If we wish only one vine, then but one bud should grow from the layer; if two vines, then two buds. The fewer buds that are permitted to grow, the stronger vines they make.

It must be remembered that this layer, for the greater part of the growing season, is drawing its sustenance from the parent plant to which it is still attached. Therefore the other branches of this vine thus called upon for unusual effort should be permitted to fruit but sparingly. We should not injure and enfeeble the original vine in order to get others like it. For this reason we advise that no more buds be permitted to grow from the layer than we actually need ourselves. To injure a good vine and deprive ourselves of fruit that we may have plants to give away, is to love one's neighbor better than one's self—a thing permitted, but not required. When our vines are pruned we can make as many cuttings as we choose, either to sell or give away.

The ground in which a layer is placed should be very rich, and its surface around the young growing vines be always kept moist and free of weeds. In the fall, after the leaves have fallen and the wood is ripe and hard, cut off the layered branch close to the vine, and with a garden fork gently and carefully lift the branch, with all its roots and young vines attached, out of the soil. First cut the young vines back to three or four buds, then separate them from the branch from which they grew, being sure to give to each plant plenty of roots, and the roots *back* of the point from which it grew—that is, those roots nearest the parent plant from which the branch was layered. All the old wood of the branch that is naked, free of roots, should be cut off. The young shoots thus separated are now independent vines, and can be set out at once where they are to fruit. If you have a variety that does not do well or that you do not like, dig it out, enrich the soil, and put one of your favorites in its place.

We will now consider briefly the diseases and insect enemies of the grape. A vine may be doomed to ill health from its very location. Mr. Hussman, a grape culturist of great experience and wide observation, writes: "Those localities may generally be considered safe for the grape in which there are no miasmatic influences. Where malaria and fevers prevail there is no safety for the crop, as the vine seems to be as susceptible to such influences as human beings."

Taking this statement literally, we may well ask, where, then, can grapes be grown? According to physicians, malaria has become one of the most generally diffused products of the country. When a man asserts that it is not in his locality, we feel sure that if pressed he will admit that it is "around the corner." Country populations still survive, however, and so does grape culture. Yet there are lowlying regions which from defective drainage are distinctively and, it would almost seem, hopelessly malarial. In such localities but few varieties of the vine will thrive. The people who are compelled to live there, or who choose to do so, should experiment until they obtain varieties so hardy and vigorous that they will triumph over everything. The best course with grape diseases is not to have them; in other words, to recognize the fact at once that certain varieties of the grape will not thrive and be productive of good fruit unless the soil and climate suit them. The proprietor of the home acre can usually learn by a little inquiry or observation whether grapes thrive in his locality. If there is much complaint of mildew, grape-rot, and general feebleness of growth, he should seek to plant only the most hardy and vigorous kinds.

As I have said before, our cultivated grapes are derived from several native species found growing wild, and some now valued highly for wine-making are nothing but wild grapes domesticated, as, for instance, Norton's Virginia, belonging to the *œstivalis* class. The original plant of this variety was found growing upon an island in the Potomac by Dr. Norton, of Virginia.

The species from which the greatest number of well known grapes is obtained is the *Vitis labrusca*, the common wild or fox grape, found growing in woods and thickets, usually where the ground is moist, from Canada to the Gulf. The dark purple berries, averaging about three-quarters of an inch in diameter, ripen in September, and they contain a tough, musky pulp. Yet this "slip of wilderness" is the parent of the refined Catawba, the delicious Brighton, and the magnificent white grape Lady Washington—indeed, of all the black, red, and white grapes with which most people are familiar. Our earliest grapes, which ripen in August, as well as some of the latest, like the Isabella, come from the *labrusca* species. It is said that the *labrusca* class will not thrive in the extreme South, and, with the exception of the high mountain slopes, this appears reasonable to the student of the vine. It is said that but few of this class will endure the long hot summers of France. But there are great differences among the varieties derived from this native species. For example, the Concord thrives almost anywhere, while even here upon the Hudson we can scarcely grow the Catawba with certainty. It is so good a grape, however, that I persist in making the effort, with varying success, but I should not recommend it or many of its class for those localities not specially suited to the grape.

I will now name a few varieties which have proved to be or promise to be the most thrifty and productive wherever grapes can be grown at all. The *labrusca* class: Black—Concord, Wilder, Worden, Amenia, Early Canada, Telegraph or Christine, Moore's Early. Red—Wyoming, Goethe, Lindley, Beauty, Brighton, Perkins (pale red), and Agawam. White—Rebecca, Martha, Allen's Hybrid, Lady Pocklington, Prentiss, Lady Washington. These are all fine grapes, and they have succeeded throughout wide areas of country. Any and all are well worth a trial, but if the grower finds that some of them are weak and diseased in his grounds, I should advise that he root them out and replace them with those which thrive. The Niagara is highly praised, and may make good all that is claimed for it.

Of the *œstivalis* class I can recommend the Cynthiana and the Herbemont or Warren for the extreme South. Both of them are black. There are new varieties of this vigorous species which promise well.

The *cordifolia* species promises to furnish some fine, hardy, and productive grapes, of which the Amber is an example. The Elvira, a pale yellow grape, is highly praised by Mr. Hussman. Although the Bacchus is distinctively a wine grape, I have already said that its flavor when fully ripe was agreeable to me. The only difficulty in growing it is to keep the ground poor and use the pruning-knife freely.

I have enlarged on this point, for I wish to direct the mind of the reader to the fact that there are many very hardy grapes. I congratulate those who, with the taste of a connoisseur, have merely to sample until they find just the varieties that suit them, and then to plant these kinds in their genial soil and favored locality. At the same time I would like to prevent others from worrying along with unsatisfactory varieties, or from reaching the conclusion that they cannot grow grapes in their region or garden. Let them rather admit that they cannot raise some kinds, but may others. If a variety was persistently diseased, feeble, and unproductive under good treatment, I would root it out rather than to continue to nurse and coddle it.

When mildew and grape-rot first appear, the evil can often be remedied in part by dusting the vines with sulphur, and continuing the process until the disease is cured, if it ever is. I have never had occasion to do this, and will not do it. A variety that often requires such nursing in this favored locality should be discarded.

There is one kind of disease, or feebleness rather, to which we are subject everywhere, and from which few varieties are exempt. It is the same kind of weakness which would be developed in a fine sound horse if we drove him until he dropped down every time we took him out. Cultivated vines are so far removed from their natural conditions that they will often bear themselves to death like a peach-tree. To permit this is a true instance of avarice overreaching itself, or the evil may result from ignorance or neglect. Close pruning in autumn and thinning out the crowding clusters soon after they have formed is the remedy. If a vine had been so enfeebled, I should cut it back rigorously, feed it well, and permit it to bear very little fruit, if any, for a year.

Of insect enemies we have the phylloxera of bad eminence, which has so dismayed Europe. The man who could discover and patent an adequate remedy in France might soon rival a Rothschild in his wealth. The remedy abroad is also ours—to plant varieties which are phylloxera-proof, or nearly so. Fortunately we have many which defy this pestiferous little rootlouse, and European vine growers have been importing them by the million. They are still used chiefly as stocks on which to graft varieties of the *vinifera* species. In California, grapes of the *vinifera* or European species are generally cultivated, but the phylloxera is at its destructive work among them. The wine grapes of the future throughout the world may be developed from the hardy *æstivalis* and *cordifolia* classes. In many localities, even in this new land, varieties like the Delaware succumb to this scourge of foreign vineyards.

The aphis, or plant-louse, sometimes attacks the young tender shoots of the vine. The moment they appear, take off the shoot, and crush it on a board with the foot. Leaf-rollers, the grape-vine sphinx, and caterpillars in general must be caught by hand and killed. Usually they are not very numerous. The horrid little rose-chafers or rose-bugs are sometimes very destructive. Our best course is to take a basin of water and jar them off into it—they fall readily—and then scald them to death. We may discover lady-bugs—small red or yellow and black beetles—among our vines, and many people, I fear, will destroy them with the rest. We should take off our hats to them and wish them godspeed. In their destruction of aphides and thrips they are among our best friends. The camel-cricket is another active destroyer of injurious insects. Why do not our schools teach a little practical natural history? Once, when walking in the Catskills, I saw the burly driver of a stage-load of ladies bound out of his vehicle to kill a garter-snake, the pallid females looking on, meanwhile, as if the earth was being rid of some terrible and venomous thing. They ought to have known that the poor little reptile was as harmless as one of their own garters, and quite as useful in its way. Every country boy and girl should be taught to recognize all our helpers in our incessant fight with insect enemies—a fight which must be maintained with more organized vigor and intelligence than at present if horticulture is ever to reach its best development.

Wasps and hornets often swarm about the sweet and early ripe varieties. A wide-mouthed bottle partially filled with molasses and water will entrap and drown great numbers of these ugly customers. Some of our favorite birds try our patience not a little. During the early summer I never wearied of watching the musical orioles flashing with their bright hues in and out of the foliage about the house, but when the early grapes were ripe they took pay for their music with the *sang-froid* of a favorite *prima donna*. On one occasion I saw three or four alight on a Diana vine, and in five minutes they had spoiled a dozen clusters. If they would only take a bunch and eat it up clean, one would readily share with them, for there would be enough for all, but the dainty little epicures puncture an indefinite number of berries, merely taking a sip from each. Then the wasps and bees come along and finish the clusters. The cardinal, cat-bird, and our unrivalled songster the wood-thrush, all help themselves in the same wasteful fashion. One can't shoot wood-thrushes. We would almost as soon think of killing off our Nilssons, Nevadas, and Carys. The only thing to do is to protect the clusters, and this can be accomplished in several ways. The most expeditious and satisfactory method is to cover the vines of early grapes with cheap mosquito netting. Another method is to make little bags of this netting and enclose each cluster. Last fall, two of my children tied up many hundreds of clusters in little paper bags, which can be procured at wholesale for a trifling sum. The two lower corners of the paper bags should be clipped off to permit the rain to pass freely through them. Clusters ripen better, last longer on the vine, and acquire a more exquisite bloom and flavor in this retirement than if exposed to light as well as to birds and wasps. Not the fruit but the foliage of the grape-vine needs the sun.

Few of the early grapes will keep long after being taken from the vine, but some of the later ones can be preserved well into the winter by putting them in small boxes and storing them where the temperature is cool, even, and dry. Some of the wine grapes, like Norton's Virginia, will keep under these conditions almost like winter apples. One October day I took a stone pot of the largest size and put in first a layer of Isabella grapes, then a double thickness of straw paper, then alternate layers of grapes and paper until the pot was full. A cloth was next pasted over the stone cover so as to make the pot water-tight. The pot was then buried on a dry knoll below the reach of frost, and dug up again on New-Year's Day. The grapes looked and tasted as if they had just been picked from the vine.

For the mysteries of hybridizing and raising new seedlings, grafting, hot-house and cold grapery culture, the reader must look in more extended works than this, and to writers who have had experience in these matters.

We shall next consider three fruits which upon the home acre may be regarded as forming a natural group—peaches, plums, and raspberries. If any one expresses surprise that the last-named fruit should be given this relationship, I have merely to reply that the raspberry thrives in the partial shade produced by such small trees as the peach and plum. Where there is need of economy of space it is well to take advantage of this fact, for but few products of the garden give any satisfaction when contending with roots below and shade above.

We have taken it for granted that some grape-vines would be planted in the two borders extending through the centre of the garden, also that there would be spaces left which might be filled with peach and plum trees and small flowering shrubs. If there is to be a good-sized poultry-yard upon the acre, we should advise that plums be planted in that; but we will speak of this fruit later, and now give our attention to that fruit which to the taste of many is unrivalled—the peach.

With the exception of the strawberry, it is perhaps the only fruit for which I prefer spring planting. At the same time, I should not hesitate to set out the trees in autumn. The ground should be good, but not too highly fertilized. I prefer young trees but one year old from the bud. If set out in the fall, I should mound up the earth eighteen inches about them to protect the roots and stem, and to keep the tree firmly in the soil. With this precaution, I am not sure but that fall planting has the greater advantage, except when the climate is very severe and subject to great alternations. Plant with the same care and on the same principles which have been already described. If a careful system of pruning is to be adopted, the trees may be set out twelve feet apart, but if they are to be left to grow at will, which I regret to say is the usual practice, they should be planted fifteen feet from each other.

There are many good reasons why the common orchard culture of the peach should not be adopted in the garden. There is no fruit more neglected and ill-treated than the beautiful and delicious peach. The trees are very cheap, usually costing but a few cents each; they are bought by the thousand from careless dealers, planted with scarcely the attention given to a cabbage plant, and too often allowed to bear themselves to death. The land, trees, and cultivation cost so little that one good crop is expected to remunerate for all outlay. If more crops are obtained, there is so much clear gain. Under this slovenly treatment there is, of course, rapid deterioration in the stamina of the peach. Pits and buds are taken from enfeebled trees for the purpose of propagation, and so tendencies to disease are perpetuated and enhanced. Little wonder that the fatal malady, the "yellows," has blighted so many hopes! I honestly believe that millions of trees have been sold in which this disease existed from the bud. If fine peaches were bred and propagated with something of the same care that is bestowed on blooded stock, the results would soon be proportionate. Gardeners abroad often give more care to one tree than hundreds receive here. Because the peach has grown so easily in our climate, we have imposed on its good-nature beyond the limits of endurance, and consequently it is not easy to get sound, healthful trees that will bear year after year under the best of treatment as they did with our fathers with no care at all. I should look to men who had made a reputation for sending out sound, healthful stock grown under their own eyes from pits and wood which they know to be free from disease. Do not try to save a few pennies on the first cost of trees, for the probabilities are that such economy will result in little more than the "yellows."

In large orchards, cultivated by horse-power, the stems of the trees are usually from four to six feet high, but in the garden this length of stem is not necessary, and the trees can be grown as dwarf standards, with stems beginning to branch two feet from the ground. A little study of the habit of growth in the peach will show that, to obtain the best results, the pruning-shears is almost as essential as in the case of the grape-vine. More than in any other fruit tree the sap tends strongly toward the ends of the shoots. Left to nature, only the terminal buds of these will grow from year to year; the other buds lower down on the shoots fail and drop off. Thus we soon have long naked reaches of unproductive wood, or sucker-like sprouts starting from the bark, which are worse than useless. Our first aim should be to form a round, open, symmetrical head, shortening in the shoots at least one-half each year, and cutting out crossing and interlacing branches. For instance, if we decide to grow our trees as dwarf standards, we will cut back the stems at a point two feet from the ground the first spring after planting, and let but three buds grow to make the first three or leading branches. The following spring we will cut back the shoots that have formed so as to make six leading branches. Thereafter we shall continue to cut out and back so as to maintain an open head for the free circulation of air and light.

To learn the importance of rigorous and careful pruning, observe the shoots of a vigorous peach-tree, say three or four years old. These shoots or sprays are long and slender, lined with fruit-buds. You will often find two fruit-buds together, with a leaf-bud between them. If the fruit-buds have been uninjured by the winter, they will nearly all form peaches, far more than the slender spray can support or mature. The sap will tend to give the most support to all growth at the end of the spray or branch. The probable result will be that you will have a score, more or less, of peaches that are little beyond skin and stones. By midsummer the brittle sprays will break or the limbs split down at the crotches. You may have myriads of peaches, but none fit for market or table. Thousands of baskets are sent to New York annually that do not pay the expenses of freight, commission, etc., while the orchards from which they come are practically ruined. I had two small trees from which, one autumn, I sold ten dollars' worth of fruit. They yielded more profit than is often obtained from a hundred trees.

Now, in the light of these facts, realize the advantages secured by cutting back the shoots or sprays so as to leave but three or four fruit-buds on each. The tree can probably mature these buds into large, beautiful peaches, and still maintain its vigor. By this shortening-in process you have less tree, but more fruit. The growth is directed and kept within proper limits, and the tree preserved for future usefulness. Thus the peach-trees of the garden will not only furnish some of the most delicious morsels of the year, but also a very agreeable and light phase of labor. They can be made pets which will amply repay all kindness, and the attentions they most appreciate, strange to say, are cutting and pinching. The pruning-shears in March and early April can cut away forming burdens which could not be borne, and pinching back during the summer can maintain beauty and symmetry in growth. When the proprietor of the home acre has learned from experience to do this work judiciously, his trees, like the grape-vines, will afford many hours of agreeable and healthful recreation. If he regards it as labor, one great, melting, luscious peach will repay him. A small apple, pear, or strawberry usually has the flavor of a large one, but a peach to be had in perfection must be fully matured to its limit of growth on a healthful tree.

Let no one imagine that the shortening in of shoots recommended consists of cutting the young sprays evenly all around the tree as one would shear a hedge. It more nearly resembles the pruning of the vine, for the peach, like the vine, bears its fruit only on the young wood of the previous summer's growth. The aim should be to have this young bearing wood distributed evenly over the tree, as should be true of a grape-vine. When the trees are kept low, as dwarf standards, the fruit is more within reach, and less liable to be blown off by high winds. Gradually, however, if the trees prove healthful, they will get high enough up in the world.

Notwithstanding the rigorous pruning recommended, the trees will often overload themselves, and thinning out the young peaches when as large as hickory nuts is almost imperative if we would secure good fruit. Men of experience say that when a tree has set too much fruit, if two-thirds of it are taken off while little, the remaining third will measure and weigh more than would the entire crop, and bring three times as much money. In flavor and beauty the gain will certainly be more than double.

Throughout its entire growth and fruiting life the peach-tree needs good cultivation, and also a good but not overstimulated soil. Well-decayed compost from the cow stable is probably the best barnyard fertilizer. Wood-ashes are peculiarly agreeable to the constitution of this tree, and tend to maintain it in health and bearing long after others not so treated are dead. I should advise that half a peck be worked in lightly every spring around each tree as far as the branches extend. When enriching the ground about a tree, never heap the fertilizer around the trunk, but spread it evenly from the stem outward as far as the branches reach, remembering that the head above is the measure of the root extension below. Air-slacked lime is also useful to the peach in small quantities, and so, no doubt, would be a little salt from time to time. Bone meal is highly recommended.

Like other fruit trees, the peach does not thrive on low, wet ground, and the fruit-buds are much more apt to be winter-killed in such localities. A light, warm soil is regarded as the most favorable.

Of course we can grow this fruit on espaliers as they do abroad, but there are few localities where any advantage is to be derived from this course. In our latitude I much prefer cool northern exposures, for the reason that the fruit-buds are kept dormant during warm spells in winter, and so late in spring that they escape injury from frost. Alternate freezing and thawing is more harmful than steady cold. The buds are seldom safe, however, at any time when the mercury sinks ten or fifteen degrees below zero.

As we have intimated, abuse of the peach-tree has developed a fatal disease known as the "yellows." It manifests itself in yellow, sickly foliage, numerous and feeble sprouts along the larger limbs and trunk, and small, miserable fruit, ripening prematurely. I can almost taste the yellows in much of the fruit bought in market. Some regard the disease as very contagious; others do not. It is best to be on the safe side. If a tree is affected generally, dig it out by the roots and burn it at once; if only a branch shows evidence of the malady, cut it off well back and commit it to the flames. The only remedy is to propagate from trees in sound health and vigor.

Like the apple, the peach-tree is everywhere subject to injury from a borer named "*exitiosa*, or the destructive." The eggs from which these little pests are hatched are laid by the moth during the summer upon the stem of the tree very near the root; the grubs bore through the outer bark, and devour the inner bark and sap-wood. Fortunately they soon reveal their evil work by the castings, and by the gum which exudes from the hole by which they entered. They cannot do much harm unless a tree is neglected; in this case, however, they will soon enfeeble and probably destroy it. When once within a tree, borers must be cut out with a sharp-pointed knife, carefully yet thoroughly. The wounds from the knife may be severe, but the ceaseless gnawing of the grub is fatal. If the tree has been lacerated to some extent, a plaster of moistened clay or cow manure makes a good salve. Keeping the borers out of the tree is far better than taking them out, and this can be effected by wrapping the stem at the ground—two inches below the surface and five above—with strong hardware or sheathing paper. If this is tied tightly about the tree, the moth cannot lay its eggs upon the stem. A neighbor of mine has used this protection not only on the peach, but also the apple, with almost complete success. Of course the pests will try to find their way under it, and it would be well to take off the wrapper occasionally and examine the trees.

In order to insure an unfailing supply of this delicious fruit I should advise that a few trees be set out every spring. The labor and expense are scarcely greater than that bestowed upon a cabbage patch, and the reward is more satisfactory.

For this latitude the following choice of varieties will prove a good one: Early Alexander, Early Rivers, Princess of Wales, Brandywine, Old Mixon Free, Stump the World, Picquet's Late, Crawford's Late, Mary's Choice, White Free Heath, Salway, and Lord Palmerston.

If the soil of one's garden is a stiff, cold, adhesive clay, the peach would succeed much better budded or grafted on plum stocks.

By easy transition we pass to the kindred fruit, the plum, which does not generally receive the attention it deserves. If one has a soil suited to it—a heavy clay or loam—it can usually be grown very easily. The fruit is so grateful to the taste and useful to the house-keeper that it should be given a fair trial, either in the garden borders or wherever a tree can be planted so as to secure plenty of light and air. The young trees may be one or two years old from the bud; I should prefer the former, if vigorous. Never be induced to purchase old trees by promises of speedy fruit. It is quite possible you may never get any fruit at all from them worth mentioning. I should allow a space of from ten to fifteen feet between the trees when they are planted together, and I should cut them back so that they would begin to branch at two feet from the ground. Long, naked stems are subject to the gum disease.

In the place of general advice in regard to this fruit I shall give the experience of Mr. T. S. Force, of Newburgh, who exhibited seventy varieties at the last annual Orange County fair.

His plum orchard is a large poultry-yard containing half an acre, of which the ground is a good loam, resting on a heavy clay subsoil. He bought trees but one year from the bud, set them out in autumn, and cut them back so that they began to form their heads at two feet from the ground. He prefers starting with strong young plants of this age, and he did not permit them to bear for the first three years, his primal aim being to develop a healthy, vigorous tree with a round, symmetrical head. During this period the ground about them was kept mellow by good cultivation, and being rich enough to start with, received no fertilizers. It is his belief that over-fertilization tends to cause the disease so well known as the black knot, which has destroyed many orchards in this vicinity. If the garden has been enriched as I have directed, the soil will probably need little if anything from the stables, and certainly will not if the trees are grown in a poultry-yard. During this growing and forming period Mr. Force gave careful attention to pruning. Budded trees are not even, symmetrical growers, but tend to send up a few very strong shoots that rob the rest of the tree of sustenance. Of course these must be cut well back in early spring, or we have long naked reaches of wood and a deformed tree. It is far better, however, not to let these rampant shoots grow to maturity, but pinch them back in early summer, thus causing them to throw out side branches. By summer pinching and rubbing off of tender shoots a tree can be made to grow in any shape we desire. When the trees receive no summer pruning, Mr. Force advises that the branches be shortened in at least one-half in the spring, while some shoots are cut back even more rigorously. At the age of four or five years, according to the vigor of the trees, he permits them to bear. Now cultivation ceases, and the ground is left to grow hard, but not weedy or grassy, beneath the boughs. Every spring, just as the blossoms are falling, he spreads evenly under the branches four quarts of salt. While the trees thrive and grow fruitful with this fertilizer, the curculio, or plum-weevil, does not appear to find it at all to his taste. As a result of his methods he has grown large and profitable crops, and his trees in the main are kept healthy and vigorous. His remedy for the black knot is to cut off and burn the small boughs and twigs affected. If the

disease appears in the side of a limb or in the stem, he cuts out all trace of it, and paints the wound with a wash of gum shel-lac and alcohol.

Trees load so heavily that the plums rest against one another. You will often find in moist warm weather decaying specimens. These should be removed at once, that the infection may not spread.

In cutting out the interfering boughs, do not take off the sharp-pointed spurs which are forming along the branches, for on these are maturing the fruit-buds.

Mr. Force recommends the following ten varieties, named in the order of ripening: Canada; Orleans, a red-cheeked plum; McLaughlin, greenish, with pink cheek; Bradshaw, large red, with lilac bloom; Smith's Orleans, purple; Green Gage; Bleeker's Gage, golden yellow; Prune d'Agen, purple; Coe's Golden Drop; and Shropshire Damson for preserves.

If we are restricted to very light soils, we shall probably have to grow some of the native varieties, of the Canada and Wild-Goose type. In regard to both this fruit and peaches we should be guided in our selection by information respecting varieties peculiarly suited to the region.

The next paper will treat of small fruits, beginning with the raspberry.

THROUGH CUMBERLAND GAP ON HORSEBACK.

BY JAMES LANE ALLEN.

I.

FRESH fields lay before us. We had left the rich, rolling plains of the blue-grass region in central Kentucky, and had set our faces toward the great Appalachian uplift on the southeastern border of the State. There Cumberland Gap, that high-swung gateway through the mountain, abides as a landmark of what Nature can do when she wishes to give an opportunity to the human race in its migrations and discoveries, without surrendering control of its liberty and its fate. Such way-side pleasures of hap and scenery as might befall us while journeying thither were ours to enjoy; but the especial quest was more knowledge of that peculiar and deeply interesting people, the Kentucky mountaineers. It can never be too clearly understood by those who are wont to speak of "the Kentuckians" that this State has within its boundaries

two entirely distinct elements of population—elements distinct in England before they came hither, distinct during more than a century of residence here, and distinct now in all that goes to constitute a separate community—occupations, manners and customs, dress, views of life, civilization. It is but a short distance from the blue-grass country to the eastern mountains; but in traversing it you detach yourself from all that you have ever experienced, and take up the history of English-speaking men and women at the point it had reached a hundred or a hundred and fifty years ago.

Leaving Lexington, then, which is in the midst of the blue-grass plateau, we were come to Burnside, a station on the Cincinnati Southern Railway some ninety miles away, where begin the navigable waters of the Cumberland River, and the foot-hills of the Cumberland Mountains.

OLD FERRY AT POINT BURNSIDE.

Burnside is not merely a station, but a sub-mountainous watering-place. The water is mostly in the bed of the river. We had come thither to get horses and saddle-bags, but to no purpose. The hotel was a sort of transition between the civili-

"BLAME ME IF THEM AIN'T THE DARNEDEST BEANS!"

zation we had left behind and the primitive society we were to enter. On the veranda were some distinctly modern and conventional red chairs; but a green and yellow gourd vine, carefully trained across so as to shut out the distant landscape, was a novel bit of local color. Under the fine beeches in the yard was swung a hammock, but it was made of boards braced between ropes, and was covered with a weather-stained piece of tarpaulin. There were electric bells in the house that did not seem to electrify anybody particularly, and near the front entrance three barrels

of Irish potatoes, with the tops off, spoke for themselves in the absence of the bill of fare. After supper, the cook, a tall, blue-eyed white fellow, walked into my room without much explanation, and carried away his guitar, showing that he had been wont to set his sighs to music in that quarter of the premises. Of a truth he was right, for the moon hung in that part of the heavens, and no doubt ogled him into many a midnight frenzy. Sitting under a beech-tree in the morning, I had watched a child from some distant city, dressed in white, and wearing a blue ribbon around her goldenish hair, amuse herself by rolling old barrels (potato barrels probably, and she may have had a motive) down the hill-side and seeing them dashed to pieces on the railway track below. By-and-by some of the staves of one fell in, the child tumbled in also, and they all rolled over together. Upon the whole, it was an odd overtopping of two worlds, and a promise of entertaining things to come. When the railway was first opened through this region a young man established a fruit store at one of the stations, and as part of his stock laid in a bunch of bananas. One day a native mountaineer entered. Arrangements generally struck him with surprise, but everything else was soon forgotten in an adhesive contemplation of the mighty aggregation of fruit. Finally he turned away with this note: "Blame me if them ain't the darnedest beans *I* ever seen!"

The scenery around Burnside is very beautiful, and the climate salubrious. In the valleys was formerly a fine growth of walnut, but the principal timbers now are oak, ash, and sycamore, with some yellow pine. I heard of a wonderful walnut-tree formerly standing, by hiring vehicles to go and see which the owner of a livery-stable made three hundred and fifty dollars. Six hundred were offered for it on the spot; but the possessor, never having read of the fatal auriferous goose, reasoned that it would bring him a fortune if cut into many pieces, and so ruined it, and sold it at a great loss. The hills are filled with the mountain limestone—that Kentucky oolite of which the new Cotton Exchange in New York is built. Here was Burnside's depot

NATIVE TYPES.

of supplies during the war, and here passed the great road—made in part a corduroy road at his order—from Somerset, Kentucky, to Jacksborough, over which countless stores were taken from central Kentucky and regions further north into Tennessee. Supplies were brought up the river in small steam-boats or through in wagons, and when the road grew impassable, pack-mules were used. Sad sights there were to be seen in those sad, sad days: the carcasses of animals at short intervals from here to Knoxville, and now and then a mule sunk up to his body in mire, and abandoned, with his pack on, to die. Here were batteries planted and rifle-pits dug, the vestiges of which yet remain; but where the forest timbers were then cut down a vigorous new growth has long been reclaiming the earth to native wildness, and altogether the aspect of the place is peaceful and serene. Doves were flying in and out of the cornfields on the hill-sides; there were green stretches in the valleys where cattle were grazing; and these, together with a single limestone road that wound upward over a distant ridge, recalled the richer scenes of the blue-grass lands.

Assured that we would find horses and saddle-bags at Cumberland Falls, we left Burnside, and were soon set down at a station some fifteen miles further along, where a hack was to convey us to another of those mountain watering-places that are being opened up in various parts of eastern Kentucky for the enjoyment of a people that has never cared to frequent in large numbers the Atlantic seaboard.

Capps stopped frequently on the road: once to halloo from the lofty ridge along which we were riding, down into a valley, to inquire of a mountain woman, sitting in her door with a baby in her arms,

CUMBERLAND FALLS.

Capps was the driver of the hack—a good-looking mulatto, wearing a faded calico shirt and a straw hat of most uncertain shape and variable colors.

whether she had any "millons"; and again at a way-side grocery to get a bushel of meal from a man who seemed to be dividing his time pretty equally between retailing meal and building himself a new house. Here we asked for a drink of water, and got it — hot from a jug, there being no spring near. Capps knew a hawk from a handsaw when it came to talking

about "moonshine" whiskey, and entered with some zest into a technical discrimination between its effects and those of "old Bourbon" on the head after imbibing incontinently. His knowledge seemed based on experience, and we waived a discussion.

MOONRISE ON CUMBERLAND RIDGE.

Meantime the darkness was falling, and the scenery along the road grew wilder and grander. A terrific storm had swept over these heights, and the great trees lay uptorn and prostrate in every direction, or reeled and fell against each other like drunken giants—a scene of fearful elemental violence. On the summits one sees the tan-bark oak; lower down, the white oak; and lower yet, fine specimens of yellow poplar; while from the valleys to the crests is a dense and varied undergrowth, save where the ground has been burnt over, year after year, to kill it out and improve the grazing. Twenty miles to the southeast we had seen through the pale-tinted air the waving line of Sellico Mountains, in Tennessee. Away to the north lay the Beaver Creek and the lower Cumberland, while in front of us rose the craggy, scowling face of Anvil Rock, commanding a view of Kentucky, Tennessee, and Virginia. The utter silence and heart-oppressing repose of primeval nature was around us. The stark white and gray trunks of the immemorial forest dead linked us to an inviolable past. The air seemed to blow upon us from over regions illimitable and unexplored, and to be fraught with unutterable suggestions. The full-moon swung itself aloft over the sharp touchings of the green with spectral pallor; and the evening-star stood lustrous on the western horizon in depths of blue as cold as a sky of Landseer, except where brushed by tremulous shadows of rose on the verge of the sunlit world. A bat wheeled upward in fantastic curves out of his undiscovered glade. And the

soft tinkle of a single cow-bell far below marked the invisible spot of some lonely human habitation. By-and-by we lost sight of the heavens altogether, so dense and interlaced the forest. The descent of the hack appeared to be into a steep abyss of gloom; then all at once we broke from the edge of the woods into a flood of moonlight; at our feet were the whirling, foaming rapids of the river; in our ears was the near roar of the cataract, where the bow-crowned mist rose and floated upward and away in long trailing shapes of ethereal lightness.

The Cumberland River runs and throws itself over the rocks here with a fall of seventy feet, or a perpendicular descent of sixty-two, making a mimic but most beautiful Niagara. Just below, Eagle Falls drops over its precipice in a lawny cascade. The roar of the cataract, under favorable conditions, may be heard up and down stream a distance of ten or twelve miles. You will not find in mountainous Kentucky a more picturesque spot. The hotel stands near the very verge of the waters; and the mountains, rising one above another around, shut it in with infinite security from all the world.

While here, we had occasion to extend our acquaintance with native types. Two young men came to the hotel, bringing a bag of small, hard peaches to sell. Slim, slab-sided, stomachless, and serene, mild and melancholy, they might have been lotos-eaters, only the suggestion of poetry was wanting, and they had probably never tasted any satisfying plant whatsoever. Their unutterable content came not from opiates, but from their souls. If they could sell their peaches, they would be happy; if not, they would be happy. What they could not sell, they could as well eat; and since no bargain was made on this occasion, they took chairs on the hotel veranda, opened the bag, and fell to. One of us tried to catch the mental attitude of the Benjamin of his tribe, while the other studied his bodily pose.

"Is that a good 'coon dog?"

"A mighty good 'coon dog. I hain't never seed him whipped by a varmint yet."

"Are there many 'coons in this country?"

"Several 'coons."

"Is this a good year for 'coons?"

"A mighty good year for 'coons. The woods is full o' varmints."

"Do 'coons eat corn?"

"'Coons is bad as hogs on corn, when they git tuk to it."

"Are there many wild turkeys in this country?"

"Several wild turkeys."

"Have you ever caught many 'coons?"

"I've cotched high as five 'coons out o' one tree."

"Are there many foxes in this country?"

"Several foxes."

"What's the best way to cook a 'coon?"

"Ketch him and parbile him, and then put him in cold water and soak him, and then put him in and bake him."

"Are there many hounds in this country?"

"Several hounds."

Here, among other discoveries, was a linguistic one—the use of "several" in the sense of a great many, probably an innumerable multitude, as in the case of the 'coons.

They hung around the hotel for hours, as beings utterly exempt from all the obligations and other phenomena of time.

"Why should we only toil, the roof and crown of things?"

True to promise, the guide bespoken the evening before had made all arrangements for our ride of some eighteen miles —was it not forty?—to Williamsburg, and in the afternoon made his appearance with three horses. Of these three horses one was a mule, with a strong lean-ing toward his father's family. Of the three saddles one was a side-saddle, and another was an army saddle with refugee stirrups. The three brutes wore among them some seven shoes. My own mincing jade had none on. Her name may have been Helen of Troy (all horses are named in Kentucky), so anciently must her great beauty have disappeared. She partook with me of the terror which her own movements inspired, and if there ever was a well-defined case, outside of literature, in which the man should have carried the beast, this was the one. While on her back I occasionally apologized for the injustice by handing her some sour apples, which she appeared never to have tasted before, just as it was told me she had never known the luxury of wearing shoes. It is often true that the owner of a horse in this region is too poor or too mean to have it shod.

Our route from Cumberland Falls lay through what is called "Little Texas," in Whitley County—a wilderness some twenty miles square. I say route, because there was not always a road; but for the guide, there would not always have been a direction. Rough as the country appears to one riding through it on horseback, it is truly called "flat woods country," and viewed from Sellico Mountains, whence the local elevations are of no account, it looks like one vast sweep of sloping, densely wooded land. Here one may see noble specimens of yellow poplar in the deeper soil at the head of the ravines; pin oak, and gum and willow, and the rarely beautiful wild-cucumber. Along the streams in the lowlands blooms the wild calacanthus, filling the air with fragrance, and here in season the wild camellia throws open its white and purple splendors. There are few traces of human presence in this great wilderness, except along the road that one comes to by-and-by; and it seems easy to believe that Williamsburg had a population of one hundred and thirty-nine in 1870, having increased fourteen souls in ten years. Since then, indeed, railway connection has caused it to double its population many times—once within in the past two years.

There is iron in Whitley County so pure as to require some poorer ore to be mixed with it to smelt it successfully, while other requires only limestone to flux it; but we did not come upon "Swift's

INTERIOR OF A MOUNTAINEER'S HOME.

Silver Mine." From the Tennessee line south to the Ohio line north one may pass through counties that claim the location of "Swift's Silver Mine"—that El Dorado spot of eastern Kentucky, where, a hundred and twenty-five years ago, one John Swift said he made silver in large quantities, burying some thirty thousand dollars and crowns on a large creek; fifteen thousand dollars a little way off, near some trees, which were duly marked; a prize of six thousand dollars close by the fork of a white oak; and three thousand dollars in the rocks of a rock house: all which, in the light of these notes, it is allowed any one who will to hunt for.

It was not until we had passed out of "Little Texas" and reached Williamsburg, had gone thence to Barbourville, the county seat of the adjoining county of Knox, and thence again into Bell County, that we stopped between Flat Lick and Cumberland Ford, on the old Wilderness road from Kentucky through Cumberland Gap. Around us were the mountains—around us the mountaineers whom we wished to meet intimately face to face.

II.

Straight, slim, angular, white bodies; average or even unusual stature, without great muscular robustness; features regular and colorless, unanimated but intelligent, in the men sometimes fierce, and in the women often sad; among the latter occasional beauty of a pure Greek type; a manner shy and deferential, but kind and fearless; eyes with a slow, long look of mild inquiry, or of general listlessness, or of unconscious and unaccountable melancholy; the key of life a low minor strain, losing itself in reverie; voices monotonous in intonation; movements uninformed by nervousness—these are characteristics of the Kentucky mountaineers. Living to-day as their forefathers lived before them a hundred years ago; hearing little of the world, caring nothing for it; responding feebly to the influences of civilization near the highways of travel in and around the towns, and latterly along the lines of railway communication, but sure to live here, if uninvaded and unaroused, in the same condition for a hundred or more years to come; utterly lacking the spirit of development from within; utterly devoid of any sympathy with that boundless and ungovernable activity which is carrying the Saxon race in America from one state to another, whether better or worse. The origin of these people, the relation they sustain to the different population of the central region—in fine, an account of them from the date of their settling in these mountains to the present time, when, as it seems, they are on the point of losing their isolation, and with it their distinctiveness—would imprison phases of life and character valuable alike to the special history of this country and to the general history of the human mind. The land in these mountains is all claimed, but it is probably not all covered by actual patent. As evidence, a company has been formed to speculate in lands not secured by title. The old careless way of marking off boundaries by going from tree to tree, by partly surveying and partly guessing, explains the present uncertainty. Many own land by right of occupancy, there being no other claim. The great body of the people live on and cultivate little patches which they either own, or hold free, or pay rent for with a third of the crop. These not unfrequently get together and trade farms as they would horses, no deed being executed. There is among them a mobile element—squatters—who make a hill-side clearing and live on it as long as it remains productive, when they move elsewhere. This accounts for the presence throughout the country of abandoned cabins, around which a dense new forest growth is springing up. Leaving out of consideration the few instances of substantial prosperity, the most of the people are abjectly poor, and they appear to have no sense of accumulation. The main crops raised on the patch are corn and potatoes. By the scant gardens will be seen little patches of cotton, sorghum, and tobacco; flax also, though less than formerly. Many make insufficient preparation for winter, laying up no meat, but buying a piece of bacon now and then, and paying for it by working. In some regions the great problem of life is to raise two dollars and a half during the year for county taxes. Being pauper counties, they are exempt from State taxation. Jury fees are highly esteemed and much sought after. The manufacture of illicit mountain whiskey—"moonshine"—was formerly, as it is now, a considerable

source of revenue to them; and a desperate self-destructive sub-source of revenue from the same business has been the betrayal of its hidden places. There is nothing harder or more dangerous to find now in the mountains than a secret still.

Formerly, also, digging "sang," as they call ginseng, was a general occupation. For this, of course, China was a great market. It has nearly all been dug out now except in the wildest parts of the country, where entire families may still be seen "out sangin'." They took it into the towns in bags, selling it at a dollar and ten cents—perhaps a dollar and a half—a pound. This was mainly the labor of the women and the children, who went to work barefooted, amid briers and chestnut burrs, copperheads and rattlesnakes. Indeed, the women prefer to go barefooted, finding shoes a trouble and constraint. It was a sad day for the people when the "sang" grew scarce. A few years ago one of the counties was nearly depopulated in consequence of a great exodus into Arkansas, whence had come the news that there "sang" was plentiful. Not long since, too, during a season of scarcity in corn, a local store-keeper told the people of a county to go out and gather all the mandrake or "May-apple" root they could find. At first only the women and children went to work, the men holding back with ridicule. By-and-by they also took part, and that year some fifteen tons were gathered, at three cents a pound, and the whole county thus got its seed-corn. Wild ginger was another root formerly much dug; also to less extent "golden-seal" and "bloodroot." The sale of feathers from a few precarious geese helps to eke out subsistence. Their methods of agriculture—if methods they may be styled—are of the most primitive sort. Ploughing is commonly done with a "bull-tongue," an implement hardly more than a sharpened stick with a metal rim; this is often drawn by an ox, or a half-yoke. But one may see women ploughing with two oxen. Traces are made of hickory or papaw, as also are bed-cords. Ropes are made of lynn bark. In some counties there is not so much as a fanning-mill, grain being winnowed by pouring it from basket to basket, after having been threshed with a flail, which is a hickory withe some seven feet long. Their threshing-floor is a clean place on the ground, and they take up grain, gravel, and some dirt

FORD ON THE CUMBERLAND.

together, not knowing or not caring for the use of a sieve. The grain is ground at their homes in a hand tub-mill, or one made by setting the nether millstone in a bee-gum, or by cutting a hole in a puncheon-log and sinking the stone into it. There are, however, other kinds of mills: the primitive little water-mill which may be considered almost characteristic of this region; in a few places improved water-mills, and small steam-mills. It is the country of mills, farm-houses being furnished with one about as frequently as with coffee-pots or spinning-wheels. A simpler way of preparing corn for bread than by even the hand-mill is used in the late summer and early autumn, while the grain is too hard for eating as roasting-ears, and too soft to be ground in a mill. On a board is tacked a piece of tin through which holes have been punched from the under side, and over this tin the ears are rubbed, producing a coarse meal, of which "gritted bread" is made. Much pleasure and doubtless much health do they get from their "gritted bread," which is withal a sweet and wholesome bit for a hungry man. Where civilization has touched on the highways and the few improved mills have been erected, one may see women going to mill with their scant sacks of grain, riding on a jack, a jennet, or a bridled ox. But this is not so bad as in North Carolina, where, Europa-like, they ride on bulls.

Aside from such occupations as have been herein pointed out, the men have nothing to do—a little work in the spring, and nine months' rest. They love to meet at the country groceries and cross-roads, to shoot matches for beef, turkeys, or liquor, and to gamble. There is with them a sort of annual succession of amusements. In its season they have the rage for pitching horseshoes, the richer ones using dollar pieces. In consequence of their abundant leisure, the loneliness of the mountains, which draws them thus together, their bravery and physical vigor, quarrels among them are frequent, and feuds are deadly. Personal enmities soon serve to array entire families in an attitude of implacable hostility, and in the course of time relatives and friends take sides, and a war of extermination ensues. The special origins of these are various: blood heated and temper lost under the influence of "moonshine"; reporting on the places and manufacturers of this; local politics; the survival of resentments engendered during the civil war—these, together with all causes that lie in the passions of the human heart and spring from the constitution of all human society, often make the remote and insulated life of these people turbulent, reckless, and distressing. But while thus bitter and cruel toward each other, they present to strangers the aspect of a polite, kind, unoffending, and most hospitable race. They will divide with you shelter and warmth and food, however scant, and will put themselves to trouble for your convenience with an unreckoning, earnest friendliness and good-nature that is touching to the last degree. No sham, no pretence; a true friend, or an open enemy. Of late they have had much occasion to regard new-comers with distrust, which, once aroused, is difficult to dispel, and now they will wish to know you and your business before treating you with that warmth which they are only too glad to show.

The women appear to do most of the work. From the few sheep, running wild, which the farm may own, they take the wool, which is carded, reeled, spun, and woven into fabrics by their own hands and on their rudest implements. One or two spinning-wheels will be found in every house. Cotton from their little patches, too, they clear by using a primitive hand cotton-gin. Flax, much spun formerly, is now less used. It is surprising to see from what appliances they will bring forth exquisite fabrics; all the garments for personal wear, bedclothes, and the like. When they can afford it they make carpets.

They have, as a rule, luxuriant hair. In some counties one is struck by the purity of the Saxon type, and their faces in early life are often very handsome. But one hears that in certain localities they are prone to lose their teeth, and that after the age of thirty-five it is a rare thing to see a woman whose front teeth are not partly or wholly wanting. The reason of this is not apparent. They appear passionately fond of dress, and array themselves in gay colors and in jewelry (pinchbeck), if so be that their worldly estate justifies the extravagance. Oftener, if young, they have a modest, shy air, as if conscious that their garb is not even decorous. Whether married or unmarried, they show much natural diffidence. It is told that in remoter districts of the mountains they are not allowed to sit at the table with the male members of the household, but serve them as in ancient societies. Commonly, too, in going to church, the men ride and carry the children, while the women walk. Dancing in some regions is hardly known, but in others is a favorite amusement, and in its movements men and women show the utmost grace. The mountain preachers oppose it as a sin.

Marriages take place early, and they are a most fecund race. I asked them time and again to fix upon the average number of children to a family, and they gave as the result seven. In case of parental opposition to wedlock, the lovers run off. There is among the people a low standard of morality in their domestic relations, the delicate privacies of home life having little appreciation where so many persons, without regard to age or sex, are crowded together within very limited quarters.

MOUNTAIN COURTSHIP.

The dwellings—often mere cabins with a single room—are built of rough-hewn logs, chinked or daubed, though not always so. Often there is a puncheon floor and no chamber roof. One of these mountaineers, called into court to testify as to the household goods of a defendant neighbor, gave in as the inventory, a string of pumpkins, a skillet without a handle, and "a wild Bill." "A wild Bill" is a bed made by boring auger-holes into a log, driving sticks into these, and overlaying them with hickory bark and sedge-grass—a favorite couch. The low chimneys, made usually of laths daubed, are so low that the saying, inelegant though true, is current, that you may sit by the fire inside and spit out over the top. The cracks in the walls give ingress and egress to a child or a dog. Even cellars are little known, their potatoes sometimes being kept during winter in a hole dug under the hearth-stone. More frequently a trap-door is made through the plank flooring in the middle of the room, and in a hole beneath are put potatoes, and, in case of some wealth, jellies and preserves. Despite the wretchedness of their habitations and all the rigors of a mountain

A MOUNTAINEER DAME.

climate, they do not suffer with cold, and one may see them out in snow knee-deep clad in low brogans, and nothing heavier than a jeans coat and hunting shirt.

The customary beverage is coffee, bitter and black, not having been roasted but burnt. All drink it from the youngest up. Another beverage is "mountain tea," which is made from the sweet-scented golden-rod and from winter-green—the New England checkerberry. These decoctions they mollify with home-made sorghum molasses, which they call "long sweetening," or with sugar, which by con-

trast is known as "short sweetening." Of home government there is little or none, boys especially setting aside at will parental authority; but a sort of traditional sense of duty and decorum restrains them by its silent power, and moulds them into respect. Children while quite young are often plump to roundness, but soon grow thin and white and meagre like the parents. There is little desire for knowledge or education. The mountain schools have sometimes less than half a dozen pupils during the few months they are in session. A gentleman who wanted a coal bank opened engaged for the work a man passing along the road. Some days later he learned that his workman was a school-teacher, who, in consideration of the seventy-five cents a day, had dismissed his academy.

Many, allured by rumors from the West, have migrated thither, but nearly all come back, from love of the mountains, from indisposition to cope with the rush and vigor and enterprise of frontier life. Theirs, they say, is a good lazy man's home.

Their customs respecting the dead are interesting. When a husband dies his funeral sermon is not preached, but the death of the wife is awaited, and *vice versa*. Then a preacher is sent for, friend and neighbor called in, and the respect is paid both together. Often two or three preachers are summoned, and each delivers a sermon. More peculiar is the custom of having the services for one person repeated; so that the dead get their funerals preached several times months and years after their burial. I heard of the unspeakably pitiful story of two sisters who had their mother's funeral preached once every summer as long as they lived. You may engage the women in mournful conversation respecting the dead, but hardly the men. In strange contrast with this regard for ceremonial observances is their neglect of the graves

A FAMILY BURYING-GROUND.

of their beloved, which they do not seem at all to visit when once closed, or to decorate with those symbols of affection which are the common indications of bereavement.

Nothing that I have ever seen in this world is so lonely, so touching in its neglect and wild irreparable solitude, as one of these mountain graveyards. On some knoll under a clump of trees, or along some hill-side where dense oak-trees make a mid-day gloom, you walk amid the unknown, undistinguishable dead. Which was father and which mother, where are lover and stricken sweetheart, whether this is the dust of laughing babe or crooning grandam, you will never know: no foot-stones, no head-stones; sometimes a few rough rails laid around as you would make a little pen for swine. In places, however, one sees a picket-fence put up, or a sort of shed built over.

Traditions and folk-lore among them are evanescent, and vary widely in different localities. It appears that in part they are sprung from the early hunters who came into the mountains when game was abundant, sport unfailing, living cheap. Among them now are still-hunters, who know the haunts of bear and deer, needing no dogs. They even now prefer wild meat—even "'possum" and "'coon" and ground-hog—to any other. In Bell County I spent the day in the house of an aged woman—eighty years old, in fact—who was a lingering representative of a nearly extinct type. She had never been out of the neighborhood of her birth, knew the mountains like a garden, had whipped men in single-handed encounter, brought down many a deer and wild turkey with her own rifle, and now, infirm, had but to sit in her cabin door and send her trained dogs into the depths of the forests to discover the wished-for game: a fiercer woman I never looked on.

III.

Our course now lay direct toward Cumberland Gap, some twenty miles southward. Our road ran along the bank of the Cumberland River to the ford, the immemorial crossing-place of early travel—and a beautiful spot—thence to Pineville, situated in that narrow opening in Pine Mountain where the river cuts it, and thence through the valley of Yellow Creek to the wonderful pass. The scenery in all this region is one succession of densely wooded mountains, blue-tinted air, small cultivated tracts in the fertile valleys, and the lovely watercourses.

Along the first part of our route the river slips crystal clear over its rocky bed, and beneath the lone green pendent branches of the trees that crowd the banks.

OLD CORN-MILL AT PINEVILLE.

Pine Mountain from "the brakes" of Sandy to the Tennessee line, and tributary to the watercourses that centre here are some five hundred thousand acres of timber land.

The ride from Pineville to the Gap, fourteen miles southward, is one of the most beautiful that may be taken. Yellow Creek becomes in local pronunciation "Yaller Crick." One cannot be long in eastern Kentucky without being struck by the number and character of the names given to the watercourses, which were the natural avenues of migratory travel. Few of the mountains have names. What a history is shut up in these names! Cutshin Creek, where some pioneer, they say, damaged those useful members; but more probably where grows a low greenbrier which cuts the aforesaid parts and riddles the pantaloons. These pioneers had humor. They named one creek "Troublesome," for reasons apparent to him who goes there; another, "No Worse Creek," on equally good grounds; another, "Defeated Creek;" and a great many, "Lost Creek." In one part of the country it is possible for one to enter "Hell fur Sartain," and get out at "Kingdom Come." Near by, strange to say, there are two liquid impersonations of Satan, "Upper Devil" and "Lower Devil." One day we went to a mountain meeting which was held in "a school-house and church-house" on "Stinking Creek." One might suppose they would have worshipped in a more fragrant locality; but the stream is very beautiful, and not malodorous. It received its name from its former canebrakes and deer licks, which made game abundant. Great numbers were killed for choice bits of venison and hides. Then there are "Ten-mile Creek" and "Sixteen-mile Creek," meaning to clinch the distance by name; and what is philologically interesting, one finds numerous "*Trace* Forks" originally "*Trail* Forks."

At the famous ford it was only two or three feet deep at the time of our crossing. This is a historic point. Here was one of the oldest settlements in the country; here the Federal army destroyed the houses and fences during the civil war; and here Zollikoffer came to protect the Kentucky gate that opens into East Tennessee. At Pineville, just beyond, we did not remain long. For some reasons not clearly understood by travellers a dead line had been drawn through the midst of the town, and not knowing on which side we were entitled to stand, we hastened on to a place where we might occupy neutral ground. The situation is strikingly picturesque: the mountain looks as if cleft sheer and fallen apart, the peaks on each side rising almost perpendicularly, with massive overhanging crests wooded to the summits, but showing gray rifts of the inexhaustible limestone. The river when lowest is here at an elevation of nine hundred and sixty feet, and the peaks leap to the height of twenty-two hundred. Here in the future will most probably pass a railroad, and be a populous town, for here is the only opening through

CUMBERLAND GAP.

Bell County and the Yellow Creek Valley serve to illustrate the incalculable mineral and timber resources of eastern Kentucky. Our road at times cut through forests of magnificent timbers—oak (black and white), walnut (black and white), poplar, maple, and chestnut, beech, lynn, gum, dogwood, and elm. Here are some of the finest coal-fields in the known world, the one on Clear Creek being fourteen feet thick. Here are exceedingly pure cannel-coals and cooking coals. At no other point in the Mississippi Valley are iron ores suitable for steel-making purposes so close to fuel so cheap. With an eastern coal-field of ten thousand square miles, with an area equally large covered with a virgin growth of the finest economic timbers, with watercourses feasible and convenient, it cannot be long before all eastern Kentucky will be opened up to the great industries of the modern world. Enterprise has already turned hither, and the distinctiveness of the mountaineer race has already begun to disappear. The two futures before them are, to be swept out of these mountains by the in-rushing spirit of contending industries, or to be aroused, civilized, and developed.

Long before you come in sight of the great Gap, the idea of it dominates the mind. At length, while yet some miles away, it looms up, sixteen hundred and seventy-five feet in elevation, some half a mile across from crest to crest, the pinnacle on the left towering to the height of twenty-five hundred.

It was late in the afternoon when our tired horses began the long, winding, rocky climb from the valley to the brow of the pass. As we stood in the passway, amid the deepening shadows of the twilight and the solemn repose of the mighty landscape, the Gap seemed to be crowded with two invisible and countless pageants of human life, the one passing in, the other passing out; and the air grew thick with ghostly utterances—primeval sounds, undistinguishable and strange, of creatures nameless and never seen by man; the wild rush and whoops of retreating and pursuing tribes; the slow steps of watchful pioneers; the wail of dying children and the songs of homeless women; the muffled tread of routed and broken armies—all the sounds of surprise and delight, victory and defeat, hunger and pain and weariness and despair, that the human heart can utter Here passed the first of all the white race who led the way into the valley of the Cumberland; here passed that small band of fearless men who gave the Gap its name; here passed the "Long Hunters"; here rushed the armies of the civil war; here has passed the wave of westerly emigration, whose force has spent itself only on the Pacific slopes; and here in the long future must flow backward and forward wealth beyond the dreams of avarice. Beneath the shadows of the pinnacle—the limit of our journey reached— we slept that night in the Poor Valley of Tennessee.

SHE STOOPS TO CONQUER;

OR, THE MISTAKES OF A NIGHT.—A COMEDY.

BY OLIVER GOLDSMITH.

ACT FIFTH.—(*Continued.*)

Scene changes to the back of the Garden.

Enter HASTINGS.

HAST. What an idiot am I, to wait here for a fellow who probably takes a delight in mortifying me! He never intended to be punctual, and I'll wait no longer. What do I see? It is he! and perhaps with news of my Constance.

Enter TONY, *booted and spattered.*

HAST. My honest 'Squire! I now find you a man of your word. This looks like friendship.

TONY. Ay, I'm your friend, and the best friend you have in the world, if you knew but all. This riding by night, by-the-bye, is cursedly tiresome. It has shook me worse than the basket of a stage-coach.

HAST. But how—where did you leave your fellow-travellers? Are they in safety? Are they housed?

TONY. Five-and-twenty miles in two hours and a half is no such bad driving. The poor beasts have smoked for it: Rabbit me, but I'd rather ride forty miles after a fox than ten with such varment.

HAST. Well, but where have you left the ladies? I die with impatience.

ENTER TONY, BOOTED AND SPATTERED.

TONY. Left them! Why, where should I leave them but where I found them?

HAST. This is a riddle.

TONY. Riddle me this, then. What's that goes round the house, and round the house, and never touches the house?

HAST. I'm still astray.

TONY. Why, that's it, mon. I have led them astray. By jingo, there's not a pond or a slough within five miles of the place but they can tell the taste of.

HAST. Ha! ha! ha! I understand: you took them in a round, while they supposed themselves going forward, and so you have at last brought them home again.

TONY. You shall hear. I first took them down Feather-bed Lane, where we stuck fast in the mud. I then rattled them crack over the stones of Up-and-down Hill. I then introduced them to the gibbet on Heavy-tree Heath; and from that, with a circumbendibus, I fairly lodged them in the horse-pond at the bottom of the garden.

HAST. But no accident, I hope?

TONY. No, no. Only mother is confoundedly frightened. She thinks herself forty miles off. She's sick of the journey; and the cattle can scarce crawl. So, if your own horses be ready, you may whip off with cousin, and I'll be bound that no soul here can budge a foot to follow you.

HAST. My dear friend, how can I be grateful?

TONY. Ay, now it's dear friend, noble 'Squire. Just now, it was all idiot, cub, and run me through the guts. Damn your way of fighting, I say. After we take a knock in this part of the country, we kiss and be friends. But if you had run me through the guts, then I should be dead, and you might go kiss the hangman.

Hast. The rebuke is just. But I must hasten to relieve Miss Neville: if you keep the old lady employed, I promise to take care of the young one.

[*Exit* Hastings.

Tony. Never fear me. Here she comes. Vanish! She's got from the pond, and draggled up to the waist, like a mermaid.

Enter Mrs. Hardcastle.

Mrs. Hard. Oh, Tony, I'm killed! Shook! Battered to death! I shall never survive it. That last jolt, that laid us against the quickset hedge, has done my business.

Tony. Alack, mamma, it was all your own fault. You would be for running away by night, without knowing one inch of the way.

Mrs. Hard. I wish we were at home again. I never met so many accidents in so short a journey. Drenched in the mud, overturned in a ditch, stuck fast in a slough, jolted to a jelly, and at last to lose our way. Whereabouts do you think we are, Tony?

Tony. By my guess we should come upon Crackskull Common, about forty miles from home.

Mrs. Hard. O lud! O lud! The most notorious spot in all the country. We only want a robbery to make a complete night on't.

Tony. Don't be afraid, mamma, don't be afraid. Two of the five that kept here are hanged, and the other three may not find us. Don't be afraid.— Is that a man that's galloping behind us? No; it's only a tree.—Don't be afraid.

Mrs. Hard. The fright will certainly kill me.

Tony. Do you see anything like a black hat moving behind the thicket?

Mrs. Hard. Oh, death!

Tony. No; it's only a cow. Don't be afraid, mamma; don't be afraid.

Mrs. Hard. As I'm alive, Tony, I see a man coming towards us. Ah! I'm sure on't. If he perceives us, we are undone.

Tony. (*Aside.*) Father-in-law, by all that's unlucky, come to take one of his night walks. (*To her.*) Ah! it's a highwayman, with pistols as long as my arm. A damn'd ill-looking fellow.

Mrs. Hard. Good Heaven defend us! He approaches.

Tony. Do you hide yourself in that thicket, and leave me to manage him. If there be any danger, I'll cough and cry hem. When I cough, be sure to keep close. [Mrs. Hardcastle *hides behind a tree in the back scene.*

Enter Hardcastle.

Hard. I'm mistaken, or I heard voices of people in want of help. Oh, Tony, is that you? I did not expect you so soon back. Are your mother and her charge in safety?

Tony. Very safe, sir, at my aunt Pedigree's. Hem!

Mrs. Hard. (*From behind.*) Ah, death! I find there's danger.

Hard. Forty miles in three hours; sure that's too much, my youngster.

Tony. Stout horses and willing minds make short journeys, as they say. Hem!

Mrs. Hard. (*From behind.*) Sure he'll do the dear boy no harm.

Hard. But I heard a voice here; I should be glad to know from whence it came.

Tony. It was I, sir, talking to myself, sir. I was saying that forty miles in four hours was very good going. Hem! As to be sure it was. Hem! I

"I'M MISTAKEN, OR I HEARD VOICES."

have got a sort of cold by being out in the air. We'll go in, if you please. Hem!

HARD. But if you talked to yourself, you did not answer yourself. I'm certain I heard two voices, and am resolved (*raising his voice*) to find the other out.

MRS. HARD. (*From behind.*) Oh! he's coming to find me out. Oh!

TONY. What need you go, sir, if I tell you? Hem! I'll lay down my life for the truth— Hem! I'll tell you all, sir.　　　　　　　[*Detaining him.*

HARD. I tell you I will not be detained. I insist on seeing. It's in vain to expect I'll believe you.

MRS. HARD. (*Running forward from behind.*) O lud! he'll murder my poor boy, my darling! Here, good gentleman, whet your rage upon me. Take my money, my life, but spare that young gentleman; spare my child, if you have any mercy.

HARD. My wife! as I'm a Christian. From whence can she come? or what does she mean?

MRS. HARD. (*Kneeling.*) Take compassion on us, good Mr. Highwayman. Take our money, our watches, all we have, but spare our lives. We will never bring you to justice; indeed we won't, good Mr. Highwayman.

HARD. I believe the woman's out of her senses. What, Dorothy, don't you know me?

MRS. HARD. Mr. Hardcastle, as I'm alive! My fears blinded me. But who, my dear, could have expected to meet you here, in this frightful place, so far from home? What has brought you to follow us?

HARD. Sure, Dorothy, you have not lost your wits? So far from home, when you are within forty yards of your own door! (*To him.*) This is one of your old tricks, you graceless rogue you. (*To her.*) Don't you know the gate, and the mulberry-tree? and don't you remember the horse-pond, my dear?

MRS. HARD. Yes, I shall remember the horse-pond as long as I live; I have caught my death in it. (*To Tony.*) And is it to you, you graceless varlet, I owe all this? I'll teach you to abuse your mother, I will!

TONY. Ecod, mother, all the parish says you have spoiled me, and so you may take the fruits on't.

MRS. HARD. I'll spoil you, I will!　　　　[*Follows him off the stage. Exit.*

HARD. There's morality, however, in his reply.　　　　　　　[*Exit.*

Enter HASTINGS *and* MISS NEVILLE.

HAST. My dear Constance, why will you deliberate thus? If we delay a moment, all is lost forever. Pluck up a little resolution, and we shall soon be out of the reach of her malignity.

MISS NEV. I find it impossible. My spirits are so sunk with the agitations I have suffered, that I am unable to face any new danger. Two or three years' patience will at last crown us with happiness.

HAST. Such a tedious delay is worse than inconstancy. Let us fly, my charmer. Let us date our happiness from this very moment. Perish fortune! Love and content will increase what we possess beyond a monarch's revenue. Let me prevail!

MISS NEV. No, Mr. Hastings, no. Prudence once more comes to my relief, and I will obey its dictates. In the moment of passion, fortune may be despised, but it ever produces a lasting repentance. I'm resolved to apply to Mr. Hardcastle's compassion and justice for redress.

HAST. But though he had the will, he has not the power to relieve you.

MISS NEV. But he has influence, and upon that I am resolved to rely.

HAST. I have no hopes. But since you persist, I must reluctantly obey you.　　　　　　　[*Exeunt.*

"MY DEAR CONSTANCE, WHY WILL YOU DELIBERATE THUS?"

A LUMP OF SUGAR.

By R. R. BOWKER.

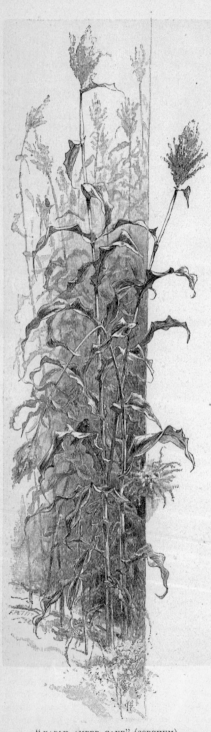

"EARLY AMBER CANE" (SORGHUM).

IT is almost impossible in these days of "sweetness and light," when the comfort and prosperity of a people are fairly tested by its consumption of sugar *per capita*, and this one article contributes more than any two or three others to the expenses of government, to look back to the times when those gracious dames our great-grandmothers, seated about the tea-table, took their delicate nibbles of the new luxury from a lump of sugar suspended in their midst by a string, or, still further in the past, to imagine a sugarless world. Yet sugar was little known to "our ancients." The Chinese date their use of sugar to that same remote and provoking antiquity which they forever fling in the face of the upstart Caucasian, and it is claimed by the apostles of the newest American industry—sorghum-growing—that it was the sorghum plant, rather than the sugar-cane proper, which furnished them with sweetness from its juice, as well as bread from its seeds. From China sugar-growing came, it would seem, to India and Arabia, and the Arabian confections were among the costly luxuries of Greece and Rome. Theophrastus mentions the juice as "honey in reeds," and the solid form is spoken of by Pliny, who describes it as a gravelly substance dissolving in the mouth, and by Dioscorides, the Greek physician who travelled about the world with the Roman armies, in his "Materia Medica," as a medicine. The inevitable Crusaders, who were to Europe what the *Mayflower* Pilgrims are to us, brought the sugar-cane to Europe amongst their many importations of antiquities and novelties, but it had probably been earlier introduced into Spain and Sicily, coming from Arabia by way of Nubia, Egypt, and Northern Africa, by the Moors and Saracens. The Venetian merchants early became interested in its product; they were probably the earliest refiners, and loaf-sugar was first made in Venice in the sixteenth century. A learned treatise on sugar-making, the "Saccharologia" of Sala, appeared in that century, and we have a notice of a refinery existing in Dresden in 1597. From the Mediterranean the sugar-cane emigrated to Madeira, and thence across the Atlantic to San Domingo and the other West Indies, probably early in the sixteenth century. About the middle of last century certain Jesuit priests, coming from San Domingo to Louisiana, are said to have brought the sugar-cane first to our own shores, but it was many years before it was grown commercially. A dramatic tradition exists at New Orleans of the first refining at a plantation near that city, which was made the occasion of a public festival, at which, when the word was given, "It grains," a shout of joy went up from the crowd. Our word "sugar" can be traced by its various forms of middle English *sugre*, French *sucre*, German *zucker*, Spanish *azucar*, Arabic *sakkar* or *sokkar*, and *assokar*, Persian *shakar* (whence the Greek *sakcharon* — Latin *saccharum*), all the way back to the Sanskrit *çarkara*, which originally meant "gravel" — a circumstance which points to the early knowledge of crystalline sugar in Asia as a "sweet gravel." "Jaggery," the name of the crude sugar imported from Asia, is another form of the same word.

Sugar is found in many plants, but the great sugar mines are the sugar-cane, the sorghum grass, and the beet root. The date-palm in the far East and our own maple-tree add to the supply, and some sugar or syrup has been made in southern California from the water-melon. Besides these natural sugars, large quantities of starch sugar or glucose are made by chemical treatment of starch. These are the great commercial sources of sweetness. A sugar which is not sweet is made in small quantities from milk, for use chiefly in medicine, milk sugar being the substance of the homœopathic powders and pellets.

The world's production of sugar is probably well toward eight million tons a year. Of this, British India and China produce and themselves consume over a million tons each of cane sugar, their exports being small, and these of very low grade sugars. The estimated product of all countries available for export was, in 1884–5, a year of large production, 2,162,000 tons of cane and no less than 2,557,800 of beet sugar. It is estimated that the cane-sugar crop marketed this year will increase to 2,218,000 tons, and that the beet-sugar crop will fall off 520,750 tons—partly the result of a lower acreage resulting from the low prices of last year. Cuba produces more than a quarter of the whole export supply of cane sugar, last year's product being 627,000

tons, while this year's will probably equal her largest crop (1875), which was 699,000 tons. Of this, more than half (in 1885, 339,536 gross tons) comes to this country, which gets nearly half its total supply for refining from that island of revolutions. Louisiana produced last year but 94,000 tons, but its normal product is nearer 125,000 tons, to which Texas, our other chief sugar-growing State, adds 10,000 tons more. Five other States contribute some cane sugar. The Sandwich Islands crop, under the stimulus of the treaty which permits its sugar to enter duty free, reaches 65,000 tons, but it is said that the use of all the available land, and the poor quality of native labor, the prohibition of Chinese, and the high price of white labor, fix the limit at the present figure. Of the beet-sugar supply, Germany produced last year 1,155,000 tons, Austria 557,000, Russia 380,000, France 325,000, Belgium 90,000, and Holland 50,000 tons. Our chief contribution to this crop is from a factory at Alvarado, California, producing about 1000 tons, but it is believed that this will become an important Pacific coast industry. Beet sugar is largely imported into this country for refining purposes, and we get also some date-palm sugar, called commercially "date jaggery." Our yield of maple sugar, in which Vermont still leads, was about 25,900 tons last year. Sorghum, although large quantities of syrup are made from the large acreage at the West, has not yet come into the market as an important commercial source of crystallizable sugar, the largest crop having been but 5000 tons; our scientific agriculturists, who give good reasons for looking to this as one of the great American crops of the future, have yet to justify their faith by their works. The manufacture of commercial glucose, or artificial starch sugar, has of late years reached enormous proportions in this country, amounting in value to a third of our cane-sugar crop.

All sugars, as well as starch and gum, belong chemically to the class of carbohydrates, that is, they are a combination of carbon (C) with hydrogen (H) and oxygen (O) already combined in the proportion in which these two form water (H_2O or Aq). There are three groups of these: the true crystalline sugars or *sucroses* ($C_{12}H_{22}O_{11}$), including cane sugar, milk sugar, maltose (the sugar of malt), etc.; the *glucoses* ($C_6H_{12}O_6$ or $C_{12}H_{24}O_{12}$),

CUTTING SUGAR-CANE.

or inverted sugars, which contain one more atom of water, including grape sugar or dextrose, fruit sugar or lævulose, etc.; and the *amyloses* ($C_6H_{10}O_5$ or $C_{12}H_{20}O_{10}$), which contain one less atom of water, and are found in irregular granules instead of crystals, including starch, dextrine (the "sticking-stuff" used for postage-stamps), the gums, and cellulose, or vegetable fibre, of which cotton is the most noteworthy example, being almost pure cellulose. Thus a lump of charcoal (C) and a glass of water (H_2O) contain together all the elements of a lump of sugar, a pint of syrup, a pound of starch, or a spool of thread. By chemical treatment either the sugar group or the starch group can be turned into the glucoses, and, by fermentation, into alcohol (C_2H_5OH). Thus a chemist will make sweetness out of your cotton handkerchief, a manufacturer will transform the starch of tons of corn into glucose, and a brewer or distiller will produce from barley malt or corn and rye gallons of beer or whiskey. Stranger still, from these same carbo-hydrates powerful explosives can be made: a mixture of sugar with chlorate of potash makes a "white gunpowder," which a drop of acid will touch off; and by soaking cotton (cellulose) with nitric and sulphuric acids, gun-cotton is produced, which may be spun and woven into unsuspicious thread or cloth or paper that will explode at a flash, or solidified into the useful but highly inflammable celluloid. Dissolved in alcohol and ether, gun-cotton becomes the collodion which on drying produces the film so useful in surgery as a temporary skin. At a temperature of 320° F. true sugar becomes the transparent substance known as barley sugar; at 400° F. it loses part of its water and becomes "caramel" or burnt sugar, the coloring matter of molasses, of brown candies, and of some liquors.

Within each of the three carbo-hydrate groups there are numerous substances, which are, as the chemists phrase it, *isomeric* (of *equal parts*), that is, containing exactly the same kind and number of atoms, but *allotropic*, that is, with these atoms arranged in *different ways*. In the "spelling game" you can arrange the same letters A, E, M, N into the quite different words, Mane, Mean, Name, Amen. Nature has the same trick. She puts her C's (carbon) together to make coal, graphite (of "lead" pencils), or the diamond. Thus out of six C's, ten H's, five O's, she makes starch, or gum, or cellulose; out of $C_{12}H_{22}O_{11}$, she makes a number of different sugars; out of $C_6H_{12}O_6$, she makes dextro-glucose or dextrose, lævo-glucose or lævulose, and still other glucoses. These have different qualities, but are chiefly to be distinguished apart by the curious effect they have in turning aside a ray of light which has first been "polarized," or made to vibrate on one plane only. Dextrose, indeed, is so called because it turns the ray to the right (*dexter*), and lævulose because, though exactly of the same atoms, it turns the ray to the left (*lævus*), or inverse direction. Cane sugar, pure, dissolved in its weight of water at a temperature of 59°, rotates the ray 73.80 to the right, whereas trehalose, a true sugar made from Turkish manna, rotates it under the

part of the instrument, and with the help of an eye-piece at the other end of the tube the degree of deviation is read off on a little scale above, marked to show the actual percentage of sugar. The key to this useful and wonderful provision of nature is probably the simple fact that the different combinations of atoms give different reflecting or refracting surfaces to the different crystals or granules.

The man who, by the patient plodding of scientific investigation, or by the inspiration of genius which is its equivalent, will some day read the secret of an atom of carbon, in its protean combinations with its intimates oxygen and hydrogen,

A PRIMITIVE SUGAR-MILL IN ARKANSAS.

same conditions 220° to the right. If the sugar is less pure, or the solution stronger, it has a different effect on the ray, and this fact is the basis of the commercial test of sugars by the scientific instrument called the polariscope, in which a ray of light, polarized as it is admitted into the instrument, passes through a solution of sugar, carefully weighed and dissolved in a definite amount of water, and placed in a long tube, closed with glass at both ends. The deflection of the ray is counteracted by interposing a wedge of quartz, forming a

will achieve one of the great triumphs of mankind. Out of the corn which gives us the daily bread for which we daily pray comes also the spirit which crazes men; out of the wholesome peach, the deadly acid one drop of which will kill. The same simple atoms are in each, and our rudest manufacturing processes can give them the change of form which is the difference between life and death; but science has not yet reached below the surface of the mystery, and to the wisest eye the transformation is still a miracle.

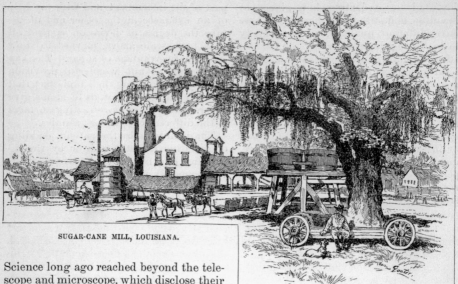

SUGAR-CANE MILL, LOUISIANA.

Science long ago reached beyond the telescope and microscope, which disclose their secrets to the eye, and turns now to the spectroscope and the polariscope, which reveal to the scientific imagination those infinitesimal secrets evident only in the effects of atoms, unknown and unseen, on the delicate and tremulous beam of light. The beam of the polariscope is not unlikely to become the divining-rod of the Columbus, yet to come, of organic chemistry, who will prove one of the great benefactors of mankind. So far, man, for the most part, has had to be content with undoing what nature has done, as in breaking up starch into glucose or alcohol. Some "organic" substances, as indigo and the aniline dyes, have, however, been made by man. When, if ever, he succeeds, directly or indirectly, in converting the carbon about us, the hydrogen and oxygen of water, the free nitrogen of the air, into the organic products we now get, in roundabout fashion, only through nature's laboratory, the plants, the whole problem of food supply will be solved.

For the plants are the great sugar-makers. By what mysterious force each extracts from the soil and the air, by help of sun and wind and rain, the exact proportions of carbon, hydrogen, and oxygen which it combines into its characteristic sugar, we can only conjecture. Still more mysterious is the transfer of "the principle of life" and of growth at certain periods of plant development from the production of fibre throughout the plant to the production of sugar in the cells, or the misdirection of that principle, under certain ill conditions of weather, to the production of "invert sugar," which provokes fermentation and the ruin of the crop.

The sugars produced by animals come chiefly, probably entirely, from the carbohydrates of the plants. The bee collects the true sugar lodged infinitesimally in two and a half millions of flowers, so it is said, to make his pound of honey, the sugar of which is really a glucose. It is a glucose also, called diabetic sugar, which is produced abnormally by the human body in the disease known as *diabetes* (or "pouring through"), from the excessive excretion of the kidneys, which holds great quantities of sugar in solution. This excessive production of sugar, which can be partially held in check by the use of non-saccharine or diabetic food, was long supposed to be a disease of the kidneys, but physicians are now inclined to consider it more a disease of the nervous system, originating at the base of the brain, which the kidneys are trying in vain to correct. In fact, it has been artificially produced in animals by experiments on the brain, and brain-workers are found to be peculiarly subject to it. Somehow or other the nerves fail to do their work, or the right orders are not given through them from the nerve centres, the processes of life go wrong, and sooner or later comes death. This is about all that medicine can tell us now; some day it will know more.

Among the sugar-producing plants, the sugar-cane, the sorghum grass, and our Indian corn, or maize, are near cousins in vegetable society, belonging all to the family of the grasses. They look down from a superior height of a dozen feet, more or less, upon their humbler second cousins twice removed, the wheat, rye, barley, oats, and common grasses of our fields, modest but very useful members of another group of the same family. There is no "set" of the vegetable kingdom to which humankind and all kinds of animal life owe more than to these humble folk and their big cousins. We get the greater part of our own food and a fiery portion of our drink from their seeds, most of the fodder for our beasts from their stalks, bedding for man and beast from the dry straw and husks, sweetness from the juice, and finally cleanliness, which is next to godliness, and so gives the family a connection with spiritual things, from the broom-corn variety of sorghum, which does most of our sweeping. The sorghum, sugar-cane, and maize are magnificent plants, with their broad green leaves, their tall stems, and the clustered spikes or tassels atop, reaching in the case of some varieties a height of thirty feet. They are distinguished from the other groups of grasses by having pithy instead of hollow stems, in which pith nature stores her sweetness. All of them require abundant moisture, more or less heat and sunshine, and a soil containing some organic matter—potash, silica, phosphoric and sulphuric acids, lime and magnesia, and oxides of iron and manganese. They seem to have the property of extracting most of their nutriment from the air, so much so that some investigators look upon them, especially maize, when ploughed in, as nature's great means of recuperating poor soil and of turning inorganic matter into organic food. Sorghum, it is said, will produce crop after crop from the same ground, and cane will grow in the tropics fifteen years consecutively without exhausting the soil.

Although sorghum is generally considered an upstart thrusting itself into sugar-cane society, it has claims to be considered the more ancient and aristocratic of the two. It is said that sorghum, which is the *durra* of the East, was the plant originally used by the Chinese in making sugar. The differences between the two plants are many and vital, despite their botanical grouping. The sugar-cane (*Saccharum officinarum*, Linn.) is a perennial plant, growing in favorable localities sometimes

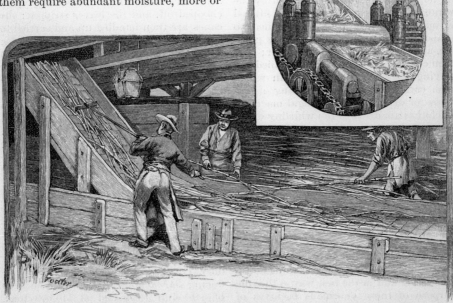

THE CRUSHERS.

for fifty years from the same roots, propagated not by seed but from cuttings, of slow growth, and requiring in the tropics often from fourteen months to two years for its development. The sorghum (*Sorghum vulgare*, Pers.), which is really a cereal, and much more like maize than like sugar-cane, is an annual, grown from seed, and maturing often within three months. The sugar-cane is of thick and sturdy growth, with a great deal of woody fibre in its outer envelope, and with a tough and dense internal structure. The sorghum is taller and more slender, of a softer outer structure, and less dense pith. The sorghum, unlike the sugar-cane, is crowned with a cluster of edible seeds, the "seed head," used as food for men as well as for cattle. There are a number of species of sugar-cane, although all are supposed to have developed by cultivation from a single progenitor, whose *habitat* is unknown; the varieties of the sorghum are less marked, and are all definitely within one species.

The process of "sugar-making," in its essentials, is a simple enough matter of cookery. The first care of the producer is to get all the sugar possible out of the cane or grass or root, either by squeezing out the juice or washing out the sugar; the sugar-maple saves the sugar-maker this trouble, delivering the sap ready for the boiler. The juice is then cleared of its impurities, as coffee is cleared by the white of an egg, or water is filtered through charcoal; it is then boiled, to evaporate as much of the water as possible, and crystallize the solid sugar; it is then cooled, and the molasses drained off, leaving the soft dark sugars, in which each crystal has its thin coating of molasses, or dried by a centrifugal machine, as clothes are dried in the whirling drier, whence the water flies out, or further clarified and left to crystallize in white loaves, which are sawed or crushed or ground or powdered into the several varieties of fine white sugar. Most of these earlier processes are performed on the plantations, but in many cases they are repeated and the sugar carried through the final process in the great refineries. "Refining" is, in fact, little more than a finer repetition of the processes of "making," and to do these simple things on a great scale and in the best way is the sole purpose of those enormous beehives of industry.

The sugar planter requires for his cane plantation a warm, moist climate, with intervals of hot, dry weather, with little danger from frost; a soil not too rich, containing lime and magnesia, and of good drainage; and the benefit of sea-breezes, salt in the air being better for him than salt in the soil. The sugar plantations of Louisiana find these conditions in the alluvial soil of the lower Mississippi Valley. In laying out an estate, drainage must be carefully provided for, and in some countries irrigation is much used. From one to four cuttings are set out together in holes about two feet apart. As the canes grow they must be well weeded and "trashed," *i. e.*, all dry, dead leaves removed. They begin to grow in Louisiana in February, and are harvested from October to January. After the first cutting of the new plants the stole or stool left sends up another growth of cane, called "ratoons," which with each cutting grow smaller in size and closer in joints, and are said to yield sweeter juice and finer sugar. The one planting will last many years, but Louisiana sugar-growers reckon only on three years' product, planting a third of the sugar ground anew each year. Rats, white ants, lice, "borers," and some minute animals producing "rust" and "must," fight against the growing plant, as also do wind and frost. When cutting-time comes, the cane is cut with a hatchet close to the stole, the top is chopped off, and the leaves stripped; the canes are then bundled up and carried to the mill, often, on the large plantations, on narrow donkey railways, or placed in windrows, on the fields, so that the juice may not ferment until they can be handled.

Louisiana plantations, when the crop is in full vigor, are indeed a lovely sight, with their broad expanse of leafy cane. Some of them are of great extent, the Magnolia Plantation, now owned by ex-Governor Warmoth, which claims to be one of the banner plantations of the State, having 492 acres in cane last year. In 1883–4 over 172,400 acres of cane were harvested in the State, the total crop of 128,000 tons of sugar being one of the best ever made in the State; but in 1884–5 floods spoiled so much of the crop that only 118,650 acres were harvested, producing 94,000 tons of sugar. The crop of 1885–6 is estimated at 110,000 tons. About 20,000 freedmen are kept busy in the sugar fields and mills. The plantations are expected to yield from twenty to twenty-five tons of cane per acre, though the average of the State in the short crop of 1884–5 was but seventeen tons. A good crop should produce 3,000,000 tons of cane, and be worth to the State from $12,500,000

the tropics, contains a much larger proportion of juice, much richer in sugar, than the Bourbon cane, commonly grown in Louisiana. It is seldom that as much as half of this sugar is utilized. The Magnolia Plantation this past year indeed produced $163\frac{3}{4}$ pounds per ton, but

WEIGHING SUGAR ON THE DOCKS.

up. To this Texas and the five other States which dabble in cane-growing add little over ten per cent.

The census returns of 1880 reported 227,776 acres in sugar-cane, of which 181,592 were in Louisiana. The crop was 178,872 hogsheads of sugar and 16,573,273 gallons of molasses, of which Louisiana's entire return was 171,706 hogsheads of sugar and 11,696,248 gallons of molasses. The cane is ninety per cent. juice, and the juice contains about fifteen per cent. of sugars, so that a hundred pounds of cane hold about thirteen and a half pounds of sugar. These figures vary greatly, however, with the variety of cane and the character of the season. The Otaheite cane, requiring a much longer hot season to ripen it, and therefore grown only in

the average for Louisiana was, with the vacuum process, 130 pounds, by other processes 87 pounds, per ton of cane. Great progress has been made in sugar-growing in recent years through an improved levee system to keep the waters of the Mississippi under control, better means of transportation, more scientific treatment of the land, and more complete processes of manufacture; but there is still an enormous margin for increased production by improved scientific methods, and an increase of half as much again in the yield of sugar per acre ought to be within the possibilities of the near future. The crop now costs $2 50 per ton of cane, or $50 or so per acre, and should yield about $500 total return. This would add over $5,000,000 yearly to the wealth of the State. So much for statistics, and their word to science.

The sugar-maker's first aim is to get from the cane as much of its percentage of juice as it can be induced to give up. The juice is enclosed in little cells of lignose, or woody fibre, which make the other tenth of the cane's weight. There are three ways of extracting the juice—by crushing, by soaking out the sugar by the process of "diffusion," or by a combination of crushing and of maceration in water. Crushing or grinding the cane is a process in use from the earliest times, as is seen in the primitive sugar-mills of the East, which consist of the hollowed stump of a tree, within which is a grinding pestle worked by oxen treading their round, driven from the arm of the bar by one man, while another feeds in pieces of cane, one by one, and takes out the crushed remains. A mill almost as primitive as this is still in use in Arkansas.

The sugar-house on a great plantation is a large, high building, the centre of the farm, to which roads or tramways lead from all directions. As a load of cane comes up, it is fed upon an endless belt or railway, which carries it up slowly to the crushing-mill, an affair of simple construction but of enormous power. The crushers are great rollers of cast-iron, in pairs or triplets, sometimes one set, sometimes more, working at a pressure of from fifty to eighty pounds to the square inch, and so arranged as to give slightly before any extraordinary strain. There are all sorts of opinions as to whether it is better to crush rapidly or slowly, and to crush once only or to repeat the operation with increasing pressures. The juice flows from the crushers in one direction; the residual cane, now known as "begass," is carried off in another by an endless belt, to be used either for dressing for the cane fields or as fuel in the heating processes which the juice is next to undergo. One of the great improvements in modern sugar-making has been the development of furnaces which get most of their fuel from the begass.

There have been several attempts to extract a greater proportion of juice by purely mechanical means, as by defibrators, shredding the cane into pulp, by raspers also tearing it into shreds, and by the curious press invented by Bessemer, but never much used, in which the canes were crushed endwise by a plunger working in a cylinder. Another method slices the canes lengthwise before crushing. The process of maceration consists in wetting or steaming the cane, either before crushing or after a first crushing.

The "diffusion" process is used somewhat in cane and commonly in beet-sugar making. Cane-cutters first slice the cane diagonally about one-sixteenth of an inch thick in pieces three or four inches long. These slices go to the diffusion "battery," a series of ten or a dozen tanks, in one of which the fresh slices are subjected to steaming and then to a flow of fresh water, which carries into the next tank the first extraction of sugar. The solution goes from tank to tank until it is nearly saturated, when it is withdrawn from the battery, while from another tank the now exhausted chips drop through a slide valve into begass carts below, and are saved for manure, or sometimes for paper-making. About eighty-three per cent. of the juice is thus saved. This process has, however, not met with favor in this country.

The juice has now to be purified (or "defecated") and clarified, going first through a preliminary straining, by means of an endless sieve of wire-gauze, which lets the strained juice through into gutters beneath, and delivers the scum at the end of the machine. It is then heated in pans or steam-coil boilers to about 210° F., "milk of lime" being added to neutralize the acid in the juice. A scum rises and a sediment falls; the cleared juice is run off by itself. An excess of lime has to be corrected by the use of acids, sulphuric or sulphurous, a delicate process known as "tempering." The liquid must then be filtered, and finally crystallized into sugar.

These processes, in the old-fashioned plantation sugar-houses, are effected by what is known as a "battery" of open pans or "taches." The first two pans are the clarifiers; below these, copper pans are set in masonry on a descending plane, the lowest of which is the "striking tache," under which is the furnace. The temperature of the upper pans is lower according to their distance from the fire. The juice is ladled from one pan to another down the scale, becoming of course more concentrated from the greater heat as it descends, until at the striking pan it is on the point of crystallization. If syrup from sour canes has got into the pan, producing a sticky proof, some buckets of lime-water are let in; on the other hand, dilute sul-

THE MIXING-ROOM.

phuric acid is introduced to clear a dark sugar. Now, after six or eight hours of boiling, the *masse-cuite* (cooked mass), as the concentrated juice is called, of a reddish gold-color, is ready for the "strike." Here the skill of the sugar-maker, standing half naked by the pan, his eye alert on the mass, must be tested. He must "strike," that is, dip off the liquid, at exactly the moment when it is ready to crystallize in the coolers. Perhaps half the contents of the pan is "struck out," or "cut." The rest is left in the pan for "doubling," or adding new syrup to make still larger crystals. Sometimes four or five cuts are made before the boiling is finished.

Most of the better plantations now use, however, the vacuum pan, which will be described as we reach the refineries. By reducing the pressure of the air, this enables the sugar to be boiled at a lower temperature, so that there is less danger of loss from burning or overheating. The "triple effect" process, very largely in use, is a combination of three steam pans, in which the pressure is less and the syrup

denser in the second than in the first, and in the third than in the second, as the liquid passes continuously through the series. As the exhaust steam of one pan is used for heating another, the saving of fuel is considerable. But the vacuum processes can best be explained by making a sudden journey (on paper) from the plantations of Louisiana to the great refineries of New York, where the methods of sugar-making are repeated on a grand scale, in the most scientific manner.

The great refineries which line the water-front of Brooklyn and Jersey City are enormous piles of brick, often more than a hundred feet high, with a dozen or more rows of windows one above the other, with no pretentions to architectural show, but by their very size and massiveness making an impressive feature of the river landscape. They are contrived so as to take the sugar as it is landed, and carry it through one process after another with the least possible waste of power, time, and space, until the "shining sand" emerges purified and ready for consumption. Accordingly the refineries are alongside deep water, and at their wharves vessels of all sorts, from West Indian coasters to the great steam "tramps" that roam the world over in search of a job, may be seen, three and four together, unloading their cargoes into the voracious maw of the great cook-shop. The dock presents a busy scene. Great hogsheads or stacks of bags are swung by derricks over the ships' sides, or a constant line of hurrying men bustle down the gang-planks with barrow-loads of bags. Uncle Sam has first to make sure that he gets his share in the shape of duties, and the refiner must also have a care that he himself gets what he is pay-ing for, and that Uncle Sam does not get more than his dues. The first work, therefore, is that of weighing and sam-pling. Two huge scale beams confront each other on the dock, one marked "U. S.," the other that of a city weigher, paid by and representing the refiner. Each hogshead is trundled along in a hurry to Uncle Sam's scale; the chain grips it; two stout pair of arms at the other end of the lever swing it into the air; a quick eye and a quick hand note the gross weight; a sampler runs his gauge through the bung, and turns out the sample into a tin can with the others, presently to be sent on to the examiners for testing. Then the cask is turned over to the second weigher, who repeats the process on the refiner's part, and compares notes with the gov-ernment's weigher. After the sugar has been turned out, one hogshead out of ev-ery three or four is weighed for "tare," and allowance made accordingly on the weigher's books.

On the wharf-level are the mixing-rooms, dark kitchens, misty and mysteri-ous with clouds of steam, where brawny men rush about half naked on the edge of seething pits of muddy broth. The floor is sloppy and treacherous, and one shudders at the horrid possibilities of a fate which has more than once overtaken the workers at this cyclopean cookery. Suddenly there comes trundling in an enormous hogshead weighing 1500 to 2000 pounds. Two men, springing fiercely at it with big hammers, knock in the head, while others attach the chains from a big derrick above, which by the pull of a lever raises the cask above the open mouth of the "mixer," and dumps its contents into the steaming syrup below. These "mix-

ers" or "blow-ups" are really great stew-pans set in the ground, heated by steam, which melt the crude sugar into a syrup, and mix together the various caskfuls and bagfuls. They are tanks made of wrought or cast iron, and inside are a vertical re-volving shaft on which are the mixing arms, and coils of steam-pipe whence live steam is blown into the seething mixture. Before the raw sugar is dumped in, clear water, or "sweet water" from the wash-ings of bags, is run in, and heated nearly to boiling. These tanks hold 3000 to 4500 gallons, and treat nine to thirteen tons of sugar at a time. The heating occupies half an hour or so, during which a scum of impurities rises to the top, and is skimmed off, while other dregs, sometimes precipi-tated, if the mixture shows a tinge of acid-ity, by a few buckets of lime-water, sink to the bottom, and are cleaned out after the liquor is run off. From the mixers run pipes connecting with force-pumps, which raise the liquid to the very top of the enor-mous building, whence, percolating down-ward, it goes through the refining process, reaching the lower stories as clear sugar.

A rude elevator takes us up to the top. For company we have the "beer man," who rings his hand-bell vigorously at each landing, and sets out a line of little pails of beer. Brawny fellows they are who come to drain them, sweating at ev-ery pore, for it is hard and hot work they do, and "moistening up" is a necessary process within as the moisture pours from them without. At last we reach the top, whence the open windows com-mand a far view of the river, the great city silent below, the two-legged midgets which skip to and fro on the wharf right beneath us. In sharp contrast with the place we have left, this is a great silent room, where nothing seems to be going on. We are in the defecating-room, fitted with banks or ranges of square tanks about six feet high, which are the "defe-cators." These are filled with the liquid pumped up from the "mixers," kept at about 170° temperature, undergoing the same process used by the house-keeper in clearing coffee with the white of an egg. What happens in the coffee-pot is simply that the albumen of the egg, as it diffuses itself and sinks slowly to the bottom, makes a kind of mesh which takes along with it the solid particles of dregs or lees which have not dissolved, leaving the coffee solution clear. Bullock's blood or

REFINING WORKS, NEW YORK HARBOR.—Drawn by Charles Graham.

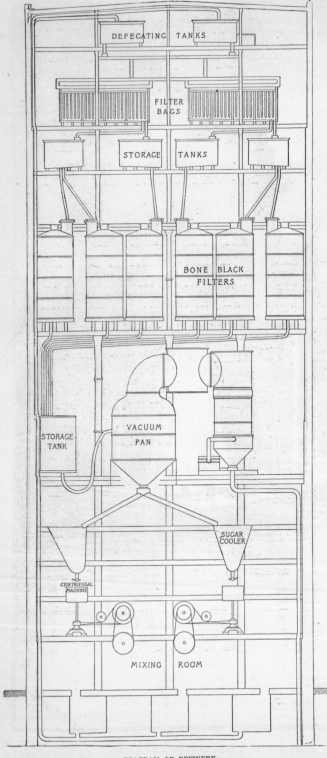

DIAGRAM OF REFINERY.

some other form of albuminous matter performs the same service for the sugar in these defecators. After from twenty minutes to half an hour the clear liquor is drawn off, and the dregs separately removed.

The good house-keeper will not only clear, but also strain her coffee; the refiner does the same with his sugar. On the next stage below, the floor seems to be a series of gutters, underneath which, it will be presently seen, hang, in great compartments holding four or five hundred bags each, the bag filters, of coarse, thick cotton twill, four or five feet long, and but a few inches round. The liquor from the defecators flows through the gutters into these filters, and thence to the floor of the compartments, where it is collected again, and carried off into vats. After the liquor has run through the bags, there remains in them much good sugar; consequently the gutters are flushed with clean warm water, which running through the bags brings the sugar with it, making a weaker liquor called "sweet water," and leaving behind only the insoluble dregs. These are washed out, by turning the bags inside out, by stout-armed washermen, whose work is not confined to Monday mornings, but lasts day in and day out.

The liquor has now been freed from its organic and insoluble matters, and is a bright but brown-colored syrup, containing still some soluble impurities. It must now be rid of these. The means employed is similar to the charcoal filter screwed on a faucet to purify drinking water, but the filter becomes a Brobdingnag affair, an enormous circular tank two stories deep (or about twenty feet) and eight feet across. Finely powdered charcoal, particularly

tom, perforated, over which a blanket is fitted to prevent the bone-black from flowing through with the liquid. A stream of bone-black is then turned on, which must be distributed evenly through the filter. To do this, a workman descends into this atmosphere of powdered blackness, first fitting a sponge over his mouth and nostrils. He fastens to the rim of the man-hole a hanging ladder of linked

THE BONE-BLACK FILTER.

the animal charcoal called bone-black, made by calcining and pulverizing bone, has a peculiar power which the most skilled chemists do not fully understand. It decolorizes syrup by retaining the soluble impurities, letting the cleared liquid pass through. The filters, of which a large refinery may contain a hundred or more, open through man-holes at the top to the filter-room floor. When a filter is to be refilled, the first work is to rinse it thoroughly clean. The tank has a false bot-

steel, takes an electric lamp suspended from a flexible wire, and disappears into the black pit. The largest filters hold thirty to forty tons of the bone-black. When they are filled, the man-hole is closed, and the syrup from the cisterns below the bag filters is turned on. It percolates slowly down, is allowed some time to settle, and after about seven hours the drawing off begins through a narrow discharge pipe. The syrup is at first crystal clear, and is discharged into a

tank from which the whitest and purest
sugars will be made. As it exhausts the
powers of the bone-black it becomes more
and more amber-colored, as is seen by the
rows of tiny glasses set in a frame against
the light, filled with samples taken at in-

eral stories of the great buildings are
given up. As a matter of fact, reburning
is just what is not done; the bone-black
is not burned, otherwise it would disappear in vapor; it is expressly prevented
from burning by being treated in red-hot

THE VACUUM PAN.

tervals from the flow. Each shelf in this
frame represents one filtering, and the
successive glasses side by side represent a
gamut of tone, from brilliant transparency
to a strong gold-color. A skilled workman, as the syrup begins to lose its clearness, turns the discharge at the fitting
moment into a second tank, and thus different grades of sugars are separated.
After about twenty hours the charge is
run out; the sugar remaining in the charcoal is washed out by running through
fresh or sweet water, and the bone-black
must be "reburned" before it can again be
used. A ton of bone-black filters about a
ton of sugar.

The "reburning" of the bone-black,
though purely a side process, is part of the
work of all large refineries, and to it sev-

pipes from which the air is carefully excluded, between which a hot flame plays.
The impurities are, however, burned, and
go off as vapor. The damp charcoal is
run out or shovelled out of the filters at
the bottom; it is washed, sometimes permitted to ferment, partly dried, and then
delivered into the burners or pipes referred to, heated by enormous fires in the
story below. It comes out "revivified"
through these cleansing fires and as good
as new, indeed better, for bone-black four
to six months in use is said to give the
best results. Some time after this it de-
teriorates, and must be mixed with new
charcoal or cast aside.

The liquor is now refined; it remains to
crystallize the sugar into solid form. This
is accomplished in the vacuum pan, or

striking pan. The principle is another application of science to kitchen cookery. The housewife who is making sugar-candy boils down her syrup till it is thick, and then lets it cool: the result is that it crystallizes more or less perfectly, and produces solid candy. If strings are strung across a pan as the mass slowly cools, large crystals of rock-candy form on them. The cook's trouble usually is that as the syrup becomes thicker, it takes a hotter fire to keep it boiling, and it is very likely to "catch" and burn. When it burns, it makes caramel; if it is not boiled enough it makes a molasses, and will not "pull" or solidify, but remains sticky.

The sugar refiner has the same difficulties to avoid and the same purposes to about forty tons of syrup. Inside the boiler are coils of steam-pipe, which do the heating. Now in boiling, the bubbles of vapor which rise to the top are kept down by the pressure of the outer air, and as a liquid grows thick these bubbles find it harder to force their way to the top, and so it requires more heat to boil a dense liquid. If, therefore, the pressure above is relieved, the bubbles rise easier, and boiling commences at a lower temperature, at which also a liquid is less likely to burn. The vacuum pan has an opening through its cover into a great pipe connected with an air-pump, which pumps the air and vapor from the top of the heated syrup, and thus permits it to boil at a lower temperature, and prevents

FILLING THE CONES.

accomplish. The vacuum pan—invented by Charles E. Howard, an Englishman, in 1813—is an enormous copper boiler, covered with a copper cover or dome, both parts being fastened together, air-tight and steam-tight, along the rim. The larger ones are twenty feet high, holding the formation of caramel. This pump is set at work, and as soon as the pressure is reduced, a feed-cock at the side is opened and syrup sufficient to cover the first coil of pipe is let in. The pipe is charged with steam, and the syrup begins to concentrate. At short intervals a new supply of syrup is let in, the upper steam coils are heated, and presently the liquid begins to "grain," or crystallize. Now comes the critical time when the skill of the sugar-maker is tested. There are several devices to show him what is going on inside the pan without breaking the vacuum: a thermometer and a vacuum gauge stand out from the top; there is a sight glass set hermetically into the side through which he may peep in; and an ingenious device, called a "proof stick," enables him to take out samples at any time. This is a hollow rod of brass or gun-metal fitting closely into a larger tube, which extends into the pan and is closed at the end by a sort of stopcock. When the proof stick is run into this tube and turned half-way round, the stopcock is opened and the stick is filled with the liquid. It is then turned back and withdrawn, and the quick eye of the sugar-maker makes "proof" by noticing against the light the crystals adhering to the stick, or by cooling the *masse-cuite* on a plate of glass. If the sugar-maker desires a large regular grain, he uses a thin syrup and concentrates it quietly and slowly. As each new charge is let in,

it boils up to the bull's-eye, or sight glass, and then subsides, adding its contribution to the existing crystals, which gradually "grow." If the sugar-maker makes mistakes, the new syrup, instead of depositing on the existing crystals, starts a new set of minute crystals of its own, making a "false grain," and injuring the quality of the sugar. When the proof will scarcely run out of the socket of the proof stick, the temperature is reduced below 150° F.; a slide at the bottom of the pan is opened, and the contents are run out into a receptacle below.

After the *masse-cuite* has left the pan, the crystallization is completed by cooling, and the sugar must then be cured. The processes are quite different for "mould" and for "soft" sugars. The best grades of syrup, boiled to an even, good-sized grain, are used for the former, whether loaf, cut, crushed, or pulverized. As the syrup cools it is run into conical moulds, with a small aperture at the bottom or smaller end, through which the uncrystallized liquid may drain off. As this drains off at the bottom, fresh liquid is poured in at the top, which washes the

SAWING SUGAR.

crystals as it slowly filters through. After some days the moulds are turned over, and the brilliant white cone of the "sugar-loaf" is turned out, solid to the last degree. This has disappeared, in its old-

is so sugary that one tastes the sweetness as he breathes. The crushed sugar is literally "crushed" by merely smashing the loaves; the pulverized sugar is simply ground fine from the dust of the other

THE DANCING BARRELS.

fashioned blue paper wrappings, from the grocer's shelves, but the finest sugars are still made from it.

The square lump-sugar is made by sawing up these loaves, first into round plates or disks, then into square rods, and then into the little cubes, by successive gang-saws, like those of a big saw-mill on a small scale, enclosed in covers like Dutch ovens to prevent waste of the sugar dust. Nevertheless, the air of the sawing-room

kinds, and sifted out by a long vibrating sieve. Granulated sugars may be made from loaf by tearing the crystals apart, but it is now mostly the product of the centrifugal machines.

The "soft" sugars are cured mostly by the centrifugal machines, which act on the familiar principle of the rotary clothes-drier. The centrifugal machines are claimed as the invention of a Massachusetts man named Hurd, in 1844, although

SORGHUM FACTORY AT HUTCHINSON, KANSAS.

it is said that the principle had previously been applied in England. They are practically two tubs or drums set one within the other, the inner one pierced with fine holes and revolving at great speed, reaching a thousand revolutions a minute. Over each centrifugal is a discharge pipe from the coolers; the brown syrup is let in, the inner drum is started, and as it whirls a change of color is seen in its inner wall, from dark to light brown, gradually to yellow, and then suddenly, if the sugar is of high grade, to brilliant white. The reason is simple. As the drum gains speed, the liquid flies off by centrifugal force, first the free liquid, and finally, as clean water is introduced for a final washing, even the delicate film of syrup or molasses coating each crystal, leaving its intrinsic whiteness to shine forth. The solid crystals remain, and fall to the bottom as the machine is stopped.

The sugar is now ready for barrelling. Most of the large refineries have cooper shops of their own, and as the barrels are delivered it is amusing to see the dexterity of those practised in handling them, as they start them spinning a hundred yards away, rounding a post or a corner, and bringing up exactly where they are wanted. The sugar is delivered slowly from spouts above the barrels, each of which "stands on its own bottom," in a separate frame, which is by eccentric machinery given just the irregular motion a man gives a barrel in "settling" it. It is droll enough to see these rows of barrels bobbing and nodding and making lunges toward each other, as though they were a set of tipsy topers holding hands in a row to keep themselves steady, and singing "We won't go home till morning!" This is the method of packing granulated sugars; the softer kinds are packed, like flour, by a screw press.

Sorghum sugar making is, in this country, rather a matter of prophecy than of experience, yet there seems to be no good reason why the work of the Department of Agriculture, of which this industry is a pet nursling, should not result in developing an important interest. The first sorghum seed was sent to this country in 1853, and the department has ever since "lent a hand" to encourage sorghum-growing, scattering over the country in a recent season, from the experimental sorghum farm established near Washington, over 60,000 pounds of seed. The growing of sorghum received its first impetus during the war, when the supply of Louisiana molasses was cut off, and all through the Western country farmers planted their half-acre of sorghum, and produced a few gallons of syrup. The first methods of manufacture were primitive enough. The first crushers were upright wooden rollers, worked by an old horse, and fed by a lad who thrust each stalk by itself through a hole in front of the rollers, dodging the beam each time the old horse went by. While it was in operation its dreadful crunching and screeching might be heard the country round, and the relief was great when, as often happened, the horse stalled and the mill stuck. Then iron mills of two-horse-power were made, and great was the demand. Farmers possessing them would "make up" their neighbors' crops on shares. The ordinary maple-sugar pans were used for boiling, and from the earliest daylight of frosty October, when the crusher would be started, until late at night, when the boiling was completed, the farmer and his men worked hard at his syrup crop. The crop was, in fact, chiefly syrup, for in the census year, 1879–80, when forty States and Territories reported sorghum, but 12,792 pounds of sugar were made, against 20,444,402 gallons of molasses. In 1881 New Jersey established a bounty of one dollar per ton of cane and one cent per pound of merchantable sugar grown in the State, and though only one establishment was the result, that at Rio Grande, this produced 375,869 pounds of sugar in 1884. The State has paid out in four years $22,275 for cane and $11,219 24 for sugar. Besides this, there are considerable factories at Sterling, Ottawa, and Hutchinson, Kansas, and as much as a million pounds of sugar has been produced in a season.

The sugar sorghum is planted from seed in April or May, and at first grows slowly, very like its cousin the broom-corn sorghum. The botanists distinguish only one species, but the farmer finds a good deal of difference between the "Early Amber cane," which is the favorite, the Orange, also much planted, Link's Hybrid,

the Honduras, Liberian, and other kinds, which ripen later than the Early Amber, and are therefore less suited to high latitudes. After the plant gets its real start, it grows wonderfully, and with remarkable independence of season and climate, in wet times or dry times, when Indian corn would be drowned out or burned up, and from Minnesota to Texas, where it has been known to develop a second crop from the stubble after the first has been cut. Profitable growing for sugar is, however, confined to lower latitudes than at first supposed, and the isothermal lines of 70° for the three summer months is now thought by the best authorities to mark the sugar limit, though syrup may be profitably made further north. This includes Missouri, Tennessee, Kentucky, Illinois—which led in syrup production in the census year in the order named—Kansas, southern Indiana, etc., as probable sugar-producing States. The crop ripens at the North in September and October, and at its maturity presents a fine picture, with its deep green leafage, and the red or dark tops of ripening seed. Its great enemies are early frosts and the equinoctial storm, which is apt to strike the plant just as it is ready to harvest, top-heavy with its cone of seed, and bend it to the ground. In 1883 the storm played sad havoc with the ripened crop. The Western farmers, who grow mostly for syrup, report a yield of from 150 gallons of syrup per acre up, costing about $24 per acre to raise, in addition to use of land and outfit. At fifty cents per gallon, this would give a profit of about $30 per acre; but the trouble is that this syrup must come into competition with other syrups selling at scarcely above half that price.

Sugar-making from sorghum follows the same processes as with cane. The most notable plantation and mill in the country is that started in 1881 at Rio Grande, New Jersey, which occupies a stretch of four miles along a narrow peninsula near Cape May. The cane is brought to the mill on a tramway, a contractor who works the plantation delivering it stripped and taking away the begass at $2 12 the ton. The begass is sent to the pig-pens, which are a most noteworthy feature of the place, where the pigs, after getting out a part of the remaining sugar, tread it into excellent manure. These pigs are fed chiefly from the sorghum seed, which is neatly chopped off the bundles of cane by a mammoth guillotine, threshed out, and boiled till the starch granules burst, making a pasty mass, which in turn makes excellent pork. This has led to the prophecy that the breakfast-table of the future may depend largely upon the sorghum plant, which supplies good bread or "cakes" and capital pork from its seed, and sugar or syrup—with a flavor of its own, easily removed, however, by bone-black—from its juice.

At Rio Grande the diffusion process now replaces crushing. The waste is still considerable, but it is claimed that the diffusion process, though costly, saves thirty per cent. more sugar, and experiments conducted at Ottawa, Kansas, last year, by Professor H. W. Wiley, of the Agricultural Department, obtained, it is claimed, ninety-eight per cent. of the sugar in the cane. How great this crop may be in the future no one can prophesy.

The beet-sugar industry has scarcely made a start yet in this country, though in Europe it has attained such proportions as to furnish half the marketed sugar of the world, and about a third of the total production. The production of beet sugar is a commercial triumph of the man of "mere science." A Berlin apothecary, Marggraf, first drew attention to the beet root as a possible sugar mine, and a Prussian chemist, Achard, first successfully extracted the sugar. It was not, however, until the Napoleonic wars and the blockade of Continental ports raised the prices of sugar that the industry was started. Napoleon in 1811 offered bounties for the production of beet sugar, and made the chemistry of the process a specialty in scientific schools. Germany followed the example, and even now the industry is fostered by the government through experimental stations and by means of bounties on sugar protection. The German law of 1869 laid a tax on beets of $4 (16 marks) per ton, to compensate for the loss of revenue from imported sugars, and gave a drawback of $42 to $47 per ton of sugar exported. As by the improved processes the yield of beet root is over nine and a half per cent. of merchantable sugar, besides more than two per cent. of molasses, this law guaranteed a profit to manufacturers for export, and the production has been very great.

The beet commonly used in Europe is the White Silesian, weighing from one and a half to two and a half pounds, and producing fifteen to twenty tons to the acre. It succeeds best where there is dry, unclouded autumn weather. The juice is extracted either by rasping the beet into shreds, and pressing out the juice, or by the diffusion process. As the beet contains much less sugar in proportion than cane, its transportation is a serious matter, and in France and Belgium under-ground pipes are in use, through which the juice is sent to a central factory. The process of extracting the sugar from the juice is essentially the same as in the treatment of cane, except that the process of carbonation, which is coming into use also with sorghum, is very generally used. The method proposed by the Department of Agriculture and practiced for one season at Ottawa, Kansas, with success, is a modification of the process used for beet juices, and consists in adding a large excess of lime to the tepid juice, and afterward precipitating the excess by carbonic acid. After passing through a filter press the clear juice is saturated with sulphurous acid, and again filtered. This process gives a juice perfectly limpid and of great purity. The production of beet sugar, where bounties are not paid, will probably be limited by the fact that, with improving scientific processes, the larger proportion of sugar in cane and sorghum will give them an increasing advantage to the planter and consumer. The census of 1880 reported four beet-root factories, with $365,000 capital, employing 350 hands, to whom it paid $62,271 wages, or $177 each, and producing $282,572 product.

Everybody has eaten maple sugar, and a good many of us have helped in sugar frolics, but few know that we produced in the census year from twenty-three States 36,576,061 pounds of sugar, besides 1,796,048 gallons of molasses, and a still larger crop in later years, reaching in 1885 25,900 tons. Vermont and New York are the States whose groves of rock or sugar maple give the chief supply. The sap begins to rise in February, after the first break-up of the long frost, and the "sap days" continue off and on for six weeks, into March or April. But the tree is like a sensitive-plant: during south winds and when a storm is coming the sap ceases to flow, and a dozen or so good sap days are a fair average. The trees are notched with an axe or tapped with an auger about three or four feet up the trunk, the sap flows into troughs, whence it is taken to open kettles in or near the grove, over fires fed with the dead branches of the maple-trees. Three gallons or more of sap will flow from a good tree during a day, producing a pound or less of sugar, but some trees have produced forty pounds of sugar in a single season. The date-palm sugar of the East is collected in much the same way. During boiling the sugar is stirred with a wooden spoon, and fresh juice added; when it thickens and becomes golden yellow, it is strained, cooled, settled with a little lime or soda, and cleared with milk or white of egg, and put in pans to crystallize. Then, as sugar or syrup, it is ready for the buckwheat cakes.

Different lines of sugar have different names, varying with the country of origin, the quality, and the process used. "Melada" is the name of the concentrated cane juice, just on the point of graining, in which shape some refining material is imported. "Jaggery" is the very crude East Indian sugar, containing a great deal of dirt. "Muscovado" sugar is that cured by simple drainage, the sticky mass from the coolers being put in casks with perforated bottoms, loosely filled with rushes, whence the molasses drains into a cask below. "A" sugar is simply a term to designate the higher grades of soft sugar, various fancy names being used by various refineries. "B" sugar is more brown.

Molasses and syrups are by-products both of the farm and the refinery in every kind of sugar-making. The molasses of the beet is too unpalatable, however, for food, and can be used only for distillation and like processes. Molasses is really a mixture of crystalline and uncrystallized sugar, with some impurities, colored by caramel or burnt sugar. The name comes by way of *melasse* (the same as *melada*), from the word *mel*, honey, and means honey-like. The sugar-maker's object is to get as much sugar and as little molasses as possible from a given quantity of juice, and with the improvement of processes the world over, less molasses is produced. The distillation of molasses makes rum, in which shape "Jamaica" in especial sends us her sugar crop. Syrup, as has been seen, is the leavings of refined sugar, that is to say, a superior grade of molasses, but most of that nowadays sold is a mixture with glucose.

Glucose, or the sugar made from starch, has become of late years an enormous industry, the chief seat of which is at Buf-

falo, New York. Thousands of bushels of corn are converted by these factories, in which the essential process is the boiling of the fresh starch of the grain, in vats holding about a ton and a half each, in water with one or two per cent. of sulphuric acid. The starch granules burst, take up the extra atom of water, and so make 238 pounds of sugar out of 220 pounds of starch. The purification of the sugar from the acid and its crystallization are processes similar to those already described. This kind of sugar can be marketed at from two to three cents, and it is much used by confectioners and brewers, as food for bees in making artificial honey, but most of all for the production of table syrups. It is simply a substitute for cane sugar, less sweet, but very much cheaper. It is probably not unhealthy, since the common notion that because acid is used in its formation it must be poisonous has no foundation, and the old objection that it is commonly sold for what it is not no longer holds true, glucose being now a recognized article of demand. The census of 1880 reported seven glucose factories, with $2,255,000 capital, employing 1193 hands, to whom it paid $605,802, or $508 each, and from material valued at $3,044,450 producing a product valued at $4,551,212, or about a third of our cane-sugar crop.

A considerable portion of the refined sugars find their way to the candy shops. The word candy comes to us from the Arabic and Persian *qand*, another name for sugar. Candy-making is a considerable trade in itself. The census of 1880 reported 13,692 confectioners. There are eight or ten large factories in New York alone, employing perhaps a hundred people each, and using a hundred barrels or more of sugar a week, besides quantities of glucose.

The "stick" candy, which seems to be an indigenous American product, is of ordinary "A" sugar, boiled down with water and a little cream of tartar to prevent crystallization. The mass is taken in batches of about fifteen pounds to a marble table, where it is kneaded like bread, and the flavoring and coloring worked in. The paste then goes to the "pulling-hooks," where for five or six minutes it is pulled and twisted and repulled and retwisted at the hands of a workman who certainly earns his living. Thence it returns to the marble table, at one end of which is a metal plate, kept hot, on which he works the candy into its final shape. Stripes are pressed into the batch, two feet long and a foot thick, and it is then drawn and twisted out till it is the proper size of the penny "stick," the right length of which is clipped off by huge scissors. Clear candy is not kneaded or pulled. Flat candy is run into pans, and a knife is run across where it is to be broken into sticks or squares. The drops, fishes, and other fancy shapes are made by passing the paste through a machine, which cuts and presses it to the proper size and shape.

Lozenges are rolled out like pie-crust, sometimes printed in carmine with a hand-stamp, and then cut out with dies. "Sugar-plums" and sugared almonds are made in a very interesting way, by throwing the nut, seed, or other nucleus with boiling sugar into great copper pans, which are shaken by hand or revolved by machinery over a hot fire. Rolled over and over in the moist sugar, the plums soon begin to grow, and are "polished off" by each other, while, above, steam-worked fans carry off the dry dust. Gum drops are made of gum-arabic and sugar, boiled and mixed, seven or eight hundred pounds at a time, in huge copper steam-kettles, whence the mixture is taken out into smaller kettles to be flavored and colored. The cheap gum drops and "marsh-mallows" are now made chiefly from glucose. Cream or soft candies are made in a simple way, from sugar mixed with cream of tartar to prevent crystallizing. To give them their fancy forms, a flat tray is filled with starch, which is pressed into moulds by a series of plaster-of-Paris models—a drop, hand, face, berry, or what it may be—arranged on a long stick. Into these starch moulds the hot cream is poured, and then allowed to dry. Some factories have as much as 50,000 pounds of starch in this use. The drying-room is kept at a high temperature, in which the "creams" soon become dry and solid. They are then separated from the starch by huge sieves. If they are to be glossed, they are placed in huge tin pans and a cold solution of sugar poured over them to stand overnight. In the morning the ice of sugar on top is broken, and the "creams" are found coated with fine crystals. The liqueur drops are a very curious product. The syrup is mixed with brandy or flavored water, and is poured into the starch

moulds. As it cools at the top and on the mould, the crystals make a continuous case, imprisoning the liquor within.

The adulteration of candy is chiefly by the use of *terra alba*, or white clay. This harmful stuff can be detected by dissolving the suspected candy in water, when the clay falls to the bottom undissolved. An ounce roll of cheap lozenges will sometimes contain three-quarters of an ounce of this injurious stuff. The coloring of candies is, for the most part, not dangerous, since a piece of red coloring matter the size of a gum drop will color 5000 pounds of candy. Unscrupulous manufacturers, however, sometimes use mineral instead of the safe vegetable colors, and cart-loads of such candy have been seized and destroyed by the health-officers in New York. For the most part, carmine and cochineal are used for red, saffron for yellow, caramel or burnt sugar for brown, and this with carmine for orange. Green and blue candies are to be avoided. These colors are used sometimes, however, in "decorating"—a surface treatment of fine candies by hand, in which a water-color artist is employed to do art work at wholesale according to the model set him. As for this purpose the proportion of coloring matter to sugar is about one-millionth, the result of swallowing paint is not so disastrous as might be expected. In flavoring, essential oils are used, about a pound to a thousand pounds of sugar, and this is worked in during the boiling or kneading. Licorice colors and flavors both at once.

The consumption of sugar is a chief test of a nation's prosperity. This country consumed of cane sugar in 1885 about 1,170,000 tons. There are no figures to show how our consumption has increased, but it is known that its use in Great Britain more than trebled in about forty years, being reported in 1846 at $20\frac{7}{5}$ pounds, and in 1882 at $70\frac{1}{2}$ pounds, per head of population. The duty was removed from sugar in that country in 1874. In our country it is the most prolific source of customs revenue, sugar and molasses constituting over 13 per cent. of our total importations, and paying 29 per cent. of all duties. The 2,578,993,335 pounds of sugar imported in 1884-5, valued at $69,078,857, produced a revenue of $50,845,916, or 73.66 per cent. The duty on sugars is, for those not above No. 13 Dutch standard in color, testing not above 75 degrees by the polariscope, $1\frac{40}{100}$ cents per pound, or if above 75 degrees, $\frac{4}{100}$ for each additional degree or part of a degree; for those above No. 13, and not above No. 16, $2\frac{75}{100}$ cents; for those not above No. 20, 3 cents; for those above No. 20, $3\frac{50}{100}$ cents per pound. The Dutch standard is an arbitrary scale of shades of brown adopted by other nations as a matter of convenience, sugars below No. 13 being the cheap, dark sugars mostly used for refining. Confectionery, or tinctured, colored, or adulterated sugar, valued at not over 30 cents a pound, pays 10 cents a pound duty; if over 30 cents, 50 per cent. *ad valorem*. Hawaiian sugar not above No. 20 is free from duty under the reciprocity treaty, but the combination of the transcontinental railroads and steam-ship lines to keep up sugar freights gave to the controllers of this crop so strong a hold that the Pacific coast has had up to this year no benefit from the remission of the duty nor from the low prices at the East. The imports of 32,183,026 gallons of molasses, valued at $4,413,492, produced, at four cents per gallon, $1,287,321, or 29.17 per cent. Molasses testing above 56° by the polariscope is subject to 8 cents per gallon duty, but this is not imported to any extent. The government pays a drawback of from $1\frac{1}{4}$ to $3\frac{18}{100}$ cents per pound on sugar exported, to encourage the importation of raw sugars for refining here, and it is alleged that this, like the German bounty, is so much above the import tax as to guarantee a profit to our refiners, who are now, in fact, doing much of the refining for England and the world. We exported of refined sugar in the year 1884–85, 252,574,335 pounds, valued at $16,071,699.

There is no industry in which the tendency to industrial concentration is more clearly shown, for whereas the census of 1880 found only 49 refineries, with a capital of $27,400,000, the product returned, $155,400,000, despite great reductions of prices, was nearly half as much again as that in 1870, when the census included the plantation mills as refineries and counted up 1091. Some of the great refineries now turn out 250,000 tons of syrup yearly. The refineries, by the census of 1880, employed 5857 hands, an average of 120 each. The ordinary hands in a New York refinery get from $35 per month up, and a sugar-boiler as much as $100 per month.

In 1864, during the war, when gold was at a premium, raw sugar averaged $17\frac{1}{4}$ cents a pound, and indeed reached 25 cents. In 1885 it averaged 5.18 cents, or in bond 3.06 cents, showing an average difference of price because of the duty of 2.12 cents per pound. The average of refined sugars in 1885 was $6\frac{1}{2}$ to 7 cents per pound, and some kinds, as granulated, fell below 6 cents during the spring. These were the lowest prices since thirty years ago, but it is to be noted that in those years raw sugar ruled on the whole as low as now, so that the demand seems to have kept fully apace with the greatly increased supply.

NOTE.—The material for the portion of this article relating to the sorghum industry has been supplied chiefly by Professor H. W. Wiley, of the Agricultural Department. Mr. Isaac A. Hedges, President of the Mississippi Valley Cane [Sorghum] Growers' Association, and a devotee of sorghum, has published a book on sorghum under the somewhat misleading title of *Sugar-canes and their Products, Culture, and Manufacture* (St. Louis, 1881); Peter Collier is the author of a later treatise on *Sorghum . . . as Source of Sugar, Syrups, and Fodder* (Cincinnati, 1884); and there are other earlier American works. The reports and bulletins of the United States Department of Agriculture, and the reports for 1883 and 1884 of the New Jersey Bureau of Labor Statistics, give valuable information as to sorghum. The most recent and highest English authority on *Sugar-growing and Refining* in general is the very comprehensive book of that title by Charles G. W. Lock, F.L.S., and others (London and New York, 1882), condensed in *Spon's Encyclopedia of the Industrial Arts, Manufactures, and Commercial Products* (London and New York, 1882), edited by the same writer. Two works on beet sugar are by E. B. Grant (Boston, 187–), and by L. S. Ware (Philadelphia, 1880). Reference may also be made to papers in this Magazine on the "Sugar Regions of Louisiana," before the war, by T. B. Thorpe (Vol. vii., p. 746); on "Sugar-making in Cuba," by H. B. Auchincloss (Vol. xxx., p. 446), and on "Sugar-making Machines," by E. H. Knight (Vol. l., p. 385). An "Annual Statement of the Sugar Trade of the United States" is issued in January of each year by the *Shipping and Commercial List*, New York.

"CULTIVATE HAPPINESS!"

IS happiness a plant of mortal birth,
 Which, shrewdly cultured, grows in gracious earth?
Rather a heavenly glory, or bright dew
Slipped from the bosom of the cloudless blue,
On some fair morning, to the soul's surprise,
Fresh with the fragrance born in Paradise.

PAUL HAMILTON HAYNES.

"THE MINISTRATION OF DEATH."

BY ANNIE PORTER.

IT was a cold, damp afternoon, and the line of carriages in front of Mrs. Henley Linden's house, at the hour for afternoon tea, grew larger every minute, and the crowd within more appreciative of warmth and comfort. The large, quaintly handsome rooms were filled, and there was a perpetual shimmering going on, the rustling, gliding, slipping of silken skirts, the waving of feathers and laces, glistening of jewels and beads, all softly visible in the shaded lamp-light and rosy fire-light which blended so becomingly. It was really a pity there were no men to be grateful for the sight, for whether from the gentle excitement of the tea, the management of the lights, the glowing effects of the weather, or some unknown cause, it is certain that the plain women were looking pretty, the pretty beautiful, the despondent bright, and the older ones young on this particular occasion. A group near the fire-place were discussing some one with great zest. Miss Delmar, stout, dark, rather masculine, but who was always spoken of as one of the cleverest women in Washington (*very satirical*, usually added in a whisper), was the speaker, and a tall woman with gray hair, a young-looking, striking face, and very bright eyes, listened eagerly.

"If there is nothing in it, why is he never seen out with her anywhere? what is the reason you never find him with her at home? Who ever heard of a young woman having to apologize for her husband's absence from his own dinner-table before? Nonsense! Of course he is jealous of her, and of course he has reason to be. No smoke without *some* fire, I say; and if she is handsome and attractive, why shouldn't she go the way of other women?"

"Other women?" interposed a young girl who was lounging in a large chair near by, and who, while surveying the scene with half-closed, near-sighted eyes, and an air of languid indifference, lost nothing of what was passing. "What do you mean, my dear Miss Delmar, by such unlimited expressions? *Some* other women may go the way of Mrs. Fitzgerald."

"Oh, then you agree with me, Lucinda, that she *is* travelling in the wrong direction, don't you? I thought you must have heard a good deal that was odd the other night at the Prendergasts', when you were sitting so near in the conservatory. She and the count were very well hidden, but I saw them, and you certainly heard them, so come and unbosom yourself. What were they saying?"

"Now did ever any one hear the equal of this creature? Fancy expecting me to overhear the conversation of other people when I was talking myself to Mr. Mallerton, and he was as near love-making as he ever gets! I not only never heard Mrs. Fitz and the count, but did not see them; and," she continued, in a lower tone, turning to a girl with pretty red hair and bright hazel eyes on the other side, "if I had heard volumes and seen folios, I should never have brought my news to your market."

"Well," said the tall lady with gray hair, "I assure you that I come down to breakfast every morning of my life expecting to hear that Mrs. Fitzgerald has eloped with Count Stanislaus during the night. Why, he is always with her."

A slight stir among the crowd by the door, and an extremely graceful woman of about thirty was seen making her way toward the hostess, who rose to receive her with effusive cordiality. There was a slight, a very slight pause in the low hum of talk, and a simultaneous flutter all over the room of heads turning to look at the new-comer, but the conversation flowed on, the pretty heads twisted this way and that again, and the scarcely perceptible effect was over before Mrs. Linden's clear, rapid words of welcome were all spoken.

"Ah, Mrs. Fitzgerald, so glad to see you! Just the weather to make one feel grateful to the good people who brave it. Don't tread on Malvina; she always makes up to you. There is no doubt that cats and dogs know their best friends. Sit down and let me give you some delicious Japanese tea."

"Mrs. Fitzgerald, is that you? Come over and sit here by the fire with us;" and Miss Delmar made room for her between herself and Mrs. Macclesfield, while two or three others who had listened with eager interest to her predictions and assertions now greeted the unconscious subject of them with the sweetest smiles. Why not? even if she and her husband were on decidedly bad terms, of which there was as yet no positive evidence. Mr. Fitzgerald was in office, rich, well born, agreeable to an uncommon degree, and universally believed in as rising fast to power.

Certainly, whatever people might say of his wife behind her back, there was no woman more courted and flattered, no one whose sayings and doings were more eagerly chronicled and admiringly interpreted. Look at her now as, laughingly declining to sit down, she stands for a few moments in front of her late critics talking and looking about her, what a blithe, proud carriage she has, how firmly and gracefully the clever little head with its close-fitting coif of braided gold is held! The face is very pale, with deep red lips, flexible lovely lips, and the prettiest white teeth in the world.

"How pretty, how very pretty she is!" murmurs an innocent débutante, watching her with deepest admiration.

"Pretty, indeed," answered her companion, "with that skin like chalk, those great black eyes and coal-black eyebrows, and all that tow-colored hair! I cannot see her beauty."

Mrs. Fitzgerald heard her, and the laugh which bubbled from her lips was as gay as a child's, while at the same moment her hand closed over a letter she was carrying in her muff, and a darting thought left a faint glow of color in her cheeks. That letter was short but pregnant with meaning; in a man's hand, but not her husband's; and her danger, in possessing it, no greater than she deserved; but if this woman belonged to the devil's kingdom, she did not yet wear his livery. Her smile was ingenuous, with all its subtlety; the purest soul could look through no purer, clearer eyes; and the cross fox-terrier followed her from group to group, and settled herself at her feet where she stood. She talked of last night's dance, of this night's ball, of Miss A.'s partners and Mrs. B.'s pearls, was witty and soft and grave by turns; but through it all there was running in her mind, as if at the bottom of her consciousness, a wonder of wonders, a surprise of questioning terror nothing could hide or quell. "Am I a lost woman or not? Shall I go back to my home and lie down in peace, the safely sheltered wife of a good man, or shall I leave husband, home, child, friends, heaven itself, behind me, to become—what?" This last question was what she could not answer, and upon which her mind was steadily at work all the time. Through everything, overpowering the lively talk within, hushing the noisy wind without, it made itself heard, and would not be denied. "What sort of creature shall I be if I do—*when* I do this thing?"

Set apart from other women only by being placed on a pedestal of love and devotion, tenderly cared for, never put aside for ambition, or neglected in the rush of public life, but always wandering through beautiful scenes, painting, singing, sharing all the delights of music and poetry with one who has true sympathy for both. Yes, that was the right answer. But she had seen something every now and then by gas-light with haggard eyes and ghastly cheeks—what folly!—as if that could ever be! No, she would shake off this foolish, superstitious dread; she had lived a life of frivolous amusement because she had fallen into the groove, but the intellectual, sympathetic life of her ideal girlish longing was now within her reach.

Again that anxious pause in all her thoughts, while the same rush of impulsive questioning, not formed, not expressed, but powerful, seemed once more to swell above every other sound. As it subsided she found these words running in her head:

> "Nay, too late for hill-mounting;
> Nay, too late for cost-counting."

"Well," she continued, thinking voluntarily and almost aloud, "if I find the burden of sin the old books tell us to be a real thing, and I cannot carry it with dignity, I can always sink beneath it with grace. It is not much to die."

As this passed through her abnormally quickened mind she was standing opposite a large mirror, and could see her own face and figure, while she laughed and chattered about the reception at the Abyssinian Embassy. How young she looked! and in spite of what that old woman had said, how pretty she was! She could not help having eyes in her head, and there was no use in pretending. She must see it if she were not a fool; she certainly did make other women look faded and coarse beside her. Curious that just at that very moment, with so much to think of, with her difficult part to play, and her whole life hanging on a thread, all of a sudden she had gone back ten years to the very morning of her wedding day, and was standing before the glass in her own bedroom waiting for her father to take her down. She glanced at herself again as the memory rushed upon her and the vision grew clearer. Surely that was the same light-hearted girl, and the interval had only been a feverish, delusive dream. She had nothing to dread in the future, or mourn in the past; her father loved and trusted her; her lover— Yes, her lover! Who was her lover? Not the hard, unresponsive husband whom she was determined to punish for all his indifference and careless neglect, and not the brilliant, many-sided Hungarian whose letter was in her hand—no, neither of these; but the thoughtful, loving gaze which the glass seemed to reflect from some one at her side was a look she had known in her sweetheart's eyes before she married him, and which alone she instinctively identified with that word "lover." What was Mrs. Drayton saying to her about the Japanese minister? She really must give up falling into reveries in public: people would think she had something on her mind. People would think, indeed! What difference would people's thoughts ever make to her again! She was soon—yes, by-the-way, *that very night*—how time does fly on!

"Is it actually six o'clock? Oh! then I must be off! We have what I call a business dinner to-night—some of Randolph's constituents—and I am always late anyway.

"Can I put you down at your door, Lucinda?"

A vague sense of saying "Good-by," then a rush of cold air, and the feeling of warm furs around her. She was in her own coupé, thank fortune! How her head was whirling! or were they only driving fast? Heavens! who was this with her? Oh, Lucinda Belden! Why, how came she here? Yes, I remember now. Did I give the order to leave her at home? "Good-night." "Good-night." Oh, for darkness and silence around me, if only for ten minutes! and if I could stop feeling so hurried, so pressingly hurried!" Mrs. Fitzgerald was at home at last, and as she walked slowly upstairs to dress for dinner, she asked a servant at what time it had been ordered. "At half past seven." She went into her dressing-room, a bright, richly glowing wood fire

was there alone, throbbing like a heart in the darkness. She bent forward and looked at her clock. Fifteen minutes past six. "Marie, you can give me my dressing-gown, and have everything ready for me to dress quickly. I must rest for half an hour; call me in that time."

At last she was alone in the dark, stretched out in the low chair where she could think comfortably and face her position. It seemed such an incredible one even now. How had it come about that she who married for love, who had been carefully taught to know the right and to do it, who was proud of her father's, yes, of her husband's, name, and who had a little son to suffer for her disgrace, should ever have come to such a pass as this, and be deliberating calmly upon whether she should leave her husband's house with another man or not? It seemed impossible that it could be true, and yet she could trace every step, remember every tiny detail which had brought her to it. Her thoughts were clear and vivid now, and worked with the force and speed of some machine. What had been the very beginning? When they first married and moved from her old home on the Hudson to Washington, she had been proud of Randolph's political life, of his being so much thought of, and taking his place easily among men much older than himself, and she had felt great sympathy with his schemes of reform. But before long it seemed to her that he thought of nothing else; she was put on one side and neglected, while he always had time for more and more work. Stop! let her be strictly honest; of course it was of very little importance now, for the main fact that he had ceased to care for her had been long established; but was she quite true in saying that he had neglected her for his work? Certainly he had sometimes refused to go out with her, but she could remember times when he *had* gone at her insistence, looking worn and tired. And she could even recall his laughing, incredulous look when she had told him he loved his work and cared for his ambition more than he loved and cared for her. He had not laughed afterward at what she said. Well, she was glad she had stung him. Nothing she had ever said would have been a real excuse for his cold, proud manner, his studied politeness, and the way he had avoided her afterward. She could have forgiven even that, if he had cared; but to see him steadily growing more absorbed in his public life, treating her always with that calm, *forgetting* indifference, not even trying to win her back, or to— Yet then, again, she could not say that. Had he not always been most kind and gentle? and how could he persist in showing her affection after the way in which she had repulsed him, and the marked manner in which she had thrown herself into a whirl of gayeties in whose midst she knew he could not pursue her? Of course she had been perfectly right. No woman should ever consent to be second in her husband's life or heart or mind to anything, no matter how worthy in itself the object may be. But hush! this is nonsense. What had she really cared for all such jealousies as these? Could she have ever really made herself miserable over such follies? No. Though the thought even from her inmost soul has been hidden away, though she has refused herself permission to dream of it even, yet to-night, at this moment of fate, she must face it, think of it, decide the question in her heart at least. Yes, this has been the real grief, the working poison, the keen-edged sword between herself and her husband; this hateful story, told so circumstantially, attested so carefully and credibly, never wholly believed, but powerful to destroy her for all that, of a rival, young, beautiful, and absorbing, who has stolen from her the best part of her life. As the vile recollection rushes unchecked upon her, its true character for the first time strikes her, and she shrinks, as if from a blow, from the conviction it brings that the whole is an invention of one whose interest it would be to make her believe it. The reaction is almost as rapid as the thought. "No, no; it must have had *some* truth. No one could have invented such a lie. Yes, it is true; it must, it shall be true. I cannot, I will not doubt it. It has tortured me for months; it has brought me to this position in which I stand. I will not doubt it to-night of all nights." Her thoughts wander on almost without volition and quite beyond control. If she had only been a religious woman, if she had ever cared to pray, perhaps all would have been different with her; but God had always been an empty name to her. She could believe in things tangible, but not in abstractions; she had "cared for none of these things," nor would she ever have known from any want in her own heart or prompting of

her own spirit that there was any God needed in the universe. It was not skepticism; it was an absolute deadness, apparently. Had all her troubles come from this? For the first time in a life which had never known real suffering she felt a wish to grasp at outside help. Should she have been a happier wife if she had been more alive to the spiritual side of her own nature? Ah! if she has really done her husband injustice—why not confess boldly to herself that she knows she has been wrong? But that is not what she wants to think of now. However *that* may be, she is not happy at home, and she must go; life is too short to waste. She wants to think of what is before her, about what she has to do to-night. The time is getting shorter and shorter. Yes, she must think of her own future, and of her relations to Count Stanislaus. There could be no doubt about *his* love. How he had followed and watched and worshipped her for three years! It was not the same kind of love as her husband's. Somehow it was a very singular thing, but while she could remember the very smallest trifle, the most minute detail, associated with Randolph Fitzgerald and his love for her, she could not remember or think about anything connected with this new lover, the count; but that would never do; if she intended to spend the rest of her life in his company, she might as well make the best of it. How the wind howls and the sleet crashes against the panes! It is warm and pleasant where she sits, and she feels unusually tired and listless to-night. It must be very nearly time for Marie's knock, but she will wait until it comes; then one more dinner under her husband's roof, one more look at his face, which never again would look upon her willingly, or upon anything belonging to her without a curse; then a farewell kiss to her sleeping boy—her boy!—and the feigned departure in evening dress for the ball she will never reach. "My God! how strangely exhausted and beaten down by fatigue even thinking of it all has made me feel! I must rouse myself; there goes the quarter again. What is this? I cannot move. There is Marie's knock. Is this a nightmare? What—what is this frightful numbness, this dead weight which prevents my moving, breathing? I am fainting." A silence, and then she hears the maid's knock, but can no more move hand or foot than the dead, while still her thoughts fly with unnatural clearness from topic to topic, and through the half-closed, lustreless eyes her sight is clearer and stronger even than usual. She feels the air blowing on her as the door opens, and in another moment sees Marie's dark shrewd face bending over her, and hears her mutter to herself: "Mais qu'est-ce qu'elle a donc? Elle est d'une pâleur! Mon Dieu! et ne respire plus! Tenez! Je n'aime pas ça, moi. Je m'en vais appeler monsieur."

"No, no, Marie," the suddenly stiffened tongue strives to say; but the effort which seems strong enough to shake the building produces not the slightest tremor, not a sign of vitality. She is as absolutely debarred from speech or motion or breath or warmth of life as any frozen corpse, while heart and mind and memory are full of surging, rushing, tumultuous activity and strength. As Marie turns to summon help, the dawning sense of horror which rose within the unhappy creature pent in such a prison overwhelms her, and she loses consciousness entirely. But what an awakening! to struggle slowly back to full life and vigor within, only to find herself apparently a stiffening corpse without. She lies upon her own bed now in her night clothes, lights burn in all directions, not only the wax candles she always used, but lamps of greater brightness, that the doctors may see more clearly. The first bustle has evidently been silenced, but there is still a subdued sound of unusual noises throughout the house, and two or three men and as many women are in the room. "Who are they all? what are they doing? Was she really dead, and could death be always like this?—the sudden horrible striking into stone of the whole body, while the spirit lives on within? Surely no; this is only some sudden form of faintness or fatigue brought on by over-excitement; and the doctors, these clever scientific physicians, will soon restore her, drive away the dumb helplessness, and give her freedom again.

Yes, freedom from this awful, awful power which has grasped her so unexpectedly and holds her so completely is all she wants. She had been thinking of all sorts of wicked things, had been very discontented and foolish, but she would never be so wicked again. Of course Randolph did not love her, and if the count did, it was perfectly natural for

her to respond; but now this little sickness had come, she supposed it would be too late for her to go out to-night anyway, even after the doctors have revived her. Oh dear! how slow, how fearfully slow they are! Why do they stand there whispering, with their heads turned to her, while she lies there in such immediate need of their services? Ah! here they come at last, and Randolph with them. How very strange and solemn they look— Dr. Lawrence, Dr. Stedman. She knows them both, and could almost predict what their greeting would be. She must speak, if only a word. God in heaven! *What* is this fearful thing which holds her in such a grasp? Can she never shake it off? But hush; listen. Dr. Lawrence is speaking, while her husband, the other doctors, Marie, and some strange woman, all stand around. Why does Randolph look at her so? "She must have died instantly, and probably without suffering. There was undoubted aneurism, but I cannot speak as positively as I would prefer to do without a more thorough investigation." That is what the doctor says. Died? she herself dead? She would laugh if she could, but she cannot. How amused they will be when she gets over this attack! But, oh! *why do they not help her?* Listen: the nurse speaks in answer to something her husband said. "We have done everything that skill can suggest; there can be no use in further effort. We have tried *everything*, and there can be no doubt *the life has left her*." Why, how long has she been unconscious? What time can it be? As she asks herself the question she hears her own little chimes ring out eleven o'clock. The last time she noticed the clock before that strange numbness seized her it was a quarter before seven, and now it is eleven. She has been unconscious for all those hours!

If so, and they have already tried every remedy, and she still lies bound hand and foot, what power is there to raise her up from among the dead? Has she not heard her death announced, the cause stated? What remains now but to

"shroud the corpse, and bury her deep;
In fathoms of grave-mould leave her to sleep"?

Where had she heard that rhyme before? "Bury her deep." Oh! yells and shrieks and screams ring, ring, ring in her head and heart and soul, and it must be that some tiny echo, *something* of these frantic dumb ravings may be ever so faintly, ever so dimly, heard! But they have gone. She sees them pass through the door, three doctors, her husband, and the strange woman, the nurse. Marie remains. She cannot turn one hair's-breadth, or wink those stiff white lids, or see more than comes into the line of her vision as she lies stark and cold upon her bed; but she can hear—oh! how she can hear! The whole of her being, all the life that throbs in her so warmly, is concentrated in hearing. The tinkle of the ashes falling, the grating of a loose bolt on the window, the rustle of Marie's dress as she moves softly about the room —she can hear all distinctly. There are two voices whispering outside the door— one is Randolph's, the other the strange woman's—a nurse, probably. What are they talking of? Another hour gone! How strange that time should fly so quickly, while she lies rigid, with nothing to check her rushing, whirling thoughts! The night flies by—a gray dawn is already struggling in. One by one the lights are extinguished, the fires replenished. Marie rises from the sofa where she has kept watch, and assists the maids to put the room in order, when the day has fully come, smoothing the snowy draperies around the couch where lies the still, frozen form, and braiding with skilful hands the heavy masses of golden hair. She crosses the hands upon the motionless breast. How natural it feels to have Marie combing her hair, and yet how horrible it seems now! This awful stillness which she cannot break, this hideous nightmare whose weight is resistless, but which leaves the mind as clear as crystal, must be a form of faintness or numbness uncommon enough to pass for death itself, and if the doctors are deceived, there can be, of course, no appeal to any one else. Perhaps, since the nurse spoke of so many and such powerful efforts having been made to rouse her, it really was the prelude to death, the dying of the body, while the departure of the soul only occurred later, and she was now awaiting that. But how long must she wait? Did all souls linger thus in their earthly houses? And if so, *for how long?* Must it be that she should lie thus until the blessed light of heaven came to be shut out by the lid of a coffin? Was it possible that such agony as this could wring a human heart and not

show itself in any way upon the surface? But here again are voices and people coming! O Christ, never believed in, never appealed to before, help this Thy most miserable creature now; grant her but one instant, one second of power to move, were it but the lifting of an eyelash, the twitching of a muscle, the faintest, weakest token of a life Thou gavest; or if that be not possible, then blot out from consciousness this poor terrified spirit which from the depths of this most awful dungeon sees and hears the torments of a twofold hell drawing near, and cannot escape!

The immortality of the spirit! What commonplace, senseless words they had always seemed!—a mere formula, a phrase without meaning; and *now* there was no truth, no fact, no reality like them; they seemed to flame in burning letters before her half-closed, motionless eyeballs. The immortality of the soul, that is, a never-dying consciousness, a *me* that must live, must suffer, must see, hear, be alive through *everything*. What was that verse she had so often read unthinkingly about fleeing to the uttermost parts of the earth without finding a refuge from the wrath to come? That was what the immortality of the soul must mean; that though the body have its own peculiar power of sinking into dust, the soul could not abate one atom of power or life or strength, but must face eternity, *the same always*. Hours have gone by again— long, fearful hours—in which no interval of unconsciousness has relieved that fearful suffering; but nature cannot always stand the same tension, and as the day declines, the minutes rushing past at lightning speed, while each minute is an endless round of torture, a merciful dulness or blunting of the senses comes to the soul in prison. She has been prepared now for the tomb, clothed in her last snowy raiment, with flowers heaped upon her; lilies-of-the-valley, white roses, hyacinths, japonicas, are on her brow, twined in her hair, clasped in her hands. As twilight draws on, and the wintry sunlight slips away, all is done, and she is left alone in the sweet-smelling, peaceful chamber, where no fire any longer twinkles on the hearth. As she thus lies, the first sensation of something that is not *all* agony comes over her, and the all-absorbing horror of the present moment fades.

There comes in its place a vision of herself in the past, and she dwells, wondering, upon the callous, light-hearted self-absorption, the delight in flattered vanity, the enjoyment of her own power, she had once called love. How could she have been so blind to the truth? Surely she must have had some true knowledge of her husband's worth. She had *once*—it must be that she had *once*—recognized his lofty nature; for she had loved him, not wisely, or nobly, or unselfishly, or even faithfully—no, that last was a lie; she had loved him faithfully *always*. Was it true that her last act on earth, her last use of the powers she had lost, had been to hide away a letter from Count Stanislaus, giving her careful directions where to meet him when she ran away from home? Count Stanislaus! why, she *hated him;* she never from the first had cared for him —his cold, hard smile, his marble gray eyes which never seemed quite human, his smoothly shaven, cruel-looking jaw— could it really be the truth that she had only been prevented by a miracle from leaving her husband, Randolph Fitzgerald, to live with Count Stanislaus?

Yes, her mind is perfectly clear; the remorseless thoughts roll on. She knows that except for this miracle she would by this time have been in that distant city by the sea whence *he* and *she* were going abroad. Her name would have been accursed in her husband's ears, her memory in his heart. Now she is still his, and in the coffin will bear his name. *In the coffin!* To wake to the knowledge that she loves him, had always loved him, could never love or like or think of any other. *In her coffin!* What had all her jealousy, her wounded pride, her cold withdrawal been worth? Nothing, and worse than nothing. Had she ever believed in his want of faith, his want of affection for her? Never; it was all of a piece with the rest. Vanity, worthless, selfish, wilful vanity; easy, shameful yielding to base insinuations, the habit of listening to vulgar, injurious gossip; the trifling with duty and truth and faith and love which all around her encouraged: love! She had never before been able to feel that God was Himself. Nothing had seemed real; she was wearied with shadows. "The fool hath said in his heart there is no God." How it all flashed through her mind at once, the long unsatisfying years full of petty weariness and complaining

coming after the love - marriage which promised such royal happiness! She saw vividly, clearly, the secret growth of all her sins and sorrow, the first yielding to foolish discontent, the pining for excitement which soon made every home occupation distasteful, the luxurious habits which swept away her time, the passion for admiration which made the society of men necessary; above all, the craving for amusement which kept her forever in a crowd, while she found herself more and more thrown with this one man, whose pursuit of her had been so stealthily progressive, so warily unalarming at first, so completely unrelenting at last.

Through it all she had been conscious of a neglected, subdued, but never-ceasing pain, of a steady inward aching, which would be made sharper at any moment by meeting her husband's eyes.

Yes, that was the marvel — how she had ever fallen apart from him; for now in this supreme last moment of her prolonged self-communing, when she must lie here face to face with life and death at once, she knows her own heart.

Ah! if she could only be raised up again to life; but God does not throw away His mercies on such a wretch as she. He had already performed a miracle in keeping her from eloping by striking her down in this terrible manner. And even lying there in the awful grasp of that living death, with the horror and agony of knowing that soon, in a few hours, she must be placed alive, conscious, full of frozen but abounding vigor, in the coffin and the tomb, to be slowly— But her thoughts went on; she could not control them, or bring them to bear steadily on that future. She could still say, "I am thankful to have been kept faithful to my husband; I am thankful to have been saved from sin."

But hark! some one is coming. It is her husband, and as he comes through the folding-door, she sees in the great mirror which is in the alcove opposite, and which has so often reflected her own graceful, perfectly dressed shape, that he is leading their little son by the hand. The room is quite dark now, except for the soft light of two wax candles which are burning at the foot of the bed, and a crimson but subdued reflection through the half-open door of the wood fire in her dressing-room, where the watchers have been sitting. Her eyes have been left as they were, and are half open; but the glassy stare of real death is absent, and though she is powerless to move them by so much as a hair's-breadth, the dark pupils, blue in health, but looking black now, are so soft and natural under the white lids that the boy's exclamation, "Papa, she is only asleep!" seems perfectly true for a moment. But his father shakes his head, and leads the little fellow to the side of the pillow. In this position it is impossible for her as she lies to see either of them. Mr. Fitzgerald lets the boy look on in silence while he gazes himself as though he would photograph that most delicately fair and touching vision upon his brain forever.

The leaves of the japonica buds are not whiter than her cheek and brow, while her lips still keep the singular red they wore in life, the coils of hair which had always been wonderful for their metallic golden shine seem even brighter and more lustrous than usual. Over the whole face, from the black upward-curling lashes and pathetic-looking eyes to the relaxed curves of the mouth, lies an indescribably touching look of humility, peace, and sadness. Young as she really is—for she has not passed her twenty-third birthday—years seem to have dropped from her like a mantle, and the very look she might have worn in her childhood is on her now. The tiny boy's wondering face, so near her own, is its very counterpart, Fitzgerald thinks, as he looks from one to the other.

"Papa," the child says, in a whisper, "is mamma dead?"

"Yes, Randolph."

"And will they bury her in the ground, papa?"

"Only her body, boy; *she* cannot be buried; she has gone to heaven."

He speaks slowly, and the child seems to ponder before he answers. At last he says (and listening with every quivering nerve on fire, his mother thinks that he touches her hair, and longs—ah! with what longing she does yearn to clasp him in her arms!):

"Papa, there's one thing I'm certain about: I would rather have had my mamma, just as she was, than all the other boys' mothers, if they do hug them and let them rumple up their clothes, and tell stories and all—you know how they do. Well, my mamma was a million hundred times the prettiest of them all, wasn't she, papa?"

"I think so, my boy—prettier, and sweeter, and—"

God! can it be a sob which chokes his voice? is it possible that her husband is weeping for her? As the questioning thought flashes through her mind she feels that he has moved from where he stood, and in another moment both he and the boy are in such a position that through her half-closed eyes, to them so glazed and cold, to her so keen with darting vision, she can drink in every detail, every line of their faces. She sees the child's awe-struck, tear-stained little visage, the chubby, rosy cheeks a little pale with excitement, the merry blue eyes honestly sad, and wide open with a child's solemn gaze; and then she sees, as he comes into her field of vision, the man whom she had thought wholly absorbed of late in his books, his professional work, and his political advancement—ay, or something worse than either. She has estranged herself from him, nursed her jealousy of his pursuits, rejected his advances, made his home unhappy, neglected his son—*and hers!*—and, last of all, she has only been prevented by a miracle, an intervention of some power not to be disputed, from disgracing, outraging him and the boy forever.

And yet he weeps for her! Weeps for her? Fool—miserable, blind, helpless fool that she has been! He has sent little Randolph out of the room, and kneeling by the bed, takes the cold, unmoving form, which within is panting and bursting with pent-up life, passion, love, remorse, and terror, into his arms—O God! in what a close, straining clasp!—and while his unaccustomed tears fall like the outpourings of a thunder-cloud upon her close-sealed face, who could have guessed that the tempest in her heart is wilder, fiercer, more deeply rending than in his own—that his strongest emotion is as nothing to the whirling rush of agony in the still form he presses to his bosom? But in that brief moment, in the short space the strong man allows himself for the full indulgence of his pain, Elsie Fitzgerald reads and understands her husband's inmost soul at last. The pale, dead woman whom he lays back on her pillow, her brow wet with his tears, even in that supreme moment, with the gates of horrible death already opening before her, feels the thrill of his kisses, the warmth of his love above and through everything, though she knows that his farewell has only been spoken then because the time of her agony is near at hand.

That time has come; the hours so long in passing have slipped away like running water, and now, clad in soft and lustrous white, Elsie lies in her last bed, covered with lilies-of-the-valley, and gazing still through those half-shut eyelids at the friends around her. She can see distinctly that she is in the centre of her own parlor, the sun shining faintly through the half-drawn curtains, and a number of people are standing about the room; she sees the end of the clergyman's long black silk robe, but not his face, while just in the line of her vision are three women who have been constant associates of hers in all kinds of amusements. They are whispering together now, and one of them is smiling maliciously. The service is evidently not to be read just yet; there is a sort of pause in the preparations, and she distinguishes the clergyman's voice conversing in a low tone with some one out of sight. Mingled with it are the murmurs of other voices equally suppressed, the rustling movement of many people, the heavy tread of servants carrying in chairs, and every few minutes the arrival of some eager late-comer. Sometimes a hand, which she knows to be that of her faithful old nurse and house-keeper, lays fresh lilies about her, or alters the position of some already there, their faint yet powerful odor breathing, it seems to her, into her very brain, and adding to the feeling of numbness, of stupefaction, which is slowly, slowly creeping over her. At last silence, and then a voice reading the old familiar words. Oh! can those be the same, the words she has heard a hundred times with indifference, with admiration, with half-poetical sentiment, but never with deep emotion before?

"I am the Resurrection and the Life."

Can it be true? can there be a new life, a new tide of full, flowing, living life coming again to *her*? Will these chains and shackles drop off, and leave her free?

Silence again, and a movement around her. The service is ended; the time is come; and though the land of deliverance, the morning of resurrection of which that voice has just spoken, lies on the other side of horror and pain unspeakable, still it will soon be over, and perhaps—

Yes, they are saying "good-by" to her now, all these friends, all these acquaintances, all these strangers. She feels a vague surprise as she mechanically classes them that any of those "newspaper women" should have been admitted, and finds herself thinking that she must warn the butler at her next reception. Then she recovers herself, and knows where she is again. It will soon be over now. She could hear the men lifting the heavy lid which was to shut her out forever from the life of earth—when a man who had slowly drawn near to that snow-white bier paused and looked down upon the breathless form within. Fairer than the daylight, the sunny braids of long thick hair framing the cold, placid face, and veiling with fold on fold the outlines of the shrouded bosom, she lay with half-open eyes, a faint, lingering smile, or shadow of a smile, parting the lips still so brightly red.

Slowly he raised his hand, this man who did not shrink from the sight, and slowly, as though to steal from her clasp a flower for good-by, he touched the waxen palm.

God of heaven! hast Thou heard to save?

The shriek that burst from those pale lips, the light that flashed from those sealed eyes!

With the gesture of one who repulses some loathsome danger the sleeper arose in her coffin, sitting there in the midst of her grave-clothes and lilies, with the sunlight streaming full upon her, and both hands outstretched to repel, while the echoes of her scream died away in the awe-struck silence. Then, with the sudden movement of a child awakened among strangers, she turned—face, figure, soul, mind, and heart one throb of ecstasy and love—to her husband, and was locked in his embrace.

That which neither love, nor fear, nor grief, nor skill could effect, the traitor's touch had done. He who would without remorse have consigned her to the death of sin, now, by the very force with which in that dread hour her nature had revolted from his sway, recalled her from her open grave. In that moment the broken shackles fell from spirit and body together, and the awakened woman knew that the "truth had made her free."

THE CITY OF IS.

BY M. J. SAVAGE.

IN the weird old days of the long agone
  Rose a city by the sea;
But the fishermen woke, one startled dawn,
  On the coast of Brittany,
To hear the white waves on the shingle hiss,
And roll out over the city of Is,
  And play with its sad débris.

For the town had sunk in a single night!
  And 'twas only yesterday
That the bride had blushed in her young delight,
  That the priest had knelt to pray,
That the fisher cried his wares in the street,
And all the life of the city complete
  Went on in its old-time way.

And still the city lies under the sea,
  With each square and dome and spire
Distinct as some cherished fair memory
  Of a vanished heart's desire,
That once like a beautiful palace stood
Rock-based to defy the wind and the flood,
  Time's crumble and tempest's ire.

And as the sweet memory, buried deep,
  O'erswept by the flooding years,
Will still all its shadowy old life keep
  With ghosts of its joys and tears,
So still, in the wave-drowned city of Is,
The people live over, in care or bliss,
  Their shadowy hopes and fears.

When the sea is rough—so the sailors say—
  And the sunny waves are green,
And the winds with the white-caps are at play,
  The tips of the spires are seen,
And peering far down through the lucent deep,
They glimpses catch of the city asleep,
  Agleam with its fairy sheen.

Or on boats becalmed, when the lazy swells
  Sleep, lulled by the idle air,
They hear, sweet-toned, the low music of bells
  Roll, calling the town to prayer.
So ever the shadowy joy of old
Rings on, and forever the bells are tolled
  To echo some soul's despair.

Each life is a sea still sweeping above
  Some sunken city of Is—
The long-cherished dream of a cherished love
  That only in dreams we kiss.
What yesterdays are sunk deep in the soul
Above whose lost treasures to-day's waves roll
  To mock what our sad hearts miss!

Oh, the glimpses rare of the submerged past!
  They gleam in the light awhile,
To mock us with visions, that may not last,
  Of faces that used to smile.
And now and then from the busy to-day
The echoing tones of the far away
  Our listening hearts beguile.

But not in the sunken city of Is
  Shall the heart its treasures see.
No pilgrims forlorn to an old-time bliss
  And a vanished past are we;
For all the glad music of olden times
Is only faint echoes of grander chimes
  That ring in the time to be!

THE ARCHER'S PRAYER.

BY J. W. DE FOREST.

YOU wouldn't shoot with me, Edith,
    When the heavens were silver and blue;
And now that the showers are falling,
  Edith Anerly, what will you do?

To linger at breakfast and dinner,
  To trifle a novelette through,
To walk in the porches with Leila,
  Will that be sufficient for you?

The evening will come, with its music,
  And feet dropping softly as dew,
Perhaps with the glances and pleadings
  Of some Douglas tender and true.

I hope it will all be delightful;
  I trust there'll be nothing to rue;
And yet I would gladly have had you
  One hour with the target and yew.

The arrows that glint through the matches
  Of life, do they all whistle true?
Are they missioned to centre the yellow,
  Or even to edge on the blue?

I trust that the shafts of your drawing
  Will fly as Maid Marian's flew,
So duly and truly and nobly
  You shall not regret that you drew.

But I shall depart and not see it,
  Leave Newport and earth before you,
Shall go unregretted, forgotten,
  And alone as the Wandering Jew.

So remember, before I have vanished,
  To do what alone you may do,
And grant me one hour of Diana,
  Lithe maid, gracious sylph, of the yew.

THEIR PILGRIMAGE.

BY CHARLES DUDLEY WARNER.

CHAPTER IV.

N the Fourth of July, at five o'clock in the morning, the porters called the sleepers out of their berths at Wickford Junction. Modern civilization offers no such test to the temper and to personal appearance as this early preparation to meet the inspection of society after a night in the stuffy and luxuriously upholstered tombs of a sleeping-car. To get into them at night one must sacrifice dignity; to get out of them in the morning, clad for the day, gives the proprieties a hard rub. It is wonderful, however, considering the twisting and scrambling in the berth and the miscellaneous and ludicrous presentation of humanity in the wash-room at the end of the car, how presentable people make themselves in a short space of time. One realizes the debt of the ordinary man to clothes, and how fortunate it is for society that commonly people do not see each other in the morning until art has done its best for them. To meet the public eye, cross and tousled and disarranged, requires either indifference or courage. It is disenchanting to some of our cherished ideals. Even the trig, irreproachable commercial drummer actually looks banged up and nothing of a man; but after a few moments, boot-blacked and paper-collared, he comes out as fresh as a daisy, and all ready to drum.

Our travellers came out quite as well as could be expected, the artist sleepy and a trifle disorganized, Mr. King in a sort of facetious humor that is more dangerous than grumbling, Mr. De Long yawning and stretching and declaring that he had not slept a wink, while Marion alighted upon the platform unruffled in plumage, greeting the morning like a bird. There were the usual early loafers at the station, hands deep in pockets, ruminant, listlessly observant. No matter at what hour of day or night a train may arrive or depart at a country station in America, the loafers are so invariably there in waiting that they seem to be a part of our railway system. There is something in the life and movement that seems to satisfy all the desire for activity they have.

Even the most sleepy tourist could not fail to be impressed with the exquisite beauty of the scene at Wickford Harbor, where the boat was taken for Newport. The slow awaking of morning life scarcely disturbed its tranquillity. Sky and sea and land blended in a tone of refined gray. The shores were silvery, a silvery light came out of the east, streamed through the entrance of the harbor, and lay molten and glowing on the water. The steamer's deck and chairs and benches were wet with dew, the noises in transferring the baggage and getting the boat under way were all muffled and echoed in the surrounding silence. The sail-boats that lay at anchor on the still silver surface sent down long shadows, and the slim masts seemed driven down into the water to hold the boats in place. The little village was still asleep. It was such a contrast, the artist was saying to Marion, as they leaned over the taffrail, to the new raw villages in the Catskills. The houses were large, and

looked solid and respectable, many of
them were shingled on the sides, a spire
peeped out over the green trees, and the
hamlet was at once home-like and picturesque. Refinement is the note of the landscape. Even the old warehouses dropping
into the water, and the decaying piles of
the wharves, have a certain grace. How
graciously the water makes into the land,
following the indentations, and flowing
in little streams, going in and withdraw-
ing gently and regretfully, and how the
shore puts itself out in low points, wooing the embrace of the sea—a lovely
union. There is no haze, but all outlines
are softened in the silver light. It is like
a dream, and there is no disturbance of
the repose when a family party, a woman, a child, and a man, come down to
the shore, slip into a boat, and scull away
out by the light-house and the rocky entrance of the harbor, off, perhaps, for a
day's pleasure. The artist has whipped
out his sketch-book to take some outlines
of the view, and his comrade, looking
that way, thinks this group a pleasing
part of the scene, and notes how the salt,
dewy morning air has brought the color
into the sensitive face of the girl. There
are not many such hours in a lifetime,
he is also thinking, when nature can be
seen in such a charming mood, and for
the moment it compensates for the night
ride.

The party indulged this feeling when
they landed, still early, at the Newport
wharf, and decided to walk through the
old town up to the hotel, perfectly well
aware that after this no money would hire
them to leave their beds and enjoy this
novel sensation at such an hour. They
had the street to themselves, and the
promenade was one of discovery, and had
much the interest of a landing in a foreign
city.

"It is so English," said the artist.

"It is so colonial," said Mr. King,
"though I've no doubt that any one of
the sleeping occupants of these houses
would be wide-awake instantly, and come
out and ask you to breakfast, if they heard
you say it is so English."

"If they were not restrained," Marion
suggested, "by the feeling that that would
not be English. How fine the shade trees,
and what brilliant banks of flowers!"

"And such lawns! We cannot make
this turf in Virginia," was the reflection
of Mr. De Long.

"Well, colonial if you like," the artist
replied to Mr. King. "What is best is in
the colonial style; but you notice that all
the new houses are built to look old, and
that they have had Queen Anne pretty
bad, though the colors are good."

"That's the way with some towns.
Queen Anne seems to strike them all of a
sudden, and become epidemic. The only
way to prevent it is to vaccinate, so to
speak, with two or three houses, and wait;
then it is not so likely to spread."

Laughing and criticising and admiring,
the party strolled along the shaded avenue to the Ocean House. There were as
yet no signs of life at the Club, or the Library, or the Casino; but the shops were
getting open, and the richness and elegance of the goods displayed in the windows were the best evidence of the wealth
and refinement of the expected customers
—culture and taste always show themselves in the shops of a town. The long
gray-brown front of the Casino, with its
shingled sides and hooded balconies and
galleries, added to the already strong foreign impression of the place. But the
artist was dissatisfied. It was not at all
his idea of Independence Day; it was like
Sunday, and Sunday without any foreign
gayety. He had expected firing of cannon and ringing of bells—there was not
even a flag out anywhere; the celebration
of the Fourth seemed to have shrunk into
a dull and decorous avoidance of all excitement. "Perhaps," suggested Miss
Lamont, "if the New-Englanders keep the
Fourth of July like Sunday, they will by-
and-by keep Sunday like the Fourth of
July. I hear it is the day for excursions
on this coast."

Mr. King was perfectly well aware that
in going to a hotel in Newport he was
putting himself out of the pale of the best
society; but he had a fancy for viewing
this society from the outside, having often
enough seen it from the inside. And perhaps he had other reasons for this eccentric conduct. He had, at any rate, declined
the invitation of his cousin, Mrs. Bartlett
Glow, to her cottage on the Point of
Rocks. It was not without regret that
he did this, for his cousin was a very
charming woman, and devoted exclusively to the most exclusive social life. Her
husband had been something in the oil
line in New York, and King had watched
with interest his evolution from the business man into the full-blown existence of

AT THE CASINO, NEWPORT.

a man of fashion. The process is perfectly charted. Success in business, membership in a good club, tandem in the Park, introduction to a good house, marriage to a pretty girl of family and not much money, a yacht, a four-in-hand, a Newport villa. His name had undergone a like evolution. It used to be written on his business card, Jacob B. Glow. It was entered at the club as J. Bartlett Glow. On the wedding invitations it was Mr. Bartlett Glow, and the dashing pair were always spoken of at Newport as the Bartlett-Glows.

When Mr. King descended from his room at the Ocean House, although it was not yet eight o'clock, he was not surprised to see Mr. Benson tilted back in one of the chairs on the long piazza, out of the way of the scrubbers, with his air of patient waiting and observation. Irene used to say that her father ought to write a book—*Life as seen from Hotel Piazzas*. His only idea of recreation when away from business seemed to be sitting about on them.

"The women-folks," he explained to Mr. King, who took a chair beside him, "won't be down for an hour yet. I like, myself, to see the show open."

"Are there many people here?"

"I guess the house is full enough. But I can't find out that anybody is actually stopping here, except ourselves and a lot of school-marms come to attend a convention. They seem to enjoy it. The rest, those I've talked with, just happen to be here for a day or so, never have been to a hotel in Newport before, always staid in a cottage, merely put up here now to visit friends in cottages. You'll see that none of them act like they belonged to the hotel. Folks are queer. At a place we were last summer all the summer boarders, in boarding-houses round, tried to act like they were staying at the big hotel, and the hotel people swelled about on the fact of being at a hotel. Here you're nobody. I hired a carriage by the week, driver in buttons, and all that. It don't make any difference. I'll bet a gold dollar every cottager knows it's hired, and probably they think by the drive."

"It's rather stupid, then, for you and the ladies."

"Not a bit of it. It's the nicest place in America: such grass, such horses, such women, and the drive round the island—there's nothing like it in the country. We take it every day. Yes, it would be a little lonesome but for the ocean. It's a good deal like a funeral procession, nobody ever recognizes you, not even the hotel people who are in hired hacks. If I were to come again, Mr. King, I'd come in a yacht, drive up from it in a box on two wheels, with a man clinging on behind with his back to me, and have a cottage with an English gardener. That would fetch 'em. Money won't do it, not at a hotel. But I'm not sure but I like this way best. It's an occupation for a man to keep up a cottage."

"And so you do not find it dull?"

"No. When we aren't out riding, she and Irene go on the cliffs, and I sit here and talk real estate. It's about all there is to talk of."

There was an awkward moment or two when the two parties met in the lobby and were introduced before going in to breakfast. There was a little putting up of guards on the part of the ladies. Between Irene and Marion passed that rapid glance of inspection, that one glance which includes a study and the passing of judgment upon family, manners, and dress, down to the least detail. It seemed to be satisfactory, for after a few words of civility the two girls walked in together, Irene a little dignified, to be sure, and Marion with her wistful, half-inquisitive expression. Mr. King could not be mistaken in thinking Irene's manner a little constrained and distant to him, and less cordial than it was to Mr. Forbes, but the mother righted the family balance.

"I'm right glad you've come, Mr. King. It's like seeing somebody from home. I told Irene that when you came I guess we should know somebody. It's an awful fashionable place."

"And you have no acquaintances here?"

"No, not really. There's Mrs. Peabody has a cottage here, what they call a cottage, but there's no such house in Cyrusville. We drove past it. Her daughter was to school with Irene. We've met 'em out riding several times, and Sally (Miss Peabody) bowed to Irene, and pa and I bowed to everybody, but they haven't called. Pa says it's because we are at a hotel, but I guess it's been company or something. They were real good friends at school."

Mr. King laughed. "Oh, Mrs. Benson, the Peabodys were nobodies only a few years ago. I remember when they used to stay at one of the smaller hotels."

"Well, they seem nice, stylish people, and I'm sorry on Irene's account."

At breakfast the party had topics enough in common to make conversation lively. The artist was sure he should be delighted with the beauty and finish of Newport. Miss Lamont doubted if she should enjoy it as much as the freedom and freshness of the Catskills. Mr. King amused himself with drawing out Miss Benson on the contrast with Atlantic City. The dining-room was full of members of the Institute, in attendance upon the annual meeting, gray-bearded, long-faced educators, devotees of theories and systems, known at a glance by a certain earnestness of manner and intensity of expression, middle-aged women of a resolute, intellectual countenance, and a great crowd of youthful school-mistresses, just on the dividing line between domestic life and self-sacrifice, still full of sentiment, and still leaning perhaps more to Tennyson and Lowell than to mathematics and Old English.

"They have a curious, mingled air of primness and gayety, as if gayety were not quite proper," the artist began. "Some of them look downright interesting, and I've no doubt they are all excellent women."

"I've no doubt they are all good as gold," put in Mr. King. "These women are the salt of New England." (Irene looked up quickly and appreciatively at the speaker.) "No fashionable nonsense about them. What's in you, Forbes, to shy so at a good woman?"

"I don't shy at a good woman—but three hundred of them! I don't want all my salt in one place. And see here —I appeal to you, Miss Lamont— why didn't these girls dress simply, as they do at home, and not attempt a sort of ill-fitting finery that is in greater contrast to Newport than simplicity would be?"

"If you were a woman," said Marion, looking demurely, not at Mr. Forbes, but at Irene, "I could explain it to you. You don't allow anything for sentiment and the natural desire to please, and it ought to be just pathetic to you that these girls, obeying a natural instinct, missed the expression of it a little."

"Men are such critics," and Irene addressed the remark to Marion, "they pretend to like intellectual women, but they can pardon anything better than an ill-fitting gown. Better be frivolous than badly dressed."

THE SHEPHERD AND HIS FLOCK.

"Well," stoutly insisted Forbes, "I'll take my chance with the well-dressed ones always; I don't believe the frumpy are the most sensible."

"No; but you make out a *prima facie* case against a woman for want of taste in dress, just as you jump at the conclusion that because a woman dresses in such a way as to show she gives her mind to it she is of the right sort. I think it's a relief to see a convention of women devoted to other things who are not thinking of their clothes."

"Pardon me; the point I made was that they are thinking of their clothes, and thinking erroneously."

"Why don't you ask leave to read a paper, Forbes, on the relation of dress to education?" asked Mr. King.

They rose from the table just as Mrs. Benson was saying that for her part she liked these girls, they were so home-like; she loved to hear them sing college songs and hymns in the parlor. To sing the songs of the students is a wild, reckless dissipation for girls in the country.

When Mr. King and Irene walked up and down the corridor after breakfast the girl's constraint seemed to have vanished, and she let it be seen that she had sincere pleasure in renewing the acquaintance. King himself began to realize how large a place the girl's image had occupied in his mind. He was not in love—that would be absurd on such short acquaintance—but a thought dropped into the mind ripens without consciousness, and he found that he had anticipated seeing Irene again with decided interest. He remembered exactly how she looked at Fortress Monroe, especially one day when she entered the parlor, bowing right and left to persons she knew, stopping to chat with one and another, tall, slender waist swelling upward in symmetrical lines, brown hair, dark gray eyes—he recalled every detail, the high-bred air (which was certainly not inherited), the unconscious perfect carriage, and his thinking in a vague way that such ease and grace meant good living and leisure and a sound body. This, at any rate, was the image in his mind—a sufficiently distracting thing for a young man to carry about with him; and now as he walked beside her he was conscious that there was something much finer in her than the image he had carried with him, that there was a charm of speech and voice and expression that made her different from any other woman he had ever seen. Who can define this charm, this difference? Some women have it for the universal man—they are desired of every man who sees them; their way to marriage (which is commonly unfortunate) is over a causeway of prostrate forms, if not of cracked hearts; a few such women light up and make the romance of history. The majority of women fortunately have it for one man only, and sometimes he never appears on the scene at all! Yet every man thinks his choice belongs to the first class; even King began to wonder that all Newport was not raving over Irene's beauty. The present writer saw her one day as she alighted from a carriage at the Ocean House, her face flushed with the sea air; and he remembers that he thought her a fine girl. "By George! that's a fine woman!" exclaimed a New York bachelor, who prided himself on knowing horses and women and all that; but the country is full of fine women—this to him was only one of a thousand.

What were this couple talking about as they promenaded, basking in each other's presence? It does not matter. They were getting to know each other, quite as much by what they did not say as by what they did say, by the thousand little exchanges of feeling and sentiment which are all important, and never appear even in a stenographer's report of a conversation. Only one thing is certain about it, that the girl could recall every word that Mr. King said, even his accent and look, long after he had forgotten even the theme of the talk. One thing, however, he did carry away with him, which set him thinking. The girl had been reading the *Life of Carlyle*, and she took up the cudgels for the old curmudgeon, as King called him, and declared that when all was said, Mrs. Carlyle was happier with him than she would have been with any other man in England. "What woman of spirit wouldn't rather mate with an eagle, and quarrel half the time, than with a humdrum barn-yard fowl?" And Mr. Stanhope King, when he went away, reflected that he who had fitted himself for the bar, and travelled extensively, and had a moderate competence, hadn't settled down to any sort of career. He had always an intention of doing something in a vague way; but now the thought that he was idle made him for the first time decidedly uneasy, for he had an indistinct notion that Irene couldn't approve of such a life.

This feeling haunted him as he was making a round of calls that day. He did not return to lunch or dinner—if he had done so he would have found that lunch was dinner and that dinner was supper—another vital distinction between the hotel and the cottage. The rest of the party had gone to the cliffs with the artist, the girls on a pretence of learning to sketch from nature. Mr. King dined with his cousin.

"You are a bad boy, Stanhope," was the greeting of Mrs. Bartlett Glow, "not to come to me. Why did you go to the hotel?"

"Oh, I thought I'd see life; I had an unaccountable feeling of independence. Besides, I've a friend with me, a very clever artist, who is reseeing his country after an absence of some years. And there are some other people."

"Oh yes. What is her name?"

"Why, there is quite a party. We met them at different places. There's a very bright New York girl, Miss Lamont, and her uncle from Richmond." ("Never heard of her," interpolated Mrs. Glow.) "And a Mr. and Mrs. Benson and their daughter, from Ohio. Mr. Benson has made money; Mrs. Benson, good-hearted old lady, rather plain and—"

"Yes, I know the sort; had a falling out with Lindley Murray in her youth and never made it up. But what I want to know is about the girl. What makes you beat about the bush so? What's her name?"

"Irene. She is an uncommonly clever girl; educated; been abroad a good deal, studying in Germany; had all advantages; and she has cultivated tastes; and the fact is that out in Cyrusville—that is where they live. You know how it is here in America when the girl is educated and the old people are not—"

"The long and short of it is, you want me to invite them here. I suppose the girl is plain too—takes after her mother?"

"Not exactly. Mr. Forbes—that's my friend—says she is a beauty. But if you don't mind, Penelope, I was going to ask you to be a little civil to them."

"Well, I'll admit she is handsome—a very striking-looking girl. I've seen them driving on the Avenue day after day. Now, Stanhope, I don't mind asking them here to a five-o'clock; I suppose the mother will have to come. If she was staying with somebody here it would be easier.

Yes, I'll do it to oblige you, if you will make yourself useful while you are here. There are some girls I want you to know, and mind, my young friend, that you don't go and fall in love with a country girl whom nobody knows, out of the set. It won't be comfortable."

"You are always giving me good advice, Penelope, and I should be a different man if I had profited by it."

"Don't be satirical, because you've coaxed me to do you a favor."

Late in the evening the gentlemen of the hotel party looked in at the skating rink, a great American institution that has for a large class taken the place of the ball, the social circle, the evening meeting. It seemed a little incongruous to find a great rink at Newport, but an epidemic is stronger than fashion, and even the most exclusive summer resort must have its rink. Roller-skating is said to be fine exercise, but the benefit of it as exercise would cease to be apparent if there was a separate rink for each sex. There is a certain exhilaration in the lights and music and the lively crowd, and always an attraction in the freedom of intercourse offered. The rink has its world as the opera has, its romances and its heroes. The frequenters of the rink know the young women and the young men who have a national reputation as adepts, and their exhibitions are advertised and talked about as are the appearances of celebrated *prime donne* and *tenori* at the opera. The visitors had an opportunity to see one of these exhibitions. After a weary watching of the monotonous and clattering round and round of the swinging couples or the stumbling single skaters, the floor was cleared, and the darling of the rink glided upon the scene. He was a slender, handsome fellow, graceful and expert to the nicest perfection in his profession. He seemed not so much to skate as to float about the floor, with no effort except volition. His rhythmic movements were followed with pleasure, but it was his feats of dexterity, which were more wonderful than graceful, that brought down the house. It was evident that he was a hero to the female part of the spectators, and no doubt his charming image continued to float round and round in the brain of many a girl when she put her head on the pillow that night. It is said that a good many matches which are not projected or registered in heaven are made at the rink.

At the breakfast table it appeared that the sketching party had been a great success—for everybody except the artist, who had only some rough memoranda, like notes for a speech, to show. The amateurs had made finished pictures.

Miss Benson had done some rocks, and had got their hardness very well. Miss Lamont's effort was more ambitious; her picture took in no less than miles of coast, as much sea as there was room for on the paper, a navy of sail boats, and all the rocks and figures that were in the foreground, and it was done with a great deal of naïveté and conscientiousness. When it was passed round the table, the comments were very flattering.

"It looks just like it," said Mrs. Benson.

"It's very comprehensive," remarked Mr. Forbes.

"What I like, Marion," said Mr. De Long, holding it out at arm's-length, "is the perspective; "it isn't an easy thing to put ships up in the sky."

"Of course," explained Irene, "it was a kind of hazy day."

"But I think Miss Lamont deserves credit for keeping the haze out of it." King was critically examining it, turning his head from side to side. "I like it; but I tell you what I think it lacks; it lacks atmosphere. Why don't you cut a hole in it, Miss Lamont, and let the air in?"

"Mr. King," replied Miss Lamont, quite seriously, "you are a real friend. I can only repay you by taking you to church this morning."

"You didn't make much that time, King," said Forbes, as he lounged out of the room.

After church King accepted a seat in the Benson carriage for a drive on the Ocean Road. He who takes this drive for the first time is enchanted with the scene, and it has so much variety, deliciousness in curve and winding, such graciousness in the union of sea and shore, such charm of color, that increased acquaintance only makes one more in love with it. A good part of its attraction lies in the fickleness of its aspect. Its serene and soft appearance might pall if it were not now and then, and often suddenly, and with little warning, transformed into a wild coast, swept by a tearing wind, enveloped in a thick fog, roaring with the noise of the angry sea slapping the rocks and break-

FIVE-O'CLOCK TEA.

ing in foam on the fragments its rage has cast down. This elementary mystery and terror is always present with one familiar with the coast, to qualify the gentleness of its lovelier aspects. It has all moods. Perhaps the most exhilarating is that on a brilliant day, when shore and sea sparkle in the sun, and the waves leap high above the cliffs, and fall in diamond showers.

This Sunday the shore was in its most gracious mood, the landscape as if newly created. There was a light, luminous fog, which revealed just enough to excite the imagination, and refined every outline and softened every color. Mr. King and Irene left the carriage to follow the road, and wandered along the sea path. What softness and tenderness of color in the gray rocks, with the browns and reds of the vines and lichens! They went out on the iron fishing stands, and looked down into the shallow water. The rocks under water took on the most exquisite shades— purple and malachite and brown; the barnacles clung to them; the long sea-weeds, in half a dozen varieties, some in vivid colors, swept over them, flowing with the restless tide, like the long locks of a drowned woman's hair. King, who had dabbled a little in natural history, took great delight in pointing out to Irene this varied and beautiful life of the sea; and the girl felt a new interest in science, for it was all pure science, and she opened her heart to it, not knowing that love can go in by the door of science as well as by any other opening. Was Irene really enraptured by the dear little barnacles and the exquisite sea-weeds? I have seen a girl all of a flutter with pleasure in a laboratory when a young chemist was showing her the retorts and the crooked tubes and the glass wool and the freaks of color which the alkalies played with the acids. God has made them so, these women, and let us be thankful for it. What a charm there was about everything! Occasionally the mist became so thin that a long line of coast and a great breadth of sea were visible, with the white sails drifting.

"There's nothing like it," said King— "there's nothing like this island. It seems as if the Creator had determined to show man, once for all, a landscape perfectly refined, you might almost say with the beauty of high-breeding, refined in outline, color, everything softened into loveliness, and yet touched with the wild quality of picturesqueness."

"It's just a dream at this moment," murmured Irene. They were standing on a promontory of rock. "See those figures of people there through the mist —silhouettes only. And look at that vessel—there—no—it has gone."

As she was speaking, a sail-vessel began to loom up large in the mysterious haze. But was it not the ghost of a ship? For an instant it was coming, coming; it was distinct; and when it was plainly in sight it faded away, like a dissolving view, and was gone. The appearance was unreal. What made it more spectral was the bell on the reefs, swinging in its triangle, always sounding, and the momentary scream of the fog-whistle. It was like an enchanted coast. Regaining the carriage, they drove out to the end, Agassiz's Point, where, when the mist lifted, they saw the sea all round dotted with sails, the irregular coasts and islands with headlands and light-houses, all the picture still, land and water in a summer swoon.

Late that afternoon all the party were out upon the cliff path in front of the cottages. There is no more lovely sea stroll in the world, the way winding over the cliff edge by the turquoise sea, where the turf, close cut and green as Erin, set with flower beds and dotted with noble trees, slopes down, a broad pleasure park, from the stately and picturesque villas. But it was a social mistake to go there on Sunday. Perhaps it is not the height of good form to walk there any day, but Mr. King did not know that the fashion had changed, and that on Sunday this lovely promenade belongs to the butlers and the upper maids, especially to the butlers, who make it resplendent on Sunday afternoons when the weather is good. As the weather had thickened in the late afternoon, our party walked in a dumb-show, listening to the soft swish of the waves on the rocks below, and watching the figures of other promenaders, who were good enough ladies and gentlemen in this friendly mist.

The next day Mr. King made a worse mistake. He remembered that at high noon everybody went down to the first beach, a charming sheltered place at the bottom of the bay, where the rollers tumble in finely from the south, to bathe or see others bathe. The beach used to be lined with carriages at that hour, and the surf, for a quarter of a mile, presented the appearance of a line of picturesquely clad skirmishers going out to battle with the surf. To-day there were not half a dozen carriages and omnibuses altogether, and the bathers were few — nursery - maids, fragments of a day-excursion, and some of the fair conventionists. Newport was not there. Mr. King had led his party into another social blunder. It has ceased to be fashionable to bathe at Newport. Strangers and servants may do so, but the cottagers have withdrawn their support from the ocean. Salt-water may be carried to the house and used without loss of caste, but bathing in the surf is vulgar. A gentleman may go down and take a dip alone—it had better be at an early hour— and the ladies of the house may be heard to apologize for his eccentricity, as if his fondness for the water were abnormal and quite out of experience. And the observer is obliged to admit that promiscuous bathing is vulgar, as it is plain enough to be seen when it becomes unfashionable. It is charitable to think also that the cottagers have made it unfashionable because it is vulgar, and not because it is a cheap and refreshing pleasure accessible to everybody.

Nevertheless, Mr. King's ideas of Newport were upset. "It's a little off color to walk much on the cliffs; you lose caste if you bathe in the surf. What can you do?"

"Oh," explained Miss Lamont, "you can make calls; go to teas and receptions and dinners; belong to the Casino, but not appear there much; and you must drive on the Ocean Road, and look as English as you can. Didn't you notice that Redfern has an establishment on the Avenue? Well, the London girls wear what Redfern tells them to wear—much to the improvement of their appearance— and so it has become possible for a New-Yorker to become partially English without sacrificing her native taste."

Before lunch Mrs. Bartlett Glow called on the Bensons, and invited them to a five-o'clock tea, and Miss Lamont, who happened to be in the parlor, was included in the invitation. Mrs. Glow was as gracious as possible, and especially attentive to the old lady, who purred with pleasure, and beamed and expanded into familiarity under the encouragement of the woman of the world. In less than ten minutes Mrs. Glow had learned the chief points in the family history, the state of health and habits of pa (Mr. Benson), and all about Cyrusville and its wonderful

growth. In all this Mrs. Glow manifested a deep interest, and learned, by observing out of the corner of her eye, that Irene was in an agony of apprehension, which she tried to conceal under an increasing coolness of civility. "A nice lady," was Mrs. Benson's comment when Mrs. Glow had taken herself away with her charmingly scented air of frank cordiality—"a real nice lady. She seemed just like our folks."

Irene heaved a deep sigh. "I suppose we shall have to go."

"Have to go, child? I should think you'd like to go. I never saw such a girl —never. Pa and me are just studying all the time to please you, and it seems as if—" And the old lady's voice broke down.

"Why, mother dear"—and the girl, with tears in her eyes, leaned over her and kissed her fondly, and stroked her gray hair—"you are just as good and sweet as you can be; and don't mind me; you know I get in moods sometimes."

The old lady pulled her down and kissed her, and looked in her face with beseeching eyes.

"What an old frump the mother is!" was Mrs. Glow's comment to Stanhope, when she next met him; "but she is immensely amusing."

"She is a kind-hearted, motherly woman," replied King, a little sharply.

"Oh, motherly! Has it come to that? I do believe you are more than half gone. The girl is pretty; she has a beautiful figure; but, my gracious! her parents are impossible—just impossible. And don't you think she's a little too intellectual for society? I don't mean too intellectual, of course, but too mental, don't you know —shows that first. You know what I mean."

"But, Penelope, I thought it was the fashion now to be intellectual—go in for reading, and literary clubs, Dante and Shakespeare, and political economy, and all that."

"Yes. I belong to three clubs. I'm going to one to-morrow morning. We are going to take up the 'Disestablishment of the English Church.' That's different; we make it fit into social life somehow, and it doesn't interfere. I'll tell you what, Stanhope, I'll take Miss Benson to the Town and County Club next Saturday."

"That will be too intellectual for Miss Benson. I suppose the topic will be Transcendentalism?"

"No; we have had that. Professor Spor, of Cambridge, is going to lecture on Bacteria—if that's the way you pronounce it—those mites that get into everything."

"I should think it would be very improving. I'll tell Miss Benson that if she stays in Newport she must improve her mind."

"You can make yourself as disagreeable as you like to me, but mind you are on your good behavior at dinner to-night, for the Misses Pelham will be here."

The five-o'clock at Mrs. Bartlett Glow's was probably an event to nobody in Newport except Mrs. Benson. To most it was only an incident in the afternoon round and drive, but everybody liked to go there, for it is one of the most charming of the moderate-sized villas. The lawn is planted in exquisite taste, and the gardener has set in the open spaces of green the most ingenious devices of flowers and foliage plants, and nothing could be more enchanting than the view from the wide veranda on the sea side. In theory, the occupants lounge there, read, embroider, and swing in hammocks; in point of fact, the breeze is usually so strong that these occupations are carried on in-doors.

The rooms were well filled with a moving, chattering crowd when the Bensons arrived, but it could not be said that their entrance was unnoticed, for Mr. Benson was conspicuous, as Irene had in vain hinted to her father that he would be, in his evening suit, and Mrs. Benson's beaming, extra-gracious manner sent a little shiver of amusement through the polite civility of the room.

"I was afraid we should be too late," was Mrs. Benson's response to the smiling greeting of the hostess, with a most friendly look toward the rest of the company. "Mr. Benson is always behindhand in getting dressed for a party, and he said he guessed the party could wait, and—"

Before the sentence was finished, Mrs. Benson found herself passed on and in charge of a certain general, who was charged by the hostess to get her a cup of tea. Her talk went right on, however, and Irene, who was still standing by the host, noticed that wherever her mother went there was a lull in the general conversation, a slight pause as if to catch what this motherly old person might be saying,

and such phrases as, "It doesn't agree with me, general; I can't eat it," "Yes, I got the rheumatiz in New Orleans, and he did too," floated over the hum of talk.

In the introduction and movement that followed, Irene became one of a group of young ladies and gentlemen who, after the first exchange of civilities, went on talking about matters of which she knew nothing, leaving her wholly out of the conversation. The matters seemed to be very important, and the conversation was animated: it was about so-and-so who was expected, or was or was not engaged, or the last evening at the Casino, or the new trap on the Avenue—the delightful little chit-chat by means of which those who are in society exchange good understandings, but which excludes one not in the circle. The young gentleman next to Irene threw in an explanation now and then, but she was becoming thoroughly uncomfortable. She could not be unconscious, either, that she was the object of polite, transient scrutiny by the ladies, and of glances of interest from gentlemen who did not approach her. She began to be annoyed by the staring (the sort of stare that a woman recognizes as impudent admiration) of a young fellow who leaned against the mantel—a youth in English clothes who had caught very successfully the air of an English groom. Two girls near her, to whom she had been talking, began speaking in lowered voices in French, but she could not help overhearing them, and her face flushed hotly when she found that her mother and her appearance were the subject of their foreign remarks.

Luckily at the moment Mr. King approached, and Irene extended her hand and said, with a laugh, "Ah, monsieur," speaking in a very pretty Paris accent, and perhaps with unnecessary distinctness, "you were quite right; the society here is very different from Cyrusville; there they all talk about each other."

Mr. King, who saw that something had occurred, was quick-witted enough to reply jestingly in French, as they moved away, but he asked, as soon as they were out of ear-shot, "What is it?"

"Nothing," said the girl, recovering her usual serenity. "I only said something for the sake of saying something; I didn't mean to speak disrespectfully of my own town. But isn't it singular how local and provincial society talk is everywhere? I must look up mother, and then I want you to take me on the veranda for some air. What a delightful house this is of your cousin's!"

The two young ladies who had dropped into French looked at each other for a moment after Irene moved away, and one of them spoke for both when she exclaimed: "Did you ever see such rudeness in a drawing-room! Who could have dreamed that she understood?" Mrs. Benson had been established very comfortably in a corner with Professor Slem, who was listening with great apparent interest to her accounts of the early life in Ohio. Irene seemed relieved to get away into the open air, but she was in a mood that Mr. King could not account for. Upon the veranda they encountered Miss Lamont and the artist, whose natural enjoyment of the scene somewhat restored her equanimity. Could there be anything more refined and charming in the world than this landscape, this hospitable, smiling house, with the throng of easy-mannered, pleasant-speaking guests, leisurely flowing along in the conventional stream of social comity. One must be a churl not to enjoy it. But Irene was not sorry when, presently, it was time to go, though she tried to extract some comfort from her mother's enjoyment of the occasion. It was beautiful. Mr. Benson was in a calculating mood. He thought it needed a great deal of money to make things run so smoothly.

Why should one inquire in such a paradise if things do run smoothly? Cannot one enjoy a rose without pulling it up by the roots? I have no patience with those people who are always looking on the seamy side. I agree with the commercial traveller who says that it will only be in the Millennium that all goods will be alike on both sides. Mr. King made the acquaintance in Newport of the great but somewhat philosophical Mr. Snodgrass, who is writing a work on *The Discomforts of the Rich*, taking a view of life which he says has been wholly overlooked. He declares that their annoyances, sufferings, mortifications, envies, jealousies, disappointments, dissatisfactions (and so on through the dictionary of disagreeable emotions), are a great deal more than those of the poor, and that they are more worthy of sympathy. Their troubles are real and unbearable, because they are largely of the mind. All these are set forth with so much powerful language and variety of illustration that King said no one could read the book without tears for the rich of Newport, and he asked Mr. Snodgrass why he did not organize a society for their relief. But the latter declared that it was not a matter for levity. The misery is real. An imaginary case would illustrate his meaning. Suppose two persons quarrel about a purchase of land, and one builds a stable on his lot so as to shut out his neighbor's view of the sea. Would not the one suffer because he could not see the ocean, and the other by reason of the revengeful state of his mind? He went on to argue that the owner of a splendid villa might have, for reasons he gave, less content in it than another person in a tiny cottage so small that it had no spare room for his mother-in-law even, and that in fact his satisfaction in his own place might be spoiled by the more showy place of his neighbor. Mr. Snodgrass attempts in his book a philosophical explanation of this. He says that if every man designed his own cottage, or had it designed as an expression of his own ideas, and developed his grounds and landscape according to his own tastes, working it out himself, with the help of specialists, he would be satisfied. But when owners have no ideas about architecture or about gardening, and their places are the creation of some experimenting architect and a foreign gardener, and the whole effort is not to express a person's individual taste and character, but to make a show, then discontent as to his own will arise whenever some new and more showy villa is built. Mr. Benson, who was poking about a good deal, strolling along the lanes and getting into the rears of the houses, said, when this book was discussed, that his impression was that the real object of these fine places was to support a lot of English gardeners, grooms, and stable-boys. They are a kind of aristocracy. They have really made Newport (that is the summer, transient Newport, for it is largely a transient Newport). "I've been inquiring," continued Mr. Benson, "and you'd be surprised to know the number of people who come here, buy or build expensive villas, splurge out for a year or two, then fail or get tired of it, and disappear."

Mr. Snodgrass devotes a chapter to the parvenues at Newport. By the parvenu —his definition may not be scientific—he seems to mean a person who is vulgar;

but has money, and tries to get into society on the strength of his money alone. He is more to be pitied than any other sort of rich man. For he not only works hard and suffers humiliation in getting his place in society, but after he is in he works just as hard, and with bitterness in his heart, to keep out other parvenues like himself. And this is misery.

But our visitors did not care for the philosophizing of Mr. Snodgrass—you can spoil almost anything by turning it wrong side out. They thought Newport the most beautiful and finished watering-place in America. Nature was in the loveliest mood when it was created, and art has generally followed her suggestions of beauty and refinement. They did not agree with the cynic who said that Newport ought to be walled in, and have a gate with an inscription, "None but Millionaires allowed here." It is very easy to get out of the artificial Newport and to come into scenery that Nature has made after artistic designs which artists are satisfied with. A favorite drive of our friends was to the Second Beach and the Purgatory Rocks overlooking it. The photographers and the water-color artists have exaggerated the Purgatory chasm into a Colorado cañon, but anybody can find it by help of a guide. The rock of this locality is a curious study. It is an agglomerate made of pebbles and cement, the pebbles being elongated as if by pressure. This rock is sometimes found in detached fragments having the form of tree trunks. Wherever it is fractured, the fracture is a clean cut, as if made by a saw, and through both pebbles and cement, and the ends present the appearance of a composite cake filled with almonds and cut with a knife. The landscape is beautiful.

"All the lines are so simple," the artist explained. "The shore, the sea, the gray rocks, with here and there the roof of a quaint cottage to enliven the effect, and few trees, only just enough for contrast with the long, sweeping lines."

"You don't like trees?" asked Miss Lamont.

"Yes, in themselves. But trees are apt to be in the way. There are too many trees in America. It is not often you can get a broad, simple effect like this."

It happened to be a day when the blue of the sea was that of the Mediterranean, and the sky and sea melted into each other, so that a distant sail-boat seemed to be climbing into the heavens. The waves rolled in blue on the white sand beach, and broke in silver. Three young girls on horseback galloping in a race along the hard beach at the moment gave the needed animation to a very pretty picture.

North of this the land comes down to the sea in knolls of rock breaking off suddenly—rocks gray with lichen, and shaded with a touch of other vegetation. Between these knife-back ledges are plots of sea-green grass and sedge, with little ponds, black, and mirroring the sky. Leaving this wild bit of nature, which has got the name of Paradise (perhaps because few people go there), the road back to town sweeps through sweet farm land; the smell of hay is in the air, loads of hay encumber the roads, flowers in profusion half smother the farm cottages, and the trees of the apple orchards are gnarled and picturesque as olives.

The younger members of the party climbed up into this Paradise one day, leaving the elders in their carriages. They came into a new world, as unlike Newport as if they had been a thousand miles away. The spot was wilder than it looked from a distance. The high ridges of rock lay parallel, with bosky valleys and ponds between, and the sea shining in the south—all in miniature. On the way to the ridges they passed clean pasture fields, bowlders, gray rocks, aged cedars with flat tops like the stone-pines of Italy. It was all wild but exquisite, a refined wildness recalling the pictures of Rousseau.

Irene and Mr. King strolled along one of the ridges, and sat down on a rock looking off upon the peaceful expanse, the silver lines of the curving shores, and the blue sea dotted with white sails.

"Ah," said the girl, with an aspiration, "this is the sort of five-o'clock I like."

"And I'm sure I'd rather be here with you than at the Blims' reception, from which we ran away."

"I thought," said Irene, not looking at him, and jabbing the point of her parasol into the ground—"I thought you liked Newport."

"So I do, or did. I thought you would like it. But, pardon me, you seem somehow different from what you were at Fortress Monroe, or even at that lovely Atlantic City," this with a rather forced laugh.

"Do I? Well, I suppose I am; that is, different from what you thought me. I should hate this place in a week more, beautiful as it is."

"Your mother is pleased here?"

The girl looked up quickly. "I forgot to tell you how much she thanked you for the invitation to your cousin's. She was delighted there."

"And you were not?"

"I didn't say so; you were very kind."

"Oh, kind! I didn't mean to be kind. I was purely selfish in wanting you to go. Cannot you believe, Miss Benson, that I had some pride in having my friends see you and know you?"

"Well, I will be as frank as you are, Mr. King. I don't like being shown off. There, don't look displeased. I didn't mean anything disagreeable."

"But I hoped you understood my motives better by this time."

"I did not think about motives, but the fact is" (another jab of the parasol), "I was made desperately uncomfortable, and always shall be under such circumstances, and, my friend—I should like to

believe you are my friend—you may as well expect I always will be."

"I cannot do that. You under—"

"I just see things as they are," Irene went on, hastily. "You think I am different here. Well, I don't mind saying that when I made your acquaintance I thought you different from any man I had met." But now it was out, she did mind saying it, and stopped, confused, as if she had confessed something. But she continued, almost immediately: "I mean that I liked your manner to women; you didn't appear to flatter, and you didn't talk complimentary nonsense."

"And now I do?"

"No. Not that. But everything is somehow changed here. Don't let's talk of it. There's the carriage."

Irene arose, a little flushed, and walked toward the point. Mr. King, picking his way along behind her over the rocks, said, with an attempt at lightening the situation, "Well, Miss Benson, I'm going to be just as different as ever a man was."

THE DEATH OF POPE ALEXANDER VI.

BY PROFESSOR T. F. CRANE.

ON the 25th of July, 1492, died Pope Innocent VIII., and on the 6th of the following month the cardinals met in conclave in the Sistine Chapel to choose his successor. The most prominent among the electors were the Cardinals Sforza, Roderick Borgia, Cibò, Riario, and Rovere. The last-named was the candidate of France, whose king had deposited 200,000 ducats in a certain bank to further the aims of his favorite. Borgia secured the influence of Sforza, who, although one of the richest prelates of the Church, did not scorn to increase his wealth, and it was said that even before the conclave Borgia had sent to his house four mules laden with money. He further promised him his own palace, the office of Vice-Chancellor, and numerous benefices. The various dependencies of the Roman state were divided among the other cardinals; even the Patriarch of Venice, an old man of ninety-five years, stretched, as Gregorovius remarks, his trembling hand out for 5000 ducats. Only five out of the twenty-five cardinals remained unbribed. In the night between the 10th and 11th of Au-

gust Roderick Borgia was unanimously elected Pope, and in the early morning the name of Alexander VI. was proclaimed from the window of the chamber where the conclave was held.* The new Pope, whose life as cardinal has already been described in these pages, was at the time he ascended the papal throne sixty-one years old, and the father of four acknowledged children, all by one mother.† He is thus described by a contemporary: "Alexander is tall, of medium color; his eyes are black, his mouth somewhat full. He is the picture of health,

* The principal sources of this article are: Gregorovius's *Geschichte der Stadt Rom*, vol. vii.; the despatches of the Venetian ambassador Giustinian: *Dispacci di Antonio Giustinian Ambasciatore veneto in Roma dal 1502 al 1505, pubblicati da P. Villari*, Florence, 1876, three volumes; and the recently published Journal of the Pope's Master of Ceremonies, John Burkhard: *Johannis Burchardi Diarium*, edited by L. Thuasne, Paris, 1883–1885, three volumes. The medallion is from the Eichler collection of casts in the Cornell University. The autograph, *Alexander Papa VI. manu propria*, is from the Este archives in Modena, reproduced in Gregorovius's *Lucrezia Borgia*.

† See articles on "Lucrezia Borgia" and "Cardinal Mephisto" in *Harper's* for March and May, 1876.

and endures fatigues of every kind beyond all conception. He is extraordinarily eloquent, and everything of an unrefined nature is repugnant to him." Another praised "the elegance of his figure, his open forehead, his kingly brows, his expression of liberality and majesty, his genius, and the beautiful and noble form of his whole body." Besides his sensuality, he was possessed of but one passion, which ruled his life, modified his reign, and affected the entire Christian world—it was his inordinate love for his children.* One of the Pope's first acts was to provide for his family: more than thirty Borgias received places of honor in the Church and state, and five were created cardinals at various times. Alexander's hopes for the future of his house rested, for its secular glory, on Lucrezia and Juan, and for its ecclesiastical on Cæsar, who was made Bishop of Valencia, and afterward cardinal. Some years later, when renouncing his Church dignities, he declared that he had always had an inclination to worldly things, and that it was only the Pope's will which had compelled him to become an ecclesiastic.† It is likely that he envied from an early date the brilliant career of his younger brother, Juan, whom his father, while cardinal, had caused to be made Duke of Gandia, in Spain, and whom he later overwhelmed with honors and principalities wrested from the old Roman nobility. One night the duke disappeared after supping with his mother and brother, and three days after, his body was found in the Tiber pierced with wounds. It was laid in a boat and carried to the Castle of St. Angelo. A contemporary who was on the bridge near by at the time says: "While I was

* Alexander VI. was moderate in but one thing, his table, which was so poor that Cæsar and the cardinals endeavored to excuse themselves when they were invited to it. The accounts of the papal stewards have recently been found in the Roman archives, and show that the monthly expense of the Pope's household was not over 700 ducats—about the same number of dollars of our money.

† While Cæsar was still an ecclesiastic, in 1497, he represented his father at the coronation of the King of Naples, and bore a ceremonial sword the blade of which was engraved with designs referring to the ancient Cæsar, and with the motto: CVM NVMINE CÆSARIS OMEN—ALEA JACTA EST. This sword and the biography of its owner are the subject of an admirable article by C. Yriarte, *L'Épée de César Borgia*, in the *Revue des Deux Mondes*, September 15, 1885. Cæsar is the hero of Mr. W. W. Astor's recent interesting historical romance, *Valentino*.

on the bridge I heard a great lamentation and crying of one person above all the rest; it was held to be the Pope, who greatly loved him." The unhappy pontiff shut himself up in his apartments, and was heard to weep and exclaim, "I know his murderer." He did not eat, drink, nor sleep from Thursday morning until Sunday. He then called the cardinals together and made an extraordinary speech, in which he said that if he had seven papacies, he would give them all for the life of his son; declared that he did not know who the murderer was; and, overcome by his feelings, promised in the future to think no more of the papacy nor of himself, but only of the reform of the Church. Unhappily all this was only a fleeting pang of remorse, and his passion for his children soon led him to forgive Cæsar's crime. The father and son met for the first time in a consistory of the cardinals. Cæsar had just returned from a legation to Naples. Burkhard, the master of ceremonies, says, "Cæsar did not speak a word to the Pope, nor the Pope to him, but he kissed him." How full the Pope's forgiveness was may be judged from the fact that he gave to Cæsar all the murdered man's jewels and treasures to hold in trust for his heir. No wonder that the people believed that the ghost of the unhappy duke went wailing through the Vatican, and compelled the terrified Pope to take refuge in the Castle of St. Angelo! The ghost, however, like the Pope's conscience, was soon quieted, and Cæsar filled completely his brother's place in his father's heart.

From this time the history of Alexander's reign is the story of Cæsar's attempt to carve out for himself an Italian state. To this end all the energies of the Pope were bent; treaties were made and broken solely to provide allies or weaken opponents; the revenues of the Church were appropriated to pay Cæsar's troops and bribe his enemies. To increase these revenues the dignities of the Church were sold to the highest bidder, and the wealthiest prelates were murdered that their property might be used to further Cæsar's designs.*

* In September, 1500, the Venetian ambassador, Paolo Capello, returned home, and reported to the senate the results of his observations during his three years' residence in Rome. He says: "The Pope loves and fears greatly his son the duke (as Cæsar is henceforth always called), who is twenty-seven years old, very handsome and tall, and of

In June, 1502, the new Venetian ambassador, Antonio Giustinian, reached Rome, where he remained three years. His despatches, written sometimes three and four a day, are a precious source of information for the last year and a half of Alexander's life. They afford an insight into the heart of the Pope to be obtained in no other way. In the light they throw upon the pontiff he is seen to contract from the colossal dimensions of guilt and power which exaggerating historians have conferred on him to the really small creature he was, the sport of his passions and the slave of his son. These despatches were written for the eye of the Doge alone, and are calm, impartial records of the events of the day. They seldom mention the scandals of the court except when necessary to explain some fact. In order, however, to arrive at the facts, the ambassador is most careful and minute in his observations, reporting not only, for instance, the Pope's words, but his manner, gestures, etc. The despatches show in a remarkable manner how absorbed the Pope was in Cæsar's undertakings. The latter was, when the Venetian ambassador arrived in Rome, engaged in his bloody conquest of the Romagna, and in proportion as he advanced in his enterprise the Pope was beside himself with joy, praised Cæsar's "magnanimity," and would not talk about anything else. After the capture of Camerino the Pope called the consistory together, but could not think of anything but his son's success. One of the cardinals reminded him that there was important news from Hungary in regard

better figure even than the King Ferdinand (of Naples). The said duke, in a place near St. Peter's, enclosed with boards, killed six wild bulls, fighting on horseback with a spear, and he cut off the head of one bull with a single stroke of his sword, which seemed a great thing to all Rome. He is most royal in his manners, rather prodigal, and this displeases the Pope. And another time he killed with his own hand Messer Pierotto, who had taken refuge under the Pope's mantle, so that his blood spirted into the face of the Pope, whose favorite he was. He also killed his brother the Duke of Gandia, and had him thrown with his throat cut into the Tiber. And every night they find in Rome four or five persons killed, viz., bishops, prelates, and others, so that all Rome trembles before this duke for fear that he will have them assassinated. The Pope is seventy years old; every day he grows younger; he never thinks of the morrow; he is of cheerful disposition, and does what is useful to himself; and his whole mind is bent on aggrandizing his children, and he has no care of anything else."

to the Turks, at that time the terror of Europe; but the Pope only said a few words about it, and sent for the letters from the Hungarian legate. When they came, however, he was so absorbed in the subject that pleased him the most that he forgot to have them read.

When the duke, to whom the Pope was sending a thousand ducats a day, did not advance rapidly enough in his enterprise, the Pope was beside himself with anger, and "with great wrath and indignation he said at least thrice, so loudly that all standing by could hear him, 'The bastard!' and other words in Spanish, all angry." After the duke had entered Sinigaglia and strangled his rebellious captains, he sent word to the Pope to arrest in Rome the heads of the Orsini family, the most prominent of whom was the Cardinal Orsini, the Pope's most intimate friend. The 29th of December, 1502, they spent the night together "in the usual enjoyments of the Pope, women being present, without whom, at the present time, in this palace (the Vatican), there is no festival that pleases; they also played for some hundreds of ducats. The cardinal has been blamed for this intimacy by many, who think he is thrusting his own head into the trap." Scarcely five days passed when the cardinal was arrested, his palace stripped of all it contained, and his mother driven into the streets with nothing but what she had on her back. In the midst of all this, while the Pope continued the arrests, and was preparing to exterminate his enemies, his mind was cheerful, his health excellent, and he gave himself up to the pleasures of the carnival, publicly gazing at the maskers from the Castle of St. Angelo, and laughing at the crowd that paused to play their tricks before him. When the *conservatori* of Rome threw themselves at his feet, asking mercy for the citizens who were in constant fear of being arrested, or strangled, or poisoned, "the Pope, to have some fun from them, told them they should be attending to making festivities and other rejoicings for the carnival." The Pope himself did not lose a single pleasure, no matter what business affairs were on hand. The 21st of February the Venetian ambassador saw him present at a comedy recited in public, "in the midst of many cardinals, some in their official robes, others in masks, with those female companions who are wont to please the

Pope, and a certain one of them was reclining at the feet of the Holy Father." What a subject for the brush of a Couture or a Makart!

The following summer (1503) was exceptionally hot and unhealthy in Rome, and the city was filled with persons stricken down by fever. The Venetian ambassador visited the Pope on the 7th of August, and found him carefully protected against the air. He said: "*Domine Orator*, the many people who are sick in Rome at present, and who are dying every day, frighten us so that we are disposed to take somewhat greater care than usual of our person." On the 12th the Pope did not receive any visitors or transact any business, and the next day Giustinian wrote that he had just learned that the Pope, the day before, had been taken ill after eating, had vomited, and been attacked by fever, which had lasted all that day and the next,* on which account the palace had been closed, and no one allowed to enter. The real reason was not, however, given, but it was merely said that his Holiness was engaged with the duke touching the latter's departure, and did not wish to be disturbed. The duke was also confined to his bed with fever, and the ambassador learned that the cause of the illness of both was that a week before they had taken supper in a vineyard belonging to the Cardinal Adrian of Corneto, and had remained there until night.† All who were present had been affected, the cardinal himself first of all. On Friday he attended mass at the chapel, and after eating was attacked by fever, which lasted until the next morning, and afterward returned. The 14th of August the Pope was bled. Giustinian heard that ten ounces had been taken from him, which he thinks a very great quantity, and remarkable in a man seventy-three years old. The blood-letting did not, however, stop the fever, which continued that day, but not as severe as before. Toward evening more blood was let.

* Burkhard, the Pope's master of ceremonies, says: "Saturday, the 12th of August, early, the Pope felt ill; after Vespers, the twenty-first or twenty-second hour (two hours before sunset), fever set in, which continued. The 15th, fourteen ounces of blood or thereabout were taken from him, and a tertian fever supervened."

† This account of a banquet in the cardinal's vineyard is confirmed by various letters written to Florence and Venice at the time. See Gregorovius's *Geschichte der Stadt Rom*, vol. vii., p. 501.

The duke grew worse, and, suspecting that the Pope's condition was dangerous, commanded his troops to concentrate in the neighborhood of Rome. It was very difficult for Giustinian to learn anything definite about the Pope, for no one was admitted to his apartment, and those who had entered were not allowed to come out again. His attendants and those who desired his health affirmed that he was well and had no fever, which, the ambassador remarks, was a thing not to be believed. The Pope and the duke were no better on the 16th, the latter having, however, more fever than the former. At midnight he had sent for his physicians, who did not reside in the Vatican, and kept them with him. The blood-letting seemed to have relieved the Pope, for before it his illness tended to his head, and he had already grown lethargic. Not only were the duke's troops observed to be approaching Rome, but various cardinals who were absent from the city were summoned back by their friends in the Vatican, who began to lose all hope of the Pope's recovery. On the 17th, Master Scipio, the Pope's physician, sent a note to the Cardinal of Naples, stating that the pontiff was still very ill with severe and continual fever, and his attendants reposed all their hope on the medicine administered that day. At a later hour that night the whole palace was upside down, every one trying to save his own, but secretly, and the adherents of the duke and Pope endeavoring as much as possible to conceal the gravity of the latter's illness; Giustinian adds: "They succeed so poorly that it would be almost better to tell the truth." The next day, the 18th of August, the Pope took communion, but in secret, and some of the cardinals were admitted to his presence. Giustinian heard, however, that early that morning, before the communion, the Bishop of Venosa (the Pope's chief physician) came from the Pope's chamber weeping and telling his friends that the danger was great, and lamenting that the medicine given the day before had not helped his Holiness as it should have done. The ambassador remarked in this despatch that the whole city was in a state of suspense, "every one desiring that this malady should put an end to the tribulations of Christianity." That same afternoon the Pope grew worse, and his attendants gave up all hope; a messenger was sent at once to the Castle of St. Angelo, which was immediately closed, the garrison put under arms, and the cannon loaded in haste. Somewhat later Giustinian saw the Master Scipio mentioned above, and received from him a full account of the Pope's illness. He says: "From what he has told me, and from the description of the whole disease, attacks, symptoms, and remedies, one would judge that the beginning of his illness was apoplexy, and of this opinion is this physician, an excellent man in his art." Master Scipio also told the ambassador that the duke was out of danger, and was preparing to betake himself that night to the Castle of St. Angelo, and there fortify himself. The Pope's child Giovanni and Lucrezia's son Rodrigo had already been sent there, and the property of the duke and his followers had been conveyed from the Vatican to the castle by the covered way which still exists, and which has often enabled a fugitive pope to take refuge in his fortress.

That same day, at the hour of vespers, the Pope died, and his death was announced an hour before sunset. The next day at noon the Pope's body was taken to St. Peter's, according to custom, and shown to the people. "Nevertheless," adds Giustinian, "on account of being the most loathsome, monstrous, and horrid corpse ever seen, without any human form or figure, from shame they kept it covered awhile, and then buried it before sunset, in the presence of two cardinals from the palace."*

Such is the careful and impartial state-

* Burkhard gives the following account: "In the evening the body was carried to the chapel by six porters and two carpenters, all jesting and laughing, and having made the coffin too short and narrow, they pounded the body with their fists until it went in: first having removed the mitre and robes, they put on it in exchange an old and dirty piece of carpet, then they placed the coffin at the left corner of the altar of St. Peter."

Gregorovius, in his *Geschichte der Stadt Rom*, vol. vii., p. 671, says: "The last Pope of the fifteenth century, Alexander VI., received no monument, not even a grave. The sarcophagus which is to-day shown as his in the crypt of the Vatican is said to be that of his uncle Calixtus III., and the marble figure reclining on it that of the same Pope. The Spaniards, who should have erected a monument to their countryman, have not done so, and the body of the terrible Borgia, together with that of his uncle, was taken to the Church of Santa Maria in Montserrat (near Barcelona, in Spain), where they are yet kept unburied in a wooden chest which bears the following inscription: 'The bones of two Popes are in this chest; they are Calixtus III. and Alexander VI., who were Spaniards.'"

ment of the illness and death of Alexander VI. by a man of deep insight into human nature, and accustomed to sift carefully the facts on which he based his belief. His account is confirmed by Burkhard and contemporary letters and despatches. In spite of all this, however, the romantic story that the Pope died of poison he had intended for another soon became circulated, and has been repeated and believed by the gravest historians, from Guicciardini to Ranke.

The favorite versions of the story are those of Tommasi and Sanuto.* The former is as follows: "Among the most recent and wealthy of the Sacred College was Adrian of Corneto, and he was therefore selected as next victim. On the 12th of August the Pope and Cæsar invited him to sup in the Belvedere casino of the Vatican, and the latter sent forward a supply of poisoned wine in charge of his butler, with strict injunctions not to serve it until specially desired by himself. Several other cardinals were to partake of the banquet, and probably were intended to share the drugged potion. Alexander had been assured by an astrologer that so long as he had about him the sacramental wafer he should not die, and accordingly he constantly carried it in a little golden box; but having on that evening forgotten it upon his toilet, he sent Monsignor Caraffa, afterward Paul IV., to fetch it. Meanwhile, overcome by the dog-day heat, he called for wine. The butler was gone to fetch a salver of peaches which had been presented to his Holiness, and his deputy, having received no instructions as to the medicated bottles, offered a draught from them to the Pope. He greedily swallowed it, and his example was more moderately followed by Cæsar. Scarcely had they taken their seats at table, when the two victims successively fell down insensible from the virulence of the poison, and were carried to bed."

Read in the light of Giustinian's despatches, it will be seen how little truth there is in the above statement; for instance, the Pope and Cæsar were not taken ill until about a week after the ban-

* Tommasi was the author of a life of Cæsar Borgia. I have taken the above translation from Dennistoun's *Memoirs of the Dukes of Urbino*, vol. ii., p. 14. Sanuto's account will be found in the same place, or, together with the original, in Ranke's *History of the Popes* (London, 1840), vol. iii., appendix, p. 5.

quet mentioned above. The account by Sanuto runs thus: "The Lord Adrian Castillense of Corneto, Cardinal Datary, having been desired by the Pope to receive him and the Duke Valentino (Cæsar) at supper in his vineyard, his Holiness supplying the eatables, this cardinal presumed the invitation to be planned for his death by poison, so that the duke might obtain his money and benefices, which were considerable. In order to save himself there seemed but one course, so watching his opportunity, he summoned the pontiff's steward, whom he knew intimately, and on his arrival received him alone in a private chamber, where 10,000 ducats were laid out. These he desired him to accept for love of him, offering him also more of his property, which he declared he could continue to enjoy only through his assistance, and adding, 'You certainly are aware of the Pope's disposition, and I know that he and the duke have designed my death by poison through you; wherefore I pray you have pity on me and spare my life.' The steward, moved with compassion on hearing this, at length avowed the plan concerted for administering the poison: that after the supper he was to serve three boxes of confections, one for the Pope, another for the duke, and a third for the cardinal, the last being poisoned. So they arranged that the service of the table should be contrived in such a way that the pontiff might eat of the cardinal's poisoned box and die. On the appointed day, the Pope having arrived at the vineyard with the duke, the cardinal begged and received permission to wait on the table of his Holiness. The supper being thus served, and the moment arrived for giving the confections, the box having been poisoned by the steward as directed by the Pope, the cardinal placed it before his Holiness, who, relying on his steward, and convinced of the cardinal's sincerity by his service, ate joyfully of this box, as did the cardinal of the other, which the pontiff believed the poisoned one. Thereafter, at the hour when from its nature the poison took effect, his Holiness began to feel it, and thus he died. The cardinal, being still alarmed, took medicine and an emetic, and was easily cured."*

This story, it will be observed, does not account for the illness of Cæsar, nor of the Cardinal Adrian. In fact, there is no foundation of truth in either story, and both rest simply on the popular belief of the day.

* This is the version, with some slight changes, followed by Mr. Astor in *Valentino.* As the readers of this article and the one on "Lucrezia Borgia" will see, Mr. Astor has observed quite closely historic truth, but with regard to the death of the Pope he has availed himself of the novelist's license, and employed the more picturesque version of popular tradition.

KING ARTHUR.
Not a Love Story.
By the Author of "John Halifax, Gentleman."

CHAPTER VII.

THERE is an old comedy entitled, *The Wonder! A Woman keeps a Secret!* Its author could have known very little of human nature. How many secrets, not always their own, do women keep every day—out of love, or a sense of honor, or even pure pity! What wonderful strength they possess in hiding what they wish to hide! able to smile with a breaking heart—to wrap their robes smoothly and even gracefully over the beast that is gnawing their vitals. Men may be very good at concealment on some affairs—especially their own; but for absolute silence—years long, life long, if necessary —there is, in spite of the old dramatist, no secret-keeper like a woman.

When Dr. Franklin made the discovery of "the woman at Andermatt"—who, by-the-bye, must have kept her secret pretty well—Mrs. Trevena, startled as she was, had strength to whisper "Hush!" for her husband was close behind them, and Arthur in front; and the good doctor had the sense to take the hint, and also to suggest that she was looking tired, and they had better go home.

"Make my excuses to Lady Damerel. She won't miss me very much," said he to the unconscious rector, and tucking

Mrs. Trevena under his arm, he walked away.

Not too soon. Susannah tottered blindly, almost without speaking a word, along the path which led to the rectory. But as soon as she got home she fainted outright.

However, it was too serious a crisis for any outward betrayal. Dr. Franklin brought her to herself without telling the servants, and by the time Mr. Trevena and Arthur came back, he and she had talked the whole thing calmly over, and made up their minds to keep it at present entirely between their two selves.

That the boy was Lady Damerel's son —her legitimate son—was more than possible—probable; but how was this to be proved? Not by herself—she dared not. Having concealed his birth so long—for Sir Charles, in speaking of his four children, was evidently quite ignorant that he had had a fifth child—to confess her folly, or wickedness, to the world and her husband, would entail an amount of scandal that few women could dare to brave. Born in wedlock the boy undoubtedly was, but what wife's fair fame could come out quite unspotted after such a disclosure?

"To run away from her husband— whether or not she went alone—to hide for months from him — to conceal her baby's birth, and then sell it for twenty pounds—phew!" said the doctor, with his low, long whistle, which meant so much. "You are quite safe, ma'am. She'll never own her son—she dare not."

Susannah looked up. She had at first been utterly stunned; now there came upon her a sort of despair, or rather desperation—the blind fury which poets describe as that of "a lioness robbed of her whelps."

"He is my son — mine! No one has any right to him but me."

"That's true," answered Dr. Franklin, soothingly. "And I doubt if Arthur would wish to have any mother but you. As for that woman there, she has tied up her own hands, cut her own throat, as one may say. He'd never care twopence for her. As for herself, it isn't a son she wants, it's an heir to the baronetcy. Let her be. It serves her right."

Such were the good doctor's arguments. Susannah's brain whirled so, that for a wonder she let another lead her, and did not attempt to think out the question for herself. When, two hours after, Arthur came in, bright and gay, having been exceedingly amused, especially by "that dreadful Lady Damerel—who is one big sham from top to toe, though she does sing so splendidly"—the whole thing seemed a ghastly nightmare, out of which she should wake soon and find it nothing.

Yet when she did wake next morning— after lying awake half the night — ah! well she understood those pathetic lines:

"The tears o' my heart fa' in showers frae my e'e
While my gudeman sleeps soun' by me"—

then Susannah found that yesterday had been not quite nothing. The mental agony, the perpetual self-restraint which it imposed, were so hard to bear that she was almost relieved when Dr. Franklin, who was obliged to leave next day, proposed taking his godson with him; and Arthur, with a boy's natural delight at the idea of seeing London, was eager to go.

"But not if you want me, mother. I'll not go anywhere, or do anything, that you don't wish."

"I only wish what is for your good, my darling!" She had of late given up all pet names, knowing how school-boys dislike them; but to-day she felt he was her darling—the very core of her heart, and the delight of her eyes—in whose figure she had reëmbarked many a ship-wrecked hope, many a broken dream. With difficulty she restrained herself from falling on Arthur's neck in a burst of bitter tears.

"It is for his good," said Dr. Franklin, with emphasis, and yet with a compassionate look in his kind eyes. "Give him a bit of pleasure with me, and then let him set to work. It's the best thing in the world for a lad to be obliged to work. Far better for him"—this was said with meaning and decision—"far better than if he were heir to a title and several thousands a year."

"Thank you — God bless you!" murmured Mrs. Trevena, as she wrung her friend's hand at parting, feeling that under his rough speech and queer un-English ways there lay hidden a heart of gold.

After a while her agony of apprehension, her feeling that the whole world was slipping away from under her feet, slowly subsided. Life at the rectory went on as usual—nothing happened—nobody came. She did not see Lady Damerel at church, for Sir Charles had caught cold at the garden party; an attack of rheumatism severer than ordinary had supervened; and the village heard, with little interest, that he and "my lady" had gone to Bath for several months. Tawton Abbas was shut up, and the rector and his wife wandered at ease about the lovely park—she with the strangest of feelings, and sometimes, in spite of what Dr. Franklin had said, with a doubt whether she were right or wrong in accepting the position of things, and letting all drift on in silence as heretofore.

It may seem almost incredible, even in this simple-minded and unworldly woman, but the last thing she thought of was the worldly benefits—the title and estate to which her Arthur might be the lawful heir. Had he been proved the legitimate son of worthy parents, she could have given him up, she thought, though it broke her heart; but to give him up to such as Lady Damerel—never!

Better that he should begin life simply as an adopted son, work his own way in the world, and win a name for himself, for which he was indebted to nobody. Unworthy parents are worse than none.

Three months had gone by, and Arthur was just coming home for Christmas—after having worked "like a brick," he wrote, and being in cheerful hope of the scholarship—before Mrs. Trevena found herself again face to face with the woman whom she believed to be her boy's mother.

It happened in this wise — apparently by accident. Lady Damerel suddenly appeared at church; having come to Tawton Abbas for three days, to order the distribution of coals, blankets, and Christmas beef — she never omitted those external duties by which many people square accounts with heaven, and keep up a good character on earth. Consequently she always went to church, rain or fair—and this day there fell a heavy storm of December rain. The rector and his wife found her lingering near the chancel door.

"Will you give me shelter for a few minutes?" she asked, in her sweetest and most condescending manner; and Mr. Trevena courteously escorted her under his umbrella to the rectory.

She had seldom been there; only for one or two formal calls; but now she sat down in the little drawing-room as if she meant friendliness rather than formality. After some courteous small-talk about Sir Charles's illness, and the cause of it, chiefly directed to Mr. Trevena—Lady Damerel was always charming to gentlemen—she said, carelessly:

"You went away from my garden party quite early, Mrs. Trevena, before I had time to speak to that tall friend of yours —Mr.— What was his name? An American, did you say? I rather like Americans."

Susannah was not a coward—her husband sometimes said of her, with his tender jesting, that she "would go up to a cannon's mouth"—if necessary. She felt something like it now. Looking full in Lady Damerel's face, she replied:

"He is not Mr. but Dr. Franklin, a countryman of yours (Sir Charles said you are American), and a physician in New York."

"Ah! New York. But I am Southern. I was born in Baltimore."

"He said you reminded him of the Baltimore belles," innocently observed the rector. "He thought he had met you somewhere. He is an excellent man. We made acquaintance with him long ago, when travelling abroad, where he once did my wife, and me too, what has turned out to be a great service. Our son, whom of course you know all about, is his godson."

"Oh, indeed," carelessly answered Lady Damerel, with the air of a person not much interested in other people's affairs. "Has your friend gone back to America?"

"He sailed yesterday—Arthur went to Liverpool to see him off."

"How kind! By-the-way, that son of yours—I must secure him as our accompanist next time I have musical people in the house. He plays extremely well. Is he to be a professional?"

"Oh no!" said the rector, with something more than distaste. "He is trying for a scholarship at New College, Oxford, which his Winchester masters think he is sure to get. He is a very clever, as well as a diligent boy."

And the good, unobservant, unreticent Austin went into details about Arthur's future university career, without noticing the absent smile with which Lady Damerel listened; most people—even parents— are indifferent enough to other people's children.

"Ah, yes—Mr. Arthur's success must be a great pleasure to his father and mother. My children were never clever, nor handsome either, poor little things! Your son is your only one, I conclude? Born late in life, and of course his parents' darling?"

All this while Susannah had sat silently observant—also, not a little amazed. First, at the extraordinary self-command of the woman, supposing she really was the woman that Dr. Franklin believed her to be; and next, that she should be so ignorant of her neighbors' affairs as never to have heard about Arthur. And yet this was not impossible. In eighteen years the story had died out; people had accepted him so completely as the rector's son—at least in the village; and beyond it the Trevenas knew almost nobody. With a sudden desperate resolve Susannah determined to put Lady Damerel to the test—to tell her the facts, which she must hear ere long, and which it was astonishing she had never heard before. "Tell the truth and shame the devil"—but it was equally to exorcise a devil—that evil spirit which prompted her, the gentle Mrs. Trevena, to fly at Lady Damerel's throat and strangle her.

Looking her full in the face, she said, distinctly: "I think you do not understand—though it is surprising you should never have heard—that Arthur is not our own son; we have no living children. Dr. Franklin found him for us, and advised us to adopt him. We do not know who were his parents, but he was born at Andermatt in Switzerland."

Human nature cannot altogether suppress itself. Whatever Lady Damerel had come to seek, she had evidently found something she neither sought nor desired. Her cheek grew ghastly under its paint. She clutched the arm of the chair as if to save herself from falling. Even the unobservant Austin could not help seeing something was amiss, and courteously observing that the room was very hot, went to open the window.

"Thank you; but I am not ill; only fatigued—worn out with nursing my husband." And then, turning round to Susannah with that mechanical smile which people learn to use in society as well as on the stage, she said: "It is kind of you to give me this confidence. I did not know the boy was not your own. He is—a fine boy—and does you great credit."

And again that ghastly pallor—was it emotion or only fear?—came over her face, till Mr. Trevena offered to fetch her a glass of wine, and looked toward his wife for sympathy and assistance.

But there was no pity—not a jot!—in Susannah's eyes, or in her hard, cold voice.

"Lady Damerel should have ordered her carriage. I am sorry I have no servant here to send. And my son is not at home."

"*My son.*" There was no mistaking the word—or its meaning—its intentional meaning. Lady Damerel removed her hand from her eyes, and the two women steadily regarded one another. In that moment both recognized, without need of words, that each was in possession of the other's secret, and that between them there was war to the knife. All the more deadly because it was a silent war—confined entirely to their two selves. The two mothers between whom King Solomon judged could not hate one another with a more deadly hatred than these—the flesh-and-blood mother who had thrown her blessing away; the real mother who had found it, and kept it—yes, and would keep it, in defiance of the whole world.

Susannah, just and tender woman as she was, could on occasion be a stern woman too. She had no belief in parental rights, or any rights at all, without their corresponding duties. Years ago she had carried off little Nanny, and would have hidden her from her father, separated them entirely, by fair means or foul, until the child was old enough not to be harmed by the man to whom she owed nothing but the mere accident of paternity. What Mrs. Trevena then did—and would have persisted in doing had not fate made it unnecessary—from pure pity, without any personal love for Nanny—would she not be ready now to do for her own Arthur?

Had Lady Damerel confessed all, and begged for the boy—perhaps even then Mrs. Trevena might have had no mercy. She might have said, with Dr. Franklin, "As you made your bed you must lie on it," and dared the unworthy mother to win one atom of either duty or affection from the son she had cast away. But if any struggle as to the right course was in Susannah's mind, she soon saw it was wholly unnecessary.

"Self-preservation is the first law of nature," says the philosopher; and though sometimes experience has contradicted this—especially in the case of mothers—it exists still.

After a minute or two Lady Damerel rose, her usual stately self, and addressed the rector:

"The rain has abated now, and I must not trouble you any longer. I will walk home, for I never like to use the carriage on Sundays, except for Sir Charles. We think of trying the German spas immediately—so this must be a farewell visit. Make my compliments to your son—I mean your adopted son—and say I congratulate him and his parents."

Evidently the so-called maternal instinct was not in the woman. Whether from conscious guilt or cowardice, she had apparently not the slightest intention of acknowledging her child. A few words of polite adieu, and she had made her escape, having betrayed absolutely nothing.

Susannah was thankful that she too had betrayed nothing—that she had had strength all these months to bear her own burden and trouble no one. The crisis had come, and passed. Now she could breathe again.

Many more weeks and months went by, in untroubled peace. Arthur was at Winchester; Sir Charles and Lady Damerel were travelling abroad. Nothing had happened: and she began to feel that nothing would happen: that she might live and die—dying did not seem so far off at nearly sixty—with her secret unrevealed, keeping Arthur as her son till death.

He seemed more than ever her son, when coming back for summer holidays—triumphant, too, for he had gained his scholarship, and was going up to Oxford next term—he found his "dear little mother" a good deal changed. Her pretty brown hair had grown silver white; her bright cheerfulness—the gayety of sound pure health, though she was never robust —had greatly departed. He could not understand it. She said she was "quite well"—"quite happy"—but she seemed so quiet, so suddenly changed from a middle-aged into an old woman. He wondered nobody saw it—not even her husband.

"Papa," he said, "I think mother wants a little nursing and companionship. When I am gone to Oxford, suppose you send for Nanny? Let her come a day or two before I leave, and I'll teach her how to take care of mother; only she is such a child still—perhaps she might not understand."

But in spite of Arthur's gentle patronizing, and firm conviction that nobody could take care of his mother except himself—it was found that Nanny did understand; that Miss Grogan had made a little woman of her already, and a capital nurse. Neat, accurate, practical; chary of words, but prompt in deeds; and doing everything necessary without making any unnecessary fuss about it—Nanny, though at first not exactly welcome to her aunt, soon became so, as well as to her uncle. And though still small, dark, and plain, there was a sweetness in her brown eyes, a fairy lightness in her dainty figure, which made her decidedly not ugly. Youth never is ugly, unless it has got an ugly soul.

"She's not so bad, is she, mother?" said Arthur, after the first two days. "She isn't a beauty, certainly; she doesn't sweep about the room like Lady Damerel—but I hate tall women!—no woman should ever be bigger than my little mother. Nanny will never be pretty—like you—but she's a nice little thing."

What mother could resist such tender flattery from a big son, not twenty yet, but fully six feet high? What mother could look into that boyish face—knowing the heart was as innocent as the face —and not feel that whatever he said was true, and whatever he did was right?

As for the "nice little thing"—was it surprising that she adored Arthur? as she had done ever since she was a small child; though she had ceased to show it now—at least, not very much—but Mrs. Trevena saw it in her eyes, and sometimes felt a little sorry for Nanny. Still, the child was only a child; and Arthur could not be expected to take much notice of her—such a man as he was grown—and just going up to Oxford. Nor did he notice her at first; being absorbed by his matriculation work.

But all young creatures like one another's company; and when of summer evenings "the children" went off for a walk together, leaving Mr. and Mrs. Trevena sitting quietly in the arbor, Susannah said to herself that it was quite natural.

She herself could not take long walks now—nor could she see to read and sew as she once did. She had made over her work-box to the busy useful fingers of Nanny. And instead of reading of evenings, she sat with her hands folded, and thought—we often like thinking as we grow old. Only it is not of ourselves we think; our day is all done—it is of other people.

Strange it was—and yet perhaps not strange—that the last subject which entered Mrs. Trevena's mind should have been that which was most probable, most natural; the story even now beginning to act itself out under her very eyes. The old story, ever new, and which will be new until the end of the world.

She had enacted it herself more than forty years ago, for she was very young when she first met Austin Trevena; and yet it never struck her to think of her boy as anything but a boy, or of Nanny except his small girl-satellite—circling round him with untiring and perfectly natural devotion, but of no importance to him whatever. That one was nearly a man, and the other—alas! — perhaps quite a woman, did not occur to Susannah.

Nor, for a good while, to the young people themselves. Their relations from childhood upward had been completely "l'un qui aime, l'autre que se laisse être aimé"—rather liked it, indeed, in an innocent way, for Arthur was neither selfish nor conceited. He had never had a sister, and honestly accepted Nanny as such: teased her, petted her, and took counsel of her by turns: ruled her, yet was led by her—for the little quiet girl had a strong will of her own, and the winning power that many plain - looking but sweet-natured women have, even over the other sex. And neither he nor any one else suspected that he was gradually slipping into what worldly mothers would call an "entanglement"—but of which the knots are often woven by a kindly Providence to be a man's protection throughout life. Especially such a one as Arthur, who, out of his very simplicity, affectionateness, and lack of personal vanity, was likely to attract every woman he came near.

It was not an ordinary "falling in love"—that headlong tumble which parents and guardians so dread: but a gradual gliding into love; love awaking so early that the young people understood neither its nature nor its name. For instance, the caress begun when, the child's poor mother lying dead in the next room, Susannah had said, "Arthur, kiss Nanny," was continued, quite naturally, at meetings and partings, until the very day that Arthur left for Oxford; when his mother noticed, with some momentary surprise, that they merely shook hands. But she soon forgot it—her own heart was so full. And when the little Nanny, who found her wandering forlornly about the empty

house—so very empty now Arthur was gone—took her hand and kissed it, Mrs. Trevena embraced her with a burst of feeling, as being the one other person who missed Arthur nearly as much as his mother did.

Shortly afterward Nanny was summoned back to Miss Grogan, who was seriously ill, and needed her sorely. Both her uncle and aunt missed her too—a good deal. Likewise at Christmas, when she had promised to return, but did not, and the rectory household had to make the best of the busy time without her. Mr. Trevena distributed his coals and blankets alone, and Arthur wandered aimlessly about the deserted park, for the Damerels were still away. Both father and son openly lamented Nanny, who was "so funny," and "so useful," to which the mother, shut helplessly in-doors, agreed with a sympathizing smile, hiding a silent pain that she could be no longer all they required to either husband or son. But it soon passed—they were both well and strong and happy—and they loved her so much that as long as she sat, even with folded hands, at the fireside, they were sure to think it bright.

After Christmas came a sudden event, ominous of changes: Miss Grogan died. Nanny was left—as she said in her sorrowful letter—"alone in the world." But, as she also said, she meant to face the world, and trouble nobody. She had had a good education—thanks to her uncle and her dear dead friend; and through all her grief there ran a thread of cheerful courage which touched everybody's heart.

"Nanny is sure to do well," said Mrs. Trevena, affectionately. "Shall we have her here for a while?"

"I wish we could have her here for always," answered the rector.

But, to the surprise of both, Nanny refused their kindness—very gratefully, yet very firmly. She wished to begin to work at once. Nothing would induce her, she said, to eat the bread of idleness. She intended to go out as a governess immediately.

"Impossible!" said her uncle, thinking of her as the last of the Trevenas. "Impossible," wrote Arthur from Oxford, assigning no reason. And "impossible," added, gravely, Mrs. Trevena, who knew what governess life is to a girl of eighteen.

But fate—in the shape of Mr. Hardy, Arthur's High-Church friend—stepped in and settled the difficulty. He had a widowed sister come to live with him, who would be most thankful to get a daily governess for her only girl. "If Miss Trevena would condescend," he said. "At least so far as to come on a visit to the rectory, and try it for the summer." Miss Trevena, being humble-minded, and strongly urged by both uncle and aunt, did condescend—and came.

She looked so sweet, with her pale face and her deep mourning, that all the curate's family fell in love with her at once; and when Arthur came home for his Easter vacation he found her quite settled: living at the rectory, and walking across the park every day to her work. It, and what she laughingly called her "parish duties" —as her aunt's substitute—absorbed her so much that, as Arthur openly complained, he saw almost nothing of her, and was left "out in the cold." At which his mother so compassionated him that she took every opportunity of sending him and Nanny for an evening walk together, rejoicing to see them come back merry and happy. Their youthful happiness was the greatest bliss she knew. It helped her to bear her own feebleness and weariness; that shadow of fast-advancing old age— which had come all the faster since the blow of last year.

Do what she would, she could not escape a perpetual fear of "something happening"—some effort on Lady Damerel's part to reclaim her son, or, worse, some discovery which might make Arthur's birth not the safe mystery that it now was, but an open disgrace that might wound him to the quick—if a man ought to be wounded by anything in which he himself is entirely innocent.

It was not difficult to divine, or at least to guess at, Lady Damerel's history. The beautiful "public" woman—half a pariah —as it was then thought, though now, thank Heaven, many a public and professional woman leads as domestic a life as any private matron who "suckles fools and chronicles small beer"—married early to a poor gentleman; resenting and hating the restraints of home; heartless, pleasure-loving, though not actually vicious; incapable of love, but too selfish to degrade herself; a "woman of genius," possibly, but with an unwomanly heart; detesting children, and the burden of them; disliking dulness and poverty, and ready always to act on impulse rather than judgment—it was easy to see how all had come about.

Not so easy to see how all would end, or how it ought to end. Sometimes Susannah thought and thought till she was half dazed—she had come to the time when one must think, for one can do little else; and all one's thoughts are for others—one's own future is of no interest now; but her thoughts all came to nothing, for she could do nothing. Also Dr. Franklin, whose wife had burned the important letter, wrote advising her to do nothing till he came back to England next year.

So she drifted on, nor noticed how other things and people were drifting on too, unto a future over which she had no jurisdiction and no claim.

That year spring came in early, deliciously; the tempting spring, when

"A young man's fancy lightly turns to thoughts of love,"

and even old men—at any rate, old women—turn half-tenderly to memories of what love was, or might have been, when the sight of a face, the touch of a hand, brought unutterable, impossible bliss. Even the rector and his wife, sitting in their lovely garden, with trees budding, primroses blooming, and thrushes singing, felt the nameless charm, and kept their silver wedding day in tender content: Susannah telling the "children," with a sweet faint blush on her old cheek, how she and papa had met when quite young, and had made a solemn vow among some gooseberry bushes—eating gooseberries plentifully meantime—that they would certainly be married some day; which vow, after half a lifetime, they kept. But she never noticed—nobody noticed—that at her innocent little story Nanny turned very pale, and Arthur very red; and they scarcely spoke to one another for the rest of the day.

It was a rather momentous day, for both inward home pleasure and outside news. Mr. Hardy appeared, in much excitement. His grateful bishop had that day rewarded his long service by an unexpected living; and though now nigh upon forty, the good curate was as happy as a boy. His vicarage was only a few miles off, so he would not lose his friends at the rectory; though, Mrs. Trevena suggested, Nanny would lose her pupil. To which, in some confusion, Mr. Hardy answered that "he was not sure."

Something constrained in his manner —and Nanny's too—startled Mrs. Trevena into remembering how very often he had been at the rectory of late, and how continually he had walked home with Nanny across the park. She smiled to herself, not ill pleased, for Mr. Hardy was an old friend, and an excellent man, young and cheerful for his age. And Nanny, though so much his junior, was such a grave, steady, reliable little thing—just the girl for a clergyman's wife. She wondered she had never thought of this before, and, woman-like, was thinking it over with unmixed satisfaction, when a name caught her ear—the name which, now she had grown weak and nervous, always seemed to go through her like a knife.

"Have you seen Lady Damerel, Arthur? I met her driving, and she asked me how all was going on at the rectory, and if you and I would come and have an evening of music—quite quietly—they have brought no company down with them. I hear Sir Charles has broken down very much, and cannot live long. Poor Lady Damerel!"

"Poor Lady Damerel indeed!" echoed Mr. Trevena. "What a change for her! And they say she hates the heir at law—a needy man with seven children. What a pity Lady Damerel has none!"

Mr. Hardy agreed, and again asked Arthur to come, as "her ladyship"—he always spoke with much awe of her ladyship—had said she especially wished for him, on account of his music.

"I won't go," said Arthur, decidedly. "I don't care for Lady Damerel, though she does sing so well. And why doesn't she invite my mother? I'll not go to Tawton Abbas, or anywhere, without my little mother," added he, caressingly.

"But your mother is not able to go, and I think you ought," said the rector, who, like most men, was not indifferent to the charming flattery of Lady Damerel.

Arthur looked at his mother.

"Yes, go," she answered—for a sudden desperation had seized her. Her boy should see with his own eyes, and judge with his own heart, between his natural, unnatural mother, and the woman who had been to him everything that a mother ought to be. "Go," she said, knotting her trembling hands together, and hoping that no one noticed in her the slightest hesitation or pain.

So it came about that during his Easter vacation Arthur went several times to Tawton Abbas, which, notwithstanding Sir Charles's critical state, was full of company—Lady Damerel would not live without it; company among whom a young Oxford man who was handsome and ready-witted, could play and sing, act and dance, with equal facility and enjoyment, was most valuable—and valued. Arthur declared it was "capital fun," and took all his "spoiling" with the most frank unconcern, coming home and joking about it to his mother and Nanny. Between the Arcadian life of mornings with Nanny, and the fashionable life of evenings, or rather nights—for he generally came back from Tawton Abbas when all the rectory had gone to bed—the young fellow seemed to be thoroughly enjoying himself—till one day.

Mr. Hardy, after a long walk with Arthur, an interview with Mr. Trevena in the study, and another with Mrs. Trevena in the garden, formally made an offer of marriage to Miss Trevena; he did it in the properest, most orthodox way—indeed, the good man's wooing seemed like a bit out of Sir Charles Grandison, only that he proved to be not the "man of men" to his Miss Byron.

Exceedingly agitated, more so than her aunt expected or could account for, the "little girl," now advanced to the dignity of a woman, declared she had never given the slightest encouragement to her suitor, and would certainly not marry him. To all arguments from Mrs. Trevena, and a few very lame ones from Arthur—whom Mr. Hardy had made his confidant, and implored to use his brotherly influence—Nanny answered, pale as death, but with firm composure, that she had made up her mind not to marry anybody, and did not wish another word said on the subject.

So, within a few hours, the thunderstorm came, broke, and passed away: but it left a troubled atmosphere in the happy family. The rector could not get over his startled perplexity at finding his little niece a woman, and Mrs. Trevena knew enough of the cares of governess-ship to regret that Nanny should not escape from them into the blessed haven of domestic life. To her, Mr. Hardy seemed very lovable; but evidently Nanny did not love him—and this wise foolish old woman, who still believed in love, had not another word to say.

The storm had passed, but it left its traces behind. Nanny looked dull and sad; and Arthur, who for some reason or other did not "go up" for a few days after term began, was not himself at all.

"Is anything vexing you, my boy?" asked his mother one night when he came in from his usual evening entertainment at Tawton Abbas. He tried to put her off—scolding her for sitting up, and declaring it was because she knew how pretty she looked in her dressing-gown and her picturesque nightcap. But she saw something was amiss, and at last, taking his candle out of his hand, and making him sit down beside her, she found it out.

"That Lady Damerel is an odd woman —a very odd woman," he said. "What do you think she wants me to do? To give up my quiet life at Oxford—I'm obliged to be a reading man, you know, or else I couldn't make ends meet—and go in for a regular jolly life. And she'd give me three hundred a year to do it with. Did you ever hear of such an offer—from a complete stranger too?"

"And you answered?"

"I said I was much obliged, of course, but that I had no idea of being a pensioner on any one's bounty. I meant to stand on my own feet and earn my own living as soon as ever I could."

"And she?"

"Oh! she took it coolly enough—as she does everything; said I might please myself, but I had better think it over—only I must speak to no one about it. 'Except my mother,' I said, and then she laughed —Lady Damerel has the most unpleasant laugh I ever heard. I can't like her, for all her kindness, and I won't try. And so I won't accept anything from her—not a thing," added Arthur, decidedly. "Don't you think I am right, mother?"

"Yes," Susannah said, beneath her breath. She was clutching her boy's hand—caressing it and patting it, as she used to do when he was a baby.

"I can't imagine why she should make such a fuss over me. It's bothering—it's humiliating. Can she do it out of compassion? or impertinent patronizing from a grand lady to— Mother," he added, abruptly, "do you think Lady Damerel knows who I am? I mean—does she know I have no right to the name I bear?"

"Everybody knows everything, my darling," said Susannah. "It was the only right, safe, and honorable way. Everybody recognizes you as our dear adopted son, who will be a credit to our name, and make a name for himself besides—as a brave man can."

"And I will. But, mother, sometimes —it's rather hard."

Susannah did not deny. She knew, to the very bottom of her soul, that it was hard.

"If I were a girl, now, it wouldn't matter. King Cophetua may woo the beggarmaid; and if she is a queenly maid, and deserves him, it's all right—nobody asks any questions. Poor old Hardy asked none about Nanny. She might never have had a father or a mother for all he cared. He loved her for herself. And he was sure of himself—that he could offer her a good income and an honest name, and creditable relations. Now, if I were to ask a girl to marry me—not that I'm going to, without one halfpenny to rub upon another—but if I were—and her father put the plain question, 'Who are you?' what should I say? It's funny, mother!—but you must allow it's a little hard."

He laughed—not without bitterness— the bitterness that she had long foreseen must come, and wondered it had not come sooner. How could she help him? By telling him the truth, which might be crueler than ignorance? And, besides, she herself did not absolutely know the truth—she only guessed at it. If she could have proved it, and thereby given her son name, fortune, every possible worldly prosperity, no matter though she robbed herself of all the joy of her life— still, Susannah was the kind of woman to have done thus.

Not now. It might be that Arthur's finding out the truth would take from him what he had, and give him nothing in return—leave him worse than nameless, worse than parentless. She looked up at him as he stood there—pale with a deeper emotion than she had ever yet seen in him, but young, strong, resolute, able to take his destiny in his own hands and carve out his own future—the best thing that can happen to any young man.

"Arthur," she said, "it is hard—in some ways; but if I were you I would not be afraid. What does your favorite poet say?

'For man is man, and master of his fate.'

So are you. And sometimes," she spoke bitterly, remembering old days, "it is almost a blessing to have no relations."

"You are thinking of papa and his brother—Nanny's father—whom I hated. He was so cruel to Nanny."

"Yes, but we have forgotten that now. Nanny has not a bit of her father in her, except his name. She is upright, honest, independent—sure to do well in the world. And so will you."

Arthur's eyes brightened. "I will try."

"And remember, my boy, every one has something to fight with—some evil fate to master. I mastered mine, and God gave me you. My dear, isn't it worth a little to you that He also gave you your mother?"

She held out her arms to him; and, big fellow as he was, the boy knelt down, laid his head on her lap, and wept like a child.

That night Susannah made up her mind. Come what might, she would be resolved; she would find out the whole truth. Her son should not be lured from her by temptations of the world, the flesh, and the devil. If he went, he should go open-eyed—choosing deliberately between her and Lady Damerel; the simple, pure, righteous life in which he had been brought up, and the shallow, worldly life they led at Tawton Abbas.

So, next day, when the rector and Nanny had gone on their parish rounds together, and Arthur was a-missing somewhere—he was often a-missing now; being restless, unhappy, weary of his own company, and other people's too—Mrs. Trevena gathered up all her feeble strength, and set out to walk alone across the park to the great house. A short stroll, yet she had not done so much for many months. But the more fast-increasing she felt her weakness, the more she was determined to conquer it, and to work while it was day.

It was a lovely morning; the sky bright with floating white clouds, the trees in the park already growing green. What a beautiful park it was! For nearly twenty years she had watched it, budding with spring, deepening into the full verdure of summer; then melting to the glowing tints of autumn, and the scarcely less lovely whiteness of winter. How she had admired and enjoyed it! much more, probably, than its successive tenants had done. Infinitely more, alas! than its owner, poor Sir Charles, whom she saw coming toward her down the path in his Bath-chair. At first she thought she would avoid him; and then—no!

Sir Charles was such a permanent invalid, such an unconsidered nothing in the Damerel establishment, that Mrs. Trevena had rarely spoken to him. The chair, with its melancholy occupant and the tall footman lounging beside it, was passing her by, when she stopped it—half ashamed of herself to think that it was not for pity she did so. She addressed the old man courteously and kindly, but vainly she tried to get a coherent word from him. He was evidently paralyzed, for his speech was thick, and his face expressionless. His hands, distorted with rheumatism, lay helpless in his lap—yet he must have been a handsome man once. He had sweet soft eyes, blue even yet—as blue as Arthur's; and the clear-cut aquiline features of the Damerels—"a nose as big as mine," she remembered Arthur had once said. Yes, withered and old as it was, the face was Arthur's face—the smile was Arthur's smile. Nature had avenged herself upon the careless wife, the unthankful mother, with circumstantial evidence stronger than any words. Mrs. Trevena saw—and wondered she had never seen it before—that if Sir Charles Damerel and Arthur were set side by side, no one could doubt that the boy was his father's son.

Well, it was good to be assured—whatever might happen; also with a sad pity that removed all conscience-stings as to any claim of the father on the son, she felt that this poor dead-alive wreck of humanity was long past being affected, for good or ill, by anything that did happen. To find a son would be to Sir Charles now neither joy nor pain. It was Lady Damerel only with whom Mrs. Trevena had to do battle; and would do it, putting herself and her feelings entirely aside—as she had had to do all her life; a curious contrast to that other woman, to whom self had been the first object always.

It was so still, to judge by the luxury of the morning-room, into which Mrs. Trevena was shown. All looked *couleur de rose*, down to the very hangings, which were so placed as to throw a becoming glow on the faded face of the *passée* beauty who was afraid to be old. Susannah, catching sight of herself in the numerous mirrors, and conscious of her trembling limbs and beating heart, knew that she was old—no doubt about that now. But she grieved not, feared not. All the more reason that she should do what she had to do, without delay.

What was there to do? Nothing, it seemed, by the easy condescending smile with which the great lady received the rector's wife, and the pleasure she expressed at Mrs. Trevena's being able to walk so far, for a mere call.

"It is not a mere call. I wanted to speak to you."

Lady Damerel started an instant—and then resumed her polite smile of attention.

"I am sure, anything I can do for you, or for our excellent rector—"

"Thank you—my husband and I want nothing. But you have offered to do something for my son, which he cannot accept—which I do not wish him to accept."

"Why not?"

"Because it is unseemly and humiliating for a young man to receive a large annual income from the bounty of—a stranger."

Lady Damerel put her fan before her face, with an air as nonchalant as it was graceful; scarcely to hide emotion: there seemed none to hide.

"I hope that Arthur"—she saw Mrs. Trevena wince—"I beg his pardon, Mr. Arthur, does not consider me quite a stranger. I like the young man; he is useful and pleasant to me—who have no children of my own. If I wish to help him, why should you hesitate to accept my offer?"

"I do not hesitate," said Susannah; "I absolutely refuse. While I live, my son shall never be indebted for a halfpenny to any one but his mother."

"I thought you told me you were not his own mother."

"I am not. Are you?"

The question was so sudden—so direct—delivered with the intensity almost of a blow, struck as it were for dear life—that it fell upon Lady Damerel like a blow. She sprang up in her chair.

"What right have you to say this—what proofs can you give?—Mrs. Trevena, how dare you—"

"I dare do anything, if it is for my son's sake, my boy, whom I took as a little baby—whom I have brought up—who has been all in all to me these twenty years—the best son that ever mother had. How dare *you* come between me and him? How can you, if, as I believe, you are the woman that deserted him, sold him, think to buy him back again with your miserable money? How dare you, I say?"

As Susannah spoke, the passion of her voice startled even herself. But it met no response either of fear or anger.

Lady Damerel sat down again, with a slight laugh. "This is—an amusing fiction. But even if it were the truth—"

"It is the truth, and you know it. And you know that Dr. Franklin knows it too. He will be coming back to England shortly; he and I between us can prove everything—everything. And we will do it."

Lady Damerel smiled still; but in somewhat ghastly fashion. "That would be unwise, Mrs. Trevena. You would lose your son, and I should not gain mine. One question: does he—the boy—know it too?"

"He does not. If he did, how he would despise you!"

There was no attempt at disguise now. The two women sat looking at one another—open enemies; tiger-like, each ready for the next spring. But both were very quiet; the one through fear, the other from speechless contempt. What would have happened next—who can tell?—but for one of those coincidences which occur sometimes, in a way so natural that we call it providential. As Susannah did, to the end of her days.

The door opened, and Arthur walked in.

"I hope I am punctual, Lady Damerel. You told me to come at eleven. What?"—seeing Mrs. Trevena—"oh, mother, how wrong of you to come alone! How tired you look! Sit down—sit down."

And he stood beside her, with his hand laid caressingly on her shoulder, and his eyes full of anxiety. He had evidently no thought of anybody but his mother. Then, with the intuition of love, he saw that something was the matter; and, with his usual frankness, faced it at once.

"I conclude, Lady Damerel, you know already what I came to tell you—that my mother would rather I did not accept your kindness. I agree with her. I wish to make my own way in the world, owing nothing to anybody—except my mother."

Was it a lingering touch of human nature—maternal jealousy if not maternal tenderness—that made Lady Damerel's lip quiver as she looked at the handsome, graceful youth, and the little old woman over whom he leant so affectionately?

"Your adopted mother, you mean. But decide as you choose. I hope you may not live to regret it."

Arthur flushed painfully. "Since you know the truth about my birth, Lady Damerel, you will allow that I am right, not only in loving, but in obeying my mother."

As Susannah clung to her boy's hand—the strong young hand which enfolded hers (and here again Nature had asserted herself, for it was the very image of Lady Damerel's)—a sudden revulsion came over her. She felt compelled by that sense of absolute right, quite irrespective of worldly wisdom or personal feeling, that stern law, "Fais ce que tu dois, advienne que pourra!" which strengthens some people—women especially—to do by impulse that which in cold blood they would perhaps have shrunk from doing.

"Thank you, my own good boy!" she said, with a sob. "You know how I have loved you. But I am not your mother. Your real mother—the woman who bore you—is—that woman there!"

Arthur sprang up as if he had been shot. "She my mother! the mother who deserted me—sold me?—oh no, mother darling!—it can't be true—it isn't true!"

"It is true. She does not deny it. Look at her."

Lady Damerel sat bolt-upright in her chair—as white and as hard as marble. Arthur took one step toward her, and then drew back.

"Thank you, mother, for telling me. I am glad I know this. It was right I should be told."

"I did not wish him to be told. No good can come of it, for his father never knew of his existence. I shall be glad to help him—with the half of my fortune if he wishes—after Sir Charles's death. But I never can acknowledge him publicly. It would ruin me."

Lady Damerel spoke in a slow, cold, impersonal voice, never looking at her son. Nor did her son look at her. Rather he turned away his eyes, as if the mere sight of her were painful to him. At last he said, very quietly—and with a strange absence of emotion which made him for the moment almost resemble her:

"You need not fear: I shall never intrude upon you. I think it would almost kill me to have to do my duty to you as your son. Good-morning, Lady Damerel. Come, mother, let us go home."

He placed Mrs. Trevena's hand within his arm, and, with a distant, stately bow —a bow worthy of the heir of all the Damerels—he quitted without another word "the woman that bore him"—who had been to him merely that and nothing more.

Lady Damerel sat, in her unshared splendor, childless and alone. Her sin *had* found her out. It was a just and a righteous retribution.

CHAPTER VIII.

FOR several days after Arthur discovered the truth about his parentage he and his "mother" never spoke on the subject. He had whispered to her on their way home from Tawton Abbas—"Please don't say a word to me—I can't bear it"—and indeed she was utterly unable to say a word. The long strain being ended, a reaction came. Ere nightfall she was so ill that Arthur silently put off his departure for Oxford; and for many days neither he nor any one at the rectory thought of aught but her—the centre of all their love and care.

When she revived she found that Arthur had told both the rector and Nanny what had happened—the bare fact—no more—"to save mother the pain of telling it"—but that he had requested of them total silence on the subject, since this discovery "made no difference in anything."

He repeated the same to herself in the few words that passed between them before he started for Oxford: she had thought it right to speak, and explain to him that even though he were the lawful heir of Tawton Abbas, unless Lady Damerel acknowledged this, it would be most difficult to prove his rights.

"It does not matter, mother," he said, calmly. "I have thought it all over, and perhaps ''Tis better as it is'—as your friend Shakespeare says. I will make my own way in the world, and be indebted to nobody. Except you—except you!"

He stooped and kissed the silver hair—whiter even within the last few weeks. Then holding his head high, though he too looked older and graver—much—he bade her and them all a cheerful good-by, and went back to his work.

From that time Arthur's letters came regularly, even more regularly than usual. But they were only to his mother—not to Nanny, who had once shared them. And they were wholly about his work—or his play, for he was equally good at both; as noted on the river as he was in the schools. But he never in the least alluded to what had occurred, or implied that he himself was in any way different from the Arthur Trevena who had been the Trevenas' only son, dearly beloved, for the last twenty years.

And Lady Damerel made no sign. She still staid on at Tawton Abbas, which, it was clear, poor Sir Charles was never likely to leave again; but she filled it with company, as usual, and lived her usual lively life there. Her sole appearance in the village was at church, where she sat, erect as ever, in her arm-chair; her cold, handsome, painted face, under the thin gauze veil which she always wore, contrasting strangely with the background of marble monuments—the old Damerels to whom her husband would soon be gathered. Sir Charles, it was rumored, would be the last of the name, though not of the race; for the next heir being by the female line, the baronetcy would become extinct. Though she was little known, and less liked, one or two of the more thoughtful of the congregation, looking at her, and recognizing what a downcome must follow her husband's death, sometimes said, "Poor Lady Damerel!"

Not Mrs. Trevena. Under all her gentleness, Susannah could, if need required, be as hard as stone and as silent. She never, in or out of the house, except upon compulsion, mentioned the name of Lady Damerel. She rose up from her illness, and went about her duties as heretofore—not even allowing Nanny to share them: Nanny, who still lived at the rectory, nominally, but was rarely at home, having obtained teaching in a neighboring town. She was cheerfully earning her honest bread, and evidently making up her mind to do this all her days, as if there had been no such person as Mr. Hardy in existence. She worked hard, poor little thing!—as her aunt had done

before her; and her aunt appreciated this, as well as the tenderness which made Nanny, whenever she was at home, as good as any daughter.

But Susannah did not want a daughter. All her heart was bound up in her son; and it was a great pang to her, even though she acknowledged it might be "all for the best," when Arthur announced his intention of spending the long vacation with a reading party in Wales. He could afford it, having earned some extra money by accidental "coaching." It was good for his health, his mother argued to herself; and would be more cheerful to him than home—which he must find rather dull now that he was a grown-up young man. So she said to Nanny, who listened and said nothing: Nanny never did speak much at any time.

Therefore it befell that for a whole year Arthur appeared at the rectory only on very short visits; between terms, or after having passed successfully all his examinations. He would never "set the Thames on fire"—as he one day bade Nanny impress upon his mother; but he had no fears of failing in his university career. Indeed, he hoped to get through it in such a way as to secure afterward his daily bread, at least, probably as an Oxford "coach." Of music, or the musical career, he now never spoke a word.

Indeed, in many ways the boy was much changed—a boy no longer, but a man. In one thing, however, there was no change, but rather a growth—his tender devotion to his mother. Ay, even though life, which with him was pouring on toward flood-tide, with her was at its quiet ebb. Though she could not share in his pleasures, could never be to him the sympathetic companion that young and active mothers often are to their boys—and a lovely sight it is!—still, to see Arthur with his little old mother, as careful as a girl, as devoted as a lover, as tender as a son, was also a sight never to be forgotten.

Lady Damerel never saw it—nor they her. Once, when walking in the park, they came across Sir Charles's wheeled chair; Arthur, taking off his hat, stood aside to let it pass, with its melancholy occupant, behind whom walked the valet, or keeper, always his sole companion.

"It's no use speaking to Sir Charles; he doesn't know anybody now," said the servant, carelessly; and they walked on. But in the blank white face of the old man, and the strongly marked profile of the young one, Susannah saw again that unmistakable likeness—fate's confirmatory evidence against the cruel bar-sinister which the world would be sure to impute to a deserted child. And though to judge a man by this, to lay to his charge his parents' sins, is wholly unjust and unchristian, still, since the world is neither christianized nor just, it will be always so.

She watched her boy as he walked on beside her, with a grave, fixed look on his face, but showing no other emotion.

"Sir Charles will not live long," she said, "and nobody could wish it."

"No; but I am glad to remember he was always kind to me."

This was all. Intercourse between Tawton Abbas and the rectory had now stopped entirely. The rector wished it to be so. Austin Trevena did not often take the law into his own hands. His own instincts had been so pure, and his life so blameless, that he did not understand sinners, and was apt to be only too lenient to them. But in this case he was very firm.

"The church door is open to any one," he said, "and I cannot refuse her the sacrament, for I know nothing against her moral character—but there it ends. I hope, Susannah, that Lady Damerel will never darken our doors again."

She did not. For a whole year no trouble entered those quiet doors, where old age was now beginning to claim its Sabbath of peace, which ought to be so welcome and so blessed. For what energetic action is to youth, so is mere rest to declining years. And at sixty—sometimes, alas! before then—we learn to say, "There is no joy but calm," and to be thankful for it if we get it.

So, when month after month slid by, and nothing happened, nothing broke the monotony of the peaceful household, except Arthur's flying visits, and his constant, comfortable letters, Susannah's worn face gradually recovered its look of sweet content, justifying her boy in telling her, as he did sometimes, that she was "the prettiest old lady that ever was seen." Or would be, one day—for he refused to allow that she was "old" yet; and often proposed the most unheard-of feats for her in the way of picnics and other expeditions with himself and Nanny. At which

she smilingly shook her head, and sent "the children" away by themselves.

Arthur, come home now for the long vacation, seemed again his merry boyish self. He had got triumphantly through his "schools," and seemed determined to enjoy himself. He went singing about the house as when he was ten years old, though now just past one-and-twenty; he walked, he fished, he bicycled; he "tramped" the parish for the rector, and visited the old women with Nanny, who was also at home for her holidays.

Nanny had changed very little within the last few years. She was still the same plain little thing, except for her great dark eyes and her exceedingly sweet-toned voice: a pleasant voice is better to live with than even a pretty face. But she had an atmosphere of prettiness about her too—exceeding neatness of dress and grace of movement; so that, though not a beauty, she could never be called decidedly ugly. Some day, perhaps, some other man—probably, her aunt thought, an elderly man—might find in her the same nameless charm that Mr. Hardy had done. Poor Mr. Hardy! He still came to the rectory sometimes, but he never said a word more to Miss Trevena. Once, when talking to Arthur about the future of "poor little Nanny," his mother suggested that perhaps she might be an old maid after all. At which the boy laughed—which Susannah thought rather unbrotherly and unkind—but he made no answer whatever.

It was August, and he had been two weeks at home; going about everywhere, except in the direction of Tawton Abbas. It was emptied of guests at last, they heard; for Sir Charles was slowly dying. Lady Damerel seldom appeared at church now; but one day a stranger gentleman was seen there, in the Damerel pew. He was stout, pompous, and common-looking. Report said he was the heir, come to pay a duty visit, and investigate the state of affairs; which made the village talk him over rather curiously, and say again, "Poor Lady Damerel!"

But nobody ever said, "Poor Mrs. Trevena!" There was little need. Though feeble and elderly now, she looked so content and at rest—so proud even, when walking into church on her tall son's arm —that no one would ever have thought of pitying her. Nor did she pity herself. Her life's storms seemed to have sunk into peace. Her boy knew everything about himself; and yet was satisfied to be still her boy. Accounts reached her on all sides of his well-doing at Oxford; where, his university curriculum being gone through, a fellowship, and possibly a tutorship, were almost sure to follow; one of the many proofs that a boy with a fair amount of brains, and the determination to use them, can make his way in the world without any extraneous help either of friends or fortune—if he so choose. "Where there's a will there's a way," Arthur used to say, as a boy; and as a man he bade fair to carry out his creed.

His mother thought of him now with that restfulness of perfect trust, not so much in his fortunes as in himself—a safer stronghold—which, God help them! not all mothers have, or deserve to have. But He had given her that blessing, and she was thankful. No doubt Arthur was not quite as perfect as she thought him; but he was a very good fellow, and a favorite with everybody—including all the young ladies of the neighborhood. For he and Nanny together had gradually brought young life about the rectory; where there were occasional garden parties, lawn-tennis meetings, and such like mild country amusements. Susannah shared them, and was amused by them; sometimes speculating upon how much her boy was admired, and wondering who would fall in love with him; and who, in some far future day, he would fall in love with himself, and marry. She would be very fond of his wife, she thought; and oh! it would be delightful to see his children.

"Only fancy! me a grandmother!" she thought, and laughed to herself at the oddness of the idea.

She was sitting, after one of these parties, in the warm August darkness, lit with stars, and fragrant with delicious scents. It was about nine o'clock; Arthur and Nanny had walked a little way down the road with their friends, and the rector was in his study. Susannah sat in the summer-house, all alone. But she did not mind solitude; she rather enjoyed it. She liked to sit and think—as now; for the scent of clematis and jasmine always brought back the August nights of her youth—when Austin came back from Oxford, and they used to walk in his father's garden together for hours. Then life was all before them; now it was behind. What matter? It had not been all she

expected; a ship or two had gone down; but much had been saved—enough to make the old scents always sweet to her, and the old days dear.

She was looking back upon them dreamily; and forward, in the days to come—not so many now!—when she heard steps upon the gravel, and there passed two figures— a man and a girl. She thought at first it was her house-maid, who she knew had a "lad"—for the man's arm was round the girl's waist, and she was sobbing on his shoulder; which kept Mrs. Trevena from speaking to them. Shortly they passed again, and then, to her utter bewilderment, she saw it was Arthur and Nanny—whom she still sometimes called "the children."

She was so accustomed to think of them as such, that at first her only feeling was a slight vexation that Nanny should be "bothering" Arthur with her troubles. She had heard him say, "Don't cry, poor little Nanny—please don't." But Nanny was a little too old to be soothed and caressed like a baby, and should be careful as to how such caresses looked outside— Arthur not being her real brother. As to anything else, Mrs. Trevena dismissed the idea as simply ridiculous. Her Arthur— such a fine young fellow, everybody's favorite; and Nanny—such an ordinary little creature—whom he had played with, petted, tyrannized over all his life—for them to be anything but brother and sister was perfect nonsense! She would not speak to Arthur, or put such a notion into his head; but she would speak to Nanny, who was a sensible girl, and would understand.

However, when she went in-doors she found Nanny had gone to bed—"very tired," Arthur explained—and that he himself, after supper and prayers, was evidently waiting for a talk with his mother—as he often did of Saturday nights when the rector was busy over his sermon.

"I have rather a serious word or two to say to you, mother darling," he whispered, as he took her hand and sat down beside her.

"Not very serious," smiled she, for his eyes were shining and his manner cheerful and happy, though a trifle nervous. At which she hardly wondered, when he came out suddenly with a startling idea.

"Mother, I want to leave you for a little. I am thinking of going to Switzerland—to Andermatt."

"To Andermatt? Why? Oh, my boy, what good would it do?"

Arthur soothed her momentary distress —he had unlimited power of soothing his mother—and then told her that in consequence of a letter from his godfather, "and for other reasons," he had lately thought it advisable to tell his whole history to a friend he had, the son of an eminent London barrister—who had taken counsel's opinion. This was that if he ever meant to claim the estate and the baronetcy, he ought immediately to take steps to obtain what is called "perpetuation of testimony;" that is, the affidavits of all those witnesses who could prove his birth and his identity; which evidence could be laid up, and would be sufficient, in case of the death of any of them before the time came for the heir to assert his rights.

"I will never do this in Sir Charles's lifetime; but afterward I may, if I can afford the money. One's birthright is one's birthright, and worth fighting for. No man could be expected not to fight, if he has the right on his side, both for his own sake and those belonging to him."

"But that is only papa and me; and we would rather keep you as our son than have you the heir of all the Damerels."

No sooner had she said this than she felt how selfish it was, and how natural, how right, that Arthur should feel as he did, and should have done what he had done—as any young man would have done—though it hurt her a little that he had done it without consulting her. But he was so tender, so thoughtful, and withal so prudent, that the feeling soon passed. If her son did what was right and wise, it mattered little whether he did it with her or without her.

So they went into the details of his proposed journey with their usual mutual confidence. He had saved enough to defray all expenses, he thought, if he travelled very economically; and when she offered him money, he refused it. He preferred being "on his own hook."

"You see, I am not doing badly, mother, for a fellow of twenty-one. It's odd, but I am really twenty-one now. I could be sued for my own debts, or for breach of promise if I had asked any one to marry me."

He said this with a laugh and a blush, but also with an anxious look out of the corners of his bright honest eyes. His mother laughed too, in unsuspicious content.

"All in good time, my dear. I hope you will marry some day, when you find anybody you care for—which you have not found yet, you know."

Arthur looked grave, and answered, very gently, "I am not sure."

A sudden wild apprehension flitted across the mother's mind. Could her boy have fallen in love? The girls of the neighborhood—she counted them over swift as thought. Not one seemed possible, probable, or desirable. "Arthur?" she cried, in an almost agonized question.

Arthur hung his head a little. "Yes, mother, it's quite true. I did really ask her—this evening. I think I must have loved her all my life, though I didn't find it out till Mr. Hardy wanted her, and couldn't get her."

"Nanny! Oh, Arthur, it isn't surely Nanny! Impossible!"

"Why impossible?" said Arthur, drawing himself up.

"Such a—" "such a plain little thing," the mother was going to say, but stopped herself—"a different kind of person from you. And she has been your cousin—almost your sister—ever since you were children together."

"But she is not my cousin, and not my sister, and I don't want her as either. I want her for my wife."

The young man—he was a man now—spoke firmly the strange new word. It went through his mother like a shaft of steel—yet she had the sense not to show it.

"You asked Nanny, you say, this evening? And she answered—"

"She would not give me any answer at all till I had told you—and her uncle. But I think—indeed, I know—" And Arthur lifted his head prouder than ever—with the honest pride of a young man who knows that the girl he loves loves him. "She is such a good girl," he added. "Nobody in the world could ever say a word against my little Nanny."

"*My*" little Nanny! the sense of possession—the passionate protection of his own against all the world—it touched the mother in spite of herself. So many lovers are such cowards—so ardent to seize, so feeble to defend! Here was the true chivalric lover, who, it was clear, meant to hold to his "little Nanny" through thick and thin.

What could Susannah say? It was the

very kind of love she most admired—the ideal of faithful tenderness which she herself had taught him; though it broke her heart, she could not but respect it. And yet—and yet—

Arthur saw her evident distress, but did not attempt to console her. There is a time —God forgive them, poor lambs!—when all young people think of themselves only. Happy for them if their elders have self-control enough to recognize this—to remember the time when they also went through the same phase of passionate egotism—or dual egotism. It cannot last long. If lovers are proverbially selfish, except to the object beloved, husbands and wives, fathers and mothers, must inevitably soon learn that self-abnegation which is the very soul of marriage and parenthood, and which often makes even the most thoughtless boy or girl into a noble man and woman.

There is much to be said for and against what the worldly-minded call "calf-love." It may not always endure—perhaps best not—for a man's last love is sometimes deeper than his first. But sometimes it does endure; and then it is the strongest thing in life: I have known people who loved one another in their teens, and loved on for sixty years.

By a sort of inspiration, Susannah's mind leaped at this truth, or at least this possibility; and it strengthened her to bear what to no mother can be a joy, and may be a sharp pang—the discovery that she has ceased to be her child's first object— that another, perhaps a total stranger, has suddenly become far closer, far dearer, far more important than she.

Restraining a sob, and compelling herself into something like a smile, Mrs. Trevena held out both her hands to her boy. He seized them, and flinging himself on his knees before her, put both his arms round her waist and kissed her again and again.

"My good mother—my kind mother!" was all he could say, almost with a sob.

She stroked his hair, and patted his shoulder.

"You silly boy—such a mere boy still! And she is such a baby—little Nanny— whom you have known all your life."

"It is because I have known her all my life, because I am quite sure of her, that I love her so. She would never despise me. She is willing to marry a man without a name—and therefore for her sake I will try to get one. I'll do nothing just yet, as I told you; I will stand on my own feet and make myself respected as I am. But by-and-by I will move heaven and earth to obtain my own. For Nanny's sake—for Nanny's sake! And if I fail, I shall still have her—and you."

"Her" first—"you" afterward. Well! it was right—it was natural; the law of nature and of God. Arthur was unconscious of having said it—nor did his mother betray that she had heard it. It was the final love-sacrifice which all mothers must make; if the smoke of it ascends to heaven, God accepts it, and that is enough.

"You are not vexed—not angry with me, mother darling?" said Arthur, anxiously.

"How could I be? You are a couple of little geese—that is all. And you will probably have to wait for years and years."

"Never mind," laughed Arthur, now quite happy—actually radiant in his happiness—so handsome, so graceful, that more than ever it was an actual amazement to her how he, her King Arthur, the cynosure of all eyes—the sort of *preux chevalier* whom most girls fall in love with—he, who might have chosen anybody, should have gone and chosen Nanny—poor little Nanny!

"You will speak to her?" pleaded he. "She is gone to bed, but she is not asleep, I am sure. You will not wait till morning—you'll go now, mother?"

"Certainly." And Mrs. Trevena rose, steadying herself by the back of her chair, and feeling blindly for the door handle. Then she turned. "I think, dear, we'll not tell papa of this just yet—not till after Sunday."

When they did tell him, Mr. Trevena was, as his wife had foreboded, a little vexed. He took the masculine and worldly view of the subject, and did not like being disturbed out of the even tenor of his way by any such youthful nonsense.

"Foolish children!—they have not a halfpenny between them," said he. "And the idea that at their age they should know their own minds—it's ridiculous!"

"We did," said Susannah, softly. And she may surely be forgiven if, looking at the Austin Trevena of to-day, she remembered the Austin Trevena of forty years ago, and thought perhaps it might have been better for both had he too been "young and foolish"—if they had trusted themselves and Providence; married as early as prudence would allow; spent the flower of their days together, not apart; fought through their cares and enjoyed their blessings; and lived to "see their children's children, and peace upon Israel." Such might be the lot of Arthur and Nanny—and, remembering her own lot, she was glad of it.

"Husband," she said, and put her arm on his shoulder with the love that had never failed him all his life—never would fail him till death—"we did not make this marriage; it made itself, or God made it—who knows? Don't you think we had better leave things alone, and let the young people settle their own affairs?"

A sentiment which coincided so much with the rector's dreamy, lazy ways that possibly he was glad in his heart to leave things alone. He told his niece "she could do as she liked," and Arthur too; went back to his books, and forgot all about it. In his gentle undemonstrative way Austin was the tenderest of husbands—the kindest of men; but with him, as was not unnatural, the days of romance were all over and done.

Were they with Susannah? are they ever with any real woman who recognizes that love is the heart of life, and, for either man or woman, its most perfect joy?

Arthur had only a few days at home before he started for Andermatt with his friend, who was also a lawyer, and capable of transacting the necessary legal business. The boy arranged all with the cleverness, shrewdness, and firmness of a man. Between whiles he went about, also like a man, with the girl he had chosen, beamingly happy, and not a bit shy or ashamed. His mother watched him with a full heart —she also "had been in Arcadia."

But it was a sore heart too. She had always liked Nanny, and been very kind to her; but kindness and liking are not necessarily love. People of wide sympathies and active benevolence are often misconceived, and supposed to love everybody. They do not. They feel kindly to everybody, but they only love one or two people in the whole course of their lives. It is like a man putting all his money in one bank: if the bank breaks— and it does break sometimes—God help him! He may carry on business very successfully outside, but at heart he is bankrupt all his days.

One of these rare loves—strong as rare —in Mrs. Trevena's life, had been the maternal passion for her adopted son. His going to school and college had made him less a part of her daily existence than if he had been a girl; but his falling in love was a greater blow to her than any daughter's would have been. In spite of the cruel jocularities against mothers-in-law, many a woman inclines tenderly to the man her daughter marries; often loving him like her own son. For "her daughter's her daughter all her life"—and she gains a son besides. But when her son marries she loses him in degree, and sometimes does not gain a daughter.

Watching Nanny, and wondering more and more how Arthur ever came to choose her—yet plain little women have ruled paramount, and for life, in the hearts of clever and handsome men—Susannah sometimes felt as if she could never love the girl; and then again as if she must love her because Arthur did. It was a desperate struggle—a small "tragedy in a teapot"—but none the less a tragedy; and all the more pathetic that it went on in the silent heart of an old woman, in whom age, which deadens most things, had never yet deadened the power of loving and of suffering.

But it could not last—it ought not to last. Best to bury it—and let the sweet charities of life grow up round it, like grass and flowers round a stone.

The household at the rectory soon found out the truth of things; so did the village, and came with its innocent congratulations to Mr. Arthur and Miss Nanny. Mr. Hardy came too—sad, but resigned—saying, with comical pathos, "It's not lost that a friend gets." By-and-by all the neighborhood brought good wishes too, except Tawton Abbas, where Sir Charles still lay in that lingering death in life which might last for months or years.

Susannah herself expected little result from Arthur's journey to Andermatt; but she thought it right he should go; and his godfather, who expected to be in England shortly, wrote, insisting on the same. Nanny said nothing—all she cared for was Arthur himself. Her absorbing and exclusive devotion to him, which had evidently existed hopelessly for years, touched his mother's heart more than anything else, and made a little easier that salutary but rather melancholy performance of "playing second fiddle," which all parents must learn, soon or late. It is the law of nature—and therefore the law of God.

Mr. Trevena was the only person in the household who dwelt much on the worldly phase of the matter; thought it possible that Arthur might one day be Sir Arthur Damerel, and suggested that the last of the Trevenas would prove a not unsuitable Lady Damerel.

"And then, my dear, you and I must make up our minds to spend our old age together. The common lot! When the young birds are flown, we must snuggle down in the empty nest. I dare say we shall bear it."

"Oh yes—we shall bear it," smiled Susannah, as she kissed him tenderly—the one man she had loved all her life through. She knew all his weaknesses, all his faults, as he knew hers; still he was himself, and she was herself—nothing could divide them but death. There is a sentence—if to quote it be not profane—and yet how can it be so to those who try in all things to imitate the Divine Master? "Having loved His own, He loved them unto the end." And in all true loves we do love—we cannot choose but love—unto the end.

Arthur wrote from Andermatt that he had "found all he hoped for, and done all he wanted to do." Nothing more. Explanations could wait. He and his companion meant to "have their fling" for a week or two—it might be many years before he could afford more foreign travelling—and then he would come home. Home to the brightest and best bit of a young man's life, or a girl's either—when their lot is all settled, their love openly acknowledged; and they start, a betrothed pair, with everybody's good wishes, to begin the journey of life together.

"My dear," said Mrs. Trevena to Nanny, as they sat at their sewing, though the younger did it chiefly now, for Susannah's eyes were fast failing her—"My dear, what day is Arthur coming home?" It was a new thing, a rather sore thing, for the mother to have to ask anybody else "when Arthur was coming home"; but the reward, to a generous heart, was Nanny's bright up-look and happy blush.

"I think, aunt, he will be here the day after to-morrow. But I told him he was not to come till he had done all he wanted to do, and seen everything he wanted to see."

This proud maidenly possession of a man, not to queen it over him in selfish vanity, but to use her influence nobly, for his good and hers—it was a pretty thing to see ; and it comforted the mother's heart. She knew well that a man's whole future often depends upon the sort of girl he falls in love with in his first youth.

"I agree with you, my dear; still, if you write again, tell him I think he should come home at once. His godfather is in England, and will be here to-day. You remember Dr. Franklin?"

"Oh yes." There was nothing connected with Arthur which Nanny did not remember. Hers was the most entire, absorbing devotion, reasonable, not blind devotion, that any girl could give, and day by day it was reconciling Arthur's mother to things as they were — even though they were wholly contrary to what she had expected or desired. She could not withstand the pathetic appeal of Nanny's dark eyes—like that of Helena to the Countess, in *All's well that ends well.*

"Let not your hate encounter with my love
For loving where you do."

Also, another thing reconciled her — a thing hard to learn, but when learnt, bringing with it a solemn peace. Dearly as she loved her own, she felt she could take care of them no more. As she watched Nanny flitting about like a little brown bird, carrying out her orders, suggesting things she had forgotten, and doing everything she was unable to do, the wife and mother learnt to say to herself, "So be it!"

When Dr. Franklin arrived she made Nanny explain to him the position of Arthur's business affairs; which the girl did so clearly and well that the old man—he was quite an old man now—patted her on the shoulder approvingly.

"My godson has fallen on his feet, whether he ever is Sir Arthur or not. When you write, tell him I say so."

But fortunately there was no need of writing. Next day Arthur came home, and Dr. Franklin's evidence, conclusive as to identity, and including Lady Damerel's own admission that the child was hers and her husband's, was formally taken.

"Depend upon it, if she finds out I'm here, she'll shake in her shoes," said the

Kentuckian, laughing his silent laugh. And truly when, the same evening, the Tawton Abbas carriage passed him, as he stood leaning on the rectory gate, the face that looked out from it turned deadly pale. But Lady Damerel made no sign of recognition. On both sides there seemed an armed truce, to last as long as fate would permit — which could not be very long, after all.

Nor was it. Two days after, when the young people, shy, but proud, and unspeakably happy, had slipped away for their daily walk together, leaving Dr. Franklin and Mrs. Trevena sitting in the garden, and the rector in his study—there came a message from Tawton Abbas. The church bell suddenly began to toll, as it had tolled for centuries on the death of any Damerel—once every minute for every year of age. They counted seventy-three strokes. It was Sir Charles Damerel, then, who had gone to his rest.

All met on the door-steps of the rectory, listening. Arthur removed his hat, and stood bareheaded, with a grave, composed air, till the bell ceased; then, taking Nanny's hand, led the way in-doors. They all followed, for they knew the crisis was come.

A long consultation followed. "Le roi est mort—vive le roi!" There could be do doubt that the heir - presumptive would immediately claim his rights, and that the heir-apparent must claim his, or else forever hold his peace.

There were two ways of procedure: one was that, supposing the remote cousin appeared at the funeral, having already taken possession, to bring an action of ejectment against him in behalf of the direct heir; the second, involving greater difficulties, was that Arthur should take possession of Tawton Abbas, and leave his opponent to bring the action of ejectment. But this could not be done without the consent and assistance of Lady Damerel, which would be equivalent to a public acknowledgment of her son.

It was decided to adopt the former course. "If I have to fight, fight I will," said Arthur, with a quiet resolution that surprised everybody. "But I will not do it untenderly. She shall not be troubled in any way till after the funeral."

This was fixed for an earlier day than the village expected. Usually the Damerels had the special honor of remaining above-ground for a week or more before being left to sleep with their fathers under Tawton church. That poor Sir Charles should be buried on the third day, looked far too unceremonious—almost as if his widow were glad to get rid of him. And when it was noised abroad that the heir was "somewhere on the Continent," taking one of his numerous sons to school in Germany, and that consequently Lady Damerel would be the only chief mourner, everybody was still more astonished.

Except Dr. Franklin. "That woman's a shrewd one," he said. "She knows on which side her bread's buttered. I shouldn't wonder—"

And there he stopped. Nobody talked very much at the rectory, except on commonplace extraneous subjects, during those three anxious days.

The funeral day was a cheerless one, such as comes sometimes in September; a settled downpour, when it appears as if the weather has broken, and the summer is gone. Nevertheless half the neighborhood assembled in the chilly church—so damp and cold that Nanny entreated her aunt not to attempt to go; and carriage after carriage rolled past the rectory gate on its way to pay respect to the last of the Damerels. It was to be a very fine funeral, everybody agreed; Lady Damerel having spared no expense to make her sorrow for her husband as public as possible.

The long procession had been already seen wending along the park, and the rector was putting on his canonicals, when Arthur came into the study, dressed in complete mourning.

"My boy?" said Mrs. Trevena, questioningly. She only questioned now—she never controlled: he had a right to judge and act for himself, and she knew he would do both rightly.

He stooped and kissed her tenderly. "You do not object? I am going to my father's funeral." It was the first time he had ever used the word: he said it now with a lingering pathos, as we speak of something wholly lost—the loss of which teaches us what it might have been. "I ought to go, I think. He was a good man. There is one thing I shall find it hard to forgive; that I was prevented—she prevented me—from ever knowing my father."

"But that gained you a mother, young fellow!" said Dr. Franklin, sharply. "You've won much more than you lost."

"I know it," said Arthur, earnestly. "And if all fails, I shall come home here, and then go to Oxford and earn my honest bread, with Nanny beside me." It was Nanny's hand he took—Nanny's eyes he looked into when he spoke. Then, as with a sudden thought, he added, "But I shall be my mother's son all my days."

Again he kissed her, and his mother kissed him back again; nor hindered him, nor grieved him, by a single look or word.

They all went to the church together, for Mrs. Trevena refused to be left behind. Arthur did not enter the rectory pew with the rest, but stood at the entrance, waiting till the body was borne in to those solemn sentences which all of us know sadly well, beginning, "Man that is born of a woman."

After it walked Lady Damerel, in her widow's weeds; erect and steady, but alone —in that utmost heart-loneliness which a woman, if she has a heart at all, can feel, when husband and children have gone to the grave before her, and she only is left, to a desolate old age. As she passed him, she looked up and saw Arthur. He did not look at her—his eyes were fixed on the coffin; but at some slight gesture she made, he stepped forward—as he might have intended to do in any case—and took his place beside her.

The service continued. The body was lowered into the vault, the solemn spadeful of "earth to earth" rattled down, heard distinctly through the dark, chilly church; there was the final pause—the last gaze into that gloomy cave of death—and Lady Damerel turned to go.

"She's fainting," Arthur heard somebody whisper. Whether she took the help, or he offered it, he never knew; but her hand was upon his arm, and leaning heavily, almost staggering sometimes, she passed through the respectful if not very sympathetic crowd to the church door. There, almost in her path, stood the gaunt figure of the Kentucky doctor, who knew —had known—everything.

Perhaps the woman felt that all was over, and determined to do with a good grace what she would soon be compelled to do; which, after all, might be the best and most prudent thing for her to do. Or—maybe—let us give her the benefit of the doubt—even thus late, nature was tugging at her heart. When Arthur had put her into the carriage, and was lifting his hat with a formal farewell bow, she leant forward and seized his hand.

"Come home with me! You must—it is necessary. I will confess; you shall claim your rights; everything will be yours."

The boy hesitated a moment—he was a man, and yet a boy; he turned very pale, and looked round—was it for his real mother? who was not the woman that bore him. But Dr. Franklin behind said, imperatively, "Go!"—and he went.

What the two said to one another when shut up in the carriage together, or what revelations were made that afternoon, when Dr. Franklin, having been sent for by the family lawyer, who of course had come for the funeral, went up to Tawton Abbas, was never clearly explained, but before nightfall the news had run like wildfire through the village that Arthur Trevena, the rector's adopted son, had been suddenly discovered to be Sir Arthur Damerel, Sir Charles's lawful heir. Of course a large amount of fiction was mingled with fact. The presumptive heir—the second cousin once removed—arrived post-haste next day—just too late for the hasty funeral—(she was a clever woman, Lady Damerel!)—and it was said he intended to fight it out by law. However, either he became convinced that litigation was hopeless, or had no money to waste among lawyers; he swallowed his disappointment and staid on placidly at Tawton Abbas. He even, some weeks after, assisted cheerfully at the ringing of bells, the roasting of oxen, and other festivities— which indicated the delight of the neighborhood that "poor Sir Charles" was not the last of the Damerels.

The strange story was a nine days' wonder; and then it all died out. It was nobody's business except the Damerels', and they were satisfied. The widow—who had been seen by nobody except the lawyers—went away "for change of air," and Sir Arthur Damerel reigned in his father's stead—the father who had never known of his existence. It was a strange chapter in human life—so strange that at first hardly anybody believed it; until, one by one, everybody got used to it, and accepted things as they were, without overmuch questioning.

As, of course, all this change was likewise accepted at the rectory. Mrs. Trevena looked a trifle paler—she had become excessively pale and thin within the past year; "worn to a shadow," people said; but she answered, with a peaceful smile, all the questions and congratulations. Only she never spoke of Sir Arthur except as "my son."

There was another thing which she had to settle, and be also congratulated upon, and that was "my son's marriage."

"You couldn't expect me to live in that big house all alone, mother," pleaded Arthur, with amusing simplicity. "And since I cannot possibly get you, why not let me have Nanny to take care of me?"

It did indeed seem the wisest plan. Though they were both so young—only nineteen and twenty-one—still they were not "foolish"; for both had already battled with the world sufficiently to gain premature wisdom. And perhaps after all, though this generation does not think so, early marriages, when not rash or improvident, are best. Our grandfathers and grandmothers, who did not wait to be rich, but began life simply, as their parents did before them, and spent together their fresh unstained hopeful youth, their busy maturity, their peaceful old age, were probably happier than we of to-day, who fritter away in idle flirting, or more harmful things, our blossoming-time; marrying late in life with all the heart gone out of us; or never marrying at all, and then arguing sagely that to "fall in love" is a folly, and to marry is little less than a crime.

Mrs. Trevena did not think so—would not have thought so even had her son been still "poor" Arthur Trevena. When, now he was Sir Arthur Damerel, he began to speak of his marriage, all she suggested was that he should wait a year, out of respect to the dead, and to gain a little experience in managing his large property, for the good of the living.

"A year is a long time," said he, disconsolately.

"Is it?" answered his mother, with a strange far-away look, which startled him a moment, till he saw it melt into her usual smile. "Then let it be six months, my dear. Leave me Nanny, and stay you beside me for just six months more. Then —do as you will."

For the young people, neither of whom had seen the world, were determined, as soon as ever they were married, to go abroad and enjoy themselves; visiting Switzerland, Italy—perhaps even going on to Constantinople! They were so happy, so full of plans, so resolved to do no end of good on their estate! but they wanted just this little bit of pleasure—a harmless frolic together before they settled down.

And so the winter passed very happily, Arthur being at the rectory almost as much as when he used to live there; but never failing to go back of nights to his large dull house. He also spent conscientiously every forenoon in his study with his steward, repairing much evil that had come about in his father's days, and planning no end of good to be done in his own. A happy time! full of hope for everybody. Nobody noticed much that Mrs. Trevena was the only one who smiled more than she spoke, and made no personal plans for the future at all.

She had had, ever since Sir Charles's funeral in the chilly church, her usual winter cold; rather worse than usual; for she ceased to fight against it, left everything to Nanny, and gradually kept entirely to the house, then to her own room —a new thing, which her husband could not understand at all. He went wandering about the rectory like a spirit in pain; or walked out into the village and wandered there, paying necessary or unnecessary pastoral visits, and telling everybody "that Mrs. Trevena had a bad cold, but would certainly be about again in a day or two." And sometimes, strong in this expectation, when he returned he would come to the foot of the stairs and call, "Susannah!" just as usual expecting her to come, as she always used to come, nobody knew from where, till he bethought himself to go in search of her to her room. There he always found her, and sat down content by her side.

But, beyond that room, always so cheerful and bright—with sunshine if there was any sun, with fire-light if there was none—the house and he had to endure her absence, to learn to do without her. Under Nanny's charge all went on as usual—"the old original clock-work way," Arthur called it, and hoped his wife would keep his big house as well as his mother had kept this little one. But day after day there was the empty chair at the head of the table, the empty sofa by the drawing-room fire, the work-box that nobody opened, the book that nobody read.

Did any of them understand? Did Susannah herself understand? Who can tell?

There comes to us all a time when we begin to say, silently of course, our *Nunc dimittis*. We are tired—so tired! Perhaps we ought not to be, and many good people would reprove us for being so, but we are tired—

"We have had all the joys that the world could bestow:
We have lived; we have loved."

Or else we have had no joys, and have long since given up the hope of any: which was scarcely Susannah's case, and yet she was tired.

When they left her alone—though they never did it for long—she would lean her head back against her pillows, with the weary look of one who waits for bedtime. All about her was so busy and bustling. One day she had watched her husband, hale and hearty, march down the garden to inquire about the first brood of chickens, and a February lamb.

"It will soon be spring," she said to herself, and listened to what seemed like a thrush's note in the garden; soon drowned by Arthur's piano below-stairs, where he sat playing, with his "little Nanny" beside him—the girl who was almost as good as a wife to him already; taking care of him, guiding him, and adoring him by turns. "How happy he is—that boy!" and a tear or two dropped from Susannah's eyes: human tears! "I should like to have seen his children—just one little baby, like himself—my little baby that I loved so. It would have been the old days over again, when I sat in the rocking-chair—he in his night-gown, sucking his thumb, with his eyes fixed on my face, and his two little feet in one of my hands. Wasn't he a pretty baby?"

The last sentence was said aloud, and in French—to Manette, now grown stout and middle-aged, but with her faithful Swiss heart still devoted to her mistress, creeping up on every excuse from her cooking to see if Madame wanted anything.

No; Susannah's wants were few—as they always had been. She was an invalid who gave no trouble to anybody. The coming Angel came so stealthily, so peacefully, that no one ever heard his step.

"Stop a minute, Manette," she said, after a few minutes' cheerful chat. "I wish you would bring the rocking-chair out of the nursery—I mean Miss Nanny's room: dear me, how stupid I am growing! I should like to have it here."

Manette brought it: and when the young people came upstairs—which they did very soon, for they were not selfish lovers—Arthur greeted it with a shout of delight, and declared it made him feel "like a little baby" once more. All that evening he insisted on sitting down on the floor at his mother's feet; and let her play with his curls, or what remained of them, for he was a fashionable young man now, and had his hair cut like other "golden youths." He told Nanny ridiculous stories of his childhood, making himself out to be twice as naughty as he ever had been; forcing even his mother to laugh, and laughing himself till the tears ran down his cheeks. In fact, cheerful and content as they always were at the rectory, they had seldom spent so merry an evening; the rector included, who came up from his Saturday night's sermon—put off as usual till the last minute—and begged to have tea in his wife's room.

"Everything seems so out of order down-stairs when you are not there, Susannah," said he, restlessly. "You really must try to come down to-morrow. Now, pour out my tea, Nanny."

"No—not Nanny this time," her aunt said, gently, and bidding Arthur move the table closer, she poured out her husband's tea, and gave it to him with her own hand—a rather shaky hand; as they remembered afterward, and wondered they had never noticed it, nor how white and quiet she sat, long after the meal was over.

When Arthur had kissed his mother and bade her good-night, and Nanny came back, extra rosy, from the other rather lengthy good-night which always took place at the hall door—she thought her aunt looked more tired than usual, and said so, offering to stay beside her for a while.

"Oh no!" Mrs. Trevena answered. "Let everybody go to bed, except Manette. She can sit with me till your uncle comes out of his study. Nanny"—holding the girl's hand, and looking hard into her face—"you'll take care of your uncle? And—no, I need not tell you to take care of Arthur. Kiss me, my dear. Good-night."

That was all.

An hour later, Nanny was startled out of her happy sleep, as sound as a child's, to see Manette standing, white with terror, at her bedside. That had happened which nobody feared or expected—except, perhaps, the sufferer herself. A sudden and violent fit of coughing had produced hemorrhage of the lungs, and Mrs. Trevena was dying.

Nanny sprang out of her bed. She had had long experience in sick-nursing—enough to know that this was a question not of days or of hours, but of minutes; that there was no time to summon anybody; that what help could be given must be given at once, by herself and Manette alone, for there was nobody to aid them, and no time to call anybody.

Susannah let them do all they could. She was quite conscious—smiled her thanks several times, but she never attempted to speak a word. Except once, when she heard Manette proposing to fetch Mr. Trevena, and motioned a feeble but decided negative.

"No, no. Save him from—from anything painful. Don't let him see me—till afterward."

And so it befell that the breast upon which the parting soul relied was, not her husband's, not Arthur's, both so tenderly beloved, but Nanny's, whom she had always been kind to, and liked much without actually loving—Nanny, the blameless daughter of her life-long foe.

There, just before midnight, while the rector was still busy over his sermon, and Arthur at Tawton Abbas was sleeping the sleep of healthy, happy youth, Susannah gradually lost all memory even of them, all consciousness of the world about her, and passed peacefully away into the world unknown.

When the two who to her had been so infinitely dear came to look at her, there was, as she had wished, "nothing painful"—only a beautiful image of eternal rest. Did she love them still? Who knows? Let us pray that it may be so.

None can mourn forever: it is not right they should. But it was a whole year before Arthur recovered from the blow, which, to him, had fallen like a thunderbolt out of a clear sky. The young seldom realize death unless it comes quite close to them. It had never entered his mind that his mother would die—until she died. He could not imagine existence without her. The shock was so great, and the change it wrought in him so piteous, that Nanny was for a time absolutely

terrified. Both the young people seemed to grow suddenly old. They spoke of love and marriage no more, but devoted themselves like a real son and daughter to the desolate man who had lost even more than they.

The rector was very quiet from first to last. Whether he grieved or not, no one could tell; from the day of her funeral he rarely mentioned his wife's name. But he often went wandering mournfully about the house as if in search of her, and then went silently back to his books, taking very little interest in anything else. He seemed to have suddenly turned into an old man—quite patient and quite helpless. It was not without cause that Nanny always answered, when questioned about the date of her marriage, "I couldn't leave him; she told me to take care of him." In truth, for a long time all that the forlorn three appeared to think of was to do exactly as she had said, or would have wished.

And they were doing it, they felt sure, when, as the primroses of the second spring began to blossom over her grave, Arthur took courage, and again asked for Nanny. The birds were singing, the little lambs bleating, the chickens chirping —all her young "family," as Susannah used to call them—the creatures whom she had so liked to see happy about her.

"She would like us to be happy, I know," Arthur said, when he urged the question, and insisted to Nanny that Manette was quite able to take charge of the rector now, and that she herself would not be more than a few minutes' walk from her uncle. When Mr. Trevena was told all this, he assented without hesitation to the marriage. It did not much matter to him who took care of him now. He might live many years yet—the bookworm's placid, self-absorbed life; but the half of himself was missing forever.

So, one bright spring day, Arthur led his bride past his mother's grave. His mother would not have grieved: she would have been glad—as is the instinct of all unselfish souls.

"On that grave drop not a tear....
Rather smile there, blessed one,
Thinking of me in the sun;
Or forget me, smiling on."

But she was not forgotten—she never could be. She had lived long enough to make her boy all that he was; to form his mind and character, heart and soul;

to fit him for the aims and duties of life—high aims and serious duties; for Sir Arthur Damerel is not the sort of man to hide himself, or submit to be hidden, under a bushel. His position must inevitably bring him many a responsibility, many a trouble and care; but he will fight through all, with his wife beside him—little Nanny, who has given the neighborhood an entirely new and revised edition of the Lady Damerels of Tawton Abbas. Active, energetic, kindly, benevolent—she is so well loved both by rich and poor that no one stops to consider whether or not she is beautiful. Nor does her husband. To him she is simply "little Nanny."

One of their duties—not always a pleasant one—is their yearly visit of a day or two to the Dowager Lady Damerel, who has turned very religious, and is made much of in a select circle who have taken the title of "Believers," one of their points of belief being that nobody can be saved except themselves. Such a creed is the natural outcome of that pleasure-loving egoism which had characterized her earlier days. The greater the sinner, the greater the saint—if such sainthood is worth anything. She takes very little interest in her son or his belongings; except perhaps in one very handsome baby granddaughter, who she declares is just like herself; but they are on terms of the utmost politeness. Only he never calls her anything but "Lady Damerel." He feels that his real mother—"*my* mother," as he always speaks of her, and scarcely a day passes that he does not speak of her—was she who sleeps in that quiet grave within sight of the dining-room window of the dear old rectory.

And Susannah, had she known this, and seen how her influence will descend through Arthur to his children's children, would have died content, feeling that those one-and-twenty years had not been thrown away; that she had not only made her own life and her husband's happy, but, as good Dr. Franklin once said, she had "saved a soul alive."

THE END.

Editor's Easy Chair.

THE return of the seasons is not surer than that of the games of boys, and there is no more interesting illustration than the recurrence of those games of what is called the law of periodicity. February is not gone before on some breezy morning the long-tailed kite is floating in the sky. Who flies it first; and what is the admonition which reminds the boy that the time of coasting is past, and that of kite-flying has come? It is an instinct as fine and as certain as the migratory instinct of the birds. Kites, tops, hoops, marbles, balls, hop-scotch, all appear in due season as regularly as the note of the frogs, the greening of the willows, the swelling of the buds, or the blossoms of the "shad," as the anemone in the woods, and the Daphne and Forsythia in the garden.

But the law is illustrated in every way. The wise man who goes out in the sunny April morning for a walk takes his umbrella with him, mindful of the showers that fall in the spring. Every year he renews his care, if not his umbrella, whose renewal depends less upon him than upon the necessities or the communistic instinct of his neighbor. There, indeed, is the law of umbrellas—but we forbear. The wisdom of the pedestrian must be shared by the editor if he would maintain the pedestrian's equanimity and sense of self-defence; for not surer are the showers of April than the complaints and queries of the cloud of authors and writers which envelops every editorial retreat, and against which the defensive umbrella of explanation is continually necessary. From time to time, probably as often as once a year, the Easy Chair has sought to correct certain popular fallacies in regard to contributions and contributors to magazines, speaking, of course, with especial knowledge of one magazine, but with the consciousness that one represents all. The fraternity has everywhere a similar experience.

Soon after the publication of the *Cornhill Magazine* began, under the editorship of Thackeray, he took all its readers into his confidence in one of the "Roundabout Papers," which he called "Thorns in the Cushion." The kindly story-teller, who was always a simple-hearted boy, revealed the fact that he was mercilessly flagellated and scored by correspondents who seemed to write, as it were, with whips of many lashes, and with steel daggers, rather than steel pens, of the sharpest point. They adjured him *per misericordiam*. They besought him to accept essays and tales and sketches and poems as pale-faced and hollow-eyed girl and boy peddlers press matches and pen-wipers and lead-pencils upon you in the busy office. You know that they are not genuine merchants; they are asking for alms. It is not trade; it is charity. You are aware that they are needy and destitute and wretched. Your heart prompts relief. "Ah, sir," they say, "this little poem is as melodious as that you published last month. I have no name, but my story is as good as anybody's. Ah! sir, please! please! I am so hungry! I have not tasted food since yesterday."

It is a thorn, says Thackeray; it pricks and wounds. The other day the Easy Chair heard the first frog of the spring, so to speak. It was the annual remark in a newspaper, evidently contributed by a sufferer, that it was useless to offer anything to any of the magazines unless you had the favor of the editorial ring. A new *Hamlet* or *L'Allegro* might be sent in anonymously, but without the word of a friend at court it would be respectfully declined. The sufferer obviously believed that the mystery of a magazine was that of the spoils system in the public service, in which success is due to favor, and not to merit. Hail! showers of spring! It is evidently beginning to rain, and the umbrella must be raised again.

Will any believer in the spoils system of magazine favor please to reflect for a moment that there are hardly a dozen miscellaneous magazines in the country which pay for contributions what may be called a living remuneration? These magazines are issued generally twelve times in the year. Each number contains every month, let us say, eighteen or twenty papers of all kinds, including serials and editorial departments. In every number there must be a suitable variety and timeliness and freshness of topic and treatment. If we allow the number of contributions besides the editorial notes to be, say sixteen every month, there will be one hundred and ninety-two published every month in the dozen magazines, and twenty-three hundred and fourteen in a year. This is the limit of the demand. What does the gentle sufferer suppose the supply to be? Not less, certainly, than fifteen or twenty thousand.

Then the contents of each number of the magazine must be determined long before the month of its issue. What follows? That at every moment the magazine has a large accumulation of papers accepted and paid for. That fact determines the acceptance of papers equally good or even better, so that the words "not available" are strictly descriptive of the situation, and are no verdict whatever upon the quality of the offering. Indeed, dear sir or madam, your sugar is undoubtedly the purest and best possible, but of that quality we have on hand a full supply, and, in the language familiar to you, we do not at present care to carry "a fuller line." In the embarrassment of riches, to command acceptance the new spice must be not only as good as that already stored in the warehouse and even better, but a great deal better. Nevertheless, even when the supply of eggs of every rare and beautiful bird seems to be as large as a wise merchant would care to hold, if some Marco Polo or Sindbad should enter with a nest of

bird-of-paradise eggs, or the eggs of the rare roc or dodo, the wise merchant will certainly secure them. But is that a reason for buying all the bantams or Shanghais or Plymouth Rocks that offer?

The generous reader sees that the Easy Chair interposes no objection to giving reasons for the executive action, but the reader, even if he winces as an author over a certain unwelcome communication that he has received from the magazine, must clear his mind of that sad stuff about personal favor. When the yachts go down the bay for the annual regatta, does anybody suppose that there is any other thought or purpose upon any craft than how to trim and sail her so as to win the cup? Does the skipper load his decks with passengers who are mere obstructions, over whom the nimble crew, who are handling the ropes and doing all the work, must needs stumble and fall? Does the sensible reader suppose that the esteemed contemporaries of this craft, which sail with it in the monthly regatta for popular favor, aim "to put it ahead" by accepting articles for sweet charity's sake or for personal partiality?

No, no; let him understand that the system which places a man in the public service because his stomach or nerves have given out, or because he treated the "boys" copiously at the polls, or because he cannot make a living at his trade, is not the system upon which a great popular magazine is prosperously conducted. Every month the public expects every magazine to do its duty, and nothing is more ludicrous than the theory that any one of them does less than its best.

BERKSHIRE, the westernmost county in Massachusetts, is full of beautiful scenery, and has been the home of some of our most famous authors. Among its charming spots many years ago—and perhaps it is so still—was the Shaker village of Tyringham, and one day a happy loiterer in the county said to his urbane host at Lenox, "There is no prettier place in Berkshire than Tyringham."

"So I am told," was the answer.

"But don't you know it?" asked his friend, with natural surprise.

"No; I have never been there. I wish to leave something for the imagination even in beautiful Berkshire."

It is a rule which some wise men observe in regard to persons as well as places. They reason, for instance, that an author gives us the best of himself in his work. If that charms us, why should we risk breaking the spell by the chance of encountering grotesque or disagreeable personal peculiarities?

"I have seen the great Mr. Pope," said one devotee of the famous poet to another.

"Ah! is it possible? And what was he like; and what was he doing?"

"Well, he is a small, sick man; and he was scratching his head."

Henry Clay was the beloved leader of a great

party, whose defeat for the Presidency affected many of his followers like a great personal misfortune. But when he lost the nomination in 1840, and Harrison was selected, Henry A. Wise says that he was with Clay when the news came, and that he strode up and down the room pouring out imprecations upon his friends and cursing his luck.

Omne ignotum pro magnifico is an old Latin saying—the unknown is magnificent. Campbell's line has the same meaning: "'Tis distance lends enchantment to the view"—a strain which echoes through the verse of many other poets. But it is a gilding of refined gold, a painting of the lily, when the mountain that we climbed is as lovely as the mountain that we saw, and when the charm of the author's page is confirmed by his presence. This happily has been true of the most eminent American men of letters, and of none of them more signally true than of Longfellow. Those who knew him were aware of it, but the great multitude to whom he was only a voice of tenderly enchanting music will find with delight in the memoir by his brother, lately published, that all which they admired in the poet they would have loved in the man.

Longfellow was so equable and serene, and his life, except for one unspeakable sorrow, seemed to be so singularly fortunate, that the force of his nature and character was not always observed, and is sometimes forgotten. But the memoir shows the depth and strength of the current of his life, which, although flowing calmly, flowed always steadily in the precise course that he designed from the first. In Longfellow's case it is especially true that the child was father of the man. The career which the youth of seventeen deliberately chose was pursued without doubt or pause, and with constant triumph and renown, until the man of seventy-five died amid universal affection and sorrow.

In 1824, when a Senior at Bowdoin College, Longfellow wrote to his father: "The fact is —and I will not disguise it in the least, for I think I ought not—the fact is, I most eagerly aspire after future eminence in literature; my whole soul burns most ardently for it, and every earthly thought centres in it." The "literary profession" was then unknown in this country. To live by literature was seemingly the maddest of dreams. But Longfellow proposed it with the most cheerful courage, founded in the confidence which he felt of ability to do it. This quiet assurance in a youth of so gentle a mould is the earliest revelation of the placid strength of his character.

His mental quality is shown also in the early letters. They are essentially youthful, warm, generous, sympathetic, sensitive; but their tone is as moderate and the expression as free from extravagance as those of any letters written at any time of his life, and always without a touch of priggishness. No man ever pursued his object with more constant devo-

tion. With a remarkable faculty for acquiring languages, he absorbed literature. His whole being was steeped in it. His whole life was literary. Literature lent an indescribable grace to his conversation, his correspondence, and his humor. The richness and accuracy of his literary accomplishment gave the mellow tone to his verse. It was never obtruded. It was too thoroughly assimilated to take any form of pedantry. But the charm which it infused into all that he wrote played exquisitely over all that he said. It supplied the ease and taste and refinement which marked every form of his personal intercourse, as the softened sunlight of a day in June touches everything with opaline light.

This complete and exclusive literary quality was held by some of the earlier critics of his works to be a serious defect. It was objected to him as a poet that his figures and allusions were not drawn from nature, but from books; and especially in the transcendental circle the tone toward him was that of Theodore Parker's question of Goethe, "What did he ever do for man?" But this was to reproach the lark that it is not a nightingale, or the pansy that it is not a tulip. He sang his own song in his own way. He brought the gift that he had. It was not the poet's fault that the critic wanted something else. But it was the critic's misfortune that because he liked rubies he looked listlessly at pearls.

The great transcendental revival, although involving many of the scholars who were Longfellow's friends and contemporaries, left him entirely untouched. He spoke his transcendental comrades fair, but he was not to be diverted from his own life. The great moral and political ground-swell of the antislavery agitation lifted him as it lifted all New England conscience and culture. He spoke his word in his own way. His sympathy was always true. His conviction was profound, his interest unswerving. But the movement was not the supreme interest and purpose of his life, as it was of his most intimate friend, Charles Sumner, to whom Longfellow's home and perfect sympathy were a haven of refuge, an atmosphere of healing and repose.

To those who knew Longfellow, the reading of the memoir, which is largely composed of extracts from his diary, is like freshening the glowing tints of a mellow picture. It is the portrait of one of the truest and most equable of men, whose perfect rectitude, modesty, simplicity, sympathetic humanity, and fidelity to the conviction and purpose and lofty ideals of his youth, the utmost gratification of a pure ambition could not affect, and whose name is cherished equally by fame and affection.

In a recent number of the Monthly one of the two thousand two hundred and thirty-three Presidential postmasters in the country gave a vivid description of his experience of the reformed system of appointment in the civil service. His paper was interesting and instructive, and was quite unique of its kind; but the author was instantly and peremptorily called to order by ex-Postmaster-General James, who was for many years the admirably efficient postmaster in New York, by Mr. Gayler, who was one of the able lieutenants of Mr. James, and by Mr. Comstock, the chairman of the Examining Board in New York, and from the organization of examinations by President Hayes a member of the Examining Board at the Custom-house.

These gentlemen with one accord denied the depreciatory charge of the author of the article that the examinations were generally pretences and shams, and satirized him for arrogating to himself the exclusive glory of a reformer. And certainly his statement was a rash generalization, but not, we are sure, designed to misrepresent, and explicable by the little that was really known to the public in regard to the examinations, and by the general skepticism which distorted in one place the truth in another. This plea is not offered in justification, but in extenuation. Generalizations upon such subjects are always dangerous, because complete and accurate information of details is always difficult. But it is easy to understand that a stranger might be misled about the perfect good faith of the examinations even in New York, since here in the city itself there was—even if we may not say is—general and profound skepticism.

Happily the Easy Chair can confirm by its own knowledge the statements made in correction of the swift generalization of the article. Less personally familiar with the course pursued at the Post-office, but knowing the deep interest in the reformed system of ex-Postmaster-General James, and aware of his early and strong representations in favor of reform to the administration at Washington, and not doubting the effectiveness of the reformed system at the Post-office, with which Mr. Eaton was constantly acquainted in detail, the Easy Chair had the fullest and most practical knowledge of the good faith and the admirable efficiency of the reform as practised at the Custom-house. It would be untrue to say that it was approved by all the chiefs, and that questions did not sometimes arise as to its scope. But it is unquestionable by the most resolute disbeliever that the examinations were in themselves perfectly appropriate, and conducted with entire good faith, and that appointments within the range of the classified service were made by the Collector, while the official reports of Postmaster James and of Collector Robertson bore unqualified official testimony to the excellent results of the reformed system.

These things, little believed even here, and actually known to very few, notwithstanding the cordial invitations to the press and to conspicuous citizens to attend the examinations, and to "see with eyes," had evidently escaped the attention of the author of the article, who was busily engaged in his own office in promoting the good work. His description of that work is very graphic, and his account of the opposition and its leaders, and of the universal scorn and incredulity which attended the beginning of reform, would be doubtless confirmed even by the gentlemen who summarily challenge that fatal generalization. But, despite all doubt and misunderstanding, they have the happy consciousness that they were the practical leaders of this great reform. They were the first to prove in detail the simplicity and practicability of the beneficent change, and to put to total rout the shadowy opposing host of ignorant objections and demagogic falsehoods.

The author of the article and his challengers and all other good citizens may well rejoice at the amazing progress of this beneficent reform. When the Senate hesitates or refuses to confirm a postmaster because he makes party use of his office, it is clear that the day when a postmaster may truthfully cry "What am I here for?" has gone forever. In such a refusal every postmaster in the land hears the new answer to that old question: "You are here to serve the public, not a party."

———

THE story of the butcher who looked out in the soft summer moonlight and announced that something ought to be done on so fine a night, and he guessed he would go and "slarter," was told to Melissa, who ejaculated pretty Ohs and Ahs, and said, "But how vulgar!" Yet had some dreadful Nathan heard the words, and beheld Melissa as she spoke, he would have raised his voice and pointed his finger and said, "Thou art the woman!" For the delicate lady was the wearer of dead birds in her hat, and encouraged the "slarter" of the loveliest and sweetest of innocent song birds merely to gratify her vanity. The butcher, madam, may be vulgar, but at least he does not kill in order to wear the horns and tails of his victims.

"How hideous!" exclaims Belinda, as she sees the pictured head of the savage islander—"rings in his nose! how hideous!" And the gentle Belinda shakes the rings in her ears in protest against such barbarism. Sylvia, too, laughs gayly at the wife of the Chinese ambassador stumping along upon invisible feet; and Sylvia would laugh more freely, except for her invisible waist. It is so preposterous to squeeze your feet, she remarks; it is a deformity; it outrages nature. And the superb and benignant Venus of Milo smiles from her pedestal in the corner, and with her eyes fixed upon Sylvia's waist, echoes Sylvia's words: "It is a deformity; it outrages nature."

The Puritan preacher who, somewhat perverting his text, cried, "Top-knot, come down!" declared war upon the innocent ribbons that, carefully trained and twisted and exalted into a towering ornament, doubtless nodded from the head of Priscilla to the heart of John Alden and melted it completely, while the preacher could not even catch his wandering eye.

The preacher's course was clear. Top-knots must come down if they allured to a sweeter worship than he inculcated. But those ribbons were made for that pretty purpose of adornment. They were not victims. They silenced no song; they hardened no heart; they rewarded no wanton cruelty; they destroyed no charm of field or wood. They were not memorials of heartless slaughter. They were simple devices by which maidenly charms were heightened, and a little grace and taste and beauty were lent to the sombre Puritan world.

But the top-knots of to-day are bought at a monstrous price. Carlyle says of certain enormous fire-flies on an island of the East Indies that, placed upon poles, they illuminate the journeys of distinguished people by night. Great honor to the fire-flies! he exclaims; but— It is great honor to the golden-winged woodpecker to be shot and then daintily poised upon the hat of Cyrilla, as, enveloped in a cloud of dudes, she promenades the Avenue on Sunday afternoon: great honor to the woodpecker, but— The naughty dog in the country which hunts and kills chickens is made to wear a dead chicken hung around his neck, and at last is shamed out of his murderous fancy. How if Cyrilla, strolling in the summer fields, haply with young Laurence hanging enthralled upon her sweet eyes, her low replies, should meet the cur disgraced with the dead chicken around her neck, she with the dead woodpecker upon her head!

The lovely lady puts a premium upon wanton slaughter and unspeakable cruelty. She incites the murderous small boy and all the idlers and vagrants to snare and shoot the singing birds, and silence the heavenly music of the summer air. She cries for "slarter," and, like the white cat enchanted into the Princess, who leaps to the floor in hot chase when the mouse appears, the Queen of Beauty, with a feathered corpse for a crown, begins to seem even to Laurence unhappily enchanted.

Henry Bergh is one of our great modern benefactors. If beasts could speak, or knew to whom they owe the deepest gratitude, his path would be hallowed by the prayers and blessings of the innocent and helpless whom he has relieved. But the birds of the air are not less our dependents than the beasts of the field. It is as plainly the duty of a humane and Christian civilization to protect the birds as we protect the beasts against the wanton cruelty of human savages. And Melissa, Belinda, Sylvia, Cyrilla, and their mates—" the rose-bud garden of girls"—will they consciously make themselves accomplices in a crime against the innocent? Let them not ask whether the pearl hanging upon their bosoms or fixed in their rings is any less a proper ornament or less beautiful because it is called "a diseased secretion." There is no cruelty in the making or taking of the pearl. It does not consciously diminish the life and beauty and melody of the world. But the dead bird upon Cyrilla's hat does all that, and it brutalizes those who do the mischief.

Like many a fashion, the wearing of dead birds is a thoughtless wrong, and the protest against it which is now not only raised, but organized, as one of the most effective methods of staying the massacre of the innocents, will suggest to many a gentle heart that unconsciously it has aided and abetted an offence against which every humane and generous feeling protests; and as the offence is swiftly removed from hat and bonnet, in the sweet and happy voices of the birds of this summer their hearts will hear a hymn of gratitude.

"Think every morning, when the sun peeps through
　　The dim, leaf-latticed windows of the grove,
How jubilant the happy birds renew
　　Their old melodious madrigals of love!
And when you think of this, remember too
'Tis always morning somewhere, and above
The awakening continents, from shore to shore,
Somewhere the birds are singing evermore."

Editor's Study.

I.

THE lectures of the Concord School of Philosophy on the *Life and Genius of Goethe* form a book which is notable for its limitations as well as its excellences, but is always curious and interesting. It is what Professor White thinks of Goethe's Youth, Mr. Albee of his Self-Culture, Professor Davidson of his Titanism, Dr. Bartol of Goethe and Schiller, Dr. Hedge of Goethe's Märchen, Mr. Sanborn of his Relation to English Literature, Mr. Partridge of his qualities as a Playwright, Mrs. Cheney of his Ewig-Weibliche, Mr. Emery of his Elective Affinities, Mrs. Sherman of his treatment of Child Life, Mr. Snider of the Faust Poem, Mrs.

Julia Ward Howe of his Women, Professor Harris of his Faust. Each of these lectures has its value, and if their fortuitous combination does not enhance their worth, we cannot say that it necessarily detracts from it. They seem to us, so far as they severally go, to embody a good deal of original if not novel impression, and to have each a certain adequacy; it is the whole book that is a little insufficient. Dr. Hedge's elucidation of the allegory which he explains is as unquestionably interesting as the Märchen itself is tiresome, even now when its cloudy prophecies concerning the rehabilitation of Germany seem fulfilled. Mr. Sanborn's inquiry as to Goethe's influence on English literature is interesting, though it fails of indicating the one certain effect which, directly or indirectly, Goethe's method in fiction is having in these latest times. He taught us, in novels otherwise now antiquated, and always full of German clumsiness, that it was false to good art—which is never anything but the reflection of life—to pursue and round the career of the persons introduced, whom he often allowed to appear and disappear in our knowledge as people in the actual world do. This is a lesson which the writers able to profit by it can never be too grateful for; and it is equally a benefaction to readers; but there is very little else in the conduct of the Goethean novels which is in advance of their time; this remains almost their sole contribution to the science of fiction. They are very primitive in certain characteristics, and unite with their calm, deep insight, an amusing helplessness in dramatization. "Wilhelm retired to his room, and indulged in the following reflections," is a mode of analysis which would not be practiced nowadays; and all that fancifulness of nomenclature in *Wilhelm Meister* is very drolly romantic and feeble. The adventures with robbers seem as if dreamed out of books of chivalry, and the tendency to allegorization affects one like an endeavor on the author's part to escape from the unrealities which he must have felt harassingly, German as he was. Mixed up with the shadows and illusions are honest, wholesome, every-day people, who have the air of wandering homelessly about among them, without definite direction; and the mists are full of a luminosity which, in spite of them, we know for common-sense and poetry. What is useful in any review of Goethe's methods is the recognition of the fact, which it must bring, that the greatest master cannot produce a masterpiece in a new kind. The novel was too recently invented in Goethe's day not to be, even in his hands, full of the faults of apprentice work.

Among these Concord essays, we believe we have liked Mrs. Howe's almost the best, because we have found it one of the clearest and frankest. She thinks that Goethe differs from most men who have written about women in not satirizing them; but she does not blink the fact that whatever Goethe's ideal women were, his treatment of real women was not ideal. To our own mind it is no defence of him to say that many other known and unknown men were as bad or worse, or to imply that much must be forgiven to his "genius." Nothing must be forgiven to a man's "genius." The greater his power, the greater his responsibility before the human conscience, which is God in us. But men come and go, and what they do in their limited physical lives is of comparatively little moment; it is what they say that really survives to bless or to ban; and we wish that some of our good Concord philosophers—pure souls and right minds as they all are—had thought it well to recognize the evil that Wordsworth felt in

Goethe, and that must long survive him. There is a kind of thing—a kind of metaphysical lie against righteousness and common-sense—which is called the Unmoral, and is supposed to be different from the Immoral; and it is this which is supposed to cover many of the faults of Goethe. His *Wilhelm Meister*, for example, is so far removed within the region of the "ideal" that its unprincipled, its evil-principled, tenor in regard to women is pronounced "unmorality," and is therefore inferably harmless. But no study of Goethe is complete without some consideration of the ethics of his great novel, and in this particular the Concord study of his life and genius is signally defective. There is no lecture on *Wilhelm Meister*, no recognition of the qualities which caused Wordsworth to hurl the book across the room with an indignant perception of its sensuality. Yet such a recognition might have come most fitly from the group who preferred rather to burn incense at his shrine. For the sins of his life Goethe was sufficiently punished in his life by his final marriage with Christiane; for the sins of his literature many others must suffer; and we think it would have been well for the worshippers of his "genius" to lift a voice of warning against them in behalf of the votaries whom they will draw to his cult. Of course people who assemble to celebrate "genius" could not be expected to interrupt the rites with too severe a scrutiny of the obliquities of the god.

II.

We do not despair, however, of the day when the poor honest herd of humankind shall give universal utterance to the universal instinct, and shall hold selfish power in politics, in art, in religion, for the devil that it is; when neither its crazy pride nor its amusing vanity shall be flattered by the puissance of the "geniuses" who have forgotten their duty to the common weakness, and have abused it to their own glory. In that day we shall shudder at many monsters of passion, of self-indulgence, of heartlessness, whom we still more or less openly adore for their "genius," and shall account no man worshipful whom we do not feel and know to be good. The spectacle of strenuous achievement will then not dazzle or mislead; it will not sanctify or palliate iniquity; it will only render it the more hideous and pitiable. A life at once good and great will no longer strike us as something so anomalous that we shall be tempted to question either its goodness or its greatness, and in that desirable time we shall know fully how to appreciate the unblotted sublimity of a career like Longfellow's. Even now the careful reader of the *Life* which the poet's brother has lately given us will feel that grandeur if he will put all the false and misshapen ideals of "genius" out of his mind. At first the story moves slowly and even coldly, but the charm of that unerring loveliness of spirit, that never-clouded right-mindedness, that unfaltering loftiness of purpose, grows upon you unawares, and it holds you closer and closer to the end. There is never anything spectacular or agonized or contorted in that life, though it knew sorrow doubly tragic by contrast with the long flow of its prosperity, and was fretted in its undercurrents, as all lives are, by the troubles which "genius" has so often exploited as its peculiar griefs.

Not much more in outline appears in Mr. Samuel Longfellow's two volumes than we knew of Longfellow already; but the detail which he loved—" Oh, give *details* of thy life, dear friend, and not generalities, which in no wise satisfy!"—is here in delightful fulness. It abounds in the letters which he wrote home on his youthful wanderings in Spain, in the journals and letters of his subsequent journeys and sojourns in Italy, in France, and in Germany, and those of the long period of his residence in Cambridge, with its manifold friendships, its beloved duties, its poetic delights, its heavy sorrow, its days of uncomplaining pain. There was nothing to be hidden, and nothing is kept from us that could throw light upon his life, whose beauty was so great, whose incidents were so simple and few. The story of his first love and marriage is given with unstudied pathos, and with the perfect taste which marks the biographer's handling of his material throughout; and then there is not much more to tell except the story of his coming to Cambridge, and of his union with the Mary Ashburton of his beautiful romance. The chief events of his life there were the poems which the world knows; and in the abundant record there is nothing to change the impression which his work gives of him, certainly none of those anomalies and contradictions of temper and performance which have made modern biography such lurid reading. He is a man to whom you have nothing to forgive, not even a feeble quality in his irreproachable goodness; for there is nothing more striking in Longfellow's life than the manly strength which governed it. He was full of fancy, and he had an optimistic gayety of heart, but neither his imagination nor his faith misled him in large things or small, personal or public, literary or moral, æsthetic or political. His philosophy of life was very simple, but entirely adequate: to do good and to be good, and then " learn to enjoy the present—that little space of time between the great past and the still greater future." There is no rancor expressed against any human creature, except " the nasty little professor in a dirty schlafrock" at Heidelberg, who, in bidding the poet farewell, " took his pipe out of his mouth and kissed" him on the lips. " I had a great mind to take him by the ears," he adds, and it must be owned the offence was great. But no one else is visited with like severity; not even Poe, whose bitterness never imparted itself to Longfellow. Now and again there is a touch of his delicate hu-

mor; and the letters and journals grow more interesting as time advances and the fermentation of youth subsides, leaving the poet clear as to his purpose and destiny. He was not always so sure of either, for in 1829 he wrote, " My poetic career is finished," and for six years after he made no verses.

While the details of his life will not change the feeling toward him, they will deepen it; for the reader will find here abundant and fresh reason to confirm himself in reverence for one of the noblest and simplest souls. Longfellow was never known, for instance, as a champion of the antislavery cause; but early in his literary career he threw down his gage in the *Poems on Slavery;* and throughout its existence he was the fast friend of those that hated it and fought it. In 1837, at the time of the Lovejoy meeting, he wrote home to his father, " The Little Peddlington community of Boston is in a great toss.... about Dr. Channing and the abolitionists; Boston is only a great village; the tyranny of public opinion there surpasses all belief"; and throughout the long struggle he stood by the righteous, and defended them, with serene dignity and courage, when scorn covered them. In the teeth of Boston respectability, which had loved him, he never faltered in his fealty. What that respectability was—its culture, its barbarism, its refinement, its meanness, its servility, its arrogance—is now pretty historical; what respectability was elsewhere in 1842 may be inferred from the fact that the editor of *Graham's Magazine* excused to Longfellow a notice of his book, which had to be made very guarded, because "the word *slavery* was never allowed to appear in a Philadelphia periodical, and the publisher objected to have even the name of the book appear in his pages." As time passed, and the infamy of Northern complicity with slavery was brought home to the North by the now incredible Fugitive Slave Law, Longfellow wrote in his journal, under date of February 15, 1851: " I learn that a fugitive slave, or a man accused of being one, escaped to-day from the court-room during the recess, aided by other blacks. Very glad of it. This government must not pass laws that outrage the sense of right in the community." This slave was Shadrach. Of the rendition of Simms he wrote, April 4th, of the same year: " There is much excitement in Boston about the capture of an alleged fugitive slave. O city without soul! When and where will this end? Shame that the great republic, the 'refuge of the oppressed,' should stoop so low as to become the hunter of slaves!.... Troops under arms in Boston; the court-house guarded; the Chief-Justice of the Supreme Court forced to stoop under chains to enter the temple of justice! ....Alas for the people who cannot feel an insult! While the 'great Webster' comes North to see that the work is done!"

To a friend who had blamed hi for his *Poems on Slavery*, he replied, declining argument, but stating his moral and political creed concerning it, which was that of Sumner and the other statesmen who first organized a practical opposition to it. But these were Longfellow's own opinions, and he based his action upon a principle that underlay his whole life. "I have great faith in doing what is righteous, and fear no evil consequences." It underlay his literature as well as his life, and it was a conscience that resulted not only in the highest conduct, but the finest art. With nothing narrow, and with finally nothing moralistic, he achieved in the poetry he has left us a blended ideal of goodness and of beauty which is incomparably perfect. It has for some time been the silly fashion in criticism to depreciate it; but those who have sneered at it have unwittingly paid it the highest tribute, for they have called it the poetry of the average human life; and this, without their knowing it, is the universal poetry.

A great part of his biography consists of passages from Longfellow's diaries, which are more interesting, because more intimate, than his letters. The records are often mere comments on the books he is reading; and these comments, without affecting profundity or finality, are often of the last wisdom. Criticism has only in these times learned to value Bulwer aright; but in 1849 Longfellow said of *The Caxtons:* "It has well-drawn characters in it, but the style produces upon me the effect of a flashy waistcoat festooned with gold chains." His judgments were seldom so harsh as these, but they were always clear and decided. He was never swayed by personal feeling, nor by that larger cockneyism which calls itself patriotism, though he was an American, zealous and strenuous to the last degree, where the good and honor of his country were concerned. He abhorred "the unrighteous Mexican war," and found it "melancholy to see how little true Christian feeling there is on the subject in the country." But even in small things he liked a thorough Americanism. When Sumner returned from his social triumphs in England in 1840, Longfellow recorded: "I fear that his head is a little turned, and no wonder; but he is a strong man, and will see in the end that there is something better than breakfasting at ten and dining at six."

Longfellow had not only great faith in men, but patience as vast and kindly as Lincoln's. Neither the foibles nor the sins of his fellow-mortals shut his heart against them, or inclined him to distinguish himself from them. He expressed in his life and in his literature that perfect toleration which was the only virtue left for the Americans to invent. Doubtless he said to himself that he too had his foibles like the rest; in fact, a tradition of his gaudiness in neck-ties and waistcoats survived his youth in Cambridge, and his biographer does not blink it. But there was nothing in that blameless life to blink, nothing to palliate, nothing to deprecate. It was filled full with a most ardent and generous love of letters, but a love of men mingled and interfused itself with this, so that it could never become reckless or cruel. He

"Whose smoothest verse was harsher-toned than he,"

left no heart to burn at the mention of his name. Yet, as we have suggested, no estimate of his character could be more mistaken than a conception of his goodness as a weak mildness, "a mush of concession." This gentlest of men was one of the manliest. It was his strength that was kind; and it not only softened him to the folly of others, but armed him with pity against their envy and malice and ingratitude, all which he felt in full measure throughout his life. It enabled him also to bear with dignity the uninstructed arrogance in criticism which found the pure and serene beauty of his work unsatisfying, and hankered for something contorted and passion-stricken.

It will be long, probably, before the Concord School of Philosophy will study Longfellow's life and genius; and perhaps it will begin by denying him the latter; but in the former it will have to leave no chapter untouched. In the mean time we can commend it to the unphilosophical without reservation, and especially we can ask the young to teach themselves from his career, not the greatness, of which he alone had the secret, but the goodness, which is open and possible to all, and which no one can read his life without feeling in supreme degree.

III.

Now that we have the new Boston translation of *César Birotteau,* we are reminded again how Balzac stood at the beginning of the great things that have followed since in fiction. There is an interesting likeness between his work in this and Nicolas Gogol's in *Dead Souls,* which serves to illustrate the simultaneity of the literary movement in men of such widely separated civilizations and conditions. Both represent their characters with the touch of exaggeration which typifies; but in bringing his story to a close, Balzac employs a beneficence unknown to the Russian, and almost as universal and as apt as that which smiles upon the fortunes of the good in the *Vicar of Wakefield.* It is not enough to have rehabilitated Birotteau pecuniarily and socially; he must make him die triumphantly, spectacularly, of an opportune hemorrhage, in the midst of the festivities which celebrate his restoration to his old home. Before this, human nature has been laid under contribution right and left for acts of generosity toward the righteous bankrupt; even the king sends him six-thousand francs. It is very pretty; it is touching, and brings the lump into the reader's throat; but it is too much, and one perceives that Balzac lived too soon to profit by

Balzac. The later men, especially the Russians, have known how to forbear the excesses of analysis, to withhold the weakly recurring descriptive and caressing epithets, to let the characters suffice for themselves. All this does not mean that *César Birotteau* is not a beautiful and pathetic story, as stainless as a French story can well be, full of shrewdly considered knowledge of men, and of a good art struggling to free itself from self-consciousness. But it does mean that Balzac at his best was under the burden of traditions which he has helped fiction to throw off. He felt obliged to construct a mechanical plot, to surcharge his characters, to moralize openly and baldly; he permitted himself to "sympathize" with certain of his people, and to point out others for the abhorrence of his readers. This is not so bad in him as it would be in a novelist of our day. It is simply primitive and inevitable, and he is not to be judged by it.

In fact, there is also something of nationality in the too visibly *operated* incidents of César Birotteau's rehabilitation, if we are to believe an eminent critic of the same nation. In his essay on *Les Grands Maîtres de la Littérature Russe*, M. Ernest Dupuy, speaking of the mechanical methods of French novelists, says: "Our good romancers are such skilful carpenters; they construct works so regular, so ingeniously arranged for effect, where the interest is managed with so much address, where the action moves with a step so sure toward a logical close suspected or desired from the first word! We find ourselves at the outset ill at ease in these Russian romances, full of art, but stripped of the little artifices; whose development resembles the course of life; where the personages hesitate, sometimes remain quiet; where the action proceeds without haste, and the author does not trouble himself to round off and finish up. It is enough for them to note facts and express character."

Monthly Record of Current Events.

POLITICAL.

OUR Record is closed on the 16th of April.— The Rhode Island State election, April 7, resulted in the return of Governor Wetmore and all the other present officers except Attorney-General Colt. The Prohibition amendment was carried by a decisive majority.

The following bills were passed in Congress during the month: Electoral Count, Senate, March 17; pension of $2000 to General Hancock's widow, both Houses; appropriating $500,000 for monument to Lincoln at Washington, Senate, April 1; Labor-Arbitration, House, April 3, by 195 to 30 (modified so that arbitration is optional, and the government pays the expense up to $1000 in each case); appropriating $550,000 for Congressional Library building, House, April 5, Senate, April 8; Mexican War Pension, House, April 5, by 158 to 68.

The bill to increase the United States army to 30,000 men was rejected by the Senate, April 7, by a vote of 19 to 31.

The Free Coinage Bill was defeated in the House, April 8, by a vote of 126 (97 Democrats and 29 Republicans) to 163 (70 Democrats and 93 Republicans).

Mr. George Hearst was appointed by Governor Stoneman United States Senator from California in place of the late John F. Miller.

Governor Murray, of Utah, resigned, and Caleb W. West, of Kentucky, was appointed in his place.

Mr. Gladstone's bill for the better government of Ireland was made public April 15. It debars the proposed Irish parliament from legislating concerning the status, dignity, or succession of the crown; from passing laws affecting peace or war, the army or navy, the militia or volunteers, or the defence of the realm, and from taking any action concerning the foreign or colonial relations of the empire. Among the other subjects placed beyond the power of the Irish government to deal with are dignities, titles, and honors, prizes and booties of war, offences against the law of nations, treason and alienage, naturalization, copyright, patents, mails, telegraphs, coinage, and weights and measures. The bill further prohibits Ireland from doing anything to establish or endow any religion, or to disturb or confer any privileges on account of religious belief, and also forbids it to impose customs or excise duties. The Queen is given the same prerogative to summon, prorogue, and dissolve the Irish legislature as she has with respect to the Imperial Parliament. To her Majesty also is reserved the power to erect forts, arsenals, magazines, and dock-yards. The Irish legislature is permitted to impose taxes to be paid into the Consolidated Fund to defray the expenses of the public service in Ireland, subject to the provisions of the Irish Land Purchase Bill, but is not to either raise or appropriate revenues without the Queen's recommendation made through the Lord-Lieutenant. The Church property in Ireland is to belong to the Irish people, subject to existing charges. The executive government of Ireland is vested by the Queen in a Lord-Lieutenant, who will govern with the aid of such officers and councils as the Queen may appoint, and will give or withhold the Queen's assent to such bills as the Irish legislature may pass.

Messrs. Chamberlain and Trevelyan resigned

from the British cabinet March 27. Messrs. James Stansfield and the Earl of Dalhousie were appointed to succeed them.

All the powers except Russia have agreed to recognize Prince Alexander as Governor of Eastern Roumelia during his life.

General Don Bernardo Soto has been elected President of Costa Rica, and Caceres President of Peru.

The Italian Ministry of Signor Depretis, formed June 29, 1885, resigned April 8.

The German Reichstag, March 27, by a vote of 181 to 3, rejected Prince Bismarck's Spirit Monopoly Bill, and on March 31, by a vote of 173 to 146, prolonged the Anti-Socialist law two years.

The Lower House of the Prussian Landtag, April 7, adopted the bill expropriating the land of the Poles in Posen, and colonizing the province with Germans.

DISASTERS.

March 15.—Steamer *Beda* foundered off Cape Perpetua. Twelve men lost.

March 20.—Steam-ship *Rapidan*, from New York for Costa Rica, February 2, given up for lost, with all hands.—Fifteen persons killed by an explosion on the steamer *Colombia* at the island of Tumaco.

April 7.—East-bound express train on the Hoosac Tunnel Railroad went over a precipice 130 feet high, near Greenfield, Massachusetts. Twelve persons killed and many injured.

April 14.—St. Cloud and Sauk Rapids, Minnesota, swept by a tornado. Seventy people killed and much property destroyed.

OBITUARY.

March 16.—In Annapolis, Maryland, Captain James J. Waddell, Commander of the Confederate ship *Shenandoah* during the civil war.

March 19.—In Berlin, Germany, Dr. Leopold Zunz, the distinguished Hebrew scholar, aged ninety-two years.

March 25.—In Paris, the Countess of Chambord, aged sixty-nine years.

March 27.—In London, Sir Henry Taylor, author of *Philip Van Artevelde*, aged eighty-six years.

March 28.—In London, Most Rev. Richard Chevenix Trench, D.D., for many years Archbishop of Dublin, in his seventy-ninth year.

April 5.—In London, Right Hon. William E. Forster, ex-Chief Secretary for Ireland, aged sixty-eight years.

April 10.—In Philadelphia, Hon. John Welsh, ex-Minister to England, aged eighty-one years.

April 12.—In St. Johnsbury, Vermont, Thaddeus Fairbanks, inventor, aged ninety years.

April 13.—At Niagara Falls, Ontario, Charles Humphrey Noyes, founder of the Oneida Community, in his seventy-fifth year.

Editor's Drawer.

AMONG the many disadvantages of civilization is the want of employment for women. In a natural state this does not arise. It is only when we get into an advanced stage of civilization that women begin to get out of employment, and become a burden to themselves and a source of solicitude to their friends. Therefore this want of employment seems to be an artificial want, and we are set thinking whether there is not something wrong in our social state that throws half our population out of working gear, and necessitates the formation of societies and attacks on social prejudice in order to give the gentler sex a sort of independent standing and an excuse for continuing in existence in this industrial age. Now in Tzintzoutzan there is no such want, and there never has been. The women have plenty to do there, and do it without loss of caste, and Tzintzoutzan is one of the oldest villages on this continent, and has in its ancient church a finer painting than can be found in any church in the United States. The intelligent reader does not need to be told that this village, on Lake Paztcuaro, was formerly the capital of the great state of Michoacan, and that it had a reputation in Europe long, long before there was a beer brewery at Ho-

boken. That was in the days when the good King Sinzicha Tangajuan Bulgo Caltzouzi reigned there, and looked down from his palace above the lake upon a prosperous community. The descendants of the subjects of King Caltzouzi still make handsome red pottery in this village—an industry carried on in nearly every house. Proper division of labor exists here. The men either draw the fish-nets or dig the clay. The women knead the clay and mould it—in short, make the pottery—while the men fire it, and transport it on their boats in big crates long distances to market. Nothing can be more felicitously domestic than to see the man squatting on the earth floor of his open-work abode, chatting with a comrade, each man wrapped to the nose in a serape, and crowned with a big hat that leaves nothing of the face visible except the black eyes, while the woman kneeling by the stone pats the red clay and deftly shapes it into plates and pans and jars. Her clothing is scant— would hardly do for Ocean Grove in the season —but a great mass of coal-black hair falls over her shoulders, and when the sun strikes it there is a red glow in it. This woman is cheerful; she smiles often, and when she smiles shows two rows of beautiful white teeth. It never has occurred to her that she is in want of employment, nor does that question disturb any man in the village concerning her. As she works she eats now and then a preserved piece of the maguey plant—a substance that looks like leather soaked in molasses. By-and-by she will crush the corn with two stones, and prepare and bake the tortilla. Some time during the day she will slip into the church, or into a little adobe chapel, and say a prayer to St. Helena, or before some other image, and at night curl up on a mat in her pottery and sleep the sleep of the employed. By-and-by, perhaps, the telegraph and the railway will come to Tzintzoutzan, and the question of the condition and position of women will be raised, and there will be at once a want of employment for women.

The Drawer expects to extract no moral out of this illustration. The season is at hand when the great mass of the unemployed, most of whom hope always to be unemployed (except, indeed, in good works), are about to take their spare time into the country to enjoy a long rest from the busy idleness of the winter. They are to leave Dante and Shakespeare and the clubs for the green fields and pastures new of Milton. Now some of these will go into the rural districts as missionaries—missionaries of the beautiful in dress, or missionaries of literary culture, or missionaries to build a hamlet chapel, with a bell in it and an embroidered pulpit cushion. All this is well. But with all these blessings they will diffuse all through the country a sense of the want of employment for women. The farmer's daughter, for instance, will suddenly discover that she has nothing to do, and that she ought to go somewhere else and do it; that is, get employment that is appropriate for woman. Now it seems to the Drawer, with all deference to civilization, that there is a great deal to do in the country, to say nothing of the villages. Did it ever strike the American mind that this United States, blessed as it is with better fruits, vegetables, meats, than any other portion of the globe, is conspicuous for poor cooking? That the most difficult thing for the traveller or the summer boarder to find is what is sometimes called a "good meal of victuals"? If all the women in the United States were to turn their attention to cooking for one year—the serious attention that they give to other things that make this world so nearly a paradise—there would be ample employment for every one of them. The Drawer yields to nobody in admiration of Dante and Browning, and the German club, and the history club, and Early English; but if the missionaries who are about to go into the country really desire to solve the problem of work for women, and to benefit their generation supremely, let them devote their summer to teaching the art of refined and wholesome cooking which they are supposed to enjoy in their city homes. If it is objected that they

themselves do not know how to cook, then there is the more reason why they should take up this branch of industry, and be able to carry into the country a blessing, instead of setting an example of discontent and the desire for some extra-domestic employment. We do waste and shorten our lives in the attempt to be good Christians on villanously cooked food. It has been said that nobody but a lady can properly prepare a piece of toast fit for another lady of dainty taste to eat. We leave one of the most important functions in life to the ignorant, the careless, the unclean. To reverse all this in our social state will be to set at rest forever the question of employment for women. It is true that many *chefs* have taken the position that it is impossible for women to attain distinction as cooks. We think that they under-estimate the artistic capability of womankind. If they will only turn their attention to this art, we shall in the course of a generation live as well as we dress in this country. They already do in Tzintzoutzan.

WHEN you are married, if a ring is required in the service, be sure the ring is where you can readily get hold of it. A widow of forty decided to marry to herself a boy of nineteen. The minister at the appropriate place asked the boy for the ring, that he might therewith endow the motherly bride with all his goods. The boy thrust his fingers in his right-hand waistcoat pocket; it seemed not to be there. He tried for it in his left-hand waistcoat pocket; his fingers clasped it not. "What can you have done with it?" asked the bride.

"Don't talk," said the boy-bridegroom. His face became eloquent with anxiety. He cast his eyes downward. He fell into a brown—or possibly a green—study. He became oblivious of his surroundings.

"Do not let us wait; we can be married without a ring," said the impatient bride.

"Don't bother me!" said the boy, who was busy exploring the realm of memory.

Some of the guests began to smile, others gave premonitions of laughter. The minister bit his lips till the blood started. Still the bridegroom pondered. At last he convulsively thrust his fingers into the corner of the right-hand pocket of his waistcoat, where he had tried for it first, and there he found the ring. The broken thread of ceremony was reunited, and the marriage knot completed. If the widow herself had taken charge of the ring, it would have been forth-coming on demand. Let your bride take care of the ring, if you are not old enough to take care of it yourself.

WHEN you go to get married, put as resolute a face as possible on the matter. Imitate the brave young country bridegroom. A party of young people went to a clergyman in central New York one evening; among the others a couple who were candidates for matrimony. They were married standing before the minister alone, the company being seated at the farther end of the room. "I have now the pleasure and honor of introducing the newly married couple to their friends; they await your greeting." No response was made; not a word was spoken. The silence became oppressive. At last the painful stillness was broken by the voice of a young countryman from the farthest corner, speaking to the bridegroom: "Jim, I say! yer did that extry. We hed an idee yer would be skittish when you was tied up; but, gosh! yer looked *bold as a sheep*."

APROPOS to the frequent divorces in some of our Western States, and the intimated fact that lawyers leave their professional card at the wedding reception, comes the following incident, related to "a country parson" by a physician, a brigade surgeon in the late war. It was after the Emancipation Proclamation, when the "contraband" began to realize his importance, and his diction took on a loftier tone. The place was Richmond, and the occasion a wedding at the most fashionable colored church. The groom and bride entered the packed church elegantly attired, and evidently realizing the profound sensation that attended their advent. The dusky clergyman in most solemn and dignified tone proceeded with the services amid a stillness that could be felt. The climax was reached with the suggestive *finale*, "I now pronounce you husband and wife *null and void*."

THE wife of a clergyman, on being interrogated as to the course her husband pursued when he had a poor sermon, naïvely replied, "Oh, he hollows it up good and loud."

IN the *Microcosm*, an Etonian monthly published when the Right Hon. George Canning was a student in Eton College, there is an article, of which Canning was the author, on "The Art of Swearing," in which the following occurs:
"I remember to have heard an honest Hibernian divine, whose zeal for morality would sometimes hurry him a little beyond the limits of good grammar or good sense, in the height of declamation declare that '*the little children that could neither speak nor walk ran about the streets blaspheming.*'"

A GOOD story was current in a quiet Vermont town, in which I was reared (writes a correspondent who got away from it early), that illustrates well the force of character and executive ability of the immediate descendants of our foremothers. It ran as follows:
The village school-house, built by the pioneers from Connecticut, fell at length into a state of dilapidation. Year after year the usual number of school meetings were holden,

but no vote was passed to build a new schoolhouse. The mothers murmured against the failure to provide suitable shelter for their children, but their complaints were unheeded. At last they determined to take the matter into their own hands, and formed and executed a plan of which only pioneer women would be capable.

A report was spread that wolves were prowling about a remote part of the town, and so many of the women were in a state of terror that a day was fixed upon for a wolf-hunt. The men rallied from far and near. I do not remember whether any wolves were killed or not. It is by no means unlikely, as they were far from scarce in those days. However that may be, when the hunters met at "the store" the next morning to talk the matter over there was another topic of interest, which threw the wolf-hunt quite out of mind—the school-house was in ruins!

I have always enjoyed the story without quite believing it true; but I fell in lately with a gentleman whose father was an honored citizen of the town, and in the course of the conversation I asked him if he ever heard the story, and whether there was any truth in it.

He smiled quietly, and said, almost too deliberately to satisfy my impatient interest, "I ought to know: I was an eye-witness of the whole affair."

He went on to say that though he was a small boy when the incident occurred, he remembered the circumstances well. His father was away from home, and his mother went out, giving him strict orders to remain in the house until her return. His curiosity was excited by the fact that she took with her a saw. He watched from the window, and saw one woman after another trudging up the street, They were carrying with them ropes, ladders. axes, and whatever implements each thought she could use most effectively in the destructive work.

At last he could endure the suspense no longer. He left the house, and crept along through the fields, hiding behind buildings and walls until he came to a high board fence in the rear of the school-house. Here he found a convenient crack, through which he watched the whole proceeding.

He laughed heartily as he recalled the scene —women chopping and sawing, pulling ropes and climbing ladders; women in every imaginable costume and attitude. He remembered particularly the presence of Mrs. Squire R——, whose husband was perhaps the most influential man in town, in spite of his blunt wit, which often hurt its luckless object.

"Thorough work they made of it," he said, in closing. "Not a post or beam was left in place, and even the timber was chopped into useless bits."

He remembered well the uproar at the store the next morning, and the towering rage in which Squire R—— went home, declaring that *his* wife never had anything to do with it. But from the time that he disappeared within his kitchen door he was never known to mention the subject.

Soon after the S——'s first baby was born Mrs. S—— went upstairs one evening and entered the room where her darling lay asleep. There she found her husband standing by the side of the crib and gazing earnestly at the child. As she stood still for a moment, touched by the sight, the tears filled her eyes, and she thought, "Oh, how dearly Charlie loves that boy!" Imagine the shock to her feelings when he suddenly turned toward her and exclaimed,

"My dear, it is incomprehensible to me how they can get up such a crib as that for two dollars and a half."

This story is told of Mr. Mac——, a well-known humorist residing at Rockliffe, Canada, on the Ottawa, who combines the duties of station agent and postmaster: Having acted for some time as master of mails at that place to the satisfaction of the community, but without pay, the M. P. for the district procured his appointment as postmaster, and the head of the department wrote him that he had much pleasure in confirming his position—"the salary to be the same as heretofore." This pleased Mac immensely, and he wrote to the chief acknowledging the honor. "I just wrote him," he says, "that I felt honored, as in duty bound, by the confirmation of my appointment, and was glad to know the salary was to be the same as heretofore, namely, nothing a year; for, says I, I'd h-h-h-hate like f-f-f-fury to have to p-p-p-pay anything!"

There was a famous character in Cincinnati in its earlier days whom we will disguise under the name of Walter Ferguson. Ferguson was of a convivial nature, and often indulged too deeply in the flowing bowl. He staggered home one time in the wee sma' hours, and was met at the door by his wife. Bracing himself against the door-jamb, he said,

"Mrs. Ferguson (hic), do you know what is the matter with me?"

"Yes, Mr. Ferguson," his wife replied—"you are drunk, sir, very drunk."

"Mrs. Ferguson (hic), you are correct," said he. "You guessed it the first time."

On another occasion Ferguson was wending his uncertain way homeward, sorely troubled in his mind over the curtain lecture he knew was in store for him, and casting about for some means of evading it. Suddenly a bright idea was evolved from his befuddled brain. He would slip quietly into the house, and get into bed without awaking his wife. Accordingly he carefully undressed in the lower hall, stole gently upstairs, and crept into bed, with his face turned toward the outside. He mentally congratulated himself upon his success thus far, and went to sleep. When he awoke in the morning he dared not look at his wife, and after lying still for a few minutes, and not hearing any noise from her, he concluded she was still asleep. He then determined to arise very quietly, carry his clothes into the hall, dress there, and go down town to business without waiting for breakfast. He was successful in this, and meeting the colored servant-girl down-stairs, he said,

"Eliza, you can tell your mistress I expect to be very busy to-day, and therefore I didn't stop to eat breakfast with her this morning."

"Law sakes, Mr. Ferguson!" said Eliza, "missus done gone 'way yesterday morning, and said she wouldn't be back till dis evening."

The family to which Johnnie Stubbs belonged lived a few years ago in Woonsocket, Rhode Island. It was rumored that the relations between Stubbs senior and his wife were not of the pleasantest, and Johnnie had doubtless heard many a family disputation, in which the father's strongest point against Mrs. Stubbs was that she was a Hicks when he raised her to her present title, and in which her collapsed and lachrymose ending was that she could expect no better treatment from one of the low-lived Stubbses. One day Johnnie took his fishing-pole and went down to the stream that ran near the house and commenced bobbing for eels. Just as he had fairly settled down to the sport, and was excited by his first nibble, he heard his mother's voice calling him loudly to come in. "There it is!" exclaimed the disgusted young philosopher. "The minnit the Stubbses begin ter fish, the Hickses begin ter holler."

Since a "Husband" has published this "memorial" in a country journal, there is no reason why it should not be passed along:

Rachel, wait until the clouds roll by,
Then we will meet thee in the sweet by-and-by,
Lida, Orlando, and I.

Methinks I see thee as beautiful as in days of yore;
But it is a dream, for thou has passed o'er.
Rachel, wait until the clouds roll by,
Then we will meet thee in the sweet by-and-by,
Lida, Orlando, and I.

A sister did care for thee in thy last hours;
May heaven be her lot as well as ours.
Rachel, wait until the clouds roll by,
Then we will meet thee in the sweet by-and-by,
Lida, Orlando, Debba, and I.

A brother-in-law also opened his heart and hand,
And bestowed on thee all the gifts of the land.
Rachel, wait until the clouds roll by,
Then we will meet thee in the sweet by-and-by,
Lida, Orlando, Debba, Charley, and I.

To err is human, to forgive is divine;
That was thy lot, and I hope it is mine.
Rachel, wait until the clouds roll by,
Then we will meet thee in the sweet by-and-by,
Lida, Orlando, Debba, Charley, Minnie, and I.

1. Mr. Bloomington wishes to join in the Doxology.

2. First he tries the bass.

3. Not succeeding in that, he decides to sing tenor. This is too high for him—

4. And he gives it up as a bad job.

NATHANIEL HAWTHORNE.
From a photograph by Mayall, London, 1860.—[See "Editor's Easy Chair."]

HARPER'S
NEW MONTHLY MAGAZINE.

VOL. LXXIII.   JULY, 1886.   No. CCCCXXXIV.

THEIR PILGRIMAGE.

BY CHARLES DUDLEY WARNER.

CHAPTER V.

WE have heard it said that one of the charms of Narragansett Pier is that you can see Newport from it. The summer dwellers at the Pier talk a good deal about liking it better than Newport; it is less artificial and more restful. The Newporters never say anything about the Pier. The Pier people say that it is not fair to judge it when you come direct from Newport, but the longer you stay there the better you like it; and if any too frank person admits that he would not stay in Narragansett a day if he could afford to live in Newport, he is suspected of aristocratic proclivities.

In a calm summer morning, such as our party of pilgrims chose for an excursion to the Pier, there is no prettier sail in the world than that out of the harbor, by Canonicut Island and Beaver-tail Light. It is a holiday harbor, all these seas are holiday seas—the yachts, the sail vessels, the puffing steamers, moving swiftly from one headland to another, or loafing about the blue smiling sea, are all on pleasure bent. The vagrant vessels that are idly watched from the rocks at the Pier may be coasters and freight schooners engaged seriously in trade, but they do not seem so. They are a part of the picture, always to be seen slowly dipping along in the horizon, and the impression is that they are manœuvred for show, arranged for picturesque effect, and that they are all taken in at night.

The visitors confessed when they landed that the Pier was a contrast to Newport. The shore below the landing is a line of broken, ragged, slimy rocks, as if they had been dumped there for a riprap wall. Fronting this unkempt shore is a line of barrack-like hotels, with a few cottages of the cheap sort. At the end of this row of hotels is a fine granite Casino, spacious, solid, with wide verandas, and a tennis-court—such a building as even Newport might envy. Then come more hotels, a cluster of cheap shops, and a long line of bath-houses facing a lovely curving beach. Bathing is the fashion, at the Pier, and everybody goes to the beach at noon. The spectators occupy chairs on the platform in front of the bath-houses, or sit under tents erected on the smooth sand. At high noon the scene is very lively, and even picturesque, for the ladies here dress for bathing with an intention of pleasing. It is generally supposed that the angels in heaven are not edified by this promiscuous bathing, and by the spectacle of a crowd of women tossing about in the surf, but an impartial angel would admit that many of the costumes here are becoming, and that the effect of the red and yellow caps, making a color line in the flashing rollers, is charming. It is true that there are odd figures in the shifting *mêlée*—one solid old gentleman, who had contrived to get his bathing suit on hind-side before, wandered along the ocean margin like a lost Ulysses; and that fat woman and fat man were never intended for this sort of exhibition; but taken all together, with its colors, and the silver flash of the breaking waves, the scene was exceedingly pretty. Not the least pretty part of it was the fringe of children tumbling on the beach, following the retreating waves, and flying from the incoming rollers with screams of delight. Children, indeed, are a characteristic of Narragansett Pier— children and mothers. It might be said to be a family place; it is a good deal so on Sundays, and occasionally when the "business men" come down from the cities to see how their wives and children get on at the hotels.

After the bathing it is the fashion to meet again at the Casino and take lunch —sometimes through a straw—and after dinner everybody goes for a stroll on the cliffs. This is a noble sea-promenade; with its handsome villas and magnificent rocks, a fair rival to Newport. The walk, as usually taken, is two or three miles along the bold rocky shore, but an ambitious pedestrian may continue it to the light on Point Judith. Nowhere on this coast are the rocks more imposing, and nowhere do they offer so many studies in color. The visitor's curiosity is excited by a massive granite tower which rises out of a mass of tangled woods planted on the crest of the hill, and his curiosity is not satisfied on nearer inspection, when he makes his way into this thick and gloomy forest, and finds a granite cottage near the tower, and the signs of neglect and wildness that might mark the home of a recluse. What is the object of this noble tower? If it was intended to adorn the landscape, why was it ruined by piercing it irregularly with square windows like those of a factory?

One has to hold himself back from being drawn into the history and romance of this Narragansett shore. Down below the bathing beach is the pretentious wooden pile called Canonicut, that already wears the air of tragedy. And here, at this end, is the mysterious tower, and an ugly unfinished dwelling-house of granite, with the legend "Druid's Dream" carved over the entrance door; and further inland, in a sandy and shrubby landscape, is Kendall Green, a private cemetery, with its granite monument, surrounded by heavy granite posts, every other one of which is hollowed in the top as a receptacle for food for birds. And one reads there these inscriptions: "Whatever their mode of faith, or creed, who feed the wandering birds, will themselves be fed." "Who helps the helpless, Heaven will help." This inland region, now apparently deserted and neglected, was once the seat of colonial aristocracy, who exercised a princely hospitality on their great plantations, exchanged visits and ran horses with the planters of Virginia and the Carolinas, and were known as far as Kentucky, and perhaps best known for their breed of Narragansett pacers. But let us get back to the shore.

In wandering along the cliff path in the afternoon, Irene and Mr. King were separated from the others, and unconsciously extended their stroll, looking for a comfortable seat in the rocks. The day was perfect. The sky had only a few fleecy, high-sailing clouds, and the great expanse of sea sparkled under the hectoring of a light breeze. The atmosphere was not too clear on the horizon for dreamy effects; all the headlands were softened and tinged with opalescent colors. As the light struck them, the sails which enlivened the scene were either dark spots or shining silver sheets on the delicate blue. At one spot on this shore rises a vast mass of detached rock, separated at low tide from the shore by irregular bowlders and a tiny thread of water. In search of a seat the two strollers made their way across this rivulet over the broken rocks, passed over the summit of the giant mass, and established themselves in a cavernous place close to the sea. Here was a natural seat, and the bulk of the seamed and colored ledge, rising above their heads and curving around them, shut them out of sight of the land, and left them alone with the dashing sea, and the gulls that circled and dipped their silver wings in their eager pursuit of prey. For a time neither spoke. Irene was looking seaward, and Mr. King, who had a lower seat, attentively watched the waves lapping the rocks at their feet, and the fine profile and trim figure of the girl against the sky. He thought he had never seen her looking more lovely, and yet he had a sense that she never was so remote from him. Here was an opportunity, to be sure, if he had anything to say, but some fine feeling of propriety restrained him from taking advantage of it. It might not be quite fair, in a place so secluded and remote, and with such sentimental influences, shut in as they were to the sea and the sky.

"It seems like a world by itself," she began, as in continuation of her thought. "They say you can see Gay Head Light from here."

"Yes. And Newport to the left there,

A CATAMARAN.

with its towers and trees rising out of the sea. It is quite like the Venice Lagoon in this light."

"I think I like Newport better at this distance. It is very poetical. I don't think I like what is called the world much, when I am close to it."

The remark seemed to ask for sympathy, and Mr. King ventured: "Are you willing to tell me, Miss Benson, why you have not seemed as happy at Newport as elsewhere? Pardon me; it is not an idle question." Irene, who seemed to be looking away beyond Gay Head, did not reply. "I should like to know if I have been in any way the cause of it. We agreed to be friends, and I think I have a friend's right to know." Still no response. "You must see—you must know," he went on, hurriedly, "that it cannot be a matter of indifference to me."

"It had better be," she said, as if speaking deliberately to herself, and still looking away. But suddenly she turned toward him, and the tears sprang to her eyes, and the words rushed out fiercely. "I wish I had never left Cyrusville. I wish I had never been abroad. I wish I had never been educated. It is all a wretched mistake."

King was unprepared for such a passionate outburst. It was like a rift in a cloud, through which he had a glimpse of her real life. Words of eager protest sprang to his lips, but, before they could be uttered, either her mood had changed or pride had come to the rescue, for she said: "How silly I am! Everybody has discontented days. Mr. King, please don't ask me such questions. If you want to be a friend, you will let me be unhappy now and then, and not say anything about it."

"But, Miss Benson—Irene—"

"There—'Miss Benson' will do very well."

"Well, Miss—Irene, then, there was something I wanted to say to you the other day in Paradise—"

"Look, Mr. King. Did you see that wave? I'm sure it is nearer our feet than when we sat down here."

"Oh, that's just an extra lift by the wind. I want to tell you. I must tell you that life—has all changed since I met you—Irene, I—"

"There! There's no mistake about that. The last wave came a foot higher than the other!"

King sprang up. "Perhaps it is the tide. I'll go and see." He ran up the rock, leaped across the fissures, and looked over on the side they had ascended. Sure enough, the tide was coming in. The stones on which they had stepped were covered, and a deep stream of water, rising with every pulsation of the sea, now, where there was only a rivulet before. He hastened back. "There is not a moment to lose. We are caught by the tide, and if we are not off in five minutes, we shall be prisoners here till the turn."

He helped her up the slope and over the chasm. The way was very plain when they came on, but now he could not find it. At the end of every attempt was a precipice. And the water was rising. A little girl on the shore shouted to them to follow along a ledge she pointed out, then descend between two bowlders to the ford. Precious minutes were lost in accomplishing this circuitous descent, and then they found the stepping-stones under water, and the sea-weed swishing about the slippery rocks with the incoming tide. It was a ridiculous position for lovers, or even "friends"—ridiculous because it had no element of danger except the ignominy of getting wet. If there was any heroism in seizing Irene before she could protest, stumbling with his burden among the slimy rocks, and depositing her, with only wet shoes, on the shore, Mr. King shared it, and gained the title of "Life-preserver." The adventure ended with a laugh.

The day after the discovery and exploration of Narragansett, Mr. King spent the morning with his cousin at the Casino. It was so pleasant that he wondered he had not gone there oftener, and that so few people frequented it. Was it that the cottagers were too strong for the

Casino also, which was built for the recreation of the cottagers, and that they found when it came to the test that they could not with comfort come into any sort of contact with popular life? It is not large, but no summer resort in Europe has a prettier place for lounging and re-union. None have such an air of refinement and exclusiveness. Indeed, one of the chief attractions and entertainments in the foreign casinos and conversation-halls is the mingling there of all sorts of peoples, and the animation arising from diversity of conditions. This popular commingling in pleasure resorts is safe enough in aristocratic countries, but it will not answer in a republic.

The Newport Casino is in the nature of a club of the best society. The building and grounds express the most refined taste. Exteriorly the house is a long, low, Queen Anne cottage, with brilliant shops on the ground-floor, and above, behind the wooded balconies, is the club-room. The tint of the shingled front is brown, and all the colors are low and blended. Within, the court is a mediæval surprise. It is a miniature castle, such as might serve for an opera scene. An extension of the galleries, an ombre, completes the circle around a plot of close-clipped green turf. The house itself is all balconies, galleries, odd windows half overgrown and hidden by ivy, and a large gilt clock face adds a touch of piquancy to the antique charm of the façade. Beyond the first court is a more spacious and less artificial lawn, set with fine trees, and at the bottom of it is the brown building containing ball-room and theatre, bowling-alley and closed tennis-court, and at an angle with the second lawn is a pretty field for lawn-tennis. Here the tournaments are held, and on these occasions, and on ball nights, the Casino is thronged.

If the Casino is then so exclusive, why is it not more used as a rendezvous and lounging-place? Alas! it must be admitted that it is not exclusive. By an astonishing concession in the organization any person can gain admittance by paying the sum of fifty cents. This tax is sufficient to exclude the deserving poor, but it is only an inducement to the vulgar rich, and it is even broken down by the prodigal excursionist, who commonly sets out from home with the intention of being reckless for one day.

CAUGHT BY THE TIDE.

It is easy to see, therefore, why the charm of this delightful place is tarnished.

The band was playing this morning—not rink music—when Mrs. Glow and King entered and took chairs on the ombre. It was a very pretty scene: more people were present than usual of a morning. Groups of half a dozen had drawn chairs together here and there, and were chatting and laughing; two or three exceedingly well preserved old bachelors, in the smart rough morning suits of the period, were entertaining their lady friends with club and horse talk; several old gentlemen were reading newspapers; and there were some dowager-looking mammas, and seated by them their cold, beautiful, high-bred daughters, who wore their visible exclusiveness like a garment, and contrasted with some other young ladies who were promenading with English-looking young men in flannel suits, who might be described as lawn-tennis young ladies conscious of being in the mode, but wanting the indescribable atmosphere of high breeding. Doubtless the most interesting persons to the student of human life were the young fellows in lawn-tennis suits. They had the languid air, which is so attractive at their age, of having found out life, and decided that it is a bore. Nothing is worth making an exertion about, not even pleasure. They had come, one could see, to a just appreciation of their value in life, and understood quite well the social manners of the mammas and girls in whose company they condescended to dawdle and make, languidly, cynical observations. They had, in truth, the manner of playing at fashion and elegance as in a stage comedy. King could not help thinking there was something theatrical about them altogether, and he fancied that when he saw them in their "traps" on the Avenue they were going through the motions for show and not for enjoyment. Probably King was mistaken in all this, having been abroad so long that he did not understand the evolution of the American gilded youth.

In a pause of the music Mrs. Bartlett Glow and Mr. King were standing with a group near the steps that led down to the inner lawn. Among them were the Postlethwaite girls, whose beauty and audacity made such a sensation in Washington last winter. They were bantering Mr. King about his Narragansett excursion, his cousin having maliciously given the party a hint of his encounter with the tide at the Pier. Just at this moment, happening to glance across the lawn, he saw the Bensons coming toward the steps. Mrs. Benson waddling over the grass and beaming toward the group, Mr. Benson carrying her shawl and looking as if he had been hired by the day, and Irene listlessly following. Mrs. Glow saw them at the same moment, but gave no other sign of her knowledge than by striking into the banter with more animation. Mr. King intended at once to detach himself and advance to meet the Bensons. But he could not rudely break away from the unfinished sentence of the younger Postlethwaite girl, and the instant that was concluded, as luck would have it, an elderly lady joined the group, and Mrs. Glow went through the formal ceremony of introducing King to her. He hardly knew how it happened, only that he made a hasty bow to the Bensons as he was shaking hands with the ceremonious old lady, and they had gone to the door of exit. He gave a little start as if to follow them, which Mrs. Glow noticed with a laugh and the remark, "You can catch them if you run," and then he weakly submitted to his fate. After all, it was only an accident, which would hardly need a word of explanation. But what Irene saw was this: a distant nod from Mrs. Glow, a cool survey and stare from the Postlethwaite girls, and the failure of Mr. King to recognize his friends any further than by an indifferent bow as he turned to speak to another lady. In the raw state of her sensitiveness she felt all this as a terrible and perhaps intended humiliation.

King did not return to the hotel till evening, and then he sent up his card to the Bensons. Word came back that the ladies were packing, and must be excused. He stood at the office desk and wrote a hasty note to Irene, attempting an expla-

nation of what might seem to her a rudeness, and asked that he might see her a moment. And then he paced the corridor waiting for a reply. In his impatience the fifteen minutes that he waited seemed an hour. Then a bell-boy handed him this note:

"DEAR MR. KING, — No explanation whatever was needed. We never shall forget your kindness. Good-by.
                         "IRENE BENSON."

He folded the note carefully and put it in his breast pocket, took it out and re-read it, lingering over the fine and dainty signature, put it back again, and walked out upon the piazza. It was a divine night, soft and sweet-scented, and all the rustling trees were luminous in the electric light. From a window opening upon a balcony overhead came the clear notes of a barytone voice enunciating the old-fashioned words of an English ballad, the refrain of which expressed hopeless separation.

The eastern coast, with its ragged outline of bays, headlands, indentations, islands, capes, and sand-spits, from Watch Hill, a favorite breezy resort, to Mount Desert, presents an almost continued chain of hotels and summer cottages. In fact, the same may be said of the whole Atlantic front from Mount Desert down to Cape May. It is to the traveller an amazing spectacle. The American people can no longer be reproached for not taking any summer recreation. The amount of money invested to meet the requirements of this vacation idleness is enormous. When one is on the coast in July or August it seems as if the whole fifty millions of people had come down to lie on the rocks, wade in the sand, and dip into the sea. But this is not the case. These crowds are only a fringe of the pleasure-seeking population. In all the mountain regions from North Carolina to the Adirondacks and the White Hills, along the St. Lawrence and the lakes away up to the Northwest, in every elevated village, on every mountain-side, about every pond, lake, and clear stream, in the wilderness and the secluded farm-house, one encounters the traveller, the summer boarder, the vacation idler, one is scarcely out of sight of the American flag flying over a summer resort. In no other nation, probably, is there such a general summer hegira, no other offers on such a vast scale such va-

"MINISTERING ANGELS" AT THE SEA-SIDE HOTEL.

riety of entertainment, and it is needless to say that history presents no parallel to this general movement of a people for a summer outing. Yet it is no doubt true that statistics, which always upset a broad, generous statement such as I have made, would show that the majority of people stay at home in the summer, and it is undeniable that the vexing question for everybody is where to go in July and August.

But there are resorts suited to all tastes, and to the economical as well as to the extravagant. Perhaps the strongest impression one has in visiting the various watering-places in the summer-time is that the multitudes of every-day folk are abroad in search of enjoyment. On the New Bedford boat for Martha's Vineyard our little party of tourists sailed quite away from Newport life—Stanhope with mingled depression and relief, the artist with some shrinking from contact with anything common, while Marion stood upon the bow beside her uncle, inhaling the salt breeze, regarding the lovely fleeting shores, her cheeks glowing and her eyes sparkling with enjoyment. The passengers and scene, Stanhope was thinking, were typically New England, until the boat made a landing at Naushon Island, when he was reminded somehow of Scotland, as much perhaps by the wild, furzy appearance of the island as by the "gentle-folks" who went ashore.

The boat lingered for the further disembarkation of a number of horses and carriages, with a piano and a cow. There was a farmer's lodge at the landing, and over the rocks and amid the trees the picturesque roof of the villa of the sole proprietor of the island appeared, and gave a feudal aspect to the domain. The sweet grass affords good picking for sheep, and besides the sheep the owner raises deer, which are destined to be chased and shot in the autumn.

The artist noted that there were several distinct types of women on board, besides the common straight-waisted, flat-chested variety. One girl, who was alone, with a city air, a neat firm figure, in a travelling suit of elegant simplicity, was fond of taking attitudes about the rails, and watching the effect produced on the spectators. There was a blue-eyed, sharp-faced, rather loose-jointed young girl, who had the manner of being familiar with the boat, and talked readily and freely with anybody, keeping an eye occasionally on her sister of eight years, a child with a serious little face in a poke-bonnet, who used the language of a young lady of sixteen, and seemed also abundantly able to take care of herself. What this mite of a child wants of all things, she confesses, is a pug-faced dog. Presently she sees one come on board in the arms of a young lady at Holmes' Holl. "No," she says, "I won't ask her for it; the lady wouldn't give it to me, and I wouldn't waste my breath;" but she draws near to the dog, and regards it with rapt attention. The owner of the dog is a very pretty black-eyed girl with banged hair, who prattles about herself and her dog with perfect freedom. She is staying at Cottage City, lives at Worcester, has been up to Boston to meet and bring down her dog, without which she couldn't live another minute. "Perhaps," she says, "you know Dr. Ridger-

ton, in Worcester; he's my brother. Don't know him? He's a chiropodist."

These girls are all types of the skating rink—an institution which is beginning to express itself in American manners.

The band was playing on the pier when the steamer landed at Cottage City (or Ball's Bluff, as it was formerly called), and the pier and the gallery leading to it were crowded with spectators, mostly women—a pleasing mingling of the skating-rink and sewing-circle varieties—and gayety was apparently about setting in with the dusk. The rink and the go-round opposite the hotel were in full tilt. After supper King and Forbes took a cursory view of this strange encampment, walking through the streets of fantastic tiny cottages among the scrub oaks, and saw something of family life in the painted little boxes, whose wide-open front doors gave to view the whole domestic economy, including the bed, centre table, and melodeon. They strolled also on the elevated plank promenade by the beach, encountering now and then a couple enjoying the lovely night. Music abounded. The circus-pumping strains burst out of the rink, calling to a gay and perhaps dissolute life. The band in the nearly empty hotel parlor, in a mournful mood, was wooing the guests who did not come to a soothing tune, something like China— "Why do we mourn departed friends?" A procession of lasses coming up the board walk, advancing out of the shadows of night, was heard afar off as the stalwart singers strode on, chanting in high nasal voices that lovely hymn, which seems to suit the rink as well as the night promenade and the camp-meeting:

" We shall me—um um—we shall me-eet, me-eet—
　　um um—we shall meet,
　In the sweet by-am-by, by-am-by—um um—
　　by-am-by,
　On the bu-u-u-u—on the bu-u-u-u—on the bu-
　　te-ful shore."

In the morning this fairy-like settlement, with its flimsy and eccentric architecture, took on more the appearance of reality. The season was late, as usual, and the hotels were still waiting for the crowds that seem to prefer to wait and make a rushing carnival of August, but the tiny cottages were nearly all occupied. At 10 A.M. the band was playing in the three-story pagoda sort of tower at the bathing-place, and the three stories were crowded with female spectators.

Below, under the bank, is a long array of bath-houses, and the shallow water was alive with floundering and screaming bathers. Anchored a little out was a raft, from which men and boys and a few

thing thought of it, as old Pepys would have said, although many of the tightly fitting costumes left less to the imagination than would have been desired by a poet describing the scene as a phase of

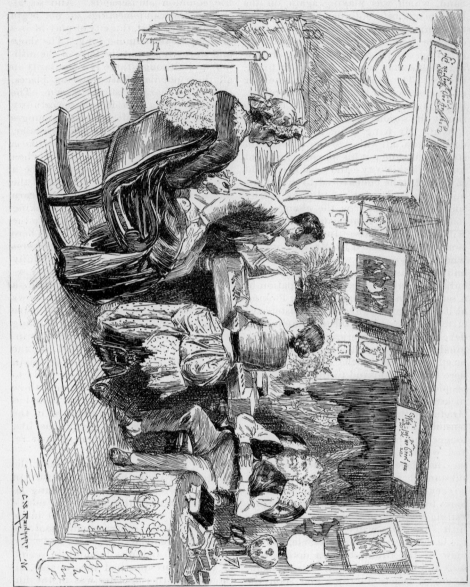

AN INTERIOR.

venturesome girls were diving, displaying the human form in graceful curves. The crowd was an immensely good-humored one, and enjoyed itself. The sexes mingled together in the water, and no-

the *comédie humaine*. The band, having played out its hour, trudged back to the hotel pier to toot while the noon steamboat landed its passengers, in order to impress the new arrivals with the mad joyousness of the place. The crowd gathered on the high gallery at the end of the pier added to this effect of reckless holiday enjoyment. Miss Lamont was infected with this gayety, and took a great deal of interest in this peripatetic band, which was playing again on the hotel piazza before dinner, with a sort of mechanical hilariousness. The rink band opposite kept up a lively competition, grinding out its go-round music, imparting, if one may say so, a glamour to existence. The band is on hand at the pier at four o'clock to toot again, and presently off, tramping to some other hotel to satisfy the serious pleasure of this people.

While Mr. King could not help wondering how all this curious life would strike Irene—he put his lonesomeness and longing in this way—and what she would say about it, he endeavored to divert his mind by a study of the conditions, and by some philosophizing on the change that had come over American summer life within a few years. In his investigations he was assisted by Mr. De Long, to whom this social life was absolutely new, and who was disposed to regard it as peculiarly Yankee—the staid dissipation of a serious-minded people. King, looking at it more broadly, found this pasteboard city by the sea one of the most interesting developments of American life. The original nucleus was the Methodist camp-meeting, which, in the season, brought here twenty thousand to thirty thousand people at a time, who camped and picnicked in a somewhat primitive style. Gradually the people who came here ostensibly for religious exercises made a longer and more permanent occupation, and, without losing its ephemeral character, the place grew and demanded more substantial accommodations. The spot is very attractive. Although the shore looks to the east, and does not get the prevailing southern breeze, and the beach has little surf, both water and air are mild, the bathing is safe and agreeable, and the view of the illimitable sea dotted with sails and fishing-boats is always pleasing. A crowd begets a crowd, and soon the world's people made a city larger than the original one, and still more fantastic, by the aid of paint and the jig-saw. The tent, however, is the type of all the dwelling-houses. The hotels, restaurants, and shops follow the usual order of flamboyant sea-side architecture. After a time

the Baptists established a camp ground on the bluffs on the opposite side of the inlet. The world's people brought in the commercial element in the way of fancy shops for the sale of all manner of cheap and bizarre "notions," and introduced the common amusements. And so, although the camp-meetings do not begin till late in August, this city of play-houses is occupied the summer long. The shops and shows represent the taste of the million, and although there is a similarity in all these popular coast watering-places, each has a characteristic of its own. The foreigner has a considerable opportunity of studying family life, whether he lounges through the narrow, sometimes circular, streets by night, when it appears like a fairy encampment, or by daylight, when there is no illusion. It seems to be a point of etiquette to show as much of the interiors as possible, and one can learn something of cooking and bed-making and mending, and the art of doing up the back hair. The photographer revels here in pictorial opportunities. The pictures of these *bizarre* cottages, with the family and friends seated in front, show very serious groups. One of the Tabernacle—a vast iron hood or dome erected over rows of benches that will seat two or three thousand people—represents the building when it is packed with an audience intent upon the preacher. Most of the faces are of a grave, severe type, plain and good, of the sort of people ready to die for a notion. The impression of these photographs is that these people abandon themselves soberly to the pleasures of the sea and of this packed, gregarious life, and get solid enjoyment out of their recreation.

Here, as elsewhere on the coast, the greater part of the population consists of women and children, and the young ladies complain of the absence of men—and, indeed, something is desirable in society besides the superannuated and the boys in roundabouts.

The artist and Miss Lamont, in search of the picturesque, had the courage, although the thermometer was in the humor to climb up to ninety degrees, to explore the Baptist encampment. They were not rewarded by anything new except at the landing, where, behind the bath-houses, the bathing suits were hung out to dry, and presented a comical spectacle, the humor of which seemed to be lost upon all except themselves. It was such a caricature of humanity! The suits hanging upon the line and distended by the wind presented the appearance of headless, bloated forms, fat men and fat women, kicking in the breeze, and vainly trying to climb over the line. It was probably merely fancy, but they declared and fantastic saw-work, explained, in a measure, the design of Providence in permitting this part of the world to be discovered; but the sandy interior had to be reconciled to the deeper divine intention, by a trial of patience and the cultivation of the heroic virtues evoked by a struggle for existence, of fitting men and women

"A CARICATURE OF HUMANITY."

that these images seemed larger, more bloated, and much livelier than those displayed on the Cottage City side. When travellers can be entertained by trifles of this kind it shows that there is an absence of more serious amusement. And, indeed, although people were not wanting, and music was in the air, and the bicycle and the tricycle stable was well patronized by men and women, and the noon bathing was well attended, it was evident that the life of Cottage City was not in full swing by the middle of July.

The morning on which our tourists took the steamer for Holmes' Holl the sea lay shimmering in the heat, only stirred a little by the land breeze, and it needed all the invigoration of the short ocean voyage to brace them up for the intolerably hot and dusty ride in the cars through the sandy part of Massachusetts. So long as the train kept by the indented shore the route was fairly picturesque; all along Buzzard Bay and Onset Bay and Monument Beach little cottages, gay with paint

for a better country. The travellers were confirmed, however, in their theory of the effect of a sandy country upon the human figure. This is not a juicy land, if the expression can be tolerated, any more than the sandy parts of New Jersey, and its unsympathetic dryness is favorable to the production—one can hardly say development—of the lean, enduring, flat-chested, and angular style of woman.

In order to reach Plymouth a wait of a couple of hours was necessary at one of the sleepy but historic villages. There was here no tavern, no restaurant, and nobody appeared to have any license to sell anything for the refreshment of the travellers. But at some distance from the station, in a two-roomed dwelling-house, a good woman was found who was willing to cook a meal of victuals, as she explained, and a sign on her front door attested, she had a right to do. What was at the bottom of the local prejudice against letting the wayfaring man have anything to eat and drink, the party could not ascertain, but the defiant air of the woman revealed the fact that there was such a prejudice. She was a noble, robust, gigantic specimen of her sex, well formed, strong as an ox, with a resolute jaw, and she talked, through tightly closed teeth, in an aggressive manner. Dinner was ordered, and the party strolled about the village pending its preparation; but it was not ready when they returned. "I ain't goin' to cook no victuals," the woman explained, not ungraciously, "till I know folks is goin' to eat it." Knowledge of the world had made her justly cautious. She intended to set out a good meal, and she had the true housewife's desire that it should be eaten, that there should be enough of it, and that the guests should like it. When she waited on the table she displayed a pair of arms that would

LAST GLIMPSE OF MARTHA'S VINEYARD.

THE MODEL HUSBAND.

discourage any approach to familiarity, and disincline a timid person to ask twice for pie; but in point of fact, as soon as the party became her *bona fide* guests, she was royally hospitable, and only displayed anxiety lest they should not eat enough.

"I like folks to be up and down and square," she began saying as she vigilantly watched the effect of her culinary skill upon the awed little party. "Yes, I've got a regular hotel license; you bet I have. There's been folks lawed in this town for sellin' a meal of victuals and not having one. I ain't goin' to be taken in by anybody. I warn't raised in New Hampshire to be scared by these Massachusetts

folks. No, I hain't got a girl now. I had one a spell, but I'd rather do my own work. You never knew what a girl was doin' or would do. After she'd left I found a broken plate tucked into the ash-barrel. Sho! you can't depend on a girl. Yes, I've got a husband. It's easier to manage him. Well, I tell you a husband is better than a girl. When you tell him to do anything, you know it's goin' to be done. He's always about, never loafin' round; he can take right hold and wash dishes, and fetch water, and anything."

King went into the kitchen after dinner and saw this model husband, who had the faculty of making himself generally useful, holding a baby on one arm, and stirring something in a pot on the stove with the other. He looked hot but resigned. There has been so much said about the position of men in Massachusetts that the travellers were glad of this evidence that husbands are beginning to be appreciated. Under proper training they are acknowledged to be "better than girls."

It was late afternoon when they reached the quiet haven of Plymouth—a place where it is apparently always afternoon, a place of memory and reminiscences, where the whole effort of the population is to hear and to tell some old thing. As the railway ends there, there is no danger of being carried beyond, and the train slowly ceases motion, and stands still in the midst of a great and welcome silence. Peace fell upon the travellers like a garment, and although they had as much difficulty in landing their baggage as the early Pilgrims had in getting theirs ashore, the circumstance was not able to disquiet them much. It seemed natural that their trunks should go astray on some of the inextricably interlocked and branching railways, and they had no doubt that when they had made the tour of the State they would be discharged, as they finally were, into this *cul-de-sac*.

The Pilgrims have made so much noise in the world, and so powerfully affected the continent, that our tourists were surprised to find they had landed in such a quiet place, and that the spirit they have left behind them is one of such tranquillity. The village has a charm all its own. The houses are old-fashioned and square, with colonial doors and porches, irregularly aligned on the main street, which is arched by ancient and stately elms. In the spacious door-yards the lindens have had room and time to expand, and in the beds of bloom the flowers, if not the very ones that our grandmothers planted, are the sorts that they loved. Showing that the town has grown in sympathy with human needs and eccentricities, and is not the work of a surveyor, the streets are irregular, forming picturesque angles and open spaces. Nothing could be imagined in greater contrast to a Western town, and a good part of the satisfaction our tourists experienced was in the absence of anything Western or "Queen Anne" in the architecture.

In the Pilgrim Hall—a stone structure with an incongruous wooden-pillared front—they came into the very presence of the early worthies, saw their portraits on the walls, sat in their chairs, admired the solidity of their shoes, and imbued themselves with the spirit of the relics of their heroic, uncomfortable lives. In the town there was nothing to disturb the serenity of mind acquired by this communion. The Puritan interdict of unseemly excitement still prevailed, and the streets were silent; the artist, who could compare it with the placidity of Holland towns, declared that he never walked in a village so silent; there was no loud talking; and even the children played without noise, like little Pilgrims. God bless such children, and increase their numbers! It might have been the approach of Sunday —if Sunday is still regarded in eastern Massachusetts—that caused this hush, for it was now toward sunset on Saturday, and the inhabitants were washing the windows and the fronts of the houses with the hose, showing how cleanliness is next to silence.

Possessed with the spirit of peace, our tourists, whose souls had been vexed with the passions of many watering-places, walked down Leyden Street (the first that was laid out), saw the site of the first house, and turned round Carver Street, walking lingeringly, so as not to break the spell, out upon the hill—Cole's Hill— where the dead during the first fearful winter were buried. This has been converted into a beautiful esplanade, grassed and gravelled and furnished with seats, and overlooks the old wharves, some coal schooners, and shabby buildings, on one of which is a sign informing the reckless that they can obtain there clam chowder and ice-cream, and the ugly, heavy granite canopy erected over the "Rock." No reverent person can see this rock for the first time without a thrill of excitement. It has the date of 1620 cut in it, and it is a good deal cracked and patched up, as if it had been much landed on, but there it is, and there it will remain a witness to a great historic event, unless somebody takes a notion to cart it off uptown again. It is said to rest on another rock, of which it formed a part before its unfortunate journey, and that lower rock, as everybody knows, rests upon the immutable principle of self-government. The stone lies too far from the water to enable anybody to land on it now, and it is protected from vandalism by an iron grating. The sentiment of the hour was disturbed by the advent of the members of a base-ball nine, who wondered why the Pilgrims did not land on the wharf, and, while thrusting their feet through the grating in a commendable desire to touch the sacred rock, expressed a doubt whether the feet of the Pilgrims were small enough to slip through the grating and land on the stone. It seems that there is nothing safe from the irreverence of American youth.

Has any other coast town besides Plymouth had the good sense and taste to utilize such an elevation by the water-side as an esplanade? It is a most charming feature of the village, and gives it what we call a foreign air. It was very lovely in the after-glow and at moonrise. Staid citizens with their families occupied the benches, groups were chatting under the spreading elm-tree at the north entrance, and young maidens in white muslin promenaded, looking seaward, as was the wont of Puritan maidens, watching a receding or coming *Mayflower*. But there were no loud talking, no laughter, no outbursts of merriment from the children. Such nice, quiet little children, all ready to be transplanted to the Puritan heaven! It was high tide, and all the bay was silvery with a tinge of color from the glowing sky. The long curved sand-spit—which was heavily wooded when the Pilgrims landed—was silvery also, and upon its northern tip glowed the white sparkle in the light-house like the evening-star. To the north, over the smooth pink water speckled with white sails, rose Captain Hill, in Duxbury, bearing the monument to Miles Standish. The three islands in sight, Clarke's (where the Pilgrims had a sermon on the first Sunday), Seguish, and Garnett (showing now twin white lights), appear like one island intersected by thin lines of blue water. The effect of these ribbons of alternate sand and water, of the lights and the ocean (or Great Bay) beyond, was exquisite.

Even the unobtrusive tavern at the rear of the esplanade, ancient, feebly lighted, and inviting, added something to the picturesqueness of the scene. The old tree by the gate—an English elm—illuminated by the street lamps and the moon, had a mysterious appearance, and the tourists were not surprised to learn that it has a romantic history. The story is that the twig or sapling from which it grew was brought over from England by a lover as a present to his mistress, that the lovers quarrelled almost immediately, that the girl in a pet threw it out of the window when she sent her lover out of the door, and that another man picked it up and planted it where it now grows. The legend provokes a good many questions. One would like to know whether this was the first case of female rebellion in Massachusetts against the common-law right of a man to correct a woman with a stick not thicker than his little finger—a rebellion which has resulted in the position of man as the tourists saw him where the New Hampshire Amazon gave them a meal of victuals—and whether the girl married the man who planted the twig, and, if so, whether he did not regret that he had not kept it by him.

This is a world of illusions. By daylight, when the tide was out, the pretty silver bay of the night before was a mud flat, and the tourists looking over it from Monument Hill lost some of their respect for the Pilgrim sagacity in selecting a landing-place. They had ascended the hill for a nearer view of the monument, King with a reverent wish to read the name of his *Mayflower* ancestor on the tablet, the others in a spirit of cold, New York criticism, for they thought the structure, which is still unfinished, would look uglier near at hand than at a distance. And it does. It is a pile of granite masonry surmounted by symbolic figures.

"It is such an unsympathetic, tasteless-looking thing!" said Miss Lamont. "Do you think it is the worst in the country?"

"I wouldn't like to say that," replied the artist, "when the competition in this direction is so lively. But just look at the drawing" (holding up his pencil with which he had intended to sketch it). "If it were quaint, now, or rude, or archaic, it might be in keeping, but bad drawing is just vulgar. I should think it had been designed by a carpenter, and executed by a stone-mason."

"Yes," said the little Lamont, who always fell in with the most abominable opinions the artist expressed; "it ought to have been made of wood, and painted and sanded."

"You will please remember," mildly suggested King, who had found the name he was in search of, "that you are trampling on my ancestral sensibilities, as might be expected of those who have no ancestors who ever landed or ever were buried anywhere in particular. I look at the commemorative spirit rather than the execution of the monument."

"So do I," retorted the girl; "and if the Pilgrims landed in such a vulgar, ostentatious spirit as this, I'm glad my name is not on the tablet."

The party were in a better mood when they had climbed up Burial Hill, back of the meeting-house, and sat down on one of the convenient benches amid the ancient gravestones, and looked upon the wide and magnificent prospect. A soft summer wind waved a little the long gray grass of the ancient resting-place, and seemed to whisper peace to the weary generation that lay there. What struggles, what heroisms, the names on the stones recalled! Here had stood the first fort of 1620, and here the watch-tower of 1642, from the top of which the warder espied the lurking savage, or hailed the expected ship from England. How much of history this view recalled, and what pathos of human life these graves made real! Read the names of those buried a couple of centuries ago—captains, elders, ministers, governors, wives well beloved, children a span long, maidens in the blush of womanhood —half the tender inscriptions are illegible; the stones are broken, sunk, slanting to fall. What a pitiful attempt to keep the world mindful of the departed!

CHAPTER VII.

MR. STANHOPE KING was not in very good spirits. Even Boston did not make him cheerful. He was half annoyed to see the artist and Miss Lamont drifting along in such laughing good-humor with the world, as if a summer holiday was just a holiday without any consequences or responsibilities. It was to him a serious affair ever since that unsatisfactory note from Miss Benson; somehow the summer had lost its sparkle. And yet was it not preposterous that a girl, just a single girl, should have the power to change for a man the aspect of a whole coast—by her presence to make it iridescent with beauty, and by her absence to take all the life out of it? And a simple girl from Ohio! She was not by any means the prettiest girl in the Newport Casino that morning, but it

was her figure that he remembered, and it was the look of hurt sensibility in her eyes that staid with him. He resented the attitude of the Casino toward her, and he hated himself for his share in it. He would write to her. He composed letter after letter in his mind, which he did not put on paper. How many millions of letters are composed in this way! It is a favorite occupation of imaginative people; and as they say that no thoughts or mental impressions are ever lost, but are all registered— made, as it were, on a "dry plate," to be developed hereafter—what a vast correspondence must be lying in the next world, in the Dead-letter Office there, waiting for the persons to whom it is addressed, who will all receive it and read it some day! How unpleasant and absurd it will be to read, much of it! I intend to be careful, for my part, about composing letters of this sort hereafter. Irene, I dare say, will find a great many of them from Mr. King, thought out in those days. But he mailed none of them to her. What should he say? Should he tell her that he didn't mind if her parents were what Mrs. Bartlett Glow called "impossible"? If he attempted any explanation, would it not involve the offensive supposition that his social rank was different from hers? Even if he convinced her that he recognized no caste in American society, what could remove from her mind the somewhat morbid impression that her education had put her in a false position? His love probably could not shield her from mortification in a society which, though indefinable in its limits and code, is an entity more vividly felt than the government of the United States.

"Don't you think the whole social atmosphere has changed," Miss Lamont suddenly asked, as they were running along in the train toward Manchester-by-the-Sea, "since we got north of Boston? I seem to find it so. Don't you think it's more refined, and, don't you know, sort of cultivated, and subdued, and Boston? You notice the gentlemen who get out at all these stations, to go to their country houses, how highly civilized they look, and ineffably respectable and intellectual, all of them presidents of colleges, and substantial bank directors, and possible ambassadors, and of a social cult (isn't that the word?) uniting brains and gentle manners."

"You must have been reading the Boston newspapers; you have hit the idea

"LOOKING SEAWARD AS WAS THE WONT OF PURITAN MAIDENS."

prevalent in these parts, at any rate. I was, however, reminded myself of an afternoon train out of London, say into Surrey, on which you are apt to encounter about as high a type of civilized men as anywhere."

"And you think this is different from a train out of New York?" asked the artist.

"Yes. New York is more mixed. No one train has this kind of tone. You see there more of the broker type and poli-

tician type, smarter apparel and nervous manners, but, dear me, not this high moral and intellectual respectability."

"Well," said the artist, "I'm changing my mind about this country. I didn't expect so much variety. I thought that all the watering-places would be pretty much alike, and that we should see the same people everywhere. But the people are quite as varied as the scenery."

"There you touch a deep question—the

refining or the vulgarizing influence of man upon nature, and the opposite. Now did the summer Bostonians make this coast refined, or did this coast refine the Bostonians who summer here ?''

"Well, this is primarily an artistic coast; I feel the influence of it; there is a refined beauty in all the lines, and residents have not vulgarized it much. But I wonder what Boston could have done for the Jersey coast ?''

In the midst of this high and useless conversation they came to the Masconomo House, a sort of concession, in this region of noble villas and private parks, to the popular desire to get to the sea. It is a long low house, with very broad passages below and above, which give lightness and cheerfulness to the interior, and each of the four corners of the entrance hall has a fireplace. The pillars of the front and back piazzas are pine stems stained, with the natural branches cut in unequal lengths, and look like the stumps for the bears to climb in the pit at Berne. Set up originally with the bark on, the worms worked underneath it in secret, at a novel sort of decoration, until the bark came off and exposed the stems most beautifully vermiculated, giving the effect of fine carving. Back of the house a meadow slopes down to a little beach in a curved bay that has rocky headlands, and is defended in part by islands of rock. The whole aspect of the place is peaceful. The hotel does not assert itself very loudly, and if occasionally transient guests appear with flash manners, they do not affect the general tone of the region.

One finds, indeed, nature and social life happily blended, the exclusiveness being rather protective than offensive. The special charm of this piece of coast is that it is bold, much broken and indented, precipices fronting the waves, promontories jutting out, high rocky points commanding extensive views, wild and picturesque, and yet softened by color and graceful shore lines, and that the forest comes down to the edge of the sea. And the occupants have heightened rather than lessened this picturesqueness by adapting their villas to a certain extent to the rocks and inequalities in color and form, and by means of roads, allées, and vistas transforming the region into a lovely park.

Here, as at Newport, is cottage life, but the contrast of the two places is immense. There is here no attempt at any assembly or congregated gayety or display. One would hesitate to say that the drives here have more beauty, but they have more variety. They seem endless, through odorous pine woods and shady lanes, by private roads among beautiful villas and exquisite grounds, with evidences everywhere of wealth to be seen, but of individual taste and refinement. How sweet and cool are these winding ways in the wonderful woods, overrun with vegetation, the bayberry, the sweet-fern, the wild roses, wood-lilies, and ferns! and it is ever a fresh surprise at a turn to find one's self so near the sea, and to open out an entrancing coast view, to emerge upon a promontory and a sight of summer isles, of light-houses, cottages, villages—Marblehead, Salem, Beverly. What a lovely coast! and how wealth and culture have set their seal on it!

It possesses essentially the same character to the north, although the shore is occasionally higher and bolder, as at the picturesque promontory of Magnolia, and Cape Ann exhibits more of the hotel and popular life. But to live in one's own cottage, to choose his calling and dining acquaintances, to make the long season contribute something to cultivation in literature, art, music—to live, in short, rather more for one's self than for society—seems the increasing tendency of the men of fortune who can afford to pay as much for an acre of rock and sand at Manchester as would build a decent house elsewhere. The tourist does not complain of this, and is grateful that individuality has expressed itself in the great variety of lovely homes, in cottages very different from those on the Jersey coast, showing more invention, and good in form and color.

There are New-Yorkers at Manchester and Bostonians at Newport; but who was it that said New York expresses itself at Newport, and Boston at Manchester and kindred coast settlements ? This may be only fancy. Where intellectual life keeps pace with the accumulation of wealth, society is likely to be more natural, simpler, less tied to artificial rules, than where wealth runs ahead. It happens that the quiet social life of Beverly, Manchester, and that region is delightful, although it is a home rather than a public life. Nowhere else at dinner and at the chance evening musical is the foreigner more likely to meet sensible men who are good

THE LAST PASSENGER.

talkers, brilliant and witty women who have the gift of being entertaining, and to have the events of the day and the social and political problems more cleverly discussed. What is the good of wealth if it does not bring one back to freedom, and the ability to live naturally and to indulge the finer tastes in vacation-time?

After all, King reflected, as the party were on their way to the Isles of Shoals, what was it that had most impressed him at Manchester? Was it not an evening spent in a cottage amid the rocks, close by the water, in the company of charming people? To be sure, there were the magical reflection of the moonlight and the bay, the points of light from cottages on the rocky shore, the hum and swell of the sea, and all the mystery of the shadowy headlands; but this was only a congenial setting for the music, the witty talk, the free play of intellectual badinage and seriousness, and the simple human cordiality that were worth all the rest.

What a kaleidoscope it is, this summer travel, and what an entertainment, if the tourist can only keep his "impression plates" fresh to take the new scenes, and not sink into the state of chronic grumbling at hotels and minor discomforts! An interview at a ticket office, a whirl of an hour on the rails, and lo! Portsmouth, anchored yet to the colonial times by a few old houses, and resisting with its respectable provincialism the encroachments of modern smartness, and the sleepy wharf in the sleepy harbor, where the little steamer is obligingly waiting for the last passenger, for the very last woman, running with a bandbox in one hand, and dragging a jerked, fretting child by the other hand, to make the hour's voyage to the Isles of Shoals.

(The shrewd reader objects to the bandbox as an anachronism: it is no longer used. If I were writing a novel, instead of a veracious chronicle, I should not have introduced it, for it is an anachronism. But I was powerless, as a mere narrator, to prevent the woman coming aboard with her bandbox. No one but a trained novelist can make a long-striding, resolute, down-East woman conform to his notions of conduct and fashion.)

If a young gentleman were in love, and the object of his adoration were beside him, he could not have chosen a lovelier day nor a prettier scene than this in which to indulge his happiness; and if he were in love, and the object absent, he could scarcely find a situation fitter to nurse his tender sentiment. Doubtless there is a stage in love when scenery of the very best quality becomes inoperative. There was a couple on board, seated in front of the pilot-house, who let the steamer float along the pretty, long, landlocked harbor, past the Kittery Navyyard, and out upon the blue sea, without taking the least notice of anything but each other. They were on a voyage of their own, Heaven help them! probably without any chart, a voyage of discovery, just as fresh and surprising as if they were the first who ever took it. It made no difference to them that there was a personally conducted excursion party on board, going, they said, to the Oceanic House on Star Island, who had out their maps and guide-books and opera-glasses, and wrung the last drop of the cost of their tickets out of every foot of the scenery. Perhaps it was to King a more sentimental journey than to anybody else, because he invoked his memory and his imagination,

and as the lovely shores opened or fell away behind the steamer in ever-shifting forms of beauty, the scene was in harmony with both his hope and his longing. As to Marion and the artist, they freely appropriated and enjoyed it. So that mediæval structure, all tower, growing out of the rock, is Stedman's Castle—just like him, to let his art spring out of nature in that way. And that is the famous Kittery Navy-yard!

"What do they do there, uncle?" asked the girl, after scanning the place in search of dry-docks and vessels and the usual accompaniments of a navy-yard.

"Oh, they make 'repairs,' principally just before an election. It is very busy then."

"What sort of repairs?"

"Why, political repairs; they call them naval in the department. They are always getting appropriations for them. I suppose that this country is better off for naval repairs than any other country in the world."

"And they are done here?"

"No; they are done in the department. Here is where the voters are. You see, we have a political navy. It costs as much as those navies that have ships and guns, but it is more in accord with the peaceful spirit of the age. Did you never hear of the leading case of 'repairs' of a government vessel here at Kittery? The 'repairs' were all done here, at Portsmouth, New Hampshire; the vessel lay all the time at Portsmouth, Virginia. How should the department know there were two places of the same name? It usually intends to have 'repairs' and the vessel in the same navy-yard."

The steamer was gliding along over smooth water toward the seven blessed isles, which lay there in the sun, masses of rock set in a sea sparkling with diamond points. There were two pretty girls in the pilot-house, and the artist thought their presence there accounted for the serene voyage, for the masts of a wrecked schooner rising out of the shallows to the north reminded him that this is a dangerous coast. But he said the passengers would have a greater sense of security if the usual placard (for the benefit of the captain) was put up: "No flirting with the girl at the wheel."

At a distance nothing could be more barren than these islands, which Captain John Smith and their native poet have

A MINIATURE HARBOR.

enveloped in a tale of romance, and it was not until the steamer was close to it that any landing-place was visible on Appledore, the largest of the group.

The boat turned into a pretty little harbor among the rocks, and the settlement was discovered: a long, low, old-fashioned hotel with piazzas, and a few cottages perched on the ledges, the door-yards of which were perfectly ablaze with patches of flowers, masses of red, yellow, purple —poppies, marigolds, nasturtiums, bachelor's-buttons, lovely splashes of color against the gray lichen-covered rock. At the landing is an interior miniature harbor, walled in, and safe for children to paddle about and sail on in tiny boats. The islands offer scarcely any other opportunity for bathing, unless one dare take a plunge off the rocks.

Talk of the kaleidoscope! At a turn of the wrist, as it were, the elements of society had taken a perfectly novel shape here. Was it only a matter of grouping and setting, or were these people different from all others the tourists had seen? There was a lively scene in the hotel corridor, the spacious office with its long counters and post-office, when the noon mail was opened and the letters called out. So many pretty girls, with pet dogs of all degrees of ugliness (dear little objects of affection overflowing and otherwise running to waste—one of the most pathetic sights in this sad world), jaunty suits with a nautical cut, for boating and rock-climbing, family groups, so much animation and excitement over the receipt of letters, so much well-bred chaffing and friendliness, such an air of refinement and "style," but withal so home-like. These people were "guests" of the proprietors, who nevertheless felt a sort of proprietorship themselves in the little island, and were very much like a company together at sea. For living on this island is very much like being on shipboard at sea, except that this rock does not heave about in a nauseous way.

Mr. King discovered by the register that the Bensons had been here (of all places in the world, he thought this would be the ideal one for a few days with her), and Miss Lamont had a letter from Irene, which she did not offer to read.

"They didn't stay long," she said, as

Mr. King seemed to expect some information out of the letter, "and they have gone on to Bar Harbor. I should like to stop here a week; wouldn't you?"

"Ye-e-s," trying to recall the mood he was in before he looked at the register; "but—but" (thinking of the words "gone on to Bar Harbor") "it is a place, after all, that you can see in a short time—go all over it in half a day."

"But you want to sit about on the rocks, and look at the sea, and dream."

"I can't dream on an island—not on a small island. It's too cooped up; you get a feeling of being a prisoner."

"I suppose you wish 'that little isle had wings, and you and I within its shady'—"

"There's one thing I will not stand, Miss Lamont, and that's Moore. Come, let's go to Star Island."

The party went in the tug *Pinafore*, which leads a restless, fussy life, puffing about among these islands, making the circuit of Appledore at fixed hours, and acting commonly as a ferry. Star Island is smaller than Appledore and more barren, but it has the big hotel (and a different class of guests from those on Appledore), and several monuments of romantic interest. There is the ancient stone church, rebuilt some time in this century; there are some gravestones; there is a monument to Captain John Smith, the only one existing anywhere to that interesting adventurer—a triangular shaft, with a long inscription that could not have been more eulogistic if he had composed it himself. There is something pathetic in this lonely monument when we recall Smith's own touching allusion to this naked rock, on which he probably landed when he once coasted along this part of New England, as being his sole possession in the world at the end of his adventurous career:

"No lot for me but Smith's Isles, which are an array of barren rocks, the most overgrown with shrubs and sharpe whins you can hardly pass them; without either grasse or wood, but three or foure short shrubby old cedars."

Every tourist goes to the south end of Star Island, and climbs down on the face of the precipice to the "Chair," a niche where a school-teacher used to sit as long ago as 1848. She was sitting there one day when a wave came up and washed her away into the ocean. She disappeared. But she who loses her life shall save it. That one thoughtless act of hers did more for her reputation than years of faithful teaching, than all her beauty, grace, and attractions. Her "Chair" is a point of pilgrimage. The tourist looks at it, guesses at its height above the water, regards the hungry sea with aversion, reënacts the drama in his imagination, sits in the chair, has his wife sit in it, has his boy and girl sit in it together, wonders what the teacher's name was, stops at the hotel and asks the photograph girl, who does not know, and the proprietor, who says it's in a book somewhere, and finally learns that it was Underhill, and straightway forgets it when he leaves the island.

What a delicious place it is, this Appledore, when the elements favor! The party were lodged in a little cottage, whence they overlooked the hotel and the little harbor, and could see all the life of the place, looking over the bank of flowers that draped the rocks of the door-yard. How charming was the miniature pond, with the children sailing round and round, and the girls in pretty costumes bathing, and sunlight lying so warm upon the greenish-gray rocks! But the night, following the glorious after-glow, the red sky, all the level sea, and the little harbor burnished gold, the rocks purple—oh! the night, when the moon came! Oh, Irene! Great heavens! why will this world fall into such a sentimental fit, when all the sweetness and the light of it are away at Bar Harbor!

Love, and moonlight, and the soft lapse of the waves, and singing? Yes, there are girls down by the landing with a banjo, and young men singing the songs of love, the modern songs of love dashed with college slang. The banjo suggests a little fastness; and this new generation carries off its sentiment with some bravado and a mocking tone. Presently the tug *Pinafore* glides up to the landing, the engineer flings open the furnace door, and the glowing fire illumines the interior, brings out forms and faces, and deepens the heavy shadows outside. It is like a cavern scene in the opera. A party of ladies in white come down to cross to Star. Some of these insist upon climbing up to the narrow deck, to sit on the roof and enjoy the moonlight and the cinders. Girls like to do these things, which are more unconventional than hazardous, at watering-places.

ARRIVAL OF THE MAIL.

What a wonderful effect it is, the masses of rock, water, sky, the night, all details lost in simple lines and forms! On the piazza of the cottage is a group of ladies and gentlemen in poses more or less graceful; one lady is in a hammock; on one side is the moonlight, on the other come gleams from the curtained windows touching here and there a white shoulder, or lighting a lovely head; the vines running up on strings and half enclosing the piazza make an exquisite tracery against the sky, and cast delicate shadow patterns on the floor; all the time music within, the piano, the violin, and the sweet waves of a woman's voice singing the songs of Schubert, floating out upon the night. A soft wind blows out of the west.

The northern part of Appledore Island is an interesting place to wander. There are no trees, but the plateau is far from barren. The gray rocks crop out among bayberry and huckleberry bushes, and the wild rose, very large and brilliant in color, fairly illuminates the landscape, massing its great bushes. Amid the chaotic desert of broken rocks further south are little valleys of deep green grass, gay with roses. On the savage precipices at the end one may sit in view of an extensive sweep of coast with a few hills, and of other rocky islands, sails, and ocean-going steamers. Here are many nooks and hidden corners to dream in and make love in, the soft sea air being favorable to that soft-hearted occupation.

One could easily get attached to the place, if duty and Irene did not call elsewhere. Those who dwell here the year round find most satisfaction when the summer guests have gone and they are alone with freaky nature. "Yes," said the woman in charge of one of the cottages, "I've lived here the year round for sixteen years, and I like it. After we get fixed up comfortable for winter, kill a critter, have pigs, and make my own sassengers, then there ain't any neighbors comin' in, and that's what I like."

"A NOOK TO DREAM IN AND MAKE LOVE IN."

THE NEW YORK PRODUCE EXCHANGE.

BY RICHARD WHEATLY.

THE New York Produce Exchange is one of the most conspicuous buildings on Manhattan Island, the seat of the most influential mercantile corporation within its limits, and the market in whose exchanges the entire national commonwealth is most deeply interested. "Like a beetling cliff commanding the eye of the home-bound mariner," it challenges the notice of travellers approaching through the Narrows, or crossing the Hudson from the further shore. Its massive campanile shares with the lace-like Brooklyn Bridge, the spire of Trinity Church, the tall tower of the *Tribune*, and the ambitious altitude of the Equitable and Western Union structures the admiration of the stranger.

Comparatively few of the busy multitudes that swarm about its base have any knowledge of the exceeding beauty visible from its summit. The White Tower of the Conqueror, the Colonne Napoléon, or the Monument on Bunker Hill offers nothing equal to the urban, rural, and marine scenery presented to the vision. East, west, north, and south the view is comparatively unobstructed. About its feet cluster the Field Building, on the site of Washington's head-quarters, Castle Garden, the United States Sub-Treasury, Assay Office, and Custom-house, the Stock, Produce, Cotton, Metal, and other exchanges, and the stately edifices in which the marvellous operations of commerce, finance, insurance, banking, railroading, and telegraphing are carried on. If Washington be the cerebrum, New York is the cerebellum of the American body-politic. Governor's Island, the pedestal of "Liberty enlightening the World," the civic municipalities of Brooklyn, Hoboken, Jersey and Long Island Cities, the distant heights in the receding country, and the shimmering waters of bay and river, mottled by craft of every civilization, invite delighted inspection.

The New York Produce Exchange stands near the spot where the boats of the adventurous Hollanders first touched the shores of Manhattan, and where the first rough ventures of commerce were made with the children of the unexplored wilderness. The courage, perseverance, and faith of the earliest European traders have lost nothing in transmission to their descendants. This massive and beautiful structure convincingly testifies that the sons are worthy of the sires, and indeed superior to them by so much as the theoretical and applied science of the present transcends that of the past. It is a speaking monument of that wise self-appreciation proper to the guardians of New York's commercial supremacy. It fully provides for present mercantile needs and for those of the near future; yields revenue from outlay sufficient to continuously advance the commercial interests of city and State, and by its architectural effects refines and educates the thinking toilers who manipulate so many of our material exchanges. The builders have evidently learned to look beyond themselves into the possibilities of the future. But little more than half a century ago the value of American exports aggregated about seventy million dollars; in 1885 it reached the sum of $742,189,755, and in 1881 the much larger amount of $902,377,346. Then thirty miles of imperfect railroad hinted at the more than 128,500 that now compose the sinews of the body-politic, and gave occult promise of the hundreds of thousands of telegraph and telephone nerves that connect the sensorium with every member.

In view of the purposes this edifice is designed to serve, it is architecturally unrivalled by any in this or any other country. Of the modern Renaissance in style, and marked by symmetrically beautiful lines, its general effect is imposing, and imparts the idea of strength and permanence. The Building Committee knew what they wanted, and were fortunate enough to find in George B. Post, the architect, a trained artist abundantly able to unite their original designs with the graces of elegance and uniformity. Begun on May 1, 1881, it was finished on May 1, 1884. Fifteen thousand and thirty-seven New England pine and spruce piles, driven through the yielding primitive soil to a solid bed, and cut off below the level of tide-water, insure the safety of the superstructure, and by their uprightness are supposed to harmonize with the mercantile men and morals they uphold. The building is fireproof throughout. Granite, brick, terracotta, and iron are piled above the cornerstone—bearing in lasting bronze the word

VIEW OF THE TOWER LOOKING SEAWARD.

"EQUITY," that was laid with imposing ceremony on the 6th of June, 1882 —and compose an edifice 300 by 150 feet in superficial area, and, with tower and terrace, of 53,779 square feet. One hundred and sixteen feet measure the distance from sidewalk to roof, 225 feet to the coping of the tower, and 306 feet to the top of the flag-staff. Of course we are not surprised when told that the flag, 50 × 20 feet, is the largest ever made. The tower clock has a face twelve feet in diameter, each number measuring a foot in length, and weighs 1500 pounds.

Entering the Exchange from Beaver Street, Broadway, the terrace, or Stone Street, the visitor finds himself in corridors from which open the doors of private offices, of the Produce Exchange Bank, a branch United States post-office, the Western Union Telegraph Company, the Pennsylvania Railroad Company, and the bustling Maritime Exchange. Four elevators near the Stone Street and five near the Beaver Street entrance facilitate passage to all the upper parts. One of the latter leaves him in a hall opposite the cloak-room, whence a sharp turn to the left leads through hurrying brokers, and men lunching at counters, or investing in fruits and confections dispensed by a typical jarl's daughter, into a series of offices devoted to the uses of president, cashier, superintendents, and the Gratuity Fund.

Retracing the path just trodden, the hum of multitudinous voices, broken by explosive jets and measureless yells of noise, allures into the Exchange Hall. Admission is contingent on member's ticket or escort. Once inside, the amplitude of space— 220 × 144 feet, with height of 47 feet 6 inches to the ceiling, and 60 feet to the skylight—compels notice. Light and ventilation are perfect. Seven thousand men would not overcrowd the 31,680 square feet of surface. Should the future bring a larger number, provision is made for adding 8000 square feet to the area, and also for the erection of other accommodations on contiguous ground owned by the corporation. On the right, attached to pillars, are black-boards reporting the prices of refined petroleum at London, Antwerp, and Bremen; and of naval stores, turpentine, and resin in London and Liverpool. Eight long tables, provided with drawers and distinct compart-

ments on the surface, afford conveniences to the flour merchants, and command a yearly rent of $10 per drawer. A premium of $200 was paid for the first choice at the opening of the Hall. One similar table supplies the needs of dealers in lard, grease, tallow, and oils. Booths belonging to the Western Union, Postal, Baltimore and Ohio, and Metropolitan telegraph and telephone companies furnish necessary means of communication to brokers; and wires, rented of different corporations, connect the telephones of private owners with their respective offices. Fifty dollars per year is the price of this privilege. The melancholy oval ring around which mercurial dealers in

MANIPULATING FLOUR.

petroleum used to gather has been removed since our illustration of the Main Hall (page 197) was prepared.

Tables scattered over the room for the use of commercial reporters accelerate the speed with which they make known what prices obtain at the tables whereon samples of barley, wheat, oats, corn, and feed are placed for examination. Not

C. M. VAIL, PRESIDENT OF THE PRODUCE EXCHANGE.

to their contents. They present the official cable report of the day's prices of provisions, naval stores, grain, flour, corn, and oils at Liverpool, and of hops in London; the bid and asking prices in the adjoining Call Room; the Beerbohm cable report of prices at London and Liverpool of 1,900,000 quarters of wheat and flour and 220,000 quarters of corn in passage to the United Kingdom, and of 280,000 quarters of wheat and 210,000 quarters of corn in passage to the European continent; the bids at call sales in the principal marts of the United States; the movement of wheat to the chief ports of the country, and the receipts on the corresponding day of last year; the receipts and shipments of grain and the stocks in store at the same points in the previous business twenty-four hours; the receipts of grain at lake and river ports, and also at Atlantic ports, during the last week, previous week, and corresponding week in 1885; the visible supply of grain in the United States and Canada in the last week, and in the corresponding weeks of 1885 and 1884; and also the grain in sight on sea and land. Thus, on January 16–17, 1886, the

	Bushels.
Visible supply of wheat in the United States and Canada was	57,108,286
On passage to the United Kingdom	14,424,000
On passage to the Continent	1,584,000
	73,116.286
The week before	73,046,176
Two weeks ago	74,237,325

The figures representing corn are also given, the quantities of wheat and maize

here, however, are the prices of all cereals determined. In that corner oval, consisting of wooden steps, rising from inside and outside one above another, and technically known as the "Pit," the prices of future deliveries, at the option of buyer or seller, are decided. Back of the "Pit" is the Call Room, in which provisions and grain are sold through the medium of the presiding callers, William L. Eichell and Edward Patterson. Five hundred seats, arranged in amphitheatrical form, ascend in concentric rows from the floor. Each bears, when so desired, the name of the owner. Five dollars per annum, plus the premium bidden at the annual auction sale in January, is the price of each seat. Those not sold are free to members of the Exchange.

Emerging from the Call Room, the little crowd of daily reporters gathered in front of the bulletin-boards calls attention

VIEW OF THE NEW YORK PRODUCE EXCHANGE FROM BOWLING GREEN.

HERMAN O. ARMOUR.

the tedium of waiting hours, and for which the ladies of the trade lords are dutifully bound to be truly grateful. One door of this spacious apartment leads into the office of the Complaint Committee, and another into the Board-Room of the managers. Interior arrangements correspond with the functions exercised in them. Similar provisions for the Arbitration Committee, whose duties are of a judicial character, furnish out their chamber. If wishful to sustain æsthetic reputation with the scores of stalwart, vigorous, and efficient merchants whose portraits adorn the pictorial representation of "Laying the Corner-Stone," by Carl J. Becker, it is well to study it in the clear gas-light that floods one end of the Reception Room. Preëminent among many whose names are lustrous in the commercial annals of the United States are David Dows, "the present patriarch of the grain trade in this city," whose "transcendent mercantile genius" has made his whole life "a prolonged story of the progressive development of this wonderful country"; Edward Hincken, who "has introduced the foreign commerce of this port into every country and almost every harbor in the world"; Herman O. Armour, whose patronymic is allied to daring commercial enterprise; Franklin Edson, thrice president, and ex-Mayor of the city, whose highest honor is held to be the fixed desire "to do the right as he had the ability and opportunity to see the right"; and others, whose energies have been reënforced by the conviction "that the sense of having lived up to the standard of the Golden Rule is better than being the objective point of a fickle fame or of popular laudation."

at the Atlantic ports, and the quantities and destinations of weekly exports of corn, wheat, and flour from the chief seaboard ports.

While on the floor a buyer may receive from Europe a cable order for a cargo of grain, flour, or provisions, may purchase what is ordered, charter a vessel for shipment, engage an elevator to load the grain, or a lighter to move provisions or flour, effect insurance, sell exchange, cable back the fact of his purchases, and write and mail his letters.

Returns of exports are obtained from the shipping offices sending out vessels, and the daily and weekly receipts of flour, grain, feed, high wines, hops, oil-cake, provisions, etc., etc., from railroad companies, steam-boat and steam-ship lines, express companies, canal lines, river boats, and barges. The collecting employés begin daily work about 7 A.M., and report to the collector of produce receipts, who collates their returns, and posts them on the bulletin-boards at 11.40 A.M.

Ascending to the third floor, and calling at the office of the statisticians, so famous for accurate and exhaustive reports, the visitor passes from thence into the elegantly furnished Reception Room, where two upright pianos stand ready to beguile

The Library, looking down upon the historic Bowling Green, and amply provided with leather-covered cherry furniture, offers a long list of foreign and domestic periodicals—the *Bangor Rustler* of Dakota included—to the choice of the reader. Seven portraits of former presidents invite criticism. The written and framed agreement, dated July 14, 1863, of many signatory members of the Produce Exchange to serve as minutemen, under command of officers of the Seventh Regiment, for the maintenance of law and order and the protection of life and property, awakens painful memories of the dark and bloody draft riots. Foreign market reports, prices current, freight reports, and shipping circulars evidently possess more interest to *habitués* of this institution than the scanty collection of volumes hidden behind the opaque glass of the cases.

A large colony of offices, in four stories of rooms devoted to mercantile uses, rises above the Exchange Hall, surrounds the entire edifice, and lends massiveness and grace to the exterior. Lavatories minister to the comfort of the occupants. Letter-openings in a conduit or "run," costing $1500, placed on each floor by the managers of the Cutler Mailing System, save weary steps to the postal depository.

In the basement are the offices of the New York Produce Exchange Safe Deposit and Storage Company, with entrance from the interior, and also from Whitehall Street. The neat and commodious Reading and Reception Room, the Ladies' Room, with parlor, toilet, and coupon-cutting conveniences attached, Trustees' Room, and thirty-seven apartments for secluded handling of documents, are all that could well be asked. The doors of the money vault, which contains 1300 safes, and has capacity for 7000 or 8000, are models of mechanical

THE WESTERN UNION BULLETIN-BOARD.

ingenuity and mathematical perfection. They have time locks set to any number of hours up to seventy, and are said to be the largest of the kind ever made, and also the safest. Each of the two outside doors weighs 7000 pounds, and each of the two inner 6000 pounds. Each outer door, hung on crane hinges, is forced bodily into position by an eccentric lever, and is thus made air-tight and powder-proof. Should the combinations of the lock be forgotten, it is said that the manufacturer's men, using all available means, would require from three to four days in which to force ingress. Seven alternate layers of steel and iron encompass the vault, and 3500-pound barred window-guards intercept the sunlight. The electric watch-clock, recording faithful guardianship, is an additional surety. In other strongly constructed vaults are stored silver plate, bulky packages, paintings, precious merchandise, books and records of firms and corporations. All are under seal, and reveal no secrets to the curious gazer.

In the Engine Room, whose presiding genius is an intelligent graduate of the Cooper Institute, are an Edison dynamo-machine of 250 light capacity, three Worthington engines for operating the elevators, two pumping engines for forcing water into tanks on roof and tower, three pneumatic engines for despatching messages from the Exchange floor to the main offices of telegraph companies by means of aerial currents generated here and driven through tubes, and a battery of three sectional boilers of 750 horse-power, which supplies motor force to the pumping engines, and also heats the building. Two thousand tons of coal annually, and 66,000 pounds of water diurnally in summer, but not in winter, owing to the peculiar method of heating, are here consumed.

The Produce Exchange, costing with land and furniture a grand total of $3,178,645 14, is a valuable index of progressive wealth and civilization. It includes 12,000,000 bricks, 15 miles of iron girders, 1¼ miles of columns, 2061 tons of terra-cotta, 7½ acres of flooring, more than 2000 windows, nearly 1000 doors, 7½ miles of sash cords and chains, over 47 tons of sash weights, ⅕ of an acre of skylight over the Exchange Room, 29 miles of steam-pipes, nearly a mile of panelled wainscoting, and weighs over 50,000 tons. Four thousand separate drawings were required for its construction. The nine hydraulic elevators carry an average of 21,500 people daily, or 6,500,000 every year. The pumping capacity is sufficient to supply water to a city of 175,000 inhabitants, and 1,194,133 horse-power is utilized annually for heat and force. All these items are of less practical interest to the members than the fact that the 190

offices rent, together with privileges, for about $180,000 per annum, not including premiums of over $24,000 paid for choice, and return about six per cent. on the entire investment. With the rents and annual dues there will be in 1886 a net surplus above interest and expenses of $40,000. This income will, of course, increase as the bonded debt decreases. When the latter is liquidated, the Exchange will enjoy a net income of about $200,000 a year, which may be applied to the reduction either of dues or of gratuity assessments.

The history of the New York Produce Exchange is far more interesting to many readers than the dry details of its structure. As an organized corporation it is of yesterday; but its beginning was in the ruggedly picturesque traders who met for the transaction of business at the "Company's store-houses" in the weekly Monday markets established by the redoubtable Governor Peter Stuyvesant in the autumn of 1648.

Rude and primitive, with sides open to the weather, and roof covered with thatch and Dutch tiles, was the edifice that housed the embryonic trade of New Amsterdam. The insignificant Marckt-velt Stegie, on which the splendid temple of trade now stands, was the cradle in which the giant American commerce was rocked.

Increasing population swept away the old market, and the dislodged merchants next met "on a bridge over a small stream at Exchange Place—the Rialto of the New World." The Broadway Shambles, situated on the present Bowling Green, were used as a market from 1658 to 1707, and again from 1720. In or about 1675 was built the Custom-house Bridge Market, almost, if not quite, on the site of the old Produce Exchange, at the corner of Pearl and Moore streets. Thence, in May, 1684, the traffickers removed to the Bowling Green. The industry and homely wealth of the period were both fitly symbolized by the figures of a beaver and a flour-barrel engraved on the seal of the colony, and representing the most important interests of the colonists. In 1690–91 the first Exchange in New York was erected. Located on the edge of the water at the foot of Broad Street, it served for a market-house as well as a business meeting-place for merchants. In January, 1727, the first authorized corn exchange, or market, was exclusively established by

THE MAIN HALL OF THE NEW YORK PRODUCE EXCHANGE.

THE LIBRARY.

corporation ordinance at the water front foot of Wall Street, "for the sale of all sorts of grain, corn, and meal." In 1739 a market-house, 42 by 25 feet, arose in the middle of Broadway, on the site of the old wagon stand opposite Liberty Street, and was also declared to be a grain and meal market in November, 1741. This hideous deformity was followed in 1754 by the New or Royal Exchange, a building raised upon arches in the middle of the street and over the canal near the foot of Broad Street. In this the merchants congregated for some years, and thence migrated to the Merchants' Exchange, now the United States Custom-house, in Wall Street.

In the fourth decade of the present century the flour trade was chiefly conducted at the foot of Cortlandt Street and at the corner of Broad and South streets, where the merchants ordinarily remained until 11 A.M. The sky was their "azure roof," and the street pavement in front of Weeks and Douglas's store, No. 19 South Street, their "tessellated floor." Colonel Edward Hincken, late of the Fourth New York Artillery, and one of the oldest veterans of the Produce Exchange, was one of the number. One day, in or about 1846, he was accosted by Alfred Barrett with the curt demand, "Hincken, give me a dollar." "What for?" was the prompt inquiry. "Buy an awning for the front of Weeks and Douglas's store," responded Barrett. The awning was bought, and under it, shielded from sun and rain, the grain and flour magnates met. There they became a "nuisance" to the occupants, whose office, pens, and paper they freely appropriated. To the credit of William H. Newman be it said, this unwarrantable intrusiveness was ended by his hiring the store No. 19 South Street from Weeks and Douglas. Like-minded associates supported him, and subscribed fifteen dollars each to defray the necessary expenditure. Organization under the title of the Corn Exchange, with Joseph Ketcham as chairman, followed. Incorporation was received from the New York Legislature in the spring of 1853, Nathaniel H. Wolfe being the presiding officer. Gatherings were informal, but grew in numbers as provision dealers, shipping merchants, and ship-owners joined them, until it became necessary to provide larger room. No. 19 South Street was purchased, and the refusal of the corner and of other property obtained. The owner of No. 17 South Street, by extravagant demands for his property, caused the Board of

Managers to select the corner of White-hall and Pearl streets for the location of a new building. On this, in 1860, the Produce Exchange was erected. Thither about seven hundred merchants removed in 1861, leaving malcontents in the old quarters, and assumed the title of the New York Commercial Association, with John B. Wright as the first president. The new organization was incorporated by the Legislature in 1862. Under the prudent management of Vice-President James P. Wallace, the entire cost of the charter, including counsel fees and several journeys to Albany, was only $96. In this new structure the two parties were reunited. Some of the opponents to removal held out until only two members — of whom Edward Hincken was one—met in the old Corn Exchange when it was last opened. "As neither could make money out of the other," the gallant colonel and his army gave in their adhesion to the new order, and were "gladly welcomed" with "loud applause" at headquarters.

Two bodies were now organized. The Produce Exchange Building Company owned the edifice, charged $20 per annum to each subscriber of the Commercial Association, and $5 per annum for other expenses; but allowed a committee to control and pay for news, police, etc., out of the proceeds—pocketing all remainders. In 1868 the title of the New York Commercial Asso-

VAULTS OF THE PRODUCE EXCHANGE SAFE DEPOSIT AND STORAGE COMPANY.

ciation was altered to that of the New York Produce Exchange by action of the Legislature.

The arrangement between the two companies—so decidedly objectionable to the tenants—under which business was carried on came to an end in 1872, by the purchase of the building for the sum of $265,000, which was raised by an assessment of $200 on each member of the Exchange.

Rapid growth required larger accommodations, and in 1880 the present site was bought. The three years intervening between conception of the new edifice and laying its foundation-stone on the 6th of June, 1882, were crowded with

FORREST H. PARKER.

"Three thousand men with one purpose, built into a living temple, whose corner-stone is integrity and equity, are here gathered to-day to inaugurate and dedicate this our visible temple of commerce." Brave words, good words, these be, and should guide judgment on what comes hereafter. They accord with those in which the charter expresses the purpose of the corporation, viz., "To inculcate just and equitable principles in trade; to establish and maintain uniformity in commercial usages; to acquire, preserve, and disseminate valuable business information; to adjust controversies and misunderstandings between persons engaged in business; and to make provision for the widows and children of deceased members."

anxieties and untiring labors. The name of Forrest H. Parker, the president, who officiated on the latter occasion, together with those of Franklin Edson, chairman, and Alexander E. Orr, secretary of the Building Committee, and of their colleagues, will always be significant of the prescience, faith, energy, and millioned liberality which, in the teeth of multitudinous discouragements and trials, wrought out so magnificent an enterprise.

On the 6th of May, 1884, possession of the new quarters was taken. Before quitting the old, Mr. James McGee delivered a valedictory address to the members.

Assembled in the main hall of the new Exchange, the members listened to speeches by Mayor Edson and President J. H. Herrick. The latter insisted that the elements of all progress are physical, intellectual, moral—and preëminently moral.

The membership of the New York Produce Exchange is limited to three thousand. To these large proportions it has grown within the memory of living and still active merchants. The lively crowd which congregated under the awning of Weeks and Douglas's store had increased to about 1000 in 1860, when they frequented the dark, dingy, and badly ventilated Corn Exchange. In 1863 the New York Commercial Association boasted 1238 members, each of whom annually paid $20 as dues. In 1870 the members of the Produce Exchange had risen to 2023, and the dues to $25. In 1872 the initiation fee rose to $300, in 1873 to $500, in 1880 to $1000, and in 1882 to $2500. Since then certificates of membership have been sold at $4800, and are now in active demand at $2750. In 1873 the members numbered 2469; in 1880, 2700; and in 1882, 3000.

What they will number in future is difficult of conjecture.

Most of the Produce Exchange traders are of American birth. The youth of the land, and especially of New England, take very kindly to commercial pursuits. But portation, finance, etc., are more frequent. All are, of necessity, keen politicians, and could supply a respectable Congress on the shortest notice. Good-humor, cordiality, and even courtliness are generic characteristics. Here and there may

DAVID DOWS.

there are many names on the roll which denote Celtic, German, Scandinavian, French, Spanish, and Slavic parentage. In *personnel* the corporation is cosmopolitan as its commerce. All grades of intellectual culture are represented in it. Men of college breeding are not infrequent. Men of bold, pushing, aggressive character, whose mental powers have been mainly employed on the facts and theories of statistics, demand and supply, trans- be one of whom the French *savant's* report on the customs and manners of the South-sea Islanders—"Customs bad; manners none"—is true; but of the overwhelming majority it may justly be said that they are exponents of the best elements in our national life. In the noisy activities of Call Room and Grain Pit the effervescent energies of younger members are amusingly apparent. Older participants, sobered by hard conflict in the

EDWARD HINCKEN.

out through the door. His back vanishes to another tremendous non-symphony: "Put —out—that—pipe!" followed by applausive laughter from the gallery.

As now constituted, the property affairs— to an amount not exceeding five million dollars—business, and concerns of the corporation are controlled by a president, vice-president, treasurer, and twelve managers, who together constitute the Board of Managers. All are gentlemen of high commercial character and standing. Vacancies are filled by the board, of whom the majority constitutes a quorum. Charles M. Vail, president, 1885–6, is a member of the firm of John S. Martin and Co., butter and cheese merchants. *Ex offi-*

changeful years, look on with complacent, half-contemptuous indifference. Boisterous play is never carried to the extreme of insult and outrage. At the Christmas festivities tooting performers on tin horns, mock traders in options, mock glove-fights with wondrously attentive seconds, practical jokers with violent animosities against straw hats, and sundry terpsichoreans whose physical force explodes through flying feet, manifest their share in the general joy.

Nicknames, mock calls, waving hats, shouts, and catcalls are concomitants of the annual sale of choice of seats in the Call Room. The surging crowd in the Wheat Pit is occasionally inspired by wild desire to emulate the sports of Crow Indians, when fair feminine faces beam upon them from the gallery. The added presence of a cockney, "just come hover, ye know," lighted pipe in mouth, and quizzing-glass screwed into one eye, evokes stentorian shout in chorus: "Put—out— that—pipe!" A second shout shoots the pipe, with strutting stranger behind it,

cio, and with the approval of the board, he appoints a standing committee for each of the trades, to which all disputes arising in it may be referred for arbitration, at a cost of from $15 to $25 to the losing party. Parties at variance may, however, settle their differences by private arbitration. The president is a member of all committees excepting that on arbitration, presides at meetings of the Exchange and of the Board of Managers, and annually, or oftener, as he deems proper, communicates to either such matters and suggestions as will, in his opinion, conduce to its usefulness and prosperity. James McGee, vice-president, is at the head of the Devoe Oil Company; Richard O. Veit, identified with the Standard Oil Company, is secretary; and John P. Townsend, of the W. J. Wilcox Company, oil refiners, treasurer. Neglect of duty vacates office.

The expenses of the Exchange are defrayed by means of an assessment of not less than $10, nor more than $30, on each certificate of membership. Non-payment is punished by suspension from all privileges, which are only restored when the delinquent foots the bill.

Under the direction of the Board of Managers eighty-four employés diligently fulfil specific tasks, graduated in importance from those of Superintendent

the building and bulletins, nominates his assistants, organizes their service, and is an administrative Briareus.

Any respectable applicant for membership, duly proposed and seconded, may be admitted if approved by the Committee on Admissions, and elected by the Board

J. H. HERRICK.

William E. Fletcher, down to those of assistant porters, coal-passers, and closet attendants. During the fiscal year ending May 16, 1885, $58,322 65 was paid for salaries, and $1330 87 for uniforms. The superintendent, aided by an assistant, L. B. Howe, records the proceedings of all meetings of the Exchange, managers, and committees; collects all moneys due to the corporation; receives, deposits—either in the Corn Exchange, Central Trust Company, Fourth National, Hanover National, Mercantile National, New York Produce Exchange, or Seaboard Bank—and pays over margins on contracts; has charge of

of Managers. Prior to this he must present a properly assigned certificate of membership, and a written application stating the nature of his business and such other facts as may be required, and must also sign an agreement to abide by the organic and statutory laws of the Exchange. Certificates of living membership are transferable only to elected persons, on payment of a fee of $5, and of any unpaid assessments. The certificate of a deceased member is transferable by his legal representatives. Nine applicants were rejected for satisfactory reasons in the year ending June 1, 1885.

WILLIAM E. FLETCHER, SUPERINTENDENT.

An Arbitration Committee, consisting of five members, not managers, elected by ballot of the board, and sworn to faithfulness in duty, hear and decide disputes between parties who have voluntarily bound themselves to acquiesce in the decision. Any controversy which might be the subject of an action at law or in equity, excepting claims to real estate, is within the jurisdiction of this committee. Judgments of the Supreme Court of the City and County of New York are rendered upon the awards made. Attendance of witnesses is compulsory. Appeal is not permissible unless fraud, collusion, or corruption be alleged against some portion of the arbitrators. The costs of these proceedings—$5 per member for each sitting—are certainly moderate. Alexander E. Orr is chairman of the committee. Hundreds of very important cases have been adjudicated. Within the past few years it is said that not a single business difference between members has sought our law courts for settlement.

The Complaint Committee is a mercantile grand-jury, which hears accusations against members, endeavors to conciliate disputants, or to induce them to arbitrate. Failing in both, the controversy is referred to the Board of Managers, whose action is final. They may censure, suspend, or expel the accused. If the accused be the scape-goat of impenitent, guilty principals outside the Exchange, they are boycotted, but he is excused.

Duly notified failures are posted in the Exchange, and all contracts of the failers, so far as may be, are closed by purchase or sale at public call, or by the Finance Committee. The law of "survival of the fittest" applies with merciless rigor. The Finance Committee audits all bills and claims against the Exchange, also the treasurer's accounts, and directs all authorized disbursements. The Floor Committee supervises the rooms used in 'Change hours, and preserves seemly order. Together with the president, treasurer, and trustees of the Gratuity Fund, they compose the Committee on Admissions. A House Committee has general supervision of the employés. That on Information and Statistics supplies all news affecting the value of articles dealt in by the members of the Exchange, and records all the useful facts of movements, prices, and transportation of products. To the Law Committee is confided all required legislation, the nomination of legal counsel, and proposed amendments to the charter or the by-laws. The duties of the Committee on Rooms and Fixtures are explained by its title. The Committee on Trade is charged with the formulation of useful regulations.

Such an organization is entitled to profound respect as the best creation of commercial genius, instructed and fructified by the experience of centuries.

Under the charter and statutes of the New York Produce Exchange, a vast and various commerce, in whose materials and methods all modern civilization is interested, is conducted. The rooms of the building are opened for business at 9 A.M. and closed at 4 P.M.—on Saturdays at 3.30 P.M. The tops of grain and provision tables freely welcome the first comers, each of whom may occupy the space over a single sample drawer for his own use. Loud and boisterous conversation, throwing of dough, corn, or other articles, is forbidden, and subjects the offender to discipline, and on very rare occasions to an imminent charge of bayonets. Smoking before 2.15 P.M. costs fifty cents for each offence, and swells the treasury of the Committee on Charities. Substitutes for sick or absent members, who are responsible for their doings, may be admitted to the floor on thirty-days renewable passes. Failure to fulfil contracts excludes both the "posted" principal and his substitute. Daily sessions, announced and ended by the deafening clangor of a soulless bell,

Exchange charges itself. Seated at the point on the Atlantic coast where all lines of travel and traffic converge, whither cereals from the boundless prairies and pastoral products from the Pacific coast are forwarded by Western merchants and packers to New York dealers and commission firms for distribution among the manufacturing millions of Europe and the several commonwealths of the American continent and archipelagoes, it presents as

THE PIT.

of the grain, lard, and provision trades are held from 10.30 A.M. to 2.15 P.M., and from 3 to 3.30 P.M. All contracts are legally enforceable. They must express the facts of transactions, and if they do not, expose the parties to penalty. Washed or fictitious sales, or false reports of sales, are also penal offences.

What shall we eat, what shall we drink, and wherewithal shall we be lighted? are the three questions with whose pleasant solution the New York Produce

various aspects as its busy traffic. This last changes characteristics with the current years. Inbound freight trains, bearing lowing cattle, bleating sheep, and disgruntled hogs, do not disquiet Bergh philanthropists as in former years. Abattoirs in Chicago, Kansas City, Cedar Rapids, and other cities silence the vocal complaints of the unwilling transports; packing-houses transfer their edible remains to boxes, barrels, and refrigerating cars for safe transit to the regions whence they pass into human consumption. Transportation of live stock, intended for export or domestic use, has not ceased, but is of smaller dimensions. Changes in the provision trade are not less noteworthy. Twenty-five years ago the multitude of drays engaged in drawing barrels and tierces from railroad termini to civic warehouses, where they were inspected and recoopered, and thence to the docks of steamers and sailing vessels, excited passing wonder. Now they are shipped at once from the railroad sidings to the holds of seagoing vessels, and sent on to foreign buyers or consignees. But enough of demand for domestic supply and export remains to sustain a vigorous trade at the Produce Exchange. Southern markets are satisfied directly from the West; those of the West Indies by New York jobbers.

Merchants either purchase in the West, or send from their own packing-houses in that region, or receive consignments, on which they make advances often equal to three-fourths the market value of the provisions here offered for sale. In the first and third cases, bills of lading accompanied by sight drafts are mailed to purchasers or consignees while the goods are on the way. Before the arrival of the latter, parties in interest not unfrequently attempt to guard against loss from fluctuation of prices by selling short in the Chicago market—a process perfectly intelligible to the "hedger" on the turf. In New York, consignments or purchases of provisions pass into the custody of licensed and responsible paid inspectors and warehousemen, of whom there are seven; and by whom the condition, quality, standard, and weight of the different lots are duly certified, or declared to be insufficient to fulfil the requirements of the contract. Each warehouse receipt must be for 250 barrels, containing an average of 200 pounds per barrel, unless otherwise stipulated. All sales contemplate merchantable meats. If 10 per cent. of a lot of dry salted meat, or 20 per cent. of other meats, be defective, they are excluded from this category. Packer's name and location, number of pieces, and weight, together with the inspector's brand, must be marked on each package. Sales, in agreed lots of any size, if for export or domestic consumption, are made upon the Exchange floor, and deliveries from warehouse or from the dock, as the goods arrive. Speculative sales are in lots of 250 barrels, or their multiples. Less business than formerly is now done in options, but the jobbing trade retains its old proportions. Official but not private sales are recorded. Receipts of provisions at New York in 1880 and 1885 were as follows:

1880.

Beef	24,478 tierces.
Beef	25,067 barrels.
Beef	713,939 cases.
Beef Hams......	18,663 tierces and barrels.
Pork	186,419 barrels.
Cut Meats.......	42,338 tierces.
Boxed Meats ....1,000,851 boxes.
Hams	54,954 tierces and barrels.
Tongues	11,138 tierces and barrels.

1885.

Beef	17,567 tierces.
Beef	31,518 barrels.
Beef	435,247 cases.
Beef Hams......	20,536 tierces and barrels.
Pork...........	182,744 barrels.
Hams	66,888 boxes.
Tongues	13,827 tierces and barrels.

Lard, "made from hog round, say head, gut, leaf, and trimmings," is mainly in demand by lard-refiners and oil-pressers, and passes through the hands of five inspectors and weighers of lard and provisions for delivery on sale or contract. The better grades are ordinarily sold from the packer's brands on the tierces, and but seldom from samples. The receipts at New York during the years 1880 and 1885 were as follows:

	Tierces and Barrels.	Kegs.	Cases.
In 1880....	733,119	171,343	25,449
In 1885....	393,040	163,288	55,906

New York and Chicago are the principal markets for farm and pastoral products in the United States. It is difficult to determine which of the two exerts the greater influence upon the values of these commodities. Formerly, under the pressure of pecuniary necessity, Chicago bent her head in respectful obedience to New York's commercial dogmatism. Now that she is financially independent she insists on leading where she was wont to follow. New York gracefully declines the leadership, listens with a spirit of maternal pride to her daughter's assumptions, and braces herself to maintain supremacy. With a population that has grown from seventy in 1830 to seven hundred thousand in 1886; with nearly twenty-three million bushels of inspected grain in her mighty elevators at one time; with an average of over 22,000 head of live stock arriving within her precincts on every day of the year; slaughtering 1,188,154 cattle in 1884, and packing 4,222,780 hogs in 1883; studying in minutest detail the wants and tastes of foreign buyers, and receiving direct orders from them—Chicago is a friendly rival that it is impossible to despise. She neglects no scientific means for facilitating business, of Chicago are represented on the floor of the New York Produce Exchange. No black-board in the elegant hall of the Chicago Board of Trade is so eagerly watched as that which, every five minutes, records the prices current in New York. New York reports only on the material of actual trade. Whatever of grain or provisions

ALEXANDER E. ORR.

saving labor, multiplying transactions, and bringing the markets of the world to her doors. Of this intense vitality, alertness, and sagacity, the splendid edifice of the Board of Trade (the interior of which is represented in our illustration on page 212) is an impressive embodiment. In design, material, and adaptation to mercantile requirements, it meets every want, and is the pride of Chicago, and indeed of the whole Northwest.

The commercial interests of these two great marts are so identified that the one is absolutely necessary to the other. All the prominent grain and provision firms passes through Chicago to various destinations is reckoned among her receipts and shipments. ("All is fish that comes to her net," even though many pass through the meshes.) This usage swells the totals of both, but does not convey an accurate idea of her trade. The following table of statistics* exhibits the amount of receipts and shipments at Chicago, in 1880 and 1885, of flour, wheat, corn, oats, rye, barley, beef, pork, other cured meats, lard, butter, seeds, live hogs, cattle, and sheep.

* Supplied by Statistician's Department of the New York Produce Exchange, and by the secretary of the Chicago Board of Trade.

Receipts, 1880.		Shipments, 1880.	
Flour	3,215,389 barrels	....	2,862,737 barrels.
Wheat	23,541,607 bushels	....	22,796,288 bushels.
Corn	97,272,844 bushels	....	93,572,934 bushels.
Oats	23,490,915 bushels	....	20,649,427 bushels.
Rye	1,869,218 bushels	....	1,365,165 bushels.
Barley	5,211,536 bushels	....	3,110,985 bushels.
Beef	6,282 packages	....	117,203 packages.
Pork	39,091 barrels	....	367,324 barrels.
Other Cured Meats	164,437,225 pounds	....	958,036,113 pounds.
Lard	68,387,204 pounds	....	333,539,138 pounds.
Butter	67,337,044 pounds	....	59,970,601 pounds.
Seeds	245,930,484 pounds	....	195,616,050 pounds.
Liquors and High Wines	127,468 barrels	....	218,582 barrels.

Receipts, 1885.		Shipments, 1885.	
Flour	5,385,772 barrels	....	5,240,199 barrels.
Wheat	18,909,717 bushels	....	13,975,032 bushels.
Corn	62,930,897 bushels	....	58,805,567 bushels.
Oats	37,678,753 bushels	....	32,426,462 bushels.
Rye	1,892,760 bushels	....	1,216,961 bushels.
Barley	10,760,127 bushels	....	5,583,003 bushels.
Beef (Dressed)	295,960 pounds	....	484,051,428 pounds.
Beef	6 packages	....	14,649 packages.
Beef	312 barrels	....	101,934 barrels.
Pork	34,959 barrels	....	393,216 barrels.
Other Cured Meats	162,540,742 pounds	....	705,365,709 pounds.
Lard	61,054,257 pounds	....	255,121,101 pounds.
Butter	92,275,988 pounds	....	96,816,686 pounds.
Seeds (Grass)	67,673,084 pounds	....	52,626,856 pounds.
Live Hogs	6,940,841	....	1,792,681
Cattle	1,906,408	....	747,983
Sheep	998,888	....	259,310

The receipts of domestic cereal produce in New York for the years 1880 and 1885 were as follows:

1880.

Wheat	59,492,246 bushels.
Corn	61,076,810 bushels.
Oats	13,997,690 bushels.
Barley	3,929,517 bushels.
Malt	2,815,853 bushels.
Rye	2,045,758 bushels.
Buckwheat	19,747 bushels.
Pease	497,896 bushels.
Beans	111,122 barrels.
Grass Seed	124,897 bags.
Flaxseed	1,020,526 bushels.

1885.

Wheat	24,329,458 bushels.
Corn	38,257,144 bushels.
Oats	26,236,970 bushels.
Barley	4,260,713 bushels.
Malt	4,264,786 bushels.
Rye	700,290 bushels.
Buckwheat	29,626 bushels.
Pease	305,116 bushels.
Beans	406,652 bushels.
Grass Seed	243,946 bushels.
Flaxseed	1,715,588 bushels.

Trade in these immense quantities of cereals begins with purchase from the producers, and continues in sale or consignment by purchasers to New York dealers. On arrival at the city they are sampled by means of a hollow iron sampling-rod, whose valve opens to admit the grain as the rod is thrust into the hatches of a vessel, or the interior of a car, and closes so as to retain the sample when it is drawn out. This process, repeated several times by responsible inspectors, in different parts of a car or boat load, secures reliable samples, which are placed in boxes on the Exchange tables. Cards affixed state the name of the seller and the quality of the cereal, and facilitate business with the miller or exporter who wishes to buy.

The relative declension of the cereal traffic at New York and its corresponding growth at other ports between the years 1866 and 1875 necessitated changes in the methods of business at this point. Vessels with incoming cargoes naturally sought ports where outgoing cargoes could best be obtained, and found them elsewhere. New York had no elevators; manual labor handled the grain; and each consignment was kept separate on canal-boats and barges, which were towed from one place to another in the harbor until all were discharged. Waste, delay, disputes between merchants and railroad companies and between buyers and sellers, followed by loss of trade, were the inevitable result. New York was the last important mart —under the lead of Franklin Edson and others—to adopt, and that in the face of

THE CALL ROOM.

FRANKLIN EDSON.

The grain trade proceeds under the supervision of a committee of five—an inspector-in-chief, a registrar, and a committee of three on the delivery of warehoused grain. The Committee on Grain, of which at the time of this writing Mr. C. R. Hickox is chairman, annually establishes the several grades, supervises the inspector-in-chief and his assistants, and fixes the fees which (below $20,000) constitute the Grain Inspection Fund, out of which salaries, audited expenses, and claims for damages are paid. Of the grades of grain established in 1884, ten were of white, amber, and red winter wheat, eight of spring, and one of State wheat. More or less of brightness, soundness, dryness, plumpness, and cleanness determines the grade. The word "Steamer" prefixed to "grade" denotes slight softness or dampness. Corn has eleven grades, oats eight, rye three, barley sixteen, pease three. Heated or unmerchantable grain is not graded at all. Standard samples of all grades of grain are kept at the Produce Exchange. The duties of the chief inspector and his deputies are to inspect, grade, and ascertain the weights of all parcels going into store as graded grain (at the owner's risk), and for which transferable warehouse receipts are given; also to inspect and ascertain the weights of all deliveries from warehouse or from railroad depot. A daily copy of his record is furnished to the registrar, and returns in duplicate to warehousemen and railroad companies of all receipts and deliveries of graded grain.

Of these warehouses, conveniently approachable by ocean vessels, having customary shipping facilities, including seventeen elevators and proper cleaning apparatus, the collective capacity is 14,110,000 bushels. The rates of storage, including weighing, are $\frac{1}{2}$ cent per bushel for 10 days, and $\frac{1}{4}$ cent per bushel for each suc-

fierce opposition, the Western system of grading grain. This enables the Western buyer who has accumulated as much wheat in his warehouses as he wishes to carry, and who knows daily and almost hourly the market prices in New York, to telegraph to any broker, and through him to sell for future delivery the amount and grade of wheat he may have on hand. He then ships it so that it may arrive in time to fulfil his contract. Certainty and precision are thus given to his business movements. He is relieved from the compulsory speculation attendant upon consignments of whose sale, price, and delivery he is perforce ignorant. The present terminal facilities for handling grain are so complete that they have restored to New York, probably for all time, the control of the grain trade on the Atlantic seaboard. True, option dealing and some objectionable practices have come in with the new system, but that is only in harmony with the universal fact that every solid good is abused by unwise and greedy men.

ceeding 10 days. Elevation from canal-boats costs ½ cent, screening and blowing ¼ cent, mixing on delivery ¼ per cent., per bushel. Consignors may have their grain kept separate if so desired, but the practice is to mix parcels of grain of the same grade together, without regard to ownership. Warehoused grain heated, but not through fault of warehouseman, is posted upon the bulletin-board of the Exchange, and made deliverable to depositors of longest date, the logical presumption being that it belongs to them. In the year ending June 30, 1885, no less than 586,699 bushels were posted as being out of condition.

The registrar keeps an exact account with each warehouse firm, and every Monday morning reports to the superintendent how many bushels of each grade of grain remained in store on the previous Saturday evening. In case of damage by fire, provision is made for the cancellation of warehouse receipts affected, and the issue of new ones covering the amount of grain injured. The tender of railroad guaranteed certificates, railroad elevator receipts, or regular warehouse receipts of the grade sold constitutes a delivery of the grain, as between buyers and sellers, in the regular course of business. Each delivery from store must be of 5000 bushels or more of oats or barley, 8000 bushels or more of wheat or corn, of 5000 bushels on boat or barge, and from cars of 500 bushels per car of all grain except oats, which must be of 900 bushels. Inspected and certified grain afloat in the port may also be delivered under the superintendence of the inspector. Demurrage at specified rates is charged to parties who fail to take pos-

session of property within defined periods. Graded grain sold on time contracts is transferred by order drawn on himself by the seller, who must issue a specific order for the delivery of the quantity named to the last receiver at the maturity of the contract. Grain bought at buyer's option is deliverable on the day or day after it is called for, and certainly at maturity of contract. Minor rules, too voluminous for notice, guard the rights of all participants in the grain trade.

Grain and feed delivered from railroad

C. R. HICKOX, CHAIRMAN OF GRAIN COMMITTEE.

tracks are under the supervision of the Produce Exchange board of weighers and measurers of track grain and feed. These furnish consignees with samples, weigh and measure the materials, issue returns in duplicate to owners (whose endorsement is needful to pass title to buyers), and also a triplicate return to the railroad company delivering the property, for the adjustment of freight and charges.

An original margin of ten cents per

INTERIOR OF THE BOARD OF TRADE, CHICAGO.

bushel on wheat, rye, and barley, and of five cents on corn and oats, may be called on all sales or purchases of grain on the spot, to arrive, or for future delivery, upon deposit of an equal amount by the caller. On all contracts for future delivery a further margin may be called to the extent of any variation of the market value from the contract price. Calls may also be made of one cent per bushel above or below current quotation, when no original margin is deposited.

The Call Room daily presents an impressive spectacle of the traffic in grain. The first call is made at 11.45 A.M., the second at 1.30 P.M. In January, 1886, the successive calls are for oats deliverable in quantities of 5000 bushels, or multiples thereof, in March, April, or May; of No. 2 corn, steamer corn, or No. 2 red winter wheat, deliverable in lots of 8000 bushels, or multiples, for cash, or in February, March, April, May, or June, at the option of the seller, unless otherwise stated. Deliveries are ordinarily made on the 1st of the month, but may be on any subsequent day. About 350 brokers are present. William L. Eichell, caller of grain, presides. In rapid, monotonous voice, drawn out at the close of each sentence, he announces: "No. 2 oats, January. What are they offered at?" A seller, in loud, explosive tones, replies, "At 34¾" (per bushel), or, "At ¾." "At ¾," jerkily echoes the caller. "What is bid? ⅛ bid, ¼, ½, ⅝ bid." "I'll take 'em," shrieks an excited individual. "Sold by Jones to Smith at ¾." Another lot is offered "at 33¾." "⅜, ½, ⅝," bid. "Sold," growls the seller. "Sold by Thomson to Johnson at ⅝." No breath is wasted. "What is offered?" (oats). "35," says one; "⅞," another. "At?" queries the caller. If so, ⅞ replies, "At;" if not so, "Give." "At ¾—any part of 5, 10, 50, 100 loads," is another offer. This holds till all are taken. Any part sold at a different rate vacates all previous bids and offers. The first offer to buy or sell at a price is accepted before subsequent offers at the same figures may be placed. If doubt arise as to whether the caller has awarded the purchase to the proper bidder, appeal is made from his decision. "Sustained or not!" is, in substance, his pithy submission to the members present. "Aye" sustains, "Nay" does not. Which is in the majority he decides, and in case of doubt, like a wise man, gives himself the benefit of

it. The call lasts ten or fifteen minutes, and occasionally has the accompaniment of callithumpian discord, blended with the fiendish screeches of a dozen frenzied locomotives. All speculative transactions are not improperly such, to be settled by the payment of differences. For example, a buyer may have an order from Liverpool for the delivery of a certain quantity of grain in three or six months' time. He buys what he wants in the Call Room. Then, chartering ship or steamer, he presents his claim at maturity to the seller, and demands the warehouse or other receipt, specifying the place where the property will be delivered. The first call in grain was on May 14, 1879. Steamer and No. 2 corn only were called; wheat and oats were added afterward. In this feverish spot the "young Napoleon of finance," Ferdinand Ward, began his meteoric career.

Speculative sales of lard in lots of 250 tierces of 320 pounds each, or multiples thereof, are also made in the Call Room, at 11 A.M. and 2 P.M., the caller of provisions and margin clerk presiding. Provisions are not now called. The original margin of $2 per tierce of lard is seldom called where parties are of known financial solvency, but margins corresponding with the fluctuations of the market may be required. Deliveries are not held to be necessary, and speculative contracts are usually settled by the payment of differences. The sales on call for the year ending June 30, 1885, were of 60,384,000 bushels of wheat, 32,597,000 of corn, 5,360,000 of oats, and 130,250 tierces of lard; in the previous year 53,480,000 bushels of wheat, 31,304,000 corn, 13,875,000 oats, and 295,750 tierces of lard. No pork was called in 1884 or 1885. Margins to the amount of $24,398,215 were deposited in the fiscal year 1885.

Option sales in the "Wheat Pit" are quite as magnetic and quite as electric as those in the Call Room. The "Pit" is the scalper's delight. He has an idea that the market is going up, buys a boatload, or any quantity of grain that may be offered, sells it at an advance of ⅛ cent per bushel, thus scalps the market, and is prouder of the exploit than a Comanche after successful pursuit of hair.

Business begins in the "Pit" at 10.30 A.M. Buyers and sellers are indiscriminately blended in the compact, throbbing, surging mass. All offers and bids are on a unit basis of 8000 bushels. Winter wheat is the only grain in mind. "I'll give 4½ [94½ cents per bushel] for May wheat," is the bid of a nervous, active broker, emphasized by uplifted hand and moving fingers. "I'll sell at 5," is the quick rejoinder of a neighbor. "I'll give ⅝." "I'll sell you at ¾." ⅛ is the only obstacle to a bargain. Long and furiously, or short and sharply, the conflict rages around that ⅛. The tug of war on the part of the seller is to pull the buyer up ⅛, and on the part of the buyer to pull the seller down ⅛. The contest is quite as exciting as aught in the intercollegiate games. But seldom is the battle drawn. Victory, hesitant in the vocal hurricane, decides for one of two parties. Bids and offers are usually regulated by telegrams from Chicago. The difference in prices between the two marts should be the cost of transmission from the latter to New York. Manipulation, or, in other words, gambling, at either point, defies all criteria of value. A "corner" in Chicago may raise wheat there above the normal price at New York; or a broken corner in New York may depress wheat below the healthful standard at Chicago.

Corners in commercial staples may be either good or evil, according to circumstances. Those of accidental character may come from the unforeseen failure of goods to arrive at New York in time for delivery. Such an event temporarily throws the command of prices into the hands of dealers who have an ample stock on hand. Corners, protective in design, may be made by persons or cliques who accept the offers made by gambling speculators on the market. These sell for future delivery what they do not own, in order to depress prices below what they sell at, and to make profit by the transaction. The protective corner arrests these "commercial pirates," and mulcts them heavily for release. Caught in their own traps, the bears howl horribly against the wickedness of corners in general. "Serve 'em right," is the only just remark. An accidental or protective corner may develop into an aggressive one; but this last is usually a conspiracy from the outset, born of cunning and overreaching, repulsive to honesty, denounced by all honorable merchants, and very injurious to commerce.

The facility with which sales and purchases for future delivery are made has enormously augmented the volume of trade. Foreign merchants avail themselves of it to provide for the prospective needs of different markets. It gives to the farmer a ready home market for his products at their full value, and affords to traders the opportunity of selling at a reasonable profit and at a moment's notice, and to deliver at option within specified times, as may be agreed. The exports of grain and grain products from the United States in the fiscal year 1885 were valued at $160,370,821. Seventy-five per cent., or more, of the whole was probably sold ten or twenty times over before it was finally shipped. Sales and purchases, charter of ships, bills of exchange for payment, sale of latter—all contemplated "future" delivery. Similar remarks are true of oil, tobacco, cotton, and other commercial staples. The system is a device of necessity, the judicious adaptation of prospective supply to probable demand, the work of foreseeing prudence. It may be, and is, abused by gambling speculators, or prostituted to assist aggressive corner conspirators, and in all such instances is shamefully demoralizing.

Settlements without actual delivery are not always obnoxious to strict probity. When honestly effected, as in the Bank Clearing-House, they are wholly concordant with it. Besides, they save much needless trouble and expense.

The Committee on Flour appoints a chief inspector and his assistants, keeps for reference a standard sample of each of the various grades of flour and meal, furnishes duplicate samples to the inspector, and causes flour and meal to be classified according to these standards. Extra No. 1, Extra No. 2, Superfine, and Fine are the established grades of wheat; Superfine and Fine, of rye flour. The committee also guards the sacredness of flour or inspection brands, provides for the inspection of barrels and bags, and designates the manner in which charges for service shall be collected. These charges, to an amount not exceeding $20,000, constitute "the flour-inspection fund," in custody of the treasurer, out of which salaries and expenses are paid.

Agents of metropolitan merchants buy of Western millers, or solicit consignments, on which advances are made. The West India, province, and general export demand is met through samples drawn by the inspector. Elasticity, color, dryness, and body in the dough are tests of quality. Much depends on the skill of the miller in dressing and cleaning the wheat. The neat, cleanly, deft manipulation of the flour expert will soon detect the quality of the work. Putting some of the flour on the palm of his hand, he applies the magnifying-glass, or the smoother, that he may examine the color, purity, and granulation. If the first and second be satisfactory, and the third sharp, there will be life in the sponge and dough. This is proven by pouring water from a handy little teapot upon the flour, mixing it, pulling it, breaking it. If the dough be short and inelastic, it is best adapted for crackers and pastry. Flours are mixed for ordinary bread, and for special purposes of the bakers.

Receipts in New York, 1880.
Flour............5,422,252 barrels.
Corn Meal........ 261,522 barrels and sacks.
Oatmeal .... 112,650 packages.
Buckwheat Flour... 72,201 sacks.

Receipts in New York, 1885.
Flour............5,970,627 barrels.
Corn Meal........ 477,196 barrels and sacks.
Oatmeal .... 99,581 packages.
Buckwheat Flour... 83,692 sacks.

Exports from New York, 1880.
Flour...................4,215,415 barrels.
Corn Meal............... 203,716 barrels.
Oatmeal .... 62,902 barrels.
Rye Flour............... 5,204 barrels.

Exports from New York, 1885.
Flour...................3,696,149 barrels.
Corn Meal............... 152,670 barrels.
Oatmeal .... 56,079 bags.
Rye Flour............... 3,811 barrels.

The Committee on Distilled Spirits licenses six inspectors and gaugers, who must make their returns of "proof," "just proof," "above proof," or "below proof," in accordance with the straight gauge rod, wantage rod, the hydrometer used by the government in the ascertainment of the tax on distilled spirits, or the Gendar hydrometer conforming in all respects to the government standard. Of whiskey 57,325, of high wines 58,247, and of alcohol 220,977 barrels were received at New York in 1880. In 1885, of whiskey 134,318, of high wines 74,304, and of alcohol 68,257 barrels arrived.

The Committee on Naval Stores licenses inspectors in New York and other cities, decides prices as a basis for business settlements, and holds a standard sample of spirits of turpentine with which all sold in shipping order must agree. Settlements

of contracts are on the basis of 310 pounds for a barrel of rosin, and 43 gallons for a barrel of spirits of turpentine. Speculation follows the usual channels, and is in quantities not less than 25 barrels of the latter, or 100 barrels of rosin or tar.

Receipts, 1880.
Turpentine, Crude........... 2,871 barrels.
Turpentine, Spirits .... 99,789 barrels.
Rosin ....389,125 barrels.
Tar........................ 21,706 barrels.

Receipts, 1885.
Turpentine, Crude........... 3,241 barrels.
Turpentine, Spirits .... 76,139 barrels.
Rosin ....318,656 barrels.
Tar........................ 23,849 barrels.

Exports from New York, 1880.
Turpentine, Crude........... 4,263 barrels.
Turpentine, Spirits .... 36,624 barrels.
Rosin ....189,419 barrels.
Tar........................ 6,883 barrels.

Exports from New York, 1885.
Turpentine, Crude........... 173 barrels.
Turpentine, Spirits .... 13,600 barrels.
Rosin ....155,123 barrels.
Tar........................ 5,714 barrels.

Connected with the natural oil industry is the Committee on Petroleum, which appoints the Petroleum Quotation Committee to quote prices for business settlements, and administer the rules of this traffic. The Committee on National Transit Certificates of crude oil is composed of members dealing in these documents. Transactions are in 1000 barrel lots, or multiples thereof; and are for Cash, Regular, or Future Delivery. The bulk of the business, whether real or fictitious, in this comparatively new but enormously valuable product, is done at the New York Consolidated Stock and Petroleum Exchange.

Its marvellous growth may be estimated by comparing the production of 82,000 barrels in 1859 with that of 21,500,000 in 1885. The computed product between and inclusive of the two years is 287,000,000 barrels. Speculation therein is rampant. There is, of course, a solid, or rather fluid, basis for the National Transit Certificates, but much of the pretended dealing in them has as little real relation to them as to the outflow of caoutchouc in Brazil. Of the production of 1885 about 70 per cent., mostly refined, was exported, partly in barrels and partly in cases. Of the latter, about 10,000,000, containing two cans of five gallons each, were shipped to China, Japan, India, Java, and Singapore. Many large cargoes are sold on the floor of the Exchange, owing to the facilities it affords for bringing buyers, sellers, and shipping agents together.

The trade in animal, vegetable, and mineral oils is supervised by the Committee on Oils, under rules which define qualities, quantities, and weights of materials; basis and price of contract settlements; size and place of deliveries; condition of packages; tares, etc.; manner of call of oils, margins, contracts, transfers, etc. Six inspectors and testers of oils are employed in conducting this department of trade. The receipts in 1880 at New York were: of lard oil 9075, of lubricating oil 34,714, of cotton-seed oil 44,084 barrels. The exports were: of lard oil 734,569, and of cotton-seed oil 1,340,709 gallons. In 1885 the receipts were: of lard oil 9234, of cotton-seed oil 67,438, and of lubricating oil 27,757 barrels. The exports were: of lard oil 579,580, of cotton-seed oil 1,351,015, and of lubricating oil 12,217,873 gallons.

The Committee on Lighterage acts under rules defining the duty of lightermen, rates of demurrage, pecuniary liability for extra towing, etc.; that on Butter consists of three receivers and two exporters, who recommend to the Board of Managers for license as inspectors of butter three members of the Exchange, whose duty it is to pass judgment on lots of real or imitation butter referred to them, and to brand such lots accordingly. An official weigher of butter is also licensed on their recommendation. The Committee on Cheese, assisted by an inspector and weigher, who is also inspector of rejections, is charged with supervision of trade in this manufacture. Two brewers and three dealers compose the Committee on Hops. These vegetable products are subject to inspection, weighing, and sundry regulations interesting to those who are engaged in dealing in them. Receipts and exports of the last three articles at New York for the years 1880 and 1885 were as follows:

Receipts, 1880.
Butter..................1,479,014 packages.
Cheese.................2,672,759 packages.
Hops................... 66,759 bales.

Receipts, 1885.
Butter..................1,733,643 packages.
Cheese.................2,191,531 packages.
Hops................... 146,209 bales.

Exports, 1880.
Butter.................. 29,030,908 pounds.
Cheese ....129,524,180 pounds.
Hops.................. 28,798 bales.

Exports, 1885.
Butter..................11,307,005 pounds.
Cheese ....91,770,106 pounds.
Hops................... 60,642 bales.

To the Committee on Maritime Affairs is confided the enforcement of the rules relative to the chartering, loading, unloading, and demurrage (or charges for delay and extra service) of sea-going vessels.

Complaint is frequently made of misrepresentations emanating "from the romancing brains of newspaper reporters, who sometimes look upon the New York Produce Exchange and the New York Stock Exchange as only a little more magnificent and a little more legalized gambling houses than some uptown"; whereas "there is more of personal honor in the keeping of contracts and engagements involving losses and profits of thousands, without regard to legal liability or compulsion, than can be found in any other equal territory on the face of the earth." That the opinion of reporters is largely that of the general public there can be no question. To what extent is it in harmony with the facts?

All business transactions are the outgrowth of intention to fulfil contracts according to terms, or not so to fulfil them. The first series is legitimate; the second illegitimate, because speculative in the gambling sense. The first necessarily accepts the risks incident to undoubted and continuous demand for consumption: the second, from motives of cupidity or love of excitement, unnecessarily accepts risks contingent upon the operation of known and unknown forces that do not essentially differ from those of the gambling table. In every legitimate business transaction each of the parties to it parts with something that he esteems of less value to himself than that which he receives. Mutual interest and obligation are essential to it. Business is not the getting of a maximum for a minimum; neither is it "the art of getting whatever you can without any consideration of equivalents." This may be the definition of "Sam'l of Posen," but never of true philosophy. Values ought to determine prices, not prices values. The fundamental consideration is what a thing is worth, and not what it can be bought or sold for. True business and gambling are opposed to each other as light and darkness; different from each other as a nursing mother from a cannibal. "Two years ago," said Chauncey M. Depew to the members of the New York Produce Exchange in 1884, "the speculators of Chicago, acting upon a theory which might have been well enough if food products could have been purchased by Europe only from America, by gigantic corners and other artificial processes drove the price of wheat up to fabulous figures." This feat awoke the slumbering energies of other nations, who became anxious to share in the wealth accruing from unusual harvests. The world went to wheatgrowing. The result, in the United States, was the exportation of gold instead of grain, and the accumulation of debts instead of dollars. The orator added: "In the Wheat Pit at Chicago in a single year was buried more of the future prosperity of this republic than the sum of all the traffic which flows through that great city in a decade." This bold statement, uttered with characteristic courage, gave no small offence to the Chicagonese, and has been challenged with a boldness and force of reasoning—that of Alexander E. Orr—not inferior to his own. All parties agree that the "Wheat Pits" of Chicago, New York, and other cities have, at times and under certain circumstances, been injurious to commercial interests; but their defenders claim that these injuries are but as "a drop in the bucket" compared with the universal benefit to all interests secured by the ability to make "future" sales of merchandise. The injury done by the Chicago operations denounced by Mr. Depew lies in the loss of control—for some time at least—of the European markets. Whether the magnitude of that injury be so large as he asserted is matter of grave doubt. The daily bank deposits and withdrawals may be accepted as representative of the traffic flowing through that city. A low estimate of their amount would be four million dollars. This sum, multiplied by 300 (business days in a year), equals $1,200,-000,000; and by 3000 (ten years), $12,000,-000,000. Gambling greed kills the geese that lay golden eggs. The damage done at the epoch in question may not amount to twelve billion dollars, but still it was enormous.

The rules of any exchange may ordain that the seller *must* deliver and the buyer *must* receive, unless the contract can be legitimately cleared in some other way. There never was a law, human or divine, but some men would try to break it. Just as there may be thieves in a church, so—and with more likelihood—there may be gamblers in a wheat pit. A million bushels of wheat at a certain price, deliverable at option in the future, may be offered in the "Pit." Some one may cry out, "I'll take it." The contract is closed. Both parties are bound by it. Both join in the declaration, "We are not gamblers—no, never." Are they not gamblers when there is no *intention* on the part of the seller to deliver or of the buyer to receive the wheat when the contract expires, but only to settle the difference between the price current when it is sold and that when it is deliverable by payment of the loser to the winner of the bet? The margin, judiciously designed to guard the interests of honest parties to equitable contracts, is converted into an instrument of gambling by those who do *not* intend the exchange of values or of their representatives. Speculative options are detrimental to beneficent business, inasmuch as they enable insufficient capital to operate largely on small margins, and thus to cause fictitious markets and deranged prices. "The American option is the curse of the world," is a *dictum* of the *Mark Lane Express* that may find some justification in this fact. All laws against washed sales and fictitious sales are inoperative where option gambling is common. Extravagance and dishonesty attend it; financial if not moral ruin is a very frequent sequence. Unwilling to accept consequences, the pallid victims—uncanny as Banquo's ghost—often reappear amidst activities where their presence is not joyously welcomed. The fact is that while legitimate business is attended by inseparable risks, much of the so-called trading in stocks and products is unmitigated gambling. It is a consuming parasitic growth on otherwise healthy commerce.

"Puts" and "calls" are subjects of so-called trading in and around the Wheat Pit from the close of business at 3.30 to 4 P.M. Brokers of all ages excitedly engage in it. Some of them may be acting in behalf of firms or persons who wish to remain unknown. He who sells a "put" collects $10 from the man to whom he sells the privilege of "putting" or selling to him 8000 bushels of wheat at a specified price on the next day, or at any period within a designated time, if he (the purchaser) wishes to do so. The price specified in the put is lower than the market price at the time the put is sold; *e. g.*, Cornheimer sells to Jackson a put—always of 8000 bushels, or multiples thereof—for one or two days at 93 when the ruling rate is 93⅜, and pockets $10 whether Jackson does put the quantity to him in that time or not. Or Cornheimer may have sold "short" 80,000 bushels at 94. He must fulfil his contract, or pay the difference between that and higher rates at maturity. He sells ten puts of 8000 bushels each at 93½, and pockets $100. He is perfectly willing to have the 80,000 bushels put to him at 93⅓, for thereby he will make ½ cent per bushel on the quantity he has contracted to supply. Whether it is put or not, he has received $100, and to that extent certainly has "hedged" himself against loss.

A "call" is the reverse of a put, and is the privilege of calling for 8000 bushels at a given price within a definite time, the price being higher than that of the last market-day. The cost of a call is also $10. The whole put and call business is simply betting on prices going up or down. It has grown to very large proportions. One dealer has been known to buy or sell to the extent of 400,000 bushels in the half-hour of active operations. The rules of the Exchange take no cognizance of the practice. It is said that it cannot be eliminated because of the difficulty of drawing a hard and fast line between the right and the wrong. A repudiating bettor may be boycotted, but cannot be disciplined.

Nothing human is physically or morally perfect. Evitable evil is to be denounced wherever it may be. But in speaking of men and of corporations just criticism requires that the good as well as the evil that is in them shall receive due recognition. The New York Produce Exchange has done immeasurable good to the commerce of the United States by simplifying and establishing its laws, gathering and disseminating all knowledge related to it, preventing its concentration in the hands of a few men of enormous wealth, and equalizing the chances of individual success. The average daily value of its business exceeds ten million dollars. The greater part of the farm products exported are handled by it. To the transportation of agricultural and mineral staples from the interior to the seaboard at minimum cost and maximum speed it has been no less serviceable. Whatever favors this, it has advocated; whatever would hinder, it has opposed. More than any other organization it contributed to the absolute freedom of the State canals from the exaction of tolls. In the development of indigenous resources it is one of the most potent factors. Its accumulations have helped to cover the land with a net-work of railways and canals. The debasement of the currency by means of the 79-cent silver dollar receives its hot condemnation. In defence of the purity of exported food products, of reciprocally beneficial commercial treaties, and of maritime rights, its stirring voice has often been heard. "The men who continually hold their fingers upon the commercial pulse of the nation are best able to detect injurious influences, and to suggest the necessary legislative remedies," is the just assertion of its members.

The Sickles Brigade—4000 strong—volunteer hospital corps, patriotic members enlisting or forming relieving committees, were the practical response of the Produce Exchange to the appeals of the heroic Hancock and others during the agony of the civil war. Organized to deal in the products of the country, it is patriotic by doing so—piratical only as some of its members gamble in them. It is one of the strongest cohesive forces of the body-politic, one of its most effective ethical teachers, and—by its system of arbitrative jurisprudence—one of the most hard-headed illustrations of corporate good sense. "We search our records in vain," said ex-President Herrick, "for one appeal of the sorrowful and suffering unheard, one cry for help unanswered."

Each of the 2900 subscribing members to the Gratuity Fund—which bears the stamp of ex-President Parker's genius—pays $3 on the death of any one of the number. Out of the proceeds a regularly increasing sum is paid to the widow, or divided among other heirs by just regulations. It is a gift, and therefore free from all legal claims—a just provision for helpless wives and dependent children. After the Exchange is freed from debt, part of the surplus revenue will swell the Gratuity Fund, which now amounts to between $800,000 and $900,000. In or about 1891 the appropriation payable to heirs of each deceased member will be about $9000. This sum, with $1000 added from the Surplus Fund, will then constitute the maximum payment of $10,000.

DIRT PIES.

BY THE AUTHOR OF "GEMINI."

I.

A GROUP of playmates, two boys, two girls, and a pair of Newfoundland puppies, were frisking about under the trees that shaded a road not far from the house at Blackheath Farm. Overhead, the young leaves at play in the sweet May air cast pretty trembling shadows on the children's happy faces, and the Newfoundland puppies—two splendid tawny creatures, so big and strong now that one wondered what they would be when they had passed the age of puppyhood—seemed to enjoy the frolic quite as much as the boys and girls. A small stream crossed the road at this place, whose current was so swift and bright that some one, in a moment of inspiration, had called it Happy Creek, and its rippling water seemed to dance to the music of its happy name. This was the children's favorite playing place, affording fine opportunities for soaking shoes and stockings, muddying jackets and trousers, and other like achievements dear to the childish heart.

Blackheath, so called from the coal mines on the place, was the country home of a family by the name of Heath, and these were the Heath children, a motherless brood, too young yet to understand the sad significance of the fact. Jack, the eldest boy, was about twelve, a well-grown lad for his age, and the king of his company; Otway, a year and a half younger, who thought the king could do no wrong; Marian, a rosy-cheeked, blond-haired girl of eight; and finally Polly, who was four, a round dot of a child, so full of spirits and so chubby as to look like an animated dumpling. She was the first to perceive a young lady coming down the road from the direction of the house, and breaking from her companions, she ran as fast as her fat little legs could carry her toward the new-comer, crying, "Kafrin! Kafrin!"

The young lady, Katharine Heath, the children's eldest sister, who filled as far as she could the place of mother to them, was a girl of about twenty, with a tall slight figure and a sweet fresh face. She held a book in her hand, which she tossed on the grassy bank that bordered the road, and catching Polly in her arms, covered the child's dimpled cheek with kisses, while the puppies, Drab and Queen, leap-

ed up about them to testify their interest in the matter.

It was a charming sight, the two blooming faces pressed close together, while Katharine's slim figure swayed lightly with the child's weight, like a slender stalk bending beneath the burden of two roses.

"Katharine," cried Marian, running to meet her sister, and looking up in her face with coaxing eyes, "it is *such* a nice day for making dirt pies!"

"Kafrin," echoed Polly, putting up her red lips to be kissed again, "dirt pies."

"Dirt pies, with those clean dresses and aprons!" exclaimed Katharine.

"We won't get a speck on them," promised Marian.

"Not a 'peck," said Polly.

"Not a peck? No; only half a peck, you little pat of butter," cried Jack, whose chief mission in life was to tease Polly.

"I ain't no pat o' butter," said Polly, doubling up her little fat fists, and stamping with one little fat foot.

The children were so bent on making mud pies in this delightful spot by the water, where the ingredients were so convenient and plentiful, that Katharine could not find it in her heart to refuse, notwithstanding the clean dresses and aprons.

An elm-tree growing in one of the Blackheath meadows cast its pleasant shade over the stream at this point, making a cool, sheltered spot, where the cattle loved to drink and the wayfarer to rest and water his horses. In the crotch of the tree whose trunk inclined over the meadow fence and dipped toward the stream, a secure and comfortable seat had been constructed years ago for Katharine, who played there with her doll. Now she found it a charming nook for reading, as secluded as a boudoir. Thus perched aloft among the leaves, she was keeping watch over the little ones, and reading her novel. They were all too much absorbed in their occupations to hear, or at least to heed, the approach of a gentleman on horseback until he had ridden into the middle of the stream, halting just under the tree, where a pool made the water deeper and stiller, and loosening his rein to let his horse drink. A cloud of white butterflies flew up from the surface of the pool; the children and dogs stopped their play to gaze at the stranger; Katharine peered down through the leaves only to catch a glimpse of a broad-brimmed straw hat that concealed the rider's face as effectually as though it had been an iron mask.

The stranger, meanwhile, was enjoying the shade, the fine air, the cool ripple of the water. His attention was attracted toward Drab and Queen; he knew a fine dog when he saw one, and he had never seen a finer brace of puppies.

While he was still admiring the dogs, a leaf from overhead fluttered down and fell softly on the pommel of his saddle. He started and looked at it with astonishment, for it was not the leaf of a tree, but of a book. He took it up, examined it attentively, and then deliberately folded it and put it in his vest pocket. This incident seemed to draw his attention to the children, who were at a little distance, where the stream was shallower, for he turned and looked at them.

"Hallo, my man!" he said.

The children stopped work and stared, that is, all except Polly, who was busy with what she called a tray of pies—a row of little round dabs of mud on a shingle.

"What is your name?" asked the stranger, looking at Jack.

Jack rose from his hands and knees, pushed back his hat, and surveyed the speaker coolly before he answered. Finally he decided that the man, especially his horse, would do. "Jack Heath, sir."

"And what is the name of this place?" indicating the meadow in which the elm-tree grew.

"Blackheath, sir."

"Humph! So you are Jack Heath of Blackheath, are you?"

"Jack Heath junior, sir."

The stranger smiled. "Those are fine dogs of yours. Good-morning."

He was riding away, when he was arrested by a scream from one of the children. He checked his horse and turned back in serious alarm.

"What is the matter?" he cried.

There stood Polly, with crimson cheeks and tearful eyes, scolding and calling him very uncomplimentary names.

When he came to understand what it was all about, he found that his horse, in stepping out of the water, had trodden on her shingle and demolished her pies. It was more than the little girl could stand, for Drab and Queen had already upset her work more than once.

Jack was adding to her discomfiture by teasing: "Come, Fatima, don't cry. There is plenty of dirt to make more pies. The whole round world is a big dirt pie."

"That's so," said Otway, laughing.

"Kafrin says you sha'n't call me Fatty," sobbed Polly.

The gentleman on horseback began to look uncomfortable. "Come, come, little girl," he said, searching his pockets, and bringing out a small paper parcel, which he gave her.

The puckers in Polly's face smoothed out, and the big tears hung on her eyelashes, while she looked with curiosity and interest, first at the giver and then at the gift, which at length she began to examine. She screamed with delight when she found that it contained ginger-cakes. She had buried her little white teeth in one when Marian arrested her.

"Oh, Polly, don't take the gentleman's cakes, maybe they are for his own little girl."

The gentleman changed color. "I haven't any little girl," he said, with a peculiar smile; then, after a pause, he added: "A kind old lady gave them to me for my own use, but as I never eat cakes, I am glad for Polly to have them. Good-by."

He rode away again, this time without being recalled.

As soon as horse and rider were quite out of sight, Katharine came down from her perch. Her face was aglow with excitement caused by the little incident of the leaf falling from her book, which the children had not perceived, and by her unavailing efforts to get a glimpse of the man's face.

"Jack," she said, abruptly, "who was that?"

"How should I know? I never saw him before," said Jack, absorbed in ginger-cakes.

"He was like General Washington," said Otway.

"He was stiff and ugly," said Jack.

"He was booful," said Polly.

"Come, children, don't be so stupid. Can't you tell me even the color of the man's eyes?"

"No," said Marian, "for he had on blue glasses."

"Blue glasses!"

II.

Katharine's father, Jack Heath of Blackheath, was well known as the finest rider, the greatest spendthrift, and the handsomest man of his day, and though he was now well advanced into middle life, being at least forty-five, his right to these distinctions had not one whit abated. It might also be added that he was the best-loved man. Everybody loved him, and he received affection with the same careless enjoyment, without too much gratitude, that he did the air, the sunlight, or any other blessing that came naturally and without effort on his part.

He was smoking his after-dinner cigar on the vine-covered portico in front of his house, stretched at ease in a deep, luxurious wicker chair. Drab was lying contentedly across his feet, while Queen bent her head to the lazy caress of his hand.

Katharine sat on a cushion on the doorstep near by, with her novel open on her lap. She was not reading, but turning over the leaves in search of the place from which one had been lost that morning.

"Papa," she was saying, "I saw such a fine horse on the road to-day."

"Finer than Firefly, Kitty?" said Mr. Heath, as with head thrown back he watched the smoke from his cigar float upward.

"No, but quite different. This was a roan."

"Not your uncle Barnard's?"

"No, indeed. A stranger, a beautiful creature, with a fine, free walk, and *such* a canter!"

Her father smiled. "I met a gentleman this morning, likewise a stranger; it may be that he and the horse had something to do with each other."

"I should not be at all surprised," said Katharine, eagerly. "What was he like? Was he like the horse?"

"I did not see the horse."

"I mean was he nice-looking," explained Katharine.

"Very."

"Where was he, papa?"

"At your uncle Barnard's. By-the-bye, I met several strangers to-day at Gresham's. You know Reverie is to be sold to-morrow, and a good many persons have been looking over the house and farm."

"Dear old Reverie!" sighed Katharine. "I do hope some nice person will buy it, though nobody could ever take the place of the Greshams."

"Yes, it is a thousand pities they are going out of the neighborhood."

Mr. Heath continued to smoke in silence. When he spoke again, Katharine knew from the inflection of his voice that he had something of importance to communicate.

"Kitty, I have invited two of the gentlemen I met at Reverie to dine here to-morrow, and I want an early dinner; we are going afterward to look at the mines."

"What do they want to see the mines for?" asked Katharine, with sudden foreboding.

"They have an idea of purchasing."

"Papa, you are not going to sell the mines?"

"If I can get my price," said Mr. Heath, quietly knocking the ashes from his cigar.

The following day the two gentlemen interested in mines came to dinner according to appointment. Katharine had looked forward to their coming with more than ordinary curiosity. She had discovered that the leaf missing from her book contained the most interesting part of the story, and she was more than ever anxious to discover who had captured it. She watched with girlish eagerness for the guests' arrival, hoping to catch a glimpse of the roan horse as the first clew toward unravelling the mystery she had created out of a trifling incident. She was disgusted to see them coming arm in arm across the fields on foot.

"The idiots! What could have possessed them to walk, a warm day like this?" turning from the window where she had been peeping from behind a climbing rose.

The children had dined early, and the party at table consisted of four—the host and hostess and the two guests. One of these, a Mr. Brown, was a good-looking young fellow. The other, with the more romantic name of Woodville, was a plain, middle-aged man with a sturdy, well-built figure and sensible face, but with eyes so near-sighted that he seemed scarcely to take in anything not directly under his nose. It was clear he thought of nothing but business, and it was not long before he and Mr. Heath were deep in mines, mining stock, and the like. Brown fell to Katharine to entertain. She led the conversation, adroitly and without difficulty, to horses. Most country-bred men know about horses, and most men like to talk about what they know.

Katharine found Brown only too willing to discuss the subject. He gave her a great deal more information than she cared to have, seeing that her curiosity was limited to one fact, the color of his own riding-horse.

After some skirmishing she ventured to narrow the subject to his individual taste. "Do you ride much? or perhaps you prefer driving?"

"No; I ride constantly."

"You walked here to-day?"

"Yes; I found that my horse had lost a shoe, and Woodville had lamed his, so we were obliged to foot it."

"Is your horse a fine one?"

"I think so. Not much for beauty, but a fine gait, and a first-rate traveller."

"Not much for beauty? Are you sure?"

"Oh yes, quite sure," said Brown, a little puzzled by the question.

"Is he a bay?"

"No; a sorrel."

A pause followed. Brown, not quick in suggesting new topics, presently resumed the one that had already been worn threadbare.

"Talking of horses, there is Woodville, now, who rides the finest horse I know."

Katharine was all interest again.

Woodville, hearing his name mentioned, turned his near-sighted eyes toward the lady's end of the table. "What are you saying about me, Brown?"

"I was telling Miss Heath about that horse you were riding this morning."

"Is he such a beauty?" asked Katharine, eagerly.

"So everybody seems to think," said Woodville. "There is a secret about my horse," added Woodville, apparently not unwilling to take a little conversational refreshment after his business talk, like sweets after meat.

"A secret!" exclaimed Katharine, her face getting uncomfortably red. Now that she had found the clew she was in search of, she was disappointed. It seemed incredible that a plain, practical man like Woodville should take a fancy to pilfer a leaf out of a love story. She did not know half the queer notions that lurk behind the grave, sensible faces of middle-aged men. Her little mystery had suddenly become commonplace.

"What is the secret?" asked Brown.

"I will tell you some day," returned the other, letting his eyes rest for a moment on Katharine's sweet, fresh face, with its varying color, with a sudden conviction that Blackheath contained something more attractive than coal mines.

"Papa," said Katharine, eager to turn the conversation, "you did not tell me who bought Reverie, or, indeed, if it was sold."

"Yes, it was sold, and brought a good price, I am glad to say. The purchaser, by an odd chance, is an old school-mate of mine, whom I have not seen for twenty years."

"I hope he is nice."

"Yes; a gentleman, at all events; a retired army officer—Major Fielding."

"I wish he had remained in the army. What made him leave it?"

"He has lately come into a great inheritance, and he says he is going to settle down into a country gentleman."

"I hope he has quantities of children," said Katharine.

"Unfortunately for you, no. He is a bachelor."

"Ah, that is too bad! And is he going to live at Reverie all by himself? Hasn't he any sisters or nieces or anything?"

"He has plenty of money," said Brown.

"Which won't do me a bit of good," said Katharine. "I had hoped that the new owner of Reverie would have some grown-up daughters, on my account, and ever so many little children to play with Jack and the others."

"You were thinking of your own comfort rather than his, Kitty. Besides, the man is only thirty-five—rather young to be endowed with such a family," said Mr. Heath.

That evening Katharine and her father met in the drawing-room before tea.

"Well, Kitty," he said, pulling the tip of her ear by way of a caress, "so you found out about the roan horse?"

"Yes, and I wish I hadn't."

"Not what you expected, eh?"

"No, indeed; I was looking for something much better."

III.

Messrs. Woodville and Brown did not decide at once in regard to the mines, and Katharine, hearing nothing more of the matter, was happy in the belief that her father had abandoned the idea of selling them. Meanwhile, in spite of Mr. Heath's desire to effect a sale quietly, it became generally known outside that the property was in the market, and other parties became interested in its purchase, but of this Katharine was ignorant.

One afternoon a young man of distinguished appearance and manners, who had called to see Mr. Heath on business, was ushered into the drawing-room, where he had to wait so long before his host made his appearance that he began to walk the floor impatiently.

The windows overlooking a garden at the back of the house were wide open. Beneath the shade of a wide-spreading mimosa-tree, with its feathery bloom, the Heath children were gathered round a basket of cherries. Jack and Otway had eaten so many that they had unbuttoned their jackets, and were lying resting from their labors on the grass. Polly, who had hung Katharine's, Marian's, and her own ears with twin cherries, was trying to decorate Queen's in the same way.

Katharine was sitting on a rustic bench near by, with an open book on her lap.

"Oh, my!" sighed Jack, partly from plethora, partly from sentiment. "Just to think, Dick and Ned Gresham won't ever eat any more of our cherries!"

"Who *has* come to live at Reverie, anyhow?" sighed Otway, similarly oppressed.

"Katharine says an old curmudgeon."

"No, Jack," said Katharine, looking up from her book; "I said a bachelor."

"I know he is a horrid snob, with nothing but money," grumbled Jack.

"No; papa says he is a gentleman," explained Katharine again.

"Well, he is a cranky old fellow without any boys," said Otway.

"And no girls," Marian chimed in.

"The worst thing about him," said Katharine, "is that he has changed the name of the place."

"What!" cried Jack and Otway simultaneously, rising at once to a sitting posture.

"Yes; he says that Reverie is silly and affected."

"The old blunderbuss! What will he call it, then?" asked Otway.

"The Growlery, I dare say," said Katharine.

The young man at the window, finding that the conversation had taken a personal turn, moved away, but he could not get beyond the sound of the voices. He was obliged to hear the young Heaths' speculations in regard to the new owner of Reverie.

While he was waiting, a servant came out of the house looking for Katharine in a great flurry.

"La! Miss Kathrin," she said, "dar is a gentleman in de drawin'-room been waitin' for ever so long, an' I can't find yo' pa nowhar. Won't you go an' see him?"

The stranger in the drawing-room, who had not witnessed this little scene, and was momentarily and impatiently expecting Mr. Heath, was surprised at the entrance of the young lady, who said, in the sweetest and freshest of voices: "I am sorry you have been kept waiting; but papa is out. Will I do?"

The gentleman, who rose as she entered, smiled at the question. He thought she would do, this tall girl with a complexion like a sweet-brier rose, clear gray eyes, and softly waving brown hair.

"I am sorry to have troubled you, Miss Heath," he said, "but I called by appointment to see your father on a matter of business. Another time will do quite as well," he hastened to add, seeing that she looked troubled.

"By appointment! Then I am afraid my father has forgotten. He does forget sometimes. Can't you leave your message with me?" she said, earnestly, trying to make up for her father's delinquency.

"Only that Major Fielding called, thank you," he said, moving to go.

"Major Fielding! Not the gentleman who lives at—at—"

"The Growlery? Yes."

Katharine blushed crimson.

"I could not help hearing, you know; but I did not object in the least. I like the name immensely," he said, with the fine rare smile of a grave man, that gave as much pleasure as it indicated.

It brought an answering smile from Katharine. "The boys and I talk a great deal of nonsense," she said, with a little apologetic shake of the head.

"The boys are very fortunate," said the gentleman, cordially.

Fielding went away wondering if Heath, who was so lax about business matters, deserved to have such a nice daughter.

When he had gone, Katharine remained standing where he had left her, the smile still on her lips, her eyes cast on the floor in deep meditation. "What a fine face!

What a distinguished bearing! Not handsome, but with something about him better than beauty," was the sum of her cogitation.

IV.

Katharine, coming down to breakfast two days later, found beside her plate two letters—a rare pleasure, for she had few correspondents. One of them proved to be only a note from her cousin Alice Barnard, which she read at once; the other, directed in an unfamiliar masculine hand, was more exciting. Like most of her sex, under similar circumstances, she did not open it immediately, but prolonged the pleasure of uncertainty by wondering from whom it came.

"Papa," she said, after a long silence, "Cousin Alice has written to ask me to come and spend a week with her."

"I am glad to hear it. You must go, by all means," said her father, promptly, demolishing his empty egg-shell with satisfaction. He had his own reasons for thinking it better for his daughter to be absent from home just now.

"Can you and the children get on without me?" she asked, nothing doubting.

"Not for long, dear," he answered, in his most caressing voice; "but nurse and I can manage to do without you for a week, and I want you to have a little change. You get moped here."

"I look like it, don't I?" she asked, her morning face shining with health and good-humor.

Breakfast came to an end at last, and then Katharine opened her letter. Her face turned furiously red, and she uttered an indignant "Pshaw!" when she found it contained only the leaf lost from her book, without note or comment. What she had expected she did not know herself. Judging from her disappointment, it would have been nothing less than an offer of marriage from a foreign prince, whereas the leaf could only have come from the rider of the roan horse, Woodville, and there was nothing of the prince about him.

The following day, Katharine, in compliance with the invitation from her cousin Alice, went to stay a week at Cheston, her uncle Barnard's place.

Her cousins—there were three of them—who were all much older than herself, enjoyed having a young thing about the house. Her fresh, breezy ways created a pleasant stir among them, and her cheerful face and temper were an especial delight to her old uncle.

Katharine was surprised to find Major Fielding an inmate of Cheston. He was a friend of the family, and had been invited to stay with them while his newly acquired house at Reverie was undergoing repairs. Remembering the impression he had made during their brief interview in the drawing-room at Blackheath, she resumed his acquaintance with more interest than she was in the habit of bestowing on her father's school-mates.

She did not see much of him except at meals, for he spent most of his time on his place, which was quite near, superintending workmen; but at table his seat was opposite hers, and it was not long before they became very good friends. Fielding was a grave, shy man, unaccustomed to ladies' society, most of his manhood having been spent on the frontier; but Katharine was so frank and unconscious that he forgot his diffidence in talking to her, nor was she afraid of him. His old reticence, that held most persons at arm's-length, did not trouble her. She asked questions, expressed her own views, and argued with him as confidently as with her father.

She was so unaffected that one felt a wholesome pleasure in admiring her youth and beauty, like that of inhaling the breath of clover fields, listening to the dash of the sea, or any simple, natural enjoyment. As he walked back from Reverie every day to dinner, Major Fielding found himself anticipating her blooming face and cheery smile, and wondering how a man who had sat opposite to them at table every day for a week could look forward to a future without them. He did not look forward.

Katharine, on her part, was not insensible to the approbation expressed in his dark eyes as they rested kindly on her from time to time during the meal. Those approving glances were the cause of a gentle exhilaration of spirits that made her more charming at dinner than at any other time. Unconsciously to themselves the sails were all set in the same direction, and it only needed a breeze to send them into port.

One day, the last but one of her visit, Fielding said: "When I have finished my alterations at 'The Growlery,' Miss Heath, I should like you to ride over some day, with your father, and give me your opinion of them."

"I should think my opinion would benefit you more if I gave it *before* you finished them," she said, with the touch of spirit which he found as agreeable as *sauce piquante*.

At this moment Uncle Barnard made an unlucky speech. "Fielding," he said, "I am glad you have bought the Blackheath Mines. It is a shame they are going out of the family; but it is better that you should have them than a stranger."

"Papa!" said Alice, in a warning voice; but it was too late; the mischief had been done.

"The mines!" exclaimed Katharine in a changed voice, the color going out of her cheeks. "Have they been sold? Poor Jack!"

Fielding lowered his eyes. He could not bear to see the change that had come over the bright face of a moment ago. Her reproachful glance seemed to accuse him of stealing Jack's heritage. Her eyes filled with tears and her lips trembled. It was impossible for her to go on with her dinner. To avoid an utter break-down she presently left the table.

"Papa—" began Alice when she was gone.

"Now, Alice," interrupted the old gentleman, testily, "there is no use saying anything. I see that I have put my foot into it; but how was I to know that the poor child was ignorant of the matter? It is just like Heath not to tell her."

"Why, didn't you know that he asked me to invite her to stay until everything was settled?"

"Never heard a word of it," said Uncle Barnard, refilling his glass. "But if this kind of thing goes on, those children will soon be beggars."

Fielding did not go back to Reverie that afternoon, as was his custom, but lingered about the house, hoping to see Katharine. The expression of her tearful eyes haunted him, and he wanted to comfort her. After a fruitless search in drawing-room, library, and veranda, he was on the point of abandoning the pursuit, with the idea that she had purposely shut herself in her room, when luckily he met Alice Barnard coming into the house with a bunch of freshly gathered roses in her hand.

"Poor Kitty! she takes it pretty hard," said Alice in passing, and Fielding rightly surmised that she had just left Katharine in the garden. He found her there,

sitting on a little grassy knoll that commanded a view of Blackheath Farm, her eyes turned wistfully toward a point where an ugly black line, just discernible in the distance, indicated the outer edge of the coal-fields.

Her dejected attitude, as she sat motionless, her hands clasped around her knees, smote his heart anew.

She did not hear his approach over the soft grass, and he, now that he had found her, did not know how to begin the subject uppermost in his mind. She started when she saw him, and turned her head away. He could see that she was feeling bitterly toward him as the owner of those coal-fields which she had been contemplating until he came. Now she pretended to be looking in quite another direction. He understood the movement; she was not willing that he should see her mourning over what was her loss and his gain. The feeling was unreasonable, but then it was natural, and he did not blame her.

"Miss Heath," he said, humbly, "I am anxious to speak to you about something, and I don't know how to begin."

His manner was so kind, and he seemed so afraid of wounding her feelings, that with an effort she forced herself to say, "Is it about the mines?"

"Yes," he answered, quickly, relieved that she could mention the subject. "I wanted to tell you that I shall never sell the mines except to your father, who hopes to be able to get them back some day."

Her face brightened—youth is so quick to hope—but it was only for a moment. Experience had taught her that Heath of Blackheath scattered abroad, and never garnered in.

"You must not think I cannot bear the trouble; but you see it took me by surprise; I was unprepared," she said, in broken sentences, unable to command her voice to speak at length.

"I know, I know. It was a cruel surprise. But you have borne it well—far better than I can bear it myself," said Fielding, vehemently.

"You know," continued Katharine, "it is not so much for myself as for Jack. We have always been taught to believe that he would be the fifth Jack Heath of Blackheath, and it is a disappointment to know that the property will never be his."

"But it shall be his," cried Fielding, joyfully, delighted at what seemed to him, in this supreme moment, an easy solution of the matter. "He can inherit from me as well as from his father, and I shall leave the mines to Jack."

To his surprise, his words seemed to increase Katharine's trouble.

"No, no!" she cried; "I did not mean that."

"I know you did not, but I mean it."

"Papa would never forgive me if he knew I had so little pride as to show you how distressed I am. He never complains; he bears his losses with a smile."

"Humph! and other people's," growled Fielding, under his breath.

"But you are very good, and I thank you very much," she continued, trying to smile. The attempt was so much sadder than her tears that Fielding became desperate.

"Katharine," he said, gently, so as not to frighten her, trying to steady his voice, that shook with an emotion so sweet and sudden that it was akin to pain, "there is another way."

She turned quickly to look at him. Her eyes fell beneath his glance. "Another way?" she faltered. "I do not understand."

"I love you, Katharine. I and all that I possess are yours to do with what you will. Be my wife, darling, and Jack will be my brother."

He stood looking at her with intense self-repression, his face pale, his eyes glowing, waiting for an answer.

A soft blush overspread her cheek, and a bashful smile began to brighten her drooping lips and sad eyes.

He drew a step nearer. The movement startled her tender mood. She sprang to her feet with the old flash.

"Be your wife for the sake of the property and poor Jack? Oh, no, no. Don't ask me that."

"Not for the sake of the property and Jack," he returned, huskily.

"For what, then?"

"For love and my sake. Can't you love me just a little, darling?" he said, removing her hands gently from her blushing face.

There was silence for a moment, which seemed an eternity to Fielding, and holding her hands in his, he could not tell whose they were that trembled.

"No," she said presently, in a scarcely audible voice—"no," turning her head shyly from him, while his cold hands released their grasp. "I cannot love you just a little, because—because that is not my way. Now if you had said much—"

His hands tightened their hold, he drew her to him, and before she could remonstrate, kissed her fresh, beautiful lips. "There!" he cried; "you deserve that for scaring me to death. What made you begin with 'No'?" he gasped, like a man suddenly saved from drowning.

"I shall never do it again; the punishment is too great," said Katharine, laughing and blushing as she drew her hands away.

V.

The following day Katharine returned to Blackheath, and in the evening Fielding made his appearance unannounced in the drawing-room, where the family were assembled for tea. Mr. Heath was delighted to see him; and Katharine, at a table pouring out tea, nodded to him from behind the steaming urn.

Marian and the boys, who only knew of Major Fielding as the man who had come to live at Gresham's old place, and whose name was a bugbear, hung back, regarding the usurper of Reverie with distrust.

Polly's instincts were surer. She ran and clasped the impressive-looking stranger around the knees, and looking up in his face with beaming eyes, said: "More dinder-takes, please."

The major blushed like a girl. Never before had a little child taken such a liberty with the shy, cold-mannered man.

Jack and Otway laughed boisterously, and Polly drew back, covered with shame.

This decided Fielding, who stooped and took the child in his arms, saying, "I haven't any ginger-cakes to-day, dear."

Polly was consoled. She threw her arms around his neck and kissed his blushing cheek.

Light struggled into Jack's countenance. "Good gracious, Otway," he whispered, "I do believe that is old Dirt Pies. That greedy little beggar Fatima spotted him as she gave him the tea."

"Did you ever happen to read a novel called *The Initials?*" asked Katharine.

"A little of it," he replied, with equal gravity, as he stirred the sugar in his cup.

"About two pages?"

"Exactly."

"Do you know that I have reason to believe that those two pages belonged to me?"

"Possibly. They came into my possession in a curious way—fluttered down into my hands from a tree. I was startled for a moment; imagined I had stumbled upon the original tree of knowledge. In all my wanderings I had never come across a tree that bore printed leaves before."

Katharine laughed. "When I saw you ride off with the prettiest part of my book, I felt like crying, 'Stop thief.'"

"When through a rent in my hat," returned Fielding, "I caught glimpses of a young lady lying in ambush, watching my movements, I wondered if she had Indian blood in her veins. I should have returned the leaf then, but I imagined that she wished to remain undiscovered."

"I noticed that rent!" said Katharine, blushing, "and I trusted to that to identify *you;* and to think, after all, that through it you found *me* out! But you are right about the Indian blood. They tell me I am descended from Pocahontas; but first of all I am descended from Mother Eve, and I confess I am dying of curiosity to know—"

"What?"

"What *did* become of the roan horse?"

"Why, the very next day I lent him to a beastly fellow who was so near-sighted that he ran the horse into a ditch, and lamed him so that he has not been fit for service since."

"So this was Woodville's secret—the horse was not his," thought Katharine. "How is it," she said, "that you never told me all this before?"

"I have been waiting for you to ask me. You like your little mysteries; why should I not enjoy mine?"

"You see I got on the wrong track," said Katharine, shrugging her shoulders at the remembrance of Woodville, "or I should have asked you. Is it true that you wore blue glasses that day?" she asked, wondering at Fielding's keen clear eyes.

"Yes; my eyes are sensitive to glare, and I had a long, sunny ride before me that morning."

"So this is the end of my mystery," said Katharine, with a happy sigh.

Fielding smiled. "I am sorry for your sake, dear, that it had not a more romantic ending than an old soldier."

"I never dreamed that it would have half so nice an ending. I like old soldiers," said Katharine.

SHE STOOPS TO CONQUER;

OR, THE MISTAKES OF A NIGHT.—A COMEDY.

BY OLIVER GOLDSMITH.

ACT FIFTH.—(*Continued.*)

Scene changes.

Enter SIR CHARLES *and* MISS HARDCASTLE.

SIR CHAS. What a situation am I in! If what you say appears, I shall then find a guilty son. If what he says be true, I shall then lose one that, of all others, I most wished for a daughter.

MISS HARD. I am proud of your approbation; and to show I merit it, if you place yourselves as I directed, you shall hear his explicit declaration. But he comes.

SIR CHAS. I'll to your father, and keep him to the appointment.

[*Exit* SIR CHARLES.

Enter MARLOW.

MARL. Though prepared for setting out, I come once more to take leave; nor did I, till this moment, know the pain I feel in the separation.

MISS HARD. (*In her own natural manner.*) I believe these sufferings cannot be very great, sir, which you can so easily remove. A day or two longer, perhaps, might lessen your uneasiness, by showing the little value of what you now think proper to regret.

MARL. (*Aside.*) This girl every moment improves upon me. (*To her.*) It must not be, madam. I have already trifled too long with my heart. My very pride begins to submit to my passion. The disparity of education and fortune, the anger of a parent, and the contempt of my equals begin to lose their weight; and nothing can restore me to myself but this painful effort of resolution.

MISS HARD. Then go, sir; I'll urge nothing more to detain you. Though my family be as good as hers you came down to visit, and my education, I hope, not inferior, what are these advantages without equal affluence? I must remain contented with the slight approbation of imputed merit; I must have only the mockery of your addresses, while all your serious aims are fixed on fortune.

Enter HARDCASTLE *and* SIR CHARLES *from behind.*

SIR CHAS. Here, behind this screen.

HARD. Ay, ay; make no noise. I'll engage my Kate covers him with confusion at last.

MARL. By heavens, madam! fortune was ever my smallest consideration. Your beauty at first caught my eye; for who could see that without emotion? But every moment that I converse with you, steals in some new grace, heightens the picture, and gives it stronger expression. What at first seemed rustic plainness, now appears refined simplicity. What seemed forward assurance, now strikes me as the result of courageous innocence and conscious virtue.

SIR CHAS. What can it mean? He amazes me!

HARD. I told you how it would be. Hush!

MARL. I am now determined to stay, madam, and I have too good an opinion of my father's discernment, when he sees you, to doubt his approbation.

MISS HARD. No, Mr. Marlow, I will not, cannot, detain you. Do you think I could suffer a connection in which there is the smallest room for repentance? Do you think I would take the mean advantage of a transient passion to load you with confusion? Do you think I could ever relish that happiness which was acquired by lessening yours?

MARL. By all that's good, I can have no happiness but what's in your power to grant me! Nor shall I ever feel repentance but in not having seen your merits before. I will stay, even contrary to your wishes; and though you should persist to shun me, I will make my respectful assiduities atone for the levity of my past conduct.

MISS HARD. Sir, I must entreat you'll desist. As our acquaintance began, so let it end, in indifference. I might have given an hour or two to levity; but seriously, Mr. Marlow, do you think I could ever submit to a connection where I must appear mercenary and you imprudent? Do you think I could ever catch at the confident addresses of a secure admirer?

MARL. (*Kneeling.*) Does this look like security? Does this look like confidence? No, madam; every moment that shows me your merit, only serves to increase my diffidence and confusion. Here let me continue—

SIR CHAS. I can hold it no longer. Charles, Charles, how hast thou deceived me! Is this your indifference, your uninteresting conversation?

HARD. Your cold contempt, your formal interview? What have you to say now?

MARL. That I'm all amazement! What can it mean?

HARD. It means that you can say and unsay things at pleasure; that you can address a lady in private, and deny it in public; that you have one story for us, and another for my daughter.

MARL. Daughter!—this lady your daughter?

HARD. Yes, sir; my only daughter; my Kate: whose else should she be?

MARL. Oh, the devil!

MISS HARD. Yes, sir, that very identical tall squinting lady you were

"HERE, BEHIND THIS SCREEN."

pleased to take me for (*courtesying*); she that you addressed as the mild, modest, sentimental man of gravity, and the bold, forward, agreeable Rattle of the Ladies' Club. Ha! ha! ha!

Marl. Zounds! there's no bearing this; it's worse than death!

Miss Hard. In which of your characters, sir, will you give us leave to address you? As the faltering gentleman, with looks on the ground, that speaks just to be heard, and hates hypocrisy; or the loud, confident creature, that keeps it up with Mrs. Mantrap and old Miss Biddy Buckskin till three in the morning? Ha! ha! ha!

Marl. Oh, curse on my noisy head! I never attempted to be impudent yet that I was not taken down! I must be gone.

Hard. By the hand of my body, but you shall not. I see it was all a mistake, and I am rejoiced to find it. You shall not, sir, I tell you. I know she'll forgive you. Won't you forgive him, Kate? We'll all forgive you. Take courage, man.   [*They retire, she tormenting him, to the back scene.*

Enter Mrs. Hardcastle, Tony.

Mrs. Hard. So, so; they're gone off. Let them go; I care not.

Hard. Who gone?

Mrs. Hard. My dutiful niece and her gentleman, Mr. Hastings, from town. He who came down with our modest visitor here.

Sir Chas. Who, my honest George Hastings? As worthy a fellow as lives; and the girl could not have made a more prudent choice.

Hard. Then, by the hand of my body, I'm proud of the connection.

Mrs. Hard. Well, if he has taken away the lady, he has not taken her fortune; that remains in this family to console us for her loss.

Hard. Sure, Dorothy, you would not be so mercenary?

Mrs. Hard. Ay, that's my affair, not yours.

Hard. But you know if your son, when of age, refuses to marry his cousin, her whole fortune is then at her own disposal.

Mrs. Hard. Ay, but he's not of age, and she has not thought proper to wait for his refusal.

Enter Hastings *and* Miss Neville.

Mrs. Hard. (*Aside.*) What, returned so soon! I begin not to like it.

Hast. (*To Hardcastle.*) For my late attempt to fly off with your niece, let my present confusion be my punishment. We are now come back, to appeal from your justice to your humanity. By her father's consent I first paid her my addresses, and our passions were first founded in duty.

Miss Nev. Since his death, I have been obliged to stoop to dissimulation to avoid oppression. In an hour of levity, I was ready to give up my fortune to secure my choice; but I am now recovered from the delusion, and hope from your tenderness what is denied me from a nearer connection.

Mrs. Hard. Pshaw, pshaw! this is all but the whining end of a modern novel.

Hard. Be it what it will, I'm glad they're come back to reclaim their due. Come hither, Tony, boy. Do you refuse this lady's hand whom I now offer you?

Tony. What signifies my refusing? You know I can't refuse her till I'm of age, father.

Hard. While I thought concealing your age, boy, was likely to conduce to your improvement, I concurred with your mother's desire to keep it secret. But since I find she turns it to a wrong use, I must now declare you have been of age these three months.

Tony. Of age! Am I of age, father?

"CHARLES, CHARLES, HOW HAST THOU DECEIVED ME?"

"TONY LUMPKIN IS HIS OWN MAN AGAIN."

HARD. Above three months.

TONY. Then you'll see the first use I'll make of my liberty. (*Taking* MISS NEVILLE's *hand.*) Witness all men by these presents, that I, Anthony Lumpkin, Esquire, of BLANK place, refuse you, Constantia Neville, spinster, of no place at all, for my true and lawful wife. So Constance Neville may marry whom she pleases, and Tony Lumpkin is his own man again.

SIR CHAS. Oh brave 'Squire!

HAST. My worthy friend!

MRS. HARD. My undutiful offspring!

MARL. Joy, my dear George, I give you joy sincerely. And could I prevail upon my little tyrant here to be less arbitrary, I should be the happiest man alive, if you would return me the favor.

HAST. (*To* MISS HARDCASTLE.) Come, Madam, you are now driven to the very last scene of all your contrivances. I know you like him, I'm sure he loves you, and you must and shall have him.

HARD. (*Joining their hands.*) And I say so too. And, Mr. Marlow, if she makes as good a wife as she has a daughter, I don't believe you'll ever repent your bargain. So now to supper. To-morrow we shall gather all the poor of the parish about us, and the mistakes of the night shall be crowned with a merry morning. So, boy, take her; and as you have been mistaken in the mistress, my wish is that you may never be mistaken in the wife.

[*Exeunt omnes.*

A NIGHT-MONKEY IN THE HOUSE.

BY OLIVE THORNE MILLER.

SO forbidding were his names that the most rabid lover of strange beasts would hesitate to introduce him into a peaceful household—night-monkey raising visions of sleepless hours and nocturnal discomfort generally, and half-monkey suggestive of a nondescript possessing neither the drollery of the monkey nor the inoffensiveness of the mere animal.

But objections vanished before the small solemn face gravely raised to survey the intruder. One steady look from the large beautiful eyes dispelled the last doubt: he came home.

A sheltered cage in which an African animal might comfortably pass the cold days and nights of a New York winter was prepared in the warmest corner of the sitting-room. Through the day he is closely covered with a double blanket, but at evening he is free to come out and wander where he will.

Naturally there are inconveniences in having for a room-mate a creature of his chilly temperament. Though clad in a thick woolly coat, which, standing out around him, would seem to be extremely warm and comfortable, he insists upon a temperature of at least 78° before he will rouse himself at all, and to be really lively the thermometer on the wall must indicate 80° at least.

Soon after the gas is lighted, therefore, the family is quieted and the cage opened. Before long the fur ball in the small round box which serves for a nest begins to uncoil; two tiny hands appear on the edge, followed by a quaint little grayish face, with a look so "uncanny" that one cannot wonder at the superstitious dread it inspires in the natives who see it in the dark peering at them with large gleaming eyes. It inspires no dread here, however, only interest, as it looks across the room to the mistress, the source of supplies. Not that he wishes to eat: he is not yet thoroughly aroused. He leans far out of the box, taking hold of the water cup across the cage, drawing his little body out in a long, long stretch, bending the back downward like a bow, at the same time opening wide his mouth, and projecting a delicate, thin tongue nearly three inches beyond his lips. Drawing back to his place, he next stretches each limb separately, expanding the fingers to their greatest extent, and being by this time fully awake, he proceeds to his toilet, which is an amusing operation. Over each long limb he passes his claws, thoroughly combing the hair the wrong way, so that it must perforce stand up; then lifting himself to an upright position, resting on feet and tail, he dresses the fur on his broad stomach, using both hands in rapid alternation on the same

fur while covered up with his blanket later in the evening, but the combing is the regular business, performed before he is ready for society.

Now he is ready for his supper—or should it be called breakfast, since he has

THE NIGHT-MONKEY.

spot, and moving them so quickly, and in so business-like a manner, that it is very funny to see. His back and head are reached by one foot or hand, in doing which he turns and twists his arms and legs over his body till it seems as if he would dislocate the joints. His face he washes as a cat does hers, and he also washes other parts of his golden-brown

eaten nothing later than the night before? A banana is peeled, a thin slice cut off, and offered to him on the point of a silver knife. He sniffs at it gently, above, below, on every side, and if exactly to his very critical taste, he gravely opens his mouth and receives it, every movement being with the utmost deliberation and dignity.

His sitting down is most curious. So flexible is his body that he can sit down at any point of his spine. He often bends at about the middle of the back, head and shoulders standing straight up without support, while he slowly despatches his food, and the rest of the body lying flat, with the two legs spread far apart to keep the balance. Not unfrequently he leans over the edge of the box, back down, eating with his head hanging wrong side up, in which position any other animal would break his back.

Slice after slice of banana disappears, till almost the whole of one is consumed, when he coolly turns his back upon the tempter, and curls down apparently for a nap. But this is merely a hint for people to withdraw, resume their ordinary occupations of book, or work, or play, and leave him in freedom, which they accordingly do.

The coast being clear—as he ascertains by cautiously peeping out—he slowly and with great deliberation prepares to come out for his evening promenade. First he reaches over to the water cup and refreshes himself with a drink, lapping it like a dog; then he quietly comes to the floor of the cage with all fours, holding tightly to his nest by the long tail. Should any one move toward him now, he would scramble back into the nest, and curl down into the smallest possible space. But no one does; and cautiously he moves around the cage, snuffing or smelling so loud that he may be heard across the room, and at last with perfect ease, although without haste, lets himself down to the floor (about two feet), and starts around the edge of the room. At every chair he rises to an erect position, smells at the cover, walking around it, and often taking two or three steps without holding on, showing that he has no difficulty in walking on two feet. Occasion-

THE KINKAJOU.—[FROM NATURE.]

ally he pulls himself up on to a chair, but it is the sofa he prefers. That has a high back, which he quickly mounts, running along the thin edge of carved wood, and standing up on the highest point to smell at a picture-frame or the wall. Sometimes he will curl down on the sofa for a nap, but usually he proceeds with his tour of the room; climbing the tall easel to the top, and there standing up to reach still higher; sliding down again by twining his tail around, and clasping the back support with his four funny little paws; mounting the mantel, if a chair has been left near enough; inspecting the bell-pull, and trying to understand the mystery of the speaking-tube. All this takes place in perfect silence with cat-like movement, never throwing a thing down, and ready on the instant to start on a clumsy run or gallop for his box if any one approaches him.

The night-monkey's tail is an interesting member, preëminently for use more than for ornament. As he walks over the floor it drags over everything with a sort of clinging feeling, and if it encounters anything like the leg of a chair, it curls around it. It is of great assistance, not only in standing up, but in steadying the body in climbing, being at least partially, if not fully, prehensile.

To find a name and place for the queer little fellow in the records of science, many books had been examined, all search being based upon the fact that he came direct from Africa, was called a night-monkey, and in looks, habits, and manners resembled the *Lemuridæ*. Scientific authorities were consulted, naturalist travellers interviewed, and all agreed he must be a lemuroid, though no one could exactly place him. But one day, in looking for something else, the searcher stumbled upon a description that suited him better than any other, though not exactly, and was consoled to find that if this be his place, we were not the first he had mystified. He has been a puzzle to naturalists by his close resemblance to the Lemuridæ of Africa, but living in America, and his teeth indicating a partially carnivorous family, he has been classed with the bear family, and called *Cercoleptes caudivolvulus*, or, by the natives, kinkajou.

African or American, lemuroid or bear, night-monkey or kinkajou—what matters? He does not the less continue to be a most attractive and interesting little beast, although if he is decided to belong to the Western continent, we shall be forced to conclude that the sailor who imported him had not the love of truth in his soul.

THE GUNPOWDER FOR BUNKER HILL.

BY BALLARD SMITH.

IT is a curious fact that the most important as well as the most dramatic incident immediately preceding the American Revolution—an incident, indeed, which directly precipitated hostilities—has but slighting mention in any of the histories. It may be well doubted whether even one in every hundred thousand Americans could recall any of the circumstances of this noteworthy event.

This was the attack upon Fort William and Mary in Portsmouth Harbor by a band of young patriots led by John Sullivan, afterward major-general in the Continental army. The assault was made in December, 1774, four months before the battle of Lexington, and six months before Bunker Hill. It was unquestionably the first act of overt treason. Singularly enough, however, Bancroft makes

but a casual reference to it, and in none of the histories is it given more than a paragraph. Yet its immediate consequences were not less momentous than those of Lexington. It was, in fact, the occasion of the conflict at Lexington, and it is more than probable that it saved Bunker Hill from proving a disastrous defeat, if not, indeed, a calamity fatal to further effort for freedom.

Amory's only reference to it in his *Military Services of General Sullivan* is this: "Soon after his return home [Sullivan had been a delegate to the Continental Congress] he planned with Thomas Pickering and John Langdon an attack, on the night of the 12th of December, upon Fort William and Mary, at Newcastle, in Portsmouth Harbor—one of the earliest acts of hostility against the mother coun-

PAUL REVERE BRINGING NEWS TO SULLIVAN.

try; and, by the aid of a portion of a force he had been for some months engaged in drilling in their military exercises in preparation for the anticipated conflict, carried ninety-seven kegs of powder and a quantity of small-arms in gondolas to Durham, where they were concealed, in part, under the pulpit of its meeting-house. Soon after the battles of Lexington and Concord had aroused the people to a realizing sense that they were actually engaged in hostilities, these much-needed supplies, or a portion of them, were brought by him to the lines at Cambridge, where he marched with his company, and were used at the battle of Bunker Hill."

This account is in some respects clearly inaccurate, and it is altogether incommensurate with the importance of the act. The assault was made, not on the 12th, but on the night of the 13th or 14th of December—for there is some conflict of authority on this point, and there is nothing to show that any act of treasonable hostility preceded it. Sparks, in his *Life of Sullivan*, gives practically the same details, and Bancroft, Botta, and Bryant make only an allusion to the event. In the course of several papers read before the Massachusetts Historical Society, defending Sullivan from aspersions of subsequent disloyalty to the American cause, Mr. Thomas C. Amory, of Boston, who is a grandnephew of the general, furnishes many additional and interesting particulars besides those already quoted; but none of these writers has correlated the facts of the attack, and the exceedingly momentous consequences that directly proceeded from it.

The little village of Durham, New Hampshire, clusters about the falls of the Oyster River, a tide-water stream that ebbs and flows through the broad and picturesque Piscataqua into Portsmouth Harbor. A century ago Durham was a flourishing ship-building town, on the highway to Portsmouth, and a "baiting-place" for the stage from Boston to Portland. Then a long bridge spanned the reach where the waters of the Oyster River and of the "Great Bay" debouch into the Piscataqua. The bridge was carried away by the ice in the first quarter of the century. Another was built from Dover Point, the course of the highway was changed, the neighboring forests were exhausted, and the shipwrights moved up to the Maine coast. The village fell into a

sleep from which it will probably never awaken; but one house, built more than a hundred years ago, still crowns one of the village hills, and before it grateful America should erect a monument, for in that house was planned the initial movement of the Revolution. On the proper site for such a monument was buried a store of powder, which, carted down to Charlestown, saved the wearied battalions of Prescott and Stark from capture or annihilation.

Sullivan was born at Somerworth, New Hampshire, in 1740. His father was in the Pretender's service, and fled from Ireland to America. His mother also emigrated from Ireland when a young girl. During the voyage a passenger laughingly asked of her, "And what do you expect to do over in America?"

"Do?" was the reply; "why, raise Governors for them, sure." (One of her sons was Governor of Massachusetts; a grandson was Governor of Maine, another was only lately a United States Senator from New Hampshire, and still another was Lieutenant-Governor of Illinois.)

The most famous of her sons, John Sullivan, was married at twenty, and opened a law office in Durham. There were then but two lawyers in the entire colony. The profession was apparently not regarded with favor, for, on the coming of Sullivan, it is a tradition that the good citizens about Durham Falls resisted his settlement among them with prompt vigor. They gathered about his house one bright evening and threatened to tear it down if he did not promise to leave. Haranguing them from an upper window, Sullivan offered to submit the question to the test of single combat. It will be remembered that New Hampshire alone of the New England colonies was settled, not by the Puritans, but by needy sons of the Cavaliers —sent out with Captain John Smith on his first voyage to these shores. There was doubtless a survival of the chivalric spirit of the tournament among the young fellows of the village, and the challenge was accepted. But John Sullivan was renowned for his strength, and it was found that no fitting opponent could be secured. Then James Sullivan—afterward successively Judge, Attorney-General, and Governor of Massachusetts—volunteered in his brother's stead, the battle was fought, and James was victor. John remained to do great honor to his adopted home; but, as John Adams afterward wrote of him that his profession had yielded him a fortune of £10,000, perhaps the fears of his village neighbors were not so groundless after all.

From the beginning of the controversies between the colonies and the mother

company died only some thirty years ago, and from his lips, shortly before his death, was obtained the story of what happened that day. Revere's horse, he said, was "nearly done" when pulled up at Sullivan's door. The rider had been despatched with all speed from Boston the day be-

GENERAL SULLIVAN'S HOME.

country, Sullivan took a most active share in the discussions, and, when the time came, was even more prominent in action. For at least a year before Lexington it is clear that he considered an armed conflict to be inevitable. He had held a royal commission on Governor Wentworth's staff, and had gathered about him and drilled thoroughly a company of young men in and about the village. In the spring of 1774 he was sent as a delegate from New Hampshire to the Congress. Returning in September, it seems that he believed the appeal to arms could not much longer be delayed.

On the afternoon of December 13, Paul Revere (the same who escaped the vigilance of Howe's guards four months later, and spread the news along the road from Boston to Lexington of Pitcairn's intended march) rode up to Sullivan's house in Durham. One of the survivors of Sullivan's

fore with messages from the Massachusetts Committee of Safety that "the King in council had prohibited the importation of arms or military stores into the colonies," and that two regiments were forthwith to march from Boston to occupy Portsmouth and the fort in its harbor. After "baiting" his wearied beast, Revere rode on to Portsmouth.

In Sullivan's mind the hour had evidently come for decisive action. The story of what followed is briefly told by Eleazer Bennett, the survivor before mentioned: "I was working for Major Sullivan," he said, "when Micah Davis came up and told me Major Sullivan wanted me to go to Portsmouth, and to get all the men I could to go with him. The men who went, as far as I can remember, were Major John Sullivan, Captain Winborn Adams, Ebenezer Thompson, John Demeritt, Alpheus and Jonathan Chesley, John

SURRENDER OF FORT WILLIAM AND MARY.

Spencer, Micah Davis, Isaac and Benjamin Small, of Durham; Ebenezer Sullivan, Captain Langdon, and Thomas Pickering, of Portsmouth; John Griffin, James Underwood, and Alexander Scammell. We took a gondola belonging to Benjamin Mathes, who was too old to go, and went down the river to Portsmouth. It was a clear, cold, moonlight night. We sailed down to the fort at the mouth of Piscataqua Harbor. The water was so shallow that we could not bring the boat to within a rod of shore. We waded through the water in perfect silence, mounted the fort, surprised the garrison, and bound the captain. In the fort we found one hundred casks of powder and one hundred small-arms, which we brought down to the boat. In wading through the water it froze upon us."

What a simple story of heroism! The men took off their boots that they might not make a noise in mounting the ramparts, and after getting back to the boat it is of record that they again took them off, "lest a spark from the iron-nailed soles might ignite the powder." And this was in December, in the severe winter of northern New England.

The "gondola"—pronounced by the natives gundolo, with accent on the first syllable—is an unwieldy sloop-rigged vessel still in use in the shallow waters of the New England coast. It is apparently named on the *lucus a non lucendo* principle, being of almost the exact shape of an old-fashioned wooden kneading-dish —broad and flat-bottomed—with bow and stern but little rounded, and carrying a large lateen-sail. Not possibly could a boat be constructed more unlike the gondola of the Venetian canals. The "gundolo" sailed quietly down with the tide to a dock in Portsmouth town, nine miles below. There perhaps half a dozen men were taken on board, including Captain Langdon, afterward first President of the United States Senate and Governor of

was awakened from sleep as the party mounted the ramparts. No blood was shed on either side. In his letter to Lord Dartmouth, Sir John (Governor) Wentworth gives some further details. "News was brought to me," he says, "that a drum was beating about the town to collect the populace together in order to take away the gunpowder and dismantle the fort. I sent the Chief-Justice to them to warn them from engaging in such an attempt. He went to them, told them it was not short of rebellion, and entreated them to desist from it and disperse. But all to no purpose. They went to the island. They forced an entrance in spite of Captain Cochran, who defended it as long as he could. They secured the captain, triumphantly gave three huzzas, and hauled down the King's colors." Captain Cochran made his report. "I told them," he wrote, " on their

TRANSPORTING POWDER FROM THE FORT.

New Hampshire. From Governor Wentworth's correspondence with the Earl of Dartmouth it would appear that he warned Captain Cochran, in command at the fort, of the intended attack; but it is a tradition in Durham that the garrison

peril not to enter. They replied they would. I immediately ordered three four-pounders to be fired on them, and then the small-arms, and before we could be ready to fire again we were stormed on all quarters, and immediately they secured me and my men, and kept us prisoners about an hour and a half, during which time they broke open the powderhouse, and took all the powder away except one barrel."

The powder being loaded aboard the "gundolo," the vessel was sailed back to Durham on the flood tide, arriving in the early morning. The larger part of the powder was buried under the pulpit of the old "meeting-house" in front of Major Sullivan's residence — under the pulpit from which venerable Parson Adams had for years back been inculcating lessons of patriotism. Two or there mounds still exist to show where the foundations of this church were laid. Over against the now vacant space, and in a little plot adjoining Sullivan's former residence, a plain marble slab gives token that the remains of the soldier-statesman were buried there.

The captured powder, as before intimated, played an important part at the battle of Bunker Hill. In the Continental army gathered about Boston there was a terrible lack of ammunition. "It is a fact," says Bancroft, referring to the day before Prescott occupied Breed's Hill, "that the Americans, after collecting all the ammunition north of the Delaware, had in their magazine, for an army engaged in a siege and preparing for fight, no more than $27\frac{1}{2}$ barrels [kegs?] of powder, with a gift from Connecticut of $36\frac{1}{2}$ barrels more." When, as the British were forming for a decisive charge on his hotly defended works, Prescott discovered that he had barely one round of ammunition among his men, and gave the order to retreat, both his and Stark's men would undoubtedly have been cut to pieces or captured except for the galling fire with which Stark, from behind the grass-stuffed fence on Bunker Hill, met the Welsh Fusileers who were marching to cut off the retreat to Cambridge. It is of tradition and some part of record that, until within even a few moments of the Fusileers' charge, Stark was no better equipped with ammunition than was Prescott. But an ample supply of powder arrived in the nick of time. It had been brought over from Durham, sixty miles away, in old John Demeritt's ox-cart, and it was a part of the store that had been buried under Parson Adams's pulpit. Failing it, Prescott might on that day have shared the martyrdom of Warren,

and Molly Stark might indeed have been a widow that night.

It is interesting to note in Sullivan's correspondence that this lack of ammunition was a grievous care to Washington after he took command. Later on in the campaign Sullivan wrote to the New Hampshire Committee of Safety: "General Washington has, I presume, already written you on the subject of this letter. We all rely upon your keeping both the contents of his letter and mine a profound secret. We had a general council day before yesterday, and, to our great surprise, discovered that we had not powder enough to furnish half a pound a man, exclusive of what the people have in their powder-horns and cartridge-boxes..... The general was so struck that he did not say a word for half an hour. Should this matter take air before a supply arrives, our army is ruined." There is apparently no record to show whether or not the New Hampshire committee responded to the call, but as old Mr. Demeritt took to Cambridge only a part of the store captured at William and Mary, it is possible that Sullivan's daring assault of the December before again served the American troops in good stead.

That act was by no means passed unnoticed by the royal authorities either at home or in the colonies. Governor Wentworth promptly issued a proclamation, "declaring the offenders guilty of treason, and offering a reward for their apprehension." But the defiant citizens of Durham "moved in procession to the common near the meeting-house, where they kindled a bonfire, and burned the commissions, uniforms, and all other insignia connecting them in any way with the royal government." And, for his part, Sullivan was no less contumacious. On December 24 he published a stirring address to the people of the province. Referring to the order which had led to his attack on the fort, he said: "I am far from wishing hostilities to commence on the part of America, but still hope that no person will at this important crisis be unprepared to act in his own defence should he be by necessity driven thereto. And I must here beg leave to recommend to the consideration of the people on this continent whether, when we are by an arbitrary decree prohibited the having of arms and ammunition by importation, we have not, by the law of self-preservation, a right to seize

BRINGING THE POWDER TO BUNKER HILL.

upon those within our power, in order to defend the liberties which God and nature have given us."

The news of the assault caused the greatest excitement in England. Parliament almost at once adopted the address to the King which was practically a declaration of war, and which was presented on February 9, 1775. "The King in his reply," says Bancroft, "pledged himself speedily and effectually to enforce obedience to the laws and the authority of the supreme legislature. His heart was hardened. Having just heard of the seizure of ammunition at the fort in New Hampshire, he intended that his 'language should open the eyes of the deluded Americans.'" Thus, while war was doubtless ultimately inevitable, Sullivan's bold action was the immediate cause that led to it. Orders were forthwith despatched from London to seize all arms to be found in the colonies, and Pitcairn's march to Lexington was the result.

Sullivan was the first man in active rebellion against the British government, and he drew with him the province he lived in. In a recent address on the history of that part of New Hampshire, the Rev. Dr. Quint, of Dover, referred briefly to the attack on the fort. "The daring character of this assault," he said, "cannot be over-estimated. It was an organized investment of a royal fortress where the King's flag was flying, and where the King's garrison met them with muskets and artillery. It was four months before Lexington, and Lexington was resistance to attack, while this was deliberate assault."

On the 13th of December, when Paul Revere rode through Durham, there was a young student in Sullivan's law office named Alexander Scammell. He accompanied his chief on the expedition to William and Mary, and it was he who pulled down the King's colors from over the fort. He became the Adjutant-General of the army, was beloved by Washington as was no other man in the command, and, it is said, no other person's quips and jokes ever brought a smile to that grave countenance during the progress of the war. Scammell fell at Yorktown almost as Cornwallis was laying down his arms. Thus, a participant in the first act of the rebellion, he died as that rebellion was crowned with perfect and fateful victory. It was a noble span of patriotic service.

SALMON FISHING—THE LANDING.

SALMON FISHING.

BY HENRY P. WELLS,

AUTHOR OF "THE AMERICAN SALMON FISHERMAN," "FLY-RODS AND FLY-TACKLE," ETC.

THAT where one fly fisherman could be found in the United States ten years ago there are ten now is a general and perhaps unexaggerated belief. That every one of them aspires to be a salmon fisherman, if not already so, may also be assumed.

But formidable obstacles oppose the realization of this aspiration by the uninitiated American angler. He neither knows where to obtain the opportunity—for salmon are not to be found in every river—nor what to do with it when it is had. The literature of the subject is either confined to the art as practised in another hemisphere, and therefore of uncertain applicability in this, or it is addressed to those already proficient in the art. The trout or black-bass fisherman who would become a salmon fisherman finds therein little to direct him at the very time and at the very stage when a guide is indispensable.

Discouraged by these considerations, many view salmon fishing in about the same light as antelope shooting on the head waters of the Congo—as something desirable indeed, but so distant and unattainable as to lie beyond reasonable hope. To remove that impression is the purpose of this paper.

When Lord Ashburton worsted us in the settlement of our northern boundary, and pushed the line so far south of the St. Lawrence River, he left us few salmon rivers on our Atlantic seaboard. What is done is done, and it is too late to remedy that now; but whenever we look at the map it is difficult to repress a sigh of regret that our commissioners were not salmon fishermen.

In the last century salmon swarmed in every river on our coast at least as far south as the Connecticut. They have disappeared. It would be well were it thoroughly and widely understood that a salmon river once thus depleted remains forever barren, unless man intervenes and restocks it by patient, protracted, and persevering effort. Nature has implanted within the salmon an impulse to breed in the river where it was itself bred, and in no other. When an artificial barrier closes the ascent of a stream, they still return till they die. But their spawn, ne-

cessarily cast in localities unsuited to its development, perishes. No other generation succeeds that in existence when the obstacle was created, and the river once swarming with fish speedily becomes sterile. And so it will remain, even though the original conditions are restored, until a new race is introduced by man.

The Penobscot, St. Croix, and Dennys rivers, all in Maine, each afforded some salmon to the fly fisherman last year. The Penobscot is a whole sermon in itself on the value of restocking exhausted rivers. Fly fishing for salmon is there in its infancy. Plenty of fish are now believed to frequent that river, and when it is thoroughly exploited, and the localities frequented by the salmon become known, there is little doubt it will rank well as a salmon stream. Information may be had of Mr. E. M. Stillwell, one of the Maine Fish and Game Commissioners, at Bangor. Should any reader be tempted to try this stream and have sport, it will not be amiss for him to remember that the fishing right costs him nothing, and that he reaps from a harvest he has not sown. He may also remember that though the importance of restocking our depleted waters is daily growing in public appreciation, still the time has not yet come when the needs of the work do not tax its available resources to the elastic limit. It will therefore be graceful, to say the least, to make some pecuniary contribution to further the work on that river in the future.

But the waters of Canada are now the real home of the salmon. The fishing there is, however, usually private property. But every property-holder does not necessarily personally occupy his possessions at all times. Some there always are who will gladly temporarily assign their rights to a stranger for a consideration.

It is a good plan to ask for what one wants but has not, and the more widely the inquiry is spread, the more certain is ultimate success. Having ascertained from some advertising agent what newspapers of Montreal, Quebec, and St. John, New Brunswick, circulate most widely among the class likely to own salmon fishings, the following advertisement may be inserted in one or more of them: "Wanted—salmon fishing. Address, with particulars, J. D., P.-o. box ——, New York city."

This will bring an abundance of answers. The following reply to the most promising will call for such further information as may be needed:

"Your answer to my advertisement in the —— has been received. Will you kindly furnish this further information in reference to your fishing? 1. Is the fishing from canoe or from bank? 2. Is wading advisable or necessary? 3. Is the water in its normal condition clear or colored? 4. What is about the average width of the stream at your fishing? 5. Do you give the right to the entire stream, or but to one side? 6. How may your fishing be best reached from Montreal [or St. John, New Brunswick, as the case may require]? 7. Are black-flies, gnats, and mosquitoes an annoyance during [state time of proposed fishing], and to what extent? 8. What are the living accommodations—camp, farm-house, hotel, or tent? If at a farm-house or hotel, what is the usual daily charge? 9. How many attendants will each rod require? 10. Where can they be obtained? 11. What wages will they require? 12. Can you place me in communication with good men familiar with your water? 13. Must we take our own supplies, or any portion of them except drink and smoke, with us? 14. If we must take any portion of our supplies with us, where would you advise us to procure them? 15. What flies and of what sizes would you recommend us to provide for the time we propose to fish? 16. Give weight of the largest fish usually taken with the fly on your water. 17. Under favorable conditions what is a fair average catch a week for an industrious and fairly skilled rod? 18. How many rods will your fishing accommodate without one inconveniencing the others? 19. Can and will you name any one in this vicinity who has fished your water?"

Human nature is weak, and one of its weaknesses is to say as little as possible of the defects, and to dilate freely on the merits, of any property in negotiation. It is so easy to overlook what one does not wish to see that it will be well to forestall such inadvertence, as far as possible, by numbering each question, and making it a paragraph by itself.

One particular will certainly appear at the outset—the price of the fishing. This will vary from a dollar a day up to twenty-five dollars a week for each rod. The latter should command a position on a really first-class river, where the fish are both abundant and large. A higher demand than this is generally considered extortionate, unless coupled with very unusual advantages outside the mere fishing right. These, too, are the prices for "casual" rods—those who come, remain a few days, and depart. The angler who wishes the water for two or three weeks or a month can usually obtain better terms, since he is a more desirable customer, especially if he is one of a party sufficient in number to occupy the entire fishing in negotiation. Then, after the number of rods the fishing will accommodate has been first ascertained, the offer of a lump sum for the exclusive use of the water for the proposed period will be judicious.

Having obtained the fishing, the next thing is the outfit. The owner of the fishing will know the kinds and sizes of salmon flies best adapted to his water. Size is quite as important as variety, larger flies being required in the first part of the season, and smaller flies toward its end. Therefore, when seeking information on this important point, the time of the proposed fishing should always be made part of the inquiry.

As to rods, one from fifteen to sixteen feet will be of sufficient length. It should have plenty of "backbone," that it may be able to handle a heavy line with ease. However the wind may be above the hills, on a salmon river, it usually draws either up or down stream, and a heavy line is necessary to cast against it with any degree of facility. That known by the letter B is the best size. A rod of domestic manufacture is altogether to be preferred to a foreign rod, except on the score of price. But I have recently seen American ash and lancewood salmon rods retailing for fifteen dollars which seem fairly to compete even in this respect. They were really excellent rods—good enough for anybody. It looks as though the present season would open with a decided drop in the cost of salmon-fishing tackle.

The reel should have capacity for 120 yards of B line without crowding, and a click sufficiently severe to render the over-running of the spool impossible, if anything but disappointment is to attend its use.

The leader should be nine or more feet long, and capable of withstanding an eight-pound pull with a spring-balance. The durability of the fly, as well as its attractiveness, is increased when it is attached to the leader by a knot rather than the customary loop. The end of the leader may be passed through the loop at the head of the fly, and be knotted upon itself so as to form a sliding knot. The "double water knot" is the best for this purpose.

Should I say I have never seen a really good gaff in a fishing-tackle store, it would be but little wide of the truth. Yet a good gaff is indispensable. See to it that it is stiff enough to resist quite a strong effort to open the hook, that the depth of the hook exceeds its greatest width, that the wire is not so thin as to cut the fish much, and that it is neither nickel-plated nor polished. Two and three-quarters to three inches across the widest part of the bend, measured inside, is the best size for general use. Those made to lash to an improvised handle are to be preferred to those furnished with a handle which must be carried with them. The gaffer can then suit himself and the water in the length and weight of the staff, and the angler is burdened only with the steel.

Mention salmon fishing to one accustomed to a single-handed rod only, and at once he doubts whether he will be able to cast with a two-handed rod without long practice. Not the slightest difficulty will be experienced if it be remembered that the lower hand must grasp the extreme butt *and be the centre of motion*, while the upper hand conforms to the movement of the rod.

That the radical difference in the manner in which the salmon and the trout take the fly be recognized and acted on is absolutely essential to success. The times when a trout manifests its presence and when it has the fly in its mouth are practically synchronous. Not so with the salmon. It rolls first and takes the fly afterward. If the angler strikes at the first indication of the presence of the fish, as does the trout fisherman, he will miss his fish every time. Though, of course, we never did it ourselves, we have during our youth seen other boys place a tempting package on the sidewalk, upon which a lien was maintained by means of a string leading to a convenient place of concealment. The wayfarer eyes the lucky find and stoops to make it his, when it vanishes from beneath his hand in obedience to a timely pull upon the string. The cases are exactly parallel, including the moral effect. A salmon thus fooled will no more notice a fly till that incident has been forgotten than would a man so deceived notice another package.

The salmon neither takes the fly nor ejects it with the promptness of the trout. There is always plenty of time to strike. When the tip is pulled downward, or the line is drawn from the reel—but not till then—if the angler will simply bend his rod, he will have done all in the way of a strike that is either necessary or advisable.

What remains to be said within the narrow limits at our disposal can be best conveyed in narrative form. The following is drawn from nature.

With Tom, the presiding genius, in the stern, the angler in the middle, and Peter in the bow, the canoe is anchored at the head of a "salmon pool." The water is from three to six feet deep, clear as crystal, and flowing at the rate of perhaps three miles an hour over a clean stony and gravelly bottom. On the right, as the angler faces down stream, the bank is perhaps a hundred feet distant, while on the other side an unbroken expanse of more or less rapid and in places deeper water extends to an island about a quarter of a mile distant. A heavy rapid, with waves about two feet high, terminates the "pool" below, while above, the water differs but little from that of the "pool" itself.

Again and again has the canoe been dropped down with the current to afford the angler a fresh field upon which he may display his fly, but without result. At last, "when he least expects it most," the water boils in the neighborhood of his "Silver Doctor," his heart gives a bound, and then seems to stop its action, for the fly is untouched. For a few seconds he moves the fly in the subsiding swirl, hoping the fish may turn and take it, but hoping in vain. The line is then drawn through the rings—not reeled in—the slack falling on the bottom of the canoe until the fly is regained.

"A fine fish," says Tom, with a disappointed air, "a fine fish altogether—altogether a fine fish," for repetition is an Indian's idea of rhetorical emphasis. "Now we rest him little bit — give him little fly, p'r'aps we get him anyhow."

Out comes the watch, and five minutes,

each seemingly of abnormal length, are allowed to elapse. Then the angler begins again, cast following cast over barren water, until the slack line is all out and the exact range of the rise is again in hand. Then follows a cast about twenty feet to one side of the appointed spot, and a smaller "Silver Doctor" careers in the most appetizing manner across the pool, passing in its orbit over the place where the rise occurred.

The fish does not take it, though he acknowledges its presence, as the disturbed state of the water shows. In with the fly; rest him five minutes more; and try him with a "Jock Scott." He will not take it. Rest him again, and try a "Durham Ranger." It is in vain. We fish over him as if he did not exist, and finish off the pool. It has been covered to its very foot without result, and three-quarters of an hour or more have elapsed. Then, making a wide circuit, we anchor well above where we had the rise, and casting but once to each side with a given length of line, we gradually work down till our old antagonist is within reach.

The fly sweeps over him, he rolls, he seizes it, and bears it downward with him. A few yards of line draw slowly from the reel, to the free action of which no impediment is offered. The rod is raised to meet the demonstration that we know, though he seems so indifferent now, will not be long postponed. The anchor is at once lifted, and the canoe is brought in close against the bank.

All is suspense—what he is about to do; for so far he has acted as though the fly had been quite forgotten. The inexperienced may wonder at his apparent apathy, but he who has been there before feels as though the heavens were about to fall, and waits for them to come. It comes; slowly the reel speaks; faster— faster; the handle becomes but a blur of light, and the voice of the click rises to a scream. The line melts away from the reel like salt in water, and the coil that was nearly four inches in diameter is now three—two—one—will he never stop? "Go for him, Tom, go for him, or the beggar will break us," and the canoe starts in pursuit with all the speed two powerful paddles can impart.

When scarcely ten yards of line out of the 120 remain in reserve, away across the river a fragment of silver apparently about a foot long soars into the air, and

falls back into the water with a splash. The line ceases to be withdrawn, and, taking immediate advantage of the possibility, it is recovered as rapidly as the handle of the reel can be manipulated, yet with every precaution that each turn is distributed evenly and solidly on the spool. For this is but the overture of the opera, so to speak, and again and again will the line be snatched from us until almost the bare axle of the reel appears.

Thus two-thirds of the line are recovered, and the angler breathes again, supporting his rod, doubled up under all the strain he dares impart, with the butt against his body.

Again the fish starts—this time up stream—the reel shrieking as it parts with the line. Wild is the angler's joy, to be succeeded by doubt, and then by anxiety, as the quantity of line in reserve grows less and less, and the fish seems to have no idea of stopping. Again the canoe is forced to follow, and again the fish concludes his run by bounding into air once —twice—thrice.

Again the line is recovered, all but about thirty yards, when away he starts across the river again, if possible more rabid than ever, finishing with another jump or two. The line is then recovered almost altogether, never omitting, no matter how hurriedly the act may be performed, so to distribute it upon the spool that it will be free to render again without the slightest hitch.

Then Tom says, "We will have to take him through the rapids — no landing-place here."

That the fish will take us up on some of the neighboring hills seems fully as probable, but the effort must be made. The canoe is run into an eddy, then shoved into the quick water, and down we go, bounding like a cork over the waves at the mercy of the fierce current.

The fish follows quietly, as though he liked it; but no, he has changed his mind; he dashes down stream and obliquely across it with the speed of a race-horse, at least it seems so, for the whizzing line trends in that direction. But what is that? Away up above us and half across the river a salmon bolts into the air. "Did you see that, Tom? We'll go for that fellow when we finish with this one." How Tom laughs—and it is not without protracted effort that he finally forces us to believe that that was the fish we are fast to. It is so very far off, and in so different a direction from that indicated by the bending rod and the running line, that it seems impossible that it can be so, though so it is.

So the canoe drops down with the swift current, halting at times as the fish becomes very obstreperous, and then resuming its course. And the salmon follows, sometimes freely, sometimes reluctantly, and sometimes in absolute rebellion, compelling us to let him have his own way for a time.

We near a landing-place. The canoe is brought to the bank, and we take to the shore, with every precaution that the pressure is not slackened upon the line for an instant, and that the foot makes no slip on the smooth stones.

The fish now exhibits symptoms of discouragement, and gradually yields, until he is not forty feet from the bank. But there he draws the line, and not another foot will he yield. Were he changed to one of the rocks embedded in the bottom of the stream, he could not seem more immovable. It is a case of the "sulks."

The rod, which heretofore has been kept in an approximately perpendicular plane, is now held almost horizontally, that the strain may as far as possible coincide with the direction in which we wish to move the fish. The bend of the rod, however, and the tension it imparts to the line, remain unchanged. We walk down below him fifteen or twenty feet. This disturbs his equilibrium. He turns his head toward the strain for a moment's respite, and instantly the implacable current sets him down and inshore. As we feel him yield we walk back from the water, thus keeping up the strain. He struggles and regains control of himself, when we first walk toward the bank, taking in the line we have gained, and then move down stream, as before. Again we work below him, with the same result, and again and again. He is now not twenty feet from the bank.

But clearly he is now of the mind that this thing has gone quite far enough, for he is as immovable as the everlasting hills. Ten, fifteen, twenty minutes pass, and it is still "pull Dick, pull devil." Our arms now ache as though they would drop off at the elbow joint. "Stone him, Tom. Do something. I can't stand this much longer." So Tom tosses in stone after stone, none of them large, and none of them thrown with violence, lest they strike

and part the leader—seemingly without effect.

At last the reel begins to move. It speaks slowly at first, like the pendulum of a clock; you can count each tooth of the ratchet-wheel by the sound; then faster, faster, till again it screams, and the line wilts away from the reel like dew before the sun.

"Quick! the canoe! the canoe!" and we shamble down the bank, one eye on the vanishing line, and one upon the slippery path we are forced to follow. At last, at the very crisis of possible defeat, the canoe reaches us. We tumble in, and are off after a fish apparently as fresh as at the very outset.

For another half-hour we fight him from the canoe, working him down stream, he running, jumping, and sulking, until we land again on the other side of the stream three-quarters of a mile below where we first took to the bank.

We again try to work him in by the same tactics, but our first effort comes to a stand at once. He begins to "jig"—a series of short, heavy, and sudden jerks fill us with apprehension, and it is plain we must wait his pleasure still. He stops, and we begin. He begins, and we stop. At last he yields, and gradually step by step swings in toward the bank. Slowly Tom approaches, gaff in hand, no part of him in motion except his feet. The salmon is now a pretty sick fish, and again and again rolls upon his side, though recovering himself almost immediately.

He sees Tom. At once he recovers, and is off again. But the pristine vigor of his rush is no longer there. He can take no more than half the line before his failing strength compels a halt. So we follow him down the bank, working him in when we can, letting him go when we cannot, playing the great game of give and take.

Once more we work him inshore, showing increased signs of distress. But again he sees Tom—it is wonderful how they hate him—and again he is off. But we are at the end of the landing-place, and so heavy a fish could not be drawn up against the current though he should remain perfectly passive. We must take to the canoe, and try him again at the next landing-place, some half-mile further down.

He is quite discouraged now, and does

as he is bid with little remonstrance. We land again, and though he sulks some, we work him slowly in without difficulty. Tom anticipates about where he will arrive, and motionless awaits him, gaff in hand. Peter hunts for a long thin stone. The exhausted fish rolls on his side, when a well-timed impulse of the rod slues him still nearer the shore and within reach. Like a flash the cruel gaff is around his backbone, he lies on the bank, the lad hammers him on the head with the stone, the scales show thirty-two pounds, and we drop the rod and sprawl out on the bank, utterly exhausted, after a contest of one hour and fifty minutes.

SOCIAL STUDIES.

BY RICHARD T. ELY.

I.—THE NATURE OF THE RAILWAY PROBLEM.

THE economic life of man is an expression used to denote those human activities which are directed to the acquisition, employment, and consumption of material good things. The character of this life has undergone radical change within one hundred years. It is not meant to imply that change is something recent in our economic life. On the contrary, this life and the various institutions through which it manifests itself have been subject to the universal law of evolution, the process of development continues in the present, and science knows no reason to apprehend a cessation of this growth at any time in the future. But recent changes have been of a specially marked significance, and have attracted the attention of all thinking people. The present transitions occasion serious disturbance in our social and industrial organism, and this is the reason why men, as they meet in public and private, are anxiously shaking their heads and whispering to one another, What does all this mean? what will be the end of it? The end of it, indeed! Thank God, there never will be an end of human development; no, not even if each birth of a new epoch takes place amid groans and shrieks and the anguish of society in travail! Such is the period in which we live. Let us not be unduly alarmed by the din of the social strife. We are even now assisting at the birth of a new civilization. There will yet gladness follow on our pain.

The fact of the transformation in economic life, as I have said, attracts universal attention, but many of its features are not at all understood. None of these is of more far-reaching import than that which we must first consider in our endeavor to understand the nature of the problem of the railway. The feature to which I refer is the increase in the economic dependence of man upon his fellows. Let us examine this more carefully.

One distinguishing characteristic of earlier production was its isolation. Goods were produced for use in the household. Few wares were exchanged. The ideal of each family was its own economic self-sufficiency. Man's labor terminated, for the most part, in the creation of values-in-use—to employ the terminology of political economy. This was the period of economic independence. Free men were dependent upon their thrift, diligence, and skill for their own well-being. Famine and flood, disease and pestilence, might destroy man and beast, but industrial crises, and the evils of stagnation and of a glut in the market, were unknown. Such a thing as modern over-production was inconceivable. The more there was produced, the more there was for man to consume. And was not man's consumption the end and purpose of all production?

As time goes on, men begin to produce more and more for others. Closer connections are formed. Trades spring up, and men are divided into ranks and classes according to occupation. The farmer grows wheat for himself and also for the shoemaker, who in turn furnishes covering for the feet of the farmer as well as for his own. A large production of values-in-use accompanies a growing production of values-in-exchange, and economic dependence becomes more marked. It does not rest with the farmer alone to say what kind of shoes he shall have, nor can the exertions of the shoemaker alone furnish him with bread. This is a beginning. The division of labor continues to increase, and large establishments finally spring into being, in each of which some one commodity, or perhaps only a part of one commodity is produced. It will often happen that the producer of the commodity will not consume one single article of his own production. A large manufacturer brings shoes on the market, but never wears a pair made in his own factory. Another directs the labor of two thousand men to the production of locomotives, but never keeps one for his own use. This evolution continues until production for others is the rule. Such is the case in our own time in all highly civilized countries. But production for others!—what does this mean? It means dependence upon others for the satisfaction of our wants. Progress and increasing economic dependence go hand in hand.

Another point of view will help us to understand the full import of this. The relations of man to man in business life continually increase in number and complexity. No fact in modern life is better known, for it is illustrated by a multiplicity of daily recurring phenomena. The vast dimensions of our postal service and the enormous use of national and international telegraph lines are outward and visible signs of an uninterrupted increase of business relations. Now relationship implies two or more, and involves a tie; in other words, dependence. Men form more truly than ever before a social and industrial organism, whose numberless parts are in infinite variety of manner interdependent. Infinite interrelations! infinite interdependences!

We may make at least a fourfold classification of this economic dependence.

Man is, as ever, dependent upon his own exertions in the production of commodities, but those commodities are now values-in-exchange.

Man is dependent upon the exertions of others to produce what he desires for his own use.

Man is dependent upon the exertions of others who produce goods of the same kind which he produces. These become rival sellers.

Finally, man is dependent upon the exertions of others who desire the articles which he desires, and thus become rival buyers.

Ruin may overtake one along any one of these four lines.

It might be supposed that this increasing dependence must be an unmixed evil, which would in the end prove intolerable. Fortunately, however, such is not necessarily the case, and it need never be the case. It seems to be the order of nature that man should associate with his fellows, and be joined with them in prosperity and evil. The truths of political science thus harmonize with the truths of religion, and emphasize the brotherhood of man. Now this never-ending variety of interrelations and interdependences becomes dangerous only when an attempt is made to deny in practice, if not in theory, this brotherhood of man, and to deny the consequences which flow therefrom. At that moment this most beneficent principle becomes revolutionary. The kingdom of God on earth, the realization of that old prayer, "Thy kingdom come," is the legitimate fruit of the practical and universal fulfilment of the duties of brotherhood. The French Revolution, with all its horrors, is the natural outcome of an attempt to break those chains of the dependency of slavery which ought to have been brotherly chords of good-will, uniting man to man in a net-work of interchanged good offices.

This feeling must spontaneously spring up in right-minded people in the performance of the duties of life in any normal condition of national economic life, for in such a state man feels that in gaining a livelihood he is rendering services for services. He wins for himself and for his family recompense, but he confers benefits on his kind. The intuitive perceptions of poets have supplied us with pictures of men working proudly in this feeling. Longfellow's "Village Blacksmith" may serve as an example.

The ordinary interdependences are scarcely felt as a burden, because they are mutual. If the farmer is dependent on the blacksmith, the relation is reciprocal, and the best feelings may prevail. Then when this dependence increases with the progress of society, man's control over nature increases, and real freedom increases. Who prefers not the dependence of well-situated citizens of a mighty capital to the independence of the savage crouching in abject fear before the unseen forces of nature, and subjected to the vicissitudes of her unregulated and cruel caprices?

But when these interrelationships become abnormal, as they do in many ways, a terrible condition of society may ensue, in which the lot of large numbers may become less enviable than that of the wild Indian roving in our primeval forests.

I propose to show in these articles that our abominable no-system of railways has brought the American people to a condition of one-sided dependence upon corporations, which too often renders our nominal freedom illusory. I propose to call the attention of my readers to the distinction between the form and the substance of liberty, and to enforce upon them the truth that the shell without the kernel is a gift to be scorned. Finally, with such means as are at my command, I desire to urge them to make a mighty effort to overthrow the power of our industrial masters, and to make them our servants, as they should ever have been, to the end that a noble democracy in social and political life may once more flourish among the American people.

What is a primary condition of the wide-spread, far-reaching division of labor which is the first feature of modern production to attract attention? Is it not the improved means of communication and transportation which the inventions and discoveries of our century have placed at our service? Undoubtedly the endless exchanges which are part and parcel of our vast system of production require a large market. Production, as has already been stated, is not carried on for one's self. But this is not all. It is largely not carried on for one's own neighborhood.

Gloversville, New York, manufactures gloves for all parts of the United States, but it is doubtful if one-thousandth part of the product of this industry is consumed in the town and its immediate environs. Westfield, Massachusetts, manufactures whips in like manner for the United States, and a few towns like Waltham and Elgin supply us with nearly all our watches. When Adam Smith wrote his *Wealth of Nations*, one hundred years ago, he assured the English farmers that they had no reason to be alarmed at his advocacy of free trade, because Irish beef was too remote ever to become a serious competitor in the English markets with English beef, as some had evidently feared. Now beef slaughtered and dressed in Chicago is eaten fresh in Baltimore and New York, and the English cattle-grower views with indignation the incursions of American beef

on the English market. The railroad thus becomes a factor in every step of production, and this so generally that it would be difficult to go into a New York market or a New York shop and pick out one single article in the price of which charges for the use of the railway did not form an element.

We discover thus a universal dependence on the railway. Does the reader remind me of other means of communication and transportation? The reply is evident on a moment's reflection. It is a law of political economy that the more perfect highway at once steps into the position of a monopolist with reference to inferior highways. But it needs no law of political economy to teach the farmer or the merchant that for most purposes he must use the railway, or entirely abandon his attempt to gain a livelihood; and when, as happened formerly more frequently than now, he was told, if not satisfied with the treatment he received, to build himself a railway, or betake himself to the ordinary wagon road, his only satisfaction lay in calling his tormentor—and that very truthfully—a fool or a knave.

We can imagine a purely hypothetical case, where this dependence would be of that beneficent kind already described. There may be some Utopia in some distant star in the heavens where railroads are split up as farms are with us, not merely among some four million owners, but some four million managers, and where farmers and railroad presidents stand on an equal footing, ready to make equitable contracts! With us there are a dozen managers of railways placed over against millions of producers. One producer in agriculture or manufactures is of small concern to a railway, but the railway may be, and often is, a matter of life and death to the producer.

Competition? Yes, competition is sometimes a blessing and sometimes a curse. It is a curse in railways, as we shall see when we come to the following article on the evils of railway management in the United States. Apart from that, what portion of the producers of the United States can ever hope to have even nominal competition? How many have effective competition?—competition, that is to say, among so many who offer their services that any combination to cease competition is altogether impracticable. Few, if any, as Mr. Hudson has abundantly shown in

his recent remarkable work on railways—
a work so admirable in needed criticism
that one feels inclined to pass lightly over
its weakness in constructive effort. Furthermore, as we can again see in Mr. Hudson's work, as well as in any even superficial survey of the history of our railways,
the most marked feature of their development is their tendency toward amalgamation and combination. Who needs to be
told this when railway advocates fill the
air with their noisy declamations for the legal recognition of the pool, a combination
among rival lines to prevent competition,
as the next step in popular reform of our
means of communication and transportation, when, furthermore, the absorption
of the two most prominent parallel lines
in the country, the West Shore and the
Nickel Plate, stands out as two of the chief
events of the railway history of recent
years?

It thus becomes already plain, and will
in the second article of this series appear
yet more conclusive, that railways have
perverted that normal and healthful dependence of man upon man which leads
to the formation of the fraternal commonwealth—a commonwealth of equal rights
and privileges such as our fathers aspired
to found. Equal and free contract between the owner of twenty acres and a
Vanderbilt or Gould who controls the sole
avenue to the market for the produce of
the humble farmer! What a simulacrum!
And I care not if we substitute for the
small farmer the owner of a thousand
acres, or a merchant with a hundred thousand in capital, or the manufacturer with
five hundred employés. There is still no
guarantee of fair treatment. If it comes,
let no one presume on it to approach on
a plane of equality the mighty magnate
rightly called king by the masses in their
natural feeling for the eternal fitness of
things. No; beware! your position is one
of grace. Presumption may ruin you.
Let me give one illustration. A miller
in the West was able to gain fifty cents,
and no more, on a certain quantity of flour
shipped to the East—the quantity escapes
my memory, but no matter. Feeling that
freights were too high, and prevented a
satisfactory return on his exertions, he
presented his case to the president of one
of the great trunk line railways. "Send
me a statement showing the details of
your business, that I may see that your
profits are not more than you represent,"

was the reply. The statement was forwarded, and the rates raised so as to absorb the entire profits of the business.
Bankruptcy was the result of his temer-
ity.

The first consideration, then, to be borne
in mind in any attempt to understand the
nature of the railway problem is this: the
railways must become still more completely our masters, or they must be reduced to complete subjection to us as their
masters; there is no middle ground. We
are dealing with the problem of economic
liberty.

The history of trades and manufactures
in the last four hundred years may be
roughly divided into two periods. The
first, called the period of restriction, is the
era of guilds and corporations. Production was regulated and controlled by select bodies, into which admission was not
free to every one. There was needed a
preparatory training and examinations to
give one the right to become a craftsman.
A general supervision of government was
also frequently exercised over producers,
and the rights of the privileged were confirmed by laws of the state. The design
was good, and the results often beneficial
in a time to which these peculiar institutions were adapted. But abuses grew up
in production, which was often limited to
benefit those who enjoyed a monopoly.
One primary object of the ancient production in guilds was to secure excellence of
work, and cities like Nuremberg in Germany to-day bear witness to the high
standard attained; but when the good of
the few was placed above the general
good, and men were for purely selfish
reasons refused entrance to the bodies of
craftsmen who alone could carry on trades
and manufactures, the time for the dissolution of the old order had arrived. Inventions and discoveries leading to production on a vast scale hastened the fall
of privilege. In France it required a terrible revolution to usher in the new era
of industrial equality, and in other countries the contest has been long and obstinate. This new era we call the period of
freedom in trades and manufactures. Its
attainment has been regarded by economists and historians as one of the greatest
achievements of modern times; but while
the jubilation over this advance is still being echoed and reëchoed, a new period of
restriction has been growing up, and that
without the justification that it meets any

special requirement of our times. The railway power is building up a class of privileged favorites in every quarter. There are men who have received special rates—and no great American city is without them—and who have been able to conquer in the competitive struggle for existence their unequally matched foes. This has proceeded to such length that it is a common saying that it is impossible "to make money" now without special favors. The avenue to success in business thus lies through the grace of a manager of a public highway, for such is the railway. And the insolence of wealth which disgusts and oppresses us is perhaps found oftenest in these newly acquired and illegitimate fortunes. The old guild-master said to the applicant for admission: "No; we are already so full that our means of livelihood might be endangered by fresh competition. We must protect ourselves." But no guilds and no laws of the Middle Ages did or could confer such outrageous privileges as the great railway magnates of this country once bestowed upon a private corporation, namely, the South Improvement Company, the infamous predecessor of the well-known Standard Oil Company. Here are the words of its special agreement with the Central, Lake Shore, Erie, and Pennsylvania railways. These corporations pledged themselves at all times to "coöperate as far as it [namely, the party of the second part] legally may with the party hereto of the first part [the South Improvement Company] to maintain the business of the party hereto of the first part against loss or injury by competition, to the end that the party hereto of the first part may keep up a remunerative and so a full and regular business, and to that end shall lower or raise the gross rates of transportation over its railroads and connections as far as it legally may, for such times and to such extent as may be necessary to overcome such competition. The rebates and drawbacks to the party of the first part to be varied *pari passu* with the gross rates." The Standard Oil Company has entered into like agreements with railway corporations, and it has been authoritatively stated that it once received ten millions of dollars in rebates in eighteen months! Is it, then, any wonder that it has crushed out competition and smothered honest industry? It is impossible in this paper to dwell longer on this, and in-

deed it is scarcely necessary, for Mr. Hudson, in the work already mentioned, has described the infamy in terms which must make the blood boil in the veins of every honest and patriotic citizen. This may serve as the chief example of a multitude of smaller outrages.

The student of the nature of the railway problem must next notice that we have to do in this with the problem of political liberty. Economic power carries with it political power. Sooner or later those who control the avenues to material well-being control the State, as matters are with us. We are not dealing with the question what ought to be, but what is and will be. Our great Hamilton well said, "A power over a man's subsistence amounts to a power over his will." It is also implied in such common assertions of every-day life as that the member of a family who carries the purse will rule the house. Now the railways represent the largest aggregations of wealth, and exercise a controlling influence in economic life. The consequences just described as inevitable have followed surely and swiftly. The King of Belgium long ago remarked that, as far as real power was concerned, he should prefer the position of president of the united Belgian railways to that he then occupied; and he spoke with a clear perception of the nature of the preponderating influences of the railway.

The political power of the railway corporations in the United States is a matter as well known as is the corruption by which it has been acquired. The State of Pennsylvania has long been regarded as the special property of the Pennsylvania Railway corporation to such an extent that, in ordinary conversation in that commonwealth, any endeavor to obtain justice in opposition to the will of that potential body is discouraged as useless; while the Supreme Court of Pennsylvania, once renowned for intelligence and integrity, is now a by-word and a reproach, and an author of a legal work finds it necessary to warn his students not to attach weight to its decisions, as it is a tool of corporations. The Supreme Court of the United States includes two judges who are regarded as railway judges. The Senate of the United States has become the stronghold of the great corporations, estimates having been made that even one-fourth of its members are railway representatives. Frequent allusions to our

"House of Lords" are heard, and in the labor press one sees references to the expediency and ultimate necessity of the abolition of this stronghold of our largest financial interests. Look to California, and you will find a Legislature which is said to be the tool of the Central Pacific, and you discover a Railway Commission unable to enforce the laws of the land. In Ohio you learn that the Standard Oil Company, a creature of the railways, controls the Legislature in opposition to the interests of the people. Nor do even our municipalities escape this malign influence. When the election of the fall of 1885 was held in Baltimore, word was sent to one of the leading politicians, who hoped to obtain a municipal office, in his campaign utterances to be sure not to touch on the subject of railways. This is the condition to which our railway kings have brought us. They are kings in very truth, and we are their subjects, to whom the right of free speech and of an independent press is denied. We read of an earlier period when America was proud of the sturdy honesty, the manly intrepidity, and the vigorous independence of her citizens. Is this passing away? In the testimony given before the Senate Committee of 1883 on Labor and Capital, one witness spoke of the subserviency of American-born laborers as a well-known fact, and no contradiction has appeared. The Germans have a forcible expression to indicate this, namely, *Hundedemuth*, the humility of a dog. Can it be that this is a characteristic of the descendants of a generation which knew Washington, Hamilton, Jefferson, and Patrick Henry, and that long line of Revolutionary heroes? Indeed, it is impossible. Our subjection will not endure forever. Our labor organizations are a pledge that it will not; and for this cause, if for no other, we may rejoice in their might.

It is a trite remark that there is at least a kernel of truth in every cause which finds its advocates. This holds even with regard to the teachings of anarchists and revolutionists. It is the kernel of truth which our own American Revolution emphasized, and which is to-day preserved intact in the Constitution of Maryland. It is the sacred right of revolution against oppressors who can be dislodged in no other way. If representatives of corporations should ever intrench themselves in our Legislatures and in our judicial service,

and pervert the will of the people and prevent its free expression, the right of revolution will become the duty of revolution. Happily affairs are not in this condition. We can by the ballot yet secure reform, and put an end to the chief causes of corporate abuses. It took the English government one hundred years to wrest political power from the East India Company, but the riotous days of the political glory of our railway corporations are, there is reason to hope, already numbered.

The railway problem is the problem of labor. No other single person, natural or artificial, employs so many men as the great railway corporation. The number of railway employés in the United States, according to the last census, was nearly 420,000.

This employment influences labor in other channels both directly and indirectly. It has more power than resides elsewhere to depress wages, to extend the hours of labor, and to subject it in other respects to abuse. Its influence for good or evil on the laboring classes exceeds any other in the United States. It might set an example in regard to kindly treatment, satisfactory tenure of office, fair wages, and wholesome environment for health of mind and body, which would speedily lead to an elevation of labor. But it is not merely as an example that the railway problem is the problem of labor. It is in many branches interested in production, and its reduction of wages will often force a reduction even upon competitors who desire to do the very best for labor. It is an unfortunate feature of our competitive economic system that meannesses are forced upon the well-meaning, and thus an ascendency is frequently given to the worst elements in industrial society. An illustration of this may again be taken from that rich storehouse of facts furnished us by Hudson. The anthracite coal combination of Pennsylvania, one of the most remarkable monopolies in the United States, comprises six railways, which own 195,000 acres of anthracite coal land out of a total 270,000 acres. Not satisfied with its oppression of the consumer, it presses with remorseless weight on the agents of production, the miners. It appears that private mine owners, after a strike of some weeks' duration, had decided to advance the wages of this wretched class; but the railways, fearing the effect on their own laborers, trebled the freight rates of these men! Thus was the matter decided against the unhappy toiler.

Again, those who do not receive special rates and rebates from the railways work at such disadvantage that at times the alternative is a cut in wages or failure in business. This is a consideration which is too often overlooked in the labor movement. Many a business man, who is pressed on the one side by the railway power and on the other by the labor power, must feel that he is ground between the upper and the nether millstone, and must be ready to welcome even socialism or any other radical reconstruction which will show him a chance of escape from the torments of business. Occasionally such a poor wretch will conclude that life is not worth living, and will put an end to his own existence.

The railway problem is the problem of coöperation and other reforms in economic life. Until those engaged in these efforts know that they can depend upon just and equitable treatment in transportation, their success will at best be but imperfect and incomplete.

The railway problem is the problem of legitimate business enterprise. John Stuart Mill, in his *Political Economy*, states forcibly that there is only one power absolutely fatal to economic progress, and that is the persistent, omnipresent oppression of a government like that of Turkey. A certain amount of inequality of taxation, certain irregularities in justice, occasional failures to repress violence —all these have been witnessed in countries rapidly progressing in wealth. Had he written in our day in America, he would have added the railway power as one which might crush enterprise. It is omnipresent. More than that: it is near the starting-point of production, and it may cut off activity at its fountain-head. You may draw off large quantities from a stream, when you approach its mouth, without affecting its mighty onward flow, whereas it can easily be diverted or dammed near its source. Transportation is an economic basis of modern production.

The railway problem is the problem of legitimate investment in the means of transportation and communication. Who now knows what he is doing in buying railway stocks or bonds? The general public does not, but managers do. Railway stocks rise and railway stocks decline,

generous railway dividends are poured into the lap of the smiling share-holder, dividends are passed altogether, prosperity and adversity in the railway world play at hide-and-seek, and amid it all the accumulations of the managers go on, until the world stares in wonder at the most monstrous fortunes of the century, and fifty men own an appreciable share of the wealth of the country.

Once more: the railway problem is the problem of the management of a large share of our national resources. Estimates such as we have are little better than shrewd guesses; but if we put the wealth of the country at forty thousand millions, and the valuation of railways at five thousand millions, and say that they represent an eighth part of our resources, we shall have a moderate estimate. A large part of the remaining wealth of the country has a direct connection with railways. Reference is made to property like rolling-mills, coal-mines, car-shops, and locomotive-works. Now the management of this wealth is a matter of vital concern to the country. Ask the most conservative political economist why the institution of private property ought to exist, and he will tell you that it is not an end in itself, but only a means to an end, which end is the welfare of the people. Private property is allowed to exist because it is thought that thus will the good of mankind be most effectively promoted. We have then to inquire how this trust is administered. Does it really justify its creation? Does it in the most effectual manner perform its proper function? It is thus seen that the management of this vast property is a matter of vital concern to the public; it is the proper concern of the public; and we reach this conclusion: the railway problem is . the problem of the management of a very large portion of our national resources.

But why should I continue? The nature of the problem with which we have to deal must now be clear to the reader. It is the problem of problems. It is the starting-point of all social reforms. The tariff, coöperation, strikes, arbitration, profit-sharing—all these are weighty topics, but they wellnigh lose their significance when placed by the side of the proper regulation, control, and ownership of our chief means of communication and transportation. Other reforms must wait on the establishment among us of satisfactorily managed highways. We desire an incorruptible civil administration: railroads can defeat our efforts to attain this. We desire a reform in the tariff: railways can render tariff laws nugatory. We desire an impartial judiciary: railways can corrupt our judges, and can take from the service of the people into their own employ those who as judges refuse to serve their purposes. A pure legislature is desired; but railways defile its purity. A better government of cities is a crying need of the hour; but in one city a great railway corporation ranges itself against reform and defeats it, while in another the officers of a street railway are under investigation for corruption of aldermen, theft, and mismanagement, and honest men long to see more than one railway man hard at work in striped garments within prison walls.

In short, the abuses which have given rise to the problem of the railway are germinal in character. They drag their slimy length over our country, and every turn in their progress is marked by a progeny of evils. Thus is our land cursed!

ROS SOLIS.

BY ANNIE FIELDS.

Paracelsus says that the herb called *Ros Solis* is at noon and under a burning sun filled with dew, while the other herbs around it are dry.—BACON.

THOU lowly herb!
The lesson thou canst teach, my heart would learn!
For the road is hot,
The centre of my being a dry spot.
I hurry and I burn,
Till by the way-side here I thee discern,
Where thou dost hold and gather to thy breast
One cool sweet drop,
While I am so opprest.

Low upon my knees I pause
To watch thee nourishing the dew that fell
In one still hour when heaven blest earth
With her cool kiss.

In that one hour of bliss
Behold a sacred birth!
What voice could tell,
As whispers this cool drop,
The body's mystery,
The spirit's prop?

Ye who have gladness known, was it a toy
Broken with years and cast away?
Or does it live, a coolness in the heat,
A resting-place for other weary feet?
Is it a song for those who cannot sing,
Turning as this flower has done,
Even in the burning sun,
The sadness of remembered joy
Into a grace no living joy can bring?

SPRINGHAVEN.

BY R. D. BLACKMORE.

CHAPTER XV.

ORDEAL OF AUDIT.

ENGLAND saw the growing danger, and prepared, with an even mind and well-girt body, to confront it. As yet stood up no other country to help or even comfort her, so cowed was all the Continent by the lash and spur of an upstart. Alone, encumbered with the pack of Ireland, pinched with hunger and dearth of victuals, and cramped with the colic of Whiggery, she set her strong shoulder to the wheel of fortune, and so kept it till the hill was behind her. Some nations (which owe their existence to her) have forgotten these things conveniently; an Englishman hates to speak of them, through his unjust abhorrence of self-praise; and so does a Frenchman, by virtue of motives equally respectable.

But now the especial danger lay in the special strength of England. Scarcely any man along the coast, who had ever come across a Frenchman, could be led (by quotations from history or even from newspapers) to believe that there was any sense in this menace of his to come and conquer us. Even if he landed, which was not likely—for none of them could box the compass—the only thing he took would be a jolly good thrashing, and a few pills of lead for his garlic. This lofty contempt on the part of the seafaring men had been enhanced by Nelson, and throve with stoutest vigour in the enlightened breasts of Springhaven.

Yet military men thought otherwise, and so did the owners of crops and ricks, and so did the dealers in bacon and eggs and crockery, and even hardware. Mr. Cheeseman, for instance, who left nothing unsold that he could turn a penny by, was anything but easy in his mind, and dreamed such dreams as he could not impart to his wife—on account of her tendency to hysterics—but told with much power to his daughter Polly, now the recognised belle of Springhaven. This vigilant grocer and butterman, tea, coffee, tobacco, and snuffman, hosier also, and general provider for the outer as well as the inner man, had much of that enterprise in his nature which the country believes to come from London. His posses-

sion of this was ascribed by all persons of a thoughtful turn to his ownership of that well-built schooner the *London Trader*. Sailing as she did, when the weather was fine, nearly every other week, for London, and returning with equal frequency, to the women who had never been ten miles from home she was a mystery and a watchword. Not one of them would allow lad of hers to join this romantic galleon, and tempt the black cloud of the distance; neither did Mr. Cheeseman yearn (for reasons of his own about city prices) to navigate this good ship with natives. Moreover, it was absurd, as he said, with a keen sense of his own cheapness, to suppose that he could find the funds to buy and ply such a ship as that!

Truth is a fugitive creature, even when she deigns to be visible, or even to exist. The truth of Mr. Cheeseman's statement had existed, but was long since flown. Such was his worth that he could now afford to buy the *London Trader* three times over, and pay ready money every time. But when he first invested hard cash in her—against the solid tears of his prudent wife—true enough it was that he could only scrape together one quarter of the sum required. Mrs. Cheeseman, who was then in a condition of absorbing interest with Polly, made it her last request in this world—for she never expected to get over it—that Jemmy should not run in debt on a goose-chase, and fetch her poor spirit from its grave again. James Cheeseman was compelled—as the noblest man may be—to dissemble and even deny his intentions until the blessed period of caudle-cup, when, the weather being pleasant and the wind along the shore, he found himself encouraged to put up the window gently. The tide was coming in with a long seesaw, and upon it, like the baby in the cradle full of sleep, lay rocking another little stranger, or rather a very big one, to the lady's conception.

Let bygones be bygones. There were some reproaches; but the weaker vessel, Mrs. Cheeseman, at last struck flag, without sinking, as she threatened to do. And when little Polly went for her first airing, the *London Trader* had accomplished her first voyage, and was sailing in triumphantly with a box of "tops and bottoms" from the ancient firm in Threadneedle Street, which has saved so many infants from the power that cuts the thread. After that, everything went as it should go, including this addition to the commercial strength of Britain, which the lady was enabled soon to talk of as "our ship," and to cite when any question rose of the latest London fashion. But even now, when a score of years, save one, had made their score and gone, Mrs. Cheeseman only guessed and doubted as to the purchase of her ship. James Cheeseman knew the value of his own counsel, and so kept it; and was patted on both shoulders by the world, while he patted his own butter.

He wore an apron of the purest white, with shoulder-straps of linen tape, and upon his counter he had a desk, with a carved oak rail in front of it and returned at either end. The joy of his life was here to stand, with goodly shirt sleeves shining, his bright cheeks also shining in the sun, unless it were hot enough to hurt his goods. He was not a great man, but a good one—in the opinion of all who owed him nothing, and even in his own estimate, though he owed so much to himself. It was enough to make any one who possessed a shilling hungry to see him so clean, so ready, and ruddy among the many good things which his looks and manner, as well as his words, commended. And as soon as he began to smack his rosy lips, which nature had fitted up on purpose, over a rasher, or a cut of gammon, or a keg of best Aylesbury, or a fine red herring, no customer having a penny in his pocket might struggle hard enough to keep it there. For the half-hearted policy of fingering one's money, and asking a price theoretically, would recoil upon the constitution of the strongest man, unless he could detach from all coöperation the congenial researches of his eyes and nose. When the weather was cool and the air full of appetite, and a fine smack of salt from the sea was sparkling on the margin of the plate of expectation, there was Mr. Cheeseman, with a knife and fork, amid a presence of hungrifying goods that beat the weak efforts of imagination. Hams of the first rank and highest education, springs of pork sweeter than the purest spring of poetry, pats of butter fragrant as the most delicious flattery, chicks with breast too ample to require to be broken, and some-

times prawns from round the headland, fresh enough to saw one another's heads off, but for being boiled already.

Memory fails to record one-tenth of all the good things gathered there. And why? Because hope was the power aroused, and how seldom can memory endorse it! Even in the case of Mr. Cheeseman's wares there were people who said, after making short work with them, that short weight had enabled them to do so. And every one living in the village was surprised to find his own scales require balancing again every time he sent his little girl to Cheeseman's.

This upright tradesman was attending to his business one cold day in May, 1803, soon after Nelson sailed from Portsmouth, and he stood with his beloved pounds of farm-house butter, bladders of lard, and new-laid eggs, and squares of cream-cheese behind him, with a broad butter-spathe of white wood in his hand, a long goose-pen tucked over his left ear, and the great copper scales hanging handy. So strict was his style, though he was not above a joke, that only his own hands might serve forth an ounce of best butter to the public. And whenever this was weighed, and the beam adjusted handsomely to the satisfaction of the purchaser, down went the butter to be packed upon a shelf uninvaded by the public eye. Persons too scantily endowed with the greatest of all Christian virtues had the hardihood to say that Mr. Cheeseman here indulged in a process of high art discovered by himself. Discoursing of the weather, or the crops, or perhaps the war, and mourning the dishonesty of statesmen nowadays, by dexterous undersweep of keen steel blade, from the bottom of the round, or pat, or roll, he would have away a thin slice, and with that motion jerk it into the barrel which he kept beneath his desk.

"Is this, then, the establishment of the illustrious Mr. Cheeseman?" The time was yet early, and the gentleman who put this question was in riding dress. The worthy tradesman looked at him, and the rosy hue upon his cheeks was marbled with a paler tint.

"This is the shop of the 'umble James Cheeseman," he answered, but not with the alacrity of business. "All things good that are in season, and nothing kept unseasonable. With what can I have the honor of serving you, sir?"

"With a little talk." The stranger's

manner was not unpleasantly contemptuous, but lofty, and such as the English
shopman loves, and calls "aristocratic."

"To talk with a gentleman is a pleasure as well as an honour," said Cheeseman.

"But not in this public establishment."
The visitor waved both hands as he spoke,
in a style not then common with Englishmen — though they are learning eloquent gesticulation now. "It is fine, Mr.
Cheeseman; but it is not—bah, I forget
your English words."

"It is fine, sir, as you are good enough
to observe"—the humble James Cheeseman was proud of his shop—"but not, as
you remarked, altogether private. That
can hardly be expected, where business is
conducted to suit universal requirements.
Polly, my dear, if your mother can spare
you, come and take my place at the desk
a few minutes. I have business inside
with this gentleman. You may sell almost anything, except butter. If any one
wants that, they must wait till I come
back."

A very pretty damsel, with a cap of
foreign lace both adorning and adorned
by her beautiful bright hair, came shyly
from a little door behind the counter, receiving with a quick blush the stranger's
earnest gaze, and returning with a curtsey the courteous flourish of his looped-up
riding-hat. "What a handsome gentleman!" said Polly to herself; "but there
is something very sad and very wild in
his appearance." Her father's conclusion was the same, and his heart misgave
him as he led in this unexpected guest.

"There is no cause for apologies. This
place is a very good one," the stranger
replied, laying down his heavy whip on
the table of a stone-floored room, to which
he had been shown. "You are a man of
business, and I am come upon dry business. You can conjecture—is it not so?
—who I am by this time, although I am
told that I do not bear any strong resemblance to my father."

He took off his hat as he spoke, shook
back his long black hair, and fixed his
jet-black eyes upon Cheeseman. That
upright dealer had not recovered his usual
self-possession yet, but managed to look
up—for he was shorter by a head than
his visitor—with a doubtful and enquiring
smile.

"I am Caryl Carne, of Carne Castle,
as you are pleased to call it. I have not
been in England these many years; from
the death of my father I have been afar;
and now, for causes of my own, I am returned, with hope of collecting the fragments of the property of my ancestors.
It appears to have been their custom to
scatter, but not gather up again. My
intention is to make a sheaf of the relics
spread by squanderers, and snapped up by
scoundrels."

"To be sure, to be sure," cried the general dealer; "this is vastly to your credit,
sir, and I wish you all success, sir, and so
will all who have so long respected your
ancient and honourable family, sir. Take
a chair, sir—please to take a chair."

"I find very little to my credit," Mr.
Carne said, dryly, as he took the offered
chair, but kept his eyes still upon Cheeseman's; "but among that little is a bond
from you, given nearly twenty years
agone, and of which you will retain, no
doubt, a vivid recollection."

"A bond, sir—a bond!" exclaimed the
other, with his bright eyes twinkling, as
in some business enterprise. "I never
signed a bond in all my life, sir. Why,
a bond requires sureties, and nobody ever
went surety for me."

"Bond may not be the proper legal
term. It is possible. I know nothing of
the English law. But a document it is,
under hand and seal, and your signature
is witnessed, Mr. Cheeseman."

"Ah well! Let me consider. I begin
to remember something. But my memory is not as it used to be, and twenty years
makes a great hole in it. Will you kindly allow me to see this paper, if you have
it with you, sir?"

"It is not a paper; it is written upon
parchment, and I have not brought it with
me. But I have written down the intention of it, and it is as follows:

"'This indenture made between James
Cheeseman (with a long description), of
the one part, and Montagu Carne (treated
likewise), of the other part, after a long
account of some arrangement made between them, witnesseth that in consideration of the sum of £300 well and truly
paid by the said Montagu Carne to Cheeseman, he, the said Cheeseman, doth assign,
transfer, set over, and so on, to the said
Carne, etc., one equal undivided moiety
and one half part of the other moiety of
and in a certain vessel, ship, trading-craft,
and so forth, known or thenceforth to be
known as the *London Trader*, of Spring-

MR. CHEESEMAN AND CARYL CARNE.

haven, in the county of Sussex, by way of security for the interest at the rate of five per cent. per annum, payable half-yearly, as well as for the principal sum of £300, so advanced as aforesaid.'"

"If it should prove, sir, that money is owing," Mr. Cheeseman said, with that exalted candour which made a weak customer condemn his own eyes and nose, "no effort on my part shall be wanting, bad as the times are, to procure it and discharge it. In every commercial transaction I have found, and my experience is now considerable, that confidence, as between man and man, is the only true footing to go upon. And how can true confidence exist, unless—"

"Unless a man shows some honesty. And a man who keeps books such as these," pursued the visitor, suggesting a small kick to a pile of ledgers, "can hardly help knowing whether he owes a large sum or whether he has paid it. But that is not the only question now. In continuation of that document I find a condition, a clause provisional, that it shall be

at the option of the aforesaid Montagu Carne, and his representatives, either to receive the interest at the rate before mentioned and thereby secured, or, if he or they should so prefer, to take for their own benefit absolutely three-fourths of the net profits, proceeds, or other increment realised by the trading ventures, or other employment from time to time, of the said *London Trader*. Also there is a covenant for the insurance of the said vessel, and a power of sale, and some other provisions about access to trading books, etc., with which you have, no doubt, a good acquaintance, Mr. Cheeseman."

That enterprising merchant, importer of commodities, and wholesale and retail dealer was fond of assuring his numerous friends that "nothing ever came amiss to him." But some of them now would have doubted about this if they had watched his face as carefully as Caryl Carne was watching it. Mr. Cheeseman could look a hundred people in the face, and with great vigour too, when a small account was running. But the sad, contemptuous, and piercing gaze — as if he were hardly worth penetrating—and the twirl of the black tuft above the lip, and the firm conviction on the broad white forehead that it was confronting a rogue too common and shallow to be worth frowning at—all these, and the facts that were under them, came amiss to the true James Cheeseman.

"I scarcely see how to take this," he said, being clever enough to suppose that a dash of candour might sweeten the embroilment. "I will not deny that I was under obligation to your highly respected father, who was greatly beloved for his good-will to his neighbours. 'Cheeseman,' he used to say, 'I will stand by you. You are the only man of enterprise in these here parts. Whatever you do is for the good of Springhaven, which belonged to my family for centuries before those new-fangled Darlings came. And, Cheeseman, you may trust to the honour of the Carnes not to grind down a poor man who has his way to make.' Them were his words, sir; how well I recollect them!"

"Too well almost," replied the young man, coldly, "considering how scanty was your memory just now. But it may save time, and painful efforts of your memory, if I tell you at once that I am not concerned in any way with the sentiments of my father. I owe him very little, as you must be well aware; and the matter betwixt you and me is strictly one of business. The position in which I am left is such that I must press every legal claim to the extremest. And having the option under this good document, I have determined to insist upon three-quarters of the clear proceeds of this trading-ship, from the date of the purchase until the present day, as well as the capital sum invested on this security."

"Very well, sir, if you do, there is only one course left me—to go into the Court of Bankruptcy, see all my little stock in trade sold up, and start in life again at the age of fifty-seven, with a curse upon all old families."

"Your curse, my good friend, will not add sixpence to your credit. And the heat you exhibit is not well adapted for calculations commercial. There is one other course which I am able to propose, though I will not give a promise yet to do so—a course which would relieve me from taking possession of this noble ship which

has made your fortune, and perhaps from enforcing the strict examination of your trading-books, to which I am entitled. But before I propose any such concession, which will be a grand abdication of rights, one or two things become necessary. For example, I must have some acquaintance with your character, some certitude that you can keep your own counsel, and not divulge everything that arrives within your knowledge; also that you have some courage, some freedom of mind from small insular sentiments, some desire to promote the true interests of mankind, and the destruction of national prejudices."

"Certainly, sir; all of those I can approve of. They are very glorious things," cried Cheeseman—a man of fine liberal vein, whenever two half-crowns were as good as a crown. "We are cramped and trampled and down-trodden by the airs big people give themselves, and the longing of such of us as thinks is to speak our minds about it. Upon that point of freedom, sir, I can heartily go with you, and every stick upon my premises is well insured."

"Including, I hope, the *London Trader*, according to your covenant. And that reminds me of another question—is it well-found, well-manned, and a good rapid ship to make the voyage? No falsehood, if you please, about this matter."

"She is the fastest sailer on the English coast, built at Dunkirk, and as sound as a bell. She could show her taffrail, in light weather, to any British cruiser in the Channel. She could run a fine cargo of French cognac and foreign laces any day."

"It is not my desire," Caryl Carne replied, "to cheat the British Revenue. For that purpose exist already plenty of British tradesmen. For the present I impress upon you one thing only, that you shall observe silence, a sacred silence, regarding this conversation. For your own sake you will be inclined to do so, and that is the only sake a man pays much attention to. But how much for your own sake you are obliged to keep your counsel, you will very soon find out if you betray it."

CHAPTER XVI.
FOX-HILL.

WHEN it was known in this fine old village that young Squire Carne from foreign parts was come back to live in the

CARNE CASTLE.

ancient castle, there was much larger outlay (both of words and thoughts) about that than about any French invasion. "Let them land if they can," said the able-bodied men, in discussion of the latter question; "they won't find it so easy to get away again as they seem to put into their reckoning. But the plague of it all is the damage to the fishing."

Not that the squadron of Captain Tugwell was shorn as yet of its number, though all the young men were under notice to hold themselves ready as "Sea-Fencibles." The injury to their trade lay rather in the difficulty of getting to their fishing-grounds, and in the disturbance of these by cruisers, with little respect for their nets and lines. Again, as the tidings of French preparation waxed more and more outrageous, Zebedee had as much as he could do to keep all his young hands loyal. All their solid interest lay (as he told them every morning) in sticking to the Springhaven flag — a pair of soles couchant, herring salient, and mackerel regardant, all upon a bright sea-green— rather than in hankering after roll of drum and Union - Jack. What could come of these but hardship, want of victuals, wounds, and death; or else to stump about on one leg, and hold out a hat for a penny with one arm? They felt that it was true; they had seen enough of that; it had happened in all their own families.

Yet such is the love of the native land and the yearning to stand in front of it, and such is the hate of being triumphed over by fellows who kiss one another and weep, and such is the tingling of the knuckles for a blow when the body has been kicked in sore places, that the heart will at last get the better of the head—or at least it used to be so in England. Wherefore Charley Bowles was in arms already against his country's enemies; and Harry Shanks waited for little except a clear proclamation of prize-money; and even young Daniel was tearing at his kedge like a lively craft riding in a brisk sea-way. He had seen Lord Nelson, and had spoken to Lord Nelson, and that great man would have patted him on the head —so patriotic were his sentiments—if the great man had been a little taller.

But the one thing that kept Dan Tugwell firm to his moorings at Springhaven was the deep hold of his steadfast heart in a love which it knew to be hopeless. To die for his country might become a stern duty, about which he would rather not be hurried; but to die for Miss Dolly would be a wild delight; and how could he do it unless he were at hand? And now there were so many young officers again, landing in boats, coming in post-chaises, or charging down the road on horseback, that Daniel, while touching up the finish of his boat with paint and varnish and Venetian Red, was not so happy as an artist should be who knows how to place the whole. Sometimes, with the paint stirred up and creaming, and the ooze of the brush trimmed warily, through the rushes and ragwort and sea-willow his keen, unconquerable eyes would spy the only figure that quelled them, far away, shown against the shining water, or shadowed upon the flat mirror of the sand. But, alas! there was always another figure near it, bigger, bulkier, framed with ugly angles, jerking about with the elbow sticking out, instead of gliding gracefully. Likely enough the lovely form, brought nearer to the eyes and heart by love, would flit about beautifully for two sweet moments, filling with rapture all the flashes of the sea and calm of the evening sky beyond; and then the third moment would be hideous. For the figure of the ungainly foe would stride across the delicious vision, huge against the waves like Cyclops, and like him gesticulant, but unhappily not so single-eyed that the slippery fair might despise him. Then away would fly all sense of art and joy in the touch of perfection, and a very nasty feeling would ensue, as if nothing were worth living for, and nobody could be believed in.

That plaguesome Polypheme was Captain Stubbard, begirt with a wife, and endowed with a family almost in excess of benediction, and dancing attendance upon Miss Dolly, too stoutly for his own comfort, in the hope of procuring for his own Penates something to eat and to sit upon. Some evil genius had whispered, or rather trumpeted, into his ear—for he had but one left, and that worked very seldom, through alarm about the bullet which had carried off its fellow—that if he desired, as he did with heart and stomach, to get a clear widening by £200 of his strait ways and restricted means, through Admiral Darling it might be done, and Miss Dolly was the proper one to make him do it. For the Inspectorship of Sea-Fencibles from Selsea-Bill to Dungeness was worth all that money in hard cash yearly; and

ON FOX-HILL.

the late Inspector having quitted this life —through pork boiled in a copper kettle— the situation was naturally vacant; and the Admiral being the man for whose check the Inspectorship was appointed, it

of the gone bones. From the ear that was gone he derived no income, having rashly compounded for £25.

In the nature of things, which the names have followed, the father is the feeder;

DAN TUGWELL.

is needless to say that (in the spirit of fair play) the appointment was vested in the Admiral.

The opinion of all who knew him was that Captain Stubbard was fairly entitled to look for something higher. And he shared that opinion, taking loftier aim than figures could be made to square with, till the latter prevailed, as they generally do, because they can work without victuals. For although the brave Captain had lost three ribs—or at any rate more than he could spare of them (not being a pig)—in the service of his country, he required as much as ever to put inside them; and his children, not having inherited that loss as scientifically as they should have done, were hard to bring up upon the £15 yearly allowed by Great Britain for each

and the world is full of remarks unless he becomes a good clothier also. But every-thing went against this father, with nine little Stubbards running after him, and no ninepence in any of his pockets, because he was shelfed upon half-pay, on account of the depression of the times and of his ribs. But Miss Dolly Darling was re-solved to see him righted, for she hated all national meanness.

"What is the use of having any influ-ence," she asked her good father, "unless you employ it for your own friends? I should be quite ashamed to have it said of me, or thought, that I could get a good thing for any one I was fond of, and was mean enough not to do it, for fear of pal-try jealousy. Mean is much too weak a word; it is downright dishonest, and what is much worse, cowardly. What is the government meant for, unless it is to do good to people?"

"Certainly, my dear child, certainly. To the people at large, that is to say, and the higher interests of the country."

"Can there be any people more at large than Captain Stubbard and his wife and children? Their elbows are coming out of their clothes, and they have scarcely got a bed to sleep upon. My income is not enough to stop to count, even when I get it paid punctually. But every farthing I receive shall go—that is to say, if it ever does come—into the lap of Mrs. Stubbard, anonymously and respectfully."

"Pay your bills, first," said the Admiral, taking the weather-gage of the discussion: "a little bird tells me that you owe a good trifle, even in Springhaven."

"Then the little bird has got a false bill," replied Dolly, who was not very easy to fluster. "Who is there to spend sixpence with in a little hole of this kind? I am not a customer for tea, coffee, tobacco, snuff, or pepper, nor even for whiting, soles, or conger. Old Cheeseman imports all the fashions, as he says; but I go by my own judgment. And trumpery as my income is, very little of it goes into his till. But I should like to know who told you such a wicked story, father?"

"Things are mentioned in confidence, and I put them together," said the Admiral. "Don't say another word, or look as if you would be happier if you had something to cry about. Your dear mother used to do it; and it beats me always. I have long had my eye upon Captain Stubbard, and I remember well that gallant action when his three ribs flew away. We called him Adam, because of his wife coming just when his middle rib went, and his name was Adam Stubbard, sure enough. Such men, in the prime of their life, should be promoted, instead of being disabled, for a scratch like that. Why, he walks every bit as well as I do, and his watch-ribbon covers it. And nine children! Lord bless my heart! I scarcely know which way to turn, with only four!"

Within a short fortnight Captain Stubbard was appointed, with an office established at the house of Widow Shanks—though his real office naturally was at the public-house—and Royal Proclamations aroused the valour of nearly everybody who could read them. Nine little Stub-

CAPTAIN STUBBARD.

bards soon were rigged too smart to know themselves, as the style is of all dandies; and even Mrs. Stubbard had a new belt made to go round her, when the weather was elastic.

"These are the things that prove the eye of an All-wise Providence over us," said the Captain to the Admiral, pointing out six pairs of short legs, galligaskined from one roll of cloth; "these are the things that make one feel the force of the words of David."

"Certainly, yes, to be sure!" replied the gallant senior officer, all at sea as to the passage suggested. "Good legs they have got, and no mistake; like the polished corners of the temple. Let them go and dip them in the sea, while you give the benefit of your opinion here. Not here, I mean, but upon Fox-hill yonder; if Mrs. Stubbard will spare you for a couple of hours, most kindly."

Of the heights that look down with a breezy air upon the snug nest of Springhaven, the fairest to see from a distance, and to tread with brisk foot, is Fox-hill. For the downs, which are channelled with the springs that form the brook, keep this for their own last spring into the air, before bathing in the vigorous composure of the sea. All the other hills fall back a little, to let Fox-hill have the first choice of aspect—or bear the first brunt, as itself would state the matter. And to anybody coming up, and ten times to a stranger, this resolute foreland offers

hill, "than any of 'they flat-bottoms,' as Swipes, my gardener, calls them, to get through these prickles, Stubbard, without Sark-blewing. Such a wonderfully thin-skinned lot they are! Did I ever tell you the story of our boatswain's mate? But

"'PAY YOUR BILLS, FIRST,' SAID THE ADMIRAL."

more invitation to go home again, than to come visiting. For the bulge of the breast is steep, and ribbed with hoops coming up in denial, concrete with chalk, muricated with flint, and thornily crested with good stout furze. And the forefront of the head, when gained, is stiff with brambles, and stubbed with sloes, and mitred with a choice band of stanch sting-nettles.

"It would take a better Frenchman," said the Admiral, with that brevity which is the happy result of stoutness up steep

that takes a better sailing breeze than I've got now. You see where we are, don't you?"

"Certainly, Admiral," replied Captain Stubbard, disdaining to lay hand to his injured side, painfully as it yearned for pressure; "we have had a long pull, and we get a fine outlook over the country for leagues, and the Channel. How close at hand everything looks! I suppose we shall have rain, and we want it. I could thump that old castle among the trees into smash, and your church looks as if I could put a shot with a rifle-gun into the bell-chamber."

"And so you could. What I want to show you is that very point, and the importance of it. With a battery of long twenty-fours up here, the landing, the bay, and all the roads are at our mercy. My dear old friend Nelson drew my attention to it."

"It is plain as a pikestaff to Tom, Dick, or Harry:" Captain Stubbard was a frank, straightforward man, and much as he owed to the Admiral's aid, not a farthing would he pay in flattery. "But why should we want to command this spot? There is nothing to protect but a few common houses, and some half-score of fishing-craft, and a schooner that trades to London, and yonder old church, and— oh yes, to be sure, your own house and property, Admiral."

"Those must take their chance, like others. I hope I know better than to think of them in comparison with the good of the country. But if we fail to occupy this important post, the enemy might take us by surprise, and do so."

"Possible, but most improbable. This little place lies, by the trend of the coast, quite out of their course from Boulogne to London; and what is there here to tempt them? No rich town to sack, no great commerce to rob, no valuable shipping to lay hands on."

"No; but there's my house and my two girls; and I don't want my old roof burned, and my daughters put to wait on Boney. But to think of self-interest is below contempt, with our country going through such trials. Neither should we add any needless expense to a treasury already overburdened."

"Certainly not. It would be absolutely wicked. We have a long and costly war before us, and not a shilling should be spent except in case of clear necessity."

"I am very glad indeed to find your opinion so decided, so untainted with petty self-interest." As Admiral Darling spoke he closed a little silver telescope, with which he had been gazing through the wooded coronet of the hill. "I thought it my duty to consult you, Stubbard, before despatching this letter, which, being backed by Nelson's opinion, would probably have received attention. If a strong battery were thrown up here, as it would be in a fortnight from the receipt of this

bit of foolscap, the appointment of commandant would rest with me, and I could appoint nobody but your good self, because of your well-known experience in earthworks. The appointment would have doubled your present pay, which, though better than nothing, is far below your merits. But your opinion settles the question otherwise, and I must burn my letter. Let us lose no more time. Mrs. Stubbard will call me a savage, for keeping you away so long."

"Important business," replied the Captain, "will not wait even for ladies, or, rather, they must try to wait for it, and give way to more reasonable urgency. Some time is required for considering this matter, and deciding what is most for the interest of the nation. Oblige me with your spy-glass, Admiral. There is one side on which I have neglected to look out, and that may of all be the most important. A conclusion arrived at by yourself and Nelson is not to be hastily set aside. Your knowledge of the country is so far beyond mine, though I may have had more to do with land-works. We ought to think twice, sir, if the government will pay for it, about a valuable job of this kind."

With these words Captain Stubbard began to use the telescope carefully, forming his opinion through it, and wisely shaking his head, now and then, with a longer and longer focus. Then he closed the glass, and his own lips firmly—whereby a man announces that no other should open his against them—and sternly striding the yard exact, took measurement for the battery. The hill was crowned with a ring of Scotch firs, casting a quiet shade upon the warlike haste of the Captain. If Admiral Darling smiled, it was to the landscape and the offing, for he knew that Stubbard was of rather touchy fibre, and relished no jokes unless of home production. His slow, solid face was enough to show this, and the squareness of his outline, and the forward thrust of his knees as he walked, and the larkspur impress of his lingering heels. And he seldom said much, without something to say.

"Well," cried the Admiral, growing tired of sitting so long upon a fallen trunk, "what conclusion do you feel inclined to come to? 'Tis a fine breezy place to clear the brain, and a briny air to sharpen the judgment."

"Only one tree need come down—this

crooked one at the southeast corner."
Captain Stubbard began to swing his
arms about, like a windmill uncertain
of the wind. "All gentlemen hate to
have a tree cut down, all blackguards
delight in the process. Admiral, we will
not hurt your trees. They will add to
our strength, by masking it. Six long
twenty-fours of the new make, here in
front, and two eighteens upon either
flank, and I should like to see the whole
of the Boulogne flotilla try to take yonder shore by daylight. That is to say,
of course, if I commanded, with good old
salts to second me. With your common
artillery officers, landlubbers, smell-the-
wicks, cross-the-braces sons of guns, there
had better not be anything at all put up.
They can't make a fortification; and
when they have made it, they can't work
it. Admiral Darling, you know that,
though you have not had the bad luck
to deal with them as I have. I may
thank one of them for being up here on
the shelf."

"Of one thing you may be quite certain," replied the commander of the sea
defence; "if we have any battery on this
Fox-hill, it shall be constructed and
manned by blue-jackets. I have a large
draft of them now at discretion. Every
man in Springhaven will lend a hand, if
paid for it. It would take at least a
twelvemonth to get it done from Woolwich. A seaman does a thing before a
landsman thinks about it."

CHAPTER XVII.
SEA-SIDE LODGINGS.

To set a dog barking is easier than to
stop him by the soundest reasoning.
Even if the roof above his honest head,
growing loose on its nails, is being mended, he comes out to ask about the matter,
and in strong terms proclaims his opinion
to the distance.

After this kind behaved the people
about to be protected by this battery.
They had dreamed of no danger till
they saw their houses beginning to be
protected, and for this—though it added
to their importance—they were not truly
thankful. They took it in various ways,
according to their rich variety of reflection; but the way in which nobody took
it was that of gratitude and humility.

"Everything upside down," they said,
"everything gone clean topsy-turvy!
And the deep meaning of it is to rob our
fishing, under pretence of the Nationals.
It may bring a good bit of money to the
place, for the lining of one or two pockets,
such as John Prater's and Cheeseman's;
but I never did hold so much with money,
when shattery ways comes along of it.
No daughter of mine stirs out-of-doors
after sundown, I can tell them."

Thus were the minds of the men disturbed, or at any rate those of the elder
ones; while the women, on the whole,
were pleased, although they pretended to
be contemptuous. "I'll tell you what I
think, ma'am," Mrs. Cheeseman said to
Widow Shanks quite early, "if you take
a farthing less than half a guinea a week
for your dimity-parlour, with the window
up the hill, and the little door under the
big sweet-briar, I shall think that you are
not as you used to be."

"And right you would be, ma'am, and
too right there;" Mrs. Shanks sighed
deeply as she thought of it. "There is
nobody but you can understand it, and I
don't mind saying it on that account to
you. Whenever I have wanted for a little bit of money, as the nature of lone
widows generally does, it has always
been out of your power, Mrs. Cheeseman,
to oblige me, and quite right of you. But
I have a good son, thank the Lord, by the
name of Harry, to provide for me; and a
guinea a week is the agreement now for
the dimity-parlour, and the three leg'd bed,
and cold dinner to be paid for extra, such
as I might send for to your good shop,
with the money ready in the hand of my
little girl, and jug below her apron for
refreshment from the Darling."

"Well, I never! My dear soul, you
have taken all my breath away. Why,
it must be the captain of all the gunners.
How gunpowder do pay, to be sure!"

"Lor, ma'am, why, don't you know,"
replied Mrs. Shanks, with some contempt,
"that the man with three ribs is the captain of the gunners—the man in my back
sitting-room? No dimity-parlour for him
with his family, not for a guinea and a
half a week. But if I was to tell you who
the gentleman is, and one of the highest all round these parts, truthful as you
know me, Mrs. Cheeseman, you would say
to yourself, what a liar she is!"

"Mrs. Shanks, I never use coarse expressions, even to myself in private. And

perhaps I could tell you a thing or two would astonish you more than me, ma'am. Suppose I should tell you, to begin with, who your guinea lodger is?"

"That you could never do, Mrs. Cheeseman, with all your time a-counting changes. He is not of the rank for a twopenny rasher, or a wedge of cheese packed in old petticoat."

These two ladies now looked at one another. They had not had a quarrel for almost three months, and a large arrear of little pricks on either side was pending. Sooner or later it would have to be fought out (like a feud between two nations), with a houseful of loss and woe to either side, but a thimbleful of pride and glory. Yet so much wiser were these women than the most sagacious nations that they put off to a cheaper time their grudge against each other.

"His rank may be royal," said the wife of Mr. Cheeseman, "though a going-down-hill kind of royalty, perhaps, and yet he might be glad, Mrs. Shanks, to come where the butter has the milk spots, and none is in the cheese, ma'am."

"If such should be his wish, ma'am, for supper or for breakfast, or even for dinner on a Sunday when the rain comes through the Castle, you may trust me to know where to send him, but not to guarantee him at all of his money."

"They high ones is very apt to slip in that," Mrs. Cheeseman answered, thoughtfully; "they seem to be less particular in paying for a thing than they was to have it good. But a burnt child dreads the fire, as they say; and a young man with a castleful of owls and rats, by reason of going for these hundred years on credit, will have it brought home to him to pay ready money. But the Lord be over us! if I don't see him a-going your way already! Good-by, my dear soul—good-by, and preserve you; and if at any time short of table or bed linen, a loan from an old friend, and coming back well washed, and it sha'n't be, as the children sing, 'A friend with a loan has the pick of your bone, and he won't let you very long alone.'"

"Many thanks to you for friendly meaning, ma'am," said the widow, as she took up her basket to go home, "and glad I may be to profit by it, with the time commanding. But as yet I have had neither sleepers or feeders in my little house, but the children. Though both of them re-serves the right to do it, if nature should so compel them—the three-ribbed gentleman with one ear, at five shillings a week, in the sitting-room, and the young man up over him. Their meaning is for business, and studying, and keeping of accounts, and having of a quiet place in bad weather, though feed they must, sooner or later, I depend; and then who is there but Mr. Cheeseman?"

"How grand he do look upon that black horse, quite as solid as if he was glued to it!" the lady of the shop replied, as she put away the money; "and to do that without victuals is beyond a young man's power. He looks like what they used to call a knight upon an errand, in the picture-books, when I was romantic, only for the hair that comes under his nose. Ah! his errand will be to break the hearts of the young ladies that goes down upon the sands in their blue gowns, I'm afraid, if they can only manage with the hair below his nose."

"And do them good, some of them, and be a judgment from the Lord, for the French style in their skirts is a shocking thing to see. What should we have said when you and I were young, my dear? But quick step is the word for me, for I expect my Jenny home on her day out from the Admiral, and no Harry in the house to look after her. Ah! dimity-parlours is a thing as may happen to cut both ways, Mrs. Cheeseman."

Widow Shanks had good cause to be proud of her cottage, which was the prettiest in Springhaven, and one of the most commodious. She had fought a hard fight, when her widowhood began, and the children were too young to help her, rather than give up the home of her love-time, and the cradle of her little ones. Some of her neighbours (who wanted the house) were sadly pained at her stubbornness, and even dishonesty, as they put it, when she knew that she never could pay her rent. But "never is a long time," according to the proverb; and with the forbearance of the Admiral, the kindness of his daughters, and the growth of her own children, she stood clear of all debt now, except the sweet one of gratitude.

And now she could listen to the moaning of the sea (which used to make her weep all night) with a milder sense of the cruel woe that it had drowned her husband, and a lull of sorrow that was almost hope; until the dark visions of wrecks and corpses melted into sweet dreams of her son upon the waters, finishing his supper, and getting ready for his pipe. For Harry was making his own track well in the wake of his dear father.

Now if she had gone inland to dwell, from the stroke of her great calamity—as most people told her to make haste and do—not only the sympathy of the sea, but many of the little cares, which are the ants that bury heavy grief, would have been wholly lost to her. And amongst these cares the foremost always, and the most distracting, was that of keeping her husband's cottage—as she still would call it—tidy, comfortable, bright, and snug, as if he were coming on Saturday.

Where the brook runs into the first hearing of the sea, to defer its own extinction it takes a lively turn inland, leaving a pleasant breadth of green between itself and its destiny. At the breath of salt the larger trees hang back, and turn their boughs up; but plenty of pretty shrubs come forth, and shade the cottage garden. Neither have the cottage walls any lack of leafy mantle, where the summer sun works his own defeat by fostering cool obstruction. For here are the tamarisk, and jasmin, and the old-fashioned corchorus flowering all the summer through, as well as the myrtle that loves the shore, with a thicket of stiff young sprigs arising, slow of growth, but hiding yearly the havoc made in its head and body by the frost of 1795, when the mark of every wave upon the sands was ice. And a vine, that seems to have been evolved from a miller, or to have prejected him, clambers with grey silver pointrels through the more glossy and darker green. And over these you behold the thatch, thick and long and parti-coloured, eaved with little windows, where a bird may nest for ever.

But it was not for this outward beauty that Widow Shanks stuck to her house, and paid the rent at intervals. To her steadfast and well-managed mind, the number of rooms, and the separate staircase which a solvent lodger might enjoy, were the choicest grant of the household gods. The times were bad—as they always are when conscientious people think of them—and poor Mrs. Shanks was desirous of paying her rent, by the payment of somebody. Every now and then some well-fed family, hungering (after long carnage) for fish, would come from village pastures or town shambles, to gaze at the sea, and to taste its contents. For in those days fish were still in their duty, to fry well, to boil well, and to go into the mouth well, instead of being dissolute—as nowadays the best is—with dirty ice, and flabby with arrested fermentation. In the pleasant dimity-parlour then, commanding a fair view of the lively sea and the stream that sparkled into it, were noble dinners of sole, and mackerel, and smelt that smelled of cucumber, and dainty dory, and pearl-buttoned turbot, and sometimes even the crisp sand-lance, happily for himself, unhappily for whitebait, still unknown in London. Then, after long rovings ashore or afloat, these diners came back with a new light shed upon them—that of the moon outside the house, of the supper candles inside. There was sure to be a crab or lobster ready, and a dish of prawns sprigged with parsley; if the sea were beginning to get cool again, a keg of philanthropic oysters; or if these were not hospitably on their hinges yet, certainly there would be choice-bodied creatures, dried with a dash of salt upon the sunny shingle, and lacking of perfection nothing more than to be warmed through upon a toasting-fork.

By none, however, of these delights was the newly won lodger tempted. All that he wanted was peace and quiet, time to go through a great trunk full of papers and parchments, which he brought with him, and a breath of fresh air from the downs on the north, and the sea to the south, to enliven him. And in good truth he wanted to be enlivened, as Widow Shanks said to her daughter Jenny; for his eyes were gloomy, and his face was stern, and he seldom said anything good-natured. He seemed to avoid all company, and to be wrapped up wholly in his own concerns, and to take little pleasure in anything. As yet he had not used the bed at his lodgings, nor broken his fast there to her knowledge, though he rode down early every morning and put up his horse at Cheeseman's, and never rode away again until the dark had fallen. Neither had he cared to make the acquaintance of Captain Stubbarb, who occupied the room beneath his for a Royal Office—as the landlady proudly entitled it; nor had he received, to the best of her knowledge, so much as a single visitor, though such might come by his private entrance among the shrubs unnoticed. All these things stirred with deep interest and wonder the enquiring mind of the widow.

"And what do they say of him up at the Hall?" she asked her daughter Jenny, who was come to spend holiday at home. "What do they say of my new gentleman, young Squire Carne from the Castle? The Carnes and the Darlings was never great friends, as every one knows in Springhaven. Still, it do seem hard and unchristianlike to keep up them old enmities; most of all, when the one side is down in the world, with the owls and the bats and the coneys."

"No, mother, no. They are not a bit like that," replied Jenny—a maid of good loyalty; "it is only that he has not called upon them. All gentlefolks have their proper rules of behaviour. You can't be expected to understand them, mother."

"But why should he go to them more than they should come to him, particular with young ladies there? And him with only one horse to their seven or eight. I am right, you may depend upon it, Jenny; and my mother, your grandmother, was a lady's-maid in a higher family than Darling—it depends upon them to come and look him up first, and he have no call to knock at their door without it. Why, it stands to reason, poor young man! And not a bit hath he eaten from Monday."

"Well, I believe I am right, but I'll ask Miss Dolly. She is that sharp, she knows everything, and I don't mind what I say to her, when she thinks that she looks handsome. And it takes a very bad dress, I can tell you, to put her out of that opinion."

"She is right enough there:" Mrs. Shanks shook her head at her daughter for speaking in this way. "The ugliest frock as ever came from France couldn't make her any but a booty. And the Lord knows the quality have come to queer shapes now. Undecent would be the name for it in our ranks of women. Why, the last of her frocks she gave you, Jenny, how much did I put on, at top and bottom, and you three inches shorter than she is! And the slips they ties round them—oh dear! oh dear! as if that was to hold them up and buckle them together! Won't they have the groanings by the time they come to my age?"

CHAPTER XVIII.

FRENCH AND ENGLISH.

ADMIRAL DARLING was now so busy, and so continually called from home by the duties of his commandership, that he could not fairly be expected to call upon Mr. Caryl Carne. Yet that gentleman, being rather sensitive—which sometimes means very spiteful—resented as a personal slight this failure; although, if the overture had been made, he would have ascribed it to intrusive curiosity, and a low desire to behold him in his ruins. But truly in the old man's kindly heart there was no sour corner for ill blood to lurk in, and no dull fibre for ill-will to feed on. He kept on meaning to go and call on Caryl Carne, and he had quite made up his mind to do it, but something always happened to prevent him.

Neither did he care a groat for his old friend Twemlow's advice upon that subject. "Don't go near him," said the Rector, taking care that his wife was quite safe out of hearing; "it would ill become me to say a word against my dear wife's own nephew, and the representative of her family. And, to the utmost of my knowledge, there is nothing to be said against him. But I can't get on with him at all. I don't know why. He has only honored us with a visit twice, and he would not even come to dinner. Nice manners they learn on the Continent! But none of us wept when he declined; not even his good aunt, my wife. Though he must have got a good deal to tell us, and an extraordinary knowledge of foreign ways. But instead of doing that, he seems to sneer at us. I can look at a question from every point of view, and I defy anybody to call me narrow-minded. But still, one must draw the line somewhere, or throw overboard all principles; and I draw it, my dear Admiral, against infidels and against Frenchmen."

"No rational person can do otherwise" —the Admiral's opinion was decisive— "but this young man is of good English birth, and one can't help feeling sorry for his circumstances. And I assure you, Twemlow, that I feel respect as well for the courage that he shows, and the perseverance, in coming home and facing those vile usurers. And your own wife's nephew! Why, you ought to take his part through thick and thin, whatever you may think of him. From all I hear he must be a young man of exceedingly high principle; and I shall make a point of calling upon him the first half-hour I get to spare. To-morrow, if possible; or if not, the day after, at the very latest."

But the needful half-hour had not yet been found; and Carne, who was wont to think the worst of everybody, concluded that the Darling race still cherished the old grudge, which had always been on his own side. For this he cared little, and perhaps was rather glad of it. For the old dwelling-place of his family (the Carne Castle besieged by the Roundheads a hundred and sixty years agone) now threatened to tumble about the ears of any one knocking at the gate too hard. Or rather the remnants of its walls did so; the greater part, having already fallen, lay harmless, and produced fine black-berries.

As a castle, it had been well respected in its day, though not of mighty bulwarks or impregnable position. Standing on a knoll, between the ramp of high land and the slope of shore, it would still have been conspicuous to traveller and to voyager but for the tall trees around it. These hid the moat, and the relics of the draw-bridge, the groined archway, and cloven tower of the keep—which had twice been struck by lightning—as well as the win-dows of the armoury, and the chapel hushed with ivy. The banqueting hall was in better repair, for the Carnes had been hospitable to the last; but the win-dows kept no wind off, neither did the roof repulse the rain. In short, all the front was in a pretty state of ruin, very nice to look at, very nasty to live in, ex-cept for toads, and bats, and owls, and rats, and efts, and brindled slugs with yel-low stripes; or on a summer eve the cock-roach and the carrion-beetle.

At the back, however, and above the road which Cheeseman travelled in his pony-chaise, was a range of rooms still fit to dwell in, though poorly furnished, and floored with stone. In better times these had been the domain of the house-keeper and the butler, the cook and the other upper servants, who had minded their duty and heeded their comfort more truly than the master and mistress did. For the downfall of this family, as of very many others, had been chiefly caused by unwise marriage. Instead of choosing sensible and active wives to look after their home affairs and regulate the house-

hold, the Carnes for several generations now had wedded flighty ladies of good birth and pretty manners, none of whom brought them a pipkinful of money, while all helped to spend a potful. Therefore their descendant was now living in the kitchens, and had no idea how to make use of them, in spite of his French educa-tion; of comfort also he had not much idea, which was all the better for him; and he scarcely knew what it was to earn and enjoy soft quietude.

One night, when the summer was in full prime, and the weather almost blameless, this young Squire Carne rode slowly back from Springhaven to his worn-out castle. The beauty of the night had kept him back, for he hated to meet people on the road. The lingering gossips, the tired fag-ot-bearers, the youths going home from the hay-rick, the man with a gun who knows where the hares play, and beyond them all the truant sweethearts, who can-not have enough of one another, and wish "good-night" at every corner of the lane, till they tumble over one another's cot-tage steps—all these to Caryl Carne were a smell to be avoided, an eyesore to shut the eyes at. He let them get home and pull their boots off, and set the frying-pan a-bubbling—for they ended the day with a bit of bacon, whenever they could cash or credit it—and then he set forth upon his lonely ride, striking fear into the heart of any bad child that lay awake.

"Almost as good as France is this," he muttered in French, though for once en-joying the pleasure of good English air; "and better than France would it be, if only it were not cut short so suddenly. There will come a cold wind by-and-by, or a chilly black cloud from the east, and then all is shivers and rawness; But if it only remained like this, I could forgive it for producing me. After all, it is my native land; and I saw the loveliest girl to-day that ever I set eyes on. None of their made-up and highly finished demoiselles is fit to look at her—such sim-ple beauty, such charms of nature, such enchanting innocence! Ah, that is where those French girls fail—they are always studying how they look, instead of leav-ing us to think of it. Bah! What odds to me? I have higher stakes to play for. But according to old Twemlow's descrip-tion, she must be the daughter of that old bear Darling, with whom I shall have to pick a bone some day. Ha! How amusing is that battery to me! How little John Bull knows the nature of French troops! To-morrow we are to have a grand practice-day; and I hope they won't shoot me in my new lodgings. Nothing is impossible to such an idiot as Stubbard. What a set of imbeciles I have found to do with! They have scarcely wit enough to amuse oneself with. Pest of my soul! Is that you, Charron? Again you have broken my orders."

"Names should be avoided in the open air," answered the man, who was swinging on a gate with the simple delight of a Picard. "The climate is of France so much to-night that I found it my duty to encourage it. For what reason shall not I do that? It is not so often that I have occasion. My dear friend, scold not, but accept the compliment very seldom truthful to your native land. There are none of your clod-pates about to-night."

"Come in at once. The mere sound of your breath is enough to set the neighbourhood wondering. Could I ever have been burdened with a more French Frenchman, though you speak as good English as I do?"

"It was all of that miserable Cheray," the French gentleman said, when they sat in the kitchen, and Jerry Bowles was feeding the fine black horse. "Fruit is a thing that my mouth prepares for, directly there is any warmth in the sun. It puts itself up, it is elevated, it will not have meat, or any substance coarse. Wine of the softest and fruit of the finest is what it must then have, or unmouth itself. That miserable Cheray, his maledictioned name put me forth to be on fire for the good thing he designs. Cherays you call them, and for cherays I despatched him, suspended between the leaves in the good sun. Bah! there is nothing ever fit to eat in England. The cherays look very fine, very fine indeed; and so many did I consume that to travel on a gate was the only palliation. Would you have me stay all day in this long cellar? No diversion, no solace, no change, no conversation! Old Cheray may sit with his hands upon his knees, but to Renaud Charron that is not sufficient. How much longer before I sally forth to do the things, to fight, to conquer the nations? Where is even my little ship of despatch?"

"Captain," answered Caryl Carne, preparing calmly for his frugal supper, "you are placed under my command, and an-other such speech will despatch you to Dunkirk, bound hand and foot, in the hold of the *Little Corporal*, with which I am now in communication. Unless by the time I have severed this bone you hand me your sword in submission, my supper will have to be postponed, while I march you to the yew-tree, signal for a boat, and lay you strapped beneath the oarsmen."

Captain Charron, who had held the command of a French corvette, stared furiously at this man, younger than himself, so strongly established over him. Carne was not concerned to look at him; all he cared about was to divide the joint of a wing-rib of cold roast beef, where some good pickings lurked in the hollow. Then the Frenchman, whose chance would have been very small in a personal encounter with his chief, arose and took a naval sword, short but rather heavy, from a hook which in better days had held a big dish-cover, and making a salute rather graceful than gracious, presented the fringed handle to the carver.

"This behaviour is sensible, my friend, and worthy of your distinguished abilities." Carne's resolute face seldom yielded to a smile, but the smile when it came was a sweet one. "Pardon me for speaking strongly, but my instructions must be the law to you. If you were my commander (as, but for local knowledge, and questions of position here, you would be), do you think then that you would allow me to rebel, to grumble, to wander, to demand my own pleasure, when you knew that it would ruin things?"

"Bravo! It is well spoken. My captain, I embrace you. In you lives the spirit of the Grand Army, which we of the sea and of the ships admire always, and always desire to emulate. Ah, if England possessed many Englishmen like you, she would be hard to conquer."

The owner of this old English castle shot a glance at the Frenchman for any sign of irony in his words. Seeing none, he continued, in the friendly vein:

"Our business here demands the greatest caution, skill, reserve, and self-denial. We are fortunate in having no man of any keen penetration in the neighbourhood, at least of those in authority and concerned with public matters. As one of an ancient family, possessing the land for centuries, I have every right to be here, and to pursue my private business in privacy. But if it once gets talked about that a French officer is with me, these stupid people will awake their suspicions more strongly by their own stupidity. In this queer island you may do what you like till the neighbourhood turns against you; and then, if you revolve upon a pin, you cannot suit them. You understand? You have heard me before. It is this that I never can knock into you."

Renaud Charron, who considered himself—as all Frenchmen did then, and perhaps do now—far swifter of intellect than any Englishman, found himself not well pleased at this, and desired to know more about it.

"Nothing can be simpler," the Englishman replied; "and therefore nothing surer. You know the old proverb—'Everything in turn, except scandal, whose turn is always.' And again another saying of our own land—'The second side of the bread takes less time to toast.' We must not let the first side of ours be toasted; we will shun all the fire of suspicion. And to do this, you must not be seen, my dear friend. I may go abroad freely; you must hide your gallant head until matters are ripe for action.

You know that you may trust me not to keep you in the dark a day longer than is needful. I have got the old shopkeeper under my thumb, and can do what I please with his trading-ship. But before I place you in command I must change some more of the crew, and do it warily. There is an obstinate Cornishman to get rid of, who sticks to the planks like a limpet. If we throw him overboard, we shall alarm the others; if we discharge him without showing cause, he will go to the old Admiral and tell all his suspicions. He must be got rid of in London with skill, and then we ship three or four Americans, first-rate seamen, afraid of nothing, who will pass here as fellows from Lancashire. After that we may run among the cruisers as we like, with the boldness and skill of a certain Captain Charron, who must be ill in his cabin when his ship is boarded."

"It is famous, it is very good, my friend. The patience I will have, and the obedience, and the courage; and so much the more readily because my pay is good, and keeps itself going on dry land as well as sea."

THE HOME ACRE.

BY E. P. ROE.

V.—THE RASPBERRY.

THE wide and favorable consideration given to small fruits clearly marks one of the changes in the world's history. This change may seem trifling indeed to the dignified chroniclers of kings and queens and others of high descent—great descent, it may be added, remembering the moral depths attained—but to those who care for the welfare of the people it is a mutation of no slight interest. I am glad to think, as has been shown in a recent novel, that Lucrezia Borgia was not so black as she has been painted, yet in the early days of June and July, when strawberries and raspberries are ripening, I fancy that most of us can dismiss her and her kin from mind as we observe nature's alchemy in our gardens. When we think of the luscious, health-imparting fruits which will grace millions of tables, and remember that until recent years they were conspicuous only by their

absence, we may not slightingly estimate a great change for the better. Once these fruits were wildings which the vast majority of our forefathers shared sparingly with the birds. Often still, unless we are careful, our share will be small indeed, for the unperverted taste of the birds discovered from the first, what men have been so slow to learn, that the ruby-like berries are the gems best worth seeking. The world is certainly progressing toward physical redemption when even the Irish laborer abridges his cabbage patch for the sake of small fruits—food which a dainty Ariel could not despise.

We have said that raspberries thrive in partial shade, and therefore some advice in regard to them naturally follows our consideration of trees. Because the raspberry is not so exacting as many other products of the garden, it does not follow that it should be marked out for neglect. As it is treated on many places, the only wonder is that even the bushes survive. Like many who try to do their best in adversity, it makes the most of what people term "a chance to get ahead."

Moreover, the raspberry is perhaps as often injured by mistaken kindness as by neglect. If we can imagine it speaking for itself, it would say: "It is not much that I want, but in the name of common-sense and nature, give me just what I do want. Then you may pick at me to your heart's content."

The first need of the raspberry is a well-drained, but not a very dry, light soil. Yet such is its adaptability that certain varieties can be grown on any land which will produce a burdock or a mullein stalk. In fact, this question of variety chiefly determines our chances of success, and the nature of our treatment of the fruit. The reader, at the start, should be enabled to distinguish the three classes of raspberries grown in this country.

As was true of grapes, our fathers first endeavored to supply their gardens from foreign nurseries, neglecting the wild species with which our woods and road-sides abounded. The raspberry of Europe (*Rubus idæus*) has been developed, and in many instances enfeebled, by ages of cultivation. Nevertheless, few other fruits have shown equal power to adapt themselves to our soil and climate, and we have obtained from foreign sources many valuable kinds, as, for instance, the Antwerp, which for weeks together annually taxed the carrying power of Hudson River steamers. In quality these foreign kinds have never been surpassed, but almost invariably they have proved tender and fastidious, thriving well in some localities, and failing utterly (except under the most skilful care) in others. The frosts of the North killed them in winter, and Southern suns shrivelled their foliage in summer. Therefore they were not raspberries for the million, but for those who resided in favored regions, and were willing to bestow upon them much care and high culture.

Eventually another process began, taking place either by chance or under the skilful manipulation of the gardener—that of hybridizing, or crossing these foreign varieties with our hardier native species. The best results have been attained more frequently, I think, by chance; that is, the bees, which get more honey from the raspberry than from most other plants, carried the pollen from a native flower to the blossom of the garden exotic. The seeds of the fruit eventually produced were endowed with characteristics of both the foreign and native strains. Occasionally these seeds fell where they had a chance to grow, and so produced a fortuitous seedling plant which soon matured into a bearing bush, differing from both of its parents, and not infrequently surpassing both in good qualities. Some one, horticulturally inclined, having observed the unusually fine fruit on the chance plant, and believing that it is a good plan to help the fittest to survive, marked the bush, and in the autumn transferred it to his garden. It speedily propagated itself by suckers, or young sprouts from the roots, and he had plants to sell or give away. Such, I believe, was the history of the Cuthbert, named after the gentleman who found it, and now probably the favorite raspberry of America.

Thus, fortuitously, or by the skill of the gardener, the foreign and our native species were crossed, and a new and hardier class of varieties obtained. The large size and richness in flavor of the European berry has been bred into and combined with our smaller and more insipid indigenous fruit. By this process the area of successful raspberry culture has been extended almost indefinitely.

Within recent years a third step forward has been taken. Some localities and soils were so unsuited to the raspberry that no variety containing even a small percentage of the foreign element could thrive. This fact led fruit-growers to give still closer attention to our native species. Wild bushes were found here and there which gave fruit of such good quality and in such large quantities that they were deemed well worthy of cultivation. Many of these wild specimens accepted cultivation gratefully, and showed such marked improvement that they were heralded over the land as of wonderful and surpassing value. Some of these pure, unmixed varieties of our native species (*Rubus strigosus*) have obtained a wide celebrity, as, for instance, the Brandywine, Highland Hardy, and, best of all, the Turner. It should be distinctly understood, however, that, with the exception of the last-named kind, these native varieties are decidedly inferior to most of the foreign berries and their hybrids, or crosses, like the Cuthbert and Marlboro. Thousands have been misled by their praise, and have planted them when they might just as easily have grown far better kinds. I suppose that many wealthy people in the latitudes of New York and Boston have told their gardeners (or, more probably, were told by them): "We do not wish any of those wild kinds. Brinckle's Orange, Franconia, and the Antwerp are good enough for us." So they should be, for they are the best, but they are all foreign varieties, and scarcely will live at all, much less be productive, in wide areas of the country.

I trust that this preliminary discussion in regard to red raspberries will prepare the way for the advice to follow, and enable the proprietor of the home acre to act intelligently. Sensible men do not like to be told, "You cannot do this, and must not do that"—in other words, to be met the moment they step into their gardens by the arbitrary dictum of A, B, or C. They wish to unite with nature in producing certain results. Understanding her simple laws, they work hopefully, confidently; and they cannot be imposed upon by those who either wittingly or unwittingly give bad advice. Having explained the natural principles on which I base my directions, I can expect the reader to follow each step, with the prospect of success and enjoyment much enhanced.

The question first arising is, What shall we plant? As before, I shall give the selection of eminent authorities, then suggest to the reader the restrictions under which he should make a choice for his own peculiar soil and climate.

Dr. F. M. Hexamer, the well-known editor of a leading horticultural journal, is recognized throughout the land as having few, if any, superiors in recent and practical acquaintance with small fruits. The following is his selection: "Cuthbert, Turner, and Marlboro." Hon. Marshall P. Wilder's choice: "Brinckle's Orange, Franconia, Cuthbert, Herstine, Shaffer." Hon. Norman J. Colman, Commissioner of Agriculture: "Turner, Marlboro, Cuthbert." P. J. Berckmans, of Georgia: "Cuthbert, Hansel, Lost Rubies, Imperial Red." A. S. Fuller: "Turner, Cuthbert, Hansel."

In analyzing this list we find three distinctly foreign kinds named, the Orange, Franconia, and Herstine. If the last is not wholly of foreign origin, the element of our native species enters into it so slightly that it will not endure winters in our latitude, or the summer sun of the South. For excellence, however, they are unsurpassed.

In the Cuthbert, Marlboro, and Lost Rubies we have hybrids of the foreign and our native species, forming the second class referred to; in the Turner and Hansel, examples of our native species unmixed. To each of these classes might be added a score of other varieties which have been more or less popular, but they would serve only to distract the reader's attention. I have tested forty or fifty kinds side by side at one time, only to be shown that four or five varieties would answer all practical purposes. I can assure the reader, however, that it will be scarcely possible to find a soil or climate where some of these approved sorts will not thrive abundantly and at slight outlay.

Throughout southern New England, along the bank of the Hudson, and westward, almost any raspberry can be grown with proper treatment. There are exceptions which are somewhat curious. For instance, the famous Hudson River Antwerp, which, until within a very few years, has been one of the great crops of the State, has never been grown successfully to any extent except on the west bank of the river, and within the limited area of Kingston on the north and Cornwall on the south. The Franconia, another foreign sort, has proved itself adapted to more extended conditions of soil and climate.

I have grown successfully nearly every well-known raspberry, and perhaps I can best give the instruction I desire to convey by describing the methods finally adopted after many years of observation, reading, and experience. I will speak of the class first named, belonging to the foreign species, of which I have tested many varieties. I expect to set out this year rows of Brinckle's Orange, Franconia, Hudson River Antwerp, and others. For this class I should make the ground very rich, deep, and mellow. I should prefer to set out the plants in the autumn, from the middle of October to the 10th of November; if not then, in early spring —the earlier the better—while the buds are dormant. I should have the rows four feet apart, and if the plants were to be grown among the smaller fruit trees, I should maintain a distance from them of at least seven feet. I should use only young plants, those of the previous summer's growth, and set them in the ground about as deeply as they stood when taken up, say three or four inches of earth above the point from which the roots branched. I should put two well-rooted plants in each hill, and this would make the hills four feet apart each way. By hills I do not mean elevations of ground. This should be kept level throughout all future cultivation. I should cut back the canes or stems of the plants to six inches. Thousands of plants are lost or put back in their growth by leaving two or three feet of the canes to grow the first year. Never do this. The little fruit gained thus prematurely always entails a hundredfold of loss. Having set out the plants, I would next scatter over and about them one or two shovelfuls of old compost or decayed manure of some kind. If the plants had been set out in the fall, I should mound the earth over them before freezing weather, so that there should be at least four inches of soil over the tops of the stems. This little mound of earth over the plants or hill would protect against all injury from frost. In the spring I should remove these mounds of earth so as to leave the ground perfectly level on all sides, and the shortened canes projecting, as at first, six inches above the surface. During the remainder of the spring and summer the soil between the plants chiefly requires to be kept open, mellow, and free from weeds. In using the hoe, be careful not to cut off the young raspberry sprouts on which the future crop depends. Do not be disappointed if the growth seems feeble the first year, for these foreign kinds are often slow in starting. In November, before there was any danger of the ground freezing, I would cut back the young canes at least one-third of their length, bend them gently down, and cover them with earth to the depth of four or five inches. It must be distinctly remembered that very few of the foreign kinds would endure our winter unprotected. Every autumn they must be covered as I have directed. Is any one aghast at this labor? Nonsense! Antwerps are covered by the acre along the Hudson. A man and boy would cover

in an hour all that are needed for a garden.

After the first year the foreign varieties, like all others, will send up too many sprouts, or suckers. Unless new plants are wanted, these should be treated as weeds, and only from three to five young canes be left to grow in each hill. This is a very important point, for too often the raspberry patch is neglected until it is a swamp of tangled bushes. Keep this simple principle in mind: there is a given amount of root-power; if this cannot be expended in making young sprouts all over the ground, it goes to produce a few strong fruit-bearing canes in the hill. In other words, you restrict the whole force of the plant to the precise work required —the giving of berries. As the original plants grow older, they will show a constantly decreasing tendency to throw up new shoots, but as long as they continue to grow, let only those survive which are designed to bear the following season.

The canes of cultivated raspberries are biennial. A young and in most varieties a fruitless cane is produced in one season; it bears in July the second year, and then its usefulness is over. It will continue to live in a half-dying way until fall, but it is a useless and unsightly life. I know that it is contended by some that the foliage on the old canes aids in nourishing the plants, but I think that, under all ordinary circumstances, the leaves on the young growth are abundantly sufficient. By removing the old canes after they have borne their fruit, an aspect of neatness is imparted, which would be conspicuously absent were they left. Every autumn, before laying the canes down, I should shorten them in one-third. The remaining two-thirds will give more fruit by actual measurement, and the berries will be finer and larger, than if the canes were left intact. From first to last the soil about the foreign varieties should be maintained in a high degree of fertility and mellowness. Of manures from the barn-yard, that from the cow stable is the best; wood-ashes, bone dust, and decayed leaves are also excellent fertilizers. During all this period the partial shade of small trees will be beneficial rather than otherwise, for it will be remembered that sheltered localities are the natural habitat of the raspberry.

By a little inquiry the reader can learn whether varieties of the foreign class are grown successfully in his vicinity. If they are, he can raise them also by following the directions which have been given. Brinckle's Orange—a buff-colored berry—is certainly one of the most beautiful, delicate, and delicious fruits in existence, and is well worth all the care it requires in the regions where it will grow; while the Franconia and others should never be permitted to die out by fruit connoisseurs. If the soil of your garden is light and sandy, or if you live much south of New York, I should not advise their trial. They may be grown far to the north, however. I am told that tender varieties of fruits that can be covered thrive even better in Canada than with us. There deep snow protects the land, and in spring and autumn they do not have long periods when the bare earth is alternately freezing and thawing.

In the second class of raspberries, the crosses between the foreign and native species, we now have such fine varieties that no one has much cause for regret if he can raise them; and I scarcely see how he can help raising them if he has sufficient energy to set out a few plants and keep them free from weeds and superabundant suckers. Take the Cuthbert, for instance; you may set it out almost anywhere, and in almost any latitude except that of the extreme Southern States. But you must reverse the conditions required for the foreign kinds. If the ground is very rich, the canes will threaten to grow out of sight. I advise that this strong-growing sort be planted in rows five feet apart. Any ordinary soil is good enough for the Cuthbert to start in, and the plants will need only a moderate degree of fertilizing as they begin to lose a little of their first vigor. Of course, if the ground is unusually light and poor, it should be enriched and maintained in a fair degree of fertility. The point I wish to make is that this variety will thrive where most others would starve, but there is plenty of land on which anything will starve. The Cuthbert is a large, late berry, which continues long in bearing, and is deserving of a place in every garden. I have grown it for many years, and have never given it any protection whatever. Occasionally there comes a winter which kills the canes to the ground. I should perhaps explain to the reader here that even in the case of the tender foreign kinds it is only the canes that are killed by the frost; the roots below the surface are uninjured, and throw up vigorous sprouts the following spring. The Cuthbert is so nearly hardy that we let it take its chances, and probably in eight winters out of ten it would stand unharmed. Its hardiness is greatly enhanced when grown on well-drained soils.

It now has a companion berry in the Marlboro, a variety but recently introduced, and therefore not thoroughly tested as yet. Its promise, however, is very fine, and it has secured the strong yet qualified approval of the best fruit critics. It requires richer soil and better treatment than the Cuthbert, and it remains to be seen whether it is equally hardy. It is well worth winter protection if it is not. It is not a suitable berry for the home garden if no other is grown, for the reason that it matures its entire crop within a brief time, and thus would give a family but a short season of raspberries. Cultivated in connection with the Cuthbert it would be admirable, for it is very early, and would produce its fruit before the Cuthberts were ripe. Unitedly the two varieties would give a family six weeks of raspberries. There are scores of other kinds in this class, and some are very good indeed, well worth a place in an amateur's collection, but the two already named are sufficient to supply a family with excellent fruit.

Of the third class of red raspberries, representing our pure native species, I should recommend only one variety, the Turner, and that is so good that it deserves a place in every collection. It is certainly a remarkable raspberry, and has an unusual history, which I have given in my work *Success with Small Fruits*. I doubt whether there is a hardier raspberry in America—one that can be grown so far to the north, and, what is still more in its favor, so far to the south. In the latter region it is known as the Southern Thornless. The fact that it is almost wholly without spines is a good quality, but it is only one among many others. The Turner requires no winter protection whatever, will grow on almost any soil in existence, and in almost any climate. It yields abundantly medium-sized berries of good flavor. The fruit begins to ripen early, and lasts throughout a somewhat extended season. It will probably give more berries, with more certainty and less trouble, than any other variety. Even its fault leans to virtue's side. Set out a single plant, leave it to nature, and in time it will cover the place with Turner raspberries, and yet it will do this in a quiet, unobtrusive way, for it is not a rampant, ugly grower. While it will persist in living under almost any circumstances, I have found no variety that responded more gratefully to good treatment. This consists simply in three things: (1) rigorous restriction of the suckers to four or five canes in the hill; (2) keeping the soil clean and mellow about the bearing plants; (3) making this soil rich. Its dwarf habit of growth, unlike that of the Cuthbert, enables one to stimulate it with any kind of manure. By this course the size of the bushes is greatly increased, and enormous crops can be obtained.

I prefer to set out all raspberries in the fall, although as a matter of convenience I often perform the task in the *early* spring. I do not believe in late spring planting, except as one takes up a young sprout, two or three inches high, and sets it out as one would a tomato plant. By this course time is often saved. When it is our wish to increase the quality and quantity of the fruit, I should advise that the canes of all varieties be cut back one-third of their length. A little observation will teach us the reason for this. Permit a long cane to bear throughout its natural length, and you will note that many buds near the ground remain dormant or make a feeble growth. The sap, following a general law of nature, pushes to the extremities, and is, moreover, too much diffused. Cut away one-third, and *all* the buds start with redoubled vigor, while more and larger fruit is the result. If, however, earliness in ripening is the chief consideration, as it often is, especially with the market-gardener, leave the canes unpruned, and the fruit ripens a few days sooner.

In purveying for the home table, white raspberries offer the attractions of variety and beauty. In the case of Brinckle's Orange, its exquisite flavor is the chief consideration; but this fastidious foreign berry is practically beyond the reach of the majority. There is, however, an excellent variety, the Caroline, which is almost as hardy as the Turner, and more easily grown. It would seem that nature designed every one to have it (if we may say *it* of Caroline), for not only does it sucker freely like the red raspberries, but the tips of the canes also bend over, take root, and form new plants. The one thing that Caroline needs is repression, the curb; she is too intense.

I am inclined to think, however, that she has had her day, even as an attendant on royalty, for a new variety, claiming the high-sounding title of Golden Queen, has mysteriously appeared. I say mysteriously, for it is difficult to account for her origin. Mr. Ezra Stokes, a fruit-grower of New Jersey, had a field of twelve acres planted with Cuthbert raspberries. In this field he found a bush producing white berries. In brief, he found an albino of the Cuthbert. Of the causes of her existence he knows nothing. All we can say, I suppose, is that the variation was produced by some unknown impulse of nature. Deriving her claims from such a source, she certainly has a better title to royalty than most of her sister queens, who, according to history, have been commonplace women, suggesting anything but nature. With the exception of the Philadelphians, perhaps, we as a people will not stand on the question of ancestry, and will be more inclined to see how she "queens it."

Of course the enthusiastic discoverer and disseminators of this variety claim that it is not only like the Cuthbert, but far better. Let us try it and see; if it is as good, we may well be content, and can grace our tables with beautiful fruit.

There is another American species of raspberry (*Rubus occidentalis*) that is almost as dear to memory as the wild strawberry—the thimble-berry, or black-cap. I confess that the wild flavor of this fruit is more to my taste than that of any other raspberry. Apparently its seeds have been sown broadcast over the continent, for it is found almost everywhere, and there have been few children in America whose lips have not been stained by the dark purple juice of its fruit. Seeds dropped in neglected pastures, by fence and road sides and along the edges of the forest, produce new varieties which do not propagate themselves by suckers like red raspberries, but in a manner quite distinct. The young purple canes bend over and take root in the soil during August, September, and October. At the extreme end of the tip from which the roots descend a bud is formed, which remains dormant until the following spring. Therefore the young plant we set out is a more or less thick mass of roots, a green bud, and usually a bit of the old parent cane, which is of no further service except as a handle and a mark indicating the location of the plant. After the ground has been prepared as one would for corn or potatoes, it should be levelled, a line stretched for the row, and the plants set four feet apart in the row. Sink the roots as straight down as possible, and let the bud point upward, covering it lightly with merely one or two inches of soil. Press the ground firmly against the roots, but not on the bud. The soil just over this should be fine and mellow, so that the young shoot can push through easily, which it will soon do if the plants were in good condition. Except in the extreme South, spring is by far the best time for planting, and it should be done early, while the buds are dormant. After these begin to grow, keep the ground mellow and free from weeds. The first effort of the young plant will be to propagate itself. It will sprawl over the ground if left to its wild impulses, and will not make an upright bearing bush. On this account put a stake down by the young sprout, and as it grows keep it tied up and away from the ground. When the side branches are eight or ten inches long, pinch them back, thus throwing the chief strength into the central cane. By keeping all the branches pinched back you form the plant into an erect, sturdy bush that will load itself with berries the following year. No fruit will be borne the first season. The young canes of the second year will incline to be more sturdy and erect in their growth, but this tendency can be greatly enhanced by clipping the long slender branches which are thrown out on every side. As soon as the old canes are through bearing they should be cut out and burned or composted with other refuse from the garden. Black-caps may be planted on any soil that is not too dry. When the plant suffers from drought, the fruit consists of little else than seeds. To escape this defect I prefer to put the black-caps in a moist location, and it is one of the few fruits that will thrive in a cold, wet soil. One can set out plants here and there in out-of-the-way corners, and they often do better than those in the garden. Indeed, unless a place is kept up very neatly, many such bushes will be found growing wild, and producing excellent fruit.

The question may arise in some minds, Why buy plants? Why not get them from the woods and fields, or let nature provide bushes for us where she will? When nature produces a bush on my place where it is not in the way, I let it grow, and pick the fruit in my rambles; but the supply would be precarious indeed for a family. By all means get plants from the woods if you have marked a bush that produced unusually fine fruit. It is by just this course that the finest varieties have been obtained. If you go a-berrying, you may light on something finer than has yet been discovered; but it is not very probable. Meanwhile, for a dollar you can get all the plants you want of the two or three best varieties that have yet been discovered from Maine to California. After testing a great many kinds, I should recommend the Souhegan for early, and the Mammoth Cluster and Gregg for late. A clean mellow soil in good condition, frequent pinchings back of the canes in summer, or a rigorous use of the pruning-shears in spring, are all that is required to secure an abundant crop from year to year. This species may also be grown among trees. I advise that every kind and description of raspberries be kept tied to stakes or a wire trellis. The wood ripens better, the fruit is cleaner and richer from exposure to air and sunshine, and the garden is far neater than if the canes are sprawling at will. I know that all horticulturists advise that the plants be pinched back so thoroughly as to form self-supporting bushes, but I have yet to see the careful fruit-grower who did this, or the bushes that some thunder gusts would not prostrate into the mud with all their precious burden, were they not well supported. Why take the risk to save a twopenny stake?

If, just before the fruit begins to ripen, a mulch of leaves, cut grass—any litter that will cover the ground slightly—is placed under and around the bushes, it may save a great deal of fruit from being spoiled. The raspberry season is also the hour and opportunity for thunder-showers, whose great slanting drops often splash the soil to surprising distances. Sugar-and-cream-coated, not mud-coated, berries, if you please.

In my remarks on raspberries I have not named many varieties, and have rather laid stress on the principles which may guide the reader in his present and future selections of kinds. Sufficient in number and variety to meet the *needs* of every family have been mentioned. The amateur may gratify his taste by testing many other sorts described in nursery-men's catalogues.

It should also be remembered that the raspberry is a Northern fruit. I am often asked in effect, What raspberries do you recommend for the Gulf States? I suppose my best reply would be, What oranges do you think best adapted to New York? Most of the foreign kinds falter and fail in New Jersey and southern Pennsylvania; the Cuthbert and its class can be grown much farther south, while the Turner and the black-caps thrive almost to Florida.

Raspberries, especially those of our native species, are comparatively free from disease. Foreign varieties and their hybrids are sometimes afflicted with the curl-leaf. The foliage crimps up, the canes are dwarfed, and the whole plant has a sickly and often yellow appearance. The only remedy is to dig up the plant, root and branch, and burn it.

A disease termed the rust not infrequently attacks old and poorly nourished black-cap bushes. The leaves take on an ochreous color, and the plant is seen to be failing. Extirpate it as directed above. If many bushes are affected, I advise that the whole patch be rooted up and healthy plants set out elsewhere.

It is a well-known law of nature that plants of nearly all kinds appear to exhaust from the soil in time the ingredients peculiarly acceptable to them. Skill can do much toward maintaining the needful supply, but the best and easiest plan is not to grow any of the small fruits too long in any one locality. By setting out new plants on different ground far better results are attained with much less trouble.

SINGING WINGS.

BY WILLIAM HAMILTON GIBSON.

WHAT a vibrant teeming chorus hovers above our meadows and pastures in the drowsy air of August! It is a whirling maze of sound, a dizzy, busy, gauzy buzz, which is like a bewildering tangle to the ear, without end or beginning—a tangle, too, so closely involved with the intricacy of its source among the weeds and grasses that the listener seldom thinks or cares to seek for a loose end.

These singing fields of ours are a suggestive heritage of the new continent. The Old World knows them not. The observant American tourist who for the first time saunters through the summer meadows of England is immediately struck with their silence. Thus Tennyson's line,

"For now the noonday quiet holds the hill,"

while truthful from the European standpoint, could never have been written on American soil. Isolated singers there are in these foreign fields, 'tis true—crickets, locusts, and grasshoppers — counterparts of American types, and these in abundance, but they do not seem exuberant; there is no such unanimous, multitudinous expression as finds escape in our pastures new. Against the background of that "noonday quiet" each individual minstrel, though unseen, betrays his portrait to the ear, and is readily recognized, as shown forth in the beautiful lines of Keats—a pretty tribute to an isolated soloist:

"The poetry of earth is never dead:
  When all the birds are faint with the hot sun,
  And hide in cooling trees, a voice will run
 From hedge to hedge about the new-mown mead;
 That is the grasshopper's; he takes the lead
  In summer luxury; he has never done
  With his delights, for when tired out with fun,
 He rests at ease beneath some pleasant weed."

There was evidently no difficulty in following the course of that song, but it would have taxed the patience of the poet to have performed a similar poetic service for the American insect, for it takes a sharp ear to separate the complete score of the individual grasshopper or cricket in our meadow orchestra. The ear must be focussed, as it were, and, moreover, equipped with the anticipation of previous familiarity with the thread of its song, ere it can be disentangled from the maze. This minstrelsy is to midsummer what the bird choral is to spring. The feathered minstrels are now silent, eclipsed, and have given place to the "joyous meadow tribes." From horizon to horizon the sunny pastures and the ripening fields resound with singing wings—the great pastoral symphony of harvest-time.

Thoreau loved to explore "the sources of the myriad sounds which crowd the summer noon." They seemed to him "the very grain and stuff of which eternity is made."

"The wide air is full of joyous wings,"

sings Bryant—a sentiment which now receives its fullest confirmation, albeit, I imagine, one not considered by the poet. The buoyancy, the joyous flight, was in his thought; the music of those wings, while doubtless quickening his own, yet prompted no expression of tribute.

Who shall draw a comparison or parallel to the bird voice of the spring, the choral of the vernal morning? Not I. There is a deep emotional and spiritual sentiment awakened by the jubilee of the returning birds which any words at my command are but paltry to express. Each voice of nature has its unison, its dear companion chord of sympathy or association in every heart; and yet there is to me in these

"Sounds that rise from the murmuring grass,"

in the sunny wing song of an insect—that strange symbolic creature, equipped for song only in its final metamorphosis, the perfect being only singing—a significance which not even the sweeter vocal charms of the birds possess.

I am never weary of renewing my acquaintance with these quaint little meadow musicians, as I stroll afield, these "high-elbowed grigs that leap in summer grass." The weedy pasture or neglected fallow is their paradise. Amid all their intense vibratory I can generally catch a certain familiar strain, and follow it to the end— *tsip, tsip, tsip, tsip, tsee-e-e-e*. It emanates apparently a rod or so in advance of me. I approach stealthily, starting up the inevitable swarms of flying locusts that pitch with headlong momentum into the quivering herbage on right and left. They certainly would break their precious necks were they not so reënforced by that stiff protecting collar—an armor in which those close-fitting, ram-shaped heads revolve as in a socket joint. The song now rises again amid the din of thousands which might be its echo, still apparently some distance in advance of me, thus with a certain alluring quality decoying me on

and on, until at last the one particular strain on which my attention has been focussed is positively approached, and seems now to rise directly from my feet. Seating myself cautiously, I await developments.

The commotion among the lively and sharp-eyed spasmodic jumpers aroused by my approach at length subsides, and the grassy jungle through which my eye now penetrates assumes its wonted equilibrium. How intricate and infinite these shadowy recesses! With what exquisite grace of motion the slender grass culms bend and sway with the tossing of their capillary plumes in the billowy breeze! How the sifting sunbeams which filter through the tangles glint and glide and play among the waving stems, with here a flash from a gauzy wing, and there a glittering spangle from some lingering dew-drop, dallying in silken gossamer, or cradled within the hollow of an envious leaf!

For a moment the identity known as "me" is annihilated. An old, strange, indefinable longing, a half-forgotten association, seems to possess me. I become a vague memory; I am a cricket again, an ant, a beetle, and fancy that the human estate knows no parallel to this luminous singing realm beneath the grasses.

Now comes a fresher billowing breeze above that works new transformations, opening up vistas hitherto unknown, and showing forth a thousandfold the limitless resources of this lowly meadow world. Just beyond, a luxuriant cluster of swamp-cabbage leaves, heretofore lost in sombre mystery, is now revealed in a burst of mellow light. It is only for an instant, while the shadow of its overhanging bush is playing elsewhere in the breeze—a brief glow of golden green, revealed just long enough to disclose the expectant toad upon the stone within its shadow, and the solitary dandelion ball floating like a puff of smoke beneath the luminous canopy.

A plumy thistle seed now floats within my realm. A huge carnivorous black fly —a bumble-bee some would call him— alights with buzzy wing upon a clover head near by. But we will not look upon him now. A history of discord is his. His hum is pitched in the minor key, and to the poor human sentiment seems ever out of unison with the harmony of nature. What have we here? What fairy creature is this, hovering in the halo of its tiny wings like an atom of down floating above the yellow toad-flax flowers? And now it settles on the golden horn of plenty, and proceeds to probe with its slender bill into the very heart of the sweets. A gnat—a snow-white gnat, in very truth—with feathery antennæ and all, transfigured and spiritualized, its old appetites renounced, and now sipping the nectar of the flowers, and singing the while with its phantom wings. One may well marvel at such an exquisite creation as this, and feelingly recall the appreciative sentiment of Pliny of old: "In these little bodies how can one comprehend the reason and the power and the inexplicable perfection that Nature hath therein showed? How hath she bestowed the five senses in a gnat? Where hath she made the seat of her eyes? where hath she set and disposed the taste? where hath she placed and

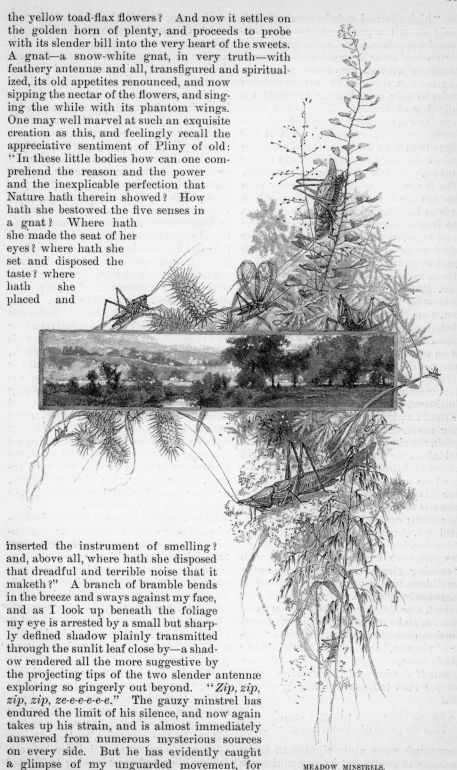

MEADOW MINSTRELS.

inserted the instrument of smelling? and, above all, where hath she disposed that dreadful and terrible noise that it maketh?" A branch of bramble bends in the breeze and sways against my face, and as I look up beneath the foliage my eye is arrested by a small but sharply defined shadow plainly transmitted through the sunlit leaf close by—a shadow rendered all the more suggestive by the projecting tips of the two slender antennæ exploring so gingerly out beyond. "*Zip, zip, zip, zip, ze-e-e-e-e-e.*" The gauzy minstrel has endured the limit of his silence, and now again takes up his strain, and is almost immediately answered from numerous mysterious sources on every side. But he has evidently caught a glimpse of my unguarded movement, for the "high-elbowed grig" kicks off suddenly from his perch and pitches haphazard into space, alighting upon a swaying stem of timothy-grass, and at length straddling with an air of comical solemnity upon a spray of capsella, where he seems to gain confidence, and permits a full view of himself. This is the common diurnal meadow grasshopper (*Orchelimum vulgare*), represented aloft in our vignette in his favorite attitude, seemingly looking down upon his fellows of the timbrel. He is a pellucid green creature, with the outline of his body readily seen through the filmy wings. He is about an inch in length, and the long legs suggest the fragile consistency of glass, and one involuntarily wonders how these slender members could have survived intact such reckless gymnastics as they are continually called upon to sustain as well as instigate. Turning upon his perch, he brings to view his "glassichord," or shrilling organ, upon his back—a glass-like spot upon his wings just behind the thorax, or what might appear to the facetiously inclined as an exceedingly uncomfortable-looking collar. Even as we take our first glimpse of this diminutive, filmy taboret, a strange tremor seems to have taken possession of the insect, the edges of the wings seem blurred and indistinct in the rapid vibratory movement, and then follow a few quick, convulsive efforts, resulting in the stridulous strain already described, and whose multitudinous repetition on every hand so saturates the quivering ether. For this is perhaps the most omnipresent meadow sound of the New England summer noon; certainly the most prominent. And yet, singularly enough, few of our entomologists seem to have discovered the fact, even associating the song with "evening gloom" and "shady places"—conditions under which my minstrel is comparatively silent. On a cloudy day, indeed, our fields emulate the downs of Britain, and are almost still, our present musician among the rest. He is a "lover of the sun," and revels in midsummer tropic heats.

But if the harp of the meadow grasshopper thus touches my willing fancy, and

> "Sweeter sound these humming wings
>   Than the proud minstrel's echoing strings,"

how much more aptly significant is the instance of another of its companions in music, the daintiest animated timbrel which this meadow orchestra can show! Fortunate are you if permitted to steal within its charmed circle and discover the pretty exhibition suggested in our vignette, an attitude assumed by the little harpist only in the act of minstrelsy, as he holds his tiny twin lyre aloft, and with deft manipulation, so rapid as almost to elude the eye, awakes "the echoes from the trembling strings"—a continuous high-keyed trill, prolonged sometimes for ten or fifteen minutes, or longer for aught I know, without intermission. But you must observe in breathless and immovable silence, for your very winking is reflected in those receptive glassy mirrors, and at the slightest surprise the music ceases and the musician is instantly transformed. The transparent taborets seem to vanish into air, and now a slender pale green creature, with flat and glistening body, dodges beneath the leaf, and is off in a twinkling, his filmy duplex theorbo neatly overlapped upon his back, with the outer half on either side closely folded against his body. This is a prominent voice of our August fields, whose commingled trills, united with the myriad murmuring fiddles of the locusts of every degree, the shrilling of the tiny brown crickets, the humming of bees, and droning of beetles, conspire to sustain and prolong the winged roundelay, and against whose continuous undertone the ringing tabors and rasping reeds of the grasshoppers recur in more or less universal accord, either rarely as a distinct feature, or as an occasional full crescendo in the great orchestral movement.

This insect is known as the broad-winged climbing cricket (*Œcanthus sapitennis*), an agile, generally pale green creature, inhabiting the higher musical plane of the meadow among the leaves and flowers of the loftier weeds and bushes. Delicate and fragile as he certainly is, he has still a striking counterpart—in every sense his superior—a yet more refined edition of himself, as it were, so nearly does the one insect suggest the other when contemplated by the eye alone.

Who has not heard that mellow rhythmical "*te-reat, te-reat, te-reat, te-reat*," the lulling, throbbing voice ever so closely associated with the late summer and autumn evenings, whose pulsating vesper chorus ushers in the sundown, and continues, without cessation, as a lullaby between the evening and the morning twilights?

A MOONLIGHT MEDLEY.

diaphanous; for the body of this vesper minstrel is almost as immaterial as its voice. It is the spectral cricket of my vocabulary, though in the more prosaic page of scientific entomology this pallid, filmy, white insect is known as the "snowy tree cricket" (*Œcanthus niveus*).

It was doubtless to the dreamy, spirit-like song of this insect that Hawthorne alluded in that happy conceit which he so generously committed to the musings of his Canterbury poet, "He listened to that most ethereal of all sounds, the song of crickets coming in full choir upon the wind, and fancied that if moonlight could be heard, it would sound just like that." Elsewhere he alludes to their song as an "audible stillness," his mind not taking note of it as an actual sound, but rather as an unobtrusive sympathetic expression of an interior sentiment—a sad foreboding of the farewell of the year. Thoreau noted the "slumbrous breathing" and the "intenser dream" of crickets. "Purring crick-

It is not the voice of the black cricket, so commonly and undeservedly associated with the sound. Approach its source. It will be found invariably to proceed from some elevated position in bush or tree, and never from the ground. No, there is no savor of the earth about that song. In comparison to the song of its sombre rival, it is as much more ethereal and spirituelle as its animated source is more subtle and

ets," Burroughs calls them, and notes that the "sound is in waves, and has a kind of rhythmic beat." How well he knows them! This "rhythmic beat" is peculiarly associated with the song of this cricket, and I have often observed, moreover, what is doubtless also signified in the above allusion, that the quality of perfect rhythm ;obtains not only to the individual song, but in a still more striking compound sense to their usually associated minstrelsy; for the positively isolated song of this cricket is rare in my experience.

The first touch of this exquisite lyre is heard about the second week in August, and from this time its music increases as the season advances, all through the late summer and autumn, mingling in discordant contrast with the "chromatic reeds" of the katydids. Indeed, long after the rasping wrangle of these latter has subsided, and the last surviving "testy little dogmatist" has had it all his own way for days, and at length succumbed, with his legs criss-crossed like a pair of scissors, even yet you may catch an occasional faint trill from the snowy cricket's spectral harp.

But it was not my intention thus long to take leave of my sunny meadow, for there yet remains another mysterious dweller therein, who claims our recognition in positive and rasping accents, "*tsip, tsip, tsip, tsip*," a continuous, rapid, exasperating stridulation, a reiterated noisy parody, simulating the prelude of the meadow grasshopper already described, always foreshadowing some musical feat that shall distance his little rival, but never getting any further than a brag. This is the loudest and most peremptory challenge we shall meet in the entire meadow, in its very grain and fibre suggestive of inordinate egotism.

After having once discussed him, and separated his green individuality from the surrounding herbage, and fully satisfied yourself that his long wings are actual insect membranes and not a brace of abbreviated blades of timothy-grass, it will interest you to observe him closely. This insect is known as the "cone-headed grasshopper" (*Conocephalus ensiger*), and may be fittingly called the clown of all this heyday.

With what an air of solemn mock-gravity he straddles around among the herbage, keeping you ever in the field of his view, with the jet-black pupil of the one white

eye turned in your direction! It matters not what his position, that pupil is incessantly riveted upon you, travelling to the upper or the lower edge of the eye, as the case may be. And if perchance he now rears up and faces you, as imperfectly indicated in our illustration, what was true of one eye is now true of both, and you are confronted with a cross-eyed grin that brings your long suppressed laugh to a final outburst, which for the time being disconcerts the merry-andrew.

Now he confronts you, "bows on," lifts one hind-leg like a mast high in the air, wriggling his long series of terminal toes as if to simulate a pennant, his slender antennæ thrown back from the apex of his long bowsprit like jib-stays. And have I not seen similar glassy bull's-eyes or light-holes in the prows of ocean craft? Yes; and look! now the machinery begins to work, you can almost hear the propeller as the hulk begins to sway and tremble, and the spinning engine lets off its noisy calliope, as already described. For it is a fact that in no other grasshopper is the sound of the shrilling mechanism so plainly perceptible beneath its song, a suggestion of axles, cogs, and cams, all the worse for wear. All through this mimetic exhibition our clown has been accomplishing the feat of looking cross-eyed over the back of his head. He would seem to afford a perfect though an exaggerated embodiment of the simile of Cicero that "the eyes are like sentinels, and occupy the highest place in the body." Nothing escapes the sentry of this watchtower, it is certain, with its two goggles suggesting prospecting windows in the summit of a minaret. But our harlequin is not yet done with us; we need not be surprised at anything. He will now perform the contortionist act. Lowering his elbowed thigh almost to a corresponding position below his wing, he will presently work the shank of the leg around beneath his body, thus bringing his jointed toes between his fore-feet. After repeating the exercise with the other leg, he next lifts his fore-foot and pulls down his long tapering antennæ into his crimson mouth, drawing them through his palpi or teeth, with the two loops gradually enlarging in front of his face. This is his magic act, for how else could those exquisitely fragile members escape unharmed the cutting edges of those hard mandibles?

And so on until the programme is finished and our cone-capped pantaloon takes a sudden notion to skip.

I am aware that this individual which I have been disclosing in my noonday haunt is more properly a nocturnal character, only by especial favor displaying his noisy resources in the daytime. He is an imp of darkness, and begins to file his saw outside your window at the approach of twilight, and may be heard in more or less incessant company with the garrulous katydids all through the night.

Recurring again to "Katy"—for how could one help recurring again and again to the noisy minstrel, when permitted to listen through the poetic fancy of "our genial autocrat," in his well-known lines inscribed to this insect, to that humorous apostrophe which begins:

"Thou testy little dogmatist!

*   *   *   *   *

"Thou mindest me of gentle-folks—
   Old gentlefolks are they—
Thou say'st an undisputed thing
   In such a solemn way.

"Thou art a female katydid;
   I know it by the trill
That quivers through thy piercing notes,
   So petulant and shrill."

What a happy, deliberate freedom with the artistic license have we here! How gladly welcome, too, when we reflect that a strict regard for scientific truth would have deprived the world of this precious bit of mother-wit. For in fact among all our insect tribes it is not the female but the male that sings, the mate, if answering audibly at all, merely with a slight rustling flirt of the voiceless wings.

There are yet many other songsters of lesser note in our New England meadows, but they must, for the present, be lost in the din.

In imputing the gift of song to these musical performers I have taken a liberty with fact, for singers in the true sense these insects are not—they are more properly minstrels—for, accurately speaking, it may be accepted, as Aristotle expressed long ago, "that no living creature hath any voice but such only as are furnished with lungs and windpipes." His context is also interesting. "The noise which we heare come from insects is no voice at all, but a very sound occasioned by the aire which gets within them, and so being enclosed makes a certain noise and resoundeth againe, and thus it is that some keep a humming or buzzing, as bees; others make a cricking with a certaine long traine, as the grasshoppers; for evident it is and well known that the aire, entering into those pipes under their breast and meeting with a certaine pellicle of thin skin, beats upon it within, by which attrition the shrill sound commeth."

When we reflect that the term "grasshopper" is here, doubtless, an instance of a common error in transla-

AN INTERRUPTED SONG.

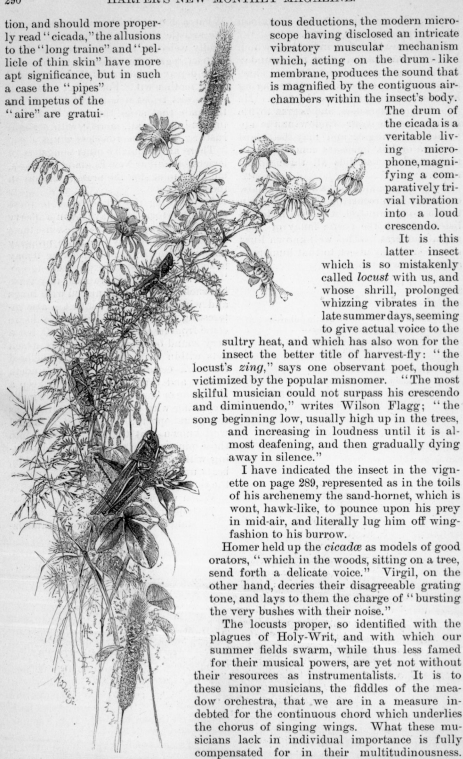

tion, and should more properly read "cicada," the allusions to the "long traine" and "pellicle of thin skin" have more apt significance, but in such a case the "pipes" and impetus of the "aire" are gratuitous deductions, the modern microscope having disclosed an intricate vibratory muscular mechanism which, acting on the drum-like membrane, produces the sound that is magnified by the contiguous air-chambers within the insect's body. The drum of the cicada is a veritable living microphone, magnifying a comparatively trivial vibration into a loud crescendo.

It is this latter insect which is so mistakenly called *locust* with us, and whose shrill, prolonged whizzing vibrates in the late summer days, seeming to give actual voice to the sultry heat, and which has also won for the insect the better title of harvest-fly: "the locust's *zing*," says one observant poet, though victimized by the popular misnomer. "The most skilful musician could not surpass his crescendo and diminuendo," writes Wilson Flagg; "the song beginning low, usually high up in the trees, and increasing in loudness until it is almost deafening, and then gradually dying away in silence."

I have indicated the insect in the vignette on page 289, represented as in the toils of his archenemy the sand-hornet, which is wont, hawk-like, to pounce upon his prey in mid-air, and literally lug him off wing-fashion to his burrow.

Homer held up the *cicadæ* as models of good orators, "which in the woods, sitting on a tree, send forth a delicate voice." Virgil, on the other hand, decries their disagreeable grating tone, and lays to them the charge of "bursting the very bushes with their noise."

The locusts proper, so identified with the plagues of Holy-Writ, and with which our summer fields swarm, while thus less famed for their musical powers, are yet not without their resources as instrumentalists. It is to these minor musicians, the fiddles of the meadow orchestra, that we are in a measure indebted for the continuous chord which underlies the chorus of singing wings. What these musicians lack in individual importance is fully compensated for in their multitudinousness. Thus the flight of an individual locust is a trifling

THREE FIDDLERS.

sound in itself, while the noise of the traditional swarm has been likened to the "roar of a wild ocean" or "fierce tempest." In less heroic comparison the consideration applies from the stand-point of their music. Barely perceptible to the ear by itself, this single diminutive "first violin," reënforced a hundred-thousandfold, asserts itself distinctly, and lends a sustained, important feature to the summer medley. In the locust the taborets of the grasshopper are wanting, the term "singing wings" being but partially applicable, the wings doing only half-duty in the musical performance as the responsive instrument, the viol, to which the insect's leg performs the office of bow. When a locust begins his "recital" he is apt to assume the attitude of the "first fiddle" among my pictured trio, the shank of his leg being drawn close within a groove beneath the thigh, evidently made to receive it.

With an air of comical solemnity the leg is now raised and lowered with more or less regular and continued motion, being pressed close against the firm edge of the wing-covers, by which contact the fiddling is accomplished. Thus a certain antique philosopher had it pretty nearly right when he affirmed, "As for locusts, it is generally believed and received that they make that sound with clapping of their feathers and thighs together." This same musical resource is known to other species of insects as well, notably many beetles, one of which, the pretty painted *clytus*, a beautiful yellow and black banded creature, may rightly claim a minor place in our orchestra as he sips and fiddles so contentedly among the goldenrod blossoms.

But there are still other voices identified with our summer fields. A few "odd ends" in this tangle of sound which we have as yet ignored, for in our compliment to the insects we have occasionally been the dupe of various little strategic shams in the way of mimetic bird-songs. Foremost among these meadow mimics is the tiny yellow-winged sparrow, and a queer little finch he is, in his feathery identity doubtless as little known as any bird in New England, and in his voice less still, for though heard the livelong day, the meadow grasshopper would be sure to get the credit. Of all our birds, even with bobolink in mind, this little sparrow is still the meadow's own. Bob

can teach him nothing of this ground. He has no points to learn from grasshopper or cricket, for his world and theirs are identical. He is the feathery counterpart of both insects; a very cricket of the shadows, threading his way among those intricate passages down deep against the mould beneath the débris of last leap-year's grasses, a complex labyrinth known else only to the field-mice and their kindred. Here he is perfectly at home; while above, again, the flitting wings of the grasshopper bound the loftier limits of his little world. The plane of his life rarely rises above the meadow-lilies—a lowly plane, but even thus it would seem the more vocal of thanksgiving. Once seen and identified with its song, this diminutive sparrow is not likely to be forgotten.

The song at a little distance almost exactly resembles the final prolonged strain of the diurnal grasshopper already described, save that it is more extended, and when in close proximity a little louder. It has, moreover, a peculiar ventriloquistic quality, which, when heard in the distance, seems to locate its origin at much closer range, this peculiarity, again, contributing to the difficulty of identity of the bird with its song, even though the former be in continual sight.

The Savannah sparrow, a streaked, speckled, terrestrial species, is a bird of much the same habits as the foregoing, and is possessed of a chirping ditty which might even deceive a cricket itself, to say nothing of the entomologist.

The third member of my mimetic trio is the diminutive field sparrow (*Spizella pusilla*), which, in addition to a sweet and varied song, has recourse to artful mimicry, and, like Irving's convivial Master Simon, we occasionally find him in "as chirping a humor as a grasshopper filled with dew."

How my ears sing! exclaims a little child to me while loitering in a sunny pasture, vibrant with the intense winged chorus. In a similar vein of thought, I doubt if the average toiling farmer ever hears the joyous din—assuming that one cannot be truly said to hear who does not listen. And yet this meadow music hath charms unknown to him. It is a generous beneficence; it sings in his ears as the undercurrent upon which he floats his fancy as he plods afield; to which his hopes, his fears, his joys, his sorrows, have

been attuned in unison through the years. How much this pastoral hymn has ministered to his life he little comprehends. We are told that the soldier may sleep soundly through the booming of artillery or the din of musketry, but starts from rest at the shock of sudden silence. Likewise the slumberer in his berth in mid-ocean awakens in apprehension at the stopping of the engine, the beating of this ponderous, palpitating heart being in

strange sympathy with his own. How many a callous, stolid toiler of the farm, apparently as innocent of sentiment as the bowlders of his boundary walls, but who through a lifetime has been soothed unaware by the music of his meadow, could he be doomed to silent harvest fields, would awaken to a consciousness that something of its beauty and sweetness had gone out of his life! Farmer, did I say? It matters not whether farmer, merchant, artist, or poet, there are none too many singing wings in his lot.

MEADOW MIMICS.

BONNE MAMAN.

BY GRACE KING.

IT was in a part of the city once truthfully, now conventionally, called "back of town," and it had been used as an obscure corner in which to thrust domestic hearths not creditable to the respectability assumed in the front part of town; where oil lamps could be safely substituted for gas, and police indifference for police protection.

The long rows of tallow-trees, with here and there an oak, shaded an unpaved street and a seemingly unbroken continuity of low cottages, with heavy green doors and windows and little wooden steps jutting out on to the banquette. Their homely architectural physiognomies were adapted to an isolated, dimly lighted locality, and were frankly devoid of any beauty or picturesqueness of expression. But as the banquette, wrinkled and corrugated from the roots beneath, retarded the steps of the passer-by, faintly asserted individualities might be discerned: declensions of one-storied degrees of prosperity, comparisons of industry and cleanliness, pretensions to social precedence inherited from the architect of a century ago, or acquired by the thrift of a present tenant. The steps were all scrubbed red with brick, or yellow with wild camomile, which, besides gilding, lent them the aromatic fragrance of antique caskets.

The quiet that reigned told that the street was still back of town in all that a corporation suggests of movement, bustle, and noise. The air of desertion which hung about the little closed cottages would have been oppressive had it not been for the children—a motley crowd, accusing an "olla podrida" parentage, chattering in tongues as varied as their complexions, and restless as if with the competing energies of hidden nationalities. They were dressed with tropical disregard of conventionality, frank, impudent, irrepressible, at all times noisy and unanimous, swooping down the street in eager response to some distant alarm, or taking swarming possession of whole rows of steps.

The delusive similarity of the blocks would generate in time the suspicion of a tread-mill under foot, did not the sharp point of a triangular enclosure furnish a landmark by cutting into the very middle of the street, parting the hitherto companion banquettes, and sending them on at divergent angles in ever-increasing separation, until they were finally arrested at unrecognizable distances apart by the banks of the bayou. The fence of this obtruding property may have been painted in front on the other street, but it degenerated to its apex through every stage of shabbiness and neglect. As a screen for the large square house, it was indebted to a hedge of orange-trees, which raised their heads proudly in the sun, illuminating the ugly spot with their golden fruit in the winter, and sanctifying it in the spring with their blossoms. The shaded banquettes along the sides of the triangle were a constant temptation to the children, alluring them, against experience, into the range of the epithets and missiles of the children-hating people within.

"Allez-vous-en!"

"Pestes de la terre!"

"Negrillons!"

"Gamins!"

"Tits démons!"

"Enfants du diable!"

The loss of a knot from one of the boards of the fence furnished a providential peep-hole into the mysteries of a "ménage" from which abnormal discoveries seemed constantly expected by the children, and if persistence of attention could have been relied upon, warnings might always have been given for timely refuge on the steps of the nearest little corner cottage. These offered an ideal juvenile place of refuge, where there were no brick or camomile scrubbings to rebuke their litter, no sudden front-door openings to sweep them away in confusion, no front-window admonitions or imprecations to disturb them, and absolutely no banquette ordinances to taunt them into wilfulness, but instead an upward glance through the small opening of the bowed shutters showed them the face of "la blanche mamzelle là-yè" at her sewing.

They were too young to appreciate the fact that the batten windows were bowed only when they were there, or to wonder why they, the children, were the only ones who ever saw her, but they did know that her face was whiter, her hair straighter and finer, than human comparison for them, and so they could not keep their eyes from looking for responses from hers, nor their lips from smiling invitingly at hers, nor their tongues from sallies of wit intended for her ear alone. To-day she paid little attention to them. They could hear her "Misères!" of impatience, and the vexatious tapping of her foot, though they could not see that she was manipulating some gaudy woollen material which gave her infinite worry with its ungracious, not to say stubborn, opposition to a necessity which ordered its stripes to go flouncing in diagonal procession round and round a skirt.

"Claire!" called a feeble voice from the back room.

She raised her head incredulously.

"Claire! Claire Blanche!"

A shade of disappointment passed over her face.

"Bonne maman!"

"Mais, Claire, fillette, where are you?"

"I am coming, bonne maman."

She caught her work together and folded it in a cloth before going into the other room.

"What are you doing, bébé?"

"But my work, bonne maman."

"Ah! I could not think where you were."

"I thought it was cooler in the other room."

"It is very warm in here."

"You are not going to get up, bonne maman? You have not finished your sleep yet."

"Have I not slept as long as usual?"

"No, indeed; only a few minutes. That was the reason I could not think it was you calling."

"Enfin, it is better for me to get up."

"But why, bonne maman? There is no necessity for you to get up earlier to-day than usual."

"As you say, it is warm here."

The old lady lay on her bed underneath the mosquito bar, the straight folds of her white "blouse volante" settled around her thin figure. Claire picked up a fan, and putting back the bar, commenced to fan her.

"Chère, bonne maman, try. Maybe you can sleep some more."

The coaxing, caressing voice and the soft motions of the fan had a soothing effect, and although the grandmother repeated, "Yes, decidedly I had better get up," she made no effort to move.

"The weather is so warm and tire-

some," continued the girl, suggesting an excuse for lethargy.

"Yes, as you say, it is warm and debilitating."

"Mais, just shut your eyes, bonne maman, and try to sleep. You have not rested at all."

"Rest," she said, catching the word. "I do not need rest; I have worked very little to-day—in fact, not at all."

"Oh, but I mean rest from thinking. Mon Dieu! if I thought as much as you, I could not keep my eyes open at all."

She turned her head on the pillow, and did close her eyes.

Claire smiled with satisfaction. Her bright face showed the reflection of cheerful interpretations alone, and her quick eyes, glancing over the surface of things, gathered only pleasant sights. She was going on tiptoe out of the room.

"Why do you not bring your work in here, Claire, where I am?"

"What, not asleep? Vilaine!"

"Mais, mon enfant, how you talk! Sleep? when I have so much to finish!"

"Oh, there is plenty of time for that, bonne maman. At least stay in bed a little longer."

"One would suppose that I was the grandchild and you the bonne maman."

Claire brought her work; not the gaudy stripes, but a piece of embroidery, and seated herself at some distance from the bed, in the path of a ray of light.

The old lady sighed heavily; her eyes were fixed on Claire.

"But what is the matter, bonne maman?"

"Oh! nothing, nothing. chérie, only, what makes you stoop so, Claire?"

"Ah, that ugly habit! Imbécile!"—slapping her forehead—"can't you cure yourself enfin? I ought to be well tapped for it, as I was at the convent."

She straightened herself up to an uncomfortable degree of rectitude, which lasted as long as the remembrance of the sigh, and she talked as if her needle could only move in unison with her tongue.

"It was funny at the convent how many bad habits I had. They seemed to grow on purpose to be corrected. And I was so young, too. Bad mark for this, en pénitence for that, fool's cap for something else, twenty-five lines by heart for something else. And all the time, 'Your grandmother never did this,' 'Your mother never did that,' 'Ah, if you had seen your tante Stephanie,' 'Look at your cousin Adelaide.' Ma foi! the first lesson I learned was that I was like no member of my family seen before. How I used to wish there had been just one lazy bad one like me! Was it that way when you were there, bonne maman?"

The old lady did not answer, but Claire showed no hesitation in summoning her thoughts from any pleasanter dallying ground.

"Hein, bonne maman?"

"What, Claire?"

"At the convent, was it that way with you? Always scolding you because you were not some one else, always punishing you because you were what you were? That was justice! And then to tell me I was lazy and could not learn! It enrages me every time I think of it. I am sure I learned very nearly the whole of the *Génie du Christianisme* in punishment. It was killing. Study! When I was thinking all the time about something else, straining my ears to listen, just to see if I could hear the cannon shooting 'way out there in the distance."

She heard another sigh, and raised her shoulders with a start.

"Pardon, bonne maman! I forget. You will see I can cure myself. Oh! I can do anything I want except be pious, as they wanted me to be at the convent. Ha! it was very easy for the sisters to say 'Study history!' 'Study geography!' and stick *La Vie des Saints* before me. Saints! It was 'ces diables de l'enfer' out there shooting their cannons that I was thinking of! Books! I hated books, and pen and ink and paper make me ill to this day; but I could embroider; that didn't prevent listening and thinking. I was only pious when the mail came in. When I remember those days, mon Dieu Seigneur! but we were frightened then! Oh, how we loved God and the saints then! and how we used to pray to them, fast, fast, fast as we could, before the letters were brought around! Getting a letter meant just the same thing as killing some one in our family. Those were times—eh, bonne maman?"

"Bonne maman!"

"Fillette!"

"But, bonne maman, you don't listen to me, you don't answer me."

"But, ma petite, I thought you wanted me to go to sleep?"

"Ah, were you going to sleep? And I woke you? What a fool I am!"

"What were you talking about, mon bébé? I will listen now."

"Ah, no, bonne maman, don't listen to me, I am so silly; indeed, I am not worth listening to. Try to go to sleep again. To think that I woke you, when I wanted you so much to sleep! I believe the sisters at the convent were right. I shall never have any sense—never; only strength. Ah, yes! they told me that often enough, and tried to shame me by pointing to the good girls—the good, weak girls. Anyhow," shrugging her shoulders, "goodness doesn't stand a convent and war as well as badness. Ma chère! when I left there you would have said that a battle had been fought in the dormitory, and the guns loaded with fevers, and all aimed at the good girls. Only the fool's-cap wearers escaped. The little cemetery was full, full, full, and the graves so even and regular, all of one size, like a patchwork quilt spread out inside the four fences."

"Now, Claire, I shall get up."

"You see, if it had not been for me you would have been sleeping; and it is so hot and tiresome to-day."

Her grandmother sat up in bed.

"Just to give me pleasure, bonne maman, stay quiet a moment longer."

"To give you pleasure—ah, well, if it gives you pleasure!" and she reclined again.

"Claire!"

"Oh, bonne maman, I forget"—sitting up with innocent egoism.

"Claire, I was thinking I would like to see my little green work-table again."

"Ah, that was what you were thinking, eh? I thought it was my shoulders."

"My little green work-table," she repeated to herself.

"Which stood in the window of your room, that looked on to the gallery, over the orange-trees, over the levee, into the river—"

"To think I should forget it until to-day! To think I could forget it!—my little green work-table."

"But, bonne maman, you have so much to forget!"

"But that was my 'corbeille de noces,' ordered from Gessler, in Paris. A corbeille de noces! how much that means! I can see the very day, the very hour, it came. First, my vexation and disappointment; there were tears in my eyes; it was so 'bourgeoise,' a work-table, with nothing but scissors and threads and needles, instead of orange flowers and lace and fans and sentiment. Eh, mon Seigneur! what ideas I had! But Aza was there! What a devil Aza was! impertinent, pushing, and perfectly fearless. I was the only one who could manage her. They said I had spoiled her, but she adored me more than she did God, and was more afraid of displeasing me too. She followed me around like a little dog. I never could put my hand out, so, without touching Aza."

Claire nodded her attention as her fingers flew backward and forward about her work.

"It seems to me," and the soft feeble voice sounded very plaintive—"it seems to me that all the bright hopes that used to fly before me, they fly behind me now as memories."

"Well, of course that is natural. We are two crabs, you and I—we walk backward. We couldn't see anything going on before us, par exemple."

"But, Claire, I keep forgetting. I must get up and finish that embroidery."

"Oh, just one moment, bonne maman —just one moment more."

"It must be finished and returned this evening."

The needle sped faster and faster, and the soothing words fell more and more disconnectedly.

"Go and fetch it to me, Claire."

"Yes, bonne maman."

"Indeed I feel quite refreshed."

"Dieu merci!" muttered the girl, and recklessly added, "Vogue la galère!"

The grandmother got very slowly out of the bed and walked to her rocking-chair.

"It is in the basket there on the mantel-piece."

Claire went for the basket, and slipped the roll of embroidery she held in it.

"Here it is, bonne maman."

"Ah! mais, this is not my embroidery."

"Si, it is your embroidery, bonne maman."

"No, my child, you have made a mistake, and put yours in my basket. Look again, and give me mine, chère."

Claire turned her head away, that her face might not discredit her voluble tongue.

"But I tell you that is your embroidery, bonne maman."

"My embroidery! Claire, how can you say so? Come and convince yourself. See! this is all done; and mine—there was a good piece to do still."

"Mais!"

"A—h! I see! Claire, it is you who have finished it for me."

"Eh, why not? I had already finished mine, and I had nothing to do—absolutely nothing. Was I to sit still and hold my hands—hein? Oh, you need not examine the stitches! I know they are not so fine, nor so smooth, nor so regular as yours, but they are good enough for that old 'chouette' Varon all the same, and—"

The grandmother jumped violently at a sudden knock at the door.

"Mais, mon Dieu! what is that?"

"À la bonne heure!" whispered Claire to herself. "It is Betsie, bonne maman, I will see what she wants."

"Ah, that Betsie! she is so badly raised. She knocks at the door as if she were a Suisse. Now, Aza—"

Claire had already left the room, and closed the door behind her.

"Mamzelle," said Betsy, standing on the step, "there's that nigger out there come for her gownd."

"Hush, Betsie! Bonne maman is awake."

"There's some frolic going on to-night, and she has set her heart on wearing her new gownd."

"But it is not finished."

"That's bad."

"I was still sewing on it when bonne maman awoke."

"I suspicioned you hadn't done it, and I tried my best to send her away; but, Lord! such a contrairy, obstreperous nigger like that!"

"If bonne maman had only slept a little while longer—"

"You couldn't baste it up any sort of fashion, right off, and let her go?"

"But how can I, Betsie? Bonne maman—"

"Couldn't you just slip out in the kitchen with it? You could say I wanted you to look after the soup while I go in the street a minute."

"Ha! you think bonne maman would not go herself to see to it?"

"That's so; the madam would come right out there herself. But that gal is so owdacious and high-minded; she has been a-jawin' out there for an hour constant, and I've been a-answering her just as fair as I could, 'cause I didn't want no fuss. I never seen anything like her brazenness all the days of my life. A-driving of white folks like they was niggers.... Couldn't you say I wanted you to cut a josie for me?"

"She would tell me to bring it to her to cut. Bonne maman is not so easy to fool, Betsie."

The bright sunlight showed lines of weariness and dejection in the girl's face which the darkness of the bedchamber had concealed. She leaned back against the closed doors and clasped her hands over her head to shelter her eyes.

"Well, I don't know. If she was not such a loud-mouthed, lazy, good-for-nothing, trolloping thing, I wish we could make an end of her!"—turning to go. "Let me see what I can do with her again."

"Ask her to wait just a little while longer; perhaps—"

"Wait! Lord bless you! she 'ain't got any idea of going. Gabriel hisself couldn't drag her away for the judgment-day withouten that gownd. I ain't afeard of her going; I'm afeard she'll holler so loud the madam will hear her."

Claire peeped anxiously through the door before entering. It was all still. She walked in on tiptoe. Her grandmother sat with her eyes closed, the embroidery in her hand.

"Ah, bonne chance!"—her face was sanguine and gay again—"bonne maman has gone to sleep at last."

The little kitchen basked in the double heat of sun and furnace, and was overcrowded with its assemblage of three. The only chair in the room was occupied by the votary of fashion, whose monotonous argument rolled on to an unresponsive audience.

"I was a-telling this lady here," she nodded to Claire with her bundle, and pointed to Betsy—"I was a-telling her I wanted my frock for to-night, for that moonlight picnic is a-coming off to-night at last. You 'ain't heerd tell of it? Me and my society gives it, and all the members is going to go, and they is bound to go. I laid off yesterday to come and tell you, but I didn't have time; and it appears to me a week's long enough to make a frock, anyhow; and if it wasn't, you should have told me so fair and square before you ever put a needle into it. The moonlight pic-

nic's done been put off long enough, the Lord knows! It did seem to me as how we never would be able to get it up. Something was always a-happening against it. Every blessed time we got all the money we'd look in the box, and, sure enough, there wouldn't be enough yet, and then it would be put off till another collection. And if it hadn't been for Sister Johnson's funeral last night it wouldn't come off now. But it's coming off this time, sure; 'cause if it had a-come off when we first started it, Sister Johnson herself could have gone to it; yes, indeed, as sure as you are standing there; and if it hadn't been for holding her funeral last night I don't believe we ever would have got it up. It was a-long past midnight when they come to me for my money, 'cause I never would have given it to 'em before; and after they had done got all the money, they said as how they had better wait for the moon; but the sisters, they just said, 'No, sir; you give that there moonlight picnic to-night, moon or no moon, 'cause it's a heap easier to give a moonlight picnic without a moon than without the money.' As I was a-telling this lady here, and if you had a-told me last week you wasn't a-going to give me that there frock there for the moonlight picnic, I could ha' given it to somebody else. Lord knows there's white people enough to do sewing, and glad to get it; and you knows yourself, after I done paid my money last night at Sister Johnson's funeral for a moonlight picnic, I'm bound to go, and I'm bound to wear a new frock if I've got one."

"Lord, child! don't you jaw so much. Don't you see the mamzelle's 'most done it? Who says you ain't gwine to git it done in time?"

"She's bound to git it done in time, if I stays here a week—she's bound to git it done in time."

It lay on the table like a heap of fresh glowing vegetables. She picked up the waist.

"And I hope to gracious you 'ain't made the josie too tight! I busts my josies awful. The color is real stylish, though. You 'ain't got a collar or some sort of neck fixin' you could sell me, have you? I could pay you cash down for it," rummaging in the privacy of her bosom; "you can see for yourself," untying the knot in a handkerchief. "Lord knows I had trouble enough getting this money after I had done worked for it! I had to jaw that white woman what owed it to me two hours incessant before she had the grace to pay me. But I was bound to get it for the moonlight picnic, and I wasn't going to wash and iron one day longer, neither, for anybody, and I told her so. Goodness knows, I ain't obliged to work for her no-how; and she flung it to me, and told me for God's sake to hush talking, and clear out and never let her lay eyes on me no more, and I ain't going to, neither; and if you've got any sort of collar or neck fixin' you could sell me cheap, I'd pay you cash down for it."

"Hein, Betsie?" asked Claire.

Betsy answered in a quick whisper, "Ef you have got some sort of little old thing you 'ain't got any use for, you know the money 'll come in mighty handy."

Claire hurried across the little yard and went into the room with the same precautions as before. Her fingers trembled as she opened the door of the armoire so near the sleeping grandmother, and she pulled from an old pasteboard box the first piece of lace that met her eye—a large antique collar of Valenciennes.

"Will this do, Betsie?" she asked, entering the kitchen.

The damage done its marketable value by the deep yellow color was painfully evident to both.

"How much you want to give for it?" asked Betsy.

"Well, I can't give you more'n I've got. I'm willing to give you all I have got, and that is the best I can do. Here's the six bits for the making of the frock, fair and square as she agreed on, out of this dollar, and here's two bits besides, and that's the last cent I've got in this world, as the Lord hears me speak; and I wouldn't have had that two bits there if I hadn't been let off last night from giving it to the collection, 'cause they didn't know I had it; and they wouldn't 'a come to me, nohow, if they hadn't found out I'd been washing by the week—"

"Six bits outen the dollar and two bits besides. How much does that make altogether?" asked Betsy of Claire.

"And that dollar there was what the white woman gave me."

"I will take it, Betsie, I will take it," said Claire, eagerly. "I assure you it is quite sufficient."

"Well, so long! I'm just a-willing to bet, now, that that moonlight picnic is put off again. I mistrusted them brothers when they come a-knocking me up last night in the middle of the night. I don't believe in moonlight picnics, nohow, and—"

"Eh, Betsie? That is plenty of money, hein? But if bonne maman finds out!"

The old lady did not open her eyes for some time after Claire returned, and then resumed, as if in continuation of her thoughts: "It is curious I never thought of my little work-table until to-day. My 'corbeille de noces.' And it was Aza the first who found it out—Aza." She shook her head meditatively as she repeated the name. "She was always pushing herself forward where I was. They told me I spoiled her; perhaps so. She was more like a doll to me than a human being. Her mother gave her to me, when she was only a day old, in my arms. It felt so grand to have a live doll, just as I was beginning to tire of the others. What plans I made for her! Enfin! it was the will of God. While I was standing, with tears in my eyes, looking at the needles and thread, Aza was feeling the green bag underneath. Do you remember the green bag, Claire?"

"Do I remember it, bonne maman? Mais sûr."

"She gave the drawer one pull, and, voilà! it was all before me."

Her thin, bluish hands, with their dark, knotted, angry veins, rubbed nervously up and down the arms of her chair, and she made frequent pauses by leaning back and closing her eyes.

"Ma foi, if Aza had waited, she would not have had to thank me for her freedom. 'Ma fille,' I used to tell her, 'it is not only the difference in our skin, but the difference in our nature.' She would have died for me—ah, yes!—but she could not be good for me. Claire, I wish I could see my little work-table again." Her voice, usually so trained, was surprisingly plaintive. "You see, so much would come back to me if I could see my little table. I think sometimes, mon enfant, that the loss of our souvenirs is the worst loss of all for us women. With them we never forget. When one is old, things get so far away. When we are young, we are like dogs: we hide away out of our provision, for the future, scraps of ribbon, lace, or a glove—no matter what—and it is very hard when, old and hungry, we come to the place and find them all gone. Of course it is all sentiment; but, 'nous autres,' we women, going through so much, we like to remember when everything happened for the first time—one's first copy-book, one's first communion, one's first ball, and when one gets married, and one's first child. Ah, mon Dieu! one can get reconciled to changes in life, but one cannot get reconciled to changes in one's self. Even when they are crumbling to dust they are fresher than we women are at the end. Mon enfant, I advise you, give up everything in life except your souvenirs; keep them for your sentiments to gnaw on, as one might say."

"Eh, grand'mère, souvenirs of what? Of the war? of the convent? Merci! I am in no danger of forgetting them. Every piece of bread I eat reminds me how hungry I used to be there, and—"

The grandmother had taken another leave of absence of mind, and Claire, having no ulterior motive for loquacity, was silent also.

The closed eyes, however, were not, had not been, sleeping; on the contrary, under their pallid lids they were looking with tense vision, in vague fear of an indeterminate something slowly evolving out of misty uncertainty into a fatal conviction.

That it had not come to her before was owing to the coercive strength of an inflexible will; that it came to her to-day with the irrefutable accumulated evidence hitherto suppressed or ignored, did not astonish, only awed, her. Women live close to nature, and are guided from initiation to initiation in life by signals and warnings which they, and only they, can see. There can be no rebellion against their own intuitions, no questioning of the credentials of the angels of the twilight who still knock at their doors, the bearers of divine commands, messengers of life or messengers of death.

She was failing—failing in physical, failing in mental, strength. The child Claire was managing her, doing her work for her surreptitiously. She would prepare for the future; but why would the past obtrude upon her, turning its corpse-lights into every nook and cranny of her memory? Regrets were useless; but why would they come, sowing discord, corroding with tardy indecision the supreme decisions of her life, arraigning, from the vantage-ground of the present, cherished feats of spent heroism, testing the metal of her approaching martyr's crown?

This was to be the end of a life conducted on principles drawn from heroic inspirations of other times. The principles were the same, but human nature had changed since women's hearts were strong enough not to break over bullet wounds, sabre cuts, and horse-hoof mutilations, when women's hands were large enough to grasp and hold the man-abandoned tiller. It had all gone wrong. The old lady spread her handkerchief over her eyes. The closed lids could not shut in all the tears. Yes, it had all gone wrong somehow. The battle turned out a defeat, not a victory; the son came back on his shield, not with it. And she? She might perhaps have done better. Death would now have been easier for her if the times and she had been different. Had it not been for overflows and disasters and disappointments, for failure of crops and epidemics of disease, for the feeding of so many useless and infirm dependents, she too might have been a successful plantation manager. As it was, when her commission merchant came to her with a statement, she frankly and firmly acknowledged that she could not rightfully claim an acre of her possessions. They came in a royal grant; they went in a royal cause. There were law quibbles; but lose a creed to grovel for coppers? She might have gone to France, as it was supposed she had done; and desert the country for which her only son had died? She was less than ever a French woman, more than ever an American. At bay, every nerve tingling with haughty defiance at the taunts and jeers of despising conquerors, every heart-throb beating accusations of womanly weakness and grief, what more effective answer to the challengers of her blood and country, what nobler one to herself, than bravely to assume the penalty she had dared? As the men had fought, let the women suffer against overpowering odds. So she left the beautiful country, her plantation, her home, her souvenirs of youth and happiness, and came to the detested city, sought out this little cabin left vacant by the death of an old slave, and with Claire commenced that life to which she had convinced herself she was committed by principle. It was an extreme of resolution to meet an extreme of disaster. Ameliorations of her lot were intolerable even in thought. She would make her destitution complete by renouncing even friends, relations, social amenities, with her humble neighbors.

She *had* lived her retaliation against fate—there was no doubt about that now —thoroughly, effectively, and death was upon her. But Claire? The handkerchief could not hide the convulsive movement of her bosom as she recognized the short range of heroic vision.

The figure of her pale, cheerful, brave, toiling granddaughter came before her with the unearthly vividness of those visions in stormy nights of her dead, helpless little children dressed in their grave-clothes. The agony she had felt in abandoning her babies to the isolation and ugliness of the tomb resuscitated poignantly at the abandonment of her last child to life.

What tomb could be lonelier or uglier than this little cabin would be to Claire when she, the grandmother, was dead?

Would the patriotic death of her father, would the martyrdom of her mother, would a proud disdain of law quibbles, would the renunciation of friends and the defiance of enemies, alleviate her affliction then, or solace her in her youthful, unaided life-struggle, for which ancestral glories, refinements, and luxuries were a poor equipment? Could enemies prepare an extremity of suffering beyond that to which Claire was predestined by her own grandmother?

The sun went down on the little back street earlier than elsewhere on account of the huge old square house blocking up the west. The windows and doors unclosed as its rays withdrew, and the hidden community finished the day's task in the publicity of the front steps, until twilight released them to indulge in the relaxation of neighborly gossip—all except the corner cottage, which maintained its distrustful reserve even through the gentle, winning shades of evening.

When others went in front to greet each other with the commonplaces of human interdependence, Claire and her grandmother went back into the contracted area between the house and kitchen, and expended their tendernesses on the mendicant groups of potted plants that formed their garden. The old lady walked this evening from shrub to shrub, laying her gentle, withered hands with maternal expertness amid the green leaves, straightening a distorted branch or searching out

diseased spots. Her own heart felt bruised and sore from suppressed emotion, and craved their fragrance, which, it seemed to her, they had never yielded so willingly or so abundantly. Did they understand all, and sympathize with her? The tears came into her eyes again, but Claire had gone to take the embroidery home, so there was no need to hide them.

The brilliant sunset sky burned overhead in deep engulfing masses, reaching down to the pointed roof of the cottage— the despised roof whose shelter she had sought as the deepest insult she could inflict upon the world. The old, worn, menial house! it also looked kindly, protectingly, at her, as if it also had penetrated her secret—the last secret of her life. An old, old sentiment thrilled in her heart as she looked through her tears at it for the first time as at a home. "Ah, mon Dieu," she thought, "everything seems to know and feel for me, just as it used to know and feel when I carried other secrets in my breast!" The youthful, timid faltering came over her once more, the virgin shudder before unknown mysteries, the same old girlish need of help and encouragement. But she overcame the expression of her face as she heard the key turn in the lock of the little back gate behind the cistern. Claire entered boisterously, followed by Betsy with a bundle. She tossed off her hat with its ugly veil of blue barége.

"Oh, bonne maman! Such a delicious walk! If I only had embroidery to take home every evening! And the old 'chouette' could not have been more amiable. Ah, it's so good to go out on the street!"

She stretched her arms over her head, tightening the faded waist around her swelling breast as she looked up in the brilliant sunset sky above.

"Mon Dieu! but it's all beautiful. I wish I could walk up there in all that pink and blue and gold; walk deeper and deeper in it, until it came up all around and over me!"

She drew a long quivering breath.

"Do you smell the night jasmine, bonne maman? I do not know how it is with you, but it is as if it came thousands and thousands of miles just to me and no one else, and it makes me feel faint with its sweetness."

She threw her arms around her grandmother and embraced her impulsively.

"You see, it is so good to go on the

street, bonne maman. It makes one feel
so gay, so fresh, so strong. Ah, you
ought to go sometimes with me, just to
see all the people. How many people
there must be in the world! And I know
only three—you, Betsie, and old Varon.
But I am glad they are there all the same,
even if I do not know them."

A loud, coarse, passionate waltz seemed
to fall in rhythmic links over the glass-
protected brick wall. She released her
grandmother and danced round and round,
as if caught in its melodious wheels, until it left her panting and glowing.

"When I hear music like that, bonne
maman, it is as if my blood would come
out of my veins and dance right there before me. Sometimes in the night I hear
it; I think at first I'm dreaming, but then
I wake and listen to it until I stop my
ears and hold myself still, for, oh, bonne
maman! I want so much to get up and
follow it, out, out, wherever it is, until I
come to the place where it begins fresh
and sweet and clear from the piano, and
then dance, dance, dance, until I cannot dance one step more!"

The words fell in unguarded fervor,
and her eyes began to burn with feverish
brightness. Betsy plucked at her dress.

"Mamzelle!"

"Sometimes I wonder whether it is in
the music or in me—"

"Mamzelle! Mamzelle!"

"Whether it is in me alone or in everybody—"

"Mamzelle Claire, just one word!"

"Decidedly that Betsie is very badly
raised," remarked bonne maman, in an
undertone.

"When I smell the night jasmine I
feel it a little, and when I look up in the
sky like awhile ago; but it's never so
strong as when I hear music. Oh, bonne
maman, can't you give me something to
make me stop feeling this way—to make
that music let me alone?"

"Mamzelle!"—the negro excitedly
placed her hand on Claire's arm to enforce
attention.

"If Aza could see that!" The old lady
turned away in disgust.

"Mamzelle! I can't stand by and see
you dancing and singing to that music
you hear over there, and hear you talk
about getting up in the night and following it." Her voice trembled, and her fingers tightened convulsively over the slim
white arm. "I don't tell the madam,

'cause it's no use bothering her; but, mamzelle, as sure as God hears me now, them
niggers over there don't play no music
excepting for devils to dance by, and that
piano don't talk nothing fittin' a young
white lady to listen to."

"Eh? What do you mean?"

"Mamzelle—"

"Does that hurt the music who plays
it? Do you think I want to dance to it,
to listen to it?" She pushed Betsy's hand
off, with her fingers grown clammy; her
cheeks were crimson, and her lips blushed
at the strange maturity of expression so
new to them.

"Did I say I was going to get up at
night and follow it? Did I say I was going on the street every evening? Did I
say I would rush up to the people to feel
them clasp my hands only once? I only"
—and her voice came in a sob—"I only
said I wanted to."

The music came now lower and sweeter.
She stopped her ears. "There! that is
what I must do—eh? Why doesn't it stop
talking to me?"

"But, mamzelle, they is—"

"It doesn't cost anything," she interrupted, furiously—"it doesn't cost anything to listen to music, to know people.
I don't have to work for it, like bread and
meat; and, grand Dieu, how much better
it is!"

Two tears rolled from her hot eyes; she
paused in startled awe and carried her
hands up to them.

"Claire! Claire Blanche! you had better come in, child."

"Yes, bonne maman."

Outside, the steps filled up with white-
sacqued women. The men tilted their
chairs back against the trees and the walls
of their houses and smoked their cigarettes. The children—and this street could
have supplied a city with children—raced
from corner to corner to dance out the
sample tunes of passing organ-grinders.
The conversation flowed in an easy murmuring tide from group to group, soared
over every now and then by a dominant
cry in pursuit of some refractory fugitive.

"You Var—iste!"

"A—na—to—le!"

"Ga cette Marie là bas!"

"Jo—seph—ine!"

"Josephine, to maman 'peler toi!"

"'Polite! tu veux pas finir?"

The lamplighter threaded his way

among the chairs, scoring off a dim record of his passage up among the green leaves of the trees. As the darkness settled over the bushy tops of the orange hedge, blotting the dim outlines of the screened house, prodigal fragments of merriment seemed to be thrown in scornful carelessness down the street—dance music with its impetuous accelerations, overtures of song and chorus, breaking off in loud laughter and the tread of dancing feet.

"They are gay over there this evening."

"When one is like that—"

The women united their heads for female comment; but the men, their cigarettes spangling the gloom, listened in silence, and cast secret wistful glances in the direction of the occult merry-making.

"They won't sleep much over there to-night," said one, pointing to the corner cottage.

"As much as any Saturday night," was answered, with a shrug.

It was long before day, when Betsy, with minute particularity, closed the little gate behind her, and started out with her stick in her hand and her sack over her shoulder. She belonged to that division of humanity who seek their daily food in the daily refuse of others. She was a rag-picker—a gleaner in the nocturnal fields of a great city. Her harvests were not beautiful nor savory; but compensations in the shape of freedom from competition, weather influences, and a stable market are not to be despised, particularly by one for whom the darkness has no terrors, the loneliness no trepidations. She had contracted a stoop in her shoulders from so much bending over barrels and buckets and tubs, and peering through dim light into the slimy bottoms of muddy gutters, so her face seldom met the glance of the passing world, in whose litter it was ordained she should seek her food; but when she did look up, there was seen no reflection of corruption or filth in her small clear black eyes; no grovelling purposes conceived in grovelling pursuits. Although dressed in a motley livery, thrown off in the night from the shoulders of vice, sin, or crime, the audible thought which fell mechanically from her lips carried the conviction that it was a harlequinade of costume only. Her twilight meanderings had taught her much of life, and while it had never been given her to look upon or appreciate the gifts of civilization, she had

not many of its banes to find out. She had more experience to hate vice than to love virtue, which with purity and goodness dwelt a long way back in her memory, or a long way forward in Biblical promise. The répertoire of her monologues was not large or varied; wherever they ended, they generally began with an early morning like this, "nigh on to three years ago," when, going forth to pick rags, she found a mistress, and in lieu of daily bread gained daily bondage. She was turning over the contents of a very destitute box indeed that morning when a gate behind her suddenly opened, and a young white girl appeared.

"A young white girl in this here quadroon faubourg! My Lord! what does this mean?" her cultivated suspicions prompted her to exclaim.

But the young girl, frankly, in the confidence of innocent childhood, said, with a polite propitiating smile, in stiff, unpractised English:

"I hear you every morning; I attended for you this morning; I want that you direct me the way of the market."

"You git up this time o' day to ask me the way to the market?"

"Yes, for my grandmother yet sleeps. I wish to go there before she wakes herself."

"Honey, 'ain't you got nobody to go for you?"

"No, nobody now, for—"

"And what could a nigger do?" muttered Betsy, in self-extenuation—"more inspecially a Baptist, a fresh-water Baptist and a cold-water Baptist, and a hanger-on of the Cross?"

It was the chance that links together husband and wife, that determines the fall of a dynasty, or directs the feet of the outcast to a loving home.

Circumstances never permitted the childish appeal for assistance to cease, and an unselfish tender heart never permitted it to meet with disappointment. For three years now the sun had measured their horizon hour by hour, and it had never shone on a moment of distrust in either to their simple confidence, or of disloyalty to the pious obligation of serving, by fair means or foul, the proud old lady glorying in her lofty ideas of self-support.

"I can see the end," Betsy told herself, fishing around in a pestiferous heap, "but I can't see after the end. The old madam's a-failing; I seen she was a-failing the first day I laid eyes on her; and the young mamzelle is a-growing and a-ripening and beginning to notice things woman-like. The old madam, she don't suspicion nothing, nor the young mamzelle neither. The end's a-coming, and it's bound to come. The laughing and the singing and the working all day and half the night ain't a-going to put it off, neither; and it's a crucifying world, any-how."

The old lady that morning, trying also to look beyond the end, was seeing Claire growing up instead of remaining forever a child—growing up in spite of tragedy, starvation, imprisonment, into beauty, gayety, joyousness; craving sympathy, companionship, mental food; throwing out woman tendrils in all directions; cut off by short-sighted precautions from friends, from relations, even from certification of her own identity. Alone, literally alone, but for the homely friend picked up out of the street. She had sent Claire to church, for the first time in her life, by herself that morning in order to carry out the one project that had come to her in her agony. She called Betsy to the side of her rocking-chair.

"Betsie, you approach me."

Her English, like most of her youthful possessions, was hers yet only by an effort of memory. She spoke very slowly, reconnoitring for equivalents for her agitated French thoughts.

"Betsie, it must we all die."

"Lord! old miss."

"Betsie, it must you die, it must me die, but more maybe me than you."

"Yes, ma'am."

"Betsie, when it comes we die, we look for friends—hein?"

"I reckon so, old miss."

"Betsie, when it comes I die, me, I look for friends, what see I? Mademoiselle Claire and you. You and Claire, nobody more—eh, Betsie?"

"Yes, ma'am."

"Betsie, all this time I have been fool; but I be fool no more. I not work for myself; no, Claire, she work for me; you, you work for me; but me, I not work for myself. Oh! I think so, I work for myself, but no. Now, I know, me. My eyes, they have been shut, but now they see everything."

There were tears of mortification in the proud old eyes, whose first coquettish scintillations lay so deep buried under the grief-drifts of a lifetime.

"Since a long time I work not. Claire Blanche, she make my 'broderie' for me."

"Please, old miss, don't you go and get mad with the mamzelle for that!"

"Me, I do nothing more; for why? I die. Since two years I die. I do not know it before; but I know it now, well, well. Betsie, you come close, close." She could not sit; standing, her face was too high up. She knelt down by the chair. "Betsie, I very sick; I die to-day or to-morrow."

"Not so bad as that, old miss."

"To-day, to-morrow, or soon. I know not when, but soon."

"Can't you take something, old miss?"

"No, Betsie. I do not need medicaments; it is death what I need. Die, Betsie, that is something terrible; no, not for the agonizing, but for the others. It lasts long sometimes—hein, Betsie?"

"God knows, ma'am."

"Betsie, when it comes I die, you stand here, so, close; Claire, she stand there"—pointing to the next room. "You here, she there; then she not see."

Her voice, obedient to the strong will, was clear, but at times a weakening tone from the heart marred its firmness, and turned the command into a petition.

"I understand, old miss."

"Betsie, in my life I have seen much die. It did me nothing. For why? I was happy. I have hold the hand; I have made the prayer. But I had much family still. Betsie, if it comes I die, like you and me we have seen some die—Betsie, ma bonne femme Betsie, you will not let ma petite Claire see. Betsie, swear me that. My good God! Betsie, you think she ever laugh like last night when she see me, her bonne maman, die? Betsie, swear me that."

"I swear you that on the Bible, old miss."

"Betsie, you will say her nothing—nothing. God, He will tell her—oh, He will tell her in time. You say I strong; you say I well—hein, Betsie?"

"Yes, ma'am."

"That is all—that is all for the moment."

"There's something else, old miss, you've done forgot," began the negro woman, still on her knees, her short thick eyelashes crystallized with tears, a surpassing pleading in her voice. "Old miss, ain't you gwine to send for none of your folks—none of your friends? Old miss, you heerd that child out there last night just a-yearning for some folks and friends. Old miss, let me go out and find 'em for you. I will search this town through from end to end, but I'll find 'em for you, old miss. For God's sake, old miss, don't leave that child here with only one poor old nigger for her friend! Old miss"—putting her eager lips close to the bleached, withered ear—"old miss, they is all out there; the earth is full of friends, old miss. Just let me go for 'em."

The bonne maman reached out her hand and laid it on Betsie's head-handkerchief. "You have reason, Betsie—you have more reason than me. You are one good woman, and I ask the good God to bless you. For me and for my grandchild. I do not know to talk it, Betsie, but"—she drew the black face to her and pressed her lips on the forehead—"that is what I would say, Betsie."

"Old miss, you will send for your folks?"

"Yes, Betsie, to-morrow. Betsie," she called again, as the woman was leaving the room, "you will tell Mademoiselle Claire nothing—nothing; it will come to her soon enough—eh?"

"'Fore God in heaven I promise you that, old miss."

But she was never strong enough to send the summons; the angel had delayed too long on the road with his warning.

The first kisses of the spring sun bring out the orange blossoms, and the first movements of the spring breeze loosen them with gentle frolickings from their stems, and then carry the sweet betrayal of their wantonness and weakness round to all the open windows of the city. The children, with their quick divinations, have the news betimes, and muster in full force on the banquettes under the trees, intrepidly braving the insulting volleys of their ambushed foes. Before the dust of the street could pollute them in their abasement, before the sun could wither their unsheltered freshness, the deft little black, brown, and yellow fingers had picked them up into high-drawn skirts, old hats, scraps of pottery, rag, or paper, and garnered them, not on their favorite steps, but in a cache selected for temporary use. For on the green doors they loved Death had affixed his standard, and the

long black crape floating with majestic solemnity in the sweet air frightened them away. The little cabin, always so dark, so quiet, so unobtrusive, thrilled the early openers of the windows with the unexpected sign of its stigmata. Sleep had lulled them all into unconscious unhelpfulness, and daylight wakened them to accusing repentance.

"La pauvre vieille madame là-yè, morte pendant la nuit."

"Ah, miséricorde!"

"Si je l'avais su."

"Et moi."

The Sunday church bells called them all to mass—all except one. It is an old-fashioned creole city, with a pompous funereal etiquette, where no dispensation is sought or given for the visit commanded by that crape scarf. Death himself had unlatched the green doors, and was host to-day. The "blanchisseuse en fin," the "coiffeuse," the "garde malade," the little hunchback who kept the "rabais," the passers-by to and from mass, the marketwoman with her basket, the paper-boy with his papers—all came, if but for a moment, to say a little prayer, or bow in respect to the conqueror and the conquered. She lay in her coffin in the bare, unfurnished room, where she had lived with her poverty, her pride, and her griefs. Through the mutilations of age and infirmity, through wrinkles, discolorations, and the stony glaze of death, she looked with the patient resignation of a marble statue reposing on the bed of a sluggish stream.

Ignorant eyes looking at her humbled aristocratic head might see a little clearer into immortality; ignorant hearts, a little deeper into the depths of divine love. The alien could feel the sympathy of a common end if not a common origin, and the prejudiced comprehend her sufferings as he could not her principles.

A large, heavy-limbed woman dressed with showy elegance moved slowly down the street, and stopped for a moment before the door, while her eyes with languid curiosity measured the length and texture of the black scarf. She was past middle age, but not past the luxuriant maturity of her prime. She held her head insolently back, challenging and defying observation, proclaiming and glorying in a pampered self-consciousness. From under the black lace of her veil jewels glistened on the soft barbaric brown skin. Pleasure had sensualized features and form into dangerous alluring harmony, and panoplied her against thought. Her sleepy large eyes rested on the door while she paused, hesitating between the instinctive craving of morbid curiosity and half-dormant reminiscences of recent gratifications. She felt it beginning to move in her, the subtle current of an untamed savagery, the precursor of desires swelling on irresistibly to satiety, and she waited until her hot blood was flush for the cannibalistic gloating which no civilization could refine from her; then, without glancing at the paper fluttering from the door, she entered the room. She bent over the coffin with its emaciated, pitiful human contents, and her eyes dilated with the fascination.

"White," she whispered in surprise, with a contemptuous smile on her voluptuous lips. What exquisite flattery to her own rich, exuberant, sumptuous flesh! What triumph for the fierce, bold blood thrilling and leaping in her veins! She raised herself with complacent comeliness, and looked again before leaving.

"Mais! I never noticed it before. It is very strange. Mais grand Dieu!" she screamed, in reckless self-abandonment. "It is she! I know it is she!" She remembered the paper at the door, and tore it off and read it. "I tell you," she screamed again to the impassive watcher, Betsy—"I tell you it is she. Mamzelle Nénaine? Mamzelle Nénaine?" she interrogated, in an agonized whisper, throwing herself on her knees by the coffin. "Is it you? Oh! is it you?" She looked around fiercely and wildly. "But what does it all mean? What can it all mean? Can't you answer me?" she demanded in English of Betsy. "Are you a fool? How did this lady come here? Who did it? I want to know who dared do it?"

Betsy had risen respectfully. She was trying, with God's help and the old lady's cold, silent presence, to see now beyond the end. In conformity with her ideas of responsibility to the dead and to the living she had put off her rags and dirt, and—the last sacrifice of her unselfish heart—had put on a new black dress, white neckerchief, and "tignon"—her own graveclothes, bought with cold and starvation, and guarded religiously through years of vagabondage.

"Who are you? What are you doing here?" demanded the imperious visitor.

"Me, ma'am; I am the madam's servant."

"You lie! You know you lie! The madam never owned a servant like you."

"I never said the madam owned me; I said I was her servant; she hired me."

It looked as if the woman could find no adequate expression for the passion that raged in her. She shook her fist at the bare cold walls, she stamped on the rough, uncovered floor, she caught sight of the jewels on her arms, and hurled the massive bracelets away from her, she tore open her dress to ease her swelling throat, and her bosom panted violently under crushed garnitures of soft white lace. She fell down by the coffin again, and, bursting into tears, hid her face in the darned, worn, white "blouse volante" shroud, moaning, with long wailing cries, "Mamzelle Nénaine! Mamzelle Nénaine!"

"Where are her friends?"

"Please, ma'am, she 'ain't got no friends, excepting the apothecary gentleman at the corner; he was mighty good and kind; he come when I went for him, and he staid all night."

"But, my God! where are her relations?"

"I 'ain't never heerd of any relations besides the mamzelle—Mamzelle Claire."

"Mademoiselle Claire! Claire Blanche? Monsieur Edgar's baby?"

She was silent again, as if unable to comprehend it.

"And God allowed this! How long have they been living here—here in this cabin?"

"I don't know, ma'am; it's nigh on to three years sence I've been with them, and they've been here all that time."

The stranger looked up to heaven with a muttered blasphemous adjuration.

Betsy had been gazing with her keen eyes as if into a murky depth; a cloud seemed to have passed away from the sun, for the room was a little lighter. "I see you now! I didn't see you before, the room was so dark." Throwing away all effort at self-restraint: "Clear out from this room! How dare you show your face here! Clear out, I tell you, before—"

"Ha!" exclaimed the woman. It had a dangerous intonation, a menace of one fearless and unscrupulous.

"Go out of that door, I tell you! Don't you dare look at the face of my madam! Don't you dare touch her again!"

"Your madam! Your madam!"

She cursed her with a French imprecation. "Don't you dare call her your madam! She was my madam! I was her Aza! I belonged to her. I was given to her before I was a day old. I slept by the side of her bed; she carried me around in her little arms like a doll; she raised me like her child; she was my godmother; she set me free. I loved her, I worshipped her. Oh God! how I worshipped her! Mamzelle Nénaine, you know it is true! Mamzelle Nénaine, if you could speak to Aza once more! Just one word!—just one word!"

A torrent of tears choked her voice. Betsy recoiled in horror.

"Your madam! Your— My God in heaven! And she lay a-dying here, and the mamzelle a-starving, and you her servant, what belonged to her, in that house over there! You! a-scandalizing, a-rioting, a-frolicking, a-flaunting yourself in carriages, you and your gals right past this house! a-carrying on your devilment right out there, and your mistress a-slaving and a-starving! You! You nigger!" The old woman's crooked back straightened until she could look the quadroon straight in the eye.

"You, you are not that—"

"Yes, I am! Yes, I am that same dirty, stinking old rag-picker what did scrubbing for you. Not for me, mind you! but to buy medicine for the poor old madam there; a-lowering myself for her, a-dying and starving and freezing, while you was throwing away in the streets the money you stole out of the pockets of them white men!"

"Hush! Oh, for God's sake, don't talk so loud!"

"And last night, when the end come, when the end come, I tell you, with the piano music a-pounding up the street, and the hollering and the laughing, and the poor mamzelle—"

"Mademoiselle Claire Blanche?" repeated the quadroon, vaguely.

Betsy misunderstood her meaning.

"The last thing before the madam there died, when your music and your devilment was going on the loudest, I told her, I told her I would look after the mamzelle the same as if I were her boughten slave; and I'm going to do it; and I tell you, nigger, standing there before me in all your brazenness and finery and sinfulness, before you so much as speak to that child, before you so much as touch the tip end of her gown, you will have to trample the life out of me under your feet."

The inspired figure of the black woman came nearer and nearer, advancing between Aza and the coffin, pointing to the door. The quadroon tried to glare back her speechless rage; but the arraignment was too crushing, the action too full of meaning. She dropped her eyes, and for the first time in her life felt ashamed.

Ashamed before whom?—a common rag-picker from the streets? How dared she steal the language and sentiments of the dead one in the coffin, and talk to her like a mistress? Her, the insubordinate, irreprovable one! With a characteristic gesture she threw her head back again; but in Betsy's fine, determined face, in the holy passion of her voice, in her firm, commanding eye, she recognized, not the stolen or borrowed principles of a white lady, but the innate virtue of all good women. She measured herself not with her dead mistress, but with Betsy, and for the first time in her wild, daring, passionate life felt the humiliation of repentance. Following the direction of the finger, she left the room.

The day wore on to the hour before the funeral. Visits had ceased, and the silence of prayer was in the room about the old lady. Black-bordered printed notices, detailing the names and dates cancelled last night by death, had been tacked on the corners of the streets and on the door of the cottage, and friends of relations, whose names were a patent of nobility in the old city, were respectfully requested to assist at the funeral obsequies.

Betsy, sitting at the head of the coffin, fanning unweariedly, heard in the other room, where Claire was, the sound of footsteps, the murmuring of voices, and her name called with a moaning cry; or she fancied she heard it, for the silence and oppression of death had benumbed her faculties, and she felt uncertain of everything. At last, to end the dream-like confusion, she went to see, and left the old lady, for the first time that day, as much alone as if she were already in her grave.

The children, a hushed, awed band crouching on the steps outside around a white tissue-paper bundle, had been peeping, and waiting long for their opportunity. It came now, to paralyze them with faintness and fear. At first they could make no impression on the green door with their trembling fingers, all holding their breath, and then it slowly opened to them the darkened chamber within. They all stood up to follow, as they promised, but when the door swung to again they were still in their places outside. All but one—an appalled, scrawny, ragged, wild little creature with black unkempt head and yellow skin, with outstretched naked arms clasping her bundle tightly, with shivering bare legs and feet clinging to the floor, with white teeth clinched, and fear-distended eyes looking anywhere but at that undefined object in the centre of the room. It took an eternity to cross the space—an eternity measured by every terror of childish imagination; still, it ended too soon. A barrier stopped her. Involuntarily she looked down. The locked teeth prevented the scream, but in the tense grip of her fingers the paper gave way, and for the second time that day the orange blossoms fell, breaking with eloquent fragrance the damp stillness of death, enshrouding the rigid form in their loveliness, and crowning with a virgin anadem the earth-worn face looking heavenward through its last human experience—of love, not hate. The door slammed behind the fleeing messenger, with her fragments of paper, and the children sped away again to their distant corner of observation.

Betsy was not mistaken; the bedchamber was filled with people—ladies and gentlemen whispering and moving around, calling Claire by name, laying caressing hands on her head and shoulders. The girl only crouched lower by the side of the bed, and pressed her closed eyes tighter against the pillow taken from under bonne maman's head, and moaned, "Ah, Betsie! Betsie!"

Betsy looked around in amazement.

"If you please to walk into the next room—" she began; seeing that they persisted in trying to arouse Claire, she pushed through them, and placing herself in front of the girl, said, querulously, "Let the mamzelle alone; she's not harming any one; what do you want to bother her for?"

She could not understand them at first, being dull and dazed with fatigue and excitement.

But then the joy in her heart weakened her. She bent over and steadied her trembling hand on Claire's head. "Child, they is all your kin; done found you out. Honey, they wants to know you. Honey, they wants to love you."

But the head only went deeper into the pillow.

"You must excuse her. You must really excuse her; she don't know herself what she's doing. She 'ain't lifted her head from that pillow sence last night."

After a pause of decorous silence, the ladies and gentlemen, as they will do at funerals, recommenced their whispering. It was excusable this time, the first gathering of a family which had been separated by the whirlwind of revolution a decade ago. There was much to talk over and a long roll of the dead to call; but chiefly there was to recount one to another, each version character-tinged, their utter dismay at the intelligence brought them by Aza that day. How like a fiery cross she had carried the tale around from one household to the other, and had rallied them once again around the old standard of family pride and family love. With what passionate eloquence had she told them of the death of bonne maman—of bonne maman whom they had supposed living at ease in France! Dead! here! a wretched, forsaken exile in their own city. Dead! in the very reach of their hand, in the sound of their voice. Dead! without a friend! she, whom living, not so very long ago after all, they had surrounded, a crowd of eager, obsequious courtiers. They spoke of the old plantation days, with its magnificent, luxurious, thoughtless hospitality; of the ancient, aristocratic distinction of a name which had been a knightly pledge in two countries; and they looked at the little room with its inexorable revelations. In the exaltation of quickening emotion they forgot to whisper. Vying in their efforts to atone for the present, they brought from their memory such glorious tributes that the old lady in her pine coffin appeared clad in garments bright enough for a bodily ascension to heaven. Pride and reserve were sacrificed, painful secrets hinted at in this holy revival that all might be said, now that it was too late for anything to be done; until it became evident, as evident as the misery surrounding them, that in their own persons or the persons of dead parents they were bonded by unpaid dues of fealty and obligation to their deceased kinswoman, or, failing her, to the shrinking, cowering fair-haired girl kneeling by the bed.

A quadroon woman in the corner, dressed in the old servile costume, listened in bitter weeping. At the grating sound of wheels outside she arose and crossed the room. Calling them by name, Master this and Mistress that, she pointed to Betsy, and in hurried, broken tones related the simple facts of her devoted service to those who owned her only by virtue of their dependence, who could pay her only with their thanks. In a wild, penitent way she was adding more, but Betsy, listening to one and to the other, tears running unheeded down her cheeks on to her white handkerchief, raised her voice also, and, after several attempts, succeeded in saying, "And the apothecary gentleman at the corner, he was mighty good and kind; he come when I went for him, and he staid all night."

The sincere tones, in which ever and anon came a chord like bonne maman's, penetrated, in spite of the pillow, to Claire's ears, and won her to listen. The glorious, tender homage to her whom she bitterly supposed unknown, uncared-for, abandoned even by God, raised her head as if by enchantment. She arose in an excitement of love and gratitude, showing them all her sad emaciated beauty, her out-worn, out-grown, wretched clothing, and when they all rushed forward impulsively to embrace her, she clung to them as indeed to the successors of bonne maman.

A pauper's funeral had been ordered, but the friends invited by Aza's notices formed a cortége that filled the little street, and the service in the mortuary chapel where Aza directed the hearse to stop was such as only the wealthiest could command. At the end of the procession walked a retinue of old slaves, the last, highest local affirmation of family worth; among them, one of them, in costume, race, condition, was Aza, bearing the conventional black and white bead memorial "Priez pour moi."

It was late in the night, when the deserted streets promised security from recognition, that she hastened through them and entered the little back gateway of the triangular fence in the slavish dress, worn for the last time.

Editor's Easy Chair.

SOME years ago there was no more attractive announcement for the theatre-goer than that of a series of the old comedies. The phrase did not mean "the artificial comedy of the last century," as Charles Lamb called the plays of Congreve and Wycherley, but the equally artificial comedy of a later day, which included Goldsmith's *She Stoops to Conquer*, and Sheridan's *School for Scandal* and *The Rivals*, and Morton's *Speed the Plough*. They were equally artificial, because the world which they depicted was a conventional world. But the tenacious traditions of the stage had given it a charming quaintness for modern taste, and largely moulded the impression of that older society.

Indeed, the general view of that society is not historical. It is derived mainly from the novels and comedies of the time, and especially from the plays. The costumes and the speech and the manners which make up the spectacle leave a vivid and unfading picture upon the mind. The old comedy is a passage of history, like Macaulay's description of the court of Charles II. on the eve of the king's death, put into actual form and color and action. Mr. Morison, indeed, in his *Life of Macaulay*, in the series of "English Men of Letters," says that the secret of Macaulay's fascination is that he writes with the rich and careful detail of the novelist rather than of the historian, so that his work is essentially pictorial. Whatever the real loveliness of Hortensia Mancini may have been, or the charms of Barbara Palmer and the Duchess of Portsmouth, it is by the glowing description of Macaulay that they will be always known, as Charles I. is inseparable from the portrait of Vandyck. So the English country squire, whatever his actual character, is fixed in tradition and universal acceptance as Addison sketched him in Sir Roger de Coverley, and Goldsmith in Hardcastle. Yet Hardcastle was but a lay figure until some admirable actor gave him the form which the stage has faithfully preserved, and which is as perfect in John Gilbert as it could have been in any predecessor.

No actor of our time recalls more certainly than Gilbert the warmth of affectionate appreciation with which Lamb expatiates upon some actors of the close of the last century whom he had seen. The swift evanescence of an actor's fame, which seems often very pathetic, as it were an unkindness of Nature that a talent whose sudden extinction eclipses the gayety of nations should leave no intelligible trace, and often but a fading name, has its compensation in the tribute of a kindred art. As the author gives the actor the opportunity to disclose his genius, so he perpetuates the story of his triumphs, and reveals his subtle and exquisite methods. Beasley and Palmer and Dodd and Dicky Suett are mere shadows of names, signifying nothing to the general reader. But they live upon the page of Elia, like "Madam Carwell," the fair Querouaille, upon the page of Macaulay. They are secure of immortality in the circle of the most cultivated and intelligent minds of successive generations. The general public does not know Munden, but every reader of Elia knows him, as the reader of to-day's newspaper and the frequenter of Wallack's Theatre knows John Gilbert.

This admirable actor has recently played Hardcastle. It is a pity that Goldsmith could not have seen him. It is doubtful whether Goldsmith had so fine and definite a conception of his own creation. The essential gentleman in Gilbert's Hardcastle contrasts most effectively with the pinchbeck gentleman of Wallack's Charles Marlow. The latter, also, is admirably done. It is a remarkable work for a man who in point of age has the advantage of Marlow. It is the rattling rake, the *vaurien* of the old comedy, who, although he is drawn as morbidly shy in the presence of a woman, has no other opinion of women than Walpole had of patriots. In contrast with this genteel swagger, what refinement and restraint and dignified courtesy Gilbert gives to Hardcastle! It is all the finer from a certain country simplicity, which is rather negative as the absence of the town air than positive as rusticity. Should the King himself enter, Hardcastle would be equal to the moment in self-respecting civility. The manner in which he submits to the insolent interruption of his stock stories by Marlow and his comrade is as inimitable as the simple pleasure with which he accepts the tribute to them of Diggory and the servants.

The whole representation of the character is delightful, and makes the spectator regret that Sir Roger de Coverley could not be delineated by the same sympathetic genius. In all the scenes in which Addison places Sir Roger, and even when the pleasant laugh turns against him, his hold upon the affection of the reader is secure. Gilbert throws the same spell upon the spectator of his Hardcastle, and much more surely than Goldsmith. Indeed, the necessity of acting to the proper effect of a play was never more conspicuously evident than in the case of *She Stoops to Conquer*. Only when well played does the humor come out, as when invisible writing is held to the fire. Even the extravagances, like the scene between Charles Marlow and Miss Hardcastle, were so well done that the scene was not extravaganza, but genuinely comical. Such overwhelming shyness in such a man is impossible. But there was a suggestion of possibility in the acting of Wallack which was incomparable. This was facilitated, as in all plays, by the fact that the world of the

theatre or of the drama is a world of itself, a little beyond the precise latitude and longitude of the familiar globe, and all that can be asked fairly is that the degree of resemblance to actual life shall be harmonious. In a world where the boorishness of Tony Lumpkin is natural, the shyness of Marlow is not caricatured.

The completeness, the ease, the symmetry, of the late performance of this play showed what a very high standard of excellence the theatre has reached in this city. No French vaudeville could be better played in Paris than *She Stoops to Conquer* was played in New York. There is no reason to suppose that Hardcastle had ever a better representative than Gilbert, and those who come after us will be fortunate if they see the character so delicately and consistently treated. The way in which it is discriminated from the same actor's Sir Peter Teazle or Sir Anthony Absolute reveals his consummate art. It is not strange that he looks askance upon six hundred consecutive nights of *Adonis*, or upon the gay nonsense of the Sullivan opera. To the sincere and earnest painter, cherishing a high view of his art, and conscious of his power, the chromo and the caricature usurping the place of legitimate picture are not pleasant sights. And certainly if such a performance as that at Wallack's of *She Stoops to Conquer* does not attract the town, it is not because of the performance, but because the "old comedies" have lost their hold for a time upon public favor, since they could not be more admirably presented.

The public, however, is not to be reasoned with upon such a point. It cannot be compelled to prefer one entertainment to another. But if the young person or the old person proposing to seek entertainment wishes not only to laugh, but to enjoy a capital and living picture of quaint manners, and of a life not beyond our knowledge and sympathy, let him go to Wallack's when Gilbert and his associates play *She Stoops to Conquer*, or some other of the old comedies.

HAWTHORNE was as "noticeable" a man as Coleridge seemed to Wordsworth. His shyness affected his movement and bearing, but without making him awkward, and his eyes seemed to be always about to glance off from those of his interlocutor. He walked rapidly, but without an air of effort, and his vigorous frame, with its swinging gait, gave the impression of massiveness, although he was not a very large man; nor would he have been called sturdy in appearance, but strong. If the Easy Chair recollects accurately, his dress was always dark. His head and face were most impressive, and his deep eye recalled Ellery Channing's line,

"The well of thy dark cold eye."

It was a singularly handsome face—the general outline full and rounded, the features symmetrical and strong, the brow broad and massive, and the dome of the brain more suggestive of Webster's than any contemporary head. Indeed, the aspect of the whole head was Websterian, but of a Webster who was poet rather than statesman. No face could be more radiant with the subtle and glancing lights that indicate genius. His smile was very sweet, and his laugh was always ready, but not extravagant. With all his shyness, his manner was self-possessed, but in no sense familiar, and it had a sense of remoteness, as if he were himself not easily accessible. In a group of persons he was generally silent, and in a *tête-à-tête* he talked quietly, without effusiveness or ardor of any kind. There was never a man who seemed to live more habitually in himself, as if, as his son Julian recently remarks, he found no better society.

The degree in which his inner world was his real sphere is shown in the best way in such a paper as the preface to *The Scarlet Letter* describing his comrades at the Customhouse in Salem, or in the *Monsieur De l'Aubepine*. He treated the figures of fact as others treat those of the fancy, and he was no more conscious of turning too strong a light upon what others might not have revealed than of describing too definitely little Pearl or the Reverend Arthur Dimmesdale. This is not to say that he was in any sense "absent-minded" or oblivious of the actual world. On the contrary, no literary man has ever shown a more comprehensive or penetrating eye for every actual object and detail.

Hawthorne's *Note-Books* reveal how thorough a literary artist he was. Everything that met his eye instinctively suggested to him its own possible artistic value and use. "Into paint will I grind thee, my bride." In strolling about the fields and in the woods, he caught from the forms and hues of flowers and trees and of all natural objects endless hints for the plastic arts as well as for his own guild. His art was as consummate as it was unconscious. It is hard to conceive a more exquisite short tale than *Rappacini's Daughter*. It is as perfect as Keats's "Ode upon a Grecian Urn," or as the urn which inspired the poet. But, like the Parthenon, the parts which are unseen are as finely finished as the most apparent parts. All the suggestions and hints and spiritual analogies of the tale are as evident as its external movement. Indeed, this is the character of every one of the wonderful minor tales as of the larger works. They are not like so many pretty stories, cut flowers, or moths or butterflies which flash and glance and vanish. They are blossoms of a weird beauty and strange perfume, with long stems and far-burrowing roots that hold by the centre, and thus draw their nourishment from unknown sources.

The Easy Chair has strayed away from the Hawthorne portraits, of which many have been published. That which is the frontispiece of this number of the Magazine Mr.

Lowell thinks to be the best that he knows. The Bennoch picture is also admirable. It represents him seated at a table with his left wrist and hand resting upon a book, and his right hand upon the side of the knee. The face is turned toward the spectator, and it is a remarkable likeness. If only there were such portraits of Shakespeare and the elders as we now have of our own famous men, the world would be richer.

To one who remembers Hawthorne in the old manse, when he was publishing an occasional story in the *Democratic Review*, edited by John L. O'Sullivan, while he was still a very obscure author; one who has seen Hawthorne and Ellery Channing departing for one of those days upon the placid river which are described in the introduction to the *Mosses from an Old Manse;* who recalls the village tragedy which gave Hawthorne the suggestion for one of his most powerful chapters, the end of *The Blithedale Romance ;* and who can still see in vivid memory the lovely face of his first child lying in her baby-wagon in the old avenue, and looking up serenely at the trees that arched over her—it is very pleasant to look upon the picture of a face once so familiarly known—the face of a man of genius in his prime—and to think that the quiet, modest author, "the artist of the beautiful," who wrought patiently and unrecognized at his marvellous work, because he did not falter or despond, nor aim lower, nor try for the easy vogue of a day, but was content to serve beauty and truth for the sake of beauty and truth, is now beheld of all men with gratitude and reverence as one of the benefactors of the world.

The circumstances attending the Mayall photograph of Hawthorne, which is the frontispiece of this number of the Magazine, are detailed in the following statement from Mr. George H. Holden, a fellow-townsman of Hawthorne, to whom we are indebted for the original from which our engraving was made:

In the work *Nathaniel Hawthorne and his Wife*, Vol. II., p. 256–8, you will find an account, by Henry A. Bright, of a sitting given by Hawthorne, May 19, 1860, at Mayall's studio, 224 Regent Street, London. Hawthorne never gave but this one sitting at Mayall's, and Mayall developed only one negative. The photo which I have sent you is a print from this negative. Some inaccuracies in Bright's story have been pointed out by the younger Mayall, but they are not essential, and the narrative may be regarded as practically correct. He says further: "I have a distinct recollection of Mr. Hawthorne—just as he sat for the photo. I remember remarking that he looked very like a Frenchman. My view of him was a momentary glance from the door of the dark room, where at that time I had charge of the chemical processes."

In another communication Mayall speaks of this photograph as "remarkably good," and adds: "Such a negative, *at that date,* could not be ordinarily produced with a less exposure than thirty or forty seconds in the camera, with the subdued light usually employed in my father's studio. Hawthorne must have remained quite still during those thirty or forty seconds, for the print shows plainly the iris of his eyes, and individual hairs in his eyebrows and mustache."

Mr. Mayall senior retired from the business in 1865, and was succeeded by the son. Many hundred negatives were removed at that time to his country residence. The son says: "A list of all the negatives removed was left in my hands, and hence I was able to trace this negative to my father's private house. When I applied to my father, he found his list, after considerable delay, and supposed, of course, that the negative was in its place, inasmuch as there was no record of its having been removed. When, however, I pressed him to let me have the negative, the box was searched, but it was not there." In explanation of this provoking discovery he goes on to say: "It would appear that somehow this negative had been taken out, and possibly the printer, knowing no more of N. Hawthorne than of the man in the moon, treated it carelessly and broke it. To prevent his being blamed, he would simply wash off the collodion, and hold his tongue about the transaction."

Let me here remark that Mr. Bright's statement to Julian Hawthorne seems to be somewhat misleading. He says: "After your father's death the photograph was engraved, and I sent other copies to your mother, Mr. Longfellow, and one or two more. The original (there was only one taken at the time) hangs in my own room." Is it not a natural and unforced interpretation of this evidently careless and hasty epistolary statement that there was but one photograph made, and that the other copies were engravings? However this may be, it is true that no photograph of Hawthorne by Mayall, and no engraving of that photograph, was received by Longfellow at the Craigie house, or by Mrs. Hawthorne at the Wayside. And it is true, furthermore, that Mayall's books show the distinct entry of a print from this same negative sent to "Mr. Motley, 31 Hertford Street, Mayfair." And this photo, I have learned, is now in the possession of Motley's daughter, Mrs. Mary Sheridan, at her house in Dorsetshire; it is, however, much faded. A third copy was made for Mayall's own collection.

When all hope of finding the negative was abandoned, diligent search was made for the senior Mayall's own copy, and it was finally discovered in an old portfolio which probably "had not been touched for more than twenty years." And it is this authentic copy, quite fresh and unfaded by reason of its prolonged seclusion, which I have had the pleasure of placing in your hands. Mayall further says: "The photo I have sent you is of extreme rarity. I have not an impression in my own collection. And before it was found I would

have wagered five pounds to a shilling that we should not have found one." It would seem, in fact, that aside from the copy now in your hands, and the two which were made for Motley and for Bright, no other impressions have been printed from the lost Mayall negative.

In the biography of Hawthorne above referred to there seems to be a remarkable error, which may as well be corrected here. It gives (Vol. II., p. 150) an exquisite etching, purporting to be made "from a photograph by Mayall." This is a mistake. The etching (which Bennoch unhesitatingly pronounces "the best book portrait of Hawthorne he has yet seen") is wholly unlike our Mayall photo. And by those who are familiar with the various portraits of Hawthorne it will be recognized immediately as a copy of the so-called "Lothrop Motley" photograph of Hawthorne.

A NOTED and successful painter recently said that he did not believe that current criticism of art and literature benefited either. It offers, indeed, an opportunity, he said, which is duly improved, of saying clever things and of showing the accomplishment and skill of writers; and it also affords opportunity, which is no less improved, of saying sharp and sarcastic things, and of ridiculing the efforts of sincere and well-meaning workers. But what criticism of pictures, for instance, since Ruskin's *Landscape Painters* has been of real service to artists? And that was serviceable, not because of its personal criticisms, but because of its large sympathy with art itself, and of the great knowledge and insight of the writer, who alluded to certain works only to illustrate great principles.

When he was asked why the critic might not to-day, also, speak of certain pictures as illustrations of great principles, and try the actual work by the highest canons, the painter replied that perhaps he might, but that he didn't; and that the general drift of criticism was to point out defects, according to some arbitrary conceit or preconceived notion of the critic, and not to attempt to ascertain what the artist intended to do, and how far he had succeeded, and how he might be aided to correct the apparent faults. Criticism, contended the painter, should be undertaken as seriously as the work criticised. But who is the critic? Disraeli says, stingingly, "The man who has failed," and who tries to avenge himself upon those who succeed. But in the daily papers how many of the men who go to the Academy and then write about the pictures have any other fitness for the task than a wish to fill a certain space and earn a certain sum? Do you think, he asked, that we are aided by that kind of performance? And that is the type of current criticism.

The Easy Chair, which has sometimes ventured to take the tone of the critic, demurred to this view. It remembered its own remarks of various kinds, which, if not *ad rem*, were at least well meant and free from all vengeful or sanguinary purpose; and what was true of one critic might very well be true of others. So it made bold to say that whatever may have been the fact in the day of limited resources, when the proprietor of a newspaper was compelled to serve also as compositor and editor and reporter and critic and pressman and office-boy, it was somewhat different now. There was a time, indeed, when the tradition of the editorial room was that of Maginn and the Mohawks of Fraser, who did execution upon every culprit they could catch, and to whom every author or artist was a criminal of the darkest dye. These terrible Jeffreyses held a perpetual bloody assize, and hanging, drawing, and quartering proceeded without pause upon all sides. Slash and dash was the cry, and the critic seemed to think himself a kind of bravo, who was to whip out his rapier and transfix every passenger who had the insolence to appear in the street.

This was at least the tradition. But it was never very well founded. Fellows like Wainwright may have done a brisk business in wanton stabbing. But yet when Wainwright wrote, Charles Lamb was writing, and Coleridge and Southey were writing; and they were not malefic critics. Father Prout was of the Maginn set, but his heart was kindly, and he had some conscience. To be "brilliant," to make a sensation, not to be dull and commonplace, this, indeed, was the aim of many a young roisterer of the pen; but this kind did not monopolize the field. It is, however, to be remembered that three of the chief modern English poets, Byron, Keats, and Tennyson, were deeply stung by the critics, and Byron and Tennyson retorted vigorously.

It is true, also, that while much critical writing to-day is intelligent and discriminating, few artists or authors probably would own that they derived much benefit from the comments upon their works. Many authors, indeed, never read the criticisms or notices of their books, and artists of all kinds are apt to recognize a personal feeling in the strictures. Yet if the person who is most interested is not benefited by the critic, the general public is hardly able to criticise him and measure the justice of his view. Indeed, the mischief done by the brilliant Mohawks, old or new, comes from the disposition to accept plausible dogmatism upon a subject little known as the conclusive opinion of a competent judge. Few readers of a newspaper know much of the "canons of art," and if a clever fencer with the pen deftly pricks a victim, or covers his work with a dazzling flash of ridicule, it is not easy for the reader to see the work except in that depreciating light.

Three or four men who write notices of the Academy exhibition, for instance, in as many leading journals, might unite in making fun of a particular picture, and it would go very hard with it in the mind of the spectator who had read the article and would not care to place his taste or knowledge against that of the critic. One of the old *Tribune* jokes was that the genuine rural reader of the paper believed that Horace Greeley wrote everything in it. And his authority was equally good with that reader, whether upon Whiggism, Henry Clay, Protection, the latest poem, or a new picture. There are many excellent persons still in the bondage of print who accept Horace Greeley as equally unquestionable an authority upon a picture or upon the duty on wool.

On the other hand, the artists would hardly prefer the absolute silence of the press to the chance of criticism; for at least the talk of the critic both shows and produces interest in the exhibition. Mr. Barnum, if asked the secret of success, would probably reply, advertising. The ingenious devices merely to secure a notice in a newspaper, almost regardless of its character, show how widely spread is the conviction that Mr. Barnum would probably express. Better, perhaps the artists would say—better misunderstanding, ignorance, praise of the bad work, and ridicule of the best work, than nothing. Silence would exclude the world. Criticism, however awry, would bring the world, and those who know could judge for themselves. Even the painter who raised the question, and who has probably suffered from the darts and quips of criticism, and who honestly doubts its usefulness in directly moulding artists happily and promoting a nobler tone in art, would admit that, indirectly by sustaining the general interest, it gives opportunity for every kind of advance.

The true critic, indeed, is rare as a bird-of-paradise. But when he appears he combines the faculty of perfect sympathy with the aim of the artist, with the power to express and interpret it to the spectator, and with the knowledge which apprehends the points at which the expression of the purpose fails, and the reasons for the failure, and those at which it is adequately conveyed. He is the interpreter of the house Beautiful, which every true work of art essentially is. Criticism is not censure, but perception and appreciation. In the case of a great artist, as when Ruskin treats of Turner, it is eulogy, but it is eulogy of the worth of the whole which comports with certain unequal details. While there are authors and artists, there will certainly be critics, and critics of every degree. We must therefore criticise the critics, not denounce them as a class, sure that in the multitude of smatterers and pretenders of every kind there will come also the eye that sees, the soul that apprehends, and the hand that records truly. This is the critic. His voice will be friendly, unflattering, but full of sympathy, and the words that it speaks will be heard in the heart of the earnest artist, "Friend, come up higher."

In his pungent and bitter preface to the "Dissertation on Parties," Bolingbroke says to Sir Robert Walpole, "If I have pressed you a little warmly, yet I have done it with the decency that every gentleman owes to another, at least to himself."

Even in that day of hot politics in England, when the nation was establishing the new Hanoverian order against the open and secret machinations of the Jacobites, and when, consequently, Whig party spirit was another name for patriotism, there was yet a certain decorum of debate. The famous attack of Sir William Wyndham upon Sir Robert Walpole in Parliament was an invective doubtless prepared by Bolingbroke, but it was delivered under the form of a supposition. "I may suppose a case, which, though it has not yet happened, may possibly happen," and the Tory leader proceeded to describe Sir Robert and his policy in the most stinging terms, and as he went on to involve the King, Wyndham again declared, "I am still not prophesying, I am only *supposing*, and the case I am going to suppose I hope never will happen." Sir Robert retorted terribly. He not only knew the voice, but he recognized the hand, and he "supposed" an "anti-minister," and laid Bolingbroke bare.

But the decency which Bolingbroke held that every gentleman owes to himself in public debate is still more comprehensive. It is a self-respect which is apt to be forgotten in a republic or in any popular government. If a courtier should profess the total surrender of his own convictions to an expression of his royal master's sovereign will, the abject tone and the unmanly servility would move the contempt of every self-respecting man who heard him. It would be a tone becoming to Siam, where courtiers and ministers lie upon their bellies before the King, to signify that in his presence they are but worms and refuse. Yet what is the indecency, to reverse Bolingbroke's phrase, of such prostration? It is that it renounces the duty which every man owes to himself. It is a surrender of that proper self-respect which belongs to him as a man. God has given every man an inner light for his own guidance. To be sure of his own respect, he must walk by his own light.

The King of Siam doubtless has power to enforce his will, and if a Siamese courtier respects his own view more than his Majesty's, the King may imprison him or behead him. That force and power, however, do not make his Majesty's view sound or wise or beneficent, and it is plain that in every country the possibility of progress lies in that decency which every man owes to himself, that self-respect which is willing to assert and maintain itself as against the will of the sovereign. It follows, therefore, that abject flattery of the sovereign is fatal to progress, because it tends to weaken manly independence, which is the only really and essentially progressive power.

The sovereign may be one or many, but he is no wiser merely because he is sovereign. In Siam the sovereign is a man; in the United States he is a majority. But it is quite as mean and servile and unmanly to crawl before a majority as before a king. When a Senator of the United States speaks of the people as the supreme sovereign to whose will he bows in humble submission, he takes the tone of the Siamese minister lying upon his belly. If the will of the people has been properly enacted into law, he will, of course, submit to it. But his tone assumes that the law is right because it is the will of the sovereign. Now, if it is not right in his judgment, every man of "decent" self-respect will do what he can to change the law.

Politicians talk of a majority as if its decisions were necessarily just and right because they are those of a majority, and the skeptic is serenely rebuked by the remark that the wisdom of ages has agreed that many are wiser than one, and that the voice of the people is the voice of God. Yes, in a proper sense it is true. But was the voice of the people the voice of God when Galileo said that the earth moves around the sun, or when Jenner began to vaccinate, or when Luther nailed his theses upon the church door, or when Adams demanded independence, or Garrison emancipation, or when the mob of Jerusalem cried, "Crucify him! crucify him!"? The sovereign people before whose ordained will a Senator professes to bow in humble submission may be as tyrannical and unjust as a single despot. Government by a majority is found by experience to be the most reasonable and convenient device for securing peace and order. But it is not because of any virtue inherent in a multitude, nor because in any particular multitude one man may not be wiser, juster, and better than all the rest. It is a convenient device for two reasons—because a majority in the long-run is amenable to intelligent persuasion, and because a majority can enforce its will against opposition.

But no divinity doth hedge a majority. The pressure of which Bolingbroke spoke in the essay was his exposition of the corruption introduced by Sir Robert Walpole into Parliament. Walpole ruled by a majority. But the will of his majority—and it is to a majority, not to its virtue or wisdom, that honorable gentlemen profess to bow in humble submission—was determined by money. "He lived in a time when a gentleman thought no more of selling his vote than he now does of selling his game or his fruit," says his latest friendly biographer. That is the way that majorities are often made. Is it, then, their roar, Mr. Senator, or the still, small voice of the unbought individual conscience, which is the voice of God?

It is not respect for the majority, but for the individual, which seems to need emphasizing in the realm of the sovereign people. You shall hear many an orator upon the stump at every election protesting that he is anxious only to know what the majority wishes, in order that he may follow and obey. He has no opinion until the caucus has spoken. What is he that he should array himself against the majority? He was inclined to another view, but the majority has spoken, and he hopes he knows his duty better than to disobey. This is the tone of Siam, not of America; of slavery, not of freedom. The majority, wherever its decision is legitimate, decides only what shall be done, not what ought to be done. It is a power to control, not to reverence. The spring of true democracy is self-respect, for from that alone comes true respect for others. Bolingbroke disdained the majority; Walpole good-naturedly despised it. But the alternative is not reverence for it, nor unquestioning obedience to it. Reform always

begins in the minority. But if reform be wise and necessary, it is demonstrated that the majority is wrong.

Which is the more American as well as the more manly attitude, that of waiting to hear what the majority decides, or that of striving to make the majority decide rightly?

But surely, Mr. Easy Chair, after all our efforts, when the majority pronounces, we must acquiesce?

Certainly, but always upon one condition, that it does not require you to blow out that light which God has kindled in you to walk by. That is the "decency" which every gentleman owes to himself.

Editor's Study.

I.

MR. SIDNEY LUSKA'S *Mrs. Peixada* is a novel so good in some things that it is a pleasure to recognize its fresh ground, its unworn *personnel*, its generous passion, its vivid incident, and the strong young *go* of the whole affair; for Mr. Luska—who is not Mr. Luska, we believe, but some one much nearer us poor Gentiles in name if not in sympathy—is clearly a young man, and has the chance of better and better work before him. He has the reasonable hope of it too; and we take all the more heart for him because in this second venture of his he has left the region of music and romance, where he dwelt in his first story, and has stepped quite out into the light of our common day, which, as we have several times assured the guests of this Study, is preferable to any manner of moonshine or alabaster lamps, or even the latest improvement in electrics. We are glad, however, that Mr. Luska has kept to his chosen people, and that he gives us Jews again in his novel. The heroine is a Jewess, and nearly all the characters in the book are New York Jews, finely distinguished one from another, and very neatly accented. In fact, Mr. Luska's mastery is in the treatment of his various Israelites, in their presentation individually, and in their collective localization here in New York. They are neither flattered nor caricatured; they are simply portrayed with truth by a hand that is already firm, and that gives promise of greater and greater skill. After them comes the plot, intricate and thrilling enough to enrapture the inexperienced, and not such as to give the old novel reader a moment's anxiety for the outcome. By-and-by Mr. Luska will probably evolve his plot from his personages, rather than involve them in it; and then he will touch hearts instead of merely shaking nerves. His present situations could all have grown out of the same number of Gentiles quite as well; but the plot is valuable because it exacts from him the study of many local

conditions and characters, and he makes this study very faithfully and graphically. His art lapses most in the narrative dramatized in the reported evidence of the murder trial, and in the autobiography of Mrs. Peixada; in these the literary man keeps coming to the front; and at other times he has a consciousness that is not altogether pleasant. His best work is in the subordinate figures; these are the *characters;* the principal people are only types of this or that passion: they do not remain in the mind like the others; they have the conventional singleness of motive noticeable in the people of a modern stage play.

II.

In fact, *Mrs. Peixada* would make into a very good play, and if as a drama it could keep the novel's variety of uncaricatured personages, and its glow of genuine, decent passion, untouched by sentimentalism, it would be a drama which would send the poor, patient metropolitan play-goer home with a real emotion under his waistcoat. He would feel that he had seen a bit of life, if the stage could show him those Beekman Place interiors, with the eating and smoking that goes on in them, and those Beekman Place figures of naturalized German Jews. If he could have also the scenes in the lonely suburban house when the tortured woman kills her hideous husband and his accomplice in self-defence, and then the scenes in court when she pleads guilty, he would have tragic "action" enough, and what such action does not always give—pathos and genuine tragedy.

Perhaps Mr. Luska's next essay may be dramatic in form as well as in spirit. Then we should have at least one phase of that American play which we are all beginning to long for, or to think we long for. In fact, with a great and unquestionable love of the theatre, we doubt if there is much love of the drama among us, and we are sure there is less knowledge. So the managers have continued to give us the theatre and not the drama; very good acting, but little or nothing worth acting. Probably if Mr. Luska wrote a very good play, fresh, native, true, he could not get it played, for there has been so little that is fresh, native, and true on the stage for so long that the managers might not know what to make of the piece; and it is to the manager, not the public, that the playwright appeals. In every other art the artist's censor is the world. He makes a statue or paints a picture, and somewhere, somehow, it meets the eye of general criticism; he writes a book, and if no publisher will have it, there are means of cheap publication by which it can still reach the light without ruining the author. But no one, unless he is rich enough to write history, can hire a theatre and produce his play. Its fate lies in the judgment, the taste, the theory, of the manager. He is eager, on his part, only too eager, to please the public, and not knowing what new thing will offend, he keeps offering it the old thing over and over in some form or other. The literary motives, outgrown and cast off in every other department of literary art, have formed so long the prosperity of the theatre, the art of the stage, that it is no wonder the manager cannot believe his public would like anything better. He knows perfectly well that it is abject trash he gives; for whatever the manager is he is very commonly not a fool. He is often a man of taste and of sufficient reading; he knows quite well what is good literature. He merely believes that it is not adapted to the stage; it might have been adapted to the stage once, he admits, but now, not. He will tell you that the public wishes merely to be amused, and does not care for the literary quality of a play. "What pleases the public, it thinks is good, and it thinks all the rest is 'rot.'" The manager is right; but the author who wishes to give his piece literary quality, to be faithful to life and to art, as he would be in writing a novel, is right too in asking the manager to let the public decide whether it likes this quality or not.

But here is another difficulty. The manager cannot afford to experiment with literary quality; for it costs so much to "stage" a play in these days of a material theatre but no drama, that he can only risk giving the old rubbish in some novel disguise. If a play could be put upon the stage cheaply, he might let a really new play make its appeal to the public; he might try half a dozen new plays during the season. But with the present expensiveness of setting, a failure is ruinous, and nothing really new can be risked. So much money has to be put into the frame of the picture that only the well-known chromo-effects in sentiment, character, and situation can be afforded in the picture. It is as if all new books were published in *éditions de luxe*, and consequently all new books were compilations and rehashes of old books. That is what he believes plays must be, compilations and rehashes of old plays, in order to stand any chance of success with the public.

III.

The outlook is not hopeless, however. We will not speak of Mr. Gilbert's exquisite ironies; he is an Englishman, and we are talking now about the American drama, or non-drama; for, in spite of theatres lavishly complete in staging, and with all the sanitary arrangements exemplary—the air changed every fifteen minutes, and artificially refrigerated in the summer—we have still no drama. Yet we have the prospect of something of the kind, and naturally we have it in accordance with the existing conditions. We have an abundance of most amusing sketches and extravaganzas, embodying more or less of our grotesque life; and amongst these, saving the respect of all the gentilities, are Mr. Hoyt's *Rag Baby*, and other absurdities. But, most hopeful of all the promises, we have the plays of Mr. Edward Harrigan. Our one original contribution and addition to histrionic art was negro minstrelsy, which, primitive, simple, elemental, was out of our own soil, and had the characteristics that distinguish autochthonic conceptions. But that is a thing almost of the past, and we have now to do with a novel contribution to the drama, and not to the art of the drama. It is peculiarly interesting, because it is morally, though not materially, the contribution most possible under our peculiar circumstances, for it is the work of a man in whom the instincts of the author combat the theatre's traditions, and the actor's experience censures the author's literary vanity. Mr. Harrigan writes, stages, and plays his pieces; he is his own playwright, manager, and comedian. He has his own theatre, and can risk his own plays in it, simply and cheaply, in contempt of the carpenter and upholsterer. Not that he does treat these useful personages with contempt, but he subordinates them. In his theatre the highly decorated husk and gilded shell are not everything, nor the kernel attenuated to the last degree of innutritiousness. But the setting is at the same time singularly perfect and entirely sufficient. Mr. Harrigan accurately realizes in his scenes what he realizes in his persons; that is, the actual life of this city. He cannot give it all; he can only give phases of it; and he has preferred to give its Irish-American phases in their rich and amusing variety, and some of its African and Teutonic phases. It is what we call low life, though whether it is essentially lower than fashionable life is another question. But what it is, it is; and it remains for others, if they can, to present other sides of our manifold life with equal perfection; Mr. Harrigan leaves a vast part of the vast field open. In his own province we think he cannot be surpassed. The art that sets before us all sorts and conditions of New York Irishmen, from the laborers in the street to the most powerful of the ward politicians and the genteelest of the ladies of that interesting race, is the art of Goldoni—the joyous yet conscientious art of the true dramatist in all times who loves the life he observes. The old Venetian filled his scene with the gondoliers, the serving-folk, the fish-women, the trades-people, the quacks, the idlers, the gamesters, of his city; and Mr. Harrigan shows us the street-cleaners and contractors, the grocery-men, the shysters, the politicians, the washer-women, the servant-girls, the truckmen, the policemen, the risen Irishman and Irish woman, of contemporary New York. Goldoni carried through scores of comedies the same characters, the masks of the older drama which he drove from the stage, and Mr. Harrigan instinctively repeats the same personages in his Mulligan series. Within his range the New-Yorker is not less admirable than the Venetian. In fact, nothing could be better than the neatness, the fineness, with which the shades of character are given in Mr. Mulligan's Irish people; and this literary conscientiousness is supplemented by acting which is worthy of it. Mr. Harrigan is himself a player of the utmost naturalness, delicate, restrained, infallibly sympathetic; and we have seen no one on his stage who did not seem to have been trained to his part through entire sympathy and intelligence. In certain moments of *Dan's Tribulations* the illusion is so perfect that you lose the sense of being in the theatre; you are out of that world of conventions and traditions, and in the presence of the facts.

All the Irish aspects of life are treated affectionately by this artist, as we might expect from one of his name; but the colored aspects do not fare so well under his touch. Not all the Irish are good Irish, but all the colored people are bad colored people. They are of the gloomy, razor-bearing variety; full of short-sighted lies and prompt dishonesties, amusing always, but truculent and tricky; and the sunny sweetness which we all know in negro character is not there. We do not wholly object to the one-sided picture; it has its historical value; and so has the contemptuous prejudice of both Irish and negroes for the Italians, which comes out in the *Leather Patch;* that marks an epoch and characterizes a condition.

The *Leather Patch* is not nearly so good as the Mulligan series, though it has very good things in it. The author seems to have labored for incident and effect in a plot, whereas all that the heart asked of him was to keep his delicious Irish folks on the scene and keep them talking. As it is, some passages of the piece are extremely good; and it is as a whole in the good direction. The material is rude, very rude; we repeat that; it is the office or it is the will of this artist to work in that material; but it is the artist and not the material which makes the work of art. The error of the dramatist has been that he has at times not known how to hold his hand; he has given us the whole truth where part of it would have been enough; he might have spared us some shocking suggestions of the undertaking

business. At other times he quite forgets his realism: the whole episode of the colored wake, with its plantation spirituals, is real and excellent; but when the old-clothes men and women of Chatham Street join in a chorus, one perceives that the theatre has come to the top, and the poet has lapsed.

In spite of such lapses, however, we recognize in Mr. Harrigan's work the spring of a true American comedy, the beginning of things which may be great things. We have more than intimated its limitations; let us say that whatever its offences, it is never, so far as we have seen it, indecent. The comedies of Edward Harrigan are, in fact, much decenter than the comedies of William Shakespeare.

They are like Shakespeare's plays, like Molière's plays, in being the work of a dramatist who is at the same time a manager and an actor. Possibly this is the only way we can have a drama of our own; it is not a bad way; and it is at least a very natural way. At any rate, loving reality as we do, we cannot do less than cordially welcome reality as we find it in Mr. Harrigan's comedies. Consciously or unconsciously, he is part of the great tendency toward the faithful representation of life which is now animating fiction.

Yet because it is so very good, one must not forget anything else that is good; and it is a pleasure to recognize the success of another playwright, who, without having the threefold qualification of those we have named, has at least worked with as intimate a relation to the theatre as Goldoni, or as the dramatists of the days when literature still found expression in the drama. Mr. Bronson Howard's *One of our Girls* touches the chord which has already vibrated in the pages of our international novelists, and contrasts the opposite civilizations of France and America in their ideal of love and marriage. It is a subject that will always interest, and Mr. Howard has handled it with distinct force. His play is extremely well knit; it is thoroughly right-minded, and it has literary quality. No one can be the worse for seeing it, and many might be very much better. It is of the good order of English plays which gave Robinson his just fame, and it is better literature, with a spirit and a nature of its own. We need not say that it proves the superiority of "the American plan" in the important matters it treats; and if its satire is rather more mordant, its irony more obvious, than the author would have found it necessary to make them in a book, we must not forget the intelligence of the ordinary play-goer. The excess will enlighten this, and it is not so great as to offend the quicker perception of others, who can enjoy the very nice work of the piece in other respects. The characterization in some of the people, while always a little too satirical, is charming; and in the performance, as we saw it at the Lyceum Theatre, the author's intention was interpreted by most of the players with the most sympathetic accuracy; there was an admirable evenness in the work, becoming truly exquisite under the touch of Mr. Sothern in his part of the slow, brave, loyal, very single-minded English captain of hussars. In fact, here as elsewhere, in our theatres, one must be struck with the enormous improvement in the average acting within a dozen years past. It is quite up to the level of Mr. Harrigan's or Mr. Howard's work for it; and it is far higher than that of most work given it to do; it is equal even to the perfect *entourage*.

IV.

But we feel that we ought to ask the reader's patience with our digression about New York theatres. The real drama is in our novels mostly. It is they chiefly which approach our actual life, and interpret it so far as it has yet been represented to the vast majority of our intelligent public; it is in them alone that a number, only a little less than that majority, will ever see it represented. The theatre is the amusement of the city, of people whose lives are crowded with pleasures and distractions; but the novel is the consolation, the refuge, of the fine spirits that pine in the dulness of small towns, or the monotony of the country, where other intellectual resources are few, and the excitements none. It is therefore of little consequence to the great mass of those who truly love literature whether the theatre is good or bad; they will never see it; they will never suffer from it, or profit by it. We in the great cities long for a renewal of the glories that surrounded it in the days when it was a living interest; but that is an affair of sentiment merely, and it would not greatly matter if the theatre remained always what it has long been—a mere diversion, neither affecting our life, nor affected by it. Perhaps the theatrical drama will never revive. We have noted some signs of renewed respiration, but we should not think it quite cataclysmal if, after a few gasps, it ceased to breathe again. We should certainly regret to see any art perish, but it is for the arts, like the interests, to assert their own vitality and maintain it; and if the drama, with all our lavish love of the theatre, cannot hold its own there, and prosper and advance, as the novel has prospered and advanced, in spite of the unfriendly literary conditions, it simply proves that the drama is an outworn literary form. It cannot be willed back to life by criticism, censured back, or coaxed back. It must take its chances; it must make them.

We do not know that we should wish Mr. Luska, for his own sake, to give his next essay dramatic form; he will meet a wider audience in the novel, and more intelligent; there can be no doubt of that. The novelist's audience is now so great and so good that it is quite worth his while to do his best for it; and we have the hope that Mr. Luska's clever work will be more than clever. We wish him a little more repose, a little more perfect dramatization, a little stronger belief that the ordinary complexion of human affairs is the thing that is now newest in fiction, and will remain so. It is not easy to catch.

For Mr. Wolcott Balestier, another young writer whom we have been reading, we could desire something of Mr. Luska's vigorous touch and security of direction from the start. A true poetical atmosphere is not wanting in his pure and sympathetically suggested story of *A Victorious Defeat;* and he has new ground among his Moravians of the early years of our century. But for a long time the figures have a teasing vagueness, and perhaps they never quite lose it. He lingers upon them with a hand that is tender and decorative, but not so sure as we hope it will be; and he has a very good, self-respectful, impersonal way of treating them. His work is suffused with a sense of what is fine and delicate in literature and in life; he has a just feeling for the value of the common materials that life is made of, and for the simple means. He has a strong situation in the attitude of the Moravian minister whom the Moravian usage of marriage by lot has given the girl he loves, and who finds it in his heart to give her up because she does not love him. That is natural and probable. It is possible, but neither natural nor probable, that he should wish afterward to marry her to the man she does love; and Mr. Balestier, with his good feeling for the minor realities, should never propose to himself anything less than nature and probability in great things. To have the minister die soon after is a concession to the weakness of novel readers; he should have lived on, as men generally do, even after signal sacrifices.

V.

We deal attentively with the work of those young writers, because if criticism is to affect literature at all, it must be through the writers who have newly left the starting-point, and are reasonably uncertain of the race, not with those who have won it again and again in their own way. Mr. Luska and Mr. Balestier may possibly think there is something in what we say; but older writers probably would not. In fact, criticism can, after all, do very little toward forming or reforming any writer; if it could, we are painfully aware that we should ourselves be very different from what we are. More and more it must content itself with ascertaining currents and tendencies, and not proposing to direct or stop them; more and more it must realize that it is not a censorship. It will not find its work lighter for this shrinkage in its apparent importance. It is so much easier to say that you like this or dislike that, than to tell why one thing is, or where another thing comes from, that many flourishing critics will have to go out of business altogether if the scientific method comes in, for then the critic will have to know something beside his own mind, which is often but a narrow field. He will have to know something of the *laws* of that mind, and of its generic history. Nothing less is required of him in the example lately set him by Mr. Hutcheson Macaulay Posnett, whose work on *Comparative Literature* is calculated, we fear, to make many complacent authorities' heads ache and hearts fail them. Before speaking of his book it is only fair to recognize what a thoroughly equipped critic of our own has done on the same lines, and to remind the reader of Mr. T. S. Perry's work in his essays on *English Literature in the Eighteenth Century*, and in his smaller volume of studies of German literature *From Opitz to Lessing*. There could not be a more interesting illustration of the principles held by both of these writers than the fact that Mr. Posnett should have been advancing contemporaneously, under the same general influences, toward the very positions taken by Mr. Perry three years ago. His field is vastly wider, for he attempts to explain and account for the whole course of literature, but we cannot see that his method is different, or that his application of scientific theories to literature is different. One in America and the other in England has been the first to respond to ideas now everywhere appealing to the human reason. "A genius," said Mr. Perry, three years ago, "in the future as in the past, is bound by the necessity of building on the foundations that society is laying every day. Every apparently insignificant action of ours contributes its mite to the sum of circumstances which inspire the writer, whose vision may be dim or inaccurate, but who can see only what exists or may exist, and is limited by experience, whether this be treated literally or be modified by imagination." "By neglecting the influences of social life on literature," says Mr. Posnett, "Greek criticism fostered the deadly theories that literature is essentially an imitation of masterpieces, that its ideals are not progressive, but permanent, that they have no dependence on particular conditions of human character, on the nature of that social instrument language, on circumscribed spheres of time and space." In other words, both of these writers, whose books will form epochs for any one who comes fresh to their principles, hold alike that literature is from life, and that it is under the law as every part of life is, and is not a series of preposterous miracles.

Mr. Posnett, for his part, is not hopeful of a ready assent to his method. But he is not dismayed for that reason: "To our friends, the men of Literature, we would say that nothing has contributed more largely to lower the value of their studies in the eyes of thinking men than the old-fashioned worship of imagination, not merely as containing an element of mystery, but as altogether superior to conditions of space and time; that, under the auspices of this irrational worship, the study of Literature tends to become a blind idolatry of the Unknown, with a priesthood of textual pedants who would sacrifice to verbalism the very deity they affect to worship; but that the comparative study of Literature not only opens an immense field of fruitful labor, but tends to foster creative imagination."

The treatise which is the fruit of this well-grounded belief is divided into five books. The first is introductory, and deals with the nature of literature, its relativity, the principle of its growth, and the comparative method. Applying this method, Mr. Posnett studies in the four succeeding books Clan Literature, the literature of the City Commonwealth, World Literature, and National Literature, with chapters subdividing each of these topics. We cannot give a just idea of the learning, the sympathy, the logic, brought to the inquiry, and we will not try. But we are sure that the book will make a fame for itself which will not suffer any lover of literature to neglect it, and we leave our readers to make its acquaintance at first hand. We can promise them that they will be much the wiser for doing so; we could even imagine an average romantic critic coming away from it with some hopeful misgivings, some vague preference of principles to impressions in considering literature. It will, of course, shake somewhat his prepossessions as to the nature and essence of literature; but he will be none the worse for that.

"The theory that literature," says Mr. Posnett, "is the detached life-work of individuals who are to be worshipped like images fallen down from heaven, not known as workers in the language and ideas of their age and place, and the kindred theory that imagination transcends the associations of space and time, have done much to conceal the relation of science to literature, and to injure the works of both. But the 'great-man theory' is really suicidal; for, while breaking up history and literature into biographies, and thus preventing the recognition of any lines of orderly development, it would logically reduce not only what is known as 'exceptional genius,' but all men and women, so far as they possess personality at all, to the unknown, the causeless—in fact, would issue in a sheer denial of human knowledge, limited or unlimited."

This is in substance what Mr. Perry has also repeatedly maintained; and these two authors stand together in a conscious perception of principles which others have been feeling more or less blindly, and which are really animating and shaping the whole future of criticism.

With their clear perception of the origin of literature comes a just and high sense of its office, which Mr. Posnett expresses in words that have the thrill and glow of a religious conviction. "It will be clear to any reader of this book that its author is far from regarding literature as the mere toy of stylists, far from advocating the 'moral indifference' of art. In his eyes literature is a very serious thing, which can become morally indifferent only in ages of moral indifference. 'Let the world go its way, and the kings and the peoples strive, and the priests and philosophers wrangle; at least to make a perfect verse is to be out of time, master of all change, and free of every creed.'* Such was Gautier's view; but it is stamped false by the whole history of literary development. Whether men like it or not, their literary efforts at ideal beauty in prose or verse must involve ideals of human conduct. Action, speech, and thought are too subtly interwoven to allow their artistic severance aught but fancied truth; if it were otherwise, literature might indeed have been the product of a Cloud-cuckoo-town in which historical science and morality would be equally out of place. But, it may be said, your science cuts at the roots of moral conduct by treating the individual as made by conditions over which he has no control. Far from it. Our science traces a growth of social and individual freedom so far as the conditions of human life have hitherto allowed them to grow together. Nothing is really gained for morality or religion by assuming that the life with which they deal is unlimited, unconditioned; nay, such limitless pretensions have hitherto proved very fatal to morality by fostering suicidal extremes of social and individual thinking. How are these suicidal extremes to be best kept in check? By insisting on the social and physiological limits within which man moves and has moved; by answering the admirers of universal shadows, in which morality itself becomes shadowy, in the words of the Hebrew prophet: 'Who hath heard such a thing? What hath seen such things? Shall a land bring forth in a day? or a people be born in a moment?'"

At the close of his preface Mr. Posnett tells us that he leaves Trinity College, Dublin, while his work is going through the press, for New Zealand, where we believe he is to have a literary professorship in a colonial university. It is one of the superb conditions of modern civilization, however, that so important a man can be equally valuable in London or New York or Auckland, and can speak as easily to the whole world from one place as the other. He must not look for ready acceptance from the Maori, anywhere; but he may be assured that the less barbarous races in different quarters of the globe will be very glad to hear from him again. In the mean time they cannot do better than study his present book.

* Dowden, *Studies in Literature*, 1789–1877, p. 401.

Monthly Record of Current Events.

POLITICAL.

OUR Record is closed on the 18th of May.— President Cleveland, April 22, sent a message to Congress recommending the creation of a Commission of Labor, consisting of three members, who shall be regular officers of the government, charged among other duties with the consideration and settlement, when possible, of all controversies between labor and capital.

The United States House of Representatives, May 6, passed the River and Harbor Bill, appropriating over $15,000,000.

The United States Senate, May 12, passed the Inter-State Commerce Bill by a vote of 47 to 4. Its chief feature is a provision for a national Commission, with a principal office at Washington.

Hon. W. C. Whitthorne has been appointed by the Governor of Tennessee to succeed Hon. Howell E. Jackson as United States Senator.

Anarchist riots took place in Chicago May 4, and in Milwaukee May 5. In Chicago a dynamite bomb was thrown among the police with murderous effect, six of the officers being killed and sixty-one wounded.

The public debt of the United States was reduced in April $10,965,387 95.

Two American schooners have been seized by the authorities of Nova Scotia for alleged infraction of the Canadian fishing laws. One of the vessels, the *David J. Adams*, was taken at Digby May 7, and the other, the *Ella M. Doughty*, at Englishtown May 17.

The Irish Land Purchase Bill, which the House of Commons, on April 16, gave Mr. Gladstone permission to introduce, was issued April 22. It is divided into five parts. There are fifty-three clauses and four schedules. The bill provides that a landlord who desires to sell his property shall apply to the state authority, who shall refer the application to a Land Commission, which, after making an inquiry, shall fix a price at which the property shall be sold, unless the landlord and the state authority have previously come to an agreement. If the landlord objects to the price fixed by the Commission, he may withdraw his application on paying the costs. When a sale of property has been effected, the Commission shall pay the creditors before making any other distribution of the purchase-money. Certain rent charges may be bought outright by the state authority, or payment may be continued from the tenants' repayments. In cases of property whereon there is reasonable cause to suppose that valuable minerals exist, the Commission shall add to the purchase-money a fair sum therefor, and the minerals realized from said property shall be vested in the state authority, or such local body as the Irish legislature may provide. The Irish Receiver-General and deputies, who are to execute the financial part of the act, shall be appointed to hold office as permanent civil servants, subject to the authority of the Treasury. The measure empowers the Treasury to create three classes of permanent annuities, bearing interest respectively at 3, 2¾, and 2½ per cent., which shall be charged to the Imperial Consolidated Fund. Strict rules are provided by the bill which forbid the subdividing or subletting of a holding so long as it is subject to any state charge; but the state authority is empowered to relax these rules where he may think it advisable.

On April 21 the powers despatched an ultimatum to Greece ordering her to disarm within eight days. To this Greece replied, April 29, that she had already notified them that she had accepted the counsel of France, thus giving formal assurance that, yielding to the desire of the powers, she would not disturb the peace. Consequently she would maintain her armaments, but would gradually reduce them. The powers considered this inadequate, and on May 6 the foreign ministers prepared to leave Athens. Three days later the foreign fleets blockaded the Greek coast, and the Greek ministry resigned. A new cabinet was formed May 12, under the leadership of M. Valvis.

The Spanish Senatorial elections resulted in the return of 128 Ministerialists, 28 Conservatives, 6 Independents, 4 Republicans, and 2 members of the Dynastic Left.

DISASTERS.

April 17.—Town of Stry, Galicia, almost destroyed by fire. One hundred and twenty-eight lives lost.

April 20.—Breaking of a reservoir dam near East Lee, Massachusetts, drowned seven persons and devastated the town.

May 6.—Terrific storm of wind, rain, and hail at Kansas City, killing twenty persons and destroying many buildings.

May 12.—Hurricane in Spain causing great destruction of life and property. In Madrid 32 persons were killed and 620 injured.—Terrific storm in Ohio and Indiana, and flood at Xenia, Ohio, killing twenty persons.

OBITUARY.

April 16.—In London, England, Sampson Low, publisher, aged eighty-nine years.

April 20.—On board a steamer bound from Calcutta for London, Lionel Tennyson, son of the Poet Laureate, aged thirty-two years.

April 27.—In Brookline, Massachusetts, Henry H. Richardson, architect, aged forty-seven years.

May 1.—In Charleston, South Carolina, Charles Franklin Robertson, Bishop of the Diocese of Missouri, aged fifty-one years.

May 2.—In London, England, Right Hon. John Thomas Freeman-Mitford, Earl of Redesdale, aged eighty-one years.

Editor's Drawer.

THE flippancy with which a portion of the press has treated the earnest discussion of *décolleté* dress is painful to every reflecting mind. It is a serious subject. No one who remembers the palace petticoat flurry in the beginning of the reign of her Majesty Queen Victoria, which for a time threatened to impair the integrity of the British Empire, would dismiss this as a question of the lowest importance. It is what may be called a constitutional question. By a sort of semi-official federal action it has become a national affair. This is greatly to be regretted; for while it may be conceded that this is a case which cannot be left to the individual conscience, since society must protect itself, it is, in the opinion of the Drawer, a State, and not a federal, question. If the neck is controlled at all, it should be controlled by State and not by federal action. To dress the neck high or low, to draw the line between that which is agreeable and that which is too agreeable, is one of the reserved rights. It is true that the women who make it a national matter take refuge behind the amendments to the Constitution, and point to the provision that the right of the people to bare arms shall not be impaired; but this is a quibble. The spirit of the Constitution leaves this an open matter, for the States

to deal with. To take the opposite view is to encourage centralization in its most dangerous form. It would necessitate a Low-neck Bureau at Washington, with branches all over the country, and commissioners (like those of the civil service) for the consideration of the merits of candidates. Now the rules which might be, or which may have been, laid down in Washington for the dress *décolleté* may be inapplicable to other parts of the country, and drawing the line for people of different temperaments and in various climates is a matter of extreme delicacy. It would interfere also with the higher law, for everybody knows that beauty is a law unto itself, and the same rule cannot be made for it as for plainness. The federal government has no power to touch this. We imagine that the most that a State could do would be to enact a law forbidding ugly women to fall below a certain pretty high line in apparel. There are some who advocate what the lawyers call, for railways, the "short-haul law"—that is, that an ugly woman should in no case cut her dress lower than a pretty woman. But this is impracticable, for Providence has so benignly ordered the world that there is scarcely a woman living who is not pretty in the eyes of somebody. And if this matter of the height of the bodice cannot be left to the taste of the women individually, it is certain that they would find or make reasons for evading any enactment.

In the desire to have an authority which shall be able to draw an exact line, so that our assemblies shall still be irradiated with loveliness, and not be of a character to take away the thoughts altogether from the higher intellectual life, it has been suggested that there be held a national woman's convention, which should consult and lay down some rules. This is an excellent suggestion, but it encounters a practical difficulty that would be raised at the outset. How should the delegates dress? If it is to be a representative body of American women, it will be very largely made up of the most beautiful women in the world. And does any one suppose that beauty would hide half its charms, and consequently surrender half its influence, in a body of this sort? Thus disarmed, the low-necks would wage a losing game from the beginning, and the result would be an alarming high-neck pronunciamento. Besides, if everybody went in high neck, there would be nothing to talk about, and the whole subject would be covered without any legislation. The fair way would be to have an equal number of delegates of the highs and the lows, who should compromise by electing a décolleté speaker and a secretary of the other persuasion, and then calmly look at the subject in a spirit of concession, with all the light that could be thrown on it.

The Drawer has not much confidence in the success of the convention scheme; and on the other hand it does not expect that any suggestions from the male sex will have, or ought to have, any weight. Interference of this sort is always resisted. In one of the large cities of the United States, several years ago, the bishop of the Catholic communion had a lovely parishioner whose dress did not meet his approval. He made the décolleté dress the subject of a sermon, and pointed his moral by such a reference to the lady before him, who was as blooming as a bank of roses in May, that the eyes of the whole congregation were turned on her, and she fainted dead away. The people were so indignant at this attack upon one so lovely and so defenceless that they rushed off in a body and mobbed the bishop's house, and forced him to leave the city.

The Drawer hopes that the great question will be settled without any violation of the Constitution, on lines that will make virtue triumphant and leave beauty regnant. But it recalls the story of the zealous bishop in order to remind man that there are some things about which he had better be blind than officious.

Does the presiding genius of the Drawer know how many monotonous hours of a sailor's life are relieved and cheered by the good things found therein? Let me add one:

Some years since. My first voyage to Bombay. When off the port, a dozen or more runners for as many Parsee merchants came on board, and with a zeal worthy of the true followers of Zoroaster began soliciting the favor of doing the ship's business while in port, each declaring that his house of Hagee, Adergee, Cowasagee, Nesserwangee, and a lot more "gees," was the best, safest, and most influential house in Bombay. When there was a slight lull—as sailors say—in the clatter of tongues, I asked one of the most respectable among them if the firm he represented was a reliable one. For a moment he did not seem to comprehend my meaning, and kept repeating the word "reliable." I was about to explain, when his features brightened, and asking me to step one side with him, said that he would tell me frankly and truly that "no man can do business in Bombay unless they lie little."

CUPID'S GARDEN.

As I weer in Cupit's garden,
  Not muoar nor heaf an hour,
'Tweer thear I zeed twa maydens,
  Zitten under Cupit's bower,
A-gathering of sweet jessamine,
  Thee lily, and thee rose—
These be thee sweetest flowers
  As in the garden grows.

I roudly stepped to one o' them;
  These words to heer I zays:
"Be you engaged to arra young man?
  Come, tell to me, I prays."
"I bean't engaged to arra young man,
  I solemnly declare;
I aims to live a mayden
  And still thee laurel wear."

Zays I: "My stars and garters!
  This hear's a pretty go,
Vor a nice young mayd as never vas
  To sarv all mankind so!"
But t'other young mayd looked sly at me
  As vrom her zeat shee risen.
Zays shee: "Let thee and I go our own way,
  And we'll let shee go shees'n."

Lest we all forget how to write vigorously, it is well to keep up occasionally with a noble specimen of newspaper English. The following is taken from the correspondence of a Western newspaper, and relates to a debate in the House at Washington last winter:

"By the courtesy of Mr. Herbert, George D. Wise of Virginia replied to Boutelle, and he did it in a way that made the fur fly, and surprised his friends. Wise jumped on Boutelle with both feet, figuratively speaking, with an avalanche of facts, sarcasm, and ridicule, and tramped the life out of him. He ripped him up the back, tore out his entrails, and, rending him limb from limb, flung the pieces all over the House. A more complete lambasting and more vigorous and thorough roasting than Wise gave Boutelle was never known. The excitement of the man as he poured forth the terrific and terrible tongue-lashing grew and augmented itself until he seemed to have turned into a very cyclone. With mighty gesticulation and in tones of wrath frightful to behold he whaled it at his opponent throughout the fifteen minutes allotted to him, while Boutelle sat pale and panting and smarting and squirming under the mighty blows of the enraged Southerner, who was skinning him from his head to his heels.

"In the course of his remarks Wise paid his compliments to William Mahone, as he called him, and made a neat cutting side stroke at Representative Brady of Virginia, disposing of him with one sharp, quick, decisive swipe. Wise vigorously and dramatically recited some facts in their order which absolutely knocked out of time every charge and allegation that Boutelle had made in his speech, and in the end landed his prey so high and dry that he could do nothing but gasp for breath."

HARRY.

My wayward, busy three-year-old
For sudden mischief loud I scold;
So carelessly my wish to dare,
He took my patience unaware.
"Oo oughtn't speak so loud at me;
I finks it isn't nice," said he.
"But mamma thinks you're to be blamed;
And, dearest, aren't you ashamed?"
Askance he turned his eyes gray-blue—
"I is ashame; I's 'shame of oo."

Nothing but an "obolus" would pay the toll required in this:

TURNPIKE NOTICE.

All persons having toll passes on the Richmond and Irvine turnpike issued by Williams and Pigg will expire January 1, 1886, and they will be required to pay toll from that date.   W. W. Pigg.

A CAPE BRETON PARSON.

He was a tall, angular parson of the old severe Presbyterian type. As the local idiom has it, "You would know by his English that he had the Gaelic." He was preaching in a brother parson's pulpit to a congregation who were strangers to him. Descanting on the *lamb* as a type of gentleness, meekness, etc., he said:

"The lamb is *quaite and kind*. The lamb is not like the other beasts, the lion and the tiger and the wolf. Ye will not be runnin' away from the lamb. No. The lamb is kaind; the lamb will not eat ye, whatever.

"And there is *food* in the lamb, too. Oh yes, you will be killin' the lamb and the sheep when the cold weather will come in the winter. You will be wantin' some good strong food in the winter, and it is then you will be killin' the lamb.

"And there is *clothing* in the lamb—he is good for the clothing. You will tek the wool off him, and you will mek clothes for yourselves. And how would you and I look without clothing?" etc.

At the close of the exercises he gave out the following very peculiar notice, to explain which I must state that ravages had been made among the Presbyterian flock by the influence of a divine of a different persuasion: "And there will most likely be a family from X. that will be baptized here after meeting on Friday night, but"—here he leaned forward, and added, in a loud stage-whisper—"*ye'll no be saying a word about it, dear brethren, as I do not think they want it known.*"

One stormy night, when the roads were wellnigh impassable, a son of Erin came into a doctor's office and desired the dispenser of physic to go to see a friend who was "jist a-dyin'." He would not take no for an answer; so, putting the saddle-bags upon his horse, the physician started out upon his journey. As soon as he saw the sick man he knew it was nearly over with him, and remarked to the courier:

"Peter, you told the truth: your friend is just at the point of death."

"Can't ye do ainytheeng for heem?" replied Peter.

"No; it is too late."

"But, docthor, ain't ye goin' to give heem ainything at all at all?"

"It will do no good."

"But, docthor, ye have come so far, it would be too bad to go back without doin' ainything."

For the peace of Peter's mind, the doctor now took a small quantity of sugar from a phial, and placed it upon the dying man's tongue just as he was drawing his last breath.

Peter, seeing his friend's head drop back, looked up to the doctor with big eyes, and said, half in a whisper, "Oh, docthor, an didn' ye do it quick!"

IS LAGER-BEER AN INTOXICANT?

A stone-cutter, whose office adjoined his stone-yard, was seated in his office when a friend called upon him, and they discussed several topics together, among them the question as to what extent lager-beer was an intoxicant. The stone-cutter maintained that beer was not intoxicating, while his friend maintained the opposite. The stone-cutter said, there is a man at work in the yard (pointing to a brawny-chested German) who could drink a bucket (three gallons) of beer at one sitting and feel none the worse for it. The friend doubted, and a wager was made and the workman called, who when asked if he could drink that bucket (pointing to a large water bucket) full of beer at one sitting, replied, "Vell, I don't know; I lets you know after a vile." The German went away, and after remaining about fifteen minutes, returned, and said, "Yes, I can trink dot peer." The bucket of beer was procured and placed before the German, who very soon absorbed the last drop, and arose from his seat, wiping his mouth with his sleeve, and was walking away with a firm step, when his employer recalled him and said to him, "See here, my friend and I have some curiosity to know why you did not drink the beer when you were first asked." The German replied, "Vell, I don'd know dot I could trink it, so I vent ont und trink a bucked, den I know I could do it." W.

A GENTLEMAN formerly a professor in Roberts College, Constantinople, relates the following travesty of justice illustrative of the law in Turkey, where an accused man must prove his innocence, or else he is declared guilty:

A convert to Christianity came to Dr. Lord, a missionary there, and asked if it was ever right to tell a lie. This was a staggerer for the doctor, and he said he would have to know the case before he could decide, although, on general principles, he did not think it was.

"The case is this," replied the seeker after truth. "A Turk, a stranger to me, living in Rustchuk, accused me of buying and receiving from him 1000 sheep. I knew of no way of proving that I did not buy and receive these sheep, and the case must certainly go against me. It came up for trial to-day, and after the charge had been made, I admitted that I had bought and received the sheep (which was a lie), and had at the same time *paid for them in full*. He couldn't prove that I had not, so the case was dismissed."

The doctor thought that if ever a lie was justifiable, this was certainly the time.

DURING a revival in Texas some years ago a negro was reputed to have had visions about heaven and hell. His boss called him up and interrogated him as to what he saw in both places, and first as to what the white men and darkies were doing in heaven. "Lord! boss, the white men was all a-tilting back in their chairs, with their heels on the banisters, a-smoking cigars, and the niggers was down on their knees a-shining up their golden slippers!" Then as to what was going on in the other place. "Ef you believe me, boss, every single white man had a nigger in his hands a-holding him up between him and the flames!"

MR. N. VICKARY, the well-known taxidermist of Lynn, tells a story of the old colored man John Johnson, a celebrated Lynn character. John happened into the shop one day just after Mr. Vickary had been skinning a large bald eagle. Thinking to have a little sport, Mr. V. asked John if he would like a nice goose for his dinner the next day.

"I tank you a hunderd million times ef you gib me de goose, 'deed I will," John exclaimed; and in due time the skinless body of the eagle was wrapped in a newspaper, and Johnson started off with it under his arm, still volubly expressing his gratitude.

About a week after, Mr. V. met Johnson on Union Street, and asked how he liked the goose he had given him.

"Dat goose," said Johnson, showing his ivories—"dat war de toughest goose. I's declar' dat mus' have bin fader to all the ganders. I biled dat goose, an' I parbiled him, den I

biled him again, but I declar' dat ar wuz de chewinest bird me an' de ole woman ever seed."

After telling him that there must have been some mistake in his method of cooking, they parted, till one day, as a large snowy owl was in preparation for stuffing, and Johnson happened to be going by, Mr. V. called to him to come in. Johnson came hobbling in, when Mr. V. asked him if he did not want another goose, pointing to the owl lying on the bench with its skin drawn over its head.

Johnson looked suspiciously from Mr. V. to the bird, and scratching his woolly pate, remarked: "See here, boss, ef 'tain't no trubble, I's like to see de feet on dat goose afore I carries him to de ole woman."

FROM an Orleans County, New York, paper:

DIED.

SOME twenty-five or thirty years ago there lived in —— County, in the State of Iowa, a young man by the name of S—— R——, at that time engaged in teaching a country school, and during leisure hours reading Blackstone in order to qualify himself for admission to the bar. Near the school-house lived two farmers, whom we shall designate as A and B. A owned a large number of hogs, which he allowed to run at large to feed on the mast. B owned a cornfield fenced with a badly dilapidated brush fence. He also owned a savage dog. When the corn began to ripen, B's hogs made frequent raids into the field, and helped themselves to the corn. B, being greatly annoyed by the hogs, finally set his dog on the hogs, and worried them considerably. When A discovered his lacerated hogs, he was full of wrath. The next morning A started, with an axe on his shoulder, to go to his timber to chop wood, which led him by B's house; and seeing B's wife inside of B's lot, about thirty or forty feet from the fence, milking a cow, he stopped at the gate and inquired for B. Being informed that B was not at home, he threatened to mash B into the earth if he ever dogged his hogs again, and to demonstrate how he would do it he brought his axe down on the fence with a fearful blow. He then left. When B returned, his wife informed him of A's threats, which filled him with wrath, and off he goes to the school-house to consult S—— R—— whether he could sue A "with the law." S—— R——, after consulting his Blackstone and the statutes, informed him that the acts constituted the offence of "assault with intent to inflict great bodily injury," and advised B to commence a criminal prosecution against A. S—— R—— drew up an information, and B took it to the nearest justice, and had a warrant issued for A's arrest. A being duly arrested, and a day set for trial, S—— R—— appeared for the prosecution, and —— Jones as attorney for the defendant. The witnesses being sworn, the facts as above stated were duly proven. S—— R—— then proceeded with a lengthy argument, not to convince the court of the defendant's guilt, but to convince the court and by-standers that he had read Blackstone, and concluded his argument with the following peroration: "May it please your Honor, the *summum bonum* of the whole business is that the defendant is guilty."

Then —— Jones, for the defence, addressed the court as follows: "Your Honor, it may be that under that old law of *summum bonum*—which was that if a man was charged with a crime, he was guilty, whether he had ever done anything wrong or not—that my client is guilty; but that law was an unjust law enacted by despots and tyrants to oppress the weak and the poor. That was the law of this country down to the time of the Revolutionary war, when our forefathers rebelled against it, and after seven long years of bloody war, finally repealed it with their swords, and enacted in its stead the great law of *E Pluribus Unum*, which is that a man is never guilty of any crime until he does something wrong. Now, since the prosecutor was not within a mile of the fence when the blow was struck, he could not have been injured; and as the blow did the fence no harm, my client did no wrong. Therefore, under the great law of *E Pluribus Unum*, which is now the law of this country, he is not guilty, and should be discharged."

The justice then summed up the case as follows: "Well, it appears by the argument that under the old law of *summum bonum* the defendant is guilty; but my father was a Revolutionary soldier, and I've hearn him tell all about the Revolutionary war, and so I know that the old law of *summum bonum* has been abolished, and the great law of *E Pluribus Unum* now waves all over this country. So I lets the defendant go."

A LAST RESORT.

"Hello, Jones! you're looking down in the mouth. How's the world treating you?"
"It isn't. I have to pay for myself."

JOSEPH JEFFERSON AS "BOB ACRES."
From the painting by J. W. Alexander.—[See page 391.]

HARPER'S
NEW MONTHLY MAGAZINE.

Vol. LXXIII.   AUGUST, 1886.   No. CCCCXXXV.

THE CITY OF THE STRAIT.

BY EDMUND KIRKE.

DETROIT is one of the oldest cities on this continent. Before Hendrik Hudson set foot on the island of Manhattan, and while Henry IV. still sat on the throne of France, the Hurons pointed out the site whereon it is built to Champlain, the founder of Quebec, as the natural gateway to "the vast seas of sweet water," and then was born in the brain of the great French navigator the dream of a "New France," which should extend from the Atlantic to the Pacific, and have Quebec and Detroit as its eastern and western fortresses.

This dream was inherited by the French monarchs; but it was not till ninety years later that one of them attempted to make it a reality. Then Louis XIV. commissioned the Sieur Antoine de la Mothe Cadillac, who from 1694 to 1699 had been in command at Mackinaw, to found at Detroit a settlement, and erect there a fort to hold the region of the Great Lakes for the French government. This was done; and Detroit, under the successive reigns of Henry IV., Louis XIII., XIV., and XV., was for nearly sixty years a French town—a bit of "sunny France" hidden away in the heart of the western wilderness; and such it might have remained to this day had not Wolfe, one dark night in September, 1759, scaled the heights of Quebec, and on the Plains of Abraham changed the fate of North America. The surrender of Detroit soon followed the conquest of Quebec; and then it became an English town, and the western head-quarters of the British power in America. It so remained—the extreme outpost of Western civilization—until July 11, 1796, when, in pursuance of the peace of 1783, it was quietly transferred to the United States. Thus we see that Detroit has had a unique history. Three times has it changed its nationality, and with each change assumed totally different characteristics. At first it was French, then English, and last of all American, and in the present town may be seen a curious blending of the traits of these various peoples. The old French *habitant* and the courtly English resident have long slumbered in their graves, but the close observer will detect that their spirits still walk abroad, and perambulate its streets arm in arm with the irrepressible Yankee, who in his seven-league boots is now striding across the continent. Brother Jonathan has everywhere the astonishing energy which, in wellnigh a single day, raised Chicago from its ashes; but here he has been held in check by those old worthies, who have now and then whispered in his ear the fable of the hare and the tortoise. This accounts for the fact that Detroit is to-day a curious compound of modern progress and old-time conservatism—a city of vast enterprises, but enterprises based on a broad, substantial, and enduring basis.

It was a sweltering day in July, 1701, when Cadillac, with his little fleet of birchbark canoes, turned southwest from Lake St. Clair, and entered the broad, clear, beautiful river now known as the Detroit. Had some native of the forest stood then upon its banks, he must have been lost in wonder at the unwonted spectacle of the strange flotilla. Twenty-five birchen boats—some measuring six feet wide and thirty-five feet long—gaudily decorated with Indian symbols, and waving gayly the flags of France, glided gracefully down the stream to the exhilarating sounds of the fife and the drum, and the joyful shout that a long journey was over. The boats were manned by fifty soldiers in "bright blue coats and white facings"; and carried four officers and fifty emigrants, with an abundant store of provisions and all the tools and utensils needed in the building and settling of a new town in the wilderness. Besides, there were on board two Roman Catholic priests, for, like all good Frenchmen, Cadillac had a tender concern for the souls of his people. He intended they should not neglect the mass, or forget their pater-noster. They had come a weary journey of forty-nine days, in those frail boats, over rough waves, the men bearing them on their shoulders on the long portage between the Ottawa River and Lake Huron, and it was but natural they should rejoice at the end of their voyage.

Where the river leaves Lake Huron it is more than half a league in width, and broken by picturesque islands; but as it flows southwestward it contracts into a single channel, and gradually narrows till at about ten miles' distance it has a breadth of only half a mile. This is the strait which was to give its name—Détroit—to both the river and the city to be built upon its northern bank. Here, at a sudden bend in the stream, the canoes were drawn up on the beach, and landing, the voyagers ascended to a level plateau which rose by successive terraces to a height of about fifty feet above the bed of the river. From this elevation they had a view of the whole broad water as it flows southward, shut in at first by steep bluffs, but then broadening out, dotted with beautiful islands, till at the distance of about twenty miles its clear green current is lost in the deep blue waves of Lake Erie. The river here is three miles wide, discharging a greater volume of water than

any other in the world, excepting only the Niagara and St. Lawrence, which receive its flow. Cadillac was a man of broad, forecasting intellect, but it may be questioned if even he would have credited a prediction that within two hundred years that river, frost-bound as it is nearly four months in the year, would give passage to a greater annual tonnage than would enter London—the largest seaport in the world. And yet such is the fact, as shown by the maritime tables for the year 1884.

Cadillac formed a temporary encampment under the great spreading trees, and, within two days, laid the foundation of a church in which to worship God after the manner of his fathers. Then he staked out the ground for a fort and a stockade, and set at work to get the settlers housed before the winter, which he knew from experience to be sometimes severe in this latitude. The stockade is supposed to have included about twenty acres. It was located on the first rise of ground near the river—in what is now the business part of the city—that the guns of the fort might command the strait and the opposite shore; and was made thus roomy to allow each settler space for a dwelling inside the pickets, safety being the thing to be first thought of by the new settlement. The settlers were but a handful, and they knew themselves surrounded by at least forty thousand savages, friendly then, but liable at any moment to become hostile upon occasion of some real or fancied injury. The area within the stockade was laid out into lots and streets, and surrounded by a lane twelve feet in width, to allow the garrison, in the event of attack, free access to every part of the enclosure. Thus Cadillac was soon in command of a walled city, built, it is true, of rough logs, and not in the latest style of European architecture, but reasonably secure, if bravely defended, against attacks from such desultory warriors as the Indians. By means of this fort the French secured control of the Great Lakes and the fur trade of the Northwest; and here the traders and soldiers of that nation congregated, and proclaimed Louis XIV. lord paramount of all the vast region that stretches away to the setting sun.

Cadillac landed on the 24th of July, and by the close of the following month the chapel, the fort, and the dwellings of the settlers were erected, and the settlement had assumed all the order of an es-

THE LANDING OF CADILLAC.

tablished community. Soon after this, Madame Cadillac, who had been left behind at Quebec, plunged into the wide wilderness to rejoin her husband. It was a thousand miles, in a birch-bark canoe, rowed by half-clad Indians or still more savage half-breeds, and the route was through a dense forest and over great seas swept by the September storms; but this brave woman undertook the journey attended by only a single female companion. When subsequently reminded of its hazards and hardships, she simply said, "A woman who loves her husband as she should has no stronger attraction than his company, wherever he may be; everything else should be indifferent to her." Cadillac has been censured for being "often involved in troubles caused by his rashness and prejudices," but whatever may have been his faults, he must have possessed noble traits of character to have inspired the strong devotion of such a woman.

The adventurous Frenchman had now built a capital, and assumed the Governorship of a vast territory. His next step was to people his settlement, and obtain the permanent good-will of the natives of the lake region. To these ends he resorted to the novel expedient of settling the Indians about him, and encouraging his soldiers to marry their young women. In this way he hoped to augment his population, and attach the aborigines to him by ties of kinship. The natives received his overtures kindly, and before long four different tribes had established settlements within cannon-shot of the fort—the Miamis and Pottawatamies within half a mile on its either side, and the Hurons and Ottawas on the opposite side of the river, near the present town of Windsor. His scheme for intermingling the white and red races was equally successful, for the Indian maiden soon learned to prefer Johnny Crapeau for a husband. He did not require her to plant his corn and dig his potatoes while he was away upon the hunt or lounging idly about the wigwam. Too highly civilized for that, he cultivated his own beets and cabbages, and arraying his dusky mate in gaudy gown and gewgaws, set her over his household to entertain his guests and preside as an in-door divinity. The extent to which this intermarrying of the French and Indians was carried may be inferred from the fact that the account-books of Judge John W. Edmonds, who, in 1837, was appointed by President Jackson to pay the Pottawatamies for their Michigan lands, show that fully one-half of that tribe bore French names, or were distinctly classed as half-breeds. The employés of the Hudson Bay Company followed the fashion thus set by Cadillac, and the result was the numerous people of mixed blood who have so recently been in rebellion against the Canadian government. But the offspring of the Detroit marriages did not become half savages. Many of them, in the second and third generation, were so highly civilized as to hold office, lead in society, and found some of the most influential families in Michigan.

To enable them to raise agricultural products, Cadillac granted the settlers land outside the fort, generally in strips having a few hundred feet of frontage upon the river, and extending back so as to form tracts of from thirty to fifty acres. He conveyed these lands in actual fee, and in some instances they were the source of large fortunes to the old families; but in every grant Cadillac reserved to himself certain rights, which curiously illustrate the sort of feudal system which he attempted to establish.* He sought to reproduce in those uncivilized wilds the system then existing where he was born, in Haute-Garonne, France—to form there a literally new France—and for a time he succeeded. But it was the France of Louis XIV., and if the system had not been annulled by the coming in of the English, it would have been swept away by the progress of the eighteenth century.

The settlement grew, and many came to it during the sixty years of French rule that followed, whose names are still borne by some of the best families of Detroit. They brought their wives with them, and formed about the commandant a select society that gave a tone of cultivation to the better part of the white community. They were a high-principled, order-loving class, and their descendants of to-day comprise the conservative element which is so distinct a feature in Detroit society. But in all these years the town was in a nebulous

* All grain was to be ground at his mill, and he exacted an annual tribute as Grand Seigneur. The curious reader will find his system fully detailed in *The History of Detroit and Michigan,* by Silas Farmer—a work recently published, which is very full and accurate in all that relates to the "past and present" of both the city and State.

GROSSE ISLE LIGHT.

state—the nucleus French, the surrounding element a dusky barbarism. In the nature of things there could be no general and thorough amalgamation of these opposite elements, and consequently the town could not crystallize into a compacted community. But with the coming in of the English a new order of things was inaugurated. The Pontiac war soon followed, and that drove the savages from the suburbs. Then the people became more homogeneous, but the French were still an important element. They still retained their own language and religion, and they never affiliated cordially with the English, though the two nationalities had enough in common to make of each other friends and neighbors. It was no longer an attempt to marry civilization and barbarism, but an endeavor to make two white races not overmuch in love with one another dwell peaceably together in one household.

The Pontiac war was a crisis in the history of Detroit, and if tradition is to be trusted, the town was then saved from destruction by one of those romantic incidents that enliven the dull record of carnage which forms so large a portion of our Western annals. It was in 1763. Pontiac had formed the extensive coalition by which he hoped to drive the English back to the east of the Alleghanies. Detroit was their western stronghold, and that taken, his purpose would be half accomplished. The fort here was therefore fixed upon for the first attack, and the wily savage sought to capture it by stratagem. He was well acquainted with the works and garrison, for his home was in the neighborhood, and he had a "summer seat" only a few miles away, at

THE RIVER AT NIGHT.

Grosse Isle, now a favorite rural resort for Detroit people.

About three o'clock on the afternoon of May 1, 1763, Pontiac made a visit to the British commandant, Major Henry Gladwin, and proposed to him a council at the fort, to which he should come with some of his principal warriors, to smoke the pipe of peace, and brighten the chain of friendship between his people and the English. Suspecting no treachery, the Englishman assented, and a date was fixed upon for the meeting. Before the appointed day arrived, Gladwin was told that the Indians were borrowing saws and files of his blacksmith, and that some of them had been observed sawing off the ends of their rifle barrels. To this, though it was a singular circumstance, he gave but little thought, until it was explained to him on the day preceding the proposed council. Then a beautiful Ojibway maiden, who is said to have been enamored of Gladwin, came to his quarters, bringing a pair of moccasins she had at his request made from an elk-skin he had furnished. He was much delighted with her beautiful workmanship, praised it highly, and requested her to make him another pair from the remainder of the peltry. She hesitated, but after a time took the skin and departed.

But she did not at once leave the fort. She lingered long about the entrance, as if uncertain whether to go or stay, until her continued hesitation attracted the attention of the sentry on duty. Who knows what struggle was then going on in the bosom of this simple child of nature —what balancing between fidelity to her race and love for the pale-face chief, whose lawful bride could not be an Indian maiden? The question of the soldier, why she was waiting, brought her to a sudden decision. Quickly she turned, and entered again the quarters of Gladwin. Holding out the pelt to him, she said, "I cannot take it; I cannot make you the moccasins."

"Why not?" he asked. "Why refuse me so small a favor?"

"Because I may not be able to bring them to you," she answered; and then, in reply to some further questions, she disclosed Pontiac's meditated treachery. Sixty of his bravest warriors had filed off the barrels of their rifles so they might be hidden under their blankets, and thus armed they would come to the council on the morrow. At a given signal from Pontiac they were to massacre the commandant, and then fall upon and slaughter the garrison, who, taken unarmed and unawares, would be able to make but fee-

THE DEPOT AT NIGHT.

ble resistance. The knives had been already sharpened to take the scalps of the Englishmen.

Pontiac had fought on the side of the French during the war which ended three years before; but he had since been on terms of close amity with the English; and, moreover, was, to all appearance, too noble a savage to be guilty of deliberate treachery. But the warning of the Indian maiden was explicit, and only a fool stops his ears at the sound of danger. Gladwin had but a slender garrison of one hundred and thirty men, and Pontiac had two thousand warriors within the sound of his rifle. The odds were terrific; but the commandant did not shut his gates upon the savages. He met them, as Pontiac proposed, in friendly council; but was prepared to officiate, in case of treachery, at an extensive Indian funeral.

On the following day—May 9, 1763— Pontiac came to the fort with sixty warriors, each having his blanket about him. Precisely at the hour appointed he entered the north gate—about where the First National Bank of Detroit is now located— and at the head of his warriors moved along a street lined on both sides with glittering ranks of redcoats, while at various points polished brass cannon glowered down upon him. At every corner he saw groups of fur traders, armed to the teeth, and every few seconds heard the measured tap of a drum, betokening warlike preparation. Astonished at the unexpected display, he was at first morose and silent; but after a few moments he turned to Gladwin and said, "Why do I see so many of my father's young men standing in the streets with their guns?" He was told it was a custom of the English at the reception of distinguished guests; and then, stately and silent, he moved on to the council-house.

Here, his warriors seated in a circle about him, he rose, and holding in his hand a belt of wampum that was to have given the fatal signal, he made to Gladwin a fervid harangue, professing great friendship to the English. But he did not give the concerted signal, and he finally sat down amid the silent astonishment of his Indians. Then Gladwin approached him, and lifting the corner of his blanket, under which his rifle was concealed, charged him with his treachery, adding that this one breach of faith would be overlooked, but swift vengeance would follow another act of duplicity or aggression. The council then suddenly broke up, the Indians hastily retired, and the Pontiac war followed.

I am persuaded there is more truth in this tradition than in much that has been written of the "queenly Pocahontas"; and if this were all that is told of the beautiful Ojibway maiden, she might be enshrined in history with Nancy Ward, the prophetess of the Cherokees. But tradition adds that she took to fire-water, and one day, when unduly under its influence, fell into a vat of boiling maple syrup, and so perished ingloriously. Alas, that so much fidelity and loveliness should come to an end in a kettle of hot molasses!

Detroit now underwent a fifteen months' siege, during which Gladwin and his men performed feats of genuine heroism. The most unfortunate event that occurred during its progress was the slaughter of Captain Dalzell, who, with a small force, had imprudently ventured from the fort to attack the Indians. He was ambushed and massacred by Pontiac near a large white-wood-tree, which still stands, not far from the centre of the city—the only remaining memorial of those years of havoc and bloodshed. If that old tree were endowed with the faculty of speech, what a tale it might tell of the heroism of the men who there, on the outer ramparts, gave up their lives for civilization!

Ten years of peace now followed, during which Detroit grew rapidly in population and prosperity. Under British enterprise it became the emporium of a vast trade in furs, and the wealth that gives leisure for cultivation soon brought its best society to a condition of refinement which rivalled that of the seaboard cities. The rough Indian trader was there, scarcely more refined than the untutored savage; but mingling with him was the cultured British officer, and the aristocratic French resident who had become rich by trade and the growth in value of his landed possessions. The extent of the trade in furs, considering that it was conducted over the lakes eastward altogether in birch-bark canoes, was a thing that strikes us with astonishment. When the English took possession, in 1760, they found on storage here furs of the value of half a million dollars; and soon the trade so increased that as many as two hundred thousand beaver-skins were shipped in a single year. Crowds of Indians, in their brightly painted bark canoes, were constantly coming and going upon the river, bringing the peltries of the deer, the otter, and the beaver, and carrying away the numerous articles of civilized production which they received in exchange; for all trade was barter. Often these gaudy craft completely lined the river bank, and the vicinity of the fort soon became the mart of a thriving commerce. The canoes were both shop

ON LAKE ST. CLAIR.

and dwelling-house for the aborigines. In them, turned bottom up, and slightly canted to one side to allow of an easy entrance, whole families lived by day and lodged by night—the copper-colored brave and his dusky mate, with the small pappoose strapped to a board upon her back, and an indefinite number of "little Injun boys" rolling in the sand at her feet, clad only in a raiment of bear's-grease to protect them from the swarms of insects that infested the quarters. Here the head of the house displayed his wares—peltries, baskets, brooms, mats, and moccasins—and exhibited a keenness at bargaining fully equal to that of his more civilized white brother. Lovers of the picturesque, no doubt, enjoyed this traffic, if not over-fastidious in the matter of dirt.

The war of the Revolution followed, during which Detroit became the centre of British operations in the West. No one locality in the East was the scene of so great activity, or witnessed so much of the horror and barbarity of war. But into the details of this period we would

not now enter. At this time, when she is harassed by foes without and within, we would speak only kindly and lovingly of our great mother across the water. She planted civilization on this continent, and she is destined to carry it around the globe, whoever and whatever may attempt to stay her progress. An irresistible moral force, her work is the uplifting of the race, and she will do this work unless the world goes backward. This is her "manifest destiny"; and if she did not see it as soon as we, it was not her fault, but that of her king and his ministers. The man the British kept in command at Detroit during the first half of the war, though born on British soil, was no true Englishman. He was a human tiger, delighting in blood, and letting loose upon the defenceless border settlements the savage knife and tomahawk, till the old council-house was piled high with the scalps of his own kindred. But he met his Nemesis in George Rogers Clark, who came upon him on March 5, 1779, when he was intrenched with a much larger force at Vincennes, and forced him to an unconditional surrender. Sent into Virginia, he was put into irons by Thomas Jefferson, and only escaped hanging through the intercession of Washington. He was finally paroled, but never afterward was a factor in the war.

A better specimen of an Englishman was Colonel Arent Schuyler De Peyster, who succeeded Hamilton in command at Detroit. He had a difficult task to perform, for the whole French population sympathized with the revolted colonies;

but he executed it with such tact, discretion, and kindness that he won "golden opinions from all sorts of people." He was constantly harassed by secret foes and open enemies—the most powerful among the latter being the indefatigable George Rogers Clark, the one dream of whose life was the capture of this stronghold. Failing in this, Clark went to a drunkard's grave, and so missed a niche in our history alongside of John Sevier and Isaac Shelby. That he failed was owing altogether to the military skill and untiring vigilance of Colonel De Peyster.

De Peyster was a thorough Englishman, though born in New York, and belonging to an old Huguenot family. He was a man of fine cultivation, and, with his accomplished lady, gave a high tone to the Detroit society of that period. After the close of the war he settled in Scotland, and became the friend of Burns, who in 1796 was a private in his regiment of Dumfries Volunteers. It was to him that Burns addressed his "Poem on Life":

> "My honored colonel, deep I feel
> Your interest in the poet's weal;
> Ah! now sma' heart hae I to speel
>   The steep Parnassus,
> Surrounded thus by bolus pill
>   And potion glasses."

De Peyster was himself a poet of some pretensions, having conducted a rhyming correspondence with Burns, and published a volume of poems.

Though a far-inland town, Detroit had, even then, the manners of the seaboard, and its fashions were those of the London and Paris of the period—somewhat late, however, to allow of a ninety days' sail from Europe, and a two months' paddle up the Mohawk and across Lake Erie. The ladies wore dresses with long skirts and short waists and still shorter sleeves, and quite as often veiled their faces as their bosoms; while the gentlemen went in shovel hats and powdered periwigs, with silk hose and knee-breeches, ornamented with broad buckles. On festive occasions, which were numerous even in the midst of the war, there was no end to the display of silk and satin gowns and gold-bespangled shoes, and costly jewels glittered in the slow and stately dance that moved through the richly furnished drawing-rooms with the solemn precision of a funeral. This was among the upper classes. The more democratic citizen went

> "In coat, no dainty cloth of France,
> Bedizened with extravagance,
> But shaped of blanket, black or blue,
> Though not unknown the scarlet hue.'
> Bound were the cuffs and pocket flap
> With fur sufficient for a cap,
> And on the collar too enough
> To make his wife a stylish muff,
> While moccasins of caribou
> Covered his feet instead of shoe.
> Gartered about his knees were seen
> Leggings of baize of lively green;
> His blanket wrapper 'twas polite
> To mention by the name of white,
> For though through darkening hues it went,
> 'Twas only time or accident;
> His mighty buck or woollen mittens
> Would hold at least a brace of kittens;
> And when he sought to cut a dash,
> He girt him with a crimson sash,
> And crowned his long and curling locks
> With spoil of woodchuck, 'coon, or fox,
> While o'er his shoulders broad the tail
> Streamed like a comet on the gale."*

The town at this time, though a century old, contained only about three hundred houses, one-half of which are supposed to have been within the stockade. A census taken July 20, 1782, shows that it had then a permanent population of 2190, 178 of whom were slaves; but a numbering of the people made in 1796 gave it only 500. This large falling off is to be attributed to the withdrawal of the British garrison and the exodus of English people which occurred with the change of government, many of them then leaving to found Amherstburg, a village lower down the river, in Upper Canada. Some Englishmen remained, but the larger portion of the citizens were now of French descent, speaking the language and clinging to the customs of their forefathers.

Soon afterward a considerable number of French immigrants arrived; but no settlers from the Eastern States came to Detroit till 1805, when a few families fixed their abode here; but they do not seem to have been accorded a very cordial welcome by either the French or English residents. The former had sympathized with the colonists in their struggle with the mother country, but they appear to have liked the Yankees best when they were at a comfortable distance. However, the latter did not thrust themselves upon the frontier settlement, being probably deterred not so much by a natural diffidence of character as by the conviction that the place was forever cut off from the seaboard by the Falls of Niagara, and consequently was no suitable field for

* Judge James V. Campbell, of Detroit.

Yankee enterprise. For "Clinton's Folly"—as the Erie Canal was termed—had not then so much as entered the dreams of its great originator.

Between 1805 and 1825—when the canal was completed—Detroit seems to have taken a Rip Van Winkle nap, during which it actually shrank in vital proportions. A census taken October 1, 1805, shows that it then had 525 heads of families—equivalent to a total population of at least 2000, while one taken as late as 1828 gives it only 1517. However, the case was not exactly one of suspended animation. It was simply a cessation of growth and shrinkage of integument, occasioned by two unfortunate occurrences—a destructive fire, and the infliction upon the town and territory of the most anomalous government ever known in this country.

In the summer of 1825 cannon planted at intervals along the line of the Erie Canal, all the way from Albany to Buffalo, announced that Clinton's great work was completed, and the West married to

FORT STREET PRESBYTERIAN CHURCH.

the East by a bond that is indissoluble. Its gates were no sooner opened than a tide of emigration set through them westward. Soon all over New England and eastern New York whole families, and in some instances whole hamlets, were on the move, and such an exodus followed as never was seen except when the Israelites came up out of Egypt, and the Kalmucks fled across the steppes of Asia. At one time it seemed that rural New England would be depopulated. Its best and youngest blood joined in the exodus; and to this fact may be traced the high character and wonderful enterprise of the West of to-day. The first wave rested for a while in western New York, and then the gathering tide swept gradually westward along the lakes and the Ohio,

and finally, in 1830, it touched the shores of Michigan. Then for the first time Detroit became in reality an American town.

In the beginning of 1830 Detroit numbered 2222 people; that is, it stood precisely where it was in 1805; and this during a quarter of a century when the population of the country generally had increased in a ratio altogether unparalleled in history. But now the old town began to feel the general impetus. It increased fourfold in the next ten years; and thus it has gone on ever since, doubling about every decade, till now it numbers, with its suburbs, fully 200,000 souls.

The acorn bears no sort of resemblance to the oak, and yet its great trunk, broad leaves, and wide-spreading branches are all enclosed in the little bowl which lies

at our feet, waiting to be fed by the juices of the earth, and invigorated by the sunshine. So in the dead-alive old French-English town we have been considering was enfolded the great city one sees now, from the dome of its City Hall stretching miles away in stately rows of brick and stone, along broad shaded avenues which branch from a central hub like the spokes of some great cart wheel. The slow-paced conservatism of its old-time residents is still seen in the modern city; but it is now so wedded to Yankee enterprise that we meet here an almost ideal community, safe but progressive, not engrossed in mere money-getting, but cultivating as well the social amenities of life, and extracting from existence, as it passes, a healthful and rational enjoyment. In proportion to its size, Detroit has a smaller foreign population than any city in the Union, and as the bulk of its people are of Eastern birth or extraction, it is to-day more truly New England in character

EXAMPLES OF DETROIT ARCHITECTURE.

than the good town of Boston itself. In no sense is it a Western town. In 1880 the numerical centre of the Union was found to be fifty-eight miles west of Cincinnati. With the speed at which population is now travelling westward, Detroit will soon be the central city of the country.

The great fire of 1805 was a present calamity but a future blessing to Detroit, for it enabled the town to escape from narrow lanes into broad open avenues stretching straight as an arrow in all directions. Those old dead and gone worthies did not, perhaps, forecast the future; but, if they did not, they planned " better than they knew," for they laid out the new town on lines that only needed to be filled up and extended to make a future city of regular yet picturesque beauty. This will strike any one who ascends to the roof of the City Hall and looks down upon the straight, symmetrical streets, crossed every now and then by broad, branching avenues. But what will surprise him most will be the great array of fine dwellings and palatial public edifices he will see in every direction. On none of the latter has so much money been squandered as on the Capitol at Albany;

but in number and uniform elegance they are not equalled by the public buildings of any city of similar size in the Union. The same remark applies generally to the private dwellings. Long vistas of West Fort Street and Jefferson and Woodward avenues are merely rows of private palaces, overhung with great trees, and seated amid beautiful grounds that are parks in miniature. Beauty, too, is blended with use in the business portions of the city. Some of the warehouses are superb structures; and Griswold Street, the financial centre, is as far in advance of State Street in Boston and Wall Street in New York as our time is of the last century. This street, beginning at the High School, and running to the river, where at the dock are moored fleets of vessels, is occupied almost exclusively by lawyers and bankers; and this has led a recent writer to apply to it the rhyme of Horace Smith:

"At the top of the street the attorneys abound,
  And down at the bottom the barges are found.
Fly, Honesty, fly to some safer retreat,
  For there's craft in the river and craft in the street."

If the observer should climb the two hundred steps that lead to the cupola of the City Hall, he would be nearly as many

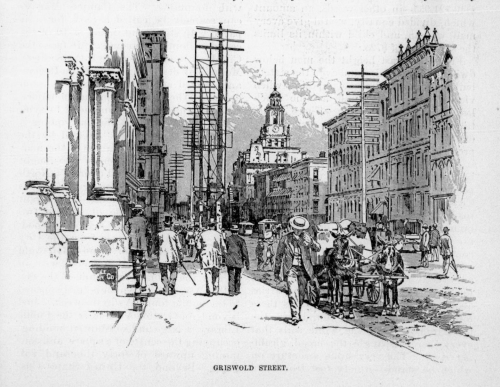

GRISWOLD STREET.

feet from the ground, and looking down from this height, he would be lost in wonder at the extent of the view, and the evidences everywhere apparent of wealth and enterprise. Whichever way he might turn, he would encounter a striking prospect. A broad panorama would be spread out below and around him—the wide river, the distant lake of St. Clair, the opposite Dominion of Canada, and the widely expanded city, extending for miles in all directions. At his very feet he would behold a vast hive of human activity—great throngs surging through the spacious streets, hundreds of furnaces belching their thick smoke to the sky, shrieking trains threading their rapid way upon the outskirts, and in the distance countless white-winged craft going and coming on the island-dotted river. Figures, it is said, do not lie; nevertheless they seldom give us as vivid ideas as the sight of the eye. And yet we may form a vague conception of the commerce of Detroit when we are told that 6000 steam and sailing vessels, manned by crews numbering 22,000 men, come and go here in a single year; and we may conceive of the wealth of the town if we understand that the assessed value of its real and personal property in 1884 was $110,721,955—in other words, an amount which, divided equally, would give every man, woman, and child within its limits the snug sum of $728.

From this vast height the men below dwindle into pigmies, and even the stately buildings, which look so imposing when viewed from the ground, assume much less striking proportions. There is nothing like a distant view to strip things of their individual magnitude. It is the prospect of the eagle when he looks down in his lofty flight and thinks upon the insignificance of man and all his puny belongings. But the dome of the Detroit City Hall is not as high up as the eagle soars, and hence the observer there catches none of the lordly bird's impressions of the littleness of human things. On the contrary, he is amazed at the evidences he everywhere sees of the mighty forces that are ever at work in the brain of man, pent up in the little globe which he carries about under his beaver. He sees these forces in the palatial buildings, the thronging avenues, the white sails that everywhere bespangle the broad, gleaming river. The very stone structure on which he stands—ninety feet front, two

hundred deep, and two hundred again to the top of its flag-staff—by the patient might of man has grown up in two hundred years from the rude log citadel where Cadillac housed his men, and Hamilton stored his human scalps, bought at so much per head, till piled so high that a tall man could not reach to their summit. Other evidences of human enterprise and energy lie below, and it may not be amiss to give them a few moments' consideration.

However, the first and most agreeable things that strike the eye are not the work of man, but of nature. These are the numerous small parks that everywhere dot the landscape—oases of green in a wide waste of brick and stone. One of these, and the most beautiful, the Grand Circus, is adorned with two fine fountains, and located in the very heart of the city. Here the tired citizen comes of sultry nights, and in the spray-laden air finds refreshing coolness. This park is semicircular, and divided into two parts by Woodward Avenue, and from it all the principal streets radiate. The avenues often intersect the streets at oblique angles, and wherever they do are smaller parks, triangular in form, and frequently adorned with fountains. The Campus Martius can scarcely be called a park, for it is paved with stone, and in the midst of the ceaseless hum of business. It faces the City Hall, and in its centre is the Soldiers' Monument, designed by Randolph Rogers, and erected at a cost of sixty thousand dollars. The figure of the Indian maiden which surmounts it is intended to symbolize the State, and the inscription it bears tells that it was "Erected by the people of Michigan in honor of the martyrs who fell and the heroes who fought in defence of Liberty and Union." North of this monument, and facing the Campus Martius, is the Opera-house—an elegant stone structure capable of seating two thousand persons. Glancing along Woodward Avenue, one block from the City Hall, is seen, at the north end of Griswold Street, the imposing High School, with, in its rear, the valuable museum of the Scientific Association, which is freely opened to the public four days in the week. Just beyond, on Gratiot Avenue, is the Public Library, a large and substantial building, occupying the centre of a square, and containing upward of forty thousand volumes. Beyond, the United States Cus-

FOUNTAIN IN THE GRAND CIRCUS.

tom-house, a large and fine building on Griswold Street, is the Michigan Central Depot, twelve hundred and fifty feet long and one hundred and two wide, with a self-supporting iron roof covering a space which is but a single room; and near it stands a grain-elevator, with a cupola that resembles the tower of a cathedral. The largest church edifice to be seen is the Roman Catholic cathedral; but there are many fine specimens of church architecture, one of which is shown in our illustration of the Fort Street Presbyterian Church.

No less than fifty miles of street railway diverge from the City Hall, and thread every portion of the city. The longest of these is the Fort Wayne line, which extends to the large fortification which now defends Detroit. The works enclose sixty-five acres, and there are

WALTER HARPER.

NANCY MARTIN.

none more substantial in the country. Near the foot are the water-works, of which a view is given on page 344. Everywhere the observer sees evidence of business enterprise and wealth almost without limit, and as he turns away to descend again to the solid earth, it may be that he will exclaim, "Surely there can here be no poverty." But should he think this, he would be mistaken. There is great wealth here, but it is not divided equally, and here, as elsewhere, are rich and poor. "As towns grow, beggars multiply," and even in Yankee towns there is poverty, and this not for the reason that Yankees are idle and thriftless, but because there are some evils inseparable from our present civilization which naturally entail want and wretchedness. We must go back to barbarism if we would have none

THE HARPER HOSPITAL.

who hunger and thirst, no naked to clothe, no sick or aged to relieve, and no prisoners to visit. In that happy state nakedness is the normal condition, the sick are left to die without the aid of doctors, and the aged are knocked on the head to help them to the hereafter. Detroit has poor, but its people have read the twenty-fifth chapter of Matthew. Last year they relieved 3569 persons, at a total expenditure of $27,429 77. It has also sick and aged and orphaned young, and for these it has provided numerous asylums, a Home for the Friendless, and various other institutions, the most notable among which is the Harper Hospital, which owes its existence to

of the poor should be taught, free of charge, the industrial arts. It does this on a large scale, and its whole working has been most satisfactory.

Within a month from the making of Mr. Harper's magnificent gift the hos-

DISTANT VIEW OF BELLE ISLE PARK.

the munificence of a benevolent but eccentric gentleman, who twenty-five years ago endowed it with his entire worldly possessions, on the curious condition that the city should pay him during his life an annuity of $2000. This, in the course of five years, he voluntarily reduced to $600. The hospital was to be not only a home for the sick, but a school where the youth

pital received a similar endowment, and on similar terms, from a Mrs. Martin, familiarly known as Nancy Martin, who at the time kept a vegetable stand in the market. She gave it all her property—

UNITED STATES SHIP-CANAL ON LAKE ST. CLAIR.

valued at the time at $15,000—with the stipulation that a small house should be built for her at an expense of $450, and she be allowed an annuity of $600. She is said to have been originally a coarse, rough-spoken woman, who, on occasions, had been known to "swear like a trooper," but the sweet influences of charity soon softened her manners. She relinquished her stand in the market, became more mild and womanly, and in 1875 died in the "full odor of sanctity." The property which these two persons thus donated is now valued at over $200,000, and the building erected upon it is probably the finest devoted to similar uses west of the Hudson. In its reception-room hang the portraits of its honored founders, Walter Harper and Nancy Martin.

The most extensive of the city's parks is situated just outside of the corporate limits, in mid-channel of the beautiful river. It comprises seven hundred acres—the whole of

Entrance to Fort Wayne.

the island of Belle Isle—and is destined to rival the Central Park of New York in rural magnificence. Seven hundred thousand dollars have already been expended upon it, and "the end is not yet." A distant view of it may be obtained from the Detroit shore, but the visitor will most probably take one of the small steamers which are constantly plying up and down the river for a nearer inspection, and in that case he would no doubt prolong his

The Water Works.

trip as far as Put-in-Bay, where Perry defeated the British squadron, and paved the way for the recapture of Detroit by Harrison and Isaac Shelby. If the trip should be on a moonlit night, it would be all the more enjoyable. Scattered through the whole course of the stream, at intervals of not more than a mile, are islands ranging in size from one acre to several thousand acres, and altogether the scenery is excelled in beauty by that of no other river, except it may be the St. Lawrence. One of the largest islands is named Grosse Isle, on which is the light-house shown in the engraving on page 332. On this island Pontiac had a summer residence, and it is a favorite resort for Detroit people in hot weather.

Probably nothing so truthfully reflects the intelligence and moral character of a city as its public journals. The press is at once the creator and reflex of public opinion, and a newspaper of high moral tone cannot long exist in a degraded community. Judged by its public journals, Detroit must therefore be a city of high moral and intellectual character. Nowhere in the country is there a press of greater ability, or one that treats current issues with more calmness and dignity, or less of acrimony and personality. Some of the journals are strongly partisan; but they conduct their controversies with courtesy—handle polished weapons with the skill and address of gentlemen. The personal relations of the leading editors are also said to be of the most friendly character; and this must be so if an anecdote current in regard to two of the most prominent of the fraternity be at all veracious. One of them, it is said, when jaded with his daily work, sent to his opposition neighbor to help him out with an editorial, saying to his Irish messenger, somewhat figuratively, "Ask him to oblige me with about half a gill of editorial." The servant repeated the message literally, when the opposition editor coolly took from the wall of his sanctum the portrait of a certain long-eared quadruped, and told the man to present it to his master with his compliments.

"But it's not that his honor is axing for, sir," answered the Hibernian. "He is wanting an editorial, and not a pictur of the editor."

The principal journals publish the news of the world at the same hour that it appears in the seaboard cities, and some of them are extensively circulated. One—the Free Press—has had the enterprise to open a branch office and issue a weekly edition in London, where it has attained a circulation of 75,000 copies, owing, no doubt, very largely to its general character, but more especially to the articles of C. B. Lewis (better known as "M. Quad"), who is perhaps the most unique and gen-

uine humorist this country has produced, excepting only Artemus Ward and Hosea Biglow.

"M. Quad" is not a humorous "artist"— a boss mechanic who manufactures jokes as a carpenter does packing-boxes, with saw and jack-plane and much exudation

C. B. LEWIS ("M. QUAD").

of perspiration. He is naturally and spontaneously funny. Humor gushes from him like champagne from an uncorked bottle, bubbling and effusive, and drenching us, whether we will or not, with laughter. And there is wisdom with his wit—strong, homely common-sense mixed with a racy, unctuous humor which makes his wisdom as grateful to our taste as whale oil is to the palate of an Esquimau. He is not a "product of the soil," with a local flavor. He is of universal relish, as is witnessed by the wide popularity that the Detroit Free Press owes to his contributions.

It is not generally known when or where he was born, nor is it a matter of much consequence, since his career did not begin till he was blown up, some fifteen years ago, on an Ohio River steamboat. He is, perhaps, the only example of a man who has been lifted into fame by being tossed a hundred feet into the

THE SOLDIERS' MONUMENT.

air, and coming down, more dead than alive, to tell the story. He did this. Standing at his printer's case, when he was so far recovered as to limp about, he put into type "How it feels to be blown up," and the whole West burst into laughter. That laugh made "M. Quad" famous. He was then transferred from the composing-room to the editorial department, and ever since short extracts from the *Free Press* have been copied into every journal throughout the country.

About ten years ago he invented—or rather created—"His Honor," and "Bijah," and "Brother Gardner," of the "Lime-kiln Club"—characters totally dissimilar, but each as natural, original, individual, and ludicrous as any in American literature. "His Honor" presides over a police court, and makes sage reflections upon men and things as they come into his field of view. "Brother Gardner" is a shrewd and quaint gentleman of color, who has all the idioms and characteristics of his race, but is not a burlesque of our colored fellow-citizens; he handles his own people gently, but satirizes the foibles, frailties, and weaknesses of the whites inimitably. His say-

ings might be termed explosive wisdom— the reader is sure to imbibe a wise thought, but it is certain to explode within him. "Artemus Ward" created one character; "M. Quad" has given birth to three, and each one has, during a period of ten years, given delight to millions.

The man is precisely what we are led to expect from his writings. He is by turns "His Honor," "Bijah," and "Brother Gardner," with the dry humor and quaint wisdom that is peculiar to each character. "If there is an odder man than he in the country," said a Detroit gentleman to me not long ago, "we would like to have him sent along with the circus." His looks, his manner, even the tones of his voice, are peculiar and eccentric. He talks as he writes, and always without any seeming premeditation. His "den," as he calls his "sanctum," in an upper story of the *Free Press* building, is a curiosity shop filled with odd mementos and knick-knacks. Here is a bit of rope that helped to hang a murderer, and a pair of shackles of the old slave time; there are bullets from Gettysburg, powder-flasks from the *Merrimac*, and swords, sabres, muskets, and shot and shell from a score of battle-fields; while around the walls, side by side with portraits of Sheridan and Custer and busts of Grant and Lee, are pictures of a dozen of the most noted criminals. But the oddest thing in the room is a slender man of about forty, with close-cropped gray hair, heavy mustache, keen, intent eyes, and an earnest, somewhat eager expression, who sits at an old-fashioned table, and looks up with a smile of welcome as a stranger enters his apartment. This is "M. Quad," known among his personal acquaintance as C. B. Lewis; and he works away at that table eight hours in a day, writing, at high pressure, short paragraphs or political leaders, and now and then seeking relaxation in a little merriment with "Bijah" and "Brother Gardner," for his best work is done as a relief from the daily drudgery of journalism.

The Revisers have not been able to amend the text, "Woe unto you when all men shall speak well of you," and if it is to be taken literally, "M. Quad" is in a bad way, as all his acquaintance unite in saying that he is temperate, social, domestic, kind-hearted, a lover of his friends, and a hater of nobody. He is also, they say, open-handed, and so given to charity that, though imposed upon sev-

en times in a day by fraudulent mendicancy, he again seven times in a day empties his pockets to the pleadings of distress. He is also said to be modest, and not at all puffed up by the fact that he has a weekly audience of a million, nearly one-half of whom are matter-of-fact Englishmen, who take him with their beefsteak and ale, as a sure help to a healthy digestion. He is spoken of as odd and eccentric, and that he may be, but I incline to the opinion that this peculiarity is due to the fact that Nature produced him in one of her genial moods, when she would do the world a kindly turn by bestowing upon it a gentle soul, who should do us good by spreading for us a wholesome feast of mingled wit and wisdom.

Considering its past progress—growing in fifty years from a town of 2000 people to a city of 200,000—it is not difficult to predict the future greatness of Detroit. It has all the elements of growth and stability—hereditary caution combined with a spirit of enterprise that is constantly pressing it onward and upward; and hence it cannot fail in another fifty years to take a front rank among American cities.

AT THE MARKET.

CATTLEYA MOSSIA ALBA.

ORCHIDS.

BY F. W. BURBIDGE, F.L.S.

SINCE the tulip-mania reached its height in the Netherlands until now, no one group of plants has taken such a firm hold on popular fancy as the orchids of to-day. Certainly other plants have enjoyed some celebrity both in England and America—cacti, ferns, roses, chrysanthemums, and palms—but orchids have represented to a great extent the horticultural respectability of our modern nineteenth-century gardens. So highly are these tropical epiphytes esteemed that on 12th May, 1885, an Orchid Conference was held in London, at which both trade and amateur cultivators met together to exhibit specimens, and to consider vital questions anent the culture and nomenclature of these lovely flowers. Botanically, the orchids belong to the petaloid division of the great endogenous group, and have a greater affinity with the *iris* than with any other common garden flower. From all other flowers they differ, however, in the total suppression of one or of two of their three anthers; their pollen for the most part is

in solid waxy masses; and one of their three inner petals is altered in shape and color, and is called the lip, its object being to attract and guide the visits of insects, which are, as a rule, necessary to fertilize these flowers. The history of orchids as popular decorative plants in Europe is a modern one. In the last edition of Miller's *Gardeners' Dictionary*, published in 1768, only thirty species of Epidendra were known in cultivation, and the great Chelsea gardener, whom Linnæus himself praised so highly as a cultivator, tells us that "as the plants cannot by any art yet known be cultivated in the ground, it would be to little purpose to enumerate them; although, could the plants be brought to thrive, many of them produce very fine flowers of uncommon forms." The earliest travellers who mention orchids are Kæmpfer (1712), who travelled in Japan, and Rumphius (1750), who visited Amboyna, while Hernandez casually mentions a few as curiosities in the quaint account of his voyage to Spanish America, and actually gives a rude wood-cut figure of the "Lynx Flower" (*Stanhopea tigrina*). Linnæus calculated that in all probability a hundred species of orchids would be found if the world was explored. Persoon, in 1807, enumerates 400 species, including the terrestrial kinds of Europe. In 1815 only 25 "air-plants" were cultivated at Kew, but Messrs. Loddige's catalogue, published in 1844, enumerates nearly 2000 species as then grown by them at Hackney, near London. In 1845 we find Lindley estimating the species at 3000, resolvable into about 400 genera. Coming down to our own era, Hooker and Bentham, in their stupendous *Genera Plantarum*, reduce the genera to 334, and at the very lowest estimate the species themselves may be placed at 10,000! The first epiphytal orchid to blossom in the Royal Gardens at Kew seems to have been *Epidendrum cochleatum*. This was in 1789, and in the following year another species, *E. fragrans*, opened its flowers. Until the year 1820 orchids were looked upon as curiosities in botanical gardens, but about that time some showy *Cattleyas* and other species produced their lovely flowers, and a more general interest was taken in their culture. Importations had been sent to Kew from India, the West Indies, and from Australia, and the Horticultural Society devoted a special hot-house to their culture at Chiswick, as had previously been done at Kew.

The wonderful *Epidendrums*, or "air-plants," as orchids generally were termed at this date, were much admired whenever they blossomed, but it was not until the Duke of Devonshire saw the Butterfly Orchid from Demerara in flower at a London exhibition that orchid culture commenced in real earnest amongst amateurs. The Duke was so delighted with the golden blossom, with its fluttering wings and long antennæ-like petals, that he set about forming a collection, and one of the first purchases was the white

CYPRIPEDIUM, OR "MOCCASIN FLOWER."

EPIDENDRUM PRISMATOCARPUM.

"Moth Orchid," from the Philippines, for which he paid one hundred guineas to the late Mr. Cuming, a noted plant collector. He also despatched the late Mr. John Gibson and other explorers to the East as collectors, and many species were thus introduced to the gardens at Chatsworth.

Harrison and Moss of Liverpool, Cattley of Barnet, Rucker of Wandsworth, Day of Tottenham, and Bateman of Knypersly were other amateurs who early took up orchid culture, and the tastefully illustrated works of the last-named, although mostly now out of print, are eagerly bought up second-hand at high prices for the sake of the beautiful hand-colored plates which they contain. After the Loddiges, the earliest trade growers in England were Messrs. Rollison, Veitch, Low, Williams, and Bull, all of London. Maule of Bristol, Backhouse of York, and more recently Messrs. Sander of St. Albans have imported many fine varieties. To the various botanical gardens rare species have been introduced from time to time, and at Kew, Manchester, Liverpool, Birmingham, Glasgow, Edinburgh, and Dublin the public of all classes can see and enjoy these curious tropical flowers; there are also small collections in the university gardens at Oxford and at Cambridge.

Orchid culture in the United States dates from about 1830, when Mr. John Wright Boott formed a small collection. This collection passed to John Amory Lowell, who was one of the first to exhibit orchids before the Massachusetts Horticultural Society. In 1854 Mr. Edward S. Rand purchased most of the best plants which had belonged to Mr. Lowell, and imported others from Europe from time to time. About 1865, however, Mr. Rand presented his collection to the botanical garden of the Harvard University at Cambridge. Mr. Thomas Hogg was one of the first to grow these plants near New York, and Mr. Isaac Buchanan, who had brought the first *Cattleya mossia* from London in 1840, grew a large number of species after Mr. Hogg's collection was broken up in 1856. Edward S. Rand, Jun., more recently grew a selection of these plants at Glen Ridge, and is also the author of a useful work on the culture of orchids in America. At the present time owners of orchid houses are so numerous in America that it would be useless trying to enumerate them, but the best trade collection is that of George Such, of South

LYCASTE.

Amboy, New Jersey, Messrs. Hovey, of Cambridge, and others having also good examples. It is a well-known fact in England that the best American growers are ever anxious to purchase good strong specimens of the rarest and most beautiful of orchids, old and new, and several English firms send over their representatives every season. Not only does Mr. Corning purchase largely from Europe, but he has directly imported many rare species from South America, having sent his own collectors there at considerable expense.

In 1881 a catalogue of Mr. Corning's collection was published, and it then consisted of about 700 species, many being in duplicate, and amongst them were some of the finest known varieties. No doubt at the present time both species and varieties are far more numerous.

On the continent of Europe the late M. Pescatore, of St. Cloud, near Paris, long ago cultivated a large collection, as also did the late Consul Schiller, of Hamburg, and the best trade collection for many years in Belgium was that of M. Linden, of Brussels, who years ago as a collector abroad introduced many rare South American plants. Orchids are naturally distributed all over the world, if we except the coldest and most arid regions, and they exist at all elevations from sea-level to 14,000 feet. Here in England we have many species of *ophrys* and *orchis*, the last common in the Avon meadows, and supposed to be the "Long Purples" of Shakespeare (*Hamlet*, act iv., scene 7).

DENDROBIUM NOBILE.

In America there are *Cypripediums*, or "Moccasin Flowers," in the woods, and tuberous-rooted species in the marshes, while one epiphyte, a kind of *Epidendrum*, is found growing on the branches of the glaucous-leaved magnolia in Texas.* The distribution of orchids is peculiarly erratic. Some genera are confined to a limited area; others, like the *Cypripediums*, are found scattered throughout Europe, Asia, and America. Even a solitary species may be as eccentric as a whole family. Thus, for example, near Bantry Bay, in the south of Ireland, grows a tiny lit-

* Those interested in the native terrestrial orchids of America will find in *The Orchids of New England*, or in the Flora of Asa Gray or that of T. Meehan, full information concerning them.

tle plant called the "Proliferous Ladies'-Tresses." Its existence there is limited to one or two wet, rushy meadows. It is known to botanists as *Spiranthes romanzoviana*, and has a three-ranked spire of sweet-scented white flowers. This particular plant is totally unknown in other parts of Ireland; it is not known in any other part of Europe, nor elsewhere in the whole world except in America, where it extends from the Atlantic to the Pacific coast. There are one or two Spanish plants found in the west of Ireland, and the American *Sisyrinchium anceps*, which now and then appears in that country, is accounted for as an immigrant with seed corn from America, but the existence of this little orchid in Ireland is a puzzle to students of geographical distribution.

Beautiful as are the ground orchids of Europe and America, it is only in the tropics that the plants of this order reach their highest development. In the great primeval forests near the equator the orchids generally cease growing in the earth, and exist in the greatest profusion high up among the branches of the trees.

One of the earliest of generic names for epiphytal orchids was *Epidendrum*, in allusion to their tree-dwelling habits, and it is self-evident that the later name of *Dendrobium* is of similar derivation and meaning. Tree trunks in a Bornean forest rise straight and tall all around you, lianas and rattans stretch from bough to bough, or sweep upward from the ground in curves as graceful as those of a ship's rigging. You are on the floor of nature's cathedral, and the giant boles rise pillar-like all around, but where, you ask, are the orchids, since nothing but a few ferns and aroid leaves grow on the ground at your feet. The truth is that the orchids and the birds, the insects, and even the snakes and the monkeys, are on the tree-tops far above you, and you feel ridiculously small and helpless as you try to catch a glimpse of the flowers so far out of your reach. Above you is a whole world of flower life basking in the sunshine, and you envy the monkeys as they swing themselves rapidly out of sight among the leafy branches overhead. Some species are very anomalous in their mode of growth. For example, the Mexican *Cattleya citrina* naturally hangs head downward, and but rarely succeeds in our hot-houses except so grown. At least two epiphytal species, viz., *Angræcum funale* and *Aerides tænale*, are absolutely *leafless*, all the usual leaf-work being carried on by the chlorophyl which exists in their band or thong like roots. Adaptive as all vegetation is now known to be under various local or climatic surroundings, we have but few examples of adaptability more striking than are these two leafless orchids. Low's "Moth Orchid" (*Phalænopsis*), which naturally exists on exposed limestone rocks in Moulmein, constantly loses its leaves during the dry monsoon every year, and even other leafy species of this genus are remarkable for the extreme vitality which exists in their fleshy roots. One of the most recent horticultural discoveries, indeed, is that, under certain conditions, the exposed roots of these "Moth Orchids" may develop adventitious buds, which in their turn produce young plants.

Remembering that the majority of tropical orchids are "tree-dwellers," or true epiphytes, the question why they are so naturally arises. In tropical countries, where heat and moisture are excessive, tree growth is rapid, and most of the trees themselves are both umbrageous and evergreen, hence it follows that all low-

MASDEVALLIA DENISONIANA.

growing plants which mainly depend on sunshine for life and strength to reproduce themselves must do one of two things, *i. e.*, either adapt themselves to the shade below, or climb to the tree-tops. Many palms, figs, and aroids actually do this by lengthening their slender stems. In cold countries the honeysuckle, or hedge-clematis, in fact, all climbing and

ODONTOGLOSSUM.

branches and into the light and sunshine, where they vegetate freely, while those which fall to the ground below are lost. The orchid-hunter abroad must face many difficulties, and often carries his life in his hand, so to speak. However successful he may be, he also runs peculiar risks which those at home can scarcely realize. In order to discover new species he must often venture where no white man's foot has been before, and must consider himself fortunate if hunger and thirst or bodily fatigue are the only difficulties he meets with. At one time drenched to the skin, at another scorched by a tropic sun, bitten by mosquitoes and jungle leeches, or stricken by fever, he must never relinquish his object. Dangerous routes must be traversed, often with the most faithless natives as guides, swollen rivers must be crossed, and all the risks from climate and wild animals and reptiles be taken as a mere matter of course, and sometimes a long and tedious journey is made only to find that a rival has been before you. As an illustration of disappointments of this kind, a collector in Ibague told me the following story:

"I was on the track of a rare *Cattleya*, and stopped that night at a little road-side posada, and for once in South America I fell among people who were the reverse of thieves. At sunrise I was awakened by a sturdy old rooster, and soon found my

trailing plants, act in the same way; but the orchids, ferns, and bromeliads seldom adopt this mode of growth. True, one curious Burmese orchid (*Erythrorchis scandens*) grows up trees to a height of fifty to one hundred feet, as do its relatives the "Vanilla" orchids; but these few exceptions only prove the rule that most orchids are comparatively dwarf and tufted in habit, and owe their elevated position to the fact that their seeds are light and easily carried upward among the

PHALÆNOPSIS SCHILLERIANA.

way outside the hut. A few minutes'
walk through the little compound brought
me to the forest I had ridden so far to explore. I followed a little path evidently
used by the residents, and soon reached a
water-fall tumbling over a mossy rock.
On a little low tree before me I suddenly
saw a sight I shall never forget—a *Cattleya*
of the most lovely flesh tints flashing and
fluttering in the early sunlight. The
gnarled old dwarf of a tree was completely
covered with plants of all sizes, and nearly
all were in bloom. The plants were in all
positions, firmly held by great thong-like
roots to the rough bark. My first resolve
was to go back and bring assistance to
cut down the tree and secure the plants.
What an act of sacrilege it seemed! No;
I would go back to breakfast first. A
morning's walk in a New Granadian forest alive with birds and insects, when every twig and leaf is dripping with dew,
is an experience no pen could describe.
Elated by my good fortune, and invigorated by the fresh air, I made short work of
my breakfast. I congratulated myself on

being the only collector who had ever seen this part of the country, when, chancing to turn my head, I was surprised to see a straight-limbed European with a troop of native followers entering the forest. 'Who is that?' said I to my man Pedro. 'Gentleman look for tree plant, sir.' Alas! it was too true; while I flattered myself that I was the only collector within a hundred leagues, here was a man who had lived for a whole week on the spot, and hearing of my arrival, he (as he afterward told me) only waited for the sun to lick up the dew a little ere he went to fetch in the *Cattleya* plants off the little tree which I fancied I had discovered this morning, but which he had really seen and purchased from a native a week ago. The plant was *Cattleya gigas*, and I often wonder under whose glass roof those identical plants are living now."

My own experience of orchids abroad is confined to the Eastern tropics, but some little time ago I was introduced to Mr. ——, a very successful South American plant collector, at a friend's house, and remembering the injunction about "gathering roses" when one may, and something about haymaking when the sun is shining, I made friends with him at once. He is a strongly built man, of forty-five, perhaps, rather above medium height, with piercing eyes and dark hair and beard. The company were on the lawn, and so I handed him a cigar, with the remark,

"Been on the Andes, I hear?"

"Thanks. Yes."

"Mining business good now."

"In some parts, yes; but I was collecting orchids, not silver."

"Ah! orchids; valuable things, now; good as gold—eh?"

"Well, you see, the thing has been overdone a bit lately; buyers are getting very cautious, and only the really good kinds pay."

"Were you up the Amazon?"

"No; I was on the Magdalena, in Bogota, Pamplona, Frontino, and Ocaña."

"Many good things in Ocaña?"

"Yes; *Odontoglossum pescatorei, O. triumphans*, and *O. phalænopsis* are among the best."

"Any bad species?"

"Yes; *O. lindleyanum*."

"And where is Ocaña?—on the western Andes?"

"Oh no; on the eastern Cordilleras. On the western side, near Frontino, *O.*

phalænopsis is replaced by *O. vexillarium, O. roezli*, and *O. warscewiczi*."

"And is there much variety among orchids of the same species abroad?"

"Oh, immense! You see, they all come from self-sown seeds, and vary as much as Chinese primulas."

"Do they hybridize abroad?"

"Now and then only a few hybrids occur between *O. pescatorei* and *O. triumphans* or *O. lindleyanum;* but between *O. alexandræ* and *O. gloriosum* there are many seedling forms; the *Cattleyas* are, however, really the most variable, and no doubt intercross naturally more frequently than most orchids."

"Where did you find *Cattleyas* most plentiful?"

"On the western Andes—Ibague, for example—where *C. aurea* and *C. gigas* are found, and near where *C. trianæ* exists in great variety."

"And you think this extreme variety due to cross-breeding?"

"Certainly."

"And what is your opinion of their specific names?"

"Well, I am only a collector; my botany is of a very practical kind; but one might just as reasonably make species of the varieties of British ferns, or of the seedling varieties of florists' flowers, as of these wild seedling *Cattleyas*."

"Where do you collect *O. alexandræ*?"

"In Bogota."

"Is it a mountain district?"

"Oh yes. *Odontoglossums* and *Masdevallias* generally are only found on the mountains at from 5000 feet to 10,000 feet elevation."

"Much rain there?"

"It comes down in torrents. At Bogota there is always rain; even in what is called the dry season there is more or less rain, and, what is nearly as bad, a thick, drizzling mist as dense as a London fog comes on at night and drenches every leaf with dew. About seven or eight o'clock in the morning, or, say, a couple of hours after sunrise, this mist 'lifts'—rises, in fact, like a muslin curtain—and floats away toward the mountaintops. Even as late as 11 o'clock A.M. my boys were drenched to the skin in five minutes after commencing their work of collecting amongst the trees."

"But I had thought these *Odontoglossums* grew on wet rocks."

ONCIDIUM PAPILIO.

"Some do so. *O. coronarium*, for example, and also *O. miniatum*."

"Are these rock-dwellers all found together?"

"Oh no. *O. coronarium* is found on dripping rocks on the eastern Andes; *O. miniatum* apparently represents it upon the western side."

"Sun or shade?"

"Both, but finest in the shade of thin, overhanging branches. *O. coronarium* creeps for yards on the rocks, producing enormous pseudo-bulbs and large leaves, the branching flower-spikes being two feet high, and bearing from twenty to forty great glossy brown flowers."

"And which are the 'tree-dwellers,' or epiphytes, among these *Odontoglossums*?"

"*O. alexandræ* and others grow upon trees of all sizes, sometimes clustering along the branches quite thickly just where the seed has fallen; at other times they occur solitary or in scattered groups.　In some cases where odd bulbs or decayed portions of masses had been thrown away by former collectors I found them growing quite freely, and making fine young growth as they lay loose upon the wet earth beneath the trees."

"Is *O. alexandræ* found most frequently in sun or in shade ?"

"Well, of course the seed blows everywhere, and I always thought the plants were finest where overhanging branches threw a light, flickering shade over them at mid-day.　I am sure that *O. alexandræ* enjoys sunshine, and would like much more than it generally gets in European gardens, and also more fresh air, especially at night."

"Would you, then, recommend an *Odontoglossum* house to be unshaded in our climate ?"

"Well, no; you see, a glass roof alters the case so much; but

LÆLIA PRÆSTANS.

with a thin canvas roof I am sure they would enjoy all our sunlight and our chilliest of summer nights with a good syringing after sundown."

"Do the plants ever suffer in the dry season ?"

"No; the heavy dews at night always are sufficient to keep their foliage fresh and green, even if no rain should fall for a few days.　That is why I have always recommended growers to syringe their *Odontoglossum* house at night, and to give more air than is generally done after sunset."

"Is there any fear of *O. alexandræ* and other species being exterminated by wholesale collecting, now that these orchids are so fashionable in Europe ?"

"I think not; a collector can cover only a comparatively small area, and there are tracts of country to which even the native collectors will not venture."

"Oh, then you employ native labor in collecting ?"

"Yes; a European could do but little unless he purchased his plants by the thousand from the natives. Of course, if novelty is desired, the white man must search the forest or mountain until he comes across a new plant to his fancy, and then he makes a bargain with the natives for as much as he wishes to secure."

"Is that the rule in collecting, then?"

"Yes; everywhere I have been, east or west, it is the same. In some places, as at Singapore, there is actually a sort of open market where *Phalœnopsids* and other East Indian orchids may be purchased, and in some parts of South America the newly arrived collector is pestered with natives desirous of selling him plants or of collecting them for him."

"Is it easy to collect the South American orchids—the *Odontoglossums*, I mean —from the trees? and how is it done?"

"Sometimes by the lasso (a cord, weighted at the end, thrown over and drawn along the branches on which the plants are growing), sometimes by climbing, while not unfrequently the whole tree is felled to the ground—a very destructive manner, since by this last method thousands of the smaller seedlings are sacrificed, and often for the sake of comparatively few salable plants."

"*Masdevallias*, you told me, were common. Are they also found on trees?"

"Generally so, but also on the ground, also on wet rocks, or creeping up the moist bases of tree trunks. *M. ignea*, for example, is frequently found among the grass and amongst rocks, *M. harryana* affects low trees, and *M. shuttleworthi* grows high up on trees also, although it is possible now and then to find a little colony or a single plant or two growing amongst the grass or on rocks below. In San Domingo, at 8000 feet or 9000 feet, *M. gustavœi*, *M. bicolor*, and its variegated-leaved form, are found on dead or fallen trees. These may be the descendants of plants which fell accidentally, or which have sprung up from the débris of former collections. *Masdevallias*, as a rule, grow in a higher zone than the *Odontoglossums* —say at 8000 feet to 10,000 feet. *Cattleyas*, on the other hand, are found at a lower level, or say at 4000 feet to 6000 feet; *Oncidiums* on ground or rocks and low trees at 5000 feet to 6000 feet; and one *Odontoglossum* (*O. lindeni*) is not uncommonly met with on rocks, or even on the moist ground level, at 6000 feet also."

"Did you find *Masdevallia veitchii* in Ocaña?"

"Oh no; it is a Peruvian plant, as is also the fine *Cypripedium caudatum;* but I found a strong-growing form of *C. schlimi* in Pamplona and La Cruz in clefts of the rocks and in the watercourses, where my men were up to their waists in water as they gathered it. This orchid does not succeed well in cultivation, because it is grown too hot and too dry, and so becomes infested with yellow thrips. It should be deluged with water; indeed, I have seen it under the current frequently during the rainy season."

"Presuming that some parts of the country are more productive than others, what parts do you prefer when exploring for orchids?"

"Well, for cool orchids, the mountains, of course, the most productive portions of which are always the gorges or gullies through which the watercourses run. Wherever possible to do so I follow the course of a mountain stream, or, if that is difficult, I make a point of 'striking' the banks as often as possible."

"And did you not find it difficult to get along in a country where only Spanish is spoken?"

"Well, not so much as one might imagine. Boys, as they are called, who speak a little English as well as Spanish are common, and can be hired for a few dollars per month, and then collectors soon find it to their interest and comfort to learn Spanish, at least colloquially, as soon as possible. In exploring, local guides are necessary, and generally easy to obtain through some one in authority."

"Now answer me one more question, please. What made you turn an orchid-hunter?"

"Well," my friend replied, smiling, "I was always hankering after 'going abroad,' and I thought I should like to see how the plants we cultivate so carefully really existed in a wild state. That was how I drifted into it; and having no domestic ties, I liked the roaming life, and so have kept to it ever since." As he knocked the ashes from his cigar he added: "But it is rather a precarious existence sometimes, and I have had a few narrow escapes from fever and accidents which I should not care to undergo again. Ah," he added, "I wonder if orchid amateurs ever give a thought as to the real price their orchids cost?" and he counted at least once or twice over his fingers such names as Bruchmueller, Zahn, Hutton, Klaboch, Endres, Chesterton, Freeman, and many others of that great army of martyrs to science who have died in the race after orchids. "And yet," he added, "there are the veterans: Roezl alive and well after all his numerous journeys, and Tom Lobb is still hale and hearty in his Cornish home."

Apart altogether from their flowers, we have many orchids which may be grown for their leaf beauty alone. The most lovely of these leaf orchids are the *Anœctochili* from Borneo, Java, the peninsula of India, and Ceylon. It is by no means easy to paint their beauty with colors, much less so with words. The plants are soft and succulent, only growing a few inches in height amongst the decaying leaves and mosses of the forest. Each leaf varies from an inch to three or four inches in length, and is generally ovate in outline, and in texture looks as if cut from the finest of velvety tissue. The color of the surface varies from the lightest to the darkest green, some are olive or of a peculiar warm and mellow brown, others richest emerald, with a lustre almost metallic. This represents only the general surface, however, for every portion is lined or laced in the most intricately beautiful and Oriental manner. Some have light green veins on a darker ground, others silvery, coppery, golden, the principal veins curved lengthwise from base to apex of the leaf, while finer cross fibres spring at various angles, and produce the general effect of the most lovely inlaid lattice-work. Sometimes you see a broad central band of lustrous bronze surface, sometimes there is the most wondrous gold-dust-like spangling, but one and all of these little leafy things are so exquisitely fashioned that Arachne herself might have wrought them when in her happiest moods.

Now, alas! comes the discord in our melody, for not only are these plants rare in our gardens, but they are ever likely to remain so, being of all orchids perhaps the most difficult of prolonged cultivation.

In addition to the great beauty and the protean variability of their blossoming, the floral mimicry of orchids was observed at an early date, even in the case of our wild British species. Thus we have the "Spider," the "Fly," the "Lizard," and the "Bee" orchids in Europe; but the weird

and curious beauty of the tropical kinds dedicated to the Moth (*Phalœnopsis*), the Butterfly (*Oncidium papilio*), the Dove (*Peristeria*), and the Swan (*Cynoches*) also attract universal admiration. The largest-flowered of all orchids is an *Angræcum* from Madagascar, with starfish-like flowers of waxy whiteness, each having a tail-like spur or nectary fifteen inches in length. A South American Lady's-Slipper (*Cypripedium*) has petals often two to three feet in length. When the flower-bud opens they are only five or six inches long, but they rapidly elongate for several days after they become liberated. The great spotted flowers of the *Stanhopeas* burst open quite suddenly, and with a somewhat startling report, and in some of the *Bolbophylla* the lip waggles about in quite a ludicrous way if you move the flower.

The cross-fertilization of orchids was one of the phenomena which attracted much attention from the late Charles Darwin, who published his views on the subject in 1868. All the epiphytal orchids, as previously observed, have their pollen grains arranged in waxy masses, and not in the dry and powdery state usual in ordinary flowers. This condition of the pollen necessitates peculiar insect aid ere the flowers can become fertilized and seed formation be insured; hence this coöperation of the insects with the flowers accounts for that protean variability observable amongst these plants. One reason why orchid flowers endure fresh and fair so long after expansion in our hot-houses is because there are no insects present, and so fertilization does not take place. A fertilized flower withers in an hour or two, even if it has but recently opened its petals. Their seeds are produced in egg-shaped capsules, and resemble the finest of mahogany or teak-wood sawdust in color and size. Darwin calculated that a single flower-spike of the common field orchis (*O. mascula*) produced nearly two hundred thousand of these seeds. Small as they are, when magnified under a low power a single orchid seed forms a beautiful object. The outer envelop is like a glossy net-work of some silky tissue, not unlike an old-fashioned ring purse, in fact, while the embryo lying in the folds seems like a gold coin in the centre. When the seeds are ripe the capsule bursts open, and the seeds gradually escape. Being extremely light, and suitably balanced for poising themselves in mid-air, the slightest breeze supports them, and they are wafted hither and thither among the branches on which their foster-parents grew. Many are lost, no doubt; nature's lavish profusion compensates for this; but hundreds find a congenial resting-place on the furrowed branches or on mossy trunks, and so grow and establish themselves high up in mid-air. They are nature's babies, kissed by the warm sunshine and bathed in nightly dews. Seeing that these plants generally must be cross-fertilized by insects in a state of nature, we have only to go a step further and the cultivator becomes the "marriage priest." But all progress is slow, even if it be sure. As a matter of fact, however, orchids were raised from seeds soon after their introduction.

In 1833 *Prescottia plantaginea* was thus raised in the Horticultural Society's garden at Chiswick, and *Paxtonia rosea* (a plant dedicated to Sir Joseph Paxton, some time gardener at Chatsworth) was found growing from seeds accidentally self-sown in Messrs. Loddige's nursery. The late Dr. Moore raised *Phaius albus* and one or two other orchids from seeds, and these flowered at Glasnevin, near Dublin, about 1850. But the actual production of artificial hybrids did not take place until 1852, in which year Mr. John Dominy commenced a series of experiments in the Exeter nursery of Messrs. Veitch, which has in recent years made his name a household word among horticulturists. Mr. Dominy's first hybrid was *Calanthe dominii*, which flowered in 1858, and was succeeded by twenty or thirty other hybrids of remarkable interest. Of these, *Calanthe veitchii, Cattleya exoniensis,* and *Lælia dominii* are perhaps best known, and it is a remarkable fact that Mr. Dominy had demonstrated the possibility of hybrid orchids being raised long ere Darwin's *Fertilization of Orchidaceous Plants* appeared. Mr. Seden, a pupil of Mr. Dominy's, has carried on the good work in the Chelsea nursery of Messrs. James Veitch and Sons, where at the present time seedlings many and various exist by the thousand. One of the most striking anomalies connected with the orchid "boom" in England is the fact that every grower and importer sends his novelties to a botanical professor in Hamburg for naming, since the death of the late Dr. Lindley, twenty years ago. It is

a singular fact that with all our great national herbaria, we have no botanical professor in England competent to name these flowers. During the last few years the race for orchids in England has been an exciting one. All the principal London nursery-men have had collectors abroad for years, but the large prices now paid for the best imported plants have stimulated them to still further exertions. Messrs. Low, of Clapton, and F. Sander, have, during recent years, quite revolutionized the orchid trade in England. Ten years ago guineas were asked for plants which shillings now would buy, but, on the other hand, there never was closer competition amongst purchasers, nor higher prices paid for novelties and rarities, than at the present time. Unique specimens of any popular orchids attract much competition and fetch high prices, while to-morrow a large importation may come in, when, of course, down fall the prices at once. As an example of this we may instance "Spicer's Lady's-Slipper" orchid, for a single plant of which £100 was paid when it was scarce in Europe, and a few weeks afterward several nursery-men were offering plants at five shillings each, so largely had it been imported in the mean time. The importers are of course anxious not to "swamp" the market, and yet competition in collecting abroad is now so keen that any one dealer rarely obtains a monopoly, and so cannot afford to hold back his stock.

It is remarkable that in a natural order so extensive there should be so few species of economic interest. The most important is "vanilla"—a product consisting of the fruit pods of a climbing epiphyte (*Vanilla planifolia*). Vanilla is cultivated in South America, its importation being very limited, and a chemical substitute has recently been obtained from the sawdust or wood fibre of coniferous trees. A starchy food called "salep" has been prepared from the tubers of *Orchis* in Europe, and of the *Eulophia* in India. The inspissated sap of some species of *Catasetum* is used in Brazil as a kind of vegetable glue, and in North America the viscid tuber of the "Putty Root" (*Aplectrum hyemale*) was formerly used as a cement for broken earthen-ware, and in Africa the leaves of *Angræcum fragrans* have been used as tea.

In London there are auction-rooms in which sales of orchids take place several times during each week of the year. Imported plants as a rule sell best, owing to the sales of "established" plants often consisting of the "weeded-out" or bad varieties of other growers, "salted," it may be, with a few good things. The prices realized are variable, of course, in proportion to the condition of the plants and their rarity or novelty. Only a few weeks ago one hundred and sixty lots of a new white variety of *Lœlia* were offered at Stevens's room, none of which sold for less than £10, and the best plants realized £50. A fine variety of *Cattleya trianœ* sold for £250, and £100 is not at all an unusual price for a particularly good variety of any really showy species. The South American *Cattleyas* are especial favorites, and the finest forms extremely valuable. *Cattleya trianœ dodgsonii* sold for 185 guineas, *C. osmanii* for 215 guineas, and the two halves of *C. percivalliana* for 220 guineas, while for a very beautiful "air-plant," or *Aërides laurenciœ*, Sir Trevor Lawrence paid 235 guineas. A single plant of the white-crested *Cœlogyne* was sold in February last for £131. Mr. Bull was the purchaser. It is now several years since he bought the original stock of this plant for £200. When it is remembered that these are not fancy or nursery-men's prices, but *bona fide* prices, actually paid at public auction sales, it will be seen that prices are as real as they are erratic. The botanical names of these plants give one but little idea of the value of any individual plant; for example, Pescatore's *Odontoglot* has been imported by the thousand for years, and one might buy plants at auction sales at a few shillings each, since no very startling variations had been observed, when quite unexpectedly a lovely form, heavily barred with purple, appeared at the Chelsea nursery, and had it been sold by auction when first it flowered, it would have brought from £50 to £100 at least. This plant was imported along with many others, and before it bloomed might have been sold for a guinea to any one who had chanced to pick it out of the batch.

It will thus be seen that one great incentive toward that popularity to which orchids have attained is the uncertainty which surrounds any collection of orchids freshly imported. Such a collection is virtually a lottery; you buy so many plants, and you have so many chances of a prize. A friend of mine, whose office is near to the orchid mart in Cheapside, went in one day to buy a few hyacinth roots for his garden. The bulb sale had not commenced, and the auctioneer, indeed, was knocking down the last lot or two of orchids offered on that day. Most of the regular orchid buyers had gone, and the last three or four lots were "hanging fire" at a few shillings, and my friend bought the lot for less than a sovereign. They were shrivelled plants of *Odontoglossums* in paper bags, and they took a good deal of skill and attention to bring them into vigor and health again. But when they bloomed some of them turned out very distinct, and an offer of £500 made for the lot as they stood, after the first five or six had bloomed, was not accepted. My friend is now a confirmed orchidophile, and has quite a small village of hot-houses near his country residence entirely devoted to these charming plants. It is nothing unusual for a London salesman to dispose of orchids valued at from £1000 to £2000 in one day, and there are collections of orchids in America as well as in Europe worth from £5000 to £50,000 at the least. In England two of the finest private collections of these plants belong to Baron Schroder, of Egham, near Windsor, and to Sir Trevor Lawrence, of Burford Lodge, near Dorking. In the United States, by far the finest and most valuable collection is that of Erastus Corning, Esq., of Albany, but General Rathbone also possesses fine specimens, and Mr. S. R. Payson recently exhibited some fine species in flower at a meeting of the Massachusetts Horticultural Society in Boston. These may be cited as representative collections in the two countries, but there are many other collections but little inferior in value and interest. It has to many been a matter of wonder that such large sums of money should be invested in rare orchids, and in erections and appliances for their cultivation. But, after all, there seems no good reason why tasteful people should not admire and value the beauty of these and other flowers, just as they admire and purchase fine pictures, rare gems, statuary, old china, antique furniture, rare books, or other works of art.

Beautiful as the large-flowered orchids certainly are, there are many of the species which are small and sombre in coloring. A large proportion of these plants have green or yellow blossoms; many are white flowered, often with rose or purple markings; a lesser proportion are of various shades of rose and purple; the yellow-flowered kinds are rarely without some brown spots or markings, the white kinds rarely without some yellow or green coloring. Bright red or scarlet flowered kinds are rare, and those of any shade of blue are the rarest in the whole family. The prevalence of green, yellow, and white flowered species seems to be suggestive of the modern origin and development of the order. Complicated as is their structure, most botanists are agreed that when compared with the "marsh horse-tails," or with the cycads, the orchids are in the infancy of their evolutionary growth. Nature is as busy in the making of new forms as ever; in a word, she is evolving new orchids in her tropical "wild garden" just as surely as our hybridizers are rearing new forms in our hot-houses at home.

AN ELECTIVE COURSE.

LINES FOUND AMONG THE PAPERS OF A HARVARD UNDERGRADUATE.

THE bloom that lies on Fanny's cheek
   Is all my Latin, all my Greek;
The only sciences I know
Are frowns that gloom and smiles that glow;
   Siberia and Italy
   Lie in her sweet geography;
No scholarship have I but such
As teaches me to love her much.

Why should I strive to read the skies,
Who know the midnight of her eyes?
No star that swims within the scope
Of Pickering's best telescope
   Ever reveals so much as when
   She stares and droops her eyes again.
Graybeards, who seek to bridge the chasm
'Twixt man to-day and protoplasm,
   How trivial your aims appear!
   Enough for me that Fanny's here.

Linnæus, avaunt! I only care
To know what flower she wants to wear.
I leave it to the addle-pated
To guess how pinks originated.
   As if it mattered! The chief thing
   Is that we have them in the spring,
And Fanny likes them. When they come,
I straightway go and purchase some.
   "The Origin of Plants"—go to!
   Their proper end I have in view.

O loveliest book that ever man
Looked into since the world began
Is Woman! As I turn those pages,
As fresh as in the primal ages,
   As day by day I scan, perplext,
   The ever subtly changing text,
I feel that I am slowly growing
To think no other book worth knowing.
   And in my copy, one of many
   (Édition de luxe called Fanny),
I find no thing set down but such
As teaches me to love it much.

DE BARBADOESA'S LITTLE HOUR.

BY LUCY C. LILLIE.

I.

IT all began on a certain December afternoon when Norris had declared he would see nobody. The decision had occurred to him when he was quite alone, and the MacFinlay, his man-servant, factotum, and sometime model, was entirely out of hearing, but the next moment he was at his studio door, and called out his idea to that faithful slave. But MacFinlay, who was trying to write a letter home to Dublin, only half heard, and misconstrued the words into meaning that his master was expecting somebody, and being in the midst of very doubtful orthography, said, "Ye', surr, ye', surr—I will, surr," and Norris went back to his sofa, where for a time he lay full length, with his hands behind his head and his eyes fixed on the tangle of green above his studio window.

He had a very pleasant occupation for his mind. His cousin Margaret was coming home after some five years' absence in Europe, and as Margaret and he had always been sworn friends, the devoted allies people with a certain bond of relationship can be, it was extremely pleasant to think of her return, and with it the picking up of their piquant intercourse of last year in Paris and London. "What fun it will be," thought Norris, "to take her about, to watch her first season in New York society!" She was sure to be admired, for Miss Fenn, although scarcely two-and-twenty, had the air of a young princess, and the type of beauty hereditary with her race. Norris's interest in Margaret was tinged by a strong sense of brotherly protection, for the young lady was nearly alone in the world—in fact, worse than alone, since her chaperon, Mrs. Troop, was for such an office possibly the least qualified woman in existence. It was a source of perpetual mystery to Norris how any Fenn could be related even distantly to so vulgar an old woman; but these curious connections occur in the most perfectly regulated families, and in this case it was chiefly exasperating because, on her father's death, Mrs. Troop had seemed to be Margaret's only friend, and as such had taken possession of the girl, and won her gratitude for kindnesses shown her in her obscurity.

Margaret's dominant trait was fidelity; gratefulness belongs to this characteristic, I believe it is allowed; so, for the sake of the past, Margaret bore with everything vulgar and wearying in the Mrs. Troop of to-day. It would undoubtedly be delightful to have Margaret in society this season, but, alas, alas, that she should be thus chaperoned! In London the old lady had been laid up with influenza half the time, and so Margaret had been taken out by Lady This or That, friends of her mother's, or by some of Norris's own acquaintances in aristocratic Bohemia; but now, here in her own home, to appear for the first time preceded, or, as Norris said, with a grim smile, battlemented, by Mrs. Troop, was hideous in the extreme. But again arose the picture of Margaret's delicate loveliness, the high-bred, simple manner which must disarm the unfriendliest criticism of her companion. After all, Norris thought, things might be worse; and at this juncture of his reflections the tread of MacFinlay was heard, and, behind his, other footsteps. Norris sprang to his feet just as the door was opened, and then remained rooted to the spot. Before him stood the most remarkable-looking man he had ever seen. MacFinlay, at one side, was struggling with the stranger's name, when the latter, in a deep voice, said, "I presume you do not know me, sir—the Count de Barbadoesa."

"I have not the pleasure, certainly, sir," said Norris, with a ghastly effort at keeping his countenance, for the man before him was as grotesque as he was singular. He was certainly over six feet in height, and if not large by nature, had been carefully expanded under the hands of his tailor. His large, melancholy face was nearly shrouded in loosely flying black locks, one of which in a wavering line hung in the middle of his forehead; his eyes were fine, but their expression of intelligence or good-will was defied by the cunning of the mouth; on his breast were innumerable decorations, and a huge topaz sparkled in a ring on his ungloved hand. With the other hand he supported his rather small waist.

The spectacle was so completely ludicrous that Norris felt he must speak or suffocate.

"May I venture to ask to what I am indebted for the pleasure—" He really could not go on, but waved the stranger to a chair, which he took without once removing his melancholy gaze from Norris's face, though he now placed his gloved hand on his knee, crooking his elbow and turning his fingers inward.

"The Count de Barbadoesa," murmured Norris, looking at him with interest.

The count bowed. "I have the honor," he began, with a partial attempt to toss back the vagrant curl—"the honor to be the bearer of a letter for your cousin, Miss Fenn."

"Miss Fenn!" Norris said, in quite another tone.

"Exactly, sir; and not finding her at home, I brought it to you," and he produced from a deep breast pocket an envelop truly enough addressed to Margaret.

Norris's face had flushed. He looked very much inclined to show the noble stranger the door.

"It is from my friend Count Giuseppe Antonini," pursued the man. "The correspondence, according to Miss Fenn's desire, is to be conducted through me. They are"—here the count again tossed the curl, which instantly returned to his left eyebrow—"they are betrothed."

"What do you mean?" half roared Norris. "What confounded nonsense are you talking? Do you know that I am Miss Fenn's cousin, sir? If there is any impertinent joke in this—"

But De Barbadoesa waved his hand and smiled. "Do not be alarmed, sir; you have only to inquire of your cousin, or the excellent Madame Troop."

"By Jove," thought Norris, "that old idiot is at the bottom of this;" and it occurred to him to take some conciliatory measures with the aristocrat before him.

"Very well," he said, rather stiffly. "I shall certainly see Miss Fenn at once on the subject, and perhaps you will call again? By-the-way, where is your friend Yussipi—what did you say his name was?"

"Giuseppe Antonini, thirteenth of the name," pronounced the stranger.

"He shall be the last of his line, then," thought Norris. But he said aloud: "Many thanks for your kind office. Shall Miss Fenn answer this—document to your address?"

De Barbadoesa drew from his card case a much emblazoned piece of pasteboard with his name rather alarmingly full upon it. This he handed with much dignity to Norris, who perceived the address to be at one of the new apartment-houses rather uptown. There seemed to be nothing more to say, and the nobleman, bowing gravely, left Norris standing in the middle of the room, a prey to perplexity and despair.

What in the name of all that was sensible did it mean? That Margaret had been doing something Quixotic or foolish he did not doubt, but that she had engaged herself to this lunatic's friend he did not credit for an instant. His first idea was to hunt the Barbadoesa up, to beard him, as it were, in his own apartment, and investigate his character. But a second's reflection showed him that would not do. Better find out the truth, or what could be told of it, from Margaret herself. She had specially requested him not to meet her at the steamer, but he knew that by this time she and Mrs. Troop were to be found at their friend Mrs. Ivors's, on Twenty-second Street, where they were to stay until Margaret's new house near the Park was entirely habitable. Yes, it was the only thing to do, and Norris, feeling his delight of an hour previous considerably dampened, sat down to await as best he might seven o'clock. On this evening, as he knew, Mrs. Ivors had invited a few friends to welcome Margaret at dinner, so there would be no chance of a *tête-à-tête* with his cousin until very late. What on earth had induced her to refuse to see him at the wharf? It was incredible in simple, honest, conscientious Margaret.

"But, after all," thought Norris, ruefully, "she's a woman; there's that to be said of it."

II.

Mrs. Ivors's guests had nearly all assembled when Dick, with a rather cynical aspect, made his way into her drawing-room. Even as he answered Mrs. Ivors's greeting his eyes searched eagerly for a glimpse of Margaret. She was standing in a little recessed window, talking to two or three reverently admiring young men, and Dick made his way quickly to the group. "Well," he exclaimed, coming forward; and Margaret, starting a little at his voice, turned her face joyfully toward him. "My dear Dick," she said, holding out her hand, and as Norris took it warmly he observed that she was prettier than ever, although a trifle thin and pale.

"It's good to see you again," she said, almost in a whisper, and her eyes were fairly shining.

"Then why couldn't you let me meet you?" Dick said, a little sharply. "You know you needed me."

A swift color came and went in Miss Fenn's cheeks.

"I—I didn't want you to, really, Dick," she murmured; "and as for needing, in one sense, you know we had Barton and my maid Alice, and they saw to the trunks."

"All the better, we could have had a little chat, and it seems odd to have to see you for the first time at a party."

Margaret laughed a little nervously, and contrived to make the conversation general; but it was some satisfaction to find himself at dinner placed next his cousin.

"And how shall I like New York?" she said to him at the first opportunity.

"Morally, mentally, or socially?" he inquired.

She laughed. "Morally, I know I shall; mentally, well, after London, Dick? Now don't think me unpatriotic, but shall I find evenings such as you remember at the Velmar-Tornes', the Von Scholtts', the—"

"I am glad you are going to be fastidious," put in Dick, "for evidently your mentally includes socially. No, my dear Meg, you will not find anything like the Tornes' or the Von Scholtts', simply because neither Torne nor Von Scholtt happens to live here, but I can promise you you will see ample material for such people to make use of—that is, if you are as keen as you used to be."

Miss Fenn opened her eyes with a little wounded look in them.

"Why, Dick," she said, "pray tell me what I have done."

He had to smile. She was so very pretty and delightful when she looked vexed.

"What you have done, Meg," he responded, gravely, "I don't pretend to fathom. It is a problem time must work out, unless you choose at once to solve the mystery."

Miss Fenn's flexible mouth curved with some disdain. "It is evident," she remarked, looking at her plate, "that there is at least a circle of advanced thinkers

over here. Pray tell me if your society is given to a very abstract way of putting things. Perhaps I shall learn to consider the charming circle at the Tornes' mere babes in wisdom."

"Go on," said Norris. Then, as a sudden idea struck him, he added: "I will promise you some foreign element. There seems to be a very distinguished nobleman over here, the Count de Barbadoesa."

As he spoke the name, Norris looked at her keenly, and across her cheeks, her brow, the bit of her soft white throat that he could see, a perfect wave of color spread, and the next instant she had averted her face and was talking to the man on her other side. Dick could have wrung his hands, have uttered loud groans and imprecations, then and there. Indeed, I believe it was only a fine sense of the fitness of things which prevented him from, in some fashion, giving vent to the anguish within. At how many such banquets, he was thinking, do guests sit longing to scream aloud?—for it was now but too plainly evident that the terrible De Barbadoesa had spoken the truth. If he had cherished the least doubt of this, his cousin had put it to flight. She turned a face quite set and hard upon him.

"May I ask," she inquired, icily, "where you have met the count?"

"He called at my studio to-day," Dick answered, quickly, and in a tone no less chilling than her own, "and he left a letter for you from his friend."

"Let me have it, if you please."

"Here—here at the table, Margaret?"

"You can slip it in beneath the table," she said, imperiously. "There, you can see I have put my hand down for it."

By this time Norris had decided that their two tragic countenances would be remarked, so with what must have appeared to the people opposite a very sinister smile, he contrived to get the note into his cousin's hidden fingers. He saw by the flutter of the roses in her gown that she sighed, but he determined not to look at her again, and turned his eyes upon the young lady he had taken in to dinner.

"I am so glad Miss Fenn has come back!" said this lady—Miss Barlow. "Isn't her house lovely?" she went on. "I hope she means to be very gay, and give us some excitement."

Dick, unable to resist his impulse, turned to Margaret with: "Margaret, here is Miss Barlow hoping you will give us some excitement in your new house. I don't doubt you will be able to satisfy her."

Miss Fenn contented herself with an oblique look of disdain from under her long lashes at her cousin, but she smiled very graciously in front of him upon Miss Barlow.

"My dear Jennie," she said, "you shall have whatever you like."

"Oh," cried Miss Barlow, "do have something dramatic!"

"Ah!" ejaculated Dick.

But Margaret's face did not betray that she heard him. It was perhaps a relief to both of the cousins when the ladies left the room. Margaret was very stately in her manner as Dick helped to move back her chair, and if the men at the table found him dull during the first few moments, he certainly showed unwonted animation later, for young Barlow began to talk of the new lion to be in society, the Count de Barbadoesa. Some of the men roared outright upon mention of his name, but an elderly gentleman named Perkins declared that the De Barbadoesas were an ancient and noble family, and this man was quite well known in foreign circles, etc., etc.

Norris listened, questioned where he could, and elicited the information that De Barbadoesa was living very sumptuously in Hotel Frothingham, and was to be taken up by society.

"Taken up!" laughed the young man; "yes, I shouldn't wonder!" and it was with a heavy heart he went into the drawing-room again. Margaret was sitting near the fire, and again came the thought to Dick's mind that she was lovelier than ever. The coil of brown hair low upon her white neck, the wide fair brow and clear eyes, the warm curves of her mouth and chin, above all the look of trustful purity and sweetness, all combined to make her fascinating even when she scorned him. What did it matter to Norris that she had unlimited thousands? To him she was only the Meg of other days. Yet, as he turned away with a sigh, he reflected that a letter from the most noble Count Antonini was in her keeping, and that such a man as De Barbadoesa had secretly conveyed it to her.

III.

It is needless to say that Richard Norris passed a night full of uncomfortable reflections. When he declared himself mys-

tified he felt cheered; but directly doubt took the form of anything like suspicion of Margaret's prudence, or even of her fine sense of propriety, then he was profoundly wretched; but no strong feeling of this kind could last when he recalled the appearance, the manner, the voice even, of his glittering guest of yesterday. Everything then merged into a laugh, hollow, perhaps, but certainly a kind of mirth, and when the sun shone in upon him the next day he had resolved that whatever folly Margaret might have been led into, he could try and lead her out of it, just as a brother would, if only she would consent to drop this air of mystery and take him into her confidence as fully as before. His doubts of her might perhaps prove morbid visions, but then De Barbadoesa was a grim reality, whoever his friend the Count Giuseppe Antonini might be. He had promised Margaret to take her to her new house that afternoon, and on this occasion he determined to talk to her with more gentleness, for he knew enough of feminine human nature to feel certain Margaret would not be driven to answer questions put with any suspicious accent.

He worked away during the next morning, using MacFinlay for a model, and quite casually inquired of that functionary what the strange gentleman who called the day before had had to say. Upon this MacFinlay laughed aloud, and instantly checking himself, apologized, but he gave his head a shake as he answered:

"Ah, Misther Dick, did iver ye see the like of him? Shure I'd like to be his barber, and paid by the hair!"

Dick was forced to smile, yet the contempt of the MacFinlay only added to his annoyance, and he went to Mrs. Ivors's in the afternoon more than ever chagrined.

Margaret came into the drawing-room with no trace of last night's hauteur, welcomed Dick cordially, and as they started up Fifth Avenue he asked her why she had tried so hard to snub him.

"My dear cousin," she said, very gravely, "I never before knew you to be so sensitive. Now"—and Margaret turned her eyes gently upon him—"now tell me what was the matter."

"I will tell you, of course," he said. "What is this man De Barbadoesa to you? where did you pick him up?—in fact, what do you know of him?"

Margaret gazed down at her muff with troubled eyes. "Very little," she said, in a low voice. "He is an Italian, we have mutual friends, but, in fact, I never saw him until yesterday, when he met us at the wharf."

"Ah," cried Dick, a light coming to him, "that is the reason you objected to my meeting you ?"

Miss Fenn remained silent until they had begun another block, then she said, deliberately, "If you must know, yes, it was."

Dick knew not what to say. His prudent resolves to be gentle with her forbade his bursting forth with impetuous warnings such as he felt he, as her nearest male relation, ought to give. But if Margaret was gentle and exquisitely womanly, she was also independent, and a trifle obstinate and proud. To push her would be, perhaps, to lose his chance of serving her, and so he determined to try a different course.

"Margaret," he said, "I want to be very good to you: tell me how I can help you."

"I will," she said, eagerly. "Promise to question me no further about the count. Dear Dick, if I need help, I promise to ask you for it."

The words stung him painfully. It had, then, come to this: *if* she needed him she would ask for help!

Dick made no answer, but walked on rather moodily at her side, until they reached the large corner house which was part of her new fortune, and which upholsterers and decorators had been long busy over, under Dick's supervision.

Mrs. Troop, large and florid as ever, was already established there, and it was some time before Dick could claim Margaret for a few words alone. They had gone to look at some stuffs sent up on approval, and which were piled up in a room intended for dancing, or other entertainments requiring space. It was a moment to seize, as they sat with the rich silks and wools between them, Margaret holding up one thing after another, anxiously, for Dick's approval.

"Very good, very good indeed," he said, absently, as she shook out a piece of dull blue silk. "Margaret," he continued, "I will not torment you about De Barbadoesa, if you will answer me one question."

She was watching him with an earnest gaze from across the rich heap of color.

"Well ?"

"This Antonini he talks of," Dick went on, hurriedly; "tell me, are you actually pledged to him ?"

The girl's breath came and went, while she still looked at her cousin fixedly.

"If I answer, will you promise to ask no more ?" she said, faintly.

Dick hesitated. "Well, I will."

"Then," with an effort, "yes, *I am.*"

The words seemed to Dick to echo on all sides of the big lonely room. Margaret had risen and was moving away.

"Stay, Margaret," he cried, springing toward her. "One thing more you must answer me. This Antonini, where is he ?"

She turned a moment and looked at him reproachfully. "In Turin," she answered, and then fled swiftly away.

Dick stood still a moment, contemplating the position ruefully. Mrs. Troop's voice was heard outside loudly clamoring for Richard Norris. Margaret's fainter tones were drowned in them, but the young man moved in their direction. "If this thing goes on," he muttered, "Miss Barlow is likely to get her theatricals."

IV.

New York received the heiress, Miss Fenn, with every mark of attention, and Dick, on going to see her, would generally find her very much engrossed by the demands of society.

"I wish people would stop inviting me," she said one morning.

"Well, you can stop going, I suppose ?" he answered, without looking up.

Margaret was pensive for a moment. "No," she said, "I can't very well. You may laugh if you like, Dick, but it so pleases Mrs. Troop!"

"Good heavens, Margaret!" exclaimed Dick, leaning back in his chair, "when are you going to give up this Quixotic notion of gratitude ? I assure you I feel like anything but laughing. I wonder what I could do to make you grateful to me ? I declare, Meg, I'd make a fine thing of it." And he did laugh, but by no means pleasantly.

Margaret looked hurt and was silent.

"I suppose it's in you, and you can't help it," he went on. "Only remember you have cast me off, in a certain sense, and therefore I don't expect to take care of you unasked. Sometimes an opinion will slip out unawares—force of habit, you see; old habits occasionally obtrude themselves."

As he looked at his cousin he saw that there were tears in her eyes, although her face was very proud.

"I think we are both changed," she said, a little hurriedly. "I certainly don't find you just the same. I feel all the time that I am challenging your good opinion; you follow me about with critical eyes as though—as though you expected something dreadful of me. The other night, for instance, at the Barlows', when I was dancing with young Mr. Perkins, you came up near us and glared at me in such a way—oh yes, you did, Dick."

"I don't like the Perkins set," remarked Dick, calmly.

"Oh, don't you?" flashed out Margaret. "And may I ask why, Richard?"

"Certainly. They are taking up that lunatic De Barbadoesa, making fools of themselves and of him—at least, if any one could improve upon that kind of thing in him."

And then Margaret was silent. It was a singular fact that the mere mention of the count's name was enough to silence her most impetuous speech. What Dick had said of the Perkins family was quite true, and might be said of others. By some singular stroke of luck or of fatuity on the part of his entertainers, De Barbadoesa had certainly been admitted within some aristocratic doorways, and on more than one occasion Dick Norris had had the anguish of seeing him talking to his cousin Margaret with an air of peculiar confidence. Useless it was to abuse him or even criticise him in Margaret's presence; she generally ignored what was said. Added to this was Mrs. Troop's loudly proclaimed championship of him—a fact that might not have worried Dick but for Margaret's association with her, and the certainty which possessed him that they shared some secret in common. An element in this affair that peculiarly tortured Norris was the manner in which men talked of the count. He had made his way into one or two clubs, and forthwith wrote notes thence in all directions. Dick had himself received one such. It was a very elaborately worded affair, requesting Dick's advice about the framing of some pictures—some little things of his own.

"Your friend the most noble count, it appears, is one of our guild," he said that evening to his cousin. She and Mrs. Ivors and Mrs. Troop were about starting to a tableaux party, where Margaret was to perform. "I had no idea he was a brother in arms."

Margaret looked at him inquiringly. "Do you mean," she said, seriously, "that he is an artist?"

"I hope not, if it is what you call the rest of us. It seems he wants my advice about frames for his little things. I hope he won't ask it for the little things themselves."

Margaret and Mrs. Ivors had to laugh, but Mrs. Troop proclaimed: "I should think he might be anything he liked, with that head of his. I do call his hair noble."

"Perhaps he bought it with the title," Dick now suggested.

"He's just a picture," Mrs. Troop said, ignoring Dick. "I do love to see him come in or out of a room."

"I'll go half-way with you there, Mrs. Troop," laughed Dick.

But as usual the topic had silenced Margaret.

Dick sought Mrs. Ivors quite early the next morning. He had asked to see her alone. "You really missed something very picturesque last night," she said. "The most noble De Barbadoesa stationed himself near the curtain, and looked as though he were giving the audience his royal permission to approve of Meg. Of course she was lovely in the tableau from *Hamlet*. He turned and said aloud, 'Brava! brava!' Mrs. Troop says there are such dulcet Italian tones in his voice." Mrs. Ivors spoke very serenely, but watched Dick with a face ready to break into smiles.

"I know what you want to talk about," she said, presently. "It would be ridiculous in me to pretend that I have not observed that something is wrong with Margaret, and that creature De Barbadoesa has something to do with it, I am certain. Now, Mr. Norris, I know equally well it is making you worried—unhappy, perhaps."

"It is," responded Dick, with dejection; "but what is to be done? She does not need our help."

"Ah!" cried Mrs. Ivors, sitting upright in her chair, "there is exactly where you are mistaken. She does—she does; but we must work cautiously. I know Margaret so well, her intense conscientiousness, her charity, her way of making herself of no account where others are concerned, and her deep capacity for loving."

As Mrs. Ivors enumerated Margaret's

virtues, a smile of intense satisfaction stole over Dick's honest face. The lady went on:

"Now I believe that she is somebody's tool or victim. Of one thing I am profoundly certain: she will never break her word. If she has made a promise, she will keep it."

"True enough," said Dick. "I would do any mortal thing to serve her," he added.

"No doubt of that; and so would I. I have a plan, and it is this: for Margaret's sake you must learn to know something more of this man. If I were you I should visit him, and invite him to visit me."

"Heavens and earth!" laughed Dick, as Mrs. Ivors launched this bolt. But a moment of shrewd reflection showed him just what she meant. "I believe I can do it," he said; "but perhaps you don't know that there's another rascally Italian in the case. He's a count also—Giuseppe Antonini."

"Goodness! Where from? and who is he?"

And Dick briefly sketched his first visit from De Barbadoesa.

"Never mind," declared Mrs. Ivors. "Only satisfy yourself as to what De Barbadoesa really is, and then we can help Margaret on some better basis. You see —pardon my plain-speaking—you have so far allowed your prejudices to stand in your way of doing this. We must now save Meg from herself and this wretched man."

It was as well that Margaret, who entered the room at this moment, was delayed by opening a letter, but she looked up and handed it to Dick with a quizzical glance.

"By all that is astonishing!" he exclaimed, and he read aloud: "'Mrs. Perkins requests the pleasure of your company on Tuesday the 19th, at 3 P.M., to view a collection of paintings by the Count de Barbadoesa.'"

V.

By the time Mrs. Perkins's reception on behalf of De Barbadoesa had come round, Dick had really learned to know something of the man—at least something of his mode of life and his personal surroundings—and we must do the count the justice to say that he received Norris with a finely hospitable manner, showed him his airy apartment, where signs of his genius were scattered about in a negligee fashion, and if he disdained talking "shop," certainly he discoursed fluently on the old masters. If his manner was insufferable to our friend, it was certainly original.

When Mrs. Ivors, with Margaret and Dick, arrived at Mrs. Perkins's house, about four o'clock, they beheld the count stationed at Mrs. Troop's side, she looking uncommonly like Mrs. Jarley with a very remarkable new wax figure in attendance. The good lady had insisted upon going earlier than either Margaret or Mrs. Ivors wished to go, and Dick might have breathed freely but that Margaret was no sooner near the count than some of their usual brief confidences were exchanged.

Mrs. Ivors and Dick enjoyed the survey of the pictures. They all presented the familiarity with common scenery which copies from poor memory might produce. Dick said they were perhaps a new kind of chromo. However, he very obligingly promised the count to call and inspect them at his leisure, the count having a very panoramic way of detailing their merits, which Dick declared would be worth a study.

Not long after, an appropriate moment occurred. Margaret had gone into her new house, and was planning a fancy-dress ball as a house-warming. The three friends were naturally very much together discussing the matter of costumes and decorations, and one afternoon Margaret, who had been much occupied over Dick's drawings for her own dress, said, suddenly: "Oh, Dick, I had nearly forgotten! Will you take a note from me to the count?"

"That he may pass judgment on my designs?" says Dick, with a grim smile.

They happened to be sitting on the top of the staircase, waiting for Mrs. Ivors to come up. Margaret leaned back wearily against the pillar of the balustrade and looked at her cousin gravely.

"You are forcing a barrier between us, my dear Dick," she said, with a smile. "Take care you do not build it too high."

Dick would have protested loudly with his voice, and perhaps even by some pressure of the hand, but the others appeared at this moment, and he went away more determined than ever to push this mystery of De Barbadoesa to its end.

"Yes," he declared to himself, "to its bitter end," for bitter he determined it should be for one person at least.

Margaret's allusions to their happier past, her sadness, perplexed, annoyed, thrilled him. As he mounted the stairs to the count's lofty nest his mind was full of this one idea, and in an absent sort of way he stood before the count's door, not knowing what he had come for. Then, with equal thoughtlessness, on seeing the door ajar, he walked in. Not a creature was there. Dick stood still a moment, wondering at the count's carelessness, and what he should do with Margaret's communication, when suddenly the sound of some one's humming a doleful Italian air caught his ear. It came from a little cupola; a door and staircase led to this small apartment, and Dick quickly turned toward them. The shrill, rather thin voice went on with "Santa Lucia," and in another moment Dick had bounded up the stairs. In relating this portion of his history Norris always says that no words can convey an idea of his feelings. He seemed, he says, at that moment to have almost a clairvoyant faculty. What he saw he as swiftly understood. Just what he saw was this: a badly lighted room, evidently the workshop of a painter; cheap chromos around the walls, one of them stuck upon a dilapidated easel. To the left of this was another easel with a half-finished sketch on it, and before it stood a man, a tall, thin, swarthy, and hungry-looking person, very unkempt and ragged, and who turned upon Dick a mournful pair of eyes. In a flash the secret of the count's art flashed upon him. This poor wretch was kept up here copying chromos, with just a dash of his very weak originality to prevent detection.

The two men looked at each other. It is a pity that no student of human nature was by to observe the scene. The contrast between Master Dick's tall, lithe, fine young figure, his clear eyes and strong features, all expressing health and an honest life, a youth not ill spent, and a prosperity not tampered with, and the lean, mournful-eyed, sorry man, with his drooping dejection of dress and manner, and doubtless of mind, was worthy of critical study; but it was not a moment for such reflections to occur to our friend. He stood still at the head of the little staircase, his hands fixed one on each rail, an instant before he spoke.

"The—count—he is not in?" Dick contrived to say at last.

The Italian shook his head with a sorrowful gesture. "No. Will you wait down-stairs? He allows no person here but myself." He beat his thin breast with the hand holding his brush, and looked at Dick above a suspended and very brilliant palette.

"And you paint—eh?" inquired Dick, to gain time.

The man nodded again, still looking anxiously.

"May I ask," Dick said, smiling as pleasantly as possible, "who you are?"

"Ah," said the man, taking a step in Dick's direction, "yes, certainly. My name is Antonini—Giuseppe Antonini."

"Then Lord help us!" said Dick, with a sensation that his last hope had now been taken from him.

VI.

(From Mr. Richard Norris to Mrs. Ivors.)

"DEAR MRS. IVORS,—Keep your courage up. I am almost certain of success. I shall be at Margaret's about 5 P.M. Show no surprise at anything you may hear me say. In haste, yours, R. N."

Mrs. Ivors arrived at Margaret's house with this letter in her pocket, and, as may be imagined, waited Dick's coming impatiently. The two ladies were in the long ball-room, discussing the question of flowers for the ball, when Dick entered, and his manner was so easy and indifferent for so long a time that Mrs. Ivors was driven to making the most exasperating signals to him behind Margaret's back. He smilingly acknowledged these, and at last, when the two ladies were at one side of the room and he was seated on one end of a table where the note-books were scattered, he said, quite carelessly,

"Oh, Margaret, by-the-way, may I bring a friend of mine to the ball?"

"Twenty, if you like," said Margaret, without looking over her shoulder at him. "Who is it?"

"Oh, an Italian friend of mine; his name—is—" Dick plunged round in his mind for a genuine name; was about to say Victor Emmanuel, and then, frightened at how near he had come to doing so, hastened to say, "Oh, Garibaldi—his name is Garibaldi—yes, Garibaldi."

"Gari—" Mrs. Ivors, in a tone of amazement, had just got so far, when Dick made an awful face at her, shook his head, and waved his hands for her to keep still.

"Of course I don't suppose he's one of the Garibaldis you know, at least not a son of the old fellow. I believe he only had two or three—didn't he, Mrs. Ivors?" he said, cheerfully. "But of course he may be a cousin or something. I'll ask him."

"Why, Dick," said Margaret, gently, and turning around with a smile, "are you picking up lions?"

"My dear Meg! The man hasn't the suspicion of a roar about him, not the least. He is only—a poor devil of an artist;" and Dick inwardly gave thanks that here, at least, he was able to tell the entire truth, for of course it will be seen that his plan was to bring the newly discovered Giuseppe Antonini with him, that he might, by the evidence of his own eyes, discover whether he were really Margaret's friend from Turin. Although he had contrived to see much of the so-called Antonini for the better furtherance of his plans, he had said little to the man himself whereby he could betray him to any one concerned. On recovering from the shock of hearing his name, Dick had wisely exchanged a few words with him, but had bidden him come to his studio that evening, on which occasion Antonini, if it were he, had actually won Dick's good-will. The sight of the comfortable studio seemed to fill him with a mournful admiration. "Ah," he had exclaimed, looking at some of Dick's appurtenances, "*I* could paint, *I*, myself, had I but any of all this;" and the poor wretch waved his hand about, shaking his head tragically.

Naturally Dick had cautioned him on no account to mention his name to De Barbadoesa, and as the Italian needed so intensely what Dick was ready to give, he made the promise, and kept to it.

Whether the man had been so long accustomed to makeshifts for life, or if he was too listless from despair to object to anything that his patron would propose, it is hard to say, but he accepted everything until it came to that unhappy question of his name. When told by what title he was to be introduced at the ball he retreated, and said, proudly: "Nevare! Nevare! Call me dog, hound, what you will, but Garibaldi, nevare!"

This was a difficulty Dick had not foreseen. It was the labor of days to overcome it, but, like other obstacles at the time, it was finally vanquished. Dick, however, feared an outburst on the night in question, and so insisted upon Antonini's accustoming himself to his new title, well knowing that the Italian temperament, in an emergency, cannot be always counted upon as cool. He would therefore desire the dejected creature to stand still while he said, "Allow me to present my friend Signor Garibaldi," an imaginary introduction being gone through with. Also Antonini was obliged to give his name to MacFinlay as that of the famous general, thereby incurring the Irishman's undying hatred. On the first occasion Dick saw the MacFinlay following him up, shaking his fist at his back, and muttering, "Ah, Garahbahldi, ahr you! Garahbahldi is it indeed!" with a smile of superior scorn.

To Mrs. Ivors Dick told as much of his discovery and his plan as he thought prudent.

VII.

Margaret's house on Fifth Avenue presented a spectacle of extraordinary gayety and splendor as Dick, with his suddenly transformed companion, arrived at the ball. Antonini's dress was one in which he was not too much disguised. Hamlet was the character, and he certainly looked like enough to so melancholy a creature. The great staircase was thronged by a very brilliant company as the two men made their way toward the small room where Margaret, Mrs. Troop, and Mrs. Ivors were receiving, and poor Antonini, suddenly delivered from his dingy, desolate surroundings, his semi-seclusion, poverty, and hunger, was pitiably bewildered, and would have escaped, I believe, had not Dick kept his eye close upon him. "For the thirteenth of his line, he has a singularly craven manner," thought Dick, as they emerged on the landing.

But all doubts on this score would soon be set at rest.

"He isn't much disguised," he thought, looking back upon the slim dark figure, whose mournful eyes were fastened upon him, as on a deliverer from this scene, should it become too dangerous. "He's only clean, and I'm sure he must have been that when Meg saw him last," for Dick's mind had refused to associate his cousin with the shiftless, dilapidated Antonini he had found.

"This way, Garibaldi," Dick said, cheerfully. At mention of the name, a few people on the staircase turned and gave a little stare, half of amazement, half of awe, and Antonini, cowering behind Dick, drew himself up with pride, and returned their glances with something so hostile in his own that Dick hurried him on all the more. Margaret was standing at one end of a room which seemed all flowers and wax-lights, and Dick felt at the doorway a tremulous beating at his heart. Mrs. Ivors certainly riveted her gaze upon the two as they approached.

"Miss Fenn, Signor Garibaldi," said Dick, in a shaking though impressive voice.

The unhappy Antonini bowed low, raised his piercing glance, and fixed it upon Margaret. Never had she seemed calmer, sweeter, more self-possessed. By not one flutter of an eyelid did she betray the least acquaintance with the man.

"Any friend of my cousin's is very welcome," she said, smiling. And then began to greet newer arrivals.

Mrs. Ivors and Dick exchanged a glance, and then the latter hurried poor Antonini away and out into the hall, whence he conducted him speedily to a small entry above the back stairs.

"Antonini," he said, sternly, "answer me one question with absolute truth— have you ever seen my cousin before?"

"Nevare," pronounced poor Hamlet, drawing himself up with pride.

"Then, come, come; we must go at once," said Dick, feeling terribly disappointed, irritated, and perhaps a little bit humiliated into the bargain, but it was not on his book that De Barbadoesa should meet Antonini there. The latter, poor man, was glad enough to be led away, even by a back entrance, and also willing to have his supper and remain for the night in Dick's apartments. Having seen him safely into his room, Dick whispered a word of warning to the MacFinlay, who was smoking a pipe in his own quarters.

"Don't let that fellow out, Mac," he said.

The MacFinlay smiled triumphantly. "Divil a step, surr. Ah, the dirty rogue! Garahbahldi, you're fixed in there this time annyhow;" and the Irishman wagged his head with glee.

Dick returned to the ball in a state of visible depression. He would not think of disturbing Margaret during the evening, but was compelled to breathe his woes to Mrs. Ivors.

"Go up to her boudoir and write a note to her," said that lady, "and I'll see that the maid gives it to her early in the morning."

Dick thought well of this, and accordingly penned the following letter:

"DEAR MARGARET,—I am sorry to have to tell you that somehow or somewhere you have been grievously imposed upon. The man I brought to your ball this evening, and whom you failed to recognize, was no other than Giuseppe Antonini. It is evident to me that some one has passed himself off upon you for such a person, unless my man is deceiving me. I found him secreted at De Barbadoesa's room, and I must say, from the little he has told me, he seems to be the genuine article. If this causes you pain and trouble, my dearest cousin, will you not confide in me, and let me take the burden of it on myself? Oh, Meg, it has grieved me so to stand by and see you swindled so shamefully! to feel that you felt yourself bound to marry a man about whom your lips were sealed! Dear, dear Margaret, let me help you. Your affectionate
"DICK."

Having delivered this into Mrs. Ivors's care, Dick took his leave, rather wearier in spirits than he had been for some time. On reaching home, he found the MacFinlay still at his pipe.

"Is he all right, MacFinlay?" Dick asked.

"Not a stirr out of him, surr," was the rejoinder. "Shure I'd the poker ready for him if I'd heard him so much as wink."

Dick contented himself with a glance into the room, where poor Antonini-Garibaldi-Hamlet lay in profound slumber.

"His conscience seems all right," thought Dick as he closed the door, and prepared to pass the night in his studio.

VIII.

By ten o'clock the next morning Dick received the following note:

"MY DEAR COUSIN,—What does all this mean? Can it be that you have really found Antonini? But why should you have called him Garibaldi? Certainly there is a mystery, if not a plot, somewhere. If the latter, I fear it is you who are the victim. Yours,

"MARGARET.

"P.S.—Dear Dick, your loving words of thought for me touch me *so much!* Pray send this man to me at once. I can explain nothing until I have seen him, and do come yourself an hour later.

"MEG."

It may easily be understood that Dick lost no time in obeying both of Margaret's commands. He found her alone, walking up and down her boudoir, looking pale and distressed, but at sight of him she sprang forward with a cry of relief.

"Tell me at once!" she exclaimed.

"No, Meg," he said, gently; "you must tell me first."

She hesitated, and walked over to the fireplace, thinking. "Yes," she said at last, "I can tell you everything."

"To whom you made the pledge you spoke of?"

"To the old Count Giuseppe Antonini in Turin."

"And of what nature was it?"

"I promised to do him a favor and to keep his secret until all was settled; and now that I am satisfied this is the Antonini for whom I have been searching, I can tell you all. The old count once did my father and myself a very great kindness, and I was only too thankful to repay it in some degree. This man is his nephew. Years ago he left the Italian army, and was lost sight of by his family. The old count, feeling certain I could discover traces of him, gave me this charge, but made me promise to speak of it to no one, as they felt their nephew might be in disgrace." There was silence. Then, "Dick, how could you think he was my lover?"

And, "What an absurd chase this has been!" was uttered simultaneously; and then Dick said,

"But De Barbadoesa told me you were betrothed?"

"That was only for his own purposes. The old count had known De Barbadoesa, and believed him to be the person most likely to find his nephew. As I heard he was to meet us at the wharf, I hoped to avoid a complication by seeing no one else. And, Dick"—she came nearer, and

put her hand on his arm—"I have been giving De Barbadoesa the most awful sums of money, for he has been pretending to find Antonini with it, and all the time he had him hidden up there painting his old pictures."

And hereupon Dick had to give vent to a loud and long laugh, in which Margaret joined.

"But, Meg," he said, finally, "did old Antonini know this idiot? Is he, then, really a count?"

"I suppose he must be," she said, "although he looks such an adventurer. Oh," she added, impatiently, "I hate the sound of his name. If only you could have suspected how I detested the man all the time!"

"But, Meg"—by this time Dick was standing very near to Margaret, and had his hands on her shoulders—"surely that couldn't have been what made you so unhappy and restless and cold to me?"

Her face was down-bent, but at these words a lovely color rose in it.

"Cold to you, Dick?" she repeated, softly.

And now she did lift her eyes, and they were shining. "Why, it was because you were so changed to me. Do you know, you nearly broke my heart."

And neither Dick nor Margaret has ever been able even to tell each other how, a few moments later, it happened that she was crying in his arms, and he was saying, "Meg, dearest, we've been stupid so long, don't let us wait for any foolish parade and ceremony." Miss Fenn was married to her second cousin Mr. Norris very quietly one morning two weeks later.

It has always been supposed that De Barbadoesa came to some knowledge of Dick's investigations, and that he considered disappearing the better part of valor. Young Antonini was sent home, liberally supplied with money by Mrs. Norris, and I believe one person only remained dissatisfied. This was MacFinlay, who has always considered himself defrauded of a "try" at the head of poor Antonini, when, as Garibaldi, he slumbered in the MacFinlay's charge. He takes it out, however, in relating the adventure to his friends, and always winds up the story with, "And wid ahl that, me sitting hours, and him in there ashlape, he died in his bed."

THE TRANSATLANTIC CAPTAINS.

BY CHARLES ALGERNON DOUGHERTY.

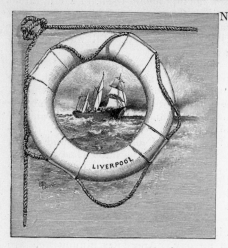

NE sees so little of the sailor that it is only natural one knows so little of him. He is here to-day, on the raging main to-morrow, and a short time afterward in a distant part of the world. And yet, regarding the master-sailors as a class, there are few sets of men to be found more worthy of admiration and esteem. They are emphatically Duty's children, and whenever she commands they obey, even if obedience be at the expense, not only of great personal comfort, but almost of life itself. A terrible affliction in the domestic circle is often obliged to restrain its claims that the tide which waits for no man may carry out to the sea him who has devoted his life in its service. They are brave men, and the record of an ocean disaster often ends thus: "The captain went down with the ship."

The mythical halo that has long encircled the sea-captain is evaporating in these days when the steam-ship service between Europe and America is developing so rapidly as to make the journey seem little longer than an ordinary land trip, and when so many persons from both sides of the sea make themselves personally ac-

THE CAPTAIN'S POST (THE BRIDGE OF THE "OREGON").
From a photograph by W. Oakley, Liverpool.

THE LATE C. H. E. JUDKINS.
From a photograph by Manchester Brothers, Providence.

quainted with a character who may long have been the subject of their wonderment. As he is divested of his mysterious functions, however, he loses nothing of his strong individuality, and gains in the esteem of those who have met him. So true is this that the officers of the different steam-ship companies will tell you that the name of the captain almost invariably influences the passengers' choice of the ship in which they are to make the voyage. As a consequence of this these transatlantic captains are becoming widely known in two continents, although Fame never praises them in her pages as she does their brethren of the navies. But they are the heroes of many anecdotes—so many, indeed, that a volume might be filled with the tales of their prowess and their bravery, but more than all of their personal peculiarities. It is by their respective dispositions and manners that the landsman measures them, and by these traits is he prepossessed or prejudiced.

"What captain sails on Tuesday?"

asks a lady passenger at the Liverpool office of one of the companies. "What! that horrid Captain Dash. I would rather swim it than cross with him again. And who leaves next week? Captain Blank? Oh, that's splendid! I'll wait and sail with him."

This illustrates the case precisely. They may all be excellent sailors and brave men, but something more than that is generally required—yes, and remembered too. The captains are by no means all of a piece as regards popularity. Some of them never make friends, and others always do. Of the latter class many instances might be given. Of the former there has never been a better illustration in the service than the late Captain Judkins, of the Cunard Line. He was highly esteemed by the company, but the bane of nine-tenths of the passengers who crossed in his day. Anecdotes innumerable are told of him, and all illustrative of his singular gruffness of manner. Perhaps the best known of all is this:

Lady passenger (advancing toward the captain, who, leaning over the rail of the *Scotia*, is looking toward Newfoundland): "Oh, captain, do tell me, is it always as foggy and nasty as this off the Banks?"

The captain (glancing briefly at his questioner, and then resuming his attitude), "How the devil do I know, madam? I don't live here."

Certain it is that the memory of this capable old salt is not cherished with much affection by transatlantic voyagers.

Captain E. G. Lott, another veteran officer of the Cunard Line, but now retired from service, was never harshspoken like Captain Judkins, but seemed almost equally averse to mingling with his passengers. He was a jolly-looking man, and usually wore a pleasant smile, which frequently emboldened passengers to address him. "I tried it once," said an Englishman who

E. G. LOTT—(CUNARD).
From a photograph by Brady, Washington.

has crossed the sea many times. "I thought I was drifting into the Gulf Stream, but I found I had struck an iceberg." Captain Lott once had the terrible misfortune of running down a ship in a fog, causing the loss of many lives. He had always been a careful man, but that calamity made him even more so, and he has been known to stay on deck constantly, never getting a moment's sleep for two days.

Captain T. Cook, the present Commodore of this line, is another type of the reserved man who does not familiarize with his passengers. He is never coarse, and will answer a simple question in a simple way. His voice is one of the low, quiet sort, but it has a solidness of sound about it that imparts an emphasis to his words. He is not one of the big, robust specimens of the mariner. He is a singular little man, who cares nothing for the *suaviter in modo*, but demands credit for his *fortiter in re*. He has been on the sea nearly all his life—a period which extends over half a century. During that time he has impressed many people with the fact that a giant's nerve and courage are not always encompassed in a colossal frame, and that men who may not provoke congeniality sometimes inspire confidence and esteem.

The three chief commanders of the Cunard Line at present were once described thus: a sailor, a social sailor, and a calico captain. It would be unfair to name the author of that definition, for he is too well known, but it may not be unjust to state that his compendium was somewhat tinctured with prejudice. However that may be, the simple sailor who is put at the head of the list, and is left adjectiveless, is Captain Cook. It is quite probable, if he chose his own epitaph, he would not desire any more mention than that one word "sailor." Not one in a hundred of his passengers possibly remembers Captain Cook as being a pleasant and agreeable gentleman, but no one can be oblivious of the fact that he is a thorough man, or fail to esteem him for being what he seems, one who can be relied upon in an emergency. Emergencies do arise at sea, and then such men are measured at their worth. In his life he has encountered many strange vicissitudes, but those that marked his earlier career are nearly all forgotten now, for he is not the man to talk, and least of all of himself.

The social sailor is Captain W. McMick-

an, of the *Umbria*. A pleasanter companion one rarely meets. You may sit in his saloon and watch his merry eye sparkle while he rattles off tales of the sea by the hour. The wind may shriek and grate through the yard-arms until

T. COOK—(CUNARD: COMMODORE).
From a photograph by Sarony, New York.

you think you hear the pinging sound of a skeleton's bones; the waves may rush over the forecastle with volcanic force, and break against his cabin door with a roar like thunder, and still you'll sit and laugh as complacently as if you rested snugly before your own fireside, while Captain McMickan spins his yarns. If there is danger, this ruddy-faced Scotchman will not be enjoying himself in his cabin, but will be facing the sea's tempest out on the bridge. He is every inch a mariner. He likes a glass of wine, an iced American beverage on a warm summer's day, or the hot spiced grog of his native land on a winter's night; he is fond of a genial companion, has an ear ever open for the last good story, and an eye of admiration for the gentle sex; but above all these charms of existence is his devotion to the capricious mistress whom he has wooed for so many years, and won at last. The sea, "than woman's love or

W. McMICKAN—(CUNARD: "UMBRIA").
From a photograph by Sarony, New York.

"encore" that ever tickled a *raconteur's* ear. He has a laughing eye, which invests his face with a kind expression, and makes him a cordial favorite with the passengers. With the lady passengers he is an especial favorite, and it was perhaps on this account he was unkindly, perhaps jealously, styled the "calico captain." It is not a pleasant-sounding adjective, and I am reluctant to repeat it; but to those who have ever met this agreeable gentleman it will lose its harsh sound, for they will take it to mean that Captain Hains is one of those men who combine courtesy with courage—qualities which win the admiration not alone of the fair sex, but of mankind as well. He is the type of man whom one admires for his suavity and kindness as well as respects for his unflinching devotion to duty. It is related of him that a few years ago he had as passengers upon his ship the Mother Superior and several nuns of a Sacred Heart convent in America. One day (so the story runs) he did what no man perhaps ever did before—he kissed the venerable Superior and all her younger nuns, and from that day to this has been a great favorite in the convent of those good women. Whenever the ship's concert is held—a fixed event upon every trip—Captain Hains endears himself to his passengers by entering heart and soul into the entertainment, and may always be depended upon to sing, "I'm afloat, I'm afloat, and the Rover is Free." These merry little eccentricities of Captain Hains are only mentioned because they well illustrate the happy-hearted humor of the man, who, besides having the skill of the best sailor afloat and the courage of a warrior, has a heart gentle and jovial as a child's.

The sea-captains, for the most part, are either one thing or the other—either of the jolly, genial type, or of the silent, retiring (I had almost said unsociable) sort. Occasionally one happens to be a little of both and not a great deal of either pattern of man. Such a one is Captain Hamilton Perry, who commands the White Star steamer *Britannic.* He looks like a mariner, and ought to, for he comes of a race of sailors. There have been and are several sea-wanderers among the family. The elder brother of the gallant commander of the *Britannic* is a captain in her Majesty's Royal Navy, and perhaps the brave Perry who will always be remembered as one of

March winds more fitful," has filled her wooing with many strange whims, but the "social sailor," an old man now, loves his heart's idol with even more devotion than in his youth, possibly because he has grown to understand her every humor.

If you have ever crossed with Captain W. H. P. Hains, you will surely remember him. He is a tall, distinguished-looking man, with one of those faces that instantly prepossess you. No mariner whose years run to their end upon the bounding deep is fonder of the sea than the gallant commander of the *Aurania;* but as life to merry men has a diversity of charms, Captain Hains loves the sea none the less in that he loves, besides, "things that are of the earth earthy." If he does not tell a story so frequently as Captain McMickan, he enjoys one just as much, and his hearty laugh is the most complimentary

America's greatest marine chieftains came from the same family of Neptunes. He is Commodore of the White Star fleet, though he looks by no means the oldest. He is about fifty years of age, the greater part of which was passed upon the bounding deep. He chose the sea as the sphere of his life, and was reared accordingly. He was educated at the Royal Naval College at Greenwich, England, and almost before his boyhood days were over began the practical part of existence for which, it might almost be said, he was born and bred. Captain Perry impresses different people differently. "It depends upon how you take him," some one once said. Yes, to a certain extent, it does. If you approach him upon the deck of his ship with one of the silly questions with which, unfortunately, too many ocean travellers are prone to harass the commanders, you will leave him presently with the notion that Captain Perry is not an agreeable man. Don't insist upon his conversing with you when there are duties calling him elsewhere, but wait until he strolls leisurely about the deck, or lolls, when the sea is calm, over the rail beneath the bridge. Then speak to him as you would to any gentleman, and you will find the *Britannic's* commander a pleasant man. He is, indeed, an agreeable man, and one who talks intelligently upon any subject, but "gushes" upon none. He has been in the service of the White Star Line for about fifteen years, but back as far as 1853 he began his transatlantic voyages, and has been crossing

W. H. P. HAINS—(CUNARD: "AURANIA").
From a photograph by Sarony.

back and forth ever since. Of course he has witnessed many strange sights and figured in not a few thrilling scenes during this long period, but even he has forgotten many of them, for it must needs be something startling and wonderful seen on the sea to impress itself upon the old mariner's mind. Souvenirs of the time, such as testimonials, medals, etc., alone recall such incidents. The British government presented him with a handsome pair of binoculars, and the Shipwrecking Humane Society of Great Britain gave him a medal for rescuing the shipwrecked crew of a vessel called the *Allen* in 1872. He found her in the dead of night, waterlogged and with a shattered rudder, in mid-ocean. The medal was "clasped" by the society for a similar act in April, 1876, when the crew of the Norwegian bark *Augusta* were saved by him.

Captain C. W. Kennedy commands a sister ship, the *Germanic*. None of the White Star captains look alike, and in some respects are as different as the sea and shore; but they are for the most part of the practical, serious mould, who rarely unbend to the average passenger's liking. They are all highly esteemed, however, as great sailors, and nearly every one has performed some gallant action and received a public reward. Like the Commodore, Captain Kennedy is best liked by those who know him best. Those who

HAMILTON PERRY—(WHITE STAR: "BRITANNIC").
From a photograph by Mora, New York.

BENJAMIN GLEADELL—(WHITE STAR: "CELTIC").
From a photograph by A. Vandyke, Liverpool.

chanced to be passengers or crew on the Newcastle steamer *Hurworth*, when she started from Montreal for Rotterdam not many years ago, may perhaps remember Captain Kennedy and the *Germanic* with gratitude. The *Hurworth* on her fatal trip had made an ordinarily good run for the first half of the journey. Then her age began to tell upon her, and, like an old charger, she tried to face the foe, but weakened herself with every struggle. The wind rent her canvas into ribbons, and cracked the big masts as if they were spider legs; the fierce waves rushed across her decks, splintering the life-boats, and crushing her cabin roof as if it were paper. The ancient hull creaked almost like a human wail. She tossed in the angry sea through one long day, and the hearts of every one aboard were despairing as the night came on. She could hold out only a little while longer, and every soul aboard knew it. The night was fiercer with the doomed craft than the day, and the winds, increased in violence, kept extinguishing the beacon lights that efforts were made to burn. Presently the red and green lamps of a vessel were seen coming nearer through the thick darkness. More beacons were ignited, and after what seemed a terrible century of anguish and suspense to every one on the Newcastle steamer, a rocket was seen to shoot up into the air from the approaching vessel. Help was coming, all knew, but all feared it would come

too late, for every instant the poor old craft shook with a tremor that seemed like a dying gasp. The stranger came on with fearful speed, and then a blue rocket went skyward. "We will stand by you," that signal meant. The rescuer was the *Germanic*. She ran as close to the disabled vessel as mariners ever find it safe to do in wrecks. So terrible was the sea that it was deemed foolhardy to attempt to get a life-boat afloat in the darkness. The same cheerful signal was again displayed, and then it was recognized by all that there was nothing to do but to wait for daylight. At last it came. The *Germanic's* decks were crowded with passengers, who had lost every desire for sleep in their anxiety for the fate of those so near and yet so far. Flying from the cracked mast-head of the wreck were signal flags which to the sailor's eye read thus: "No boats serviceable; in great distress; send assistance." Long before the sun was up that morning a life-boat was manned by a volunteer crew of the White Star steamer. Captain Bence, now of the *Baltic*, was the chief officer of the *Germanic*, and commanded the relief party. Ten persons were brought back on the first trip. Again the little boat bounded toward the breaking ship, and another load was saved. A third time she made the dangerous journey. All that remained were rescued, but not before the little life-boat had her stem splintered by being dashed by the heavy sea with great force against the sinking hull. Captain Kennedy and Mr. Bence were both highly commended for that gallant rescue, and can show to-day medals which commemorate the incident.

Both officers had a similar previous experience in the same relative positions in 1872, when they (it is fair to say "they," for one deserved and received as much credit as the other) rescued the crew of the ship *Assyrian* in mid-ocean. The sea was, if possible, even rougher than on the winter night when the *Hurworth* tossed in its trough. It was so rough, indeed, that even the old seamen who manned the life-boat were frightened, and mutinied against making another trip to the wreck, after they had brought one boat's load to safety. Then it was that the brave first officer showed the stuff of which he was made. He calmly turned in his seat, and pulling the tiller from its groove, raised it above his head, and in a quiet voice threatened to brain the first man who refused to join in the rescue. That deed was one that many men lived to praise, for all that had been left to rescue or to perish on the *Assyrian* were brought off and safely disposed on the *Germanic*.

Captain Benjamin Gleadell is another illustration of the silent type. He commands the *Celtic*, and as its chief officer has distinguished himself for thorough seamanship and bravery, as he has frequently done during the many years he has been in the service of the White Star Line. He notes the flight of time by a handsome watch presented to him by the President of the United States for saving an American vessel and the lives of all her crew. In his room you may see—but you will have to ask, for he is not the man to display such things—medals presented to him by individuals and associations for similar deeds of humanity, and testimonials prepared and signed by passengers to testify their admiration for the gallant officer. He is, nevertheless, not the man to whom the average passenger takes a fancy. He is strangely reserved, and rarely in a trip ventures upon more than an occasional "Good-morning" as he passes an early riser on the deck. "I won't say he's a darned disagreeable cuss, but he's too dignified

PETER J. IRVING—(WHITE STAR: "REPUBLIC").
From a photograph by A. Vandyke, Liverpool.

to suit me," a traveller from a Western State once said of Captain Gleadell. He is a man of about fifty-four now, and an Englishman by birth. When he dons his uniform and goes up on the bridge he looks every inch a sailor, and a fine specimen of physical manhood.

Captain Peter J. Irving, of the *Republic*, is still another of the White Star's galaxy of quiet men, and yet he is the sort of officer that always favorably impresses those who meet him. He is scarcely more than forty years of age, but in that time has climbed the ladder, or perhaps it would be more applicable to say has mounted to the topmast of position step by step upon the riggings of merit. He is what is described among seamen as a "*Conway* boy"; that is, he acquired his rudimentary knowledge of navigation on the old training ship whose name gives a special distinction to her alumni. He, like nearly all his fellow-captains of the line, has figured in not a few gallant rescues at sea.

Captain Parsell, of the *Adriatic*, is unlike all the other commanders of Messrs. Ismay and Imrie's fleet. He has a distinct personality about him which makes one glad to know him and likely to remem-

FREDERICK WATKINS—(INMAN: "CITY OF CHICAGO").
From a photograph by Mora, New York.

FRANCIS S. LAND—(INMAN : "CITY OF BERLIN").
From a photograph by Messrs. Brown, Barnes, and Bell, Liverpool.

HENRY CONDRON—(INMAN : "CITY OF CHESTER").
From a photograph by Mora, New York.

ber him. His age is not so easy to guess as most men's, because when he smiles — as he frequently does — his face is as frank and merry as that of a school-boy; but when he falls into a reverie and talks of his wanderings on icy seas so many years ago, you can't help thinking that this young-looking man must really be almost a patriarch. Nothing will better indicate the man than by saying he enjoys the esteem of everybody who has ever met him, and possesses the entire confidence of the company. So strong, indeed, is he in the confidence and good graces of the line that he has always been the pioneer officer in any new development of the White Star service. There is not a sea on the planet he has not navigated. He has sailed upon the Arctic as well as upon the Antarctic, and all the big streams that flow between the two. He is an intelligent man, and of so genial a type that he never gets out of patience with a passenger even if he is stormed with an arsenal of such landsmen's questions as would drive many a mariner to distraction.

The minute you set foot upon the deck of the *City of Chicago* you will like Captain Frederick Watkins. If you, as some people do, make the very first duty aboard ship to see what sort of a man you have for captain, and try the experiment of exchanging a word with him, you may rest assured you won't go away grumbling at

his lack of courtesy when you have spoken to the Commodore of the Inman fleet. Pleasanter men are not to be found either on sea or shore. "He's made of the right sort of stuff for a mariner," one of his seamen once said to me. All his sailors like him, and it is much the same quality of polite consideration which has made him one of the most popular of all the trans-atlantic captains. In his uniform he looks every inch the sailor. When he has doffed the "gilded blue" for street apparel he would never be taken for one whose days and nights, year in and year out, are passed upon the bounding billow. Some one has called the commander of the *Chicago* the "gentleman captain." There is no man who sails the Atlantic who has received more testimonials from his passengers than Captain Watkins has elicited by his unchanging good temper and constant urbanity.

If you are a believer in physiognomy, look at Captain Francis S. Land's portrait, and you will know him to be, as he is, a man of the kindest instincts, and yet of the strongest force of character. Possibly better than any officer who can be named in this sketch he illustrates the popular idea of the sea-captain. He is a big man, of the hearty, robust type; he looks a giant in his uniform. You say, as you gaze upon him, "Here's a man such as one looks for upon the sea; he is approachable by a child, but he secures and retains the respect of every one." He has hosts of friends, whom he has won by his geniality and retains by his high character. It is related that some such conversation as this once occurred, of which Captain Land was the subject:

"He's a splendid, warm-hearted fellow."

"Warm-hearted, did you say? Why, he's the coolest man I ever knew. You ought to see him sometimes."

He is both. That he is warm-hearted, the average uneventful trip will show. That he is "cool," only becomes manifest upon certain occasions. A recent incident well demonstrates the fact. A few months ago Captain Land's vessel, the *City of Berlin*, collided with an iceberg. It was in the night-time, and no blame at-

JAMES PRICE—(GUION: PORT ADMIRAL).
From a photograph by Messrs. Brown, Barnes, and Bell, Liverpool.

GEORGE S. MURRAY—(GUION: "ALASKA").
From a photograph by Rockwood, New York.

Lewis, of the *City of Richmond*, and Redford, of the *City of Montreal*, are perhaps still younger. They form a trio of agreeable men and thorough sailors, and it is said of them all that they have "lowered their boats" many a time.

Some people say of the Guion Line that it is particularly fortunate in having such a staff of universally popular commanders. Captain James Price is distinctively an Atlantic veteran. He has crossed 'twixt shore and shore times without number. He has commanded all the crack "greyhounds" of the company, and has perhaps ferried ten thousand people over the wide stream. When it is considered that this jolly, amiable Welshman, with a kind word for everybody, has left his like-

taches to any one for the accident. The berg was almost as hard as the iron ship, and much larger. Both opposing bodies were sadly damaged, and at one time affairs looked serious for the passengers aboard the steamer, but the gallant mariner with the anomalous name carried his boat through dangerous seas to the port of New York. A handsome watch and chain are his souvenirs of those trying days. They were presented to Captain Land, in the language of the gentleman who spoke in behalf of his fellow-passengers, "for being cooler than the iceberg."

The Inman officers are all comparatively young men. Captain Condron, of the *City of Chester*, is about forty-two or forty-three years of age, and Captains

SAMUEL BROOKS—(GUION: "ARIZONA").
From a photograph by R. A. Lewis, New York.

R. D. MUNRO—(ANCHOR: "CITY OF ROME").
From a photograph by Joseph Hall, Brooklyn.

ness in many minds, and perhaps a more lasting impression upon almost as many hearts, it is natural to presume that in two continents Captain Price, as good a sailor as he is a pleasant man, will not soon be forgotten. He is now the line's Port Admiral at Liverpool.

Captain George Siddons Murray commands the *Alaska*. He is a Scotchman by birth, and as big, robust a son of Caledonia as ever came out of the Highlands or Lowlands. He is about five-and-forty years of age, of handsome appearance, and fine bearing. He is popular with passengers, although never effusive in his manner.

Captain Samuel Brooks, of the *Arizona*, is another example of the colossal captain. He is a man of powerful frame, but scarcely so tall as Captain Murray. He is about five years the senior of the *Alaska's* commander, and wears a full gray beard most becomingly. He is a man of distinguished appearance, who blends suavity with a dignity that never repels, but prevents intrusive familiarity. He is a favorite with every passenger. Madame Patti almost invariably crosses the Atlantic on Captain Brooks's steamer. Mrs. Langtry, Henry Irving, and a host of other people known as well on one side of the sea as the other, speak in terms of admiration of this popular officer. He has been twenty-eight years in the Atlantic service.

His record shows that he has crossed the ocean 540 times, without the loss of a single life on his vessel. In this time he has added extra laurels to his wreath by rescuing many persons.

Captain R. D. Munro is Commodore of the Anchor Line fleet, and commander of that great ship the *City of Rome*, which has grown to be known as the Leviathan of the Atlantic. His is the only vessel of the line which sails between Liverpool and New York. Glasgow is the home port of all the other Anchors. Munro is a veteran. He is sixty or thereabouts, although he doesn't look it, which is all the more surprising when one thinks that for nearly a half-century the Atlantic has been hurling her biting winds and salty spray in the old tar's face. Like all the Anchor's commanders, he is a Scotchman. He can say a funny thing in a funny way, but is not so fond of getting convivial spirits about him and reeling off yarns by the yard as some of his countrymen. His line inclines rather to the ladies, to whom he devotes himself when off watch. He has crossed the sea about five hundred times.

Captain John J. Small, of the *Anchoria*, doesn't look like Captain Munro, but the same general description will fit both. He is of nearly the same age, of the same short, thickset figure, and has a weather-beaten complexion and grayish beard like Munro. Unlike the Commodore, however, he is rather indifferent to the society of lady passengers. A few pleasant fellows around the whist table in his cabin comes nearer his notion of comfort.

JAMES SUMNER—(NATIONAL: "EGYPT").
From a photograph by Messrs. Brown, Barnes, and Bell, Liverpool.

Captain John Hedderwick, of the *Furnessia*, is different from both in appearance, and a sort of link between the two in his tastes. His strong right arm has escorted many a lady across slippery and rocking decks, and many of them will always remember the captain as a pleasant man. "Black Jock" is the familiar title he is known by. He is dark as a Spaniard in skin, eyes, and hair, and of a good height. He is a cool, courageous man. One foggy day, some years ago, another steamer collided with his vessel. There was an immediate panic. Even the sailors were frightened, and jumped into the life-boats. Hedderwick grabbed an axe and a pistol, and brought his crew to a sense of their duties. A man of nerve is needed at such times, and "Black Jock" was such a one.

The National Line is justly proud of her captains. She has a big fleet of stanch ships, to each of which the name of one of the great nations of the earth is given. The line is a British corporation, and hence no selfish partiality is responsible for the fact that the largest, newest, and best of the baker's dozen of splendid vessels is called the *America*. It may have been a mere coincidence in its christening, but it is a compliment none the less to what the patriotic American would call the largest, newest, and best of the nations. The command of this fine steamer has been given to Captain R. W. Grace, who ranks as the Commodore of the line. He has been temporarily deprived of the guardianship of this youngest sea child of the National by her British Majesty's government, who have enrolled the *America* into the military transport service. It is expected that she will soon resume her usual sphere of existence as one of the monarchs of the Atlantic. Captain Grace is as proud of his ship as the line is of him. Unlike his vessel, he is neither the largest nor the newest of his colleague captains, but there are many people who persist that he is the best. In point of length of service and varied experience on the sea, he is unquestionably the patriarch. He is in his fifty-seventh year, and looks every inch a gallant mariner. He has been a National captain for twenty years. If he wore on his breast all the medals he has won for fearless deeds and humane actions, his coat would look like a jeweller's shop case. A hale, jovial, and genial man, always courteous and considerate, one is never at a loss to understand, when speaking to him, why Commodore Grace is so popular with ocean travellers.

Next to him in order of seniority is Captain James Sumner, of the *Egypt*. There is nearly 1000 tons difference in the size of the *America* and the *Egypt*. The same relative difference of weight prevails in the case of the two commanders.

REDFORD W. SARGENT—(AMERICAN: "INDIANA").
From a photograph by A. Vandyke, Liverpool.

Sumner is short of stature, though not slight of build. He is twelve years the junior of Grace, and runs the latter a hard race for general popularity. He has been in the employ of the company ever since it was established, and has made a name for himself as a thorough sailor and a pleasant man which seems to grow and expand with each succeeding year. A passenger would never die of *ennui* while Captain Sumner is near at hand. The other vessels of the National fleet are officered by good men, not, however, generally known, for their ships do not usually carry saloon passengers; but when any one of them, like Captain Heely, the big, energetic commander of the *England*, happens to rescue a shipwrecked crew, as he did not long ago, the newspapers make the public acquainted with their sterling traits.

PATRICK URQUHART—(AMERICAN: "LORD CLIVE").
From a photograph by Messrs. Brown, Barnes, and Bell, Liverpool.

Captain Redford W. Sargent commands the American Line steam-ship *Indiana*, which runs between Liverpool and Philadelphia. The *Indiana* is only a freight-carrier now, but a few years ago she and her three sister ships, the *Pennsylvania*, *Illinois*, and *Ohio*, were the only vessels in the ocean ferrying trade which sailed under the American flag. There are not a few people on both sides of the sea who sincerely regret the change, for it prevents their having the pleasure of sailing with Captain Sargent—one of the pleasantest men who ever helped to make the long, tedious journey seem all too short. He is only a young man now, but he carries a sailor's head on his thickset shoulders, and knows every wave of the sea as well as he knows every rope of his ship. He is perhaps not as spontaneously genial as either Captain McMickan or Captain Hains, but he impresses one first as a courteous gentleman, and the more one sees of him the better one grows to like him. He is a New-Englander, and although quite a young man at the time, rendered distinguished service to his country during the late war. He served in the Union fleet which advanced up the James River to Richmond, and was subsequently an officer on different vessels of the blockading fleet engaged along the coast of the Southern States. He has several times been instrumental in saving life at sea. The Ca-

nadian government conferred a certificate of honor upon him for saving the crew of the schooner *Wild Rose*, and the United States government presented him with a valuable telescope for rescuing the shipwrecked crew of the *Forest State*. Since he has been in the service of the American Line he has been rewarded for similar feats, and received a medal from the Royal Humane Society of Great Britain for rescuing the crew of the bark *Avon* in 1874.

Captain Sargent is the Commodore of the "Quartette"—embracing four distinct branches under the same general management—the other three captains having more recently succeeded to their posts, either through the retirement or death of predecessors. Captain Shackford formerly commanded the *Illinois*, but retired from the transatlantic service to accept the command of Mr. Jay Gould's yacht. Shackford was universally popular, and is remembered by many ocean voyagers as being for many years first officer on a Cunarder before he joined the *Illinois*. He was voted by the ladies the handsomest of Neptune's Atlantic sons.

Since the American Line was established two deaths have occurred among her commanders. The first captain of the *Pennsylvania* was lost overboard during a gale at sea on, if not the first, at least

W. G. RANDLE—(RED STAR: "WESTERNLAND").
From a photograph by Gutekunst, Philadelphia.

one of the earliest trips made by that ship. Another captain died of illness when a few days out from Philadelphia. The two officers named above, as indeed have been nearly all the captains of the "Keystoners," are Americans. The English ships, however, which are chartered by the same company are officered by citizens of Great Britain. Captain Patrick Urquhart, of the *Lord Clive*, and Captain E. H. Freeth, of the *British Princess*, are subjects of the Queen. The company considers them both capable officers, and the travelling public goes a little further, and looks upon them as attractive men. Captain Urquhart is a few years the senior of Captain Sargent. He has served his company as a commander for eleven years, but his life on other seas runs far beyond his term upon the Atlantic. He was for many years in Papayam's Greek service. He is different from Captain Freeth in being a sailor of the quiet, retiring, and almost shy stamp. The man who guides the *British Princess* through trackless seas is a second edition of Captain Shackford. He is only three-and-thirty, and if ever another Andromeda is chained to an ocean rock, this handsome young *Conway* sailor is the man to enact Perseus. Like the late commander of the *Illinois*, he is a favorite with every one, and promises in a few years to be one of the best-known men who sail the Altantic.

Captain William G. Randle, of the Red Star branch of the American Line, commands the *Westernland*. The home port of his vessel, unlike that of his three brethren, Sargent, Urquhart, and Freeth, is New York. No, on second thought, this is not exactly the fact. The home port of the Red Star ships is Antwerp, since the line is distinctly more Belgian than American in its *personnel*. One hardly knows just how to describe it, but it may not be improper to speak of the Red Star as one of the branches of the American Line. In all its features and peculiarities it partakes of two nationalities more than any line which traverses the Atlantic. Some of its officers are Belgians, while others are citizens of the United States. The Commodore of the fleet, Captain W. G. Randle, is a Pennsylvanian by birth. He was born and still has his home in that thriving little ship-building town on the Delaware River, Chester. I have met lots of old ocean travellers who declare that Ran-

dle is "the pleasantest captain who crosses the sea."

The captains of the North German Lloyd Line are well known now in three of the greatest nations of the earth, and the growing prosperity of this company will soon expand still more their modest fame. Their vessels touch three ports,

E. H. FREETH—(AMERICAN: "BRITISH PRINCESS").
From a photograph by Messrs. Brown, Barnes, and Bell, Liverpool.

German, English, and American, on each oceanic journey. From Bremen they carry to the Western world hundreds of German travellers, whose number is reënforced at Southampton by many Britishers who dread the long rail ride from London to Liverpool. It may not be proper here to say that the Bremen steamers are of themselves especially attractive to the average transatlantic traveller, but this fact may with propriety and truth be emphasized—that the North German Lloyd captains for seamanship and social qualities are the peers of any men who sail the sea. Look at the portraits of the four German captains on the next page. You will find that they look like sailors, and you needn't be told that they know how to manage their ships in the heaviest gale. Each of the four has likewise his host of friends, won by his sterling worth and genial ways. Captain Christoph Leist

RICHARD BUSSIUS—(NORTH GERMAN LLOYD:
"WERRA").

From a photograph by Emil Tiedemann, Bremen.

CHRISTOPH LEIST—(NORTH GERMAN LLOYD:
SUPERINTENDENT-CAPTAIN).

From a photograph by Emil Tiedemann, Bremen.

is the youngest of the quartette, being now in the forty-third year of his age. He is a practical sailor in more ways than one. Added to his skill as a navigator—for he has been a captain in the company's service for seventeen years—he has a complete knowledge of the art of ship-building. He superintended the construction of the five latest additions to the fleet at the shipyard in Scotland, and is well known in Glasgow. He now holds the honorable post of Superintendent-Captain. Unlike him, the three other captains still have command of vessels.

Captain Richard Bussius is commander of the *Werra*. Like Captain Barre, he is

JULIUS BARRE—(NORTH GERMAN LLOYD).

From a photograph by Emil Tiedemann, Bremen.

WILHELM WILLIGEROD—(NORTH GERMAN LLOYD).

From a photograph by Emil Tiedemann, Bremen.

two years older than the Superintendent-Captain. He was born in Brunswick. He has a good voice, is fond of music, brimful of anecdotes, and is universally popular. In November last he was entertained at a banquet on the steamer *Elbe* by the directors of the line, in honor of his having concluded his one-hundredth round voyage across the Atlantic. On that occasion he received from the German Emperor the knighthood of the Prussian Crown Order of the Fourth Class. He is highly esteemed as a sailor, and as a man he is cordially liked, for he takes pains to see that all who cross with him are comfortable and happy.

Captain Wilhelm Willigerod, who formerly commanded the *Ems*, and will control one of the three new steamers which Messrs. John Elder and Co. are constructing, is the oldest of this group of captains, although only forty-seven himself. And he doesn't even look that old. He is a man of a hardy, robust physique.

Captain Julius Barre hails from Westphalia. He commanded the *Werra* until recently, but will soon assume charge of one of the company's new steamers now building. Captain Barre is a living proof that the strictest disciplinarian may be a jolly, genial companion.

So much for the Germans. Now what about the French captains? Here is the condensed essence of an old ocean traveller's opinions, as he expressed them recently to me:

"You know that I am not the sort of a man to be deceived by the superficial appearance of any one, and that surface politeness is a thing I abhor. Moreover, I have crossed this sea as many times as most of the veterans who live upon it, and therefore I think my opinion upon a line is entitled to some respect. Well, this I can say for the Compagnie Générale Transatlantique: their ships— Oh! you don't want to hear about the ships; it's only about the captains that you want me to talk. Very well. I have crossed with them all, and know them pretty intimately. Individually they are all entirely different. Collectively they are as courteous a set of men as I have ever known. They are as kind-hearted and gentle as school-girls, and, despite what you may hear occasionally, they are as good seamen and as brave and cool in danger as you will find anywhere. They assure your safety by their constant watchfulness, and your

ALPHONSE P. M. PERIER D'HAUTERIVE—(COMPAGNIE GÉNÉRALE TRANSATLANTIQUE: "LABRADOR").
From a photograph by A. Caccia, Havre.

comfort and contentment by their polite attention. What more could I say of any man or men?"

I have found by personal investigation that this statement is true as gospel. In the first place, they have been proven to be skilled navigators. Four out of the six are officers of the French navy, and all but one are Chevaliers of the Legion of Honor. The single exception, it is thought, will soon be awarded this distinction, for, besides being highly esteem-

E. FRANGEUL—(COMPAGNIE GÉNÉRALE TRANSATLANTIQUE: "LA NORMANDIE").
From a photograph by Fredericks, New York.

S. SANTELLI—(COMPAGNIE GÉNÉRALE TRANSATLANTIQUE:
"AMÉRIQUE").

From a photograph by A. Caccia, Havre.

G. A. M. S. DE KERSABIEC—(COMPAGNIE GÉNÉRALE
TRANSATLANTIQUE: "CANADA").

From a photograph by M. Van Bosch, Paris.

ed as a mariner, he (Perier d'Hauterive) bears a name honored in the naval history of France. I have heard numerous incidents from passengers which show that the exuberant, emotional nature of the Frenchman can be as phlegmatic and passionless in times of danger at sea as the coldest Scottish tar. And they are highly esteemed. This is especially true of Captain E. Frangeul, commander of *La Normandie* and Commodore of the fleet. Everybody likes him. He is a man under the average height, and of slight frame, and just in the prime of life, for he is approaching his fiftieth year. When the sun is dancing on the water, the waves are smooth, and the breeze is rushing, trap-like, into the sails, Frangeul is the lightest-hearted, merriest man aboard, and his voice may be heard singing, laughing,

EDOUARD G. TRAUB—(COMPAGNIE GÉNÉRALE
TRANSATLANTIQUE: "ST. GERMAIN").

From a photograph by Louis Martin, Nantes.

or spinning a yarn. Even the sea-sick passengers try to be near him to catch the contagion of his merriment. When sun, waves, and wind are different—well, Frangeul is different too, and from the pleasant companion is changed to the severe sailor. As a mariner, his record is an enviable one. One instance may serve to show him as a navigator. A few years ago the *Amérique* broke a shaft when nearly in mid-ocean. A passing vessel brought the news to Havre. The latitude and longitude of the disabled ship were given him, and Frangeul, with the *Ville de Brest*, a much smaller steamer, went out to search for her. Of course he had to calculate how the shaftless ship might drift. He calculated well, for more than a week later, in the dead of night, the vessels met, "nose to nose," as the sailors say. Of course this showed Frangeul's mettle, and it is only one of many similar feats that help to make his record.

Captain S. Santelli is next in order. His ship is the *Amérique*. Though holding a commission in the French navy, he has served as a merchantman in the company's service for years. He is a handsome little man, an excellent sailor, and very popular with passengers. Captain Alphonse P. M. Perier d'Hauterive, of the *Labrador*, is not an ordinary-looking man. He is rather tall for a Frenchman, and wears a full beard. He is of slight frame, but it is his eyes which make him rather conspicuous. One is of Italian darkness, and the other of the light hue peculiar to the Saxon. As if jealous of each other, each eye renders its owner all the service possible. The consequence is that the *Labrador's* commander is a marvel as to his wonderful sight. And if the eyes be the windows of the soul, it is fair to presume that in his nature Perier d'Hauterive blends the characteristics of the people of sunny skies with those of the land of fog, for he is both genial and cool, as occasions demand. He is the nephew of the late distinguished French admiral who bore the same name.

Captain Edouard G. Traub, of the *St. Germain*, Captain De Jousselin, of the *St. Laurent*, and Captain G. A. M. S. De Kersabiec, of the *Canada*, are the three remaining commanders of the French fleet. They are all comparatively young men. Traub is looked upon as a wonderful mathematician. Unlike the others, he does not care to mingle much with the passengers. De Jousselin is a Vendean and a marquis. He is a fine-looking man, with excellent address. De Kersabiec, as his name indicates, is a native of vine-clad Brittany. Like the wine of his country, he is sparkling, bright, and effervescent.

Besides the lines named above there are several others running between European and United States ports. Among their respective staffs of commanders may be found several who in recent years have proved themselves made of the metal of which Fate moulds heroes. It is impossible, however, in the limited space of a magazine sketch to speak separately of all the Atlantic's great sons, brave men and true, whose sunshiny days and blackest nights will come and go like so many waves of the ocean, whose billows to come will rush after those that have passed, and from whose life wind and wave will never vanish until the old tar has finished his last round voyage, and anchored his ancient craft in a tempestless port.

JOSEPH JEFFERSON.
BY WILLIAM WINTER.

JOSEPH JEFFERSON, the comedian, now in the fifty-eighth year of his age, and at the zenith of his professional career, is one of the most famous and one of the best beloved of actors, whether at home or abroad. The first thought that naturally occurs to the observer of his renown is the thought of its singular beauty, tranquillity, and beneficence. Mr. Jefferson has been a long time in public life, and he has made his way to eminence and fortune through a period marked by the uncommonly fierce strife of conflicting ambitions; but probably he never had an enemy in the world. Simply to mention his name is to conjure up pleasant memories and awaken feelings of kindness. He has been seen far and wide, in all parts of the United States, in Canada, in Australia and New Zealand, and throughout the British Isles, and the influence that he has everywhere diffused has been bright, gentle, and pure. It is not alone the exquisite finish of his dramatic art that has prevailed with the world, gaining for Mr. Jefferson a first place in the public mind: the tender sympathetic spirit of humanity and the sweet poetic charm that radiate from his spirit and suffuse his acting with kindly warmth and mysterious fascination have equally endeared him to the public heart.

It has sometimes been asserted that judgment of an actor cannot be wise and impartial unless it separates the artist from the man—that the less you know about the nature of the actor himself, the better are you fitted to analyze and estimate his art. But this is a mistaken doctrine. The beauties of an actor's art are technical only up to a certain point. Riding, swimming, skating, fencing, playing whist, playing chess—these, and all such arts as these, are to be viewed simply and solely with reference to method. Acting is a far greater art, involving much more than clearness of design, competent force, precision of touch, and grace of execution. The informing vitality and the crowning charm of an actor's art reside in attributes that flow out of an actor's spiritual nature; and the true excellence of the one is clearly seen and rightly appreciated only by those observers who can see into the constitution and resources of the other. Every truth that can be discerned as to the soul of the actor helps such an observer more justly to comprehend and more deeply to feel the power and the loveliness of his work. Superficial knowledge of surroundings and habiliments is not denoted as essential, although, to some extent, this also may help. The vital thing is a deep and true perception of the soul. The more you know about the actor in this sense, the better are you qualified to estimate his acting. In fact, unless you know him in this way, you can know his acting merely as mechanism. In the case of Mr. Jefferson, the man and the actor are so inextricably blended that in any disquisition upon his art it is wellnigh impossible to dissever them. This comedian, indeed, has completely and accurately assumed many different identities; few actors have equalled him in abundance of the resources of technical skill; but the felicitous precision, the truth to nature, with which he has portrayed these identities, and the magical charm, whether of grace, humor, tenderness, eccentricity, or genius, with which he has suffused them, arise out of attributes in the spiritual constitution of the man himself, and are not referable to his dramatic art.

Mr. Jefferson comes of a theatrical lineage in both branches of his ancestry. The Jefferson family of actors was founded by Thomas Jefferson, born about the year 1728, a native of the township of Ripon, Yorkshire, England, who went up to London, probably in 1746, when a youth of about eighteen, became a member of Garrick's company at Drury Lane Theatre, and subsequently had a career of about sixty years on the English stage. Old dramatic records give but meagre information about this actor; but he seems to have attained to a good position. He was esteemed the equal, in comedy, of so fine an actor as Spranger Barry, and the superior, in this field, of Mossop, Reddish,

and the elder Sheridan. His tragic performances, if less meritorious, were accounted to be equal with those of Macklin, the first true Shylock of the English theatre. He is mentioned as "Garrick's favorite Horatio." He was even accepted sometimes as a substitute for that brilliant genius; and in one of the accounts of him that were published immediately after his death—which occurred in 1807—he is described as "the friend, contemporary, and exact prototype of the immortal Garrick."

Thomas Jefferson was on the stage from 1746 till almost the day of his death in 1807. He managed theatres in England at Richmond, Exeter, Plymouth, and other cities, but chiefly at Plymouth. His career might be told in much more detail, and with the picture of the whole brilliant Garrick period as a background, although, of course, Thomas Jefferson was not, and should not be made, the chief figure in that resplendent picture. But he lived in a remarkable dramatic era, and he was associated with many of the finest intellects, the loveliest faces, and the brightest reputations of the eighteenth century.

Joseph Jefferson, second in the Jefferson family of actors, was born at Plymouth, England, in 1774 or 1776. There is some uncertainty as to the date of his birth. He was carefully educated for the stage, and he appeared at the Plymouth theatre while yet a youth, under his father's direction. As soon as he had attained to manhood, however, he emigrated to America, and he never returned to his native land. He came over in 1795, under engagement to Charles Stuart Powell, first manager of the theatre in Federal Street, Boston—a house that was opened on February 3, 1794. Powell agreed to pay the young actor's passage, and a salary of seventeen dollars a week. On reaching Boston, Jefferson found that Powell had been unfortunate, and had been obliged to shut the theatre (June 19, 1795). Left thus adrift, he engaged with Hallam and Hodgkinson, who were on a professional visit to Boston, from the John Street Theatre, New York, and with those managers he performed at Boston, Providence, and Hartford, and finally came to the metropolis. His first appearance in New York was made on February 10, 1796, at the theatre in John Street, and the part he played was Squire Richard, in *The Provoked Husband*. He was of small stature, slight in figure, well formed, and graceful. He had a Grecian nose, and his eyes were blue and full of laughter. The John Street Theatre, precursor to the old Park, was first opened December 7, 1767, and it was finally closed on January 13, 1798. Jefferson was connected with it for nearly the whole period of its last two years, and when it closed he went to the Park, at first styled "The New Theatre," or simply "The Theatre." Jefferson's career at the Park Theatre extended through five regular seasons, ending in the spring of 1803, when he accepted an engagement with Mrs. Wignell, who just then had succeeded, by the sudden death of her husband, to the management of the Chestnut Street Theatre, in Philadelphia. The detailed story of the rest of his life would be the story of that theatre. There he developed his powers, there he accomplished his best works, and there he acquired his great fame. Making allowance for the differences existent between the conditions of publicity in those days and in ours, he had a career as prominent, though not as well known, as that of his famous grandson, and in much the same spirit he was honored and beloved. His rank and position were much the same as those in the present day of Mr. John Gilbert. He had the friendship of President Jefferson, and the two were of opinion that they had sprung from the same stock; but the relationship was never directly traced. The President was of Welsh extraction, the comedian of English. It is recorded of Jefferson and his wife that they were born on the same day of the same month and year, one in America, the other in England. They had nine children, all but two of whom adopted the stage. Jefferson was a man of sweet but formal character and polished, punctilious manners, of absolute integrity, and of pure and exemplary life. As an actor he was remarkable for nature and variety. It is said he never twice gave a scene in precisely the same manner. His humor was involuntary and exceedingly fascinating. He never used grimace. He may be traced through more than 200 characters. "He played everything that was comic," said John P. Kennedy, the novelist, "and always made people laugh till the tears came in their eyes. . . . When he acted, families all went together, old and young. Smiles were on every face; the town was happy." The latter days of his life were

sorely overwhelmed with calamity and sorrow. He died at Harrisburg in 1832.

The third Jefferson, father of our comedian, was born in Philadelphia in 1804. He was a man of most serene and gentle nature, and of simple, blameless life. He was an inveterate quiz, a good scene-painter, and a good actor of old men; but he did not make an important figure on the stage.

The maternal ancestry of our present representative American comedian, Joseph Jefferson, is also dramatic, his mother having adopted the stage when a child, and subsequently risen to distinction as an actress, and to special eminence as a singer. This lady was the only child of a French gentleman, M. Thomas, resident for some time at San Domingo, from which place, however, he fled with his wife and daughter, the latter then only three or four years of age, at the time of the second revolt of the negroes against the French government in 1803, when a massacre of the white population was ordered, and to some extent accomplished, by those fierce insurgents. The refugees had a narrow escape. One of M. Thomas's slaves, more faithful than the rest to his master's fortunes, gave information of the intended slaughter, so that the planter was enabled just in time to make his escape. The fugitives decamped by night, and hid themselves among dense thickets adjacent to their home. The house was pillaged and burnt, and the whole place was devastated. Jefferson remembers having heard his mother speak of this experience, saying that, although then only a little child, she could recollect something of the fright and horror of the time—the concealment by night, the warning not to utter a sound, the suspense, the cries of the negroes as they went about beating the bushes in their murderous quest, which proved in vain. Fortunately the child did not cry, and M. Thomas, with his living treasures, at length got safely away from the island.

Joseph Jefferson, the fourth of this distinguished dynasty, was born at Philadelphia on February 20, 1829. The home of his birth is still standing, at the southwest corner of Spruce and Sixth streets. He was reared by theatrical parents and among theatrical friends and the surroundings of the theatre, and he was embarked upon his theatrical career while yet a little child. His first appearance upon the stage was made in 1833, when he was only four years old, at a theatre in Washington. The negro comedian Thomas D. Rice (1808–60), once and for a long time known and popular as "Jim Crow," carried him on in a bag or basket, and at a certain point, while singing the song of "Jim Crow," emptied from it this youngster, blackened and "made up" as a fac-simile of himself, who immediately struck the attitude of Rice, and danced and sung in exact imitation of the long, lank, ungainly, humorous original. Four years later this lad was at the Franklin Theatre, in New York, with his parents, and he appeared there on September 30, that year, in a sword combat with one Master Titus, whom it was his business to discomfit, and over whom he triumphed in good old bravado manner. Early in 1838 young Jefferson was taken to Chicago, together with his half-brother, Charles Burke, and both of them were there kept in continual practice on the stage. The whole family, indeed, went wandering into the West and South, and many and varied were the adventures through which they passed, earning a precarious livelihood by the practice of an art almost unrecognized as yet in those regions.

A glimpse of Jefferson as he appeared in the early days of his professional career, which were also the early days of the American theatre, more particularly in the West, was afforded not long since at a meeting of the Historical Society of Chicago, at which the veteran theatrical manager Mr. James H. McVickar read a paper descriptive of the origin and growth of the theatre in that city. The first entertainment for which an admission fee was charged in Chicago occurred in 1834. The first theatre there was established in 1837, by Henry Isherwood and Alexander McKenzie. It stood on the southeast corner of Lake and Market streets. Isherwood is remembered as long a scenic artist at Wallack's Theatre, a man of signal talent and of interesting character. Mr. McVickar expatiated agreeably upon these and kindred details, and read this letter from the comedian:

" I am not quite sure that I remember dates and circumstances in their exact form, but will give you the benefit of all I know relating to Chicago theatricals. My father and his family arrived in Chicago by way of the lakes, in a steamer, somewhere about May, in the year 1838. He came to join Alexander McKenzie

(my uncle) in the management of his new theatre. McKenzie had been manager of the old one the season before. I think the new theatre was the old one refitted. [This is an error.] I know it was the pride of the city and the ideal of the new managers, for it had one tier of boxes and a gallery at the back. I don't think that the seats of the dress circle were stuffed, but I am almost sure that they were planed. The company consisted of William Leicester, William Warren, James Wright, Charles Burke, Joseph Jefferson, Thomas Sankey, William Childs, H. Isherwood (artist), Joseph Jefferson, Jun., Mrs. McKenzie, Mrs. J. Jefferson (my mother), Mrs. Ingersoll, and Jane Germon. I was the comic singer of this party, making myself useful in small parts and first villagers, now and then doing duty as a Roman Senator, at the back, wrapped in a clean hotel sheet, with my head just peering over the profile banquet tables. I was just nine years old. I was found useful as Albert and Duke of York. In those days the audience used to throw money on the stage, either for comic songs or dances; and oh, with that thoughtful prudence which has characterized my after-life, how I used to lengthen out the verses! The stars during the season were Mrs. McClure, Dan Marble, and A. A. Addams. Some of the plays acted were *Lady of Lyons, Stranger, Rob Roy, Damon and Pythias, Wives as They Were—Maids as They Are, Sam Patch*, etc. The theatre was in Randolph Street—at least it strikes me that was the name. [It was in Dearborn Street.] The city about that time had from three to four thousand inhabitants. I can remember following my father along the shore, when he went shooting, on what is now Michigan Avenue.   JOSEPH JEFFERSON."

During the progress of the Mexican war the Jeffersons followed, in company with other players, in the track of General Taylor's army, giving performances to please a military and boisterous audience. Those were the rough and wild days of the American provincial theatre. Readers of such records as Ludlow's *Dramatic Life* and Sol Smith's *Reminiscences* may therein catch impressive glimpses of this period in our theatrical history, and they will find it recorded that the pioneers of the profession in the West often had to pursue their journeys in flat-boats down the great rivers, from town to town, living on fish and birds, sometimes shooting wild animals on the river-banks, and stopping at intervals to act in the settlements. Land journeys were frequently made by the poor player in wagons or ox carts, and sometimes he travelled on foot. Jefferson had experience of all these itinerant methods, and so it was in the school of hardship that he acquired his thorough professional training. He saw General Taylor on the banks of the Rio Grande. He was sufficiently near at the battle of Palo Alto, May 8, 1846, to hear the report of the cannon. He saw the bombardment of Matamoras, and he acted in that city, in the Spanish theatre, two nights after the capture of the place by the American forces. At one time in the course of this gypsy period he was so "hard up" that he was constrained to diversify the avocation of acting by opening a coffee and cake stall as one of the camp followers of General Taylor. But when adverting to this incident, in a talk with the present writer, he indicated what has been the law of his life and the secret of his success in all things. "I sold good coffee and good cakes," he said, "and the little stall was not a failure." Jefferson did not return to the New York stage until 1849, when, on September 10, he came out at Chanfrau's National Theatre, acting Jack Rackbottle, in the play of *Jonathan Bradford*. Here he met Miss Margaret Lockyer, a native of Burnham, Somersetshire, England, to whom subsequently (May 19, 1850) he was married. From 1849 onward he drifted about the country during several years. At one time he was in partnership with Mr. John Ellsler, now a prominent manager and admired comedian at Cleveland, and together they took a dramatic company through the chief cities of the Southern States. At another time he was settled in Philadelphia, and later in Baltimore. In the latter city he was allied with that eminent manager, since so intimately associated with some of the brightest and saddest pages of American theatrical history, Mr. John T. Ford; and Jefferson was there the manager of the Baltimore Museum. In 1856 he made a summer trip to Europe, in order to observe and study the art of acting as exemplified on the stage in London and Paris. A poor man then, but then, as always, devoted to his art as to a sacred religion, he could face hardship and endure trouble and pain for the accomplishment of a high purpose: one of the ocean voyages he made in the steerage of a packet. But all things come round at last to those who wait, making ready to improve opportunity when it arrives, and Jefferson's time came in good season, after much privation and many disappointments. On August 31, 1857, Laura Keene opened her theatre

in New York at No. 622 Broadway, and her company included Jefferson, who on the first night made a hit as Dr. Pangloss, in *The Heir at Law*. But it was not till the 18th of October following, when for the first time on any stage was presented Tom Taylor's comedy of *Our American Cousin*, that Jefferson gained his first permanent laurel, and established himself in the judicious thought and the popular favor of his time as a great comedian. This victory was obtained by his matchless performance of Asa Trenchard. The piece had a run of 140 nights. Sothern was in the cast as Lord Dundreary, and that was the beginning of the almost world-wide success afterward gained by him. Jefferson remained at Laura Keene's Theatre till July, 1859, when the season ended. He was a member of Mr. Boucicault's company and stage-manager of the Winter Garden Theatre—on the west side of Broadway, opposite to the end of Bond Street—in the season of 1859-60; but he withdrew from that theatre in the spring of 1860, and on May 16 opened Laura Keene's Theatre for a summer season, which lasted till August 31. There he presented *The Invisible Prince, The Tycoon, Our American Cousin,* and other plays, with a company that included Edward A. Sothern, Charles W. Couldock, Mrs. John Wood, Mrs. Henrietta Chanfrau, Cornelia Jefferson (his only sister), Mrs. H. Vincent, Hetty Warren, James H. Stoddart, and James G. Burnett. That part of Jefferson's professional life is particularly well remembered. The performances then given were of singular brilliancy, and the foundations of his own reputation were at that time securely laid. Early in 1861 he had the afflicting misfortune to lose his wife, who died suddenly, and thereafter he fell into infirm health, so that for some time his own death seemed imminent; but a trip across the continent to San Francisco, a voyage thence to Australia, and the good influence of the climate of that country, where he passed four years, restored him to hope and vigor. He was married again, in 1867, to his third cousin, Miss Sarah Warren, of Chicago. In Australia he increased his reputation by the excellence of his professional efforts. He there acted Asa Trenchard, Caleb Plummer, Bob Brierly, Dogberry, and other characters, and especially Rip Van Winkle. His popularity in that country was prodigious. Once, at Hobart Town, in Tasmania, among a people whom the late Henry J. Byron used to call the Tasmaniacs, he acted Bob Brierly, the rustic hero of Tom Taylor's play of *The Ticket-of-leave Man*, in presence of about 600 ticket-of-leave men, and this formidable concourse of capable critics, at first hostile, ended by accepting him with delighted acclamation. He visited the Pacific coast of South America and the Isthmus of Panama on leaving Australia, and from the latter place he went directly to London, where he induced Mr. Boucicault to rearrange and rewrite the play of *Rip Van Winkle*, and where he came out, giving his exquisite performance of Rip, in September, 1865, at the Adelphi Theatre. "In Mr. Jefferson's hands," wrote John Oxenford, of the London *Times*, "the character of Rip Van Winkle becomes the vehicle for an extremely fine psychological exhibition." The comedian's success was great, and it prepared the way for great and continuous triumph upon the American stage after he came home. Jefferson reappeared in New York, August 13, 1866, at the Olympic Theatre, and afterward traversed the principal cities of the republic, being everywhere received with intellectual appreciation and the admiring plaudits of the public. He has since then made another visit to the English capital, acting in London and in other cities of the British Isles. He reappeared at the Princess's Theatre November 1, 1875, and acted until April 29, 1876. He appeared at the same theatre at Easter, 1877, and remained there until midsummer, when he went to the Haymarket with Mr. John S. Clarke, and acted for several weeks Mr. Golightly, in *Lend Me Five Shillings*, and Hugh De Brass, in *A Regular Fix*. He arrived home that year on October 17, and all his engagements since then have been played in America. His repertory has been confined to Rip Van Winkle, Caleb Plummer, Mr. Golightly, Bob Acres, and occasionally Dr. Ollapod.

Of late years Jefferson has acted but a small part of each season, preferring to live mostly at home, and devote his attention to the art of painting. All his life an amateur in water-colors, he developed some years ago not only an ardent passion, but a remarkable talent, for oil-painting in the department of landscape. Several of his works have been exhibited. Many of them are suffused with a mysterious and tender charm of feeling, much like the imaginative quality in the paintings of Corot. In this field Jefferson has accomplished more than society is aware of, and more than perhaps his contemporaries will consent to recognize. No man must succeed in more than one art if he would satisfy the standard of the age in which he lives.

Mr. Jefferson's power has been exerted and his position has been gained chiefly by means of the performance of Rip Van Winkle. In his time, indeed, he has played many parts. More than a hundred of them could be mentioned, and in several of them his acting has been so fine that he would have been recognized with admiration even though he had never played Rip Van Winkle at all. It is, accordingly, either ignorance or injustice that describes him as "a one-part actor." Yet certainly he has obtained his fame and influence mainly by acting one part. This fact has been noticed by various observers in various moods. "I am glad to see you making your fortune, Jefferson," the late Mr. Charles Mathews said to him, "but I don't like to see you doing it with a carpet-bag." Mr. Mathews was obliged to play many parts, and therefore to travel about the world with many trunks full of wardrobe, whereas the blue shirt, the old leather jacket, the red-brown breeches, the stained leggings, the old shoes, the torn red and white silk handkerchief, the tattered old hat, the guns and bottle, and the two wigs for Rip Van Winkle can be carried in a single box. The remark of Mr. Mathews, however, was meant to glance at the "one-part" custom, and Mr. Jefferson's reply to this ebullition was at once good-humored and significant. "It is perhaps better," he said, "to play one part in different ways than to play many parts all in one way." The explanation of his artistic victory is indicated here. Mr. Jefferson found in the old play of *Rip Van Winkle* a subject with reference to which he could freely and fully express not only his own human nature at its highest and best, but his ideas as to human nature and human life in general. The part of Rip, indeed, as set forth in the pages of Washington Irving and in the ancient and clumsy play which Jefferson derived from his half-brother Charles Burke, amounts to nothing; but the part as Mr. Jefferson conceived it and built it up amounts to an epitome of human life, and in that respect it is one of the most valuable parts in the range of the acting drama. Mr. Jefferson was exceedingly fond of it while yet he was a youth, and long before the arrival of that happy time when he was privileged to attempt it on the stage. It was his custom to dress himself as Rip Van Winkle and to act the part alone in his lodgings, and for his own edification and the purposes of study and experiment, years before he acted it in public. His mind instinctively recognized its value. It is a part that contains all of the great extremes of human experience — youth and age, mirth and sadness, humor and pathos, loss and gain, the natural and the supernatural, man in his relations to his fellow-men, and man in his relation to the world of spirits. It is domestic without insipidity, and it is romantic without extravagance. In a remote way it is even suggestive of " the sceptred pall of tragedy." Yet it is perfectly simple, and it is sweet, pure, and deeply and richly fraught with the sympathetic emotion of powerful and tender humanity.

About ten years ago Mr. Jefferson bought a large estate west of Iberia, in Louisiana, and there he has established his residence. He possesses, indeed, a Northern retreat, a fine dwelling and picturesque grounds, at Hohokus, New Jersey, but his Southern plantation is his preferred and permanent home. It is a place where any man might be happy. It is an island in the prairie, but high and variegated, containing more than six hundred acres of land, and isolated by a broad, shining, steel-blue lake, and by an arm of one of the bayous of that well-watered country—the country associated with Longfellow's " Evangeline," and in which still may be found the race of the exiled Acadians. It is ten miles from the nearest neighbor. Almost every kind of wood that grows may be found growing upon this estate. Some of its trees are nearly three hundred years old, and in summer the great spreading boughs of these giants are profusely draped, in many a green dell, not only with the long, funereal moss of the South, but with brilliant and odorous tropical flowers. Six or eight orange groves are scattered over the place. Many kinds of wild fowl live in the woods and swamps and on the lake, and often the blue waters are cleft by the rapid canoe of the sportsman in pursuit of this delicate and delicious game. In one wild part of this gorgeous solitude an eagle has made his nest on the peak of a tall stalwart pine-tree. Jefferson's dwelling, a spacious mansion embowered by large trees, stands upon a gentle eminence, looking southward, and commands an unbroken prospect of miles and miles of lonely prairie, over which the dark buzzards slowly sail and the small birds flit merrily about, and through which herds of roving cattle, seen in the distance as black and formless shapes, roam lazily around, making a changeful picture of commingled motion and peace. Here, with his wife and children, his books, his pictures, the art of painting for an occupation, and the memories of a good and honored life for a solace, he reaps "the harvest of a quiet mind," and calmly looks onward to the sunset of life.

AN INVITATION.

BY ANNIE FIELDS.

WHEN in the house the day is warm,
  And dogs lie stretched before the door,
Come out to my neglected farm,
  And sit upon the grassy floor.

Under the apple-trees' green roof,
  Laced with the yellow light of morn,
Share nature's joy without reproof,
  Thou man who art to trouble born!

Alas! 'tis said for price of gold
  The axe shall hew these leafy towers;
The spade shall trample in the mould
  This fragrant grass, these dewy flowers;

And when this pleasure-house is waste,
  A mansion built for earthly care,

For waiting days, and tiresome haste,
  Shall lift a stately front in air.

Then come, before the day declines,
  And hear the bees among the boughs;
See where the early moon entwines
  Her crescent in my bloomy house.

Perhaps before the spade shall wound
  This turf, to plant the cares of earth,
A smaller plot of turf be found
  More green, to tell our nobler birth.

Then hasten ere the day shall die,
  And lay thy heart to summer's bliss,
And learn, whatever joys may fly,
  To know the permanence of this.

VERONICA.

A ROMAN LEGEND.

BY THE AUTHOR OF "JOHN HALIFAX, GENTLEMAN."

Cecilia, a noble Roman lady, young, wealthy, beautiful, with a voice so divine that an angel came down to listen to her singing, converted to Christianity her husband, Valerian, and his brother, Tiburtius. They suffered martyrdom, and she afterward, by order of the Emperor Alexander Severus. Attempts were made first to suffocate her in her bath, and then to behead her, but she lived for three days with the death-wound in her neck, and brought many souls to Christ. The persecution ceasing, Pope Urban built a church over her house, which still exists, with the bath-chamber and heating apparatus, and the marble table on which she laid her head to receive the fatal blow. About A.D. 817 her remains, and those of her husband and his brother, were discovered in the catacombs of St. Calixtus, and transferred to the church. There, in the sixteenth century, the tomb was opened, and the embalmed body found lying there, where it was seen by a sculptor, Stefano Maderno, who modelled from it a marble statue, now placed under the altar of the church of Santa Cecilia at Rome. It bears an inscription: "*Behold the body of the most holy Cecilia, whom I myself saw lying uncorrupt in her tomb, and have in this marble expressed the same saint in the very same posture of body*"—a posture so natural, so difficult to invent, and yet so exactly that into which the martyred body might have fallen, and, the limbs stiffening, been obliged to be buried as it lay, that it furnishes circumstantial evidence of the truth—at least the foundation truth—of the legend.

The following story was told me at Rome of another saint. But a most heavenly voice which I heard at vespers in the church of the Trinità del Monte gave me the idea of Veronica, and that of St. Cecilia naturally resulted.

HER eyes are depths of dark delight;
  Her lips, twin roses closely prest
    In rapture of contented rest,
From night till morn, from morn till
    night;
Her hair, that fell in dusky clouds,
The soft black veil forever shrouds.

The convent walls are high and strong,
  But fair the convent garden flowers,
    And swiftly pass the busy hours
From matins until even-song;
And last to mourn and first to pray
Is the young nun Veronica.

Within her cell she keeps alway
  That lovely marble saint, who lies
    As in the tomb for centuries
The sweet, pure, martyred body lay;
With heart-warm love oft murmurs
    she,
"Santa Cecilia, pray for me!"

And when at vespers heavenly clear
  Her voice rings out above the rest,
  "Santa Cecilia sure has blest,"
Say the proud nuns, "our sister dear.
What joy, did listening angel come,
As to the noble lady of Rome!"

No angel came. Veronica
  Sang on unto herself alone,
  Or silent saints in sculptured stone,
Or sisters white and cold as they,

And gazed up to the impassive blue,
Where not one heavenly face looked
    through.

But youthful blood runs hot and fast,
  And narrow are the convent walls,
  And wild ambition leaps and falls,
And leaps again. "At last! at last!"—
Loathing the pale life that can tend
To no beginning and no end.

She walks beneath the ilex-trees,
  Watching the dull suns rise and set.
  Her days are filled with vague regret;
In the long nights strange dreams she sees,
And wakes in terror. "Must this be?
Santa Cecilia, pity me!

"Dear saint, who hadst all that I lack—
  Wealth, love, hope, joy — O martyr
    sweet!
  By thy dead hands, and straight, dead
    feet
Now walking safe the heavenly track,
And woman's soul, from flesh set free—
Santa Cecilia, come to me!"

Was it a vision? Close beside
  There stands a Presence in the cell;
  The white shroud round her limbs that
    fell
Shines like the garment of a bride.
The blood marks on her neck yet stay.
It is the saint Cecilia.

Few are her words, but soft as rain
  Down-falling on long-thirsty soil:
  "Sister, go forth. Live, love, and toil.
I in thy stead will here remain.
Farewell." And broken are all bands;
Outside the gate the young nun stands.

O Fame, how grand thy empty sound!
  O Love, how sweet thy treacherous
    breath!
  Youth, strong in life, thinks not of
    death.
She climbs the hill-top, looks around.
Her eager feet have reached their goal;
Earth-satisfied is her full soul.

"Santa Cecilia" oft they call
  The heavenly singer, human yet.
  Midst home and babes does she forget
The narrow cell, the convent wall,
Or through applauding crowds can hear
The nuns' meek voices chanting clear?

Who knows? She lived her life, they say,
  Serene, contented, proudly pure,
  Of earth and heaven alike secure,
Till out of her blue sky one day
The bolt fell. Childless, widowed, lone,
Earth faded. Is heaven also gone?

"O Christ," she prayed, "of martyrs Lord,
  Whose service only cannot tire,
  Who only fill'st the heart's desire,
I will arise and hear Thy Word,
Who am as truly slain as she,
Thy dead Cecilia. Comfort me!"

One May morn at the convent gate
  A pale, gaunt woman knocked, and
    cried:
  "Open! Oh, let me here abide;
I am so very desolate."
"Who art thou?" "That young sister
    gay,
The singer called Veronica."

Laughed the good nun: "Our sister dear
  Has never left these peaceful walls;
  Each morn and eve her sweet voice calls
To prayer, and saints and angels hear.
Her face is lovely, as of yore.
But thine? Begone!" She shut the door.

In her old cell that even-tide
  Veronica awoke, and saw,
  With a strange quiet, mixed with awe,
Her old self sitting by her side,
But sweeter, holier, calmer made,
As pure souls grow whose bodies fade.

Slowly it changed. Upright and fair,
  In her celestial youth, there stands
  The statue with the linkèd hands,
And straight dead feet, and folded hair,
And virginal soft raiment, white
And shining in the Lamb's own light.

"Welcome!"—those silver accents fall.
  "God proved thee as strong souls are
    proved.
  Thou in the world hast lived, worked,
    loved,
And suffered. Sister, is it well?
The path desired thy feet have trod;
Is aught enduring, except God?"

A low sob thrilled the convent cell;
  The gray hair swept the convent floor.
  Veronica arose once more.
"Ay, all was best as it befell;
But all is past. I trust His word.
Deal with me as Thou wilt, O Lord!"

Next morning on the pallet-bed
  They found a woman wan and gray.
  "Can this be our Veronica,
Who was so fair last night?" they said.
"And will she rise once more, and sing
God's praises, like the birds in spring?"

She rose; she sang. Her step was slow;
  Feeble her voice, like songs in dreams.
  The same, yet not the same, she seems:
As when some face we used to know
We sudden meet, and on it see
The shadow of eternity.

Yet still she went her daily round
  Of humble duties, dear as joys,
  And still the music of her voice
Rejoiced the convent's narrow bound.
Outside, the world went on its way;
Forgotten was Veronica.

Her cell the silent secret kept
  Years long. At last they found her
    there,
  The sainted nun with silver hair,
Soft smiling, like a child that slept,
Only the dream of life was o'er;
They knew that she would wake no
    more.

And as they mourned above her bier,
  They felt a sudden sweet perfume,
  And through the stillness of the room
They heard *two* voices singing clear,
Then fading, pass far, far away.
So lived, so died, Veronica.

SPRINGHAVEN.

BY R. D. BLACKMORE.

CHAPTER XIX.

IN THE LINE OF FIRE.

NO wonder there had been a great deal of talking in the village all that evening, for the following notice had appeared in a dozen conspicuous places, beginning with the gate of the church-yard, and ending with two of the biggest mooring-posts, and not even sparing the Admiral's white gate, where it flapped between the two upper rails. It was not printed, but written in round hand, with a liberal supply of capitals, on a stiff sheet of official paper, stamped with the Royal Arms at the top. And those who were in the secret knew that Master Bob Stubbard, the Captain's eldest son, had accomplished this great literary feat at a guerdon of one shilling from the public service funds every time he sucked his pen at the end of it.

"By order of His Majesty King George III. To-morrow being Wednesday, and the fishing-boats at sea, Artillery practice from Fox-hill fort will be carried on from twelve at noon until three P.M. at a mark-boat moored half a mile from the shore. Therefore His Majesty's loyal subjects are warned to avoid the beach westward of the brook between the white flagstaffs, as well as the sea in front of it, and not to cross the line of fire below the village but at their own risk and peril.

"(Signed) ADAM JACKSON STUBBARD, R.N., commanding Fox-hill Battery."

Some indignation was aroused by this; for Mrs. Caper junior (who was Mrs. Prater's cousin) had been confined, out of proper calculation, and for the very first time, the moment the boats were gone on Monday; and her house, being nearest to the fort, and in a hollow where the noise would be certain to keep going round and round, the effect upon her head, not to mention the dear baby's, was more than any one dared to think of, with the poor father so far away. And if Squire Darling had only been at home, not a woman who could walk would have thought twice about it, but gone all together to insist upon it that he should stop this wicked bombardment. And this was most unselfish

of all of them, they were sure, because they had so long looked forward to putting cotton-wool in their ears, and seeing how all the enemies of England would be demolished. But Mrs. Caper junior, and Caper, *natu minimus*, fell fast asleep together, as things turned out, and heard not a single bang of it.

And so it turned out, in another line of life, with things against all calculation, resenting to be reckoned as they always do, like the countless children of Israel. For Admiral Darling was gone far away inspecting, leaving his daughters to inspect themselves.

"You may just say exactly what you consider right, dear," said Miss Dolly Darling to her sister Faith; "and I dare say it makes you more comfortable. But you know as well as I do, that there is no reason in it. Father is a darling; but he must be wrong sometimes. And how can he tell whether he is wrong or right, when he goes away fifty miles to attend to other people? Of course I would never disobey his orders, any more than you would. But facts change according to circumstances, and I feel convinced that if he were here he would say, 'Go down and see it, Dolly.'"

"We have no right to speculate as to what he might say," replied Faith, who was very clear-headed. "His orders were definite: 'Keep within the grounds, when notice is given of artillery practice.' And those orders I mean to obey."

"And so do I; but not to misunderstand them. The beach is a part of our grounds, as I have heard him say fifty times in argument, when people tried to come encroaching. And I mean to go on that part of his grounds, because I can't see well from the other part. That is clearly what he meant; and he would laugh at us, if we could tell him nothing when he comes home. Why, he promised to take us as far as Portsmouth to see some artillery practice."

"That is a different thing altogether, because we should be under his control. If you disobey him, it is at your own risk, and I shall not let one of the servants go with you, for I am mistress of the household, if not of you."

"What trumpery airs you do give yourself! One would think you were fifty years old at least. Stay at home, if you are such a coward! I am sure dear daddy would be quite ashamed of you. They are popping already, and I mean to watch them."

"You won't go so very far, I am quite sure of that," answered Faith, who understood her sister. "You know your own value, darling Dolly, and you would not go at all, if you had not been forbidden."

"When people talk like that, it goads me up to almost anything. I intend to go, and stand, as near as can be, in the middle of the space that is marked off 'dangerous.'"

"Do, that's a dear. I will lend you my shell - silk that measures twenty yards, that you may be sure of being hit, dear."

"Inhuman, selfish, wicked creature!" cried Dolly, and it was almost crying; "you shall see what comes of your cold-bloodedness! I shall pace to and fro in the direct line of fire, and hang on my back the king's proclamation, inside out, and written on it in large letters—'By order of my sister I do this.' Then what will be said of you, if they only kill me? My feelings might be very sad, but I should not envy yours, Faith."

"Kiss me, at any rate, before you perish, in token of forgiveness;" and Dolly (who dearly loved her sister at the keenest height of rebellion) ran up and kissed Faith, with a smile for her, and a tear for her own self-sacrifice. "I shall put on my shell-pink," she said, "and they won't have the heart to fire shells at it."

The dress of the ladies of the present passing period had been largely affected by the recent peace, which allowed the "French babies"—as the milliners' dolls were called—to come in as quickly as they were conceived. In war time scores of these "doxy-dummies"—as the rough tars called them—were tossed overboard from captured vessels or set up as a mark for tobacco-juice, while sweet eyes in London wept for want of them. And even Mr. Cheeseman had failed to bring any type genuinely French from the wholesale house in St. Mary's Axe, which was famed for canonical issue. But blessed are the patient, if their patience lasts long enough. The ladies of England were now in full enjoyment of all the new French discoveries, which proved to be

the right name, inasmuch as they banished all reputable forms of covering. At least, so Mrs. Twemlow said; and the Rector went further than she did, obtaining for his sympathy a recommendation to attend to his own business. But when he showed the Admiral his wife's last book of patterns—from a drawer which he had no right to go to—great laughter was held between the twain, with some glancing over shoulders, and much dread of bad example. "Whatever you do, don't let my girls see it; I'll be bound you won't let your Eliza," said the Admiral, after a pinch of snuff to restore the true balance of his principles; "Faith would pitch it straight into the fire; but I am not quite so sure that my Dolly would. She loves a bit of finery, and she looks well in it."

"Tonnish females," as the magazine of fashion called the higher class of popinjays, would have stared with contempt at both Faith and Dolly Darling in their simple walking-dress that day. Dowdies would have been the name for them, or frumps, or frights, or country gawks, because their attire was not statuesque or classic, as it should have been, which means that they were not half naked.

Faith, the eldest sister, had meant to let young Dolly take the course of her own stubbornness; but no sooner did she see her go forth alone than she threw on cloak and hat, and followed. The day was unsuited for classic apparel, as English days are apt to be, and a lady of fashion would have looked more foolish, and even more indecent, than usual. A brisk and rather crisp east wind had arisen, which had no respect for persons, and even Faith and Dolly in their high-necked country dresses had to handle their tackle warily.

Dolly had a good start, and growing much excited with the petulance of the wind and with her own audacity, crossed the mouth of the brook at a very fine pace, with the easterly gusts to second her. She could see the little mark-boat well out in the offing, with a red flag flaring merrily, defying all the efforts of the gunners on the hill to plunge it into the bright dance of the waves. And now and then she heard what she knew to be the rush of a round shot far above her head, and following the sound saw a little silver fountain leap up into the sunshine and skim before the breeze; then glancing up the hill she saw the gray puff drifting, and presently felt the dull rumble of the air. At the root of the smoke-puffs, once or twice, she descried a stocky figure moving leisurely, and in spite of the distance and huddle of vapour could declare that it was Captain Stubbard. Then a dense mass of smoke was brought down by an eddy of wind, and set her coughing.

"Come away, come away this very moment, Dolly," cried Faith, who had hurried up and seized her hand; "you are past the danger-post, and I met a man back there who says they are going to fire shells, and they have got two short guns on purpose. He says it will be very dangerous till they get the range, and he begged me most earnestly not to come on here. If I were anybody else, he said, he would lay hands on me and hold me back."

"Some old fisherman, no doubt. What do they know about gun practice? I can see Captain Stubbard up there; he would rather shoot himself than me, he said yesterday."

While Dolly was repeating this assurance, the following words were being exchanged upon the smoky parapet: "If you please, sir, I can see two women on the beach, half-way between the posts a'most." "Can't help it—wouldn't stop for all the petticoats in the kingdom. If they choose to go there, they must take their chance. A bit more up, and to you, my good man. Are you sure you put in twenty-three? Steady! so, so — that's beautiful."

"What a noisy thing! What does it come here for? I never saw it fall. There must be some mistake. I hope there's nothing nasty inside it. Run for your life, Faith; it means to burst, I do believe."

"Down on your faces!" cried a loud, stern voice; and Dolly obeyed in an instant. But Faith stood calmly, and said to the man who rushed past her, "I trust in the Lord, sir."

There was no time to answer. The shell had left off rolling, and sputtered more fiercely as the fuse thickened. The man laid hold of this, and tried to pull it out, but could not, and jumped with both feet on it; while Faith, who quite expected to be blown to pieces, said to herself, "What pretty boots he has!"

"A fine bit of gunnery!" said the young man, stooping over it, after treading the last spark into the springy sand. "The little artillery man is wanted here. Ladies, you may safely stay here now. They will not make two hits in proximity to each other."

"You shall not go," said Faith, as he was hurrying away, "until we know who has been so reckless of his life, to save the lives of others. Both your hands are burned—very seriously, I fear."

"And your clothes, sir," cried Dolly, running up in hot terror, as soon as the danger was over; "your clothes are spoiled sadly. Oh, how good it was of you! And the whole fault was mine—or at least Captain Stubbard's. He will never dare to face me again, I should hope."

"Young ladies, if I have been of any service to you," said the stranger, with a smile at their excitement, "I beg you to be silent to the Captain Stubbard concerning my share in this occasion. He would not be gratified by the interest I feel in his beautiful little bombardments, especially that of fair ladies. Ha, there goes another shell! They will make better aim now; but you must not delay. I beseech you to hasten home, if you would do me kindness."

The fair daughters of the Admiral had enjoyed enough of warfare to last them till the end of their honeymoon, and they could not reject the entreaty of a man who had risked his life to save them. Trembling and bewildered, they made off at the quickest step permitted by maiden dignity, with one or two kindly turns of neck, to show that he was meant to follow them. But another sulphurous cloud rushed down from the indefatigable Stubbard, and when it had passed them, they looked back vainly for the gentleman who had spoiled his boots.

CHAPTER XX.

AMONG THE LADIES.

IT would have surprised the stout Captain Stubbard, who thought no small beer of his gunnery, to hear that it was held in very light esteem by the "Frenchified young man overhead," as he called Caryl Carne, to his landlady. And it would have amazed him to learn that this young man was a captain of artillery, in the grand army mustering across the sea, and one of the most able among plenty of ability, and favoured by the great First Consul.

In the gully where the Tugwell boats were built, behind a fringe of rough long-shore growth, young Carne had been sitting with a good field-glass, observing the practice of the battery. He had also been able to observe unseen the disobedient practices of young ladies, when their father is widely out of sight. Upon Faith, however, no blame could fall, for she went against her wish, and only to retrieve the rebellious Dolly.

Secure from the danger, these two held council in the comfort of the Admiral's Round-house. There Miss Dolly, who considered it her domain, kept sundry snug appliances congenial to young ladies, for removing all traces of sudden excitement, and making them fit to be seen again. Simple and unfashionable as they were in dress, they were sure to have something to do to themselves after the late derangement, ere ever they could run the risk of meeting any of the brave young officers, who were so mysteriously fond of coming for orders to Springhaven Hall.

"You look well enough, dear," said Faith at last, "and much better than you deserve to look, after leading me such a dance by your self-will. But one thing must be settled before we go back—are we to speak of this matter, or not?"

"How can you ask such a question, Faith?" Miss Dolly loved a bit of secrecy. "Of course we must rather bite our tongues out, than break the solemn pledges which we have given." She had cried a good deal, and she began to cry again.

"Don't cry, that's a darling," said the simple-hearted sister. "You make the whole world seem so cruel when you cry, because you look so innocent. It shall be as you please, if I can only think it right. But I cannot see how we gave a pledge of any sort, considering that we ran away without speaking. The question is—have we any right to conceal it, when father has a right to know everything?"

"He would be in such a sad passion," pleaded Dolly, with a stock of fresh tears only waiting, "and he never would look again at poor Captain Stubbard, and what would become of all his family?"

"Father is a just and conscientious man," replied the daughter who inherited those qualities; "he would not blame Captain Stubbard; he would blame us, and no others."

"Oh, I could not bear to hear you blamed, Faith. I should have to say that it was all my fault. And then how I should catch it, and be punished for a month! Confined to the grounds for a month at least, and never have a bit of appetite. But I am not thinking of myself, I am quite sure of that. You know that I never do that much. I am thinking of that heroic gentleman, who stamped out the sparks so cleverly. All the time I lay on the sand I watched him, though I expected to be blown to pieces every single moment. Oh! what a nasty sensation it was! I expected to find all my hair turned grey. But, thank Heaven, I don't see a streak in it!" To make sure of that, she went to the glass again.

"If all mine had turned grey, 'twould be no odds to nobody—as Captain Zeb says about his income—because I am intended for an old maid." Miss Darling, whose beauty still lacked many years of its prime, turned away for a moment, because her eyes were glistening, and her sister was tired of the subject. "But for yours there are fifty to weep, Dolly. Especially perhaps this young gentleman, towards whom you feel so much gratitude."

"How unkind you are, Faith! All the gratitude I owe him is for saving your life. As for myself, I was flat upon the sand, with a heap of sea-weed between me and the thing. If it had gone off, it would have gone over me; but you chose to stand up, like a stupid. Your life was saved, beyond all doubt, by him; and the way you acknowledge it is to go and tell his chief enemy that he was there observing him!"

"Well, I never!" Faith exclaimed, with more vigour than grace of language. "A minute ago you knew nothing of him, and even wondered who he was, and now you know all about his enemies! I am afraid that you stick at nothing."

"I don't stick thinking, as you do, Miss," Dolly answered, without abashment, and knowing that the elder hated to be so addressed; "but things come to me by the light of nature, without a twelvemonth of brown-study. When I said what you remind me of, in such a hurry, it was perfectly true—so true that you need have no trouble about it, with all your truth. But since that, a sudden idea flashed across me, the sort of idea that proves itself. Your hero you are in such a hurry to betray can be nobody but the mysterious lodger in Widow Shanks' dimity-parlour, as she calls it; and Jenny has told me all she knows about him, which is a great deal less than she ought to know. I meant to have told you, but you are so grand in your lofty contempt of what you call gossip, but which I call good neighbourly intercourse! You know that he is Mr. Caryl Carne, of course. Everybody knows that, and there the knowledge seems to terminate. Even the Twemlows, his own aunt and uncle, are scarcely ever favoured with his company; and I, who am always on the beach, or in the village, have never had the honour of beholding him, until — until it came to this"—here she imitated with her lips the spluttering of the fuse so well that her sister could not keep from laughing. "He never goes out, and he never asks questions, any more than he answers them, and he never cares to hear what fish they have caught, or anything else, about anybody. He never eats or drinks, and he never says a word about the flowers they put upon his table; and what he does all day long nobody knows, except that he has a lot of books with him. Widow Shanks, who has the best right to know all about him, has made up her mind that his head has been turned by the troubles of his family, except for his going without dinner, which no lunatic ever does, according to her knowledge. And he seems to have got 'Butter Cheeseman,' as they call him, entirely at his beck and call. He leaves his black horse there every morning, and rides home at night to his ancestral ruins. There, now, you know as much as I do."

"There is mischief at the bottom of all this," said Faith; "in these dangerous times, it must not be neglected. We are bound, as you say, to consider his wishes, after all that he has done for us. But the tale about us will be over the place in a few hours, at the latest. The gunners will have known where their bad shot fell, and perhaps they will have seen us with their glasses. How will it be possible to keep this affair from gossip?"

"They may have seen us, without seeing him at all, on account of the smoke that came afterwards. At any rate, let us say nothing about it until we hear what other people say. The shell will be washed away or buried in the sand, for it fell upon the shingle, and then rolled towards the sea; and there need be no fuss unless we choose to make it, and so perhaps ruin Captain Stubbard and his family. And his wife has made such pretty things for us. If he knew what he had done, he would go and shoot himself. He is so excessively humane and kind."

"We will not urge his humanity to that extreme. I hate all mystery, as you know well. But about this affair I will say nothing, unless there is cause to do so, at least until father comes back; and then I shall tell him if it seems to be my duty."

"It won't be your duty, it can't be your duty, to get good people into trouble, Faith. I find it my duty to keep out of trouble, and I like to treat others the same as myself."

"You are such a lover of duty, dear Dolly, because everything you like becomes your duty. And now your next duty is to your dinner. Mrs. Twemlow is coming—I forgot to tell you—as well as Eliza, and Mrs. Stubbard. And if Johnny comes home in time from Harrow, to be Jack among the ladies, we shall hear some wonders, you may be quite sure."

"Oh, I vow, I forgot all about that wicked Johnny. What a blessing that he was not here just now! It is my black Monday when his holidays begin. Instead of getting steadier, he grows more plaguesome. And the wonder of it is that he would tie your kid shoes; while he pulls out my jaconet, and sits on my French hat. How I wish he was old enough for his commission! To-morrow he will be dancing in and out of every cottage, boat, or gun, or rabbit-hole, and nothing shall be hidden from his eyes and ears. Let him come. 'I am accustomed to have all things go awry,' as somebody says in some tragedy. The only chance is to make him fall in love, deeply in love, with Miss Stubbard. He did it with somebody for his Easter week, and became as harmless as a sucking dove, till he found his nymph eating onions raw with a pocketful of boiled limpets. Maggie Stubbard is too perfect in her style for that. She is twelve years old, and has lots of hair, and eyes as large as oysters. I shall introduce Johnny to-morrow, and hope to keep him melancholy all his holidays."

"Perhaps it will be for his good," said Faith, "because, without some high ideas, he gets into such dreadful scrapes; and certainly it will be for our good."

After making light of young love thus, these girls deserved the shafts of Cupid, in addition to Captain Stubbard's shells. And it would have been hard to find fairer marks when they came down dressed for dinner. Mrs. Twemlow arrived with her daughter Eliza, but without her husband, who was to fetch her in the evening; and Mrs. Stubbard came quite alone, for her walkable children—as she called them—were all up at the battery. "Can't smell powder too young in such days as these," was the Captain's utterance; and, sure enough, they took to it, like sons of guns.

"I should be so frightened," Mrs. Twemlow said, when Johnny (who sat at the foot of the table representing his father most gallantly) had said grace in Latin, to astonish their weak minds, "so nervous all the time, so excessively anxious, the whole time that dreadful din was proceeding! It is over now, thank goodness! But how can you have endured it, how can you have gone about your household duties calmly, with seven of your children—I think you said—going about in that fiery furnace?"

"Because, ma'am," replied Mrs. Stubbard, who was dry of speech, and fit mother of heroes, "the cannons are so made, if you can understand, that they do not shoot out of their back ends."

"We are quite aware of that"—Miss Twemlow came to her mother's relief very sharply—"but still they are apt to burst, or to be overloaded, or badly directed, or even to fly back suddenly, as I have heard on good authority."

"Very likely, miss, when they are commanded by young women."

Eliza Twemlow coloured, for she was rather quick of temper; but she did not condescend to pay rudeness in kind.

"It would hardly be a lady-like position, I suppose," she answered, with a curve of her graceful neck—the Carnes had been celebrated for their necks, which were longer than those of the Darlings; "but even under the command of a most skilful man, for instance Captain Stubbard, little accidents will happen, like the fall of a shell upon the beach this afternoon. Some people were close to it, according to the rumour; but luckily it did not explode."

"How providential!" cried Mrs. Twemlow; "but the stupid people would have gone without much pity, whatever had befallen them, unless they were blind, or too ignorant to read. Don't you think so, Faith, my dear?"

"I don't believe a single word of that story," Mrs. Stubbard cut short the question; "for the simple reason that it never could have happened. My husband was to direct every gun himself. Is it likely he would have shelled the beach?"

"Well, the beach is the proper place for shells; but if I had only known it, wouldn't I have come a few hours earlier?" said Johnny. "Even now there must be something left to see; and I am bound to understand that sort of thing. Ladies, I entreat you not to think me rude, if I go as soon as ever you can do without me. I think I have got you nearly everything you want; and perhaps you would rather be without me."

With many thanks and compliments— such a pretty boy he was—the ladies released him gladly; and then Mrs. Twemlow, having reasons of her own, drew nigh to Mrs. Stubbard with lively interest in her children. At first, she received short answers only; for the Captain's wife had drawn more sour juices than sweet uses from adversity. But the wife of the man of peace outflanked the better half of the man of war, drove in her outposts, and secured the key of all her communications.

"I can scarcely believe that you are so kind. My dear Mrs. Twemlow, how good you are! My Bob is a nice boy, so manly and clever, so gentle and well-behaved, even when he knows that I am not likely to find him out. But that you should have noticed it, is what surprises me—so few people now know the difference! But in the House of God—as you so well observe — you can very soon see what a boy is. When I tell him that he may ride your grey pony, I wish you could be there to watch the fine expression of his face. How he does love dumb animals! It was only last Saturday, he knocked down a boy nearly three times his own size for poking a pin into a poor donkey with the fish. And Maggie to have a flower-bed on your front lawn! They won't let her touch a plant, at our

cottage, though she understands gardening so thoroughly. She won't sleep a
wink to-night, if I tell her, and I had better keep that for the morning. Poor
children! They have had a hard time of
it; but they have come out like pure gold
from the fire—I mean as many of them as
can use their legs. But to be on horseback—what will Bob say?"

"You must have met with very little
kindness, Mrs. Stubbard, to attach any importance to such mere trifles. It makes
me blush to think that there can be a spot
in England where such children as yours
could pass unnoticed. It is not a question
of religious feeling only. Far from it; in
fact, quite the opposite; though my husband, of course, is quite right in insisting
that all our opinions and actions must be
referred to that one standard. But I look
at things also from a motherly point of
view, because I have suffered such sad
trials. Three dear ones in the church-
yard, and the dearest of all—the Almighty
only knows where he is. Sometimes it is
more than I can bear, to live on in this
dark and most dreadful uncertainty. My
medical man has forbidden me to speak
of it. But how can he know what it is
to be a mother? But hush! Or darling
Faith may hear me. Sometimes I lose all
self-command."

Mrs. Twemlow's eyes were in need of
wiping, and stout Mrs. Stubbard's in the
same condition. "How I wish I could
help you," said the latter, softly: "is
there anything in the world that I can
do?"

"No, my dear friend; I wish there was,
for I'm sure that it would be a pleasure
to you. But another anxiety, though far
less painful, is worrying me as well just
now. My poor brother's son is behaving
most strangely. He hardly ever comes
near us, and he seems to dislike my dear
husband. He has taken rooms over your
brave husband's Office, and he comes and
goes very mysteriously. It is my duty to
know something about this; but I dare
not ask Captain Stubbard."

"My dear Mrs. Twemlow, it has puzzled
me too. But thinking that you knew all
about it, I concluded that everything must
be quite right. What you tell me has surprised me more than I can tell. I shall
go to work quietly to find out all about
it. Mystery and secrecy are such hateful
things; and a woman is always the best
hand at either."

CHAPTER XXI.

A GRACIOUS MERCY.

As a matter of course, every gunner at
the fort was ready to make oath by every
colour of the rainbow, that never shot,
shell, wad, sponge, or even powder-flake
could by any possibility have fallen on the
beach. And before they had time to grow
much more than doubly positive—that is
to say, within three days' time—the sound
of guns fired in earnest drowned all questions of bad practice.

For the following Sunday beheld Springhaven in a state of excitement beyond the
memory of the very oldest inhabitant, or
the imagination of the youngest. Excitement is a crop that, to be large, must grow
—though it thrives all the better without
much root—and in this particular field it
began to grow before noon of Saturday.
For the men who were too old to go to sea,
and the boys who were too young, and the
women who were never of the proper age,
all these kept looking from the best look-
outs, but nothing could they see to enable
them to say when the kettle, or the frying-
pan, or gridiron, would be wanted. They
rubbed their eyes grievously, and spun
round three times, if time had brought or
left them the power so to spin; and they
pulled an Irish halfpenny, with the harp
on, from their pockets, and moistened it
with saliva—which in English means spat
on it—and then threw it into the pocket on
the other side of body. But none of these
accredited appeals to heaven put a speck
upon the sea where the boats ought to
have been, or cast upon the clouds a shade
of any sail approaching. Uneasily wondering, the grannies, wives, and little ones
went home, when the nightfall quenched
all eyesight, and told one another ancient
tales of woe.

Yet there is a salve for every sore, a
bung for every bunghole. Upon the Sunday morning, when the tide was coming
in, and a golden haze hung upon the peaceful sea, and the seven bells of the old grey
church were speaking of the service cheerfully, suddenly a deep boom moved the
bosom of distance, and palpitated all along
the shore. Six or seven hale old gaffers
(not too stiff to walk, with the help of a
staff, a little further than the rest) were
coming to hear parson by the path below the warren, where a smack of salt
would season them for doctrine. They
knew from long experience, the grand-

mother of science, that the mist of the sea, coming on at breakfast-time, in the month of August (with the wind where it was and the tides as they were), would be sure to hold fast until dinner-time. Else, good as they were, and preparing punctually once a week for a better world, the hind buttons of their Sunday coats would have been towards the church, and the front ones to the headland. For the bodies of their sons were dearer to them, substantially dearer, than their own old souls.

They were all beginning to be deaf, or rather going on with it very agreeably, losing thereby a great deal of disturbance, and gaining great room for reflection. And now when the sound of a gun from the sea hung shaking in the web of vapour, each of these wise men gazed steadfastly at the rest, to see his own conclusion reflected, or concluded. A gun it was indeed—a big well-shotted gun, and no deafness could throw any doubt on it. There might not be anything to see, but still there would be plenty to hear at the headland—a sound more arousing than the parson's voice, a roar beyond that of all the gallery. "'Tis a battle!" said one, and his neighbour cried, "A rare one!" They turned to the parish church the quarters of farewell, and those of salutation to the battle out at sea.

It was all over the village, in the time it takes to put a hat on, that the British and the French fleets were hammer and tongs at it, within the distance you may throw an apple off Springhaven headland. Even the young women knew that this was quite impossible, because there was no water there for a collier-brig to anchor; nevertheless, in the hurry and scare, the thoughts of that new battery and Lord Nelson, and above all in the fog, they believed it. So that there was scarcely any room to stand, at the Watch-point, inside the Shag-rock; while in church there was

"HOW I WISH I COULD HELP YOU!"

no one who could help being there, by force of holy office, or example.

These latter were not in a devout frame of mind, and (but for the look of it) would have done more good by joining the other congregation. For the sound of cannon-shot came into their ears, like balls of unadulterated pepper, and every report made them look at one another, and whisper—"Ah! there goes some poor fellow's head." For the sacred building was constructed so that the sounds outside of it had more power than the good things offered in the inside.

However, as many, or as few, as did their duty, by joining the good company of the minister, found themselves all the better for it, and more fresh for a start than the runagates. Inasmuch as these latter had nearly got enough of listening without seeing anything, while the steady church-goers had refreshed the entire system by looking about without listening. And to show the truant people where their duty should have bound them, the haze had been thickening all over the sea, while the sun kept the time on the old church dial. This was spoken of for many years, throughout the village, as a Scriptural token of the proper thing to do.

"Well, and what have 'e seen?" asked the senior church-warden—not Cheeseman, who was only the junior, and had neither been at church nor on the headland—but Farmer Graves, the tenant of the Glebe and of Up-farm, the Admiral's best holding; "what have 'e seen, good people all, to leave parson to prache to hisself a'most a.sarmon as he's hathn't prached for five year, to my knowledge? Have 'e seen fat bulls of Basan?"

"Naw; but us have heer'd un roar," replied one who was sure to say something. "Wust of it is, there be no making out what language un do roar in."

"One Englishman, I tell 'e, and two Frenchmen," said an ancient tar who had served under Keppel; "by the ring of the guns I could swear to that much. And they loads them so different, that they do."

Before the others had well finished laughing at him, it became his turn to laugh at them. The wind was in the east, and the weather set fair, and but for the sea-mist the power of the sun would have been enough to dazzle all beholders. Already this vapour was beginning to clear off, coiling up in fleecy wisps above the glistening water, but clinging still to any bluff or cliff it could lay hold on.

"Halloa, Jem! Where be going of now?" shouted one or two voices from the Oar-stone point, the furthest outlook of the Havenhead hill.

"To see them Frenchy hoppers get a jolly hiding," Jem Prater replied, without easing his sculls. He was John Prater's nephew, of the "Darling Arms," and had stopped behind the fishing to see his uncle's monthly beer in. "You can't see up there, I reckon, the same as I do here. One English ship have got a job to.tackle two Crappos. But, by George! she'll do it, mates. Good bye, and the Lord defend you!"

He had nobody but his little brother Sam, who was holding the tiller, to help him, and his uncle's boat (which he had taken without leave) was neither stout nor handy. But the stir of the battle had fetched him forth, and he meant to see the whole of it without taking harm. Every Englishman had a full right to do this, in a case of such French audacity, and the English sea and air began to give him fair occasion. For now the sun had swept the mist with a besom of gold wire, widening every sweep, and throw-

ing brilliant prospect down it. The gentle heave of the sea flashed forth with the white birds hovering over it, and the curdles of fugitive vapour glowed like pillars of fire as they floated off. Then out of the drift appeared three ships, partly shrouded in their own fog.

The wind was too light for manœuvring much, and the combatants swung to their broadsides, having taken the breath of the air away by the fury of their fire. All three were standing to the north-north-west, under easy sail, and on the starboard tack, but scarcely holding steerage-way, and taking little heed of it. Close quarters, closer and closer still, muzzle to muzzle, and beard to beard, clinched teeth, and hard pounding, were the order of the day, with the crash of shattered timber and the cries of dying men. And still the ships came onward, forgetting where they were, heaving too much iron to have thought of heaving lead, ready to be shipwrecks, if they could but wreck the enemy.

Between the bulky curls of smoke could be seen the scars of furious battle, splintered masts and shivered yards, tattered sails and yawning bulwarks, and great gaps even of the solid side; and above the ruck of smoke appeared the tricolor flag upon the right hand and the left, and the Union-jack in the middle.

"She've a'got more than she can do, I reckon," said an old man famous in the lobster line; "other a one of they is as big as she be, and two to one seemeth onfair odds. Wish her well out of it—that's all as can be done."

"Kelks, you're a fool," replied the ancient navyman, steadying his spy-glass upon a ledge of rock. "In my time we made very little of that; and the breed may be slacked off a little, but not quite so bad as that would be. Ah! you should a' heard what old Keppel—on the twenty-seventh day of July it was, in the year of our Lord 1778. Talk about Nelson! to my mind old Keppel could have boxed his compass backward. Not but what these men know how to fight quite as well as need be nowadays. Why, if I was aboard of that there frigate, I couldn't do much more than she have done. She'll have one of them, you see if she don't, though she look to have the worst of it, till you comes to understand. The *Leader* her name is, of thirty-eight guns, and she'll lead one of they into Portsmouth, to refit."

LOOKING AT THE BATTLE FROM THE WATCH POINT.

It was hard to understand the matter, in its present aspect, at all as the ancient sailor did; for the fire of the *Leda* ceased suddenly, and she fell behind the others, as if hampered with her canvas. A thrill of pain ran through all the gazing Britons.

"How now, old Navy-Mike?" cried the lobster man. "Strike is the word, and no mistake. And small blame to her either. She hathn't got a sound thread to draw, I do believe. Who is the fool now, Mike? Though vexed I be to ask it."

"Wait a bit, old lobster-pot. Ah, there now, she breezes! Whistle for a wind, lads, whistle, whistle. Sure as I'm a sinner, yes! She's laying her course to board the Frenchman on the weather quarter. With a slant of wind she'll do it, too, if it only holds two minutes. Whistle on your nails, my boys, for the glory of old England."

In reply to their shrill appeal—for even the women tried to whistle—or perhaps in compulsory sequence of the sun, the wind freshened briskly from the sunny side of east. The tattered sails of the brave ship filled, with the light falling through them upon one another, the head swung round at the command of helm, the pennons flew gaily and the ensign flapped, and she bore down smoothly on the outer and therefore unwounded side of the enemy.

"That's what I call judgmatical," old Mike shouted, with a voice that rivalled cannon; "whoever thought of that deserves three epulets, one on each shoulder and one upon his head. Doubt if old Keppel would have thought of that, now. You see, mates, the other Crappo can't fire at her without first hitting of her own consort. And better than that—ever so much better—the tilt of the charge will throw her over on her wounds. Master Muncher hath two great holes 'twixt wind and water on his larboard side, and won't they suck the briny, with the weight of our bows upon the starboard beam? 'Twill take fifty hands to stop leaks, instead of stopping boarders."

The smoke was drifting off, and the sun shone bravely. The battle had been gliding toward the feet of the spectators; and now from the height of the cliff they could descry the decks, the guns, the coils of rope, the turmoil, and dark rush of men to their fate. Small fights, man to man, demanded still the power of a telescope, and distance made the trenchant arms of heroes, working right and left, appear like the nippers of an earwig. The only thing certain was that men were being killed, and glory was being manufactured largely.

"She've a doed it, she've a doed it rarely. There's not a d——d froggy left to go to heaven; or if there be so he's a' battened down below," old Mike shouted, flourishing his spy-glass, which rattled in its joints as much as he did; "down comes the blood, froth, and blue blazes, as they call the Republican emrods, and up goes the Union-jack, my hearties. Three cheers! three cheers! Again! again! again!"

From the sea far below, and far away, came also the volume of a noble English shout, as the flag began to flutter in the quickening breeze, and the sea arose and danced with sunshine. No one, who had got all his blood left in him, could think of anything but glory.

"My certy, they had better mind their soundings, though!" said the old navy-man, with a stitch in his side and a lump in his throat, from loud utterance; "five fathoms is every inch of it where they be now, and the tide making strong, and precious little wind to claw off with. Jem Prater! Jem Prater! Oar up, and give signal. Ah, he's too far off to do any good. In five minutes more they'll be on the White Pig, where no ship ever got off again. Oh, thank the Lord, mates, thank the Lord, for his mercy endureth forever! The other froggy is stuck hard and fast, and our lads will just fetch out in time."

Old Navy-Mike had made no mistake. The consort of the captured frigate, a corvette of twenty-four guns, had boldly stood on with the intention of rounding to the wind, crossing the bows of the other twain, and retrieving the fortunes of the day perhaps, by a broadside into the shattered upper works of the terribly hampered British ship. The idea was clever and spirited, and had a very fair chance of success; but the land below the sea forefended it. Full of fine ardour and the noble thirst for fame, speeding on for the palm of high enterprise and the glory of the native land, alas, they stuck fast in a soft bit of English sand! It was in their power now to swear by all they disbelieved in, and in everything visible and too tangible; but their power was limited strictly to that; and the faster they swore, the faster they were bound to stick.

Springhaven dined well, with its enemy

"WAIT A BIT, OLD LOBSTER-POT."

so placed, and a message from the *Leda* by Jem Prater, that the fishing fleet was rescued, and would be home to early supper, and so much to be talked about all dinner-time, that for once in his life nearly everybody found it more expedient to eat with his fork than his knife. Then all who could be spared from washing up, and getting ready for further cookery, went duly to church in the afternoon, to hear the good rector return humble thanks for a Gracious Mercy to the British arms, and to see a young man, who had landed with despatches, put a face full of gunpowder in at window, to learn whether Admiral Darling was there.

CHAPTER XXII.

A SPECIAL URGENCY.

ADMIRAL DARLING was not in church. His duty to his country kept him up the hill, and in close consultation with Captain Stubbard, who was burning to fire his battery.

"I never knew such bad luck in all my life. The devil has been appointed First Lord of the weather ever since I came to Springhaven." As Stubbard declared these great truths he strode about in his little fortress, delivering a kick at the heels of things which had no right to be lumbering there. "To think that I should never have seen those beggars, when but for the fog I could have smashed them right and left. Admiral, these things make a Christian an infidel."

"Nonsense, sir!" said the Admiral, sternly, for a man of his kind nature; "you forget that without the fog, or rather the mist—for it was only that—those fellows would never have come within range. We have very great blessings to be thankful for, though the credit falls not to our battery. The Frenchmen fought wonderfully well, as well as the best Englishman could have done, and to capture them both is a miracle of luck, if indeed we can manage to secure them. My friend, young Honyman, of the *Leda*, has proved himself just what I said he would be; and has performed a very gallant exploit, though I fear he is severely wounded. But we shall know more now, for I see a young fellow jumping up the hill, like a kangaroo, and probably he comes for orders. One thing we have learned, Stubbard, and must take the hint to-morrow—put a hut on the Haven head, and keep a watchman there. Why, bless my heart, it is Blyth Scudamore that's coming! There is nobody else that can skip like that."

The young lieutenant entered between two guns—the gunners were dismissed in great disgust to dinner—with his pleasant face still a little grimed with gunpowder, and flushed by his hurry up the steep hill-side.

"This for you, sir," he said, saluting the Admiral, presenting his letter, and then drawing back; "and I am to wait your convenience for reply."

"What next will the service come to," asked the Admiral of Captain Stubbard, "when a young man just commissioned gives himself such mighty airs? Shake hands, Blyth, and promise you will come and dine with us, unless you are ordered to return on board at once. How is your good captain? I knew him when he wore Nankins. Jem Prater brought word that he was wounded. I hope it is not serious."

"No, sir; not much to speak of. He has only lost three fingers. That was why I wrote this letter—or report, I ought to call it, if anybody else had written it. Oh, sir! I cannot bear to think of it! I was fifth luff when the fight began, and now there is only one left above me, and he is in command of our biggest prize, the *Ville d'Anvers*. But, Admiral, here you will find it all, as I wrote it, from the lips, when they tied up the fingers, of Captain Honyman."

"How could you tie them up when they were gone?" Captain Stubbard enquired, with a sneer at such a youth. He had got on very slowly in his early days, and could not bear to see a young man with such vacancies before him. "Why, you are the luckiest lad I ever saw! Sure to go up at least three steps. How well you must have kept out of it! And how happy you must feel, Lieutenant Scudamore!"

"I am not at all happy at losing dear friends," the young man answered, gently, as he turned away and patted the breech of a gun, upon which there was a little rust next day; "that feeling comes later in life, I suppose."

The Admiral was not attending to them now, but absorbed in the brief account of the conflict, begun by Captain Honyman in his own handwriting, and finished by his voice, but not his pen. Any one desirous to read this may do so in the proper place. For the present purpose it is enough to say that the modesty of the language was scarcely surpassed by the brilliancy of the exploit. And if anything were needed to commend the writer

to the deepest good will of the reader, it was found in the fact that this enterprise sprang from warm zeal for the commerce of Springhaven. The *Leda* had been ordered on Friday last to protect the peaceful little fishing fleet from a crafty design for their capture, and this she had done with good effect, having justice on her side, and fortune. The particulars of the combat were not so clear, after the captain's three fingers were gone; but if one made proper allowance for that, there was not very much to complain of. The Admiral considered it a very good report; and then put on his spectacles, and thought it still better.

"Why! why! why!" he said—for without affectation many officers had caught the style of His then Gracious Majesty—"What's this? what's this? Something on the other side, in a different man's handwriting, and mighty difficult to read, in my opinion. Stubbard, did you ever see such a scrawl? Make it out for me. You have good eyes, like a hawk, or the man who saw through a milestone. Scudamore, what was his name? You know."

"Three fingers at five pounds apiece per annum as long as he lives!" Captain Stubbard computed on his own: "fifteen pounds a year perhaps for forty years, as you seem to say how young he is; that comes to just £600, and his hand as good as ever"—("I'll be hanged if it is, if he wrote this!" the Admiral interjected)—"and better, I must say, from a selfish point of view, because of only two nails left to clean, and his other hand increased in value; why, the scale is disgraceful, iniquitous, boobyish, and made without any knowledge of the human frame, and the comparative value of its members. Lieutenant Scudamore, look at me. Here you see me without an ear, damaged in the fore-hatch, and with the larboard bow stove in—and how much do I get, though so much older?"

"Well, if you won't help me, Stubbard," said the Admiral, who knew how long his friend would carry on upon that tack, "I must even get Scudamore to read it, though it seems to have been written on purpose to elude him. Blyth, my dear boy, can you explain it?"

"It was—it was only something, sir" —the lieutenant blushed, and hesitated, and looked away unmanfully—"which I asked Captain Honyman to leave out, because—because it had nothing to do with

"I AM NOT AT ALL HAPPY AT LOSING DEAR FRIENDS."

it. I mean, because it was of no impor- tance, even if he happened to have that opinion. His hand was tied up so, that I did not like to say too much, and I thought that he would go to sleep, be- cause the doctor had made him drink a poppy head boiled down with pigtail. But it seems as if he had got up after that —for he always will have his own way— while I was gone to put this coat on; and perhaps he wrote that with his left hand, sir. But it is no part of the business."

"Then we will leave it," said Admiral Darling, "for younger eyes than mine to read. Nelson wrote better with his left hand than ever he did with his right, to my thinking, the very first time that he tried it. But we can't expect everybody to do that. There is no sign of any change of weather, is there, Stubbard? My or- ders will depend very much upon that. I must go home and look at the quick- silver before I know what is best to do. You had better come with me, Scuda- more."

Admiral Darling was quite right in this. Everything depended upon the wea- ther; and although the rough autumn was not come yet, the prime of the hope- ful year was past. The summer had not been a grand one, such as we get about once in a decade, but of loose and uncer- tain character, such as an Englishman

has to make the best of. It might be tak- ing up for a golden autumn, ripening corn, and fruit, and tree, or it might break up into shower and tempest, sodden earth, and weltering sky.

"Your captain refers to me for orders," said Admiral Darling to Scudamore, while they were hastening to the Hall, "as Com- mander of the Coast Defence, because he has been brought too far inshore, and one of the Frenchmen is stranded. The frig- ate you boarded and carried is the *Ville d'Anvers*, of forty guns. The corvette that took the ground, so luckily for you, when half of your hands were aboard the prize, is the *Blonde*, teak-built, and only launched last year. We must try to have her, whatever happens. She won't hurt where she is, unless it comes on to blow. Our sands hold fast without nipping, as you know, like a well-bred sheep-dog, and the White Pig is the toughest of all of them. She may stay there till the equi- nox, without much mischief, if the pre- sent light airs continue. But the worst job will be with the prisoners; they are the plague of all these affairs, and we can't imitate Boney by poisoning them. On the whole, it had better not have hap- pened, perhaps. Though you must not tell Honyman that I said so. It was a very gallant action, very skilful, very beau- tiful; and I hope he will get a fine lift for it; and you too, my dear Blyth, for you must have fought well."

"But, Admiral, surely you would have been grieved if so many of your tenants, and their boats as well, had been swept away into a French harbour. What would Springhaven be without its Captain Zebedee?"

"You are right, Blyth; I forgot that for the moment. There would have been weeping and wailing indeed, even in our own household. But they could not have kept them long, though the loss of their boats would have been most terrible. But I cannot make out why the French should have wanted to catch a few harmless fishing-smacks. *Aquila non captat muscas*, as you taught the boys at Stonnington. And two ships despatched upon a paltry job of that sort! Either Captain Honyman was strangely misinformed, or there is something in the background, entirely beyond our knowledge. Pay attention to this matter, and let me know what you hear of it—as a friend, Blyth, as a friend, I mean. But here we are! You must want feeding. Mrs. Cloam will take care of you, and find all that is needful for a warrior's clean-up. I must look at the barometer, and consider my despatches. Let us have dinner, Mrs. Cloam, in twenty minutes, if possible. For we stand in real need of it."

Concerning that there could be no doubt. Glory, as all English officers know, is no durable stay for the stomach. The urgency of mankind for victuals may roughly be gauged by the length of the jaw. Captain Stubbard had jaws of tremendous length, and always carried a bag of captain's biscuits, to which he was obliged to have recourse in the height of the hottest engagement. Scudamore had short jaws, well set up, and powerful, without rapacity. But even these, after twelve hours of fasting, demanded something better than gunpowder. He could not help thinking that his host was regarding the condition of affairs very calmly, until he remembered that the day was Sunday, when no Briton has any call to be disturbed by any but sacred insistency. At any rate, he was under orders now, and those orders were entirely to his liking. So he freshened up his cheerful and simple-minded face, put his sailor-knot neckcloth askew, as usual, and with some trepidation went down to dinner.

The young ladies would not have been

young women if they had not received him warmly. Kind Faith, who loved him as a sister might—for she had long discovered his good qualities—had tears in her beautiful eyes, as she gave him both hands, and smiled sweetly at his bashfulness. And even the critical Dolly, who looked so sharply at the outside of everything, allowed her fair hand to stay well in his, and said something which was melody to him. Then Johnny, who was of a warlike cast, and hoped soon to destroy the French nation, shook hands with this public benefactor already employed in that great work.

"I shall scarcely have time for a bit of dinner," said Admiral Darling, as they sat down. "I have sent word to have the *Protector* launched, and to give little Billy a feed of corn. All you young people may take your leisure. Youth is the time that commands time and space. But for my part, if I can only manage this plate of soup, and a slice of that fish, and then one help of mutton, and just an apple-fritter, or some trifle of that sort, I shall be quite as lucky as I can hope to be. Duty perpetually spoils my dinner, and I must get some clever fellow to invent a plate that will keep as hot as duty is in these volcanic times. But I never complain; I am so used to it. Eat your dinners, children, and don't think of mine."

Having scarcely afforded himself an hour, the Admiral, in full uniform, embarked upon little Billy, a gentle-minded pony from the west country, who conducted his own digestion while he consulted that of his rider. At the haven they found the *Protector* ready, a ten-oared galley manned by Captain Stubbard's men, good samples of Sea-Fencibles. And the Captain himself was there, to take the tiller, and do any fighting if the chance should arise, for he had been disappointed all the morning. The boat which brought Scudamore had been recalled by signal from the *Leda*, and that active young officer having sought her vainly, and thereby missed the *Protector*, followed steadily in Mr. Prater's boat, with the nephew, Jem, pulling the other oar, and Johnny Darling, who raged at the thought of being left behind, steering vaguely. And just as they rounded the harbour-head, the long glassy sweep of the palpitating sea bore inward and homeward the peaceful squadron, so wistfully watched for and so dearly welcome.

EPILOGUE TO "SHE STOOPS TO CONQUER."

Spoken by Mrs. Bulkley in the character of MISS HARDCASTLE.

WELL, having stoop'd to conquer with success,
    And gain'd a husband without aid from dress,
Still, as a bar-maid, I could wish it too,
As I have conquer'd him, to conquer you;
And let me say, for all your resolution,
That pretty bar-maids have done execution.
Our life is all a play, composed to please;
"We have our exits and our entrances."
The first act shows the simple country maid,
Harmless and young, of everything afraid;
Blushes when hired, and, with unmeaning action,
"I hopes as how to give you satisfaction."
Her second act displays a livelier scene—
The unblushing bar-maid of a country inn,

Who whisks about the house, at market caters,
Talks loud, coquets the guests, and scolds the waiters.
Next the scene shifts to town, and there she soars,
The chop-house toast of ogling connoisseurs.
On squires and cits she there displays her arts,
And on the gridiron broils her lovers' hearts;
And as she smiles, her triumphs to complete,
E'en common-councilmen forget to eat.
The fourth act shows her wedded to the squire,
And madam now begins to hold it higher;
Pretends to taste, at operas cries Caro!
And quits her Nancy Dawson for Che Faro;
Dotes upon dancing, and in all her pride
Swims round the room, the Heinel of Cheapside;
Ogles and leers with artificial skill,
Till, having lost in age the power to kill,
She sits all night at cards, and ogles at spadille.
Such through our lives the eventful history.
The fifth and last act still remains for me:
The bar-maid now for your protection prays,
Turns female barrister, and pleads for Bayes.

THEIR PILGRIMAGE.

BY CHARLES DUDLEY WARNER.

CHAPTER VIII.

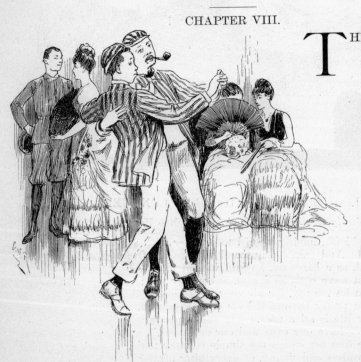

THE attraction of Bar Harbor is in the union of mountain and sea; the mountains rise in granite majesty right out of the ocean.

The genesis of Bar Harbor is curious and instructive. For many years, like other settlements on Mount Desert Island, it had been frequented by people who have more fondness for nature than they have money, and who were willing to put up with wretched accommodations, and enjoyed a wild sort of "roughing it."

But some society people in New York, who have the reputation of setting the mode, chanced to go there; they declared in favor of it; and instantly, by an occult law which governs fashionable life, Bar Harbor became the fashion. Everybody could

ON THE PIAZZA AT RODICK'S.

see its preëminent attractions. The word was passed along by the Boudoir Telephone from Boston to New Orleans, and soon it was a matter of necessity for a *débutante*, or a woman of fashion, or a man of the world, or a *blasé* boy, to show themselves there during the season. It became the scene of summer romances; the student of manners went there to study the "American girl." The notion spread that it was the finest sanitarium on the continent for flirtations; and as trade is said to follow the flag, so in this case real estate speculation rioted in the wake of beauty and fashion.

Our tourists passed a weary, hot day on the coast railway of Maine. Notwithstanding the high temperature the country seemed cheerless, the sunlight to fall less genially than in more fertile regions to the south, upon a landscape stripped of its forests, naked, and unpicturesque.

They were plunged into a cold bath on the steamer in the half-hour's sail from the end of the rail to Bar Harbor. The wind was fresh, white-caps enlivened the scene, the spray dashed over the huge pile of baggage on the bow, the passengers shivered, and could little enjoy the islands and the picturesque shore, but fixed eyes of hope upon the electric lights which showed above the headlands, and marked the site of the hotels and the town in the hidden harbor. Spits of rain dashed in their faces, and in some discomfort they came to the wharf, which was alive with vehicles and tooters for the hotels. In short, with its lights and noise, it had every appearance of being an important place, and when our party, holding on to their seats in a buck-board, were whirled at a gallop up to Rodick's, and ushered into a spacious office swarming with people, they realized that they were entering upon a lively if somewhat hap-hazard life. The first confused impression was of a bewildering number of slim, pretty girls, nonchalant young fellows in lawn-tennis suits, and indefinite opportunities in the halls and parlors and wide piazzas for promenades and flirtations.

Rodick's is a sort of big boarding-house, hesitating whether to be a hotel or not, no bells in the rooms, no bills of fare (or rarely one), no wine list, a go-as-you-please, help-yourself sort of place, which is popular because it has its own character, and everybody drifts into it first or last. Some say it is an acquired taste; that people do not take to it at first. The big office is a sort of assembly-room, where new arrivals are scanned and discovered, and it is unblushingly called the "fish-pond" by the young ladies who daily angle there.

Bar Harbor was indeed an interesting society study. Except in some of the cottages, it might be said that society was on a lark. With all the manners of the world and the freemasonry of fashionable life, it had elected to be unconventional. The young ladies liked to appear in nautical and lawn-tennis toilet, carried so far that one might refer to the "cut of their jib," and their minds were not much given to any elaborate dressing for evening. As to the young gentlemen, if there were any dress-coats on the island, they took pains not to display them, but delighted in appearing in the evening promenade, and even in the ball-room, in the nondescript suits that made them so conspicuous in the morning, the favorite being a dress of stripes, with striped jockey cap to match, that did not suggest the penitentiary uniform, because in State-prisons the stripes run round. This *négligé* costume was adhered to even in the ball-room. To be sure, the ball-room was little frequented, only an adventurous couple now and then gliding over the floor, and affording scant amusement to the throng gathered on the piazza and about the open windows. Mrs. Montrose, a stately dame of the old school, whose standard was the court in the days of Calhoun, Clay, and Webster, disapproved of this laxity, and when a couple of young fellows in striped array one evening whirled round the room together, with brier-wood pipes in their mouths, she was scandalized. If the young ladies shared her sentiments, they made no resolute protests, remembering perhaps the scarcity of young men elsewhere, and thinking that it is better to be loved by a lawn-ten-

nis suit than not to be loved at all. The daughters of Mrs. Montrose thought they should draw the line on the brier-wood pipe.

But the principal occupation at Bar Harbor was not dancing. It was outdoor exercise, incessant activity in driving, walking, boating—rowing and sailing—bowling, tennis, and flirtation. There was always an excursion somewhere, by land or sea, watermelon parties, races in the harbor in which the girls took part, drives in buck-boards which they organized—indeed, the canoe and the buck-board were in constant demand. In all this there was a pleasing freedom—of course under proper chaperonage. And such delightful chaperons as they were, their business being to promote and not to hinder the intercourse of the sexes!

This activity, this desire to row and walk and drive and to become acquainted, was all due to the air. It has a peculiar quality. Even the skeptic has to admit this. It composes his nerves to sleep, it stimulates to unwonted exertion. The fanatics of the place declare that the fogs are not damp as at other resorts on the coast. Fashion can make even a fog dry. But the air is delicious. In this latitude, and by reason of the hills, the atmosphere is pure and elastic and stimulating, and it is softened by the presence of the sea.

"Everybody" was at Bar Harbor, or would be there in course of the season. Mrs. Cortlandt was there, and Mrs. Pendragon of New Orleans, one of the most brilliant, amiable, and charming of women. I remember her as far back as the seventies. A young man like Mr. King, if he could be called young, could not have a safer and more sympathetic social adviser. Why are not all handsome women cordial, good-tempered, and well-bred? And there were the Ashleys—clever mother and three daughters, *au fait* girls, racy and witty talkers: I forget whether they were last from Paris, Washington, or San Francisco. Family motto—"Don't be dull." All the Van Dams from New York, and the Sleider-heifers and Mulligrubs of New Jersey, were there for the season, some of them in cottages. These families are intimate, even connected by marriage, with the Bayardiers of South Carolina and the Lontoons of Louisiana. The girls are handsome, dashing women, without much

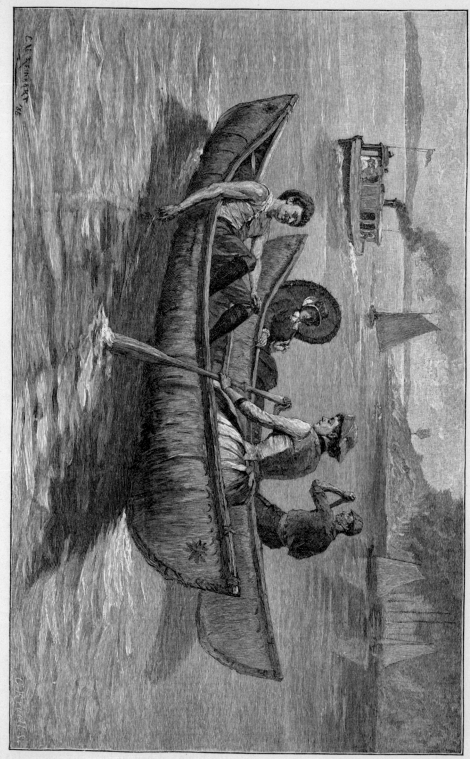

information, but rattling talkers, and so exclusive! and the young men, with a Piccadilly air, fancy that they belong to the "Prince of Wales set," you know. There is a good deal of monarchical simplicity in our heterogeneous society.

Mrs. Cortlandt was quite in her element here as director-general of expeditions and promoter of social activity. "I have been expecting you," she was kind enough to say to Mr. King the morning after his arrival. "Kitty Van Sandford spied you last night, and exclaimed, 'There, now, is a real reënforcement!' You see that you are mortgaged already."

"It's very kind of you to expect me. Is there anybody else here I know?"

"Several hundreds, I should say. If you cannot find friends here, you are a subject for an orphans' asylum. And you have not seen anybody?"

"Well, I was late at breakfast."

"And you have looked on the register?"

"Yes, I did run my eye over the register."

"And you are standing right before me and trying to look as if you did not know that Irene Benson is in the house. I didn't think, Mr. King, it had gone that far—indeed I didn't. You know I'm in a manner responsible for it. And I heard all about you at Newport. She's a heart of gold, that girl."

"Did she—did Miss Benson say anything about Newport?"

"No. Why?"

"Oh, I didn't know but she might have mentioned how she liked it."

"I don't think she liked it as much as her mother did. Mrs. Benson talks of nothing else. Irene said nothing special to me. I don't know what she may have said to Mr. Meigs," this wily woman added, in the most natural manner.

"Who is Mr. Meigs?"

"Mr. Alfred Meigs, Boston. He is a rich widower, about forty—the most fascinating age for a widower, you know. I think he is conceited, but he is really a most entertaining man; has travelled all over the world—Egypt, Persia—lived in Japan, prides himself a little on never having been in Colorado or Florida."

"What does he do?"

"Do? He drives Miss Benson to Otter Cliffs, and out on the Cornice Road, about seven days in the week, and gets up sailing parties and all that in the intervals."

"I mean his occupation."

"Isn't that occupation enough? Well, he has a library and a little archæological museum, and prints monographs on art now and then. If he were a New-Yorker, you know, he would have a yacht instead of a library. There they are now."

A carriage with a pair of spirited horses stood at the bottom of the steps on the entrance side. Mrs. Cortlandt and King turned the corner of the piazza and walked that way. On the back seat were Mrs. Benson and Mrs. Simpkins. The gentleman holding the reins was just helping Irene to the high seat in front. Mr. King was running down the long flight of steps. Mrs. Benson saw him, bowed most cordially, and called his name. Irene, turning quickly, also bowed—he thought there was a flush on her face. The gentleman, in the act of starting the horses, raised his hat. King was delighted to notice that he was bald. He had a round head, snugly trimmed beard slightly dashed with gray, was short and a trifle stout—King thought dumpy. "I suppose women like that kind of man," he said to Mrs. Cortlandt when the carriage was out of sight.

"Why not? He has perfect manners; he knows the world—that is a great point I can tell you in the imagination of a girl; he is rich; and he is no end obliging."

"How long has he been here?"

"Several days. They happened to come up from the Isles of Shoals together. He is somehow related to the Simpkinses. There! I've wasted time enough on you. I must go and see Mrs. Pendragon about a watermelon party to Jordan Pond. You'll see, I'll arrange something."

King had no idea what a watermelon party was, but he was pleased to think that it was just the sort of thing that Mr. Meigs would shine in. He said to himself that he hated dilettante snobs. His bitter reflections were interrupted by the appearance of Miss Lamont and the artist, and with them Mr. Benson. The men shook hands with downright heartiness. Here is a genuine man, King was thinking.

"Yes. We are still at it," he said, with his humorous air of resignation. "I tell my wife that I'm beginning to understand how old Christian felt going through Vanity Fair. We ought to be pretty near the Heavenly Gates by this time. I reckoned she thought they opened into Newport. She said I ought to be ashamed to ridicule the Bible. I had to have my joke. It's

CLIMBING UP NEWPORT.

queer how different the world looks to women."

"And how does it look to men?" asked Miss Lamont.

"Well, my dear young lady, it looks like a good deal of fuss, and tolerably large bills."

"But what does it matter about the bills if you enjoy yourself?"

"That's just it. Folks work harder to enjoy themselves than at anything else I know. Half of them spend more money than they can afford to, and keep under the harrow all the time, just because they see others spend money."

"I saw your wife and daughter driving away just now," said King, shifting the conversation to a more interesting topic.

"Yes. They have gone to take a ride over what they call here the Cornneechy. It's a pretty enough road along the bay, but Irene says it's about as much like the road in Europe they name it from as Green Mountain is like Mount Blanck. Our folks seem possessed to stick a foreign name on to everything. And the road round through the scrub to Eagle Lake they call Norway. If Norway is like that, it's pretty short of timber. If there hadn't been so much lumbering here, I should like it better. There is hardly a decent pine-tree left. Mr. Meigs—they have gone riding with Mr. Meigs—says the Maine government ought to have a Maine law that amounts to something—one that will protect the forests, and start up some trees on the coast."

"Is Mr. Meigs in the lumber business?" asked King.

"Only for scenery, I guess. He is great on scenery. He's a Boston man. I tell the women he is what I call a bric-er-brac man. But you come to sit right down with him, away from women, and he talks just as sensible as anybody. He is shrewd enough. It beats all how men are with men and with women."

Mr. Benson was capable of going on in this way all day. But the artist proposed a walk up Newport, and Mr. King getting Mrs. Pendragon to accompany them, the party set out. It is a very agreeable climb up Newport, and not difficult; but if the sun is out, one feels, after scrambling over the rocks and walking home by the dusty road, like taking a long pull at a cup of shandygaff. The mountain is a solid mass of granite, bare on top, and commands a noble view of islands and ocean, of the gorge separating it from Green Mountain, and of that respectable hill. For this reason, because it is some two or three hundred feet lower than Green Mountain, and includes that scarred eminence in its view, it is the most picturesque and pleasing elevation on the island. It also has the recommendation of being nearer to the sea than its sister mountain. On the south side, by a long slope, it comes nearly to the water, and the longing that the visitor to Bar Harbor has to see the ocean is moderately gratified. The prospect is at once noble and poetic.

Mrs. Pendragon informed Mr. King that he and Miss Lamont and Mr. Forbes were included in the watermelon party that was to start that afternoon at five o'clock. The plan was for the party to go in buckboards to Eagle Lake, cross that in the steamer, scramble on foot over the "carry" to Jordan Pond, take row-boats to the foot of that, and find at a farm-house there the watermelons and other refreshments, which would be sent by the shorter road, and then all return by moonlight in the buck-boards.

This plan was carried out. Mrs. Cortlandt, Mrs. Pendragon, and Mrs. Simpkins were to go as chaperons. And Mr. Meigs had been invited by Mrs. Cortlandt, King learned to his disgust, also to act as a chaperon. All the proprieties are observed at Bar Harbor. Half a dozen long buck-boards were loaded with their merry freight. At the last Mrs. Pendragon pleaded a headache, and could not go. Mr. King was wandering about among the buck-boards to find an eligible seat. He was not put in good-humor by finding that Mr. Meigs had ensconced himself beside Irene, and he was about crowding in with the Ashley girls—not a bad fate—when word was passed down the line from Mrs. Cortlandt, who was the autocrat of the expedition, that Mr. Meigs was to come back and take a seat with Mrs. Simpkins in the buck-board with the watermelons. She could not walk

A BAR HARBOR BUCK-BOARD.

INDIAN VILLAGE, BAR HARBOR.

around the "carry"; she must go by the direct road, and of course she couldn't go alone. There was no help for it, and Mr. Meigs, looking as pleased as an undertaker in a healthy season, got down from his seat and trudged back. Thus two chaperons were disposed of at a stroke, and the young men all said that they hated to assume so much responsibility. Mr. King didn't need prompting in this emergency; the wagons were already moving, and before Irene knew exactly what had happened, Mr. King was begging her pardon for the change, and seating himself beside her. And he was thinking, "What a confoundedly clever woman Mrs. Cortlandt is!"

There is an informality about a buckboard that communicates itself at once to conduct. The exhilaration of the long spring-board, the necessity of holding on to something or somebody to prevent being tossed overboard, put occupants in a larkish mood that they might never attain in an ordinary vehicle. All this was favorable to King, and it relieved Irene from an embarrassment she might have

felt in meeting him under ordinary circumstances. And King had the tact to treat himself and their meeting merely as accidents.

"The American youth seem to have invented a novel way of disposing of chaperons," he said. "To send them in one direction and the party chaperoned in another is certainly original."

"I'm not sure the chaperons like it. And I doubt if it is proper to pack them off by themselves, especially when one is a widow and the other is a widower."

"It's a case of chaperon eat chaperon. I hope your friend didn't mind it. I had nearly despaired of finding a seat."

"Mr. Meigs? He did not say he liked it, but he is the most obliging of men."

"I suppose you have pretty well seen the island?"

"We have driven about a good deal. We have seen Southwest Harbor, and Somes's Sound and Schooner Head, and the Ovens and Otter Cliffs—there's no end of things to see; it needs a month. I suppose you have been up Green Mountain?"

"No. I sent Mr. Forbes."

"You ought to go. It saves buying a map. Yes, I like the place immensely. You mustn't judge of the variety here by the table at Rodick's. I don't suppose there's a place on the coast that compares with it in interest; I mean variety of effects and natural beauty. If the writers wouldn't exaggerate so, talk about 'the sublimity of the mountains challenging the eternal grandeur of the sea'!"

"Don't use such strong language there on the back seat," cried Miss Lamont. "This is a pleasure party. Mr. Van Dusen wants to know why Maud S. is like a salamander?"

"He is not to be gratified, Marion. If it is conundrums, I shall get out and walk."

Before the conundrum was guessed, the volatile Van Dusen broke out into, "Here's a how d'e do!" One of the Ashley girls in the next wagon caught up the word with, "Here's a state of things!" and the two buck-boards went rattling down the hill to Eagle Lake in a *Mikado* chorus.

On the steamer crossing the lake, King hoped for an opportunity to make an explanation to Irene. But when the opportunity came, he found it very difficult to tell what it was he wanted to explain, and so blundered on in commonplaces.

"You like Bar Harbor so well," he said, "that I suppose your father will be buying a cottage here?"

"Hardly. Mr. Meigs" (King thought there was too much Meigs in the conversation) "said that he had once thought of doing so, but he likes the place too well for that. He prefers to come here voluntarily. The trouble about owning a cottage at a watering-place is that it makes a duty of a pleasure. You can always rent, father says. He has noticed that usually when a person gets comfortably established in a summer cottage he wants to rent it."

"And you like it better than Newport?"

"On some accounts—the air, you know, and—"

"I want to tell you," he said, breaking in most illogically—"I want to tell you, Miss Benson, that it was all a wretched mistake at Newport that morning. I don't suppose you care, but I'm afraid you are not quite just to me."

"I don't think I was unjust." The girl's voice was low, and she spoke slow-

ly. "You couldn't help it. We can't any of us help it. We cannot make the world over, you know." And she looked up at him with a faint little smile.

"But you didn't understand. I didn't care for any of those people. It was just an accident. Won't you believe me? I do not ask much. But I cannot have you think I'm a coward."

"I never did, Mr. King. Perhaps you do not see what society is as I do. People think they can face it when they cannot. I can't say what I mean, and I think we'd better not talk about it."

The boat was landing; and the party streamed up into the woods, and with jest and laughter and feigned anxiety about danger and assistance, picked its way over the rough, stony path. It was such a scramble as young ladies enjoy, especially if they are city bred, for it seems to them an achievement of more magnitude than to the country lasses who see nothing uncommon or heroic in following a cow path. And the young men like it because it brings out the trusting, dependent, clinging nature of girls. King wished it had been five miles long instead of a mile and a half. It gave him an opportunity to show his helpful, considerate spirit. It was necessary to take her hand to help her over the bad spots, and either the bad spots increased as they went on, or Irene was deceived about it. What makes a path of this sort so perilous to a woman's heart? Is it because it is an excuse for doing what she longs to do? Taking her hand recalled the day on the rocks at Narragansett, and the nervous clutch of her little fingers, when the footing failed, sent a delicious thrill through her lover.

At Jordan Pond boats were waiting. It is a pretty fresh-water pond between high sloping hills, and twin peaks at the north end give it even picturesqueness. There are a good many trout in it—at least that is the supposition, for the visitors very seldom get them out. When the boats with their chattering passengers had pushed out into the lake and accomplished a third of the voyage, they were met by a skiff containing the faithful chaperons Mrs. Simpkins and Mr. Meigs. They hailed, but Mr. King, who was rowing his boat, did not slacken speed. "Are you much tired, Miss Benson?" shouted Mr. Meigs. King didn't like this assumption of protection. "I've brought you a shawl."

THE WATERMELON PARTY.

"Hang his paternal impudence!" growled King, under his breath, as he threw himself back with a jerk on the oars that nearly sent Irene over the stern of the boat.

Evidently the boat-load, of which the Ashley girls and Mr. Van Dusen were a part, had taken the sense of this little comedy, for immediately they struck up:

"For he is going to marry Yum-Yum—
            Yum-Yum!
For he is going to marry Yum-Yum—
            Yum-Yum!"

This pleasantry passed entirely over the head of Irene, who had not heard the *Mikado*, but King accepted it as a good omen, and forgave its impudence. It set Mr. Meigs thinking that he had a rival.

At the landing, however, Mr. Meigs was on hand to help Irene out, and a presentation of Mr. King followed. Mr. Meigs was polite even to cordiality, and thanked him for taking such good care of her. Men will make such blunders sometimes.

"Oh, we are old friends," she said, carelessly.

Mr. Meigs tried to mend matters by saying that he had promised Mrs. Benson, you know, to look after her. There was

that in Irene's manner that said she was not to be appropriated without leave. But the consciousness that her look betrayed this softened her at once toward Mr. Meigs, and decidedly improved his chances for the evening. The philosopher says that women are cruelest when they set out to be kind.

The supper was an *al fresco* affair, the party being seated about on rocks and logs and shawls spread upon the grass near the farmer's house. The scene was a very pretty one, at least the artist thought so, and Miss Lamont said it was lovely, and the Ashley girls declared it was just divine. There was no reason why King should not enjoy the chaff and merriment and the sunset light which touched the group, except that the one woman he cared to serve was enveloped in the attentions of Mr. Meigs. The drive home in the moonlight was the best part of the excursion, or it would have been if there had not been a general change of seats ordered, altogether, as Mr. King thought, for the accommodation of the Boston man. It nettled him that Irene let herself fall to the escort of Mr. Meigs, for women can always arrange these things if they choose, and he had only a melancholy satisfaction in the college songs and conundrums that enlivened the festive buckboard in which he was a passenger. Not that he did not join in the hilarity, but it seemed only a poor imitation of pleasure. Alas, that the tone of one woman's voice, the touch of her hand, the glance of her eye, should outweigh the world!

Somehow, with all the opportunities, the suit of our friend did not advance beyond a certain point. Irene was always cordial, always friendly, but he tried in vain to ascertain whether the middle-aged man from Boston had touched her imagination. There was a boating party the next evening in Frenchman's Bay, and King had the pleasure of pulling Miss Benson and Miss Lamont out seaward under the dark frowning cliffs until they felt the ocean swell, and then of making the circuit of Porcupine Island. It was an enchanting night, full of mystery. The rock face of the Porcupine glistened white in the moonlight as if it were encrusted with salt, the waves beat in a continuous roar against its base, which is honey-combed by the action of the waves, and when the boat glided into its shadow it loomed up vast and wonderful. Seaward were the harbor lights, the phosphorescent glisten of the waves, the dim forms of other islands; all about in the bay row-boats darted in and out of the moonlight, voices were heard calling from boat to boat, songs floated over the water, and the huge Portland steamer came plunging in out of the night, a blazing, trembling monster. Not much was said in the boat, but the impression of such a night goes far in the romance of real life.

Perhaps it was this impression that made her assent readily to walk next morning with Mr. King along the bay. The shore is nearly all occupied by private cottages, with little lawns running down to the granite edge of the water. It is a favorite place for strolling; couples establish themselves with books and umbrellas on the rocks, children are dabbling in the coves, sails enliven the bay, row-boats dart about, the cawing of crows is heard in the still air. Irene declared that the scene was idyllic. The girl was in a most gracious humor, and opened her life more to King than she had ever done before. By such confidences usually women invite avowals, and as the two passed along,

King felt the moment approach when there would be the most natural chance in the world for him to tell this woman what she was to him; at the next turn in the shore, by that rock, surely the moment would come. What is this airy nothing by which women protect themselves in such emergencies, by a question, by a tone, an invisible strong barrier that the most impetuous dare not attempt to break? King felt the subtle restraint which he could not define or explain. And before he could speak she said,

"We are going away to-morrow."

"We? And who are we?"

"Oh, the Simpkinses and our whole family, and Mr. Meigs."

"And where?"

"Mr. Meigs has persuaded mother into the wildest scheme. It is nothing less than to leap from here across all the intervening States to the White Sulphur Springs in Virginia. Father falls into the notion because he wants to see more of the Southerners, Mrs. Simpkins and her daughter are crazy to go, and Mr. Meigs says he has been trying to get there all his life, and in August the season is at its height. It was all arranged before I was consulted, but I confess I rather like it. It will be a change."

"Yes, I should think it would be delightful," King replied, rather absent-mindedly. "It's a long journey, a very long journey. I should think it would be too long a journey for Mr. Meigs—at his time of life."

It was not a fortunate remark, and still it might be; for who could tell whether Irene would not be flattered by this declaration of his jealousy of Mr. Meigs. But she passed it over as not serious, with the remark that the going did not seem to be beyond the strength of her father.

The introduction of Mr. Meigs in the guise of an accepted family friend and travelling companion chilled King and cast a gloom over the landscape. Afterward he knew that he ought to have dashed in and scattered this encompassing network of Meigs, disregarded the girl's fence of reserve, and avowed his love. More women are won by a single charge at the right moment than by a whole campaign of strategy.

On the way back to the hotel he was absorbed in thought, and he burst into the room where Forbes was touching up one of his sketches, with a fully formed plan. "Old fellow, what do you say to going to Virginia?"

Forbes put in a few deliberate touches, moving his head from side to side, and with aggravating slowness said, "What do you want to go to Virginia for?"

"Why, White Sulphur, of course; the most characteristic watering-place in America. See the whole Southern life there in August; and there's the Natural Bridge."

"I've seen pictures of the Natural Bridge. I don't know as I care much" (still contemplating the sketch from different points of view, and softly whistling) "for the whole of Southern life."

"See here, Forbes, you must have some deep design to make you take that attitude."

"Deep design!" replied Forbes, facing round. "I'll be hanged if I see what you are driving at. I thought it was Saratoga and Richfield, and mild things of that sort."

"And the little Lamont. I know we talked of going there with her and her uncle; but we can go there afterward. I tell you what I'll do: I'll go to Richfield, and stay till snow comes, if you will take a dip with me down into Virginia first. You ought to do it for your art. It's something new, picturesque — negroes, Southern belles, old-time manners. You cannot afford to neglect it."

"I don't see the fun in being yanked all over the United States territory in August."

"You want shaking up. You've been drawing sea-shores with one figure in them till your pictures all look like— well, like Lamont and water."

"That's better," Forbes retorted, "than Benson and gruel."

NEGRO WAITER.

And the two got into a huff. The artist took his sketch-book and went out-doors, and King went to his room to study the guide-books and the map of Virginia. The result was that when the friends met for dinner, King said,

"I thought you might do it for me, old boy."

And Forbes replied: "Why didn't you say so? I don't care a rap where I go. But it's Richfield afterward."

CHAPTER IX.

What occurred at the parting between the artist and the little Lamont at Bar Harbor I never knew. There was that good comradeship between the two, that frank enjoyment of each other's society, without any sentimental nonsense, so often seen between two young people in America, which may end in a friendship of a summer, or extend to the cordial esteem of a lifetime, or result in marriage. I always liked the girl; she had such a sunny temper, such a flow of originality in her mental attitude toward people and things without being a wit or a critic, and so much piquancy in all her little

"HAVEN'T I WAITED ON YOU BEFO', SAH?"—[SEE PAGE 430.]

nuded of its trees! By afternoon they were far down the east valley of the Shenandoah, between the Blue Ridge and the Massanutten range, in a country broken, picturesque, fertile, so attractive that they wondered there were so few villages on the route, and only now and then a cheap shanty in sight; and crossing the divide to the waters of the James, at sundown, in the midst of a splendid effect of mountains and clouds in a thunder-storm, they came to Natural Bridge station, where a coach awaited them. This was old ground to King, who had been telling the artist that the two natural objects east of the Rocky Mountains that he thought entitled to the epithet "sublime" were Niagara Falls and the Natural Bridge; and as for scenery, he did not know of any more noble and refined than this region of the Blue Ridge. Take away the Bridge altogether, which is a mere freak, and the place would still possess, he said, a charm unique. Since the enlargement of hotel facilities and the conversion of this princely domain into a grand park, it has become a favorite summer resort. The gorge of the Bridge is a botanical storehouse, greater variety of evergreens cannot be found together anywhere else in the country, and the hills are still clad with stately forests. In opening drives, and cutting roads and vistas to give views, the proprietor has shown a skill and taste in dealing with natural resources, both in regard to form and the development of contrasts of color in foliage, which are rare in landscape gardening on this side of the Atlantic. Here is the highest part of the Blue Ridge, and from the gentle summit of Mount Jefferson the spectator has in view a hundred miles of this remarkable range, this ribbed mountain structure,

ways. She would take to matrimony, I should say, like a duck to water, with unruffled plumage, but as a wife she would never be commonplace, or anything but engaging, and, as the saying is, she could make almost any man happy.

If Marion had shed any tears overnight, say on account of a little lonesomeness because her friend was speeding away from her southward, there were no traces of them when she met her uncle at the breakfast table, as bright and chatty as usual, and in as high spirits as one can maintain with the Rodick coffee.

What a world of shifting scenes it is! Forbes had picked up his traps and gone off with his unreasonable companion like a soldier. The day after, when he looked out of the window of his sleeping compartment at half past four, he saw the red sky of morning, and against it the spires of Philadelphia. At ten o'clock the two friends were breakfasting comfortably in the car, and running along down the lovely Cumberland Valley. What a contrast was this rich country, warm with color and suggestive of abundance, to the pale and scrimped coast land of Maine de-

which always wears a mantle of beauty, changeable purple and violet.

After supper there was an illumination of the cascade, and the ancient gnarled arbor-vitæ trees that lean over it—perhaps the largest known specimens of this species —of the gorge and the Bridge. Nature is apt to be belittled by this sort of display, but the noble dignity of the vast arch of stone was superior to this trifling, and even had a sort of mystery added to its imposing grandeur.

of all the muscles of the body, as if in response to the twang of a banjo; they do nothing without excessive motion and flourish. The gestures and good-humored vitality expended in changing plates would become the leader of an orchestra. Many of them, besides, have the expression of class-leaders—of a worldly sort. There were the aristocratic chamber-maid and porter, who had the air of never having waited on any but the first families. And what clever flatterers and readers of hu-

POLITICS AND CIGARS.

The presence of the colored brother in force distinguished this from provincial resorts at the North, even those that employ this color as servants. The flavor of Old Virginia is unmistakable, and life drops into an easy-going pace under this influence. What fine manners, to be sure! The waiters in the dining-room, in white ties and dress-coats, move on springs, starting even to walk with a complicated use

man nature! They can tell in a moment whether a man will be complimented by the remark, "I tuk you for a Richmond gemman, never sho'd have know'd you was frum de Norf," or whether it is best to say, "We depen's on de gemmen frum de Norf; folks down hyer never gives noffin; is too pore." But to a Richmond man it is always, "The Yankee is mighty keerful of his money; we depen's on the old sort, marse." A fine specimen of the "Richmond darky" of the old school—polite, flattering, with a venerable head of gray wool, was the bar-tender, who mixed his juleps with a flourish as if keeping time to music. "Haven't I waited on you befo', sah? At Capon Springs? Sorry, sah, but tho't I knowed you when you come in. Sorry, but glad to know you now, sah. If that julep don't suit you, sah, throw it in my face."

A friendly, restful, family sort of place, with music, a little mild dancing, mostly performed by children, in the pavilion, driving and riding—in short, peace in the midst of noble scenery. No display of fashion, the artist soon discovered, and he said he longed to give the pretty girls some instruction in the art of dress. Forbes was a missionary of "style." It hurt his sense of the fitness of things to see women without it. He used to say that an ill-dressed woman would spoil the finest landscape. For such a man, with an artistic feeling so sensitive, the White Sulphur Springs is a natural goal. And he and his friend hastened thither with as much speed as the Virginia railways, whose time-tables are carefully adjusted to miss all connections, permit.

"What do you think of a place," he wrote Miss Lamont—the girl read me a portion of his lively letter that summer at Saratoga—"into which you come by a belated train at half past eleven at night, find friends waiting up for you in evening costume, are taken to a champagne supper at twelve, get to your quarters at one, and have your baggage delivered to you at two o'clock in the morning?" The friends were lodged in "Paradise Row"—a whimsical name given to one of the quarters assigned to single gentlemen. Put into these single-room barracks, which were neat but exceedingly primitive in their accommodations, by hilarious negro attendants who appeared to regard life as one prolonged lark, and who avowed that there was no time of day or night when a mint-julep or any other necessary of life would not be forth-coming at a moment's warning, the beginning of their sojourn at "The White" took on an air of adventure, and the two strangers had the impression of having dropped into a garrison somewhere on the frontier. But when King stepped out upon the gallery in the fresh summer morning, the scene that met his eyes was one of such peaceful dignity, and so different from any in his experience, that he was aware that he had come upon an original development of watering-place life.

The White Sulphur has been for the better part of a century, as everybody knows, the typical Southern resort, the rendezvous of all that was most characteristic in the society of the whole South, the meeting-place of its politicians, the haunt of its belles, the arena of gayety, intrigue, and fashion. If tradition is to be believed, here in years gone by were concocted the measures that were subsequently deployed for the government of the country at Washington, here historic matches were made, here beauty had triumphs that were the talk of a generation, here hearts were broken at a ball and mended in Lovers' Walk, and here fortunes were nightly lost and won. It must have been in its material conditions a primitive place in the days of its greatest fame. Visitors came to it in their carriages and unwieldy four-horse chariots, attended by troops of servants, making slow but most enjoyable pilgrimages over the mountain roads, journeys that lasted a week or a fortnight, and were every day enlivened by jovial adventure. They came for the season. They were all of one social order, and needed no introduction; those from Virginia were all related to each other, and though life there was somewhat in the nature of a picnic, it had its very well defined and ceremonious code of etiquette. In the memory of its old *habitués* it was at once the freest and the most aristocratic assembly in the world. The hotel was small and its arrangements primitive; a good many of the visitors had their own cottages, and the rows of these cheap structures took their names from their occupants. The Southern Presidents, the Senators and statesmen, the rich planters, lived in cottages which still have a historic interest in their memory. But cottage life was never the exclusive affair that it is elsewhere; the society was one body, and the hotel was the centre.

Time has greatly changed the White Sulphur; doubtless in its physical aspect it never was so beautiful and attractive as it is to-day, but all the modern improvements have not destroyed the character of the resort, which possesses a great many of its primitive and old-time peculiarities.

Briefly, the White is in an elevated and charming mountain region, so cool, in

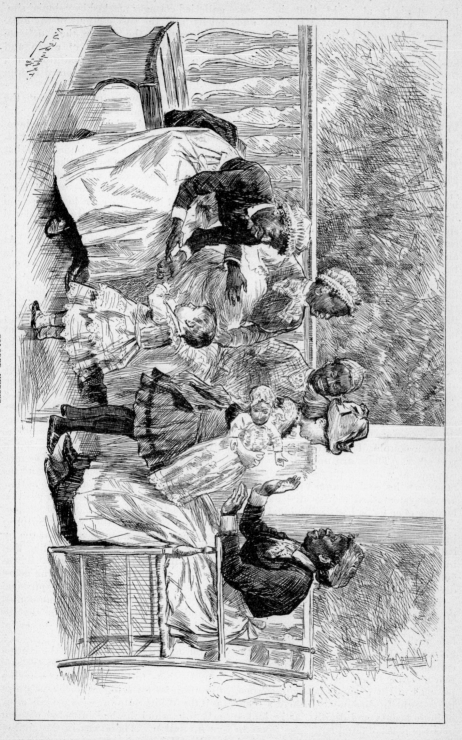

fact, especially at night, that the "season" is practically limited to July and August, although I am not sure but a quiet person, who likes invigorating air, and has no daughters to marry off, would find it equally attractive in September and October, when the autumn foliage is in its glory. In a green rolling interval, planted with noble trees and flanked by moderate hills, stands the vast white caravansary, having wide galleries and big pillars running round three sides. The front and two sides are elevated, the galleries being reached by flights of steps, and affording room underneath for the large billiard and bar rooms. From the hotel the ground slopes down to the spring, which is surmounted by a round canopy on white columns, and below is an opening across the stream to the race-track, the servants' quarters, and a fine view of receding hills. Three sides of this charming park are enclosed by the cottages and cabins, which back against the hills, and are more or less embowered in trees. Most of these cottages are built in blocks and rows, some single rooms, others large enough to accommodate a family, but all reached by flights of steps, all with verandas, and most of them connected by galleries. Occasionally the forest trees have been left, and the galleries built around them. Included in the premises are two churches, a gambling-house, a couple of country stores, and a post-office. There are none of the shops common at watering-places for the sale of fancy articles, and, strange to say, flowers are not systematically cultivated, and very few are ever to be had. The hotel has a vast dining-room, besides the minor eating-rooms for children and nurses, a large ball-room, and a drawing-room of imposing dimensions. Hotel and cottages together, it is said, can lodge fifteen hundred guests.

The natural beauty of the place is very great, and fortunately there is not much smart and fantastic architecture to interfere with it. I cannot say whether the knowledge that Irene was in one of the cottages affected King's judgment, but that morning, when he strolled to the upper part of the grounds before breakfast, he thought he had never beheld a scene of more beauty and dignity, as he looked over the mass of hotel buildings, upon the park set with a wonderful variety of dark green foliage, upon the elevated rows of galleried cottages marked by colonial simplicity, and the soft contour of the hills, which satisfy the eye in their delicate blending of every shade of green and brown. And after an acquaintance of a couple of weeks the place seemed to him ravishingly beautiful.

King was always raving about the White Sulphur after he came North, and one never could tell how much his judgment was colored by his peculiar experiences there. It was my impression that if he had spent those two weeks on a barren rock in the ocean, with only one fair spirit for his minister, he would have sworn that it was the most lovely spot on the face of the earth. He always declared that it was the most friendly, cordial society at this resort in the country. At breakfast he knew scarcely any one in the vast dining-room, except the New Orleans and Richmond friends with whom he had a seat at table. But their acquaintance sufficed to establish his position. Before dinner-time he knew half a hundred; in the evening his introductions had run up into the hundreds, and he felt that he had potential friends in every Southern city; and before the week was over there was not one of the thousand guests he did not know or might not know. At his table he heard Irene spoken of and her beauty commented on. Two or three days had been enough to give her a reputation in a society that is exceedingly sensitive to beauty. The men were all ready to do her homage, and the women took her into favor as soon as they saw that Mr. Meigs, whose social position was perfectly well known, was of her party. The society at the White Sulphur seems perfectly easy of access, but the ineligible will find that it is able, like that of Washington, to protect itself. It was not without a little shock that King heard the good points, the style, the physical perfections, of Irene so fully commented on, and not without some alarm that he heard predicted for her a very successful career as a belle.

Coming out from breakfast, the Benson party were encountered on the gallery, and introductions followed. It was a trying five minutes for King, who felt as guilty as if the White Sulphur were private property into which he had intruded without an invitation. There was in the civility of Mr. Meigs no sign of an invitation. Mrs. Benson said she was never so sur-

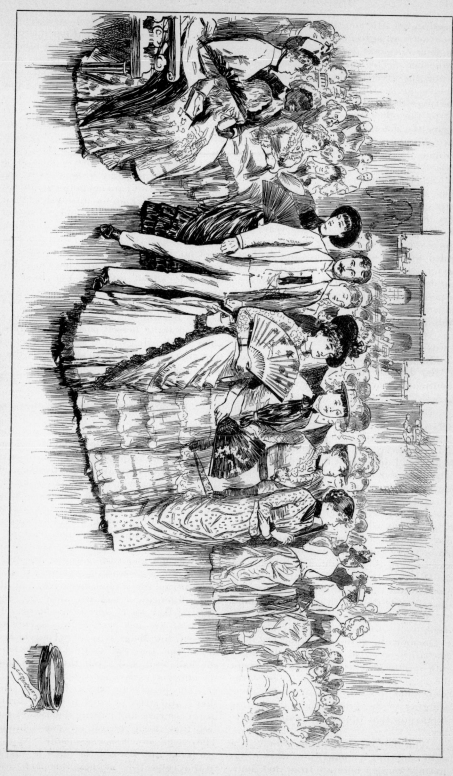

prised in her life, and the surprise seemed not exactly an agreeable one, but Mr. Benson looked a great deal more pleased than astonished. The slight flush in Irene's face as she greeted him might have been wholly due to the unexpectedness of the meeting. Some of the gentlemen lounged off to the office region for politics and cigars, the elderly ladies took seats upon the gallery, and the rest of the party strolled down to the benches under the trees.

"So Miss Benson was expecting you!" said Mrs. Farquhar, who was walking with King. It is enough to mention Mrs. Farquhar's name to an *habitué* of the Springs. It is not so many years ago since she was a reigning belle, and as noted for her wit and sparkling raillery as for her beauty. She was still a very handsome woman, whose original cleverness had been cultivated by a considerable experience of social life in this country as well as in London and Paris.

"Was she? I'm sure I never told her I was coming here."

"No, simple man. You were with her at Bar Harbor, and I suppose she never mentioned to you that she was coming here?"

"But why did you think she expected me?"

"You men are too aggravatingly stupid. I never saw astonishment better feigned. I dare say it imposed upon that other admirer of hers also. Well, I like her, and I am going to be good to her." This meant a good deal. Mrs. Farquhar was related to everybody in Virginia—that is, everybody who was anybody before the war—and she could count at that moment seventy-five cousins, some of them first and some of them double-first cousins, at the White Sulphur. Mrs. Farquhar's remark meant that all these cousins and all their friends the South over would stand by Miss Benson socially from that moment.

The morning german had just begun in the ball-room. The gallery was thronged with spectators, clustering like bees about the large windows, and the notes of the band came floating out over the lawn, bringing to the groups there the lulling impression that life is all a summer holiday.

"And they say she is from Ohio. It is right odd, isn't it? but two or three of the prettiest women here are from that State.

There is Mrs. Martin, sweet as a jacqueminot. I'd introduce you if her husband were here. Ohio! Well, we get used to it. I should have known the father and mother were corn-fed. I suppose you prefer the corn-feds to the Confeds. But there's homespun and homespun. You see those under the trees yonder? Georgia homespun! Perhaps you don't see the difference. I do."

"I suppose you mean provincial."

"Oh dear no. I'm provincial. It is the most difficult thing to be in these levelling days. But I am not going to interest you in myself. I am too unselfish. Your Miss Benson is a fine girl, and it does not matter about her parents. Since you Yankees upset everything by the war, it is really of no importance who one's mother is. But, mind, this is not my opinion. I'm trying to adjust myself. You have no idea how reconstructed I am."

And with this Mrs. Farquhar went over to Miss Benson, and chatted for a few moments, making herself particularly agreeable to Mr. Meigs, and actually carried that gentleman off to the spring, and then as an escort to her cottage, shaking her fan as she went away at Mr. King and Irene, and saying, "It is a waste of time for you youngsters not to be in the german."

The german was just ended, and the participants were grouping themselves on the gallery to be photographed, the usual custom for perpetuating the memory of these exercises, which only take place every other morning. And since something must be done, as there are only six nights for dancing in the week, on the off mornings there are champagne and fruit parties on the lawn.

It was not about the german, however, that King was thinking. He was once more beside the woman he loved, and all the influences of summer and the very spirit of this resort were in his favor. If I cannot win her here, he was saying to himself, the Meigs is in it. They talked about the journey, about Luray, where she had been, and about the Bridge, and the abnormal gayety of the Springs.

"The people are all so friendly," she said, "and strive so much to put the stranger at his ease, and putting themselves out lest time hang heavy on one's hands. They seem somehow responsible."

"Yes," said King, "the place is unique in that respect. I suppose it is partly ow-

FLIRTATION ON THE LAWN.

ing to the concentration of the company in and around the hotel."

"But the sole object appears to me to be agreeable, and make a real social life. At other like places nobody seems to care what becomes of anybody else."

"Doubtless the cordiality and good-feeling are spontaneous, though something is due to manner, and a habit of expressing the feeling that arises. Still, I do not expect to find any watering-place a paradise. This must be vastly different from any other if it is not full of cliques and gossip and envy underneath. But we do not go to a summer resort to philosophize. A market is a market, you know."

"I don't know anything about markets, and this cordiality may all be on the sur-

face, but it makes life very agreeable, and I wish our Northerners would catch the Southern habit of showing sympathy where it exists."

"Well, I'm free to say that I like the place, and all its easy-going ways, and I have to thank you for a new experience."

"Me? Why so?"

"Oh, I wouldn't have come if it had not been for your suggestion—I mean for your —your saying that you were coming here reminded me that it was a place I ought to see."

"I'm glad to have served you as a guide-book."

"And I hope you are not sorry that I—"

At this moment Mrs. Benson and Mr. Meigs came down with the announcement of the dinner hour, and the latter marched off with the ladies with a "one-of-the-family" air.

The party did not meet again until evening in the great drawing-room. The busi-ness at the White Sulphur is pleasure. And this is about the order of proceedings: A few conscientious people take an early glass at the spring, and later patronize the baths, and there is a crowd at the post-office; a late breakfast; lounging and gossip on the galleries and in the parlor; politics and old-fogy talk in the reading-room and in the piazza corners; flirtation on the lawn; a german every other morning at eleven; wine parties under the trees; morning calls at the cottages; servants running hither and thither with cooling drinks; the bar-room not absolutely deserted and cheerless at any hour, day or night; dinner from two to four; occasionally a riding par-ty; some driving; though there were charming drives in every direction, few private carriages, and no display of turn-outs; strolls in Lovers' Walk and in the pretty hill paths; supper at eight, and then the full-dress assembly in the draw-ing-room, and a "walk around" while the chil-dren have their hour in the ball-room; the night-ly dance, witnessed by a crowd on the veranda, followed frequently by a private german and a sup-per given by some lover of his kind, lasting till all hours in the morning; and while the majority of the vast encampment reposes in slumber, some resolute spirits are fighting the ti-ger, and a light gleaming from one cottage and an-other shows where devo-tees of science are back-ing their opinion of the relative value of chance bits of pasteboard, in cer-tain combinations, with a liberality and faith for which the world gives

COLONEL FANE.

"THE ANXIOUS FACES OF THE MOTHERS."—[SEE PAGE 440.]

them no credit. And lest their life should become monotonous, the enterprising young men are continually organizing entertainments, mock races, comical games. The idea seems to prevail that a summer resort ought to be a place of enjoyment.

The White Sulphur is the only watering-place remaining in the United States where there is what may be called an "assembly," such as might formerly be seen at Saratoga or at Ballston Spa in Irving's young days. Everybody is in the drawing-room in the evening, and although, in the freedom of the place, full dress is not exacted, the habit of parade in full toilet prevails. When King entered the room the scene might well be called brilliant, and even bewildering, so that in the maze of beauty and the babble of talk he was glad to obtain the services of Mrs. Farquhar as cicerone. Between the rim of people next the walls and the elliptical centre was an open space for promenading, and in this beauty and its attendant cavalier went round and round in unending show. This is called the "tread-mill." But for the seriousness of this frank display, and the unflagging interest of the spectators, there would have been an element of high comedy in it. It was an education to join a wall group and hear the free and critical comments on the style, the dress, the physical perfection, of the charming procession. When Mrs. Farquhar and King had taken a turn or two, they stood one side to enjoy the scene.

"Did you ever see so many pretty girls

"SHE WAS IN HIS ARMS."—[SEE PAGE 443.]

together before? If you did, don't you dare say so."

"But at the North the pretty women are scattered in a thousand places. You have here the whole South to draw on. Are they elected as representatives from the various districts, Mrs. Farquhar?"

"Certainly. By an election that your clumsy device of the ballot is not equal to. Why shouldn't beauty have a reputation? You see that old lady in the corner? Well, forty years ago the Springs just raved over her; everybody in the South knew her; I suppose she had an average of seven proposals a week; the young men went wild about her, followed her, toasted her, and fought duels for her possession—you don't like duels?—why, she was engaged to three men at one time, and after all she went off with a worthless fellow."

"That seems to me rather a melancholy history."

"Well, she is a most charming old lady; just as entertaining! I must introduce you. But this is history. Now look! There's the belle of Mobile, that tall, stately brunette. And that superb figure, you wouldn't guess she is the belle of Selma. There is a fascinating girl. What a mixture of languor and vivacity! Creole, you know; full blood. She is the belle of New Orleans—or one of them. Oh! do you see that Paris dress? I must look at it again when it comes round; she carries it well, too—belle of Richmond. And, see there; there's one of the prettiest girls in the South—belle of Macon. And that handsome woman — Nashville?— Louisville? See, that's the new-comer from Ohio." And so the procession went on, and the enumeration—belle of Montgomery, belle of Augusta, belle of Charleston, belle of Savannah, belle of Atlanta—always the belle of some place.

"No, I don't expect you to say that these are prettier than Northern women; but just between friends, Mr. King, don't you think the North might make a little more of their beautiful women? Yes, you are right: she is handsome" (King was bowing to Irene, who was on the arm of Mr. Meigs), "and has something besides beauty. I see what you mean" (King had not intimated that he meant anything), "but don't you dare to say it."

"Oh, I'm quite subdued."

"I wouldn't trust you. I suppose you Yankees cannot help your critical spirit."

"Critical? Why, I've heard more criticism in the last half-hour from these spectators than in a year before. And—I wonder if you will let me say it?"

"Say on."

"Seems to me that the chief topic here is physical beauty—about the shape, the style, the dress, of women, and whether this or that one is well made and handsome."

"Well, suppose beauty is worshipped in the South—we worship what we have; we haven't much money now, you know. Would you mind my saying that Mr. Meigs is a very presentable man?"

"You may say what you like about Mr. Meigs."

"That's the reason I took him away this morning."

"Thank you."

"He is full of information, and so unobtrusive—"

"I hadn't noticed that."

"And I think he ought to be encouraged. I'll tell you what you ought to do, Mr. King: you ought to give a german. If you do not, I shall put Mr. Meigs up to it—it is the thing to do here."

"Mr. Meigs give a german!"

"Why not? You see that old beau there, the one smiling and bending toward her as he walks with the belle of Macon? He does not look any older than Mr. Meigs. He has been coming here for fifty years; he owns up to sixty-five and the Mexican war; it's my firm belief that he was out in 1812. Well, he has led the german here for years. You will find Colonel Fane in the ball-room every night. Yes, I shall speak to Mr. Meigs."

The room was thinning out. King found himself in front of a row of dowagers, whose tongues were still going about the departing beauties. "No mercy there," he heard a lady say to her companion; "that's a jury for conviction every time." What confidential communication Mrs. Farquhar made to Mr. Meigs, King never knew, but he took advantage of the diversion in his favor to lead Miss Benson off to the ball-room.

CHAPTER X.

THE days went by at the White Sulphur on the wings of incessant gayety. Literally the nights were filled with music, and the only cares that infested the day appeared in the anxious faces of the mothers as the campaign became more intricate and uncertain. King watched this with the double interest of spectator and player. The artist threw himself into the *mêlée* with abandon, and pacified his conscience by an occasional letter to Miss Lamont, in which he confessed just as many of his conquests and defeats as he thought it would be good for her to know.

The colored people, who are a conspicuous part of the establishment, are a source of never-failing interest and amusement. Every morning the mammies and nurses with their charges were seated in a long shining row on a part of the veranda where there was most passing and repassing, holding a sort of baby show, the social consequence of each one depending upon the rank of the family who employed her, and the dress of the children in her charge. High-toned conversation on these topics occupied these dignified and faithful mammies, upon whom seemed to rest to a considerable extent the maintenance of the aristocratic social traditions. Forbes had heard that while the colored people of the South had suspended several of the ten commandments, the eighth was especially regarded as non-applicable in the present state of society. But he was compelled to revise this opinion as to the White Sulphur. Nobody ever locked a door or closed a window. Cottages most remote were left for hours open and without guard, miscellaneous articles of the toilet were left about, trunks were not locked, waiters, chamber-maids, porters, washer-women, were constantly coming and going, having access to the rooms at all hours, and yet no guest ever lost so much as a hair-pin or a cigar.

Sports of a colonial and old English flavor that have fallen into disuse elsewhere varied the life at the White. One day the gentlemen rode in a mule-race, the slowest mule to win, and this feat was followed by an exhibition of negro agility in climbing the greased pole and catching the greased pig; another day the cavaliers contended on the green field, surrounded by a brilliant array of beauty and costume, as two Amazon base-ball nines, the one nine arrayed in yellow cambric frocks and sun-bonnets, and the other in bright red gowns, the whiskers and big boots and trousers adding nothing whatever to the illusion of the female battle.

The two tables, King's and the Bensons', united in an expedition to the Old Sweet, a drive of eighteen miles. Mrs. Farquhar arranged the affair, and assigned the seats in the carriages. It is a very picturesque drive, as are all the drives in this region, and if King did not enjoy it, it was not because Mrs. Farquhar was not even more entertaining than usual. The truth is that a young man in love is poor company for himself and for everybody else. Even the object of his passion could not tolerate him unless she returned it. Irene and Mr. Meigs rode in the carriage in advance of his, and King thought the scenery about the tamest he had ever seen, the roads bad, the horses slow. His ill-humor, however, was concentrated on one spot; that was Mr. Meigs's back; he thought he had never seen a more disagreeable back, a more conceited back. It ought to have been a delightful day; in his imagination it was to be an eventful day. Indeed, why shouldn't the opportunity come at the Old Sweet, at the end of the drive ?—there was something promising in the name. Mrs. Farquhar was in a mocking mood all the way. She liked to go to the Old Sweet, she said, because it was so intolerably dull; it was a sensation. She thought, too, that it might please Miss Benson, there was such a fitness in the thing—the old sweet to the Old Sweet. "And he is not so very old either," she added: "just the age young girls like. I should think Miss Benson in danger—seriously, now—if she were three or four years younger."

The Old Sweet is, in fact, a delightful old-fashioned resort, respectable and dull, with a pretty park, and a crystal pond that stimulates the bather like a glass of champagne, and perhaps has the property of restoring youth. King tried the spring, which he heard Mrs. Farquhar soberly commending to Mr. Meigs; and after dinner he manœuvred for a half-hour alone with Irene. But the fates and the women were against him. He had the mortification to see her stroll away with Mr. Meigs to a distant part of the grounds, where they remained in confidential discourse until it was time to return.

In the rearrangement of seats Mrs. Farquhar exchanged with Irene. Mrs. Farquhar said that it was very much like going to a funeral each way. As for Irene, she was in high, even feverish spirits, and rattled away in a manner that convinced King that she was almost too happy to contain herself.

Notwithstanding the general chaff, the singing, and the gayety of Irene, the drive seemed to him intolerably long. At the half-way house, where in the moonlight the horses drank from a shallow stream, Mr. Meigs came forward to the carriage and inquired if Miss Benson was sufficiently protected against the chilliness of the night. King had an impulse to offer to change seats with him; but no, he would not surrender in the face of the enemy. It would be more dignified to quietly leave the Springs the next day.

It was late at night when the party returned. The carriage drove to the Benson cottage; King helped Irene to alight, coolly bade her good-night, and went to his barracks. But it was not a good night to sleep. He tossed about, he counted every step of the late night birds on his gallery; he got up and lighted a cigar, and tried dispassionately to think the matter over. But thinking was of no use. He took pen and paper; he would write a chill letter of farewell; he would write a manly avowal of his passion; he would make such an appeal that no woman could resist it. She must know, she did know—what was the use of writing? He sat staring at the blank prospect. Great heavens! what would become of his life if he lost the only woman in the world? Probably the world would go on much the same. Why, listen to it! The band was playing on the lawn at four o'clock in the morning. A party was breaking up after a night of german and a supper, and the revellers were dispersing. The lively tunes of "Dixie," "Marching through Georgia," and "Home, sweet Home," awoke the echoes in all the galleries and corridors, and filled the whole encampment with a sad gayety. Dawn was approaching. Good-nights and farewells and laughter were heard, and the voice of a wanderer explaining to the trees, with more or less broken melody, his fixed purpose not to go home till morning.

Stanhope King might have had a better though still a sleepless night if he had known that Mr. Meigs was packing his trunks at that hour to the tune of "Home, sweet Home," and if he had been aware of the scene at the Benson cottage after he bade Irene good-night. Mrs. Benson had a light burning, and the noise of the carriage awakened her. Irene entered the room, saw that her mother was awake, shut the door carefully, sat down on the foot of the bed, said, "It's all over, mother," and burst into the tears of a long-repressed nervous excitement.

"What's over, child?" cried Mrs. Benson, sitting bolt-upright in bed.

"Mr. Meigs. I had to tell him that it couldn't be. And he is one of the best men I ever knew."

"You don't tell me you've gone and refused him, Irene?"

"Please don't scold me. It was no use. He ought to have seen that I did not care for him, except as a friend. I'm so sorry!"

"You are the strangest girl I ever saw." And Mrs. Benson dropped back on the pillow again, crying herself now, and muttering, "I'm sure I don't know what you do want."

When King came out to breakfast he encountered Mr. Benson, who told him that their friend Mr. Meigs had gone off that morning—had a sudden business call to Boston. Mr. Benson did not seem to be depressed about it. Irene did not appear, and King idled away the hours with his equally industrious companions under the trees. There was no german that morning, and the hotel band was going through its *répertoire* for the benefit of a champagne party on the lawn. There was nothing melancholy about this party; and King couldn't help saying to Mrs. Farquhar that it hardly represented his idea of the destitution and depression resulting from the war; but she replied that they must do something to keep up their spirits.

"And I think," said the artist, who had been watching, from the little distance at which they sat, the table of the revellers, "that they will succeed. Twenty-six bottles of champagne, and not many more guests! What a happy people, to be able to enjoy champagne before twelve o'clock!"

"Oh, you never will understand us!" said Mrs. Farquhar; "there is nothing spontaneous in you."

"We do not begin to be spontaneous till after dinner," said King.

"And then it is all calculated. Think of Mr. Forbes counting the bottles! Such a dreadfully mercenary spirit! Oh, I have been North. Because you are not so open as we are, you set up for being more virtuous."

"And you mean," said King, "that frankness and impulse cover a multitude of—"

"I don't mean anything of the sort. I just mean that conventionality isn't virtue. You yourself confessed that you like the Southern openness right much, and you like to come here, and you like the Southern people as they are at home."

"Well?"

"And now will you tell me, Mr. Prim, why it is that almost all Northern people who come South to live become more Southern than the Southerners themselves; and that almost all Southern people who go North to live remain just as Southern as ever?"

"No. Nor do I understand any more than Dr. Johnson did why the Scotch, who couldn't scratch a living at home, and came up to London, always kept on bragging about their native land and abused the metropolis."

This sort of sparring went on daily, with the result of increasing friendship between the representatives of the two geographical sections, and commonly ended with the declaration on Mrs. Farquhar's part that she should never know that King was not born in the South except for his accent; and on his part that if Mrs. Farquhar would conceal her delightful Virginia inflection she would pass everywhere at the North for a Northern woman.

"I hear," she said, later, as they sat alone, "that Mr. Meigs has beat a retreat, saving nothing but his personal baggage. I think Miss Benson is a great goose. Such a chance for an establishment and a position! You didn't half appreciate him."

"I'm afraid I did not."

"Well, it is none of my business; but I hope you understand the responsibility of the situation. If you do not, I want to warn you about one thing: don't go strolling off before sunset in the Lovers' Walk. It is the most dangerous place. It is a fatal place. I suppose every turn in it, every tree that has a knoll at the foot where two persons can sit, has witnessed a tragedy, or, what is worse, a comedy. There are legends enough about it to fill a book. Maybe there is not a Southern woman living who has not been engaged there once at least. I'll tell you a little story for a warning. Some years ago there was a famous belle here who had the Springs at her feet, and half a dozen determined suitors. One of them, who had been unable to make the least impression on her heart, resolved to win her by a stratagem. Walking one evening on

the hill with her, the two stopped just at a turn in the walk—I can show you the exact spot, with a chaperon—and he fell into earnest discourse with her. She was as cool and repellent as usual. Just then he heard a party approaching; his chance had come. The moment the party came in sight he suddenly kissed her. Everybody saw it. The witnesses discreetly turned back. The girl was indignant. But the deed was done. In half an hour the whole Springs would know it. She was compromised. No explanation could do away with the fact that she had been kissed in Lovers' Walk. But the girl was game, and that evening the engagement was announced in the drawing-room. Isn't that a pretty story?"

However much Stanhope might have been alarmed at this recital, he betrayed nothing of his fear that evening when, after walking to the spring with Irene, the two sauntered along, and unconsciously, as it seemed, turned up the hill into that winding path which has been trodden by generations of lovers with loitering steps—steps easy to take and so hard to retrace! It is a delightful forest, the walk winding about on the edge of the hill, and giving charming prospects of intervals, stream, and mountains. To one in the mood for a quiet hour with nature, no scene could be more attractive.

The couple walked on, attempting little conversation, both apparently prepossessed and constrained. The sunset was spoken of, and when Irene at length suggested turning back, that was declared to be King's object in ascending the hill to a particular point; but whether either of them saw the sunset, or would have known it from a sunrise, I cannot say. The drive to the Old Sweet was pleasant. Yes, but rather tiresome. Mr. Meigs had gone away suddenly. Yes; Irene was sorry his business should have called him away. Was she very sorry? She wouldn't lie awake at night over it, but he was a good friend. The time passed very quickly here. Yes; one couldn't tell how it went; the days just melted away; the two weeks seemed like a day. They were going away the next day. King said he was going also.

"And," he added, as if with an effort, "when the season is over, Miss Benson, I am going to settle down to work."

"I'm glad of that," she said, turning upon him a face glowing with approval.

"Yes, I have arranged to go on with

practice in my uncle's office. I remember what you said about a dilettante life."

"Why, I never said anything of the kind!"

"But you looked it. It is all the same."

They had come to the crown of the hill, and stood looking over the intervals to the purple mountains. Irene was deeply occupied in tying up with grass a bunch of wild flowers. Suddenly he seized her hand.

"Irene!"

"No, no," she cried, turning away. The flowers dropped from her hands.

"You must listen, Irene. I love you— I love you."

She turned her face toward him; her lips trembled; her eyes were full of tears; there was a great look of wonder and tenderness in her face.

"Is it all true?"

She was in his arms. He kissed her hair, her eyes—ah me! it is the old story. It had always been true. He loved her from the first, at Fortress Monroe, every minute since. And she—well, perhaps she could learn to love him in time, if he was very good; yes, maybe she had loved him a little at Fortress Monroe. How could he? what was there in her to attract him? What a wonder it was that she could tolerate him! What could she see in him?

So this impossible thing, this miracle, was explained? No, indeed! It had to be inquired into and explained over and over again, this absolutely new experience of two people loving each other.

She could speak now of herself, of her doubt that he could know his own heart and be stronger than the social traditions, and would not mind, as she thought he did at Newport—just a little bit—the opinions of other people. I do not by any means imply that she said all this bluntly, or that she took at all the tone of apology; but she contrived, as a woman can without saying much, to let him see why she had distrusted, not the sincerity, but the perseverance of his love. There would never be any more doubt now. What a wonder it all is!

The two parted—alas! alas! till supper-time!—I don't know why scoffers make so light of these partings—at the foot of the main stairs of the hotel gallery, just as Mrs. Farquhar was descending. Irene's face was radiant as she ran away from Mrs. Farquhar.

"Bless you, my children! I see my warning was in vain, Mr. King. It is a fatal walk. It always was in our family. Oh, youth! youth!" A shade of melancholy came over her charming face as she turned alone toward the spring.

THE HOME ACRE.

BY E. P. ROE.

VI. — THE CURRANT.

WHO that has ever lived in the country does not remember the old straggling currant bushes that disputed their existence with grass, docks, and other coarse-growing weeds along some ancient fence? Many also can recall the weary task of gathering a quart or two of the diminutive fruit for pies, and the endless picking required to obtain enough for the annual jelly-making. Nor is this condition of affairs a thing of the past. Drive through the land where you will in early July, and you will see farmers mowing around the venerable Red Dutch currants "to give the women-folks a chance at 'em." The average farmer still bestows upon this fruit about as much attention as the aborigines gave to their patches of maize. This seems very absurd when we remember the important place held in the domestic economy by the currant, and how greatly it improves under decent treatment. If it demanded the attention which a cabbage plant requires, it would be given, but the currant belongs to that small class of creatures who permit themselves to be used when wanted, and snubbed, neglected, and imposed upon at other times. It is known that the bushes will manage to exist, and do the very best they can, no matter how badly treated; and average human nature has ever taken advantage of such traits, to its continuous loss.

The patience of the currant is due perhaps to its origin, for it grows wild around the northern hemisphere, its chief haunts being the dim, cold, damp woods of the high latitudes. You may tame, modify, and vastly change anything possessing life, but original traits are scarcely ever wholly eradicated. Therefore the natural habitat and primal qualities of the currant indicate the true lines of development, its capabilities and limitations. It is essentially a Northern fruit, requiring coolness, moisture, and alluvial soils. It begins to falter and look homesick even in New Jersey, and one does not have to go far down the Atlantic coast to pass beyond the range of its successful culture. I do not see why it should not thrive much farther south on the northern slopes of the mountains. From Philadelphia northward, however, except on light dry soils and in sunny exposures, there is no reason why it should not give ample returns for the attention it requires.

I shall not lay stress on the old, well-known uses to which this fruit is put, but I do think its value is but half appreciated. People rush around in July in search of health: let me recommend the currant cure. If any one is languid, depressed in spirits, inclined to headaches, and generally "out of sorts," let him finish his breakfast daily for a month with a dish of freshly picked currants. He will soon almost doubt his own identity, and may even begin to think that he is becoming a good man. He will be more gallant to his wife, kinder to his children, friendlier to his neighbors, and more open-handed to every good cause. Work will soon seem play, and play fun. In brief, the truth of the ancient pun will be verified that "the power to live a good life depends largely upon the *liver*." Out upon the nonsense of taking medicine and nostrums during the currant season! Let it be taught at theological seminaries that the currant is a "means of grace." It is a corrective, and that is what average humanity most needs.

The currant, like the raspberry, is willing to keep shady, but only because it is modest. It is one of the fruits that thrive better among trees than in too dry and sunny exposures. Therefore, in economizing space on the home acre, it may be grown among smaller trees, or, better still, on the northern or eastern side of a wall or hedge. But shade is not essential except as we go south; then the requisites of moisture and shelter from the burning rays of the sun should be complied with as far as possible. In giving this and kindred fruits partial shade they should not be compelled to contend to any extent with the roots of trees. This will ever prove an unequal contest. No fruit can thrive in dense shade or find sustenance among the voracious roots of a tree.

Select, therefore, if possible, heavy, deep, moist, yet well-drained soil, and do not fear to make and keep it very rich. If you are restricted to sandy or gravelly soils, correct their defects with compost, decayed leaves and sods, muck, manure from the cow stable, and other fertilizers with staying rather than stimulating qualities. Either by ploughing or forking, deepen as well as enrich the soil. It is then ready for the plants, which may be set out either in the fall or in early spring. I prefer the autumn—any time after the leaves have fallen—but spring answers almost as well, while buds are dormant or partially so. It should be remembered that the currant starts very early, and is in full foliage before some people are fairly wakened to garden interests. It would, in this case, be better to wait until October, unless the plants can be obtained from a neighbor on a cloudy day; then they should be cut back two-thirds of their length before being removed, and the transfer made as quickly as possible. Under any circumstances take off half of the wood from the plants bought. This need not be thrown away. Every cutting of young wood six inches long will make a new plant in a single season. All that is needful is to keep the wood moist until ready to put it in the ground, or, better still, a cool, damp place in the garden can be selected at once, and the cuttings sunk two-thirds of their length into the ground, and the soil pressed firm around them. By fall they will have a good supply of roots, and by the following autumn be ready to be set out wherever you wish them to fruit.

Currant bushes may be planted five feet apart each way, and at the same distance if they are to line a fence. They should be sunk a few inches deeper in the soil than they stood before, and the locality be such as to admit of good culture. The soil should never be permitted to become hard, weedy, or grass-grown. As a rule I prefer two-year-old plants, while those of one year's growth answer nearly as well, if vigorous. If in haste for fruit, it may be well to get three-year-old plants, unless they have been dwarfed and enfeebled by neglect. Subsequent culture consists chiefly in keeping the soil clean, mellow, rich, and therefore moist. I have named the best fertilizers for the currant; but if the product of the horse stable is employed, use it first as a mulch. It will thus gradually reach the roots. Otherwise it is too stimulating, and produces a rampant growth of wood rather than fruit.

Under any circumstances this tendency to produce an undue amount of wood must be repressed almost as rigorously as in the grape-vine. The secret of successful currant culture is richness beneath and restriction above. English gardeners are said to have as complete and minute systems of pruning and training currants as the grape, but we do not seem to have patience for such detail. Nor do I regard it as necessary. Our object is an abundant supply of excellent fruit, and this result can be obtained at a surprisingly small outlay of time and money if they are expended judiciously.

The art of trimming a currant bush, like that of pruning a grape-vine, is best learned by observation and experience. One can give principles rather than lay down rules. Like the vine, the currant tends to choke itself with a superabundance of wood, which soon becomes more or less barren. This is truer of some varieties than of others, but in all instances the judicious use of the pruning-knife doubles the yield. In view of the supposition that the leading shoot and all the branches were shortened in one-half when the plant was set out, I will suggest that early in June it will be observed that much more wood is forming than can be permitted to remain. There are weak, crowding shoots which never can be of any use. If these are cut out at this time, the sap which would go to mature them will be directed into the valuable parts of the forming bush. Summer pruning prevents misspent force, and it may be kept up with great advantage from year to year. This is rarely done, however; therefore early in spring the bushes must receive a good annual pruning, and the long shoots and branches be cut well back, so as to prevent naked reaches of wood. Observe a very productive bush, and you will see that there are many points abounding in little side branches. It is upon these that the fruit is chiefly borne.

A bush left to itself is soon a mass of long, slender, almost naked stalks, with a little fruit at the ends. The ideal bush is stocky, open, well branched, admitting light, air, and sun in every part. There is no crowding and smothering of the fruit by the foliage. But few clusters are borne on very young wood, and when this grows old and black the clusters are small. Therefore new wood should always be coming on and kept well cut back, so as to form joints and side branches, and as other parts grow old and feeble they should be cut out. Observation and experience will teach the gardener more than all the rules that could be written, for he will perceive that he must prune each bush according to its own individuality.

For practical purposes the bush form is the best in which to grow currants, but they can easily be made to form pretty little trees with tops shaped like an umbrella, or any other form we desire. For instance, I found, one autumn, a shoot about three feet long. I rubbed off all the buds except the terminal one and three or four just beneath it, then sunk the lower end of the shoot six inches into the soil, and tied the part above the ground to a short stake. The following spring the lower end took root, and the few buds at the top developed into a small bushy head. Clumps of miniature currant-trees would make as pretty an ornament for the garden border as one would wish to see. It should be remembered that there is a currant as well as an apple borer, but the pests are not very numerous or destructive, and such little trees can easily be grown by the hundred.

Clean culture has one disadvantage which must be guarded against. If the ground under bushes is loose, heavy rains will sometimes so splash up the soil as to muddy the greater part of the fruit. I once suffered serious loss in this way, and deserved it, for a little grass mown from the lawn or any other litter spread under and around the bushes just before the fruit ripened would have prevented it. It will require but a very few minutes to insure a clean crop.

I imagine that if these pages are ever read, and such advice as I can give is followed, it will be more often by the mistress than the master of the home acre. I address him, but quite as often I mean her, and just at this point I am able to give "the power behind the throne" a useful hint. Miss Alcott, in her immortal *Little Women*, has given an instance of what dire results may follow if the "jelly won't jell." Let me hasten to insure domestic peace by telling my fair reader (who will also be, if the jelly turns out of the tumblers tremulous yet firm, a gentle reader) that if she will have the currants picked just as soon as they are fully ripe, and before they have been drenched by a heavy rain, she will find that the jelly will jell. It is over-ripe, water-soaked currants that break up families and demolish household gods.

In passing to the consideration of varieties it is quite natural in this connection to mention the white sorts first. I know that people are not yet sufficiently educated to demand white currants of their grocers; but the home garden is as much beyond the grocer's stall as the home is better than a boarding-house. There is no reason why free people in the country should be slaves to conventionalities, prejudices, and traditions. If white currants *are* sweeter, more delicious and beautiful than the red, why, so they are. Therefore let us plant them abundantly.

If there is to be a queen among the currants, the White Grape is entitled to the crown. When placed upon the table the dish appears heaped with translucent pearls. The sharp acid of the red varieties is absent, and you feel that if you could live upon them for a time, your blood would grow pure if not "blue."

The bush producing this exquisite fruit is like an uncouth-looking poet who gives beauty from an inner life, but disappoints in externals. It is low-branching and unshapely, and must be forced into good form — the bush, not the poet — by the pruning-knife. If this is done judiciously, no other variety will bear more profusely or present a fairer object on a July day.

The White Dutch has the well-known characteristics in growth of the common Red Dutch currant, and is only inferior to the White Grape in size. The fruit is equally transparent, beautiful, mild, and agreeable in flavor, while the bush is enormously productive and shapely in form, if properly trained and fertilized.

While the white currants are such favorites, I do not undervalue the red. Indeed, were I restricted to one variety, it should be the old Dutch Red of our fathers, or, more properly, of our grandmothers. For general house uses I do not think it has yet been surpassed. It is not so mild in flavor as the white varieties, but there is a richness and sprightliness in its acid that are grateful indeed on a sultry day. Mingled with the white berries it makes a beautiful dish, while it has all culinary qualities which the house-keeper can desire. If the bush is rigorously pruned and generously enriched, it is unsurpassed in productiveness, and the fruit approaches very nearly to the Cherry currant in size.

I do not recommend the last-named kind for the home garden unless large, showy fruit counts for more than flavor. The acid of the Cherry currant, unless very ripe, is harsh and watery. At best, it never acquires an agreeable mildness, to my taste. The bushes also are not so certainly productive, and usually require skilful pruning and constant fertilizing to be profitable. For the market, which demands size above all things, the Cherry is the kind to grow, but in the home garden flavor and productiveness are the more important qualities. Fay's Prolific is a new sort that has been very highly praised.

The Victoria is an excellent late variety, which, if planted in a sheltered place, prolongs the currant season well into the autumn. Spurious kinds are sold under this name. The true Victoria produces a pale red fruit with tapering clusters or racemes of berries. This variety, with the three others recommended, gives the family two red and two white kinds—all that are needed. Those who are fond of black currants can, at almost any nursery, procure the Black Naples and Lee's Prolific. Either variety will answer all practical purposes. I confess they are not at all to my taste.

From the currant we pass on naturally to the gooseberry, for in origin and requirements it is very similar. Both belong to the *Ribes* family of plants, and they are to be cultivated on the same general principles. What I have written in regard to partial shade, cool, sheltered localities, rich, heavy soils, good culture, and especially rigorous pruning, applies with even greater force to this fruit, especially if we endeavor to raise the foreign varieties. In cultivating this fruit it is even more important than was true of raspberries that the reader should distinguish between the native and foreign species. The latter are so inclined to mildew in almost every locality that there is rarely any certainty of satisfactory fruit. The same evil pursues the seedling children of the foreign sorts, and I have never seen a hybrid or cross between the English and native species that was with any certainty free from a brown disfiguring rust wholly or partially enveloping the berries. Here and there the fruit in some gardens will escape year after year; again, on places not far away, the blighting mildew is sure to appear before the berries are fully grown. Nevertheless, the foreign varieties are so fine that it is well to give them a fair trial. The three kinds which appear best adapted to our climate are Crown Bob, Roaring Lion, and Whitesmith. A new large variety, named Industry, is now being introduced, and if half of what is claimed for it is true, it is worth a place in all gardens.

In order to be certain of clean, fair gooseberries every year, we must turn to our native species, which has already given us several good varieties. The Downing is the largest and best, and the Houghton the hardiest, most productive, and easily raised. When we remember the superb fruit which English gardeners have developed from wild kinds inferior to ours, we can well understand that the true American gooseberries are yet to be developed. In my work *Success with Small Fruits* those who are interested in this fruit will find much fuller treatment than is warranted in these papers.

Not only do currants and gooseberries require similar treatment and cultivation, but they also have a common enemy that must be vigilantly guarded against, or the bushes will be defoliated in many localities almost before its existence is known. After an absence of a few days I have found some of my bushes stripped of every leaf. When this happens, the fruit is comparatively worthless. Foliage is as necessary to a plant as lungs to a man. It is not essential that I should go into the natural history of the currant worm and moth. Having once seen the yellowish-green caterpillars at their destructive work, the reader's thoughts will not revert to the science of entomology, but will at once become bloody and implacable. I hasten to suggest the means of rescue and vengeance. The moment these worms appear, be on your guard, for they usually spread like fire in stubble. Procure of

your druggist white hellebore, scald and mix a tablespoonful in a bowl of hot water, and then pour it in a full watering-can. This gives you an infusion of about a tablespoonful to an ordinary pail of water at its ordinary summer temperature. Sprinkle the infected bushes with this as often as there is a worm to be seen. I have never failed in destroying the pests by this course. It should be remembered, however, that new eggs are often hatched out daily. You may kill every worm to-day, yet find plenty on the morrow. Vigilance, however, will soon so check the evil that your currants are safe, and if every one would fight the pests, they would eventually be almost exterminated. The trouble is that, while you do your duty, your next-door neighbor may grow nothing on his bushes but currant worms. Thus the evil is continued, and even increased, in spite of all that you can do; but by a little vigilance and the use of hellebore you can always save *your* currants. I have kept my bushes green, luxuriant, and loaded with fruit when, at a short distance, the patches of careless neighbors were rendered utterly worthless. Our laws but half protect the birds, the best insecticides, and there is no law to prevent a man from allowing his acres to be the breeding-place of every pest prevailing.

There are three species of the currant borer, and their presence is indicated by yellow foliage and shrivelling fruit. The only remedy is to cut out and burn the affected stems. These pests are not often sufficiently numerous to do much harm.

I earnestly urge that virulent poisons like Paris green, London purple, etc., never be used on fruit or edible vegetables. There cannot be safety in this course. I never heard of any one that was injured by white hellebore, used as I have directed, and I have found that if the worms were kept off until the fruit began to ripen, the danger was practically over. If I had to use hellebore after the fruit was fit to use, I should first kill the worms and then cleanse the bushes thoroughly by spraying them with clean water.

In treating the two remaining small fruits, blackberries and strawberries, we pass wholly out of the shade and away from trees. Sunshine and open ground are now required. Another important difference can also be mentioned, reversing former experience. America is the home of these fruits. The wild species of the blackberry abroad has never, as far as I can learn, been developed into varieties worthy of cultivation; and before importations from North and South America began, the only strawberry of Europe was the Alpine, with its slight variations, and the musky Hautbois.

I do not know whether any of our fine varieties of blackberries are cultivated abroad, but I am perfectly certain that they are worthy of the slight attention required to raise them in perfection here.

Like the blackcaps, all our best varieties are the spontaneous products of nature, first discovered growing wild, and transferred to the garden. It is a fruit that takes kindly to cultivation, and improves under it.

The proper treatment is management rather than cultivation and stimulation. It requires a sunny exposure and a light warm soil, yet not so dry as to prevent the fruit from maturing into juicy berries. If possible, locate the blackberries off by themselves, for it is hard to prevent the strong roots from travelling all over the garden. It likes a rich, moist, mellow soil, and, finding it, some varieties will give you canes sixteen feet high. You do not want rank, thorny brambles, however, but berries. Therefore the blackberry should be put where it can do no harm, and, by a little judicious repression, a great deal of good. A gravelly or sandy knoll, with a chance to mow all around the patch, is the best place. The blackberry needs a deep loose soil rather than a rich one. Then the roots will luxuriate to unknown depths, the wood ripen thoroughly, and the fruit be correspondingly abundant.

Let the rows be six feet apart; set out the plants in fall, if possible, or *early* spring; put two plants in the hills, which may be four feet apart. If the ground is very poor, give the young plants a shovelful of old compost, decayed leaves, etc. Any fertilizer will answer, so that it is spread just over the roots to give the plants a good send-off.

As a rule, complete success in blackberry culture consists in a little judicious work performed in May, June, and July. The plants, having been set out as I have advised in the case of raspberries, throw up the first season strong green shoots. When these shoots are three feet high, pinch off the top, so as to stop upward

growth. The result of this is that branches start on every side, and the plant forms a low, stocky, self-supporting bush, which will be loaded with fruit the following season.

The second year the plants in the hill will send up stronger canes, and there will be plenty of sprouts or suckers in the intervening spaces. When very young, these useless sprouts can be pulled out with the least possible trouble. Left to mature, they make a thorny wilderness which will cause bleeding hands and faces when attacked, and add largely to the family mending. That which a child could do as play, when the suckers were just coming through the ground, is now a formidable task for any man. In early summer you can keep every useless blackberry sprout from growing with the utmost ease. More canes, also, will usually start from the hill than are needed. Leave but three strong shoots, and this year pinch them back as soon as they are four feet high, thus producing three stocky, well-branched bushes, which in sheltered places will be self-supporting. Should there be the slightest danger of their breaking down with their load of fruit, tie them to stakes by all means. I do not believe in that kind of economy which tries to save a penny at the risk of a dollar.

I believe that better and larger fruit is always secured by shortening in the side branches one-third of their length in spring. Fine varieties like the Kittatinny are not entirely hardy in all localities. The snow will protect the lower branches, and the upper ones can usually be kept uninjured by throwing over them some very light litter, like old pea or bean vines, etc.—nothing heavy enough to break them down. As soon as the old canes are through bearing, they should be cut out. If the blackberry patch has been left to its own wild will, there is nothing left for us but to attack it, well gloved, in April, with the pruning-shears, and cut out everything except three or four young canes in the hill. These will probably be tall, slender, and branchless, therefore comparatively unproductive. In order to have any fruit at all, we must shorten them one-third, and tie them to stakes. It thus may be clearly seen that with blackberries "a stitch in time" saves almost ninety-nine. Keep out coarse weeds and grass, and give fertilizers only when the plants show signs of feebleness and lack of nutrition.

A rust similar to that which attacks the blackcap is about the only disease we have to contend with. The remedy is the same—extirpation of the plant, root and branch.

After testing a great many kinds, I recommend the three following varieties, ripening in succession for the family—the Early Harvest, Snyder, and Kittatinny. These all produce rich, high-flavored berries, and, under the treatment suggested, will prove hardy in nearly all localities. This fruit is not ripe as soon as it is black, and it is rarely left on the bushes until the hard core in the centre is mellowed by complete maturity. I have found that berries picked in the evening and stood in a cool place were in excellent condition for breakfast. To have them in perfection, however, they must be so ripe as to drop into the basket at the slightest touch. Then, as Donald Mitchell says, they are "bloated bubbles of forest honey."

I fancy the reader is as impatient to reach the strawberry as I am myself. "Doubtless God could have made a better berry"—but I forbear. This saying has been quoted by the greater part of the human race, and attributed to nearly every prominent man, from Adam to Mr. Beecher. There are said to be unfortunates whom the strawberry poisons. The majority of us feel as if we could attain Methuselah's age if we had nothing worse to contend with. Praising the strawberry is like "painting the lily"; therefore let us give our attention at once to the essential details of its successful culture.

As we have intimated before, this fruit as we find it in our gardens, even though we raise foreign kinds, came originally from America. The two great species, *Fragaria chilensis*, found on the Pacific slope from Oregon to Chili, and *Fragaria virginiana*, growing wild in all parts of North America east of the Rocky Mountains, are the sources of all the fine varieties that have been named and cultivated. The Alpine strawberry (*Fragaria vesca*), which grows wild throughout the northern hemisphere, does not appear capable of much variation and development under cultivation. Its seeds, sown under all possible conditions, reproduce the parent plant. Foreign gardeners eventually learned, however, that seeds of the Chili and Virginia strawberry produced new varieties, which were often much better than their parents. As time passed, and more attention was drawn to this subject, superb varieties were originated abroad, many of them acquiring a wide celebrity. In this case, as has been true of nearly all other fruits, our nurserymen and fruit-growers first looked to Europe for improved varieties. Horticulturists were slow to learn that in our own native species were the possibilities of the best success. The Chili strawberry, brought directly from the Pacific coast to the East, is not at home in our climate, and is still more unfitted to contend with it after generations of culture in Europe. Even our hardier Virginia strawberry, coming back to us from England after many years of high stimulation in a moist, mild climate, is unequal to the harsher conditions of life here. They are like native Americans who have lived and been pampered abroad so long that they find this country "quite too rude, you know—beastly climate." Therefore, in the choice varieties, and in developing new ones, the nearer we can keep to vigorous strains of our own hardy Virginia species the better. From it have proceeded and will continue to come the finest kinds that can be grown east of the Rockies. Nevertheless, what was said of foreign raspberries is almost equally true of European strawberries like the Triomphe de Gand and Jucunda, and hybrids like the Wilder. In localities where they can be grown, their beauty and fine flavor repay for the high culture and careful winter protection required. But they can scarcely be made to thrive on light soils and very far to the south.

So many varieties are offered for sale that the question of choice is a bewildering one. I have therefore sought to meet it, as before, by giving the advice of those whose opinions are well entitled to respect.

Dr. Hexamer, who has had great and varied experience, writes as follows: "A neighbor of mine who has for years bought nearly every new strawberry when first introduced has settled on the Duchess and Cumberland as the only varieties he will grow in the future, and thinks it not worth while to seek for something better. Confined to two varieties, a more satisfactory selection could scarcely be made. But you want six or seven, either being, I think, about the right number for the home garden. I will give them in the order of desirability according to my judgment—

Cumberland, Charles Downing, Duchess, Mount Vernon, Warren, Sharpless, Jewell."

The selection which places the Cumberland Triumph at the head of the list is but another proof how kinds differ under varied conditions. On my place this highly praised sort is but moderately productive and not high-flavored, although the fruit is very large and handsome. I regard the list, however, as a most excellent one for most localities.

Hon. Marshall P. Wilder's choice, for the latitude of Massachusetts: "Charles Downing, Wilder, Hervey Davis, Sharpless, Cumberland, Kentucky. Jewell is very promising." A. S. Fuller, for latitude of New York: "Charles Downing, Sharpless, Miner's Prolific, Wilson's Albany, Champion." P. C. Berckmans, for the latitude of Georgia: "Wilson, Sharpless, Charles Downing, Triomphe de Gand, Glendale." Hon. Norman J. Coleman's choice, for Missouri and the West: "Crescent, Captain Jack, Cumberland, Champion, Hart's Minnesota, Cornelia."

If I gave a hundred other lists, no two of them probably would agree in all respects. Mr. Downing often said to me, "Soil, climate, and locality make greater differences with the strawberry than with any other fruit." This is far more true of some varieties than others. I believe that the excellent kind named after Mr. Downing, if given proper treatment, will do well almost anywhere on the continent. It will be noted that it is on all the lists except one. I should place it at the head of garden strawberries. It is a kind that will endure much neglect, and it responds splendidly to generous, sensible treatment. Its delicious flavor is its chief recommendation, as it should be that of every berry for the home garden.

I have tested many hundreds of kinds, and have grown scores and scores that were so praised when first sent out that the novice might be tempted to dig up and throw away everything except the wonderful novelty pressed upon his attention. There is one quiet, effective way of meeting all this heralding and laudation, and that is to make trial beds. For instance, I have put out as many as seventy kinds at nearly the same time, and grown them under precisely the same conditions. Some of the much-vaunted new-comers were found to be old varieties renamed, others, although sold at high prices and asserted to be prodigies, were seen to be comparatively worthless when growing by the side of good old standard sorts; the majority never rose above mediocrity under ordinary treatment, but now and then one, like the Sharpless, fulfilled the promises made for it.

In my next paper I shall venture to recommend those varieties which my own experience and observation have shown to be best adapted to various soils and localities, and shall also seek to prove that proper cultivation has more to do with success than even the selection of favored kinds.

Nor would I seek to dissuade the proprietor of the home acre from testing the many novelties offered. He will be sure to get a fair return in strawberries, and to his interest in his garden will add the pleasure and anticipation which accompany uncertain experiment. In brief, he has found an innocent form of gambling, which will injure neither pocket nor morals. In slow-maturing fruits we cannot afford to make mistakes; in strawberries, one prize out of a dozen blanks repays for everything.

SOCIAL STUDIES.

BY RICHARD T. ELY.

II.—THE ECONOMIC EVILS IN AMERICAN RAILWAY METHODS.

A RECENT article in *Harper's Magazine* on "English and American Railways," as seen from the stand-point of the traveller, was a revelation to large numbers. Our railways have so long sung their own praises, and a subservient press has so readily reëchoed these boastful strains, that we have been deluded into the belief that we possessed the fastest trains, the finest passenger coaches, the largest supply of conveniences, the grandest stations, and the cheapest rates to be found in the world. Now it ought not to be necessary to say that the reason why one rejoices to see the publication of an article designed to dispel such illusions is not that one likes to see the institutions of one's own country decried. No; the reason is the hope that an insight into the actual condition of things may lead to an improvement in these institutions.

The articles in the present series have chiefly to do with railways as factors in production, and in production the railway, as a means for the transportation of passengers, plays a subordinate part. It is not, then, necessary in this place to emphasize and reënforce the statements in the article on "English and American Railways." It may be remarked, however, that a residence of several years in Europe leads me to the belief that the author of that article has given even too favorable a view of our railways as compared with European railways. The reader will find it an interesting and profitable pastime to compare the railway time-tables of fifteen or twenty typical American railways with the time-tables of as many European railways. He will then obtain some idea of the slow average rate of travel with us.

Other features of our railways do not fare better in the comparison. Our stations are inconvenient and ugly, sometimes even filthy. Our cars are uncomfortable, and it is difficult to see how one who has lived long enough in Germany to become accustomed to her institutions should not prefer second-class travel in that country to first-class in the ordinary American railway, although the average charge is thirty, forty, and occasionally even more than fifty per centum lower.

A still more important element is the safety of travel, and it can be said without fear of successful contradiction that the reckless prodigality of human life, which as part of our railway history has astonished foreigners, is elsewhere unknown.*

But the chief evils of American railways appear when we come to treat of them as performing economic services in the transportation of goods, and when we view railway property as an important element in our national resources. It is then difficult to tell where to begin or where to end an account of abuses, as they are so numerous and momentous.

* Mulhall in his *Dictionary of Statistics* gives the number of killed and wounded on the railways of the United States as 41.1 per million passengers, whereas in Europe it is only 10.8.

Equally difficult is it to find language in which to portray the sober scientific truth in regard to these abuses, for their enormity is such as almost to baffle description.

In 1879 the Assembly of the State of New York passed a resolution for the appointment of a special committee to investigate the methods of the railways in that State, which from the name of its chairman is usually called the Hepburn Committee, though it was under the guidance of Mr. Simon Sterne, of New York city. The investigation forms an epoch in the economic history of the United States, and the American people owe a debt of gratitude to Mr. Sterne for the ability, fearlessness, and self-sacrificing fidelity with which he conducted the difficult inquiry. The magnitude and true nature of the evils which we had been suffering from railway domination then for the first time became fully known, and the committee in their report are compelled to say that the abuses are "so glaring in their proportions as to savor of fiction rather than actual history." The reader who would know all the prominent details of the railway methods of the country may find them in a copy of this report with testimony, and in other reports of committees like the present Senate Committee on Inter-State Commerce, or he can find a good *résumé* in one of these two works, *Die Nordamerikanischen Eisenbahnen*, by that excellent German authority Alfred von der Leyen, and Hudson's *Railways and the Republic*. Personal intercourse with honest and intelligent business men and railway employés will add to the fulness and vividness of his knowledge.

Some evils of railways have been touched upon, and one or two briefly described in the first article in this series. This present article will treat of a few points selected out of the vast number which present themselves, either because they have not generally received satisfactory treatment hitherto, or because they are specially weighty in a consideration of railways from an economic point of view. These points are the waste of national resources in the railway world, the evils in the manner in which railway shares are bought and sold for speculative, or perhaps more properly gambling, purposes, and finally the great injury to our economic life by discriminations in railway charges.

More than two thousand years ago Aristotle uttered words which in our age sound almost prophetic. This wise philosopher defended slavery on broad humanitarian grounds as an institution required to keep alive the culture which alone rendered the advance of mankind a possibility, for he held that in no other way could the choice spirits among men secure leisure for higher pursuits; but, added he, if the time should ever come "when the shuttle would move of itself, and plectra of themselves strike the lyre, we should need no more slaves." What would he have thought could he have foreseen the marvellous inventions and discoveries of the past century, which have led to such utilization of the elementary powers of nature that it is scarcely an exaggeration to say that the largest portion of material products is the creation of self-acting machinery? Had he known that in a future age one man in various leading branches would produce as much as thirty, one hundred and fifty, three hundred, five hundred, and even a thousand in his day, would he not have painted in glowing colors the high and universal culture which could then be attained? It can scarcely be doubted that Aristotle would have taken it as an indisputable fact that universal freedom, leisure for higher pursuits, and an abundance of all needed economic good would become the property of all the sons of men. Alas! how different is the reality, not from dreams, but even from the actual anticipations of the past generation! There may have been improvement, and shallow optimists paint it as all that we could desire; but truth compels us to acknowledge that it is not so marked as to be beyond controversy. There has been undoubted advance in certain quarters, and undoubted deterioration in others, but what has been the change in the average condition of the masses? Who can tell? That man who in spite of all his faults still retains his reputation as the most distinguished English economist of his day considers it "questionable if all the mechanical inventions yet made have lightened the day's toil of any human being," while the most careful English student of economic facts now before the public leaves one with the impression that on the whole the lot of the English laboring class might have been more desirable some four centuries ago. And in

the United States, this most favored land, economic distress now vexes us, and a tinge of pessimism mingled with surprise characterizes the thoughts of intelligent and feeling Americans.

Now it is manifestly out of the question—even if it were in my power, which it is not—to attempt to explain all this in one article like the present, but it is well to call attention to a partial explanation. The question is this: What has become of the fruits of the material progress of our time? It is undoubtedly true that they are largely absorbed by the needless waste of competition, and it is likewise beyond controversy that no other one economic factor causes so much of this needless waste with us as the railway. Fifty years ago we went mad with the idea that universal competition was a panacea for all social evils, and the man would have received no attention who suggested that there were certain territories in our economic life which in their nature were not adapted to competition. Some of us have not yet recovered from this madness, but the time has now come for discrimination. Let us examine very briefly what unregulated railway competition has brought us.

My thesis is this: the needless waste of railway competition has been sufficient to provide good, comfortable homes—a whole house to a family—for that part of the entire population of the United States not already provided with such homes.

The first item in the count is needless expenditure in railway construction. This has been estimated at one thousand millions of dollars, and it is certainly a low estimate, for two needless railways, the West Shore and the Nickel Plate, alone account for one-fifth of this sum. It must be borne in mind that needless expenditure is waste of national resources which ought to have benefited the people. This is very simple, yet it is often necessary to repeat it. Now, one thousand millions of dollars is a sum sufficient to build homes for one million families, or five million people.

Second, every needless train is a waste, and parallel and competing roads necessitate a vast number of them daily.

Third, our railways have not been planned according to any intelligent scheme, so that they should become part of one grand system of means of communication and transportation, supplementing our natural and artificial waterways and other highways. On the contrary, they were often designed to injure other public highways, and are still managed with that view. Railways run along by the side of canals, and drive them out of existence. At times they buy the canal and stop using it, lest it should longer render any service to anybody. The Richmond and Alleghany Railroad of Virginia is an example. Here is a great waste of resources expended in canals. Railways prevent the use of natural waterways. Thus the Pennsylvania Railroad and the Pacific railways discriminate against those who use the Ohio River and the Atlantic and Pacific oceans respectively. These are examples of a waste of nature's bounty.

Freight rates are often so much cheaper between competing points than from an intermediate point that freight frequently passes twice over the same track—a waste of labor and capital. Freight is thus sent from Pittsburgh to Philadelphia and New York, and then right back through Pittsburgh to a Western point, so as to get the competition rate from one of the large cities. Freight has likewise been sent from Rochester, New York, to New York city, then back again over the same tracks through Rochester to the West. Last winter freight was sent from Baltimore to New York, then back through Baltimore to the West. These examples might be multiplied indefinitely.

Another variety of waste is illustrated by the anthracite coal combination, which stops production at intervals in order to maintain high prices. Capital power and labor power meantime remain idle, and other industries are injured.

But why continue this, as one easily might? It is impossible to express with mathematical accuracy all this enormous waste of national resources, but no one will be likely to deny that I have more than proved my thesis.

The transactions of the Stock Exchange, which has to do largely with the purchase and sale of railway shares, are not altogether illegitimate by any means. Railway property is sold honestly, as other property is, in order to obtain money for other purposes, and it is bought legitimately for investment. But a great part of the transactions are of a speculative character; in other words, property is bought and sold, not for the sake of realizing on the shares, or for the sake of an investment, but in order to get gain out of the fluctuation in value of railway property. This leads naturally to attempts to promote fluctuations. A railway manager may desire to depress the property committed to his care, in order to buy the shares of others at a low price. The devices to which recourse is had for this purpose by the management in such cases are varied. The property may be neglected, so that dividends will not be earned, dividends may be passed needlessly, groundless rumors may be circulated calculated to injure the railway, fictitious sales at low figures may be effected. These are simple processes, but one familiar with the transactions of the Stock Exchange could readily fill many pages of this Magazine in the description of devices used to depreciate property unduly. Even easier to understand are the methods used to inflate property, of which the most common, at any rate the best known, is the declaration of unearned dividends, which must then be paid out of capital.

Of course this is morally no better than highway robbery, while it is far more contemptible. It gives a false impression of the value of property, which is then sold to the community at an inflated valuation. It is a method by which corporate managers have enriched themselves, and plundered the widow, the orphan, and the thrifty hard-working citizen. It establishes that diversity of interest between the management of railways and the great body of shareholders which is one of the most marked features of our railway history. This is well illustrated in the graphically narrated account of the rise and progress of the Camden and Amboy Transportation Company, which is found in Alfred von der Leyen's work; and it may be remarked in passing that this company, of odious memory, whose history is marked not only by theft, wholesale bribery, and legislative corruption, but even by violence and murder, furnishes examples of all abuses known to the railway world. But another view of the effect of speculation in railway shares is as important as, and possibly less generally mentioned than, that which has just received our attention. The large fortunes which have been made in this way, and still more the immense possibilities of this species of gambling, are seducing the youth of the country from the paths of honest industry. This is a matter frequently bewailed almost in terms of despair by President Andrew D. White, certainly one of the most experienced and distinguished educators of the country. It ruins daily bright and promising careers, and is a curse to the land. In what does this all-pervading speculation in business differ from theft? Is it not trying to obtain something for nothing, trying to coax the property of your neighbor into your pocket without a return? and is not that the essence of theft? Should it be a matter of surprise, with the railway transactions in the Stock Exchange constantly before the eyes of the public, that these methods should extend to all spheres of business life? Or ought it to astonish one that the more vulgar, like our New York aldermen, should resort to more direct and old-fashioned methods of robbing the people whose property they ought to protect? When, in the winter of 1879–80, a measure was brought forward in the Prussian Parliament for the purchase of the private railways in Prussia, some allusion was made to the injury that this might do to the Stock Exchange; but the Minister of Public Works, or Railway Minister, as he is frequently called, Herr Maybach, replied: "Yes, gentlemen, if we shall be able to restrict the operations of this exchange by removing from it altogether this kind of property, we shall consider it a great advantage. It will indeed give me peculiar pleasure to lop off some of the branches of this upas-tree." *Gift-baum* was the word used, and it is more expressive than our English word— a poison tree, a tree poisonous in nature, and whose fruit must be poisonous. Yes, and if in any manner we in America shall be able to hew off a great branch from our *Gift-baum*, it would be a blessing to our youth, and to all who desire to live honestly and uprightly—a blessing of such proportions that it could not be easily overestimated. A curse to us is our *Gift-baum*.

Discriminations in railway charges mean a difference of treatment in favor of one party or thing and against another party or thing. They are of three principal kinds, namely: first, between places, as, for example, in favor of Boston and against New York, or in favor of New York and against Rochester; second, between things, as in favor of wheat and

against iron; third, between individuals. Only the third will be treated in this place, as it is of chief importance from a general economic stand-point.

To understand the real gravity of this evil it is necessary to consider the nature of competition, or the struggle for existence in the economic world. Men offer services or goods at varying rates, and each tries to underbid the other, and that offer is accepted which, all things considered, is the lowest. Now this is not the universal rule of business, but it is a very general one, and in the great business transactions of our time it prevails to such an extent as to be decisive, provided these transactions are honest. The largest number of exceptions may be found in the remuneration for personal services, but the force of competition is indirectly becoming more and more felt, and it is increasingly difficult to escape from its control. When Mill wrote his treatise on political economy, forty years ago, he could say that custom, not competition, fixed prices in retail trade. It is doubtful if this can now be said of that trade in any of the large centres in Europe or America—certainly not without serious modification. In an ideal condition of things, such as the old political economy presupposed, there are excellent sides to this competitive struggle, as it then gives a stimulus to individual initiative and activity, each one trying to offer superior services or goods, or endeavoring to devise methods whereby production may be cheapened; and cheapened production means a saving of capital force and labor force—a benefit to the world. It can perhaps be said with slight qualification that this economic struggle produces a near approximation to justice when it is between equals. But how is this affected by railway discriminations? It has already been stated that they are not merely in favor of one, but against another, and the latter proposition is as important as the first. Its truth follows inevitably from the nature of competition. These favors to the friends of the railway power, or to those who have in some way secured an exceptional position, who have, to use an expression becoming classic with us, gotten in "on the ground-floor," are an external force against which all their competitors must contend. Their rivals enter into the struggle carrying a weight, a weight varying in amount, but at times great enough to bear down even those who would otherwise be the strongest. Where competition is sharp—and it is sharp in these days for nearly all outside of rings and combinations—the freight on goods is frequently far greater than the profit on them, and a slight variation in charges in favor of one party is all that is needed to make the fortune of that one and to ruin competitors.

It is stated that even such delay in shipment and such annoyance as a railway can inflict on a business man not in favor is at times sufficient to cause his bankruptcy. All this involves immense waste of economic resources. Talent in business, accumulation of capital in various forms, and organizations extending over a wide area, all of which ought to have been a blessing to the laboring population and the entire country, are annihilated. The best known example is the Standard Oil Company. It received, as already stated, $10,000,000 in eighteen months in rebates. If it had done business at what would have been cost for others, it would still have had that enormous sum as profit. If it had transacted its business at such terms as would have involved a loss of $5,000,000 for others on the same amount of business, there would still have been an equal sum for distribution among the members of the company. It is a matter of course that its competitors were ruined, and idle factories, old pipe lines no longer used, and business wrecks throughout the country give evidence of enormous economic waste. It is not to the point to urge that the quality of oil has been improving, and that the price of oil has been declining, any more than it is to the point to urge the alleged chivalry of the Italian brigands as a plea for highway robbery. Doubtless the managers of this company have not been altogether blind to their permanent interests, and may have given the public some of the advantages of improvements in oil production, while the enormous increased supply of oil was such as to force down prices if the oil was to be disposed of. It is a well-known fact that millions of barrels in reservoirs have been held from the market in order to raise prices. Furthermore, it is worthy of notice that Russian petroleum is now a competitor of American petroleum, although the crude Russian oil contains only thirty per centum of refined oil, while the American contains eighty per centum. It must be admitted that there are at times savings in the transactions of business by a monopoly, but when these are desired it is essential that this line of business should be made a public undertaking, in order that it may be regulated, and that the entire public may participate in all these advantages. What we have to look at in this case is the ruin of men engaged in honorable and legitimate business. These men form part of the commonwealth, and the body cannot thrive when its members are in a diseased condition. It must be inquired, what would be the logical outcome of the extension of such methods?

What is the extent of these discriminations? It is such as to affect seriously our entire economic life. At the time of the investigation of the New York Hepburn committee it was found that special rates were the rule, and the regular tariff existed only for the weak and inexperienced. Notorious is the contract with Schoellkopf and Matthews, millers, of Buffalo, New York, which enabled them to continue business when other millers were obliged to suspend operations. A vivid light is thrown on the true character of the agreement by one clause in this contract, which reads as follows: "Provided, however, and this agreement is made upon the express understanding and consideration that said second party [*i. e.*, Messrs. Schoellkopf and Matthews] shall regard and treat this agreement as confidential, and will use all reasonable precaution to keep the same secret."

Not long ago a merchant of Baltimore attempted to do a comparatively small business in the purchase and sale of cotton. "I thought," said he, "that I would not attempt any business so large that I could not keep it all under my own immediate supervision, and would thus be able to effect savings impossible to the large dealers who are obliged to rely on agents. These small economies were to constitute my profit." With this in view he went South to the cotton regions, but what was the result? His calculations were sound until it came to the shipments of cotton, when he found that he could not obtain the rebates given to the large dealers, and was obliged to retire from the field of competition. Because of these discriminations in this line of business it is confined to ten or a dozen houses.

It is asserted in favor of the pools, or

railway combinations, that they prevent discriminations; but Mr. Hudson has shown that they do not affect the most notorious examples of discriminations, and one of the shrewdest business men it has been my pleasure to know explains the practice of railways during the existence of a pool thus: "If you go into a freight office, and are unknown, there is one general rate for freight shown you. You may argue and plead as long as you will, and enlarge upon the great amount of freight you expect to send, and the advantages which will accrue to the railway from the formation of a connection with you, but it will be quite useless; the schedule rates will be maintained. Are you, however, an old friend whose secrecy and discretion can be trusted? Then it is a different matter. You are taken aside into a little room, the doors are closed, and no one knows what is said, but you will doubtless leave with contentment expressed on your countenance." This same gentleman informed me that he could not understand how a certain Chicago dealer could put goods on the market which had been supplied by himself, at figures much lower than his Chicago competitors, until by accident he discovered that this Chicago merchant received a special secret rate.

The uncertainty and inequality of rates produce in many quarters a kind of paralysis in our economic life. Individual initiative, energy, and activity give place to a feeling of helplessness and prostration.

In speaking of railway charges and discriminations, Mr. Charles Francis Adams, Jun., said, in 1880: "In regard to these things I consider the existing system nearly as bad as any system can be. Studying its operations, as I have long and patiently, I am ready to repeat now what I have repeatedly said before, that the most surprising thing about it to me is that the business community sustains itself under such conditions."

Another abuse closely connected with this is the management of railways for the outside interests of managers and their friends. This takes at times the precise form just described. It can be readily understood that the interests of a railway director as a dealer in coal can far outweigh his interests as an owner of railway stock, so that he may be well content to forego dividends on his shares for the sake of special rates. Here there is a double robbery. The other stockholders are robbed and business competitors are robbed by those who are faithless to their trust as managers of a public highway. But this is only one form of this kind of robbery. Directors may have interests in various corporations, as freight transportation companies, express companies, sleeping-car companies, and may sacrifice the railway to these external corporations. The Hepburn committee found the Erie Railway covered in this manner with barnacles.

Another abuse of moment is the peculiar methods of construction companies, whereby men in their capacity as railroad officials enter into contracts with themselves in another capacity, and reap a rich harvest from the harmony between the two parties to the contract.

The abuse of railway power in stock-watering, and the present and still graver evils for the future in the immense empires of land owned by railways, must be passed over with a bare reference to the fact of their existence.

Still more serious are the moral evils connected with corporate management. Under this head effective essays might be written with such titles as, "Corruption no Harm," "Lying no Sin," "Theft no Crime." No one feels this more keenly than the upright business man. It is useless to deny any part of this impeachment, for proofs lie on every hand; and our popular heroes are becoming dishonest and successful adventurers. Even ministers of the Christian religion can be found to whiten their characters, and present them in the light of public benefactors; and did not the people of New York a few years ago propose to erect a statue to a man who ended his life a convict? Did not that same population recently gaze with a kind of admiration upon a man who perpetrated a successful robbery, and plundered the city of New York of several millions of dollars? Yes; we are rapidly supplying interesting and dramatic material for the future historian, who will therefrom paint startling pictures for the instruction and amusement of his readers.

There are many things which the railway advocate will urge in favor of our railways. He will endeavor to show that rates are lower in America than in Europe; but there are three things he will fail to mention in his comparison. First, our railways have been built at a low cost, owing to inferior quality of construction, and still more owing to the cheapness of right of way—often, indeed, costing nothing—in a new country, and to the level and otherwise favorable surface of our country. If we estimate the average cost of our railways at $35,000 per mile, it is a generous figure, whereas the European railways with which comparison is made will probably average $140,000 per mile. Second, no attention will be paid to the fact that terminal charges constitute a large part of freight expenses, and that these are lower with us per mile on account of our long distances. Third, you will not be informed that quality of service is a vital element in reasonable charges. What probability is there that your freight will be shipped promptly, that it will move rapidly, and that it will arrive in safety? What percentage of freight is injured or destroyed in a country like Germany, and what in America?

Comparisons are difficult in freight charges; in passenger charges easy. No one disputes that charges for passenger service are far higher in America, and there can scarcely be a doubt that, when all elements are properly considered, freight charges will be found relatively lower elsewhere, and particularly in Belgium and Germany. The charges now under consideration are the rates for the ordinary average shipper between two average points.

After all, the vital question in the comparison is whether rates are as low as they ought to be with us, and the enormous waste in our methods shows that they cannot be.

But the question of low rates is a minor one. The low rates which we do enjoy are not infrequently established at the expense of the owners of railway property, and there is cause for regret when people do not obtain a return on legitimate investments. Unless we are a nation of paupers, we desire those to receive a return who invest their means in railways. Are they not a part of the commonwealth? And do we not desire the prosperity of the commonwealth?

Still more vital is the question of economic liberty, which, as our first article has abundantly shown, is involved in the problem of the railway; equally vital are good morals and political integrity.

It has not been thought necessary to dwell on the inestimable benefits which our railways have brought us, for this is a too familiar topic. This new means of communication and transportation has added to the material resources of the country, has brought man near to his fellows in all parts of the world, and has thus promoted a beneficent kind of internationalism, while it has at the same time strengthened national bonds; it has facilitated the spread of knowledge, and in many ways tended to the ethical elevation of the race. We must regret that its beneficent features and its ideal democratic character have not been still better developed, while for the good it has brought we should remember in profound gratitude the devotion to the welfare of humanity of Watt, of Fulton, and of George Stephenson, and of a long line of scientific investigators and discoverers who preceded them and prepared the way for them, and who since their time have continued their labors. Many of these worked without hope of pecuniary reward for the love of their kind. These are our true heroes. To our railway kings we owe nothing. More than ample compensation have they received for such doubtful services as they have rendered.

THE PENALTIES OF AUTHORSHIP.

MANY years ago, before I had learned to profit by the experience of others, I wrote a story. There was nothing wonderful in this, for young people are continually ruining good paper, ink, and time in a similar manner. Neither was there anything wonderful in the story, yet it found a publisher. The title was, *The Smithton Swains*, and the publisher who accepted the manuscript, after several firms had declined it, said that perhaps his judgment had been warped in favor of the book by the startling resemblance between some portions of the plot and a bit of village romance in which he had once been an actor.

When the book reached that stage of manufacture known as "in press," and I saw it in the cold print of the proof-sheets, it seemed so slight and colorless, compared with what I had intended it, that I begged the publisher not to use my name on the title-page. My request was granted, the publisher frankly saying he did not see that my name could do the book any good commercially, while, if published anonymously, the story might be attributed to any one of several noted authors, suggestions of whose styles might be caught from my pages. But I had another reason besides dissatisfaction with my work for wanting my name suppressed; I was doing so well at the time as a salesman of hardware that I had hopes of one day becoming junior partner in our firm —Hobbs, Tobbs, and Co.—and I feared the result of either member learning that any of my time had been spent in book-writing.

I spare the reader a recital of my own sensations when I saw my book in print. It is necessary, however, to say that the general public was affected just as the publisher had been; every reader seemed to have known among his acquaintances or in his native town just such people and incidents as appeared in *The Smithton Swains;* so very soon the publisher began to receive letters from different parts of the Union asking if the scene of the book was not laid in towns specified by the writers, and whether the author was not Mr. —— or Miss ——. The publisher professed to be a truthful man, but he answered all those letters in such a way that the writers felt assured their surmises were correct. A consequence of this was that during a single trip for our firm I was introduced three several times, in three different towns, to the author of *The Smithton Swains,* and, still more startling, each of the three persons to whom was attributed the doubtful honor accepted without the faintest perceptible sign of guilt the congratulations which I offered. The humorous aspect of the blundering amused me greatly, but I must confess that my fun was short-lived, for there was always present some one who was fiercely jealous of the supposed author, and who would explain privately that the book was such wretched twaddle that it seemed strange how people could read it at all. Although I never openly disagreed with these persons, their confidences always made me angry.

The number of towns and social circles that imagined themselves the scene of *The Smithton Swains* increased so rapidly

and piqued curiosity so much that the book began to sell far in excess of the publisher's expectations. But one day I was found out. The book chanced to fall into the hands of a friend in the city in which I was born; he recognized in one of the chapters a story told word for word as I had once told it to him; so he sat down at once and wrote a two-column letter to his favorite newspaper, in which he announced his discovery in a few lines, and then consumed the remaining space by giving a minute biographical sketch of me, my tastes and peculiarities. He even caused my portrait to be engraved, from an old photograph, and printed at the head of the article; then he bought several hundred copies of the paper and sent them, carefully marked, to leading newspapers throughout the country. He wrote me of what he had done, and said he was sure it would do me a great deal of good. As for me, I kept out of sight as much as possible, and grew a beard so that I should not be recognized through the medium of the newspaper cut.

The revelation of the authorship of *The Smithton Swains* soon reached New York, and those of my business friends who first heard it came to our store to ask who was making fun of me. None of them seemed for a moment to imagine that I had written the book, or that I could write a book of any kind, so I frequently lost my temper, and did not find it again until I met some lady acquaintances—members of that delightful variety of their sex that believes whatever it hears, and thinks the writer of the most insignificant story or poem greater than any statesman or warrior that the world ever knew.

But my gentle acquaintances were not restricted to these ladies. There were others, highly intelligent and educated, whom I had always been glad to meet, and who had not seemed averse to me. But now their manner became strangely distant. I did not long have to wonder why, for a voluble damsel who knew them well told me in strict confidence that they too had written stories, stories which any one could see—so they said—were vastly superior to *The Smithton Swains,* yet for which they could not find publishers. They were not exactly jealous of me—no one could be jealous of such a trashy book, they said; still, they could not help feeling hurt at the lack of appreciation in the world, and they could not help showing it in the presence of one who was a constant reminder of the low tastes of publishers and the reading community. To reinstate myself, if possible, in the esteem of these injured damsels, I severely berated my own work when I talked with them, and wished aloud that publishers would give the public something better. This course had the effect of restoring confidence; it also caused me to be charged with the friendly service of reading their manuscripts and pressing them upon my own publisher. As this astute literary purveyor declined each and every dainty package of sentiment I carried him, the maidens again lapsed into frigidity, from which I never was able to rouse them.

Meanwhile the fact that I was an author became known through my entire circle of acquaintance, and although the knowledge brought me congratulations from a few big-hearted fellows, the general results were by turns enraging and depressing. I began to imagine that nearly everybody had written books and failed to find publishers, and that the remainder regarded an author as a member of a new, peculiar, and somewhat unpleasing order of animals. What hurt me most, however, was the sudden quiet—almost a chill—that would come over company whenever I entered a parlor. I was only five-and-twenty, and no more fond than other young people of conversation that was not trifling; but now my own old set of youths of both sexes seemed to imagine that my mind was continually soaring in the empyrean of literature, so they would hold their tongues until some one—generally the oldest, homeliest, and most affected damsel in the room—would engage me in close conversation about Browning's poetry, or some logical stickler recalled from Kames's *Elements of Criticism*. I am sure that after I became known as an author the girls in our set even waltzed less gracefully with me than with any other young man.

Then some critics began to pay me attention—in print. While I was anonymous, I suppose the book was beneath notice, but now that everybody knew who wrote it, and felt they could say what they pleased without offending any author about whom the world knew anything, they had a real good time in vivisecting me and *The Smithton Swains*. As I knew what I would have said about the book had I been a reviewer, I careful-

ly avoided the literary columns of the newspapers. But my friends did not; they carefully cut out every scathing notice, and read them all aloud to me, for fear I might accidentally lay them aside unread.

About this time I had a call from my brother Ben, who had been preaching the gospel many years with great success and small pay. Ben was twenty times as wise as I; he knew Greek and Hebrew better than I knew English; so when he heard that I had written a successful book, he hurried to New York with half a hundred poems which he had hastily written.

"You see, Charley," he said, with brotherly frankness, "if people will read with avidity so trifling a sketch as yours, what will they not do to get such a volume as these poems will make?—a volume bearing on every page evidences of scholarship and earnest thought. I think I ought to clear enough to build a house for myself, so I need no longer be shifted from one cottage to another according to the condition of the parish purse."

I thought so too as I read the poems. The publishers thought differently; so I guaranteed one of them against loss, and had the book produced in good style. But the publishers were right; Ben's poems, although some critics spoke highly of them, did not sell a thousand copies, and I never was able to fully persuade the dear old author that I had not conspired with the publisher to kill the book. Even when I lent Ben money enough to start the desired house, I believe my checks were regarded somewhat in the light of conscience money.

But whatever else happened, *The Smithton Swains* continued to sell, so people came slowly to tell one another that I was making a great deal of money. I learned this by the great increase in the number of persons who wanted to borrow money of me, and the large sums that were asked for, by the variety of subscription papers that were brought to me, and the number of business schemes with which enterprising fellows assailed me. I was also "invited out" a great deal by families which until then had barely noticed me. All this was embarrassing, for I had no right, under the terms of my contract with my publisher, to expect any money from my book for many months to come. How much I was reputed to be worth I did not learn until I was called upon by a lady member of the church to which I belonged; she was soliciting contributions to the fund being raised by the congregation for the endowment of a professorship in a theological seminary.

"We have agreed, after consultation with our husbands," said the lady, "that as the older members have sustained the entire burden of building the church, the younger men should be urged to assume this new and special duty. We have farther resolved to ask each young man to give one-tenth of this year's income, according to the ancient custom of our denomination."

This was somewhat staggering, but as I knew that a few months after the year's end I should receive a large sum from my publisher, I hastily concluded the interview, and promised to accede to the fair petitioner's request.

"What a splendid beginning!" exclaimed the lady. "It is really true, isn't it, Mr. Smith, that fifty thousand copies of *The Smithton Swains* have been sold?"

"I believe so."

"Dear me!" She pencilled rapidly on the cover of her subscription book for a moment, and then continued : "Fifty thousand copies at a dollar each come to fifty thousand dollars, one-tenth of which is five thousand dollars. Now, Mr. Smith, if you will kindly add one-tenth of your salary to the amount, I will know exactly how much to write down as your subscription."

"But I have not offered you any part of the income of my book," I gasped, "for I have not received a penny of it yet, and will not for at least half a year. I may never receive any. My publisher may fail, or I may die, or—something else may happen. Besides, I do not get all the money which people pay for the books; I get but a small percentage of it."

My visitor arose, flushed and evidently angry.

"It is all simple enough, Mr. Smith," she said, showing the figuring on her book cover. "Fifty thousand copies, fifty thousand dollars, ten per cent. of which is five thousand dollars. I believe you business men say that figures can't lie. Still, if your conscience will allow you to defraud a holy cause by subterfuge, I do not know what I can do to prevent, except report the matter to the deacons as a probable case for discipline."

"But, my dear madam—" I began. It was too late; she was half-way to the door; and one of my employers, noting the haste and manner of her departure, called me aside, and gravely expressed a hope that I had not forgotten myself so far as to make love to another man's wife. A day or two afterward I heard from the deacons through one of their number, who called at the office in the capacity of peacemaker. I was very glad to see him, for he was a business man. I explained my position, but, to my amazement, he failed to understand me. He said that he had always regarded what he had earned as his own, and really it seemed to him that the lady's view was quite correct. I am happy to say that the deacon's firm failed within a year, and the assignee reported that the book-keeping was a marvel of contradictions. This revelation, however, came too late to be used as evidence in my favor before the board of deacons; the old gentlemen adopted the visiting member's view; and although they did not formally discipline me, their wives carefully avoided assigning me any prominent and pleasing position in subsequent church sociables.

A month or two later the firm for which I had worked many years was reorganized, on the death of the widow of one of its founders. The old lady had owned a one-fifth interest in the business, and I proposed to the remaining partners that I should buy this, paying on account several thousand dollars that I had saved, and assigning my copyright contract with my publisher as security for the remainder. But Mr. Hobbs, the senior partner, startled me by saying, in a most chilling manner, "Your offer may be safe enough financially for us to accept, Mr. Smith, but I can scarcely feel that our interests would be safe in the care of a man whose tastes lead him to give part of his time to a different line of business."

Then Mr. Tobbs looked meditatively out of the dingy window of the office, clasping his left hand with his right, and said, in a far-away voice, "Literature is death to the business faculty; it impels young men to late dinners, and freethinking, and Paris, and such things."

This was more than my self-respect could endure. I withdrew at once and unconditionally from the employ of Hobbs, Tobbs, and Co., saying, as I left the office, that they could at their leisure send me their check for the balance due me.

"You'll at least take your letters, won't you, Mr. Smith?" asked Mr. Hobbs, with a peculiar grin, as he passed over the rail a note which he knew, by the writing and post-mark, to be from a young lady with whom I had corresponded industriously for a year. "Dear Nellie," I murmured to myself as I broke the seal, "you at least know me well enough to trust me." I read as I walked; but by the time I reached the store door my head was so light and my heart so heavy that I needed support. Nellie's letter was by turns sarcastic and indignant. The dear creature complained that I had never confided to her that I had written a book, that I had never acknowledged the authorship in confidence, when I knew that every girl in the country was dying to know who wrote *The Smithton Swains*, and that I had not even sent her a copy, anonymously or otherwise, when the book was published.

But the most serious grievance was reserved for the last. During the development of *The Smithton Swains* it had become necessary that one of the lovers should be extremely romantic, so I had compelled him to write some verses. These Miss Nellie dignified as "poetry," and said that if admiration for an imaginary heroine had inspired me more than affection for her—to whom I had never written poetry—it would be better if all were over between us. She was strengthened in her opinion, she said, by her pastor, who had declared that the character of the one villain in the story was too powerful and realistic not to have been drawn from the author's own life.

Nellie married her pastor. I wrote no more books. I have immured myself in the wilds of the West as keeper of a country store; I am also the village postmaster. I do not concern myself with the mail matter of my fellow-townsmen, except when I receive a bulky package addressed to a publisher. In such a case I strive industriously to seek out the writer, to work myself into his (or her) confidence, and to say, with all the earnestness of my nature, "Don't!"

SOME FRENCH MINERAL SPRINGS.

BY TITUS MUNSON COAN, M.D.

IT would not be an easy task to give an accurate count of all the mineral waters of Europe, or even of any leading country of Europe. Germany has over a hundred springs, with establishments of greater or less importance. France has probably two hundred. Spain, Italy, Switzerland, England, follow in the order named, according to the number of their establishments. Happily the number of chronic diseases is greatly less than the number of mineral springs, or, I should rather say, the springs far outnumber the *classes* of disease which are cured or relieved by their waters. For the ailment of every sufferer, if not a malignant entity, as the old physicians taught, is at least an individuality which requires individual knowledge and treatment. And for such individual curative agency the multitude of mineral springs, whether at home or abroad, offers a most precious resource, and one that physicians are yearly appreciating more and more. The object of this paper is to describe some of the best mineral waters of France, and especially those that are the less known even by those that travel for health's sake, and to point out such as have especial curative values for particular classes and varieties of disease.

In this matter "the field is the world." It is the duty, often the serious responsibility, of the consulting physician to choose among the many springs which form his therapeutic armament.

How is this choice to be made? What are the conditions of fitness for a cure? This question is often a complex one. First of all comes the strictly medicinal question, that of the nature of the spring. What class of mineral waters has been found useful in the particular ailment? Is a saline, an iron, a sulphur water indicated? This much is not hard to know. The next step is to choose among many iron, saline, or sulphur waters the particular kind that is best suited to the particular case. But this is only the beginning of the problem for the consulting physician. What sort of a climate will best suit the invalid? What are its winds, rains, exposure, sunlight? When do the fruits ripen? When will cold weather send you away? The topography of the region is also an important thing to know. Is the country hilly, or plain, or mountain? What kind of excursions may be taken? What attractions have the neighboring regions? Then the size and character of the place, as village, town, or city, as lively or quiet, as centrally or remotely situated—all these elements bear upon the patient's welfare, and choice among them can only be made by means of fitting knowledge. Much of this knowledge, indeed, the physician may acquire from books, though hardly with the clearness of personal experience. But several things remain for him to know, and these things, among the most important of all for the patient whom he may send abroad, he will never learn from books. They are what kind of hotels, boarding-houses, or furnished apartments the place can boast; what the comforts are or the discomforts of the place; what kind of people the invalid will meet during his sojourn; what sort of life in general is led at the given station, and what it will cost him to lead it? All these things the consulting physician should know by experience, for all these things go to determine the choice and the effectiveness of a cure. Neither for physician nor patient is it enough to know that one water is tonic and another alterative. The question is, what particular iron water, or saline, or calcic, or sulphur, in what particular place, cures any particular ailment? The value of the watering-place for an invalid, its working force, as the mechanician might call it, thus depends upon many factors, and it is their nice adaptation that promotes the cure. And the likelihood of a correct answer to these questions is determined mainly by the historic method; not by the fact that such and such waters ought to cure such and such complaints, but that a given case was actually cured by the specified water.

There are a hundred springs, as I have just said, for each and every class of chronic invalidism. I shall speak here of but a few of those that I have seen. And in what I am about to say I shall not direct the reader to the more crowded and expensive, but to the quieter watering-places; not because the crowded watering-places are less desirable for some—indeed, their stir and bustle are for many patients a needed element in the cure—not because they lack virtue (the waters of Vichy, Carlsbad, and Aix-les-Bains are among the most potent or "serious" of waters for their appointed cases), but simply because they are already well known. This paper I reserve for places that should be better known because of their special virtues.

I will begin with the mineral waters of a region that is in itself in the highest degree attractive on the account of beautiful scenery and healthful climate, but that is little known to American tourists —eastern France, and particularly the departments of the Jura, the Doubs, and the Vosges. The currents of travel are constantly flowing through this lovely country toward Strasburg or Geneva, but very few of my countrymen stop to know it better than through the windows of the railway car. For most of us the Swiss Alps are all of Europe for landscape, as Paris is all of France; but either of these postulates is a great mistake.

Salins, in the mountain outposts of the Jura, is a town of six thousand people. Its white houses, covered with brown tiles, cling along the banks of the Furieuse for three miles. There is only one street to speak of; but the valley itself is spacious and full of sunlight, and slopes away on either side to the summits of fortified mountains, St. André and Belin, respectively a little less and a little more than two thousand feet high, and unimaginably picturesque. A few miles to the east the summit of Mont Poupet rises 2800 feet; it is the farthest westward buttress of the chain of the Jura. Its form is not fine, yet in the twilight the outlines of its rugged crags have a wild grandeur.

The waters of Salins have been known and used from time immemorial; but the present establishment dates from 1855, when an energetic citizen, M. Grimaldi, began to erect it.* The springs indicate their character by their name; they are very strongly saline (150 grains of salt

---

* Two years later, in 1857, the same energetic citizen procured the construction of a railroad to Dôle, giving to Salins its first steam communication with the outer world; and in 1864 his townsmen, mindful of these benefits, made him their mayor. He proved a little too autocratic, however, even for the office of a French mayor, which carries great power with it, and he was displaced by a subsequent election.

to the pint), cold, having a temperature of 11.5° C. = 53° F. at the source, and abundant in quantity, supplying one large salt manufactory on the spot and another eleven miles away at the village of Arc-et-Senans.

They are salter than sea-water, but not like the sea in their saltness, for in addition they contain a large quantity of the bromide of potassium. A bath of fifty-two gallons (200 litres) contains seventeen pounds of salt and two ounces of the bromide of potassium; their intimate chemical composition resembles that of the springs at Nauheim and at Kreuznach in Germany, but these latter have more calcic salts. The manufacture of table salt is carried on in large buildings near the bathing establishment. The visitor descends many feet into the excavations, where immense wooden wheels, turned by the waters of the Furieuse, pump up the brine and discharge it into the vats above. Nothing can be weirder than these subterranean sights and sounds—the slow turning of the great wheels, the motion of great pumps and levers, and the rush of the river-waters into the works far overhead, as if they were to flood the salt caverns where you wander darkling.

What are they good for, these ocean waters springing out of the Jura Mountains? Their action is tonic and stimulating. They are especially adapted to the scrofulous temperament and to its diseases. The glandular and ganglionic swellings, the discolored skin, both the anæmia and the uterine disorders which often accompany this temperament, and even white swelling, Pott's disease, and other affections of the joints, provided they have passed the acute period, find in these waters an excellent means of cure. Dr. Dumoulin, the resident inspector, has found them serviceable in the early stages of diabetes. Dr. Guyenot prescribes them for every variety of anæmia.

Both internal and external use of the waters is made. The baths are perfectly appointed; the marble bathing pool, or *piscine*, is one of the largest in Europe, containing 22,400 gallons of water, which is warmed to a temperature of from 83° to 86° F. Every bath has faucets for warm and for cold water, and there are douches of every description.

The bathing establishment accommodates about one hundred and fifty guests. It is beautifully appointed, being a fine hotel, with concert-room and theatre in addition, and it stands in a pretty but narrow garden, which has long deserved more room at the hands of the company who own it. The needed extensions were being made in August, 1885, when I last saw the place. The good people of Salins, however, are anything but progressive. They have taken hardly any pains to advertise their springs, and in consequence, though they are much frequented by the French, these excellent waters are little known to others.

The establishment is a quiet one, yet there is a patient now and then who needs still greater quiet. For such a one there is abundance of furnished apartments, where, if he chooses, he may hear nothing but the mountain breeze blowing, and the slow rumbling of the ox-drawn trucks that bring down the hundred-year-old pines of the Jura to the saw-mills on the outskirts of the town. The surrounding country is extremely beautiful, and offers tempting excursions. The mountains stand all around the little town. The climb to the forts, the view of Mont Blanc from Fort Belin, the higher ascent to the top of Mont Poupet and the wonderful panoramic view from its summit, the fairy valley of Nans, the Source du Lison, and the Grotte Sarrazine—these are among the most beautiful trips in a land of lovely scenery.

There are several excellent physicians. From Dr. A. Dumoulin, the inspector, and Dr. T. Guyenot, the patient will receive the most skilful treatment. Each of these gentlemen has written at length and very learnedly upon the waters of the place. Dr. Compagnon, a younger man, is also a man to trust. I must not leave Salins without remarking that it is the home of an eminent and charming artist, Max Claudet, the sculptor. His beautiful house on the hill-side, the ideal of an artist's home, has proved the most attractive spot in Salins to many a visitor of artistic and literary tastes. The home of Pasteur, his friend and crony, is but a few miles away.

There is another Salins not very far away, and its waters are not dissimilar to those that we have seen. Salins-Moutiers, in Savoy, is in the high mountains, at the end of a charming ride in the diligence. Its waters are rich in salt, and have the advantage over those of Salins in the Jura of being warm. They are also given in baths and internally, and for the same ailments; besides which they have been found powerfully curative in chronic troubles of the genito-urinary system.

Not far away in miles, but on the northward of the mighty ranges of the Alps, lies Evian, on the French or southern side of Lake Geneva. It is a charming place, and in sharp contrast as to its situation with the mountain-builded towns that we have just left. Six thousand people come here every year to try its pure, cool, bicarbonated waters, which are especially adapted to dyspepsia, gravel, and inflammation of the bladder. They are very lightly mineralized, and are taken in abundant quantity. Evian is on the cool side of the lake, and is a much quieter place than the towns on the opposite or Swiss side. The pretty and aristocratic casino, formerly the residence of the Baron de Blonay, was bequeathed by him to the city, of which he had been mayor. Among the physicians, either Dr. Taberly or Dr. Flotard, both very competent men, may be consulted.

Turning now to the northeast, let us examine the springs of the Vosges, beginning with the ancient station of Luxeuil. Its waters are either mildly saline, or contain iron and manganese; the latter combination occurs nowhere else in the warm mineral waters of Europe. Each of its fifteen springs contains considerable silex; they vary in temperature from 82° to 124° F. The establishment belongs to the government; like Salins, it is not advertised, and is less frequented than it deserves to be. Situated in a beautiful park, and walled in on the south by the finest plane-trees I have ever seen, the spacious building, erected in 1768 and enlarged in 1853, contains every appliance that is needed for bathers. The Bain des Bénédictins, the Bain des Fleurs, the Bain des Dames, the Bain des Capucins, are among the most frequented; the current of warm water moves constantly through the marble basins, and thus remains pure however many bathers there may be, and however long their baths; and there is now a tendency to the old system of long soaking. Men and women bathe together at Luxeuil—a fashion which has gone out of use in nearly all the other baths of France. The custom is a social one, and produces beneficent results in the cure of nervous or melancholy patients. In a famous establishment, which I will not mention by name, but it is near Luxeuil,

the bathing of the sexes in common had to be stopped a few years ago, because some of the men took liberties with the ladies—by splashing water in their faces across the marble partition that separated them.

The mild but efficacious waters of Luxeuil are given for three classes of ailments: 1, anæmia; 2, leucorrhœa depending upon anæmia (for this the iron-manganese waters are the most efficient of cures; and 3, for all the nerve derangements that follow uterine disease, as hysteria, the waters of Luxeuil are unsurpassed. I must add that the place is quiet and inexpensive. It is a town of 3700 inhabitants, in an open rolling country, 1325 feet above sea-level. The climate is, in French phrase, a little "of the mountains"; that is to say, variable, according to their standard; but compared with the performances of our American summer, the variations of heat and cold are far from excessive. There are charming walks in the neighborhood and toward the Vosges Mountains. A fine old street remains in the town itself, which is as old at least as the Roman time. At the bathing establishment a collection of Roman remains has been made. The visitor will find the lovely face of the Roman dancing girl on the north side of the court—a thing worth going miles to see. The Romans had a fine establishment here, and some of their inscriptions have been restored to the walls of the modern establishment. Dr. Champouillon, a man of great ability, discrimination, and courtesy, and Dr. Gauthier, should be consulted.

For board and lodging the guest will not go amiss. At the Hôtel des Thermes, the largest in Luxeuil, he will find a pretty court-yard, a beautiful view, and a well-appointed house. The Hôtel du Lion Vert is also good. Among the many *chambres garnies* he can live to his own taste at a very moderate expense. Luxeuil in any case, like all of the spas in the Vosges, is not dear. Of the *maisons meublées* those of MM. Colard, Ganneval, Magny, Philippon, and Thomas are well spoken of.

Near Luxeuil, at most an hour or so by train, is Plombières, where the railroad abandons the attempt to climb the beautiful valley any further. An excellent spring it is for the cure of nervous affections and of anæmia; but the place is so well known that I need not do more than mention it here. Plombières, with its warm waters, its "Roman" steam baths, where they still show you the masonry of Marcus Aurelius's time, and the plumbing of the third century—or it may be a little later, but it is certainly more solid plumbing than that of the nineteenth—Plombières, with its splendid establishment built by Napoleon III., whose name on the façade of the building is still dimly visible under the title that effaces it—all this and much more is known to the public. I must not forget to name the courteous Dr. Gustave Liétard, one of the two inspecting physicians of the place, and one of the skilled doctors at this very attractive and curative thermal station.

Farthest to the east in our tour, surrounded by the green mountains of the Vosges, and hidden in the very heart of their elevated valleys, is the greenest spot among their watering-places, at once the most charming and the least known of them all—Bussang. What mountains surround it, and what views from their summits! Standing on the top of the Ballon d'Alsace, a few miles away, I saw all the snow-clad peaks of western Switzerland rising before me in soft yellow lights and blue shadows; on the top of Mont Blanc, 138 miles away as the crow flies, the snows of France and Italy shone together in the morning sunlight, with the still vaster glaciers of the Bernese Alps ranging to still vaster distances in the east. No part of Mont Blanc, the reader will remember, is in Switzerland; the Swiss boundary at its nearest point is near Mont Dolent, eleven miles to the east of the summit. Another boundary passes over the Ballon d'Alsace; the granite pillar that marks the summit marks the new line between France and Alsace — between the German *militarismus* and the French kindliness. In the rear of the establishment at Bussang this line runs over the hill, and its plane is indicated by a granite post in the middle of the tunnel. The tourist thus has two countries at hand for his rambles.

But I am speaking too soon of the environs; let us come to the springs themselves. At the town of Bussang itself we need not linger; it is twenty minutes' ride in the diligence beyond Saint-Maurice, where we leave the railroad. Except that it has grown to contain 2000 people, one doubts whether it has greatly changed during three centuries past, for Montaigne in his journal, written on his way to Ger-

many, speaks of "Bossan, petit méchant village, le dernier français." And now again, after the German conquest of Alsace, it has become once more "the last French village."

About a mile beyond this "petit méchant village," on a hill 2188 feet above sea-level, and surrounded by the living green of the Vosges Mountains, stands the new hotel. A quarter of a mile farther up the Col de Bussang the pure spring of the Moselle breaks out of the hill-side. The mineral waters flow from a point close to the establishment, where packers work all day long bottling them. As much as 3400 tons are shipped by railroad every year. The waters are clear, cold (52° F.), sparkling, and as delicious as the Bohemian Giesshübel, which is the highest praise I know to give their taste. They contain manganese, bicarbonate of iron, and a little arsenic.

But who shall drink of the springs of Bussang? Though they are the most tempting of table waters, they should not be used indiscriminately. They are classed as mild waters, yet they are a little too strong to take without medical advice. They are especially a digestive water; they are tonic and laxative, and act promptly upon the digestive tract. Anæmia depending upon impaired digestion, or any other consequence of an impaired digestive power, is here treated with great success. This is no place to recite cases that have come under my observation, but I may say that the results leave no doubt as to who should come to Bussang. Delicate persons, anæmic and nervous, and especially delicate persons of the lymphatic temperament, who have tried iron tonics and found themselves unable to digest them—such persons will find in the waters of Bussang a gentle tonic that is both digestible and digestive. Cases of chronic diarrhœa that have resisted every other treatment are frequently cured at these springs.

A bathing establishment has been constructed, and will soon be available for patients. The place is of the quietest, and visitors must depend upon the society of the mountains and of their fellow-visitors for their company. The place is well adapted for the sojourn of small families. The hotel has a Swiss air about it; it is new, perfectly appointed, clean, and well managed, and the cooking is excellent— no small consideration for the delicate invalids who seek their cure in this beautiful spot. The climate is variable—that is to say, considerably cooler by night than by day—but not more variable than that of our own inland towns; and the air is so clear that the setting planets often move down in their full brightness to the valley horizon, and suddenly go out behind it with the soft swift extinction of falling stars, not the sullen fire of setting upon a murky horizon. A stroll on the heights behind the hotel, among the cow-herds' *chalets*, after sunset, is a thing that one will long remember.

I now come to a group of springs, still in the Vosges, that are near each other, and similar in character—Contrexéville, Vittel, and Martigny. They all emerge from the triassic rocks, and are all calcic waters, with other less prominent ingredients. Quitting the mountains for the elevated plateau which forms the eastern and central parts of France, we find Vittel first in order among these allied waters. The town has 1400 inhabitants, and lies 1100 feet above sea-level, in the valley of the Vair. It is a rolling country, full of wheat; vineyards are few, owing to the elevation. The climate is somewhat of the mountains, but the air is pure and not untempered. The waters have been known since 1860. The beautiful establishment is mostly new. Baths, saloons, covered galleries, courts, theatre, all things that look toward comfort, are there. And for health, the sufferers from gravel, from enlargement of the liver, and from the gout of anæmia will seek these cold and abundant springs, which are of two kinds, calcic and iron. They have little taste, but the iron waters throw down an abundant deposit in their marble basins. The calcic waters are of great value in cases of obstinate constipation. They purge actively, but they do not purge by indigestion, as some calcic waters do; it is rather by direct medicinal action upon the torpid organs. Like the waters of Vichy, they have been called a milder Carlsbad. Dr. Bouloumié, the physician of the establishment, speaks English. He is a highly cultivated man, and one whom it is a pleasure to meet, either socially or professionally. The visitor at Vittel will find every accommodation in the establishment, with the choice of furnished apartments if he prefers it.

Contrexéville is another town in the valley of the Vair, an hour's drive from Vittel; a valley somewhat narrow, and crowded by the fine establishment, yet not too deep for abundant sunlight; it is a hot place in summer, but it is 1148 feet above sea-level, and has cool nights. The waters are much like those of Vittel and Martigny, yet to be mentioned; and like those they are given successfully for gravel and gout, but they have a special value in cases of vesical catarrh and in enlargements of the prostate gland. There is no lack of excellent doctors at Contrexéville, among whom I will name two, Doctors Brongniard and Thiéry. I may add that the cooks of Contrexéville are famous. You may find better dinners there than at Paris—if your physician will permit you to eat them. Contrexéville is a lively little place, and the visitor is sometimes tempted to entertain himself in ways that are not strictly in accordance with ascetic principles of treatment.

At Martigny, the third in this group of neighboring and related waters, all is new, both the commodious establishment and the use of its excellent waters. The place, widely known to the French, is as yet little known outside of France. It amply deserves to be known, for gout and gravel find here certain relief and frequent cure. The baths are well appointed, and the establishment is adding constantly to its accommodations. In Dr. Bridou, the physician of the establishment, the visitor will find a most competent and faithful physician. The prices of board are moderate.

Taking horse and carriage at Martigny, and driving thirteen miles due southward into the Haute-Marne, one passes through quiet uplands not yet invaded by the railroad engineer, and covered with wondrously beautiful wheat; the country makes one think of the fields of Galilee; it is the picture of absolute peace. A long white road leads down to the town of Bourbonne-les-Bains, which appears against a long hill that extends from east to west, its thermal establishment resting against the slope. A little higher up are the great reservoirs into which the hot mineral water is pumped in order that it may cool down overnight to a temperature at which it can be used for baths and drinking. These are saline waters, known and used since the time of the Romans, and now employed in every form known to science, as by baths, by drinking, in vapor, in fomentations, in spraying or "pulverization," and in mud baths. There are seven springs, their temperature ranging from 149° to 151° F. The waters are tonic and exciting, and their taste is not disagreeable. They are especially used for the cure of rheumatism and of wounds, and they have, like other saline waters, the most beneficial effect as a tonic for scrofulous cases, and in the anæmia resulting from scrofula.

Bourbonne is a town of 4000 people, and the visitor will have no difficulty in suiting himself among the excellent hotels and furnished apartments that may be found. The Maison Beaurain, near the establishment, is one of the best; its courteous proprietor speaks English fluently, and one will meet many people of distinction among his guests. The Hôtel des Bains is also to be commended. Among the older physicians I may mention Dr. Cabrol and Dr. Magnin, the inspector; among the younger, Dr. Magnin, Jun., and Drs. Bougard and Causard.

We will now turn from eastern to central France, and to a famous group of mineral waters which, in spite of their fame, are but little visited by Americans. They are the springs of Auvergne, the richest group of mineral springs in the world. Every variety of water, except the soda and the sulphur waters, is represented among them; and on Dr. Petit's beautiful chart of the Puy-de-Dôme no less than two hundred and ninety separate springs are indicated. The number of establishments is considerable. Those of Mont Dore and of La Bourboule are, perhaps, better known to Americans than any others among them; but of these, in their distinctive character of arsenical waters, I will speak on another occasion.

The visitor to Auvergne will usually arrive by Clermont-Ferrand, the principal city of the region—a fine old place, with a fine cathedral, finished within a year or two, five centuries after it was begun. The soil of the city is in parts impregnated with carbonic acid gas, and so lately as the summer of 1885, when I was first there, a lady was suffocated by remaining too long in her own cellar. Close by Clermont stands the lovely new town of Royat. Its springs were frequented by the Romans. Then, during the long centuries that followed the overthrow of the Roman civilization—the greatest misfortune that has ever happen-

ed to men, and a misfortune still uncompensated by what the later centuries have given us—they were forgotten. Of late years they have been successively rediscovered, the ancient plumbing even remaining in places, as at Plombières; and now Royat is one of the most important and most frequented stations of central France, the visitors ranging from 6000 to 7000 every summer.

It is eminently a place to charm the lover of natural beauty; a more delightful valley it would be hard to find anywhere. The type of scenery in Auvergne is different from that of any other part of Europe, that I know; it more resembles that presented by the picturesque hills and valleys of Hilo in the Hawaiian Islands, with the important difference, however, that in Auvergne the ocean forms no part of the view. The likeness is based upon the fact that both regions are of volcanic formation, and one that is, geologically speaking, comparatively recent. But while the higher stations, like Mont Dore, La Bourboule, Saint-Nectaire, have a severe mountain beauty, Royat is all smiles; in Royat whatever charm nature can put forth is at its fullest. The country is extremely varied in contour, or *accidenté*, as the French say; each house almost stands upon its own hill, or against it in such way that you may enter a magnificent hotel at the level of the lower street in the valley, and climb four stories before reaching the rear basement and the terrace on the crest of the hill.

The valley and the old village of Royat, with its church of the twelfth century, the latter situated half a mile above the splendid thermal establishment, are very picturesque. The little neighboring village of Fontanat, on the route to the Puy-de-Dôme, commands a fine view of the magnificent plain of the Limagne, and the whole hill-side is full of water running musically. The sweet springs of Fontanat! how they flow away sounding in their rocky channels, or following the roadside with companionable babble, or speeding softly over the hill-side grass, or bursting up unexpectedly from the forest path! There are no such springs elsewhere. They turn old mill-wheels, centuries old, one would say, their wheels laden with green moss, more moss than wood; and in the dusty milling-room, quite untended, you see the grain slowly pulverizing under the old-fashioned millstones as if by some gentle primordial force. The strange old church, the deep ravine and dark forest of Vaucluse, the rolling hills and wild uplands all abloom with heather, the musical current of the Tiretaine in the gorge below, and in the distance the wild outlines of the mountains of the Puy-de-Dôme standing against the pure horizon in spectral blue—Europe does not offer a more fascinating picture.

The springs at Royat are four in number, all warm:

The Cæsar, rediscovered in 1822, iron and carbonic acid, 29° Cent. =84° Fah.

The Eugénie, 1843–53, alkaline and chlorinated, 35° C. =95° F.

The St. Mart, 1875, alkaline and chlorinated, 31° C. =88° F.

The St. Victor, 1875, iron, carbonate of lime, potash, and a little arsenic, 20° C. = 68° F.

The Cæsar is very useful in dyspepsia, chlorosis, and in nervous affections. It is a delicious table water.

The Eugénie is one of the most abundant mineral springs, not only in Europe, but in the world. It pours forth a noble jet of 2700 gallons per minute at 95° F., and supplies no less than eighty-five baths with flowing water—a great advantage in using the "live bath," as the French physicians call it. The saline constituents of the waters and their carbonic acid gas all reach the bather exactly as they leave nature's laboratory.

The St. Mart has a great reputation, and a deserved one, in the case of bronchitis, laryngitis, and uterine affections.

The St. Victor is especially useful in chlorosis, amenorrhœa, and leucorrhœa.

These waters, very complicated in their constitution, have one remarkable quality. They contain nearly all the constituents of the serum of the blood, and in nearly the proportion in which it is found in the human body. They are a natural mineral lymph: two pints of the waters of Royat represent almost exactly one pint of serum. They are, as one might expect, of the highest value in diseases which depend upon impoverishment of the blood.

A few other mineral springs share in a certain degree with Royat the invaluable constitution of mineral lymph. Such are those of Châteauneuf, of Saint-Nectaire, and of Vic-sur-Cère in Auvergne, and of Ems in Germany, the nearest congener, medicinally speaking, to Royat. But Ems

has not the iron of Royat, nor is its climate, like that of Royat, invigorating.

Who, in fine, should go to Royat? Invalids of these three classes should go:

1. Those who suffer from affections of the respiratory tract—chronic laryngitis, bronchitis, asthma, catarrh, and even the first stages of phthisis.

2. Those who suffer from the manifestations of the arthritic diathesis; from gout, rheumatism, sciatica, gravel, or eczema and acne, which are allied skin diseases.

3. Those who suffer from chloro-anæmic and nervous affections resulting from uterine derangements; women who suffer from any impoverishment of the blood and its consequences; the chlorotic young girl; the anæmic and the nervous invalid of whatever age—these are patients for the pure springs of Royat. Let them put themselves under the care of one of the excellent physicians there, and they will return cured after four or five weeks' trial of the waters and of the enchanting mountain rambles. I must mention two among those good doctors—Dr. Boucomont, the inspector, and Dr. Alexander Petit. The learning and the courtesy of these gentlemen, the latter of whom speaks English, made my stay in Royat one of the pleasantest experiences in the memory of one who has seen more than a few pleasant places in distant countries. I must name, too, among the hotels of a town that is full of hotels, villas, and maisons meublées, the Grand Hôtel, kept by M. Servant. It is all that cleanliness, good cooking, and unfailing courtesy can make it, plus the noble views of mountain, plain, and valley that expand, as at the establishment of Bussang, before every window. The Prince of Wales has put up here, and naturally the Grand Hôtel is a favorite resort with English guests.

Seventy-five miles from Clermont-Ferrand lies Saint-Nectaire, a village of a thousand people. It is at the head of a wild valley, with fine mountains closing it in; the excursions lead into the smiling country beyond. More than forty springs flow down the valley, leaving a red ochreous deposit as they flow. They are all hot; ten or twelve of them are used medicinally. There are three well-managed establishments. The waters are the strongest in Auvergne, and they contain all the mineral elements of the other springs, from carbonic acid to arsenic.

They are strong waters, and can only be used safely under strict medical supervision, but they are admirable for one large class of diseases—in the condition known as lymphatism. For scrofulous and lymphatic patients, and especially for the earlier stages of scrofula, the waters of Saint-Nectaire are strongly tonic. They are much given in baths and douches.

In Châteauneuf we come again upon mineral waters of the very first importance. With Dr. Boucomont of Royat I am inclined to rank them among the most valuable, not merely of Auvergne, but of all France. Fifteen springs offer to the physician in their varied warmth and chemical composition an extended gamut of qualities for his prescription. They are either predominantly iron, magnesian, or bicarbonated waters, more alkaline than those of Royat, less so than those of Vals, and laxative in sufficient doses. They are especially adapted to those dyspeptic, anæmic, and chlorotic sufferers for whom the waters of Vichy are too strong, and who find in those of Royat a too urgent tonic effect. But these waters are also true mineral lymphs; their iron, lime, chloride of sodium are mingled nearly as in the human blood. Châteauneuf is among the most important of all stations for the cure of chlorosis, anæmia, and the resulting neuroses. The thermal establishments are less complete than most of those that I have already described; but the cure, the one thing needful, is to be had, and it will be not a little aided by the walks and drives in the neighborhood. The situation in the valley of the Sioule is one of ravishing beauty. Placed at the extremity of Auvergne, this landscape will leave an ineffaceable impression upon the mind of the departing traveller.

Coming back from the mountain fastnesses, Châtelguyon, near Riom, is a village of two thousand people. It is situated on the Sardon, and many of its warm mineral springs join themselves to the current of the stream. So bountiful is their flow that at some places, if you will put your ear to the ground, you will hear the waters boiling far down in profound channels in the earth. Their mineralization is very complex, but they have a definite effect; they are cathartic, and more strongly so than one would anticipate from the most careful study of their composition. They may be described as tonic-purgative

waters; they resemble in many respects those of Kissingen, but they are better supported by the stomach, and their temperature (34° C. = 93° F.) adapts them, like those of Royat, to immediate use as they emerge from the ground as a "live bath," while the waters of Kissingen require to be heated. In their double properties of tonic and purgative the waters of Châtelguyon are unsurpassed by any in the cure of anæmic and lymphatic patients. The tonic effect quietly repairs the purgative. They are excellent for anæmia, gout, rheumatism, malarious fevers, chlorosis, leucorrhœa, dyspepsia, and the restoration after hemiplegic paralysis.

Rouzat, four miles from Riom, stands 1312 feet above sea-level, upon the slope of the Dôme mountains. It has a fine establishment. The waters are chloro-bicarbonated and warm (31° C. = 88° F.), and especially fitted for the cure of lymphatism and anæmia. Taken in moderation, these highly mineralized waters will cure the dyspepsia of lymphatic persons, but a nervous dyspeptic will not be benefited here. Congestive or catarrhal ailments of the uterus are also sure to find relief or cure at this station.

Sainte-Marguerite, on the Allier, one hour by railroad from Clermont-Ferrand, has a veritable geyser in its "wonderful" spring, the Source Merveilleuse. An intermittent jet of carbonated water spouts forth every three or four minutes, but twice a day a furious burst of water at 31° C. = 88° F. breaks from the fountain, flinging itself to a height of twenty-three feet, and deluging everything around. The water, saturated with carbonic acid gas, is used in baths and as a drink. There are two other springs similar in composition, but cooler, having a temperature of only 13°–14° C. = 55°–57° F., but all are alike chloro-carbonated. They are essentially plastic, blood-forming, reconstituent; they stimulate the digestion, repair the blood, and restore the anæmic and the chlorotic to health. These excellent waters have been known for at least three hundred years, and their modest but comfortable establishment deserves a greater vogue than it possesses to-day.

Such are a few of the more valuable of the healing springs of central and eastern France. But it must be remembered that what I have said will not enable the invalid to choose among them without the aid of a competent consulting physician.

Editor's Easy Chair.

IT was said of Lord John Russell that his self-confidence was such that if suddenly summoned to take command of the Channel fleet, he would not hesitate to do it. Lord John's name is legion. It is the name of those excellent persons who give the conduct of their neighbors the benefit of their comment and criticism, and who gladly volunteer "to steer other people's canoes." There is a saying about old maids' children which imports that women who have no actual maternal responsibility know—or suppose that they know—precisely how that responsibility should be discharged, and have no reluctance in pointing out how the most troublesome child might have been made decorous and sweet-mannered, and how sadly remiss parents are in doing their duty.

These instructive people have a deep impression of the wastefulness of nature or the fatuity of fate in failing to call into activity the guiding genius which in their cases is apparently a mere superfluity. Nature with unpardonable remissness accumulates children to be trained upon the hands of the poor mothers which are already more than full, and leaves empty of candidates for training the willing hands of the mentors which are aching for that very employment. It should be borne in mind, therefore, by the benevolent, that the good people who point out to others how they might do their duty more effectively have no impertinent intention, but are merely springs that overflow from too copious and undesired a supply, and so moisten the adjacent ground beyond reason.

If this great truth had been constantly remembered, the familiar remark would hardly have been made to the mentor overflowing with counsel to his neighbor that there was once a man who made a large fortune by minding his own business. The truth is that this remark, so far as it implies that a man should interest himself only in what concerns himself exclusively and personally, inculcates by sarcastic indirection a mischievous selfishness. If, as the remark intends, everybody should mind only his own business, who would mind everybody's business? And this question, of course, suggests the further question whether the tendency of which we are speaking is not really a perversion or a diversion of the instinct which produces public spirit.

If, for instance, you live in the country, which Ignatius informs the Easy Chair is his happy lot, and the roads are covered with large cracked stones, and these covered again with earth, which makes a good road impossible, because it prevents crushing and packing, what shall Ignatius do? It is a question which he propounds to the Easy Chair. He can remonstrate with the local officers, or he can write tremendous letters to the village

paper and sign them "Junius," and "Vindex," and "Boanerges," and "A Taxpayer," and "A Patriot," and "Sentinel," and "Cincinnatus," or he can do nothing. Now Ignatius says that if he takes the first course he is asked pleasantly on all sides if he proposes to run the village, and to attend to everybody else's business, and to earn the title of the village busybody, and whether he really supposes that he can do other people's work as well as his own? If he takes the other course, there is an equal host of critics who declare that his conduct is like that of all other men, and that it is no wonder the village languishes.

If Ignatius is to take counsel of the spirit which extols the man who made a fortune by minding his own business, he will conclude that the care of the streets is the business of the overseer appointed to that office, and that he has no more interest in the matter than all his neighbors. Then it will appear that what is everybody's business is nobody's, and the wisdom of minding your own business will be illustrated by abominable roads. It will be objected that this is not the same case as that of the superserviceable neighbor, or of the excellent maiden lady who seeks to regulate her married friend's nursery. But is it not very much the same? If Ignatius lifts up his voice against the road, what does he do? He says to the village overseer that he knows better than the overseer how to make a road. Is not that what Diana says to Cornelia when she instructs her in training her children, or what Tityrus says to Melibœus when he advises him how to plant trees?

Lord John's willingness to take command of the Channel fleet is akin to the readiness with which many good people who have little experience, or even none at all, offer to edit magazines and newspapers. Whether they also bestow their counsel upon the family physician as to the conduct of his practice, or kindly volunteer to superintend the business of others with whom they deal, does not appear. But as there is as much reason for the action in one case as in the others, it is to be assumed that they propose a general management of the business of other people. They will expect, therefore, and naturally, that others will do the same friendly office for them, and the vivacious Cato, who recently favored an editor, who tells us the story, with his views of the proper management of the editor's journal, was not surprised by the editor's rejoinder.

Cato thought, and said to the editor in substance, that if a new lock, stock, and barrel were provided, the musket would be a tolerable weapon. Cato was a lawyer, and the editor, without referring to the letter of his correspondent, replied at length and in detail, admonishing Cato that his knowledge of law was very imperfect, that as an advocate he apparently lacked every qualification, that he was singularly destitute of tact, and that his manners were so offensive that they repelled clients and discredited his profession. He added that he wrote as a friend, and with sole regard to Cato's success at the bar. Cato made no reply, but he said to his friends that the editor was the most impudent fellow of his acquaintance—an opinion which, by a singular coincidence, the editor had freely expressed to his friends in regard to Cato.

Cato, who is not an ill-disposed, but also not a very perceptive person, meant no mischief, and wrote in good faith. But the wise dame said to her infant pupil, "My dear, you must not only not mean to; you must mean not to." The pupil who pondered and applied that saying was a much happier man than the one who never understood it. Probably Cato will not write to that editor again, and possibly he will spare other editors. Indeed, the editorial reply may have suggested to him that editors are quite as likely to be capable of managing their own business as lawyers or doctors, and hereafter before Lord John advises the admiral how to handle his squadron to the best advantage, he will be inclined to remember the good advice to Tattycoram, who was inclined suddenly to burst into explosive speech, "Count twenty-four, Tattycoram."

THE virtue and the duty of hospitality are celebrated in the most ancient records. But the hospitality of a tribe and a tent, the virtue of washing the feet and cooling the brow of the travel-worn wayfarer, are very different from the duty of surrendering your time to the demand of anybody who chooses to knock at your door. "Ah, Charles," said Longfellow to his friend Professor Norton, "if I were not kind to that poor fellow, who would be?" Longfellow was the most generous and patient of men. But his time was like an orchard of noble fruit by the road-side, and every tramp felt at liberty to jump over the fence and help himself. Emerson in one of his poems exclaims:

> "Askest 'how long thou shalt stay'?
> Devastator of the day!....
> Speeding Saturn cannot halt;
> Linger—thou shalt rue the fault;
> If Love his moment overstay,
> Hatred's swift repulsions play."

The thief of time, that is to say, of another's time, is a gross offender. He assumes that the man whom he makes his involuntary host can have no pleasure greater and no occupation more pressing than seeing and amusing him. He takes his victim in a way that prevents self-defence. He has him at a frightful disadvantage, namely, the inability imposed by hospitality to express impatience or sense of wrong. Why should a man of the English-speaking race try to console himself with the assurance that a man's house is his castle, if the airy idler passes the bridge, penetrates the portcullis, and quietly occupies the citadel, while the dismayed lord of the domain is paralyzed by the ancient virtue of hospitality, and can only smile weakly upon the foe in full possession?

But the devastator of the day is found upon both sides of the door. If the airy idler enters and lays waste the precious hours within, there is also the watchful spider in the parlor who entices the innocent fly upon the wing. The most valuable of all possessions is time. Life itself is measured by it. Whoever steals or wastes it, wastes and steals so much inestimable treasure. Yet the lady Avaricia is a kind of spider—enchanted, of course, into that charming form, like the white cat into the princess. But she glides up and down the pavement, and a fly, earnestly intent upon his own private buzz, comes humming by, and Avaricia whispers to him to walk into her parlor. She whispers every day. Her voice is persuasive at first, then it modulates into the key of surprise, of reproach, of indignation. "Won't you come? Why do you never come? Do you know how long it is since you came? I heard of you at Portia's. Is my house so repulsive? Why do you slight me so? Your conduct is insulting. It implies that I am too stupid to waste an hour upon. You think me a fool. Fly! you are no gentleman."

Good heavens! Is a fly bound to walk in and be consumed? Does the eager spider—that is to say, Avaricia—suppose her house to be the garden of Eden? Is there no joy comparable to an hour in her drawing-room? Is she a houri of houris that all true believers in calling upon her are imparadised? Is a man necessarily so unhappy in his own society? Does it never occur to her that the thin scum of tittle-tattle which she skims for all comers is not nutritious? Can anything be more ludicrous than to assume to the point of anger that you are a delightful person whom everybody must gladly see? Yet this is what Avaricia does in her wearisome urgency that you shall come to her house.

Such urgency is not hospitality. The secret of hospitality is perfect freedom for the guest—freedom to come or not to come, to stay or not to stay, and, when actually within your domain, freedom from incessant prods of service of every kind. Hospitality says to the guest, in a sense more sincere than that of Spanish courtesy, this house is yours. That phrase means that you will do precisely as you do at home, and if you shrink from receiving the offer as it is made, it is because you do not understand the nature of hospitality. But hospitality does not say to every invader of the household, This house is yours. On the contrary, to the devastators of the day it says emphatically, This house is mine. When Montaigne went down into Italy from France he stopped at all the fine châteaux, and claimed hospitality of the lord as one gentleman of another. If you are Montaigne, you can likewise knock at every door and be sure of your welcome. But if you are not Montaigne—?

You ask in return whether Montaigne shall be a churl, and shut his door in the face of the ingenuous disciple or mere admirer who would fain pay homage of respect to the kindly author who has cheered his life, or consoled his affliction, or resolved his doubts? No; not at all. Montaigne doubtless enjoys the tributes of friendly regard and obligation which the pilgrim brings. The Autocrat in England receives with the keenest pleasure the practical assurance that he has heightened the gayety of nations. Longfellow at the Craigie house sat sublimely to be bored. Such gracious natures are always patient. This is only a plea in abatement. He *was* bored, and haply this word may fall gently upon some borer, and remind him to be merciful, whether he bores by penetrating the house of another or by compelling another to penetrate his house.

Let us resolve that this shall still be a land of liberty, and that even if a man has charmed us with his song, or guided us by his wisdom, or lifted us by his fervor, or has proved himself in any way to be a public benefactor, he shall not be condemned to too severe a penalty. He shall not be sentenced, for instance, to confiscation of all his time, nor stripped wholly of that protection which home secures to other people who are not guilty of public benefits. Undoubtedly a man who makes himself favorably known, and becomes a popular favorite, takes a great risk. But let us have mercy. If we are really grateful to him, if we truly honor him, and would show our regard, let us remember that to rob him of his time is to deprive a captive song-bird of fresh air.

THE press, that vigilant sentinel upon the watch-tower of civil and religious liberty, like Sister Anne upon Blue-beard's turret, descried something wrong in the ceremony of the President's wedding. It whispered audibly that the Reverend Doctor omitted from the service the word "obey," and that the lady therefore became a wife without the vow of obedience to a husband. This incident seriously disturbed certain newspapers whose course for many years has shown their profound concern for the interests of religion, and many excellent persons also have been anxious to know whether, under such circumstances, the wife has been married properly. Indeed, there are said to be some young women who suppose that the vow of obedience is the essential marriage vow—a view in which they are resolutely supported by many very young gentlemen who are not very long emancipated from maternal control.

It may allay these tender apprehensions to know not only that the word obey is often omitted from the marriage ceremony, but that many veiled ladies, in wreaths of orange flowers, insist upon the omission. In fact, to use diplomatic language, the concession of the omission has been known to be held in many

cases to be a preliminary *sine qua non* upon the part of one of the high contracting parties. The word was introduced into the ceremony by men to express and emphasize the view of men that the man is the head of the woman. Indeed, the interested inquirer will find that most of the traditional theories of the relations of the sexes which are often quoted as indisputable and conclusive arguments represent merely the views of men. The laws which regulate these relations—the laws of divorce, of the rights and the control of property, of the disposition and care of children—are the work of men, and simply express their will. More than a quarter of a century ago Mr. Gladstone said the divorce laws in England were a shame to civilization and humanity.

The ladies, therefore, who suppose that these laws and traditions and ceremonial vows rest upon a divine sanction, and who are consequently solicitous to wear the yoke of unquestioning subjugation, not of choice, but as a religious duty, need bend no longer for that reason. If they prefer to obey, indeed, they are not restrained by any religious obligation, nor if they prefer to command. "But," interposes at this point the youthful casuist of the other sex, "surely exigencies of difference arise when there must be a decisive will, and, of course, that will must be the man's." Yes; so men have generally said, and their views have generally prevailed. But the general prevalence of ignorance was not a sound argument against the introduction of general education, and in the republic of reason and matrimony the general assent of husbands cannot conclude the rights of wives.

In a matrimonial difference some one must decide. Granted; and what should determine the decision? Plainly, the right of the case. Now a wife is quite as likely—upon the whole, indeed, more likely—to be right upon a family question than the husband. Still, says the casuist, he must decide, because he is the bread-winner, and because he is the stronger and can enforce his will. Very well; then the reason disappears when the woman is the bread-winner, and in that case it is plainly not as a man that the husband must decide, which ends the merely masculine pretension. The other reason, that he can enforce his will, is applicable to the control of a brute or of a slave, but is it applicable to that of a wife? Moreover, when we speak of right, we do not mean brute force. That one man may be able to knock another man down, or to beat a woman, establishes no right to do so. The casuist must look further if he would justify himself.

In the matrimonial republic, indeed, as in all other communities, undoubtedly force will decide many a difference. It is notorious that the English law—made by men, and interpreted by men—authorized the husband to correct the wife with a stick of reasonable thickness, and upon appeal the judge, who was presumably a husband, decided that reasonable thickness was about the thickness of a thumb. The British usage also permitted the sale of the wife by the husband, a logical deduction from the theory of the right of the husband as founded in strength of muscle. If the wife be bound to obey the husband, certainly the husband is authorized to enforce obedience, and if the contumacy of the wife compels resort to the stick of a thumb's thickness, it may be very painful to Romeo to adjust his relations with Juliet in that emphatic manner, but who can deny the right of the husband to compel the obedience which he has the right to demand?

Does Romeo suppose, perhaps, that if his bride promises to obey, her promise will make the stick unnecessary? The answer to his supposition is printed every day in the police reports. Romeo, if he be a sensible man—and for such men only is this debate opened—will see that all differences between Juliet and himself will be determined, not by her vow of obedience or submission to his will, however unwise or dangerous or criminal his will may be, but by their common good sense. In the happy realm of conjugal affection the stronger nature will rule, however mild and feminine its expression may be, as the moon, "sweet regent of the sky," sways the ocean tides. However that gentle regent may have vowed to follow the whims of the restless sea, and however the raging sea may toss and roar, her vows will be resistlessly forsworn, and all his fury vain, as she moves softly on, and he up every cove and bay runs obediently after.

As the eternal and divine laws assert themselves in the happy realm, Romeo the husband will perceive that marriage vows are not promises to be enforced, but lovers' protestations to be fulfilled. They are very solemn, and of mighty import. They unite two lives for better or worse. But the vow to love, the vow to honor, how shall they be enforced when love has fled and honor is no longer possible? A vow is a form of words, a heart-felt purpose. But has it "a charm to stay the morning-star"? Has it the power to hold a heart to its betrayer, or honor to the dishonored? The downy-bearded casuist, therefore, need not insist ardently that there shall be a vow of obedience as binding his Dulcinea to do what ought not to be done whether he commands it or not. But, on the other hand, the sweet regent "that shall be" need not hesitate to promise to obey, since she gladly promises to love and honor. Obedience is of the will, but love is beyond it. She may obey when she can no longer love, and if she hesitates at all, it should be at the promise which eludes her power to fulfil.

No New-Yorker need longer be ignorant of what a Kirmess actually is, although the exact significance of the word may be unknown to him. It is a kind of open-air fair, or a fair within a hall which properly should be held without it. But whatever the word may precisely mean, and wherever a fair ought to be held, whoever was fortunate enough to see the Kirmess of a month ago on Staten Island and saw a very beautiful and memorable spectacle. Staten Island is a pleasant suburb of the city, whose long slumber was never disturbed until it was suddenly and finally broken by the rapid transit railroad, which abruptly ended all the traditions of the island by superseding both lines of ferry—the old Quarantine ferry, whose establishment reaches back to the time of Governor Tompkins and to the youth of Cornelius Vanderbilt, and the North Shore ferry, which pleasantly skirted the margin of the island along the Kill von Kull.

All this is changed. There is now one ferry, with a boat every half-hour, from the end of the Battery to the nearest point of the island, which has been "made" out into the bay, and the new land bears the new name of St. George, probably of Cappadocia—certainly not of Staten Island; for that island, St. Patrick or St. Nicholas among foreign saints, and St. Base-Ball or St. Buffalo Bill among domestic deities, would seem to be the tutelary genius.—But the rapid transit shall not whirl us away from the Kirmess. Indeed, it whirled many an islander and some ex-islanders from the city to that pretty and pleasant scene on two soft evenings in May.

There is a hall on Staten Island unusually spacious and convenient for a suburb, in which the Kirmess was held. A stage at one end is fitted for concerts and plays, and upon this happy occasion a large space upon the floor in front was corded off from the rest of the hall in which the audience sat. In one corner of the hall, by the stage, was Lander's band, beloved of the flying feet of gay young New York, and when the chairs were full and expectation was eager—even as when "the elephant now goes round, goes round"—the band began to play. Up rose the drop-curtain, and revealed a stage massed with figures in the most brilliant and various costumes, with the stage behind set with decorated and illuminated booths, a booth of flowers, of Japan and its treasures, all felicitously combined in a beautiful effect, as of a peopled scene from the happy islands lying enchanted and far, far away beyond care and weariness, and Wall Street and Buffalo Bill.

The music still sounded as the curtain fell amid the eager applause of the audience, charmed with the suggestive and sparkling prelude, and while the pleased murmur filled the room the music modulated into the marked measure of a national dance, and the prettiest procession of Dutch maidens emerged from the anteroom into the hall within the enclosed space, their heads bending from side to side, and their movement keeping time with the melody of the dance. They were dressed in Dutch costume, and in every variety and degree of quaintness—the staidest of caps, the snuggest of kirtles, and the brightest of ribbons. Many of the costumes were those in which the Dutch belles of an earlier day in New York and upon the banks of the upper Hudson had danced as demurely as their lovely descendants, and captured young hearts that long since grew old, but beat none the less true, and which now for many a year have ceased to beat.

Thus in a soft perspective of tender association the Dutch maidens danced, swayed by the buoyant impulse of the music, interlacing, interlocked, banded and dispersed, now advancing, now retreating, still with the measured fall of accordant feet, a picture, a memory, a poem—or, as Mr. Whistler might say, a characteristic symphony in color and form and motion—until, amid cheers and plaudits, the retiring column of happy youth, sporting coyly in its May and palpitating with its own pleasure, danced gayly off and disappeared.

Meanwhile, as the Dutch maidens entered, the drop-curtain rose, and the stage, with its booths and a few gay groups gracefully disposed, made a most fitting background for the dance. Then upon the floor came the Spaniards, dark-haired, dark-eyed, with dusky veils and beautiful costumes of Basque and Andalusia, with graceful abandon, lithe forms bending low and rising proudly erect, with stately movement stepping to the stately rhythm, marked by the clicking castanet, queenly, disdainful, passionate, fascinating. So might Cleopatra have enchanted Antony and drawn him on to his doom, or Xarifa have arisen, laying her golden cushion down, and with imperial grace and yearning pathos of romantic motion have dared Abdallah to be false. It was a captivating dance; but the Spanish houris vanished too swiftly, like the Dutch maidens, and were followed by the gypsies with tinkling tambourines. The swift and intricate movement of flying figures in glittering costumes was greeted with continual gusts of applause, and as the gypsies disappeared the delighted spectators felt that every successive dance was better than every other.

The Dresden china set was a group of Louis Quinze costumes, of demoiselles in brocade and chevaliers in flowered satin, who, with elaborate artificiality of decorous dignity, loftily bowed and courtesied the minuet, in striking contrast with the breezy rush of the gypsies. The music of the dance from *Don Giovanni* gave a pathos to the scene, which the glances of smiling eyes from under powdered hair did not confirm, and for a moment there was a bewildering glimpse of that old heartless society in which politeness took the place of principle, and reckless and splendid luxury concealed decay. Then while the vision of Dutch maidenhood and Spanish romance and gypsy gayety and the powdered pomp of Versailles still lingered, loath to go, suddenly all vanished in the modern moment and the familiar simple dress of the lawn-tennis players carrying their rackets, and in the mazes

of a dance enclosing their grouped partners in the net. It was the happy end of the spectacle of characteristic dances which for two hours had charmed the eye; but the Kirmess continued in visits to the booths, and traffic in dainty wares, and the waltz and Lancers upon the floor.

The Kirmess is a Dutch festival. But never could Dutch and Spanish and gypsy and French maidens have been fairer, nor all the gay pageant of dances and costumes more brilliant and beautiful, than they were that evening upon Staten Island.

JENKINS appearing in the form of a public benefactor is a very comical figure, and Jenkins posing as a patriotic asserter of the right of the public to inspect the tooth-brushes of public men, and to contemplate the towels upon which they have wiped their hands, and taking the air of a tribune of the people as he reports through the key-hole or from his own nimble invention the remarks of a public man to his secretary or his wife, is one of the most absurd objects conceivable. That the clown should take himself seriously is a jest beyond all the rest. But this is what Jenkins has recently done with an earnestness that is ludicrous.

The marriage of an eminent man who occupies a conspicuous public position is an essentially private event. But his official dignity gives to it a certain degree of public interest, so that if he be a President of the United States, the Queen of England and other official personages and authorities naturally send to him respectful messages of congratulation. His fellow-citizens hear with universal interest of the contemplated event, and wish him well, and when the marriage occurs it is an occasion which is noted with pleasure. But official position does not authorize impertinent scrutiny of private life, and an American citizen does not lose the right of privacy because he is called to the discharge of certain public duties.

This is an elementary axiom which Jenkins regards very much as certain politicians regard what they call Sunday-school politics. Jenkins disdainfully pities those who suppose that public men are not at every moment and in every relation the lawful prey of morbid curiosity. He holds that when a man has voted for a public officer who has been elected, he has a right to know how often the officer's boots are blacked, and with what blacking, and whether the blacking is sold to him at higher or lower rates because of his official position. If such an official declines to admit Jenkins to see him wash his hands or brush his teeth, Jenkins, as a vigilant guardian of public liberty, will denounce him to the country as a peacock and an upstart, an aristocrat and enemy of the people, a dude of Anglomaniac tendencies, and an assassin of free institutions.

But when it is surmised that such an officer

is to be married, Jenkins, so to speak, appears in arms all along the line. From that moment nothing that he can ascertain or invent concerning the lady shall be withheld from exposure to the public in Jenkins's most glowing style. Her appearance, her manner, her dress, her conversation, shall all be described in the utmost detail, and with all luxuriance of fancy and falsehood that Jenkins can command. The trousseau, the wedding dress, her favorite dishes at table, anecdotes of her school years, the number of dresses and the size of her shoes, shall all be mingled, as it were, in a savory mess, and served by *Chef* Jenkins, piping hot and spiced to the utmost for Jenkins's palpitating public. This shall be done day after day, and at endless length and in elaborate detail. It shall be seasoned also with insinuations and gibes and mock compliments and congratulations, for Jenkins has the soul of a true valet; and the performance shall not stop with the wedding. By no means; Jenkins hopes that he understands his business better than that.

If during this tremendous bombardment of impertinence, against which a gentleman, being a public man, has really no defence, except in the instincts of other gentlemen, a suspicion crosses the mind of Jenkins that the whole business is base and contemptible and inexcusable, he is quite equal to the occasion. With a fine air he exclaims: "Why does the public man try to make a mystery of this thing? Does he acknowledge no duty to the country? to himself? above all, to the lady? Jenkins 1st declares that it is Miss Dobb; Jenkins 2d insists that it is Mrs. Cobb; Jenkins 3d telegraphs from Timbuctoo that the whole story is false, and that no marriage is contem-

plated. What has the gentleman most concerned to say? Has any man in any position a right thus to trifle with the anxiety of a whole country? Honorable consideration for ladies demands that this suspicious and outrageous reticence shall end. The conduct of the public officer is unpardonable. He has himself only to blame if the most injurious construction is placed upon all the circumstances." Jenkins then resumes his daily volley of twaddle, and informs us, what we all know to be untrue, that the American people are profoundly agitated by the event, and desire, before all things, to know whether the lady takes strawberries with sugar, or with cream, or both, or without either.

But he is not content with the sloppy pen; he takes to the dirty pencil, and degrades the American press with the coarsest and most vulgar cuts. The newspaper which could be guilty of issuing some of the pictures which were recently published under pretence of gratifying public interest in a marriage deserves the scorn of every honorable man and woman. The mighty press, fed by Jenkins with daily columns of the lowest kitchen ribaldry, and "illustrated" with shameful pictures, is a national disgrace. If there be really a demand for such things, it is only among a kind of people to which no decent paper appeals, and if money is actually made by pandering to their tastes, it is money as deeply tainted as the booty of a pirate or any other wages of sin.

Jenkins has been hitherto a mere snob and clown and booby. But he has shown signs recently both of malignant and contemptible knavery. Let him return to his proper function of admiring valet.

Editor's Study.

I.

ONE of the minor regrets which the observer of contemporary literature must feel in view of the fact that he will probably not be alive a hundred years hence is that he cannot know what is to become of all the estimable books which the press is now pouring out. If he is himself an author, he knows that his own books must at least perish in the second glacial epoch; and he cannot help the foreboding that much besides which is excellent and much which is beautiful will be lost before that time in the mere excess of beauty and excellence. The greatest excellence and the greatest beauty are still perhaps as rare as in the past, but we think that the literary average is in some ways higher than ever it was. More honest and faithful and skilful work is done, and more of it. The penetrating spirit of democracy has found its expression in the very quality of literature; the old oligarchic

republic of letters is passing; already we have glimpses of the Commune. If the reader has noted the optimistic tone of these essays he will conceive that we are not wholly dismayed at the prospect, and that we find a consolation in recognizing what seems good now, when the difficult business of forecasting its future perplexes and saddens. Our chief concern is that we cannot recognize all the good there is in all the books that come to us; but if the public will keep our secret, we will confess that we believe this will have very little to do with their destiny. The fittest, in literature as in everything else, will survive, as it has always done; and for all our confident air in saying this is well and that is ill, we understand perfectly that we are not dealing final doom. We are saying what our experience of literature and of life has persuaded us is the truth; but these books are also the expression of literature and of life, and we will confess again, if again the public will keep our secret, that sometimes the crudest expression in that sort seems better than the finest comment upon it. We have sometimes suspected that more thinking, more feeling certainly, goes to the creation of a poor novel than to the production of a brilliant criticism; and if any novel of our time fails to live a hundred years, will any censure of it live? Who can endure to read old reviews? One can hardly read them if they are in praise of one's own books. It is not, then, with a wholly impersonal pang, dearly beloved brother immortals, that we sit here in our Study sorrowfully regarding your multitude, and misgiving which of you shall survive. You cannot all, that is certain; and more and more pensively we perceive that it is not absolutely for us to say which; but to use what patience we may if the poets, the historians, the novelists, the essayists, are not able to keep their number within bounds. It is vain, at any rate, to preach Malthusianism to them, and we willingly relinquish to the reader the problem of their future, if, as seems very likely, they should multiply rather than decrease. It is already quite impossible to do more than touch contemporary literature at a few points, to speak of what seems characteristic, or what seems promising; but the author neglected or overlooked need not despair for that reason, if he will reflect that criticism can neither make nor unmake authors; that there have not been greater books since criticism became an art than there were before; that in fact the greatest books seem to have come much earlier.

II.

That which criticism seems most certainly to have done is to have put a literary consciousness into books unfelt in the early masterpieces, but unfelt now only in the books of men whose lives have been passed in activities, who have been used to employing language as they would have employed any implement, to effect an object, who have regarded a thing to be said as in no wise different from a thing to be done. In this sort we have seen no modern book so unconscious as *General Grant's Personal Memoirs*, which is now complete in its second volume. We have already spoken of the first volume, and of the simplicity which distinguished it. The same unimpassioned, singular directness characterizes the story to its end. The author's one end and aim is to get the facts out in words. He does not cast about for phrases, but takes the word, whatever it is, that will best give his meaning, as if it were a man or a force of men for the accomplishment of a feat of arms. There is not a moment wasted in preening and prettifying, after the fashion of literary men; there is no thought of style, and so the style is good as it is in the Book of Chronicles, as it is in the *Pilgrim's Progress*, or in a novel of De Foe's, with a peculiar, almost plebeian, plainness at times. There is no more attempt at dramatic effect than there is at ceremonious pose; things happen in that tale of a mighty

war as they happened in the mighty war itself, without setting, without artificial reliefs, one after another, as if they were all of one quality and degree. Judgments are delivered with the same unimposing quiet; no awe surrounds the tribunal except that which comes from the weight and justice of the opinions; it is always an unaffected, unpretentious man who is talking; and throughout he prefers to wear the uniform of a private, with nothing of the general about him but the shoulder-straps, which he sometimes forgets.

We have heard a great deal about what the American was to be in literature when he once got there. What if this were he—this good form without formality, this inner dignity, this straightforward arrival, this mid-day clearness? We find much of these qualities in the two large volumes of Lieutenant Greely's *Three Years of Arctic Service;* so much that we are not sure but West Point might be a good training school for our literati, as it has certainly been for our soldiers. The annual appointment of a literary cadet from each Congressional district would probably give us a permanent body of writers whom we could draw upon for all departments, with a reasonable assurance that they had been rigidly trained to express themselves with distinctness and sincerity; and this our present happy-go-lucky fashion of getting our literary men hardly does. The idea is one which must not be pressed too far, or suffered to interfere with a more serious expression of the respect we feel for Lieutenant Greely's telling of his wonderful story; but still we think there must be something due to the high and wholesome discipline of two men, alike in little else in their past, when they come to the same effect in their reader's mind. The effect is all the more noticeable because the method of the books is so different. Lieutenant Greely's story is not a continuous, full narrative, told without stopping, as it were, from memory. Some day, we hope, he will give us this, or something like it in unity and compactness; but for the present we have a mass of details, patched and pieced together from various diaries, with loose threads of statement, and weighted with facts of scientific interest only, from which, however, the heroic experience of that three years' service disentangles itself in the retrospect, and remains an impression as clear as that given by Grant's unbroken memories of the war. We do not know why this should be unless it is from the same habit, inbred in both writers, of looking to one end only—the presentation of the facts without regard to the effects. In this way their work has the advantage over literary writing that scientific writing must always have: they are both possessed of their subject rather than possessed of their manner.

It is not strange that Lieutenant Greely's narrative should have the fascination it has; a potent charm always invests the experience of a life or a group of lives isolated from all others, and striving to be self-sufficient in circumstances that forbid hope or help from without. When the exploring party are settled for the first winter at Fort Conger, one feels a sort of pleasure in their snug security, with their forays into the realms of cold and night, a sense of cosiness expanding into sympathetic rapture when the brief arctic summer drops suddenly upon them, and fills the air with birds, and floods the waste with blooming grasses and wild flowers. We think Lieutenant Greely, more than any former explorer, realizes to the reader this brief flush of glowing and throbbing vitality in regions which the fancy had delivered over to perpetual death and "ever-during dark"; but he uses no rhetoric upon it, and it becomes of itself a tragic light and color in the background when the retreat begins, when the pleasant safety and plenty of Fort Conger are abandoned for the struggle southward through the freezing wilderness to the famine and despair of Cape Sabine. It is in this part of the story that the observer interested to know how simply great things happen, how hunger, cold, and death are really met by the human weakness and the human will confronted with them, will find the greatest instruction. It is not all one uninterrupted course toward the catastrophe, spectacular, with an exterior of impressive dramatic unity; it is relieved by little respites, by little reversions of prosperity; even at the worst, hope remains, and character and discipline persist. The gay young fellow who lies dying in the arms of his comrade, far from the wretched camp, in the midst of an arctic storm, keeps up his American habit of joking to his last breath; certain men are helpful to the rest as naturally and unconsciously as women in a sick-room; there is weakness and selfishness of the sort we find everywhere; the "villain" is as absent as the "hero," but there is a starving thief who is found stealing the portions of his companions, and will not stop; he is sentenced, and two dying men put him to death, in a perfectly business-like way. All goes on orderly, and with a ghastly conformity to the life-long usages and habits. The hunters kill a little game, and the doom is stayed a while. They catch shrimps and live on them till their bait fails; then they live on boiled lichens, and the cripple who has lost both his hands and feet by freezing is quite cheerful when one of the others ties the spoon to the stump of his wrist, so that he can help himself to the stew of lichens and seal-skin. At last the seven men left out of twenty-five lie pinned to the ground in their sleeping-bags, under their fallen tent, waiting for death, when rescue comes instead. We need not recite the points of the story so well known; and for a full sense of what that tremendous passage of human experience was we must send the reader to the book itself.

What chiefly strikes one in it is that everything seems like everything else; that neither this thing nor that has projection or relief. Given the conditions, the events seem to proceed naturally and in a proper sequence. It seems in keeping with all the rest that the welcome home of the leader of the expedition should have been imbittered by calumny, and that the soldiers who suffered with him should still be the objects of private charity, disabled for life, their allowances for arctic service unpaid, and their pensions not awarded.

III.

Upon the whole, the effect is something like the effect studied in the best modern novels; only the reality takes all the color out of realism, and we should be doing injustice to the most vivid invention if we placed it beside such experience. The reader will therefore kindly suppose a considerable interval of time and space between the consideration of Lieutenant Greely's history of *Three Years of Arctic Service* and Miss Woolson's story of *East Angels*, though, after all, if he likes to bathe his fancy immediately in the warm air and tepid sea of the Florida coast, there are reasons why he may do so without prejudice to the first great romance of that region. He will find himself in a peculiar atmosphere, very faithfully and perfectly rendered, and amidst interesting groups of the sex necessarily excluded from arctic adventure; and that will be certainly a pleasure if not wholly an advantage. Of the ladies of East Angels several are freshly and singularly charming, whom the reader will like if he is a man, and there is at least one very heroic, whom she may adore if she is a woman. Margaret Harold, martyr-wife of that chief of scapegraces Lansing Harold, is a figure that ought to console such of her sex as have heart-hungered for grand and perfect women in fiction perhaps ever since George Eliot drew Romola. She not only dedicates her life to the invalided age of the unloved husband who has insulted her by the precept as well as the example of gross indifference, she not only very rightly drives from her the man she loves, but she proposes to the young widow who jilted him that she shall try to get him back and marry him, and promises that their children shall be a consolation to her. If this is not enough for the worshippers of grand and perfect women, we cannot imagine what they want more.

For ourselves we will confess that it is too much, and that we are better satisfied with the man who guesses this plan for his consolation, and finds it revolting, though he is too much in love with Margaret Harold to feel its absurdity. It was perhaps the supposed necessity of keeping the chief person exemplary and sublime which caused the error. Neither Margaret nor Winthrop her lover appeals to our sympathy, perhaps because we cannot believe in them; they form for us the one false note of the book. The other people, men and women, are all better, and they are for the most part, in mood and motive, like people one meets. The least important figure among them is sketched with a feeling for character which leaves it distinct and memorable. Many of the studies in this sort have an uncommon value, like Mrs. Thorne, the poor little lady who supposed she had lived English and Southern, but who perceives in dying that she has always been immutably New England and Northern. There is a delicate pathos in the treatment of her character which moves the heart, and is the right complement of the delicate humor which differentiates the comic points of the two young Spaniards, Ernesto de Torres and Manuel Ruiz, without caricaturing either of them, and depicts the intellectual commonplace of the Rev. Mr. Moore while divining his rare and exalted goodness. A purely artistic temperament like Lucian Spenser is caught as unerringly as if by some instantaneous process, and a big, dull girl, like Rosalie Bogardus, even more difficult to catch, is given again to the reader with none of her compensating traits and qualities forgotten. We speak of these minor persons in the book because it is in the excellence of all the minor persons that the charming mastery of the author is shown. She cannot do an injustice, and this keeps her faithful and patient with Garda Thorne, and will not suffer her to make that light, chameleon nature merely typical of a race or a latitude, but exacts in it the representation of a distinct, individual life, which has nothing of flirtation's badness, and, slight as it is, wishes to be generous, and is sincere. Garda is a masterpiece, and the triumph of the book. For our own selfish pleasure we prefer a novel where there is less going and coming, and there are fewer people, and the webs of so many different lives are not intertangled. Yet we are obliged to own that the small isolated group is less life-like, and that if Miss Woolson can paint a multitude of figures so well, that is a sufficient reason for her introducing them. The story is full of delightful moments, of interesting moments, and there are great moments in it. But, above all, there is, except in the heroine, the respect for probability, the fidelity to conditions, human and social, which can alone justify the reading or writing of novels; there is the artistic conscience, and the other conscience without which art is merely pernicious.

Both kinds of conscience are felt also in *Constance of Acadia*, a romance which an unknown hand gives us. Whether it is an unpractised hand we are not so sure, nor whether it is the hand of a man or of a woman; but this does not matter if it is apt and true. The story is that of Constance, the Huguenot wife of Charles la Tour, Governor of Acadia under Louis XIII. He is Huguenot too, but primarily ambitious trader and wily politician; and by her help holds his own against his father, coming from the English to take his fort from him, and against Charnacé, who comes from the Jesuits with designs upon both his fort and his wife; for Charnacé, who has not completed his ecclesiastical vows, loved Constance in La Rochelle long before, and has not ceased to love her. Acadia, apparently, is not only inexhaustible in romance, but it has a history that blends so happily with its romance that in this writer's hands it is all one web, and the less-learned reader will do well not to attempt to say which is which. What strikes one no less than the poetic beauty of the book is this mastery of the historical situation. The thoroughness with which the author has assimilated the facts of that remote time and scene is of the same effect in his art as close observation of contemporary life would be, and there is a comfortable reality in the people very uncommon in historical fiction. The La Tours, father and son, are admirably of their time, and Charnacé, wavering between passion and devotion, and now man and now Jesuit, is a peculiarly seventeenth-century personage. Some passages, fundamentally historical, lift the curtain upon the Boston and the Boston traits of that day, and there is a very pleasant humor mixed with the more heroic strain of the book. This strain is single only in the character of Constance, which is yet so well managed that it does not lose in probability or lovableness. The figures are not always distinctly outlined; and withdrawn so far into the past, the action has a dimness except in certain details upon which the light is strongly thrown. Yet within the vague you are somehow assured of a veritable human life, and we welcome in the book a fresh and brilliant achievement in a sort that has long seemed obsolescent, if not obsolete. It is a pleasure to come upon good work in any direction, and if the direction of the historical romance is one which fiction seems not likely to explore again very extensively, still we must admire the success of an occasional daring foray like this. We do not know that we should altogether regret it if this were the precursor of adventure by other and lesser talents. Perhaps the whole region of historical romance might be reopened with advantage to readers and writers who cannot bear to be brought face to face with human nature, but require a mist of distance or a far perspective, in which all the disagreeable details shall be lost. There is no good reason why these harmless people should not be amused, or their little preferences indulged. In the mean time we can praise *Constance of Acadia* as a beautiful and touching story.

IV.

Mr. H. H. Boyesen's *Story of Norway* reads like another historical romance, so picturesque and poetic is the wild past of the land of fiords and mountains. We do not know that it would have been possible to treat it in the modern spirit which presents historical events as illustrations of conditions, and gives greater prominence to peoples than to heroes; but it is certain that the author has not chosen to do this. He has, however, supplied such abundant material that the reader can philosophize the facts for himself, and arrive at the solution of all the problems involved. They are not very intricate, for the story is that of a rude race living in almost incomparable degree in an imagination stormily sublime and grotesque, and striving to realize their tremendous dreams in their deeds. They had an ideal of valor, of endurance, of power, which Mr. Boyesen lets declare itself in that texture of record and legend forming his story. This is the poet's way, and Mr. Boyesen is first of all a poet, and delights in the feats he recounts as if he had invented them. His book is the prose epic of his race—a race so passionately enamored of individual liberty that it could not fail in time to submit itself to law for the sake of freedom to all, and in this way emerge from war and barbarism into peace and civilization. Mr. Boyesen does not fail to claim as a final expression of this once turbulent and always mighty passion of the Norsemen the glory of constitutional freedom in England and America; and we do not know that the claim can be altogether denied: our German kindred have never known freedom or unity at home, and, as he points out, they exist nationally now only as a great military despotism.

A very interesting inquiry into the operation of the political instinct in the Anglo-Saxon race, wherever that instinct comes from, is to be found in Professor Josiah Royce's *History of California*, in Mr. Scudder's "American Commonwealth Series." His method is so exactly opposite that of Mr. Boyesen that we could almost wish it were less so. It seems to us that the early life of California could have been advantageously painted to the exclusion of great part of that painfully traced coil of intrigue and violence by which, to be sure, Spanish California came to be American, but which the reader follows with difficulty and impatience, feeling that it could all be much more briefly and distinctly told. No doubt it helps to give effect to the spectacle of the rise of a civilized state from conditions of as rascally barbarism as an educated race could well lapse into; but the absence of background is felt throughout till we come to the story of the great Vigilance Committee, which marked a final phase in the evolution of order. Professor Royce frankly calls his volume a study of American character, and doubtless did not feel at all bound to present a dramatic synthesis. This final passage, however, as compared with the rest of the book, illustrates the difference between history and a historical study, and the vastly greater advantage of the former to the reader. It is a beautifully compact, vigorous, and effective piece of writing, and embodies the action and its significance in thoroughly vivid form. There is, indeed, hardly a page of the book which is not illuminated by shrewd and just thinking; and there is always frank courage of statement and characterization. It is the story of a community clothing itself anew in civilization and decency, after a debauch of disorder. The reader never fails of the author's intention, and if he feels that he is made too much a partner in the enterprise, as a French critic acutely said of the poetry of Mr. Walt Whitman, that is at least a tribute to his intelligence. In a fair half of the volume, from where the study of " The Struggle for Order" begins, to the end, his complicity is not invoked, and the volume closes with a passage or two which are as characteristic of the author as they are true:

" The race that has since grown up in California, as the outcome of these early struggles, is characterized by very marked qualities of strength and weakness, some of which, perchance, even a native Californian like the author, who neither can nor would outgrow his healthy local traits, may still be able to note and confess. A general sense of social irresponsibility is, even to-day, the average Californian's easiest failing. Like his father, he is probably a born wanderer, who will feel as restless in his farm life, or in his own town, as his father felt in his. He will have little or no sense of social or of material barriers, he will perchance hunt for himself a new home somewhere else in the world, or in the old home will long for some speculative business that promises easy wealth, or, again, on the other hand, he will undertake some great material labor that attracts him by its imposing difficulty. His training at home gives him a curious union of provincial prejudice with a varied if not very exact knowledge of the sorts of things that there are in the world. For his surroundings from infancy have been in one sense of a cosmopolitan character, while much of his training has been rigidly or even narrowly American. He is apt to lack a little, moreover, complete devotion to the life within the household, because, as people so often have pointed out, the fireside, an essential institution of our English race, is of such small significance in the climate of California. In short, the Californian has too often come to love mere fulness of life, and to lack reverence for the relations of life.

" And yet, as we have seen, the whole lesson of his early history, rightly read, is a lesson in reverence for the relations of life. It was by despising, or at least by forgetting them, that the early community entered into the valley of the shadow of death; and there was salvation for the community in those days only by virtue of its final and hard-learned submission to what it had despised and forgotten. This lesson, I confess, has come home to me personally, as I have studied this early history, with a quite unexpected force. I had always thought of the old days as times of fine and rough labors, amusements, and crimes, but not as a very rational historical process. I have learned, as I have toiled for a while over the sources, to see in these days a process of divinely moral significance. And, as a Californian, I am glad to be able to suggest what I have found, plain and simple as it is, to any fellow-Californian who may perchance note in himself the faults of which I make confession. Here in the early history are these faults, writ large, with their penalties, and the only possible salvation from them.

"After all, however, our lesson is an old and simple one. It is the State, the Social Order, that is divine. We are all but dust, save as this social order gives us life. When we think it our instrument, our plaything, and make our private fortunes the one object, then this social order rapidly becomes vile to us; we call it sordid, degraded, corrupt, unspiritual, and ask how we may escape from it forever. But if we turn again and serve the social order, and not merely ourselves, we soon find that what we are serving is simply our own highest spiritual destiny in bodily form. It is never truly sordid or corrupt or unspiritual; it is only we that are so when we neglect our duty."

Here, it seems to us, are not only right feeling and plain speaking, but thinking of a sort which is likely to invite the reader to do some thinking of his own. There is a ring of earnestness unafraid and unashamed in it all, which is the key-note of the best modern writing in all kinds, and which, more than anything else, characterizes the real literary endeavor of an epoch serious, sympathetic, and conscientious beyond those that have gone before it.

Monthly Record of Current Events.

POLITICAL.

OUR Record is closed on the 18th of June.— The following are the most important matters of business transacted by Congress: Both Houses passed the Shipping Bill, with the Frye amendment empowering the President to deny to the vessels of other nations such privileges as they deny to ours.— The Senate, May 19, by a vote of 34 to 14, passed the Pension Bill, so amended as to provide that "no pension paid under any law to any soldier, sailor, or marine hereafter shall be rated at less than $4 a month," and to cover men who served only three months.—The Senate, May 20, and the House, June 7, passed the Arthur Kill Bridge Bill. The House, the same day, by a vote of 178 nays to 80 yeas, defeated the $800,000 mail subsidy.—The Senate, June 4, passed the Chinese Indemnity Bill by a vote of 31 to 9.—The bill taxing oleomargarine five cents per pound passed the House June 3, by 177 to 101.—The House, June 7, by a vote of 183 to 40, passed a bill repealing the preëmption, timber culture, and desert land laws, and so modifying the homestead law that the settler is not entitled to a patent until thirty months after the filing of his claim, and six months after the presentation of proof of settlement and cultivation.—The Tariff Bill was defeated in the House June 17, on a call for the yeas and nays on a motion to consider.

The Hon. Nelson Aldrich was reëlected United States Senator from Rhode Island June 9.

President Grover Cleveland was married at the White House June 2, to Miss Frances Folsom. Owing to the recent death of the grandfather of the bride the wedding was a quiet one, only near relatives and the members of the cabinet and their wives being invited. The ceremony was performed by the Rev. Dr. Sunderland, of the First Presbyterian Church of Washington, D. C. Queen Victoria sent the following cable message to the President·

"Pray accept my sincere congratulations on your marriage, and my best wishes for your happiness."

The following nominations for Governors have been made by State Conventions: New Jersey Prohibition, May 28, General Clinton B. Fisk; Maine Democratic, June 2, Colonel C. S. Edwards; Maine Republican, June 9, Hon. J. R. Bodwell; Alabama Democratic, June 11, Thomas Seay; Vermont Republican, June 16, E. J. Ormsbee.

The Oregon State election, June 7, resulted in a Democratic victory, with a majority for Governor of about 1800.

The New York State Legislature adjourned *sine die* May 20.

The official report of the Minister of Militia, presented to the Canadian Parliament May 21, shows that the total cost of the half-breed rebellion was $4,700,000, and the casualties 26 men killed and 206 wounded.

In the British House of Commons, May 19, the bill providing for the election by ballot of the Poor-law Guardians in Ireland passed its second reading by a vote of 207 to 105.—In the House of Commons, May 28, the Arms Bill passed its third reading by a vote of 156 to 65. The House of Lords, May 24, by a vote of 149 to 127, rejected the second reading of the bill legalizing marriage with a deceased wife's sister. The Prince of Wales supported the bill. The Duke of Connaught, who was in favor of the bill, paired. Nineteen bishops voted with the majority.

Mr. Gladstone's Home Rule Bill was defeated in the House of Commons June 8, by a majority of 30. The vote was 311 to 341. Of those voting against the bill 94 were Liberals.

General Caceres took his seat as President of Peru June 3.

M. Tricoupis, May 21, formed a new Greek ministry. He assumed provisionally the offices of Minister of War and Minister of Finance.

The French Chamber of Deputies, June 11, passed the government's bill prohibiting the chief pretender of the families which formerly reigned in France from remaining within the country, under a penalty of five years' imprisonment.

Ludwig II., the deposed King of Bavaria, committed suicide June 13, by drowning himself in Lake Starnberg, near Berg Castle, whither he had been taken. Dr. Gudden, his attendant physician, lost his life, it is supposed, in trying to prevent his patient from committing the rash act. Both bodies were recovered.

DISASTERS.

May 27.—Austrian ship *Miroslav*, from Philadelphia February 17, with twenty men, given up for lost.

May 31.—News of the loss of the steamer *Lyeemoon*, from Melbourne for Sydney, with seventy persons on board.

June 2.—News of almost complete destruction by fire of town of Akita, Japan, early in May. Over three thousand houses burned.

OBITUARY.

May 17.—In London, England, Lord Farnborough, Sir Thomas Erskine May, Clerk of the House of Commons since 1871, aged seventy-one years.

May 19.—In New York, Arthur Quartley, marine painter, aged forty-seven years.

May 21.—In Yonkers, New York, Dr. Dio Lewis, hygiene reformer, aged sixty-three years.—In Albany, New York, Hon. Samuel Hand, ex-Judge of the Court of Appeals, aged fifty-two years.

May 22.—In Lebanon, Ohio, General Durbin Ward, aged sixty-seven years.

May 23.—In Berlin, Germany, Leopold von Ranke, historian, aged ninety-one years.

May 28.—In Providence, Rhode Island, John Russell Bartlett, ex-Secretary of State for Rhode Island, aged eighty-one years.

June 1.—In New York city, Hon. John Kelly, aged sixty-four years.

June 6.—In Lancaster, Pennsylvania, Rev. John W. Nevin, D.D., LL.D., for many years President of Franklin and Marshall College, aged eighty-three years.

June 7.—In Florence, Italy, Richard M. Hoe, aged seventy-four years.

June 10.—In Fordham, New York, Robert Barry Coffin ("Barry Gray"), author, aged sixty years.

June 16.—In Boston, Massachusetts, Edwin Percy Whipple, author, aged sixty-seven years.

Editor's Drawer.

IS truth better than fiction; that is, better for ordinary purposes? Is Julius Cæsar any more real to us than Ulysses, or would he be any less to us if he and his deeds were simply creations like Ulysses and Hamlet? Mr. Froude says he has many times puzzled himself to sleep with Kant's question whether to have had a being subject to space and time is a necessary condition of existence. To pursue this suggestion, we may say that we are sure of the characters of Hamlet and Ulysses, but how do we know that the real Julius Cæsar was like the conception of him that remains in the world through the medium of human testimony and tradition? Was Zachary Taylor the rough-and-ready, plantation-mannered, rather illiterate person who went through the campaign of 1848 so triumphantly in a popular belief in his uncultivated, homespun qualities? Who created the General Jackson, the "Old Hickory," of the popular imagination—the blunt, uncivil, swearing Executive? Was it Major Jack Downing and the gentlemen of the press of the period who supplied the public with a hero to their liking? The real General Jackson was one of the most courtly men of his time, and a devout man besides; it is the testimony of Mr. Bancroft, whose recollection goes back to President Jackson and his cabinet, that he never swore—that he never used that expletive, so dear to his worshippers, "By the Eternal!" How near to the real persons is the popular conception of most of our public men? The present cabinet has a newspaper existence which seems to satisfy the public just as well as the real qualities and personalities of its members.

This question of Kant is revived in the circumstances attending the marriage of the President. It seems to have been the theory of the President that, while he is a public man, he has a private life and feelings, sentiments and experiences, like other men, which he is not bound to make public as he does executive acts and his political views in messages and vetoes; that his privacy ought to be respected. This weak theory, of course, could not stand against the well-defined modern idea that no man has any private affairs that ought to be respected, and that he justly falls under suspicion if he shuts his mouth or his bedroom door against any inquisition. When, therefore, the President refused to take the public into his confidence about his intended marriage, and it was suspected that he had been for months living a life of duplicity toward the reporters of personalities, the newspapers were obliged to take steps commensurate to the emergency. It is not to be supposed that there is anything that the newspapers do not know or cannot find out, and it will not do for them to disappoint the public of full details of all matters in which it has any curiosity. And it can be boasted that the newspapers were equal to the occasion. Probably there never was a marriage whose antecedent circumstances and collateral relations were so freely and graphically reported. No ingenuity has been spared to fill the public ear with the minutest and most trivial details concerning it and everybody who had the remotest connection with the parties to it. That the facts in the case were not forth-coming was not the fault of the newspapers, and that the public have been served from day to day with details of the progress of the affair is one of the most marvellous achievements of modern journalism.

There is a disposition in some quarters to reproach the newspapers for the course they have taken. This arises from a misapprehension of the philosophic system of the reporters. They are humble disciples of the idea of Kant, and they act upon their belief that time and space are subjective, forms imposed upon existence by the human understanding. They have been true to this large-minded cosmic notion. The fault has been in the application of their theory, in the want of unity and agreement among themselves, and this has resulted in a sort of confusion, so that the future historian may accuse them of the error of "obscurantism," and they will not know how to defend themselves. Any one must acknowledge that, failing the real person, there should have been only one created image of Miss Folsom presented to the public mind, whereas there were a dozen. Admitting the public right to be told what constituted the breakfast of the bride-elect the morning after her landing, it is perplexing to read in one account of that meal that she took coffee, in another that she took tea, in another that she took chocolate, and in another that she allowed all those exciting things, and simply sipped a glass of milk while opening half a bushel of letters and telegrams. Brethren and sisters! this is bungling work. It might have been mended by a little consultation in the lobby. Again, did the President on that fateful morning eat his breakfast on the railway car, and put red pepper on his eggs, as one of the Kant men said, or did he breakfast at the White House, as another, just as well informed, asserts, or did he eat two breakfasts that day? These varying statements do not at all affect this system of making history, but they show that its practice is very imperfect. Our public is not a difficult one. Demanding news, it is satisfied with almost anything, but its capacity and credulity ought not to be overstrained.

GREENMOUNT CEMETERY, Baltimore, has an oddity in the tombstone line which would be hard to equal on the score of evidently unconscious grotesqueness. In a centrally located lot are to be found three simple stones. On the first of these, in addition to the usual inscription for a deceased wife, has been chiselled an index hand. It points diagonally downward toward the base of the central stone, and surmounts the information

" *Hier ruht mein Mann*" (Here rests my husband).

The third stone, to the memory of a second wife, differs from the first in the mere matter of detail; a similar hand points downward to the same interior spot, and beneath it runs an inscription equally laconic:

" *Mein ist er auch*" (He is mine too).

The climax of absurdity, however, is reserved for the middle stone, where crossed hands point serenely to the two outlying mounds, and beneath it the husband informs the curious:

" *Diese beiden sind mein*" (These two are mine).

The fact that said husband is still a resident of Baltimore, with many years, in all probability, between himself and this final resting-place, does not detract appreciably from the humor which invests the whole arrangement.

THESE lines, written upon the tombstone of Margaret Scott, who died at Dalkeith, Scotland, April 9, 1738, will be new to many readers:

Stop, courteous passenger, till thou hast read:
The living may gain knowledge by the dead.
Five times five years I lived a virgin's life.
Ten times five years I lived a virtuous wife.
Ten times five years I wept a widow's woes.
Now, tired of mortal life, I here repose.
Eight mighty kings of Scotland and one queen
I 'twixt my cradle and my grave have seen.
Four times five years the Commonwealth I saw;
Ten times the subjects rise against the law;
Twice have I seen old Prelacy pulled down,
And twice the cloak was humbled by the gown;
I saw my country sold for English ore;
And Stuart race destroyed to rise no more.
Such desolations in my time have been,
I have an end of all perfection seen.

IT was a banker in Pennsylvania, who never made or saw a joke, aged seventy (no doubt he was as bright as the other "four-year-olds" who write to the Drawer), that came in one day from dinner and began to tell the cashier about seeing a man arrested in front of a store for stealing a pair of pantaloons. He drawled the narrative along in his hesitating way for an hour, till the cashier was exhausted, when the book-keeper, having overheard the thrilling tale, poked his head in at the door and asked:

"What did they do with him?"

"They arrested him, of course."

"But can they do anything to him?"

"Certainly; bring suit against him."

"Oh, they can? I didn't know they could make a suit out of a pair of pants."

And the good old banker never knew that anything had happened.

À propos de bottes, and of some recent discussion of the nude in art, is a remark heard in North Carolina last Christmas. A card of the Venus de Milo having been brought for a Christmas gift, and having, after much discussion, been appropriately placed, the family assembled to admire. Among them was the darky servant, who, after testifying her approbation, turned suddenly to her mistress to ask, with an expression of earnest curiosity, "Is that the fashion now—no arms and no clo's?"

EPITAPH.

HERE does the body of Mary Anne rest,
With her head on Abraham's breast.
It's a very good thing for Mary Anne,
But it's very hard lines on Abraham.

THE following bayou version of one of the negro folk-lore stories is translated by a lady on Petite Anse Island, Louisiana:

"TROUBLE, BRUDDER ALLIGATOR, TROUBLE!"

Laws-a-massy! honey, mammy beleebs she 'mos' dun forgit dat story hersef. Lemme see. Yer know de rabbit is jes de mischeevusest critter in de woods, an' is a-fureber gittin hissef inter trouble. Well, he used ter be mighty fond of playin' Mr. Alligator; so one day he went down ter de bayou ter hab some fun wid dat 'spectable ole gemman; but he was takin' a nap in his hole; so Mr. Rabbit he sot ter work foolin' de crabs by stickin' his yurs in de water an' makin' de crabs b'leeb dey was beef meat. Well, terrectly he got tired ob dat sorter play, an' turned roun' fer ter go home, but all de marsh was on fire! Some folks had comed out ter hunt Mr. Deer, an' sot de marsh on fire to run him out. Well, sir, Mr. Rabbit was 'mos' skeert out ob his wits, an' he jes hollered, "Trouble, Brudder Alligator, trouble!" an' kep' a-hollerin' it till Mr. Alligator comed out ob his hole ter see what was de matter. Den Mr. Rabbit he say, "Brudder Alligator, ef yer will jes take me on yer back an' cross me ober de bayou so de fire won't ketch me, I'll thank yer as long as I lib, an' all my family 'll thank yer too, an' I'll neber scratch no mo' ob yer eggs out ob yer nes'."

"Oh no," sez Mr. Alligator; "I don't do nuffin like dat widout pay."

Mr. Rabbit he say, "All right, den; you tote me ober, an' I'll send you my great-grandmudder fur yer breakfuss to-morrow mornin'."

Mr. Alligator he fought dat was mighty slim rations, but he knowed he could make Mr. Rabbit promise more as soon as he got him in de bayou, so he tole Mr. Rabbit ter git on his back; but when he got in de middle ob de bayou he commence a-gwine under, an' Mr. Rabbit he hollered:

"Oh, trouble, Brudder Alligator, trouble! My foots is gittin wet."

"Climb up on my neck, den," sez Mr. Alligator; but he kep' a-gwine under. So Mr. Rabbit hollered out agin:

"Oh, trouble, Brudder Alligator, trouble! My foots is gittin wet."

"Well," says Mr. Alligator, "climb up on my head."

So he clum up on his head; but Mr. Alligator was a-sinkin' under so fas' dat Mr. Rabbit he got more skeert; so he sez, "Brudder Alligator, ef you jes carry me ober safe, I'll let yer eat my great-grandfader."

But Mr. Alligator say, "Dat ain't ernuff;" an' he kep' a-sinkin'. An' Mr. Rabbit say:

"Den I'll let yer eat up my wife's mudder." But as Mr. Alligator didn't stop a-gwine under, he hollered out, "Wait a minit, Brudder Alligator, an' I promise you 'fore goodness I'll git you all my 'lations fur breakfuss."

Well, dat was jes too much fur Brudder Alligator, an' he tuk Mr. Rabbit ober ter de udder side all right; but as soon as he got on dry lan' Mr. Rabbit say:

"I's much obleegt ter yer, Mr. Alligator; but ef yer finks yer a-gwine ter eat up any a my kinfolks, you's mighty mistaken;" an' he jes lay back his yurs an' jes flewed home.

An' Mr. Alligator he say to hissef: "Well, dat's jes de meanest trick dat leetle creetur eber did play me! I alwus knowed he was tricky, but when he promised me all his 'lations, bless yer heart! I b'leebed him."

ANYTHING FOR QUIET.

JOHN came home and found his boy
Filling all the house with riot,
Banging madly on his drum,
While his mother in the room
Sat serenely, unmoved by it.

"Madam," said the irate sire,
"I would stop this noise—or try it."
"No, you wouldn't," answered she;
"Were you vext all day like me,
You'd do *anything for quiet*."
MRS. GEORGE ARCHIBALD.

A DINNER WITH A CHORUS.

THE many instances and anecdotes of the late war with which the papers teem remind the writer of the following, heard during a recent visit to Virginia:

Very soon after peace had been declared, two gentlemen high in authority in the North had occasion to go to Richmond. They brought with them letters of introduction from Jefferson Davis to General A——, one of the most prominent citizens of the place, asking that particular attention and courtesy be shown the Northern visitors, as they had been very kind to him at a time when kindness was specially appreciated; in other words, during his imprisonment. General A—— immediately made preparations for a large dinner party the following evening, to show all possible respect to the request of the late Confederate President, and every attention to those who had treated him with sympathy and consideration, and also to maintain Virginia's reputation for hospitality, of which General A—— was very proud. His invitation was accepted, and in due time the guests arrived. Dinner was soon announced, and proceeded with all form and ceremony, while many reminiscences of the war were indulged in, and guests and host vied with each other in telling stories illustrating the bravery and magnanimity of their late opponents. Indeed, it seemed a veritable love-feast. Finally, as the wine went round, and good feeling flowed with it, General A——, lifting his glass of old Madiera, a remnant of former prosperity, proposed a toast:

"A speedy cessation to all ill feeling—a union of hearts as well as of States."

At the supreme moment, and mingling with the clink of the glasses, a childish treble came from an adjoining pantry:

"I am a good old rebel, and that is what I am,
And for the Yankee nation I do not care a dam."

His father, being very deaf, did not hear a word of it, bowed low, and drank the toast, while wondering in what he could have offended that the cordial manner of his guests so suddenly changed. However, he but redoubled his courteous attentions, not knowing that every few moments the above refrain floated into the room in decided contrast to his expressions of kindly feeling.

The hostess cast despairing glances at the servants, who in expressive pantomime declared they could do nothing, though doubtless, in point of fact, they were encouraging the young rascal, and greatly enjoying the consternation in the dining-room.

Many years passed before it was thought expedient to explain the sudden stiffening of the company on that memorable occasion, for General A—— held discourtesy to a guest as the blackest of social sins, and would have deemed no punishment too severe for the young scapegrace. The lady of the house has been frequently heard to declare that the most violent Northern patriots would have surely admitted she had more than atoned for her disloyalty to the Union by her sufferings during the concluding courses of that dinner of good-will.   M.

A COUNTRY boy was given a sentence to translate into French and write upon the blackboard in one of our co-educational colleges. When he made a mistake the professor requested another pupil to write it as he thought right. After he had done so, the teacher turned to one of the young ladies, and asked, innocently, "Which will you accept?" When she blushed and answered, "The latter," a voice called from the back of the room, "He is already taken."

THE TRANSLATING MACHINE.

IT was some years ago, when type-writers were just being introduced, and one of them had been placed on trial in the office of a leading life-insurance company of which I was an employé. Having reached the office at an early hour, anxious to finish some work which had annoyed me for some time, fairly seated at my desk, I was suddenly interrupted by the janitor, who informed me that there were parties desirous of taking a look at the office.

Sure enough, and there they came, four in number—two ladies and two gentlemen—sailing down the office toward my desk.

Who were they? Well, the names of the men might readily have been Moses, Levi, Abraham, or Isaac. They must have been in the clothing business, and their appearance reminded one forcibly that it must have been a second-hand clothing business at that. The ladies—ah, the ladies! they were adorned with diamonds, rings, and gold chains; wore dresses of expensive material, poorly made, and ill fitting.

The spokesman—a little bit of a man, all nose—in a voice which was as shrill as it was thin, addressed me: "I am intschured here, and dees is my brodher-in-law from New York und his wife und dauder. I dell dem dees building is schost so goot as dose wat is in New York, und I vant you to have de kindliness to show dem aboud."

There was nothing to be done but to show them about. At first, rather annoyed, I may have betrayed my displeasure, but soon warmed to my task, followed from desk to desk and room to room by the quartette, answering, as cheerfully as the circumstances would permit, the various conundrums they propounded. Very soon my visitors began chatting among themselves (they probably had run dry their stock of inquiries), and now, to my great amusement, conversed in German—a German tinged by an accent which had its origin in Palestine.

Finally we reached the room in which was placed the type-writer, and then it was that I casually observed, "Have you ever seen a translating machine?" The answer being quite unanimous in the negative, I explained that if only some one present were conversant with a foreign tongue, a sentence might be dictated in English, and translated by the machine into any desired language. Encouraged by a firm avowal that there was nothing in the way of testing the instrument, inasmuch as all of them understood German, matters began to shape themselves as I had foreseen. Having spent half of my life in Germany, fully conversant with the language, I had no odds to ask. Each visitor then began in the most polite manner and deferential way to urge upon the other the naming of the sentence to be translated. After a lively debate it was decided that the spokesman—my little friend with the preponderance of nose—should propound something nice. He cleared his throat, placed the back of the right-hand index finger on such a portion of the left side of his nose as it was able to cover, wrinkled his noble brow, looked wise, and said, "Make him say dees in Tscherman: Dees is my brodher-in-law von New York; he like dees office very much, und his wife und dauder also find it fine."

The translating of this sentence into German, while the group of strangers, following my every movement in breathless suspense, jumping at every ring of the bell, was accomplished in less time than it takes to tell it.

Before submitting the document I explained that I was not in the habit of running the translator, and probably the blame for any mistakes, if there were such, would attach to me rather than to the instrument; that my visitors would be able to tell me whether or not the machine was capable of performing what was claimed for it. A chorus of voices shouted, "Let us see; ve vill dell you." Fearing that in facing my guests I might be unable to control my features, and so betray the joke, I handed the sheet over my shoulder without turning.

I could fairly feel the quiver of quickening pulses as my New York friend in a low, solemn, and awe-stricken voice read what to all appeared a most wonderful transformation of the English sentence.

"Dies ist mein Schwager aus New York, ihm gefaellt dies Comptoir sehr gut, und seine Frau und Tochter finden es auch schoen."

For a few seconds you might have heard a pin drop, but shortly a reaction set in, and exclamations were at a discount; they bubbled forth in two languages: Himmel, grashus, saprament, oh my, na nu, grand, Donnerwetter, schblendid, wunderbar, etc. The privilege asked and readily granted to take away the "most brizeless broduction," with many a bow, thanking me again and again, my friends made ready for their departure. Arrived at the office door, my New York friend turned once more and said, "Abrobo, wat does this insehdrument cost?" I answered, "It costs about $125." He declared he would have one right off, at "any brize"; then, upon reflection, he added, "Maybe I get some gommischuns off." The ladies bade me a fond farewell, and my little friend, pressing my hand, whispered hoarsely that he would buy a translator as soon as he could afford it, but that "pischness vas bretty guiet schoost now." With another shake of the hand he said, "Goot-by; I alvays vill remember you mit great pleascherableness," and coming close to my ear, with a tremor in his voice he expressed the opinion, "I dell you vat, if dees ding hafe its existence in de days of Moses, by Himmel dey schwear it vas one mirragle!" — A. C. L.

A PAIR OF THEM.

I MUST tell you of something I heard about a lady from the South (I can't believe from Georgia), who, the other day, was chaperoning a young female friend from her section in Washington. In the Corcoran Gallery the lady, after other sights, led her élève to the statues of Apollo and Diana.

"Now here, my dear Bessie," she said, with as much spirit as was possible to a rather languid person who had so much of that sort of work on hand—"here is one of the very *splen-didest* things in this whole town. *That* is the celebrated Apollo, and *that*," she said, pointing to his no less famous sister, "is—Appolinaris."

This reminded me of a scene I witnessed at the Centennial. I was standing before the statue of "The Young Achilles" in the Annex, when a portly lady, accompanied by a couple of grown-up girls (I hope they were not Vermonters), came up. After reading the card, she said: "Ah, now! Yes; that's the young Archilus! Now *don't* he look sweet?"

THE following is sent as an indication of the cheerful resignation of some of the itinerants, by the pastor of the Methodist Episcopal church in an inland town, who says:

Not long since one of the preachers in this district of the Illinois Conference sent the following quaint epistle to his Presiding Elder. The writer of the poem is a genius in his way. He himself built the wagon in which he travels his circuit, and has invented a fly brush which works with a treadle for the table, and the table itself is made with two circular tops, the lower one stationary, and the upper one revolving, whenever one of his children desires anything opposite him, by simply giving it a whirl. I think this ought to be interesting, as I have found nothing so quaint for a long time:

B——, ILLINOIS, *March*, ——.

Rev. ——:

DEAR BROTHER,—I have received since Conference from Bath Society, $1; from Union, $1. No one makes any effort in that direction. I can only trust and wait. I have added the following to my prayers:

Since all my money now is gone,
And I have naught to live upon,
Grant me, O Lord, the special grace
For meat and bread to run my face.

As I have followed, at Thy call,
To preach the Gospel unto all,
Give me, O Lord, for every day
My bread, for which I can not pay.

I must depend, O Lord, on Thee;
The stewards can't collect for me,
For people have to pay their tax,
No matter what Thy kingdom lacks.

I am trying to raise the deficit on your claim, but don't have much encouragement. Will do my best.

Your brother in Christ, —— ——.

AN Irish aborigine not only serves in Mrs. A——'s kitchen, but diverts the whole family with her perfectly original remarks. When Mrs. A——'s grandmother died, and she had gone to assist in the last sad offices, a lady friend called during her absence. Ellen opened the door, and the lady said, "Is Mrs. A—— at home?"

"Oh no, mum," replied Ellen; "her grandmudther's dead, and she's to the *corpse's house.*"

She confidentially remarked on another occasion: "Well, mum, Bridget's got a new set of teeth, and I tould her if ever she was going to get married, now's the time. Why, mum, she's got *a set overhead and a set undther foot!*"

Mrs. A—— went into the kitchen one morning and informed Ellen that Mr. Thompson, a neighbor, and a prominent resident, had committed suicide. Ellen looked at her with an expression of mingled astonishment and disgust, and said: "Oh–h–h, mum, *has* he? *Wid who?*"

THE following poem appears in the obituary columns of a Baltimore newspaper under the death notice of a husband and father, born in Ireland, aged fifty-four:

He heard the angels calling him
    From that celestial shore;
He flopped his wings, and away he went
    To make one angel more.   BY HIS SON.

IN 1881, in the Sagadahoc County court, held in the city of Bath, Maine, a case for assault and battery came up for trial; Mrs. O. *v.* Mr. O.; Judge G. for plaintiff and Lawyer L. for defendant. Mr. O., by-the-way, kept a grocery store in a small country town, also the post-office in his dining and sitting room.

Mrs. O. had testified that Mr. O. had pushed her with such violence that she fell from a platform to the ground, and injured her side in consequence of the fall, etc.

When Mr. O. came upon the stand, he swore that Mrs. O. first pushed him.

As Judge G. arose to begin the cross-examination of the defendant, Mr. O. braced up with an evident determination that the lawyer should not "browbeat" him.

JUDGE G. "Mr. O., what is your business or profession?"

MR. O. "I am a merchant, sir, and a government officer, sir."

JUDGE G. "What office do you hold under the government?"

MR. O. "I am the postmaster in my own town, sir."

JUDGE G. "Did I understand you to say that you pushed Mrs. O. down?"

MR. O. "No, sir. I said that I pushed her, and she *fell down.* But she first pushed me."

JUDGE G. "How hard did she push you?"

MR. O. "She pushed me as hard as I pushed her, sir."

JUDGE G. "Did you lose your equilibrium when she pushed you?"

MR. O. "No, sir, I did *not* lose my equilibrium; I had no equilibrium to lose, for I *never had* any, sir [very emphatic], *and I don't think that you as a lawyer have any right to ask me any such question, sir.*"

Judge G. simply replied: "Oh, I beg pardon! I was not aware that you hadn't any equilibrium."

TOMMY (*who has just received a severe scolding*). "Am I really so bad, mamma?"
MAMMA. "Yes, Tommy, you are a very bad boy."
TOMMY (*reflectively*). "Well, anyway, mamma, I think you ought to be real darn glad I ain't twins!"

SAINTS IN THE SURF, OCEAN GROVE.—[See "Their Pilgrimage."]
From a painting by C. S. Reinhart.

FERDINAND BARBEDIENNE.
ARTISTIC BRONZE.
BY THEODORE CHILD.

THE name of M. Ferdinand Barbedienne is that of a great reformer of the industrial arts. In no country has any man won by the same means the fame which he enjoys, and only a few of the most favored handicraftsmen have ever had the privilege, and that, too, after their death, of such renown as this illustrious innovator has acquired during his life. Let us reflect for a moment what abominations were accepted as artistic bronzes fifty years ago. Let us remember even the productions which figured at the first universal exhibition at London in 1851. By comparison the present state will seem to be the last word of progress and the ideal of perfection. The decorative arts have been veritably revived and enriched from all the sources of beauty; the masterpieces of the plastic artists of antiquity, of the Renaissance, and of the eighteenth century have been reproduced in such a manner that they can henceforward enter the most modest homes; while the works of our modern sculptors no longer exist for the exclusive joy of a single possessor, but in their turn also contribute to the pleasure of our daily life. Public taste has been revolutionized and purified; and renewed acquaintance with the immortal majesty of the works of antiquity has rendered it necessary for the industry of bronze in all its branches to demand the best only of modern work. The artists have recognized the fact with joy. The artisans have followed suit, and sought to educate themselves up to the dignity of their task. Even the manufacturers themselves, in spite of inevitable economical considerations and anti-artistic prejudices, have not escaped the salutary influence of the respect for beauty. The history of this revolution of taste, and of

this magnificent growth of the Parisian industry of artistic bronze, is to a large extent the history of the life and work of M. Ferdinand Barbedienne, which it is proposed to sketch in the following pages.

The transformation of the bronze industry is due almost entirely to an ingenious invention of Achille Collas, of which M. Barbedienne was the first to foresee the future. Collas, who was born in 1795, and who died in 1859, was the veritable type of the inventor, thoroughly unpractical, neglectful of pecuniary interests, bending to no authority, gentle, taciturn, distrustful. He was by trade a mechanician. He worked first on clock-makers' tools, and then on surgical instruments. At the end of the First Empire he served for some time in the army; at the beginning of the Restoration he established himself modestly as a small tool-maker, and for the rest of his days he lived all alone, with no company but his dog and an old woman-servant, and proceeded to invent and take out patents for all sorts of things, from buckle-making machines down to hollow bricks and drain-pipes. His attention, however, was principally turned to mechanical engraving, for which he took out his first patent in 1825, and which he rapidly perfected, and applied not merely to the engraving of bank-notes and to all kinds of industrial engraving on metal, wood, leather, and paper, but also to artistic engraving in the mezzotint style.

In 1836 Collas succeeded in applying the principles of the diagraph and the pantograph, which form the basis of his engraving machines, to the reproduction and reduction of sculpture in relief and in the round. At the same time Frédéric Sauvage, the inventor of the screw-propeller, having started from a different point, arrived by different methods at a similar result, and the two men, almost within the same month, took out patents for the mechanical and mathematical reproduction of sculpture. The system of Sauvage was subsequently adopted by several Parisian houses, where it is still in use.

In 1839 Collas became the partner of M. Barbedienne, and his machine, improved and in many respects perfected since his death, will remain for some years the exclusive property of his survivor. Into the details of the delicate mechanism of the Collas reducing lathe I have no right to enter; the principle of the machine is, however, common property, and may therefore be summarily described without prejudice to the interest of any one. At the end of a horizontal bench suppose a fixed point, to which is attached by a universal joint the extremity of a long wooden bar or arm, provided with a longitudinal groove in which run two carriages, bearing, the one a stump or runner, the other a graving point. To this arm is attached a stem of steel pierced with holes, and this stem is itself connected with the tool-carriages by two other steel rods likewise pierced with holes, by means of which the distances and relative proportions may be graduated. This bar with its stem and two connecting rods always forms two equiangular triangles, described one within the other. On the bench, at a distance which can be varied at will, are placed two round tables or supports, geared together by an endless screw so that they can revolve while retaining the same relative position. These supports are fixed opposite the tool-carriages, and one receives the model and the other the block of plaster or other material which is to be transformed into a reproduction of the model on a reduced scale. The operator holds the wooden bar lightly, and makes the dulled point or runner pass over the whole surface of the model, while at the same time the sharp steel graver cuts into the plaster block, and reproduces mathematically the trajectory described by the dulled point, inasmuch as both tools work from the same centre. The proportions of the reduction are fixed by the mathematical adjustment of the proportions of the equiangular triangles above described, and by the corresponding adjustment of the model and the block of plaster on the revolving tables. It is obvious that in a

complete revolution of the tables it will be possible to trace on the two surfaces an infinity of similar curves in the meridian planes of the model and of the reduction; and by repeating the operation in an infinity of planes, which the universal joint of the bar allows, and by turning the model and the plaster block, it will be possible to obtain the reduced reproduction of the whole surface of the model. This reduction is not only theoretically exact, but, inasmuch as it is obtained by the reduction of the lines of grand curvature traced by the tool, it also gives the finest results, because there are the lines which best represent the surface, and whose perfection, above all other things, gives its artistic value to a statue or group. For the reduction of low reliefs Collas invented a self-acting machine, driven by steam-power, which is an application of the same principle; that is to say, the design is graven by a point following and repeating with an automatic and synchronous movement all the movements effected by another point or runner which traverses the whole surface of the model in relief. Naturally the reducing lathes may be also used for the reverse process of enlarging, and the reproduction may be made not only in plaster, but also in wood, ivory, marble, malachite, and all other plastic materials which the steel point of the graver can attack.

M. Barbedienne, before he entered into partnership with Collas, was a simple dealer in wall-paper. Born in Normandy in 1810, he came to Paris to make himself a position in the world, bringing with him little except the astuteness and obstinate will of his countrymen, rare natural taste, and a broad appreciation of beauty. While he was in the wall-paper business his suggestions and demands contributed to arouse the manufacturers from their lethargic state of mere mechanical production, and to make them look upon wall-paper really as a decoration, and not a mere covering of wall surface. His dream already was to direct the decorative arts into a new and healthy way, but the dream was as yet little more than a vague aspiration. He felt that he had an innate appreciation of the beautiful; but he had never travelled; he had seen little; he was not even quite sure of his vocation until the day when he bought Decamps's splendid study for "The Defeat of the Cimbrians," exhibited in the Salon

PORTRAIT BUST OF ACHILLE COLLAS.

of 1834. He was not rich enough to pay for the work except by instalments: even thus the sacrifice was a great one for a young man in his position; but the temptation was irresistible, and so the picture was deposited in the hands of a banker until the whole debt was discharged. This purchase was the beginning of a collection of pictures which has since become precious, and it served to confirm M. Barbedienne in his pursuit of beauty in all the forms of art.

Innate taste, power of initiative, a moderate, equable, and sure temperament, strong will, a comprehension of the talents of others, the faculty of unifying those talents, of inspiring them with his own taste, and of making them work together in the *ensemble* of the execution of his plans and ideas by some undefinable moral and personal impulse—such are the qualities which have enabled M. Barbedienne to create the vast establishment over which he now presides, and which began in a very modest way in the year 1839.

A reduction in plaster of the Venus of Milo, obtained by the primitive Collas lathe, was the first and for some years the only production of the new firm. Then followed the Diana of Gabii and other antiques from the Louvre; a foundery and finishing shops were gradually added; and after vegetating for ten years, M. Barbedienne, unknown, but confident of the excellence of his effort, sent to the exhibition at London in 1851, besides the reductions of antique statuary and various decorative bronzes, a reproduction of Lorenzo Ghiberti's principal door of the Baptistery of Florence, reduced to the scale of one-half by the Collas process, together with a magnificent book-case of ebony, decorated with bronze ornaments, reduced from works of the Italian Renaissance. This exhibit was a triumph; the firm of Collas and Barbedienne received the highest special medal, and the fortune of the house was assured. At the universal exhibition at Paris in 1855, Achille Collas received the grand medal of honor for his reducing lathe, and at the universal exhibitions at London in 1862, at Paris in 1867, at Vienna in 1873, and at Paris in 1878, M. Barbedienne and his collaborators received the highest recompenses for work which had become year by year more and more excellent and more and more varied.

Thanks to the wonderful invention of Collas, who was, as one may say, the Gutenberg of statuary, M. Barbedienne drove out of the market the wretched models of the Empire and the Restoration, which could not for a moment bear comparison with the reproductions of the fine works of antiquity which he was placing within the reach of the general public. Then followed reproductions of the great works of the Italian Renaissance, and of the French sculptors Germain Pilon, Coysevox, Couston, Caffieri, and Clodion. Furthermore, considering justly that art would become mummified if it were forced to live entirely in the past, M. Barbedienne gradually extended the advantages of the Collas process to the finest productions of modern art, and admitted to the illustrious company of their great ancestors of Greece, Italy, and France, works like Rude's "Mercury," Pradier's "Sapho," Aizelin's "Mignon," Chapu's "Youth," Mercié's "David," and Paul Dubois's "Military Courage." The multiplication of such works as these naturally influenced the accessories and surroundings of daily life, and to meet the demand for beautiful objects, and to show the way to others, M. Barbedienne executed those monumental pieces of furniture which have at each universal exhibition been examples of taste in design and perfection in execution. At the same time Falguière, Guillemin, Carrier-Belleuse, Constant Sévin, Claudius Popelin, Serre, and other artists were called upon to design torchères, lampadaria, vases, jewel caskets, clocks, and all kinds of ornamental bronzes for house decoration, while from the ovens of the enamel department artists like Thesmar were succeeding in introducing into our habitations some of the harmonies of colors familiar to Eastern people. The beautiful in all its manifestations has been the constant concern of M. Barbedienne. What the hand of man has done, the hand of man can do. Such has been his conviction in that never-resting initiative which has made him a pioneer in the revival and continuation of so many branches of the industrial arts.

M. Barbedienne's countrymen have been the first to recognize his merits and the importance of his life-work. He has received all the official honors that a Frenchman can obtain, but of all these distinctions the one perhaps which he values

SMALL OVENS IN ENAMEL SHOP.

most highly is the respect of his colleagues, who at the exhibition of 1878
proclaimed him the father of their industry—*le père du bronze.*

At the present day the manufactory of
M. Barbedienne in the Rue de Lanery
gives employment to some 450 workmen,
and is the most complete establishment of
the kind in France, for it comprises in its
various departments all the branches of
the bronze industry, from the formation
of the alloy in ingots to the gilding and
burnishing of the finished metal, and its
application to the rational adornment of
cabinet-work—reduction, moulding, casting, chiselling, turning, mounting, bronz-
ing, gilding, galvanoplasty, marble - cutting, glass-engraving, *cloisonné* and *champlevé* enamel, photography, designing—
all these operations are brought together

in a series of workshops, in a visit to the principal of which I shall ask the reader to accompany me. By this means, and with the aid of brief general explanations of the different processes, I shall hope to convey some impression of the difficulties which the production of artistic bronze offers, and of the qualities which it is sought to obtain. Within the limited space allotted to me I make no pretence to give more than a very general outline of my subject, each section of which would require a whole volume for its complete treatment.

The general aspect of the manufactory has nothing particularly striking. Like almost all Parisian manufactories, it is an agglomeration of old houses and buildings which have been transformed and more or less successfully adapted to their present use, and which are connected by a labyrinth of tortuous passages and queer staircases. The workshops are utterly without uniformity, and full of picturesque and interesting corners, and, above all, full of interesting faces. Amongst the proverbially intelligent Parisian workmen you will find none more intelligent than the metal-workers, none more artistic in sentiment, and none more gifted with that faculty of rapid assimilation which renders the Parisian workman so susceptible to the influence of his surroundings. The whole establishment is a sort of republic, receiving supreme direction from its president, M. Barbedienne, who reserves for himself the right of initiative, but otherwise leaves his ministers and his collaborators free. As regards execution and means and methods of working, each man is his own master, and each department is independent. If any man has improvements to recommend or experiments to make, he is free to do so. No one's activity is absolutely circumscribed. "We all belong," says M. Barbedienne, "to the great family of workmen who from century to century form a continuous chain to hand on to future ages the work of the past incessantly augmented. Each of us has, therefore, the right to express himself without being hampered by any routine." Within practical limits this doctrine is carried out in all the workshops. The men respect their president, esteem him as the director of their artistic consciences, and honor him as a patriot who has devoted his whole life and his whole thought to the resuscitation and glorifica-

tion of his industry. There is something touching in the relations of these men and their austere chief, who, by a strange coincidence, has many points of resemblance, both physically and morally, to the great sculptor Barye, of whom he is an ardent admirer. They know that he has always restricted his personal wants within the severest limits; that he has lived all his life as the most modest of bachelors, and imposed upon himself every sacrifice in order to aggrandize his industry, and in order to represent his country worthily at the great international competitions.

Let us visit the workshops, and watch the production of a bronze statue through its various stages. We will take, for instance, Antonin Mercié's group "Gloria Victis." The sculptor's clay model is first reproduced in plaster, in which form it is taken to the reducing department—a long room where a dozen men are working at Collas lathes, under the inspiration of the honored shade of the inventor, whose bust in bronze occupies a niche at one end of the shop. The foreman caster and the foreman mounter consult together with the foreman of the reducing department, and the plaster model is cut into sections in the manner which is considered by them to be most advantageous. Each fragment is coated with stearine to protect it, and to enable the runner of the Collas lathe to glide over it smoothly. The measurements are taken; the proportions of the reduction decided upon; and blocks of plaster are cut and sculped approximately to the form of each section which has to be reduced. The section of the model and the corresponding block of plaster, or *poupée*, as it is called, are placed on the revolving tables of the lathe; the machine is adjusted, and the model is reproduced in the manner already mentioned above in the description of the apparatus. Simple as it may seem, this process of reduction requires great skill and delicacy of touch; it is a veritable art in itself, full of minutiæ and details which we need not dwell upon here, but which must not be neglected in our appreciation of the difficulty of the work. The original group, "Gloria Victis," is 10 feet 6 inches high. By the Collas machine it has been reduced to four sizes, respectively $\frac{3}{5}$, $\frac{9}{20}$, $\frac{3}{10}$, $\frac{2}{10}$ of the original. The reduction to $\frac{3}{5}$ can be made by the Collas machines in two months, supposing five or

six men to be working at it.
It is needless to say that
the artist could not model
a copy of his group in the
same space of time, or with
the same accuracy, to say
nothing of the cost.

The next operation is
making the mould for the
casting. This is done by
workmen who are purely
specialists, rough-looking
men who form a class by
themselves, unpolished in
their manners compared
with the chisellers and
mounters, but who never-
theless do astonishingly delicate work with their enormous hands and thick fin-
gers. In order to insure
the success of the operation
a statue is generally cast in
several pieces, which are fitted together by the mounter
afterward. Thus the group
"Gloria Victis" is cast in ten
sections. The reduced plaster sections, each with the
points of correspondence
carefully marked, are carried from the reducing shop
into the moulding depart-
ment. The mould is made
of fine sand obtained at
Fontenay-aux-Roses, a village near Paris, which during the past two centuries
has been famous for the excellence of its casting sand.
This sand is sifted and
ground in a mill, and mixed
in equal parts with sand
which has already served
for moulding. This mix-
ture is tenacious and fine
enough to take and retain
the imprint of the most delicately modelled surfaces,
and sufficiently refractory
to resist the contact of the
molten metal. The moulder
with his spatulæ, his trow-
els, his smoothers and cutters, his bellows and brushes
and other tools before him,
places the model on a provisional bed of sand maintained in position by iron

MONUMENTAL CLOCK.

MAKING A MOULD OF THE "GLORIA VICTIS."

frames; he beats down the sand to an arbitrary level, and from this level he starts the formation of the different pieces of his mould. These pieces, formed simply by beating and pressing the sand over the model, are calculated, as regards shape, size, and number, in such a manner that they can be easily removed from the model without breaking. The model itself is dusted over with talc before the sand is pressed over it, and the joints of the mould are sprinkled with potato fecula in order to prevent the adherence of the different pieces. The portion of the model above the arbitrary line having been moulded, each piece dovetailing into its neighbor, and the necessary vents having been formed, more iron frames are placed round it and filled with sand. The whole is then turned over, the first bed of sand is cleared away, and the rest of the model thus uncovered is provided in turn with a series of pieces of beaten sand as above described. The mould is thus complete. This assemblage of juxtaposited pieces is surrounded by a filling in composed likewise of sand, and, for large work, of plaster on the outside. This outer casing is called the *chape*. The next operation is the removal of the model from the inside of this articulated mass of compressed sand. The *chape* is removed piece by piece, the different sections being strengthened by wires which form a loop in the middle and facilitate handling. The mould is likewise removed piece by piece, and *chape* and mould are reconstructed in the iron frames or chases, after having been dried in an oven. In the hollow mould thus obtained a core, or *noyau*, is formed

of sand, in which the proportion of old sand is less than it is in the mixture used for the outer mould, and which is consequently more porous. This core is strengthened by an *armature*, or bracing of iron rods, and traversed by strings dipped in tallow and resin, which evaporate the moment the hot metal penetrates the mould, and form passages which give a certain elasticity to the consistency of the sand of the core, and prevent it offering too great resistance to the bronze during the process of contraction. These passages serve also for the escape of air and gases. The next operation is the removal from the entire surface of this sand core of a thin and equal coating of from $\frac{1}{16}$ to $\frac{1}{8}$ of an inch, or from 2 to 3 millimetres thick. The core is then dried in the oven, and replaced in the hollow mould, where it is held in position by rods running through and through. Finally, the feeders for conveying the metal into the mould and the vent-holes for the issue of the air and gas having been provided for, the mould is closed, packed round with sand in the chases, braced up with screws and bolts, and passed on to the caster. How complicated and delicate is this operation of moulding the reader will perhaps be able to comprehend even from this summary description. From the choice of the sand to the perfect regularity of the peeling of the core every detail requires skill, attention, experience, and infinite patience. It must be remembered, also, that mould and core serve only once; each copy of a model requires the formation of a new mould and a new core; and to make merely the exterior mould of a simple figure like Mercié's "David," four feet high, requires a week's work. A complicated group like Paul Dubois's "Charity," 30 inches high, requires three weeks' work to make the outer mould and the core.

About the operation of casting I need say little. For small statues the metal is melted in crucibles, and either poured directly into the feeders, or, if the piece is of some size, into a basin communicating by a hole with the principal feeder. This hole is fitted with a stopper, which is pulled up when the necessary amount of metal has been poured into the basin. The molten bronze rushes into the mould by all the feeders that have been prepared, the gases escape by the vents, and the waste metal by the passage reserved for it. The space of two or three millimetres left between the outer mould and the peeled core is filled with metal. The statue is cast. When the statue is of large dimensions the mould is buried in a pit at the side of the reverberatory furnace, in which the bronze is in that case melted. This process of casting in piece moulds of Fontenay sand is alone in use in M. Barbedienne's foundery and in all other Parisian founderies. There is another process of casting with a wax model, *moulage*

à cire perdue, as it is called, which was practised by the sculptors of the Renaissance and of the last century, and which is still practised in Paris by M. Eugène Gonon, not without success. This process is profoundly interesting, as, indeed, is the whole art of casting, but it is not employed in M. Barbedienne's establishment. Certainly the founders of the Renaissance, many of the old French founders, and the prodigious metal-workers of China and Japan had processes and *tours de main* which remain a secret to us, and by which they obtained, as the Japanese

THE FOUNDERY.

do at the present day, results which we can only admire without being able to rival them. However, the question has not yet been definitely settled, and very serious efforts are now being made in Belgium to render casting by the *cire perdue* process at once sure, practical, and economical. Meanwhile the Parisian founders obtain admirable results with their sand moulds, and although for general purposes the casting is made in several pieces, there is no reason why it should not be cast in one piece by means of sand moulds just as well as by the *cire perdue* process. It is simply a matter of greater risk and of greater cost. The Barye "Lion" in Mount Vernon Place, Baltimore, was cast in one piece in M. Barbedienne's foundery. Barye's "Theseus and the Minotaur," the "Wrestlers" of the Museum of Florence, Lepautre's "Æneas and Anchises," Coysevox's "Flute-players," and other equally difficult pieces have been cast in one piece also, and with a perfection which leaves nothing to be desired, and with a surface so clean that the use of the chisel is scarcely needed at all, which is really the ideal of casting. As for the grain of the bronze, it is exquisite. The alloy used in all the Barbedienne bronzes is the same as that which Barye fixed upon as fulfilling all requirements, namely, ninety parts best red copper, seven parts zinc, and three parts tin. The metal practically fused in the crucible is composed half of new bronze and half of waste bronze which has already been moulded once. This alloy gives that fineness of epiderm which is the characteristic of good casting, and which is visible even beneath that patina or oxidation with which time covers it, as it were, with a magnificent varnish, varying from dark blue to turquoise. This epiderm, it may be added, is all the finer the thinner the metal is, while at the same time the lightness and regularity of the thickness of the casting is the best guarantee of the conservation of the form of the model.

We now have our specimen group, "Gloria Victis," reproduced in bronze and in ten separate pieces. The moulds have been broken off and the cores extracted, and each section appears in metal of a yellowish color, disfigured with iridescent patches, and with seams wherever the pieces of the mould were joined, and encumbered with a net-work of branches formed by the superfluous metal which

has run into the feeders and vent-holes. These pieces have next to be cleaned in acid baths, freed from all superfluous metal by the chisellers, and then adjusted by the mounters by means of screws, dovetails, rivets, and cold-hammered joints, for soldering can only be used when the piece is destined to be gilded or silvered, otherwise the difference in the color of the bronze and of the soldering alloy would be visible and mar the whole. The last operation is the patina, the primitive meaning of which word is the coating of oxidation which atmospheric influences produce in course of time on the surface of bronze. At the present day the patina is obtained artificially by means of acetic acid, sulpho-hydrate of ammonia, salts of antimony, and other mordants, and of coloring substances more or less liquid, and applied with a brush. The recipes for the production of antique green, Florentine bronze, black, red, and other patens will be found in special treatises, but in this, as in all other details of the treatment of metal, personal skill and sentimental experience play a large rôle.

We have indicated the various operations necessary for reproducing in bronze the sculptor's model. But here we may note, in a parenthesis, that when once the "Gloria Victis," or any other group, has been cast in bronze, the first proof is very carefully chiselled under the supervision of the artist, and all succeeding proofs are moulded, not from the plaster reductions, but from this finished bronze, which is left in sections simply pinned together, and which henceforward serves as the model. We will now pay a visit to the workshops where the chiselling is done. No less than six rooms are devoted to this department, and nearly two hundred men are employed in the delicate work of finishing the statuary and ornamental bronzes which are sent up in the rough from the foundery. The workshops, which have received the characteristic names of the Chamber, the Senate, the Capitole, the Belvédère, the Big Bath, and the Campana, are full of vises, tables, and benches, all strewn with tools and fragments of bronze, and reëchoing with the din of sharp hammer strokes and clicking chisels. In our illustration, taken in the Capitole, an expert workman is seen chiselling the main section of "Gloria Victis," and removing with firm stroke some excrescence or fault which the casting has left. The operation is indeed so important in the production of artistic bronze that we shall need to consider it in some detail.

However excellent may be the reproduction in metal of the artist's model, and whatever the method of casting, the bronze before it can truly be said to be finished generally requires very careful and almost minute work, which gives to the execution its fineness, its character, and its value. The very nature of the alloy commands this careful finish. The tenacity of bronze enables the sculptor to give more action and independence to the object represented than if he employed marble or stone; its density imposes delicate finish; its color requires the accentuation of hollows and reliefs, and makes the contours predominate. The resources for expression offered by bronze and marble are different. In a nude statue in marble the light and shade can be rendered as they are in flesh itself, by gentle gradations, by lights that fade into shadows, and by shadows that brighten into lights.

CHISELLING THE "GLORIA VICTIS."

The light and shade combine harmoniously on the pure white surfaces of marble, and become, as it were, incorporated with the material which reproduces so marvellously the transparency and *morbidezza* of the tissues. In a bronze statue the effect is one of extremes of light and shade; a neutral and opaque tone envelops the whole group; and whereas marble seems to absorb and retain the light, bronze reflects it. Hence the art of the statuary in bronze resides, above all things, in the lines, and the perfection of his modelling consists in the precision of the contours. In the execution of a bronze statue there must therefore be nothing vague, nothing exuberant, and nothing that indicates indolence or indecision. As has been well observed by M. Eugène Guillaume the sculptor, and Member of the Institute of France, in all the fine works of the ancients we can see that the chiseller has accomplished his task rigorously and in all parts. The planes and surfaces are developed without any uncertainty or vagueness—

determined even with apparent aridity; the reliefs and the hollows are sharply rendered; and throughout the traces of the process of casting have disappeared, and allow us to admire the diligent attention and energetic action of the scrupulous artist, indefatigable in the care of purging his work, not merely from the accidents of moulding and casting, but also from the weaknesses and defects that he may have discovered in his model. Thanks to this perfecting labor, the eye at once perceives the silhouette of the statue in all the purity of its contours, and the patina is developed equally and smoothly over the metal thus freed from the coating of foreign matter deposited over the surface by the contact of the metal with the moulding sand. Chiselling, therefore, is generally indispensable, and it is equally indispensable that this final working of the bronze should have all the excellence possible. From the point of view of simple reasoning one might well fail to understand how an artist, after having conceived a work, and seen it in his imagination clothed with a certain perfection, can entrust the realization of all that is most delicate and subtle in this perfection to the care of a man who is a stranger to him, and generally not under his control. But it is not merely a false sentiment of dignity which prevents artists from handling the metal themselves. The great masters of the Renaissance, we are told, modelled, cast, and chiselled their bronzes in person. True. The great Florentines handled the chisel readily for the simple reason that they invariably began their artistic education by being apprenticed to goldsmiths and workers in the precious metals. Nevertheless, there can be no doubt that there were professional chisellers in those days, just as there were in the seventeenth and eighteenth centuries, and there is no reason why the creative sculptors should not have taken advantage of their skill. Then, again, let us reflect for a moment how completely the conditions of production have changed. Each work of the Florentines is unique. Even up to the middle of the present century a work of sculpture remained practically unique, and did not become vulgarized, as it does nowadays, by means of graduated reductions which preserve exactly the proportions, the lines, the form, and the spirit of the original. Certainly there is nothing to prevent the

sculptor from becoming a chiseller, but it is only natural that he should prefer to devote his time to the more fertile function of creation rather than to the task of repeating himself and of reproducing his works for commercial diffusion.

The chiseller on his side can educate himself at the same sources as the sculptor, and acquire the same knowledge and the same taste in discerning the composition, even if he cannot create that composition. He becomes in a measure the collaborator of the sculptor, for in order to preserve the true accent and to revive the spirit of the work, which has been inevitably dulled by the fusion of the metal, the chiseller must be thoroughly penetrated with the spirit of the author, and this result cannot be obtained by mere mechanical labor. The chiseller works with the artist's original model before his eyes, as far as this is possible, or at any rate with a plaster cast of the model, but in all careful work it is useful, not to say indispensable, that the chiseller should be able to refer to the original model, at least for the accents, which, one may say, constitute the spirit of the work. Then, again, besides this modest function of bringing into light the skill of the sculptor, of developing the expression, and of determining the form of the bronze as it comes from the foundery, the chiseller must be prepared to carry out the intentions of the artist if he wishes to change or modify details of his work after it is cast, or if he demands a finish which the plastic matter of his model could not render—for instance, the details of lace, of embroidery, of furs, or the alternate burnished and dull ornaments of armor. Often a model which has been made with a view to reproduction in marble loses when transposed into bronze, and in such cases the chiseller who is called upon to accentuate the work anew becomes really the collaborator of the sculptor, and displays a taste and an artistic sentiment which are most widely removed from mere mechanical labor.

From what I have said above, the reader must not conclude that the perfection of chiselling consists, as some think, in the multiplication of details, in polish and smoothness, or even in removing certain little accidents which are due to the sculptor's very touch, and which in no way impair the general effect, any more than certain roughnesses of the casting or of the strokes of the modelling brush. Too

THE MODEL-ROOM, SHOWING COLOSSAL STATUE OF AUGUSTUS.

POTASH BATH IN GILDING SHOP.

led form in all its suppleness and purity, and, furthermore, to impart to that form the sharpness, the crispness, and energy which form the peculiar characteristic of chiselled bronze." Thanks to the transformation of the bronze industry by the invention of Achille Collas, and thanks to the influence of his own enlightened taste, M. Barbedienne was able to record, in 1867, a capital improvement in the artistic value of the models, but at the same time he had to confess the superiority of Oriental, Greek, Roman, and Renaissance bronzes from the point of view of artistic workmanship. "It is absolutely necessary," he says, "to teach drawing and modelling in order to form the new generation of workmen, without whom the bronze industry cannot progress. In the history of industrial art the merit of the present generation will be, above all things, the fact that it has freed itself from routine, and courageously prepared the way for a new and stronger generation. But in order to march surely and safely in the upward path, all of us, manufacturers, artists, and workmen alike, must know how to treat the metal in accordance with its peculiar qualities."

great minuteness in chiselling tends to produce confusion and falsification.

During the long period which saw the exclusive triumph of the tool, before M. Barbedienne succeeded in regenerating the chiseller's art, the accessories and details of a composition became the principal point; their importance broke up the broad spaces, destroyed the proportions of the whole, and left the eye no repose. In the first half of this century, and even up to within twenty years ago, the more overcharged and minute the chiselling was the better it pleased. It was against this unreasoning minuteness that Barye was one of the first to protest by his practice, and by his influence over the workmen whom he employed. It is against this monotonous over-finish that M. Barbedienne himself protests in his admirable report on the section of artistic bronze at the exhibition of 1867. "The chiseller," says M. Barbedienne, "ought to have two objects in view—first of all to respect the form which is intrusted to him, and secondly to bring into evidence the qualities peculiar to the metal. Good chiselling ought, therefore, to reproduce the model-

The outcome of M. Barbedienne's exhortations was the foundation of periodical competitions in the various branches of the industry by the society of the "Réunion des Fabricants de Bronze," of which M. Barbedienne is the president, while in the different departments of the establishment of the Rue de Lanery renewed efforts were made to achieve perfection.

An indefatigable searcher, always observing and always studying, M. Barbedienne has discovered new patens which neither the ancients nor the artists of the Renaissance possessed. Such is that warm finish called *frotté d'or*, which consists in rubbing with gold the salient parts of the drapery on which the light is to be concentrated; such, too, are various new red, brown, brick, and clay colored patens which have no special names. The general characteristic of all these modern patinas employed by M. Barbedienne is their relative transparency compared with the uniform brown patinas of the eighteenth century, and the dark and often heavy patinas of the Florentines. In this research of transparency we detect once more M. Barbedienne's excellent principle of bringing into relief all the qualities of the metal, and at the same time of respecting most minutely the modelling and touch of the artist.

In this wonderful art city in the Rue de Lanery we might still spend many hours in visiting the quaint workshops where the various processes of chemical gilding, mercury gilding, and burnishing are conducted; in the galvanoplastic room; in the marble works; in the cabinet-making department; and, above all, in those fascinating rooms where the enamellers prepare their brilliant plaques and vases for the capricious trial of the furnace. But within the limits of a magazine article it would be absurd to attempt to imitate that worthy mediæval monk Theophilus, whose multifarious *Schedula diversarum artium* has been of such great avail to the historians of the decorative arts. I will merely add that M. Barbedienne was one of the first in modern times to appreciate the enamels and metalwork of the extreme East, and to form a collection of fine specimens. He enjoys also the still greater honor of having been the first to mount a laboratory for experimenting and adapting the Oriental processes to European production. This new venture, like all M. Barbedienne's artistic enterprises, has been crowned with success, and now the enamel department of his establishment produces currently not only *cloisonné* enamels after the Japanese method, but also a novel kind of *champlevé* enamel, in which the alveoles or compartments are

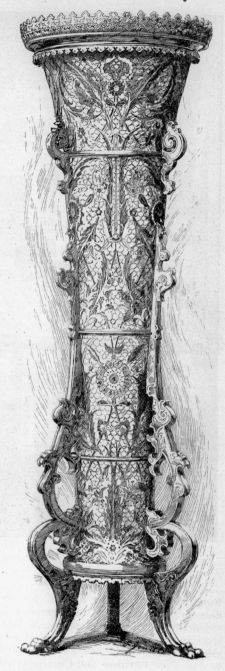

CLOISONNÉ ENAMEL VASE.

not dug out of the metal laboriously with a chisel or graver, but moulded in plaster and cast in solid metal. This system of *cloisonné sur fonte*, with its rather heavy metallic outlines, is admirably adapted for ornamentation in the Persian taste.

CLOISONNÉ ENAMEL SHOP.

Finally, let us remark that in his endeavors to acclimatize in Europe this Oriental art of cloisonné enamel, M. Barbedienne has avoided the error of servilely copying. He has not attempted to reproduce Japanese and Chinese types or designs without regard to differences of manners and of national ideal, according to that system of blind imitation which has produced such sad results in ceramics, silver-ware, and even furniture both in Europe and America. On the contrary, he has contented himself with assimilating the general scheme of decoration and the means of executing it, and with taking suggestions from certain broad novelties in color and in symmetry. M. Barbedienne is right; the imitation of exotic forms is not what we need to seek in our study of Chinese and Japanese art, but rather the secrets of their exquisite colorations of enamel, of their perfect castings, of their methods of inlaying metal upon metal, of their free and firm chiselling, and of their mysterious alloys.

WORKING-MEN IN THE BRITISH PARLIAMENT.

BY EDWARD BROWN, F. L. S.

"NO one can have watched the leaders of the working-men for the last ten years without finding among them men capable of commanding the attention and respect of the House of Commons, not merely for their eloquence, surprising as that is, but for their good sense, good feeling, and good-breeding." Such were the words of the late Charles Kingsley twenty years ago.

The prophecy has been abundantly verified. Nearly ten years, however, elapsed after these words were uttered ere a working-man member was found in the House of Commons, though several determined attempts had been made. Mr. Burt, who has occupied a place in the Parliaments of 1874 and 1880, the late Mr. Alexander Macdonald, who was in the House from 1874 until his death in 1881, and Mr. Broadhurst, who was elected in 1880, were the first to wear the honor, and each has "commanded the attention and respect of the House of Commons," so much so that Mr. Broadhurst is now a member of Mr. Gladstone's cabinet. Now that several colleagues have been given to them by the recent elections, the influence of the working-man member may be expected to increase rather than diminish.

The advent of *bona fide* working-men to seats in the British legislature only marks a phase in that vast, though, as far as England is concerned, peaceable revolution which will ever be regarded as one of the distinguishing features of the nineteenth century. During the early decades of the century the laboring classes were politically, and in many respects socially, under the heavy heel of a tyrannical or indifferent aristocracy; their voice was unheard or unheeded, save when, as in 1832, the voice was mingled with the stern rumblings of revolution. Intellectually the working classes then were far behind the standard of to-day; socially they had no influence; politically they were regarded as outside the pale, and unfitted to exercise even the power contained in a vote. The time was a weary one for the laboring-man, and justice was apparently slow to make its advent. But delay had its advantages. The working-men of Great Britain received a much-needed education in the management of their trades-unions and in many

HENRY BROADHURST.
From a photograph by Barraud, London.

other directions—a training that matured the judgment and self-control of those whose vote in future days will be so powerful for good or ill.

The social and political improvement in the industrial population has been most clearly discernible during the last twenty or thirty years. Fifty years ago a working-man would have been ostracized even if he had obtained election to Parliament; now he is received there as an equal. Before the reform bill of 1867 the voting power of workmen was comparatively small, and few of the middle classes would have listened to a request for a workmen's representative, had there been no property qualification to stand in the way of such an election. With the passage of that act the condition of things was changed in the great centres of population. It is not, therefore, a matter for surprise that there should be a wish on the part of those to whom political power has been committed to have a direct voice in the making of the laws in which as citizens they are so deeply interested. Ardently, however, as working-men members might be wished for by their class, a greater difficulty still blocked the way—

the want of money to sustain them in Parliamentary life. This difficulty has, however, been overcome by the nomination to Parliament of the men who are leaders in the unions, and who are being maintained by the funds of these societies.

The first *bona fide* working-man to enter the British Parliament was Mr. Thomas Burt. He was the elect of Morpeth in the new Parliament of 1874. He was born at Colliery Row, Northumberland, in 1837. At that time the houses of the miners were bad throughout the northern coal-field. But the Northumbrian miners' wives were a grand race of women, and their homes, as a rule, were pictures of comfort and cleanliness. The inborn pride and self-respect of both men and women enabled them to make their dwellings centres of peace and happiness. Under such conditions Thomas Burt was born. His father, who died in 1882, was a remarkable man. He was original and quaint in his speech, and his dialect was of the broadest Northumbrian *patois*. He was enthusiastic in any work he took up, and full of a humor which was more dry than boisterous. During the struggles between masters and men in the thirties and forties Peter Burt took a leading part.

After the strike of 1844 Peter Burt took his family across the Tyne into the county of Durham, settling at Hetton colliery for a year. He then removed to Haswell, a few miles from Hetton, and it was here, at the age of ten years, that Thomas entered the pit as a "trapper-boy." At one time children at the age of five or six years were sent down the mines amidst every kind of foul conditions to work for a miserable pittance. But this practice for some time had been abolished. Yet it was a hard life for boys of ten to spend twelve hours a day, sitting for the most part in a dismal hole, dark save for a feeble glimmer from a lamp or candle, and only gaining a glimpse of any human being when a few tubs were passing. The Burt family returned to Northumberland in 1851, first to New Hartley, afterward to Cramlington, and then to Seaton Delaval.

The daily life of Thomas Burt as a miner contains no special features. He lived as did his class. His contemporaries tell us that he was an average workman and reliable; but in a branch of work where distinction comes chiefly through physical strength his somewhat delicate

frame prevented him winning fame by doing more work than his neighbors. As a lad he was not of robust constitution, and now it is impossible to conceive how he bore the confinement underground during the period of over eighteen years which he spent in the pits. The Sunday-school was one of Burt's sources of education, and as scholar and teacher he enjoyed its benefits many years. At fifteen he became a teetotaler, and has ever since remained an abstainer. His first speech was on the temperance platform. The member for Morpeth is now spoken of as the probable leader of the temperance party in the new Parliament, consequent upon the defeat of Sir Wilfred Lawson. In early days his library was small, but choice. Channing was his father's favorite author, and the son read his works with pleasure and avidity. To these were added such others as his means would permit, his good sense leading him to choose the best within his reach. The boy was father to the man. The member for Morpeth has now in his home at Newcastle a splendid library, large beyond his most ardent youthful aspirations, filled with some of the best modern works. The young pitman's study was the little "garret" up the ladder. Here he spent his time learning Latin and French, reading history, poetry, and political economy. By such labor and perseverance he made himself an effective speaker, and his language to-day is as refined as though there were no Northumbrian burr in his pronunciation. Valuing education so highly, it is but natural that his desire to promote it should be strong. At Seaton Delaval he was one of the earliest supporters of the Mechanics' Institute. Afterward, at Choppington, he was appointed the first secretary of the Educational Society, and throughout that district he was ever ready by speech and work to help forward questions tending to the advancement and improvement of his order.

In 1860 Thomas Burt removed from Seaton Delaval to Choppington, a colliery village three miles from Morpeth, and part of the borough which he now represents in the House of Commons. Ere this he had married. His choice was a cousin, Mary, the daughter of Thomas Weatherburn, of Cowpen, and in her he has found a true helpmeet. Mrs. Burt has been the stay of his home in all its varied fortunes. As a miner's wife she fulfilled her duties well; and now, when the mistress of a more pretentious home, she wins the affection and esteem of all who know her. The true woman is not hidden by any veneer of social conventionalities, but her whole bearing is dignified by a noble spirit of humble independence.

The life at Choppington colliery extended over five years. Mr. Burt was soon appointed Choppington delegate to the Union of the Northumberland and Durham miners formed in 1882. In the early part of 1865 the Northumberland miners seceded from the joint counties' Union, and formed a society of their own. Mr. William Crawford, who is now M.P. for Mid-Durham, and has been for some years secretary of the Durham Miners' Association, was the first secretary, which office he retained only for a few months, and Thomas Burt was appointed his successor. Burt's work as a miner was now over. He bade farewell to the pick and the shovel, and took to the pen and the platform as the methods of his future life's work.

Matters were not in a very promising condition when Mr. Burt assumed the reins of office. His powers of organization, however, soon made themselves felt. A strike was in progress at Cramlington colliery. It had already lasted eight weeks, with no prospect of a speedy termination. The treasury was almost empty, and there were nearly six hundred men out of work. Ere long the masters began to evict the men from their homes, and scenes were enacted which happily have never since been witnessed in the district. The new secretary set himself to foster a better state of feeling between the masters and men. The former found that they had a man to deal with who was fair-minded and just, who would ask nothing he did not believe to be right. The result of such conduct was that in a few years strikes became almost unknown. At one colliery there had been twenty-three strikes in twenty-six years. Now disputes are referred to the Board of Conciliation, established in 1873, mainly through Mr. Burt's efforts, and they seldom assume an acute form. Before passing to the more public work of Mr. Burt, it should be mentioned that he has not held his position in the miners' union by blindly yielding to the wishes of the members. He has never feared to speak his mind, and more than once has found himself

THOMAS BURT.
From a photograph by A. and C. Taylor, Newcastle-on-Tyne.

opposed to the miners. At such times he has spoken out honestly. Unfair demands have received opposition impartially, whether they came from the masters or the men. His sense of justice has never been blinded by prejudice or interest.

The reform bill of 1867 extended household suffrage to the borough constituencies, and among the alterations made by that act was the incorporation of Blyth and Bedlington into the old borough of Morpeth. The new portion was largely inhabited by miners, who, however, from the conditions under which they held their houses, were not placed upon the register as voters. In 1872 a meeting was held at Choppington with the object of instituting legal proceedings to secure the enfranchisement of miners within the borough. It was decided that if this first step succeeded, a miners' representative should be nominated at the next election. The first step was successful, a candidate was selected, and when Mr. Gladstone suddenly dissolved Parliament in January, 1874, Thomas Burt was that candidate. His election was a triumph. Mr. Burt received 3332 votes, against 585 given to his opponent, Major Duncan, R.A. Since 1874 the miners have voluntarily taxed themselves to the extent of £500 a year to support their representative. During the years of depression which have intervened

THE LATE ALEXANDER MACDONALD.
From a photograph by Lock and Whitfield, London.

they have cheerfully paid their individual share.

From the outset the member for Morpeth won the good opinion of all parties in the House of Commons. He has ever been ready to uphold his views, but never loquacious. Flattery has fallen unheeded upon him, and he has not gone out of his way to seek the company of aristocrats. As the first *bona fide* working-man member, prejudice was arrayed against him, but prejudice soon died down in the presence of his modest, manly bearing and speech. In the House of Commons Mr. Burt has taken his full share of work. His speeches have not been very numerous, but they have commanded attention. Perhaps the most important of these was that in 1878 on the Afghan war, which conflict he unsparingly condemned, characterizing it as "a war that is needless, that is unjust, and that is utterly indefensible." He has seconded more than once Sir Wilfred Lawson's local option resolutions. He took a leading part in the debates of the Employers' Liability Act of 1880, securing several important amendments thereto, and in 1884 he obtained the appointment of additional mines inspectors. He served on the City Livery Commission, and has recently been on the Royal Commission on accidents in mines, and that on loss of life at sea. Since 1881 he has been president of the National Miners' Union, a federation of the various miners' societies.

In the Parliament of 1874 there also appeared Alexander Macdonald, the representative of Stafford, for which constituency he sat until his death, October 31, 1881. No name is regarded with greater affection by the working classes, and especially the miners, of Great Britain, than his, whose life was shortened by his herculean labors on behalf of the mining population. This affection was somewhat surprising to those who did not know the real worth of the man, for Macdonald was at times unfortunate in rousing opposition.

Macdonald was a descendant of the old Highland clan Macdonald. He was born in 1821. He went to work in the mine early in his eighth year, and his period of labor was from twelve to seventeen hours per day. Before he was ten years old, being able to read the newspapers, he devoured with avidity the reports of meetings held at that time on behalf of factory children, and also the accounts of what was being done by the then Lord Ashley (the late Earl of Shaftesbury) on behalf of children and females employed in mines. The movements, together with his own experience, led him to the determination that as far as was possible he would work for the elevation of his class. In those days unions were scarcely known, but the spirit of resistance to tyranny was growing rapidly.

A thirst for knowledge is inborn among Scotchmen. Much of this is due to the influence of Scottish mothers. It was so in the case of Alexander Macdonald. His mother fostered the ambition for learning within him. She worked to help in overcoming the difficulties in his way. And though his hours of labor were so long, much of his leisure was spent in studying grammar, Latin, Greek, and mathematics. But this was not enough. From his earnings and by his mother's help he saved enough to maintain himself at Glasgow University during two sessions. In 1851 he left actual work underground, taking up the duties of a village school-master, in which capacity he remained six years, but never failing to advocate the claims of his old compatriots by voice and pen, or to work on their behalf. In 1857 he gave up teaching and devoted himself to the service of the miners.

Much of the labor of the ex-Lanarkshire miner is to be seen in the various acts of Parliament passed since 1855 for the elevation and protection of the working classes. The measures enacted in 1855, 1860, 1862, and 1872 were largely due to his efforts, and when the select committee appointed in 1865 to inquire into the condition and complaints of the miners was sitting, he attended all the meetings, and such questions were put as he thought would be of service to the miners. The acts for the amendment of the labor law and the abolition of the truck system owed much to his instigation. In 1876 he and Mr. Burt were members of the Labor Laws Commission.

During the great strike of 1868 Mr. Macdonald chartered two of the Anchor Line steamers, in which he took men and their families to America, chiefly to the mining districts of Pennsylvania. He had visited the States the previous year, and he visited the emigrants in 1869 and again in 1876. His wanderings over the continent extended to California, and he was the first Briton who crossed the entire continent by rail. He ever had a warm affection for America. Several of his relatives reside in the States, and one of his brothers, Captain Charles Macdonald, was engaged on the national side during the civil war.

In 1868 Mr. Macdonald was nominated as candidate for the Kilmarnock Burghs, but he retired rather than divide the Liberal vote. At the general election of 1874 Stafford chose him as its member, and again in 1880. This connection was only terminated by his death. The portrait which accompanies this sketch was taken but two months before he passed away. The day of his funeral was a time of general mourning in the pit districts. The blinds of all the miners' cottages in South Durham were drawn for several hours, and now the front of the Durham miners' offices in the city of Durham is graced by an admirable statue of him, "who, being dead, yet speaketh."

After the general election of 1880 another working-man M. P. appeared in the House of Commons, in the person of Mr. Henry Broadhurst, who was then elected as representative of Stoke-upon-Trent. Mr. Broadhurst had been for five years, and he still is, secretary of the Parliamentary Committee of the Trades-Union Congress. Up to 1872 Mr. Broadhurst had been a working stone-mason. In appearance he is a burly, well-made man, whose limbs show capacity for wielding the hammer and lifting heavy weights.

He is essentially a man of action, with a keen, piercing eye which seems to read men as a book; in his appearance and methods he is as unlike Thomas Burt as possible. One is a student, the other a worker. His speeches are full of practical common-sense, and he is a very popular speaker. During the few weeks prior to and at the general election Mr. Broadhurst was in great request throughout the kingdom in support of Liberal candidates, and when the Gladstone government was formed, in February last, he was appointed Undersecretary for Home Affairs.

Mr. Broadhurst can show a remarkable record of Parliamentary work during the five years he has been in the House of Commons. Whilst Mr. Burt and himself work well together, they hold different opinions on some subjects, and act as their own consciences dictate. For instance, Mr. Burt supports the Sunday opening of museums, whilst Mr. Broadhurst strenuously opposes it. Mr. Broadhurst has been actively engaged in the promotion of bills for the welfare of the people. The Employers' Liability Act, passed in 1880, was largely the bill introduced at the instigation of the Parliamentary Committee of the Trades-Union Congress, and was then taken up by the Home Secretary, Sir William Harcourt, on behalf of the government. In the session of 1884 the then member for Stoke took charge of the motion in favor of legalizing marriage with a deceased wife's sister, and successfully carried it by a majority of 111 in the House of Commons. But the bill, introduced into the House of Lords, was thrown out by that august body.

Mr. Broadhurst has also introduced bills for the enfranchisement of leaseholds, for the payment of returning officers' expenses at elections, and for compulsory powers to purchase sites for places of worship. Perhaps the most important work in which he is now engaged is as a member of the Royal Commission on the housing of the poor. Two years ago the country was roused by revelations as to the herding together of the poor in London and other centres of population. A Royal Commission was appointed to inquire into the whole question. The Prince of Wales being a diligent member of this commission as well as Mr. Broadhurst, we have the happy combination of the prince and the ex-stone-mason working together in the arduous task of seeking a solution of this terrible problem.

London sent four working-men members at the recent election to the House of Commons. The best known of these is Mr. George Howell, to whom must be

GEORGE HOWELL.
From a photograph by Barraud, London.

given a leading position, and who ought to make his mark inside, as he has outside, the House. He was born in 1833, at Wrington, Somerset. He was the eldest son of a builder and contractor. For thirty years he has been before the public in one capacity or another. But the fortunes of war, as far as Parliamentary life is concerned, have been against him. Six years before Mr. Burt was selected by the borough of Morpeth, Mr. Howell was a candidate for Parliamentary honors. He contested Aylesbury in 1868, and again in 1874, each time, however, without success. On the death of Mr. Alexander Macdonald, in 1881, he contested Stafford, but was again defeated, by the Irish vote being transferred to the Conservative party. And now, after seventeen years' persevering labor, Mr. Howell has attained the honor of being an M.P. His constituency is the northeastern division of Bethnal Green, one of the most populous districts of eastern London. Mr. Howell is an earnest, active Radical. He is a quondam Chartist, though but a youth during the later years of the Chartist agitation. The reform movements of the last generation have received great assistance at his hand. He acted as organizer of the London demonstrations of 1866, 1867, and 1884. Italian unity, Polish liberty, Hungarian freedom, found in him a warm supporter, and during the American struggle he was one of the strongest upholders of the North. At the great meeting in St. James's Hall, London, presided over by John Bright, Mr. Howell proposed the first resolution. It was his pen that wrote the address to the people of England asking their sympathy with the cause of American freedom, and that also to the American people on the overthrow of slavery. Charles Sumner and others of the Union leaders wrote letters to Mr. Howell expressing their appreciation of what he had done. These letters, it need scarcely be said, have a high place assigned to them amongst his treasures. He was also a member of the Garibaldian committee, a personal friend of Mazzini, and one of the founders of the International Workingmen's Association. Mr. Howell is thus one of the best known men in western Europe, so far as popular movements are concerned. Nor has his activity been confined to organization and speech. He is an able writer, and a contributor to some of the best reviews. He has also written two valuable works, which have been accepted as authorities on their special subjects. The first, *The Handy Book of the Labor Laws*, published in 1876; the other, *The Conflicts of Capital and Labor*, published in 1876.

Like other of the working-men leaders, Mr. Howell was connected with the International Working-men's Association during the early years of its career. Charges of intended revolution, of a desire to promote strife, were freely circulated. Had there been such a desire, abundant opportunity was afforded. During the Fenian disturbances in 1867, the French General Cluseret came to Mr. Howell with letters of introduction from several well-known European and American politicians, including Charles Sumner, Garibaldi, and Mazzini, asking for a meeting with the working-class leaders. This meeting was held in the little room on the first floor, nearest to Oxford Street, of the Black Horse Hotel in Rathbone Place. Here Cluseret unfolded his plans for a general insurrection. Money, arms, and men were promised. But the late George Odger said at once: "Oh, this is not in our line," and rang the bell for the waiter. The thing was treated as a joke. When the Tuileries at Paris was burnt down by the Commune, of which this General Cluseret was a leading spirit, a report of this meeting was found in Napoleon's bureau.* Whether it was a plot of the Emperor to involve Britain in internal difficulties, or a police scheme to entrap these men worked through the French government, has yet to be proved. That those who gave the letters of introduction knew the object for which they were to be used cannot be credited. The English working-men have ever been opposed to violence. Mr. Howell and others withdrew from the International because of its tendency to measures involving force.

The second of the labor candidates elected by metropolitan constituencies was Mr. W. R. Cremer, who represented the Haggerston division of Shoreditch. Mr. Cremer is not an unknown man, and like Mr. Howell he was an unsuccessful candidate at the general election of 1868, when he contested Warwick. He was secretary of the Working-men's International As-

JOSEPH LEICESTER.
From a photograph by Barraud, London.

Karl Marx, the English leaders withdrew from the association. The great meeting held March, 1863, in St. James's Hall, to which reference has already been made, was organized by Mr. Cremer.

War was brought within a short distance of the British shores during the terrible conflict between Germany and France in 1870–71, and there was grave danger more than once that England might be involved in the struggle. This led to the formation of a committee of working-men to protest against English interference in the war. From this committee grew the Working-men's Peace Association, the object of which is to promote peaceable arbitration between nations, and to prevent useless wars or the risk of useless wars. Of that association Mr. Cremer has been secretary for fifteen years, and is editor of the *Arbitrator*, which publishes these principles. He has visited several parts of the continent of Europe in the interests of this society.

Of the labor members who have most recently worked at their respective trades one is Mr. Joseph Leicester, representative of the South Westham division. Up to the time of his accepting the invitation to contest that constituency he was working for his daily bread as a glass-blower. He had intended to give up this work if elected to Parliament, but he was compelled to do so earlier than he wished, and in a way not at all creditable to those whom he had

W. R. CREMER.
From a photograph by Barraud, London.

sociation, with his old friend the late George Odger as president. So soon as other and more dangerous influences came uppermost, such as were represented by

* See *Nineteenth Century*, July, 1878.

J. C. DURANT.
From a photograph by Barraud, London.

faithfully served for so many years. Mr.
Leicester's career has been remarkable.
He possesses great force of character, and
a determined adherence to principle. He
was born at Warrington, in Lancashire,
and is now fifty-eight years of age. He
has, until the time of his election, remained connected with his own trade, of which
he is regarded as one of the best workmen,
and in addition to this he has done a considerable amount of public work. On three
occasions he has won the first prizes offered
by the Society of Arts for artistic work in
glass. At the Paris exhibitions of 1867
and 1878 Mr. Leicester was commissioned
to report on the glass industries, and to
generally represent the interests of English glass-blowing. On the former occasion he was objected to on the ground
that he was too dangerous a revolutionist
to be admitted into the presence of Napoleon III. His visit to the exhibition
would have been prevented but for the
testimony as to his irreproachable character and exceptional fitness for the work,
given him by his employers, with whom
he obtained employment on his first arrival in London, and with whom he remained nearly thirty-five years. He also
served on the jury of the international
exhibition at Islington some years ago.
During Sir Charles Dilke's negotiations
to effect a new commercial treaty with

France, Joseph Leicester was appointed to
represent the glass trade before the French
commission, and the forcible speech which
he then delivered is a model of terse and
powerful argument against protection.

Regarded strictly, Mr. J. C. Durant, who
sits for the London constituency of Mile
End West, cannot be included among the
working-men M.P.'s, for he is an employer, and not himself a workman. But as
he has ever been an ardent upholder of
trades-unions, and a supporter of the extension on a wider scale of rights hitherto
enjoyed by the few, Mr. Durant has so
maintained the good opinion of those from
whom he has risen that his candidature was
recognized by the Labor Representation
Union. He is now forty years old, and
was born at Fordingbridge, in Hampshire,
close to the New Forest. When the Hyde
Park railings fell in 1866 he was one of
those who suffered from the police batons,
and his head still bears the record of that
conflict. Mr. Durant has for many years
been a local preacher, and at one time
contemplated entering the ministry. Of
late years he has been a strong supporter
of Mr. Henry George, and was one of the
founders of the Land National Society, as

WILLIAM CRAWFORD.
From a photograph by A. and C. Taylor, Newcastle-on-Tyne.

well as of the English Land Restoration
Society. He first published George's book
Progress and Poverty, and has been an
ardent upholder of the crofter movement
in the western Highlands of Scotland.

The great mining interest is now represented by six members of Parliament. Thus half of the working-men M.P.'s have been pitmen. This may appear an undue proportion, but it is not difficult to see how it arises. The miners' unions are very powerful, and since the extension of the franchise the congregation of this class of the community in certain districts gives them the dominant influence there.

Of the new members not the least known are the two leaders of the Durham Miners' Association, William Crawford, the secretary, who sits for Mid-Durham, and John Wilson, the treasurer, and the elect of the Houghton-le-Spring division. William Crawford's name is "familiar as household words" in the north of England; and though it may not be so well known elsewhere, it is very familiar to the working-men, especially the miners, of Great Britain. He has been leader in several stout industrial conflicts, and his monthly circular, though addressed to the members of his own organization, is widely read and quoted beyond the confines of the county, dealing as it does with political as well as labor topics. For nearly twenty-five years Mr. Crawford has been earnest in his efforts to secure the rights of the class whence he sprang, and of which he is a true representative in opinions, speech, and style.

John Wilson is another man from whom much is expected. His appearance indicates great force of mind, and he has that calm, conscious strength which is a vast power. He is an orator of no mean ability, a most effective platform speaker, and yet knows how to listen. Words are used by him as tools are by a skilled workman —they are used, not played with. Though forty-eight years of age, Mr. Wilson shows little of the strong Durham intonation of speech. This is to be accounted for by the fact that he has travelled much, and travel in youth and early manhood has polished his tongue. He was born in 1837, at the sea-side village of Greatham, in the county of Durham, six miles south of Hartlepool. When thirteen years of age he entered Ludworth pit as a trapper-boy. Here and at Sherburn Hill colliery he worked until nineteen years of age, when, tiring of under-ground life, he went to sea for nearly four years. The sea was abandoned and the mine entered again in 1859, at Haswell colliery. In 1862 Mr. Wilson married, and the following year emigrated to America,

where he lived for three and a half years, working as a miner in Pennsylvania and Illinois, chiefly at Pittsburgh and Peoria. Here two of his five children were born. Mr. Wilson has therefore some strong ties connecting him with the

JOHN WILSON.
From a photograph by A. and C. Taylor, Newcastle-on-Tyne.

Western republic. Returning to the old country in 1867, the Wilsons settled at Haswell, where they continued to dwell until the last yearly binding, in 1871. For the part John Wilson took in the agitation for the abolition of that bond system he became a marked man, and was refused work by the owners of the pit. Mr. Wilson was appointed treasurer of the Miners' Association in 1882. This office does not merely involve caring for the money of that society, but there is much to do in local arbitrations—a work wherein Wilson has gained the confidence of both employers and employed. During the sad accidents at Seaham colliery in 1879, Trimdon Grange in 1880, and Usworth in 1885 he was foremost in the work of rescue, and he still shows with a pathetic interest a miner's lamp picked up from the side of its dead owner after the Trimdon Grange explosion. He has been a member of the Primitive Methodist community since 1863, and for seventeen years a local preacher in connection with that section of Christians. He is also a teetotaler.

Glancing for a moment across the Tyne, we find from that locality Mr. Burt has had a working-man colleague sent to him in the person of Charles Fenwick, who within three months of the date of his election for the Wansbeck division of Northum-

CHARLES FENWICK.
From a photograph by A. and C. Taylor, Newcastle-on-Tyne.

berland was hewing coals in the Bebside colliery. Like Joseph Leicester, Mr. Fenwick has gone direct from daily toil to the House of Commons. Even after he had become a candidate for Parliament he continued to work in the mine, and the future M.P. might have been found hewing coals in the morning and addressing his fellow-electors in the afternoon. Charles Fenwick has the great advantage of being one of the youngest working-men members of Parliament. That this is an advantage none will dispute; it gives him that early acquaintance with leading men and political movements which would have been impossible had he been born half a generation before; or, if possible, such a position could only have been attained by great expenditure of time, close application, and conflict. His strong mental qualities, excellent memory, sound judgment, and honesty of purpose will, as they have already done, win him the confidence and esteem of all who associate with him.

The mining interest in the south and southwest of Yorkshire is one of the most important in the country, and it is not surprising that so powerful an organization

as the Yorkshire Miners' Association should desire direct representation in Parliament. This has found expression in the election of the secretary, Mr. Benjamin Picard, for the Normanton division of the county. Like all of his colleagues who represent mining districts, Mr. Picard actually worked in the pits until he entered the service of his fellow-workmen as an official of their union. This took place in 1873, when he was appointed assistant secretary of the West Yorkshire Union, succeeding to the secretaryship on the death of Mr. John Dixon, in 1876. When the West and the South Yorkshire associations were amalgamated in 1881, Mr. Picard was made secretary of the joint union. In 1883 he was elected a member of the Wakefield School Board, and he has been for several years vice-president of the Miners' National Union.

With one exception all the labor candidates have been elected by English constituencies. The exception is William Abraham, or "Mabon," as he is known throughout South Wales, who represents the Rhondda Valley district of Glamorganshire. "Mabon" is one of the most interesting figures amongst the working-men members, and, in fact, of the whole House, for he is a poet and a songster of no mean order, and a remarkable orator in his native tongue. All who hear him addressing vast masses in the vernacular are struck with the copiousness of his Cymric vocabulary. He is blessed with a fine tenor voice, approaching very near to a barytone, and it is a treat to hear him in a rich accent pouring forth his eloquence. He is a most popular orator on the temperance platform, and up to the time of his election to Parliament he taught the choir and was leader of the congregational singing at Nazareth Calvinistic Methodist Chapel, Pentre, near Pontypridd. He is a member of the Calvinistic Methodist body, in connection with which he has been brought up from childhood. "Mabon" will therefore be a unique figure in the House of Commons. He was born at Cwmafon, in the county of Glamorgan, in 1842, and is the son of a working miner.

If the Parliament of 1874 is to be remembered as that in which a pitman was first found, and that of 1880 because a mason found a seat, the Parliament of 1885 will be equally remarkable for the fact that the other great branch of industry, agriculture, found for itself direct representation. Thus the great departments of labor — mining, manufacture, and agriculture—have now a voice in making those laws which so nearly concern them. Of these three interests the last-named has been the slowest to shake off the yoke, and the fact of its being the last to find a voice at St. Stephen's is indicative of the slower progress it has made generally toward a better state of things. When miners and industrial trades were struggling for what they regarded as liberty, the agricultural laborers in the midlands and the south of England were yet steeped in a fatal lethargy. The dependence upon those above them which had been inculcated as a religious duty for generations, and rebellion against which was taught to be sinful in the sight of God and man, had sapped the spirit of the rural population. Poor-laws and the action of land-owners had tended to the same end. Those who had a spirit above this kind of life moved away into the towns, leaving behind such only as were too timid to venture on an unknown course, or too supine to seek to improve their position. The condition of the rural laborers is now vastly improved. Wages

WILLIAM ABRAHAM.
From a photograph by A. Freke, Cardiff.

BENJAMIN PICARD.
From a photograph by W. Gothard, Barnsley and Wakefield.

are higher, houses are better, education is spreading, and whatever may be the position of the farmers, that of their workmen is much superior now as compared with fifteen years ago. Much of this improvement is due to Joseph Arch, the Warwick-

shire laborer, who now enters Parliament for the northwest division of the royal and aristocratic county of Norfolk, where he has defeated the heir to a dukedom, Lord Henry Bentinck. The Prince of Wales is numbered amongst the constituents of Joseph Arch.

Joseph Arch, before he became president of the Agricultural Laborers' Union, was an ordinary farm laborer, and the son of a farm laborer, though happily he had raised himself above the level of his class. He therefore knew accurately the condition of things around him. He was born in Barford, a charming Warwickshire village on the banks of Shakespeare's Avon. He still resides there, in a small but cosy cottage. Here by the "ingle nook" of the living-room have been developed those plans which have so greatly assisted in altering the condition of rural English life.

Joseph Arch's mother died when he was sixteen years old, and to her he owes much of what is best in his character. She was an earnest Christian, a Methodist, and she imbued his mind with those sentiments and principles of truth which are the most notable characteristics of his later manhood. She also taught him how to read and write, and fostered his taste for reading and mental application.

As was usual in those days, and is yet to a limited extent, young Arch was sent into the fields to scare birds when eight and a half years old. Later he became ploughboy, and passed through the usual

JOSEPH ARCH.
From a photograph by Elliott and Fry, London.

grades of an agricultural laborer's life, until he reached manhood, when he was able to earn the munificent sum of eleven shillings a week. Ere this he had become a member of the Methodist chapel, and at nineteen began work as a local preacher, which work he has continued through life. Arch married before he was twenty-one years of age. His father and he had been alone since his mother's death, and this loneliness hastened the marriage. His wife has been a great help in all his work, a stimulus to self-improvement, and a supporter amidst the labors of his life. A woman of the people, her hand, through that of her husband, has fought valiantly for their elevation. Six children have been born to them, of which five live, all doing well in the world. Arch is now sixty years of age.

When the first two children were born in the Arch cottage the young laborer received notice that his wages were to be reduced one shilling and sixpence per week. This was an unwelcome change in the face of new responsibilities. But it set him thinking. He began through this apparent reverse to seek for more remunerative work, following work wherever it was most profitable, and, turning his attention to hedging, became ere long the champion hedger of England. This proved to be his opportunity. He had accepted ordinary prices until this time, but when he became champion his charges were raised. The farmers grumbled, and wished they had not let him attain the dignity, but in the end they had to pay. Thus, owner of his little home, and able to com-

mand good wages, with plenty of work, Arch was in a comfortable position, could save money, and obtain comforts which were out of reach of his fellows. This state of things continued till 1872, and Arch says it was the happiest time of his life. On the 7th of February in that year he was working in his garden, when Mrs. Arch came to him and said two men wished to see him about forming a union. His first remark was, "They have not spirit enough to do it," but she said he had better see them. They were men he knew, laborers from the village of Wellesbourne, four miles distant, working on the estate of the Charlecote Lucys—descendants of Shakespeare's Justice Shallow. The men were gaunt in frame, and clothed in veritable coats of many colors. Their garments had been patched and mended until there was barely a trace of the original left. Their story was soon told. Life had been hard, and they had just managed to live, but now a notice of reduction had been given. Everything was dear, and if the reduction were made, it meant starvation. Half a dozen of them, the bolder spirits, had met to talk the matter over, and as a result these two had come as a deputation to ask the Barford hedge-cutter to take up their cause, help them to form a union, and, in short, to become their leader. Arch hesitated. His customers would be the men against whom the fight would be waged. If he took up the laborers' cause, it meant that his living would be gone. But the men, with tears in their eyes, pleaded for help, and he, flinging prudence to the winds, agreed to attend a meeting at Wellesbourne the following week. The only promise he exacted was that the men should pledge themselves to stick together. He expected to see a dozen men at the meeting, but no fewer than fifteen hundred, from all parts of that and the adjoining counties, were gathered together. The inhabitants of the quiet village were terrified. Doors and windows were barricaded. This was the celebrated gathering "under the spreading chestnut-tree." Arch says that when he saw the number of men present he felt the responsibility to be enormous. His first words in speaking to them were to ask a promise that no injury should be done to property or person, and he told his hearers that if they did not keep within the limits of the law he would never stir another finger to help them. This has been his policy throughout. The union was formed. Between six and seven hundred men joined it that night, and by the time another meeting was held, a fortnight afterward, at which over two thousand were present, the movement had spread greatly. Then a demand for a small rise of wages was made, in consequence of which came the Warwickshire lock-out. The union had but five shillings in the treasury to meet the demands upon it, but an appeal was made to trades-unions and members of Parliament, to which there came a noble response. At the end of the lock-out, six months afterward, during which time all those involved received an allowance of nine shillings per week, there was a balance of £800 in hand. No time was lost. A great meeting was held at Leamington on the Good-Friday, and another in May, Branches of the union were formed all over the country. For fifteen weeks Arch went about the country on this work at his own cost, until all his available savings and his watch were gone. He never touched a penny of the money which came to the funds. Then he was elected president, with a small salary—a position which is yet held by him, and is never likely to be wrested from him as long as he lives. From that time forward the movement has grown, and it is growing yet.

Other work has come within the scope of the union. In 1873 the president visited America, not with the object of encouraging emigration, but of assisting laborers if they wished to emigrate. He spent ten weeks in the States and Canada, visiting Boston, New York, and Albany. He was warmly received at Cambridge by Longfellow, by Senator Sumner, and in Boston was welcomed at a dinner at which the Mayor of the city presided, and at a great meeting in Faneuil Hall, where Wendell Phillips was chairman. Early in the conflict Arch saw that it was necessary for the laborers to acquire political power in order to win their rights, and he began to advocate an extension of the franchise. This step alienated many supporters, and subjected the advocate to much calumny and opposition. But its justification has come in recent legislation.

In previous agitations the arguments that had been used were of a physical kind, such as the destruction of crops and fences, but this was peaceful throughout. Very few outrages have marked its course, thanks to the influence of the president and the growing intelligence of the men. The movement has to a large extent been a religious one. Arch, though brought up a Methodist, was excommunicated by the older communion for his sympathy with the reform movement, and is now another Primitive Methodist M.P. added to the list. The union has held several great camp-meetings. At one of these, in Dorsetshire, twelve thousand persons were present, and two services were held on the Sunday.

Mr. Arch contested Wilton against Mr. Sydney Herbert in 1880, but that being a pocket borough, he failed. This is now happily extinguished. An interesting fact of the contest in northwest Norfolk is that the Prince of Wales gave instructions for every one on his Sandringham estates to be permitted perfect freedom in the matter of voting, and that no influence was to be brought upon the workmen by those above them—an example which ought in future to be copied by landowners generally.

BROTHER ANGELAN.

BY HAROLD FREDERIC.

IT will be the easier for me to tell this story succinctly because it is the only romance I know. My years are so few, and save for the few days of which I write my cloistered life has been so serene and uneventful, that it is small wonder the strange things which came so suddenly upon me last summer should have left exceedingly sharp and minute outlines in my mind. During the year already passed I seem not to have lost an iota of the acute vividness of this recollection; I doubt if I ever shall.

The summer was the fierce, parched, windy, suffocating season of the lower Hérault. In the old college of St. Hippolyte, where many generations of lazy, shrewd, fortunate boys of Provence had been trained for the conquest of Paris, there were but three of us brothers left to kill time in utter idleness and seclusion by ourselves. All the pupils had been

sent home, of course, even before the
cholera reached Cette, and eighteen brothers, including our Director, had been
summoned to Paris. We three, left in
charge either as a favor or a slight, I have
never known which, did not repine. The
ancient buildings of which we took up a
little corner were sufficiently near the
main road to Béziers to keep us within
touch of the outside world. From time
to time we heard news of the plague at
Marseilles, Toulon, Aix, and also tidings
of our friends in community elsewhere.
What more could we desire? And as for
our home, there was surely no other place
in all the littoral where one might feel less
the discomforts of the season. The high,
spacious, stone-bound rooms, darkened all
day against the sun, retained always a
grateful coolness; the great garden, with
its fountain in the bathing basin which
kept the leaves above continually moist,
and its thick shade of mulberry and soft
maple, had even at noonday its comfortable nooks, where one could pleasantly
pass time in reading a good book or doz-
ing over its pages.

I am not at all indolent by nature, but I
assuredly enjoyed those somnolent summer months far beyond my wont. Something of this satisfaction was due, no
doubt, to the material pleasures of my
environment, but much more to my companionship. I do not speak so much of
old Brother Mandalus, our Infirmarian,
who presumably had been left as a professional guard against the epidemic, although he was an amiable and considerate
man. It is Brother Angelan, the Subdirector, who rises always in my thoughts
as the one monopolizing feature of our
convent life that summer, as the pivot
upon which everything turned.

I cannot say, certainly I did not feel,
that I knew Angelan very well. There
seemed to be a restraint upon me in talking with him which I never knew with
others, yet I was conspicuously his favorite among all the brothers in the house.
Almost from our first meeting he had
seemed to like me, and soon allowed me
to walk and sit in the garden with him.
I was very young, and combined great eagerness to learn with a naturally deferential manner, which doubtless pleased him.
Looking back, it appears to me that everything I know is due to the wisdom of his
words. Not that he was at all a talker;
often we were together hours with scarce-

ly a word. But when he spoke—although,
as became a man versed in high mathematics and astronomy, and, so it was said,
in all those hidden links which bind us to
the magic of the pyramid-builders, this
was rarely—every word had a strength,
suggestiveness, fibre, which made for it a
lasting place in my mind. The brothers
used to imagine me his confidant. Ah!
that I never was, at least in those days.
I only saw something more than did the
others of the sweetness and depth of his
nature, and guessed somewhat more closely the limits and quality of his disposition. For Angelan was what is called a
sad man, and not all in community got
on perfectly with his moods.

He was not strictly, I suppose, a handsome man, although, until I come to consider the word on paper, I am conscious
of having always *thought* it in connection
with him. He was a tall, fair man, with
lightish brown hair well tinged with
gray, though still much under forty.
Almost alone among all the brothers I
have known, he was so graceful that he
carried our shapeless gown as if it had
been invented to become him, instead of
being an awkward encumbrance. His face
I find it most difficult to describe, save as
that of a serious, reserved, and very capable man, not especially regular or notable, but with fine eyes, blue and full,
and a thin, tight-shut mouth, which could
smile most winningly at times, but was
habitually bent down at the corners as in
grief or self-repression. I have said that
he was a sad and silent brother. He never talked of himself, and there was an un-
objectionable something about him which
made personal questions difficult. I think
no one in the house knew more of him
than that he was from the north, near
Lille, and that he was a teacher before he
entered the brotherhood. Every one felt
his to be our wisest, most elevated mind,
and I fancied that his friendship even reflected a sort of pale dignity upon me in
the eyes of my fellows.

If now or hereafter I seem to speak
with the enthusiasm of undiscriminating
youth, pardon my fondness. My heart
will never grow old enough to throb less
warmly when the name of Brother Angelan is mentioned.

We three came through the dormitory
one morning in August, when prayers were
over, to go down to our coffee and the

day's easy tasks. It was a long, low, des-olate room, with many rows of empty lit-tle white cots, recalling to me only the boyish pupils who had been sent off six weeks before, but to Brother Mandalus suggesting also the host of young Mobiles lodged in turn there when France was last at war, about whom he was never wearied of telling. At the northern end of this room, almost over the staircase, was a narrow casement, the only window not closed overnight against the morning sun. Angelan, as usual, led the way, and, as was his daily habit, leaned out through the casement to view the already sultry morning and report to us. This time he drew back into the room, after a moment, and looked at us with a puzzled air; then gave another, more searching glance through the garden below, and held his head attentively on one side as if listen-ing; then said, as he followed us down the stone stairs, "The birds have all gone."

This may have seemed strange to Man-dalus and me, for the sweet happy matin concert from the shrubbery was as much a part of the daily beginning of life as our prayers or our coffee, but neither of us thought of connecting it with anything else, any more than as if he had said, "The acacia blossoms have withered." When we entered the refectory, Pepin, our lame, crusty old house-servant, was absent, and no amount of ringing across the garden to his quarters could raise an answer; but as he had made some prepa-rations for the morning meal, and, more-over, was at best an erratic fellow, we thought nothing strange of this. Nor, later, after Mandalus had made the cof-fee, and we sat in the droll solitude at one end of the vast table, chatting over our bowls and rolls, did we two dull ones at-tach any special significance to Angelan's queries about the villages nearest to us. Although he had been at St. Hippolyte's more than a year, he knew nothing of the country roundabout, being a bookman, and indifferent enough about his health to hate walking for the sake of exercise; so I fancy it was genuine news to him to learn that our nearest neighbors were in the valley four miles above, in the hamlet of Vorsalçon, and that on the high-road there were three villages nearer than the market-town of Béziers, and in the oppo-site direction two others within a dozen miles.

"Why do you ask?" asked the Infirma-rian, breaking bread lazily in his coffee. "Are you thinking of an excursion? It is fully hot enough here in the shade for me."

I looked up with some vague idea that he might have a long walk in mind, and would invite me to accompany him.

"I ask," he said, quite calmly, "be-cause the cholera is here, within a few miles of us, somewhere. It is from the pest in the air that our birds, wiser than human beings, have fled."

Even while he spoke there came to our ears the faint sound of a voice shouting from the highway. Without a word, and, I should think, obeying some almost me-chanical impulse, Mandalus and I rose and hurried through the front garden to the gate.

Through the arched portal we could see a cart, piled high in air with bedding, furniture, clothes, all sorts of household goods. Its owner, a worthy villager, stood gesticulating wildly at us. His eyes seemed starting from his head with excitement as he waved his hands to keep us back from him, and shouted with trem-ulous energy:

"Come no nearer, brothers. Who knows?—perhaps it is on me. Ah, Sainte Ursule! Twenty souls dead since milk-ing-time at Plessine! They drop like sheep in a murrain over in the valley of the Orb. Death's angel stands at every cor-ner of Béziers. It is the pestilence. At Vorsalçon all who are not dead are dy-ing. All night long the plain has been covered with men, women, children—all in flight. Do you fly also, brothers. I am among the last, because of my bad shoulder, but please the good Sainte Ur-sule, I still shall sleep in Olargues to-night, or kill my horse."

He stopped, breathless. The fat horse, whose high, conical collar with crimson tassels, and straw hat through which his ears protruded, I can still recall best of all in the scene, shook his full sides and made a movement to start, as if impressed by the sinister allusion to himself.

"Of the places nearest us, which suffers the most?" It was Brother Angelan, who had followed us, and stood now domi-nating the short villager, his pale hair glistening from under his cap in the high morning sun.

"Ah, brother, who can say with which hand the devil strikes hardest? From

"I CAUGHT ONLY THE GLIMPSE OF A YOUNG WOMAN'S BLANCHED FACE ON THE PILLOW OF AN
EXTEMPORIZED BED."—[SEE PAGE 524.]

every side one hears stories, each worse than the other. In my village, Saint-Pré, eight died between mass and vespers, and so at Cerel. My shoulder has kept me back, so I do not know the tales from the other side of the hills. But the worst? Surely it must be Vorsalçon, where they say every house has its death-bed, and that none will escape. Already the curé has fled, and no man is left to bury the dead, let alone comfort the dying. But do you fly at once, brothers. Lose no time. I promised your Pepin, whom I met two hours ago scurrying over the road with his limping leg, that I would warn you. Poor faithful fellow! he seemed much distressed for your safety."

"Yes, Pepin has a large heart," said the Subdirector, dryly, as the farmer remounted his perch and rattled off. As he disappeared we turned toward the house in silence. Brother Mandalus, who seemed to breathe heavily, and in other ways not to bear his flesh as easily as usual, broke this silence as we neared the refectory door, which still stood open as in our haste we had left it.

"If we were sure of getting a wagon at Puisserguier, and could count on there being no quarantine, Milhau would be perhaps the best place to go to."

"I have in mind a better place to go to," said Angelan, who stood now in the vine-shaded porch, and turned to look at us—"a much better place."

"Very well, then, Subdirector," replied Mandalus, speaking somewhat testily, for Angelan's ignorance of Southern geography was a byword in the house, "if it is certain that we can make connections, if the air is specially salubrious, if it is easier to reach than Milhau—it is for you to say, of course, not me. Of what place do you speak?"

"Oh, it is very near; one can get there more easily than anywhere else."

"What is this place?"

"Vorsalçon."

Little Mandalus nearly toppled over into my arms. He stared at us both; he clutched his gown nervously with his pursy fingers; he took off his cap in an absent way, and put it back again much out of place. "We go—to—Vorsalçon?" he stammered, as if asking a question in a dream.

"I have not said 'we,' brother," replied Angelan, with a faint smile. "I know that this disease has an exceptional terror for you. Therefore it would be wiser for you to stay. A fearful heart makes a faint stomach. But I certainly shall go; and you, Brother Imbert, I think you will like to accompany me?"

I take no credit to myself for having said "Yes, Subdirector," in a voice which was neither low nor broken, for in truth I spoke mechanically, with a tongue which seemed released from the control of my brain.

During the hour which followed this decision, and which was consumed in preparation, I do not remember having said anything. Brother Mandalus, I know, had a great deal to say about the criminal folly of the venture. To him, he felt free to say, it seemed utterly scandalous, not to say irreligious. He called us to witness that he was no coward, for he had risen at two in the morning daily from August, 1870, to March, 1871, and cooked breakfast for from one to four hundred Mobiles, all as hungry as flames in the dry grass, and Heaven knows it would have been no more wearying work to nurse the wounded on the field of battle, after all the fighting was over, and this he would have unquestionably done had the Prussians not perversely staid in the North. But then, mind you, war was one thing, and pestilence another. The Church had many noble and venerated fraternities for nursing the sick. Every one to his trade. It was our mission, as trained educators, to live for the youth of France, not to put ourselves in the way of dying like flies. Besides, the plague was sent of God— But here Angelan stopped the worthy man's babble by a firm word or two, and the Infirmarian packed the remainder of the opiates, cordials, drugs, and supplies in the two baskets without further ado, only grumbling to himself occasionally.

The Subdirector had made few replies to all these remonstrances and arguments. Doubtless he felt grieved that Mandalus should have made no better showing of courage. But he was not angry, for when we were quite ready to start, with our thick shoes, and our skirts well tucked up, and the last words about laudanum and ammoniac and filters and cooling bandages had been spoken, he went up to the Infirmarian and kissed him on both cheeks. The poor old man, his weak nature already sorely tried by the shocks of the morning, nearly broke down at this. He bade us a most feeling adieu—it was a real effort for him not to say farewell instead—beseeching us to

take all manner of precautions, and, almost in tears, intimating that he was ashamed of having suggested flight, and that he would surely stay to welcome us back. I know that I felt all this to be grievously weak in old Mandalus, who should have been firmer. Yet I doubt not Brother Imbert, in a silent way, quaked quite as ingloriously just then.

So we started. The heat was already considerable, and, perhaps because my fancy was so keenly at work, the morning air seemed tainted and stifling. Each bore a basket, such as Pepin used for bringing eggs and the like from neighboring markets; but these were not heavy, and we should have made good progress had the way been less difficult. But there was no road leading to the doomed hamlet, and our course lay up the valley of a little river—the same which, wider and more imposing, crossed our highway not far from the college under the ancient arches of a Roman bridge. The bed of the stream was nearly dry now, under the fierce August sun, and the gray limestones were even at that hour warm beneath our feet. The leaves of the few trees which found root on the inhospitable sides of the valley hung parched and motionless in the hot air. The ceaseless cry of the insects in the brown grass seemed one of suffering, and jarred painfully on the nerves. The thin rivulet of water, which found its way to the Orb sluggishly here and there between bowlders and over the slimy pebbles, looked black and bad. Angelan said that doubtless in this water the whole mischief lay.

Once, when we stopped for a minute's rest in the shade of a great, jagged, overhanging rock, such as I have seen nowhere in France save in these southern valleys, where ungovernable mountain torrents eat capriciously through the soft stone, he looked in my face curiously, and asked, "Art thou afraid, little one?" This was his caressing name for me in affectionate moments, though I was nearly his equal in stature, and was much larger in bone.

I made answer: "If we were going to the hospital of some great city, I should not fear in the least, for my uncle, who is a physician in Marseilles, says there is no danger of infection there. Witness the case of the Duc de Chartres, who last month went through all these hospitals without injury. But you won't misunderstand me if I say that the prospect of penetrating into a wretched little village where every cottage is a pest-house, where all the unknown elements of contagion are focussed, so to speak, makes me nervous. I am not afraid; no; but I am apprehensive."

I said this timidly yet frankly, seeking for words which should not make me seem a poltroon in his eyes, yet should honestly portray my state of mind—if anything so chaotic could be called a state. I still found it impossible to actually realize what I was doing, where I was going.

He smiled on me in a fatherly way, and said, as we lifted our baskets for another start, "Keep up thy courage, Imbert; there will be no need of undue exposure for thee."

It must have taken us fully two hours to reach Vorsalçon. As we gained the plateau, where cultivation began again, and bent our steps across the dry fields toward the tiny church spire in the distance, not a soul was to be seen. The hamlet, with its flat-gabled, tile-roofed, Spanish-looking houses showing irregular outlines through the dark shadows of pomegranate-trees in rich, full bloom; the long straight rows of short, square-cut olive-trees, their silver-green leaves so much like the willows of spring-time on my native Oise, stretching away on either side of our foot-path to converge to the eye with geometrical precision in the distance; the neat little walls, whose white stones shone in the strong light like our snow of the North beneath the thick creeping vines—these bespoke human toil, human hopes; but for all the signs of human life we saw our progress might have been through a desert. On the whole broad slope of hill land above and beyond the village; through the low avenues between the olives, which seemed to be moving in procession as we walked through them; over the smooth expanse of unbroken meadow which led off toward the château—no living thing was in sight. Even the insects' shrill chirrup was hushed here. I shuddered at the awful significance of this sunlit solitude.

Our path broadened into a lane as we neared the first straggling houses of Vorsalçon, and the centre upon which we walked had become bare and white with use. A goat, crouched in the shelter of the wall and its dusty overhanging verd-

ure, bleated piteously to us as we passed. Its plaint conveyed no meaning to me; but Angelan went to the suffering animal and relieved its swollen udder. We entered the high-road of the hamlet, the goat following at our heels.

In the centre of this wide, irregular street, which here had the air of a place because destitute of the shade that narrowed the thoroughfare further on, there stood some sort of ancient monument, part cross, part image, worn and defaced to shapelessness through centuries, and about which to this day antiquarians are no wiser than I am.

At the foot of this monument, seated on its pedestal, was a man, his elbows on his knees, his face hidden in his hands, the whole as lifeless to appearance as the scene of which he seemed so fit a part. We came close to him without his making a movement, and as Angelan touched him on the shoulder, the sickening fear that I was looking on a corpse chilled my stomach. But no, he raised his head, and one could see at a glance that he was not a sick man. His dress was that of a miller, but showed that he had not recently been in the floury air. He was well along in years, with iron-gray beard and hair, big and rather fierce black eyebrows, sharp eyes, and mouth bent down at the corners in a resolute fashion. He had evidently been asleep, and he studied us for an instant before he seemed to collect himself. Then he scowled, and, with a repellent gesture, said to us in a rough voice:

"Here you! *calotins!* While one is in the business he may as well save your lives along with those of honest men. Go back! Get out! The air here makes dead men every little hour. Don't you understand? The plague is here."

Angelan replied, gently: "We know the plague is here. That is why we came. And don't call us *calotins*, my friend, for our house-caps may cover the heads of good men as well as millers' hats. Rather tell us, if you belong to this place, what hopes and means of help there are here."

The miller looked him in the eye, still scowling. "I am not your friend, nor the friend of any black-gown. You don't know me. I am called the impious miller, because I hate all you shavelings. Mothers here would let their children starve rather than eat my flour, because it is cursed, do you see. Luckily, in the cities they are not all idiots, or it is I who would starve." Then, with a stormier accent: "Why don't you run, I say, like that fine cousin of yours, Monsieur le Curé, while there is still time? He waited no urging, I can tell you. Or do you want to fill your baskets before you go?"

Angelan looked vexed and discouraged. "You are either a very bad man or a great fool," he said, raising his voice as he went on. "Don't you see we have come here to try and save lives, to be of use, and have brought medicines with us? and you, *misérable*, waste precious time with your silly talk!" The Subdirector's blue eyes flashed as he spoke, and his fists clinched with the fire of the old Adam.

The miller had gazed at us very steadily from the first, or rather at my companion, and now turned his deep eyes on me. If he had any mind-reading gifts, he must have divined that I thought him a wretched fellow. While I was still striving to properly express my indignation on my face, he shut his eyes for a moment, stretched his arms and yawned, looked us all over again, and then said, "Truly, now, have you come to help?"

"For what else, simpleton?" demanded Angelan, still sharply.

"Ah! pardon, messieurs," the miller replied, straightening himself, and speaking more at his ease. "I begin to understand you better. But you do not understand me when you call me a simpleton. I have read many more books, and more sensible ones too, than the curé. But, you see, I show badly because of my weariness. I have been at work most of the night burying the dead as well as I could. Poor souls, how religious they were! even after death they struggled against burial at the hands of the impious miller." (He alluded to the *post-mortem* agitation in cholera subjects, which few villagers knew aught about at this time; so that, worthy man, he had his superstitions as well as the rest, proud as he was of his superiority.) "I am the only well man left. All the terrible labor has been mine, single-handed. At dawn I came here to warn back the farmers of Ville du Pont and Beyralle, who pass through here Thursday mornings on their way to market. I must have been too tired to keep awake, and I was still drowsy when I spoke to you."

Brother Angelan held out his hand, saying: "You are an honest man, and I was much in the wrong to speak harshly

to you. But your speech was none of the softest either."

They shook hands frankly.

The miller's eyes twinkled with a melancholy sort of amusement. "No," he said. "I woke up with a feud against all churchmen. Even in my dreams here I did not forget my wrath at the curé, who packed off his valuables yesterday morning, and, so they say, even galloped through mass that he might fly before the sun was high. *He!* the very rascal who had cried so loudly that Marseilles and Toulon were being punished by the pest for their infidelity, and who told old Mother Panet yesterday that my irreligion —*mine*, do you hear?—had very likely provoked God to strike this region also! But—pardon, messieurs—did I tell you that I was irreligious?"

"Next autumn will do to talk of that," said Angelan—wisely, I suppose. "Now tell me the state of the village—where the sick are which need help first, what you have done, and all. I know something of this class of disease. We have drugs, and we have courage."

It was a gloomy story which we heard, the while Brother Angelan, listening carefully, opened his basket, and broke an egg in a glass of wine for each of us. There were scarcely any sick left. From almost every house the devoted miller during the evening and night had drawn some dread addition to his lonely task. Some had even died in their gardens or on their door-steps; and of this latter we saw an instance, which I shall never forget. The panic had been sudden, scandalous, awful. When the curé set the example, it had become a rout. Parents had fled, leaving their children behind to die. A wife whose husband was seized with death had locked him out in the stable that she might have an uninfected bed to carry with her in her flight. So the hideous recital went on, the old man's right hand locating each cruel incident for us as our eyes followed up the street. There were in all some dozen people who had been living at three that morning, when he came down here to watch. Of these he assumed some were dead, while it was probable that all would die, save perhaps in one house at the very end of the hamlet, where the plague seemed to have softened its blow, doubtless because the inmates were of gentle blood, and where there was no immediate danger, he thought.

"And you?" asked Angelan, as he took the miller's hand again on parting. "Are you in no need of aid? Shall you escape?"

"Ah, thanks to that precious curé, I am much too angry to be ill. Do not fear for me."

It would in no way help my story, and would only give unnecessary pain, to recount the terrors of the two hours which followed, as we went from house to house up the village highway, with open, vacant doors and windows where there were not the still more suggestive closed shutters, on either side, and the smell and sinister silence of death all about us. I am afraid that I hung back a good deal; certainly nowhere did I take the initiative; and though after the first few minutes of real trial I gained some sort of control of my nerves, the heart that I bore about in my breast weighed like platinum. As for my companion, I have no words to describe what he seemed to me in those hours, so gentle, so resourceful, so handsome!

We had been in some half-dozen of these rudely built, ancient, rustic houses, never, I should think, very inviting, and now unspeakably otherwise, but, alas! with no good results beyond lightening an irrevocable doom by religious words and soothing opiate drinks, when we came to the dwelling which the miller had specially indicated as the one where lives might be saved. Angelan had originally thought of coming here first of all, but could not bring himself to pass the other and meaner habitations in which helpless wretches lay without solace or succor.

The dwelling which we approached was not conspicuously larger or better than the others, perhaps, but it bore all those hundred and one external signs which, without defining themselves to the mind, betoken none the less surely inhabitants of a superior class. There was more set pretence of a flower garden than one commonly sees in the South. The wall was tidily kept. The carmine blossoms in the trees overhead seemed larger and more lustrous than elsewhere. The fields back and on the side away from the hamlet, which by their extent argued affluence beyond that of the mere villager, were spick and span in the cleanliness of the stubble and the pruned regularity of the hedge-rows. The lower shutters in the front of the house were closed, but in the small windows under the eaves there were curtains, surely a rare thing in Vorsalçon. The door-stone was bright with careful polishing.

Angelan knocked at the unfastened door; then pushed it open and entered. I was following him, but as the door opened, the vast contrast between the chilling, fatal darkness within and the beauty and rich joy of life outside in the sunshine seemed all at once to appeal to and overcome me. I caught only the glimpse of a young woman's blanched face on the pillow of an extemporized bed through the blackness of the shadows, when this feeling of faintness came over me. I leaned against the doorway, trying, I remember, to breathe deep enough to draw down some fragrance from the fruit flowers above, and thus save my reeling senses. How long this state had continued I know not, when I heard Angelan's voice, raised in a strange, startled cry, "Constance! you here!"

A moment later, as I was collecting my wits under the spur of curiosity, and beginning to feel strong enough to enter, the Subdirector came to the door, excitedly, I thought, and with some hesitancy made known his wish that I should expose myself no more—he had been extremely careful of me from the beginning —but should wait outside in the cool shade. I am now ashamed to recall the secret joy with which I felt myself assenting, though I was not without some worldly wonderment about his desire to be alone in this special house of death, where he seemed to be acquainted.

As I paced to and fro on the shaded side of the building, musing upon the great experiences of the morning, I heard a voice as of a child singing in doleful, crooning measure to itself, in the open air and not far away. Tracing the sound, as well as I could, to a little goat shelter at the rear of the house, I came upon a tiny girl of three or four years, enthroned in the clean straw, and plaiting a necklace of flowers for a pretty kid which lay curled at her knees. She sang softly meantime, while the eyes of the pet followed hers intently.

Ah, what a sweet sight, after all the squalid, tragic scenes of the day! She was a wonderfully dark child, with a skin like dusky Siena marble, and great deep black eyes, and she fondled her docile playmate with a rapt Oriental tenderness one may imagine in a Cleopatra. So I fancied, at least, and I stood watching her for some time before she saw me or I spoke. When at last she caught sight of me she seemed less embarrassed than myself, and asked me calmly who I was. In the conversation which ensued, drolly old-fashioned on her part, she told me nothing save that her name was Constance, that this was her kid, that she had been put out to sleep with it here all night, with some bread, a crust of which lay on the straw, and that papa and mamma were both ill—very ill.

While I stood thus gravely conversing with this swarthy mite, Angelan came to us. Without a word he lifted the child up from the straw into his arms, and kissed her a dozen times, I should think, with a moaning, caressing sound. "These are your mother's last kisses, my poor baby," he murmured, sobs breaking the words.

When he finally, still holding the child in his arms, turned his face to me, I saw that it was ashen in color, with a great sadness in the eyes, and with what seemed to be new lines graven about the mouth.

"Imbert," he said, still in a tear-choked voice, "I have just been through a most sorrowful experience—sadder than anything you can imagine. I cannot tell you about it now; some time you shall know it all—all; but now like a friend you will help me, won't you, in some things I am sworn to do?"

"Ah, how can you ask me?" I broke in, profoundly moved, yet knowing nothing of what so deeply stirred me.

As we walked toward the front again he briefly told me that he would carry the child to the college. She had escaped contagion thus far, and doubtless would altogether, if removed. Some other task he began to outline to me, and then abruptly stopped. I do not like to think that he failed to trust me wholly, but rather that his own mind was not entirely clear about this proposed action.

I carried both the lightened baskets now, while the Subdirector bore the child. She seemed not unwilling to come, stipulating only that the kid should also be brought. When we had passed into the high-road Angelan stopped, turned toward the house, and, still with little Constance in his arms, knelt in the white dust for a prayer. I knelt also. There were real tears in his eyes as he gave his parting look toward the closed shutters.

At the monument the brave miller was still posted. He had finished the food we gave him, and was smoking placidly. The black outlines of a cart and horse hurrying away on the distant horizon of hill testified to his latest public service. The Subdirector recounted to him briefly what had been done and what remained to be done in the dwellings this side of little Constance's stricken home. Then with a gesture he led him aside, and the two men talked in low tones for a few moments, of course about this last visit of ours. I won't pretend that I did not feel piqued at this exclusion, but that doesn't matter. Soon they moved toward me again, and Angelan, who had never once put the child aside, said we would start.

The old miller had taken off his hat, with an awkward, unaccustomed gesture, and stood before us. "Messieurs," he said, with a bow which included us both, but looking only at the Subdirector, "I travelled out of my way this morning to inform you that I was not religious. Since I have said it, let it pass as true. I do not attend the services of M. le Curé, who just now happens to be absent"—(he could not forget his hatred of this bad priest even while struggling with a compliment to the Church)—"and I am a Radical—against all black-gowns in politics. But you must not go before I say to you that if religion meant men like you, if to be religious meant to believe in you and try to imitate you and obey you, why, then no one would have intentions more holy than mine."

The sorrowful look faded from Angelan's face for the moment, and he almost smiled. "Tut! tut!" he said, "there are good and bad, weak and strong, everywhere. The brave, devoted priests in other villages more than atone for one coward at Vorsalçon. You old Frenchmen are only irreligious in your fancy, because of your vanity, and you desire to make a grand impression on one another. You forget us all when you are well, but in the hour of trial, on the battle-field, in the pest-house, the old childish love and faith always return. Do not be deceived about yourself. I think you are in fact about the most religious man I ever knew. If you were not, I shouldn't be as fond of you as I am." The words do not seem especially gracious as I have put them down, but I shall not soon forget the delighted face of the miller as he shook us by the hand again and again, and, after we started, called out to Angelan that he would not fail to remember their arrangement.

Thus we started down the valley on our homeward way, the baby girl asleep on Angelan's shoulder, the little kid ambling behind us, the loose bottles clinking in my baskets at every step. Dark clouds had leaped over the sky; a cold, penetrating, dust-laden mistral was blowing with a sough through the olives like a moan from last night's graves. The Subdirector never spoke during the journey.

At the extreme end of the spacious garden of the college, and nearest the little gate by which we had started for Vorsalçon, was a small building in which I have already mentioned that our single servant, the scamp, had quarters. When school was full, four other servants had slept there—for we had never had brother servitors here—but they had left at vacation, and now cowardly Pepin too was gone. On the ground-floor was a kind of shop, where repairs and tinkering of all sorts were done, and a rough staircase led to the two plain, low dormitories into which the upper floor was divided. It was here that Angelan installed little Constance, and that same day, from some place, I never knew where, he managed to bring an old peasant woman to care for her. This I learned afterward.

Very little—in fact, next to nothing—were we allowed to know of his movements at the time. He did not enter the college buildings at all on our return, but spoke to unhappy Mandalus through the doorway, telling him not to go near the servants' quarters—he laid the same injunction on me—as there might be danger, and not to be disturbed in mind if for the next week or so he should be absent, as there was work he must do. To me Brother Angelan said, before I left him to go into the house:

"My dear Imbert, the risks are greater for you, with your lack of mature strength, than I supposed. I hope you have not already received injury. I will not have you expose yourself again. Change at once all your clothes, and have these boiled thoroughly before they are worn again. Do you too stay away from the servants' house; you can do no good there, and harm may come to you. It is my wish." He must have seen the look of pain in my face, for he added

quickly, and oh! with what an affectionate tone: "Do not think, little one, that I am not wholly pleased with thee, or that I do not love thee very dearly. But thou must please me in this too, and—and I promise if the slightest need arises, thou shalt be sent for." He made as if to kiss me, then drew back with a haste which I did not then understand, pressed my hand in both his, and so sent me in to Mandalus.

Poor old Infirmarian! from his melancholy visage and deep sighs one would have thought his heart was breaking. Indeed, for both of us what remained of the day was a long, wearisome affair, and the sleep-broken night insufferable. All the next day we had but a single thought; every few minutes we cast anxious glances through the thick foliage over the fountain to the servants' house. Some few patches of its gray stones we could see through the leaves, but no sign of life. It seemed as if the day would never end. Once a peasant on horseback stopped in front, and called us out to tell us that the plague was raging fiercely in Béziers and Agde, and that in almost all the villages of the lower Hérault utter panic reigned. We heard him without interest, and returned dejectedly to the house. How hateful and stupid its bare white walls, stone floors, and hard narrow benches seemed! "He said a week," thought I; "how shall I ever get through a whole week like this?" But we were not to wait so long.

On the second day the miller came to the refectory door, saw Mandalus, held a long conversation with him about certain drugs and their effects, got some provisions and linen, and went away again into the rear of the garden. I saw him from an upstairs window, and hurried to meet him, but he was gone when I reached the door, and dull Mandalus had asked him nothing!

It was near the evening of the third day—that is, on Sunday following the Thursday of our visit to Vorsalçon—that the old miller came again to the door, and this time he asked for the young brother —for me! Judge with what haste I ran to him, how gladly I would have taken him by the hand! But he held back, and, while asking me to walk in the garden with him, said it would be better for me to keep on the other side of the path. Considering that I had been through the most desperate forms of exposure, and that he had come, though I knew it not, to conduct me to a cholera chamber, this precaution was rather ridiculous, I see now, but I was too impatient then to think of it. So we walked slowly, a yard apart, to and from the fountain, with poor Brother Mandalus eagerly watching us from the window.

"I have come to tell you a story—a true story," whispered this strange miller across the gravel. "I suppose it was told me only in order that you might know it—for he said he had promised to tell you, and that is out of the question now."

"Oh, our Lady! Then is he—"

"'Sh-h! Wait first for the story. Then you are to go to him. It is not long, and I will tell it as briefly as may be. A young gentleman, an orphan, with high position but little fortune, loved a young lady in Orleans. He was a teacher, the youngest in the university, but among the ablest; she was much younger, childish, perhaps silly. Their love dream of a year was very sweet—you don't know anything about these matters, but you can see by the sequel how he loved her. Her mother, a wealthy widow, was not favorable to his suit, because of his poverty, but still did not say 'no,' and he knew the young lady loved him. Suddenly he had news of the death of some forgotten relative in Lille, which gave him a fortune as large as it was unexpected. With eyes brimming with joy, for he could not pretend to be a mourner, he went to the widow, and was accepted as the betrothed of her daughter. He pressed a kiss upon the lips of this daughter; it was the first, and also the last—or no, there was one other long afterward. It was necessary for him to leave at once for Lille to settle the estate, and the happy day was fixed for only two months ahead.

"He left behind him a rich young Greek, as beautiful, as cunning, as wicked, as a serpent, who also loved this young lady, and with that furious Oriental love which knows no obstacles. This Greek forged two lying letters, one to him from Orleans, one to her from Lille, and with the cleverness of sin arranged a series which, in the minds of each, fitted the other's perfidy. Then, with the witchcraft of his dark beauty over her, he played upon the passions and jealousies of her young heart, how you would not under-stand, until he induced her madly to fly with him. That was seven years ago."

Fancy hearing all this, whispered in the queer Provençal dialect, across three feet of path! I could see no earthly relevancy in it, so slow of wit was I, and once the thought occurred to me that much suffering had turned the miller's head. He went on:

"The young professor was ill for a time, heart-broken for years. He found consolation, as it is called, finally in religion. He became a brother of the Christian schools."

Ah! it came clearly enough to me now, and the shock stopped my breath.

"Meanwhile," continued the miller, "the Greek and his wife—they were married—came to Marseilles. There a child was born to them. By accumulated ill-luck—a ship sinking now, then an olive crop failing—they became reduced, until nothing available was left but a village plantation in the Hérault, which his father, a usurer, had taken for debt, and which they had never seen. They moved to this village last spring.

"Your God, young brother, does strange things. One day He smote the house of this Greek with pestilence, and the same day He filled the heart of the wronged Christian brother with a yearning to go forth and succor the afflicted, and led him to that very house."

He stopped short. I was so filled with amazement at this astonishing story, so like a dream of fiction, yet almost a part of my own life, that I could say nothing. We were again turned toward the servants' house, and this time, by silent consent, we passed the fountain and walked toward it. At the door I found my tongue to ask two questions—alas! the great question of all I instinctively felt it was useless to ask.

"And the—the woman. Is she dead?"

"We buried her the night of the day you were at Vorsalçon."

"Did the Greek die?"

"No, curses on him!"

The profanity of this rejoinder passed without attracting my attention, so proper a part did it seem of the narrative which it concluded. The miller had been much excited at the close of his recital, and he panted now for breath as we climbed the dark stairs. I heard him mutter to himself, as he fumbled with a key at the door, which it seemed odd that he should have locked, "At all events, if he leaves here alive, the brother's word will have been kept."

As we entered the first of the two chambers I was surprised to see there, sitting dressed on the edge of the pallet, a man I did not know—a tall, athletic, dark man, with straight, handsome features and a glossy, short beard. He looked up at us for a moment—it was a disagreeable look, as from eyes not rightly placed together —and then turned his head away with an indifferent air.

"This is the Greek," said the miller, in a voice too low for the further room, but perfectly audible throughout ours. "This is the descendant of all those grand heroes we read about. You are astonished to see him here? On my honor I too am amazed whenever I look at him. Yet I helped bring him here none the less. It was about that we talked apart at the village cross the other day. We two, the brother and I, bore him on a litter that very night, after we had buried *her*. The brother had promised her, I think; at least, excellent man, he felt it to be his duty. Yet both the brother and she had known of this creature's treachery for years, and he had ill-treated her besides. Ah, who knows! Doubtless it is because I am not religious that *I* seem to have no duty toward people like him, except to— to throttle them."

The Greek did not appear to be disturbed by either the miller's scowling regard or his contemptuous words. He rose, stretched himself carelessly, and sauntered to the window, without paying further attention to us. I remember very well that he had a tread like a cat, easy and noiseless.

"The brother nursed him well, you see," continued the miller, still with his scowling eyes fastened on him, and in the same low tones of concentrated rage. "*He* is quite well again, you see—quite strong and hearty, the scoundrel. It does not at all worry him that his family should die. Oh no; it rather agrees with his health."

Still the Greek was silent. This strange encounter, if it did not annoy him, was certainly painful to me, as one can easily comprehend, and I was glad when my guide gave a signal that it was at an end by moving toward the closed door leading to the other room.

Ah! the sight! I saw first of all a

priest, a grave, white-haired curé, brought from I know not where during the day by the indefatigable miller. The window by which he sat, deep in his breviary, was open, and the faint first breath of the mistral stirred softly, and spread into the air in transparent waves a thin column of smoke rising from some pastilles in a brazier on the floor near us. Through this pale haze, and, as it were, transfigured by it, I saw Brother Angelan, and knew in an instant that he was dying. There was nothing dread or ghastly in his face. It seemed, as I stole nearer the bed, even sweeter and nobler than the face I had known—a face upon which the very light of heaven was shining. He lay with eyes closed, one arm above the sheet. I had never seen him in white before, and this added to the effect of gentle purity in the sight. Yes, he was dying; and the little girl, whose tiny, dusky form lay beside him, upon his arm, she also was dying.

"He asked to have her brought to him just before he sent for you," softly whispered the miller. "Hush! he sees you."

My dear friend was indeed looking at me, with wide, appealing eyes. I stood at his side, taking his thin, fevered hand in mine. He uttered to me, speaking without much effort, but with great weakness, some very precious personal words, which do not belong to this story. Then came a pause, during which I stroked his hand gently, and tried in vain to keep the hot tears back. But now his regard seemed upon some distant object, still directed toward me, it is true, but as if seeing something far, far beyond. His lips—nay, his whole face—melted into a most tender smile, and he murmured,

"But, Constance, if it be true that I die because I kissed you, still it was right; for without the kiss you would have died doubting my forgiveness."

His eyelids closed wearily. For some minutes he was silent: they seemed hours. Then his hand stirred in mine, and a movement, as if of a great change, ran through his frame. He spoke again, in a clearer voice, with infinite peace in its tones:

"In te, Domine, speravi; non confundar in æternum."

Some one touched my shoulder. It was the venerable priest, and I read in his sad eyes that what remained belonged to him and to God. Thus I parted forever on earth from Brother Angelan.

THE HOME ACRE.

BY E. P. ROE.

VII.—STRAWBERRIES.

THERE is a very general impression that light, dry, sandy soils are the best for the strawberry. Just the reverse of this is true. In its desire for moisture it is almost an aquatic plant. Experienced horticulturists have learned to recognize this truth, which the Hon. Marshall P. Wilder has suggested in the following piquant manner: "In the first place, the strawberry's chief need is a great deal of water. In the second place, it needs more water. In the third place, I think I would give it a great deal more water."

While emphasizing this truth the reader should at the same time be warned against land whereon water stands above the surface in winter and spring, or stagnates beneath the surface at any time. Moisture is essential to the best results; good drainage is equally so. The marvellous crops of strawberries raised in California under well-directed systems of irrigation should teach us useful lessons. The plants, instead of producing a partially developed crop within a few brief days, continue in bearing through weeks and months. It may often be possible to supply abundantly on the home acre this vital requirement of moisture, and I shall refer to this point further on.

My first advice in regard to strawberries is to set them out immediately almost anywhere except upon land so recently in grass that the sod is still undecayed. This course is better than not to have the fruit at all, or to wait for it. A year without strawberries is a lost year in one serious respect. While there is a wide difference between what plants can do under unfavorable conditions and what they can be made to do when their needs are fully met, they will probably in any event yield a fair supply of delicious fruit. Secure this as soon as possible. At the same time remember that a plant of a good variety is a genius capable of wonderful development. In ordinary circumstances it is like the "mute, inglorious poets" whose enforced limitations were lamented by the poet Gray; but when its innate powers and gifts are fully nourished it expands into surprising proportions, sends up hundreds of flowers, which are followed by ruby gems of fruit whose exquisite flavor is only surpassed by its beauty. No such concentrated ambrosia ever graced the feasts of the Olympian gods, for they were restricted to the humble *Fragaria vesca*, or Alpine species. In discovering the New World, Columbus also discovered the true strawberry, and died without knowledge of this result of his achievement.

I can imagine the expression on the faces of those who buy the "sour, crude, half-ripe Wilsons," against which the poet Bryant inveighed so justly. The market is flooded with this fruit, because it bears transportation about as well as would marbles. Yes, they are strawberries; choke-pears and Seckels belong to the same species. There is truth enough in my exaggeration to warrant the assertion that if we would enjoy the possible strawberry we must raise it ourselves, and pick it when fully matured—ready for the table and not for market. Then any man's garden can furnish something better than was found in Eden.

Having started a strawberry patch without loss of time wherever it was handiest, we can now give our attention to the formation of an ideal bed. In this instance we must shun the shade of trees above and their roots beneath. The land should be open to the sky, and the sun free to practise his alchemy on the fruit the greater part of the day. The most favorable soil is a sandy loam, verging toward clay, and it should have been under cultivation sufficiently long to destroy all roots of grass and perennial weeds. Put on the fertilizer with a free hand. If it is barnyard manure, the rate of sixty tons to the acre is not in excess. A strawberry plant has a large appetite and excellent digestion. It prefers decidedly manure from the cow stable, but that from the horse stable answers very well, but it is not advisable to incorporate it with the soil in its raw, unfermented state, and then to plant immediately. The ground can scarcely be too rich for strawberries, but it can easily be overheated and stimulated. In fertilizing ever keep in mind the two great requisites, moisture and coolness. Manure from the horse stable, therefore, is about doubled in value as well as bulk if composted with leaves, muck, or sods, and allowed to decay before being used.

Next to enriching the soil the most important step is to deepen it. If a plough is used, sink it to the beam, run it twice in a furrow. If a lifting subsoil-plough can follow, all the better. Strawberry roots have been traced two feet below the surface.

If the location of the plot does not admit the use of a plough, let the gardener begin at one side and trench the area to at least the depth of eighteen inches, taking pains to mix the surface, subsoil, and fertilizer evenly and thoroughly. A small plot thus treated will yield as much as one three or four times as large. One of the chief advantages of thus deepening the soil is that the plants are insured against their worst enemy—drought. How often I have seen beds in early June languishing for moisture, the fruit trusses lying on the ground, fainting under the burden, and the berries ripening prematurely into little more than diminutive collections of seeds! When ground has been deepened as I have said, the drought must be almost unparalleled to resist the development of the fruit. Even in the most favorable seasons, hard, shallow soils give but a brief period of strawberries; the fruit ripens all at once, and although the first berries may be of good size, the later ones dwindle until they are scarcely larger than peas. Be sure to have a deep, mellow soil beneath the plants.

Such a bed can be made in either spring or fall; indeed, at any time when the soil is free from frost, and neither too wet nor dry. I do not believe in preparing and fertilizing ground during a period of drought.

We will suppose the work has been done in the spring, as early as the earth was dry enough to crumble freely, and that the surface of the bed is smooth, mellow, and ready for the plants. Stretch a garden line down the length of the plot two feet from the outer edge, and set the plants along the line one foot apart from each other. Let the roots be spread out, and not buried in a mat, the earth pressed *firmly* against them, and the crown of the plant be exactly even with the surface of the soil, which should also be pressed closely around it with the fingers. This

may seem minute detail, yet much dismal experience proves it to be essential. I have employed scores of men, and the great majority at first would either bury the crowns out of sight or else leave part of the roots exposed, and the remainder so loose in the soil that a sharp gale would blow the plants away. There is no one so economical of time as the hired man whose time is paid for. He is ever bent on saving a minute or half-minute in this kind of work. On one occasion I had to reset a good part of an acre on which my men had saved time in planting. If I had asked them to save the plants in the year of '86, they might have "struck."

The first row having been set out, I advise that the line be moved forward three feet. This would make the rows three feet apart—not too far in ground prepared as described, and in view of the subsequent method of cultivation. The bed may therefore be filled up in this ratio, the plants one foot apart in the row, and the rows three feet apart. The next point in my system, for the kind of soil named (for light sandy soils another plan will be indicated), is to regard each plant as an individual that is to be developed to the utmost. Of course only young plants of the previous season's growth should be used. If a plant has old, woody, black roots, throw it away. Plants set out in April will begin to blossom in May. These buds and blossoms should be picked off ruthlessly as soon as they appear. Never does avarice overreach itself more completely than when plants are permitted to bear the same season in which they are set out. The young, half-established plant is drained of its vitality in producing a little imperfect fruit, yet this is permitted even by farmers who would hold up their hands at the idea of harnessing a colt to a plough.

The plants do not know anything about our purpose in regard to them. They merely seek to follow the law of nature to propagate themselves, first by seeds which, strictly speaking, are the fruit, and then by runners. These slender tendril-like growths begin to appear early in summer, and if left unchecked will mat the ground about the parent with young plants by late autumn. If we wish plants, let them grow by all means; but if fruit is our object, why should we let them grow? Because nearly every one seems to do it, would be, perhaps, the most rational answer. This is a mistake, for many are beginning to take just the opposite course even when growing strawberries by the acre.

Let us fix our attention on a single plant. It has a certain amount of root pasturage and space in which to grow. Since it is not permitted to produce an indefinite number of young plants, it begins to develop itself. The soil is rich, the roots are busy, and there must be an outlet. The original plant cannot form others, and therefore begins to produce fruit crowns for the coming year. All the sap, all the increasing power of root and foliage, is directed to preparation for fruit. In brief, we have got the plant in traces; it is pulling in the direction we wish; it will eventually deliver a load of berries which would surprise those who trust simply to nature unguided.

Some one may object that this is a troublesome and expensive way of growing strawberries. Do not the facts in the case prove the reverse? A plant restricted to a single root can be hoed and worked around like a hill of corn or a currant bush. With comparatively little trouble the ground between the rows can be kept clean and mellow. Under the common system, which allows the runners to interlace and mat the ground, you soon have an almost endless amount of hand-weeding to do, and even this fails if white clover, sorrel, and certain grasses once get a start. The system I advocate forbids neglect; the runners must be clipped off as fast as they appear, and they continue to grow from June till frost; but the actual labor of the year is reduced to a minimum. A little boy or girl could keep a large bed clipped by the occasional use of a shears or knife before breakfast, and if the ground between the plants is free of runners, it can be hoed over in an hour. Considering, therefore, merely the trouble and expense, the single-plant system has the facts in its favor. But our object is not to grow strawberry plants with the least trouble, but to have strawberries of the largest and finest quality.

In addition to ease and thoroughness of cultivation there are other important advantages. The single narrow row of plants is more easily protected against winter's frosts. Light strawy manure from the horse stable serves well for this purpose, but it should be light and free from heat. I have seen beds destroyed by too heavy a covering of chunky, rank manure. It is not our purpose to keep the beds and plants from freezing, but from alternately freezing and thawing. If snow fell on the bed in December and lasted till April, no other protection would be needed. Nature, in this latitude, has no sympathy for the careless man. Last winter, during January, and again in February and March, the ground was bare, unprotected plants were badly frozen, and in many instances lifted partly out of the ground by mid-day thawing and night freezing. The only safe course is to cover the rows thoroughly, but not heavily, early in December. If then light stable manure is not at hand, leaves, old bean vines, or any dry refuse from the garden not containing injurious seeds will answer. Do not employ asparagus tops which contain seed. Of course we wish this vegetable, but not in the strawberry bed. Like some people out of their proper sphere, asparagus may easily become a nuisance, and it will dispossess other growths of their rights and places as serenely as a Knight of Labor. The proper balance must be kept in the garden as well as in society, and therefore it is important to cover our plants with something that will not speedily become a usurper. Let it be a settled point, then, that the narrow rows must be covered thoroughly out of sight with some light material which will not rest with smothering weight on the plants or leave among them injurious seeds. Light stable manure is often objected to for the reason that employing it is like sowing the ground with grass seed. If the plants had been allowed to grow in matted beds I would not use this material for a winter covering unless it had been allowed to heat sufficiently to destroy the grass and clover seed contained in it. I have seen matted beds protected with stable manure that were fit to mow by June, the plants and fruit having been swamped with grass. No such result need follow if the plants are cultivated in a single line, for then the manure can be raked off in early spring—first of April in our latitude—and the ground cultivated. There is a great advantage in employing light manure if the system I advocate is followed, for the melting snows and rains carry the richness of the fertilizer to the roots, and winter protection serves a double purpose.

We will now consider the proper management for the second year, when a full crop should be yielded. I know that many authorities frown upon cultivation during the second spring, before plants bear their fruit. I cannot agree with this view, except in regard to very light soils, and look upon it as a relic of the old theory that sandy land was the best for strawberries. Take the soil under consideration, a sandy loam, for instance. After the frost is out, the earth settled, and the winter covering raked off, the soil under the spring sun grows hard, and by June is almost as solid as a road-bed. Every one knows that land in such condition suffers tenfold more severely from drought than if it were light and mellow from cultivation. Perennial weeds that sprouted late in the fall or early spring get a start, and by fruiting time are rampant. I do advocate *early* spring cultivation, and by it I almost double my crop, while at the same time maintaining a mastery over the weeds.

As soon as the severe frosts are over, in April, I rake the coarsest of the stable manure from the plants, leaving the finer and decayed portions as a fertilizer. Then, when the ground is dry enough to work, I have a man weed out the rows, and if there are vacant spaces, fill in the rows with young plants. The man then forks the ground lightly between the rows, and stirs the surface merely among the plants. Thus all the hard, sodden surface is loosened or scarified, opened to the reception of air and light, dew and rain. The man is charged emphatically that in this cultivation he must not lift the plants or disturb the roots to any extent. If I find a plant with its hold upon the ground loosened, I know there has been careless work. Before digging along the row the fork is sunk beside the plants to prevent the soil from lifting in cakes, and the plants with them. In brief, pains are taken that the plants should be just as firm in the soil after cultivation as before. Let the reader carefully observe that this work is done *early* in April, while the plants are comparatively *dormant*. Most emphatically it should not be done in May, after the blossoms begin to appear. If the bed has been neglected till that time, the *surface merely* can be cultivated with a hoe. When the plants have approached so near to the fruiting, the roots must not be disturbed at all. *Early* cultivation gives time for new roots to grow, and

stimulates such growth. Where the rows are sufficiently long, and the ground permits it, this early loosening of the soil is accomplished with a horse-cultivator better than with a fork, the hoe following, and levelling the soil and taking out all weeds.

My next step during the second season is to mulch the plants in order to keep the fruit clean. Without this mulch the fruit is usually unfit for the table. A dashing shower splashes the berries with mud and grit, the fruit must be washed before it is eaten, and strawberries with their sun-bestowed beauty and flavor washed away are as ridiculous as mere noise from musical instruments.

At least mulch as soon as possible after the plants begin to blossom, and also after a good soaking rain. In this case the litter keeps the ground moist. If the soil immediately about the plants is covered when dry, the mulch may keep it dry, to the great detriment of the forming berries. It is usually best to put on the mulch as soon as the early cultivation is over in April, and then the bed can be left till the fruit is picked. Of course it may be necessary to pull out some rank-growing weeds from time to time. If the hired man is left to do the mulching very late in the season, he will probably cover much of the green fruit and blossoms as well as the ground.

After the berries have been picked, the remaining treatment of the year is very simple. Rake out the mulch, cultivate the soil, keep the plants free of weeds and runners as during the previous year. Before hard freezing weather protect again as before, and give the plants similar treatment the following spring and summer. Under this system the same plants can be kept in bearing three, four, and five years, according to the variety. Some kinds maintain their vigor longer than others. After the first year the disposition to run declines, and with the third year, in most instances, deterioration in the plant itself begins. I would therefore advise that under this system a new bed be made, as described, every third year, for, it should be remembered, the new bed is unproductive the first year. This should never be forgotten if one would maintain a continuous supply of berries, or otherwise he will be like those born on the 29th of February, and have only occasional birthdays.

If the old bed is just where you wish, and has been prepared in the thorough manner described, it can be renewed in the following manner: When the old plants begin to decline in vigor, say the third or fourth spring, a line of well-decayed compost and manure from the cow stable a foot wide can be spread thickly down between the rows, dug under deeply, and young plants set out just over the fertilizer. The old plants can be treated as has already been described, and, as soon as they are through bearing, dug under. This would leave the young plants in full possession of the ground, and the cultivation and management for three or more years would go on as already directed. This course involves no loss of time or change of ground for a long period. If, however, a new bed can be made somewhere else, the plants will thrive better upon it. Unless there are serious objections, a change of ground is always advantageous, for no matter how lavishly the plot is enriched, the strawberry appears to exhaust certain required constituents in the soil; continued vigor is better maintained by wood-ashes perhaps than by any other fertilizer, after the soil is once deepened and enriched, and it may be regarded as one of the very best tonics for the strawberry plant. Bone meal is almost equally good. Guano and kindred fertilizers are too stimulating, and have not the staying qualities required.

As has been intimated before, the strawberry bed may often be so located on the home acre as to permit of irrigation. This does not mean sprinkling and splattering with water, but the continuous maintenance of abundant moisture during the critical period from the time the fruit begins to grow until it ripens. Partial watering during a drought is very injurious; so also would be too frequent watering. If the ground could be soaked twice a week in the evening, and then left to the hardening and maturing influence of the sun and wind, the finest results would be secured. I am satisfied that in most localities the size of the berries and the number of quarts produced could be doubled by judicious irrigation.

The system given above applies not only to sandy loam, but also to all varieties of clay, even the most stubborn. In the latter instance it would be well to employ stable manure in the initial enriching, for this would tend to lighten and warm the soil. Care also must be exercised in not working clay when it is too wet or too dry. Mulch also plays an important part on heavy clay, for it prevents the soil from baking and cracking. One of the best methods of preventing this is to top-dress the ground with stable manure, and hoe it in from time to time when fighting the weeds. This keeps the surface open and mellow—a vital necessity for vigorous growth. Few plants will thrive when the surface is hard and baked. Nevertheless, if I had to choose between heavy clay and light sand for strawberries, I should much prefer the clay. On the last-named soil an abundant winter protection is absolutely necessary, or else the plants will freeze entirely out of the ground.

The native strain of cultivated strawberries has so much vigor and adaptation that plenty of excellent varieties can be grown on the lightest soil. In this instance, however, we would suggest important modifications in preparation and culture. The soil, as has been already shown, must be treated like a spendthrift. Deep ploughing or spading should be avoided, as the subsoil is too loose and leachy already. The initial enriching of the bed should be generous, but not lavish. You cannot deposit fertilizers for long-continued use. I should prefer to harrow or rake in the manure, leaving it near the surface. The rains will carry it down fast enough. One of the very best methods is to open furrows, three feet apart, with a light corn plough, half fill them with decayed compost, again run the plough through to mix the fertilizer with the soil; then level the ground, and set out the plants immediately over the manure. They thus get the benefit of it before it can leach away. The accomplished horticulturist Mr. P. T. Quinn, of Newark, New Jersey, has achieved remarkable success by this plan.

It is a well-known fact that on light land strawberry plants are not so long-lived, and do not develop or "stool out," as it is termed, as on heavier land. In order to secure the largest and best possible crop, therefore, I should not advise a single line of plants, but rather a narrow bed of plants, say eighteen inches wide, leaving eighteen inches for a walk. I should not allow this bed to be matted with an indefinite number of little plants crowding each other into feeble life, but would leave only those runners which had taken root early, and destroy the rest. A plant which forms in June and the first weeks in July has time to mature good-sized fruit buds before winter, especially if given space in which to develop. This, however, would be impossible if the runners were allowed to sod the ground thickly. In principle I should carry out the first system, and give each plant space in which to grow upon its own root as large as it naturally would in a light soil, and I would have a sufficient number of plants to supply the deficiency in growth. On good loamy soil the foliage of single lines of plants, three feet apart, will grow so large as to touch across the spaces; but this could scarcely be expected on light soil unless irrigation was combined with great fertility. Nevertheless, a bed with plants standing not too thickly upon it will give an abundance of superb fruit.

Strawberries grown in beds may not require so much spring mulching to keep the fruit clean, but should carefully receive all that is needed. Winter protection also is not so indispensable as on heavier soils, but it always well repays. A thick bed of plants should never be protected by any kind of litter which would leave seeds of various kinds, for under this system of culture weeds must be taken out by hand, and this is always slow, back-aching work.

When plants are grown in beds it does not pay to continue them after fruiting the third year. For instance, they are set out in spring, and during the first season they are permitted to make a limited number of runners, and prepare to fruit the following year. After the berries are picked the third year, dig the plants under, and occupy the ground with something else. On light soils, and when the plants are grown in beds instead of narrow rows, new beds should be set out every alternate year.

In order to have an abundant supply of young plants it is only necessary to let one end of a row or a small portion of a bed run at will. Then new plants can be set out as desired.

While more strawberries are planted in spring than at any other time, certain advantages are secured by summer and fall setting. This is especially true of the gardens wherein early crops are maturing, leaving the ground vacant. For instance,

there are areas from which early peas, beans, or potatoes have been gathered. Suppose such a plot is ready for something else in July or August, the earlier the better. Unless the ground is very dry, a bed can be prepared as has been described. If the soil is in good condition, rich and deep, it can be dug thoroughly, and the plants set out at once in the cool of the evening, or just before a shower. During the hot season a great advantage is secured if the plants are set immediately after the ground is prepared, and while the surface is still moist. It is unfortunate if ground is made ready and then permitted to dry out before planting takes place, for watering, no matter how thorough, has not so good an influence in starting new growth as the natural moisture of the soil. It would be better, therefore, to dig the ground late in the afternoon, and set out the plants the same evening. Watering, however, should never be dispensed with during warm weather, unless there is a certainty of rain, and even then it does no harm.

Suppose one wishes to set a new bed in July. If he has strawberries growing on his place, his course would be to let some of his favorite varieties make new runners as early as possible. These should be well-rooted young plants by the middle of the month. After the new ground is prepared, these can be taken up, with a ball of earth attached to their roots, and carried carefully to their new starting-place. If they are removed so gently as not to shake off the earth from the roots, they will not know they have been moved, but continue to thrive without wilting a leaf. If such transplanting is done immediately after a soaking rain, the soil will cling to the roots so tenaciously as to insure a transfer that will not cause any check of growth. But it is not necessary to wait for rain. At five in the afternoon soak with water the ground in which the young plants are standing, and by six o'clock you can take up the plants with their roots encased in clinging earth just as successfully as after a rain. Plants thus transferred, and watered after being set out, will not wilt although the thermometer is in the nineties the following day. If young plants are scarce, take up the strongest and best-rooted ones, and leave the runner attached; set out such plants with their balls of earth four feet apart in the row, and with a lump of earth fasten down the runners along the line. Within a month these runners will fill up the new rows as closely as is desirable. Then all propagation in the new beds should be checked, and the plants compelled to develop for fruiting in the coming season. In this latitude a plant thus transferred in July or August will bear a very good crop the following June, and the berries will probably be larger than in the following years. This tendency to produce very large fruit is characteristic of young plants set out in summer. It thus may be seen that plants set in spring cannot produce a good crop of fruit under about fourteen months, while others, set in summer, will yield in nine or ten months. I have set out many acres in summer and early autumn with the most satisfactory results. Thereafter the plants were treated in precisely the same manner as those set in spring.

If the plants must be bought and transported from a distance during hot weather, I should not advise the purchase of any except those grown in pots. Nursery-men have made us familiar with pot-grown plants, for we fill our flower beds with them. In like manner strawberry plants are grown and sold. Little pots, three inches across at the top, are sunk in the earth along a strawberry row, and the runners so fastened down that they take root in these pots. In about two weeks the young plant will fill a pot with roots. It may then be severed from the parent, and transported almost any distance, like a verbena. Usually the ball of earth and roots is separated from the pot, and is then wrapped in paper before being packed in the shallow box employed for shipping purposes. A nursery-man once distributed in a summer throughout the country a hundred thousand plants of one variety grown in this manner. The earth encasing the roots sustained the plants during transportation and after setting sufficiently to prevent any loss worth mentioning.

Some have adopted this system in raising strawberries for market. They prepare very rich beds, fill them with pot-grown plants in June or July, take from these plants one crop the following June, then plough them under. As a rule, however, such plants cannot be bought in quantities before August and September.

As we go south, September, October, and November, according to lowness of latitude, are the favorite months for planting. I have had excellent success on the Hudson in late autumn planting. My method has been to cover the young plants, just before the ground froze, with two or three inches of clean earth, and then to rake it off again early in April. The roots of such plants become thoroughly established during the winter, and start with double vigor. Plants set out in *late* autumn do best on light, dry soils. On heavy soils they will be frozen out unless well covered. They should not be allowed to bear the following season. A late-set plant cannot before winter in our climate become strong and sturdy enough to produce much fruit the following season. I make it a rule not to permit plants set out after the 1st of October to bear fruit until a year from the following June.

In setting out plants, the principle of sex should be remembered. The majority of our favorite varieties are bisexual; that is, the blossoms are furnished with both stamens and pistils. A variety with this organization, as the Sharpless, for instance, will bear alone with no other kind near it. But if one set out a bed of Champions—another fine variety—well apart from any staminate kind, it would blossom profusely, but produce no fruit. When I was a boy, Hovey's Seedling was the great strawberry of the day, and marvellous stories were told of the productiveness of the plants and the size of the berries. How well I remember the disappointment and wrath of people who bought the plants at a high price, and set them out with no staminate varieties near to fertilize the pistillate blossoms! Expectations were raised to the highest pitch by profuse blossoming in May, but not a berry could be found the ensuing June. The vigorous plants were only a mockery, and the people who sold them were berated as humbugs. To-day the most highly praised strawberry is the Jewell. The originator, Mr. P. M. Augur, writes me that "plants set two feet by eighteen inches apart, August 1, 1884, in June, 1885, completely covered the ground, touching both ways, and averaged little over a quart to the plant for the entire patch." All runners were kept off, in accordance with the system advocated in this paper. "At Boston a silver medal was awarded to this variety as the best new strawberry introduced within five years." People reading such laudation—well deserved, I believe— might conclude the best is good enough for us, and send for enough Jewell plants to set out a bed. If they set no others near it, their experience would be similar to that which I witnessed in the case of Hovey's' Seedling thirty odd years ago. The blossom of the Jewell contains pistils only, and will produce no fruit unless a staminate variety is planted near. I have never considered this an objection against a variety; for why should any one wish to raise only one variety of strawberry? All danger of barrenness in pistillate kinds is removed absolutely by planting stami- nate sorts in the same bed. In nursery- men's catalogues pistillate varieties are marked "P.," and the purchaser has mere- ly to set out the plants within a few feet of some perfect-flowering kind to secure abundant fruit.

As a result of much experience, I will now make some suggestions as to varie- ties. In a former paper I have given the opinions of others upon this important subject, and one can follow the advice of such eminent authorities without misgiv- ing. The earliest strawberry that I have ever raised, and one of the best flavored, is the Crystal City. It is evidently a wild variety domesticated, and it has the ex- quisite flavor and perfume of the field berry. It rarely fails to give us fruit in May, and my children, with the unerring taste of connoisseurs, follow it up until the last berry is picked. It would run all over the garden unchecked, and this pro- pensity must be severely curbed to render a bed productive. Keeping earliness and high flavor in view, I would next recom- mend the Black Defiance. It is not re- markably productive on many soils, but the fruit is so delicious that it well de- serves a place. The Duchess and Bidwell follow in the order of ripening. On my grounds they have always made enormous plants, and yielded an abundance of good- flavored berries. The Downing is early to medium in the season of ripening, and should be in every collection. The Indi- ana is said to resemble this kind, and to be an improvement upon it. Miner's Pro- lific is another kindred berry, and a most excellent one. Among the latest berries I recommend the Sharpless, Champion, or Windsor Chief, and Parry. If one wishes to raise a very large late, showy berry, let him try the Longfellow. The Cornelia is said to grow very large and ripen late, but

I have not yet fruited it. As I said fifteen or twenty years ago, if I were restricted to but one variety, I would choose the Tri- omphe de Gand, a foreign kind, but well adapted to rich heavy soils. The berries begin to ripen early, and last very late. The Memphis Late has always been the last to mature on my grounds, and, like the Crystal City, is either a wild variety or else but slightly removed. The Wilson is the great berry of commerce. It is not ripe when it is red, and therefore is rarely eaten in perfection. Let it get almost black in its ripeness, and it is one of the richest berries in existence. With a lib- eral allowance of sugar and cream, it makes a dish much too good for an aver- age king. It is also the best variety for preserving.

It should be remembered that all straw- berries, unlike pears, should be allowed to mature fully before being picked. Many a variety is condemned because the fruit is eaten prematurely. There is no richer berry in existence than the Windsor Chief, yet the fruit, when merely red, is decided- ly disagreeable.

The reader can now make a selection of kinds which should give him six weeks of strawberries. At the same time he must be warned that plants growing in a hard, dry, poor soil, and in matted beds, yield their fruit almost together, no mat- ter how many varieties may have been set out. Under such conditions the straw- berry season is brief indeed.

While I was writing this paper the chief enemy of the strawberry came blundering and bumping about my lamp—the May- beetle. The larva of this insect, the well- known white grub, has an insatiable ap- petite for strawberry roots, and in some localities and seasons is very destructive. One year I lost at least one hundred thou- sand plants by this pest. This beetle does not often lay its egg in well-cultivated ground, and we may reasonably hope to escape its ravages in a garden. If, when preparing for a bed, many white grubs are found in the soil, I should certainly ad- vise that another locality be chosen. The only remedy is to dig out the larvæ and kill them. If you find a plant wilting without apparent cause, you may be sure that a grub is feeding on the roots. The strawberry plant is comparatively free from insect enemies and disease, and rare- ly disappoints any one who gives it a tithe of the attention it deserves.

SHORT-HORN CATTLE.

BY LEWIS F. ALLEN.

THIS noble breed of bovines is of remote origin. For some centuries previous to the conquest of England by the first William, in the year 1066, the warlike Scandinavians of Denmark and Sweden had made frequent predatory incursions into Northumbria. The object of these incursions was conquest, plunder, trade, and subjection of the Britons to their rule and domination. Many of the marauders settled in Northumbria, and became incorporated with the natives by marriage and succession of their families, and so remained until the invading forces were driven back to their own shores under the power of the new conqueror. As a consequence of the Scandinavian invasions commerce between them and the Northumbrians became frequent, and the cattle of the neighboring continent were more or less introduced on to British soil. So far as we can learn from imperfect history and tradition, those cattle were large in size, short in the horns, rather coarse frames, the cows giving abundance of milk, and, when fatted for slaughter, heavy weights of beef

of rather coarse quality. Their colors were either pure white, or pale red, or red and white more or less intermixed into roan, or brindled, sometimes red, no other colors prevailing.

It has been from that ancient stock, in all probability, that the grand breed of improved short-horns has descended. The ancestors of them trace to no other parts of England than the counties of ancient Northumbria, where the Scandinavians held rule previous to the Norman Conquest. A striking evidence of the existence of these cattle at an early date is now seen in a piece of statuary in an arched niche of Durham Cathedral, twenty feet or more above the ground. The figures are a fair resemblance of a short-horn cow of her day with two milkmaids attending. The present sculpture is of comparatively modern date, probably between the years 1790 and 1800, when some parts of the tower were taken out and repaired. The original statue was too much broken to be replaced, and the present one is said to be an exact copy of the original. Even this has been somewhat mutilated. The

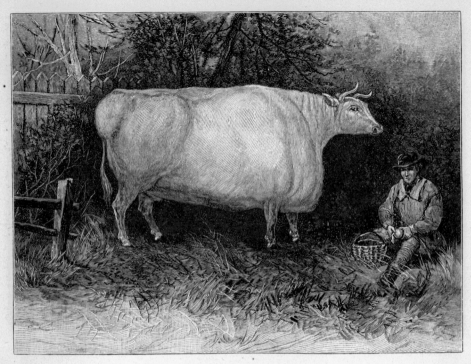

"THE WHITE HEIFER THAT TRAVELLED."

cathedral was finished about the year 1300.

Why the statue was so inserted in the tower is explained by an ancient monkish legend existing some centuries previous to its original erection. Its condensed account may be given as follows:

"St. Cuthbert, famed for royal descent and many great virtues, died on the 20th of March, 687, and was buried in Holy Island—a meet place for so worthy and sanctified a man. There his body rested for two hundred years, but fearing it would be disturbed by the devastations of the Danes, it was exhumed for reinterment a few miles from Dunholme (now Durham), where it remained for one hundred and thirteen years. Then the remains were removed to Ripon, in Yorkshire, and after four months again taken for a final resting-place to Dunholme. On their way thither, Bishop Aldwinus and the monks having charge of the removal, when a few miles from their destination, lost their way, when they stopped in despair, not knowing exactly where Dunholme lay. Soon, however, they heard a woman calling to another whom she met that her cow had strayed away, and asked if she had seen her. 'Yes,' was the reply; 'just beyond Dunholme.' Thus guided by the wo-

men, they found their way, and deposited the remains in a rude temporary cathedral, constructed for the purpose, until the year 1093, when the corner-stone of the present cathedral was laid."

This statue may be criticised as not representing correctly a modern short-horn cow, but as it does not represent one of any other known breed, it affords quite probable evidence of that at an early period. The agriculture of England for some centuries after the Conquest was rude, and progressive stock-breeding was in a like condition. The clergy and monks of those early days were altogether superior in learning to the better classes of the people or even the nobility, and as they had appropriated many of the choicest selections of land on which to build the monasteries and abbeys, it may be supposed that the limited agriculture in which they engaged was of a much higher order than that of the rude peasantry around them, that they also cultivated a better taste in their domesticated animals, and adopting the short-horn cattle as their models, improved their qualities to a considerable extent. The noblemen of their vicinities may have profited by their example, and, as time progressed, an increase in the good qualities of their cattle might have followed to a time when subsequent history could give truthful chronicles of their condition.

We have traditional reports of the ex- of short-horns, descending to the present day.

Down to the year 1780 many conspicuous breeders of short-horns were scattered through the Northumbrian counties, yet their cattle, with all their excellent qualities, had not attained a wide notoriety in England. About that year two brothers,

DUCHESS, BY DAISY BULL.

cellences of many of these cattle so far back as the seventeenth century, in which their great weights were known. More or less of the nobility had engaged in their breeding and cultivation, and their progress was onward. In the year 1737 was born a remarkably fine animal, Studley Bull (626), recorded in the first volume of the English Short-horn Herd-book, published in the year 1822. No pedigree is given to him, and he is only described as "red and white, bred by Mr. Sharter, of Chilton."

In the year 1739 the cow Tripes, daughter of Studley Bull, was born, "bred by Mr. Stephenson, of Ketton." She was the ancestor of the numerous "Princess" tribe

Robert and Charles Colling, sons of a short-horn breeder, began their vocation in that line, and settled on two neighboring farms in Yorkshire, near the river Tees. They were enterprising young men, and selected their animals from among the best herds of the neighboring breeders. Determined to spread the reputation of the breed broadly through the adjoining counties, Charles bred "The Durham Ox," and fed him until five years old, when he had attained the weight of 3024 pounds. In the year 1801 he sold him for £140 ($700). A carriage was made for him, and after travelling and exhibiting him for five weeks, he was again sold, to John Day, for £250 ($1250). Two months

COMET.

afterward Mr. Day was offered and refused £2000 ($10,000) for him as an exhibiting value. Mr. Day travelled with him nearly six years through the principal counties of England and Scotland, till at Oxford the ox dislocated his hipbone, and continued in that state eight weeks, when he was slaughtered. He lost considerable flesh after the injury, yet his dead weight was, in his four quarters of beef, 2322 pounds; tallow, 156 pounds; hide, 142 pounds—profitable weights. At ten years his live weight was 3400 pounds.

About the year 1806 Robert Colling bred "The White Heifer that Travelled," which, not proving a breeder, was fed and sent out for exhibition through various counties for some years. Her live weight was estimated at 2300 pounds, and, when slaughtered, her profitable dead weight at 1820 pounds.

There were other extraordinary weights of short-horn cattle bred by contemporaries of the Collings, not important to be recorded. The milking quality of many of the cows of those days was remarkable, many of them yielding thirty quarts (Eng-lish measure) daily, on good pasturage, in their full season, of good butter quality. Duchess, by Daisy Bull, bred by Charles Colling, was noted as one of them. A constant breeder, she was slaughtered at seventeen years old, and made an excellent carcass of beef.

Large numbers of cattle reared by breeders in the counties of Northumberland, Durham, York, and Lincoln were of superlative excellence and form. The most remarkable bull of his day was Comet (155), bred by Charles Colling in the year 1804, and sold at his great sale in 1810 for 1000 guineas (upward of $5000), the highest price yet obtained.

These portraits are of nearly eighty years ago, and the excellence of their originals is proven by the fact that many noted bulls and cows of the time of the Collings were sold at prices ranging from £100 to £500, and even larger sums. They were reared by the eminent breeders Mason, Wetherell, Maynard, Sir Henry V. Tempest, Booth, and others, and the popularity which they had achieved created a demand through many counties of England richly remunerative to their propagators. So progressed the English short-horns until their early introduction to the United States.

and Miller, of Virginia, into Baltimore, Maryland. What were the exact genealogies of the cattle is not known. Some

A SHORT-HORN BULL.

It has been asserted, no doubt truthfully, that soon after our Revolutionary war, and previous to 1790, a few short-horns of both sexes were imported by Messrs. Goff of their descendants were a few years afterward taken to Kentucky, where they were highly approved, and bred to the native cows of the "blue-grass" counties.

They much improved the progeny of the cattle where they were bred. Soon after the war, also, a few short-horns were imported from England to the city of New York by a Mr. Hustler. From them we have no accurate account; but in a short time he returned to England with one of the young cows, and there she became celebrated as "The American Cow," and the ancestress of many valuable animals of the present day, both in England and America.

In the year 1815 Mr. Samuel Miles Hopkins, an eminent lawyer of New York, imported a bull and two cows, and placed them on his farm in Livingston County. Their descendants proved of valuable service in the herds of that vicinity. In the year 1816 an Englishman, Mr. Cox, imported a few short-horns to the vicinity of Albany, New York, where they were bred, and many good animals descended from them. In 1817 Colonel Lewis Sanders, of Kentucky, imported three bulls and three cows, certified in their bills of sale to be thorough-bred short-horns; but as the English Herd-book was not published until the year 1822, no record of their pedigrees was established. They were received with great favor in Kentucky, and numerous descendants from them, of excellent quality, with pedigrees, have been recorded both in the English and American Herd-books. In the years from 1817 to 1830 several wealthy merchants and other enterprising gentlemen in Massachusetts, New York, Pennsylvania, and Maryland made importations of well-bred pedigreed short-horns. From 1824 to 1826 Colonel John Hare Powell, of Philadelphia, made the larger number of these importations, chiefly from the extensive herd of Jonas Whitaker, of Yorkshire. They were first-class animals, and of the best pedigree. Some of the cows proved extraordinary milkers, giving nearly twenty pounds of butter per week, on grass pasture, in the height of the season. Several of the descendants from them were taken to Kentucky and other States, until the herd was dispersed. The prices paid for these imported cattle are not accurately known, but are supposed to have been from $300 to $500 each.

Stimulated by the success of short-horns in Kentucky, Mr. Walter Dun, of that State, in 1833-6, imported several fine ones, and soon afterward some of them were sold for from $450 to nearly $1500

each. In 1834 to 1836 a company of breeders in the Scioto Valley, Ohio, made three importations of upward of forty head. They were kept and bred together until the latter part of the year 1836 and early in 1837, when they were sold at public auction, and distributed mostly among the stockholders, though more than sixty went to Kentucky. Their prices ranged from $300 to $1500 each, while two of the bulls brought $2500 each.

In the years 1835 to 1840 several importations were made into New York and Kentucky. Mr. Weddle, an English immigrant, brought a dozen or more into Ontario County, New York. Mr. Ezra P. Prentice, of Albany, and Mr. George Vail, of Troy, New York, each imported as many as Mr. Weddle, all first-quality animals, those of Mr. Vail being chiefly from the herd of the noted breeder Thomas Bates, of Kirkleavington. In 1836 Messrs. Le Roy and Newbould imported several excellent short-horns, and bred them successfully on their broad farms in the Genesee Valley, New York. In 1837 to 1839 the distinguished English breeder Jonas Whitaker of Yorkshire sent a considerable number to Philadelphia, where they sold at prices averaging $353 for bulls and $480 for cows. In the years 1837 and 1839 Messrs. James Shelby and Henry Clay, Jun., jointly, and Dr. S. D. Martin, of Kentucky, imported several well-selected animals, most of which were soon afterward sold and distributed in that State. About the same years Mr. William Gibbons imported some short-horns for his farm in Madison, New Jersey. At about this time also Mr. John Fisher Sheafe and Mr. James Lenox, of New York city, imported several choice animals, and placed them on their fine estates at New Hamburg, Dutchess County. In 1839 Rev. T. Dillard and Mr. Nelson J. Dudley, of Lexington, Kentucky, imported a considerable number, which in July, 1840, were sold at auction, averaging $422 each for eleven bulls, and $620 each for twenty females. A few other small herds were imported at this time, after which there were no further importations for several years. The calamitous financial condition throughout our States following 1837 had stopped all cattle enterprises, and depressed the value of agricultural products at large to the lowest extremity. The raising of short-horns lay dormant for even a longer period than agriculture.

ROMEO'S OXFORD AT EIGHT YEARS.
From a lithograph.

But after several slumberous years the wheels of industry had gradually renewed active business, and short-horn breeders again anticipated brighter days. In 1849, and again in 1851, Mr. Ambrose Stevens, of Batavia, New York, brought from England several well-bred bulls and cows of the Princess tribe, on account of himself and Colonel John M. Sherwood, of Auburn, New York, as also the bull 3d Duke of Cambridge, bred by Mr. Bates. These animals were successfully bred for some years—the cows noted for superior milking quality—and finally dispersed. Many valuable descendants of them still exist. In 1851 or 1852 Mr. Lorillard Spencer, of New York city, imported several animals, chiefly of "Bates blood," and bred them for a few years, when they were sold and dispersed. And now has to be noticed a new era in American enterprise, more marked in its influence than any previous effort in America's short-horn annals.

In the year 1849, at his home in Kirkleavington, England, died Thomas Bates, at nearly eighty years of age, a leading short-horn breeder, whose herd, from a life-long assiduity in breeding, had progressed to the highest excellence then attainable. Of good estate, honest in character, but of strong prejudices and partialities, he had combated his way in competition with others, and reared several different families of short-horn blood, individualizing them to his own tastes, and running their pedigrees back to what

he considered the best of their kind. During his many years' course of breeding he had sold many animals of both sexes, and let out on hire numerous bulls for service, at high prices, to other breeders. He was acknowledged a leading breeder of his time. The choicest of them he called "Duchess" blood, and the next in merit "Oxford." A bachelor during life, and no direct heirs following, his property was left in the hands of an executor, who made a catalogue of the herd and advertised it for sale in May, 1850. The executor, knowing little of cattle, had partially neglected their keeping, and prices then ruling low, they were brought to the auction block under adverse circumstances. Yet their high quality gathered a large array of leading breeders. Colonel Lewis G. Morris, for some years a short-horn breeder at Mount Fordham, near New York city, and Mr. Noel J. Becar, a New York merchant, were the only Americans who attended the sale. They jointly purchased one Oxford cow and two Oxford heifers at an average price of $322 each. Colonel Morris also purchased the bull Balco 227 (9918), of the Duchess and Wild Eyes tribes, for $1050. After the sale they purchased of other breeders several animals of high quality, males and females, and on their return home distributed them on their several farms, Colonel Morris's at Mount Fordham, and Mr. Becar's on his Long Island estate, where they were successfully bred. Sixty-eight animals composed the sale of Mr. Bates's herd: 14 Duchesses, of both sexes, averaging $581 each; 13 Oxfords, $313; 6 Waterloos, $297 50; 3 Cambridge Roses, $245; 25 Wild Eyes, $241; and 7 Foggathorpes, $231: the sixty-eight averaging $327, all from Duke and Oxford sires—a striking contrast to what the same bloods a few years afterward attained.

At the sale three female Duchesses, 55th, 59th, and 64th, at an average price of $801, two Oxford females, at $656 each, and Duchess bull 4th Duke of York, at $1050, were purchased by Earl Ducie, of Tortworth Court. The remainder of the herd went into the hands of different leading English breeders, each one of whom afterward diligently attended to their propagation, assured as they were of their rising value and importance. Among the purchasers Lord Ducie was one of the most spirited and enterprising. With ample means and enthusiastic love for his animals, during the three years following he nourished them with painstaking care. He died about three years after their purchase, and in August, 1853, his executors made a public sale of his herd, containing many valuable animals aside from those of his Bates purchases. They had been widely advertised, in the United States as in Great Britain, and so rapidly had short-horns generally risen in value, and the reputation of "Bates blood" following, that the attention of American as well as English breeders was eagerly attracted to the sale. The attendance there was the largest ever collected since the famous sale of Charles Colling in 1810. Colonel Morris, Mr. Becar, and Mr. Samuel Thorne, of Thornedale, New York, were among the attendants whose presence as expectant purchasers no doubt stimulated the zeal of English breeders to pay extreme prices for favorite choices. Colonel Morris bought Duchess 66th, three years old, for $3675, and bull Duke of Gloster 2763 (11,382), three years old, for $3412. Mr. Thorne bought Duchess 59th, five years old, at $1837; Duchess 64th, four years old, at $3150; and Duchess 68th, one year old, at $1575, which last was killed by the falling of a mast on shipboard on her passage to America. Mr. Thorne also bought of Mr. Bolden the bull Grand Duke 545 (10,284) for $5000, and at his death, some years afterward, 2d Grand Duke (12,961), bred by Earl Ducie, for $5000. Mr. George

Vail, of Troy, New York, and General Cadwalader, of Philadelphia, jointly bought 4th Duke of York, six years old, at Earl Ducie's sale, for $2625, but he unfortunately died on his passage across the ocean. The other animals of the Duchess and Oxford tribes passed into the hands of English breeders at similar prices. Several of the descendants of the Duchesses and Oxfords soon afterward came to America. Among them were Duchess of Atholl and her son Duke of Airdrie 9798 (12,730), which came to Mr. R. A. Alexander, of Kentucky, and later three heifers, Duchess 97th, 101st, and 103d, to Mr. M. H. Cochrane, Quebec, and afterward bull Grand Duke of Oxford 3988 (16,184), to Mr. James O. Sheldon, Geneva, New York. Of the Duchess and Oxford tribes, male and female, there are now some scores both in America and England in possession of various breeders.

The extraordinary sale of Lord Ducie's herd added to the rapidly increasing demand for fresh blood by American breeders. Several associations were soon formed in the States of Kentucky, Ohio, Illinois, and New York, who sent their agents to England in the years 1852 extending to 1857, bringing out several hundred well-selected bulls and cows in the aggregate, most of which were sold at auction soon after their arrival, and distributed in their several States. Some of the females sold as high as $2000 and bulls for $1000 each and upward, while two individual bulls in Kentucky sold at $4000 and $6000 each. Several separate breeders, in person or by their agent, also made large importations of both sexes. About sixty were obtained by Mr. Alexander of Kentucky, some scores by Mr. Thorne of New York and Mr. Cochrane of Quebec, and smaller numbers by several others. The spread of these new importations, together with the mingling of their blood among the previously established herds of their owners, stimulated the short-horn demand among numerous new breeders. Prices continued good, from a few hundred up to one thousand dollars each, for individual animals of both sexes, until the outbreak of the civil war in 1861. That event was immediately followed by a decline in short-horn values, which continued until the restoration of peace in 1865. Few importations were made during that period, and although previous prices were partially maintained for thorough-bred

GROUP OF SHORT-HORNS.

cattle, sales were less frequent. During the years 1867 to 1872 Mr. Cochrane imported sixty-eight well-selected bulls and cows to his Canadian farm, including two Bates Duchess heifers at the cost of $6250 each, and several bulls and cows from the celebrated English Booth herds.

Reference is made to the purchase of Duchess and Oxford animals by Messrs. Morris, Becar, and Thorne at the Tortworth sale in 1853, and afterward by Messrs. Alexander, Cochrane, and others, simply to note the most remarkable phase in short-horn progress and values which has occurred in their history. Not the slightest reflection is intended on any other tribes of 1857, when Mr. Thorne made a purchase of the entire herd, and transferred them to Thornedale. Ten years afterward, in the year 1867, he sold his herd, about forty in all, to Mr. Sheldon, of Geneva, New York, for $42,300, several Duchesses, Oxfords, and others of near affinity of blood among them. Messrs. Morris, Becar, and Thorne, during the years of their breeding, had sold numerous animals both in their own and neighboring States, as well as of the Duchess and Oxford tribes to England. Mr. Sheldon, previous to his purchase of the herd of Mr. Thorne, had become possessed of some of the Duchesses, Oxfords, and others, that

SIXTH DUKE OF GENEVA AT TWO YEARS.
From a lithograph.

or families or bloods of the breed, all of which are embraced in the general category of short-horns, and in their superior qualities have produced and are still producing excellent descendants. Settled in their new American homes, the Duchess, Oxford, and their nearly affiliated relatives, invigorated by changes of climate, food, and skilful attention, have, in their descendants, improved beyond their progenitors.

Mr. Becar died in the year 1854, after bestowing excellent care on his increasing stock. A few months later Colonel Morris purchased his entire herd, and consolidated it with his own at Mount Fordham, where he successfully bred and sold many of them, until the spring had formerly belonged to the herd. So high had the value and quality of those choice families continued in the esteem of English breeders that a demand was made from the American cattle to renovate their own herds. Mr. Thorne sold nine young Duchess and Oxford bulls and heifers to go to England at prices ranging from $2500 to $3000 each. In 1867 Mr. Sheldon sold to English buyers the young bull 3d Duke of Geneva 5563 for 550 guineas (upward of $2750), the white heifer 7th Duchess of Geneva for 700 guineas (more than $3500), and six Oxford heifers at an average of $2290 each. And again, in 1870, he sold the roan bull-calf 8th Duke of Geneva for 800 guineas, and two heifer Duchesses of Ge-

EIGHTH DUCHESS OF GENEVA AT THREE YEARS.
From a lithograph.

neva for 500 guineas each in gold coin (gold was then at forty per cent. premium over American currency), delivered on shipboard in the city of New York.

In 1871 Mr. Cochrane sold to English breeders an Oxford heifer at 750 guineas, and bull Duke of Hillhurst 9862, at eleven months old, for 800 guineas; also two young Duchesses of Hillhurst for 1250 guineas each, and cow 8th Maid of Oxford, with her heifer calf, for 1300 guineas, and some time afterward 6th Duke of Geneva 7933, bred by Mr. Sheldon, for $6400.

Late in the year 1870 Messrs. Walcott and Campbell, at New York Mills, Oneida County, New York, purchased the entire herd of Mr. Sheldon, about eighty in number, at an average price of $1000 each. In 1871 they sold to Lord Skelmersdale, in England, the young bull 1st Duke of Oneida for 850 guineas, and to other English breeders a young Oxford bull and three Oxford heifers at the average prices of Oxfords sold to England by Mr. Sheldon. About these years Mr. Alexander of Kentucky sold two or three heifer descendants of his Duchess of Atholl to English breeders, and a young Duke of Airdrie or two at good prices, not exactly known to the writer. A few heifers, descendants of The American Cow, long ago imported to New York by Mr. Hustler, were also bought and sent abroad by Eng-

lish purchasers. Ever since the sale of Lord Ducie's herd the prices of Duchess and Oxford cattle and other distinguished tribes had gradually advanced both in England and America, as has been related.

An event occurred in September, 1873, the most remarkable which had ever been recorded in the history of short-horns, and which perhaps may never again occur. Messrs. Walcott and Campbell, a few years previous to their large purchase of Mr. Sheldon, had imported several fashionable high-bred short-horns from the celebrated Booth and other English herds. The addition of the Sheldon herd to them gave them a larger number of well-bred short-horns than any other breeder either in America or England then possessed. Mr. Samuel Campbell, early in the summer of 1873, bought the interest of his partner, Mr. Walcott, in the herd, and soon after advertised the entire number for public sale at auction in the month of September of that year. Catalogues of the cattle with their pedigrees were published and widely sent out in the United States and in England. So large a proposed sale of first-class animals immediately aroused the attention of breeders on both sides of the Atlantic, and brought out several English breeders, either in person or by their agents, to attend it. The interest created by inspection of the animals in their well-

BARON OF OXFORD AT THIRTEEN YEARS.
From a lithograph.

finished sale condition was probably never exceeded, if equalled, on a like occasion. The herd numbered 108 animals. The bull 2d Duke of Oneida, two years old, was first offered, and started by an opening bid of $10,000. He was bought by Mr. Megibben, of Cynthiana, Kentucky, at $12,000. The next, 7th Duke of Oneida, four or five months old, went to Mr. A. W. Griswold, of New York city, at $4000. Twelve Duchess cows and heifers—the latter not arrived at breeding age—next followed, three of the cows at an average of $30,600 each, the entire number averaging $20,900 each. Five of them went to England, and six remained in the United States. 8th Duchess of Geneva, six years old, was considered the best of the lot. Her portrait is here given. Following them were several Oxford cows, heifers, and young bulls. One Oxford cow at $7000, one Gwynne cow at $2000, and two Lady Worcesters at $6200 (for both) went to English buyers. The remainder of the herd were taken by purchasers in the States of New York, Vermont, Minnesota, Kentucky, Pennsylvania, Ohio, Virginia, Michigan, and two or three for Canada. The entire sale amounted to nearly $380,000, the most remarkable in numbers and prices which had ever occurred in any country. All the Duchess tribe, bulls and cows, were descended from Duchess 66th, imported

by Colonel Morris from the Tortworth sale in 1853; the Oxfords descended from the Oxford females bought by Messrs. Morris and Becar at the Bates sale in 1850. A majority of all the stock were deeply bred from Duke and Oxford bulls, which, in the estimation of the purchasers, added largely to their value. In Mr. Megibben's possession three years, 2d Duke of Oneida earned in service more than his cost, unfortunately dying at five years old. The cows exported to England proved successful breeders and profitable to their owners, while those remaining in the United States were less fortunate in production.

During two or three years after the Campbell sale Mr. Cochrane sold several Duchess cows and bulls, chiefly bred by himself, to English purchasers, at prices over $20,000 each. As the numbers of American short-horns increased in the hands of their several proprietors, values gradually lowered in general average. Still the most fashionable strains of blood and pedigree maintained their ascendency. Even to the present time importations of Dukes, Duchesses, and Oxfords, male and female, and others of high celebrity, are occasionally made by several enterprising breeders, such as Mr. H. Y. Atrill, at Goderich, the Bow Park Association, and individual breeders in Canada. Mr. Bronson C. Rumsey, Buffalo, New York, made importations in 1880, 1882, and 1883 from England of fifteen to twenty of the best Duchess and Oxford descent, among them Knight of Oxford 2d 39,549 (43,440), and several cows inheriting largely their blood. Messrs. Hill and others in Minnesota, and a few other States and Canada, imported several animals of Duchess, Oxford, and closely related bloods in 1885.

The integrity of pedigrees of short-horn cattle in the United States has been well sustained by the publication of the American Herd-book, founded by the writer of this article in the year 1846, and continued through twenty-four successive volumes, containing pedigrees of more than 125,000

safely estimated at full four thousand, with herds of half a dozen to several scores of cattle each. They extend all over North America between the Atlantic and Pacific shores, and to the lower Southern States, Texas, and New Mexico, wherever climate and soil are suitable and proper forage is produced for their sustenance, and in numbers too large for accurate estimate. Although considerable numbers of other good flesh-producing breeds for several years past have been imported from abroad and successfully bred, chiefly in the Western States, in competition with the short-horns, the demand for short-horn bulls is greater than that for all

DUCHESS OF NIAGARA AT TEN MONTHS.
From a lithograph.

animals of both sexes, when in the year 1883 it was transferred by sale to the Short-horn Breeders' Association, located at Chicago, Illinois, where it has been continued, in its twenty-ninth volume, to 72,271 bulls and a much larger number of cows, to August 31, 1885.

The number of breeders of thoroughbred pedigree short-horns in the United States, its Territories, and Canada may be

other breeds, to cross upon and elevate the quality of common cattle, not only in their own localities, but also for the extensive grazing ranches of the farther West, to improve the beef quality of the coarse bovines long existing there. Many hundreds of young short-horn bulls are annually taken to the ranches for breeding purposes.

The quality of the flesh of short-horns is

superior. When not fatted to excess, it is distributed all over the carcass, finely marbled in combination of fat and lean. They mature to profitable slaughter as veal calves at six or eight weeks old of much greater weight than common ones on equal supplies of milk from the udders of their dams. The steers at two and a half years old, when properly fed, attain a live weight of 1500 to 1600 pounds, and are ripe for the shambles. At three to three and a half years they attain a live weight of even 2000 pounds, after which longer feeding is seldom profitable. The American exports to Europe—Great Britain chiefly—for the first six months of the year 1885 of live bullocks was more than 82,000 head, aside from the largely increased weight of dead carcasses in quarters of fresh beef, almost exclusively of short-horn blood, the quality most salable in foreign markets. The best beef for consumption in our American cities and towns is also of short-horn blood, and commands a price considerably above that of common cattle.

For longevity and hardihood in all climates where used they are remarkable in both sexes. Numerous bulls both in England and America might be named which have continued successful sires to twelve, fifteen, and even more years of age. The American bull Baron of Oxford 2525, bred by Mr. Becar on Long Island, one of the most successful sires, maintained his vigor until nearly fourteen years old, when a fatal accident befell him. His annexed portrait, by the artist Mr. John R. Page, at thirteen years old, in low condition of flesh, shows his grand anatomy.

The cows, as milkers, when bred and educated for the dairy, have proved equal to any other breeds, their docility of disposition and lymphatic temperament highly promoting their lacteal product. In England from their earliest days large numbers of them have proved extraordinary milkers and butter yielders, and in the metropolitan dairies for milk supply, as well as on farms for cheese and butter production, they are extensively used. In their earlier importations to America, the cows, as a rule, were abundant milkers, as many now continue to be; but their early and rapid tendency to flesh, more particularly in the Western beef-producing States, has led to a neglect of their dairy qualities, butter and cheese production there being less followed

than in many other localities. Yet in thorough-breds, or high grades from native cows, they are largely bred and kept for dairy use in many of our States, and profitable through life on average pasture in summer and wholesome keep in the colder months. Many cows might be named as continuing constant breeders and large milkers until fifteen, even twenty, years old, and fatted into profitable carcasses of beef at the end. The precocity and tendency to early maturity in the females is illustrated by a portrait of Duchess of Niagara at ten months old, bred by Mr. B. C. Rumsey, Buffalo, N. Y.

We place every animal of true blood on an equality of excellence, so far as merit can be shown. Fashion and preferences in all domestic animals more or less prevail among those who are partial to them. The "Bates blood," it is not unjust to say, with the leading English as well as American breeders, is almost universally sought, particularly in bulls, to cross upon other breeds. The numerous public auctions and private sales in select herds of the kind thoroughly testify to the prevailing taste for those bloods. Nearly all the importations of late years made by our spirited breeders have been of selections from the most aristocratic herds, tracing their pedigree to the Bates Duchesses and Oxfords.

It may be asked, Where is now the necessity of such fresh importations? The answer can only be given by those who import them. No better animals or better blood exists in the short-horns of any part of Great Britain than, during the last thirty years, have existed in the United States. English breeders have drawn numerous samples of favorite bloods from American herds in years past to improve the quality of their own, based probably on the opinion that a change in our climate and food has added a new element to their quality and value. At all events, the English progeny derived from the American exportations have met with high favor there, and the experiment has been successful.

Our engravings of a short-horn cow, short-horn bull, and group of short-horns, are from photographs of the Millburn herd of Mr. R. H. Allen, to whose courtesy we are also indebted for the paintings from which were engraved the portraits of "The White Heifer that Travelled," "Duchess, by Daisy Bull," and "Comet."

PLACES OF WORSHIP.

BY WILLIAM WORDSWORTH.

AS star that shines dependent upon star
   Is to the sky while we look up in love;
As to the deep fair ships, which though they
     move
Seem fixed, to eyes that watch them from afar;
As to the sandy desert fountains are,
With palm groves shaded at wide intervals,
Whose fruit around the sun-burnt Native falls,

Of roving tired or desultory war—
Such to this British Isle her Christian Fanes,
Each linked to each for kindred services;
Her Spires, her Steeple-towers with glittering
     vanes
Far-kenned, her Chapels lurking among trees,
Where a few villagers on bended knees
Find solace which a busy world disdains.

"AND HERE IS A COPY OF THE WORDS."

SPRINGHAVEN.

BY R. D. BLACKMORE.

CHAPTER XXIII.

YOH-HEAVE-OH!

"HER condition was very bad, as bad as could be, without going straight to the bottom," the Admiral said to the Rector that night, as they smoked a pipe together; "and to the bottom she must have gone, if the sea had got up, before we thrummed her. Honyman wanted to have her brought inside the Head; but even if we could have got there, she would ground at low water and fill with the tide. And what could we do with all those prisoners? With our fresh hands at the pumps, we very soon fetched the water out of her, and made her as tight as we could; and I think they will manage to take her to Portsmouth. She has beautiful lines. I never saw a smarter ship. How she came to the wind, with all that water in her! The wind is all right for Portsmouth, and she will be a fine addition to the Navy."

"But what is become of the other vessel, craft, corvette, or whatever you call her? You say that she is scarcely hurt at all. And if she gets off the White Pig's back in the night, she may come up and bombard us. Not that I am afraid; but my wife is nervous, and the Rectory faces the sea so much. If you have ordered away the *Leda*, which seems to have conquered both of them, the least you can do is to keep Captain Stubbard under arms all night in his battery."

"I have a great mind to do so; it would be a good idea, for he was very much inclined to cut up rough to-day. But he never would forgive me, he is such a hog at hammock—as we used to say, until we grew too elegant. And he knows that the *Blonde* has hauled down her colours, and Scudamore is now prize-captain. I have sent away most of her crew in the *Leda*, and I am not at all sure that we ought not to blow her up. In the end, we shall have to do so, no doubt; for nothing larger than a smack has ever got off that sand, and floated. But let our young friend try; let him have a fair trial. He has the stuff of a very fine seaman in him. And if he should succeed, it would be scored with a long leg for him. Halloa! Why, I thought the girls were fast asleep long ago!"

"As if we could sleep, papa, with this upon our minds!" Dolly waved an open letter in the air, and then presented it. "Perhaps Faith might, but I am sure I never could. You defied us to make out this, which is on the other leaf; and then, without giving us fair play, you took it to the desk in your Oak-room, and there you left it. Well, I took the liberty of going there for it, for there can't be any secret about a thing that will be printed; and how are they to print it, if they can't contrive to read it? How much will you pay me for interpreting, papa? Mr. Twemlow, I think I ought to have a guinea. Can you read it, now, with all your learning, and knowledge of dead languages?"

"My dear, it is not my duty to read it, and not at all my business. It seems to be written with the end of a stick, by a boy who was learning his letters. If you can interpret it, you must be almost a Daniel."

"Do you hear that, papa, you who think I am so stupid? Faith gave it up; she has no perseverance, or perhaps no curiosity. And I was very nearly beaten

too, till a very fine idea came into my head, and I have made out every word except three, and perhaps even those three, if Captain Honyman is not very particular in his spelling. Can you tell me anything about that, papa?"

"Yes, Dolly, just what you have heard from me before. Honyman is a good officer; a very good one, as he has just proved. No good officer ever spells well, whether in the army or the navy. Look at Nelson's letters. I am inclined to ascribe my own slow promotion to the unnatural accuracy of my spelling, which offended my lords, because it puzzled them."

"Then all is straight sailing, as you say, papa. But I must tell you first how I found it out, or perhaps you won't believe me. I knew that Captain Honyman wrote this postscript, or whatever it is, with his left hand, so I took a pen in my own left hand, and practised all the letters, and the way they join, which is quite different from the other hand. And here is the copy of the words, as my left hand taught my right to put them down, after inking ever so many fingers:

"'We never could have done it without Scudamore. He jumped a most wonderful jump from our jib-boom into her mizzen chains, when our grapples had slipped, and we could get no nearer, and there he made fast, though the enemy came at him with cutlasses, pikes, and muskets. By this means we borded and carried the ship, with a loss as above reported. When I grew faint from a trifling wound, Luff Scudamore led the borders with a cool courage that discomfited the fo.'"

"Robert Honyman all over!" cried the Admiral, with delight. "I could swear that he wrote it, if it was written with his toes. 'Twas an old joke against him, when he was lieutenant, that he never could spell his own title; and he never would put an e after an o in any word. He is far too straightforward a man to spell well; and now the loss of three fingers will cut his words shorter than ever, and be a fine excuse for him. He was faint again, when I boarded the *Leda*, partly no doubt through strong medical measures; for the doctor, who is an ornament to his profession, had cauterised his stumps with a marlinspike, for fear of inflammation. And I heard that he had singed the other finger off. But I hope that may prove incorrect. At any rate, I could not bear to disturb him, but left written orders with Scudamore; for the senior was on board the prize. Dolly, be off to bed, this moment."

"Well, now," said the Rector, drawing near, and filling another deliberative pipe, "I have no right to ask what your orders were, and perhaps you have no right to tell me. But as to the ship that remains in my parish, or at any rate on its borders, if you can tell me anything, I shall be very grateful, both as a question of parochial duty, and also because of the many questions I am sure to have to answer from my wife and daughter."

"There is no cause for secrecy; I will tell you everything:" the Admiral hated mystery. "Why, the London papers will publish the whole of it, and a great deal more than that, in three days' time. I have sent off the *Leda* with her prize to Portsmouth. With this easterly breeze and smooth water, they will get there, crippled as they are, in some twenty-four hours. There the wounded will be cared for, and the prisoners drafted off. The *Blonde*, the corvette which is aground, surrendered, as you know, when she found herself helpless, and within range of our new battery. Stubbard's men longed to have a few shots at her; but of course we stopped any such outrage. Nearly all her officers and most of her crew are on board the *Leda*, having given their parole to attempt no rising; and Frenchmen are always honourable, unless they have some very wicked leader. But we left in the corvette her captain, an exceedingly fine fellow, and about a score of hands who volunteered to stay to help to work the ship, upon condition that if we can float her, they shall have their freedom. And we put a prize crew from the *Leda* on board her, only eight-and-twenty hands, which was all that could be spared, and in command of them our friend Blyth Scudamore. I sent him to ask Robert Honyman about it, when he managed to survive the doctor, for a captain is the master of his own luffs; and he answered that it was exactly what he wished. Our gallant frigate lost three lieutenants in this very spirited action, two killed and one heavily wounded. And the first is in charge of the *Ville d'Anvers*, so there was nobody for this enterprise except the gentle Scuddy, as they call him. He is very young for such a business, and we must do all we can to help him."

"I have confidence in that young man," said Mr. Twemlow, as if it were a question of theology; "he has very sound views, and his principles are high; and he would have taken holy orders, I believe, if his father's assets had permitted it. He perceives all the rapidly growing dangers with which the Church is surrounded, and when I was in doubt about a line of Horace, he showed the finest diffidence, and yet proved that I was right. The 'White Pig,' as the name of a submarine bank, is most clearly of classic origin. We find it in Homer, and in Virgil too; and probably the Romans, who undoubtedly had a naval station in Springhaven, and exterminated the oyster, as they always did—"

"Come, come, Twemlow," said the Admiral, with a smile which smoothed the breach of interruption, "you carry me out of my depth so far that I long to be stranded on my pillow. When your great book comes out, we shall have in perfect form all the pile of your discoveries, which you break up into little bits too liberally. The *Blonde* on the Pig is like Beauty and the Beast. If gentle Scuddy rescues her, it won't be by Homer, or Horace, or even holy orders, but by hard tugs and stout seamanship."

"With the blessing of the Lord, it shall be done," said the Rector, knocking his pipe out; "and I trust that Providence may see fit to have it done very speedily; for I dread the effect which so many gallant strangers, all working hard and apparently in peril, may produce upon the females of this parish."

But the Admiral laughed, and said, "Pooh, pooh!" for he had faith in the maids of Springhaven.

For these there was a fine time now in store—young men up and down everywhere, people running in and out with some new news, before they could get their hats on, the kettle to boil half a dozen times a day, and almost as much to see as they could talk of. At every highwater that came by daylight—and sometimes there were two of them—every maid in the parish was bound to run to the top of a sand-hill high enough to see over the neck of the Head, and there to be up among the rushes all together, and repulse disdainfully the society of lads. These took the matter in a very different light, and thought it quite a pity and a piece of fickle-mindedness, that they might go the round of crab-pots, or of inshore lug-lines, without anybody to watch them off, or come down with a basket to meet them.

For be it understood that the great fishing fleet had not launched forth upon its labours. Their narrow escape from the two French cruisers would last them a long time to think over, and to say the same thing to each other about it that each other had said to them every time they met. And they knew that they could not do this so well as to make a new credit of it every time, when once they were in the same craft together, and could not go asunder more than ten yards and a half. And better, far better, than all these reasons for staying at home and enjoying themselves, was the great fact that they could make more money by leisure than by labour, in this nobly golden time.

Luck fostered skill in this great affair, which deserves to be recorded for the good of any village gifted with like opportunity. It appears that the British Admiralty had long been eager for the capture of the *Blonde*, because of her speed and strength and beauty, and the mischief she had done to English trade. To destroy her would be a great comfort, but to employ her aright would be glorious; and her proper employment was to serve as a model for English frigates first, and then to fight against her native land. Therefore, no sooner did their lordships hear what had happened at Springhaven than they sent down a rider express, to say that the ship must be saved at any price. And as nothing could be spared from the blockading force, or the fleet in the Downs, or the cruising squadron, the Commander of the coast-defence was instructed to enrol, impress, or adapt somehow all the men and the matter available. Something was said about free use of money in the service of His Majesty, but not a penny was sent to begin upon. But Admiral Darling carried out his orders, as if he had received them framed in gold. "They are pretty sure to pay me in the end," he said; "and if they don't, it won't break me. I would give £500 on my own account, to carry that corvette to Spithead. And it would be the making of Scudamore, who reminds me of his father more and more, every time I come across him."

The fleet under Captain Tugwell had quite lately fallen off from seven to five, through the fierce patriotism of some younger members, and their sanguine belief in bounty-money. Captain Zeb had presented them with his experience in a long harangue—nearly fifty words long—and they looked as if they were convinced by it. However, in the morning they were gone, having mostly had tiffs with their sweethearts—which are fervent incentives to patriotism—and they chartered themselves, and their boats were numbered for the service of their Country. They had done their work well, because they had none to do, except to draw small wages, and they found themselves qualified now for more money, and came home at the earliest chance of it.

Two guineas a day for each smack and four hands, were the terms offered by the Admiral, whose hard-working conscience was twitched into herring-bones by the strife between native land and native spot. "I have had many tussles with uncertainty before," he told Dolly, going down one evening, "but never such vexation of the mind as now. All our people expect to get more for a day, than a month of fine fishing would bring them; while the Government goes by the worst time they make, and expects them to throw in their boats for nothing. 'The same as our breeches,' Tugwell said to me; 'whenever we works, we throws in they, and we ought to do the very same with our boats.' This makes it very hard for me."

But by doing his best, he got over the hardship, as people generally do. He settled the daily wages as above, with a bonus of double that amount for the day that saw the *Blonde* upon her legs again. Indignation prevailed, or pretended to do so; but common-sense conquered, and all set to work. Hawsers, and chains, and buoys, and all other needful gear and tackle were provided by the Admiralty from the store-house built not long ago for the Fencibles. And Zebedee Tugwell, by right of position, and without a word said for it—because who could say a word against it?—became the commander of the Rescue fleet, and drew double pay naturally for himself and family.

"I does it," he said, "if you ask me why I does it, without any intention of bettering myself, for the Lord hath placed me above need of that; but mainly for the sake of discipline, and the respectability of things. Suppose I was under you, sir, and knew you was getting no more than I was, why, my stomach would fly every time that you gave me an order without a 'Please, Zebedee!' But as soon as I feels that you pocket a shilling, in the time I take pocketing twopence, the value of your brain ariseth plain before me; and instead of thinking what you says, I does it."

CHAPTER XXIV.

ACCORDING TO CONTRACT.

WHEN the *Blonde* had been on the White Pig for a week, in spite of all the science of Scudamore, ready money of the Admiral, and efforts of the natives, there began to be signs of a change in the weather. The sea was as smooth, and the sky as bright, and the land as brown as ever; but the feel of the air was not the same, and the sounds that came through it were different. "Rain afore Friday," said Captain Zeb, "and a blow from sowwest afore Sunday. 'Twill break up the *Blunder*, I reckon, my lads."

With various aspects they looked at him, all holding sweet converse at the *Darling Arms*, after the manifold struggles of the day. The eyes of the younger men were filled with disappointment and anger, as at a sure seer of evil; the elder, to whom cash was more important, gazed with anxiety and dismay; while a pair, old enough to be sires of Zebedee, nodded approval, and looked at one another, expecting to receive, but too discreet to give, a wink. Then a lively discourse arose and throve among the younger; and the elders let them hold it, while they talked of something else.

On the following morning two dialogues were held upon different parts of Springhaven shore, but each of great import to the beautiful captive still fast aground in the offing. The first was between Captain Zebedee Tugwell and Lieutenant Scudamore. The gentle Scuddy, still hoping against hope, had stuck fast to his charge, upon whose fortunes so much of his own depended. If he could only succeed in floating and carrying her into Portsmouth, his mark would be made, his position secured far quicker than by ten gallant actions; and that which he cared for a hundredfold, the comfort of his widowed mother, would be advanced and established. For, upon the valuation of the prizes, a considerable sum would fall to him, and every farthing of it would be sent to her. Bright with youthful hope, and trustful in the rising spring of tide, which had all but released them yesterday, according to his firm belief, he ran from the Hall through the Admiral's grounds, to meet the boat which was waiting for him, while he was having breakfast and council with his chief. Between the Round-house and the old white gate he heard a low whistle from a clump of shrubs, and turning that way, met Tugwell. With that prince of fishermen he shook hands, according to the manner of Springhaven, for he had learned to admire the brave habit of the man, his strong mind, and frank taciturnity. And Tugwell on his part had taken a liking to the simple and cheerful young officer, who received his suggestions, was kind to all hands, and so manfully bore the daily disappointment.

"Nobody in there?" asked Zeb, with one finger pointing to the Round-house; "then sit down on this bit of bank, sir, a minute. Less chance to be shot at by any French ship."

The bit of bank really was a bit of hollow, where no one could see them from the beach, or lane, or even from the Round-house. Scudamore, who understood his man, obeyed; and Tugwell came to his bearings on a clump of fern before him.

"How much will Government pay the chaps as fetches her out of that snug little berth? For division to self and partners, how much? For division to self and family, how much?"

"I have thought about that," the lieutenant answered, with little surprise at the question, but much at the secrecy thrown around it; "and I think it would be very unsafe to count upon getting a penny beyond the Admiral's terms—double pay for the day that we float her."

Captain Zebedee shook his head, and the golden sheaf of his Olympian beard ruffled and crisped, as to an adverse wind.

"Can't a'most believe it," he replied, with his bright eyes steadily settled on Scudamore's; "the English country, as I belongs to, can't quite 'a coom to that yet!"

"I fear that it has indeed," Blyth answered, very gravely; "at least I am sure of this, Master Tugwell, that you must not look forward to any bounty, bonus, or premium, or whatever it is called, from the Authorities who should provide it. But for myself, and the difference it will make to me whether we succeed or fail, I shall be happy, and will give my word, to send you £50, to be divided at your discretion among the smacks. I mean, of course, as soon as I get paid."

Scudamore was frightened by the size of his own promise; for he had never yet owned £50 in the solid. And then he was scared at the wholesale loss of so large a sum to his mother.

"Never fear, lad," honest Tugwell replied, for the young man's face was fair to read; "we'll not take a farden of thy hard airnings, not a brass farden, so help me Bob! Gentlefolks has so much call for money, as none of us know nothing of. And thou hast helped to save all the lot of us from Frenchies, and been the most forwardest, as I hear tell. But if us could 'a got £50 out of Government, why so much more for us, and none the less for they. But a Englishman must do his duty, in reason, and when 'a don't hurt his self by the same. There's a change in the weather, as forbids more sport. You shall have the *Blunder* off to-morrow, lad. Wouldn't do to be too sudden like."

"I fear I am very stupid, Master Tugwell. But I don't see how you can manage it so surely, after labouring nine days all in vain."

Zebedee hesitated half a moment, betwixt discretion and the pride of knowledge. Then the latter vanquished and relieved his mind.

"I trust in your honour, sir, of course, to keep me clear. I might have brought 'e off the Pig, first day, or second to the latest, if it were sound business. But with winter time coming, and the week's fishing lost, our duty to our families and this place was to pull 'e on harder, sir, to pull 'e aground firmer; and with the help of the Lord we have a-doed it well. We wasn't a-going to kill the goose as laid the golden eggs. No offence to you, sir; it wasn't you as was the goose."

Master Tugwell rubbed his pockets with a very pleasant smile, and then put his elbows on his great square knees, and complacently studied the lieutenant's smaller mind.

"I can understand how you could do such a thing," said Scudamore, after he had rubbed his eyes, and then looked away for fear of laughing, "but I cannot understand by what power on earth you are enabled to look at me and tell me this.

For nine days you have been paid every night, and paid pretty well, as you yourself acknowledge, to haul a ship off a shoal; and all the time you have been hauling her harder upon it!"

"Young man," replied Tugwell, with just indignation, "a hofficer should be above such words. But I forgive 'e, and hope the Lord will do the same, with allowance for youth and ill-convenience. I might 'a knowed no better, at your age and training."

"But what were you paid for, just answer me that, unless it was to pull the *Blonde* off the sand-bank? And how can you pretend that you have done an honest thing by pulling her further upon the bank?"

"I won't ask 'e, sir, to beg my pardon for saying what never man said to me, without reading the words of the contraction;" Zeb pulled out a paper from his hat, and spread it, and laid a stone at every corner; "this contraction was signed by yourself and Squire Darling, for and on behalf of the kingdom; and the words are for us to give our services, to pull, haul, tow, warp, or otherwise as directed, release, relieve, set free, and rescue the aforesaid ship, or bark, or vessel, craft, or—"

"Please not to read all that," cried Scuddy, "or a gale of wind may come before you are half-way through. It was Admiral Darling's lawyer, Mr. Furkettle, who prepared it, to prevent any chance of misunderstanding."

"Provided always," continued Tugwell, slowly, "and the meaning, condition, purport, object, sense, and intention of this agreement is, that the aforesaid Zebedee Tugwell shall submit in everything to the orders, commands, instructions, counsel, directions, injunctions, authority, or discretion, whether in writing or otherwise, of the aforesaid—"

"I would not interrupt you if I could help it"—Scudamore had a large stock of patience (enhanced by laborious practice at Stonnington), but who might abide, when time was precious, to see Zebedee feeling his way with his fingers along the bottom and to the end of every word, and then stopping to congratulate himself at the conquest of every one over two syllables? "But excuse me for saying that I know all these conditions; and the tide will be lost, if we stop here."

"Very good, sir; then you see how it

standeth. Who hath broken them? Not us! We was paid for to haul; and haul we did, according to superior orders. She grounded from the south, with the tide making upp'ard, somewhere about three-quarter flow; and the Squire, and you, and all the rest of 'e, without no knowledge of the Pig whatsomever, fastens all your pulley-haulies by the starn, and says, ' now pull!' And pull we did, to the tune of sixteen guineas a day for the good of Springhaven."

"And you knew all the time that it was wrong! Well, I never came across such people. But surely some one of you would have had the honesty—I beg pardon, I mean the good-will—to tell us. I can scarcely imagine some forty men and boys preserving such a secret for nine whole days, hauling for their lives in the wrong direction, and never even by a wink or smile—"

"Springhaven is like that," said Master Tugwell, proudly; "we does a thing one and all together, even if us reasons consarning it. And over and above that, sir, there is but two men in Springhaven as understands the White Pig, barring my own self. The young 'uns might 'a smelt a rat, but they knew better than to say so. Where the *Blunder* grounded—and she hath airned her name, for the good of the dwellers in this village—is the chine of the Pig; and he hath a double back, with the outer side higher than the inner one. She came through a narrow nick in his outer back, and then plumped, stem on, upon the inner one. You may haul at her forever by the starn, and there she'll 'bide, or lay up again on the other back. But bring her weight forrard, and tackle her by the head, and off she comes, the very next fair tide; for she hath berthed herself over the biggest of it, and there bain't but a basketful under her forefoot."

"Then, Master Tugwell, let us lose no time, but have at her at once, and be done with it." Scudamore jumped up, to give action to his words; but Tugwell sate aground still, as firmly as the *Blonde*.

" Begging of your pardon, sir, I would invite of you not to be in no sart of hurry hasting forwardly. Us must come off gradual, after holding on so long there, and better to have Squire Darling round the corner first, sir. Not that he knoweth much about it, but 'a might make believe to do so. And when 'a hath seen us pull

wrong ways, a hundred and twenty guineas' worth, a' might grudge us the reward for pulling right ways. I've a-knowed 'un get into that state of mind, although it was his own tenants."

The lieutenant was at length compelled to laugh, though for many reasons loth to do so. But the quiet contempt for the Admiral's skill, and the brief hint about his character, touched his sense of the ludicrous more softly than the explanation of his own mishaps. Then the Captain of Springhaven smiled almost imperceptibly; for he was a serious man, and his smiles were accustomed to be interior.

" I did hear tell," he said, stroking his beard, for fear of having discomposed it, "that the Squire were under compulsion to go a bit westward again to-morrow. And when he cometh back he would be glad to find us had managed the job without him. No fear of the weather breaking up afore Friday, and her can't take no harm for a tide or two. If you thinks well, sir, let us heave at her to-day, as afore, by superior orders. Then it come into your mind to try t'other end a bit, and you shift all the guns and heavy lumber forrard to give weight to the bows and lift the starn, and off her will glide at the first tug to-morrow, so sure as my name is Zebedee. But mind one thing, sir, that you keep her, when you've got her. She hath too many furriner natives aboard of her, to be any way to my liking."

"Oh, there need be no doubt about them," replied Blyth; "we treat them like ourselves, and they are all upon their honour, which no Frenchman ever thinks of breaking. But my men will be tired of waiting for me. I shall leave you to your plans, Tugwell."

"Ah, I know the natur' of they young men," Captain Zebedee mused, as he sate in his hollow, till Scudamore's boat was far away; "they be full of scruples for themselves and faith in other fellows. He'll never tell Squire, nor no one else here, what I laid him under, and the laugh would go again' him, if he did. We shall get to-day's money, I reckon, as well as double pay to-morrow, and airn it. Well, it might 'a been better, and it might be wuss."

About two miles westward of the brook, some rocks marked the end of the fine Springhaven sands and the beginning of a far more rugged beach, the shingles and flint shelves of Pebbleridge. Here the chalk of the Sussex backbone (which has been plumped over and sleeked by the flesh of the valley) juts forth, like the scrags of a skeleton, and crumbles in low but rugged cliffs into the flat domain of sea. Here the landing is bad, and the anchorage worse, for a slippery shale rejects the fluke, and the water is usually kept in a fidget between the orders of the west wind and scurry of the tide.

This very quiet morning, with the wind off shore, and scarcely enough of it to comb the sea, four smart-looking Frenchmen, with red caps on their heads, were barely holding way upon the light gig of the *Blonde*, while their Captain was keeping an appointment with a stranger, not far from the weed-strewn line of waves. In a deep rocky channel where a land-spring rose (which was still-born except at low water), and laver and dilsk and claw-coral showed that the sea had more dominion there than the sky, two men stood facing each other; and their words, though belonging to the most polite of tongues, were not so courteous as might be. Each man stood with his back to a rock—not touching it, however, because it was too wet—one was as cold and as firm as the rock, the other like the sea, tumultuous. The passionate man was Captain Desportes, and the cold one Caryl Carne.

"Then you wish me to conclude, monsieur," Carne spoke as one offering repentance, "that you will not do your duty to your country, in the subject set before you? I pray you to deliberate, because your position hangs upon it."

"Never! Never! Once more, Captain, with all thanks for your consideration, I refuse. My duty to my own honour has first place. After that my duty to my country. Speak of it no more, sir; it quite is to insult me."

"No, Captain Desportes, it is nothing of that kind, or I should not be here to propose it. Your parole is given only as long as your ship continues upon the sand. The moment she floats, you are liberated. Then is the time for a noble stroke of fortune. Is it not so, my dear friend?"

"No, sir. This affair is impossible. My honour has been pledged, not until the ship is floating, but until I am myself set free in France. I am sorry not to see things as you see them for me; but the question is for my own consideration."

Captain Desportes had resented, as an honest man must do, especially when more advanced in years, the other's calm settlement, without invitation, of matters which concerned his own conscience. And as most mankind—if at all perceptive—like or dislike one another at a glance, Desportes, being very quick and warm of nature, had felt at first sight a strong repulsion from the cold and arrogant man who faced him. His age was at least twice that of Carne, he had seen much service in the better days of France, and had risen slowly by his own skill and valour; he knew that his future in the service depended upon his decision in this matter, and he had a large family to maintain. But his honour was pledged, and he held fast by it.

"There is one consideration," Carne replied, with rancour slowly kindling in his great black eyes, "which precedes all others, even that of honour, in the mind of a trusted officer. It is not that of patriotism—which has not its usual weight with monsieur—but it is that of obedience, discipline, loyalty, faith, towards those who have placed faith in him. Captain Desportes, as commander of a ship, is entrusted with property; and that confidence is the first debt upon his honour."

To Desportes, as to most men of action, the right was plainer than the reason. He knew that this final plea was unsound, but he did not see how to contest it. So he came back to fact, which was easier for him.

"How am I to know, monsieur, what would be the wishes of those who have entrusted me with my position? You are placed in authority by some means here, in your own country, but against it. That much you have proved to me, by papers. But your credentials are general only. They do not apply to this especial case. If the Chief of the State knew my position, he would wish me to act as I mean to act, for the honour and credit of our nation."

"Are you then acquainted with his signature? If so, perhaps you will verify this, even if you are resolved to reject it."

Carne drew a letter from an inner pocket, and carefully unfolded it. There were many words and minute directions upon various subjects, written by the hand of the most minute, and yet most comprehensive, of mankind.

"There is nothing in this that concerns

you," he said, after showing the date, only four days old, "except these few words at the end, which perhaps you may like to read, before you make final decision. The signature of the Chief is clear."

Captain Desportes read aloud—"It is of the utmost importance to me, that the *Blonde* should not be captured by the enemy, as the *Ville d'Anvers* has been. You tell me that it is ashore near you, and the Captain and crew upon parole, to be liberated if they assist in the extrication of the vessel. This must not be. In the service of the State, I demand that they consider not at all their parole. The well-known speed and light draught of that vessel have rendered her almost indispensable to me. When the vessel is free, they must rise upon the enemy, and make for the nearest of our ports without delay. Upon this I insist, and place confidence in your established courage and management, to accomplish it to my satisfaction."

"Your orders are clear enough," said Caryl Carne. "What reason can you give, as an officer of the Republic, for disobeying them?"

Desportes looked at his ship in the distance, and then at the sea and the sky, with a groan, as if he were bidding farewell to them. Carne felt sure that he had prevailed, and a smile shed light, but not a soft light, on his hard pale countenance.

"Be in no rash haste," said the French sea-captain, and he could not have found words more annoying to the cold proud man before him; "I do not recognise in this mandate the voice of my country, of the honourable France, which would never say, 'Let my sons break their word of honour!' This man speaks, not as Chief of a grand State, not as leader of noble gentlemen, but as Emperor of a society of serfs. France is no empire; she is a grand nation of spirit, of valour, above all, of honour. The English have treated me, as I would treat them, with kindness, with largeness, with confidence. In the name of fair France, I will not do this thing."

Carne was naturally pale, but now he grew white with rage, and his black eyes flashed.

"France will be an empire within six months; and your honour will be put upon prison diet, while your family starve for the sake of it."

"If I ever meet you under other cir-

cumstances," replied the brave Frenchman, now equally pale, "I shall demand reparation, sir."

"With great pleasure," replied Carne, contemptuously; "meanwhile monsieur will have enough to do to repair his broken fortunes."

Captain Desportes turned his back, and gave a whistle for his crew, then stepped with much dignity into his boat. "To the *Blonde*, lads," he cried, "to the unsullied *Blonde!*" Then he sate, looking at her, and stroked his grizzled beard, into which there came trickling a bitter tear or two, as he thought of his wife and family. He had acted well; but, according to the measure of the present world, unwisely.

CHAPTER XXV.
NO CONCERN OF OURS.

THE very next morning it was known to the faithful of Springhaven that the glory of the place would be trebled that day, and its income increased desirably. That day, the fair stranger (which had so long awakened the admiration of the women, and the jealousy of the men) would by the consummate skill of Captain Zeb—who had triumphed over all the officers of the British Navy—float forth magnificently from her narrow bed, hoist her white sails, and under British ensign salute the new fort, and shape a course for Portsmouth. That she had stuck fast and in danger so long was simply because the cocked hats were too proud to give ear to the wisdom in an old otter-skin. Now Admiral Darling was baffled and gone; and Captain Tugwell would show the world what he could do, and what stuff his men were made of, if they only had their way. From old Daddy Stakes, the bald father of the village, to Mrs. Caper junior's baby—equally bald, but with a crop as sure of coming as mustard and cress beneath his flannel—some in arms, some on legs, some upon brave crutches, all were abroad in the soft air from the west, which had stolen up under the stiff steel skirt of the east wind, exactly as wise Captain Zeb predicted.

"My dear," said Mrs. Twemlow to the solid Mrs. Stubbard, for a very sweet friendship had sprung up between these ladies, and would last until their interests should happen to diverge, "this will be a

"A FAVOURITE PLACE FOR A SAGE COCK-PHEASANT."—[SEE PAGE 564.]

great day for my dear husband's parish. Perhaps there is no other parish in the kingdom capable of acting as Springhaven has, so obedient, so disciplined, so faithful to their contract! I am told that they even pulled the vessel more aground, in preference to setting up their own opinions. I am told that as soon as the Admiral was gone—for between you and me he is a little overbearing, with the very best intentions in the world, but too confident in his own sagacity—then that clever but exceedingly modest young man, Lieutenant Scudamore, was allowed at last to listen to our great man Tugwell, who has long been the oracle of the neighbourhood about the sea, and the weather, and all questions of that kind. And between you and me, my dear, the poor old Admiral seems a little bit jealous of his reputation. And what do you think he said before he went, which shows his high opinion of his own abilities? Tugwell said something in his rough and ready way, which, I suppose, put his mightiness upon the high ropes, for he shouted out in everybody's hearing, 'I'll tell you what it is, my man, if you can get her off, by any of your'—something I must not repeat—'devices, I'll give you fifty guineas, five-and-twenty for yourself, and the rest to be divided among these other fellows.' Then Zebedee pulled out a Testament from his pocket, for he is a man of deep religious convictions, and can read almost all the easy places, though he thinks most of the hard ones, and he made his son Dan (who is a great scholar, as they say, and a very fine-looking youth as well) put down at the end what the Admiral had said. Now, what do you think of that, dear Mrs. Stubbard?"

"I think," replied that strong-minded lady, "that Tugwell is an arrant old fox; and if he gets the fifty guineas, he will put every farthing into his own pocket."

"Oh, no! He is honest as the day itself. He will take his own twenty-five, and then leave the rest to settle whether he should share in their twenty-five. But we must be quick, or we shall lose the sight. Quite a number of people are come from inland. How wonderfully quickly these things spread! They came the first day, and then made up their minds that nothing could be done, and so they stopped at home. But now, here they are again, as if by magic! If the ship gets off, it will be known half-way to London before nightfall. But I see Captain Stubbard going up the hill to your charming battery. That shows implicit faith in Tugwell, to return the salute of the fair captive! It is indeed a proud day for Springhaven!"

"But it isn't done yet. And perhaps it won't be done. I would rather trust officers of the navy than people who catch crabs and oysters. I would go up to the battery, to laugh at my husband, but for the tricks the children play me. My authority is gone, at the very first puff of smoke. How children do delight in that vile gunpowder!"

"So they ought, in the present state of our country, with five hundred thousand of Frenchmen coming. My dear Mrs. Stubbard, how thankful we should be to have children who love gunpowder!"

"But not when they blow up their mother, ma'am."

"Oh, here comes Eliza!" cried Mrs. Twemlow. "I am so glad, because she knows everything. I thought we had missed her. My dear child, where are Faith and Dolly Darling gone? There are so many strangers about to-day that the better class should keep together."

"Here are three of us at any rate," replied the young lady, who considered her mother old-fashioned: "enough to secure one another's sanctity from the lower orders. Faith has gone on to the headland, with that heroic mannikin, Johnny. Dolly was to follow, with that Shanks maid to protect her, as soon as her hat was trimmed, or some such era. But I'll answer for it that she loses herself in the crowd, or some fib of that sort."

"Eliza!" said her mother, and very severely, because Mrs. Stubbard was present, "I am quite astonished at your talking so. You might do the greatest injury to a very lively and harmless, but not overprudent girl, if any one heard you who would repeat it. We all know that the Admiral is so wrapped up in Dolly that he lets her do many things which a mother would forbid. But that is no concern of ours; and once for all, if such things must be said, I beg that they may not be said by you."

In the present age, Mrs. Twemlow would have got sharp answer. But her daughter only looked aggrieved, and glanced at Mrs. Stubbard, as if to say, "Well, time will show whether I deserve it." And then they hastened on, among the worse class, to the headland.

Not only all the fishing-smacks, and Captain Stubbard's galley, but every boat half as sound as a hat, might now be seen near the grounded vessel, preparing to labour or look on. And though the White Pig was allowed to be three-quarters of a mile from the nearest point, the mighty voice of Captain Zeb rode over the flickering breadth of sea, and through the soft babble of the waves ashore. The wind was light from southwest, and the warp being nearly in the same direction now, the *Blonde* began to set her

"THERE WAS NO ONE WHO COULD SAY HER NAY."

courses, to catch a lift of air, when the tide should come busily working under her. And this would be the best tide since she took the ground, last Sunday week, when the springs were going off. As soon as the hawsers were made fast, and the shouts of Zebedee redoubled with great strength (both of sound and of language), and the long ropes lifted with a flash of splashes, and a creak of heavy wood, and the cry was, "With a will! with a will, my gay lads!" every body having a sound eye in it was gazing intently, and every heart was fluttering, except the loveliest eyes and quickest heart in all Springhaven.

Miss Dolly had made up her mind to go, and would have had warm words ready for any one rash enough to try to prevent her. But a very short note

which was put into her hand about 10 A.M. distracted her.

"If you wish to do me a real service, according to your kind words of Saturday, be in the upper shrubbery at half past eleven; but tell no one except the bearer. You will see all that happens better there than on the beach, and I will bring a telescope."

Dolly knew at once who had written this, and admired it all the more because it was followed by no signature. For years she had longed for a bit of romance; and the common-sense of all the world irked her. She knew as well as possible that what she ought to do was to take this letter to her sister Faith, and be guided by her advice about it. Faith was her elder by three years or more, and as steadfast as a rock, yet as tender as young moss. There was no fear that Faith would ride the high horse with her, or lay down the law severely; she was much more likely to be too indulgent, though certain not to play with wrong.

All this the younger sister knew, and therefore resolved to eschew that knowledge. She liked her own way, and she meant to have it, in a harmless sort of way; her own high spirit should be her guide, and she was old enough now to be her own judge. Mr. Carne had saved her sister's life, when she stood up in that senseless way; and if Faith had no gratitude, Dolly must feel, and endeavour to express it for her.

Reasoning thus, and much better than this, she was very particular about her hat, and French pelerine of fluted lawn, and frock of pale violet trimmed on either side with gathered muslin. Her little heart fluttered at being drawn in, when it should have been plumped up to her neck, and very nearly displayed to the public; but her father was stern upon some points, and never would hear of the classic discoveries. She had not even Grecian sandals, nor a "surprise fan" to flutter from her wrist, nor hair oiled into flat Lesbian coils, but freedom of rich young tresses, and of graceful figure, and taper limbs. There was no one who could say her nay, of the lovers of maiden nature.

However, maidens must be discreet, even when most adventurous; and so she took another maid to help her, of respected but not romantic name—Jenny Shanks, who had brought her that letter. Jenny was much prettier than her name, and the ground she trod on was worshipped by many, even when her shoes were down at heel. Especially in this track remained the finer part of Charley Bowles's heart (while the coarser was up against the Frenchmen), as well as a good deal of Mr. Prater's nephew's, and of several other sole-fishers. This enabled Jenny to enter kindly into tender questions. And she fetched her Sunday bonnet down the trap-ladder where she kept it—because the other maids were so nasty—as soon as her letter was delivered.

"Your place, Jenny, is to go behind," Miss Dolly said, with no small dignity, as this zealous attendant kept step for step with her, and swung her red arm against the lady's fair one. "I am come upon important business, Jenny, such as you cannot understand, but may stay at a proper distance."

"Lor, miss, I am sure I begs your pardon. I thought it was a kind of coorting-match, and you might be glad of my experience."

"Such things I never do, and have no idea what you mean. I shall be much obliged to you, Jenny, if you will hold your tongue."

"Oh yes, miss; no fear of my telling anybody. Wild horses would never pull a syllable out of me. The young men is so aggravating that I keep my proper distance from them. But the mind must be made up, at one time or other."

Dolly looked down at her with vast contempt, which she would not lower herself by expressing, even with favour of time and place. Then turning a corner of the grassy walk, between ground-ash and young larches, they came upon an opening planted round with ilex, arbutus, juniper, and laurel, and backed by one of the rocks which form the outworks of the valley. From a niche in this rock, like the port-hole of a ship, a rill of sparkling water poured, and beginning to make a noise already, cut corners—of its own production—short, in its hurry to be a brook, and then to help the sea. And across its exit from the rock (like a measure of its insignificance) a very comfortable seat was fixed, so that any gentleman —or even a lady with divided skirts— might freely sit with one foot on either bank of this menacing but not yet very formidable stream. So that on the whole this nook of shelter under the coronet of rock was a favourite place for a sage cock-

pheasant, or even a woodcock in wintry weather.

Upon that bench (where the Admiral loved to sit, in the afternoon of peace and leisure, observing with a spy-glass the manœuvres of his tranquil fishing fleet) Caryl Carne was sitting now, with his long and strong legs well spread out, his shoulders comfortably settled back, and his head cast a little on one side, as if he were trying to compute his property. Then, as Dolly came into the opening, he arose, made a bow beyond the compass of any true Briton, and swinging his hat, came to meet her. Dolly made a curtsey in the style impressed upon her by her last governess but one—a French lady of exceedingly high ancestry and manners—and Carne recognised it as a fine thing out of date.

"Jenny, get away!" said Dolly—words not meant for him to hear, but he had grave command of countenance.

"This lays me under one more obligation:" Carne spoke in a low voice, and with a smile of diffidence which reminded her of Scudamore, though the two smiles were as different as night and day. "I have taken a great liberty in asking you to come, and that multiplies my gratitude for your good-will. For my own sake alone I would not have dared to sue this great favour from you, though I put it so, in terror of alarming you. But it is for my own sake also, since anything evil to you would be terrible to me."

"No one can wish to hurt me," she answered, looking up at him bravely, and yet frightened by his gaze, "because I have never harmed any one. And I assure you, sir, that I have many to defend me, even when my father is gone from home."

"It is beyond doubt. Who would not rush to do so? But it is from those who are least suspected that the danger comes the worst. The most modest of all gentlemen, who blushes like a damsel, or the gallant officer devoted to his wife and children, or the simple veteran with his stars, and scars, and downright speech— these are the people that do the wrong, because no one believes it is in them."

"Then which of the three is to carry me off from home, and friends, and family—Lieutenant Scudamore, Captain Stubbard, or my own godfather, Lord Nelson?"

This young man nourished a large contempt for the intellect of women, and was

"LOR, MISS, I AM SURE I BEGS YOUR PARDON."

therefore surprised at the quickness and spirit of the girl whom he wished to terrify. A sterner tone must be used with her.

"I never deal in jokes," he said, with a smile of sad sympathy for those who do; "my life is one perpetual peril, and that restrains facetiousness. But I can make allowance for those who like it."

Miss Dolly, the pet child of the house, and all the people round it—except the gardener, Mr. Swipes, who found her too inquisitive—quick as she was, could not realise at once the possibility of being looked down upon.

"I am sorry that you have to be so grave," she said, "because it prevents all enjoyment. But why should you be in such continual danger? You promised to explain it, on Saturday, only you had no time then. We are all in danger from the French, of course, if they ever should succeed in landing. But you mean something more than that; and it seems so hard, after all your losses, that you should not be safe from harm."

With all her many faults—many more than she dreamed of—fair Dolly had a warm and gentle heart, which filled her eyes with tender loveliness, whenever it obtained command of them. Carne, who was watching them steadfastly for his own purpose, forgot that purpose, and dropped his dark eyes, and lost the way to tell a lie.

"If I may ask you," he said, almost stammering, and longing without knowledge for the blessing of her touch, "to—to allow me just to lead you to this seat, I may perhaps be able—I will not take the liberty of sitting at your side—but I may perhaps be able to explain as much of my affairs as you can wish to hear of them, and a great deal more, I fear, a great deal more, Miss Darling."

Dolly blushed at the rich tone in which he pronounced her name, almost as if it were an adjective; but she allowed him to take her hand, and lead her to the bench beneath the rock. Then, regardless of his breeches, although of fine padusoy, and his coat, though of purple velvet, he sate down on the bank of the rill at her feet, and waited for her to say something. The young lady loved mainly to take the lead, but would liefer have followed suit just now.

"You have promised to tell me," she said, very softly, and with an unusual timidity, which added to her face and manner almost the only charm they lacked, "some things which I do not understand, and which I have no right to ask you of, except for your own offer. Why should you, without injuring any one, but only having suffered loss of all your family property, and of all your rights and comforts, and living in that lonely place which used to be full of company—why should you be in danger now, when you have nothing more to be robbed of? I beg your pardon—I mean when all your enemies must have done their worst."

"You are too young yet to understand the world," he answered, with a well-drawn sigh; "and I hope most truly that you may never do so. In your gentle

presence I cannot speak with bitterness, even if I could feel it. I will not speak harshly of any one, however I may have been treated. But you will understand that my life alone remains betwixt the plunderers and their prey, and that my errand here prevents them from legally swallowing up the spoil."

Miss Dolly's idea of the law, in common with that of most young ladies, suggested a horrible monster ravening to devour the fallen. And the fall of the Carnes had long been a subject of romantic interest to her.

"Oh, I see!" she exclaimed, with a look of deep wisdom. "I can quite understand a thing like that, from what I have heard about witnesses. I hope you will be very careful. My sister owes so much to you, and so do I."

"You must never speak of that again, unless you wish to grieve me. I know that I have said too much about myself; but you alone care to know anything about me; and that beguiles one out—out of one's wits. If I speak bad English, you will forgive me. I have passed so many years on the Continent, and am picking up the language of my childhood very slowly. You will pardon me, when I am misled by—by my own signification."

"Well done!" cried the innocent Dolly. "Now that is the very first piece of bad English you have used, to the best of my belief, and I am rather quick in that. But you have not yet explained to me my own danger, though you asked me to come here for that purpose, I believe."

"But you shall not be so; you shall not be in danger. My life shall be given for your defence. What imports my peril compared with yours? I am not of cold blood. I will sacrifice all. Have faith in me purely, and all shall be done."

"All what?" Dolly asked, with a turn of common-sense, which is the most provoking of all things sometimes; and she looked at him steadily, to follow up her question.

"You cannot be persuaded that you are in any danger. It is possible that I have been too anxious. Do you speak the French language easily? Do you comprehend it, when spoken quickly?"

"Not a word of it. I have had to learn, of course, and can pronounce very well, my last mistress said; but I cannot make it out at all in the way the French people pronounce it, when one comes to talk with them."

"It is very wrong of them, and the loss is theirs. They expect us to copy them even in their language, because we do it in everything else. Pardon me—one moment. May I look at the great enterprise which is to glorify Springhaven? It is more than kind of you to be here instead of there. But this, as I ventured to say, is a far better place to observe the operation. Your words reminded me of Captain Desportes, who has been, I think, your father's guest. A very gallant sailor, and famed for the most unexpected exploits. Without doubt, he would have captured all three ships, if he had not contrived to run his own aground."

"How could he capture his own ship? I thought that you never dealt in jokes. But if you dislike them, you seem to be fond of a little mystery. I like the French captain very much, and he took the trouble to speak slowly for me. My father says that he bears his misfortune nobly, and like a perfect gentleman. Mr. Scudamore admires him, and they are great friends. And yet, sir, you seem inclined to hint that I am in danger from Captain Desportes!"

"Ha! she is afloat! They have succeeded. I thought that they had so arranged it. The brave ship spreads her pinions. How clever the people of Springhaven are! If you will condescend to look through this glass, you will see much embracing of the Saxon and the Gaul, or rather, I should say, of the Saxon by the Gaul. Old Tugwell is not fond to be embraced."

"Oh, let me see that! I must see that!" cried Dolly, with all reserve and caution flown; "to see Capp'en Zeb in the arms of a Frenchman—yes, I declare, two have got him, if not three, and he puts his great back against the mast to disentangle it. Oh, what will he do next? He has knocked down two, in reply to excessive cordiality. What wonderful creatures Frenchmen are! How kind it is of you to show me this! But excuse me, Mr. Carne; there will be twenty people coming to the house before I can get back almost. And the ship will salute the battery, and the battery will return it. Look! there goes a great puff of smoke already. They can see me up here, when they get to that corner."

"But this spot is not private? I trust that I have not intruded. Your father

allows a sort of foot-path through this upper end of his grounds?"

"Yes, to all the villagers, and you are almost one of them; there is no right of way at all; and they very seldom come this way, because it leads to nowhere. Faith is fond of sitting here, to watch the sea, and think of things. And so am I—sometimes, I mean."

CHAPTER XXVI.

LONG-PIPE TIMES.

DAILY now the roar and clank of war grew loud and louder, across the narrow seas, and up the rivers, and around the quiet homes of England. If any unusual cloud of dust, any moving shade, appeared afar, if the tramp of horses in the lane were heard, or neigh of a colt from the four-cross roads, people at dinner would start up and cry, "The French, the French have landed!" while the men in the fields would get nearer the hedge to peep through it, and then run away down the ditch.

But the nation at large, and the governing powers, certainly were not in any great fright. Nay, rather they erred, if at all, on the side of tranquillity and self-confidence; as one who has been fired at with blank-cartridge forgets that the click of the trigger will not tell him when the bullet has been dropped in. The bullet was there this time; and it missed the heart of Britannia, only through the failure of the powder to explode all at once.

It was some years before all this was known; even Nelson had no perception of it; and although much alarm was indulged in on the sly, the few who gave voice to it were condemned as faint-hearted fellows and "alarmists." How then could Springhaven, which never had feared any enemies, or even neighbours, depart from its habits, while still an eye-witness of what had befallen the Frenchman? And in this state of mind, having plenty to talk of, it did not (as otherwise must have been done) attach any deep importance to the strange vagaries of the *London Trader*.

That great Institution, and Royal Exchange, as well as central embassy of Fashion, had lately become most uncertain in its dates, which for years had announced to loose-reckoning housewives the day of the week and the hour to buy candles. Instead of coming home on a Saturday eve, in the van of all the fishing fleet, returning their cheers and those of customers on the beach, the *London Trader* arrived anywhen, as often in the dark as daylight, never took the ground at all, and gave a very wide berth to Captain Zeb Tugwell, his craft, and his crews. At times she landed packages big and bulky, which would have been searched (in spite of London bills of lading) if there had been any Custom-house here, or any keen Officer of Customs. But these were delivered by daylight always, and carted by Mr. Cheeseman's horse direct to his master's cellars; and Cheeseman had told everybody that his wife, having come into a little legacy, was resolved in spite of his advice to try a bit of speculation in hardware, through her sister miles away at Uckfield. Most of the neighbours liked Mrs. Cheeseman, because she gave good weight (scarcely half an ounce short, with her conscience to her family thrown in against it), as well as the soundest piece of gossip to be had for the money in Springhaven. And therefore they wished her well, and boxed their children's ears if they found them poking nose into her packages. Mrs. Cheeseman shook her head when enquired of on the subject, and said with grave truth that the Lord alone can tell how any of poor people's doings may turn out.

Some other things puzzled the village, and would in more sensible times have produced a sensation. Why did Mr. Cheeseman now think nothing of as much as three spots on his white linen apron, even in the first half of the week? Why was he seldom at John Prater's now, and silent in a corner even when he did appear? What was become of the ruddy polish, like that of a Winter Redstrake, on his cheeks, which made a man long for a slice of his ham? Why, the only joke he had made for the last three months was a terrible one at his own expense. He had rushed down the street about ten o'clock one morning, at a pace quite insane for a middle-aged man, with no hat on his head and no coat on his back, but the strings of his apron dashed wild on the breeze, and his biggest ham-carver making flashes in his hand. It was thought that some boy must have run off with a penny, or some visitor changed a bad shilling; but no, there was no such good reason to give for it.

The yearning of all ages, especially dotage, is for a relapse to the infantile state when all playthings were held in common. And this wisest of all places (in its own opinion) had a certain eccentric inclination towards the poetic perfection when it will be impossible to steal, because there will be nothing left worth stealing. Still everybody here stuck to his own rights, and would knock down anybody across them, though finding it very nice to talk as if others could have no such standing-point. Moreover, they had sufficient common-sense to begin with the right end foremost, and to take a tender interest in one another's goods, moveable, handy, and divisible; instead of hungering after hungry land, which feeds nobody, until itself well fed and tended, and is as useless without a master as a donkey or a man is. The knowledge of these rudiments of civilization was not yet lost at Springhaven; and while everybody felt and even proved his desire to share a neighbour's trouble, nobody meddled with any right of his, save his right to be assisted.

Among them throve the old English feeling of respect for ancient families, which is nowadays called "toadyism" by those whom it baulks of robbery. To trade upon this good-will is almost as low a thing as any man can do, even when he does it for good uses. But to trade upon it, for the harm of those who feel it, and the ruin of his country, is without exception the very lowest—and this was what Caryl Carne was at.

He looked at the matter in a wholly different light, and would have stabbed any man who put it as above; for his sense of honour was as quick and hot as it was crooked and misguided. His father had been a true Carne, of the old stamp —hot-blooded, headstrong, stubborn, wayward, narrow-minded, and often arrogant; but—to balance these faults and many others—truthful, generous, kind-hearted, affectionate, staunch to his friends, to his inferiors genial, loyal to his country, and respectful to religion. And he might have done well, but for two sad evils—he took a burdened property, and he plunged into a bad marriage.

His wife, on the other hand, might have done well, if she had married almost anybody else. But her nature was too like his own, with feminine vanity and caprice, French conceit, and the pride of noble birth—in the proudest age of nobility—hardening all her faults, and hammering the rivets of her strong self-will. To these little difficulties must be added the difference of religion; and though neither of them cared two pins for that, it was a matter for crossed daggers. A pound of feathers weighs as much as (and in some poise more than) a pound of lead, and the leaden-headed Squire and the feather-headed Madame swung always at opposite ends of the beam, until it broke between them. Tales of rough conflict, imprisonment, starvation, and even vile blows, were told about them for several years; and then "Madame la Comtesse" (as her husband disdainfully called her) disappeared, carrying off her one child, Caryl. She was still of very comely face and form; and the Squire made known to all whom it concerned, and many whom it did not concern, that his French wife had run away with a young Frenchman, according to the habit of her race and kind. In support of this charge he had nothing whatever to show, and his friends disbelieved it, knowing him to be the last man in the world to leave such a wrong unresented.

During the last three generations the fortunes of the Carnes had been declining, slowly at first, and then faster and faster; and now they fell with the final crash. The lady of high birth and great beauty had brought nothing else into the family, but rather had impoverished it by her settlement, and wild extravagance afterwards. Her husband Montagu Carne staved off the evil day just for the present, by raising a large sum upon second mortgage and the security of a trustful friend. But this sum was dissipated, like the rest; for the Squire, being deeply wounded by his wife's desertion, proved to the world his indifference about it by plunging into still more reckless ways. He had none to succeed him; for he vowed that the son of the adulteress—as he called her—should never have Carne Castle; and his last mad act was to buy five-and-twenty barrels of powder, wherewith to blow up his ancestral home. But ere he could accomplish that stroke of business he stumbled and fell down the old chapel steps, and was found the next morning by faithful Jeremiah, as cold as the ivy which had caught his feet, and as dead as the stones he would have sent to heaven.

No marvel that his son had no love for his memory, and little for the land that gave him birth. In very early days this boy had shown that his French blood was predominant. He would bite, and kick, and scratch, instead of striking, as an English child does, and he never cared for dogs or horses, neither worshipped he the gamekeeper. France was the proper land for him, as his mother always said with a sweet proud smile, and his father with a sneer, or a brief word now condemned. And France was the land for him (as facts ordained) to be nourished, and taught, and grown into tall manhood, and formed into the principles and habitude and character which every nation stamps upon the nature of its members.

However, our strong point—like that of all others—is absolute freedom from prejudice; and the few English people who met Caryl Carne were well pleased with his difference from themselves. Even the enlightened fishermen, imbued with a due contempt for Crappos, felt a kindly will towards him, and were touched by his return to a ruined home and a lonely life. But the women, romantic as they ought to be, felt a tender interest in a young man so handsome and so unlucky, who lifted his hat to them, and paid his way.

Among the rising spirits of the place, who liked to take a larger view, on the strength of more education, than their fathers had found confirmed by life, Dan Tugwell was perhaps the foremost. In the present days he might have been a hot radical, even a socialist; but things were not come to that pass yet among people brought up to their duty. And Dan's free sentiments had not been worked by those who make a trade of such work now. So that he was pleased and respectful, instead of carping and contradictory, when persons of higher position than his own would discuss the condition of the times with him. Carne had discovered this, although as a rule he said little to his neighbours, and for reasons of his own he was striving to get a good hold upon this young fellow. He knew that it could not be done in a moment, nor by any common corruption; the mind of the youth being keen, clear-sighted, and simple—by reason of soundness. Then Carne accidentally heard of something, which encouraged and helped him in his design upon Dan.

Business was slack upon the sea just

now, but unusually active upon land, a tide of gold having flowed into Springhaven, and bubbled up in frying-pans and sparkled in new bonnets. The fishing fleet had captured the finest French frigate—according to feminine history—that ever endeavoured to capture them. After such a prisoner, let the fish go free, till hunger should spring again in the human breast, or the part that stands up under it. The hero of the whole (unlike most heroes) had not succeeded in ruining himself by his services to his country, but was able to go about patting his pocket, with an echo in his heart, every time it tinkled, that a quantity more to come into it was lying locked up in a drawer at home. These are the things that breed present happiness in a noble human nature, all else being either of the future or the past; and this is the reason why gold outweighs everything that can be said against it.

Captain Tugwell, in his pithy style, was wont to divide all human life into two distinctive tenses—the long-pipe time and the short-pipe time. The long-pipe time was of ease and leisure, comfort in the way of hot victuals and cool pots, the stretching of legs without strain of muscle, and that ever-fresh well-spring of delight to the hard worker, the censorial but not censorious contemplation of equally fine fellows, equally lazy, yet pegging hard, because of nothing in their pockets to tap. Such were the golden periods of standing, or, still better, sitting with his back against a tree, and a cool yard of clay between his gently smiling lips, shaving with his girdle-knife a cake of rich tobacco, and then milling it complacently betwixt his horny palms, with his resolute eyes relaxing into a gentle gaze at the labouring sea, and the part (where his supper soon would be) warming into a fine condition for it, by good-will towards all the world. As for the short-pipe times, with a bitter gale dashing the cold spray into his eyes, legs drenched with sleet, and shivering to the fork, and shoulders racked with rheumatism against the groaning mast, and the stump of a pipe keeping chatter with his teeth—away with all thought of such hardship now, except what would serve to fatten present comfort.

But fatherly feeling and sense of right compelled Captain Zeb to check idle enjoyment from going too far—i. e., further than himself. Every other member of

his family but himself, however good the times might be, must work away as hard as ever, and earn whatever victuals it should please the Lord to send them. There was always a job to be found, he knew that, if a young man or maid had a mind for it; and "no silver no supper" was the order of his house. His eldest son Dan was the first to be driven—for a good example to the younger ones—and now he was set to work full time and overtime, upon a heavy job at Pebbleridge.

Young Daniel was not at all afraid of work, whenever there was any kind of skill to be shown, or bodily strength to be proved by it. But the present task was hateful to him; for any big-armed yokel, or common wood-hewer, might have done as much as he could do, and perhaps more, at it, and could have taken the same wage over it. Mr. Coggs, of Pebbleridge, the only wheelwright within ten miles of Springhaven, had taken a Government contract to supply within a certain time five hundred spoke-wheels for ammunition tumbrils, and as many block-wheels for small artillery; and to hack out these latter for better men to finish was the daily task of Dan Tugwell.

This job swelled his muscles and enlarged his calves, and fetched away all the fat he had been enabled to form in loftier walks of art; but these outward improvements were made at the expense of his inner and nobler qualities. To hack and hew timber by the cubic foot, without any growing pleasure of proportion or design, to knit the brows hard for a struggle with knots, and smile the stern smile of destruction; and then, after a long and rough walk in the dark—for the equinox now was impending—to be joked at by his father (who had lounged about all day), and have all his money told into the paternal pocket, with narrow enquiries, each Saturday night. But worst of all to know that because he was not born with a silver spoon in his mouth, he had no heart—no heart that he could offer where he laid it; but there it must lie, and be trodden on in silence, while rakish-looking popinjays— But this reflection stopped him, for it was too bitter to be thought out, and fetched down his quivering hand upon his axe. Enough that these things did not tend to a healthy condition of mind, or the proper worship of the British Constitution. However, he was not quite a Radical yet.

III.—THE REFORM OF RAILWAY ABUSES.

THERE are certain things which individuals can do for themselves. There are other things which they cannot do as individuals, but only as members of some body. This common body may be a voluntary combination, like the ordinary coöperative enterprise and the joint-stock corporation, or it may be a compulsory organization, like the state.* Now this state is also a coöperative concern backed by force to compel action. It has industrial as well as social and moral functions, and it must perform all these to furnish a suitable basis for individual effort. The state must provide means for the development of the individual, and encourage the individual to make use of these means. True development is an internal growth, and is impossible without the effort of the person who is developed, but this effort can be encouraged or discouraged. Moreover, development comes as well from associated effort as from private action.

This leads naturally to the observation that state help is only one form of self-help, for the state is not something apart from the people, but is the people in their organic capacity. Associated effort through the state will best promote the growth of certain faculties.

Voluntary coöperative exertion will be found most efficient in the development of others, while family and individual industry will prove the most advantageous aid in the formation of still others. The public need at all times is to draw the line properly between individual and coöperative enterprises and the various kinds of coöperative enterprises, not between state help and self-help, for, as just seen, that implies a distinction which does not exist. What are some of these things which must be performed by men acting coöperatively? Sanitary arrangements are one class. The individual may control partially the sanitary arrangements of his own property, but even then only

partially, and when we have to do with a whole town or a larger area, there is required such a compulsory coöperative institution as we find in the state or some of its political subdivisions. Education of the masses is another case in point. The one who specially needs mental training is a child, and is, on that account, unable to guard his own interests. The modern community also imperatively requires the education of all its members, but can secure this only by compulsory coöperation. Repression of crime and the preservation of public peace likewise come under this head. So do such economic functions as care for the harbors of a country, the provision of proper drainage and river improvements, and the construction of canals and highways of all sorts. These all stand on precisely the same footing, for there is no more reason in the nature of things why the state should punish murder than there is why it should coin money; no more reason why it should send a thief to prison than why it should control a steam railway. There may be a difference in the degree of utility, but that is all.

We now find the place of railways in economic life. A little reflection renders it as obvious that a voluntary association of private individuals cannot provide themselves with railways as it is that each individual cannot do this. No railway can be constructed without a compulsory seizure of private property by exercise of the right of eminent domain; but the right of eminent domain is one of the highest attributes of sovereignty, and can be used only by a public body. The delegation of this right to a company of individuals is allowable only for a public purpose, and when they exercise this right they necessarily cease to be a private body. But there are even stronger reasons than this why one ought to regard railways as public, not private, undertakings. The railway is in its nature a monopoly. It could only be a competitive undertaking were it possible to multiply the number of railways between all centres with ease and rapidity, and without limit, so as to render any permanent

* Whenever the word state is used in this general way in the present paper, it is equivalent to political organizations of the people in the broad sense. It includes the federal state as well as the individual states of a federation, and their various subordinate parts, as city, town, and county.

combinations impossible, in order that each person might have the choice between two or more real competitors. This will never be the case anywhere, for the multiplication of railways is hindered by the enormous expenditure of labor and capital required, and also by such physical limitations as the absorption of available space by existing railways and their freight and passenger stations and other appendages. There are at times three or more parallel railways, but the advantages of combination are so great as always to lead to it sooner or later, not only between parallel lines, but between railways which may together constitute a railway system.

There are in England eleven great companies, but these were formed of two hundred and sixty-two companies, while the six great companies of France have absorbed forty-eight companies. When the New York Central Railway was formed in 1853, it consisted of a union of eleven railways. It takes twenty-five pages in *Poor's Manual of Railroads for* 1885 merely to give a list of railways in the United States which have been merged in other lines. This shows in marked manner the tendency toward consolidation. There is no exception. It is a phenomenon common to all countries.

When the number of railways has been needlessly great, there is a correspondingly increased capital on which dividends must be earned, if these unnecessary lines are to be remunerative enterprises. It is easier to see the legitimate outcome of useless railways in older countries, where railway development has nearly reached its conclusion. England is an example, and it is a well-ascertained fact that the regular effect of attempts at railway competition in England has been an ultimate increase of charges.

By means of combination and concentration of railway property the railway business of the country can be conducted most effectively. It is an improvement in economic methods of large proportions. The experience of the world has demonstrated this so conclusively that it admits of no doubt, and a very little reflection on the nature of the economic functions of the railway will render it clear to the reader. When the general public and the press resist this tendency, or cry out in childish indignation because Mr. Vanderbilt bought the West Shore Railway in the interest of the New York Central and Hudson River Railway, they are more foolish than laboring-men who resist the introduction of new and improved machinery. The latter have at least the excuse that changed methods of production often occasion the bitterest distress, and injure permanently some few laboring-men, and it is hard to appreciate a permanent advantage which must be acquired by severe present suffering. The impulse to such great economies as can be secured by combination is so strong as to be irresistible. It is one of those forces which overwhelm the man who puts himself against them, though they may be guided and directed, will one but put one's self in the stream and move with it.

George Stephenson, in the very beginning of railway construction, declared, with wonderful insight into the nature of railways, that there would never be competition where combination was possible; and a few years later Mr. James Morrison, one of England's wealthiest merchants, attempted to teach Parliament the same truth. In vain; stock phrases about free competition, the play of natural forces, and the like, blinded men. Experience, however, at length demonstrated it so conclusively that in 1872 even Mr. John Bright, extremest of economic doctrinaires, no longer objected to the establishment of a railway commission. In this country railways have managed their own affairs so poorly that they are now clamoring for legislation to protect themselves from one another. When an English Parliamentary commission, after protracted inquiry, abandon an economic theory which had long been one of the most cherished superstitions of English thought, and declare that "no means have yet been devised by which competition can be permanently maintained," and when American railway directors renounce their most valued tradition, and pronounce competition a failure in railway management, it is time to accept the lesson long ago taught by the very nature of railways, and look to some other force than free competition for deliverance from the abuses of railway power. The first conclusion to be borne in mind in a discussion of remedies is, then, this: the tendency of railways toward monopoly is in the long-run irresistible.

The second observation of a general nature upon which emphasis must be laid is this: competition in railways is not only impossible, but undesirable. It is the proper business of each nation to develop most completely all national resources, and to promote the spiritual, mental, and physical welfare of the people in the most efficient manner. In this matter, as in others, duty knows no limit save that of possibility, and whatever can be done ought to be done. We, as a people, must not tolerate such waste of power as attempts at railway competition involve. We should, on the contrary, endeavor to encourage the use of the most improved economic methods.

We not only have to do with a monopoly in the railway problem, but we desire a monopoly. Can a monopoly of such fundamental importance be left to private individuals? As we love liberty, we must reply, No. The railway problem is an affair which concerns the entire people of the United States in the most vital manner. We thus again arrive at the same conclusion reached earlier in this article. The railway is a public undertaking.

Does it follow necessarily that railways are to be owned and managed by the state? No. Public functions are sometimes delegated to bodies of citizens. The collection of taxes is a public affair, but from time immemorial governments have sold certain sources of revenue to private parties, and allowed these to collect the taxes and derive whatever profit they could from the operation. Who has not heard of the farmers-general in pre-revolutionary France?

Messrs. Vanderbilt and Jewett, in their letter to the Hepburn Committee, very properly took the ground that the construction and management of railways are an affair of the state, and that as railway officials they were performing public functions which had been committed to them.

There are two, and only two, alternatives. We must regard our railways—these modern highways—as a public undertaking managed by delegated authority, and develop all the possibilities of this thought, or we must pass over to a system of state ownership and control. The present tendency in the development of American railways is to correct abuses by recourse to the possibilities of delegated action. Something may be done in this direction, and perhaps France is the land which can teach us most about these possibilities. The idea that railways are

public highways seems to have actuated legislators from the beginning of railway construction in France. Railways have consequently there been built according to a well-defined plan; a persistent attempt has been made to subordinate them to the public interest by careful state supervision, the evils of competition have for the most part been avoided, and charters have been so granted that at the expiration of ninety-nine years all railway property reverts to the state without any compensation whatever, while the right of purchase in the mean time is reserved. Should we decide to adopt this idea in the United States, it would be necessary to extend our system of State railway commissions, and to supplement it by a national commission. This movement could then be followed by the preparation of a carefully drawn federal and State railway map, giving the location of actual and proposed railways, so that they might form one harmonious system, supplementing all other highways. No railways not embraced in the plan of construction could be built. Elaborate forms of charters, State and federal, would have to be devised, and it should be decided once for all to let each generation manage its own affairs; in other words, no more grants of perpetual charters or corporate rights for any purpose whatever ought to be made either by the United States or any individual State. A further protection both to the general public and to the owners of railway property might be afforded by a much needed change in our general corporation laws, which would give a representation in the management to a minority. The principle of one vote to a share ought to be abolished. Another necessary step in this programme is to clothe the State and federal commissions with the same power to make rates which the Georgia commission now enjoys. The most complete publicity of the accounts of railway corporations follows as a matter of course. A model can be found in the administration of national banks. Not only should railway accounts drawn up on a required plan and sworn to by directors be examined at short and regular intervals, but at every step in their career they should be subjected to that closest scrutiny which has enabled us to replace the worst banking system in the world, the old State banks, by one of the very best, our present national banks.

Two plans which have been prepared for railway reform may be dismissed in a few words. One is a law regulating charges and railway conduct, and allowing an aggrieved party recourse to the courts. This is the character of the well-known Reagan bills which have been before Congress for some time. This plan is chimerical. Railway management is so complicated a matter that minute regulations cannot be given long in advance. If charges are limited by law, it is as a rule necessary to place the charges so high that the law is valueless. Improvements in technical railway processes are continually making, and how can the law anticipate reductions which ought to follow these? Railway experience has sufficiently demonstrated that railway management must be intrusted to those who have power to decide on details from time to time, though it is easily possible to map out a general line of policy. All this decides the question apart from the enormous expense of railway litigation, and the fear of the railway power which now intimidates business men.

The second plan is that of Mr. Hudson—the separation of railway ownership from the business of transportation.

The idea is that the railway should become a public highway,· and should be compelled to allow all persons to run freight and passenger cars with locomotives over it, provided only that these be placed under proper supervision to prevent accident, and that a reasonable toll be paid. This is the theory that obtained universally in the first days of the railway, and it is doubtless this theory that led to the decision in Holland to intrust to the state the construction of the railway, and to allow private parties to take charge of the transportation of passengers and goods. Perhaps the strongest plea in favor of this theory is to be found in Mr. Hudson's book, but no instance can be adduced of any practical success in the application of this proposed method, and it is difficult to see anything further in this restatement of the arguments for a separation between the ownership of the highway and the business of a common carrier than the lengths to which an able man may be driven who once determines to adhere at all costs to the doctrines of universal competition. How is one to gain control of the railways? it may be asked. It is easy to pass laws, but will

the managers of railways not continue to defy them? Why is there not now competition in the express business? We observe a monopoly, express companies having divided territory, although this does not at all seem to be due to the character of our laws. Competition has been attempted between Baltimore and New York, but the Adams Express Company has crushed it. An old-established company with wide ramifications and large capital will even do business for nothing, between two main points, for a time, to ruin an obnoxious rival, and will maintain its life from other revenues, and look to a free field in the future for profits. If the separation suggested was effected, what guarantee have we that similar phenomena in the transportation of freight would not manifest themselves? Again, there is great economy and convenience in the conduct of the transportation of freight and passengers by those operating on a vast scale, whether they own the tracks or not, and this gives to that industry its inherent and irresistible impulse toward monopoly, and, as already remarked, we desire these advantages. It is not clear that the technical difficulties of railway management do not interpose other and insuperable obstacles to the plan proposed by Mr. Hudson.

Something may be done in the direction in which we are now moving, but the prospect is not encouraging. State railway commissions have done some good, and may effect more in the future, but no government has ever been strong enough to gain complete control over a system of private railways. English railways have been known to defy even the War Department. In Canada the question has been raised whether the state should absorb the railways, or the railways the state; in France no one of the various governments which have come and gone since railway construction began has shown adequate power to subordinate the railways to the people; and in Germany, Bismarck, backed by the mighty German Empire, and aided by the most magnificent civil service the world has ever seen, gave up the problem as a hopeless one. An Imperial Railway Office was created in 1873, and under this were placed the comparatively insignificant imperial railways of Alsace and Lorraine. The purpose of this office was to exercise a general control over the German railways in accordance with the provisions of the imperial constitution. But it could not be effected. The office remained an ornamental appendage to the imperial government. "The imperial constitution," said Bismarck, in a speech on April 26, 1876, "attributes to the empire the duty of a general supervision over all German railways, a certain control over tariffs, etc. An Imperial Railway Office has been called into existence with the view of carrying out the provisions of the constitution. The experience of the office has manifested, however, the impotence of the empire.... The Imperial Railway Office has become a council, which gives good advice, and prefaces its requests with 'if you please.' It writes a great deal and makes much ado, but no one heeds its behests."

It may be well to explain that the empire was obliged to contend against the private and state railway systems of the various states, like Prussia, Bavaria, Saxony, etc., and that up to the present time it has never been supported by any substantial economic railway power of its own.

What evidence is there that we in this country shall in the future be able to control the railway power? We never have done it. Save in Georgia it does not appear that State commissions have ever forced the railways to do anything of great moment which they did not desire. It is considered a wonderful thing in New York State if the Railway Commissioners can induce the railways to give even an indifferent sort of heed to the wishes of the public, and no one seriously expects the railways to obey the laws like a private individual. In Georgia the power against which the commission contends still lives, and even threatens its existence. It is its perpetual foe.

Our present system of commissions is one which confers responsibility without adequate power, and the entire history of administration in this and other countries condemns such a course.

Another grave objection to be urged against the development of the idea of delegated authority along the lines which have been marked out in this paper is that it violates the well-established and weighty principle that corporate rights either should not be conferred at all, or should be conferred by a general law upon all alike who fulfil certain required conditions.

It ought to be remarked, in regard to our existing railways, that the blame which attaches to managers has in some respects been unduly magnified by good people who do not appreciate the almost irresistible temptations to which railway authorities are exposed. It is our vicious system which fairly forces some of these evils described even upon unwilling men, and for this system the public must bear its share of blame.

If it should prove impossible in this country to develop a thoroughly satisfactory system of railway control through delegated authority, there will remain only the one alternative—State and federal railways; and men of great ability have long predicted that the nature of things would inevitably force us to this sooner or later. While we are not prepared to say, here and now, that the system of government ownership is the best, yet the inquiry upon which we have entered cannot be dismissed without giving this system a careful consideration.

The advantages of state railways, when properly managed, are obvious. They become a basis of economic life, upon which each one can with confidence devote himself to the construction of his own fortune. The most reasonable of the objections against what is called a "paternal" government is that it is opposed to the highest development of individual enterprise. But it may be found that such a development will become possible only through as immediate and efficient control by the government over telegraphs and railways as it now exercises over the post-office.

But one great good which they would bring us is so little understood that it requires a moment's attention. They would mitigate industrial crises which are due largely to the irregular methods of corporate enterprises, as Colonel Wright, Commissioner of Labor, has endeavored to show in his recent report. The feverish development and subsequent prostration in our economic life thus caused have deranged our industrial system and brought upon us grave evils. There is reason to believe that even our Chinese question is largely due to this feature of our economic life, as has been well shown by a writer in the Australian press, who thus explains why Australia has not encountered a problem of such dimensions in the Chinese: "The smallness of the Mongolian element existing in Australia as compared with that in the United States may be ascribed to the steadier and less spasmodic development of these colonies, in which public works are not, as a rule, the outcome of lobbying, and are, when decided upon, constructed methodically and with due regard to financial considerations, instead of being rushed through by a 'ring.'"

It is also important to notice that periods of stagnation in commerce and industry are those most favorable to the construction of public works, as capital is seeking investment, interest is low, material cheap, and labor abundant. Government might well improve these circumstances to relieve distress and remove many of the dangers and sufferings of "hard times."

It likewise deserves attention that the centralization in the natural development of railway management is preparing the way for an easy transfer of the railways to the state.

The arguments employed against state railways are familiar.

It is said that private parties can manage a business undertaking better than government, but this is an assertion which experience has not borne out. Private enterprise had an opportunity to do what it could in the management of the post-office, and competition was carried so far that at one time there were nine or ten post-office stations on one block in the city of Hamburg. The world over, private enterprise has yielded to public enterprise in the post-office, and that with such excellent results that there has been no serious proposal to return to old methods. The express business is analogous; and will any one claim that it is so well managed for the people by private enterprise as it would be by the public? A conclusive answer seems to be afforded by the rapidity with which, in spite of serious opposition, the post-office is everywhere absorbing the express business.

Gas supply serves as another illustration. This has been almost universally better managed by municipalities than by private parties. There were few improvements in this industry in England until the municipalities took hold of it, since which time improvements have been rapid, price has fallen until it is now proposed in one place in Scotland to place it at twenty-five cents a thousand. The muni-

cipalities derive a profit from the manufacture of gas, and such private companies as still exist have at length been forced to follow the public works in the adoption of improved methods. New York and Baltimore, on the other hand, are conspicuous illustrations of the evils of a private gas supply. Probably no municipality ever managed this branch of industry so badly. Political corruption has also been a prominent factor in private management.*

It is clearly necessary to discriminate between those things which the state should do and those which it should not do, and it is perhaps more unfortunate for it to do too little than too much. At any rate, the evil consequences of both errors are serious. People talk about the stimulus of private interest, and forget that corporate property, like state enterprises, is managed by delegated authority, not directly by the owners of the stock, and experience tends to confirm the view that those chosen by governmental agency are even more likely to perform their duties with an eye single to the permanent prosperity of the railways which they manage than are directors of railway corporations. Does some person suggest that political corruption might be connected with public highways? That is not impossible, but could it well be worse than the political corruption which private railways have fostered? The one who thinks so may safely be defied to produce instances of such corruption under a system of state railways as we have seen in the United States. Indeed, there is good reason to believe that our political life would never have sunk to such low depths had we known only state railways. This matter was brought up in the debate on the purchase of private railways in Prussia in the session of Parliament for 1879–80, when the frank statement made by Minister Maybach produced a favorable impression. It was in substance about as follows: "Gentlemen, it may be that government will be able to exert some influence over the employés of state railways. But what is the present condition of things? I will tell you, gentlemen. Railways continually want favors of governments, and

---

* This entire subject has received satisfactory treatment in the admirable monograph by Dr. E. J. James, on "The Relation of the Modern Municipality to the Gas Supply," just published in Baltimore by the American Economic Association.

are willing to promise votes as a *quid pro quo.* At the present time we can get the votes of railway employés through railway presidents. When the railways become state property, these men will at least have the protection of the civil service law. Now they have none."

There is reason to believe that the increase of civil service employés through the purchase of our railways by the state would be the best thing which could happen to us. It would bring the question of administrative reforms to a head at once, and settle it forever. When sound principles of administration are so vital as they would be then, public sentiment insists upon them. Two illustrations are much to the point. The colonial governors sent out by England are usually men who have become bankrupt as politicians, or party hacks who must be rewarded, or at best noble figure-heads, and it is a matter which attracts little attention, for the position is one of minor importance; but when the time comes for the selection of a Governor-General of India, totally different principles prevail. With a realization of the enormous responsibility which devolves upon this official, it is the practice to select men who are among the ablest English administrative officers to be found. The New York Post-office affords the second illustration. This became so important some time ago that the commercial interests of New York demanded that it should be managed on sound administrative principles, and as a result it was the first large post-office in the country to be removed from the sphere of partisan politics. To-day we witness what has been a notable phenomenon—a Republican postmaster in New York under a Democratic President.

It would be too hasty a generalization—though no more hasty than those which we see every day—to attempt to lay it down as a law that the larger the functions of government, the smaller the amount of patronage; yet there is weighty experience to corroborate this hypothesis. America, England, and Prussia are examples. The truth probably is that, other things being equal, there is least corruption and smallest room for the spoils system when government performs its legitimate industrial functions, neither too little nor too much.

The successful experiment of Prussia is instructive. One might have heard all sorts of apprehensions expressed in 1879 about the change from private to state railways, but now the sentiment of the Prussian people is overwhelmingly in their favor. A well-known German economist expressed grave fears about the contemplated change in 1877, but the year 1882 found him an enthusiastic adherent of state railways. There is an English school of economists in Germany, composed of those called the Manchester men, who were very generally opposed to the state railways before they came; but the *Frankfort Gazette*, a bitter opponent of Bismarck, was able to state in 1885 that one of this school could not be found who desired a return to private railways, while business men are gratified by the stability, impartiality, and publicity of railway charges. It is, indeed, possible to observe a marked progress among German business men in initiative and enterprise in recent years, and these qualities have evidently been stimulated by the encouragement which they have received from a good railway system. It requires no prophet to foresee a great industrial future for Germany, and many careful men expect to see her outstrip England as an economic power. There is a return of commerce to the old route through central Europe since the Suez Canal has been constructed, and there is prospect of a revival of the ancient glory of the German cities, and the state railways that the country now enjoys place her in a position to improve every opportunity for commercial and industrial greatness. Even this same *Frankfort Gazette*, which, as one can imagine, does not represent the German, possibly still less the Prussian, government in too favorable a light, acknowledges that the financial success of the state railways has surpassed the anticipations of government.

A careful student of recent Prussian administration will notice the following coincidence as a most interesting and important fact. The increase of economic functions and improvements in administrative methods has accompanied a steady decentralization of government, and a vast increase in local self-government. This is the true significance of the changes in the Prussian administration of the Interior which have been in progress since 1872, and which have been so little understood abroad.

Our country is in many respects better

fitted to receive the full fruits of the beneficent change from private to state railways than is Germany. We need improvement in administration, but this will surely come; in fact, is already coming. What we want is a democratic administration, not a despotic administration like the present. This is a point too little understood, though it ought not to be necessary to enlarge on it now, after the excellent work our civil service reformers have been doing. People say, "We don't want Prussian administration in America," and overlook the fact that that is the one chief democratic and redeeming feature in Prussian government. Prussian civil service denotes a downfall of privilege, for when the people at length wrested a constitution from the Hohenzollerns, one of the guaranteed rights of all Prussians was equal access to all offices. There was no longer a privileged class of appointed office-holders. So in England administrative reform has gone hand in hand with the progress of democracy. Thus will it be with us. It will come in with the dawn of economic liberty.

North and South found renowned generals to win grand victories in time of war, but peace has her victories. And when the people will it, we shall find our generals in industry who will win very different but no less glorious victories in the field of economic life, and restore to the people their own.

There is talk of progress in many branches of science and in every industrial pursuit, but we are witnesses of progress in the art of administration, and we may be sure that our government will be able to perform its legitimate functions. It is not unnatural that so many are looking forward with hope and enthusiasm to state railways, for they will abolish the supremacy of the railway king, and help to restore among us a cherished democracy, the rule "of the people, by the people, and for the people." The idea has taken firm hold of the masses, and is working among them. It may be but a germ now, but everything points to its rapid growth, and certainly the end will not come until our railways are really the people's highways.

THE END OF A LOVE-MATCH.

BY JULIA D. WHITING.

"WAL, what I say," said old Mr. Graves, shifting his quid to his other cheek, and contemplating the side of his cowhide boot, "is that gals ought to git married. They're better off, and happier. We hev authority for't. Watts sez,

'Birds in their little nests agree,'

and it's jest so with human critters, and I hate to see a pretty, hulsome gal turnin' inter a cross-grained old maid. 'Tain't nateral, and 'tain't right. Why, I *know* folks is happier. Wife, she hain't never left me by myself, as you may say, but once sence we was married, twenty-seven year ago, and that was the time when her sister Olive, over to Norridge, hed the black janders. That 'ere was a kind of myster'ous disease, Mis' Elder. No one knowed how she got it nor why she hed it. Wal, Jane, she was sent for, and went to nuss her sister, and she staid and staid, and I was lunsomer than a owl, and finally, thinks to me, 'I can't stand this no longer!' I tackled up and went after her, and brought her home, and I don't

cal'late ever to be left so agin. I'm willin' she should go. 'Yes,' I tell her, 'she's free to go,' and she is; but I must tag along. I can't stand it to be left. Mis' Elder, I d'know as you ever see any one with the black janders, did you?"

"Yes, I have," said Mrs. Elder, working away on a braided mat.

"Wal," said Mr. Graves, "it doos beat all how a critter can look that's got it. Why, Olive, she's middlin' fair complected, but when she was down with that spell her face looked jest like a piece of cloth that's hed coffee spilled onto it—jest that same brown kind of look."

"Brown," snapped Mrs. Elder, holding up her mat, and viewing it critically to see if the last row sewed on didn't pucker a little: "I should admire to know what your coffee is made of. Reel old Javy don't make no brown stain."

"Wal, now, Mis' Elder," Mr. Graves remonstrated, "I *do* know something, and if you'd asked pleasanter, I should just as soon told you that we use dandelion coffee. I git the roots, and wife browns 'em and grinds 'em, and it makes amazin' good coffee, and now dandelion coffee *doos* make a brown stain, and that's jest the way Olive's face looked. Wal, now, I forgit what we was talkin' about."

"Jane Morril's not gittin married was what you *started* on," observed Mrs. Elder, who had laid down her mat, and was moulding bread.

"Yes, so it was. Wal, now, what makes *you* think she won't?"

"Oh, well, 'cause I do."

"Want to know! Wal, now, it's my belief she hain't never had no chance. I don't believe any gal would live single if she could help it: stands to reason."

"Now, Mr. Graves, that 'ere remark shows just how much you know about it. There's some girls that ain't such fools but what they know better than to marry a poor stick, jest so as to say they're married, and don't think a crooked stick is better than none, and Jane's one of them. Why, Jane told me—" But here Mrs. Elder broke off, and dumping the last loaf into a pan, set all before the fire to rise, and began industriously washing the baking dishes.

"Wal, Mis' Elder," said Mr. Graves, who had perforce taken down his feet from the stove hearth to make way for the bread, and was now tilted back against the wall.

"Well, what?"

"What did Jane tell you?"

"Nothing she wanted you to know. Was you cal'latin' to go to mill this mornin'?"

"Why, yes, I was. Why, was you wantin' to send by me to git some meal, Mis' Elder?"

"No, I wa'n't; but if you hev any idee of gittin home so as not to keep dinner waitin', you'd better be goin'."

"Wal, wal, perhaps I hed. I'd no idee it was so late," apologized the old farmer, slowly rising and buttoning up his old overcoat. "Pooty tejus weather. Do you know how the mercury stood this morning? Six below, to our house. I call that pooty snug."

As the farmer slowly clumped his way down the path, Mrs. Elder, after watching him for a moment, stepped across the floor, and opening the sitting-room door, looked in and said: "What! you here, Miss Snow, settin' in the cold? How long you've ben here? Why didn't you fetch your knittin' out inter the kitchen?

There wan't nobody to hurt you. Nothin' but Mr. Graves holdin' forth as usual. The most shif'less creeter I ever see. Willin', but hain't no more jas'm than a dead corn-stalk, and *so* curious! Now I s'pose he'll keep harpin' on Jane Morril's not bein' married till we're all sick on't."

"Who is this Jane Morril?" inquired Miss Snow (an elderly but not unpleasant maiden lady, who was visiting the Elders). "Is there anything strange about her?"

"Strange? No; not unless to be remarkable pretty and takin' is strange; and I guess it is. If Jane has a fault, it's pride, and, for that matter, the hull family are as proud as you ever see folks. I don't understand Jane, and I don't pretend to; and I hain't always known her. Her folks come here about six year ago. There's her pa, and her ma, and her sister Eudoxy, and the little boys. Eudoxy ain't much to look at, but she's as proud as if she was Cleopatry. I think that reely they set a sight by Jane, but they don't act as if they did; and then, they're driven to work; at least Eudoxy and her pa are. I don't know what her ma was, because she's got spinal disease, and sets in one postur' in her chair the whole during time; and it don't make her sweet-tempered. Wal, Jane is first-rate to entertain company, and she reads a sight. Mrs. Browning, now, is one of her favorites; but I s'pose she don't do as much as she might round the house. And there's considerable *to* do; and she's careless—dreadful careless. I d'know as I ever see her when she looked reel slick; but then she's reel pretty."

"It is rather strange so pretty a girl wasn't snapped up before this," said Miss Snow.

"I hain't a doubt," observed Mrs. Elder, hanging up her dish-pan, and resuming work on her mat, "but what she's had offers enough; but I don't know certain, and I wouldn't dast to ask; but I could 'a told Mr. Graves of *one* chance I was knowin' to. I had it on my tongue's end to speak out, but I knew 'twa'n't right. I used to wonder why she didn't git married, and finally I up and asked her. 'Jane,' sez I (she was settin' right there on the lounge, and lookin' her prettiest, and it set me thinkin')—'Jane,' sez I, 'why don't you git married?' She didn't say nothin' for a minute, but her eyes kinder danced, and the corners of her mouth kep' quirkin'. Finally sez she,

"'Well, Mis' Elder, 'tain't because I don't have no chance.'

"'Land, no!' sez I; 'I didn't think *that*.'

"'No,' sez she. 'I had an offer yes'-day,' she sez, 'and a real steady man.'

"'Do tell!' sez I. "Who was it?'

"She burst out laughin', and said, 'It was old Job Giddings that made me an offer—at least ma said it was an offer.'

"'Land of compassion!' sez I, 'you ain't a-goin'—'

"'I'm not, indeed,' sez she. 'Do you think I'd marry that wretched, sordid old man?'

"I see she was kinder riled, and I told her that I never thought on it for a minute, that it was just as unsuitable as it could be, and got her smoothed down, and then I asked her how 'twas, but she wouldn't tell me no particulars; she was awful 'shamed of it. I kinder mistrust that Jane has hed a reel serious affair, though. I d'know, but I kinder think so."

"Who is it? Any one I know? Not Deacon Chadwick's boy? I always thought he'd be quite a beau."

"Mercy sakes, no! It's some one you don't know; it's a cousin of hers, Jerome Warner. He come here about a year ago, and hez been clerkin' it ever sence. He's got a drea'ful good education, I s'pose; but he's high-strung, and couldn't get on with his folks, I guess. He hain't let on much about his affairs, but that's what people say, and so he left home in a huff, and come here, and—and before he'd been here long, any one could see how 'twas goin'. He was allers with her when he could git out of the store, and when I met 'em out walkin' they was all bound up in each other, so's they couldn't see nor hear no one but themselves, and I thought it was comin' to something sure enough, when his folks sent for him all of a sudden, and he went off, and Jane's been reel kinder down ever sence. It's as much as two months sence he went off, and I hain't scurcely seen Jane sence.

"Wonder if that ain't *him* comin' up now? I never heerd him hurry so before. I hope there hain't nothing happened to the oxen." And Mrs. Elder hurried to the door, but before she could lift the latch, it flew open, and Mr. Graves flew in, all out of breath.

"Well, Nathan Graves, for the mercy's sake, what is the matter? Hez that 'ere off ox of his'n been cuttin' up agin?

Where is he? Why don't you say something?" demanded exasperated and frightened Mrs. Elder. "There you stand gaspin' at me! If they're bringin' him home 'most dead, I want to know it. *Will* you speak?"

"Why, Mis' Elder," remonstrated poor Mr. Graves, "how you do go on! Well, there hain't anything happened to your man, and I shouldn't come to tell you you was a widder if you was. *He's* all right. But I tell you, Mis' Elder, I've heerd news that beats the beater! Now who do you s'pose has left town sudden?—run off to git married too? I don't believe you could guess if you kep' at it for a fortnight."

"I don't want to guess," said Mrs. Elder, with some sourness; "but if you want to tell your news, do it and hev done. I don't believe it will prove anything very amazin'."

"You don't! Well, sometimes you're mistaken, same as other folks. Wal—it's Jane Morril."

"It ain't possible!" said Mrs. Elder, excitedly. "Jane's no such girl; and her folks know where she is. I see her ma yes'day, and she was tellin' me that Jane was gone to Newton Four Corners to help her aunt, now that Malvy is down with the fever, and she some expected her home yes'day afternoon."

"Wal, they can keep expectin', I s'pose; 'twon't hurt 'em none, nor change nothing; but Jane's Mis' Jerome Warner as sure as guns!" and Mr. Graves left the support of the door-jamb for a chair before the fire.

"Well, now, Nathan Graves, for the mercy's sake! How are you so knowin' to this, over and above all of Jane's friends?"

"Why, I heerd it. You see, I was waitin' to the mill to hev my corn ground, and there come a feller ridin' up, and come to look and see who 'twas, turned out to be Ed Pillsbury to the Corners—doctor's son, you know. He was ridin' that 'ere sorrel hoss that the doctor bought of your brother two year ago; and I guess Ed is rather hard on hosses; looked as if he run him consid'able; amazin' thin. Hate to see a smart hoss kinder run down like that 'ere. You remember that hoss, don't you, Mis' Elder?"

"Mr. Graves, did you come to talk about hosses, or to tell me what you heerd? You're enough to try the patience of Job!"

"Wal, wal, I was gittin to it. Wal, you see, Ed rode up, and sez he: 'Good-mornin', Mr. Graves. Smart frosty mornin'. How's your folks?'"

"Look here, Nathan Graves, *I* don't want to know what you said back agin, nor nothin' about your folks. For pity's sake come to the gist of the matter," said Mrs. Elder, completely out of patience.

"Wal, Mis' Elder, you git me all flustrated, takin' me up so. I was gittin round."

"Well, I want you to *git* there some time. If you're all day tellin' me, you won't hev no chance to tell the neighborhood."

"Wal, Ed, he talked a while, and then he sez, 'How do the folks like Jane's gittin' married this way?' I didn't know what he meant, and told him so, and then it all come out. Come to find out, it seems that she set out sure enough for her aunt's, but never went there. She stopped at the tavern, and Jerome joined her there, and they took the cars and went to Schenectady—(what do you s'pose they went *there* for, Mis' Elder?)—and got married; then they went on to Buffalo, and spent the week, and finally brought up to the Corners last night. Ed said that Jerome's folks were so put out (Jane bein' his own cousin so, and expectin' of her there, bein' sickness in the house so, doos make it seem kinder unfeelin', don't it?) that they wouldn't hev no part nor lot with 'em—wouldn't hev 'em in the house; and they went to the tavern and staid, and I s'pose they're comin' home to-day. I guess her folks will be hoppin'. Ed said he heerd that Malvy was a great deal worse than what she had been. I s'pose they had pooty hot words right there in the settin-room, and Malvy's room opens right off of it, and she heerd it all. Wal, I must be goin'. Wife will want to hear the news, and I guess I'll stop and let the widder Stow know about it. There won't be nobody to tell her, and widders want to know as much as any one;" and off he went.

"First time I ever see that man hurry," observed Mrs. Elder. "Well, now you've heerd the upshot of Jane's story, Miss Snow."

Ten years afterward, one cold rainy night, in the latter part of April, brought Miss Snow again to Mrs. Elder's door. It was past eight o'clock; the train was late, and she knew no one expected her, but was sure of a welcome; so she walked around to the kitchen door and knocked.

Mrs. Elder opened the door, and shading her eyes with one hand while she held out the kerosene lamp with the other, looked sharply at her late visitor.

"I want to know, now, if this is Miss Snow? I'm dreadful glad to see you. Step right in. But where under the canopy did you drop from? Well, I *be* surprised!"

"I came up just now from the station; I've been visiting friends in Westbrook," quietly observed Miss Snow, walking in and setting down her hand-bag.

"Well, this *is* an onexpected pleasure. *He'll* be amazin' glad to see you. You was allers a favorite with him; but I guess I won't let him know to-night. He's been layin' stone wall all day, and come supper-time he was so beat out that I told him the best place for him was bed, and so, as quick as supper was down, he went. But where are your things? Round in the front yard? Slocum bring you up? Well, Abner and Joel, you go and git 'em in. Be sure and wipe your feet onto the mat before you go upstairs, and try and step kinder softly, so as not to wake your pa."

Abner and Joel, great boys of sixteen and eighteen, who had been shyly grinning at the visitor, gladly obeyed the order, and left Miss Snow with their mother.

"Come, Miss Snow, let me take your things, and you set right up to the fire, and I'll get you something to stay your stummick."

The cloth was laid, the table set, and Mrs. Elder, superintending the frying of some ham and eggs, surveyed her friend.

"Well, I see Time has been workin' at you, same as he has at the rest of us; not but what your new teeth are more becomin' than what your own was, and I judge you're usin' hair-dye. *I* would if the boys didn't pester me so. They will have it that they like my hair gray; but I hate to look older than what I be. Hev you had your health?"

"Pretty well, thank you. Have you?"

"I have, since that sickness of mine. You recollect it was three year ago I hed that fever. I'm sure I wrote to you about it. That *was* a tejus time, and the only consolin' thing I could think on when I was burnin' and tossin' was that if I didn't git well I shouldn't hev to make no more cheeses, turnin' of 'em was so hard for my wrists. I worried through, and here I be as tough as ever; but there's been changes here, same as everywhere. Now, if you feel like eatin', Miss Snow, set right up to the table. I hain't nothing extra to offer you, but the ham is some of our own raisin', and good."

"While I am eating, Mrs. Elder, I wish you'd tell me how the neighbors have been getting on all this time," said Miss Snow.

"Well, perhaps I'd better begin to home. *He's* middlin' smart. Doos as big a day's work as he ever did. I tell him he ain't rustin' out, anyway. The boys are reel good, and help, and Mary is married, and lives about half a mile this side of the Holler. She's doin' well; got a reel smart go-ahead man.

"You don't remember Nathan Graves, do you? I want to know! Well, he and his wife are both gone. Died in one week, of pneumony. She was took a Thursday, and he come down on Saturday, and come next Thursday mornin' they see she was goin', and they went in and told him. You know he was allers sayin' he couldn't be left, and he was amazin' fond of his wife. Well, they said he didn't sense it at first, but when he see how it was, he just smiled and said, 'I must go too,' and turned over, and was gone, jest as sudden as that. Well, she was a good Christian woman, and he allers *meant* well.

"I'm afraid you ain't a-goin' to make out a supper, Miss Snow. Wouldn't you like another pickle for a relish? Don't tell me you're through. I used to think you had consid'able appetite. Well, if you won't eat no more, let me git you another chair, so you can set more comfortable;" and she went out, and soon returned with a rocker. "There, Miss Snow, what do you think of that? Mary beats all for patchin', and she made that log-cabin cushion for a surprise for me. Looks kinder gay, don't it?"

"Very nice indeed," said Miss Snow.

"You set up to the fire and rest while I do the dishes."

Abner and Joel had come in from doing their evening work at the barn, and gone upstairs to bed. Mrs. Elder, having set aside the dishes, took her knitting-work and sat down by her friend.

"After all, come to look at you agin,

you ain't changed so much as what I thought you was. You've had an easier life than what I have."

A long pause followed Mrs. Elder's last words, broken at last by Miss Snow: "Just before I left here, ten years ago, there was a girl that made a runaway match—married her cousin, I think. I've often wondered how that affair turned out."

"Oh, Jane? You can see her that was Miss Jane Morril any day. She teaches school in that little new building just below here, and you'll see her goin' by with her boys about half after eight in the mornin'. It hain't turned out as Jane s'posed it would. You see, Jane's folks were riled consid'able, and they didn't want 'em, and they was both high-strung, and didn't want to be beholden to any one; but finally Malvy interceded with her folks (you know she was Jerome's twin, and felt just as twins allers do), and his pa gave him a farm that he held down in the Holler.

"Well, they was pleased enough, and set up house-keepin', and nothing would do but Jerome must try scientific farmin'. Of course, if he'd a-been rich, it would done well enough; but he wa'n't—hadn't nothin'—and that kind of farmin' costs a sight; and after a spell his folks got tired of lendin' him money, and they run in debt, and there was hard feelin's, and first I knew they was movin'."

"Why, where did they go?"

"Well, he tried school-keepin' a spell, and she did dress-makin', but she wa'n't a first-rate fitter, and they didn't neither of 'em know how to make their money last. If they hed some, jest as like as not he'd buy some book on scientific farmin' (he was allers harpin' on that), when he'd oughter got some flour; and they owed, and that wa'n't pleasant. Finally he out with a new plan.

"He was possessed to get a cattle ranch out to Colorado. He *knew* he should make his fortin, and Jane was just as fierce as he was; and so his pa let him have some money, and off they went.

"Jane's oldest boy was a year old by that time, and she wa'n't reel well. Well, they went, and first they wrote home that it was beautiful—climate and critters and everything. Then Jane hed her other boy, and before long Jerome took cold out herdin' cattle, and hed rheumatiz awful, so's it drored up one leg some, and made him lame, and I guess it was about then he began to git discouraged and let things go; and I knew well enough, without lookin' inter her butt'ry, that Jane was an awful slack house-keeper, and she was sick a good deal too.

"They hed been there about five years when Tom Hawkins was out in that section of the country (he's a dreadful rovin' kind), and he heerd, I forgit how, there was Eastern folks by the name of Warner on a ranch there, and he went and see 'em."

"Did he know them?" inquired Miss Snow.

"Why, yes, he did; that is, he hed allers known Jane—went to school with her. He was born and brought up in this town. His mother was the widder Hawkins. I guess you never see her."

"Oh yes, he knowed Jane well, and Jerome some. They was pleased, and so was he, and they asked him to stay, and he did. They was short of hands, and finally he was there as much as six months. I do' know but he'd 'a staid longer if things hed been pleasant, but they wa'n't.

"You see, Jerome's health wa'n't so good, and he was kinder soured, and was dreadful uncomfortable. Some days, Tom said, he'd seem to be so fond of the children and Jane, and she'd chipper up and fix up what she could, and everything would be reel pleasant, seems so; then agin he'd be as glum, and push the children out of the way, and snap at Jane, and nothing would suit. He'd take his gun and off he'd go, and be gone a week, maybe; and Jane would be round with her eyes all swelled up, jest as worried as she could live; but she never let on a word to Tom.

"There was another thing. Jane used to write poems, you know; she was a reel good poetry-maker, and she'd send 'em East, and sometimes the magazines would take 'em and send her a little money, and more times they didn't; whichever way it was made Jerome mad, and he was allers flingin' at her.

"But the wust on't was when he found ore. Well, Tom said he thought he was possessed. He was certain it would be a payin' mine, and was all for workin' it. He sent home for money, but his folks wa'n't so ridiculous as what he was, and they wouldn't send him none; nor would her folks; so there he was!

"He was left to himself, I guess, if a man ever was. He wouldn't hear to Jane nor Tom, but he was *set* to work that mine;

and he sold his critters, all but some oxen, and everything he could; sold the crops, what they had, standin'. Tom said, if he'd had his way, he'd 'a clapped Jerome inter a 'sylum till his senses come back to him.

"I do s'pose Jane has seen sorrer over and above what most folks hez. I declare! it's kep' me in more times than a few. When I get frettin', then I think to myself, 'what's your trouble to what some folks' is?' Why, if my husband was so panicky and wild, I don' know what I should do."

"Sorrow—do you call that sorrow, Mrs. Elder? I should call it trouble—serious trouble; but sorrow is more for the loss of friends. Had Jane sorrow of that kind?'

"Well, Miss Snow, you're older than what I be, and you've been round and seen livin' that's different from what I have; but *I* call that sorrer, or cause for it. Jane had lost friends, same as other folks, and she'd lost a little child that died before it could walk, but she never was reel unhappy until that minin' fever struck him.

"Why, Tom said he reely was afraid for Jerome some of the time after they got to minin'. If they found a little mite of ore, or what Tom called 'indications' (*I* do' know what that means), Jerome would come in the house and plan how they was goin' to be rich right off, and tell what hosses he'd buy and houses he'd build, and lay out all their lives; and Tom said it would beat Solomon in all his glory, if it had turned out so, and he'd get as fierce, and talk as fast, and his eyes would sparkle; and Jane would set with her eyes on the floor till she couldn't stan' it, and she'd say something kinder throwin' doubts on it, you know, and Jerome would grind out a swear word, and fling out of the house. And then they was gittin poorer and poorer.

"Well, Tom, he got tired, finally, of stayin'; things was so unpleasant, and he up and told 'em he should hev to quit. They was both sorry. I guess they both liked him, and then they'd kinder fling at each other over his shoulders, as you might say, and it was kinder of an accommodation.

"Well, he was goin' pretty soon, when one day Jerome took the youngest child, little Homer, out with him when he started out in the mornin'. He was allers fond of Homer, Tom said, let his temper be what it might.

"Well, he went off a piece with him, lookin' after the oxen that hed strayed, and they got out in one of them gullies, and they s'pose Jerome thought he see ore, and he was all took up with it, and forgot the child, and it fell down one of them precipitous places, and its little head struck onto a stone; the upshot on't was that the child was dead when his father picked him up."

"Poor man!" said Miss Snow, "how I pity him!"

"That's what I say," rejoined Mrs. Elder, wiping her eyes with the corner of her gingham apron; "it *was* unfortinate; and Tom said, if he ever see a man *look* as if he was struck with death, Jerome did when he come up to the house carryin' the body. Jane happened to be out hangin' up some clo'es, and she seemed to see in a minute how 'twas, and she dropped the clo'es and run up and took the child out of his father's arms, and looked at it, and see it was dead, and screamed right out, 'You've murdered him!' and fell right down in a dead faint, and Tom said, as quick as she came out of that she went inter hysterics, and screamed and raved and kep' a-callin' out, 'You've murdered him!' the whole during time.

"Well, I do s'pose they hed an awful time. Tom said he never felt so sorry for any one as what he did for that poor man. Then he, sure enough, was the means of the little boy's death, and then to hear them words soundin' in his ears the whole time!

"The child was in its grave before she come round so as to have her mind, and then she was as hard and set, and Tom said he heard her tellin' Jerome she was goin' to take the children and go home. Tom said Jerome pled with Jane, but 'twa'n't no good. She heard him through, and then she says, 'You nigh broke my heart with your unkindness; but I'd have overlooked all that; but now you've murdered my child, and *that* I'll never forgive.' Tom said it broke Jerome all down, and he'd beg and plead with her and make promises, but she allers answered him the same way. Tom said seemed as if she wa'n't herself at all, she was so changed; didn't seem to have no feelin's at all. Now don't you think it was hard on Jerome, Miss Snow? Of course if it hadn't been for his bein' taken up so with minin', it wouldn't 'a happened; but he wouldn't 'a harmed a

hair on that child's head no more than I would, and I guess he suffered same as she. Of course 'twa'n't the *same* as if he'd been the child's mother, but it was worse; seems so.

"Well, it wa'n't a week after the child was buried before she was all packed up and gone. Tom said when Jerome see she was bent on goin', and he couldn't do nothing with her, he jest took his gun and left. Well, she come home and shut herself up, and see no one, and I do s'pose her folks thought her mind was goin'."

"What became of her most unfortunate husband?" inquired Miss Snow.

"Oh, well, I hate to tell you, it's so kind of dreadful. You see, they was Injuns around there. Jane wrote home, first on't, about their comin' to the house to beg; but they never did no harm. Well, nobody knew how it come about, only, about five months after Jane come home, some men was out huntin', and they come across Jane's house, and see the door was open, and went in, and looked round, and finally come to the bedroom, and found Jerome layin' on the bed, and, come to look at him, he was dead, and had been for a long time."

"What had that to do with Indians, Mrs. Elder?"

"Why, I do' know, only they see he'd been shot, and they mistrusted he'd met some of them 'ere Injuns, and they shot him, and he got away, and got home to die. They said he wa'n't hurt so bad but what he might 'a lived if he'd been took care of; but I cal'late he was all beat out and willin' to die, and didn't try to live at all. Jane, she's teachin' school; and there's what them two lives have come to!"

"Does Jane know of her husband's tragical fate?" said Miss Snow.

"Why, yes, I s'pose she does. Word was brought her about it, but there don't no one know how she took it. She never said nothing. Well, well, and Jane was as likely a girl as ever lived here, let the other be who she may;" and Mrs. Elder let her knitting-work fall on her knee, and rocked slowly back and forth until roused by the clock striking ten.

"Well, I declare! I'd no idee it was so late. I allers forgit what time it is when I git talkin'. There, Miss Snow, I'll git your lamp for you. You look reel beat out and tired. Good-night. Don't git up to early breakfast unless you feel like it."

AT THE RACES.

THEIR PILGRIMAGE.

BY CHARLES DUDLEY WARNER.

CHAPTER XI.

MRS. FARQUHAR, Colonel Fane, and a great many of their first and second cousins were at the station the morning the Bensons and King and Forbes departed for the North. The gallant colonel was foremost in his expressions of regret, and if he had been the proprietor of Virginia, and of the entire South added

thereto, and had been anxious to close out the whole lot on favorable terms to the purchaser, he would not have exhibited greater solicitude as to the impression the visitors had received. This solicitude was, however, wholly in his manner—and it is the traditional manner that has nearly passed away—for underneath all this humility it was plain to be seen that the South had conferred a great favor, sir, upon these persons by a recognition of their merits.

"I am not come to give you good-by, but *au revoir*," said Mrs. Farquhar to Stanhope and Irene, who were standing apart. "I hate to go North in the summer, it is so hot and crowded and snobbish, but I dare say I shall meet you somewhere, for I confess I don't like to lose sight of so much happiness. No, no, Miss Benson, you need not thank me, even with a blush; I am not responsible for this state of things. I did all I could to warn you, and I tell you now that my sympathy is with Mr. Meigs, who never did either of you any harm, and I think has been very badly treated."

"I don't know any one, Mrs. Farquhar, who is so capable of repairing his injuries as yourself," said King.

"Thank you; I'm not used to such delicate, elephantine compliments. It is just like a man, Miss Benson, to try to kill two birds with one stone—get rid of a rival by sacrificing a useless friend. All the same, *au revoir*."

"We shall be glad to see you," replied Irene, "you know that, wherever we are; and we will try to make the North tolerable for you."

"Oh, I shall hide my pride and go. If you were not all so rich up there! Not that I object to wealth; I enjoy it. I think I shall take to that old prayer—'May my lot be with the rich in this world, and with the South in the next!'"

I suppose there never was such a journey as that from the White Sulphur to New York. If the Virginia scenery had seemed to King beautiful when he came down, it was now transcendently lovely. He raved about it when I saw him afterward—the Blue Ridge, the wheat valleys, the commercial advantages, the mineral resources of the State, the grand old traditional Heaven knows what of the Old Dominion; as to details he was obscure, and when I pinned him down, he was not certain which route they took. It is my opinion that the most costly scenery in the world is thrown away upon a pair of newly plighted lovers.

The rest of the party were in good spirits. Even Mrs. Benson, who was at first a little bewildered at the failure of her admirably planned campaign, accepted the situation with serenity.

"So you are engaged!" she said, when Irene went to her with the story of the little affair in Lovers' Walk. "I suppose he'll like it. He always took a fancy to Mr. King. No, I haven't any objections, Irene, and I hope you'll be happy. Mr. King was always very polite to me—only he didn't never seem exactly like our folks. We only want you to be happy." And the old lady declared with a shaky voice, and tears streaming down her cheeks, that she was perfectly happy if Irene was.

Mr. Meigs, the refined, the fastidious, the man of the world, who had known how to adapt himself perfectly to Mrs. Benson, might nevertheless have been surprised at her implication that he was "like our folks."

At the station in Jersey City—a place suggestive of love and romance and full of tender associations—the party separated for a few days, the Bensons going to Saratoga, and King accompanying Forbes to Long Branch, in pursuance of an agreement which, not being in writing, he was unable to break. As the two friends went in the early morning down to the coast over the level salt meadows, cut by bayous and intersected by canals, they were curiously reminded both of the Venice lagoons and the plains of the Teche; and the artist went into raptures over the colors of the landscape, which he declared was Oriental in softness and blending. He was to discover afterward other features in this region still more Oriental.

Long Branch and its adjuncts were planned for New York excursionists who are content with the ocean and the salt air, and do not care much for the picturesque. It can be described in a phrase: a straight line of sandy coast with a high bank, parallel to it a driveway, and an endless row of hotels and cottages. Knowing what the American sea-side cottage and hotel are, it is unnecessary to go to Long Branch to have an accurate picture of it in the mind. Seen from the end of the pier, the coast appears to be all built up—a thin, straggling city by the sea. The line of buildings is continuous for two miles, from Long Branch to Elberon; midway is the West End, where our tourists were advised to go as the best post of observation, a medium point of respectability between the excursion medley of one extremity and the cottage refinement of the other, and equally convenient to the races, which attract crowds of metropolitan betting men and betting women.

The fine toilets of these children of fortune are not less admired than their fashionable race-course manners. The satirist who said that Atlantic City is typical of Philadelphia, said also that Long Branch is typical of New York. What Mr. King said was that the satirist was not acquainted with the good society of either place.

All the summer resorts get somehow a certain character, but it is not easy always to say how it is produced. The Long Branch region was the resort of politicians, and of persons of some fortune who connect politics with speculation. Society, which in America does not identify itself with politics as it does in England, was not specially attracted

would not have bathed in public if Nature had made them self-conscious. All down the shore were pavilions and bath-houses, and the scene at a distance was not unlike that when the water is occupied by schools of leaping mackerel. An excursion steamer from New York landed at the pier. The passengers were not of any recognized American type, but mixed foreign races— a crowd of respectable people who take their rare holidays rather seriously, and offer little of interest to an artist. The boats that arrive at night are said to bring a less respectable cargo.

It is a pleasant walk or drive down to Elberon when there is a sea-breeze, especially if there happen to be a dozen yachts

A DRIVE TO ELBERON.

by the newspaper notoriety of the place, although fashion to some extent declared in favor of Elberon.

In the morning the artist went up to the pier at the bathing hour. Thousands of men, women, and children were tossing about in the lively surf promiscuously, revealing to the spectators such forms as Nature had given them, with a modest confidence in her handiwork. It seemed to the artist, who was a student of the human figure, that many of these people

in the offing. Such elegance as this watering-place has lies in this direction; the Elberon is a refined sort of hotel, and has near it a group of pretty cottages, not too fantastic for holiday residences, and even the "greeny-yellowy" ones do not much offend, for eccentricities of color are toned down by the sea atmosphere. These cottages have excellent lawns set with brilliant beds of flowers, and the turf rivals that at Newport; but without a tree or shrub anywhere along the shore the aspect is too unrelieved and photographically distinct. Here as elsewhere the cottage life is taking the place of hotel life.

There were few handsome turnouts on the main drive, and perhaps the popular character of the place was indicated by the use of omnibuses instead of carriages. For, notwithstanding Elberon and such fashion as is there gathered, Long Branch lacks "style." After the White Sulphur, it did not seem to King alive with gayety, nor has it any society. In the hotel parlors there is music in the evenings, but little dancing except by children. Large women, offensively dressed, sit about the veranda, and give a heavy and "company" air to the drawing-rooms. No, the place is not gay. The people come here to eat, to bathe, to take the air; and these are reasons enough for being here. Upon the artist, alert for social peculiarities, the scene made only two impressions, and these were the Oriental features heretofore alluded to—he was strongly impressed by the noses and the diamonds.

It was in search of something different from this that King and Forbes took the train and travelled six miles south to Asbury Park and Ocean Grove. These great summer settlements are separated by a sheet of fresh-water three-quarters of a mile long; its sloping banks are studded with pretty cottages, its surface is alive with boats gay with awnings of red and blue and green and seats of motley color, and is altogether a fairy spectacle. Asbury Park is the worldly correlative of Ocean Grove, and esteems itself a notch above it in social tone. Each is a city of small houses, and each is teeming with life, but Ocean Grove, whose centre is the camp-meeting tabernacle, lodges its devotees in tents as well as cottages, and copies the architecture of Oak Bluffs. The inhabitants of the two cities meet on the two-mile-long plank promenade by the sea.

Perhaps there is no place on the coast that would more astonish the foreigner than Ocean Grove, and if he should describe it faithfully he would be unpopular with its inhabitants. He would be astonished at the crowds at the station, the throngs in the streets, the shops and stores for supplying the wants of the religious pilgrims, and used as he might be to the promiscuous bathing along our coast, would inevitably comment upon the freedom existing here. He would see women

in their bathing dresses, wet and clinging, walking in the streets of the town, and he would read notices posted up by the camp-meeting authorities forbidding women so clad to come upon the tabernacle ground. He would also read placards along the beach explaining the reason why decency in bathing suits is desirable, and he would wonder why such notices should be necessary. If, however, he walked along the shore at bathing times he might be enlightened, and he would see besides a certain simplicity of social life which sophisticated Europe has no parallel for. A peculiar custom here is sand-burrowing. To lie in the warm sand, which accommodates itself to any position of the body, and listen to the dash of the waves, is a dreamy and delightful way of spending a summer day. The beach for miles is strewn with these sand-burrowers, in groups of two or three or half a dozen, or single figures laid out like the effigies of Crusaders. One encounters these groups sprawling in all attitudes, and frequently asleep in their promiscuous beds. The foreigner is forced to see all this, because it is a public exhibition. A couple in bathing suits take a dip together in the sea, and then lie down in the sand. The artist proposed to make a sketch of one of these primitive couples, but it was impossible to do so, because they lay in a trench which they had scooped in the sand two feet deep, and had hoisted an umbrella over their heads. The position was novel and artistic, but beyond the reach of the artist. It was a great pity, because art is never more agreeable than when it concerns itself with domestic life.

While this charming spectacle was exhibited at the beach, afternoon service was going on in the tabernacle, and King sought that in preference. The vast audience under the canopy directed its eyes to a man on the platform, who was violently gesticulating and shouting at the top of his voice. King, fresh from the scenes of the beach, listened a long time, expecting to hear some close counsel on the conduct of life, but he heard nothing except the vaguest emotional exhortation. By this the audience were apparently unmoved, for it was only when the preacher paused to get his breath on some word on which he could dwell by reason of its vowels, like w-o-r-l-d or a-n-d, that he awoke any response from his hearers. The spiritual exercise of prayer which fol-

"SOLEMN MEN WHO SAID LITTLE, BUT LOOKED RICH."

lowed was even more of a physical demonstration, and it aroused more response. The officiating minister, kneeling at the desk, gesticulated furiously, doubled up his fists and shook them on high, stretched out both arms, and pounded the pulpit. Among people of his own race King had never before seen anything like this, and he went away a sadder if not a wiser man, having at least learned one lesson of charity—never again to speak lightly of a negro religious meeting.

This vast city of the sea has many charms, and is the resort of thousands of people, who find here health and repose. But King, who was immensely interested in it all as one phase of American summer life, was glad that Irene was not at Ocean Grove.

CHAPTER XII.

IT was the 22d of August, and the height of the season at Saratoga. Familiar as King had been with these Springs, accustomed as the artist was to foreign Spas, the scene was a surprise to both. They had been told that fashion had ceased to patronize it, and that its old-time character was gone. But Saratoga is too strong for the whims of fashion; its existence does not depend upon its decrees; it has reached the point where it cannot be killed by the inroads of Jew or Gentile. In ceasing to be a society centre, it has become in a manner metropolitan; for the season it is no longer a provincial village, but the meeting-place of as mixed and heterogeneous a throng as flows into New York from all the Union in the autumn shopping period.

It was race week, but the sporting men did not give Saratoga their complexion. It was convention time, but except in the hotel corridors politicians were not the feature of the place. One of the great hotels was almost exclusively occupied by the descendants of Abraham, but the town did not at all resemble Jerusalem. Innumerable boarding-houses swarmed with city and country clergymen, who have a well-founded impression that the waters of the springs have a beneficent relation to the bilious secretions of the year, but the resort had not an oppressive air of sanctity. Nearly every prominent politician in the State and a good many from other States registered at the hotels, but no one seemed to think that the country was in danger. Hundreds of men and women Saratoga to study the fashions. Perhaps the most impressive spectacle in this lowly world was the row of millionaires sunning themselves every morning on the piazza of the States, solemn men in black broadcloth and white hats, who said little, but looked rich; visitors used to pass that way casually, and the towns-people regarded them with a kind of awe, as if they

AN "OFFICER."—[SEE PAGE 594.]

were there because they had been there every year for thirty or forty years back, and they have no doubt that their health absolutely requires a week at Saratoga, yet the village has not the aspect of a sanitarium. The hotel dining-rooms and galleries were thronged with large overdressed women who glittered with diamonds and looked uncomfortable in silks and velvets, and Broadway was gay with elegant equipages, but nobody would go to were the king-pins of the whole social fabric; but even these magnates were only pleasing incidents in the kaleidoscopic show.

The first person King encountered on the piazza of the Grand Union was not the one he most wished to see, although it could never be otherwise than agreeable to meet his fair cousin, Mrs. Bartlett-Glow. She was in a fresh morning toilet, dainty, *comme il faut*, radiant, with that unobtru-

MORNING AT THE SPRINGS

ON THE BOAT, LAKE GEORGE.—[SEE PAGE 599.]

sive manner of "society" which made the present surroundings appear a trifle vulgar to King, and to his self-disgust forced upon him the image of Mrs. Benson.

"You here!" was his abrupt and involuntary exclamation.

"Yes—why not?" And then she added, as if from the Newport point of view some explanation was necessary: "My husband thinks he must come here for a week every year to take the waters; it's an old habit, and I find it amusing for a few days. Of course there is nobody here. Will you take me to the spring?—Yes, Congress. I'm too old to change. If I believed the pamphlets the proprietors write about each other's springs, I should never go to either of them."

Mrs. Bartlett-Glow was not alone in say-

ing that nobody was there. There were scores of ladies at each hotel who said the same thing, and who accounted for their own presence there in the way she did. And they were not there at all in the same way they would be later at Lenox. Mrs. Pendragon, of New Orleans, who was at the United States, would have said the same thing, remembering the time when the Southern colony made a very distinct impression upon the social life of the place; and the Ashleys, who had put up at the Congress Hall in company with an old friend, a returned foreign minister, who stuck to the old traditions—even the Ashleys said they were only lookers-on at the pageant.

Paying their entrance, and passing through the turnstile in the pretty pavilion gate, they stood in the Congress Spring Park. The band was playing in the kiosk; the dew still lay on the flowers and the green turf; the miniature lake sparkled in the sun. It is one of the most pleasing artificial scenes in the world; to be sure, nature set the great pine-trees on the hills, and made the graceful little valley, but art and exquisite taste have increased the apparent size of the small plot of ground, and filled it with beauty. It is a gem of a place with a character of its own, although its prettiness suggests some foreign Spa. Groups of people, having taken the water, were strolling about the gravelled paths, sitting on the slopes overlooking the pond, or wandering up the glen to the tiny deer park.

"So you have been at the White Sulphur," said Mrs. Glow. "How did you like it?"

"Immensely. It's the only place left where there is a congregate social life."

"You mean provincial life. Everybody knows everybody else."

"Well," King retorted, with some spirit, "it is not a place where people pretend not to know each other, as if their salvation depended on it."

"Oh, I see; hospitable, frank, cordial—all that. Stanhope, do you know, I think you are a little demoralized this summer. Did you fall in love with a Southern belle? Who was there?"

"Well, all the South, pretty much. I didn't fall in love with all the belles: we were there only two weeks. Oh! there was a Mrs. Farquhar there."

"Georgiana Randolph! Georgie! How did she look? We were at Madame Sequin's together, and a couple of seasons in Paris. Georgie! She was the handsomest, the wittiest, the most fascinating woman I ever saw. I hope she didn't give you a turn?"

"Oh no. But we were very good friends. She is a very handsome woman —perhaps you would expect me to say handsome still; but that seems a sort of treason to her mature beauty."

"And who else?"

"Oh, the Storbes from New Orleans, the Slifers from Mobile—no end of people —some from Philadelphia—and Ohio."

"Ohio? Those Bensons?" said she, turning sharply on him.

"Yes, those Bensons, Penelope. Why not?"

"Oh, nothing. It's a free country. I

hope, Stanhope, you didn't encourage her. You might make her very unhappy."

"I trust not," said King, stoutly. "We are engaged."

"Engaged!" repeated Mrs. Glow, in a tone that implied a whole world of astonishment and improbability.

"Yes, and you are just in time to congratulate us. There they are!"

Mr. Benson, Mrs. Benson, and Irene were coming down the walk from the deer park. King turned to meet them, but Mrs. Glow was close at his side, and apparently as pleased at seeing them again as the lover. Nothing could be more charming than the grace and welcome she threw into her salutations. She shook hands with Mr. Benson; she was delighted to meet Mrs. Benson again, and gave her both her little hands; she almost embraced Irene, placed a hand on each shoulder, kissed her on the cheek, and said something in a low voice that brought the blood to the girl's face and suffused her eyes with tenderness.

When the party returned to the hotel the two women were walking lovingly arm in arm, and King was following after, in the more prosaic atmosphere of Cyrusville, Ohio. The good old lady began at once to treat King like one of the family; she took his arm, and leaned heavily on it, as they walked, and confided to him all her complaints. The White Sulphur waters, she said, had not done her a mite of good; she didn't know but she'd oughter see a doctor, but he said that it warn't nothing but indigestion. Now the White Sulphur agreed with Irene better than any other place, and I guess that I know the reason why, Mr. King, she said, with a faintly facetious smile. Meantime Mrs. Glow was talking to Irene on the one topic that a maiden is never weary of, her lover; and so adroitly mingled praises of him with flattery of herself that the girl's heart went out to her in entire trust.

"She is a charming girl," said Mrs. Glow to King, later. "She needs a little forming, but that will be easy when she is separated from her family. Don't interrupt me. I like her. I don't say I like it. But if you will go out of your set, you might do a great deal worse. Have you written to your uncle and to your aunt?"

"No: I don't know why, in a matter

wholly personal to myself, I should call a family council. You represent the family completely, Penelope."

"Yes. Thanks to my happening to be here. Well, I wouldn't write to them if I were you. It's no use to disturb the whole connection now. By-the-way, Imogene Cypher was at Newport after you left; she is more beautiful than ever—just lovely; no other girl there had half the attention."

"I am glad to hear it," said King, who did not fancy the drift their conversation was taking. "I hope she will make a good match. Brains are not necessary, you know."

"Stanhope, I never said that—never. I might have said she wasn't a *bas bleu.* No more is she. But she has beauty, and a good temper, and money. It isn't the cleverest women who make the best wives, sir."

"Well, I'm not objecting to her being a wife. Only it does not follow that, because my uncle and aunts are in love with her, I should want to marry her."

"I said nothing about marriage, my touchy friend. I am not advising you to be engaged to two women at the same time. And I like Irene immensely."

It was evident that she had taken a great fancy to the girl. They were always together; it seemed to happen so, and King could hardly admit to himself that Mrs. Glow was *de trop* as a third. Mr. Bartlett-Glow was very polite to King and his friend, and forever had one excuse and another for taking them off with him—the races or a lounge about town. He showed them one night, I am sorry to say, the inside of the Temple of Chance and its decorous society, its splendid buffet, the quiet tables of *rouge et noir*, and the highly respectable attendants—aged men, white-haired, in evening costume, devout and almost godly in appearance, with faces chastened to resignation and patience with a wicked world, sedate and venerable as the deacons in a Presbyterian church. He was lonesome and wanted company, and, besides, the women liked to be by themselves occasionally.

One might be amused at the Saratoga show without taking an active part in it, and indeed nobody did seem to take a very active part in it. Everybody was looking on. People drove, visited the springs—in a vain expectation that excessive drinking of the medicated waters would counteract the effect of excessive gormandizing at the hotels—sat about in the endless rows of arm-chairs on the piazzas, crowded the heavily upholstered parlors, promenaded in the corridors, listened to the music in the morning, and again in the afternoon, and thronged the stairways and passages, and blocked up the entrance to the ball-rooms. Balls? Yes, with dress *de rigueur*, many beautiful women in wonderful toilets, a few *débutantes*, a scarcity of young men, and a delicious band—much better music than that at the White Sulphur.

And yet no society. But a wonderful agglomeration, the artist was saying. It is a robust sort of place. If Newport is the queen of the watering-places, this is the king. See how well fed and fat the people are, men and women large and expansive, richly dressed, prosperous-looking! What a contrast to the family sort of life at the White Sulphur! Here nobody, apparently, cares for anybody else—not much; it is not to be expected that people should know each other in such a heterogeneous concern; you see how comparatively few greetings there are on the piazzas and in the parlors. You notice, too, that the types are not so distinctively American as at the Southern resort—full faces, thick necks—more like Germans than Americans. And then the everlasting white hats. And I suppose it is not certain that every man in a tall white hat is a politician, or a railway magnate, or a sporting man.

These big hotels are an epitome of expansive, gorgeous American life. At the Grand Union, King was No. 1710, and it seemed to him that he walked the length of the town to get to his room after ascending four stories. He might as well, so far as exercise was concerned, have taken an apartment outside. And the dining-room. Standing at the door, he had a vista of an eighth of a mile of small tables, sparkling with brilliant service of glass and porcelain, chandeliers and frescoed ceiling. What perfect appointments! what well-trained waiters!—perhaps they were not waiters, for he was passed from one "officer" to another "officer" down to his place. At the tables silent couples and restrained family parties, no hilarity, little talking; and what a contrast this was to the happy-go-lucky service and jollity of the White Sulphur! Then the interior parks of the United

States and the Grand Union, with corridors and cottages, close-clipped turf, banks of flowers, forest trees, fountains, and at night, when the band filled all the air with seductive strains, the electric and the colored lights, gleaming through the foliage and dancing on fountains and greensward, made a scene of enchantment. Each hotel was a village in itself, and the thousands of guests had no more in common than the frequenters of New York hotels and theatres. But what a paradise for lovers!

"It would be lonesome enough but for you, Irene," Stanhope said, as they sat one night on the inner piazza of the Grand Union, surrendering themselves to all the charms of the scene.

"I love it all," she said, in the full tide of her happiness.

On another evening they were at the illumination of the Congress Spring Park. The scene seemed the creation of magic. By a skilful arrangement of the colored globes an illusion of vastness was created, and the little enclosure, with its glowing lights, was like the starry heavens for extent. In the mass of white globes and colored lanterns of paper the eye was deceived as to distances. The *allées* stretched away interminably, the pines seemed enormous, and the green hill-sides mountainous. Nor were charming single effects wanting. Down the winding walk from the hill, touched by a distant electric light, the loitering people, in couples and in groups, seemed no more in real life than the supernumeraries in a scene at the opera. Above, in the illuminated foliage, were doubtless a castle and a broad terrace, with a row of statues, and these gay promenaders were ladies and cavaliers in an old-time masquerade. The gilded kiosk on the island in the centre of the miniature lake and the fairy bridge that leads to it were outlined by colored globes; and the lake, itself set about with brilliants, reflected kiosk and bridge and lights, repeating a hundredfold the fantastic scene, while from their island retreat the band sent out through the illumined night strains of sentiment and gayety and sadness. In the intervals of the music there was silence, as if the great throng were too deeply enjoying this feast of the senses to speak. Perhaps a foreigner would have been impressed with the decorous respectability of the assembly; he would have remarked that there were no little tables scattered about the ground, no boys running about with foaming mugs of beer, no noise, no loud talking; and how restful to all the senses!

Mrs. Bartlett-Glow had the whim to devote herself to Mrs. Benson, and was repaid by the acquisition of a great deal of information concerning the social and domestic life in Cyrusville, Ohio, and the maternal ambition for Irene. Stanhope and Irene sat a little apart from the others, and gave themselves up to the witchery of the hour. It would not be easy to reproduce in type all that they said; and what was most important to them, and would be most interesting to the reader, are the things they did not say—the half exclamations, the delightful silences, the tones, the looks, that are the sign language of lovers. It was Irene who first broke the spell of this delightful mode of communication, and in a pause of the music said, "Your cousin has been telling me of your relatives in New York, and she told me more of yourself than you ever did."

"Very likely. Trust your friends for that. I hope she gave me a good character."

"Oh, she has the greatest admiration for you, and she said the family have the highest expectations of your career. Why didn't you tell me you were the child of such hopes? It half frightened me."

"It must be appalling. What did she say of my uncle and aunts?"

"Oh, I cannot tell you, except that she raised an image in my mind of an awful hierarchy of ancient family and exclusiveness, the most fastidious, delightful, conventional people, she said, very old family, looked down upon Washington Irving, don't you know, because he wrote. I suppose she wanted to impress me with the value of the prize I've drawn, dear. But I should like you just as well if your connections had not looked down on Irving. Are they so very high and mighty?"

"Oh dear no. Much like other people. My aunts are the dearest old ladies, just a little near-sighted, you know, about seeing people that are not—well, of course, they live in a rather small world. My uncle is a bachelor, rather particular, not what you would call a genial old man; been abroad a good deal, and moved mostly in our set; sometimes I think he cares more for his descent than for his position at the bar, which is a very respectable one, by-the-way. You know what an old bachelor is who never has had anybody to shake him out of his contemplation of his family?"

"Do you think," said Irene, a little anxiously, letting her hand rest a moment upon Stanhope's, "that they will like poor little me? I believe I am more afraid of the aunts than of the uncle. I don't believe they will be as nice as your cousin."

"Of course they will like you. Everybody likes you. The aunts are just a little old-fashioned, that is all. Habit has made them draw a social circle with a small radius. Some have one kind of circle, some another. Of course my aunts are sorry for any one who is not descended from the Van Schlovenhovens—the old Van Schlovenhoven had the first brewery of the colony in the time of Peter Stuyvesant. In New York it's a family matter, in Philadelphia it's geographical. There it's a question whether you live within the lines of Chestnut Street and Spruce Street—outside of these in the city you are socially impossible. Mrs. Courtlandt told me that two Philadelphia ladies who had become great friends at a summer resort—one lived within and the other without the charmed lines—went back to town together in the autumn. At the station when they parted, the 'inside' lady said to the other: 'Good-by. It has been such a pleasure to know you! I suppose I shall see you sometimes at Moneymaker's!' Moneymaker's is the *Bon Marché* of Philadelphia."

The music ceased; the band were hurrying away; the people all over the grounds were rising to go, lingering a little, reluctant to leave the enchanting scene. Irene wished, with a sigh, that it might never end; unreal as it was, it was more native to her spirit than that future which her talk with Stanhope had opened to her contemplation. An ill-defined apprehension possessed her in spite of the reassuring presence of her lover and her perfect confidence in the sincerity of his passion; and this feeling was somehow increased by the appearance of Mrs. Glow with her mother; she could not shake off the uneasy suggestion of the contrast.

At the hour when the ladies went to their rooms the day was just beginning for a certain class of the *habitués*. The parlors were nearly deserted, and few chairs were occupied on the piazzas, but the ghosts of another generation seemed to linger, especially in the offices and barroom. Flitting about were to be seen the social heroes who had a notoriety thirty and forty years ago in the newspapers. This dried-up old man in a bronze wig, scuffling along in list slippers, was a famous criminal lawyer in his day; this gentleman, who still wears an air of gallantry, and is addressed as General, had once a reputation for successes in the drawing-room as well as on the field of Mars; here is a genuine old beau, with the unmistakable self-consciousness of one who has been a favorite of the sex, but who has slowly decayed in the midst of his cosmetics; here saunter along a couple of actors with the air of being on the stage. These people all have the "nightcap" habit, and drift along toward the bar-room—the last brilliant scene in the drama of the idle day, the necessary portal to the realm of silence and sleep.

This is a large apartment, brightly lighted, with a bar extending across one end of it. Modern taste is conspicuous here, nothing is gaudy, colors are subdued, and its decorations are simple—even the bar itself is refined, substantial, decorous, wanting entirely the meretricious glitter and barbarous ornamentation of the old structures of this sort, and the attendants have wholly laid aside the smart antics of the former bar-tender, and the customers are swiftly and silently served by the deferential waiters. This is one of the most striking changes that King noticed in American life.

There is a certain sort of life—whether it is worth seeing is a question—that we can see nowhere else, and for an hour Mr. Glow and King and Forbes, sipping their raspberry shrub in a retired corner of the bar-room, were interested spectators of the scene. Through the padded swinging doors entered, as in a play, character after character. Each actor as he entered stopped for a moment and stared about him, and in this act revealed his character —his conceit, his slyness, his bravado, his self-importance. There was great variety, but practically one prevailing type, and that the New York politician. Most of them were from the city, though the country politician apes the city politician as much as possible, but he lacks the exact air, notwithstanding the black broadcloth and the white hat. The city men are of two varieties—the smart, perky-nosed, vulgar young ward worker, and the heavy-featured, gross, fat old fellow. One after another they glide in, with an always conscious air, swagger off to the bar, strike attitudes in groups, one with his legs spread, another with a foot behind on tip-toe, another leaning against the counter, and so pose, and drink—"My respects"—all rather solemn and stiff, impressed perhaps by the decorousness of the place, and conscious of their good clothes. Enter together three stout men, a yard across the shoulders, each with an enormous development in front, waddle up to the bar, attempt to form a triangular group for conversation, but find themselves too far apart to talk in that position, and so arrange themselves side by side—a most distinguished-looking party, like a portion of a swell-front street in Boston. To them swaggers up a young sport, like one of Thackeray's figures in the *Irish Sketch-Book*—short, in a white hat, poor face, impudent manner, poses before the swell fronts, and tosses off his glass. About a little table in one corner are three excessively "ugly mugs," leering at each other and pouring down champagne. These men are all dressed as nearly like gentlemen as the tailor can make them, but even he cannot change their hard, brutal faces. It is not their fault that money and clothes do not make a gentleman; they are well fed and vulgarly prosperous, and if you inquire you will find that their women are in silks and laces. This is a good place to study the rulers of New York; and impressive as they are in appearance, it is a relief to notice that they unbend to each other, and hail one another familiarly as "Billy" and "Tommy." Do they not ape what is most prosperous and successful in American life? There is one who in make-up, form, and air, even to the cut of his side whiskers, is an exact counterpart of the great railway king. Here is a heavy-faced young fellow in evening dress, perhaps endeavoring to act the part of a gentleman, who has come from an evening party unfortunately a little "slewed," but who does not know how to sustain the character, for presently he becomes very familiar and confidential with the dignified colored waiter at the buffet, who requires all his native politeness to maintain the character of a gentleman for two.

If these men had millions, could they get any more enjoyment out of life? To have fine clothes, drink champagne, and pose in a fashionable bar-room in the height of the season—is not this the apotheosis of the "heeler" and the ward "worker?" The scene had a fascination for the artist, who declared that he never tired watching the evolutions of the foreign element into the full bloom of American citizenship.

CHAPTER XIII.

THE intimacy between Mrs. Bartlett-Glow and Irene increased as the days went by. The woman of society was always devising plans for Irene's entertainment, and winning her confidence by a thousand evidences of interest and affection. Pleased as King was with this at first, he began to be annoyed at a devotion to which he could have no objection except that it often came between him and the enjoyment of the girl's society alone; and latterly he had noticed that her manner was more grave when they were together, and that a little something of reserve mingled with her tenderness.

They made an excursion one day to Lake George—a poetical pilgrimage that recalled to some of the party (which included some New Orleans friends) the romance of early days. To the Bensons and the artist it was all new, and to King it was seen for the first time in the transforming atmosphere of love. To men of sentiment its beauties will never be exhausted; but to the elderly and perhaps rheumatic tourist the draughty steamboats do not always bring back the remembered delight of youth. There is no pleasanter place in the North for a summer residence, but there is a certain element of monotony and weariness inseparable from an excursion: travellers have been known to yawn even on the Rhine. It was a gray day, the country began to show the approach of autumn, and the view from the landing at Caldwell's, the foot of the lake, was never more pleasing. In the marshes the cat-tails and the faint flush of color on the alders and soft maples gave a character to the low shore, and the gentle rise of the hills from the water's edge combined to make a sweet and peaceful landscape.

The tourists find the steamer waiting for them at the end of the rail, and if they are indifferent to the war romances of the place, as most of them are, they hurry on without a glance at the sites of the famous old forts St. George and William Henry. Yet the foot of the lake might well detain them a few hours though they do not care for the scalping Indians and their sometime allies the French or the English. On the east side the lake is wooded to the shore, and the jutting points and charming bays make a pleasant outline to the eye. Crosbyside is the ideal of a summer retreat, nestled in foliage on a pretty point, with its great trees on a sloping lawn, boat-houses and innumerable row and sail boats, and a lovely view, over the blue waters, of a fine range of hills. Caldwell itself, on the west side, is a pretty tree-planted village in a break in the hills, and a point above it shaded with great pines is a favorite rendezvous for pleasure parties, who leave the ground strewn with egg-shells and newspapers. The Fort William Henry Hotel was formerly the chief resort on the lake. It is a long, handsome structure, with broad piazzas, and low evergreens and flowers planted in front. The view from it, under the great pines, of the lake and the northern purple hills is lovely. But the tide of travel passes it by, and the few people who were there seemed lonesome. The victorious race who conquered Canaan have invaded the Fort William Henry, and planted their flag there, and the weaker Christians have moved on. Our travellers, who dined there, were pleased to see, however, that the proprietors are determined to maintain themselves, having learned from their conquerors how to charge.

Lake George has changed very much within ten years; hotels and great boarding-houses line the shores; but the marked difference is in the increase of cottage life. As our tourists sailed up the lake they were surprised by the number of pretty villas with red roofs peeping out from the trees, and the occupation of every island and headland by gay and often fantastic summer residences. King had heard this lake compared with Como and Maggiore, and as a patriot he endeavored to think that its wild and sylvan loveliness was more pleasing than the romantic beauty of the Italian lakes. But the effort failed. In this climate it is impossible that Horicon should ever be like Como. Pretty hills and forests and tem-

porary summer structures cannot have the poetic or the substantial interest of the ancient villages and towns clinging to the hills, the old stone houses, the vines, the ruins, the atmosphere of a long civilization. They do the lovely Horicon no service who provoke such comparisons.

The lake has a character of its own. As the traveller sails north and approaches the middle of the lake, the gems of green islands multiply, the mountains rise higher, and shouldering up in the sky seem to bar a further advance; toward sunset the hills, which are stately but lovely, a silent assembly of round and sharp peaks, with long graceful slopes, take on exquisite colors, violet, bronze, and green, and now and again a bold rocky bluff shines like a ruby in the ruddy light. Just at dusk the steamer landed midway in the lake at Green Island, where the scenery is the boldest and most romantic; from the landing a park-like lawn, planted with big trees, slopes up to a picturesque hotel. Lights twinkled from many a cottage window and from boats in the bay, and strains of music saluted the travellers. It was an enchanting scene.

The genius of Philadelphia again claims the gratitude of the tourist, for the Sagamore Hotel is one of the most delightful hostelries in the world. A peculiar, interesting building, rambling up the slope on different levels, so contrived that all the rooms are outside, and having a delightful irregularity, as if the house had been a growth. Naturally a hotel so dainty in its service and furniture, and so refined, was crowded to its utmost capacity. The artist could find nothing to complain of in the morning except that the incandescent electric light in his chamber went out suddenly at midnight and left him in blank darkness in the most exciting crisis of a novel. Green Island is perhaps a mile long. A bridge connects it with the mainland, and besides the hotel it has a couple of picturesque stone and timber cottages. At the north end are the remains of the English intrenchments of 1755—signs of war and hate which kindly nature has almost obliterated with sturdy trees. With the natural beauty of the island art has little interfered; near the hotel is the most stately grove of white birches anywhere to be seen, and their silvery sheen, with occasional patches of sedge, and the tender sort of foliage that Corot liked to paint, gives an exceptional refinement to the landscape. One needs, indeed, to be toned up by the glimpses, under the trees, over the blue water, of the wooded craggy hills, with their shelf-like ledges, which are full of strength and character. The charm of the place is due to this combination of loveliness and granitic strength.

Irene long remembered the sail of that morning, seated in the bow of the steamer with King, through scenes of ever-changing beauty, as the boat wound about the headlands and made its calls, now on one side and now on the other, at the pretty landings and decorated hotels. On every hand was the gayety of summer life—a striped tent on a rocky point with a platform erected for dancing, a miniature bark hut on an island, and a rustic arched bridge to the mainland, gaudy little hotels with winding paths along the shore, and at all the landings groups of pretty girls and college lads in boating costume. It was wonderful how much these holiday-makers were willing to do for the entertainment of the passing travellers. A favorite pastime in this peaceful region was the broom drill, and its execution gave an operatic character to the voyage. When the steamer approaches, a band of young ladies in military ranks, clad in light marching costume, each with a broom in place of a musket, descend to the landing, and delight the spectators with their warlike manœuvres. The march in the broom drill is two steps forward and one step back, a mode of progression that conveys the notion of a pleasing indecision of purpose, which is foreign to the character of these handsome Amazons, who are quite able to hold the wharf against all comers. This act of war in fancy dress, with its two steps forward and one back, and the singing of a song, is one of the most fatal to the masculine peace of mind in the whole history of carnage.

Mrs. Bartlett-Glow, to be sure, thought it would be out of place at the Casino; but even she had to admit that the American girl who would bewitch the foreigner with her one, two, and one, and her flourish of broom, on Lake George was capable of freezing his ardor by her cool good-breeding at Newport.

There was not much more to be done at Saratoga. Mrs. Benson had tried every spring in the valley, and thus anticipated a remedy, as Mr. Benson said, for any

possible "complaint" that might visit her in the future. Mr. Benson himself said that he thought it was time for him to move to a new piazza, as he had worn out half the chairs at the Grand Union. The Bartlett-Glows were already due at Richfield; in fact, Penelope was impatient to go, now that she had persuaded the Bensons to accompany her; and the artist, who had been for some time grumbling that there was nothing left in Saratoga to draw except corks, reminded King of his agreement at Bar Harbor, and the necessity he felt for rural retirement after having been dragged all over the continent.

On the last day Mr. Glow took King and Forbes off to the races, and Penelope and the Bensons drove to the Lake. King never could tell why he consented to this arrangement, but he knew in a vague way that it is useless to attempt to resist feminine power, that shapes our destiny in spite of all our roughhewing of its outlines. He had become very uneasy at the friendship between Irene and Penelope, but he could give no reason for his suspicion, for it was the most natural thing in the world for his cousin to be interested in the girl who was about to come into the family. It seemed also natural that Penelope should be attracted by her nobility of nature. He did not know till afterward that it was this very nobility and unselfishness which Penelope saw could be turned to account for her own purposes. Mrs. Bartlett-Glow herself would have said that she was very much attached to Irene, and this would have been true; she would have said also that she pitied her, and this would have been true; but she was a woman whose world was bounded by her own social order, and she had no doubt in her own mind that she was loyal to the best prospects of her cousin, and what was of more importance, that she was protecting her little world from a *mésalliance* when she preferred Imogene Cypher to Irene Benson. In fact, the Bensons in her set were simply an unthinkable element. It disturbed the established order of things. If any one thinks meanly of Penelope for counting upon the heroism of Irene to effect her unhappiness, let him reflect of how little consequence is the temporary happiness of one or two individuals compared with the peace and comfort of a whole social order. And she might also well make herself believe that she was consulting the best interests of Irene in keeping her out of a position where she might be subject to so many humiliations. She was capable of crying over the social adventures of the heroine of a love story, and taking sides with her against the world, but as to the actual world itself, her practical philosophy taught her that it was much better always, even at the cost of a little heartache in youth, to go with the stream than against it.

The Lake at Saratoga is the most picturesque feature of the region, and would alone make the fortune of any other watering-place. It is always a surprise to the stranger, who has bowled along the broad drive of five miles through a pleasing but not striking landscape, to come suddenly, when he alights at the hotel, upon what seems to be a "fault," a sunken valley, and to look down a precipitous, grassy, tree-planted slope upon a lake sparkling at the bottom and reflecting the enclosing steep shores. It is like an aquamarine gem countersunk in the green landscape. Many an hour had Irene and Stanhope passed in dreamy contemplation of it. They had sailed down the lake in the little steamer, they had whimsically speculated about this and that couple who took their ices or juleps under the trees or on the piazza of the hotel, and the spot had for them a thousand tender associations. It was here that Stanhope had told her very fully the uneventful story of his life, and it was here that she had grown into full sympathy with his aspirations for the future.

It was of all this that Irene thought as she sat talking that day with Penelope on a bench at the foot of the hill by the steam-boat landing. It was this very future that the woman of the world was using to raise in the mind of Irene a morbid sense of her duty. Skilfully with this was insinuated the notion of the false and contemptible social pride and exclusiveness of Stanhope's relations, which Mrs. Bartlett-Glow represented as implacable while she condemned it as absurd. There was not a word of opposition to the union of Irene and Stanhope: Penelope was not such a bungler as to make that mistake. It was not her cue to definitely suggest a sacrifice for the welfare of her cousin. If she let Irene perceive that she admired the courage in her that could face all these adverse social conditions that were con-

jured up before her, Irene could never say that Penelope had expressed anything of the sort. Her manner was affectionate, almost caressing; she declared that she felt a sisterly interest in her. This was genuine enough. I am not sure that Mrs. Bartlett-Glow did not sometimes waver in her purpose when she was in the immediate influence of the girl's genuine charm, and felt how sincere she was. She even went so far as to wish to herself that Irene had been born in her own world.

It was not at all unnatural that Irene should have been charmed by Penelope, and that the latter should gradually have established an influence over her. She was certainly kind-hearted, amiable, bright, engaging. I think all those who have known her at Newport, or in her New York home, regard her as one of the most charming women in the world. Nor is she artificial, except as society requires her to be, and if she regards the conventions of her own set as the most important things in life, therein she does not differ from hosts of excellent wives and mothers. Irene, being utterly candid herself, never suspected that Penelope had at all exaggerated the family and social obstacles, nor did it occur to her to doubt Penelope's affection for her. But she was not blind. Being a woman, she comprehended perfectly the indirection of a woman's approaches, and knew well enough by this time that Penelope, whatever her personal leanings, must feel with her family in regard to this engagement. And that she, who was apparently her friend, and who had Stanhope's welfare so much at heart, did so feel was an added reason why she was drifting toward a purpose of self-sacrifice. When she was with Stanhope, such a sacrifice seemed as impossible as it would be cruel, but when she was with Mrs. Bartlett-Glow or alone, the subject took another aspect. There is nothing more attractive to a noble woman of tender heart than a duty the performance of which will make her suffer. A false notion of duty has to account for much of the misery in life.

It was under this impression that Irene passed the last evening at Saratoga with Stanhope on the piazza of the hotel—an evening that the latter long remembered as giving him the sweetest and the most contradictory and perplexing glimpses of a woman's heart.

CROWNINSHIELD WHARF DURING EMBARGO TIMES.
From a painting by George Ropes, Jun., 1806, in the Essex Institute, Salem.

OLD SALEM SEA-CAPTAINS.

BY THOMAS WENTWORTH HIGGINSON.

THOSE who may have had occasion, thirty or forty years ago, to visit the custom-houses of the New England coast may remember certain typical figures now vanished—a race of quiet, elderly men, who came and went about their monotonous duties, bearing no trace of stormy and adventurous careers, except a certain slight deference from those around them, and the title of "Captain." The voice that quavered as it slowly read aloud a column of figures had once shouted forth the order to cut away the masts in a hurricane, or to open fire upon a Spanish fort; hands that trembled as they unfolded a manifest had once struck down a Malay pirate with a cutlass, or steered a sinking vessel into an unknown harbor in the Indian Ocean. These men were the humbler Drakes, the Cavendishes, of their day; they had carried the American flag where it was an unknown ensign; they had voyaged from distant island on to island without chart or light-house; they had made and lost great fortunes—made them commonly for others, lost them for themselves. At twenty they had been ship-masters; at fifty they were stranded hulks. They were like those other seaside products, those floating and homeless jelly-fishes that at first are borne wherever ocean wills, and then change into a fixed, clinging creature that rests in some secluded custom-house in a cleft of rock, thenceforth to move no more.

These were the less fortunate but not less heroic type of Salem sea-captains, the men who could say to their children, as Virgil's Æneas says to Iulus:

"Disce, puer, virtutem ex me, verumque laborem,
    Fortunam ex aliis."

There were others who added good fortune to courage and industry; men like Nathaniel Silsbee, who was for years the associate of Daniel Webster in the Senate of the United States, or like the Crowninshields and Derbys and Grays, who bequeathed large estates to their descendants. These were the conspicuous instances of success; those of financial failure were more frequent. The old sea-captains were more commonly men who, like Dogberry, had had losses, or who, like great inventors, enriched all but themselves. Captain Richard Cleveland left home at twenty-three with $2000 invested, and after twice circumnavigating the globe, returned at thirty with what was then regarded as a comfortable fortune—$70,000. This he naturally invested in the voyages of others; they naturally lost it; and after sacrificing, as he estimates it, $200,000 in all, he brought up in a custom-house at last.

Successful or unsuccessful, the centre and head-quarters of these retired navigators was Salem, Massachusetts. The very seal of that now quiet city drew its proud motto, "*Divitis Indiæ usque ad ultimum sinum*," from their unwearied labors. There is nothing more brilliant in American history than the brief career of maritime adventure which made the name of Salem synonymous with that of America in many a distant port. The period bridged the interval between two wars: the American Revolution laid its foundation; the later war with England saw its last trophies. Its evolution was very simple. When the chief ports of the colonies were closed and their commerce ruined, the group of ports around Salem became the head-quarters of privateers; and when the Revolutionary war was over, those vessels, being too large for the coasting trade, sought a new outlet, and could not find it short of the Pacific and the southeastern archipelago. By their daring and adventure those who owned

vard College, and Governor of the English colony of Madras—the home-keeping brother suggests that the ex-Governor should make the Massachusetts colony the seat of an Oriental commerce by way of London, and thus enumerates the resources of such a traffic:

HOUSE OF BENJAMIN PICKMAN, BUILT IN 1740.

and sailed these vessels became for a time the heroes of the sea; they competed single-handed with the great chartered companies of European nations; they ventured freely between the giant forces of England and France, both ready to swallow them up. Even when finally crushed between French "decrees" and English "orders in council," they retained vitality enough to lead up to the naval glories of the war of 1812.

Yet long before the Revolution a plan had been vaguely sketched out by which Salem was to obtain something of that share in the India trade which later events brought to her. In an old letter-book containing part of the correspondence that passed in 1669 between Lieutenant-Colonel John Higginson, of Salem, and his brother Nathaniel—graduate of Har-

"All sorts of calicoes, aligers, remwalls, muslin, silks for clothing and linings; all sorts of drugs proper for the apothecaries, and all sorts of spice, are vendible with us, and the prices of them alter much according as they were plenty or scarce. In the late war time all East India goods were extremely dear. Muslins of the best sort, plain, striped, and flowered, were sold for £10 per piece, and some more. Pepper, 3s. per pound; nuts [nutmegs], 10s. per pound; cloves, 20s.; mace, 30s.; but now are abated about a quarter part in value. Some of the china ware, toys, and lacquer ware will sell well, but no great quantity. As for ambergris, we often have it from the West Indies, and it is sold for about 3 per ounce. For musk, pearl, and diamond, I believe some of them may sell well, but I understand not their value."

Thus early, it seems, was the taste for Chinese and Japanese goods—germ of future æstheticism—implanted in the American colonies; but when it comes to pearls and diamonds, the quiet Salem burgher, descendant of three generations of devout clergymen, "understands not their value." Yet he believes that some of them will sell well, even in 1669!

In the early commerce of Salem the whale-fishery took the lead, and this same John Higginson at one time petitioned the General Court (or State Legislature) to recover the value of a whale which was proved to have had a harpoon sticking in it and bearing his mark, but which had afterward been harpooned and brought in by some one else. Later the West India trade flourished, the chief imports being sugar and molasses, and these being very much checked by the arbitrary taxes imposed by the British government. It was on a petition of the Salem collector for a warrant to search after smuggled molasses that James Otis made his celebrated plea against Writs of Assistance. These were among the imports, and they were paid for, first and chiefly, by the historic codfish, the fish whose effigy still adorns the Massachusetts Representatives' Hall, and which the old Salem merchant Benjamin Pickman also commemorated with carving and gilding on each stair of his mansion in Salem—a house built in 1740, and still standing. Like the pious Bishop Willegis, who took for his crest the wheel, his early labors on which were regarded as plebeian by his rivals, so Benjamin Pickman exalted the codfish. Other merchants used for the same purpose the symbolic pineapple, which may be found so frequently carved on old stairways and bureaus; and possibly the scallop-shell which so often appears on colonial furniture or cornices may have had a similar association, and suggested "treasures hid in the sands."

But it took the great stress of the Revolutionary war to evolve the old Salem sea-captain. During that war it is hard to tell how the intercourse between Europe and the colonies would have been kept up—with Boston, Newport, New York, Philadelphia, Charleston, and Savannah successively in the hands of the enemy—but for the merchants and mariners of Salem, Beverly, and Marblehead. Salem alone sent out 158 armed vessels, carrying in all more than 2000 guns, each vessel having twelve or fourteen. They took 445 prizes, 54 out of their own fleet being lost.

The loss of the vessels was to be expected; but the loss from history of all detailed memorial of these daring men is more serious. What is fame that preserves of all that period only the madcap daring of Paul Jones, and forgets the solid heroism of Jonathan Haraden?

Jonathan Haraden was born in Gloucester, but was taken early to Salem in the employ of Richard Cabot, father of the celebrated president of the Hartford Convention. He first went to sea as lieutenant, then as captain of a fourteen-gun sloop built for the State of Massachusetts, and bearing a name that would have delighted Wendell Phillips—the *Tyrannicide*. In her he helped capture a British naval vessel, that was carried in triumph into Salem Harbor. Afterward Haraden was put in command of the *General Pickering*, a Salem privateer of 180 tons, carrying fourteen six-pounders, and a crew of forty-five men and boys. He sailed in 1780 with a cargo of sugar for Bilboa, then a resort for American privateers and prize vessels. On his passage he had a two hours' fight with a British cutter of twenty guns, and beat her off, but on entering the Bay of Biscay found opportunity for an exploit more daring. Running by night alongside a British privateer carrying twenty-two guns and sixty men, he ordered her, through his trumpet, to "surrender to an American frigate or be sunk." The astonished Englishman yielded, and came on board to find himself outgeneralled. A prize crew was put on the captured vessel, and both made sail for Bilboa, when they were met by a king's ship, which, as the captured captain told Haraden with delight, was the *Achilles*, another English privateer, with forty-two guns and 140 men. "I sha'n't run from her," said Haraden, coolly. At once the scene changed; the big Englishman recaptured the little one, then lay alongside Haraden's ship all night to fight her next day. Haraden took a sound night's sleep, and recruited a boatswain and eight sailors from his prisoners in the morning, when they went to work.

The American ship seemed, said an eye-witness, like a long-boat beside a man-of-war; many of the Englishman's shot went over her opponent, while she herself was always hit below the water-line—this modern Achilles, like the ancient, proving vulnerable in the heel. A final broadside of crow-bars from Haraden had great effect, and Achilles fled. The *Pick-ering* gave chase, and Haraden offered a large reward to his gunner if he would carry away a spar, but no such luck occurred, and the Englishman got off. Haraden recaptured his first prize, which had thus changed hands thrice in twenty-four hours, and went into port with her. The battle had lasted three hours, being fought so near the Spanish coast that a hundred thousand spectators, it was said, lined the shores; and it was also said that, before the *Pickering* and her prize had been half an hour at anchor, one could have walked a mile over the water by stepping from boat to boat; and when the captain landed he was borne in triumph through the city on men's shoulders. This is but a sample of this bold sailor's adventures. On another occasion still, in the *Pickering*, he fell in with three armed Englishmen in company, carrying respectively twelve, fourteen, and sixteen guns; and he captured each in succession with his vessel, he carrying just as many guns as the largest of the enemy.

Haraden alone took more than a thousand guns from the British during the war. The Salem ships intercepted the vessels which carried supplies from England or Nova Scotia to the garrisons in New York and Boston; they cruised in

GEORGE CABOT IN YOUTH.
From the painting owned by Mr. H. C. Lodge, Boston.

the Bay of Biscay, and in the English and Irish channels; they raised the insurance on British ships to twenty-three per cent., and obliged a large naval force to be constantly employed in convoying merchantmen; they, moreover, brought munitions of war from the French islands. Some sailed as privateers pure and simple; others under "letters of marque," in voyages whose privateering was incidental, but where the dangers incurred were much the same. Joseph Peabody, for instance, sailed from Salem in the winter of 1781 as second mate of the letter-of-marque *Ranger*, Captain Simmons, carrying seven guns. They took a cargo of salt, sold it at Richmond, Virginia, and at Alexandria loaded with flour for Havana. Part of the cargo, being from General Washington's plantation, was received at Havana at the marked weight; all was sold, and the *Ranger* returned to Alexandria for another freight. Anchoring at the mouth of the Potomac because of headwinds, the officers turned in, but were roused before midnight by the watch, with news that large boats were coming toward the ship from different directions. Simmons and Peabody rushed to the deck, the latter in his night clothes. As they reached it, a volley of musketry met them, and the captain fell wounded. Peabody ran forward, shouting for the crew to

JOSEPH PEABODY.
From the painting in the East India Marine Society, Salem.

ELIAS HASKET DERBY.
From the painting in the East India Marine Society, Salem.

seize the boarding pikes, and he himself attacked some men who were climbing on board. Meantime another strange boat opened fire from another quarter. All was confusion; they knew not who were their assailants or whence; the captain lay helpless, the first officer was serving out ammunition, and Peabody, still conspicuous in his white raiment, had command of the deck. Two boats were already grappled to the *Ranger ;* he ordered cold shot to be dropped into them, and frightened one crew so that it cast off; then he ordered his men against the other boat, shouting, "We have sunk one, boys; now let us sink the other!" His men cheered, and presently both boats dropped astern, leaving one of the *Ranger's* crew dead and three wounded. Peabody himself was hurt in three places, not counting the loss of his club of hair, worn in the fashion of those days, which had been shot clean off, and was found on deck the next morning. The enemy proved to be a guerrilla band of Tories, whose rendezvous was at St. George's Island, near where the *Ranger* lay at anchor. There had been sixty men in their boats, while the crew of the *Ranger* numbered twenty; and the same guerrillas had lately captured a brig of seven guns and thirty men by the same tactics, which the promptness of Peabody had foiled.

On such tales as these was the youth of Salem nourished during the bitter period

of the American Revolution. That once over, the same bold spirits sought wider adventure. Joseph Peabody himself lived to own, first and last, eighty-three ships, which he freighted himself; he shipped 7000 seamen, and promoted forty-five men to be captains who had first shipped with him as boys. Other merchants, of whom Elias Hasket Derby was the chief, were constantly projecting distant voyages, and taking pains to bring forward enterprising young men, who were given ventures of their own as captain or supercargo. These were often the sons of the ship-owners, and, aided by the excellent public schools of Salem, became officers at an age that seems surprisingly early. Nathaniel Silsbee, the eldest son of a sea-captain, went to sea as captain's clerk at fourteen, his brother William did the same at fifteen, and his brother Zachariah at sixteen. The eldest brother was in command of a vessel before he was nineteen, and the two others before they were twenty. All three retired from the sea when under twenty-nine. Captain Nathaniel Silsbee sailed one East India voyage of nineteen months, at the beginning of which neither he, nor his first mate (Charles Derby), nor his second mate (Richard Cleveland), was twenty years old. My own grandfather, Stephen Higginson—afterward member of the Continental Congress—commanded one of his father's ships at twenty-one. His double-first cousin, George Cabot—afterward the first Secretary of the Navy, and the president of the Hartford Convention—left Harvard College and went to sea at sixteen as cabin-boy under his brother-in-law, Joseph Lee, the traditional opinion expressed in the family being that "Cap'n Joe would put George Cabot's nose to the grindstone," which was doubtless done. At twenty he was himself a captain. In the slower development of the present day there is something amusing in this carnival of youth.

While still too young to vote, these boys were deemed old enough to open new channels of trade, penetrate unknown seas, and risk collision with the great naval nations of Europe. They had to make their own charts, as, for instance, of the coast of Sumatra, where Captain Jonathan Carnes, of Salem, first discovered that pepper grew wild, and then made his way thither on a secret voyage. The private charts of this difficult coast, prepared on "pepper voyages" by Captain Charles M. Endicott and Captain James D. Gillis, were recognized and used by the United States navy as a sufficient guide; and when Commodore Wilkes went on his famous exploring expedition he took with him a Salem sea-captain as pilot, Captain Benjamin Vanderford. But in the earlier voyages there were still greater difficulties than these. Ships were then rarely coppered; mathematical instruments were imperfect, and the rig of vessels was such as is now almost vanished from the seas—as, for instance, that of the old-fashioned cutter, in which the jib was reefed by sliding the whole bowsprit inboard. Bowditch—himself a Salem sea-captain—had not yet prepared his *Practical Navigator*, but the favorite encyclopædia among East India traders was Guthrie's *Geographical Grammar*—a quaint old book, which I remember in my grandfather's library, and which contained the vaguest descriptions of all the remoter countries of the earth.

There exists an impression, not wholly unfounded, that these ship-masters derived some advantage from the fact that, sailing in American vessels, they at least had American crews. This was true, no doubt, when they first left home; but as the voyages lasted for a year or two, and often involved transshipment, or even the sale and purchase of vessels in foreign ports, the more difficult part of the trip was usually made without this advantage. From the manuscripts of a typical Salem sea-captain — Captain Richard J. Cleveland, for which I am indebted to his son, H. W. S. Cleveland, of Minneapolis—it is easy to show with what kind of material these men had to deal. Writing of a voyage from Havre to the Isle of France in 1798, he says:

"It was not till the last hour that I was in Havre (even while the visiting officers were on board) that I finally shipped my crew. Fortunately they were all so much in debt as not to want any time to spend their advance, but were ready at the instant, and with this motley crew (who for aught I knew were robbers or pirates) I put to sea. That you may form some idea of the fatigue and trouble I have had I will attempt to describe them to you.

"At the head of the list is my mate, a Nantucket lad, whom I persuaded the captain of a ship to discharge from before the mast, and who knew little or nothing of navigation, but is now capable of conducting the vessel in case of accident to me. The first of my foremast

hands is a great surly, crabbed, rawboned, ignorant Prussian, who is so timid aloft that the mate has frequently been obliged to do his duty there. I believe him to be more of a soldier than a sailor, though he has often assured me that he has been boatswain's mate of a Dutch Indiaman, which I do not believe, as he hardly knows how to put two ends of a rope together. He speaks enough English to be

NATHANIEL SILSBEE.
From the painting in the Massachusetts Senate Chamber.

tolerably understood. The next in point of consequence is my cook—a good-natured negro and a tolerable cook, so unused to a vessel that in the smoothest weather he cannot walk fore and aft without holding on to something with both hands. This fear proceeds from the fact that he is so tall and slim that, if he should get a cant, it might be fatal to him. I did not think America could furnish such a specimen of the negro race (he is a native of Savannah), nor did I ever see such a perfect simpleton. It is impossible to teach him anything, and notwithstanding the frequency with which we have been obliged to take in and make sail on this long voyage, he can hardly tell the main halyards from the main-stay. He one day took it into his head to learn the compass, and not being permitted to come on the quarter-deck to learn by the one in the binnacle, he took off the cover of the till of his chest, and with his knife cut out something that looked like a cart-wheel, and wanted me to let him nail it on the deck to steer by, insisting that he could 'teer by him better'n tudder one.'

"Next is an English boy of seventeen years old, who, from having lately had the small-pox, is feeble and almost blind—a miserable object, but pity for his misfortunes induces me to make his duty as easy as possible. Finally, I have a little ugly French boy, the very image of a baboon, who, from having served for some time on different privateers, has all the tricks of a veteran man-of-war's man, though only thirteen years old, and by having been in an English prison has learned enough of the language to be a proficient in swearing. To hear all these fellows quarrelling (which from not understanding each other they are very apt to do) serves to give one a realizing conception of the confusion of tongues at the tower of Babel. Nobody need envy me my four months' experience with such a set, though they are now far better than when I first took them."

The skill and tact shown by the commanders in handling these motley crews are well illustrated by this extract from the manuscripts of another typical Salem sea-captain, Nathaniel Silsbee. The scene is on board a ship bought by himself at the Isle of France, and on the homeward trip to Salem in 1795. The whole crew except himself and his younger brother—both being then under the age of twenty-three—had been shipped at the Isle of France, and was made up " of all the nations of the earth." The greater part of the voyage having been made in safety, he found himself in this critical position :

"A short time before our arrival at Boston we were for two days in company with and but a few miles from a schooner which we suspected to be a privateer watching for a favorable opportunity to attack us. Having on board the ship six guns and twenty-five men, I was determined to resist, as far as practicable, the attack of any small vessel. On the afternoon of the second day that this vessel had been dogging us she bore down upon us, with an apparent intention of executing what we had supposed to be her purpose, and which we were, as I had imagined, prepared to meet ; but on calling our crew to the quarters which had previously been assigned to them, I was informed by one of my officers that there were four or five of the seamen who were unwilling thus to expose themselves, alleging that they had neither engaged nor expected to 'fight.' On hearing this, all hands being on deck, I ordered every passageway which led below-deck, excepting that leading to the cabin, to be securely fastened, then calling to me such of the crew as *had not engaged to fight*, I immediately sent them up the shrouds to repair the ratlines, and to perform other duties which they *had engaged to do*, in the most exposed parts of the ship.

"Finding themselves thus exposed to greater danger than their shipmates, they requested, before the schooner had come within gunshot of us, to be recalled from their then situation and allowed to participate in the defence of the ship, which request was granted. All our six guns were placed on one side of the ship, and we succeeded, by a simultaneous discharge of the whole of them, as soon as the schooner had approached within the reach of their contents, in causing her to haul off and hasten from us ; but whether this was caused by an unexpected resistance on our part, or by any damage caused by that resistance, we could not ascertain. I felt quite as willing to be rid of her, however, as any one of her crew could have been to be rid of us."

But it was not so much in dealing with their own men that the qualities of manhood were tested in these sea-captains as in encountering the insolence of foreign officials, and the attempts of warring nations to crush out these daring invaders. There was as yet no powerful nationality to appeal to, no naval squadron at their back. No other ship within five hundred miles, perhaps, carried the United States flag. They must rely, in order to be respected, on their own address and courage alone. When Captain Nathaniel Silsbee, on his way to India in the ship *Portland*, in 1798, put in at Cadiz, he heard for the first time of the "decrees" of the French government making liable to condemnation any vessel, of whatever nation, having on board any article grown or manufactured in Great Britain or any of its colonies. This greatly enhanced all prices in Mediterranean ports, as well as the risk of capture ; and Silsbee at once sold half his cargo, to be delivered, at the risk of the purchaser, at Leghorn or Genoa. He then laid his plans to deliver it, put on shore some English coal he had, and all his English books ; erased the name of the English maker from his nautical instruments, and cautioned the crew, if questioned, "to say, what was the truth," that they were not taken on board until after the cargo was put in, and therefore did not know whence it came. He was captured by a French privateer off Malaga, and was carried before the French consul in that city. The consul, before whom the Spanish authorities were utterly prostrate, asked him a dozen questions, and demanded an answer "in five words." Silsbee replied that this was impossible, and called for an immediate and thorough investigation, which, he said, would not take long, and would undoubtedly clear him. The consul said that there were a number of prizes in harbor, and that his case probably would not come on for two months. Silsbee informed him that this was the extreme of injustice, and that he should not leave the consular office, except by force, until his case had been settled. He accordingly sat in his chair, without sleep or food, for more than twenty-four hours, after which the consul, either admiring his pluck or exhausted by his obstinacy, gave him, rather to his astonishment, a free discharge. He learned afterward that the consul, when asked, "Why did you discharge the Yankee so quickly?" had answered, "I found that I must either dismiss him or bury him, and I preferred the former."

The mere accident of keeping a diary is often a preservative of fame, and the best type of these adventurous Salem sailors will always be Captain Richard J. Cleveland, who was just now mentioned. The first instalment of his own reminiscences was given in the *North American Review* for October, 1827, and his *Voyages and Commercial Enterprises* were first published collectively in 1842, and afterward reprinted in 1850. There lies before me a farther collection of manuscript extracts from his diaries and letters, and the same Defoe-like quality runs through them all. He was my father's own cousin, and I remember him well in my childhood, when he had reached the haven of the custom-house, after occupying for a time the temporary retreat, for which every sailor sighs, of a small farm in the country. He was then a serene old man, with a round apple-shaped head, a complexion indelibly sunburnt, and a freshness of look which bore testimony to the abstemiousness of his life; for he asserts that he never had tasted spirituous liquors, or, indeed, anything stronger than tea and coffee, nor had he ever used tobacco. In his mouth a single clove-pink was forever carried. I remember him as habitually silent, yielding admiringly to the superior colloquial powers of a very lively wife, yet easily lured into the most delightful yarns when she happened to be absent. Then he became our Ulysses and our Robinson Crusoe in one. The whole globe had been his home. It could be said of him, as Thoreau says of the sailor brother in a country farmhouse, that he knew only how far it was

to the nearest port, no more distances, all the rest being only seas and distant capes. He had grown to be a perfect, practical philosopher; Epictetus or Seneca could have taught him no farther lessons as to acquiescence in the inevitable; and yet there was an unquenched fire in his quiet eyes that showed him still to have the qualities of his youth. It was easy to fancy him issuing from his sheltered nook to

> "point the guns upon the chase
> Or bid the deadly cutlass shine,"

as in those adventurous early days.

One of Cleveland's best feats was the performance of a voyage, then unexampled, from Macao to the northwest coast of America and back, for the purchase of furs—a voyage made the more remarkable by the fact that it was achieved in a cutter-sloop of fifty tons, with a crew of the worst description, without any printed chart of the coast, and in the teeth of the monsoon. It was essential to his success to reach his destination before the arrival of certain ships that had been despatched from Boston round Cape Horn;

SANDWICH ISLANDS IDOL, IN THE ESSEX INSTITUTE, SALEM.

RICHARD J. CLEVELAND.

and his plan was to procure a vessel small enough to keep near the coast, sometimes taking advantage of a favorable current, and making a port, although an unknown one, every night. In his letters to his father he frankly says that his plan is pronounced impracticable by all experienced ship-masters at the port; but since nobody has ever tried it, how can it be asserted to be impracticable? They all predicted that he might sail a month without making any progress, and would then return, if at all, with sails and rigging torn to pieces. "I was," he coolly says, "not pleased with such gloomy prospects, but concluded that if I was to meet ruin, it might as well be by being torn to pieces on the China coast as to arrive on the coast of America after the object of my voyage had been secured by other vessels." So he sailed January 30, 1799, with twenty-five on board—two Americans, the rest Irish, Swedes, French, and chiefly English, the last mostly deserters from men-of-war and Botany Bay ships—"a list of as accomplished villains as ever disgraced a country." The work was so hard that the precious crew soon mutinied, and refused one morning to weigh anchor. In preparation for this he had stored all provisions near the cabin, and he coolly informed them that they could

not eat until they worked; and so mounted guard for twenty-four hours, with two or three men, including the black cook. His muskets were flintlocks, and revolvers were not yet introduced; but he had two four-pound cannon loaded with grape. It then occurred to him that if he offered to set them on shore, they would soon have enough of it. They caught at the proposal; but the Chinese would not keep or feed them on land, nor the captain take them on board next day: pointing a cannon, he bade them keep off. He then went to the shore in an armed boat, and offered to take them on board one by one. Several came eagerly; but when it turned out that the boatswain and one other ringleader were not to be taken back on any terms, these two desperadoes presented their knives at the breasts of the others, and swore that they should not stir. Some yielded; others were sullenly indifferent; one lay intoxicated on the beach. It was like one of the mutineering scenes in Stevenson's *Treasure Island*. At last all but six were brought on board, and thenceforth behaved well, having probably coincided by this time with their young captain, who quietly writes to his father, "No grosser miscalculation of character was ever made than by these men in supposing that they could accomplish their object by threats or intimidations."

They kept on their formidable voyage, often finding themselves, after a toilsome day, set back leagues on their way; grazing on rocks, caught in whirlpools, threatened by pirates. The diminished crew proved an advantage, as they had to be put on allowance of provisions at any rate. In thirty days they sighted the north end of Formosa, and had performed that part of the trip deemed impracticable; then they crossed the North Pacific amid constant storms, and anchored in Norfolk Sound on March 30, 1799, after a voyage of two months, and in advance of almost all competing vessels. Even those which had arrived from Boston were at disadvantage, being much larger, and unable to penetrate the innumerable bays and inlets on the northwest coast. Putting up a screen of hides round the deck, and never letting more than one native on board at once, Cleveland concealed the smallness of his crew, and eluded attack, though the Indian canoes were often larger than his little vessel. On one occasion his cutter ran on a rock, and lay there twenty-four hours, at such an angle that no one could stand on deck, the Indians fortunately not discovering his plight. At last the vessel floated with returning tide, and after two months' traffic they reached China, September 15, by way of the Sandwich Islands, laden with a cargo worth $60,000, the sea-otter skins that had been bought at the rate of eight for a musket selling for $36 apiece. His deserters had reached Wampoa before him, and all Cleveland's friends had believed their assertion that he was dead.

The youthfulness of these men gave a flavor of impulse and adventure to the soberest mercantile enterprises. They made up their plans for some voyage round the the oldest of the three not being yet thirty years old. In these days, when every little remote port of the globe has been visited and described in full, its manners sketched, its channels laid down in a chart, and its commercial resources fully known, it is impossible to appreciate the uncertain and vague delights of such an expedition. Every entry into a new harbor might imply a fortune or a prison, for Spain had not yet lost its control of the regions they were to visit, but claimed the right to monopolize the commerce of all. For each port there was some pompous official to be managed or bribed, and in general, where any injustice had been done to them, the pluck and ready wit of the young Americans carried the

PUNCH-BOWL PRESENTED TO THE EAST INDIA MARINE SOCIETY BY CAPTAIN BENJAMIN HODGES IN 1800, SHOWING SALEM SHIP-YARD.

globe as blithely as if it were a yachting trip. It seemed like commerce on a lark, and yet there was always a keen eye to business. Cleveland and his friend Shaler—whose *Sketches of Algiers* has still a place in the literature of travel—having come together from the Isle of France to Copenhagen, formed the project of a voyage round Cape Horn. They bought at Hamburg an American brig of 175 tons, the *Lelia Byrd*, tossed up a coin to decide which should go as captain and which as supercargo, invited a delightful young Polish nobleman, the Count de Rouissillon, to accompany them, and sailed November 8, 1801, for a two years' voyage, day. More than once, after being actually imprisoned and ordered out of the port, they quietly refused to weigh anchor until their wrongs had been redressed and an apology made. On one occasion, after going on shore with a boat's crew to rescue some of their own men who had been improperly detained, they carried off the Spanish guard also; and then sailed within musket-shot of a fort garrisoned by a hundred men, compelling their prisoners to stand conspicuously by the bulwarks, in order to ward off the fire from the battery. Nevertheless they were under fire for half an hour. One shot struck them just above the water-line, and several cut the sails and rigging. The Spaniards had eight nine-pound guns, the Americans had only three-pounders, but when the latter got within range, the Spanish soldiers fled, and in ten minutes the fight was done. This was at San Diego, California, and we have the testimony of Mr. Richard H. Dana that it was still vividly remembered upon that coast thirty years later. When the *Lelia Byrd* was safe the prisoners were set on shore, and the Americans had soon after a several days' visit from the "jolly padres," as Cleveland calls them, of the old Spanish missions, who took uproarious satisfaction in the whole affair, and agreed that the Spanish commandant, Don Manuel Rodriguez, ought to be sent back to the mother country as a poltroon.

The pioneer Salem vessel in the Eastern trade was apparently the *Grand Turk*—a ship of 300 tons, built for a privateer by Elias Hasket Derby. She carried twenty-two guns, and took many prizes. The war being over, she was sent by her owner on the first American voyage to the Cape of Good Hope in 1781, the cargo consisting largely of rum. The voyage proved profitable, and Captain Jonathan Ingersoll, her commander, bought in the West Indies on his return enough of Grenada rum to load two vessels, sent home the *Grand Turk*, and came himself in the *Atlantic*. On the way he rescued the captain and mate of an English schooner, the *Amity*, whose crew had mutinied and set them adrift in a boat. By one of those singular coincidences of which maritime life then seemed to yield so many, this very schooner was afterward recaptured in Salem Harbor in this way: after their arrival the captain of the *Amity* was sitting with Mr. Derby in his counting-room, and presently saw through the spy-glass his own vessel in the offing. Mr. Derby promptly put two pieces of ordnance on board one of his brigs, and gave the English captain the unlooked-for pleasure of recapturing the *Amity*, whose mutineers had no reason to suppose that they should happen upon the precise port into which their victims had been carried.

This was not the only pioneer expedition of the *Grand Turk*, which also made, in 1785-6, the first voyage direct from New England to the Isle of France and China. There exists a picture of this celebrated vessel on a punch-bowl made for

Mr. Derby in China, and still preserved in the collections of the East India Marine Society at Salem, side by side with what may be called the official punch-bowl of the society itself, bearing the date of 1800, and adorned with a graphic design representing the ship-building of that period. Another similar design may be found on the quaint certificates of membership of the same society, dated in 1796; and many memorials of the maritime life of those days are preserved by this honored association itself and by the Essex Institute. Some of these are here reproduced, through the kindness of the officers of this last association, and of the Peabody Academy of Science, to which the remarkable collections of the East India Marine Society are now transferred. For more than half a century the merchants and ship-masters of Salem vied with each other in bringing home Oriental curiosities for this museum—weapons, costumes, musical instruments, carriages, models of ships, culminating in a great wooden idol that once stood alone in a desert on the Sandwich Islands. This unique collection is now, through the wide munificence of George Peabody, preserved for all future generations.

Another ship of "King" Derby's, the *Astræa*, was the first to make the direct voyage to Canton, in 1789; and his ship the *Atlantic* first displayed the American flag at Bombay and Calcutta in 1788, and the brig *Sally* first did the same at Batavia in 1796. A Salem captain, James Devereux, on a Boston vessel, first visited Japan in 1799, and the Salem ship *Margaret* went there two years later, half a century before the country was freely opened to commerce by Commodore Perry. The schooner *Rajah*, from Salem, first reached Sumatra in 1793. The *Astræa* from Salem entered the port of Manila in 1796, and there exists a manuscript log-book of her voyage, by Nathaniel Bowditch, the mathematician, who was on board. The stars and stripes were first floated at Mocha by Captain Joseph Ropes, of the ship *Recovery*, in 1798. The authorities of the place could not be made to understand whence she came, or how many moons she had been sailing, but they readily took their share, perhaps, of the $50,000 which he carried with him in specie to invest in coffee. The trade with the Feejee Islands, Madagascar, and Zanzibar was opened later, and that with Surinam,

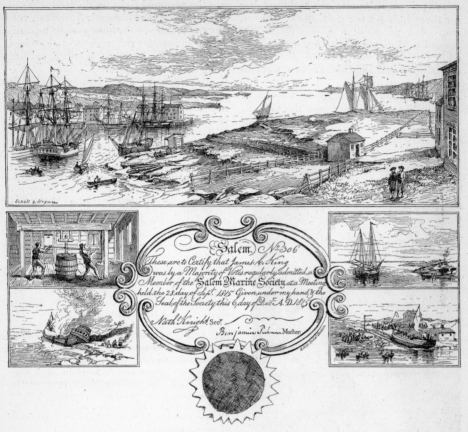

CERTIFICATE OF MEMBERSHIP OF EAST INDIA MARINE SOCIETY, SHOWING SALEM HARBOR, 1797.
From the original in the Essex Institute, Salem.

Cayenne, and other South American ports was carried on during all this period. With Senegal and the west coast of Africa the Salem trade began in 1789, the two schooners *Sally* and *Polly* — seductive creatures — first teaching the poor Africans the taste of rum. It must be remembered that the exportation of cotton had not then begun; it was even imported in small quantities from the West Indies and Demerara; and the cargoes brought from the East Indies were at first chiefly paid for in furs from the northwest coast and in Spanish dollars.

Mr. Derby alone, according to Osgood and Batchelder's *Historical Sketches of Salem*, caused one hundred and twenty-five voyages to be made in fourteen years (1785–99) by thirty-seven different vessels, forty-five of these voyages being to the East Indies or China. He rarely bought or sold on credit, and there were then no banks; so that, while his large ships were on their Oriental voyages, his smaller ones were sent to Gottenburg and St. Petersburg for iron, duck, and hemp; to France, Spain, and Madeira for wine and lead; to the West Indies for spirits; and to New York, Philadelphia, and Richmond for flour, provisions, iron, and tobacco. Accumulating for himself the largest fortune left in this country during the last century—a million dollars—he obtained also the more important memorial of gratitude and affection from the young men whom he trained and encouraged. To him primarily the nation also owed the building of the frigate *Essex*, the pride of the earlier navy. When, in 1798, we were apparently about to engage in a war with France, and had no naval force, Congress authorized President Adams to accept such vessels as private citizens might build, paying for them in a six per cent. stock. Salem responded at once; a subscription was opened by Mr. Derby with $10,000, followed by William Gray with the same sum; others put down smaller amounts, some in money, some in work, till $75,000 were raised, and the frigate *Essex* was built. Among her contractors was the veteran Captain Haraden, who supplied a part of

STEPHEN HIGGINSON.

From the painting by Stuart in possession of George Higginson, Esq., Boston.

the cordage, her large cables being borne in procession to the ship, attended by martial music. She was launched September 30, 1799, carried thirty-two guns, and proved the fastest ship in the navy, as well as one of the cheapest. Captain Edward Preble was her first actual commander, and Farragut served as a midshipman on board. She was credited with taking two millions of dollars in prizes from the enemy during the subsequent war with England, in which she was captured at last, while the stock in which she was paid for fell to fifty cents on the dollar before the war was over, with but few purchasers. In other words, half her value was practically given to the government by the citizens of Salem.

It will be remembered that the prime cause of the war of 1812 against England

was the assumed right on the part of English naval officers to search American vessels for seamen. In how utterly unscrupulous a manner this right was exercised is well shown in the following extract from the manuscript recollections of Nathaniel Silsbee. The narrative makes it also clear with what zeal the Salem men, who had heard the tale of Edward Hulen, must have shipped on board the Salem privateers when it came to open war. The events here described took place in 1796:

"In the course of the few days that I remained at Madras, one of those occurrences took place which more than any and all others led to the late war between the United States and Great Britain. I received a note early one morning from my chief mate, apprising me that one of my sailors (Edward Hulen, a fellow-townsman whom I had known from boyhood) had been impressed and taken on board of a British frigate then lying in port. On receiving this intelligence I immediately went on board my ship, and having there learnt all the facts in the case, proceeded to the frigate, where I found Hulen, and in his presence was informed by the first lieutenant of the frigate that he had taken Hulen from my ship under a peremptory order from his commander ' to visit every American ship in port, and to take from each of them one or more of their seamen.' With that information I returned to the shore, and called upon Captain Cook, who commanded the frigate, and sought, first by all the persuasive means that I was capable of using, and ultimately by threats to appeal to the government of the place, to obtain Hulen's release, but in vain. I then, with the aid of the senior partner of one of the first commercial houses of the place, sought the interference and assistance of the civil authorities of the port, but without success, it being a case in which they said they could not interfere.

"In the course of the day I went again to the frigate, and in the presence of the lieutenant tendered to Hulen the amount of his wages, of which he requested me to give him only ten dollars, and to take the residue to his mother in Salem, on hearing which the lieutenant expressed his perfect conviction that Hulen was an American citizen, accompanied by a strong assurance that if it was in *his* power to release him he should not suffer another moment's detention, adding at the same time that he doubted if this or any other circumstance would induce Captain Cook to permit his return to my ship. It remained for me only to recommend Hulen to that protection of the lieutenant which a good seaman deserves, and to submit to the high-handed insult thus offered to the flag of my country, which I had no means of either preventing or resisting, beyond the expression of my opinion of it to the said Captain Cook, which took place in the presence of

LAUNCH OF THE SHIP "FAME," NEAR CROWNINSHIELD'S WHARF, 1802.
From the painting in Essex Institute, Salem.

other British officers, and in terms dictated by the then excited state of my feelings. After several years' detention in the British navy, and after the peace of Amiens, Hulen returned to Salem, and lived to perform services on board privateers owned in Salem, in the late war between this country and England."

Of the 250 privateers sent out during the war of 1812, Salem furnished forty, Baltimore and New York alone exceeding her. The Salem fleet carried in all 189 cannon. Of these the schooner *Fame*, a mere fishing-boat of thirty tons, with two guns and thirty men, received her commission at noon, sailed in the afternoon, and sent the first prize into Salem. The second prize was sent in by the *Jefferson*, a boat of only fourteen tons, carrying one gun and twenty men. The *America*, belonging to George Crowninshield and Sons, was claimed to be the swiftest vessel afloat during the war—a ship of 350 tons, carrying twenty guns and 150 men, and capturing twenty-six prizes with more than a million dollars. She was commanded successively by Captain Joseph Ropes and Captain Benjamin Chever, Jun. With this war the palmy days of Salem seafaring substantially closed, although this narrative might well be expanded to take in the description of *Cleopatra's Barge*, a pleasure yacht of 197 tons built in 1816 by George Crowninshield, and once sent by him to St. Helena,

with several ladies of the Bonaparte family on board, in the abortive design of rescuing the Emperor Napoleon. She was the first American yacht to cross the Atlantic; and is a curious illustration of the Salem nautical training that the black cook on this yacht, who had sailed under Bowditch, was found as capable of keeping a ship's reckoning as any of the officers.

A type of character so strong as that of the old Salem sea-captains could not well pass away in America without making its final mark on the politics as well as the business of the nation. In the fierce strife between Federalists and Democrats these men not only took the Federalist side as a body, but it was for a time recognized as incarnated in them. A few of them, indeed, were followers of Jefferson, and it is an interesting fact that Captain Richard Cleveland himself, writing to his father from off the Cape of Good Hope, early in 1798, thus indicated the very point of view that led within a few years to the famous embargo for which the New England ship-owners reproached Jefferson so bitterly. "You may perhaps laugh at me," he said, "and call it quixotism, but I believe, if we would keep our ships at home and entirely withhold our supplies, we could be more than a match for these two noisy powers united [England and France]. I see no reason why we can't live for a time without foreign commerce." Again, Nathaniel Silsbee, when first chosen to Congress, was nominated against Timothy Pickering as a Democrat (or, as it was then called, Republican); yet he records in his autobiography that he was opposed in this respect to nearly all his circle of friends; and it is well understood that "Billy" Gray, who was, after Derby, the most important of the Salem merchants, left that town in 1809 to reside in Boston, because of his unpopularity with the Federalists as a supporter of the embargo. Two of the Crowninshield brothers were Secretaries of the Navy under Jefferson and Madison. These were the exceptions that proved the rule. Salem was Federalist, and the head-quarters of Federalism was Salem. The strength of that strong and concentrated party was in the merchants of Essex County, almost all of whom had been ship-masters in their youth. This fact is forever established by the very

phrase "Essex Junto." Timothy Pickering says that the first time he heard this phrase was from President John Adams, in 1797, and that the three men whom he named as constituting the clique were George Cabot, Stephen Higginson, and Theophilus Parsons—in other words, two ex-sea-captains and the chief maritime lawyer of his time. The habit of the quarter-deck went all through the Federalist party of Massachusetts; the slave-holders themselves did not more firmly believe that they constituted the nation. To the "Essex Junto" Jefferson himself seemed but a mutineering first mate, and his "rights of man" but the black flag of a rebellious crew. They paid the penalty of their own autocratic habit; they lived to see their cause lost; but they went down with their flags flying, having had the satisfaction—if satisfaction it was—to see most of their cargo of political principles transferred bodily to the hold of their victor.

UNITED STATES DOCKS AND NAVY-YARDS.

BY REAR-ADMIRAL EDWARD SIMPSON, U.S.N.

IN the course of the rehabilitation of the United States navy, docks and navy-yards require very serious consideration, for, after ships and guns, there are no requirements of more importance for naval purposes. The capacity of the government yards for dockage is very insignificant, owing to which the bottoms of our ships are but seldom subjected to scrutiny, and this, above all others, is the part of the integrity of which we need to be most assured. The few docks that we have are generally appropriated by vessels under repair, and the cruising ship is debarred the use of this means of guarding her safety and providing for her speed. A very slight accident may disturb the copper on the bottom of a wooden ship, which may result in serious consequences if she be sent to cruise in waters where she will be exposed to the influence of the teredo, and the neglect to clean the bottom when loaded with grass or barnacles might so impair speed as to make the difference between capture and failure in a chase. Docking for such purposes as inspecting and cleaning the bottom is the exception in our practice,

as the demands of repairs are considered paramount. A ship in which the repairs approach or lie below the water-line must be placed in a dock, and months being often required to complete the work, the dock is closed to all other purposes, and our ships are frequently sent from one navy-yard to another to take advantage of a dock that may be vacant.

The embarrassments that have attended this course in the past, while our fleet has consisted of copper-sheathed wooden ships, will be increased by the introduction of iron and steel hulls, which demand much more care and more frequent removals of such hinderances to speed as will attach themselves to their bottoms.

The government has at present but three stone dry-docks and one floating-dock. The latter is in use at Portsmouth, New Hampshire; the stone docks are at the navy-yards in Boston, New York, and Norfolk.

The first dock built by the government was constructed at Boston. It was commenced in 1827 and completed in 1834, thus occupying seven years in its construction. This length of period was due much to the novel character of the work, and to delays caused by the failure of contractors to deliver the stone as rapidly as it could have been used.

The difficulties encountered were not great; the ground was found to be very suitable at the site that was selected. The first eighteen inches in depth excavated consisted of marsh mud; then five feet of blue clay; then thirteen feet of yellow sand and gravel mixed with large stones; then hard blue clay to the bottom of the foundation pit, interspersed with strata of hard and loose sand and gravel with bowlders. This made irregular the length of the piles driven for the foundation, as some would reach rock in eight or ten feet, while others were driven to thirty feet, but all reached hard, firm bottom.

The length of this dock is 379 feet, its breadth is 60 feet, the depth of water over the sill is 25 feet, and the extreme length of ship that can be accommodated in it is 354 feet. The total cost of the dock was $677,089 50.

The stone dock at the Norfolk yard was commenced in the same year as the Boston dock, 1827, and completed in 1834, a few months after it. The site, though not as well adapted as the one in Boston, was favorable for the work of excavation. The first eleven feet was composed of yellow sand and loam; then two feet of red and yellow wet sand; then one foot of red sand and gravel; then two feet of blue clay and sand; then eighteen inches of blue clay and oyster shells. At this depth a very firm, compact blue clay was found, which continued to the bottom of the excavation; and under this clay there was a stratum of hard gravel into which an auger would not penetrate. The foundation piles reach the hard gravel, being at the entrance of the dock about thirty feet long, diminishing very gradually in length toward the head of the dock, where they are about fifteen feet in length. After they reached the stratum of gravel it was impossible to force them into it more than a few inches.

The length of this dock is 320 feet, its breadth is 60 feet, and the depth of water over the sill is 25 feet; the extreme length of ship that can be accommodated is 290 feet. The total cost was $943,676 73.

The history of the construction of the stone dry-dock at the Brooklyn Navy-

yard, New York, is an exhibition of persistence in an effort to overcome natural obstacles. The site was examined in 1824, but no steps were taken until 1835, when an appropriation of $100,000 was made, of which $5000 was expended in making examinations for a definite location; the balance of this money reverted to the Treasury. The differences about locating the site continued until 1841, when $50,000 was appropriated for commencing the work. In 1842, the site being definitely fixed, an appropriation of $100,000 was made, followed in 1845 by an appropriation of $150,000, from which time the work went on to completion in 1851.

The soil was very unsuitable. The superstratum was formed by vegetable decomposition to a depth of ten feet; below this there was an impalpable quicksand, containing large portions of mica; this material, when confined and not mixed with water, was very firm, but when saturated with water assumed a semi-fluid form. When within six feet of the required excavation for the foundation, small veins of sand were encountered, through which flowed springs of fresh-water. These natural obstacles were the cause of great embarrassment during the progress of the work, endangering at times the safety of life and the permanence of material, requiring an exceptional character of continuous work. The successful completion of the work was regarded as a remarkable engineering triumph.

The length of the dock is 350 feet, its breadth is 66 feet, and the depth of water over the sill is 25 feet; the extreme length of ship that can be accommodated is 327 feet. The difficulties attending the construction are made very apparent in the cost of the work, which amounted to $2,151,173 60.

A stone dock is in process of construction at Mare Island, California; this is of dimensions capable of receiving ships of the first class. Its length is 530 feet; breadth, 79 feet; depth of water over the sill, 27.6 feet; and it will admit a ship of 460 feet in length. When completed it will supply a great want on the Pacific coast.

It requires no argument to show that the government needs a great increase in its facilities for dockage; the necessity of a plentiful supply of docks is recognized by all powers, and we cannot pretend to be blind to our own deficiency. This is a want that must be provided for, but it is well to study all points that bear on the subject, and to mature some plan of operations before we embark in work which involves great expense, and the success of which must depend on the thoroughness with which all the factors are considered beforehand.

A stone dry-dock is a construction requiring engineering skill, and involves great expense. The same may be said of any other kind of dock for naval purposes. When such a work is contemplated, it should be accepted that the structure is to endure permanently, for all time, and the location or navy-yard in which the site is selected should be regarded in the same light; that is, it should be the deliberate opinion of the authorities that it will be to the advantage of the country to perpetuate that location for its present uses. It is not sufficient reason to justify expenditure to say that because we already have a dock at a certain place we will increase our resources there; there may have been a time when that location was the best under the then existing condition of things, but circumstances may be now very different, and the condition of things may be such as to make the old site objectionable, making any further development of it inconsistent with good judgment.

Circumstances had, no doubt, much to do with the completion of our dry-dock at the Brooklyn Navy-yard, where, it is seen, the ground was very unsuitable, resulting in an enormous expenditure of money, more than three times the amount expended for the same purpose at Boston, where a dock of larger dimensions was built at the reduced cost. The yard had been established, machinery and ship-houses had been erected, a dock was necessary, and it, perforce, must have its site in the government grounds. The suitability of the ground for excavations had not been well considered when the yard was located; but, this being done, all other considerations were forced to yield, and no matter what difficulties presented themselves subsequently, they had to be overcome at any cost. The location of the Boston and Norfolk yards was most fortunate; the soil was suitable for dock excavations. The selection at New York was not so; and at this time, in considering the matter of increasing the number of our docks, it is important to reconsider the locations of the yards themselves.

Another reason for reverting thus to first principles is that experience has shown that for an economical performance of the current work of the navy we have too many yards. The expenditures are out of all proportion to the results obtained. This arises much from the organization that obtains in them, by which each bureau in the Navy Department has its own independent shops, triplicating sometimes the same character of work in one yard; this can be corrected by concentrating these shops; but apart from this, and supposing this concentration to be effected, certain shop organizations will still be constantly preserved in each yard, no matter how unimportant, and irrespective of work going on or not. In these, in order to secure the services of good foremen, they must be retained permanently on pay, machinists must be kept on the pay-roll if only to care for tools, and the numerous current expenses for maintaining a shop must be incurred; in fact, the support of a skeleton organization producing nothing costs as much as if many workmen are employed.

If it should be decided to retain possession of all the sites now owned by the government, many could be permanently closed, to be reserved for emergencies; but for the practical purposes of our navy the work will be better done by limiting it to two yards on the Atlantic coast, one on the coast of the Gulf of Mexico, and one on the Pacific, and these should be selected on grounds of a purely physical and strategic character. By thus concentrating the work opportunity will be afforded of providing at a comparatively moderate cost new tools and appliances suited to the developments in modern naval architecture, and to the change which has taken place in the material for construction. To supply these implements to all our present yards would be a great and useless expenditure, and to retain yards in commission which were not supplied with them would be a waste of public money.

The question, then, of providing increased facilities for dockage assumes the form of the selection of the best site for a navy-yard suited to all the purposes of modern naval development.

Judgment in selecting a site for a navy-yard will be clouded if too many conditions are considered as essential; many desirable features not natural to a site can be provided artificially, proving as effective practically as if they had originally existed; the want of these should not be allowed to affect a decision if other more essential characteristics can be secured which no artificial means can supply. These only should be considered. They can be summarized as follows:

1. Ample depth of water in a channel not subject to shoaling caused by deposits.

2. Solid ground capable of affording good foundations for the heaviest structures and tools.

3. Facility of ingress from and egress to the sea.

4. Abundant supply of good fresh-water.

5. Absence of rapid currents.

6. Healthy climate.

These are the essential conditions for a good site for a navy-yard; they should be natural to the location.

As to the question of defensibility, it must always be recognized that a navy-yard is a point of weakness in itself, as it invites attack. The fact of establishing a navy-yard at any point carries with it as a necessary corollary the construction of defences for its protection, and these must be adequate for the purpose.

The question of facility of procuring supplies is one that is often urged as necessarily indicating that a navy-yard should be established in or near a large city, from which workmen as well as material can be procured. This had an important bearing on the question when the country was sparsely settled, and communication between distant points was established over country roads; but the annihilation of space by rapid railroad transit robs this proposition of all force. In fact, at the present time the location of a government establishment at a large city is objectionable, for with the rapid development of the trades, and the ever-growing proportions of our private industries, the necessity of more and more space in cities is felt for private accommodation, and the government establishment, instead of being as formerly an aid, proves an obstacle to the expansion of local interests, and the water-fronts which are required for the navy-yards grow to be of such value that the loss of them becomes a serious deprivation to the transportation facilities of the manufacturers and merchants.

Very decided testimony bearing on the injury caused to private establishments by the proximity of government works was given by Mr. Charles Cramp, one of the leading ship-builders in the United States, before the Naval Committee of the House of the present Congress. Mr. Cramp says: "The effect of a navy-yard is to demoralize ship-building labor in its vicinity." He says further: "If there are to be navy-yards for ship-building purposes, they should be located at points where there is no private ship-building industry to be demoralized and ruined by them." And making a direct application, he says: "To build a steam-ship in the League Island Navy-yard would immediately create a complete demoralization in the private yards of the Delaware—at Wilmington of Harlan and Hollingsworth, the Pusey and Janes Company yard at Kaighn's Point, Mr. Dialogue's, and two or three places in Philadelphia, including our own. We do not know why the government of the United States should punish us by demoralizing our business."

At whatever spot a navy-yard may be located, if work is carried on continuously, as would be the case in a first-class yard established with the view of carrying out such a system as now seems to be determined on by Congress, the needed workmen will be forth-coming, they will make their homes in the neighborhood, and the character of the employés will be better than that of men exposed to the temptations of a large city. The contrast also will be avoided between the administrations of the government and private establishments which works to the injury of the private manufacturer, who demands more hours for a day's work than does the government, and whose employés are, as a rule, not treated with the consideration that one obtains in government shops.

In the matter of separate locations for government and private establishments, the experience abroad has resulted in the adoption of the rule that Mr. Cramp would lay down for our guidance. In Great Britain the cities of Glasgow, Dumbarton, and others on the Clyde, Newcastle, and both banks of the Tyne, the shores of the Wear, the Teese, and the Humber, are monopolized by private establishments, while all the government works are at Chatham, Devonport, Pembroke, Portsmouth, and Sheerness, far removed, in districts peopled to a more limited degree. The same rule obtains in France and other countries on the continent of Europe.

The selection of a site for a first-class yard should be confined, if possible, to property now owned by the government. To go outside of this would open up the whole question of local claims. In considering the sites already occupied, some will need but a passing allusion.

The navy-yard at Portsmouth, New Hampshire, is of little or no use. The site presents but few advantages, the disadvantages far outweighing them. It is unfit for purposes of docking.

The navy-yard at Boston was an admirable selection in every way, for the construction of docks as well as for other purposes; but the new conditions of things, notably those relating to ordnance, rob it of its advantages, and there is no room for expansion. It is now crowded in by the business of the community, and is closely surrounded by buildings which increase the risk of loss of public property by fire. The site is much needed for commercial purposes, and the sale of it might reimburse the government for a large portion of its outlay. The dry-dock is a very valuable one, the largest in the possession of the government, and should be retained until others are built at more suitable sites. After this is done, it would be well to dispose of the yard, dock included. This dock is smaller in dimensions than would be constructed in the present day.

The character of the ground at the Brooklyn Navy-yard, New York, was sufficiently demonstrated during the construction of the dry-dock at that place, showing it to be unfit for the purpose. The yard has very little useful waterfront, which is near to rapid currents. The expansion of this yard and additional docks would involve the expenditure of large sums of money; it is crowded in now by a community which needs the space for private and mercantile purposes. After the establishment of a first-class yard elsewhere, a large portion of the ground now held by the government could be disposed of, and what now constitutes the yard proper should be retained, but with no effort at further expansion. It could continue of service to its present capacity, and will be important in time of war as the rendezvous for coast-defence vessels assigned to the protection of the entrance to the Narrows.

The navy-yard at Norfolk, Virginia,

may be said to have the unanimous support and approval of those who have considered the subject. The depth of water is good, and the channel is narrow, which is a great point in defence. The ground where the dry-dock is built proved to be very good for the purpose, and though the expansion of the yard to first-class capacity and the increase of the facilities of dockage will involve much work and expense, the return will more than compensate. The strategic position is remarkable, and cannot be disregarded, being at the entrance of one of our most important sheets of inland waters. It is at this point that the navy would be called upon to occupy a prominent position in the defence of the coast, and it is here that a powerful force of "floating batteries" (coast-defence vessels) would be concentrated to dispute the possession of the Chesapeake Bay. Nature has clearly indicated this site as one for a first-class yard.

The navy-yard at Pensacola is entirely untenable in view of modern artillery, is deficient in depth of water, and unsuited for purposes of dockage. It is very desirable that a good site should be found for a large yard on the Gulf coast, but until that is done a suitable site for a naval station might be found in the neighborhood of Pensacola for the storage of coal and other consumable articles, but nothing on a large scale should be attempted. The same may be said of the small station now established at Key West.

The necessities of the coast-defence vessels that should be assigned to the defence of New Orleans might involve the establishment of a naval station at that place for the storage of consumable articles and the erection of small shops, but the establishment of a first-class yard would not be advisable at this place.

We have, then, on our Atlantic coast one site which is, we may say, universally recognized as suitable for a first-class yard. This is not sufficient; we need one more. Where shall it be located?

This question came up in 1862, when it was under consideration whether or not the public interest would be promoted by acquiring the title to League Island, Pennsylvania, for naval purposes.

There was at the same time a project on foot to induce the Navy Department to favor the establishment of a navy-yard at a site on the Thames River near New London, Connecticut, and a site on Narragansett Bay was also being urged.

In consequence of these influences, and with a view to procuring a report on the comparative merits of the sites proposed, Congress authorized the Secretary of the Navy to appoint a board of competent officers to examine the harbor of New London, Narragansett Bay, and League Island, and to report by the selection of which the public interests would be best promoted.

This board reported in October, 1862. Narragansett Bay was the first visited; a careful examination was made of all the localities suggested, resulting in an adverse opinion, in which all the members of the board concurred.

The selection was thus restricted to a choice between League Island and a site on the Thames. On this subject there was a difference of opinion in the board, resulting in a majority and minority report, the majority, consisting of Rear-Admiral Stringham, Commodores Gardner and Van Brunt, and Civil Engineer Sanger, reporting strongly in favor of the site on the Thames, the minority, consisting of Captain Marston, U.S.N., and Professor A. D. Bache, reporting in favor of League Island. By a singular coincidence, the dissenting members who presented the minority report were Philadelphians.

These reports were submitted to Congress, and were referred to the Committee on Naval Affairs in the House of Representatives for consideration, which committee made a thorough investigation and personal examination of both sites, and reported its conclusions to the House in 1864, a majority reporting in favor of New London, a minority of two members in favor of League Island, while one member, agreeing to the preference declared by the minority for League Island, stated that there were many substantial reasons in favor of the location at New London.

Notwithstanding the adverse reports, League Island, as well as a site on the Thames, became the property of the government, under authority of acts of Congress passed in 1867, and as such they should be considered as on the list from which selection can be made for the location of a first-class yard. The effort at selection between these two sites, which resulted in an impotent conclusion in 1864, should now be renewed and decided on

their merits, and this can best be done by referring to the exhaustive report made by those who were charged with the study of the subject.

The majority report of the Naval Committee on League Island shows that it is situated at the confluence of the Schuylkill and Delaware rivers, about one hundred miles from the ocean, that the island is really a flat from three to four feet below the level of mean high water, and that but for a "stone wall backed by an embankment of earth," it would be under water at each recurring tide. The soil is described as of the character found in the bottom-lands of alluvial rivers, borings in which show a depth of from twenty to fifty-five feet before a solid bed is reached, and in expressing their disapproval of such a character of soil for foundations for heavy structures the committee cite the instance of Fort Delaware, in the vicinity, the foundations of which, upon an island not flowed by the tide, and resting upon piles, settled in a few years to such an extent as to render its lower tier of port-holes useless.

In addition to the want of solid ground for foundations, the committee point to the large amount of filling that must be done to raise the island to such a level as the grade may require, and to the necessity of importing all the necessary material; they submit a probable estimate of $10,000 an acre for this work, and as the area to be filled embraces four hundred or five hundred acres, they demur to the expense, especially as the additional cost of piling will be added to that of all structures that may be erected.

The disadvantage of the distance from the ocean is dwelt on by the committee, and they find that in addition to the tortuous character of the channel, making it one of the most difficult streams to navigate in the United States, the depth of water over the shoalest bars is not adequate for the passage of large vessels at all periods of the tide, and that these dangers are increased by the deposits and the changes constantly taking place in the channel.

The committee refer to the damage and obstruction to navigation occasioned by ice, fast and floating, in the winter season, and make copious citations from insurance companies, marine offices, reports of the Philadelphia Corn Exchange, and cases of damage and detention to men-of-war, to show that the navigation of the Delaware in the winter season is regarded as full of danger, and to be avoided if possible. They show the practical effect of this danger by citing the fact that the increase of navigation for the summer months over the winter months is six hundred per cent., which is mentioned as "a very significant evidence of the extent of this obstruction to navigation in the estimation of the practical ship masters and owners of the United States."

The majority report condemns League Island as deficient in the essential characteristics for a good site for a navy-yard, not having an ample depth of water, not having soil fit for solid foundations, not having facility for rapid egress to and ingress from the sea, not free from rapid currents and dangerous obstructions to navigation, and not having a climate free from malarial influences.

The minority report, signed by two members of the committee, in the personality of which Philadelphia was strongly represented, does not dispute the depth of water as stated by the majority, but takes the ground that the excessive draught of water of ships cited is abnormal, "not in harmony with the forces and properties of nature," and that the Delaware has adequate depth of water for the largest vessels contemplated by the United States government, and the prophecy was made (1864) that no more ships of this abnormal draught of water will be built—a prophecy which has failed of fulfilment.

The minority do not reply to the difficulties shown to exist from deposits and shifting channels, but undertake to defend the character of the ground for foundations by arguing for the necessity of elasticity under heavy tools, such as a steam-hammer. The effort is sadly strained, and in the light of modern experience is ridiculous; but it shows the determination to make a case for the defence of a bad cause. In refutation of this point made by the minority it is well to state that in the foundation of the anvil under the 100-ton hammer at Le Creuzot, in France, the foundation of which is on bed-rock at a depth of eleven yards, on which is raised a mass of masonry laid in cement, there is placed under the anvil block of cast-iron a layer of oak timbers about one yard in thickness; this is all the elasticity that is needed for the perfect working of this the largest hammer in the world; the

energy of this hammer is 1640 foot-tons. It is safe to assert that no foundation could be erected on League Island to withstand this blow.

The minority do not deal with the subject of ready egress to and ingress from the sea, their idea evidently being that the farther from the sea a navy-yard is established the better.

The presence of a fresh-water river and proximity to supplies are the only tenable grounds advanced by the minorities either of the board of officers or of the Congressional committee in favor of League Island.

The committee, in reporting favorably on the site on the Thames near New London, call attention to the fact that after emerging from our Revolutionary struggle, when it was in contemplation to establish "one grand yard and depot for the entire American navy," a commission formed of the senior officers of the navy recommended New London "as the best harbor in the United States for that purpose," "which judgment was afterward confirmed by Commanders Hull, Rodgers, Decatur, Jones, Morris, and Biddle, and later by Admirals Stringham, Paulding, and Gregory, and Commanders Van Brunt, Gardner, and Ringgold."

The majority recognized at this location all the characteristics essential for a good site for a yard, and pointed to its important strategic position, its proximity to the "Race," the eastern entrance to Long Island Sound, the defence of which the committee regarded as vital to the protection of the coast cities of Connecticut, the manufacturing interests of New England, and the city of New York.

The committee found that the brackish water in the Thames "answers all the conditions required for the safe-keeping of iron and iron-clad vessels."

The work of the board presided over by Rear-Admiral Stringham and that of the Congressional committee was supplemented by that of boards of civil engineers of the navy, who were directed to prepare plans for the future development of League Island and the site on the Thames.

These had no orders to report on the suitability of the sites, but their statements of what is required for the development of each, when placed in parallel columns, show a striking contrast in favor of the site on the Thames.

The engineers' report on League Island, made in 1872, after stating the character of the soil, the necessity of filling and piling for foundations, and of enclosing the island in a quay wall, shows the necessity of raising the height of the wall to 10.5 feet above mean low water, though the ordinary rise and fall of the tide is about six and a half feet. This precaution is necessary to provide against freshets; and the wisdom of this recommendation was made very apparent in 1878, when the autumnal freshet raised the water in the Delaware to such a height as to overflow the dikes and inundate the unfilled portions of the island, washing away 1396 feet of the dikes and wall, causing the inhabitants to seek safety in boats.

This report further states that in winter vessels cannot lie in safety at the quay wall, for which reason "harbors of safety" must be provided, and the "back channel" between the island and the mainland is indicated as the locality for the largest of these harbors. Since the time of the report the deposits have accumulated so rapidly in this "back channel" as to make its use for this purpose quite impossible without much dredging, which would have to be a continuous operation to preserve any depth of water.

The plan for a first-class yard, comprehending the entire area of the island, was elaborated by this board of engineers, but no estimate is hazarded of the cost of all or of a part of the labor and material needed. An approximate estimate can be made, however, of the cost of one important part of the work, founded on expenditures to the present time. The cost of filling to date has been $440,028. The area filled up to grade is thirty-five acres, the portion partially filled is equivalent to about five acres; thus we have forty acres of filling, costing $440,028—an average of $11,000 per acre. At present an area of 410 acres is included in the dikes, but the position of the quay wall will be outside the dikes, advanced to the Port Warden's line, which will add 170 acres to the area to be filled. We will thus have 580 acres to be filled; this, at $11,000 an acre, will cost $6,380,000.

It is estimated that a quay wall to enclose this will cost about the same amount, raising the cost of preparing the site to over $12,000,000, and every foot of this on which a structure is to be raised must be piled. Is the game worth the candle?

The board of civil engineers appointed to present a plan for the future development of the site on the Thames, in establishing the line of quay wall half-way between the shore and the channel, found that the excavations needed for grading the yard would provide material for filling between the shore and the quay wall, so as to make the cut and fill about equally divided, with no necessity of importing any. The ground is reported as very suitable for roads and drainage, the stone and gravel being very abundant, affording good material for macadamizing, and sand for building purposes is present in large quantities. The proximity of ledges of stratified granite is also referred to as a ready and economical source from which to draw a supply of building material.

The deposit in the river is said to be on an average of one inch in four years, the current is very moderate, and the site is protected from the effect of gales of wind. The climate is stated as remarkably healthful, and the engineers conclude their report by bearing testimony to the freedom from danger caused by ice, saying, "The unusually severe winter of 1874–5, which closed more southern harbors, scarcely interrupted the navigation of the Thames."

If this site shall be developed in the future to a first-class yard, it will be necessary to increase the amount of territory, which can be done by purchase on very easy terms, and to increase the width of the channel, which can be readily accomplished, and which when once widened will retain its dimensions for all time, as it is evident that the deposit in the river is virtually nil. The increase of territory will naturally be to the north and east, and the opportunity will thus be afforded of constructing a series of stone or Simpson docks on ground well suited for their construction. If it should be decided to proceed at once to the construction of docks within the limits of the present site, an admirable location for two such docks will be found about half-way of the river front, where very little rock will be encountered; but, considering the present want of the service in this respect, it would seem more judicious to adopt the proposition of the board of civil engineers for a system of docking by floating-dock and shallow basins, as it can be the most promptly brought to a condition of practical utility. To each of the shallow basins there are attached eight railways; thus, if both basins were in use, there would be capacity for hauling out sixteen ships at one time, another one being accommodated on the floating dock itself, and it requires but a short time and an expenditure of a comparatively small amount of money to enable us to avail of this advantage.

With a view to an advance in this direction an approximate estimate has been made of the cost of developing the plan of this yard so far as to build the southern shallow basin, and to prepare it for work. In the estimate there are no allowances made for cost of anything except what is absolutely necessary to achieve the object in view.

The estimate is as follows:

Excavations	$113,000
Coffer-dam	129,000
Foundation for basin walls	40,000
Foundations in basin for bearings	42,000
Timber flooring in basin	60,000
Bearings in basin of granite	90,000
Basin walls of granite	200,000
Foundations for railways and shoring	45,000
Stone foundations and shoring	100,000
Timber for railways and tracks	100,000
Two piers and foundations	41,000
Floating-dock	400,000
Hydraulic	20,000
Iron, iron bolts, and smith's work	10,000
Clearing away coffer-dam, etc	20,000
Cradles, turn-tables, rigging, tools, etc	50,000
	$1,460,000
Add ten per cent. for superintendence, machinery, pumping, etc	146,000
	$1,606,000

For this comparatively small sum of money we have it in our power to provide ourselves in a short space of time with such facilities for dockage as will treble our present means, and this can be done at no other site in the possession of the government. We have here ample depth of water (thirty feet), with virtually no deposit in the river; we have a stream of brackish water, with a gentle current, not strong enough to swing a ship at her anchor against a light breeze; we have protection against high winds (a three-inch rope will hold a frigate at the wharf); and we have ground the best suited for the character of the work required. We have here at this site on the Thames the solution of the problem how to provide the navy with docking facilities. It needs but recognition, and we can profit by the value of what we now possess.

The establishment of a first-class yard at New London would lead naturally to the consideration of the defence at that the most vital point on the whole coast of the United States, the entrance to the inland waters of Long Island Sound, the real deep-water channel to the harbor and city of New York. In these days, when the efficiency of a vessel of war may be said to depend on a consumable article, such as coal, it becomes necessary for an enemy to be able to establish depots on the coast where such articles can be accumulated. If this is rendered impossible, his visits can be but transitory, and if delayed or repulsed in an attack, he must withdraw to great distances to renew his supplies. Long Island Sound and Chesapeake Bay are the two locations that would be most desired. The occupation of these by an enemy would be fraught with most disastrous results, and should be prevented at all hazards.

We have all-sufficient testimony as to the practicability of defending the harbor of New London, but the defence at this point should include the entrance to the Sound, and prevent the occupation of Gardiner's Bay, on the east end of Long Island, and for this a fleet of floating batteries, torpedo-boats, etc., should be concentrated in the vicinity, not only to supplement the defence in the rear of or in line with the permanent fortifications, but for the purpose of sallying out and disputing the approach of the attacking fleet. The possession of Gardiner's Bay would be practically as valuable to an enemy for depot purposes as would be an entrance to the Sound itself, and the chief defence at this point would rest with our force afloat. As a rendezvous for this force, where it could remain concentrated until the moment for action, constantly, daily if necessary, renewing its consumable stores, the New London Navy-yard is indispensable. As a shelter for repairs it is equally necessary; and as a ready provider of docking facilities for a sinking vessel it would afford the only available means of relief.

Nature has contracted the eastern entrance to the Sound, making it defensible, and the Thames River supplements these defences by providing a site where all that a naval arsenal can supply can be kept available for use, out of range of the fire of the enemy, but at a convenient distance from the field of action for the relief of our own forces. It is difficult to conceive of an arrangement for defence where the parts could more fitly join together; ingenuity could not conceive of a more perfect combination of the needed elements than are supplied by nature at the eastern entrance of the Sound; it needs but to equip each point with its appropriate appliances, and a perfect defence will result. In this the navy must bear a very important part, and its depot must be near at hand; and thus are the advantages of a navy - yard affording "ready egress to and ingress from the sea" exhibited over one remote from the coast.

There are indications that Congress recognizes the need of increased facilities for dockage; the first impulse has suggested the navy-yards at New York, Norfolk, and League Island as the places where additional docks should be located: would it be wise to carry out this plan without first deciding on their suitability for permanent occupation ?

From what has been shówn of the characteristics of League Island it ought to be evident that a great mistake would be made if this site were selected for further development. The depth of water is deficient on bars in the Delaware between the island and the sea; the soil of the island is mud, varying from twenty to fifty-five feet in depth; the channel is shifting, and the deposits very rapid; it is far from the sea, making ready egress to and ingress from it impossible; ships cannot remain at the quay wall in the winter season; it has no supply of potable water; the atmosphere is charged with malarial influences; its establishment is an interference with private ship-building interests on the Delaware; the cost of its development to a first-class yard would be fabulous, and the time required perfectly

indefinable. It possesses the single advantage of being near a coal and iron region, which, in these days of rapid transit, is one hardly practical in effect.

A new dock at New York will also be a mistake, if the development of the site on the Thames shall be determined on. The dock now in use was built under great difficulties, at great expense; the ground is not well suited, and the permanence of the yard is doubtful.

As to Norfolk, there is no reason to delay a system of steady development at that site. It has natural advantages, and occupies a most important strategic position. Here is a point where the facilities for dockage can be multiplied without fear of misapplication of the public money. This yard should be regarded as permanent; constructions at this place should be considered as built to endure, for as long as the waters of the Chesapeake Bay need protection, the Norfolk yard must be the depot for the naval defence.

Meantime, Long Island Sound, "the Mediterranean of the Western hemisphere," remains undefended, ready to welcome an enemy to a hospitable anchorage, where he can establish his depots, and from which he can sally forth for the destruction of coast trade, and to lay cities under contribution. If we will make use of the means that nature has supplied to our hands, all this can be changed, and with guns at the proper points on shore, and a fleet of coast-defence vessels concentrated at their naval depot on the Thames, the fancied shelter which was held as promise to the ear may be broken to the hope, and wreck and disaster may be the penalty of invasion. We shall be wise if, in the rehabilitation of the navy, we refer all our acts to the standard of national defence, and see to it that in all ways possible we make the one accord with the other.

THE CENTRAL ENGINE OF THE SOLAR SYSTEM.

BY RICHARD A. PROCTOR.

THE visible globe of the sun is 1,250,000 times as large as the earth; within the surface so seen there lies a mass exceeding the earth's 320,000 times; the materials present in the sun's globe are the same as those which form the globe of our earth —at least we know that iron, copper, zinc, sodium, magnesium, calcium, titanium,

and a number of other metallic elements are present; hydrogen is certainly there in enormous quantities, and Dr. Henry Draper proved also that oxygen is present, while no astronomer doubts that those other elements which have not as yet been detected in the sun are really present in his mass.

Now have we any evidence as to the way in which the mighty mass of the sun is disposed within that surface which encloses what we term his volume?—though in reality one can hardly say what his volume is, seeing that there are portions of his mass outside the surface which bounds his *visible* globe. Is the sun's mass uniformly distributed throughout that visible globe, 1,250,000 times as large as our earth? or is it concentrated toward the centre? or, on the other hand, is the denser part near the surface, so that the sun is what Professor Young once suggested, a gigantic bubble?

There are three lines on which we can seek for an answer to these questions.

First, we may ask whether the visible surface behaves as if it were (i.) close to the real globe of the sun, or (ii.) close to an outer shell constituting the greater part of the sun's mass, or (iii.) far away from the real globe. *Secondly,* we may inquire whether the shape of what we call the sun's globe is that which he would have if (i.) of nearly uniform density throughout, (ii.) a mere shell of denser matter enclosing a gaseous interior, or (iii.) a comparatively small globe of considerable density, surrounded to a vast depth by vaporous matter, the outskirts of this vaporous region forming (by condensation into clouds) the sun's apparent surface. *Thirdly,* we may ask whether there is any evidence derived from the solar emission of light and heat, now and in past times, to indicate the arrangement of the matter forming his mass within the globular veil which we call the photosphere.

These questions have been asked and answered. The same answer comes to all three of them. Probably, then, that answer may be trusted.

First, we find that the visible surface of the sun behaves in a manner utterly inconsistent alike with the idea that this surface is near the real surface of an inferior globe, and with the idea that the visible surface is part of a mighty vesicle or bubble. The spot zones are carried around at different rates, according to their distance from the equatorial solar regions. Not to follow Faye and others in niceties of calculation (far from justified by the evidence we have), I may say that the equatorial zone gains about one rotation in seven on the spot zones, or, roughly, some 2,700,000 miles in 200 days—say 13,500 miles per day. Such a velocity as

this, close on ten miles in a minute, could not possibly exist in a cloud-laden region (such as the visible surface of the sun undoubtedly is), and as affecting regions exceeding the whole surface of the earth thousands of times, unless that cloud-laden region were very far away from the real surface of the sun, and therefore from the frictional effects of the true solar rotation. The real mass of the sun, however distributed, can only rotate as *one;* the visible cloud surface has *many* rates of rotation; therefore there must be an enormous distance between the two.

Secondly, calculation has been made by competent mathematicians respecting the amount of polar compression which would arise from the rotation of a globe such as the sun appears to be, at the average rate of rotation indicated by the solar spots. It is found that the polar flattening would be well within the measuring capacity of our best instruments. But if there is one thing certain about the sun, it is that (within such capacity) his apparent globe is not flattened at all. It is absolutely certain, then, that the real globe of the sun lies far within the surface of flowing clouds which we see and measure.

Thirdly, our earth has her story to tell about the sun's interior. We know from the earth's crust that, for periods of time which geologists now estimate by tens of millions of years, the sun's power has been at work on the earth's crust, by rain, wind, and storm, fashioning and refashioning the structure of that crust, now forming layers, anon cutting them up, but throughout leaving clear traces of his handiwork. Croll estimates the duration of this part of the earth's history—that is, of the time during which the earth's crust has been forming under solar action—at fully one hundred millions of years. In other words, our earth tells us of at least one hundred millions of years of sun work, at the sun's present rate of working. It is a matter of no importance whether we suppose that the sun has worked all the time at his present rate, or has sometimes worked with more energy, sometimes with less. It is the quantity of sun work, not the way in which the work has been done, which alone has to be considered. Now all physicists and astronomers are agreed in regarding the sun's emission of heat as due wholly or almost wholly to solar gravitation, resulting in the steady contraction of the sun's mass. To get from the sun of past ages the amount of work which our earth tells us he has actually done, we must suppose him once to have been very much larger than he is now—*how* much larger we cannot say. But suppose him to have been as large as we please, as large as "all outside," if we will, there is yet a limit to the amount of work he *could* have done by contracting to his present size. It is absolutely impossible, if his apparent size is his real size—in other words, if his substance is pretty uniformly distributed through a globe about 840,000 miles in diameter—that he could have done more than twenty millions of years' work at his present rate of emission of light and heat. How are we going to reconcile the apparent contradiction between the earth and the sun? Not assuredly in the wild way suggested by Dr. Croll, who imagines that the excess of work actually done by the sun over that due to contraction to his present size may be accounted for by imagining that his frame was formed by the collision of mighty masses which had been rushing with enormous velocities through space. For it is certain that all the heat generated in that way would have been dissipated long before the solar system, with its present symmetry of shape and uniformity of motion, had begun to be formed. It appears to me that we have no resource but to accept in explanation of the apparent discrepancy the very result to which we have already been led by two distinct lines of reasoning, each, like this third line, demonstrative. The work of solar contraction has gone on much farther than it seems to have done; the sun's mass has been compressed into a globe much smaller than that orb, 840,000 miles in diameter, which we call the sun. Instead of being of small density, as (judging by his size) the sun had seemed to be —barely one-fourth the earth's—the sun's real globe is much denser than the earth's. Tens of thousands of miles separate the surface of the sun's real globe from those resplendent layers of cloud, themselves thousands of miles in depth, which form what we call the solar photosphere.

But this being so, we can have no doubt as to the real origin of all the various forms of solar energy. Our evidence respecting solar energy seems to come from the sun's bright surface; but the real region where all the work is done can be no other than the surface of the sun's hidden globe, far within the bright surface we see. It is within that comparatively small globe that the mighty force of gravity resides, which is the true source of solar light and heat. In that globe there must take place the chief manifestations of solar energy, the most tremendous forms of solar disturbance.

It is remarkable how, so soon as we have thus sought far below the photosphere for the origin of solar activity, the various phenomena presented by the sun seem to find a natural interpretation, and to admit of orderly arrangement as parts of one grand process of mechanism.

Thus, regarding the sun spots (and many do thus regard them) as due to action from without, the downfall of meteor flights, rush of solar cyclones, and so forth, the features of the sun spots seem in no sense explicable. One would say that the photosphere would be irregularly disturbed at first by the action of any such forces as might thus affect it from without, and that if at any time a spot or region of disturbance became regular in shape, it would be after it had existed several days, and the forces at work upon it had time to steady their action. The reverse is actually the case. A spot begins as a circular or nearly circular opening in the photosphere, and only becomes irregular in shape when nearing the end of its existence. Now this regularity of shape in a spot at the very beginning of its career is a feature which deserves more attention than it has usually received. A symmetrical region of disturbance in a cloud-laden envelop implies that there are forces at work all round a centre, expanding their range of action from that centre with a certain uniformity in all directions around it. If now we imagine some kind of eruptive action at the real surface of the sun, and a vaporous mass, necessarily much compressed at that low interior level, to be flung upward toward the cloud-laden envelops which form the photosphere, it is evident that, as it rushes upward, that vaporous mass would rapidly expand as the pressure around it diminished. As it impinged on the inner layers of the cloud envelop it would be already large, and so would make a wide opening there; but when it had passed onward to the outer layers it would be still more expanded, and so would form a larger opening in the outermost cloud layers than in the lower ones. This would explain the fact that in the case of every spot at the beginning of its career the sides of the opening through the cloud envelop (some ten thousand miles in thickness) are shelving, the widest opening being in the outer layers and the narrowest opening in the lowermost layers.

In passing it may be asked whether this explanation of the origin of a spot affords any explanation of the striation of the spot's penumbral region. This striation is a very remarkable feature. When a spot is as yet in the earlier stages of its career, the penumbral fringe of nearly uniform width seems to be marked by a series of radial bright lines. Imagine a saucer the inside of which is colored a light yellowish-brown from the outer rim to the circular bottom, this being dark brown; now suppose that with a paint-brush full of Chinese white you pass round the edge, leaving a series of drops of the white liquid close to each other all round the rim, and that the liquid presently runs down from each drop to the edge of the dark brown floor of the saucer; then the series of parallel white streaks over the sides of the saucer would represent fairly in general character the striations of the penumbra of a sun spot. Your saucer, held at a suitable distance, and tilted in various ways, would give you a fair idea of the appearance of a spot, if the right tints of brown had been used; though it is hardly necessary to say the picture would be but rough and in many respects imperfect.

The question is, How are we to account for these radial striations? Various explanations have been suggested, one of the favorite ones being that the rounded clouds covering the general surface of the sun become elongated in the neighborhood of a spot as they are drawn in toward the centre, and that these striations are simply stretched-out clouds. As the clouds are but two or three hundred miles in diameter, and the striations often several thousand miles in length, this explanation seems fanciful, and, in fact, untenable. If we remember that in a sun spot we get a side view of the solar cloud layers to a depth of from six or seven to nine or ten thousand miles, we shall probably be able to form a better idea of the meaning of the striations. The clouds near the surface have been thrust far away all round the region of disturbance, what-

ever theory we form respecting the origin of the solar spots; the parts of the cloud layer lower down have been thrust away to a less distance; thus we have a side view of a range in depth which had originally extended vertically downward. This side view seems to show that the rounded clouds, where the surface is quiescent, are simply the "capitals" of vertical luminous columns several thousand miles in height, and that we get side views of these luminous columns when they are slanted over by the forces which produce sun-spot disturbance. The case may be compared to that of a corn-field (my English ideas present a field of wheat, which in England we always call "corn," but a field of Indian-corn will do equally well). In such a field the ears are the capitals of vertical stalks when the field is undisturbed. But imagine a small whirlwind to traverse such a field, and that you look down on the corn from the car of a balloon above it; then you would see the slanted stalks looking like a series of radial streaks all round the region of disturbance. It appears to me that the radial striation of a young spot as certainly proves that the solar clouds are the capitals of vertical luminous columns, which become slant luminous columns at a time of disturbance, as the radially situated streaks would prove to our observer in a balloon that corn ears are at the tops of stalks, supposing he had not known this before, or regarding him for the nonce as a visitor from another world, unacquainted with maize and wheat and all the forms of corn we terrestrials have.

But we may here reason also on *a priori* grounds. (It is always safest, despite the names, to take *a priori* reasoning last and *a posteriori* reasoning first.) If the roundish white specks we see all over the sun's surface are really clouds, as they seem to be, and as reasoning assures us they *ought* to be, if that counts for anything, then we may reason respecting them from what we know about our own clouds. Now our rounded summer clouds are the capitals of vertical columns, though these are not luminous or even visible. Ascending streams of aqueous vapor expanding, and therefore cooling, as they rise, condense high in air into the form of visible clouds. Our rain clouds, again, when rain is falling from them, may be regarded as the capitals of vertical streams of falling rain; at least the streams are vertical when the air is undisturbed. Most probably, then, the solar clouds are capitals either of ascending columns of vapor or of descending columns of solar rain, or, far more probably, of *both*. In either case the columns would be luminous, and therefore though they would be hidden below the clouds when the sun's surface is undisturbed, they would be visible when thrust aslant by the disturbing forces, whatever they may be, which produce the great openings we call sun spots. They would also present such an appearance as is actually observed.

When *a priori* and *a posteriori* reasonings about observed appearances thus agree in suggesting and supporting the same theory, it may usually be taken for granted that the theory is sound.

The general explanation of the striations to which we have thus been led seems to correspond with any theory of sun spots which explains the saucer shape of spots in their earlier stages. But a theory which is really reconcilable with the configuration of the streaks actually observed must explain a spot as the origin of central forces. A storm from without, even if it were cyclonic, could not possibly account for the radial disposition of the streaks. In our illustration from a corn-field there is a circumstance which certainly has no analogue in the case of the sun—*the corn-stalks are all held to the ground*. Yet even the corn-stalks would not be truly radial, though thus held at the part nearest the centre of disturbance. Much less could the solar luminous columns, whatever their real nature, be radial under cyclonic action. It is absolutely certain that the force at work in opening out a spot region must at the beginning, when the striation is radial, act from the centre outward. It seems absolutely impossible, moreover, that any force acting from outside the sun can thus operate radially from the centre of the disturbed region. But such a cause as has been suggested above, viz., the expansion of vaporous masses flung from the sun's real surface deep down below the visible surface or photosphere, would inevitably act in just this way. The relatively small and compressed mass of vapor would expand energetically as it rose, and urge the streams of luminous vapor or of metallic rains aslant radially just as the luminous striations are seen actually to lie.

But a volcanic outburst such as we have imagined cannot last forever. At last there would cease to be a supply of compressed vapor from the sun's interior at this particular centre of disturbance. Not only would there cease to be a thrusting away of the solar cloud masses all round the spot region, but the balance of energy would now be the other way. The region of disturbance would no longer be adequately occupied by vaporous matter; it would be a region of rarefaction surrounded by a region of compression. The vaporous, cloud-laden masses around would now begin to make their way back toward the spot region—gradually at first, but more energetically and tumultuously afterward. There would be what the late Father Secchi described as a pell-mell rush toward the centre of the spot. Let us see what might be expected to happen as this rush continued.

In the first place, as the rush would be from the surface regions on a spot formed from below, and as the surface regions necessarily move more rapidly, owing to solar rotation, than the lower regions, the rush might be expected to take place most energetically from east to west, that being the direction of rotation, though cloud masses would break in also from north and south. The eastern side of a spot would be most markedly affected by the in-rush, the northern and southern sides less, the western side least of all. Necessarily, also, the photosphere would be most disturbed outside the eastern part of the spot, and least disturbed outside the western part.

Now this is precisely what we find. The western side of a spot retains its symmetry of form and the neatness of its penumbra long after the eastern side has been thoroughly broken up. Look, for instance, at the fine drawing of a typical spot by Professor Langley which adorns the later editions of my treatise on the sun. Here the western side of the spot is still regular in shape, and the striations there are almost all radial or nearly so. But on the eastern side there is no penumbra at all, but, instead, a flocculent mass of the photosphere has broken its way in, and been flung (by the westwardly hurricanes bearing it onward) right over the central part of the spot. The northern and southern sides of the spot, though much more disturbed than the western, still have penumbral striations, though these are slanted westward far away from the radial direction. Outside the eastern side of the spot the solar photosphere is broken up so remarkably that large openings have been formed around the masses of cloud which are breaking away to follow their forerunners on to the spot's centre. Around these openings streaks or filaments, such as are seen in the penumbra, are brought into view, as we might expect from the way in which the cloud masses are disturbed. Professor Young, whose bubble theory of the sun is quite distinct from, and in fact contrary to, the theory we are now considering, so that his evidence will appear so much the more trustworthy, says of this later stage of a spot's career, "Very often a large spot is followed upon the eastern side by a train of smaller ones, many of which, in such a case, are apt to be very imperfect in structure, sometimes showing no umbra at all, often having a penumbra only upon one side, and usually irregular in form." In fact, they are only openings in the disturbed cloud envelop outside the main spot. "It is noticeable, also, that in such cases, when any considerable change of form or structure shows itself in the principal spot of a group, it" (the spot) "seems to rush forward (westward) upon the solar surface, leaving its attendants trailing behind." It is, in fact, by this westwardly rush of vaporous matter and cloud masses from outside that the "considerable changes of form" attending the dissolution of a spot are brought about.

It is at this stage of a spot's career that the spot seems to break up into parts. So striking is the illusion that many observers seem unable to dispossess themselves of the idea that a spot really is an entity which can be divided into parts, instead of being a vacuity which becomes partially filled. The process is in reality the converse of that carried out by the Irishman who, having to pay so much for the repair of each hole in his coat, turned the holes into one by an extra tear; and it would, in fact, be as absurd to consider Pat's action a partial repair of the coat as it is to describe a sun spot as breaking into parts. Yet we find Wollaston describing a spot as being shivered into fragments (!); and every student of the sun knows how natural it is to speak of a spot as breaking up. Professor Young allows the illusion to carry him even far-

ther. "When a large spot divides into two or more, as often happens," he says, "the parts usually seem to repel each other, and fly asunder with great velocity—velocities of three or four hundred miles an hour are usual, and velocities of one thousand miles, and even more, are by no means exceptional." What, however, is really happening when a spot is thus broken up, and when the parts of a spot seem thus to repel each other? Manifestly a stream of photospheral clouds has sailed in across the spot, or two streams have come in from opposite sides. This explains the apparent breaking up of the spot. And then, as more and more of the cloud-laden outer atmosphere is thus brought in, the dividing streak gets wider and wider, accounting for the apparent recession of the parts of the spot from each other. It affords a grand idea of the tumultuous nature of the pell-mell rush of cloud matter into the spot region that the bridges across the spots should grow in breadth at the rate of several hundred, or even more than a thousand, miles an hour. For the motion of the cloud-laden matter in the direction or directions of in-rush must be very much more rapid than the mere rate at which the stream of clouds increases in breadth. Imagine the tremendous rate at which water would have to flow into a channel that the channel should widen at the rate of even a few yards per minute, and one can conceive the fearful onrush of the cloud masses which could alone produce a widening at the rate of several hundred miles per hour.

It appears, then, that all the changes taking place in a spot, from the time of its first appearance until it is broken up by in-rushes from the cloud-laden atmosphere outside, are such as correspond with the idea that spots are formed by eruptional action from the real surface of the sun deep below the surface we see. But it is essential to inquire whether the searching analysis of the spectroscope confirms this theory.

Now if this theory is sound, the vapors flung up from below drive away the solar cloud masses all around by their expansion. In expanding and in doing this work of driving away the cloud masses, the vapors necessarily lose heat, the thermal equivalent of this mechanical work (to use the pleasing language of the theory of the correlation of forces). Therefore we should expect, first, that whatever luminous matter of solid or liquid nature, as in the clouds, remained in the spot region, would lose lustre, being cooled by the surrounding vapors. Next, the vapors within a spot, being thus cooled, would exercise a powerful absorptive action. But lastly, assuming that in these mighty solar eruptions solid or liquid masses would be ejected with enormous velocity (so as to pass far beyond the ejected vapors), such masses in the rush through the outer vapors of the solar atmosphere would cause such vapors to glow with intense lustre. According to the principles of spectroscopic analysis, then we should expect the following three phenomena to present themselves in the spectrum of a sun spot: First, a darkened general spectrum (compared with the spectrum of the photosphere); secondly, that the dark lines of the ejected vapors would be very much stronger than in the spectrum of the photosphere; and thirdly, that the dark lines due to the vapors outside the photosphere would at times be changed into bright lines. Of course, also, if any vapors present in considerable quantities in the solar atmosphere were not so largely present in the ejected vapors, we might expect the dark lines of such vapors to be less marked or altogether wanting in the spectrum of a spot.

Comparing this with what is actually observed, we find the most marked correspondence. Thus, Professor Young writes as follows respecting sun-spot spectra: "Along its whole length the background is darkened, showing a general absorption. Many of the dark lines of the ordinary spectrum are wholly unmodified in the spectrum of the spot; in fact, this seems the case with the majority of them. Others, however, are much widened and darkened, and some, which are hardly visible at all in the ordinary spectrum, are so strong and black in the penumbra even as to be very conspicuous. Certain other lines, which are strong in the ordinary spectrum, thin out and almost disappear in the spot spectrum, and some are even reversed at times. There are also a number of *bright* lines, not very brilliant, to be sure, but still unmistakable, and there are some dark shadings of peculiar appearance."

But perhaps the strongest evidence we have to show how deep-seated are the forces to which the solar spots are due is to be found in the so-called colored prominences—really vast volumes of glowing gas. These prove beyond all possibility of doubt or question that the sun possesses enormous eruptional energies, and they go so far toward proving that the spots are due to these energies as to leave scarcely any room for doubt, even though their evidence stood alone; combined as it is with what we have learned from the spots themselves, and other circumstances presently to be considered, the evidence of the prominences appears to me absolutely decisive.

The mere existence of masses of glowing gas in the sun's neighborhood proves little. If all the colored flames were like those first noticed, resembling great floating clouds high above the solar surface, we might fairly explain them as due to the uprising of the lighter gases—hydrogen and the as yet undetermined gas *helium*—above the level of the complex vaporous envelop which lies immediately above the photosphere. But it was soon discovered, after the method of observing the prominences without the aid of an eclipse had been invented, that the prominences can be divided into two distinct classes—the cloud-like and the jet-like. The former resemble vast clouds of varied forms; they are often very large, but seldom very lustrous; they are much more frequently seen than the jet prominences, and they appear with almost equal frequency around all parts of the solar disk, the equatorial regions, the spot zones, and the polar regions. It is otherwise with the jet-like prominences. They are never seen except when spots are present on the sun's face, and they are only to be looked for opposite the two spot zones, so that their connection in some way or other with the spots can hardly be doubted. They resemble jets of glowing, ruddy matter, and often attain an enormous visible distance from the surface; they are sometimes exceedingly bright, much brighter than their cloud-like fellows, whence we may infer that their substance is much more intensely heated.

No one who considers any of the more striking examples of these jet-like prominences can doubt that they are really, as they seem, phenomena of eruption. Respighi was once disposed to attribute them to electrical action, but that was when as yet all the peculiarities of these tremendous outbursts had not been recognized. Zöllner long since held that they are akin to terrestrial volcanic outbursts, though not, as I would explain them, to outbursts occurring far below the visible surface of the sun. Professor Young adopted a similar view. "The eruptions which are all the time occurring on the sun's surface," he wrote, "almost compel the supposition that there is a crust of some kind which restrains the imprisoned gases, and through which they force their way with great violence. This crust may consist," he proceeds, "of a more or less continuous sheet of rain—not of water, of course, but of materials whose vapors are shown by means of the spectroscope to exist in the solar atmosphere, and whose condensation and combinations are supposed to furnish the solar heat. As this tremendous rain descends, the velocity of the falling drops would be retarded by the resistance of the denser gases underneath, the drops would coalesce until continuous sheets would be formed, and the sheets would unite and form a sort of bottomless ocean, resting upon the compressed vapors beneath, and pierced by innumerable ascending jets and bubbles.....*In other words, the sun, according to this view*, is a gigantic bubble, whose walls are gradually thickening and its diameter diminishing at a rate determined by its loss of heat; it differs, however, from ordinary bubbles in the fact that its skin is constantly penetrated by blasts and jets from within."

This theory—which has been confounded with the one I have advocated—and Zöllner's are alike inconsistent with the practically demonstrated fact that the mass of the sun, whatever its condition, is gathered in the main near the centre, and is neither, as in Professor Young's theory, near the photosphere, nor, as in Zöllner's, reaches close up to that visible surface. But both theories recognize what must be regarded as undoubtedly demonstrated—the existence of eruptive or rather explosional forces within the sun's interior. When we consider the tremendous velocities indicated by the movements of some of these eruptive prominences we cannot escape the conclusion that they have their origin in regions where the pressures and densities are such as to supply immense powers of repression. For, as I have elsewhere pointed out, the velocity with which matter is ejected in an explosion indicates the extent of the repression which had been exerted on the exploding matter before its

outburst. I apprehend that we have here an additional argument, and one of some force, in favor of the belief that the real origin of the disturbances by which the sun's surface and the region just outside it are disturbed must lie deep down below that visible surface.

It is certain that the ejectional force in some of these eruptions is so enormous that we are almost forced to look for its origin much nearer the sun's centre than either Young's or Zöllner's theory would allow. In the great eruption of September, 1871, the observed rate of advance of the hydrogen streaks averaged more than 200 miles a second, and from a calculation which I made and published at the time, it followed that the matter ejected on that occasion must have crossed the visible surface of the sun at a rate of certainly not less than 400 miles per second—a velocity so great that the ejected matter would never return to the sun, but must be passing away at this moment toward the interstellar depths.

I take it also that the change which takes place in the aspect of the sun's corona as the number of sun spots varies, and the alteration of the physical condition of the corona—in such sort that when there are many spots, its spectrum indicates the presence of glowing hydrogen, whereas, when there are few, the lines of hydrogen are few or wanting—correspond also with the theory that the time of sun spots is a time of great eruptional activity. For the rush of ejected masses through the coronal region would cause the hydrogen present there (not as an atmosphere, but irregularly distributed and moving around the sun) to glow with greater lustre, so as to show the lines of hydrogen in the spectrum of the corona.

It is, at any rate, remarkable that all the facts known to us in regard to the sun spots themselves, to the colored flames, and to the corona, should agree in confirming that which is already all but demonstrated by three strong lines of evidence, that the real working mass of the sun is very much smaller than the globe we measure as his, and that all the phenomena which give so great an interest to the study of the sun are due to tremendous forces at work tens of thousands of miles below the surface which limits our view of his globe, and hides from us the processes by which the life of the solar system is maintained.

Editor's Easy Chair.

AT the Williams College Commencement this summer, Dr. Mark Hopkins, the ex-President of the college, delivered a discourse upon the fiftieth anniversary of his inauguration. It was a discourse of interesting local reminiscence and practical scholarly suggestion, and it was pleasantly prefaced by comments upon the American fondness for celebrating anniversaries. But there could be no better holidays than those which commemorate significant and beneficent historic events. Italy is in continual festival. But the days which the masked balls and the pretty processions and the picturesque pageants celebrate are generally ecclesiastical feasts and saints' days, and the human interest in the older saints is not very warm or vital. But the anniversary of the Plymouth landing, of Penn's treaty, of the Fourth of July, are anniversaries that appeal strongly to patriotism, to the love of liberty, to the historic sense. Congress and the Chamber of Commerce in New York are already contemplating a fitting celebration of the centenary of the Constitution, and Congress also forecasts the observance of the four-hundredth anniversary of the discovery of America.

No great nation is so heterogeneous as the American, and nowhere, therefore, are historic celebrations more valuable and desirable than here. In 1858 Palfrey computed that one-third of the population of the country at that time was sprung from the twenty thousand Englishmen who came to New England in the twenty years from 1620 to 1640. But 1858 was only about the middle of the great epoch of immigration ending this year, the latter part of which has been much the largest. Since 1820 the Irish immigration alone has been more than 3,300,000, and of this number nearly 2,600,000 came between 1840 and 1870. The proportion of heterogeneity is therefore very much larger than when Palfrey wrote. The anniversary celebrations are necessarily instructive. They teach a great multitude of celebrants what the celebration means. On such days throngs of "Americans" learn for the first time something of the history of the country in which they live. In the city of New York the number of persons who see the celebration of the Fourth of July, and who know no more of the day and its meaning than the Yankee knows of St. Ambrose or St. Januarius, is enormous. A worthy son of St. Patrick said that he believed the Fourth of July commemorated the arrival of Irishmen in America. To such patriots the lesson of the day is of the highest importance.

This heterogeneity and the character of American life are shown in the most unexpected way in the anniversary celebrations of the founding of our cities. Springfield and Providence have each recently observed the two hundred-and-fiftieth anniversary of its settlement, and Albany the two-hundredth of its incorporation as a city. But although Albany and Providence are reckoned among the more conservative and homogeneous American communities, it was remarked that in Albany the preparations for the great day were mainly in the hands of new-comers to the city, while in Providence a very considerable part of the civic procession was composed of French Canadians, to whom Roger Williams and the principles and practices of American liberty were virtually unknown. Indeed, the day for the French Canadians was a saint's day, but a very fitting saint for a State in which the Baptists lay especial claim to Roger Williams; for the day of the celebration was Midsummer Day, the feast of St. John the Baptist, and the French societies were all marshalled in societies bearing the saint's name. The original Rhode-Islanders were honoring Roger Williams. The throng of new-comers celebrated St. John the Baptist.

The spectacle strongly emphasized the value of such holidays. At least they awaken curiosity in the minds of the semi-Americans, and plant the seeds of necessary knowledge. Some of them would inevitably, and for Rhode-Islanders very properly, ask who was Roger Williams, the founder of the State in which we live? If, indeed, they could understand the language of the State, they might have learned who he was from the masterly discourse of Chief-Justice Durfee. But they must have been born in Rhode Island, and have been bred in its traditions, fully to comprehend the delight of the great Rhode Island audience as the intolerance and sophistry of Massachusetts Bay were pitilessly scourged and satirized by the imperturbable orator. As the part of the procession that bore a banner with its legend in the French language could not comprehend the discourse, so the church in which it was delivered was to the Canadian but a sectarian meeting-house. But to every born Rhode-Islander no building in the city of Providence is more intimately associated with great days and patriotic occasions. For a midsummer meeting it is incomparable. Standing separate upon an ample green, and open upon every side, it is full of light and air, and orators and audience are both conscious of that vast and invisible presence of departed generations which consecrates an ancient temple of popular assembly.

The cities which, with Walt Whitman, have justly and proudly celebrated themselves this summer, have their individual distinction. The story of each of them is suggestive and inspiring, and in each one it was admirably told. The distance from Narragansett Bay to the Connecticut and from the Connecticut to the Hudson is inconsiderable. But the difference in the annals of the settlements upon the three waters is very striking. The glory of early Providence, however, no city in the world disputes. It is its settlement by the man who first among the builders of great states proclaimed and practised the doctrine of soul liberty. It is, indeed, a principle much more comprehensive than he knew. It is a sun which he saw as a star. But it was a polestar for him, as it has been for American civilization.

The city of Roger Williams has been slow to build him a monument. Mr. Guild, the librarian of Brown University, in his *Footprints of Roger Williams*, says that he has now been dead two hundred and three years. There have been much discussion and reproach and resolution upon the subject of a monument, and a small subscription. There have been votes of the town, and organizations of committees, and appeals to the public, and at the end of two hundred and three years there are three funds amounting to $6695 91. In fifty years, as Mr. Guild computes, they will amount, at six per cent. interest, to $150,000, and then perhaps a monument may be erected. But it must not be supposed from this statement that the memory of Roger Williams is neglected in the city and the State that he founded. America is not a builder of monuments. It is not the way in which American respect and gratitude generally express themselves. The Central Park in New York yet wants statues of the two most famous sons of the city—John Jay and Washington Irving. But Jay and Irving are not forgotten.

The name of Roger Williams appears everywhere in his State, and his character and his wisdom are the conscious pride of every native Rhode-Islander. The most becoming monument or memorial would have been a park composed of the tract immediately around State Rock, where he stepped ashore for a conference with the Indians. There is, indeed, a spacious Roger Williams Park at the opposite end of the city. But the site has no association with the man. A few acres upon the banks of the Seekonk, where the famous Indian greeting, "What cheer?" was spoken, and a statue in the sylvan shade, would have well commemorated the greatest man among the fathers of New England.

THAT the Americans are a good-natured people is always conceded. There is always room in an American omnibus for the thirteenth or fourteenth man, who makes everybody else uncomfortable. The railroad conductor always steps politely over obstructing bundles. The passengers smile upon the spoiled children who transform the peaceful car into a riotous nursery unchecked by the parent. In country communities the willingness of everybody to lend everything is assumed, and "'Tis just as well," and "'Tisn't worth making a fuss about," are characteristic and familiar expressions. It is certainly not to be denied that good-nature is very much better than petulance and a quarrelsome dis-

position, and it is wiser to make the best of everything rather than the worst of everything.

But that is not the whole statement of the case. It is not better to like a poor thing as much as a good thing, nor to think that an old towel stuffed into the place of a broken pane in the window is as good as glass. It is not "just as well" that a boy should be inaccurate in his Latin grammar, or that a girl should be untidy and bold. It is "worth making a fuss about" if the village authorities leave holes in the roads unguarded, and if your neighbors' cows and cocks rouse the whole neighborhood at daybreak. Good-nature is a capital quality, but cowardice is the gift of the wicked fairy, and the disposition to accept superficiality for thoroughness, and botching and shirking for honest work, and laziness for industry, and inaccuracy for precision, is not good-nature, but weakness and lack of courage. Lying of every kind, in word and in work, evasion and shutting your eyes to the fact, do not save trouble. They make trouble. Everything has its price, which, sooner or later, you must pay, and to say that ninety cents is "just as good" as a dollar will not make it so, nor relieve you from payment.

The good-nature in which we have all taken pride as a virtue is now challenged as cowardice. It is denounced as the feeble smile of the boy who does not dare to say no. It is scorned as the mask of indolence. Philosophically, it is thought to be the natural consequence of deference to the majority, so that, according to the philosophers, you may safely assume that in a republic work will be "scamped," and instead of an honest result there will be a result that will "pass muster." Thirty years ago a newly arrived Englishman said that he had not seen an honest table or bureau in "the States." The tables all "teetered" on their legs, and the bureau drawers opened and shut only by jerks, and at a great outlay of bad language. In a land of the majority, says the skeptic, the standard of everything is not the best of the kind, it is merely whatever will do. The majority, he argues, are ignorant, and as their approval is the object, it is not necessary to cultivate wisdom.

This mischief extends to public life, and the man who is politically ambitious does not ask, what ought I to do? what does the public welfare, in my opinion, require? but what does the majority wish, or think that it wishes, to have done? His aim, therefore, is to guess the will of the majority, instead of following his own conviction, which is the only guide that he can really understand or follow with self-respect. One fatal but inevitable result of this situation is that he constantly substitutes an unknown for a known quantity, and conforms his action, not to what he thinks and knows, but to what he supposes that he knows. Public men are constantly saying that public opinion will not sustain this measure or that policy, and that you must not outstrip the public. That means merely that they suppose the public to hold a certain opinion, and it is the inevitable consequence of this condition of mind that it believes the opinion to be more ignorant and degraded than it is, so that such a standard of action is politically low and mean.

Courageous confidence in the intelligence of the community, instead of contempt for its ignorance, is the sign of a true leadership and success. To get place is not a proof of eminence, or of the success that attends real ability. Few statesmen who have appealed to the higher sentiment of a country have been ultimately disappointed. Sam Adams in our early Revolutionary contest, Seward and Sumner in a later day, Cobden and Bright and Sir Robert Peel in the corn-law debate, were really leaders because they were the foremost representatives of a great and general tendency of opinion. They did not lag behind, and wait upon the probable ignorance of the majority. They assumed its intelligence and its ready comprehension of truth and argument.

Indeed, in a land ruled by the majority, progress would be impossible if every man should conform his speech and action to the supposed present opinion of the majority. Content does not wish for change. Progress begins with the minority. It is completed by persuading the majority, by showing the reason and the advantage of the step forward, and that is accomplished by appealing to the intelligence of the majority. It is a fine definition of the poet that he sings what everybody thinks and feels, but did not know it until he heard the song. That also is leadership. It is showing the way so clearly that every man sees that it is the very way for which he was looking. Men are better than they are believed to be by those who make the supposed will of the majority their rule of action.

A man who had some popularity as a public lecturer, but who aimed to make people laugh rather than to make them think, and whose popularity therefore was that of a clown rather than of a teacher, advised a younger orator when he rose to speak to reassure himself with the thought that nobody in the audience could do as well as he. But the younger orator, if his self-respect had not admonished him differently, would have been warned by the fate of his Mentor. For people laughed at him, not with him, until he disappeared from the platform. The younger orator felt instinctively that the secret of success in any work for which you prepare yourself is always to do your best. And the rule is sound, because experience shows that the majority, the multitude, will respond accordingly.

But that response must be the incident or consequence, not the object. The fact serves to cheer the self-reliance of the individual, but he should cultivate that self-reliance even if the fact were otherwise. It is not the slave of the majority, but the leader of them, whom the majority respect, and no man is their leader who tries constantly to propitiate their most sweet voices. Such an endeavor is the danger of public men and the corruption of public action. How often we read the speech of an intelligent Senator, and before we have advanced far we perceive that he is not speaking as a man, but as a partisan. He is saying what he believes the multitude of his party probably think, and his object is to commend himself to that multitude, not to tell the truth. It was therefore pleasant to read the words of a Senator during a debate this summer: "The people expect to hold their legislators to their constitutional functions and sworn constitutional duty of doing what they shall themselves believe is best for the public interest. There is but one method by which the Senator or the Representative is to ascertain the sentiment of the people, and that is by finding out what is right. The mistakes and the misfortunes of the public men of this country have arisen, not from a disregard of public sentiment, but from a disregard of their own sense of right in the endeavor to please a temporary popular demand, and a loss of public confidence in so doing. The man who loses the habit of seeking for what is right loses with it the capacity to form a correct judgment of the true opinion of the American people."

But the more usual strain is that of another Senator, who in a college address advised young men, not that they should seek first of all good government and honest governors, but attach themselves to a multitude or party, and when the party went wrong, to go with it, trying to persuade it to go right. It was advice natural to a public man who had not learned the primary truth of great statesmanship:

"He is free who dares to be
In the right with two or three."

How different was it from the counsel of a great scholar and one of the noblest of men, who spoke fifty years ago at Dartmouth College to young men who are now old! "When you shall say, As others do, so must I; I renounce, I am sorry for it, the dreams of my youth; I must eat the fat of the land, and let learning and romantic expectation go till a more convenient season—then dies the man in you, then perish the buds of art and poetry and science, as they have died already in a thousand, thousand men." Just in the degree that this lofty admonition has been the rule of their lives have those young men grown old nobly. Just in the degree that the other advice is followed will the lives of young men morally dwindle and shrivel.

It is a fatal cowardice which asks, not what is right, but what says the majority. It is asserting in grave and public affairs the sovereignty which is known in the private circle as Mrs. Grundy. But if that potentate is despicable in the drawing-room, how much more so is she in the Capitol and in public life!

When Columbia College makes a Wellesley Bachelor of the gentler sex a Doctor, and Yale signalizes her new departure as a university by making a maiden a Bachelor, it is useless to call the college the last refuge of conservatism. Yale, indeed, shuddered at her own act, which a true sense of honor extorted from her, and, shuddering, she whispered that her courses of instruction are open only to the male sex—meaning, we presume, men. But much must be pardoned to sudden alarm. Brown, however, meanwhile, proposes that, under certain conditions, women shall share her instruction. The phrase "last refuge of conservatism" implies a conservatism hopeless and obdurate. But a conservatism which yields graciously to the softening touch of wise progress, like a slope of evergreens to the south wind, is not an obstacle to progress, but an auxiliary. None the less, however, the spectacle of the mediæval cap and scholar's gown in which the willing President of Columbia sat repeating the Latin form of presentation, and of the young woman who stood before him to receive the diploma, was a happy blending of the old and the new.

The elder sons of Columbia, chiefs among the great Revolutionary leaders, might have gazed amazed at this later revolution, and have bethought themselves of certain Scriptural texts and familiar theories of the "place" and "sphere" of women. But had they been actually present upon the platform, and observed the composed grace and maidenly reserve of the young candidate for the degree, and, above all, if they had known how amply fitted was that bonneted Bachelor for the Doctorate, they would all of them, Clinton and Livingston, Jay and Morris, Hamilton and Van Cortland, Benson and Rutgers, have risen with the senior and beloved Professor Drisler in his academic robe, and have hastened with him, amid thunders of applause and the staccato cheer C-o-l-u-m-b-i-a, to aid the overladen Doctor to bear away her heaped tributes of flowers.

The incident was a sign of that gradual advance and amelioration of opinion which constitutes the progress of civilization. The test of civilization is the estimate of woman. Among savages she is a slave. In the dark ages of Christendom she is a toy and a sentimental goddess. With increasing moral light, and larger liberty, and more universal justice, she begins to develop as an equal human being. The last century has witnessed the repeal of laws that restrained her development and denied to her fair play. Like snow and ice before the increasing sun of spring, prejudice and ignorance and consequent injustice have melted in the glow of a truer view of human society. The same wisdom which in England has modified penal laws, and emancipated Catholics and Jews, and enlarged the suffrage, and repealed the corn-laws, has also emancipated women, not only from unequal laws, but from the unjust views out of which the laws sprang.

In nothing more than in the general view of the education of women has this advance been shown. A century ago the standard of "female education" was ludicrous. Within the century Sydney Smith tells us how absurd it was. But the simple and obvious law of liberty has rapidly raised the standard to its natural height. It is now seen that the sphere of men and women is not determined by an arbitrary edict or an ignorant assumption of the other sex, but as all spheres are determined, namely, by natural development. Before we can assert that nature intends that women shall do this and be that, we must stop insisting that our theory of nature shall be accepted as the will of nature, and permit nature to speak for herself.

There need be no fear that the richest resources for the study of music will tempt a boy who has no ear for time or tune to devote himself to the study of the science of harmony, nor will a blind man pursue painting as his profession. A man who has no taste for philosophical study, and no means to gratify it if he had the taste, will not betake himself to the pursuit of philosophy merely because the opportunity of study is offered to him. Still less do men desert the mechanical trades and manual labor and the professions simply because they may, if they will, in order to undertake the work for which women are naturally more adapted. Nor will women leave their congenial pursuits merely because of the conceded liberty of choice.

Opening to women every opportunity of instruction will not change the nature of woman, as it does not change the nature of man. It will only enable her, as it enables him, to become more truly that which she is made to be, and to do more efficiently what she is made to do. The Doctorate conferred by Columbia upon that gentle Bachelor was only a certificate of devoted study and of the ability to pass successfully a severe examination. It was not an act of gallantry, but of justice. Columbia College testified that the young woman had acquired a certain degree of knowledge, let us say, of astronomy. If a young woman has proved it to the satisfaction of Columbia, why should Columbia refuse to attest it to the world, any more than she would refuse to attest the same proficiency in the case of a young man? It is the knowledge, not the age, or color, or sex, or nativity, or previous condition, of the proficient which the diploma certifies. Nor will Columbia refuse to teach any applicant who shows the required qualifications for a pupil. She reserves to herself, as Oxford and Cambridge and Harvard and Yale and Cornell and Brown reserve to themselves, the decision in what way, whether in association with young men or not, she will impart her instruction.

Even the most absolute of Tories, good old Sir Roger de Coverley himself, need not fear that the young daughter of his house will now desert all other avocations which please her genius and her taste and immerse herself in mathematics in order to win a Doctorate of Philosophy or to proceed Bachelor of Laws. The world to-day is a richer and a riper world than that of the troubadour and the crusader. There was no dream then of learned women, although learned women there had been. Women did not stray beyond the pale of what seems to some dreamers of to-day to be their "natural sphere." Behold, a little later, the women of the English plays and of the English and French novels. Surely they are not dreadful Doctors of Science nor unsexed Bachelors of Art. They are, in fact, the women who are always the ideal women in the minds of those who exclaim with caustic sarcasm, as they contemplate the modern woman, A Doctor? a Bachelor?

But do any of us believe that women, so far as they are now—to use the word that puts men to flight — emancipated, are less lovely and feminine than the women of the troubadours, of the knights of Cœur de Lion, or of the cavalieri serventi? In any time or in any country were there ever women who could be more truly described in Shelley's phrase as Shakespeare's women, so feminine and fair are they, than those who may to-day compete for the Doctorate or receive the diploma of the Bachelor? Has the opportunity of larger knowledge, of more various employment, of legal equality, tended to degrade in any least degree all that is finest and rarest and most poetic and enchanting in womanly nature or womanly manner?

No, no, Sir Roger, it is not that the young woman who knows more of astronomy and Greek than you and I is less womanly than Juliet, or the "dear dead women" who danced to Galuppi's toccata, but that the old barbarian still survives in us, and tries to imprison them in what we choose to call their sphere, instead of leaving them to the same freedom of choice that we demand for ourselves, and so enabling them to be what Providence designed them to be.

————

THERE are still villages among the hills in New England—we cannot call them remote hills, because the locomotive darts up every valley and fills the woods upon the highest hillside with the shrill, eager cry of hurrying life and bustling human society, but even where the steam scream is heard softened and far away—there are yet villages nestling in the hills in which also the old New England Sabbath lingers and nestles. The village street, broad and arched with thick-foliaged sugar-maples, is always still. In the warm silence of a summer noon, as you sit reading upon the piazza or in the shade of a tree, the only moving object in the street is a load of hay slowly passing under the maples, drawn by oxen, or a group of loiterers in front of the village store pitching quoits. The creak of the wagon, the ring of the quoits, or the laugh and exclamation of the players are the only sounds, except, indeed, the musical clangor of the blacksmith's anvil as his quick hammer moulds the sparkling horseshoe or beats out the bar.

These are drowsy summer sounds that only emphasize the stillness of the week-day. But the stillness of Sunday is startling. A faint tinkle of cows in the early morning filing to the pasture, and the warning shout of the barefooted boy who drives them, are the only sounds that break the Sabbath silence, except, again, the chirp and song of birds in the trees, which are no respecters of days, and which sing as blithely, even in the deacon's maples, on "Sabbath morning," as in the tavern ash on the Fourth of July. The cows pass, and all is still. The street is deserted, save at intervals a solitary figure upon some small errand. The sun lies hot upon the pastures and hillsides. There is no mail on Sunday, no newspaper, no barber to visit. Now and then men in their daily dress are seen at the barn door or in the shed or yard doing their chores. They are bringing wood, milking, feeding the cattle. But all is spectral. There is no sound. Even the wind in summer fears to be a Sabbath-breaker. It is an enchanted realm. Have the blue-laws such vitality? Are we still held by that grim spell?

It is nine o'clock, and the meeting-house bell, with a bold voice of authority, as if it had the sole right to disturb the silence and to speak out, warns the village and the outlying farms that it is the Sabbath, and everybody must prepare to come to meeting; and little children hear the bell with awe as if it were a living voice, and sacred as a part of the Sabbath, and to be heeded under unknown penalties. Obey thy father and mother; thou shalt not lie; thou shalt not steal; thou shalt go to meeting—seem to them all commandments of the first table. The sound of the bell lingers in their ears and hearts as a Thus saith the Lord. And lo! at the second bell, the men, who have changed the daily dress and put on their Sabbath clothes, issue from the houses on the village street with their wives and children, and through the street, closely following each other, and pounding along in a cloud of dust, comes the long line of wagons from the farms. The sun beats down remorselessly, and the man in heavy woollens, such as he wears in the sleigh in January, sits between two women in their Sabbath garments, and the horses trot with a Sabbath jog, and all turn up to the stone platform by the meeting-house, upon which the women alight, and the man drives the horse under the shed, and then chats soberly with the others at the door.

But the minister passes in, not clad in gown and bands and cocked hat as in the older day, but in plain black clothes. The chatting loiterers follow him in. The bell which has gathered the village into the sacred fold rests from its labors. There is no one in the street. There is no sound. But after a few moments the music of "Old Hundred" pours out of the open doors and windows of the meeting-house, sung by a well-balanced and well-trained choir.

It is the opening hymn, and it has a full, vigorous, triumphant sound. Once more Thus saith the Lord. There is another interval of silence, but at a little distance you can hear the voice of reading and prayer. Hark! another hymn. It is "Federal Street," or "Coronation," or "Dundee," but whatever it is, it is a strain from other years; and voices and faces and scenes and days that are no more all blend in the familiar music, and a Sabbath benediction rests upon the listener's soul.

A longer silence follows, broken by fragmentary sounds of energetic speech. Is the preacher emphasizing and elucidating the five points? Is he denouncing and alarming that tough regiment in woollen, or winning the wandering and doubting mind? Is his sermon an official and perfunctory discourse by which the little children are soothed to sleep, and in which the elders like unqualified damnation and the hottest fire, as a toper likes "power" in his dram? Or is his pure and manly life and conversation his true preaching, and the Sabbath sermon only a statement of the principles of such holy living, and a revival of the colors in the immortal portrait of the holy life of the Gospel?

Before we can answer there is a burst of singing, then two strokes of the bell to announce that "meeting is out," then an issue of the congregation, a procession homeward, a driving away of wagons, and soon, once more, the silent, solitary street. In the afternoon there is the Sabbath-school, and the good pastor preaches at one of the school-houses in the farther parts of the town. But it is always the Sabbath, in every sight and sound, until the sun has set, and then from the neighboring house upon the hill above the village street comes a clear, resonant soprano voice singing hymns and prolonging the solemn spell of the holy day. The tithing-men are gone, and the deacons do not sit severe and conspicuous in the meeting-house, and the minister has not the air of a lord spiritual of the village, and the genius of modern times and the spirit of the age are entertained with full consciousness of what they are. But it is still the sober and restrained and decorous New England Sabbath which recurs every seventh day, and the honest, industrious, intelligent, self-respecting, plain-living village recalls remotely the day of the severer dispensation, and illustrates the noble manhood that the severe dispensation fostered.

SOME months ago when we said that Mr. Parnell was not merely a political leader, but one of the most marked personages of the time, it did not seem that his plan of home rule would be so soon submitted to the vote of the English people. But even the most tranquil of Easy Chairs has been rocked a little by the universal storm of political excitement in Great Britain. Since the days of Waterloo there has been nothing comparable to it. The reform bill of '32, and the agitation for the repeal of the corn-laws a dozen years later, stirred the kingdom greatly. But they were local storms, and the infrequency of communication even then with the rest of the world limited the area of immediate and active interest. Waterloo, indeed, interested Christendom, and Byron expressed the general feeling in his famous lines:

> "The desolator desolate,
> The victor overthrown,
> The arbiter of others' fate
> A suppliant for his own."

Bonaparte seemed to every country an incubus upon civilization, a kind of moral glacier gradually overspreading the green world. It was a relief to know that at last it was melted.

The excitement of the spring and summer has been very different, but in England, at least, not less general and intense. When John Bright publicly speaks of his political and personal estrangement from his old friend the Liberal leader, whom he says he has not followed, but by whose side he has gladly marched, and when Mr. Gladstone in a public letter reproaches John Bright not only with abandoning the principles of his life, but with deliberate misrepresentation, the incident is more pathetic than the separation of Burke and Fox, as the question is much more momentous.

Throughout the great controversy the one conspicuous fact more striking than any other has been the personality of Gladstone. The only individual ascendency in modern English history with which it is comparable is that of Chatham in the middle of the last century, when his lofty will and high intelligence and dauntless persistence restored the glory of the English military name, and girdled the globe with British victories. Mr. Gladstone's answer to the accusation of his old Liberal associates who opposed him, and which was reiterated in every form, that he sprang the Irish issue suddenly upon Parliament and the country, seemed to be complete. The Liberal dissenters declared that the question was not presented at the election last autumn, and that Mr. Gladstone by introducing his measure had broken with his party, and was himself the dissenter, while Mr. Bright and Lord Hartington and Mr. Chamberlain had been the orthodox Liberals.

But Mr. Gladstone replied promptly that on the 9th of last November he had stated emphatically to his constituents at Edinburgh that if the Irish elections went as he expected, and as they did go, the magnitude of the subject they would bring forward would throw all others in the shade, and that it went down to the very roots and foundations of our whole civil and political constitution. This was certainly plain, and no statement could have been more decisive and emphatic. Moreover, that, if successful, he would necessarily introduce some comprehensive Irish scheme was obvious and well known, and it is not a fair objection that its extent and scope were indefinite and unanticipated. But his ascendency was shown by the evidently sincere feeling of the great body of the Liberals that Liberalism is what Mr. Gladstone says, and the true Liberal policy what he demands. It is a loyalty which acknowledges him as the party. *L'état c'est moi.*

That this individual ascendency asserts its supremacy at the age of seventy-six, and asserts it not only by the accumulated wisdom of more than half a century of official public life, but with a general accomplishment in every branch of knowledge, and with a power and art of oratory unsurpassed among English-speaking men, is one of the most interesting and commanding facts of the situation. The hold which he still has even upon some of the most active leaders of the Liberal opposition has been one of the striking evidences of the masterful nature of the man. This has been shown especially in the tone of Lord Hartington's speeches. The secession of Lord Hartington was the most significant and injurious blow to the Gladstone policy. It was the departure of the Whigs, with all their immense influence and wealth, from the Liberal camp. But although for months constantly speaking upon the subject in Parliament and throughout England, Lord Hartington never mentioned Mr. Gladstone but with tender and reverent respect, and even after the voting had begun, in the last speech of the canvass, he said, "We respect the sincerity of Mr. Gladstone's dreams, but we cannot dream with him."

On the other hand, the Tory vituperation, and even some Liberal invective, have surpassed any electoral blackguardism in this country. There are, indeed, certain newspapers which become mere sluices of lies and scandal in our campaigns. But American candidates and the better kind of speakers maintain a courteous personal tone, unless, as sometimes, but happily seldom, happens, the personal record is of such a kind that even truth-telling seems to be abuse and aspersion. The most amusing of the flings at Mr. Gladstone was the assertion that he had entered upon the Irish agitation as a last desperate course to retain office a little longer. This theory supposed that he feared the Irish Parliamentary vote would ally itself with the Tory vote upon an Irish policy and so turn him out. But it appeared, on the one hand, that Mr. Gladstone had told Lord Salisbury that he would support him in a wise Irish policy, while on the other, Lord Salisbury stoutly denied that the Tories would have tolerated the thought of any concession to home rule. This effectually disposed of the theory.

Another striking inconsistency in the opposition to Mr. Gladstone was the assertion that there was no Irish grievance, and that the whole trouble was due to the agitation of Mr. Parnell and his friends for their own purposes of separation. But when Mr. Parnell pledged himself and his friends to satisfaction with the Gladstone settlement, the same objectors retorted that he was but a chip upon the torrent of Irish hatred, which would sweep him aside and push on for independence. Of course this was the admission that there was a general sense of grievance and wrong, and that Mr. Parnell, instead of fomenting agitation for his own ends, was simply the voice of a national feeling.

Discussion of the merits of the question lies beyond the domain of the Easy Chair, which merely notes the fact of the general excitement and of the vast importance of the issue. Whether, as Mr. Gladstone asserted, his policy would close forever the most prolonged, bitter, disturbing, and shameful of British controversies, or, as his opponents declared, it would end in the dissolution of the British Empire, it is certainly the greatest British question of our time, and its central and towering figure has been one of the greatest in the long line of great British statesmen.

Editor's Study.

I.

THE readers of Tourguéneff and of Tolstoï must now add Dostoïevsky to their list if they wish to understand the reasons for the supremacy of the Russians in modern fiction; and we think they must put him beside these two, and not below either, in moral and artistic qualities. They are all so very much more than realists that this name, never satisfactory in regard to any school of writers, seems altogether insufficient for them. They are realists in ascertaining an entire probability of motive and situation in their work; but with them this is only the beginning; they go so far beyond it in purpose and effect that one must cast about for some other word if one would try to define them. Perhaps humanist would be the best phrase in which to clothe the idea of their literary office, if it could be limited to mean their simply, almost humbly, fraternal attitude toward the persons and conditions with which they deal, and again extended to include a profound sense of that individual responsibility from which the common responsibility can free no one. The phrase does not express that artistry which one feels in them, and it can only group them loosely in a single characteristic; but it certainly hints at what one feels most of all in the latest known of these great masters. At the same time, if it suggests anything of sentimentality, it is wholly and mischievously false. For instance, in *Le Crime et le Châtiment*, which we have just been reading, and which, besides *Les Humiliés et Offensés*, is the only book of Dostoïevsky's yet given in French, the author studies the effect of murder in the assassin, who is brought to confession and repentance by a hapless creature whom poverty has forced to a life of shame. Yet there is nothing of the maudlin glamour of heroism thrown about this pair; Raskolnikoff is the only man who has not been merely brutal to Sonia, and she divines his misery through her gratitude; this done, her one thought, her only hope, is not to help him hide his crime, but to help him own it to the law and to expiate it. She sees that there is no escape for him but this, and her inspiration is not superior to her; it is not from her mind, but from her soul, primitively good and incorrupt, amidst the hideous facts of her life, which, by-the-way, are in nowise brought forward or exploited in the story. Raskolnikoff is not her lover; he becomes so only when his expiation has begun; and the reader is scarcely allowed to see beyond the first breaking down of his egotistic self-justification in the Siberian prison. He has done the murder for which he suffers upon a theory, if not a principle: the theory that the greatest heroes and even benefactors of the race have not hesitated at crime when it would advance their extraordinary purposes or promote their development. He is a student, forced to quit the university by his poverty, and he reasons that it is better he should complete his career, destined, as he feels, to be useful and splendid, than that a certain old woman who keeps a pawnbroker's shop should continue to live and to prey upon the necessities of others. He asks himself which of the extraordinary men who have set the world forward would have stopped at putting her out of his way if he had found it to his advantage, and he kills her and robs her; he kills her half-witted sister too, the harmless thing that comes in upon him and his first victim through the door he has forgotten to lock. His punishment begins with this deed, which he had never counted upon, for the wickedness of the old usuress was largely his defence for taking her off; but it cannot properly be said that Raskolnikoff feels regret or even remorse for his crime until he has confessed it. Till then his terrible secret, which all the accidents and endeavors of the world seem conspiring to tear from him, forms his torment, and almost this alone. His repentance and his redemption begin with his penalty. The truth is a very old one, but what makes this book so wonderful is the power with which it is set forth. The story is not merely an accumulation of incident upon incident, a collection of significant anecdotes, as it might be in the hands of an inferior artist, but a mounting drama, to the catastrophe of which all the facts and characters tend, not mechanically or intentionally, but in the natural and providential way; it is only in the latter half of the story that you suspect a temptation in the author to intensify and to operate. At moments the stress of the story is almost intolerable; the misery of Raskolnikoff is such that you suffer all Sonia's despair when he comes back from the police office without having confessed, and you scarcely breathe till he makes the second attempt and succeeds.

The arrival of his mother and sister in the midst of his wretchedness, to be the loving and trusting witnesses of suffering of which they cannot understand the cause, is merely one of the episodes of the book which penetrate the soul by their reality, by their unsparing yet compassionate truth. But the impressive scenes abound so that it is hard to name one without having seemed to leave a finer one unmentioned. Perhaps there is nothing of higher and nobler strain than that series of passages in which the Judge of Instruction, softened and humanized by the familiarity with crime which hardens so many, tries to bring Raskolnikoff to confess for his own sake the murder which the Judge is sure he committed. Other passages are of a pathos intense beyond anything else that we can remember in fiction, and chief among them, perhaps, are those in which Sonia's stepmother goes mad after her drunken husband's death, and leads her little children, fantastically tricked out in tattered finery, through the street to sing and dance. She is herself dying of consumption; terrible fits of coughing interrupt her ravings, and the weird escapade is the precursor of her death; she ceases to live the same night. Between her and her step-daughter, whom her wild appeal drove to ruin that the others might not starve, there exists an affection which no sense of wrong done and wrong suffered can weaken; their love for each other is a consolation when they have no friend or helper but the impenitent assassin who wreaks upon them the desire to do good, to help some one, which is one of the most subtly divined traits of a soul at war with itself.

It is a lurid chapter of human life certainly, but the light of truth is in it; and in the ghastliest picture which it presents there is the hope, the relief, that human sympathy gives, and everywhere there is recognition of the fact that behind the supreme law is the supreme love, and only there. It is therefore by no means a desperate book, nor a wholly depressing book. It not only clearly indicates the consequences of sin, but it attempts to define their bounds, the limits at which they seem to cease. Raskolnikoff suffers, but we reach the point at which he begins not to suffer. He makes others suffer, but we see where the suffering which his guilt inflicts must naturally end. It leaves him at the outset of a new life, the life of a man who has submitted to punishment, and has thereby won the privilege to repent. It is the reverse of a pessimistic book.

II.

The reader of such a story will hardly be satisfied without knowing something of the author, and in an article of the *Revue des Deux Mondes* for January 15, 1885, M. Eugène-Melchoir de Vogüé will tell him the hardly less tragical story of Dostoïevsky's own life. It seems that he was born at Moscow, in a charity hospital, in 1821, and to the day of his death he struggled with poverty, injustice, and disease. His first book, *Poor People*, which won him reputation and the hope of better things, was followed within a few years by his arrest for Socialism. He was not really concerned in Socialism, except through his friendship for some of the Socialists, but he was imprisoned with them, and after eight months of solitude in the casemate of a fortress—solitude unrelieved by the sight of a friendly human face, or a book, or a pen—he was led out to receive his sentence. All the prisoners had been condemned to death; the muskets were loaded in their presence, and levelled at their breasts; then the muzzles were struck up, and the Czar's commutation of their sentence was read. They were sent to Siberia, where Dostoïevsky spent six years at hard labor. There he made his studies among the prisoners for his book *The Humiliated and the Wronged*, which the French have now translated with *The Crime and the Punishment*. At the end of this time he returned to St. Petersburg, famous, beloved, adored, to continue his struggle with poverty and disease. The struggle was long, for he died only five years ago, when his body was followed to the grave by such a mighty concourse of all manner of people as never assembled at the funeral of any author before: "Priests chanting prayers; the students of the universities; the children of the schools; the young girl medical students; the Nihilists, distinguishable by their eccentricities of costume and bearing—the men with their shawls, and the women with their spectacles and close-clipped hair; all the literary and scientific societies; deputations from all parts of the empire—old Muscovite merchants, peasants, servants, beggars; in the church waited the official dignitaries, the Minister of Public Instruction, and the young princes of the imperial family. A forest of banners, of crosses, and of crowns waved over this army in its march; and while these different fragments of Russia passed, you could distinguish the gentle and sinister faces, tears, prayers, sneers, and silences, tranquil or ferocious.... What passed was the spectacle of this man's own work, formidable and disquieting, with its weakness and its grandeur; in the first rank, without doubt, and the most numerous, his favorite clients, the *Poor People, The Humiliated and the Wronged*, even *The Bedeviled*"—these are all titles of his books—"wretched beings happy to have their day, and to bear their defender on the path of glory, but with them and enveloping them

all that uncertainty and confusion of the national life such as he has painted it, all the vague hopes that he had roused in all. As the czars of old were said to gather together the Russian earth, this royal spirit had assembled the Russian soul."

III.

M. Vogüé writes with perhaps too breathless a fervor, but his article is valuable for the light it casts upon the origins of Dostoïevsky's work, and its inspirations and motives. It was the natural expression of such a life and such conditions. But it is useful to observe that while *The Crime and the Punishment* may be read with the deepest sympathy and interest, and may enforce with unique power the lessons which it teaches, it is to be praised only in its place, and its message is to be received with allowances by readers exterior to the social and political circumstances in which it was conceived. It used to be one of the disadvantages of the practice of romance in America, which Hawthorne more or less whimsically lamented, that there were so few shadows and inequalities in our broad level of prosperity; and it is one of the reflections suggested by Dostoïevsky's book that whoever struck a note so profoundly tragic in American fiction would do a false and mistaken thing—as false and as mistaken in its way as dealing in American fiction with certain nudities which the Latin peoples seem to find edifying. Whatever their deserts, very few American novelists have been led out to be shot, or finally exiled to the rigors of a winter at Duluth; one might make Herr Most the hero of a labor-question romance with perfect impunity; and in a land where journeymen carpenters and plumbers strike for four dollars a day the sum of hunger and cold is certainly very small, and the wrong from class to class is almost inappreciable. We invite our novelists, therefore, to concern themselves with the more smiling aspects of life, which are the more American, and to seek the universal in the individual rather than the social interests. It is worth while, even at the risk of being called commonplace, to be true to our well-to-do actualities; the very passions themselves seem to be softened and modified by conditions which cannot be said to wrong any one, to cramp endeavor, or to cross lawful desire. Sin and suffering and shame there must always be in the world, we suppose, but we believe that in this new world of ours it is mainly from one to another one, and oftener still from one to one's self. We have death too in America, and a great deal of disagreeable and painful disease, which the multiplicity of our patent medicines does not seem to cure; but this is tragedy that comes in the very nature of things, and is not peculiarly American, as the large, cheerful average of health and success and happy life is. It will not do to boast, but it is well to be true to the facts, and to see that, apart from these purely mortal troubles, the race here enjoys conditions in which most of the ills that have darkened its annals may be averted by honest work and unselfish behavior.

It is only now and then, when some dark shadow of our shameful past appears, that we can believe there ever was a tragic element in our prosperity. Even then, when we read such an artlessly impressive sketch as Mrs. Sarah Bradford writes of Harriet Tubman—once famous as the Moses of her people—the self-freed bondwoman who led three hundred of her brethren out of slavery, and with a price set upon her head, risked her life and liberty nineteen times in this cause; even then it affects us like a tale

"Of old, unhappy, far-off things,
And battles long ago,"

and nothing within the date of actual history. We cannot realize that most of the men and women now living were once commanded by the law of the land to turn and hunt such fugitives back into slavery, and to deliver such an outlaw as Harriet over to her owner; that those who abetted such outlaws were sometimes mulcted to the last dollar of their substance in fines. We can hardly imagine such things now for the purposes of fiction; all troubles that now hurt and threaten us are as crumpled rose leaves in our couch. But we may nevertheless read Dostoïevsky, and especially our novelists may read him, to advantage, for in spite of his terrible picture of a soul's agony he is hopeful and wholesome, and teaches in every page patience, merciful judgment, humble helpfulness, and that brotherly responsibility, that duty of man to man, from which not even the Americans are emancipated.

IV.

There are some very interesting passages concerning this obligation in Vernon Lee's last book, *Baldwin*, where she speaks through several dialogic personages about novels, and claims for them an influence in deepening and refining human feeling which we suppose no one can successfully deny. "They have, by playing upon our emotions, immensely increased the sensitiveness, the richness of this living key-board, even as a singing-master, by playing on his pupil's throat, increases the number of the musical intervals which he can intone.... Believing as I do in the power of directing human feeling into certain channels rather than certain others, believing especially in the power of reiteration of emotion in constituting our emotional selves, in digging by a constant drop, drop, such moral channels as have been already traced, I must necessarily also believe that the modern human being has been largely fashioned in all his more delicate peculiarities by those who have written about him, and most of all, therefore, by the novelist. I believe that were the majority of us educated and sensitive men and women able to analyze what we call our almost in-

born, nay, automatic, views of life, character, and feeling, able to scientifically assign its origin to each and trace its modifications—I believe that were this possible, we should find that a good third of what we take to be instinctive knowledge, or knowledge vaguely acquired from personal experience, is really obtained from the novels which we or our friends have read."

There are a great many just and true things in this talk about novels, as there are in the other papers which discuss such topics as the responsibilities of unbelief and the consolations of belief, vivisection, the value of the ideal, and doubts and pessimism; and we think there is sense, if not final wisdom, in this conclusion: "To make the shrewd and tolerant a little less shrewd and tolerant, to make the generous and austere a little more skeptical and easy-going, this seems to me pretty well the chief problem of life, and also the chief use of the novel."

V.

It is an interesting proof of the intimate hold which fiction has taken upon life that when we wish to praise a true story we say that it reads like a novel. By this we do not at all mean always that it is very exciting or very romantic, but often merely that it is ideally charming. This is the quality of Miss Louise Livingston Hunt's memoir of her great-aunt, Mrs. Edward Livingston, the daughter of an old and noble French house, colonialized in San Domingo, and surrounded there by all that we fancy of tropical ease and state. The patriarchal family dwelt in a white marble palace, surrounded by a village of eight hundred slaves, to whom harshness was unknown, and among whom they led such lives of dreamful splendor as are dreamily suggested in the enchanted pages of *Prue and I.* Her daughter was a widow of sixteen—she was a bride three years earlier—when the insurrection of the blacks broke out; and she escaped to New Orleans in time to see the transfer of Louisiana to the United States. Life in the old Franco-Spanish town was then hardly less idyllic (with the plague-spot of slavery on it, of course) than it had been in San Domingo, and the memoir offers quaint glimpses of the simple, sensuous, pleasure-loving society, in which the ladies walked to balls in their "white satin slippers behind slaves carrying lanterns; .... when it rained, or the weather was bad, the ball did not take place," and "this was announced by a crier through the streets to the sound of a drum." The young widow from San Domingo married the most brilliant of the young Americans who came in with the new rule, and she saw the success of the young Republic's arms in the defeat of the British in 1815.

Thereafter, as the wife of a rising statesman, great part of her life was passed in Washington, where she was a leader while her husband was Secretary of State under Jackson. Life in Washington was then as simple, if not as idyllic, as in New Orleans, and Mrs. Livingston's friends were charming and cultivated people, who founded the tradition of social freedom and equality which makes Washington still the most delightful city in the world. There is no doubt but Jackson, who broke up the old official life, and has the shame of introducing the spoils system, should have the credit of liberating society from the trammels of etiquette that even Jefferson had left. The reader of this memoir will find some letters of the old warrior in it which will show him in a new light, for one thinks of his saying things roughly and forcibly rather than with the delicacy and dignity which these letters attest. Mrs. Livingston afterward shone at the French court, when her husband was sent thither as minister, and she died, an old woman, in 1860, at her country place on the Hudson. An attractive feature of the memoir is in the letters given of those which she and her husband daily exchanged in their frequent separations: hers especially have a literary grace which, if a little studied, a little academic, is very, very lovely. In her whole character were united that elegance and strength which were the best effect of the best eighteenth-century education in women, and one cannot read of it without a sense of its refining and ennobling influence, or without a sigh for an amiable type which is necessarily extinct.

VI.

It was an aristocratic type, adapting itself sincerely and patriotically to our conditions, but not springing from them, nor from such aristocratic conditions as are known to our rude Anglo-Saxon race elsewhere. What types these produce the reader may learn from General Adam Badeau's very entertaining, if perhaps a little too gossipy, study of *Aristocracy in England*. It is, of course, imprudent to prophesy anything in particular of human nature, but it does not seem as though this ugly relic of feudalism, if it should ever be cast down, could be regretted by the fondest of its idolaters. One fancies the thing itself feeling a sort of relief if its reign were once well over, and it were reduced to its merely human elements once more.

In General Badeau's book, which does not differ from other impartial observers' accounts of the English social system, we see how very much less respectable than ordinary human beings men are apt to become by assuming to be something more. Not that he paints the English aristocracy very black or intentionally bad; it is probably bad, where it is bad, in spite of a great deal of personal good intention. But he shows satisfactorily that the so-called aristocratic virtues do not exist, and there really never were any virtues which society would not have had without the aristocracy. The aristocrats have been supposed to be preëminently courageous; but Thackeray noticed long ago that the plough-boy seemed to die

quite as bravely as the lord who led him into battle. They have been honored for their veracity and generosity; but wealth need not deny itself to give, and generosity is self-denial; as for lies, why should a man tell them whose standing and prosperity could hardly be imperiled by speaking the truth? We are brave and true when we are so to our possible ruin, and what aristocracy was ever more so than the lowest democracy? An undoubted frankness the English aristocrats seem, from General Badeau and other students of them, to have; they do not trouble themselves to hide their bad qualities. They would probably not be worse than the average of society if public opinion forbade them; but the corrosion of English life by snobbishness is the great mischief resulting from their existence, and it is certain that public opinion spoils them. When it comes to a question of rank, the natural self-respect of the English people seems eaten away, from the highest to the lowest; and the meanest lackey is not of a meaner soul before a lord than the lord is before royalty. This spiritual abasement is open and undeniable; it is defended and perpetuated by the whole ecclesiastical and political civilization of England; and probably General Badeau touches the very heart of the matter, the vital difference between English and American things, when he says that though with us some people may look down upon their fellows, their fellows (who feel that they are only the other fellows) do not look up. As long as this is the fact we are safe; and till a thoroughly stupid millionaire can inspire social reverence, or anything but a more or less jocular curiosity, in most Americans, we can still hold up our heads. Till then we need only hang them in shame for the truly great Englishmen, the princes of letters and of arts, who tell us that it refines people to revere rank, to exalt a class of titled persons necessarily their intellectual and moral inferiors, and worship them as their betters, because reverence is a good thing. Reverence for good is a good thing, but even then it had better be good in the abstract, lest at the very best it savor of that respect to persons abhorred of the apostle. This is the important lesson which General Badeau's book teaches; and it might be a very much less admirable book than it is and still be commendable for teaching it. As it is, it groups a great number of facts together, and reasons justly and good-humoredly enough from them. If the facts were less notorious, if they did not qualify the whole of English life and literature, if they were told of some unknown people otherwise great and noble, they would simply seem preposterous. Such a story as Dostoïevsky's leaves one braced and strong by a sense of the self-help in human nature; but General Badeau's study is curiously depressing. It is not even a comfort to feel that one has not a part in that particular squalor.

Monthly Record of Current Events.

POLITICAL.

OUR Record is closed on the 15th of July.— The following bills and resolutions were passed by the United States Congress: Senate, June 18, Mr. Frye's bill "for the encouragement of the American merchant marine, and to promote postal and commercial relations with foreign countries" (to subsidize American vessels carrying the United States mails); Senate, June 18, by a two-thirds vote, the joint resolution for the submission to the several States of a Constitutional amendment extending the period of the President's term and the session of the Fiftieth Congress until April 30, 1889, and substituting April 30 for March 4 as the commencement in future of the Presidential and Congressional terms; House, June 21, Naval Appropriation Bill, amounting to $12,930,034; on July 3 the same bill was reported in the Senate with a reduction of $46,800; Senate, June 25, by a vote of 30 to 17, the House bill for the relief of General Fitz-John Porter. On July 1 the bill was signed by President Cleveland.

The United States Senate, June 18, by a vote of 33 to 6, indefinitely postponed Mr. Vance's bill to repeal the civil service law.

The extradition treaty with Japan, and one for the resurvey of the boundary line between the United States and Mexico, were ratified by the United States Senate June 21.

The following nominations for Governors were made by State Conventions: Tennessee Republican, June 16, Alfred A. Taylor; Maine Prohibition, June 17, Aaron Clark; New Hampshire Democratic, June 29, Thomas Cogswell; Pennsylvania Republican, June 30, General James A. Beaver (by acclamation); Arkansas Democratic, June 30, S. P. Hughes; Minnesota Prohibition, July 7, J. E. Childs; Kansas Republican, July 8, John A. Martin (renominated by acclamation); Kansas Prohibition, July 14, C. H. Branscomb.

The British Parliament was prorogued June 25. The Queen in the royal speech gave notice of her intention to dissolve that body in order to test the sense of the people on the proposed Irish home rule question.

The British Parliamentary elections began July 1. Up to midnight of the 14th all but thirty-seven constituencies had been heard from. The totals at that time were: Conservatives and Unionists, 386; Gladstonians, 252.

President Caceres of Peru has assumed office.

King Ludwig of Bavaria was buried in Munich June 20, with great pomp.

Prince Luitpold, June 28, was formally declared Regent of Bavaria, to administer the affairs of the kingdom during the occupation of the throne by King Otto.

The French Senate, June 22, passed the Princes Expulsion Bill by a vote of 141 to 107. A decree of banishment followed the next day, and soon afterward Prince Victor Napoleon went to Brussels, Prince Jerome Napoleon to Geneva, and the Comte de Paris to England. The Comte de Paris issued a manifesto protesting against the violence done him, and declaring that in the decisive hour he should be ready.—On July 13 President Grévy signed a decree for the expulsion of the Duke d'Aumale.

The French Chamber of Deputies, June 22, notwithstanding the objections of the government, decided, by a vote of 302 to 227, in favor of a sur-tax on cereals. On June 26 the Chamber, by a vote of 242 to 216, rejected M. Blanquier's proposal to abolish the use of titles of nobility.

The final act of the German Reichstag before the close of the session, June 26, was the rejection of the Brandy Tax Bill. A bill to form a literary convention with England was passed on the previous day.

The Spanish Cortes, by a majority of 200 votes, has declared that no government of Spain will ever give autonomy to Cuba.

The elections in Holland resulted in the return of 47 Liberals and 39 anti-Liberals. The previous Chamber was a tie.

DISASTERS.

June 25.—Twenty-four men killed by an explosion in the colliery at Rochamp, France.

July 2.—Ten workmen blown to atoms by dynamite in the Atlantic Company's works, near McCainsville, New Jersey.

July 2.—News of the loss of eight French torpedo-boats in a storm on the Atlantic. Fifty men drowned.

July 11.—News received of fearful volcanic eruptions in New Zealand in June. Twenty-one persons killed and much property destroyed.

OBITUARY.

June 19.—At Milan, Italy, Hobart Pasha (the Hon. Augustus Charles Hobart), Marshal of the Turkish Empire, aged sixty-four years. —In London, England, Sir Charles Edward Trevelyan, Bart., in his eightieth year.

June 20.—In Braintree, England, Benjamin Moran, ex-United States Minister to Portugal, aged sixty-six years.

June 22.—In London, England, Daniel D. Home, spiritualist, aged fifty-three years.—In Charlestown, Massachusetts, Moses A. Dow, proprietor of the *Waverley Magazine*, aged seventy-six years.

June 26.—At Bloomington, Illinois, Hon. David Davis, aged seventy-one years.

July 6.—At Copse Hill, near Grovetown, Georgia, Paul H. Hayne, poet, in his fifty-seventh year.

July 8.—In Paris, France, Joseph Hippolyte Guibert, Archbishop of Paris, in his eighty-fourth year.

Editor's Drawer.

SO many women are about to change their names (as a result of the summer campaign, let us suppose and hope) that it is proper to make a suggestion, or to renew it if the Drawer has made it before, in regard to baptismal and married appellations. It cannot escape the observation of the most careless that the names of women, standing for distinct entities in the world, are daily becoming of more importance. Woman, in the mass, has always been regarded with favor, and her position in the economy of life has been cheerfully acknowledged, but her distinctive individuality in a public way has not been much insisted on. There has been an occasional Helen who has set the world by the ears, but it is comparatively a modern notion that women's names need to stand out with individual emphasis. But this is a necessary result of the women themselves standing out so conspicuously in various occupations and enterprises. It has ceased to be necessary for silk manufacturers in the United States to put foreign names on their fabrics in order to sell them, and in the same way the time has gone by when women need to masquerade under masculine names on the title-pages of books they write. Since women write our books, and teach our schools, and practice our laws, and ride in gigs, and send our messages by telegraph, and "hello" from one end of the country to the other through the telephone, and write after their names "M.D.," and "A.B.," and "A.M.," and nearly all the letters of the alphabet, and even "LL.D."—thanks to the Smith College appreciation of Miss Amelia B. Edwards—it is necessary that woman should have a name that will be inalienable and her own through life. Of course the time may come when the relations of the sexes before the public will be reversed, and man will have to fight for his name. Revolutions are said not to revolve backward, and a witty righter of wrongs has already declared that she will never be satisfied with the position of her sex until she can go into a graveyard and read on a head-stone some such sentiment as this, "Here lies Samuel Johnson, relict of Mary Johnson."

Now, however good a woman's name may be, she is in danger—except, they say, in Massachusetts—of losing it, and commonly in the change she blots out all traces of her former existence and even identity. In royal and noble families the attempt has been made to pile on so many names upon the female infant that some of them should stick through life, and we have to some extent imitated this in our republic by giving girls two and three names, sometimes a string of very pretty appellations taken out of novels; and especially if the child is poor, she will be rich in names. This is all very well so long as the girl remains Clarissa Elvira Euphemia Hoskins; but when it would become Clarissa Elvira Euphemia Hoskins Pond, it is too much, and either the surname or some of the baptismal names have to be thrown overboard. Usually the surname goes, and the others are left dangling about uselessly. The girl has cut herself off from her family, and, in fact, has quite lost her identity in the world. There must be some way devised by which the young lady can "keep her cake and eat it too." The present system has other inconveniences. If one receives a letter in the beautiful spider hand-writing, with the signature in two or three or four names, it is impossible to tell whether to address the writer as Miss or as Mrs. And such is the peculiarity of human nature that a mistake in this matter is sure to be offensive; somehow neither the Miss nor the Mrs. is complimented by having her status in life misapprehended. Whichever way she would like to change it, she has no mind to have the world think she would like to change it.

All these and many other inconveniences can be avoided, and the personal identity of a woman be secured through all changes, by a very simple device. In the first place, give the girl in baptism only one name. She will be perfectly content with it. Her lover never requires, never uses, but one of her names, if she has half a dozen. In the height of his tenderness he never says, "Amelia Jane, come to my arms!" He simply extends his arms and cries, "Jane!" In the second place, when the girl marries let her always keep her surname. Then, whenever we see a woman's name, we shall know whether she is married or single; and if she is married, we shall know what her family name is. If she has earned a reputation as a writer or a doctor or an LL.D. as Mary Brown, she will carry that with her as Mary Brown Johnson; and in all cases there will be spared an infinite amount of talk and inquiry as to who she was before she was married. In the opinion of the Drawer, this system is essential to the "cause" of woman. It may be said that it lacks perfection in two respects: we could not tell from the three names whether the bearer of them might not be a widow; and it makes no provision for a second marriage. These are delicate questions. In regard to the first, it is nobody's business to know whether the woman is or is not a widow, unless she chooses to make that fact prominent, and then she has ways enough to emphasize it. And in the second place (in case the woman does not marry her Deceased Husband's Brother, by permission of Congress), it does not at all matter what becomes of the name of the first husband. It is the woman's identity that is to be preserved. And she cannot be required to set up mile-stones all along her life.

THE Rev. —— (or "Father" ——, as he was called) was life-long pastor of the Congregational church in ——, Massachusetts. He was a man of great sobriety of deportment, yet was noted for a dry humor, which, though chiefly exercised in private, sometimes cropped out in public. His people were fond of him, and when the fiftieth year of his ministry was completed, made a grand celebration in honor of the event. He preached a sermon on the occasion. In this sermon he made an extensive review of the half-century that had passed since his ordination. He spoke first of the changes it had witnessed there in the town. It was a very different town from what it was when he came there. Then there was only one house that had a carpet, and no house that had a piano, or even so much as a melodeon, etc., etc. Next he spoke of changes in the State, illustrating in a variety of ways the contrast between the Massachusetts of former times and the Massachusetts of the present. Then he spoke of the country in the same strain, and finally of the world, showing how fifty years had in the case of both wrought wonderful transformations. "But," he added, "there is one thing, my dear friends, that has *not* changed—that through all these fifty years gone by has been the same. Empires, as I have described, have risen and fallen; kings have been born, and reigned, and died; great men have had their day, and passed from the stage, to be succeeded by other great men, who in their turn have sunk from view. There is one thing, I repeat, that has *not* changed [pause and stillness] *and that is my salary. It was six hundred dollars fifty years ago; it is six hundred dollars now."*

A TEACHER, in catechising her class of boys at Sunday-school, asked, "Who was the strongest man?" A little chap of eight years answered, without a moment's hesitation: "*Sullivan.* Now ask me who is the best rower."

THERE seems to be some sense in the remark of the young Irishman whose father was trying to coax him out of a drinking saloon, and at length, losing patience, threatened him with, "You Tim, ye come out now; if ye don't come out now I'll give yez a dale of a batin'"—the remark being, "Och, faith, an' I wouldn't come out if ye'd give me two of 'em; ye mind that, now."

RELIGIOUS TOLERANCE.

DEACON PETTYBONE (*to twenty-year-old son*): "James, you know my love of liberty, right of conscience, freedom of speech and worship; you have heard me proclaim them in public time and time again. You seem to prefer the other church to our own, notwithstanding my arguments and persuasions. Well, this is a free country, you are a free citizen; far be it from me to coerce or influence you in any way. Go, my son, go; if your heart tells you you are seeking the right path, GO. *But if you do go,*

may I be struck deaf, dumb, and blind if I don't drive you from my house like a dog. I'll follow your path, and take from you all means of earning an honest livelihood. I'll drive you to want and crime, and I'll die cursing you with my last breath. I am determined to do my whole duty as a Christian."

E. REED.

DER DEUTSCHER'S MAXIM.

DHERE vas vot you call a maxim
    Dot I hear der oder day,
Und I wride id in mine album,
    So id don'd could got avay;
Und I dells mine leedle Yawcob
    He moost mind vot he's aboudt:
"'Tis too late to lock der shtable
    Vhen der horse he vas gone oudt."

Vhen I see ubon der corners
    Off der shtreets, most efry night,
Der loafers und der hoodlums,
    Who do nix but shvear und fight,
I says to mine Katrina:
    "Let us make home bright und gay;
Ve had petter lock der shtable,
    So our colts don'd got avay."

Vhen you see dhose leedle urchins,
    Not mooch ofer knee-high tall,
Shump rightd indo der melon patch,
    Shust owf der garden vall,
Und vatch each leedle rashkell
    Vhen he cooms back mit hees "boodle,"
Look oudt und lock your shtable,
    So your own nag don'd shkydoodle!

Vhen der young man at der counter
    Vants to shpecgulate in shtocks,
Und buys hees girl some timond rings,
    Und piles rightd oup der rocks,
Look oudt for dot young feller;
    Id vas safe enuff to say
Dot der shtable id vas empty,
    Und der horse vas gone avay.

Dhen dake Time by der fetlock;
    Don'd hurry droo life's courses,
Rememper vot der poet says,
    "Life's but a shpan"—off horses;
Der poy he vas der comin' man;
    Be careful vhile you may;
Shust keep der shtable bolted,
    Und der horse don'd got avay.

CHARLES FOLLEN ADAMS.

PROPER NAMES.

THIS is the name of a man living near our South Carolina correspondent: Harmon Diveover Jump-under Come-hither-to-me Out-yonder Go-fetch-it Jehu Joshua William Hugh Hall Hiram Harvey Kiziah Jones.

This last one is from a tombstone near Wetumpka, Alabama: "Henri Ritter Demi Ritter Emmi Ritter Sweet-Potato Cream-Tartar Caroline Bostwick, infant daughter of Bob and Sukey Catlin." It was the name of a little negro girl.

FOR a year past a pair of souls in Flushing, Long Island, have been accustomed to share a thought between them, and two devoted hearts have beat in such close and perfect unison as to produce but one rounded and complete throb. Now, alas! they do so no more forever, and all on account of a cough.

Miss C—— and her *fiancé* Mr. L—— attended the sociable at the Baptist church parlors recently, and were happy as usual in each other's society, except that Mr. L—— was somewhat disturbed by a hacking cough with which Miss C—— was suffering. When at last the sociable was over, and the pair started on the three-quarter-mile lap to Miss C——'s house—which, it being moonlight and not too late, it is safe to assume was not to be covered too quickly—the lady was seized with a violent paroxysm of coughing. In great distress, Mr. L—— supported her tenderly, wishing he might cough for her, when a happy thought struck him. He always carried troches in his pocket; possibly one was about him then. A quick search filled him with triumph.

"Take this," he said, pressing it upon her; "it will give you relief, I am sure;" and the young woman gratefully put the small flat disk upon her tongue.

They walked on. Miss C—— sucked upon the troche and hung upon her lover's words, and one or the other acted so soothingly that her coughing spells were few and far between. Several times Mr. L—— inquired with solicitude if the troche were dissolved, receiving each time the assurance that it was not yet, coupled with the pleasing announcement that its efficacy was very apparent.

There was a prolonged and interesting farewell at the door, in which, for the time, both cough and remedy were forgotten. As Mr. L—— moved away, however, his anxiety returned, and he called back, "Shall I leave another troche?" And in the light of later events it struck Miss C—— there was a mocking cadence in his tone.

She lightly declined his offer, and entered the house. A few moments afterward, by the light of her bedroom lamp, a discovery took place which so aroused her indignation that in a moment Cupid fled, and before she slept the letter containing the fatal words "all is over" was written.

In his anxiety he had unwittingly given her a trousers button.

———

THE Rev. Dr. ——, a prominent New York clergyman, relates with much gusto the following story about himself. The present Mrs. Rev. Dr. ——, by-the-way, is not the wife of the doctor's youth, nor yet of his early manhood, but is the lady of his third choice, and as a consequence the Doctor's set of olive branches spring from diverse maternal ancestry. "Such a condition of affairs," says the Doctor, as *raconteur*, "might at times become embarrassing except for the thorough amiability of all concerned. I confess, however, to a slightly disconcerted feeling when shortly before my third marriage I was approached by one of my daughters, a girl of nine, and one

who called my second wife mother, with, 'Papa, will you let me go to see you married? I have never been at any of your weddings.'"

———

A LACONIC LETTER.

"IN the days of '49" a member of a party of miners strayed away from his companions and was destroyed by wild beasts. The friend upon whom it devolved to "break the news gently" to the bereaved parents showed himself equal to the occasion by writing the following letter:

MISTER SMITH DEER SUR the Kiotes has ete yur sun's hed off　　　Yurs　　　JOHN JONES.

———

EXPRESSING HIS FEELINGS.

A—— man whose matrimonial life had been anything but happy in consequence of the quarrelsome habits of his wife, who thus contrived to keep him constantly in hot water with the neighbors, was at last relieved of her company by death. As the widower's means were limited, the funeral was plain, but respectable enough to satisfy any reasonable relative. The brother of the deceased lady, however, was not a reasonable man; and on the return of the mourners to the house he ridiculed the funeral, said that it was mean, undemonstrative, and so quiet that all the neighbors must have considered it niggardly.

"Yes, it was rather quiet," responded the widower; "but what did you expect? Did you want me to show my submission to the decree of Providence in removing my late lamented spouse by closing the funeral with a display of fire-works? I did think of a cheerful display of some sort, but abandoned the idea because I feared the neighbors might talk about it, and say that I was giving too much expression to my feelings."

———

LITTLE Sam Bonsall is three years old, and formerly lived at Portsmouth, Ohio. His parents are now living at Elizabeth, New York. The other day Sam's disposition for fun and mischief led him to commit some little depredation, for which his mother gave him a talking to. She dwelt upon the idea of God's seeing us and knowing what we were doing here, which set Sam to thinking. Pretty soon he asked: "Mamma, do God see eberyting we do here?" "Yes," replied his mother; to which the little rascal immediately replied, "Oh, pshaw! den let's move back to Ports'uth."

———

A GENTLEMAN travelling through the mountainous and thinly settled districts of North Carolina was overtaken by a severe storm. As he was on horseback, and therefore quite unprotected, he beheld with delight a log cabin in the distance, and speedily betook himself thither. The old farmer greeted him with true Southern hospitality, and he soon found himself seated at the dinner-table beside "the old 'ooman," as his host designated his wife, while one by one a seemingly endless file of daughters entered the room. Turning to the farmer, he mildly observed, "You have a fine family of daughters, sir."

"Well," said the old man, mournfully, "we've been kinder unfort'nate with our darters. The chimbly fell in and killed all but nine on 'em."

The historian dares not guess how many there were at first.

A NEWLY married couple were spending a few days with friends in one of our cities. One morning they were heard to have some pretty loud words together. Soon the husband left the house for a stroll. Not long after, the friends discovered the bride lying upon the bed, apparently dead. Dr. Q—— was summoned without delay. He was a very precise gentleman, and a strict observer of the code of ethics. He detected no pulsation of the heart, nor any sign of breathing. He decided that the lady was dead. Remembering, however, a similar case in which the patient was in a trance, and learning that the patient had had asthma, he delayed a few moments to make sure of the result. While he was noting the surroundings in the room, expecting at least

to be called before a coroner's court, the door opened, and a tall, seedy-looking individual came in, whom the doctor recognized as a "corn-doctor," a genuine quack. Of course he would not deign to notice such a character, and he could not see why the family should allow him in the house. The seedy-looking individual slid around the side of the room up to the corpse, and began gently to rub her hands between his own. Then he carefully chafed her fore-arm. When, however, he continued his work upon the lady's arm the precise doctor could stand it no longer, and, after sharply rebuking the quack for thus sacrilegiously treating a corpse, he departed. The next morning the husband of the deceased came to his office. He knew what the gentleman wanted. He took out his book of death certificates, and began to ask the necessary questions as to age, birth, etc. After filling out all the blanks and signing his name, the physician folded the certificate and handed it to the gentleman. Up to this time the gentleman had not had a chance to say anything of his own accord. He asked how much he should pay. "Two dollars." While the doctor was writing a receipt the gentleman remarked, "My wife is better to-day, and we are going to resume our journey."

THE PEOPLE WE MEET IN THE COUNTRY.

LADY. "No, I don't know Victor Hugo's works well. I've only read ''93.'"
ALDERMAN'S DAUGHTER. "Only ninety-three! Why, I haven't read more than seventy or eighty of them."

"PERSICOS ODI."—Horace's Odes, I., 38.
From a drawing by J. R. Weguelin.—[See page 709.]

HARPER'S
NEW MONTHLY MAGAZINE.

VOL. LXXIII.   OCTOBER, 1886.   No. CCCCXXXVII.

AUTUMN IN ENGLAND

BY LUCY C. LILLIE.

THERE are certain days in northern America which strikingly reproduce the aspect of an English autumn. These are the days when the last of the goldenrod has vanished; when even Indian-pipe is a matter of uncertainty; when the last red and yellow of the sumac have been strewn, and over all the land has come a tinge of brown, touched here and there with some faint lingering green; when the mornings and evenings are chill, but with a delicious chilliness; when after a walk through the broken woodlands or along some hilly road a wood fire is a cheerful friend; and yet when the sky holds something of its soft, summer-like blue, with the gray lines that speak of November.

Only rarely do such days occur, and resembling the English autumn, they come bringing back innumerable memories, and make one wonder at the prevalent opinion among Americans that theirs is the only country where September, October, and November are seen in their perfection.

True it is that few know how and where to find the glories of the English autumn. Let the wanderer find himself in a Lon-

don fog, and his memorandum, "The English climate at this season is detestable," is by no means unjustifiable, for nothing, I believe, that nature ever produced is more depressing, bewildering, or exasperating than a London fog. I knew a young American lady who staid on perversely in London just to see a fog; it would be *so* like something in one of Dickens's novels, she thought; so delightfully English an experience to go about with a boy carrying a torch to guide her uncertain steps. But when one morning this spirited young person opened her eyes upon a day that was all indescribable yellow mist; when it settled into almost a black vapor; when she went out in search of adventure and absolutely lost her way, and was assisted over a crossing by a totally invisible individual—then she decided that a fog was better to read about, and that one strip of the blue sky at home, one gleam of the sunshine of New York, would be welcomed like the flowers of May.

London, therefore, is, or ought to be, forbidden ground during the autumn. The whole wide country lies open to the tourist, and he who has friends with hos-

DRIVING AT TWILIGHT FROM THE STATION.

pitable firesides "down" in some good county may consider himself a blessed individual.

Any reader of English novels knows, of course, how the upper ten thousand go to their country houses about September, and also how forthwith go out those select invitations, the method of which is so admirable, and the tact and discernment so subtle. How they contrive to do it all so well is a mystery to me. How they arrange things to such a nicety that the autumn visits are all fascination to guests, and not special matter of weariness to the host and hostess, is marvellous, unless one stops to reflect on the traditional *savoir-faire* of an English household, the perfect system of domestic service, and the mixture of formality and freedom which inspires both host and guest, and to understand which it is necessary to absorb a sort of appreciation of the intention, or perhaps I should say *raison d'être*, of country-house ways and manners.

And how delightful such experiences are! How agreeable, and at the same time, from an American point of view, how singular, a side of life is presented, for a round of visits during the autumn in England shows the whole scheme of English society in its most varied, definite, and perplexing forms, and while we

admire, we can also wonder, and perhaps vaguely smile, just a very little, over our discoveries, and learn to feel that those who occupy debatable ground, the so-called middle class, are unquestionably the happiest, heartiest, and worthiest society.

This, however, is not the subject in hand; rather have we to think of certain glorious autumn days, mellow, luminous, and cheering; of a country where the brown and yellow tints were delightful harmonies, where the roads were capital for walking, riding, or driving, and where the rich undulations of the country showed to almost finer advantage than in the days of deep green verdure and summer blossom.

Who that has once experienced it but recalls with pleasure the arrival at a country house in England somewhere between twilight and darkness? There is the long drive from the station, the turn into a park, the opening of the hospitable doorway, and the welcome of host and hostess; and if it be September, there will be in the drawing-room a five-o'clock tea party, where the gentlemen are discussing the day's shooting, and the ladies, sitting about in pretty tea-gowns, listening, talking, perhaps now and then in some shadowy window indulging in the quiet bits of flirtation which, in the English country house full of guests, is, I believe, absolutely indispensable.

Such houses are scattered over every county in England. Some are opened solely for the entertainment of autumn or winter guests; others lie deserted all the year round, either because the owners do not care to inhabit them or cannot afford the immense expense entailed; and in many cases where a shooting property is very good it is "let" at a pretty round sum during the season, the tenant having all the privileges of the landlord, and none of the disagreeable duties so often incurred by actual ownership of a property which needs "watching" and "keeping" and "preserving."

Madame Merle, in one of Mr. Henry James's most delightful novels, is described as having divested herself of every remnant of that tonic wildness which we may assume to have belonged even to the most amiable persons in the ages before country-house life was the fashion, and, to the experienced or acute observer, therein might lie the theme of a long discourse, for genuine country-house life in

England means much more than the actual habitation of the mansion by its owners and their friends for a specified portion of the year; in fact, it is emphatically necessary to the scheme of English social life, if by "social" we mean the governing portion of the community. The squire in any English country village, the earl, the duke, who occupy their country houses, have actual duties to perform while there. The movements, well-being, progress, and, we may add, happiness of the people depend so largely upon the great land-owners of the country that the period of country living cannot conscientiously be considered as entirely one of amusement; of course it does not follow that these responsibilities are always felt or held sacredly; in many cases they are entirely disregarded; but certainly the moral or political aspect is not the one we have to consider; rather do we think of English autumns from the point of view of a well-entertained, kindly considered guest.

The first object in going down to the country seems to be the shooting, and perhaps this idle paper might have been called "The Fox and the Pheasant," since its main object is to treat of the sports of an English autumn. But personal experiences which have had their fascination are sure to creep in, however didactic or instructive one's impulse may be; and for myself, when I think of the shooting season, there rises to my mind the picture of a quaint little town, with zigzag, hilly streets, a long country road leading to a manor-house, set deeply in its park, and overlooking a rolling country, richly diversified, wooded, and populous with the game so dear to the sportsman's bag after the last day of August.

There is a certain routine of life in English country houses which is always maintained in spite of any variations in out-door life. Whether this is the result of careful domestic management or the outcome of persistent habit, one need not inquire. The result is certainly very agreeable. As soon as a guest arrives, an invisible agency seems to be at work for his comfort. As such arrivals are apt to take place late in the afternoon, it is customary for the guest to go at once into the drawing-room, where tea is waiting. No "effect" can be prettier than that produced by the five-o'clock tea-table in the drawing-room of an English country house. Formality is dispensed with; the gentlemen are in their shooting costume; the business of the day is over. This hour seems to be one in which the individual self may be asserted with no feeling that any conventionality or matter of etiquette is trenched upon. An hour later, and the scene is changed. The company reassemble with the solemnity of dinner before them, that august meal at which no Englishman dares seat himself without a full sense of its importance. And after dinner the recreations of the evening vary according to the place and the people. There are always billiards, there is sure to be some music, and occasionally a variety in the way of charades or a dance, but every one may follow his or her inclination about leaving the company.

In the hall a table containing bedroom candlesticks is always provided. You may take your candle and go your way whenever you feel inclined, so simple and at the same time so luxurious is this form of English hospitality.

Breakfast is a sort of movable feast. Unless absolutely necessary, the servants are not kept in the room. On the sideboard are placed all the cold dishes, which the gentlemen carve and hand about informally. It is at breakfast that the day's work or pleasure is discussed.

Until after October, shooting and cub-hunting are the only sports, and the former is sure to be in the ascendant. Hares and partridges are to be had earliest in the season, and I believe that they can be found on open ground. Moors are often let for the purpose of such shooting, but what is directly called "covert shooting" is a different matter, and it is here that the pheasant asserts itself as an aristocratic bird. The pheasant is not supposed to be as injurious to the preserving of foxes as other game, but it costs a great deal more to keep up. It is generally understood that any gentleman preserving pheasants pays for them at the rate of five dollars a head, at the very time they are sold in London at half the price. The reasons for this are various, and I suppose that the iniquities of the poacher are chief among them. It is usual for any shooting party to go out about ten o'clock in the morning, arranging for the ladies of the household to meet them at noontime for luncheon at the "covert side." This means somewhere near the place of successful work. I can well remember an occasion of this kind during which there hovered in the background a very gloomy figure. This was a keeper of precisely the type which Mr. Anthony Trollope so cleverly portrayed. He could restrain neither his indignation nor his thirst for vengeance. He was quite certain that poaching to an alarming extent had been done, and we, as Americans, wished to understand exactly what this kind of villany meant.

As the game-laws of England prohibit any kind of shooting of game unless authorized by the owner of the land, temptation to the poacher is very great. The word itself had always seemed to us to mean something vaguely terrible—some one who went out by night to do some indescribably dark deed. Of course the work of such a one is really thieving, yet it may be understood how the rural mind in England may fail to fully take this in. I once talked to a young man about it, and his reiterated remark, "Ah, well, I sees un a-flyin'," seemed to contain excuse enough for his depredations. When poaching is suspected, very careful and adroit watch is set upon the ground, and the keeper triumphs who can detect the thief in the act. The habitual poacher is usually a very miserable sort of creature. Since his business is carried on at night, he has neither heart nor strength for work in the daytime, and usually spends his morning hours in sleep. Occasionally a very clever poacher applies for the position of keeper, and if he be found honest in other ways, he does well at this work, his own experiences furnishing him with useful clews. I believe the law allows a punishment of from three months to two years for poaching.

One of the most beautiful estates I have ever seen had famous pheasant coverts; they were situated about two miles from the house, and in the care of a most intelligent keeper. The man had a nice house on the grounds, and his two sons worked under him. The shooting done on that place was genuine work, although on one occasion they shot what is called "a battue." This is considered a very lazy form of sport, although a great many people delight to indulge in it, because it is well known to be a most costly amusement. I dare not pretend to enter into details concerning it. The object, so far as I could understand, was to draw into the covert as many pheasants as possible, careful preparations having been made some time in advance. The shooting party are stationed at different points, and fire upon the game as they rise, with a continual bang, bang, which brings down in a short time several hundreds—a result which can scarcely seem amusing to any one who cares for the excitement of ordinary shooting. There is a sense of luxury in this kind of work, but no glory.

One has to wonder, after the day's sport, how the guests in a country house find animation for other amusements; yet they are always ready, even eager, for anything in the form of entertainment, from a dance to a church festival, and private theatricals are a never-failing resource. And such things go on so easily! There are always "people" who can be "had down" from London to do the drudgery—costumers, prompters, managers, and the like —even, if it be necessary, a stray professional or two to help out the work. And the amateur acting on such occasions is apt to be very good. The amount of time and thought and expense bestowed upon such performances ought, it is true, to produce a gratifying result, and sometimes it happens that from just such occasions comes an impulse for the real stage, so that a great success has its disadvantages.

The church interests are so many in English country life that the ladies of the household need never be unemployed. It is not for us to say how complicated or how simple is the question of church livings, vicarages, curacies, etc., but the parson is a strong figure socially, and his grade is as pronounced as if he were in the army. The rector in any good parish is a man well enough off to be eligible socially and matrimonially, but his curate is in rather a hopeless position, unless he has ahead of him the promise of a "living," and the peculiarity of his case is added to by the fact that he is on terms of sufficient intimacy with his superiors to run all sorts of risks of unhappiness. How dangerous are the hours of companionship with the fair Lady Marys and Honorable Miss Janes, who delight in parish work, and break his heart while they console the people! If he "speaks," sentence of exile is pronounced, unless his case be a rare one, which includes a pri-

EARTH-STOPPING.

vate fortune; and if he marries in his own class, how dull and weary a life he is apt to lead! Josiah Crawley, perpetual curate of Hogglestock, is no uncommon character. But there is undeniably a fascination about English church work on those crisp autumn days when sometimes an hour or two hangs heavily upon one's hands. The cottage visiting it includes, the school treats, the glimpses into humble life, all so strongly English that they characterize experience and reminiscence in a picturesque way, and have the powerful charm of being exactly like what one has read and imagined.

Occasionally some village seems almost too well cared for, too perfect to be interesting. I recall one such, where the cottages were such models, the people so industrious, so indulged by their landlords, the roads so perfect, the growth so sure, that a little irregularity would have been a great relief, and I am inclined to think the people felt life rather burdened with content. The ladies of the manor took great pride and satisfaction in this perfect state of things, and at Christmas were compelled to think a long time as to what gifts or distributions would be novel and worthy their giving. A contrast to that happy valley was a small place near to a great duke's castle, where want and cold, hunger and idleness, stared you in the face. The people were wretchedly unhappy, and seemed to have settled down into a kind of despair over life. They cared for nothing but the chance to drink, and drink they did, from the youngest to the oldest, letting desolation come in upon them, sickness, death—all the miseries of life accumulating while they endured existence with the stolidity of despair. It was a rich and fertile part of the country. The drives in every direction were beautiful, and the great duke's house, though rarely inhabited, formed a striking feature in a landscape which has been painted many times. The house was well worthy of a visit. We went there one quiet October day when the park was all strewn with leaves, and the air melancholy with a touch of something wintry. The housekeeper seemed rather startled by our arrival, and indeed everything about the place was so still and lonely that one could not wonder at it. We went through the great faded-looking rooms, trying to realize that once, a century or so ago, they had been brilliantly hospitable and full of good cheer. The pictures were very fine, the staircase lined with them, and they suggested the curious histories belonging to people of that house. Romance, beauty, misfortune, all have characterized the race, and the gloom settling down over the splendid mansion seemed to be a natural outcome of the story of its past. The house-keeper gradually came out of her startled mood, and became communicative and even confidential, showed us the rooms supposed to haunted, which were solemn and stately enough for a ducal ghost, and were, she told us, rarely occupied. We asked her if she had ever seen or heard anything of this intruder, and she became very impressive in tone and manner as she said, "Yes, when she was a girl."

This was really interesting.

"Where did you see it?" asked the most indefatigable of our party, whose curiosity was never sufficiently appeased on such topics. The good woman stood still, grew thoughtful, and gave a careful glance all about her before she spoke.

We were standing in the small corridor leading to the rooms, and from a large and dusty window could look out across the park. It was mournfully autumnal in its aspect, rigid in its air of seclusion, and perhaps fast approaching decay; indeed, one might think even a ghost would have been unhappy in such a place.

The timid-looking house-keeper went on. "It was the night of a ball here," she said, "and we'd a deal to do upstairs. I was lady's-maid then, and I had been helping one of the house-maids in these very rooms. It was about ten o'clock, and I came in just to see that all was right, when I felt a sort of chill. I looked over to see if the windows were open, but it was all shut up close, and then—I can't just say how or where it came from—it was standing right in the middle of the room."

"What?"

I think two or three of us asked this question in an awe-struck whisper.

The house-keeper shook her head very slowly, and looked very dejected. "It was the figure of a young girl in a long blue cloak. It didn't speak, but just walked over to the press at the side of the room, and stood there a moment with such a wild look—and then it was gone."

"Were you frightened?"

"Oh, ma'am, I thought I'd never get out into the hall again. And her picture's down on the staircase. She lived here in the time of Charles I.'"*

The house-keeper's tone had gained some animation as she said this. She was again in her character of guide.

We paused on the staircase a moment to look at the portrait. It was that of a very lovely girl in seventeenth-century costume, with the arch smile and slim figure which seem to belong to maidens of that day.

It was disappointing not to hear more of her story, yet the very vagueness surrounding her ghostly appearances gave something to think of. *Why* did she wear a blue cloak? *Why* did she go over to that press? *Why* was her expression tragic? We pondered over all this as we drove away from the castle, the sadness of the weather urging on such conjectures, and I suppose a ghost, to be really

---

* The truth of this story, of course, I cannot vouch for, but I have told it exactly as it was told me.

COTTAGE VISITING.

worth while, ought not to be very definite or give entire satisfaction in regard to its movements; directly anything of that kind settles itself into something comprehensive, the weirdness is lost; so that the young lady of Charles the First's court was wise to haunt the house in a way which would give no one any right to decide about her life or the misery which kept her out of her grave.

It was down in this very county that our first active interest in fox-hunting commenced.

Where there is good feeling in the county and an interest in the work, the foxes can be admirably kept up, and the Master of the hounds and his men have little trouble in finding their game. The Master is chosen entirely because of his ability to do his work, although he must be a gentleman of leisure and of means. A certain sum is paid in by the gentlemen of the hunt for its support, and anything over and above must come out of the Master's own pocket. The cleverest man at this sort of work we ever saw was one who had very little else in common with his friends and neighbors, but, as the saying is, he "kept things together" in a wonderful way. Instead of occupying his inherited property, where there was a lovely house, he lived in a small comfortless place, entirely for the sake of superintending the kennels for himself. No order could have been more perfect than that which regulated those kennels. They were beautifully tiled, well ventilated, and as cleanly as a carefully swept room. The hounds themselves were not only perfect in breed, but beautiful to look at, and Colonel ——, I believe, cared for them more tenderly than for anything else on earth. There were some seven or eight men in charge, all of whom had the keenest interest in their work. The actual number of men needed is about six.

There must be a huntsman, and his essential quality is his voice. The hounds have to know it; and although he has, perhaps, less to do with them than any other servant on the field, yet his voice of authority must be paramount. Next come the whippers-in, or "whips," as they are sometimes called.* Their duty is to keep the hounds together, and their work is

* This term is also used in Parliament. The whips or whippers-in are those who go about in the lobbies for votes. The term was used originally in connection with hunting.

real activity. Next to these men come what are called earth-stoppers, and to them is intrusted a really great responsibility. It is their duty to take care of the fox. If they perform it badly, he is not "found." The earths are the fox's hiding-places, and before the day of the meet these must be stopped, because not only would it affect the finding of a fox, but in the run he might get away to one of his habitations. The idea to be carried out is that the fox shall be "found," and then chased up hill and down dale, the riders taking everything, fence or ditch, in their pursuit of this wily creature.

I remember on one occasion speaking compassionately of the animal to a man whose life had been devoted to a fox-hunting district. Although I had enjoyed my own ride, I did feel that there was some philanthropy to be exercised for the fox himself; but on expressing it, S—— remarked, looking at me with the most curious expression: "Why, ma'am, they foxes they wouldn't know wot to do without the 'unt. Why, they likes it, they does. It's all the fun they gets out of life"—an argument that sounded irresistible; still, having seen the startled creature rise out of the wood and dash off pursued by two or three hundred people and half as many dogs, the humane sense of view had to linger.

It was, I think, on this very occasion that S—— pointed out to us the scene of one of the most famous runs ever made in the county—a place sadly significant, since there three of the riders lost their lives. The fox had been started in a wood about five miles distant, and when this awful declivity was reached, he darted down, and, under pressure of excitement, half the riders followed. The result may easily be imagined, and those who witnessed it say it was a sight that seemed to burn itself upon their minds. How any one escaped death seemed almost miraculous, but those who told the tale in calmer moments could not do so without a shudder, and the place has always gone by a name significant of that one day's adventure. S—— regarded it with a solemn kind of pride; it was much to him that the gentlemen of his county had risked their lives so nobly. The place itself presented only the aspect of a neglected hillside, the underbrush tangled, the weeds coming up in a grim sort of fashion, and nothing reaching anything but a stunted

THE MEET.

growth. It was said that every one avoided the place, the glory of its one day's success having been all lost in the tragedy which it entailed.

Notices of the hunt are always published in the newspapers, and if one is staying at a country house, information is given more definitely. When ways and manners in any place are novel, all sorts of trifles become interesting, and I can recall a feeling of intense interest on discovering in my room at —— Manor a little card on which was printed the time and place of the next meet. Such cards of notification are sent about to every one of consequence, or any one who is likely to wish to ride. To me the fascination of the bit of pasteboard was positively exhilarating. It really seemed to put me into the delightful region of Barsetshire. Mentioning this at dinner to my neighbor, I found that it excited quite a keen interest in him. It never had occurred to him to think that the detail of country life in England could have any glamour, and he expressed himself with a great many "Why, reallys," and "Dear me, only fancys." However, he obligingly gave me a great deal of information.

It seemed to me that I should have liked to have had the meet held at some place called something Spinnies or Trumpeton Woods, that I might feel it entirely characteristic; unfortunately for such sentiments, the place had a most ordinary name, but it was five miles away, and the drive would include a fine part of the county. My companion was eagerly inquisitive about hunting in America; he did not cherish the idea prevalent some twenty years since that the buffalo was to be found on Broadway, nor did he feel that in a chase in America the red man could be hunted; still, his ideas of prairie shooting were about as misty as mine of hunting in England; he had an idea, he said, of taking a little run across Colorado, and thought perhaps three weeks would do it nicely. Perhaps I ought to record of him that he went on his little run, taking six months for the journey, and investing in good Western property.

Every one who intends to ride must appear early at the breakfast table, and the scene is a most interesting one; the pink coats are a charming variety, and make many ordinary-looking people picturesque for the time being. Only those whose station warrants them can wear

pink; occasionally a well-to-do farmer may be seen thus arrayed, but in every case there is a tax of several pounds a year for wearing it; besides this there are fees to keepers and the like, and if any man's country is too well ridden over, that is to say, if a farmer's crops suffer, it is always customary to make up a purse for him. Now and then some one rebels against his ground being used, and as the laws of the hunting field are entirely unwritten ones, it is difficult to decide in such a matter; but the voice of the people is always loud against anything which interferes with the fox. I knew of one case where the animal was hunted across a lawn and garden beds, and killed almost at the door of a rectory. The rector was not a hunting man himself, but it never occurred to him to object to this intrusion. Not only does the interest taken in the sport affect the results, but the county itself makes a great difference. Leicestershire is considered the best, including as it does both Market-Harborough and Melton-Mowbray. In the middle of the last century very little interest was taken in this sport. Foxes could be trapped with impunity. In Leicestershire an enterprising rider named Meynell tried to rouse some enthusiasm, and was so far successful that at this day the following couplet is constantly quoted:

"Talk of horses and hounds and the system of kennel,
Give me Leicestershire nags and the hounds of old Meynell."

Mr. Meynell's hounds were quite famous, but he worked hard to keep them up to the mark. One of his associates was a man who was called "Prince Boothby," famous as a beau and wit, and who ended a life of frivolity by committing suicide, because, he said, he was "tired of the bore of dressing and undressing so many times."

Leicestershire is a different county today, so far as the hunting is concerned. The sport is most beautifully cared for. The North Pytchley pack, under the Mastership of Mr. Langham, is out three days a week, their huntsman being the Earl of Lonsdale,* and the Quorn pack (Mr. Coupland, Master) has a world-wide celebrity. About two years since, some of the most famous runs ever recorded were made at Melton-Mowbray, and although I

---

* It is frequently the case that gentlemen, from love of it, perform the duties of huntsmen.

THROWING THE FOX TO THE DOGS.

did not see them myself, I had the benefit of full descriptions, given in the most graphic style by "a young lady of high degree," who was the antitype of Lady Gay Spanker.

The reasons, as I have suggested, are many why hunting differs in different counties, but chief among them is the scent. There are some places where, no matter how well up to their work the hounds and officials are, it is almost impossible to get a good scent. Both the climate and the ground have to do with this, and as nothing can be accomplished unless the fox is started, and as he cannot be started or "found" without the scent, it may easily be seen of what importance this is. One will see at a country house a doleful expression settling down upon more faces than one if the air be not favorable; and if a frost comes up suddenly, how wretched all the company can appear, for a frost is the death of good sport.

"There's a tone in the wind which seems clearly
    to say,
  We shall soon go a-hunting—hurrah, boys,
    hurrah!"

These old-time lines are as applicable to-day as when they were written, and I may be pardoned for another quotation from the same period, as it is equally characteristic :

  "Hounds stout and horses healthy,
    Earths stopped, and foxes plenty."

Once the earths are well stopped, the fox may be considered as above-ground and to be hunted out, unless the awful crime of trapping has been committed. I believe that there are various ways of trapping, but unless in a county where no hunting is done, it is always supposed to be the result of malice. The game-keepers in any good shooting country are tempted to set traps for the foxes, as the latter so often destroy the birds; but no gentleman is supposed to keep a game-keeper who will do this. The trap is made, as a general thing, by digging a hole in the ground which the fox will run to, and setting within it a snare. When one such trapped animal is found in a wood, there arises a general wail among the hunting people, and the traitor must be found; particularly if the Master is like Lord Chiltern, of whom, as we all remember, his wife said, "You can't alter a man's nature; Oswald was born to be a Master of Hounds"; and to continue a quotation from the same book :

"Lady Chiltern was probably right when she declared that her husband must have been made to be a Master of Hounds —presuming it to be granted that somebody must be Master of Hounds. Such necessity certainly does exist in this the present condition of England. Hunting prevails; hunting men increase in numbers; foxes are preserved; farmers do not rebel; owners of coverts, even when they are not hunting men themselves, acknowledge the fact, and do not dare maintain their pheasants at the expense of the much better beloved four-footed animal. Hounds are bred and horses are trained specially to the work. A master of fox-hounds is a necessity of the period. Allowing so much, we cannot but allow also that Lord Chiltern must have been made to fill the situation. He understood hunting, and perhaps there was nothing else requiring acute intelligence that he did understand. And he understood hunting not only as a huntsman understands it—in that branch of the science which refers simply to the judicious pursuit of the fox, being probably inferior to his own huntsman in that respect—but he knew exactly what men should do and what they should not. In regard to all those various interests with which he was brought in contact, he knew when to hold fast to his own claims, and when to make no claims at all. He was afraid of no one, but he was possessed of a sense of justice which induced him to acknowledge the rights of those around him. When he found the earths were not stopped in Trumpeton Wood—from which he judged that the keeper would complain that the hounds would not or could not kill any of the cubs found there —he wrote in very round terms to the duke who owned it. If his Grace did not want to have the woods drawn, let him say so; if he did, let him have the earths stopped. . . .

"It is essential that a Master of Hounds should be somewhat feared by the men who ride with him. There should be much awe mixed with the love felt for him. He should be a man with whom other men will not care to argue; an irrational cut and thrust, unscrupulous, but yet distinctly honest man; one who can be tyrannical, but will tyrannize only over evil spirits; a man capable of intense cruelty to those alongside of him, but who will know whether his victim does in truth deserve scalping before he draws

THE FOX'S TAIL.

his knife. He should be savage and yet good-humored, severe and yet forbearing, turbulent and pleasant, in the same moment. He should exercise unflinching authority, but should do so with the consciousness that he can support it only by his own popularity. His speech should be short, incisive, always to the point, but never founded on argument. His rules are based on no reason, and will never bear discussion. He must be the most candid of men, also the most close—and yet never a hypocrite. He must condescend to no explanation, and yet must impress men with an assurance that his decisions will certainly be right. He must rule all as though no man's special welfare were of any account, and yet administer all so as to offend none. Friends he must have, but not favorites. He must be self-sacrificing, diligent, eager, and watchful. He must be strong in health, strong in heart, strong in purpose, and strong in purse. He must be economical and yet lavish, generous as the wind and yet obdurate as the frost. He should be assured that of all human pursuits hunting is the best, and that of all living things a fox is the most valuable. He must so train his heart as to feel for the fox a mingled tenderness and cruelty which is inexplicable to ordinary men and women. His desire to preserve the brute and then to kill him should be equally intense and passionate, and he should do it all in accordance with a code of unwritten laws which cannot be learned without profound study."

Whoever wishes to ride, goes to the place appointed as meeting, generally some short time in advance of the hour, but prompt on time the huntsman, the whips, and the hounds arrive. The Master's appearance is eagerly looked for, and it is a beautiful sight to see the hounds welcome him. I think the prettiest picture I ever saw connected with sport was the assembling of the South Devon pack one clear autumn morning. As the Master rode into the field, the hounds rushed forward and settled themselves on their haunches in circles around his horse. As far as the eye could see, the country was rich and beautiful, with enough of wood, enough of meadow, enough of undulation, to make the picture well worth remembering, and in the field the hunting party were waiting their word of command. This given, off they started to "draw" the wood to the left.* On this day, delightful as were all the elements—a combination which seemed to insure success—there was not a fox to be found, and it was rumored that at the next meeting what is called a "bagman" would be brought. This term is applied to a fox which is brought in a bag to the hunt, and then let out and away—a kind of hunting much despised by genuine sportsmen.

It is interesting to observe the ways and manners of different people in the field. Those new to the sport are so anxious to be conspicuous, to cry out on every provocation, and nine times out of ten to bring down the wrath of the Master on their heads by so doing. Even one of the "whips" will show his indignation when some young rider is "too forward," and sometimes it seems as if the dogs themselves knew just who had a right to speak and who had not.

Those magical words, "in at the death!" how seldom are they used satisfactorily! But since the animal has to be run down, this is a fine sight. As a general rule, the huntsman or one of the men seizes the fox as soon as it is killed, and holds it high above the hounds, whose notes of triumph are tremendous. When it is quite certain that all have seen it, the body is thrown to the dogs and quickly devoured, the "brush," or tail, being presented to the first lady on the spot.

* Drawing means looking for the fox. To draw a wood blank means finding no fox.

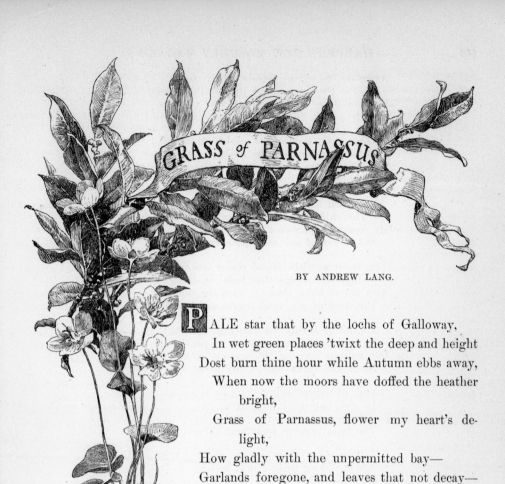

GRASS OF PARNASSUS

BY ANDREW LANG.

PALE star that by the lochs of Galloway,
    In wet green places 'twixt the deep and height
Dost burn thine hour while Autumn ebbs away,
    When now the moors have doffed the heather
        bright,
        Grass of Parnassus, flower my heart's de-
            light,
How gladly with the unpermitted bay—
Garlands foregone, and leaves that not decay—
    How gladly would I twine thee if I might!

The bays are out of reach! But far below
    The peaks forbidden of the muses' hill,
Grass of Parnassus, thy returning glow
    Between September and October chill
Doth speak to me of Autumns long ago,
    And my old memories are with me still.

INDIAN SUMMER.

QUEEN of the seasons, grave yet tender!
    What revellers were thy sylvan gods,
That late ran riot with cups of splendor,
    Overspilled on the golden-rods!

A banquet, a Bacchanal march of color!
    Opaline tints as of wine and flame!
In rivalry rosy Spring were duller,
    And Summer in all her pomp were tame.

After the revel, the woods grown sober,
　Feel'st thou regret for that brilliant rout
Held in thine honor ?　Doth sere October
　Sigh, joy is fled, and the play played out,

O Queen! O Goddess! O mighty Mother!
　Whom ancient sorrow hath made so wise
That the shows of Time and the world are other
　To thee than their seeming to mortal eyes ?

"Ah! with me," she rebukes my question,
　"The shifting scenery ends no play;
My heart keeps sweet through its inexhaustion,
　Whatever of joy may pass away."

Yea, from a misty cloud comes answer:
　"Only the things that fade are fair;
And lo! as from many a burning censer,
　The dust of my dead leaves smokes in air!

"All things lovely are flowing, flowing:
　Be not disconsolate: let them pass!
The seasons coming, the seasons going,
　Birth and bereavement, my great eyes glass;

"And, unremembering tears or laughter,
　In resignation of long ago,
In like regard are before and after,
　The festal groves and their shroud of snow.

"I sit in my veils while the sugar-maples
　Are shedding their glory, leaf by leaf;
My hands ambrosial let fall their apples
　And bread for man in the withering sheaf;

"As warm light lingers a silent actor
　In the after-glow and the after-math,
I still am the mother and benefactor,
　Though ravished Beauty be bride of Death.

"She, my child, whom with iridescence
　I dowered, and fragrance and grace withal,
And song—or divinity's floating presence
　Expressed in song—to interpret all,

"Seems stripped of charm.　There will no bird carol
　Of love to the scentless chrysanthemum.
I weave of the mist the world's apparel,
　And sink into dream—　But is music dumb ?

"As thoughts of the poet, in solitude springing,
　Are shaped and move to an underflow
Of melody sweeter than any singing,
　Till simplest words into beauty grow,

"So to the finer sense, in the pregnant
　Womb of darkness beneath the sod,
The strain of the sphere is rhythmical, regnant,
　Shaping to measure the thoughts of God!"
　　　　　　　　COMMANDER WILLIAM GIBSON, U.S.N.

THEIR PILGRIMAGE.

BY CHARLES DUDLEY WARNER.

CHAPTER XIV.

AFTER weeks of the din of Strauss and Gungl, the soothing strains of the Pastoral Symphony. Now no more the kettle-drum and the ceaseless promenade in showy corridors, but the oaten pipe under the spreading maples, the sheep feeding on the gentle hills of Otsego, the carnival of the hop-pickers. It is time to be rural, to adore the country, to speak about the dew on the upland pasture, and the exquisite view from Sunset Hill. It is quite English, is it not? this passion for quiet,

refined country life, which attacks all the summer revellers at certain periods in the season, and sends them in troops to Richfield or Lenox or some other peaceful retreat, with their simple apparel bestowed in modest four-story trunks. Come, gentle shepherdesses, come, sweet youths in white flannel, let us tread a measure on the greensward, let us wander down the lane, let us pass under the festoons of the hop-vines, let us saunter in the paths of sentiment, that lead to love in a cottage and a house in town.

Every watering-place has a character of

its own, and those who have given little thought to this are surprised at the endless variety in the American resorts. But what is even more surprising is the influence that these places have upon the people that frequent them, who appear to change their characters with their surroundings. One woman in her season plays many parts, dashing in one place, reserved in another, now gay and active, now listless and sentimental, not at all the same woman at Newport that she is in the Adirondack camps, one thing at Bar Harbor and quite another at Saratoga or at Richfield. Different tastes, to be sure, are suited at different resorts, but fashion sends a steady procession of the same people on the round of all.

The charm of Richfield Springs is in the character of the landscape. It is a limestone region of gentle slopes and fine lines; and although it is elevated, the general character is refined rather than bold, the fertile valleys in pleasing irregularity falling away from rounded wooded hills in a manner to produce the impression of peace and repose. The lay of the land is such that an elevation of a few hundred feet gives a most extensive prospect, a view of meadows and upland pastures, of lakes and ponds, of forests hanging in dark masses on the limestone summits, of fields of wheat and hops, and of distant mountain ranges. It is scenery that one grows to love, and that responds to one's every mood in variety and beauty. In a whole summer the pedestrian will not exhaust the inspiring views, and the drives through the gracious land, over hills, round the lakes, by woods and farms, increase in interest as one knows them better. The *habitués* of the place, year after year, are at a loss for words to convey their peaceful satisfaction.

In this smiling country lies the pretty village of Richfield, the rural character of which is not entirely lost by reason of the hotels, cottages, and boarding-houses which line the broad principal street. The centre of the town is the old Spring House and grounds. When our travellers alighted in the evening at this mansion, they were reminded of an English inn, though it is not at all like an inn in England except in its atmosphere of comfort. The building has rather a colonial character, with its long corridors and pillared piazzas; built at different times, and without any particular plans except to remain old-fashioned, it is now a big rambling white mass of buildings in the midst of maple-trees, with so many stairs and passages on different levels, and so many nooks and corners, that the stranger is always getting lost in it—turning up in the luxurious smoking-room when he wants to dine, and opening a door that lets him out into the park when he is trying to go to bed. But there are few hotels in the country where the guests are so well taken care of.

This was the unbought testimony of Miss Lamont, who, with her uncle, had been there long enough to acquire the common anxiety of sojourners that the new-comers should be pleased, and who superfluously explained the attractions of the place to the artist, as if in his eyes, that rested on her, more than one attraction was needed. It was very pleasant to see the good comradeship that existed between these two, and the frank expression of their delight in meeting again. Here was a friendship without any reserve, or any rueful misunderstandings, or necessity for explanations. Irene's eyes followed them with a wistful look as they went off together round the piazza and through the parlors, the girl playing the part of the hostess, and inducting him in the mild gayeties of the place. The height of the season was over, she said; there had been tableaux and charades, and broom-drills, and readings, and charity concerts. Now the season was on the sentimental wane; every night the rooms were full of whist-players, and the days were occupied in quiet strolling over the hills, and excursions to Cooperstown and Cherry Valley and "points of view," and visits to the fields to see the hop-pickers at work. If there were a little larking about the piazzas in the evening, and a group here and there pretending to be merry over tall glasses with ice and straws in them, and lingering goodnights at the stairways, why should the aged and rheumatic make a note of it? Did they not also once prefer the dance to hobbling to the spring, and the taste of ginger to sulphur?

Of course the *raison d'être* of being here is the sulphur spring. There is no doubt of its efficacy. I suppose it is as unpleasant as any in the country. Everybody smells it, and a great many drink it. The artist said that after using it a week the blind walk, the lame see,

"LET US PASS UNDER THE FESTOONS OF THE HOP-VINES."

and the dumb swear. It renews youth, and although the analyzer does not say that it is a "love philter," the statistics kept by the colored autocrat who ladles out the fluid show that there are made as many engagements at Richfield as at any other summer fair in the country.

There is not much to chronicle in the peaceful flow of domestic life, and, truth to say, the charm of Richfield is largely in its restfulness. Those who go there year after year converse a great deal about their liking for it, and think the time well spent in persuading new arrivals to take certain walks and drives. It was impressed upon King that he must upon no account omit a visit to Rum Hill, from the summit of which is had a noble prospect, including the Adirondack Mountains. He tried this with a walking party, was driven back when near the summit by a thunder-storm, which offered a series of grand pictures in the sky and on the hills, and took refuge in a farm-house which was occupied by a band of hop-pickers. These adventurers are mostly young girls and young men from the cities and factory villages, to whom this is the only holiday of the year. Many of the pickers, however, are veterans. At this season one meets them on all the roads, driving from farm to farm in lumber wagons, carrying into the dull rural life their slang, and "Captain Jinks" songs, and shocking free manners. At the great hop fields they lodge all together in big barracks, and they make lively for the time whatever farm-house they occupy. They are a "rough lot," and need very much the attention of the poet and the novelist, who might (if they shut their eyes) make this season as romantic as vintage-time on the Rhine, or "moon-shining" on the Southern mountains. The hop field itself, with its tall poles draped in graceful vines which reach from pole to pole, and hang their yellowing fruit in pretty festoons and arbors, is much more picturesque than the vine-clad hills.

Mrs. Bartlett-Glow found many acquaintances here from New York and Philadelphia and Newport, and, to do her justice, she introduced Irene to them, and presently involved her in so many pleasure parties and excursions that she and King were scarcely ever alone together. When opportunity offered for a stroll à deux, the girl's manner was so constrained that King was compelled to ask the reason

of it. He got very little satisfaction, and the puzzle of her conduct was increased by her confession that she loved him just the same, and always should.

"But something has come between us," he said. "I think I have the right to be treated with perfect frankness."

"So you have," she replied. "There is nothing—nothing at least that changes my feeling toward you."

"But you think that mine is changed for you?"

"No, not that, either, never that;" and her voice showed excitement as she turned away her head. "But don't you know, Stanhope, you have not known me very long, and perhaps you have been a little hasty, and—how shall I say it?—if you had more time to reflect, when you go back to your associates and your active life, it might somehow look differently to you, and your prospects—"

"Why, Irene, I have no prospects without you. I love you; you are my life. I don't understand. I am just yours, and nothing you can do will ever make it any different for me; but if you want to be free—"

"No, no," cried the girl, trying in vain to restrain her agitation and her tears, "not that. I don't want to be free. But you will not understand. Circumstances are so cruel, and if, Stanhope, you ever should regret when it is too late! It would kill me. I want you to be happy. And, Stanhope, promise me that, whatever happens, you will not think ill of me."

Of course he promised, he declared that nothing could happen, he vowed, and he protested against this ridiculous phantom in her mind. To a man, used to straightforward cuts in love as in any other object of his desire, this feminine exaggeration of conscientiousness is wholly incomprehensible. How under heavens a woman could get a kink of duty in her mind which involved the sacrifice of herself and her lover was past his fathoming.

The morning after this conversation, the most of which the reader has been spared, there was an excursion to Cooperstown. The early start of the Tally-ho coaches for this trip is one of the chief sensations of the quiet village. The bustle to collect the laggards, the importance of the conductors and drivers, the scramble up the ladders, the ruses to get congenial seat-neighbors, the fine spirits of everybody evoked by the fresh morning

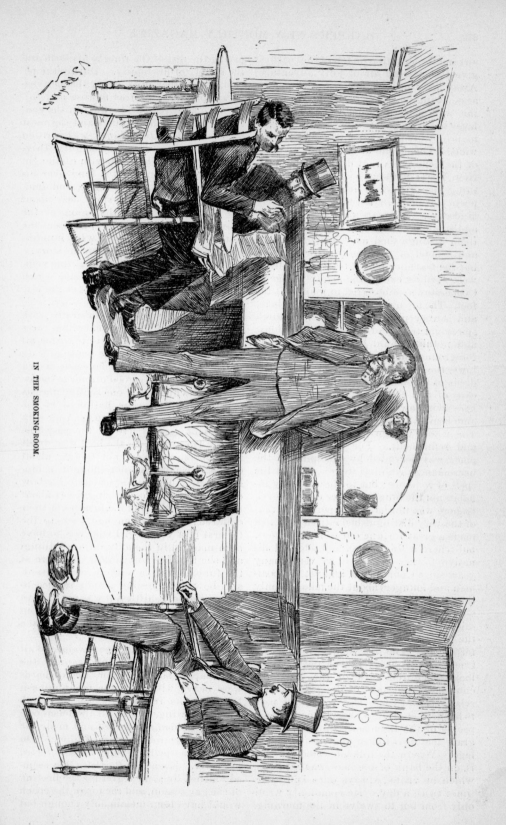

IN THE SMOKING-ROOM.

air, and the elevation on top of the coaches, give the start an air of jolly adventure. Away they go, the big red and yellow arks, swinging over the hills and along the well-watered valleys, past the twin lakes to Otsego, over which hangs the romance of Cooper's tales, where a steamer waits. This is one of the most charming of the little lakes that dot the interior of New York; without bold shores or anything sensational in its scenery, it is a poetic element in a refined and lovely landscape. There are a few fishing lodges and summer cottages on its banks (one of them distinguished as "Sinners' Rest"), and a hotel or two famous for dinners; but the traveller would be repaid if there were nothing except the lovely village of Cooperstown embowered in maples at the foot. The town rises gently from the lake, and is very picturesque with its church spires and trees and handsome mansions; and nothing could be prettier than the foreground, the gardens, the *allées* of willows, the long boat wharves with hundreds of row-boats and sail-boats, and the exit of the Susquehanna River, which here swirls away under drooping foliage, and begins its long journey to the sea. The whole village has an air of leisure and refinement. For our tourists the place was pervaded by the spirit of the necromancer who has woven about it the spell of romance; but to the ordinary inhabitants the long residence of the novelist here was not half so important as that of the very distinguished citizen who had made a great fortune out of some patent, built here a fine house, and adorned his native town. It is not so very many years since Cooper died, and yet the boatmen and loungers about the lake had only the faintest impression of the man—there was a writer by that name, one of them said, and some of his family lived near the house of the great man already referred to. The magician who created Cooperstown sleeps in the old English-looking church-yard of the Episcopal church, in the midst of the graves of his relations, and there is a well-worn path to his head-stone. Whatever the common people of the town may think, it is that grave that draws most pilgrims to the village. Where the hill-side cemetery now is, on the bank of the lake, was his farm, which he visited always once and sometimes twice a day. He commonly wrote only from ten to twelve in the morning,

giving the rest of the time to his farm and the society of his family. During the period of his libel suits, when the newspapers represented him as morose and sullen in his retirement, he was, on the contrary, in the highest spirits and the most genial mood. *Deerslayer* was written while this contest was at its height. Driving one day from his farm with his daughter, he stopped and looked long over his favorite prospect on the lake, and said, "I must write one more story, dear, about our little lake." At that moment the *Deerslayer* was born. He was silent the rest of the way home, and went immediately to his library and began the story.

The party returned in a moralizing vein. How vague already in the village which his genius has made known over the civilized world is the fame of Cooper! To our tourists the place was saturated with his presence, but the new generation cares more for its smart prosperity than for all his romance. Many of the passengers on the boat had stopped at a lake-side tavern to dine, preferring a good dinner to the associations which drew our sentimentalists to the spots that were hallowed by the necromancer's imagination. And why not? One cannot live in the past forever. The people on the boat who dwelt in Cooperstown were not talking about Cooper, perhaps had not thought of him for a year. The ladies, seated in the bow of the boat, were comparing notes about their rheumatism and the measles of their children; one of them had been to the funeral of a young girl who was to have been married in the autumn, poor thing, and she told her companion who were at the funeral, and how they were dressed, and how little feeling Nancy seemed to show, and how shiftless it was not to have more flowers, and how the bridegroom bore up—well, perhaps it's an escape, she was so weakly.

The day lent a certain pensiveness to all this; the season was visibly waning; the soft maples showed color, the orchards were heavy with fruit, the mountain-ash hung out its red signals, the hop-vines were yellowing, and in all the fence corners the golden-rod flamed and made the meanest high-road a way of glory. On Irene fell a spell of sadness that affected her lover. Even Mrs. Bartlett-Glow seemed touched by some regret for the fleeting of the gay season, and the top of the coach would have been melancholy enough but

"WHY, WHAT HAS COME OVER YOU, OLD MAN?"—[SEE NEXT PAGE.]

for the high spirits of Marion and the artist, whose gayety expanded in the abundance of the harvest season. Happy natures, unrestrained by the subtle melancholy of a decaying year!

The summer was really going. On Sunday the weather broke in a violent storm
of wind and rain, and at sunset, when it
abated, there were portentous gleams on
the hills, and threatening clouds lurking

about the sky. It was time to go. Few
people have the courage to abide the breaking of the serenity of summer, and remain
in the country for the more glorious autumn days that are to follow. The Glows
must hurry back to Newport. The Bensons would not be persuaded out of their
fixed plan to "take in," as Mr. Benson expressed it, the White Mountains. The
others were going to Niagara and the

Thousand Islands, and when King told Irene that he would much rather change his route and accompany her, he saw by the girl's manner that it was best not to press the subject. He dreaded to push an explanation, and, foolish as lovers are, he was wise for once in trusting to time. But he had a miserable evening. He let himself be irritated by the light-heartedness of Forbes. He objected to the latter's whistling as he went about his room packing up his traps. He hated a fellow that was always in high spirits. "Why, what has come over you, old man?" queried the artist, stopping to take a critical look at his comrade. "Do you want to get out of it? It's my impression that you haven't taken sulphur water enough."

On Monday morning there was a general clearing out. The platform at the station was crowded. The palace-cars for New York, for Niagara, for Albany, for the West, were overflowing. There was a pile of trunks as big as a city dwelling-house. Baby-carriages cumbered the way; dogs were under foot, yelping and rending the tender hearts of their owners; the porters staggered about under their loads, and shouted till they were hoarse; farewells were said; rendezvous made—alas! how many half-fledged hopes came to an end on that platform! The artist thought he had never seen so many pretty girls together in his life before, and each one had in her belt a bunch of golden-rod. Summer was over, sure enough.

At Utica the train was broken up, and its cars despatched in various directions. King remembered that it was at Utica that the younger Cato sacrificed himself. In the presence of all the world Irene bade him good-by. "It will not be for long," said King, with an attempt at gayety. "Nothing is for long," she said, with the same manner. And then added in a low tone, as she slipped a note into his hand, "Do not think ill of me."

King opened the note as soon as he found his seat in the car, and this was what he read as the train rushed westward toward the Great Fall:

"MY DEAR FRIEND,—How can I ever say it? It is best that we separate. I have thought and thought; I have struggled with myself. I think that I know it is best for you. I have been happy—ah me! Dear, we must look at the world as it is. We cannot change it—if we

break our hearts, we cannot. Don't blame your cousin. It is nothing that she has done. She has been as sweet and kind to me as possible, but I have seen through her what I feared, just how it is. Don't reproach me. It is hard now. I know it. But I believe that you will come to see it as I do. If it was any sacrifice that I could make, that would be easy. But to think that I had sacrificed you, and that you should some day become aware of it! You are free. I am not silly. It is the future I am thinking of. You must take your place in the world where your lot is cast. Don't think I have a foolish pride. Perhaps it *is* pride that tells me not to put myself in a false position; perhaps it is something else. Never think it is want of heart in IRENE.

"Good-by."

As King finished this he looked out of the window. The landscape was black.

CHAPTER XV.

IN the car for Niagara was an Englishman of the receptive, guileless, thin type, inquisitive, and overflowing with approval of everything American—a type which has now become one of the common features of travel in this country. He had light hair, sandy side-whiskers, a face that looked as if it had been scrubbed with soap and sand-paper, and he wore a sickly yellow travelling suit. He was accompanied by his wife, a stout, resolute matron, in heavy boots, a sensible stuff gown, with a lot of cotton lace fudged about her neck, and a broad-brimmed hat with a vegetable garden on top. The little man was always in pursuit of information, in his guide-book or from his fellow-passengers, and whenever he obtained any he invariably repeated it to his wife, who said, "Fancy!" and "Now, really!" in a rising inflection that expressed surprise and expectation.

The conceited American, who commonly draws himself into a shell when he travels, and affects indifference, and seems to be losing all natural curiosity, receptivity, and the power of observation, is pretty certain to undervalue the intelligence of this class of English travellers, and get amusement out of their peculiarities instead of learning from them how to

"WHO SAID, 'FANCY!' AND 'NOW, REALLY!'"

make every day of life interesting. Even King, who, besides his national crust of exclusiveness, was to-day wrapped in the gloom of Irene's letter, was gradually drawn to these simple, unpretending people. He took for granted their ignorance of America—ignorance of America being one of the branches taught in the English schools—and he soon discovered that they were citizens of the world. They not only knew the Continent very well, but they had spent a winter in Egypt, lived a year in India, and seen something of China and much of Japan. Although they had been scarcely a fortnight in the United States, King doubted if there were ten women in the State of New York, not professional teachers, who knew as much of the flora of the country as this plain-featured, rich-voiced woman. They called King's attention to a great many features of the landscape he had never noticed before, and asked him a great many questions about farming and stock and wages that he could not answer. It appeared that Mr. Stanley Stubbs, Stoke-Cruden—for that was the name and address of the present

discoverers of America—had a herd of short-horns, and that Mrs. Stubbs was even more familiar with the herd-book than her husband. But before the fact had enabled King to settle the position of his new acquaintance satisfactorily to himself, Mrs. Stubbs upset his estimate by quoting Tennyson.

"Your great English poet is very much read here," King said, by way of being agreeable.

"So we have heard," replied Mrs. Stubbs. "Mr. Stubbs reads Tennyson beautifully. He has thought of giving some readings while we are here. We have been told that the Americans are very fond of readings."

"Yes," said King, "they are devoted to them, especially readings by Englishmen in their native tongue. There is a great rage now for everything English; at Newport hardly anything else is spoken."

Mrs. Stubbs looked for a moment as if this might be an American joke; but there was no smile upon King's face, and she only said, "Fancy! You must make a note of Newport, dear. That is one of the places we must see. Of course Mr. Stubbs has never read in public, you know. But I suppose that would make no difference, the Americans are so kind and so appreciative."

"Not the least difference," replied King. "They are used to it."

"It is a wonderful country," said Mr. Stubbs.

"Most interesting," chimed in Mrs. Stubbs; "and so odd!"

"You know, Mr. King, we find some of the Americans so clever. We have been surprised, really. It makes us feel quite at home. At the hotels and everywhere, most obliging."

"Do you make a long stay?"

"Oh no. We just want to study the people and the government, and see the principal places. We were told that Albany is the capital, instead of New York; it's so odd, you know. And Washington is another capital. And there is Boston. It must be very confusing." King began to suspect that he must be talking with the editor of the *Saturday Review*. Mr. Stubbs continued: "They told us in New York that we ought to go to Paterson, on the island of Jersey, I believe. I suppose it is as interesting as Niagara. We shall visit it on our return. But we came over more to see Niagara than anything else. And from there we shall run over to Chicago and the Yosemite. Now we are here, we could not think of going back without a look at the Yosemite."

King said that thus far he had existed without seeing the Yosemite, but he believed that next to Chicago it was the most attractive place in the country.

It was dark when they came into the station at Niagara—dark and silent. Our American tourists, who were accustomed to the clamor of the hackmen here, and expected to be assaulted by a horde of wild Comanches in plain clothes, and torn limb from baggage, if not limb from limb, were unable to account for this silence, and the absence of the common highwaymen, until they remembered that the State had bought the Falls, and the agents of the government had suppressed many of the old nuisances. It was possible now to hear the roar of the cataract.

This unaccustomed human stillness was ominous to King. He would have welcomed a Niagara of importunity and imprecations; he was bursting with impatience to express himself; it seemed as if he would die if he were silent an hour longer under that letter. Of course the usual American relief of irritability and impatience suggested itself. He would telegraph; only electricity was quick enough and fiery enough for his mood. But what should he telegraph? The telegraph was not invented for love-making, and is not adapted to it. It is ridiculous to make love by wire. How was it possible to frame a message that should be commercial on its face, and yet convey the deepest agony and devotion of the sender's heart? King stood at the little telegraph window, looking at the despatcher who was to send it, and thought of this. Depressed and intent as he was, the whimsicality of the situation struck him. What could he say? It illustrates our sheep-like habit of expressing ourselves in the familiar phrase or popular slang of the day that at the instant the only thing King could think of to send was this: "Hold the fort, for I am coming." The incongruity of this made him smile, and he did not write it. Finally he composed this message, which seemed to him to have a business-like and innocent aspect: "Too late. Impossible for me to change. Have invested everything. Expect letter." Mechanically he counted the words when he had written this. On the fair presumption that the company would send "everything" as one word, there were still two more than the conventional ten, and, from force of habit, he struck out the words "for me." But he had no sooner done this than he felt a sense of shame. It was contemptible for a man in love to count his words, and it was intolerable to be haggling with himself at such a crisis over the expense of a despatch. He got cold over the thought that Irene might also count them, and see that the cost of this message of passion had been calculated. And with recklessness he added: "We reach the Profile House next week, and I am sure I can convince you I am right."

King found Niagara pitched to the key of his lacerated and tumultuous feelings. There were few people at the Cataract House, and either the bridal season had not set in, or in America a bride has been evolved who does not show any consciousness of her new position. In his present mood the place seemed deserted, the figures of the few visitors gliding

MUZZLED HACKMEN.

about as in a dream, as if they too had been subdued by the recent commission which had silenced the drivers, and stopped the mills, and made the park free, and was tearing down the presumptuous structures along the bank. In this silence, which emphasized the quaking of the earth and air, there was a sense of unknown, impending disaster. It was not to be borne in-doors, and the two friends went out into the night.

On the edge of the rapids, above the hotel, the old bath-house was in process of demolition, its shaking piazza almost over-hanging the flood. Not much could be seen from it, but it was in the midst of an elemental uproar. Some electric lamps shining through the trees made high lights on the crests of the rapids, while others near were in shadow and dark. The black mass of Goat Island appeared under the lightning flashes in the north-west sky, and whenever these quick gleams pierced the gloom, the frail bridge to the island was outlined for a moment, and then vanished as if it had been swept away, and there could only be seen sparks of light in the houses on the Canadian shore, which seemed very near. In this unknown, which was rather felt than seen, there was a sense of power and of mystery which overcame the mind; and in the black night the roar, the cruel haste of the rapids, tossing white gleams and hurrying to the fatal plunge, begat a sort of terror in the spectators. It was a power implacable, vengeful, not to be measured. They strolled down to Prospect Park. The gate was closed; it had been the scene of an awful tragedy but a few minutes before. They did not know it, but they knew that the air shuddered, and as they skirted the grounds along the way to the foot-bridge, the roar grew in their stunned ears. There, projected out into the night, were the cables of steel holding the frail platform over the abyss of night and terror. Beyond was Canada. There was light enough in the sky to reveal, but not to dissipate, the appalling insecurity. What an impious thing it seemed to them, this trembling structure across the chasm! They advanced upon it. There were gleams on the mill cascades below, and on the mass of the American Fall. Below, down in the gloom, were patches of foam, slowly circling around in the eddy—no haste now, just sullen and black satisfaction in the awful tragedy of the fall. The whole was vague, fearful. Always the roar, the shuddering of the air. I think that a man placed on this bridge at night, and ignorant of the cause of the aerial agitation and the wild uproar, could almost lose his reason in the panic of the scene.

They walked on; they set foot on her Majesty's dominions; they entered the Clifton House—quite American, you know, with its new bar and office. A subdued air about everybody here also, and the same quaking, shivering, and impending sense of irresponsible force. Even "two fingers," said the artist, standing at the bar, had little effect in allaying the impression of the terror out there. When they returned, the moon was coming up, rising and struggling and making its way slowly through ragged masses of colored clouds. The river could be plainly seen now, smooth, deep, treacherous; the falls on the American side showed fitfully like patches of light and foam; the Horseshoe, mostly hidden by a cold silver mist, occasionally loomed up a white and ghastly mass. They stood for a long time looking down at the foot of the American

Fall, the moon now showing clearly the plunge of the heavy columns—a column as stiff as if it were melted silver—hushed and frightened by the weird and appalling scene. They did not know at that moment that there where their eyes were riveted, there at the base of the fall, a man's body was churning about, plunged down and cast up, and beaten and whirled, imprisoned in the refluent eddy. But a body was there. In the morning a man's overcoat was found on the parapet at the angle of the fall. Some one then remembered that in the evening, just before the park gate closed, he had seen a man approach the angle of the wall where the overcoat was found. The man was never seen after that. Night first, and then the hungry water, swallowed him. One pictures the fearful leap into the dark, the midway repentance, perhaps, the despair of the plunge. A body cast in here is likely to tarry for days, eddying round and round, and tossed in that terrible maelstrom, before a chance current ejects it, and sends it down the fierce rapids below. King went back to the hotel in a terror of the place, which did not leave him so long as he remained. His room quivered, the roar filled all the air. Is not life real and terrible enough, he asked himself, but that brides must cast this experience also into their honeymoon?

The morning light did not efface the impressions of the night, the dominating presence of a gigantic, pitiless force, a blind passion of nature, uncontrolled and uncontrollable. Shut the windows and lock the door, you could not shut out the terror of it. The town did not seem safe; the bridges, the buildings on the edge of the precipices with their shaking casements, the islands, might at any moment be engulfed and disappear. It was a thing to flee from.

I suspect King was in a very sensitive mood; the world seemed for the moment devoid of human sympathy, and the savageness and turmoil played upon his bare nerves. The artist himself shrank from contact with this overpowering display, and said that he could not endure more than a day or two of it. It needed all the sunshine in the face of Miss Lamont and the serenity of her cheerful nature to make the situation tolerable, and even her sprightliness was somewhat subdued. It was a day of big, broken, high-sailing clouds, with a deep blue sky and strong sunlight. The slight bridge to Goat Island appeared more presumptuous by daylight, and the sharp slope of the rapids above it gave a new sense of the impetuosity of the torrent. As they walked slowly on, past the now abandoned paper-mills and the other human impertinences, the elemental turmoil increased, and they seemed entering a world the foundations of which were broken up. This must have been a good deal a matter of impression, for other parties of sight-seers were coming and going, apparently unawed, and intent simply on visiting every point spoken of in the guide-book, and probably unconscious of the all-pervading terror. But King could not escape it, even in the throng descending and ascending the stairway to Luna Island. Standing upon the platform at the top, he realized for the first time the immense might of the downpour of the American Fall, and noted the pale green color, with here and there a violet tone, and the white cloud mass spurting out from the solid color. On the foam-crested river lay a rainbow forming nearly a complete circle. The little steamer *Maid of the Mist* was coming up, riding the waves, dashed here and there by conflicting currents, but resolutely steaming on—such is the audacity of man—and poking her venturesome nose into the boiling foam under the Horseshoe. On the deck are pigmy passengers in oil-skin suits, clumsy figures, like arctic explorers. The boat tosses about like a chip, it hesitates and quivers, and then slowly swinging, darts away down the current, fleeing from the wrath of the waters, and pursued by the angry roar.

Surely it is an island of magic, unsubstantial, liable to go adrift and plunge into the cañon. Even in the forest path, where the great tree trunks assure one of stability and long immunity, this feeling cannot be shaken off. Our party descended the winding staircase in the tower, and walked on the shelf under the mighty ledge to the entrance of the Cave of the Winds. The curtain of water covering this entrance was blown back and forth by the wind, now leaving the platform dry and now deluging it. A woman in the pathway was beckoning frantically and calling to a man who stood on the platform, entirely unconscious of danger, looking up to the green curtain and down

into the boiling mist. It was Mrs. Stubbs; but she was shouting against Niagara, and her husband mistook her pantomime for gestures of wonder and admiration. Some moments passed, and then the curtain swung in, and tons of water drenched the Englishman, and for an instant hid him from sight. Then, as the curtain swung back, he was seen clinging to the hand-rail, sputtering and astonished at such treatment. He came up the bank dripping, and declaring that it was extraordinary, most extraordinary, but he wouldn't have missed it for the world. From this platform one looks down the narrow slippery stairs that are lost in the boiling mist, and wonders at the daring that built these steps down into that hell, and carried the frail walk of planks over the bowlders outside the fall. A party in oil-skins, making their way there, looked like lost men and women in a Dante Inferno. The turbulent waters dashed all about them; the mist occasionally wrapped them from sight; they clung to the rails, they tried to speak to each other; their gestures seemed motions of despair. Could that be·Eurydice whom the rough guide was tenderly dragging out of the hell of waters, up the stony path, that singular figure in oil-skin trousers, who disclosed a pretty face inside her hood as she emerged? One might venture into the infernal regions to rescue such a woman; but why take her there? The group of adventurers stopped a moment on the platform, with the opening into the misty cavern for a background, and the artist said that the picture was, beyond all power of the pencil, strange and fantastic. There is nothing, after all, that the human race will not dare for a new sensation.

The walk around Goat Island is probably unsurpassed in the world for wonder and beauty. The Americans have every reason to be satisfied with their share of the fall; they get nowhere one single grand view like that from the Canada side, but infinitely the deepest impression of majesty and power is obtained on Goat Island. There the spectator is in the midst of the war of nature. From the point over the Horseshoe Fall our friends, speaking not much, but more and more deeply moved, strolled along in the lovely forest, in a rural solemnity, in a local calm, almost a seclusion, except for the ever-present shuddering roar in the air. On the shore above the Horseshoe they first comprehended the breadth, the great sweep, of the rapids. The white crests of the waves in the west were coming out from under a black, lowering sky; all the foreground was in bright sunlight, dancing, sparkling, leaping, hurrying on, converging to the angle where the water becomes a deep emerald at the break and plunge. The rapids above are a series of shelves, bristling with jutting rocks and lodged trunks of trees, and the wildness of the scene is intensified by the ragged fringe of evergreens on the opposite shore.

Over the whole island the mist, rising from the caldron, drifts in spray when the wind is favorable; but on this day the forest was bright and cheerful, and as the strollers went farther away from the Great Fall, the beauty of the scene began to steal away its terror. The roar was still dominant, but far off and softened, and did not crush the ear. The triple islands, the Three Sisters, in their picturesque wildness appeared like playful freaks of nature in a momentary relaxation of the savage mood. Here is the finest view of the river; to one standing on the outermost island the great flood seems tumbling out of the sky. They continued along the bank of the river. The shallow stream races by headlong, but close to the edge are numerous eddies, and places where one might step in and not be swept away. At length they reached the point where the river divides, and the water stands for an instant almost still, hesitating whether to take the Canadian or the American plunge. Out a little way from the shore the waves leap and tumble, and the two currents are like race-horses parted on two ways to the goal. Just at this point the water swirls and lingers, having lost all its fierceness and haste, and spreads itself out placidly, dimpling in the sun. It may be a treacherous pause, this water may be as cruel as that which rages below and exults in catching a boat or a man and bounding with the victim over the cataract; but the calm was very grateful to the stunned and buffeted visitors; upon their jarred nerves it was like the peace of God.

"The preacher might moralize here," said King. "Here are the parting of the ways for the young man; here is a moment of calm in which he can decide which course he will take. See, with my hand I can turn the waters to Canada or to America! So momentous is the easy decision of the moment."

"Yes," said the artist, "your figure is perfect. Whichever side the young man takes, he goes to destruction."

"Or," continued King, appealing to Miss Lamont against this illogical construction, "this is the maiden at the crucial instant of choosing between two impetuous suitors."

"You mean she will be sorry, whichever she chooses?"

"You two practical people would spoil any illustration in the world. You would divest the impressive drop of water on the mountain summit, which might go to the Atlantic or to the Pacific, of all moral character by saying that it makes no difference which ocean it falls into."

The relief from the dread of Niagara felt at this point of peace was only temporary. The dread returned when the party approached again the turmoil of the American Fall, and fell again under the influence of the merciless haste of the flood. And there every islet, every rock, every point, has its legend of terror; here a boat lodged with a man in it, and after a day and night of vain attempts to rescue him, thousands of people saw him take the frightful leap, throwing up his arms as he went over; here a young woman slipped, and was instantly whirled away out of life; and from that point more than one dazed or frantic visitor had taken the suicidal leap. Death was so near here and so easy!

One seems in less personal peril on the Canadian side, and has more the feeling of a spectator, and less that of a participant in the wild uproar. Perhaps there is more sense of force, but the majesty of the scene is relieved by a hundred shifting effects of light and color. In the afternoon, under a broken sky, the rapids above the Horseshoe reminded one of the sea-shore on a very stormy day. Impeded by the rocks, the flood hesitated and even ran back, as if reluctant to take the final plunge! The sienna-color of the water on the table contrasted sharply with the emerald at the break of the fall. A rainbow springing out of the centre of the caldron arched clear over the American cataract, and was one moment bright and the next dimly seen through the mist, which boiled up out of the hell of waters and swayed in the wind. Through this veil darted adventurous birds, flashing their wings in the prismatic colors, and circling about as if fascinated by the aw-

A PARTY IN OIL-SKINS.

ful rush and thunder. With the shifting wind and the passing clouds the scene was in perpetual change; now the American Fall was creamy white, and the mist below dark, and again the heavy mass was gray and sullen, and the mist like silver spray. Perhaps nowhere else in the world is the force of nature so overpowering to the mind, and as the eye wanders from the chaos of the fall to the far horizon, where the vast rivers of rapids are poured out of the sky, one feels that this force is inexhaustible and eternal.

If our travellers expected to escape the impression they were under by driving down to the rapids and whirlpool below, they were mistaken. Nowhere is the river so terrible as where it rushes, as if maddened by its narrow bondage, through the cañon. Flung down the precipice and forced into this contracted space, it fumes and tosses and rages with vindictive fury, driving on in a passion that has almost a human quality in it. Restrained by the walls of stone from being destructive, it seems to rave at its own impotence, and when it reaches the whirlpool it is like a hungry animal, returning and licking the shore for the prey it has missed. But it has not always wanted a prey. Now and again it has a wreck or a dead body to toss and fling about. Although it does not need the human element of disaster

to make this cañon grewsome, the keepers of the show places make the most of the late Captain Webb. So vivid were their narratives that our sympathetic party felt his presence continually, saw the strong swimmer tossed like a chip, saw him throw up his hands, saw the agony in his face at the spot where he was last seen. There are several places where he disappeared, each vouched for by credible witnesses, so that the horror of the scene is multiplied for the tourist. The late afternoon had turned gray and cold, and dashes of rain fell as our party descended to the whirlpool. As they looked over the heaped-up and foaming waters in this eddy they almost expected to see Captain Webb or the suicide of the night before circling round in the maelstrom. They came up out of the gorge silent, and drove back to the hotel full of nervous apprehension.

King found no telegram from Irene, and the place seemed to him intolerable. The artist was quite ready to go on in the morning; indeed, the whole party, although they said it was unreasonable, confessed that they were almost afraid to stay longer; the roar, the trembling, the pervading sense of a blind force and rage, inspired a nameless dread. The artist said, the next morning at the station, that he understood the feelings of Lot.

TO FAME.

BY R. D. BLACKMORE.

"BRIGHT fairy of the morn, with flowers arrayed,
  Whose beauties to thy young pursuer seem
  Beyond the ecstasy of poet's dream—
Shall I o'ertake thee, ere thy lustre fade?

"Ripe glory of the noon, to dazzled eyes
  A pageant of delight and power and gold,
  Dissolving into mirage manifold—
Do I o'ertake thee, or mistake my prize?

"Dull shadow of the evening, gaunt and gray,
  At random thrown, beyond me, or above,
  And cold as memory in the arms of love—
Have I o'erta'en thee, but to cast away?"

"No morn, or noon, or eve, am I," she said,
  "But night, the depth of night behind the sun;
  By all mankind pursued, but never won,
Until my shadow falls upon a shade."

THE NATIONAL HOME FOR DISABLED VOLUNTEER SOLDIERS.

BY MARIA BARRETT BUTLER.

AFTER twenty years of garnered harvests from intrenched battle-fields, and of steadily abating sectional feeling, there is little left to sharply remind one of the fratricidal conflict, save the invalid and disabled soldiers gathered together, under the auspices of the government, into a stupendous institution, designed by special enactment to be considered as a home, in contradistinction to the asylums founded by charitable or legislative policy. The magnitude of this achievement justifies a brief review of what so entirely relates to the soldier and to the nation's interest in his behalf.

The whole number of Federal soldiers engaged in the civil war was 2,778,304. Of these the colored troops numbered 178,975, while the Indian nations furnished 3530 men. The aggregate of deaths, from all causes, up to the time that the different armies were disbanded, was 359,528. By culling the tables of statistical exhibit of deaths a brief schedule of striking interest is obtained.

Killed in Action.

Officers........ 4,142
Men 62,916

Died of Wounds received in Action.

Officers........ 2,223
Men 40,789

INCOMPLETE RETURNS OF PRISONERS.

Died of Wounds received in Action.

Officers................... 99
Men 1,973

Died of Disease in Prison.

Officers................... 83
Men 24,783

Inasmuch as it is not only the soldier living, but the soldier dead, that the na-

HOSPITAL, EASTERN BRANCH.

tion aims to provide for, a few items relative to the eighty-two national cemeteries may be given here as a fitting sequel to the foregoing. The alphabetical list from which these results are obtained was copied by special favor from records in the "Office of National Cemeteries" at Washington. Eleven of these are in Virginia (besides the one in West Virginia), seven in Tennessee, four each in North Carolina and Kentucky, and three each in Mississippi and Louisiana. The others are variously distributed in twenty-one States and Territories, including one at Washington, D. C., and another at Mexico city, Mexico. Twenty-one of these cemeteries have over 2000, not exceeding 5000 interments; nine cemeteries have 5000, not exceeding 10,000; and eleven cemeteries

NATIONAL CEMETERY, SOUTHERN BRANCH.

have over 10,000, as designated in the following table. A marble head-stone marks each grave, bearing the name and rank of the occupant, when known, the same standing also on the register of the cemetery. Salaried men have care of the na-

COLONEL ANDREW J. SMITH, GOVERNOR OF THE
WESTERN BRANCH.

tion's dead, and visitors are shown the grounds free of charge.

LOCATION OF CEMETERIES WITH OVER TEN THOUSAND INTERMENTS.

Name.	Known.	Unknown.	Total.
Marietta, Georgia	7,192	2,963	10,155
Jefferson Barracks, Missouri	8,647	2,906	11,553
Salisbury, North Carolina ..	97	12,032	12,129
Chalmetto, Louisiana........	6,851	5,674	12,525
Chattanooga, Tennessee....	8,012	4,963	12,975
Andersonville, Georgia	12,781	921	13,702
Memphis, Tennessee	5,163	8,818	13,981
Fredericksburg, Virginia ...	2,487	12,771	15,258
Arlington, Virginia	11,853	4,349	16,202
Nashville, Tennessee	11,825	4,701	16,526
Vicksburg, Mississippi	3,899	12,710	16,609

The total number of interments in all the national cemeteries is 322,851. Of these, 9438 were Confederates.

At the cessation of hostilities in 1865 the government had in charge 204 hospitals, with capacity for 136,894 beds. The returns of sick and wounded show that the total of cases treated up to that time was 1,057,423. At the end of eight months there were yet in existence thirty-four government hospitals, besides the State hospitals and soldiers' retreats, which had been temporarily established in most of the Northern States for immediate use upon the disbanding of the armies. These gradually disappeared upon the carrying into effect of an act of Congress, approved March 31, 1865, for the establishment of a National Home. The Board of Managers was to comprise one hundred men; but after twice failing to secure a quorum, its bulk was found to paralyze its efficiency. But government looked after the maimed soldiers, and during the year 6410 artificial limbs were supplied to them without charge.

In the mean time a great Sanitary Commission, conducted by the people, was doing its beneficent work. With head-quarters at Washington, its ramifications extending to every community on Union soil, it was the largest and most efficient organization of the kind ever known. Not only were the inmates of hospitals looked after, and supplies of every needed comfort systematically furnished them, but when the time came for still other help, bureaus of information and employment were established in all the principal cities for those needing such aid; as also were claim agencies, for collecting, free of charge, their back pay, pensions, and bounties. So fully had public confidence been secured that large donations of goods, clothing, and moneys were constantly received by the Commission for its work. An official exhibit in April, 1865, showed that the contributions from California alone to that date amounted to $1,199,675, and from the sparsely populated States of Nevada and Oregon the sums of $99,512 and $20,733 respectively had been received. Metropolitan fairs of almost fabulous magnitude were conducted for the same

GENERAL LUTHER STEPHENSON, JUN., GOVERNOR
OF THE EASTERN BRANCH.

purpose, and became a feature of the times. A notable one in New York city yielded a profit of $1,184,145, and the net proceeds of the Central Fair of Philadelphia amounted to $1,035,398. These fairs, aside from their financial significance, proved a fitting outlet for the repressed impulsion of thousands of men and wo-

BARRACK BUILDINGS, WESTERN BRANCH.

men compelled to remain at home and to hold themselves still—the hardest of all things to do, when the leading spirit of the hour almost impelled to action. The Sanitary Commission recognized and took advantage of this state of feeling by conducting still other fairs, under its own auspices, with the most satisfactory results, the one held at Cincinnati having been especially notable.

When finally the disbanded armies were homeward bound, hundreds of thousands of soldiers, left at stations and landings for change of transportation, were met by emissaries of the Commission, supplied with all necessities, and forwarded each one toward his point of destination. The Commission having decided that the claim agencies and others of equal import must still be continued for a time, a fair to meet this additional expenditure was opened up at Chicago, from which was realized the sum of $325,000. Thus did a grateful people extend to the defenders of the Union most generous and unstinted aid, to be more directly dispensed where most needed than could be the government supplies, always retarded as they were in their channels of transit by the complicities of official red tape.

Finally, on April 21, 1866, by a joint resolution of the two Houses of Congress, a Board of Managers for the Soldiers' National Home was appointed, of nine citizens of the United States, not members of Congress, no two of whom could be residents of the same State, nor residents of any State other than those which furnished organized bodies in the late war. The *ex officio* members of the board, during their terms of office, are the President of the United States, the Secretary of War, and the Chief-Justice. This board was vested with authority to establish, besides a central Home for the Middle States, sectional branches thereto, in view of the wide extent of territory to be represented by the just claimants of such a benefice.

The board, keenly appreciating the great responsibility of the work before it, looked abroad for successful precedent. The great naval hospital at Greenwich, England, which for one hundred and sixty years had been an asylum for disabled and superannuated seamen, had just dismissed its inmates, making them all "out-pensioners," and was then being converted into a Royal Naval College, the

reasons therefor being that "it came to be doubted whether the stupendous charity were not, after all, a mistake. As far as the pensioners were concerned, it was a monastery, without the soul-sustaining convictions of monasticism."

The military asylum at Chelsea was built to accommodate only 500 pensioners, and its administrative management as an asylum differed so widely from that held in contemplation by the board in the organization of a Home that it seemed undesirable as a model in any respect.

Turning to France, there was the Hôtel des Invalides at Paris—a vast military asylum designed to accommodate 5000 soldiers, and covering sixteen acres of ground, affording an existence to its inmates more restricted, with all its amplitude, than that of people living within the walls of a fortified city under military surveillance. Therefore, all things considered, the Board of Managers—a majority of whom were men of large military experience, and all of well-known executive ability—fell back upon their own resources, and proceeded to give shape to their concerted plans, according to the exigencies and demands of the situation. By mid-November of the same year the Eastern Branch was opened for applicants, and the Central and Northwestern branches were soon after established. The location of a Southern Branch three years later was fully justified, not only by the greatly increased number of beneficiaries, but by the necessity felt for a milder climate for certain classes of disease.

An act of Congress, approved July 5, 1884, authorizing still another branch Home, was in part the result of a sectional clause of that act, which directs the admission to the Home of "all United States soldiers of any war who are incapable of earning a living, whether the incapacity resulted from their service or not." This law has opened the Home to a large class of men who were hitherto ineligible.

The Western Branch was located under the provisions of a bill passed by Congress to establish a Branch of the Home west of the Mississippi River. The city of Leavenworth, Kansas, made a munificent donation to the government of 640 acres of land, and $50,000 for embellishment, which secured to them the location of the new Branch, which was opened for applicants during the spring of 1886. The

READY FOR REVIEW—EASTERN BRANCH.

CAPTAIN P. T. WOODFIN, GOVERNOR OF THE
SOUTHERN BRANCH.

Unfortunately the early history of this Branch was marked by two destructive fires. The first occurred in midwinter of 1868, and caused the total loss of the main building (hotel). The nine-o'clock tattoo had been sounded, and the half past nine "taps for lights out and all in bed" had been responded to, when the alarm of fire was given. The sick were hastily carried out on their mattresses, and laid on the snow of that rigorous climate. Couriers were despatched to Augusta for aid, and citizens and firemen promptly responded, the former with teams which conveyed the sick to private houses, while the others were temporarily quartered in public buildings. The second fire occurred three years later, and destroyed Amusement Hall, involving a loss of $20,000. This building was replaced by a smaller one at less outlay; but in place of the main building there had been erected three large brick structures, so arranged that with the hospital they formed a hollow square, comprising the present main building—the most economical arrangement.

This Branch was originally intended only for applicants from the State of New York and the New England States. But notwithstanding the final "muster out" at all the Branches of large numbers of veterans full of years, and others who were victims of fatal wounds and disease, the passage of time brought old age and increasing infirmities upon still other hundreds who had hitherto supported themselves outside the Home. This great accession of numbers resulted in the general distribution being governed mainly by the relative facilities of the different Branches, and by climatic considerations, so that of late years this Branch has represented a score or more of different States.

On June 1, 1886, the number of "members" present and living in this Home was 1224, while 464 were absent on furlough, most of whom would return with cold weather, making a total of 1698. The whole number "cared for" during the year ending June 30, 1885, was 2621. Quite a number of the men live in cottages near the Home, receiving their rations in common with the others, and carrying them to their homes to be eaten. Still others hire themselves to farmers, and draw rations as the cheapest way of obtaining board. No new members are now admitted on these conditions, however.

As at all the Branches, admissions, fur-

grounds are located about two miles below Leavenworth, Kansas, bordering the river, in the midst of beautiful scenery. Eight barrack buildings, to accommodate 120 men each, have recently been completed, and a large dining-hall with a seating capacity of 2000 men. Over 1000 members are cared for now.

The Eastern Branch of the National Home is located about five miles from Augusta, Maine, on a tract of land originally comprising 1100 acres. This had been reclaimed from a wilderness of thickets and bowlders by private enterprise, and converted into a summer resort known as Togus Spring, at an estimated outlay of $200,000, because of supposed medicinal virtue in the waters of the spring. The structural improvements consisted in part of a hotel of capacity to accommodate 300 guests, a farm-house, stables, and bowling-alleys. The grounds were ornamented by shade trees, and laid out with walks and drives; the spring was enclosed in a bowery arbor, a race-course told of past excitements of the turf, and a young orchard of five acres gave fair promise for the future. This property was thought none too choice, and was purchased entire for $50,000; and to this beautiful retreat was sent the first instalment of soldiers on November 10, 1866.

loughs, discharges, and readmissions are continually going on, and the pensioners, all alike, "are jealous of what they call their 'blood-money,' most of them preferring privation outside the Home rather than consent to its confiscation." Congress therefore secures the pensions to all having near dependent relatives.

At the close of the war there was clothing in the Quartermaster's Department sufficient for an army of 1,500,000 men. Of

coast. It commands an unobstructed view of the fashionable resort at Old Point Comfort, famous for its beautiful scenery, invigorating air, and historic interest. The climate is everything to be desired for those classes of disease in which extremes of temperature are inimical, while "malarial fevers are unknown. The records of the meteorological observatory for the last ten years give an average temperature of 74° in summer and 44° in winter." A mag-

MAIN BUILDING, SOUTHERN BRANCH.

course distributions from this supply were made to the Home as needed. Not only are food and raiment thus provided for these honored guests of the nation, but a spacious and beautifully finished auditorium affords facilities for lectures and theatrical entertainments, while billiards, bowling, and the smaller games are free to all. The library, always an important feature, contains nearly 6000 volumes, and is supplied with numerous papers and periodicals, the foreign inmates being furnished with reading in the German, French, and Italian languages.

The Southern Branch of the National Home is located in Hampton, Virginia, about two miles from Fortress Monroe, with a water-front on Hampton Roads, one of the finest harbors on the American

nificent array of 150 flower beds adorns the premises. The large greenhouses are stocked with "4400 new and rare plants"; while a rose-house stands unrivalled by them all.

The main building of this Branch, whose broad avenue leads directly through the embellished grounds to the terraced water-front, was originally an educational institution, and used as such until the encroachment of hostilities compelled its desertion. Remaining intact after fire and cannon had demolished its surroundings, it was appropriated as a Union hospital, while its bullet-scarred walls mutely offered shelter alike to the wearers of the blue and the gray, as they were deposited, wounded and dying, under its roof, soon to be borne thence, in common brotherhood at last, to the national cemetery hard by. Cherished as a relic of the past, there now stands on a gallery of the building a marble slab with this inscription, "Chesapeake Female Seminary, 1854." A constant reminder, this, of the blooming girlhood, happy voices, and merry laughter of the youthful maidens once trooping through those halls, with no thought of blood and carnage coming nearer to their lives than the bare recital of such horrors from their pages of history.

In 1870 the building was purchased by the government for its present use. Only 50 veterans were accommodated at first.

GENERAL JACOB SHARPE, GOVERNOR OF THE NORTHWESTERN BRANCH.

Captain P. T. Woodfin, the present Governor of the Branch, took charge in 1873. The institution at once became popular with old soldiers, and it has been crowded ever since. The number of members now amounts to 1800. About one-fourth of the roll are mild-weather absentees, away on furlough during summer to earn wages at light employment. During the Christmas holidays all who have homes or friends are likely to seek them if able; and about one-fifth of the whole number are absent, one may pleasantly imagine, enjoying the season with outside friends, though a sorry percentage at best of so large a number of once stalwart men.

The amount of pension money received here for the fiscal year ending June 30, 1884, was $121,344; remitted to families, $20,786; held at interest for pensioners, $13,806; value of farm products, $10,031; number of books in library, 4384; number published in German, 380; number published in French, 91; number of issues of books, 22,305; number of papers and magazines, 160. The total number of members "cared for" during the year, including "out-door relief," was 2182. Of these, 1193 were of foreign birth.

Several religious sects are alternately represented here; and added to the usual range of amusements are such as the proximity to water naturally affords; while the manifold interests of the institution and surroundings attract frequent visitors from all States of the Union, with quite a percentage of foreigners.

The national cemetery adjoins the Home, and forms the northern boundary. Many Union and Confederate soldiers were buried here in war time, and this is the last resting-place of the inmates.

The Northwestern Branch, near Milwaukee, Wisconsin, justly claiming one of the most beautiful sites in the State, is located about three miles west of Lake Michigan, and one from the city limits. The original purchase of 440 acres of land for $100,000—the proceeds of a sanitary fair—was made by the ladies of Milwaukee, and donated to the government as an inducement for the location thereon of the projected Soldiers' Home for the Northwest. By this stroke of enterprise the competitive claims of some other cities were thrown in the shade.

The Chicago, Milwaukee, and St. Paul Railway runs through the grounds, bringing excursionists from every part of the country—the station being a unique department in the "Ward" Memorial Hall. This building, it may be explained, is the result—in common with those so called at other Branches—of a bequest to the National Home by Horatio Ward. One floor in each of the buildings is occupied by a beautiful theatre for dramatic and other entertainments.

The forest trees in this vicinity are among the most majestic to be found in this country, attesting by their size to the strength of the soil. This is also evident

Hospital N W Branch

Main Building N.W. Branch

Memorial Hall N.W. Branch.

in the "returns" of agricultural products of the Home farm as given in the last report, the "cash value of crop sold" showing a total of $15,544—a pertinent item with the social economist. All the floral decorations of the grounds are supplied by the greenhouses.

The main building is a noble structure of 300 feet in length, with a central tower of 180 feet. Its spacious compartments comprised the Home proper upon the first establishment of this Branch, affording space for hospital, dining hall, and barracks. But all is now changed, and various buildings are required, as at the other

DINING HALL, CENTRAL BRANCH.

Branches, to furnish accommodations and supply the necessary workshops for so large a community of soldiers. But other than actual wants and needs are met; and the most critical visitor may search in vain for anything here that will conflict with the statement made by the Board of Managers in their last annual report to Congress, to wit:

"The Board calls attention to the fact that its endeavor has constantly been to make the institution as nearly as possible a home for the members, and not a mere asylum. To attain this end, chapels, libraries, reading-rooms, objects of amusement of various kinds, theatres, greenhouses, etc., have been furnished."

On June 30, 1884, the number of members, as per last published report, was:

Present and absent 1370
Total cared for during the year 2088
Of native birth........................ 622
Foreign birth 1466

Disabilities.

Loss of limbs......................... 171
Wounds 739
Disease..............................1099
Blindness 52
Other causes 27

Of the former occupations represented by the members, those in excess of forty of one class rate as follows:

Blacksmiths ......41 | Shoemakers...... 64
Clerks ....46 | Carpenters....... 83
Tailors ....46 | Farmers.........436
Painters.........49 | Laborers 702

Of the whole number, 268 could neither read nor write. Of these, 16 were natives, and 252 of foreign birth. The amount of fines imposed was $738 20 during the fiscal year, while 75 per cent. of the whole number committed no offence. The average number employed per month for pay was 246, and the pay-rolls amounted to $28,593. Besides this sum earned at the Home by the members, their families were paid $2289 for work on under-garments and bed-furnishings made here for the different Branches.

"No permanent diet list is prepared at this Branch, but a bill of fare adapted to the season is prepared daily for the general kitchen by the governor, and the commissary employés and cooks are required to conform to it. In the hospital the bill of fare is prescribed by the surgeon." Including the regimen of both, the average cost of the daily ration per hundred men was $16 28. The cost for the same in 1870 was $23 62; in 1875, $21 61; and for the year ending June 30, 1880, the cost was only $14 31, showing a variation corresponding with the varying cost of provisions. It is interesting to know that these estimates not only cover the first cost of food supplies, but include all contingent expenses, as cost of transportation, fuel consumed, pay-roll of employés, etc.

In order to convey a comprehensive idea of the actual workings of so vast an institution, a few of the more pertinent details of each Branch thus far noticed have been interspersed with the general description, as calculated to give a clearer idea of the daily life of the disabled soldier than if only ponderous generalizations had been given. The general estimates already presented apply with more or less accuracy to all the Branches, any prominence given by either to certain conditions or interests being chiefly due to local differences, and obviously in a slight degree to the particular cast of *personnel* comprising the administrative force of the respective Branches.

In relation to the foreign element in the Home, it seems proper to state that this class predominates in nearly the same proportion at all the Branches, and an impression has prevailed that by reason of temperament and native precedent they are more ready to accept a condition of dependence than are our own countrymen. This is unjust. Let it be remembered that a large proportion of the foreign-born were yet without homes of their own in their newly adopted country, and many without family ties, and therefore, when disabled in service, were without resource, and doubly entitled, as loyal foster-sons of the mother republic, to a full share of her bounties. Be it also borne in mind that nine-tenths of this class represent England, Ireland, and Germany, and that these are not the countries that supply the world with paupers.

The Central Branch, for the Middle States, is located in the Miami Valley, near Dayton, Ohio, about midway between Columbus and Cincinnati. Besides the large area of choice farming land on its 627 acres, there were originally natural advantages of upland and glen, mineral and other springs, rendering it susceptible of charming possibilities—a result long since realized—making it to-day one of the most inviting places of resort.

Its central location renders it the largest Branch of the National Home—the total of present members being almost equal to the number designed to be accommodated by the great French military asylum. The buildings required for this soldier community—including hotel, restaurant, and the dwellings of officers in charge—form by their numbers and structure an imposing array. These include and are surrounded by an extent of ground—known in military parlance as "the camp"—under the special supervision of a landscape gardener, the same being intersected by thirty-two miles of broad avenues, each one named for a State of the Union—a statement conveying some conception of the inadequate idea of details

IN THE HOSPITAL, CENTRAL BRANCH.

that the average visitor of a day is likely to bear away with him.

Not first in importance by any means, but in this connection, comes the unique glen garden, or garden in the glen. It is reached from different points by descending stone stairways, flanked on either side by gay platoons of witching growths. Its shaded banks, cropping out with continual surprises of fresh exuberance, enclose various attractions of cascade, springs, and floral splendors, as well as scores of tropical marvels, including stately palms and a purple - green grove of bananas. The loiterer and lounger may find embowered seats and shady nooks, while the curious plant-lover, ever on the alert, may quietly pursue his rounds, and finally, if he choose, ascend by steps directly into a conservatory, whose strange company of extraordinary growths may somehow remind him of jungles, and if he stumble against a spotted coil of boa-like cactus, he may think he is in one; but happily, being on the second floor, he will find ready escape to the common level of the earth again. Near at hand rises a palm-house thirty-five feet in height and ninety feet long. The total area of conservatory space outside of this is covered by 25,000 feet of glass.

SOLDIERS' MONUMENT, CENTRAL BRANCH.

We turn next to the hospital building. The helpless invalids are secured against the perils of conflagration by a fire-proof arrangement, consisting of a tunnel 200 feet in length, and over seven feet square, which connects the hospital with the building containing steam - boilers and fuel deposit. Through this channel run the steam and water pipes and the railway for conveying coal.

Soon after the occupancy of the building by patients, the Northern Ohio Soldiers' Aid Society presented an elegant carriage and horses for their exclusive use. There are usually from 300 to 400 patients here, assigned, according to disability, to the upper and lower wards. Passing through the latter, one may see the invalids variously occupied, some deftly making work-baskets of self-binding bits of wood, and other useful and ornamental articles.

The crowded condition of this large hospital has been recently relieved by the erection of four additional wards, and by the removal to the government hospital at Washington of the insane patients.

The barracks, comprising thirty-five or more three-story buildings, no longer furnish ample accommodations, while the numbers to be fed were long ago quite beyond the comfortable seating capacity of the grand dining-hall building, as shown by the report of the governor for the year 1882–3.

"......Our facilities for handling over 3000 men at the great dining hall are very imperfect. We are obliged to seat, say, 1100 men three times at each meal. To do this, the employés at the kitchen and dining-room must be up a large portion of the night, and the men must turn out very early in the morning in order that the third table may get through breakfast in any reasonable time for work."

Since then, the men occupying the large hall above the dining-room have been removed to a new barrack building, and that room converted into a dining hall, so that now, by having two sittings at each meal in both halls the men are amply accommodated. But a still further improvement on all this is hoped for with the opening of the new Western Branch. To convey an idea of the amount of food consumed at this one boarding-house of Uncle Sam's, the quantity furnished for a recent dinner for 4300 men may be given as a fair sample. Of beef there were over 2000 pounds; of bread, 2700 pounds; of sugar, 240 pounds; of potatoes, 50 bushels; of coffee, 1200 gallons, and 900 pies.

The library, comprising 14,800 volumes, is in two divisions, known as the Putnam and Thomas libraries. Contributions to both are being constantly made—in the former case by the Lady Bountiful herself, and in the latter "by its many friends." This library has also become the repository of many interesting relics and trophies of the war, as well as numerous others of various significance.

The magazines and papers handled here by hungry readers are of 258 varieties, and the issues of books now amount to nearly 53,000.

A peculiar interest attaches to the chaste monument near the cemetery, from its having been erected by the officers and men of the National Home as a memorial tribute to their honored dead. "To Our Fallen Comrades" is one of the four inscriptions on the pedestal. The marble shaft is surmounted by a soldier "on guard." The figures below, typical of the army and navy, were sculptured in Rome, and in every detail are most exquisitely wrought. The device of giving the effect of color to wide-open eyes by simply hollowing the pupils is wonderfully effective in these faces.

The post-office, where the United States mail is delivered direct, is always a gathering-place before mail-time for the soldiers anxious to be first served. Under the shady trees, or in a sunny corner, as the weather may incline, they engage in social exchange or sit in silent expectancy while thus waiting for the mail.

The number of letters and cards mailed here during the year, as per last report, was 134,590, the number received being 131,460.

The various appliances of steam and machinery render it possible to accomplish marvels here in the line of domestic labor, as shown by the one item of laundry-work, there being an average of 36,000 pieces in the weekly wash.

Of the different trades carried on at the several Branches there are from ten to thirteen, including printing and bookbinding. Such men as are able to work are always glad to avail themselves of employment within the Home.

The number of soldiers "cared for" at this Branch for the year ending June 30, 1884, was 7146. Of these, 4357 were of foreign birth; 2238 were from Germany and Prussia, 1403 from Ireland, and 259 from England.

The mortuary returns since 1867 show the total deaths in the Central Branch of National Home to have been 4517. The annual percentage of death rate during that period is remarkably low, considering the age and debility of the subjects, having reached 6 per cent. in one year only.

For each of the three fiscal years ending June, 1884, the amount appropriated by Congress for the support of this Branch averages $1,138,046 65, while the estimate

GENERAL M. R. PATRICK, GOVERNOR OF THE CENTRAL BRANCH.

for the last fiscal year was $1,237,134—an increase proportionate to the increase of members.

The number of "present and absent" in June, 1886, was 5244, and the actual number present 4157, a pitiful showing, in view of the delightful season, when furloughs are in request by all who are able to use them. Private official returns from the other Branches give us a total of over 10,000 members of the National Military Home; and it is estimated there will be no decrease in number for some time to come, in view of the large class hitherto able to take care of themselves, but who now are becoming dependent by reason of age and infirmity.

NOTE.—Limited space has excluded the worthy mention of many names most honorably connected with the projection and development of the institution thus briefly reviewed. But they are well known, and need no trumpeting here. The soldier himself, his daily life in the Home, and what government is doing for him, have been the leading interest of this writing.

For efficient aid rendered in the preparation of the same, thanks are due to Brigadier-General Richard C. Drum, Adjutant-General United States Army, and to Lieutenant-Colonel R. N. Batchelder, Deputy Quartermaster-General, both of the War Department. Also, for favors conferred, thanks are tendered to General Luther Stephenson, Captain P. T. Woodfin, General Jacob Sharpe, Colonel Andrew J. Smith, and to General M. R. Patrick, governors respectively of the Eastern, Southern, Northwestern, Western, and Central Branches of the National Home for Disabled Volunteer Soldiers.

OLE 'STRACTED.

BY THOMAS NELSON PAGE.

"AWE, little Ephum! *awe*, little Ephum! ef you don' come 'long heah,
boy, an' rock dis chile, I'll buss you haid
open!" screamed the high-pitched voice
of a woman, breaking the stillness of the
summer evening. She had just come to
the door of the little cabin, where she was
now standing, anxiously scanning the
space before her, while a baby's plaintive
wail rose and fell within with wearying
monotony. The log cabin, set in a gall
in the middle of an old field all grown up
in sassafras, was not a very inviting-look-
ing place; a few hens loitering about the
new hen-house, a brood of half-grown
chickens picking in the grass and watching the door, and a runty pig tied to a
"stob," were the only signs of thrift; yet
the face of the woman cleared up as she
gazed about her, and afar off where the
gleam of green made a pleasant spot,
where the corn grew in the river-bottom,
for it was her home, and the best of all
was she thought it belonged to them.

A rumble of distant thunder caught her
ear, and she stepped down and took a well-
worn garment from the clothes-line,
stretched between two dogwood forks, and
having, after a keen glance down the path
through the bushes, satisfied herself that
no one was in sight, she returned to the
house, and the baby's voice rose louder
than before. The mother, as she set out
her ironing table, raised a dirge-like hymn,
which she chanted, partly from habit and
partly in self-defence. She ironed carefully the ragged shirt she had just taken
from the line, and then, after some search,
finding a needle and cotton, she drew a
chair to the door and proceeded to mend
the garment.

"Dis de on'ies' shut Ole 'Stracted got,"
she said, as if in apology to herself for being so careful.

The cloud slowly gathered over the pines
in the direction of the path; the fowls
carefully tripped up the path, and after
a prudent pause at the hole, disappeared
one by one within; the chickens picked
in a gradually contracting circuit, and
finally one or two stole furtively to the
cabin door, and after a brief recognizance
came in, and fluttered up the ladder to the
loft, where they had been born, and yet
roosted. Once more the baby's voice pre-

vailed, and once more the woman went to
the door, and, looking down the path,
screamed, "Awe, little Ephum! awe, little Ephum!"

"Mam," came the not very distant answer from the bushes.

"Why 'n't you come 'long heah, boy,
an' rock dis chile?"

"Yes, 'm, I comin'," came the answer.
She waited, watching, until there emerged
from the bushes a queer little caravan,
headed by a small brat, who staggered
under the weight of another apparently
nearly as large and quite as black as himself, while several more of various degrees of diminutiveness struggled along
behind.

"Ain't you heah me callin' you, boy?
You better come when I call you. I'll
tyah you all to pieces!" pursued the woman, in the angriest of keys, her countenance, however, appearing unruffled. The
head of the caravan stooped and deposited his burden carefully on the ground;
then, with a comical look of mingled
alarm and penitence, he slowly approached the door, keeping his eye watchfully
on his mother, and picking his opportunity, slipped in past her, dodging skilfully
just enough to escape a blow which she
aimed at him, and which would have
"slapped him flat" had it struck him, but
which, in truth, was intended merely to
warn and keep him in wholesome fear,
and was purposely aimed high enough to
miss him, allowing for the certain dodge.

The culprit, having stifled the whimper
with which he was prepared, flung himself on to the foot of the rough plank cradle, and began to rock it violently and
noisily, using one leg as a lever, and singing an accompaniment, of which the only
words that rose above the noise of the
rockers were, "By-a-by, don't you cry;
go to sleep, little baby;" and sure enough
the baby stopped crying and went to
sleep.

Eph watched his mammy furtively as
she scraped away the ashes and laid the
thick pone of dough on the hearth, and
shovelled the hot ashes upon it. Supper
would be ready directly, and it was time
to propitiate her. He bethought himself
of a message.

"Mammy, Ole 'Stracted say you must

bring he shut; he say he marster comin' to-night."

"How he say he is?" inquired the woman, with some interest.

"He ain' say—jes say he want he shut. He sutny is comical—he layin' down in de baid." Then having relieved his mind, Eph went to sleep in the cradle.

"'Layin' down in de baid?'" quoted the woman to herself as she moved about the room. "I 'ain' nuver hearn 'bout dat befo'. Dat sutny is a comical ole man anyways. He say he used to live on dis plantation, an' yit he al'ays talkin' 'bout de gret house an' de fine kerridges dee used to have, an' 'bout he marster comin' to buy him back. De 'ain' nuver been no gret house on dis place, not sence I know nuttin 'bout it, 'sep de overseer house whar dat man live. I heah Ephum say Aunt Dinah tell him de ole house whar used to be on de hill whar dat gret oak-tree is in de pines bu'nt down de year he wuz born, an' he ole marster had to live in de overseer house, an' hit break he heart, an' dee teck all he niggers, an' dat's de way *he* come to blongst to we all; but dat ole man ain' know nuttin 'bout dat house, 'cause hit bu'nt down. I wonder whar he did come from?" she pursued, "an' what he sho' 'nough name? He sholy couldn' been named 'Ole 'Stracted,' jes so; dat ain' no name 'tall. Yit ef he ain' 'stracted, 'tain' nobody is. He ain' even know he own name," she continued, presently. "Say he marster 'll know him when he come—ain' know de folks is free; say he marster gwi buy him back in de summer an' kyar him home, an' 'bout de money he gwine gi' him. Ef he got any money, I wonder he live down dyah in dat evil-sperit hole." And the woman glanced around with great complacency on the picture-pasted walls of her own by no means sumptuously furnished house. "Money!" she repeated aloud, as she began to rake in the ashes. "He 'ain' got nuttin. I got to kyar him piece o' dis bread now," and she went off into a dream of what they would do when the big crop on their land should be all in, and the last payment made on the house; of what she would wear, and how she would dress the children, and the appearance she would make at meeting, not reflecting that the sum they had paid on the property had never, even with all their stinting, amounted in any one year to more than a few dollars over the rent charged for the place, and that the eight hundred

dollars yet due on it was more than they could make at the present rate in a lifetime.

"Ef Ephum jes had a mule, or even somebody to help him," she thought, "but he 'ain' got nuttin. De chil'n ain' big 'nough to do nuttin but eat; he 'ain' got no brurrs, an' he deddy took 'way an' sold down Souf de same time my ole marster whar dead buy him; dat's what I al'ays heah 'em say, an' I know he's dead long befo' dis, 'cause I heah em say dese Virginia niggers carn stan' hit long deah, hit so hot, hit frizzle 'em up, an' I reckon he die befo' he ole marster, whar I heah say die of a broked heart torectly after dee teck he niggers an' sell 'em befo' he face. I heah Aunt Dinah say dat, an' dat he might'ly sot on he ole servants, spressaly on Ephum deddy, whar named Little Ephum, an' whar used to wait on him. Dis mus' 'a been a gret place dem days, 'cordin' to what dee say." She went on: "Dee say he sutny live strong, wuz jes rich as cream, an' weahed he blue coat an' brass buttons, an' lived in dat ole house whar wuz up whar de pines is now, an' whar bu'nt down, like he owned de wull. An' now look at it; dat man own it all, an' cuttin' all de woods off it. He don' know nuttin 'bout black folks, ain' nuver been fotch up wid him. Who ever heah he name 'fo' he come heah an' buy de place, an' move in de overseer house, an' charge we all eight hundred dollars for dis land, jes 'cause it got little piece o' bottom on it, and forty-eight dollars rent besides, wid he ole stingy wife whar oon' even gi' 'way buttermilk!" An expression of mingled disgust and contempt concluded the reflection.

She took the ash-cake out of the ashes, slapped it first on one side, then on the other, with her hand, dusted it with her apron, and walked to the door and poured a gourd of water from the piggin over it. Then she divided it in half; one half she set up against the side of the chimney, the other she broke up into smaller pieces and distributed among the children, dragging the sleeping Eph, limp and soaked with sleep, from the cradle to receive his share. Her manner was not rough—was perhaps even tender—but she used no caresses, as a white woman would have done under the circumstances. It was only toward the baby at the breast that she exhibited any endearments. Her nearest approach to it with the others was when she told them, as she portioned out the ash-cake, "Mam-

"THEY WERE AT THE CABIN NOW, AND A BRIEF PAUSE OF DOUBT ENSUED."—[SEE PAGE 701.]

my 'ain' got nuttin else; but nuver min', she gwine have plenty o' good meat next year, when deddy done pay for he land."

"Hi! who dat out dyah?" she said, suddenly. "Run to de do', son, an' see who dat comin'," and the whole tribe rushed to inspect the new-comer.

It was, as she suspected, her husband, and as soon as he entered she saw that something was wrong. He dropped into a chair, and sat in moody silence, the picture of fatigue, physical and mental. After waiting for some time, she asked, indifferently, "What de matter?"

"Dat man."

"What he done do now?" The query was sharp with suspicion.

"He say he ain' gwine let me have my land."

"He's a half-strainer," said the woman, with sudden anger. "How he gwine help it? 'Ain' you got crap on it?" She felt that there must be a defence against such an outrage.

"He say he ain' gwine wait no longer; dat I wuz to have tell Christmas to finish payin' for it, an' I 'ain' do it, an' now he done change he min'."

"Tell dis Christmas comin'," said his wife, with the positiveness of one accustomed to expound contracts.

"Yes; but I tell you he say he done change he min'." The man had evidently given up all hope; he was dead beat.

"De crap's yourn," said she, affected by his surrender, but prepared only to compromise.

"He say he gwine teck all dat for de rent, an' dat he gwine drive Ole 'Stracted 'way too."

"He ain' nuttin but po' white trash!" It expressed her supreme contempt.

"He say he'll gi' me jes one week mo' to pay him all he ax for it," continued he, forced to a correction by her intense feeling, and the instinct of a man to defend the absent from a woman's attack, and perhaps in the hope that she might suggest some escape.

"He ain' nuttin sep po' white trash!" she repeated. "How you gwine raise eight hunderd dollars at once? Dee kyarn nobody do dat. Gord mout! He 'ain' got good sense."

"You 'ain' see dat corn lately, is you?" he asked. "Hit jes as rank! You can almos' see it growin' ef you look at it good. Dat's strong land. I know dat when I buy it."

He knew it was gone now, but he had been in the habit of calling it his in the past three years, and it did him good to claim the ownership a little longer.

"I wonder whar Marse Johnny is?" said the woman. He was the son of her former owner; and now, finding her proper support failing her, she instinctively turned to him. "He wouldn' let him turn we all out."

"He 'ain' got nuttin, an' ef he is, he kyarn git it in a week," said Ephraim.

"Kyarn you teck it in de co't?"

"Dat's whar he say he gwine have it ef I don' git out," said her husband, despairingly.

Her last defence was gone.

"Ain' you hongry?" she inquired.

"What you got?"

"I jes gwine kill a chicken for you." It was her nearest approach to tenderness, and he knew it was a mark of special attention, for all the chickens and eggs had for the past three years gone to swell the fund which was to buy the home, and it was only on special occasions that one was spared for food.

The news that he was to be turned out of his home had fallen on him like a blow, and had stunned him; he could make no resistance, he could form no plans. He went into a rough estimate as he waited.

"Le' me see: I done wuck for it three years dis Christmas done gone; how much does dat meck?"

"An' fo' dollars, an' five dollars, an' two dollars an' a half last Christmas from de chickens, an' all dem ducks I done sell he wife, an' de washin' I been doin' for 'em; how much is dat?" supplemented his wife.

"Dat's what I say!"

His wife endeavored vainly to remember the amount she had been told it was; but the unaccounted-for washing changed the sum and destroyed her reliance on the result. And as the chicken was now approaching perfection, and required her undivided attention, she gave up the arithmetic and applied herself to her culinary duties.

Ephraim also abandoned the attempt, and waited in a reverie, in which he saw corn stand so high and rank over his land that he could scarcely distinguish the balk, and a stable and barn and a mule, or may be two—it was a possibility—and two cows which his wife would milk, and a green wagon driven by his boys, while he took it easy and gave orders like a master, and a clover patch, and wheat, and he saw the yellow grain waving, and heard his sons sing the old harvest song of "Cool Water" while they swung their cradles, and—

"You say he gwine turn Ole 'Stracted out too ?" inquired his wife, breaking the spell. The chicken was done now, and her mind reverted to the all-engrossing subject.

"Yes; say he tired o' ole 'stracted nigger livin' on he place an' payin' no rent."

"Good Gord A'mighty! Pay rent for dat ole pile o' logs! 'Ain't he been mendin' he shoes an' harness for rent all dese years ?"

"'Twill kill dat ole man to tu'n him out dat house," said Ephraim; "he 'ain' nuver stay away from dyah a hour sence he come heah."

"Sutny 'twill," assented his wife; then she added, in reply to the rest of the remark, "Nuver min', den; we'll see what he got in dyah." To a woman, that was at least some compensation. Ephraim's thoughts had taken a new direction.

"He al'ays feared he marster 'd come for him while he 'way," he said, in mere continuance of his last remark.

"He sen' me wud he marster comin' to-night, an' he want he shut," said his wife, as she handed him his supper. Ephraim's face expressed more than interest; it was tenderness which softened the rugged lines as he sat looking into the fire. Perhaps he thought of the old man's loneliness, and of his own father torn away and sold so long ago, before he could even remember, and perhaps very dimly of the beauty of the sublime devotion of this poor old creature to his love and his trust, holding steadfast beyond memory, beyond reason, after the knowledge even of his own identity and of his very name was lost.

The woman caught the contagion of his sympathy.

"De chil'n say he mighty comical, an' he layin' down in de baid," she said.

Ephraim rose from his seat.

"Whar you gwine ?"

"I mus' go to see 'bout him," he said, simply.

"Ain' you gwine finish eatin' ?"

"I gwine kyar dis to him."

"Well, I kin cook you anurr when we come back," said his wife, with ready acquiescence.

In a few minutes they were on the way, going single file down the path through the sassafras, along which little Eph and his followers had come an hour before, the man in the lead and his wife following, and according to the custom of their race, carrying the bundles, one the surrendered supper, and the other the neatly folded and well patched shirt in which Ole 'Stracted hoped to meet his long-expected loved ones.

As they came in sight of the ruinous little hut which had been the old man's abode since his sudden appearance in the neighborhood a few years after the war, they observed that the bench beside the door was deserted, and that the door stood ajar—two circumstances which neither of them remembered ever to have seen before; for in all the years in which he had been their neighbor Ole 'Stracted had never admitted any one within his door, and had never been known to leave it open. In mild weather he occupied a bench outside, where he either cobbled shoes for his neighbors, accepting without question anything they paid him, or else sat perfectly quiet with the air of a person waiting for some one. He held only the briefest communication with anybody, and was believed by some to have intimate relations with the evil one, and his tumble-down hut, which he was particular to keep closely daubed, was thought by such as took this view of the matter to be the temple where he practised his unholy rites. For this reason, and because the little cabin, surrounded by dense pines and covered with vines which the popular belief held "pizonous," was the most desolate abode a human being could have selected, most of the dwellers in that section gave the place a wide berth, especially toward nightfall, and Ole 'Stracted would probably have suffered but for the charity of Ephraim and his wife, who, although often wanting the necessaries of life themselves, had long divided it with their strange neighbor. Yet even they had never been admitted inside his door, and knew no more of him than the other people about the settlement knew.

His advent in the neighborhood had been mysterious. The first that was known of him was one summer morning, when he was found sitting on the bench beside the door of this cabin, which had long been unoccupied and left to decay.

He was unable to give any account of himself, except that he always declared that he had been sold by some one other than his master from that plantation, that his wife and boy had been sold to some other person at the same time for $1200 (he was particular as to the amount), and that his master was coming in the summer to buy him back and take him home, and would bring him his wife and child when he came. Everything since that day was a blank to him, and as he could not tell the name of his master or wife, or even his own name, and as no one was left old enough to remember him, the neighborhood having been entirely deserted after the war, he simply passed as a harmless old lunatic laboring under a delusion. He was devoted to children, and Ephraim's small brood were his chief delight. They were not at all afraid of him, and whenever they got a chance they would slip off and steal down to his house, where they might be found any time squatting about his feet listening to his accounts of his expected visit from his master, and what he was going to do afterward. It was all of a great plantation, and fine carriages and horses, and a house with his wife and the boy.

This was all that was known of him, except that once a stranger, passing through the country, and hearing the name Ole 'Stracted, said that he heard a similar one once, long before the war, in one of the Louisiana parishes, where the man roamed at will, having been bought of the trader by the gentleman who owned him, for a small price, on account of his infirmity.

"Is you gwine in dyah?" asked the woman as they approached the hut.

"Hi! yes; 'tain' nuttin gwine hu't you; an' you say Ephum say he layin' in de baid?" he replied, his mind having evidently been busy on the subject.

"An' mighty comical," she corrected him, with exactness born of apprehension.

"Well? I 'feared he sick."

"I 'ain' nuver been in dyah," she persisted.

"'Ain' de chil'n been in dyah?"

"Dee say 'stracted folks oon hu't chil'n."

"Dat ole man oon hu't nobody; he jes tame as a ole tomcat."

"I wonder he ain' feared to live in dat lonesome ole house by hisself. I jes lieve stay in a graveyard at once. I ain' won-

der folks say he see sperrits in dat hanty-lookin' place." She came up by her husband's side at the suggestion. "I wonder he don' go home?"

"Whar he got any home to go to sep heaven?" said Ephraim.

"What was you mammy name, Ephum?"

"Mymy," said he, simply.

They were at the cabin now, and a brief pause of doubt ensued. It was perfectly dark inside the door, and there was not a sound. The bench where they had heretofore held their only communication with their strange neighbor was lying on its side in the weeds which grew up to the very walls of the ruinous cabin, and a lizard suddenly ran over it, and with a little rustle disappeared under the rotting ground-sill. To the woman it was an ill omen. She glanced furtively behind her, and moved nearer her husband's side. She noticed that the cloud above the pines was getting a faint yellow tinge on its lower border, while it was very black above them. It filled her with dread, and she was about to call her husband's notice to it, when a voice within arrested their attention. It was very low, and they both listened in awed silence, watching the door meanwhile as if they expected to see something supernatural spring from it.

"Nem min'— jes wait — 'tain' so long now — he'll be heah torectly," said the voice. "Dat's what he say—gwine come an' buy me back—den we gwine home."

In their endeavor to catch the words they moved nearer, and made a slight noise. Suddenly the low earnest tone changed to one full of eagerness.

"Who dat?" was called in sharp inquiry.

"'Tain' nobody but me an' Polly, Ole 'Stracted," said Ephraim, pushing the door slightly wider open and stepping in. They had an indistinct idea that the poor deluded creature had fancied them his longed-for loved ones, yet it was a relief to see him bodily.

"Who you say you is?" inquired the old man, feebly.

"Me an' Polly."

"I done bring you shut home," said the woman, as if supplementing her husband's reply. "Hit all bran' clean, an' I done patch it."

"Oh, I thought—" said the voice, sadly.

They knew what he thought. Their

eyes were now accustomed to the darkness, and they saw that the only article of furniture which the room contained was the wretched bed or bench on which the old man was stretched. The light sifting through the chinks in the roof enabled them to see his face, and that it had changed much in the last twenty-four hours, and an instinct told them that he was near the end of his long waiting.

"How is you, Ole 'Stracted?" asked the woman.

"Dat ain' my name," answered the old man, promptly. It was the first time he had ever disowned the name.

"Well, how is you, Ole— What I gwine call you?" asked she, with feeble finesse.

"I don' know—he kin tell you."

"Who?"

"Who? Marster. He know it. Ole 'Stracted ain' know it; but dat ain' nuttin. *He* know it—got it set down in de book. I jes waitin' for em now."

A hush fell on the little audience—they were in full sympathy with him, and knowing no way of expressing it, kept silence. Only the breathing of the old man was audible in the room. He was evidently nearing the end. "I mighty tired of waitin'," he said, pathetically. "Look out dyah and see ef you see anybody," he added, suddenly.

Both of them obeyed, and then returned and stood silent; they could not tell him no.

Presently the woman said, "Don' you warn put you' shut on?"

"What did you say my name was?" he said.

"Ole 'Str—" She paused at the look of pain on his face, shifted uneasily from one foot to the other, and relapsed into embarrassed silence.

"Nem min'! dee'll know it—dee'll know me 'dout any name, oon dee?" He appealed wistfully to them both. The woman for answer unfolded the shirt. He moved feebly as if in assent.

"I so tired waitin'," he whispered— "done 'mos' gin out, an' he oon come; but I thought I heah little Eph to-day?" There was a faint inquiry in his voice.

"Yes, he wuz heah."

"Wuz he?" The languid form became instantly alert, the tired face took on a look of eager expectancy. "Heah, gi' m'y shut quick. I knowed it. Wait; go over dyah, son, and git me dat money. He'll be heah torectly." They thought his mind wandered, and merely followed the direction of his eyes with theirs. "Go over dyah quick—don't you heah me?"

And to humor him Ephraim went over to the corner indicated.

"Retch up dyah, an' run you' hand in onder de second jice. It's all in dyah," he said to the woman—"twelve hundred dollars—dat's what dee went for. I wucked night an' day forty year to save dat money for marster: you know dee teck all he land an' all he niggers an' tu'n him out in de ole fiel'? I put 'tin dyah 'ginst he come. You ain' know he comin' dis evenin' is you? Heah, help me on wid dat shut, gal—I stan'in' heah talkin' an' maybe ole marster waitin'. Push de do' open so you kin see. Forty year ago," he murmured, as Polly jambed the door back and returned to his side—"forty year ago dee come an' levelled on me: marster sutny did cry. 'Nem min',' he say, 'I comin' right down in de summer to buy you back an' bring you home. He's comin', too—nuver tol' me a lie in he life —comin' dis evenin'. Make 'aste." This in tremulous eagerness to the woman, who had involuntarily caught the feeling, and was now with eager and ineffectual haste trying to button his shirt.

An exclamation from her husband caused her to turn around, as he stepped into the light and held up an old sock filled with something.

"Heah, hol' you' apron," said the old man to Polly, who gathered up the lower corners of her apron and stood nearer the bed.

"Po' it in dyah." This to Ephraim, who mechanically obeyed. He pulled off the string, and poured into his wife's lap the heap of glittering coin—gold and silver more than their eyes had ever seen before.

"Hit's all dyah," said the old man, confidentially, as if he were rendering an account. "I been savin' it ever sence dee took me 'way. I so busy savin' it I 'ain' had time to eat, but I ain' hongry now; have plenty when I git home." He sank back exhausted. "Oon marster be glad to see me?" he asked, presently, in pathetic simplicity. "You know we growed up togerr? I been waitin' so long I 'feared dee 'mos' done forgit me. You reckon dee is?" he asked the woman, appealingly.

"No, suh, dee 'ain' forgit you," she said, comfortingly.

"I know dee 'ain'," he said, reassured. "Dat's what he tell me—he ain' nuver gwine forgit me." The reaction had set in, and his voice was so feeble now it was scarcely audible. He was talking rather to himself than to them, and finally he sank into a doze. A painful silence reigned in the little hut, in which the only sound was the breathing of the dying man. A single shaft of light stole down under the edge of the slowly passing cloud and slipped up to the door. Suddenly the sleeper waked with a start, and gazed around.

"Hit gittin' mighty dark," he whispered, faintly. "You reckon dee'll git heah 'fo' dark ?"

The light was dying from his eyes.

"Ephum," said the woman, softly, to her husband.

The effect was electrical.

"Heish ! you heah dat ?" exclaimed the dying man, eagerly.

"Ephum"—she repeated. The rest was drowned by Ole 'Stracted's joyous exclamation.

"Gord ! I knowed it !" he cried, suddenly rising upright, and, with beaming face, stretching both arms toward the door. "Dyah dee come ! Now watch 'em smile. All y'all jes stand back. Heah de one you lookin' for. Marster—Mymy—heah's little Ephum !" And with a smile on his face he sank back into his son's arms.

The evening sun, dropping on the instant to his setting, flooded the room with light; but as Ephraim gently eased him down and drew his arm from around him, it was the light of the unending morning that was on his face. His Master had at last come for him, and after his long waiting, Ole 'Stracted had indeed gone home.

THE HOME ACRE.

BY E. P. ROE.

VIII.—THE KITCHEN-GARDEN.

THE garden should be open to the sky, and as far as possible unshaded by adjacent trees from the morning and afternoon sun. It is even more essential that the trees be not so near that their voracious roots can make their way to the rich loam of the garden.

Now for the soil. We would naturally suppose that that of Eden was a deep sandy loam, with not too porous a subsoil. As we have already seen again and again, such a soil appears to be the laboratory in which we can assist Nature to develop her best products. But Nature has a profound respect for skill, and when she recognizes it, "lends a hand" in securing excellent crops from almost drifting sand or stubborn clay. She has even assisted the Hollander in wresting from the ocean one of the gardens of the world.

We must again dwell on the principles already emphasized, that soils must be treated according to their nature. If too damp, they must be drained; if of the fortunate quality of a sandy loam resting on a clay subsoil, they can be abundantly deepened and enriched from the start; if of a heavy clay, inclined to be cold and

wet in spring, and to bake and crack in summer, skill should aim to lighten it and remove its inertia; finally, as we have shown, a light porous soil should be treated like a spendthrift. All soils, except the last-named, are much the better for being enriched and deeply ploughed or forked in October or November. This exposes the mould to the sweetening and mechanical action of the frost, and the fertilizers incorporated with it are gradually transformed into just that condition of plant food which the rootlets take up with the greatest ease and rapidity. A light soil, on the contrary, should not be worked in autumn, but be left intact after the crops are taken from it.

In one respect a light soil and a stiff heavy one should be treated in the same way, but for different reasons. In the first instance fertilizers should be applied in moderation to the surface, and rains and the cultivation of the growing crops depended upon to carry the richness downward to the roots. The porous nature of the earth must ever be borne in mind; fertilizers pass through it and disappear, and therefore are applied to the surface to delay this process and enable the roots to obtain as much nutriment as possible during the passage. Equal and even greater advantages are secured by a top-dressing of barnyard manures and composts to the heaviest of clay. The surface of such soils, left to nature, becomes in hot dry weather like pottery, baking and cracking, shielding from dew and shower, and preventing all circulation of air about the roots. A top-dressing prevents all this, keeps the surface open and mellow, and supplies not only fertility, but the mechanical conditions that are essential.

If we are now ready to begin, let us begin right. I have not much sympathy with finical, fussy gardening. One of the chief fascinations of gardening is the endless field it affords for skilful sleight of hand, short-cuts, unconventional methods, and experiments. The true gardener soon ceases to be a man of rules, and becomes one of strategy, of expedients. He is prompt to act at the right moment. Like the artist, he is ever seeking and acting upon hints from nature. The man of rules says the 1st of July is the time to set out winter cabbage, and out the plants go, though the sky be brazen and the mercury in the nineties. The gardener has his plants ready, and for a few days watches the sky. At last he perceives that rain is coming; then he sets out his plants, and nature's watering starts them, unwilted, on their new growth.

At the same time I protest against careless, slovenly gardening—ground imperfectly prepared, crooked rows, seed half covered, or covered so deeply that the germs are discouraged long before they reach light. One of the best aids to success is a small compost heap composed equally of manure from the horse-stable, the cow-stable, and of leaves. This should be allowed to stand so long, and be cut down and turned so often, that it becomes like a fine black powder, and is much the better for being kept under shelter from sun and rain.

All who hope to have a permanent garden will naturally think first of asparagus, one of the vegetables that have been longest in cultivation, and one which is justly among the most valued. It was cultivated hundreds of years before the Christian era, and is to-day growing in popular esteem among civilized peoples.

In the matter of preparation I shall take issue with many of the authorities. I have read and known of instances wherein extraordinary expense and pains have been bestowed upon the asparagus bed. The soil has been dug out to the depth of two or more feet, the bottom paved, and the homely, hardy roots, accustomed to roughing it the world over, set out and tended with a care which, if given to a potato, would make it open its eyes. There are few more hardy and widely distributed species of vegetables than asparagus. It is "a native of the sea-coasts of various countries of Europe and Asia." According to Loudon, it is abundant on the sandy steppes in the interior of Russia. In southern Russia and Poland the horses and cows feed upon it. It grows freely in the fens of Lincolnshire, and is indigenous to Cornwall. On the borders of the Euphrates the shoots are so extraordinarily large and vigorous that Thompson thinks that it would be to the advantage of gardeners to import roots from that region. These facts may indicate that too much stress may have been laid on its character as a marine plant. Yet it is true that it grows naturally on the coast of Holland, in the sandy valleys and on the downs, while off Lizard Point it flourishes naturally on an island where, in gales, the sea breaks over the roots. In this country also it has escaped cultivation, and is establishing itself along our coasts. The truth is that it is a plant endowed with a remarkable power of adaptation to all soils and climates, and does not need the extravagant petting often given it. On different portions of my place chance seeds have fallen, and annually produce almost as fine heads as are cut from the garden. Nature therefore teaches what experience verifies, that asparagus is one of the most easily grown and inexpensive vegetables of the garden. From two small beds we have raised during the past eight years twice as much as we could use, and at the cost of very little trouble either in planting or cultivation.

In my effort to show, from the hardy nature of the asparagus plant, that extravagant preparation is unnecessary, let no one conclude that I am opposed to a good thorough preparation that accords with common-sense. It is not for one year's crop that you are preparing, but for a vegetable that should be productive on the same ground thirty or forty years. What I said of strawberries applies here. A fair yield of fruit can be expected from plants set out on ordinary corn ground, but more than double the crop would be secured from ground generously prepared.

When I first came to Cornwall, about twelve years since, I determined to have an asparagus bed as soon as possible. I selected a plot 80 feet long by 30 wide, of sandy loam, sloping to the southwest. It had been used as a garden before, but was greatly impoverished. I gave it a good top-dressing of barn-yard manure in the autumn, and ploughed it deeply; another top-dressing of fine yard manure and a deep forking in the early spring. Then, raking the surface smooth, I set a line along its length on one side. A man took a spade, sunk its length in the soil, and pushed it forward strongly. This action made an almost perpendicular wedge-shaped aperture just back of the spade. The asparagus plant, with its roots spread out fan-shape, was sunk in this opening to a depth that left the crown of the plant between three and four inches below the surface. Then the spade was drawn out, and the soil left to fall over the crown of the plant. Rapidly repeating this simple process, the whole plot was soon set out. The entire bed was then raked smooth. The rows were three feet apart, and plants one foot apart in the row. A similar plot could scarcely have been planted with potatoes more quickly or at less expense, and a good crop of potatoes could not have been raised on that poor land with less preparation. A few years later I made another and smaller bed in the same way. The results have been entirely satisfactory. I secured my object, and had plenty of asparagus at slight cost, and have also sold and given away large quantities. A bit of experience is often worth much more than theory.

At the same time it is proper that some suggestions should follow this brief record. The asparagus bed should be in well-drained soil, for while the plant will grow on wet land, it will start late, and our aim is to have it early.

Again, with asparagus as with nearly everything else, the deeper and richer the soil, the larger and more luxuriant the crop. Listen to Thompson, the great English gardener: "If the ground has been drained, trenched, or made good to the depth of *three* feet, as directed for the kitchen-garden generally (!), that depth will suffice for the growth of asparagus." We should think so; yet I am fast reaching the conclusion that under most circumstances it would in the end repay us to secure that depth of rich soil throughout our gardens, not only for asparagus, but for everything else. Few of the hasty, slipshod gardeners of America have any idea of the results secured by extending root pasturage to the depth of three feet instead of six or seven inches; soil thus prepared would defy flood and drought, and everything planted therein would attain almost perfection, asparagus included. But who has not seen little gardens by the road-side in which all the esculents seemed growing together much as they would be blended in the pot thereafter? Yet from such patches, half snatched from barrenness, many a hearty, wholesome dinner results. Let us have a garden at once, then improve it indefinitely.

I will give in brief just what is essential to secure a good and lasting asparagus bed. We can if we choose grow our own plants, and thus be sure of good ones. The seed can be sown in late October or *early* spring on light rich soil in rows eighteen inches apart. An ounce of seed will sow fifty feet of drill. If the soil is light, cover the seed one inch deep; if heavy, half an inch, pack the ground lightly, and cover the drill with a good dusting of that fine compost we spoke of, or any fine manure. This gives the young plants a good send-off. By the use of the hoe and hand-weeding keep them scrupulously clean during the growing season, and when the tops are killed by frost mow them off. I should advise sowing two or three seeds to the inch, and then when the plants are three inches high, thinning them out so that they stand four inches apart. You thus insure almost the certainty of good strong plants by autumn, for plants raised as directed are ready to be set out after one season's growth, and by most gardeners are preferred.

In most instances good plants can be bought for a small sum from nurserymen, who usually offer for sale those that are two years old. Strong one-year-olds are just as good, but under ordinary culture are rarely large enough until two years of age. I would not set out three-year-old plants, for they are apt to be stunted and enfeebled. You can easily calculate how many plants you require by remembering that the rows are to be three feet apart, and the plants one foot apart in the row.

Now whether you have raised the plants yourself or have bought them, you are ready to put them where they will grow, and yield to the end of your life probably. Again I substantiate my position by quoting from the well-known gardener and writer Mr. Joseph Harris: "The old directions for planting an asparagus bed were well calculated to deter any one from making the attempt. I can recollect the first I made. The labor and manure must have cost at the rate of a thousand dollars an acre, and, after all was done, no better results were obtained than we now secure at one-tenth of the expense."

If the ground selected for the bed is a well-drained sandy loam, is clean, free from sod, roots, stones, etc., I would give it a top-dressing of six inches of good barn-yard manure, which by trenching or ploughing I would thoroughly mix with the soil to the depth of at least two feet. If the ground is not free from stones, roots, and sod, I should put on the manure, as directed, in the autumn, and begin on one side of the prospective bed and trench it all over, mingling the fertilizer through the soil. The trencher can throw out on the surface back of him every stone, root, and weed, so that by the time he is through there is a sufficient space of ground amply prepared.

On all soils except a wet, heavy clay I prefer autumn planting. During the latter part of October or early November, put in the plants as explained above, or else make a straight trench that will give room for the spreading of the roots, and leave the crowns between three and four inches below the surface. Then level the ground, and cover the row with a light mulch of stable manure as you would strawberries. If more convenient to set out the plants in spring, do so as soon as the ground is dry enough to crumble freely when worked. In the spring rake off the mulch, and as early as possible fork the ground over lightly, taking pains not to touch or wound the crowns of the plants. The young, slender shoots will soon appear, and slender enough they will be at first. Keep them free of weeds and let them grow uncut all through the first year; mow off the tops in late October, and cover the entire bed with three or four inches of coarse barn-yard manure. In spring rake off the coarsest of this mulch, from which the rains and melting snows have been carrying down richness, dig the bed over lightly once (never wounding the roots and crowns of the plants), and then sow salt over the bed till it is barely white. Let the tops grow naturally and uncut the second year, and merely keep clean. Take precisely the same action again in the autumn and the following spring. During the latter part of April and May a few of the strongest shoots can be cut for the table. This should be done with a sharp knife a little below the surface, so that the soil may heal the wound, and carefully, lest other heads just beneath the surface will be clipped prematurely. Cut from the bed very sparingly, however, the third year, and let vigorous foliage form corresponding root power. In the autumn of the third and the spring of the fourth year the treatment is precisely the same. In the fourth season, however, the shoots may be used freely to, say, about June 20, after which the plants should be permitted to grow unchecked till fall, in order to maintain and increase the root-power. Every year thereafter there should be an abundant top-dressing of manure in the fall and a careful digging of the ground in the early spring.

Light, sandy soil, clear of stones, is well adapted to asparagus, but should be treated on the principles already indicated in these papers. There should be no attempt, by trenching, to render a porous subsoil more leaky. It is useless to give the bed a thorough initial enriching. Put on a generous top-dressing every autumn and leave the rains to do their work, and good crops will result.

If, on the contrary, a cold, heavy clay must be dealt with, every effort should be made to ameliorate it. Work in a large quantity of sand at first, if possible; employ manures from the horse-stable, or other light and exciting fertilizers, and there will be no failure.

In regard to the use of salt, Mr. Harris writes: "It is a popular notion that common salt is exceedingly beneficial to asparagus. I do not know that there is any positive proof of this, but, at any rate, salt will do no harm, even if applied thick enough to kill many of our common weeds. Salt is usually sown broadcast, at the rate of ten bushels to the acre."

Until recently I have grown asparagus without salt. Hereafter I shall employ it in sufficient degree to kill all weeds except the strongest. I shall sow it every spring after the bed is dug until the ground is as white as if a flurry of snow had passed over it. I think salt *is* a good manure for asparagus, and many other things. At any rate, we secure a great advantage in keeping our beds free of weeds.

I have written thus fully of asparagus because when a man makes a bed as directed he makes it for a lifetime. He can scarcely find another investment that will yield a larger return. We have asparagus on our table every day from the middle of April to July 1, and the annual care of the crop is far less than that of a cabbage patch. I do not advise severe cutting, however, after the middle of June, and for this reason: it is well known that the most pestiferous perennial weed can be killed utterly if never allowed to make foliage. As foliage depends upon the root, so the root depends on foliage. The roots of asparagus may therefore be greatly enfeebled by too severe and long-continued cutting. Avarice always over-reaches itself.

In some localities the asparagus beetle destroys whole plantations. Thompson, the English authority, says: "The larvæ, beetles, and eggs are found from June to the end of September. Picking off the larvæ and beetles, or shaking them into receptacles, appears to be the only remedy."

Peter Henderson, in his valuable book *Gardening for Profit*, figures this insect and its larvæ accurately, and says: "Whenever the eggs or larvæ appear, cut and burn the plants as long as any traces of the insect are seen. This must be done, if it destroys every vestige of vegetation." He and other authorities speak of the advantage of cooping a hen and chickens in the bed. Most emphatically would I recommend this latter course, for I have tried it with various vegetables. Active broods of little chickens here and there in the garden are the best of insecticides, and pay for themselves twice over in this service alone.

We will next speak of the *onion*, because it is so hardy that the earlier it is planted in spring the better. Indeed, I have often, with great advantage, sown the seed on light soils the 1st of September, and wintered over the young plants in the open ground. Nature evidently intended the onion for humanity in general, for she has endowed the plant with the power to flourish from the tropics to the coldest limit of the temperate zone.

While onions are grown in all sorts of careless ways, like other vegetables, it is by far the best plan to select a space for an annual and permanent bed, just as we do for asparagus. Unlike most other crops, the onion does not require change of ground, but usually does better on the same soil for an indefinite number of years. Therefore I would advise that upon the home acre the onion, like the asparagus bed, should be made with a view to permanence.

Not much success can be hoped for on rough, poor land. The onion, like the asparagus bed, should be made and maintained with some care. If possible, select a light, well-drained, but not dry plot. Make the soil rich, deep, mellow, to the depth of twenty inches, taking out all stones, roots, etc.; cover the land with at least six inches of good strong barn-yard manure. This should be done in the autumn. Sow the ground white with salt, as in the case of asparagus, and then mingle these fertilizers thoroughly with the soil by forking or ploughing it at once, leaving the surface as rough as possible, so that the frost can penetrate deeply. Just as soon as the ground is dry enough to work in the spring, fork or plough again, breaking every lump and raking all smooth, so that the surface is as fine as the soil in a hot-bed. You cannot hope for much in heavy, lumpy ground. Sow at least three seeds to the inch in a shallow drill one inch deep, and spat the earth firmly over the seed with the back of a spade or with your hand. In subsequent culture little more is required than keeping the *mere surface* stirred with a hoe and the rows clean of weeds. Onions are not benefited by deep stirring of the soil, but the surface, from the start, should be kept clean and scarified an inch or two deep between the rows during the growing season. I prefer to have my onions growing at the rate of one or two to every inch of row, for I do not like large bulbs. I think that moderate-sized onions are better for the table. Those who value largeness should thin out the plants to three or four inches apart, but even in the market there is less demand for large, coarse onions. When the tops begin to fall over from their own weight, in August or September, leave them to mature and ripen naturally.

When the tops begin to dry up, pull them from the soil, let them dry thoroughly in the sun, and then spread them thinly in a dry loft till there is danger of their freezing. Even there they will keep better, if covered deeply with straw, hay, etc., than in a damp cellar. Wherever the air is damp and a little too warm, onions will speedily start to grow again, and soon become worthless. After the crop has been taken, the ground should be treated as at first — thoroughly enriched and pulverized late in autumn, and left to lie in a rough state during the winter, then prepared for planting as early as possible. I prefer March sowing of the seed to April, and April, by far, to May. In England they try to plant in February. Indeed, as I have said, I have had excellent success by sowing the seed early in September on light soils and letting the plants grow during all the mild days of fall, winter, and early spring. By this course we have onions fit for the table and market the following May. In this latitude they need the protection of a little coarse litter from December 1 to about the middle of March. Only the very severest frost injures them. Most of us have seen onions, overlooked in the fall gathering, growing vigorously as soon as the thaws began in spring. This fact contains all the hint we need in wintering over the vegetable in the open ground. If the seed is sown late in September, the plants do not usually acquire sufficient strength in this latitude to resist the frost. It is necessary, therefore, to secure our main crop by very early spring sowings, and it may be said here that after the second thorough pulverization of the soil in spring, the ground will be in such good condition that, if well enriched and stirred late in autumn, it will only need levelling down and smoothing off before the spring sowing. Onions appear to do best on a compact soil, if rich, deep, and clean. It is the *surface* merely that needs to be stirred lightly and frequently.

If young green onions with thin succulent tops are desired very early in spring, it will be an interesting experiment to sow the seed the latter part of August or early in September. Another method is to leave a row of onions in the garden where they ripened. When the autumn rains begin, they will start to grow again. The winter will not harm them, and even in April there will be a strong growth of green tops. The seed stalk should be picked off as soon as it appears in spring, or else the whole strength will speedily go to the formation of the seed.

It should be remembered that good onions cannot be produced very far to the south by sowing the small gunpowder-like seed. In our own, and especially in warmer climates, a great advantage is secured by employing what are known as "onion sets." These are produced by sowing the ordinary black seed very thickly on light poor land. Being much crowded, and not having much nutriment, the seed develop into little onions from the size of a pea to that of a walnut, the smaller the better, if they are solid and plump. These, pressed or sunk, about three inches apart, into rich garden soil about an inch deep, just as soon as the frost is out, make fine bulbs by the middle of June. For instance, we had in our garden plenty of onions three inches in diameter from these little sets, while the seed, sown at the same time, will not yield good bulbs before August. There is but little need of raising these sets, for it is rather difficult to keep them in good condition over the winter. Any seedsman can furnish them, and they are usually on sale at country stores. Three or four quarts, if in good condition, will supply a family abundantly, and leave many to be used dry during the autumn. Insist on plump little bulbs. If you plant them early, as you should, you will be more apt to get good sets. Many neglect the planting till the sets are half dried up, or so badly sprouted as to be wellnigh worthless. They usually come in the form of white and yellow sets, and I plant an equal number of each.

The chief insect enemy is the onion maggot, the larvæ of the onion fly. These bore through the outer leaf and down into the bulb, which they soon destroy. I know of no remedy but to pull up the yellow and sickly plants and burn them and the pests together. The free use of salt in the fall, and a light top-dressing of wood-ashes at the time of planting, tend to subdue these insects, but the best course is prevention by deeply cultivating and thoroughly enriching in the fall, leaving the ground rough and uneven for the deep action of frost, and by sowing the seed *very early* in spring. I have found that the insect usually attacks late-sown and feeble plants. If the maggot was in my garden, I should use the little sets only.

Some special manures have been employed in attaining the greatest success with this vegetable. In England, pigeon dung and the cleanings of the pigsty are extensively employed. In this country the sweepings of the hen-roost are generally recommended. It should be remembered that all these are strong agents, and if brought in contact with the roots of any vegetable while in a crude, undiluted state, burn like fire, especially in our climate. What can be done in safety in England will not answer under our vivid sun and in our frequent droughts. These strong fertilizers could be doubled in value as well as bulk by being composted with sods, leaves, etc., and then, after having been mixed, allowed to decay thoroughly. Then the compost can be used with great advantage as a top-dressing directly over the drills when either sets or seeds are planted. The spring rains will carry the richness from the surface to the roots, and insure a very vigorous growth. When the compost named in the early part of this paper is used I sow it thickly *in* the drill, draw a pointed hoe through once more to mingle the fertilizer with the soil, then sow the seeds or put in the sets one inch deep at once, and the result is immediate and vigorous growth. Wood ashes and bone-dust are excellent fertilizers, and should be sown on the surface on the row as soon as planted, and gradually worked in by weeding and cultivation during the growing season. Manure from the pigsty, wherein weeds, litter, sods, muck, etc., have been thrown freely during the summer, can be spread broadcast over the onion bed in the autumn, and worked in deeply like the product of the barn-yard. The onion bed can scarcely be made too rich as long as the manure is not applied in its crude, unfermented state at the time of planting. Then, if the seed is put in very early, it grows too strongly and quickly for insects to do much damage.

Varieties.—Thompson in his English work names nineteen varieties with many synonyms; Henderson offers the seed of thirteen varieties; Gregory, of seventeen kinds. There is no need of our being confused by this latitude of choice. We find it in the great majority of fruits and vegetables offered by nursery-men and seedsmen. Each of the old varieties that have survived the test of years has certain good qualities which make it valuable, especially in certain localities. Many of the novelties in vegetables, as among fruits, will soon disappear; a few will take their place among the standard sorts. In the case of the kitchen, as well as in the fruit garden, I shall give the opinion of men who have a celebrity as wide as the continent for actual experience, and modestly add occasionally some views of my own which are the result of observation.

As a choice for the home garden Mr. Peter recommends the following varieties of onions: Extra Early Red, Yellow Globe Danvers, White Portugal or Silver Skin, and Southport Yellow Globe. Mr. Joseph Harris, the well-known and practical author: Yellow Danvers, Extra Early Large Red, and White Globe. Mr. J. J. H. Gregory: New Queen, Early Yellow Acker, Yellow Danvers, Early Red Globe Danvers, Large Red Wethersfield. They all recommend onion sets. The Queen onion is quite distinct. I have already from the black seed snow-white onions nearly ripe, and about the size of a quarter of a dollar. For the home table, where earliness, as well as quality, size, and quantity, is desired, I think the Queen deserves a place. They are admirably fitted for pickling. I have tried all the varieties named with good success, and grown some of the largest kinds to six inches in diameter.

PERSICOS ODI.

HORACE'S ODES, I., 38.

TRANSLATED BY SIR STEPHEN E. DE VERE, BART.

NO pomp of Persian feasts for me;
   No garland woven curiously
With linden bark !* Nor seek where blows
The dying summer's lingering rose.

Bind round my brow, and round thine own,
My boy, the myrtle wreath alone,
And 'neath the overarching vine
Pour forth full cups of ruby wine.

* The ancients knitted together their most sumptuous festal garlands from a fibre made out of the inner bark of the "tilia," or linden-tree.

THE STORY OF TANIS.

BY AMELIA B. EDWARDS.

"Tsaru or Tanis, called also T'san, or Zoan."—BIRCH.

"*Tsoan* de l'Hébreu, *Djani* du Copte, et *Tanis* du Grec, sont une seule et même ville."—MARIETTE.

THERE is a *terra incognita* in Lower Egypt. Untraversed by railroads, untrodden by tourists, this region, which may be described as an irregular pentagon, is bounded on the north by the Mediterranean Sea, on the east by the Suez Canal, and on the south, southwest, and northwest by three conterminous lines of railway. The vast space thus enclosed—commonly called "the Menzaleh district" —comprises nearly one fifth part of the whole Delta of the Nile. It contains as much lake as land, and nearly as much mud as either. The boundaries of both land and lake are practically interchangeable, and vary with the seasons. In winter, when rains are heavy, the lower flats and smaller islets disappear, and the whole district becomes one net-work of lagoons and swamps. In spring and summer the waters subside, the land emerges, the mud swamps turn to tracts of sunbaked clay, and the great salt lake, evaporating over a surface of some 500,000 acres, shrinks in its shallow bed, and simmers all day long in a mist of silvery mirage.

The inhabitants of these wastes—a race of fishers—share the characteristics of their native province. Catching fish, curing fish, selling fish, eating fish, they live half their lives upon the water. Wherever a spit of barren desert rises above the level of the annual floods, there they congregate in clusters of mud-built hovels, each cluster a village governed by its local sheik. These villages, which in winter are for the most part accessible only by boat, are in summer islanded amid seas of rippling barley. When the barley ripens, every fisher turns husbandman. Boats are hauled up, nets brought in, doors bolted, dogs let loose, and whole villages turn out to camp in the open fields and bring in the harvest.

That this *terra incognita* should remain a *terra incognita* is not surprising, for a visit to the Menzaleh district is in truth beset by more difficulties than would be encountered in a trip to the Second Cataract. Roads, public conveyances, hotels, there are none. The adventurous traveller must consequently provide himself with stores, tent, bedding, and a boat expressly built for the navigation of very shallow waters. Such travellers are either sportsmen keen upon aquatic birds or archæologists in quest of relics of the past. For no others do these treeless flats and monotonous lagoons possess any attraction; and even sportsmen and archæologists are few and far between.

Toward the centre of this pentagon, as shown upon the map, and about midway of the marshes which divide lake from land, the wide monotony is broken by an extensive sand-hill and a broad canal. The sand-hill rises from the flats like an island from the ocean. Other and lesser islets—the nearest two miles and a half away, the farthest a blue profile against the horizon—are seen dotted here and there over the vast plain. Though curiously like artificial tumuli, these are natural hillocks, ranging from fifteen to fifty feet in height, and averaging from four hundred to a thousand feet in diameter. The great "gezîreh"*—bigger than all the rest put together—skirts the right bank of the canal, lying due north and south, and rising at its highest level to 117 feet above the plain. In superficial extent it covers about four hundred and forty-five acres. Seen from afar—and it is a conspicuous object for miles in every direction —it looks like a little mountain, abrupt, isolated, its jagged ridge fantastically outlined against the sky. On nearer inspection, however, this ridge proves to be no part of the original elevation, which was much less lofty when the first settlers pitched upon it as a convenient platform for habitation. The great "gezîreh" is, in fact, artificially raised, being heaped far and wide with mounds of crumbled and crumbling brick. Thus also the smaller hills are crested with ancient camps and honey-combed with tombs. Those mounds, those camps, those tombs, are the unmistakable hieroglyphs in which the history of ancient Egypt is written all over the face of the country. It needs no scholarship to interpret them.

* *Arabic:* gezîreh—island. The Arabs employ this word to express either an island surrounded by water or a natural elevation in the desert.

They tell of an important centre of civilization long since abandoned. Here, what was once a crowded city; yonder, its cemeteries and military outposts. For, as there was once a time when all this littoral district was sea, followed by a time when it was being slowly converted into land, so also there was a period when it was fertile and populous; when these wastes of mud and sand were rich in corn-lands and vineyards; when this slow canal was a mighty arm of the Nile, charged once a year with the wealth of the inundation; when, in place of a miserable fishing village and a wilderness of ruin, there stood upon this spot a city famous not only in the annals of Egypt, but in the history of all the nations of the ancient East.

Like every Egyptian town, great or small, this city had many names—some sacred, some civil; some native, some foreign; some so old that their origin is lost in the obscurity of time past, and some comparatively modern. Certain of its sacred names—and doubtless it had more—have come down to us in contemporary inscriptions; as "The Place of the Leg,"* "The Winged Disk of the North," and "The Cradle of Lower Egypt." Of the first we shall have more to say presently. The last two relate to the great Horus myth, or legendary life of the divine son of Osiris and Isis, who was one of the gods here especially worshipped. The winged disk, a familiar and beautiful emblem typifying the sun in his daily course from east to west, is a special symbol of Horus, who, when he combated Set and his followers, assumed this form. So also "The Cradle of Lower Egypt" points to the tradition of his birth, which was supposed to have taken place in the marsh-lands of the Delta. "The Teb of Lower Egypt" is another name containing a similar reference, "Teb" being the Egyptian name of the city of Edfoo in Upper Egypt, where Harhut, or "Horus of the Winged Disk," was adored in the most magnificent temple of Ptolemaic times. "Zal," or "Zar," T'a, T'an, and T'sān, were the secular names of our dead city. All may perhaps be echoes of one yet earlier, and long forgotten. Transmuted into other tongues, T'san,

or T'ān, became "Zoan" in Hebrew, "Tsânu" in Assyrian, "Tanis" in Greek, "Tani" in Coptic, and in Arabic "Sān." As "Zoan," the place is familiar to every Bible student; as "Tanis," it is known to every reader of classical history. In early Christian times it became the nominal seat of a bishopric,* and so occupies a niche in the history of the Coptic Church; while to this day, as "Sān-el-Hagar" (Sān of the Stones), the ruins preserve their ancient name unchanged. Thus, through every vicissitude of rule, of faith, of fortune, the topographical identity of the site has never been obscured; neither has a single link in the chain of historic and philological evidence been lost. No Bible commentator, no historian, no Egyptologist, has ever questioned the continuity of its traditions or rejected the overwhelming testimony of its ruins. Authorities might be quoted, and proof be piled on proof, to show that T'ān, T'san, Zoan, Tsânu, Tanis, Tani, and Sān are one and the same; but a single verse from the 78th Psalm is enough.

"Marvellous things did He in the sight of their fathers, in the land of Egypt, in the field of Zoan," wrote the inspired singer, and so it reads in the original Hebrew. Translating the Hebrew Scriptures into Greek some seven hundred years later, while T'san was yet a populous provincial capital, the Septuagint thus rendered the above passage: "Marvellous things did He in the sight of their fathers, in the land of Egypt, in the field of Tanis." The force of contemporary evidence can no further go.

To assign a date to the beginnings of Tanis is impossible. In the Book of Numbers (chapter xiii., verse 22) it is said to have been founded "seven years after Hebron," but this reference shifts the problem to Hebron without solving it. By some, the foundation of the city is conjecturally ascribed to Pepi, a great king of the old Pyramid period, whose name and titles occur on a stone discovered in the ruins; but there is good reason to believe that this particular stone originally belonged to another sanctuary in another part of

---

* *Ha-uar*, also pronounced *Ha-Tān:* this name signifies the "Place (or House) of the Leg," or, according to another rendering, "The Place of the Flight." Professor Maspero assigns this name to an incident in the great mythic legend of Osiris and Typhon.

* Coptic tradition identifies Tanis with the birthplace of Moses; hence, perhaps, its selection as a titular see. No Coptic settlement, however, occupied the site, and there are no remains of Coptic buildings among the ruins. The place had undoubtedly been deserted for nearly 300 years when Apollonius, "Bishop of Tanis," assisted in A.D. 451 at the Council of Chalcedon.

the country, and that it was brought to Tanis as mere building material during the time of Rameses II. It therefore proves nothing.* The excavations of 1884 may, however, yield a more trustworthy clew, for among a mass of papyri discovered by Mr. Flinders Petrie in the ruins of two private houses belonging to citizens of Tanis of the time of Marcus Aurelius, there occurs a Calendar of Temple Festivals wherein the name of Khufu (Cheops), the builder of the Great Pyramid, is entered in connection, apparently, with certain local feast-days. It would be premature to hazard conjectures before the papyrus is fully translated; but were Khufu seen to be in any way connected with the building or endowment of the Great Temple of Tanis, it would carry back the date of that famous structure to about B.C. 4000.

The story of an ancient Egyptian city may be sketched in a few lines. What is true of one is for the most part true of all. Upon some spot of rising ground above the level of the annual inundation a few mud huts cluster round a rude sanctuary. The hut-dwellers multiply; the village spreads; the sanctuary is enlarged or rebuilt. As time goes on, the village becomes a town; the town becomes a city; and the temple, enriched by successive generations of kings, governors, and pious donors, becomes a vast historical aggregate of chapels, halls, courts, avenues, pylons, and sacred enclosures. By-and-by, whether ravaged by foreign foes or shattered by some convulsion of nature, the splendid structure falls into partial ruin. Hereupon the degenerate princes of a later age, careless of the past and eager to raise some memorial of their own uneventful rule, lay profane hands upon the monuments of their great predecessors, cut them up for building material, and use them in the construction of debased imitations of earlier schools. This process, in all probability, is again and again repeated. Not merely stones, but statues, sphinxes, obelisks, are appropriated and reappropriated, worked and reworked, till at last there comes a time of disruption and change, when the old religion is abolished, and the images of the gods are cast down, and the very language of the inscriptions is forgotten. After this, the sacred places become quarries for the builders of Coptic churches, Arab mosques, and the palaces of Turkish governors. Meanwhile the actual city, consisting of labyrinthine lanes of mud-built dwellings, gradually disappears. The spacious houses of the rich, the hovels of the poor, crumble, collapse, and resolve themselves into mounds of dust and potsherds. Such is the local history of hundreds of ancient Egyptian sites, and such is the history of Tanis.

A hundred years ago, the grave of this dead city was yet inviolate. Then, as now, the great sand island was heaped high with desolate piles of reddish-brown rubbish. Then, as now, those mounds enclosed a low, level area of large extent like the bed of a dry lake, or the crater of an extinct volcano. The traveller who—once, perchance, in a decade—scaled those crumbling slopes and looked down into that area, beheld at his feet an undulating waste enclosed by what at first sight looked like a quadrangular rampart of earthworks, but which proved, on closer inspection, to be the remains of an extraordinarily massive wall built of sun-dried bricks. The space thus bounded was strewn with ruins. Here were the shattered shafts of a double line of obelisks, two mountainous piles of sculptured blocks, a couple of mutilated statues, a broken shrine, and a number of carved capitals. These fragments identified the site of the great temple. Here was the temenos, or sacred enclosure. That avenue of obelisks marked the approach to the portico. That shrine once stood within the holy precincts. So much was certain; and the irregularities of the ground suggested the rest. What sculptures, what inscriptions, what treasures of art and history, might not there lie buried!

Such was the aspect of the place when surveyed in 1798 by the engineers of the great French expedition.* Meanwhile there was war in Egypt, in India, in Europe, on land, on sea—universal war, followed, in 1815, by universal peace. Peace meant public security, the revival of commerce, the encouragement of the arts. The rich, the learned, the adventurous, the speculative, were once more free to travel, and the world was speedily over-

* Mr. Petrie shows good reason for supposing that this stone was brought from some very ancient ruined temple near Denderah. See *Tanis*, Part I., page 4.

* *Description des Ruines de San, Tanis des Anciens*, par Louis Cordier. *Description de l'Egypte*, Vol. V., chap. XXIII. Paris: 1829.

run by tourists and traders. The picture market and the antiquity market, both long dormant, started into new and vigorous life. In Egypt the soil was strewn with treasures which it was not only profitable but praiseworthy to rescue from the destructive propensities of native fellaheen and Turkish pashas. Drovetti, Salt, Minutoli, Belzoni, Ricci, Passalacqua, Anastasi, Hay, and a host of lesser depredators laid hands accordingly upon every movable object within their reach, and the collections so amassed were sold for enormous sums to crowned heads and wealthy *virtuosi*. Thus were founded the great Egyptian galleries of our European museums. The plunder shipped by Salt, Belzoni, and others, together with a precious store of objects wrested from the French army on the capitulation of Alexandria, went to the British Museum; the Minutoli collection was bought for Berlin by the Prussian government; the Grand Duke of Tuscany purchased the Ricci collection for the Museum of Florence; and (most magnificent and valuable of all) the Drovetti spoils were mainly acquired by the King of Sardinia. Of the Hay collection, part was purchased for the British Museum, and part found its way to the United States, where it now forms the main wealth of the Egyptian department in the Museum of Fine Arts at Boston.

In the course of this great raid, not even so remote and inhospitable a place as Sān escaped the greed of the treasure-seekers. In 1836, M. Prisse d'Avennes revisited the spot, and witnessed the ravage that had been wrought.* He found the temple area pitted with excavations and strewn with plinths, pedestals, fragments of obelisks and mutilated colossi, the heads of which had been sawn off "to adorn European museums." This was the work of the two Consuls-General Drovetti and Salt,† whose barbarous practice it was to smash up whatever was too large or too heavy for transport. Sān, unfortunately, was one of their happy hunting grounds; and when the bulk of Drovetti's spoils passed into the possession of Carlo Felice, many of the noblest ornaments of what was once the great temple of Tanis found their last refuge at Turin.

From Drovetti to Mariette—that is, from about 1820 to 1860—the place seems to have been left to its fate. Meanwhile the salt vapors from Lake Menzaleh corroded the glassy surfaces of the sculptures; the winter floods submerged them; the drifted sands of the desert reburied them. The great wall of circuit, moreover, was perpetually crumbling away in dry weather, and washing away in wet, thereby contributing a steady deposit of dust and mud to the level of the enclosed area. As for the fishermen of the neighboring hamlet, they, of course, went thither as to a quarry, whenever they wanted stones. To this scene of desolation came Auguste Mariette in 1860; and again the grave of Tanis was summoned to render up its dead. But the treasure-seeker this time was no mere greedy plunderer. His object was not to put money in his purse, but to recover the lost links of history. Guided by the line of the obelisk avenue, he unburied the temple ruins for a distance of 1050 feet from west to east, thus laying bare an unparalleled profusion of inscribed stones, columns, bass-reliefs, obelisks, and works of sculpture, all piled together in unimaginable confusion. Never was so rich an archæological discovery made at one blow.* He conveyed a few of the more valuable monuments to Boulak. Some, for their better preservation, he reburied; and for some he made the Sheiks of Sān responsible. The rest were left upon the ground.

While he lived, Mariette never abandoned the hope of going farther and deeper into the mounds of Tanis. In his last discourse delivered before the French Academy—that discourse which has been aptly defined as his "archæological will" —he emphatically pleaded the necessity of prosecuting these excavations. But nevermore was Mariette destined to labor in "the field of Zoan." The hand of death was already upon him; and he passed away, self-martyred in the cause of science, on the 19th of January, 1881.

Meanwhile, however, there were some whose eyes had long been turned toward the Delta, looking for "more light." M. Naville, who in 1879 had drawn attention to Mariette's Academic discourse in the *Journal de Genève*, took occasion two years later to survey and report upon the

---

* See *Miscellanea Ægyptiaca*, Vol. I., Part I., p. 42. Alexandria: 1842.

† Signor Drovetti was Consul-General for France, and Mr. Salt was Consul-General for England.

* See Mariette's letters from Tanis addressed to De Rougé. *Revue Archéologique*, Nouvelle Série. Vol. III. and Vol. V.

ruins of Sän. He describes them as surpassing in severe grandeur and solemnity even the ruins of Karnak. "Herodotus," he says, "who had never seen Tanis, expatiated at much length upon the beauty of Bubastis. To judge by what is left of the one and of the other, Tanis must have greatly surpassed its rival. Supposing that some part at least was left standing —that all was not, as now it is, overthrown and shattered—I have no hesitation in saying that Tanis must have been the most beautiful ruin in Egypt."

Though not yet a regularly organized society, there existed at the time a little English coterie, the members of which were anxious to promote the progress of discovery in Egypt. Upon these persons M. Naville's picturesque narrative made so lively an impression that, when "The Egypt Exploration Fund" became an accomplished fact, they hastened to invite him to make Tanis the scene of the young society's first venture. M. Naville accepted that invitation, and went out accordingly. Arrived in Egypt, however, and having but a few weeks at his disposal, he came to the conclusion that his time was too short for the commencement of any very large undertaking. He therefore decided in favor of the Wady Tûmilat; excavated the much-disputed mound of Maskhûtah ; and by discovering the long-sought "treasure city" of Pithom, achieved the most brilliant Biblical identification of modern times.* It is not, however, generally known that M. Naville, when he started for Egypt in 1883, was actually bound for Tanis, and that but for his unexpected change of plan Pithom might have remained undiscovered to this day. Thus, by a turn of the scale, the excavation of Tanis was deferred till 1884, when it fell to the lot of Mr. W. M. Flinders Petrie.

From the advent of this latest comer dates the first and only scientific exploration of the site. Mr. Petrie went thither with advantages such as Mariette never enjoyed. His time was his own, and his expenditure was unrestricted. Already acclimatized, he feared neither winter rains nor summer heats; and he took with him two faithful Arab overseers who had served him through his work at the Great Pyramid. No man living is more indifferent to creature comforts than Mr. Petrie, but he who proposes to sojourn for months in a place where there is neither lodging for hire nor food for sale must perforce build and provision his castle like Robinson Crusoe.

Preserved meats and vegetables, biscuits and mineral waters, scientific instruments, photographic apparatus, carpenters' tools, bedding, books, a tent, and a goodly store of iron roofing were therefore actual necessities. Thus burdened, the explorer reached his inhospitable haven in February, 1884, after eleven hours of canal trip in a Menzaleh row-boat. It was midnight, and bitter cold. When day broke he jumped ashore, climbed the crumbling mounds, and looked down upon what was once the sacred place of Tanis. There, massed along the centre of a vast area, lay the débris of the temple—sculptured blocks, columns, obelisks, architraves, statues and parts of statues, heads, trunks, and colossal limbs in countless profusion. Seen in the mysterious morning light, it looked like a place that had been carried by assault, victors and vanquished yet lying where they fell. Enclosing this battle ground of giants he beheld the remains of the great wall; beyond the wall, covering about a mile from north to south, and three-quarters of a mile from east to west, the desolate rubbish mounds of the ancient city; beyond these again a boundless flat, all swamp, sand, and solitude. Yonder, to the southward, the convergence of two silvery lines marked the meeting point of the canals Bahr Sän-el-Hagar and Bahr Fakûs, while a shimmering haze to the northward indicated the whereabouts of Lake Menzaleh. As for the modern village, it lay down by the water-

* See *The Store City of Pithom and the Route of the Exodus*, by E. Naville. Published by order of The Egypt Exploration Fund. 1885.

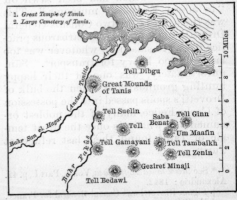

PLAN OF THE SITE OF TANIS AND ITS NEIGHBORHOOD.

SĀN VILLAGE.

side, a mere congeries of mud huts clustered about a tiny mosque, with a score or so of long-masted fishing-boats drawn up alongside the bank.

The scene was one of indescribable monotony and barrenness. Not a blade of grass was visible, and but one tree. That tree—the solitary sycamore of Sān—stands on the opposite side of the canal, facing the village.

Such was the place of Mr. Petrie's exile. Uninviting enough at first sight, it failed to improve upon acquaintance. He lived there, nevertheless, for five months, till driven away by the approach of Ramadân. What he accomplished during those five months should be read in his own narrative,* and can be but lightly touched upon in these pages. Enough that in addition to all his other labors he did actually turn every stone and copy every inscription, thus fulfilling Mariette's programme to the letter.†

The chronicles of Tanis are her ruins. Fragmentary passages of her history are found scattered up and down the annals

* *Tanis.* Part I. By W. M. Flinders Petrie. Published by order of the committee of the Egypt Exploration Fund. Trübner and Co. 1885.

† Mr. Petrie not only turned, cleaned, and dated every inscribed stone and copied the inscriptions, but also photographed and measured every object of interest in the ruins, his photographs being over 120 in number. He made a trigonometrical survey of the site, and drew three plans to scale. He excavated no less than 35 trenches, ranging from 7 to 24 feet in depth, and from 50 to 400 feet in length; he also sunk 12 great shafts. He discovered the remains of a large Ptolemaic temple, a small Ptolemaic chapel with its contents intact, three sphinxes, many important stelæ, and a great treasure of domestic relics in private houses of various periods. He also discovered and excavated three extra-mural cemeteries in the neighborhood of Tanis, in one of which alone he opened no less than 150 pits.

of the ancient world; but we look in vain for any such description as Herodotus gives of Bubastis in her prime, or as Abdel-Latif wrote sixteen centuries later of Memphis in ruins. Had the stones of Tanis been carried away to build an Arab city, like the stones of Bubastis and Memphis, there would now remain scarcely a tradition of the civic splendor of the capital of the eastern Delta. But the place tells its own story, and tells it with a twofold tongue. Every stone is history, and the vehicle of history. Every stone is history, because the stone reveals the quarry, and the use or disuse of certain quarries not unfrequently stamps the political condition of the country. And every stone, as it may be inscribed, or as it forms part of this or that portion of this or that structure, is the vehicle of history. Thus each fragment has its message. Some stones have been erased and reëngraved by successive kings; while others, diverted from their original purpose, have been cut up, turned, and used again and again. This is message upon message, history upon history. The monks of the middle ages, when they effaced Cicero and Plautus to make room for Augustine and Jerome, merely plagiarized on parchment the barbarisms perpetrated on basalt and granite by the dynasts of Tanis.

It is only by interrogating the stones and the mounds that we can now hope to recover more fragments of these lost chronicles. Of the primitive settlement there remains but the casual record already quoted from the Book of Numbers. "(Now Zoan was built seven years after Hebron.)" Brief as it is, this parenthesis surely conveys more than meets the eye at first reading. Hebron and Zoan are

IN THE LAND OF GOSHEN.

not thus bracketed by the Mosaic scribe in mere discursive idleness. The connection implies that both were Semitic colonies, and, possibly, that both had a common origin. In this case Zoan, like Hebron, would be of Hittite foundation. The question of date, as already pointed out, is one of insuperable difficulty. As regards Hebron, we at all events know that it was a place of some importance—a walled city with gates—when Abraham purchased the cave of the field of Machpelah for four hundred shekels of silver from Ephron the Hittite; and Tanis may by that time have been scarcely less flourishing. Abraham, when he went up out of Egypt, might very possibly have tarried within its gates before setting off upon his long journey through the northeastern desert. Even in his time, however, we are evidently far removed from that fateful dawn when the unknown founder marked out the ground, and the first stone of the first altar was laid. We know not to what God that altar was dedicated. We know not even by what name the new-comers called the new city. Every vestige of that primitive town must, however, have been swept away when the great Pharaohs of the Twelfth Dynasty, recognizing the strategic importance of the site, fortified the place and raised it to the dignity of a royal city.

The monumental history of Tanis begins with the first king of this heroic line, Amenemhat I., whose magnificent colossal portrait-statue in red granite—broken in three pieces, head, trunk, and throne—yet lies amid the ruins. This statue and the prince whom it commemorates date back, according to the chronological system of Mariette (based upon that of Manetho), to about B.C. 3064. He came to the throne in troubled times. We read of conspiracies against his person, of revolt in Lower Egypt, of risings along the frontiers. His reign was one long effort to restore order and repel invasion. He conquered the Ethiopians on the south and the Libyans on the west. To the eastward he repaired the great border wall, and the chain of fortified posts built by the kings of the ancient empire for the protection of those fertile districts known in later days as the "Field of Zoan," the "Land of Goshen," and the "Land of Rameses." "I conquered the Ethiopians," he says, in a treatise which purports to be written by his own hand for the instruction of his son and successor; "I led the Libyans into captivity; I made the Asiatics run before me like greyhounds."* The Egyp-

* The papyrus containing this treatise is in the British Museum. It is translated into English by Maspero, under the title of "The Instructions of

tian word here used for Asiatics is "*Sati*," a generic term for all nations north of the Syrian border. Now the Semite squatters on the sand island beside the great northeastern river branch would certainly have come under the head of "*Sati*"; and although we have no record of their expulsion from this particular spot, it is very certain that Amenemhat I. would have driven them out beyond the Great Wall when he fortified the place and consecrated it to the gods of his forefathers.* Some magnificent remains of the temple of Amenemhat, consisting principally of clustered lotus columns exquisitely sculptured in the beautiful rose-granite of Syene, are yet extant. That he should have elected to construct his work in that material is proof sufficient of his power and splendor. The whole territory of Egypt to its southernmost boundary on the Nubian border lies between the place where that granite was quarried and the place where it was erected.

From this time forth the XIIth-Dynasty Pharaohs delighted to honor the provincial sanctuary founded by their great ancestor. They enriched it; they enlarged it; they peopled it with statues of themselves, their queens, their heirs and princesses. Like the memorial chapel of the Ramessides at Koorneh, the red granite temple of Tanis became a family portrait gallery; but it was a gallery in some respects unequalled at any epoch of Egyptian history. Other dynasties were as lavish of sculpture, as ambitious of immortality in granite and basalt, but the art which they commanded was not the art of the great school of the Usertesens and Amenemhats.

Amenemhat I. to his son Usertesen I." See *Records of the Past*. Vol. II. 1874.

* It is, of course, possible that Amenemhat I. may not have been the earliest royal builder on the site of historic Tanis. The Semites *may* have been expelled, and the first Egyptian sanctuary *may* have been erected by some king of a foregone dynasty; but if so, that earliest structure has been completely demolished. Meanwhile the presence of a portrait-statue of the founder of the XIIth Dynasty implies a temple wherein it was dedicated, and the earliest architectural remains are of the well-known XIIth Dynasty type.

That school represents the heroic age of Egyptian sculpture. It lacks the startling naturalism of the school of the Pyramid period; it never aspired to the giant scale of the XVIIIth and XIXth dynasties; but it excels all in monumental majesty. And not only the artist's work but the craftsman's skill is seen at its best during this age. No details are so finely cut, no surfaces glow with so lustrous and indestructible a polish, as those wrought by the lapidaries of the XIIth and XIIIth dynasties. They finished their colossi as fastidiously as a gem engraver finishes a cameo. They even polished the sunk sur-

HEAD OF AMENEMHAT I.—(RED GRANITE.)

faces of their hieroglyphs in incuse inscriptions.

The accompanying illustrations, engraved on wood after photographs taken by Mr. Petrie, convey a vivid impression of these admirable works. The red granite head of Amenemhat I. gives the ethnic type of the dynasty—a type which is to this day characteristic of Upper Egypt. The cheek-bones are high; the eyes prominent and heavy-lidded; the nostrils open; the lips full, smiling, and defined by a slight ridge at the edges; the frontal bone is wide, and the chin small and shapely;

COLOSSUS OF MERMASHIU.—(BLACK SYENITE.)

the ears are set curiously high. Such faces may be seen by the score on a market-day in the villages between Thebes and Assuân. To find a nobler example of form and finish than the black granite "Mermashiu" would be impossible. If upright, this grand statue and its fellow—for there are two—would stand twelve feet high from head to heel, without the plinth. The modelling of the arm, the knee, and the fore part of the body is as subtle and learned as the most exacting anatomist could desire; while the steely lustre of the surface, perfect as when it left the studio of the patient polisher, flashes back the sunlight like a mirror.*

* Mermashiu is known only by these twin colossi, and his place in history is conjectural. His name signifies "general." It perhaps indicates a military adventurer, who at some political crisis seized upon the double crown by a *coup de main;* but whether he achieved greatness when the direct male line of the Amenemhat family expired, or whether he was intermediate between the XIIIth and XIVth dynasties, is unknown. This use of a military title in a royal oval finds an interesting parallel in the similar use of a sacerdotal title by the founder of the dynasty of priest-kings, Se-Amen.

The XIIIth Dynasty is represented by a line of princes whose monuments are found from the Delta to farthest Ethiopia, but whose political history is a blank. They largely contributed to the great votive sculpture gallery of Tanis, and they raised the city to the dignity of a royal residence; but only a few of their statues have escaped the ravages of time and plunder. One superb sitting colossus of Sebakhotep III. lies, snapped in twain, among the ruins. The companion statue, purchased more than fifty years ago, is in the Louvre. Others at Turin and elsewhere may well have been among the spoils carried off by the chartered raiders of the first quarter of the present century, but there remains no clew by which to trace their history. The royal and noble virtuosi of that time collected works of antique art for the mere gratification of their personal taste, a granite Pharaoh being a splendid curiosity, and nothing more. It never occurred to these so-called "patrons of the arts" that such monuments are concrete history, and that it is of especial importance to identify every object with the place of its discovery. Schools, periods, dynasties, were nothing to them. They paid, and asked no questions, and it was to the dealer's interest to keep silence. Thus it happens that, although our European collections are crowded with precious specimens of Egyptian art, the curators of those collections are for the most part unable to classify them topographically.*

* De Rougé's two catalogues of Egyptian antiquities in the Museum of the Louvre repeatedly refer to objects as being "probably from Tanis," but betray complete uncertainty as to the actual *provenance* of some of the most important works of the early schools in that collection. The same want of positive information prevails not only at the British Museum, but even at Turin, whither it is very certain that a large number of the choicest Tanite monuments were transported by Drovetti, whose collection was purchased by Carlo Felice in 1822. The present writer, being anxious to identify the Tanis colossi in the Turin Museum, recently addressed some inquiries to Signor Lanzone, the learned and courteous director of that famous collection, to which he replied that he was "quite unable to give the desired information as regarded the antiquities proceeding from Tanis, as he possessed no catalogue or inventory which gave the slightest clew to the localities in which the objects were dis-

The lower half of the broken Sebakhotep* of Tanis is a conspicuous object in the annexed illustration, the upper half, which lies near by, not being in view. In a line with this fine fragment are seen the feet, legs, and throne of Amenemhat I.; while in the middle distance, half embedded in the sand, lie the crowned head and beautifully modelled shoulders of Usertesen I. The obelisk, broken in five pieces, bears a boldly cut inscription of Rameses II. down the face of the shaft.

covered." To which he adds, significantly, "Ma pur troppo quasi tutti i musei d' Europa si trovano nella stessa condizione."

* Sebakhotep means "united to Sebak," or "peace of Sebak," Sebak being the crocodile god of the Ombite Nome and of the Fayoom. It will be noted that the throne is covered with hieroglyphic inscriptions, in which the royal throne name and proper name are enclosed in ovals representing the king's signet. In these inscriptions he is styled "The Good God, Lord of the Two Lands [Upper and Lower Egypt], Ra-Nefer-a-ka, Son of Ra, of his very substance, his Beloved, Sebakhotep," etc., etc. Mariette discovered a colossus of this king's son, Mentuhotep, and one of Sebakhotep VI., both in granite, which he reburied, and which have not been again disinterred.

BROKEN COLOSSUS OF SEBAKHOTEP III.—(BROWN-RED GRANITE.)

From the colossus of Sebakhotep to the obelisk of Rameses the distance is but a few yards, yet between those two monuments there lies a mysterious gulf of some nine hundred years. Setting aside the obscure "Hyksôs sculptures," which scarcely admit of chronological classification, Tanis has not one stone to show which can be positively assigned to any intermediate reign or line. The XIVth Dynasty passed and left no trace, and, save the catastrophe which put its latest princes to flight, and prostrated Lower Egypt beneath the heel of the Hyksôs, we know nothing of its history. Of these same Hyksòs and their famous invasion we are, in truth, almost as ignorant. No Hyksôs inscription other than a mere name and title is known to science. No Hyksòs grave has ever been discovered. The very term "Hyksòs" is unsatisfactory from the philological stand-point, and has never yet been identified, even in an equivalent form, in any Egyptian document.* Manetho, in a fragment quoted by Josephus, describes the invaders as base-born barbarians who came "from the eastward," slaughtering, plundering, burning cities, destroying temples, and encountering no resistance from the Egyptians. "From the eastward" is vague, and might apply to any nation on the farther side of the Isthmus of Suez. No one people would, however, have ventured at that time to challenge Egypt to single combat. Such attacks under the Ramesside dynasties were always made by the united forces of confederate princes, and we may be certain that this earliest invasion was an onslaught of many nations. Maspero's striking theory of an immense westward movement of Mesopotamian tribes, driven out from Chaldæa and Babylonia by the irruption of the Elamites under Kudur-nan-khundi the First, fits the epoch and the events.† The Hyksôs, it is clear, were not an army, but a rabble, and the Mesopotamian fugi-

tives would be just such a rabble. Sweeping onward like a cloud of locusts, their path scathed by fire and rapine, their ranks continually swelled by bands of predatory nomads, they were irresistible by mere force of numbers.

The fragment quoted by Josephus goes on to say that after a time the barbarians elected one of themselves, named Salatis, to be king over the East. This Salatis (or "Shalit") posted garrisons in various parts of Lower Egypt, and being especially careful to guard the way by which himself and his hordes had entered the country, he rebuilt and fortified a certain city of the eastern Delta which "after an ancient religious tradition" was called Avaris (Ha-uar). Here he installed a standing force of 240,000 men.* Now we have already seen that "Ha-uar" was also pronounced "Ha-Tân"; that its meaning is "the Place of the Leg" (or perhaps "the Place of the Flight"); and that Ha-Tân is identical with T'an, T'sân, Zoan, and Tanis. Thus, by an evil turn of Fortune's wheel, Tanis became the stronghold of the Hyksòs power.

To this great camp of Ha-uar, Salatis came once a year for the purpose of reviewing and paying his soldiers; but he lived at Memphis. His successors more prudently elected to reside where their military strength was concentrated; they therefore made Tanis their capital, and so founded the first "Tanite dynasties."†

Whether the famous camp was actually contained within the city precincts we know not. Future explorations may throw light upon this point; but most probably a part of the Hyksôs garrison was lodged inside the walls, the rest occupying forts and outposts on the neighboring hills, of which there are no less than twelve within a radius of eight miles. As for the fortifications of Tanis, they must be sought in the great outer circuit of mounds, no part of which is yet excavated.

---

* When referred to by the national scribes of later times, these alien conquerors are called "The Scourge," and sometimes the "Amû" (Asiatics), such a compound word as "Hiq-Shasu" (Ruler of Shasu) for the Greek "Hyksôs" or "Hykoussòs" being apparently unknown.

† See Maspero's *Histoire Ancienne des Peuples de l'Orient*. Chap. IV., p. 161 *et seq.* Fourth Edition: 1886. Kudur-nan-khundi I. was a predecessor of that Kudur-Lagamar (Chedorlaomer) whom Abraham pursued and vanquished some generations later.

* This is a number not to be taken too literally, but rather as expressing a very large but undetermined force. The Greek soldiers who deserted to Ethiopia in the reign of Psammetichus I. are stated by Herodotus to have numbered 240,000, which is as evidently a gross exaggeration.

† For tables of the Tanite dynasties see Lepsius's *Königsbuch*, plates 42, 43, and 46; Sayce's "Dynastic Tables," appended to his new edition of *Herodotus*, pp. 461–470; also Mariette's "Tableau des Dynasties Egyptiennes," in *Notice des Monuments*, Ed. 4, p. 15, etc., etc.

The rule of the Hyksôs lasted for 511 years,* and the history of those 511 years is again a blank. The first three Tanite dynasties, classified as the XVth, XVIth, and XVIIth, fall into this period. The first line ruled only in the Delta; the second was supreme over all Egypt; the third, confronted by a patriot league of Theban princes, fought obstinately for the possession of the Delta till expelled by Aahmes I., who founded the XVIIIth (Theban) Dynasty.

Of all these alien despots three only can be said to have left "foot-prints on posterity. Apepi II., less, yet more, than a shadow, bequeaths his name and titles to the celebrated "Mathematical Papyrus" of the British Museum, which, according to the testimony of its writer, Aahmesu the scribe, was copied from a yet earlier MS. in the thirty-third year of the King Ra-ââ-user Apepi. The next of this name, Ra-ââ-ab-taui Apepi, heads the third and last Hyksôs Dynasty. He is divided from Salatis by some three and a half centuries, during which time the conquerors had adopted the language, arts, and manners of the conquered. If

HYKSÔS SPHINXES AND BROKEN OBELISK OF RAMESES II.

the sands of time." Those three are Salatis (the barbarian leader), Apepi II., and Apepi III. The rest have gone into oblivion, leaving at the most some three or four names of uncertain etymology embedded, fossil-like, in the works of early Greek writers. Salatis (a sinister shadow momentarily projected against a background of smoke and flame) darkens the page of Josephus, vanishes, and leaves only an illegible inscription† to puzzle

Salatis was an unlettered savage, Apepi III. was a highly civilized prince, surrounded in his Tanite capital by a court modelled after the splendid courts of the old national Pharaohs. The central figure of his time, he comes before us not only as a focus of Biblical and historical tradition, but as the typical tyrant of romance. By early Christian writers he is identified with the Pharaoh of Joseph, who enriched himself in time of famine at the cost of a starving people; while according to an ancient popular tale, pre-

* According to Manetho, 511 years; according to Africanus, 958 years.

† In a broken and illegible oval engraved upon the Hyksôs sphinx discovered at Tell Mokhdam the name of Salatis has been conjecturally read by some

Egyptologists, but the identification is not generally accepted. See Ebers's *Ægypten und die Bücher Moses*, p. 202.

served in a papyrus of the time of Rameses II., he figures as a mocking and bigoted despot, who seeks to impose the worship of his own national god, Sutehk of the Hyksôs, upon Ra-Sekenen, prince of the Thebaid.

Apepi and Ra-Sekenen are characters as substantially authentic as Guthrum and Alfred. It was during the rule of Apepi that Ra-Sekenen raised the standard of national independence, and it is probable enough that some religious dispute as to the supremacy of Sutehk, Lord of Ha-uar, or Amen of Thebes may have precipitated the armed strife which ended a century later in the restoration of the legitimate monarchy. In his inscriptions Apepi is invariably distinguished as the devotee of Sutehk;* and although no architectural remains of the temple built "to last eternally" can now be identified, some at least of the sentinel sphinxes which once guarded its gates have survived the wreck of ages. Two of the most perfect have been removed to Boulak; six others— all more or less shattered—still keep watch among the ruins of Tanis.

Two fine fragments couchant in a wilderness of ruin are seen in our illustration of the Hyksôs sphinxes on the preceding page. They are human-headed, maned like lions, bearded like gods, crowned with the klaft and basilisk like kings. Though the faces are the faces of men, the ears are the ears of lions. The shaggy mane which covers the shoulders and chest is gathered in a thick short roll at the back of the head, like a pigtail. The noses and ears of all these sphinxes have

been systematically smashed, probably at the time of the Hyksôs expulsion. Some, like the foreground sphinx in our illustration, have suffered further indignity in the mutilation of the beard and the basilisk. To solve the problem of a noseless face is always difficult; but these hard-featured, morose-looking, hollow-cheeked sphinxes, with their prominent jaws, high cheek-bones, and mouths curving sternly downward at the corners, perplex us with a riddle harder to guess than that of their mythic descendant. The same ethnic type is unmistakably stamped upon such few fragments of portrait sculpture as are known to belong to this period. The "Fish-Offerers," the Mit-Farès bust, the Ludovisi head, have one and all the same furrowed, square-cut, truculent visage. Even the fashion of the sphinx mane reappears in the heavy beards, long curls, and plaited pigtails of the Hyksôs warriors.* The question of the type remains unanswered. It is neither Egyptian, nor Ethiopic, nor Semitic. It bears a more Northern stamp. It reminds us that those early Chaldæans who were driven out by the Elamites under Kudur-nan-khundi spoke and wrote a Turanian dialect, and that their blood was akin to that of the yellow races which we now call Tartar and Mongolian.

These Hyksôs sphinxes are superbly sculptured in black granite. The modelling is as learned as that of the finest periods of Egyptian art, and the execution as masterly. While, however, the lion body is duly rendered with conventional severity, the faces are treated with a realism that is all the more startling by reason of the unaccustomed type. That type is

---

* On the upper part of the right arm of each black granite colossus of Mermashiu (see previous illustration), Apepi has engraved his own name and titles, thus: " *The good God, Ra-āā-ab-taui, Son of Ra, Apepi, the Life-giver, the Beloved of Sutehk.*" Also he has in like manner usurped two large red granite sphinxes, apparently of the XIIth Dynasty—one still at San, the other at the Louvre. As Apepi was the first to appropriate the monuments of his predecessors, so, according to the law of poetical justice, he was destined to be himself the greatest sufferer at the hands of his successors, who not only appropriated and reappropriated his works, but almost invariably erased his inscriptions. Those on the Mermashiu colossi are, in fact, the only examples which have entirely escaped. Only recently it has been discovered by Dr. Wiedemann that a fine colossus, hitherto believed to be of Amenhotep III., in the gallery of the Louvre, bore originally the name and style of Apepi, whose inscription has been erased and surcharged by the great XVIIIth-Dynasty Pharaoh. It therefore results from this interesting discovery that we possibly possess in that colossus a portrait statue of Apepi.

* For an excellent series of heads illustrating all the types of Hyksôs sculpture as yet discovered, see Plates 9, 10, 12, and 13, in Tomkins's *Studies of the Times of Abraham.* London: 1878. See also illustrations of Hyksôs sculptures in Perrot and Chipiez's *Histoire de l'Art dans l'Antiquité. L'Egypte.* Vol. I. The Mit-Farès bust (found at Mit-Farès in the Fayoom) is figured in the last-named work; and the Ludovisi head (so called because it is in the Ludovisi Collection, Rome) is reproduced in Mr. Tomkins's learned and interesting work above mentioned. It is worth noting in this connection that Heliodorus and Achilles Tatius (A.D. 400–500) describe the Bucolic population (Bashmourites) of this district as a fierce and lawless race of great size and strength, who went bareheaded, and wore their hair hanging in long locks to their shoulders; these Bashmourites being the descendants of the Hyksôs of ancient time. Some modern travellers, including Mariette and Ebers, believe the type to be not yet extinct in the district.

TANIS AS IT APPEARED IN THE DAYS OF MOSES.

HEAD OF RAMESES II.—(FROM A GROUP IN RED GRANITE.)

ken, "the Victorious"; and Kames, the husband of Queen Aah-hotep—all brave and steadfast princes who disputed the ground foot by foot, ever driving the foe farther to the northward, till the Hyksôs made their last desperate stand behind the walls of Tanis. These Theban patriots are very real personages, and bring us back to the firm footing of history. From that famous ancient police report known as the "Abbott Papyrus"* we learn that the tombs of three among them (Taä I., Taä II., and Kames) were examined by a royal commission in the sixteenth year of Rameses IX., and "found intact," while the mummy and mummy case of Taä III. (Taä-ken) and the feather-fan of King Kames may be seen by all the world at the Boulak Museum.†

It was by Taä-ken, in alliance with Kames and all the princes of the Upper Country, that the Hyksôs were expelled from Memphis and forced back toward the eastern Delta; and it was by Ahmes I., son of Kames and founder of the XVIIIth Dynasty, that they were besieged in Tanis.

Finally Tanis was taken. Then came the sack and the slaughter, the destruction of the temple of Sutehk, the mutilation of the black granite sphinxes, the burning of houses and palaces, the desecration of every emblem and image and shrine that the Hyksôs held sacred. Nothing escaped save those pre-Hyksôs monuments which the barbarians themselves had respected—the noble red granite temple of Amenemhat I., and the statues and obelisks with which it had been adorned by a long line

well seen in the features of the foreground sphinx. His rugged face is instinct with life. Upon his chest is carved the oval of Pisebkhanu, an obscure king of the XXIst Dynasty, and along the side of the plinth runs a largely cut inscription of Rameses II. The names and titles of Menepthah, the supposed Pharaoh of the Exodus, deface the lustrous left shoulder of the farther sphinx. Besides being thus charged and surcharged with the signatures of later Pharaohs, the Hyksôs sphinxes have one and all an erased inscription on the right shoulder, and under some of these erasures the name of Apepi can yet be deciphered.

That Apepi ruled at Tanis, and Ra-Sekenen at Thebes, what time the nation arose and cast off the yoke of the Hyksôs, is about the sum of our knowledge in regard of this great historical event. How long the war lasted, who fought, who fell, we know not. Apepi may have died fighting. He at all events disappears, and is heard of no more. Ra-Sekenen, meanwhile, founds a new native dynasty, and assumes the style and title of Taä the First. To Taä I. succeeded Taä II., called "the Great"; Taä III., best known as Taä-

* I have already had occasion to refer to the "Abbott Papyrus" (which, it may be remembered, contains the minutes of an official inquiry into certain tomb robberies committed during the sixteenth year of the reign of Rameses IX.) in a previous number of *Harper's Magazine*. See "Lying in State in Cairo," July, 1882.

† For a full account of the discovery of this mummy, which was discovered with the mummies of many other royal or noble personages of various epochs, see the same article, *Harper's Magazine*, July, 1882.

of Pharaohs. Meanwhile the remnant of the vanquished fled over the Syrian border, and took refuge in Sharahana, where they were again besieged and again conquered. Henceforth they disappear and are heard of no more. Now and then, in after-times, we read of a raid into Syria, and of the return of a triumphant general with a herd of "Shasu" captives; but these are mere slave hunts, and "Shasu" (a generic term like "Sati") would apply to any nomadic tribe north of the frontier.

And now, for the space of some three hundred years, Tanis is blotted out from history. Neither by Mariette nor by Pe-

stronghold regained its importance as a strategic position.

It was Rameses II. who reëdified Tanis —that Rameses popularly known as "the Great," whom Egyptologists agree in identifying with the oppressor of the Hebrews, and whom the ancients called "Sesostris." He found the place given over to "the abomination of desolation"; he left it one of the most magnificent of Egyptian cities. Three-fourths of the ruins which yet bestrew the temple area are the work of his architects and sculptors. What he found ready to his hand he appropriated; for the rest, he laid all the quarries of Egypt

GREAT SCULPTURED SHRINE OF RAMESES II.—(SANDSTONE.)

trie has there been found any inscription, however fragmentary, any relic, however trivial, which bears the stamp of the XVIIIth Dynasty. Either the place was held accursed, and therefore abandoned, or it was not deemed worth the cost of restoration. The Tanitic Nome had ceased, in fact, to be a frontier province, and Hauar was no longer a frontier post. Ahmes had incorporated southern Syria with the eastern Delta, and the Egyptian garrisons of Raphia and Gaza were now the real outposts of the mother country. It was not till the lustre of the new régime began to pale and the inevitable turn of the tide had actually set in that the ruined

under contribution, bringing red granite from Syene and black from the valley of Hammamat, sandstone from Silsilis, and limestone from Toorah. Then a new temple uprose amid the ruins, larger and more splendid than ever yet graced the Delta. This temple, ostensibly consecrate to the worship of Ra, Horus, and other gods, was in truth erected to the glory and honor of Rameses himself. His name and titles, cut in gigantic hieroglyphs, were everywhere conspicuous. His victories were commemorated in innumerable bass-relief tableaux and in hundreds of high-sounding phrases. His portrait-statues, in all sizes and all materials,

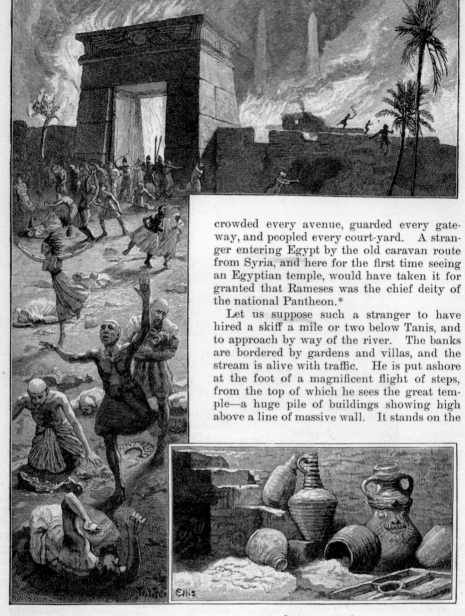

FIRE AND SWORD—THE END OF TANIS.—[SEE PAGE 737.]

crowded every avenue, guarded every gateway, and peopled every court-yard. A stranger entering Egypt by the old caravan route from Syria, and here for the first time seeing an Egyptian temple, would have taken it for granted that Rameses was the chief deity of the national Pantheon.*

Let us suppose such a stranger to have hired a skiff a mile or two below Tanis, and to approach by way of the river. The banks are bordered by gardens and villas, and the stream is alive with traffic. He is put ashore at the foot of a magnificent flight of steps, from the top of which he sees the great temple—a huge pile of buildings showing high above a line of massive wall. It stands on the east bank of the Nile, facing westward. A paved roadway leads from the landing-place to the gateway. This pile of buildings—more like a huge fortress than a

* And, in truth, he would not have been far wrong in his conjecture. Strange as the belief seems to us, every Egyptian monarch was a demi-god in the eyes of his people. The legitimate line of Pharaohs claimed to be the actual descendants of Ra, the great solar deity, and were so accepted. Rameses II. carried this fiction so far that he frequently introduced his own image as one of a divine triad, and he is even represented (during his lifetime) as both king and deity, Rameses the Pharaoh burning incense before Rameses the god.

temple — looks quite near; but it is full half a mile from the water-side. Around it, beyond it, lies a flat, verdant, limitless panorama divided by the broad river. This plain is dotted with villages, each embowered in clumps of sycamores and palms. Here and there a gliding sail betrays the course of an unseen canal, while far away to the northward, whence a mass of storm-cloud is driving up from the coast, a pallid, far-distant gleam tells the story of the sea. As yet there is no Lake Menzaleh; as yet there is no desert. The great natural dike which shuts out the waters of the Mediterranean on the one hand is still intact; the bounteous Nile is not yet canalized on the other. A time will come when the one shall be let in and the other shall be barred out, but for the present all is corn-land and meadow-grass where hereafter there shall be salt lake and sand.

Even at this distance the stranger's quick sight detects the tops of a forest of tapering obelisks, and the twin towers of a series of massive pylons. One object, shining, solitary, towering high above the temple and its surroundings, fixes his attention. It is ruddy, as if touched by sunset; it glitters as though the surface were of glass. It is not an obelisk; neither is it a tower. It cannot be a statue; that is impossible. Yet, as he draws nearer, his shadow lengthening before him, the paved dromos blinding white beneath his feet, that glowing, glittering, perplexing Thing grows more distinct, more shapely, more like that into which it presently resolves itself—a god-like, gigantic figure, crowned, erect, majestic, watching over the temple and the city.

And now, as the new-comer draws nearer, the dromos begins to be bordered with couchant sphinxes. Then come two colossal red granite statues of Rameses II., standing like sentinels on either side. Then more sphinxes, and another pair of colossi, twin brethren of the first; and then the first pylon, an immense double-towered gateway, beyond which there is another, and yet another, to pass ere he shall come into the presence of that marvel, that colossus of colossi, which never had, and never will have, a rival. And now he is there, standing in the shadow of it, looking up to it from below, as one stands at the foot of a great perpendicular cliff, looking up to the top where it shows against the sky. Yes, a marvel!

A single figure fourteen times the height of the living man—a single figure cut from a single stone of the precious red granite of Syene.

The giant stands alone, not in the middle but to the side of a large court-yard, so leaving an unbroken vista from the door of the first pylon to the door of the sanctuary. His attitude is that of walking, with the left foot forward. His right hand grasps a short truncheon, his left holds a massive staff of state. The face

UNFINISHED STATUETTE, FROM THE HOUSE OF A TANITE SCULPTOR.—(B.C. 300.)

is serene and noble, and on the head towers high the double crown of Upper and Lower Egypt. The figure alone, with its crown, stands over 90 feet in height, and weighs at the least 900 tons. Crown, plinth, and pedestal all counted, it stands 120 feet above the level of the pavement.* After this no miracle of art, no pomp of decoration, can greatly move the wonder

* The feet of this colossus measured four feet nine inches and two-eighths in diameter, and the great toe was one foot two inches and seven-eighths across. The rest of the figure was proportionately gigantic, being probably from thirteen to fifteen times the size and height of a living man. The crown upon its head must have stood at least fourteen and a half feet high, and the royal ovals (carved, doubtless, on the upper part of the arms and on the breast) were one yard in diameter.

Desert Hare.   Piece of Porcelain Sceptre.   Isis and Infant Horus.   Shu,
Kohl Pot   Alabaster Capital.   Rain;   Knum.   Ta-ur.—(Pottery).
          Apis Amulet.—(Pottery.)   Bowl.—(Greenstone-ware.)
Infant Horus.—(Bronze.)   Calyx Capital.—(Bronze.)   Ceramic Jar.   Calyx Capital.—(Bronze.)   Tahuti (Thoth).—(Greenstone-ware.)

GROUP OF OBJECTS DISCOVERED IN A PRIVATE HOUSE AT TANIS (PERIOD, XXXTH DYNASTY), NOW IN THE
MUSEUM OF FINE ARTS, BOSTON.—[SEE PAGE 734].

of the pilgrim stranger. He goes on through a court-yard surrounded by a colonnade, and bisected by an avenue of single-stone columns thirty-six feet high; thence through another gateway, across an open space, and along a magnificent avenue bordered on both sides by monuments of many kinds and many ages. This avenue is the Via Sacra of Tanis. It is about 375 feet in length, and within that comparatively short distance, arranged so as to produce the subtlest play of color and the greatest diversity of effect, are ranged a multitude of red granite obelisks, yellow sandstone colossi, por-trait-statues in red, black, and gray granite, shrines, sphinxes, and doubtless many smaller works in the more rare materials, such as diorite, alabaster, green serpentine, and the like.

Here, too, are the great red granite sphinxes of the old XIIth Dynasty temple; and here, about midway of the avenue, are the Hyksôs sculptures, all together, and all in black granite—two groups of "Fish-offerers,"* and the eight

* The group of "Fish-offerers" at Boulak is the most singular of all the Hyksôs monuments. It represents two Hyksôs warriors standing side by side, holding sacrificial trays containing fish, aquat-

famous sphinxes, four on each side of the road. Such is this splendid Sacred Way up which the stranger advances. Still more splendid is the surprise which awaits him when, arrived at the end, he finds himself face to face with a long array of colossal statues, some seated, some standing, all ranged in one magnificent line, fronting the spectator. Here, transferred from their original places in the early temple, stand the great Pharaohs of the olden time—the Amenemhats and Usertesens, the Sebakhoteps and Mentuhoteps, and the two colossi of Mermashiu—a royal and stately company, representing all the glory of the Theban line. Among them Rameses has installed four more colossal statues of himself, two seated, two standing; and upon most of the effigies of his illustrious predecessors his own names and titles are conspicuously carved. Ten to the right, ten to the left, they occupy a broad space of basalt pavement, leaving still a passage between the two central statues leading direct to the colonnade in front of the sanctuary. This colonnade is composed in part of the fine old red granite columns of Amenemhat I., and in part of new circular columns sculptured with figures of Rameses and the gods. In the centre—never opened unless to admit Pharaoh in person—is the great door of cedar-wood plated with gold and bronze. No profane foot may cross that threshold or tread the dimly lighted halls and obscure chambers which surround the holy of holies.* Robing rooms, anointing rooms, rooms for the storage of vestments and sacred vessels, rooms for the preparation of unguents, perfumes, and various kinds of offerings, rooms for the safe custody of title-deeds, charters, records, and other precious documents—these, and the mysterious subterranean crypts in which are kept the golden images and emblems of the gods, are accessible only to the king and the priests.

ic birds, and water plants. The mutilated features of these figures are precisely like those of the Hyksôs sphinxes, and their plaited beards, ropy curls, and massive pigtails look curiously like the shaggy manes of those andro-lions. They are sculptured in the same dark gray, almost black, granite. The broken fragments of a similar group are yet at Tanis.

* For the best description ever written of the interior of an Egyptian temple, see the "Avant-propos," to Mariette's *Denderah*. Paris: 1873–5.

But it is when Rameses himself comes hither, returning perhaps from an expedition against the people of Ruten, in northern Syria, that one should see Tanis and its temple. Then the streets are decked with green boughs, and the houses with hangings of many-colored stuffs; and before all the temple pylons and in front of every great man's gates long streamers float from painted flag-staffs. The citizens, we may be sure, are in holiday garb; and there is hurrying to and fro, and music everywhere, and the river is as crowded and as gay as the town. Writing of a festival day in another city not far dis-

TERMINAL BUST (DECORATIVE ART: WHITE MARBLE: SECOND CENTURY A.D.)—[SEE PAGE 430.]

tant, a poet of the time tells how the young girls gather on the thresholds of their homes, laden with flowers, to see the king go by:

" Lo, the maidens of Aanekht are in holiday attire;
   Their locks are redolent of perfumed oil;
   They stand in their doorways,
   Their hands full of nosegays,
   And of green boughs of Pa-Hathor,
   And garlands of Lake Pahura,
   On the day of the entry of
   Ra-user-ma Sotep-en-Ra!"*

* The poetical letter of Panbesa (Anastasi Pa-

PORTRAIT-STATUE OF BAKAKHIN, WITH HIS HOUSEHOLD GOODS AND GODS (SECOND CENTURY A.D.).
ALSO ROYAL STATUE AND TABLETS OF EARLIER DATE (THIRD CENTURY B.C.).—[SEE PAGE 735.]

The procession, however, is the march past of an army, and the maidens must wait while battalion after battalion streams through the narrow streets. Here are foot - soldiers bearing palm branches; archers armed with bow and boomerang; light runners with javelin and dagger ; Nubians with clubs and hatchets ; and fair - skinned Sardinian mercenaries with short swords, round bucklers, and close-fitting casques ornamented with a ball and spikes. Next come squadrons of two-horse chariots, each containing warrior and driver; and next after these the prisoners and the booty. Here are sallow-faced, bearded Asiatics, in long fringed robes, tied neck and neck in strings of ten or a dozen, their arms fast bound behind their backs; women and children on mules and asses; horses and chariots taken in battle, each led by a couple of soldiers; camels laden with stuffs, skins, tents, weapons, furniture, and vessels of gold and silver; more male prisoners, more trophies, more plunder, more infantry, more squadrons of armed chariot-fighters; and so on, hour after hour, till at last a flourish of clarions announces the approach of the king. He is preceded by a glittering phalanx of officers and standard-bearers, by a detachment of the royal body-guard, and by the court scribes, whose duty it is in time of war to catalogue the prisoners and the spoils, and record the prowess of the conqueror. Last of all comes the officiating priest, walking backward, and burning incense as before a god.

Clad in a loose robe of fine muslin, girdled by a jewelled belt, on his head a

pyri, No. 111, British Museum), translated into French by Maspero (see *Du Genre Epistolaire*), and into English by Goodwin (see *Records of the Past*, Vol. VI.). "Ra-user-ma Sotep-en-Ra" (Ra Strong in Divine Law, Elect of Ra) is the throne or solar name of Rameses II.

helmet covered with leopard-skin, on his neck and arms rich collars and bracelets set with gems, in his left hand a bow, in his right a curved scimitar, the Son of Ra stands in his gorgeous chariot, upright, haughty, immovable as one of his own statues. Upon his horses' heads are nodding plumes; his young sons, carrying aloft great fans of ostrich feathers, walk beside his chariot wheels; his tame lion follows after. And now the maidens fling their flowers, and the children clap their hands, and the men prostrate themselves, and, amid a great roar of acclamation, Pharaoh passes.

The priests in robes of ceremony are waiting at the temple gates. They receive him with divine honors; they salute him as the lineal descendant of the gods, as the veritable Son of Ra. With harp and flute, cymbal and sistrum, with chanting of hymns and the sweet savor of frankincense, they precede him to the door of the sanctuary, which now stands wide open. Here the king makes his offering of captives and booty—princes and nobles of Ruten for temple slaves, and treasure for the service of the gods. What follows is best told in the words of a famous hieroglyphic tablet now in the Boulak Museum. Though made for a very different personage, and in a later age, this important inscription relates the order of ceremonial observed on the occasion of a royal visit to a renowned temple; it also possesses the peculiar interest of being an ancient Egyptian "state paper" of unquestionable authenticity:*

"He went in procession to the great Sanctuary with solemn adoration. Then the Chief Priest offered supplications to ward off calamity from the King, performing the rite of lustration girded with the sacred vestments. He then purified him [the King] with incense and sprinkling, and brought him garlands from the Temple of Obelisks.

"When the garlands were brought to him, he as-

* The great red granite stela of Piankhi Mer-Amen, discovered at Gebel Barkal, the ancient Napata, in 1863, now No. 98 in the Boulak Museum, Salle historique de l'Ouest. The text is published in Mariette's *Monuments Divers*, 1872. The inscription records the conquest of Egypt by Piankhi, King of Ethiopia, himself a descendant of the Amenide family, or priest-kings, of the XXIst Theban Dynasty. This event took place some 600 years later than the time of Rameses II., under the XXIVth (Saïte) Dynasty. The whole stela has been translated into German by Brugsch (*Geschichte Ægyptens unter den Pharaonen*, 1878), and into English by Canon Cook (*Records of the Past*, Vol. II.). The above short quotation is slightly altered from Canon Cook's version.

cended the flight of steps to the great Shrine, to behold Ra in the Temple of Obelisks.*

"The King himself stood there, he the great one, he alone. He drew the bolt; he opened the folding doors; he beheld his Father Ra in the Temple of Obelisks, and the bark of Ra, and the bark of Tum.†

"Then he closed the doors, and he impressed sealing-clay upon them, and he sealed it with his royal signet;‡ and he commanded the priests, saying: 'I have set my seal. Let no other Prince whatsoever enter herein.'

"And he stood while they prostrated themselves before his Majesty, crying:

"'All hail to thee, O Horus,§ the Immortal One! Thou who ministerest to the images of the Gods!'"

Such was Tanis in the day of her resurrection; such was her principal temple when remodelled and adorned by Rameses II. Like the "restorers" of our own time, the architects of the imperial builder took, however, unwarrantable liberties with the works of their predecessors. They scraped down the delicately incised obelisks of the Amenemhats and Usertesens, and reëngraved them with the monotonous legends of Rameses II. They took a noble statue of a XIIth Dynasty princess in black granite, altered her hair and head-dress, grooved a hideous striped pattern upon her simple antique robe, and falsified history by inscribing her throne with the names and titles of the mother of Rameses.‖ On every monument of every pre-

* That is, the temple of Heliopolis, in which Piankhi performed the above ceremonies. The description, however, applies equally to the great temple of Tanis.

† Every god in an Egyptian temple had his sacred bark (*bari*), or ark, in which his image or emblem was placed (in a curtained shrine), and borne on the shoulders of priests in festival processions. These barks were made of cedar-wood, ebony, etc., set with precious metals. The prow of one, representing a hawk-head in bronze superbly inlaid with gold, was presented by Mr. Flinders Petrie last year to the British Museum. For some excellent illustrations of sacred barks with shrines, and of the way in which they were carried, see the large folding plate to Naville's *Inscription Historique de Pinodjem III.*: 1883.

‡ Moist clay impressed with a seal was commonly used to fasten doors, lids of boxes, etc., and specimens of these are to be seen in many Egyptian collections. The broken clay seal of King Menkheperra (XXIst Dynasty) was found on the door jambs of the entrance to the vault at Dayr-el-Bahari, and the king's seal upon the hamper containing the funerary feast of Queen Isi-em-kheb was discovered intact. (See "Lying in State in Cairo," p. 189 of *Harper's Monthly* for July, 1882.)

§ "Horus" is here used in the same sense as "Son of Ra." The Pharaoh was always "the Golden Horus," and was thus identified as the Son of Osiris as well as the Son of Ra.

‖ For a full account of the barbarisms committed

ceding dynasty, with scarcely an exception, they emblazoned the ovals and praises of "The Powerful Bull, the Golden Horus, the Elect of Ra, the Beloved of Amen, of Tum, of Ptah, of Sutekh, of Seb, of Har, of Khnum, the Lord of the Two Lands, Rameses Mer-Amen." The result, nevertheless, was magnificent, and the great Colossus, towering half his height above the roof of the temple, was the wonder of the age.

The subsequent history of Tanis relapses into obscurity. Menepthah, the Exodus Pharaoh, before whom, in "the field of Zoan," and within the gates of this very city, Moses wrought the miracles of murrain and darkness, of plague and death*— Menepthah, the son and successor of Rameses II., merely superadded his names and titles to the monuments of the early dynasties, and left an unimportant portrait-statue among the débris of the great avenue. One fragmentary block bears the name of his son, Seti II., while the next royal line (XXth Dynasty) is represented by a headless Rameses III. in gray granite.

From Rameses III., second Pharaoh of the XXth Dynasty, to Se-Amen, first priest-king of the XXIst Dynasty, all is blank. What befell during that century of silence? We know not. Yet some great catastrophe had happened, for Se-Amen found the temple in ruins. He has left abundant evidence of work, but it is such work as a builder would class under the head of "necessary repairs." He had, for instance, to reërect the colonnade in front of the sanctuary, putting bases inscribed with his own name and titles under the columns of Amenhotep and Rameses II., which must therefore have been overthrown. These new bases are roughly made from sculptured blocks of Ramesside date. An important series of historical tables appears to have been cut up at about the same time for building slabs.† These facts are significant. They point not to decay, but to destruction.

The fall of one obelisk may imply the fall of all, and with the obelisks we may suppose the great Colossus and the line of historical statues to have crashed down in simultaneous ruin. So tremendous a disaster occurring in an age of peace can scarcely be accounted for except by natural causes; that is to say, by an upheaval or a subsidence of the soil. Either hypothesis is probable. Egypt undoubtedly suffered from seismic disturbances in ancient times,* while as regards the alternative proposition, a very considerable subsidence has actually taken place, the soil of "the field of Zoan" having, according to Mr. Petrie's observations, sunk to a depth of ten feet below its original level.

After Se-Amen, the next name found is that of Pisebkhanu, a later king of the same dynasty, who repaved the sanctuary,† inscribed his ovals on the Hyksôs monuments, and surrounded the temple enclosure with a stupendous crude-brick wall eighty feet in thickness. Despite the ravages of war and weather, this wall, which is estimated to have contained 25,000,000 large bricks, still retains from twenty to twenty-five feet of its original height.

With the advent of the XXIIId Dynasty Bubastis became the seat of government, and Tanis again sank to the level of a provincial town. It was one of these Bubastite kings, namely, Sheshonk III., who committed the astonishing barbarism

at Tanis by the "restorers" of Rameses II., see Mr. Petrie's second chapter of *Tanis*, Part I.

* Tanis was unquestionably the city in which Menepthah was residing when Moses and Aaron went up with their demand for a free passage for their people. They must have seen all the splendor of the great temple as here described.

† The celebrated "tablet of 400 years" was one of these, and Mr. Petrie found the remains of a large number of others, all much worn and weathered.

* The great earthquake of B.C. 27, which shattered the northernmost colossus of the plain of Thebes, is of course a well-worn case in point, but there was another great earthquake of which no written record survives, but which, as I have elsewhere shown, must have occurred during the lifetime of Rameses II. This great wave of earthquake passed along the left bank of the Nile in Nubia, doing great injury to the temples of Wady Sabooah, Derr, and Gerf Hossayn, and so severely shaking the mountain of the great temple at Aboo-Simbel that it shattered one of the four sitting colossi of the façade, more or less injured the other three, and cracked one of the Osiride columns in the first great hall. The proof that it happened during the life of Rameses II. is sufficiently clear, a wall having been built up to support the last two pillars to the left at the upper end of the hall, on which wall is a large stela sculptured with a long hieroglyphic inscription dated the 13th day of the month Tybi, in the 35th year of Rameses II. See *A Thousand Miles up the Nile*, chap. xviii., p. 515 et seq.

† To record this circumstance, a number of small glazed pottery tablets bearing this king's royal titles were strewn in the sand under the pavement Mr. Petrie found fragments of two or three of these tablets, one of which is now in the Museum of Fine Arts, Boston.

of converting Rameses II. into a pylon. Till Mr. Petrie discovered from what a royal quarry the Bubastite had derived his ill-gotten material, the very existence of that granite giant was undreamed of. It had been cut up, reworked, and forgotten long enough before the time when travelling came into fashion, and neither Herodotus nor Diodorus heard so much as a tradition of its splendor. The sensation created on both sides of the Atlantic by the announcement of Mr. Petrie's discovery in 1884 is not yet forgotten. When the Bubastites had ruled for about one hundred and seventy years, fortune deserted them, and a prince of Tanite blood, Petsebast by name, seized the reins of power. And now for a short time—for the last time—Tanis once more became, in name at all events, the capital of Egypt. But Petsebast and his descendants were

NOTE.—The very beautiful red granite head shown in our illustration on page 724—a portrait of Rameses II. at the age of perhaps fifteen years—evidently belonged to a group, as shown by the hand to the left of the head. This hand, uplifted as if in protection or blessing, belonged probably to some deity. The softness of the youthful face, the sweetness of the expression, and the exquisite delicacy of the execution combine to make this one of the most interesting portrait-heads of Rameses II. which have come down to the present time. It is to be noted also that it is evidently a good likeness. The mummy of this Pharaoh has recently been unbandaged at the Boulak Museum by Professor Maspero, who especially dwells in his official report upon the prominent "frontal ridge" and "high cheek-bones" of the great autocrat, as well as upon his large round ears, described as standing out well from the head, all features distinctly recognizable in the above portrait, though softened by the contours of youth. This group occupied a place in the Via Sacra of Tanis in close proximity to the Hyksôs monuments.

The splendid shrine of Rameses II. shown on page 725 was another ornament of the great Via Sacra, and stood apparently between the third and fourth pairs of obelisks. It was one of a pair placed on opposite sides of the avenue. The material is quartzite sandstone, each shrine being cut from a single block nine feet in length. The above illustration represents the northern shrine, which is nearly perfect. The surface is very delicately sculptured with groups and hieroglyphic texts in bass-relief; while inside, at the upper end, is a small seated triad of deities—Amen, Maut, and Tum. The roof is patterned with bands of royal ovals and titles, and symbolic vultures with outstretched wings, emblematic of Maut. On the outer end of the shrine, as seen in our illustration, Rameses is represented in the act of offering vases of perfume to the gods Seb (the earth) and Shu (the light of the sun); on the side, here seen in perspective, the king makes similar offerings to Seb, Tum (the setting sun), and Ra (the sun personified). The companion or southern shrine has been mercilessly smashed, and only the back remains.

suzerains rather than sovereigns, and the XXIIId Dynasty would be best described as a protectorate line presiding over some eighteen or twenty semi-independent princes.

Henceforth the story of the old historic capital becomes a fragmentary record of decadence. Foes from the south and foes from the east trample in turn upon her liberties. The tablets of Napata and the clay cylinders of Nineveh tell how the Tanite province was administered, now by an Ethiopian and now by an Assyrian governor; while Assurbanipal himself relates in his famous *Annals** that he took Memphis, Saïs, Mendes, and Tanis† by storm, and put their inhabitants, "both small and great," to the sword. Three hundred years later, when the star of Assyria had set and the power of Persia was in the ascendant, Nectanebo II. (XXXth Dynasty, B.C. 360) assembled his forces at Tanis, and there, with the help of Agesilaus and a Spartan contingent, sustained a siege conducted by the Prince of Mendes and his Persian allies. Plutarch, in his narrative of this siege, refers to Tanis as being then "a large and strongly fortified town."‡ He also tells, in his simple and striking way, how, by a skilful stratagem, Agesilaus trapped and slew the blockaders in their own earthworks, and so saved the king and the city.

Nectanebo was the last legitimate Pharaoh of the last native dynasty, and Plutarch's story of the siege is the last chronicle of Tanis. Thus, by a dramatic coincidence, the immemorial line of Pharaohs and the most ancient city of the Delta disappear together from the stage of history. Tanis, however, did not become extinct. Tanis merely passed into oblivion, and as a frontier garrison long plodded on its uneventful way. Meanwhile, by a process analogous to the formation of a coral reef, the level of the city and its cemeteries continued to be raised by successive generations, houses being erected on the ruins of houses, and graves being superimposed upon graves. So, in like manner, the annual rains periodically washed away the surface of the great crude-brick

* See *The Annals of Assurbanipal*, translated by G. Smith. *Records of the Past*. Vol. I. 1873.

† The cylinder gives it Tsa-an-nu, *i. e.*, Tsânu.

‡ See Plutarch's *Life of Agesilaus*. Diodorus, treating of the same event (Book XV., chapter 93), also speaks of the place as "a large city." Singularly enough, neither Plutarch nor Diodorus mentions Tanis by name.

wall of Pisebkhanu, and deposited layer after layer of mud upon the surface of the sacred enclosure. By-and-by (a new temple having been built outside the fortifications by one of the Ptolemies) the old historic structure was deserted, and houses were built in the shelter of the pylon, inside the precincts of the temple enclosure, and even on the top of the great wall. By this time the ruins had become a public quarry. Prostrate pillars and colossi disappeared under heaps of chips and floods of mud, and at last only two or three obelisks and one solitary column remained standing.

There seems no reason to conclude that the political extinction of Tanis caused any decrease in its population. Strabo, writing probably about A.D. 15 or 18, speaks of it as "a large city," and a well-known medal of the Emperor Hadrian was struck here just a century later. Mr. Petrie's recent excavations also show that Tanis had a resident aristocracy of some importance up to the time of its final destruction—a catastrophe which the silent testimony of coins, gems, proper names, and the like enables us to ascribe to the reign of Marcus Aurelius. In other words, Tanis perished by fire at the time of the so-called "Bucolic Revolt," in A.D. 174, when the herdsmen of the Delta marsh lands—a mongrel and turbulent race, supposed to be in part descended from the ancient Hyksôs—ravaged the littoral provinces with a savagery worthy of their reputed ancestors.

The Tanite aristocracy lived in large mansions in and about the temple enclosure, which was evidently a privileged quarter. These mansions were plundered and burned; but the plundering seems to have been hastily done, as if the looters were disturbed in their work or driven off by the approaching flames; for although they swept away everything they could find in the shape of money, jewelry, and the like, they took no objects of secondary value. When, therefore, the upper timbers burned through, the houses fell in, burying household goods and household gods under the charred and smoking débris. All the more perishable furniture was, of course, consumed; but a large variety of beautiful and interesting things, chiefly articles of domestic utility and decorative art, in bronze, basalt, marble, alabaster, faience, terra-cotta, and even glass, were fortunately protect-

ed by the superincumbent rubbish. Thus for seventeen hundred and ten years they lay in unsuspected safety, to be at last recovered by Mr. Petrie in the interests of the Egypt Exploration Fund. Having been exhibited in London, together with a large number of objects found in the neighboring cemeteries and in other parts of the Delta, these relics were divided among various public collections at home and abroad, the British Museum and the Museum of Fine Arts at Boston (U. S. A.) receiving, as was their just due, the largest share of the spoil.[*]

Many of the objects discovered in the above-named private houses being here reproduced after photographs taken by Mr. Petrie, it will be convenient to localize them by calling certain of the more important dwellings after the antiquities found in their ruins—as the "House of the Statuettes," the "House of the Sculptor," the "House of the Painter," and the "House of the Greek Term." Another house is best known by the name of its owner, one Bakakhin.

Taken chronologically, the earliest of these is the "House of the Statuettes,"[†] so called from the number and excellence of the sacred images which it contained. The house and its belongings date from the XXXth Dynasty, while the pure style and high finish of the statuettes point to the reign of Nectanebo II. (Nekhtnebf), the Pharaoh of the siege, in whose time there was a remarkable, though brief, renaissance of the best traditions of Egyptian art. One hundred and twelve relics from this house (small, it is true, but exceptionally interesting, inasmuch as they represent the last survival of national freedom) are now in the Museum of Fine Arts at Boston.

Our illustration on page 728 gives a group of sixteen objects selected from this special lot,[‡] the scale reduced to about half

[*] The first exhibition of objects from San (Tanis) here referred to was held at the rooms of the Royal Archæological Institute, Oxford Mansion, London, in September and October, 1884. See report in *The Academy*, September 20, and ditto in *The Athenæum* of the same date, 1884. See also various reports by Mr. W. M. F. Petrie, M. Naville, and Amelia B. Edwards in *The Academy* during the months of March, April, May, June, and July, 1884; also see more particularly Mr. Petrie's *Tanis*, Part I., 1885.

[†] This is the house which Mr. Petrie classifies as No. 20 (see *Tanis*, Part I., p. 29 *et seq.*), and which is marked G in his smaller plan at the end of the volume.

[‡] 1. A bulbous-shaped jar, unfortunately broken

the actual size. Of other objects not shown in the group, three iron knives and two small silver gods must be noted for their extreme rarity, iron and silver being the

two scarcest metals of Pharaonic Egypt.* The knives are the first ever found; and Mr. Petrie says of the silver deities, "Such images are very rare; no silver of Bes was known at Boulak, and there are no such figures in the Louvre."

at the neck, stands in the centre foreground. This fine specimen measures 4½ inches in height, and is coated with a peculiar tint of green glaze, much esteemed by the Egyptians of all periods. To the right and left of this jar (3 and 4) are placed two very interesting objects, namely, a pair of bronze capitals, the surface of the metal corroded by the brilliant green rust of antiquity. Six of these capitals were found in the House of Statuettes, being evidently designed as a finish to wooden supports, charred wood having been found in them when discovered. They probably ornamented the legs of a piece of furniture. Their effect in our engraving is somewhat marred by being placed upside down; but if reversed, the popular calyx capital of Egyptian architecture is immediately recognized. Less corroded, though a little granulated upon the surface, is the admirable statuette (5) to the extreme left. This represents the divine son of Isis and Osiris, called in Egyptian *Har-pa-khrat*, literally "Har the Child," infancy, according to the simple symbolism of that early art, being indicated by the finger in, or uplifted toward, the mouth. The Greeks, mistaking this action for the finger *on* the lip, made him their god of silence, and rendered his name by Harpocrates. This statuette measures 5½ inches high. The eyes are gold inlaid, and the modelling, especially of the torso, is very free, fleshy, and unconventional. A large Thoth (6), in Egyptian, "Tahuti," occupies the opposite corner. This figure, moulded in a very hard stone-ware, is almost as good in its way as the Har-pa-khrat. Though injured by the action of fire, it is a fine specimen, and of good execution. Thoth was "Lord of Divine Words and of Sacred Writings"—that is, he personified the divine intelligence, and presided over literature and letters. The ibis was sacred to him, and he is always represented with the head of the bird and the body of a man. The bird head is well modelled in the Boston example, but the beak is unfortunately lost. The figure stands 5½ inches high, and is coated with a thin green glaze. The bowl (7) immediately behind the head of Thoth is of the same ware and color, and measures 3½ inches in diameter. The centre group (8) represents Isis with the infant Horus (Har-pa-khrat) on her knees. The features, hands, and feet are carefully defined; the child wears the side-lock still the distinctive characteristic of little boys in Egypt and Nubia, and the goddess is crowned with the emblematic throne, her special symbol. The coloring of this group is cold green and Venetian red, the sides of the throne being patterned with alternate green and red leaves. The height of the piece is 4½ inches. It is a subject of which the British Museum possesses many examples, but the Boston group excels them all in delicacy and finish. Close behind it, standing apparently on the upturned base of the bronze capital, we see a small amulet in the form of a bull (9), with the solar disk between his horns. Also two more of the same size, one at the top left-hand corner representing a couchant hare with long ears (10), and another of a couchant ram (11), near the Isis and Horus group. These three little objects (each with a pierced loop for suspension) represent three of the mightiest Egyptian deities. The bull is Apis, the great god of Memphis, in whom Osiris was believed to be incarnate. From the colossal stone Apis discovered by Mariette at the Serapeum of Sakkarah, down to the tiniest amulet in carnelian or pottery, the bull is invariably represented in the same attitude, and with the same attributes; and it was in the image of this little Apis of the Boston collection that the Hebrews modelled their golden calf when they relapsed into the idolatry of the land of bondage. The couchant hare represents the pretty little desert hare of Egypt, which was sacred to Osiris; while the couchant ram is emblematic of the god Knum, or Kneph, the principal deity of Elephantine, the great god of the Cataracts, the creator of mankind, and the spirit or soul of the gods. To the right of this amulet, and on the same level, stands a small green pottery image of the same divinity (12), represented as a ram-headed man walking, height 2¾ inches. Facing him we see an amulet of the same height, color, and material, representing the hippopotamus goddess, Ta-ur, "the Great," a beneficent lunar deity who presided over births. She wears the skin and tail of a crocodile trailing down her back, and she stood for Ursa Major in the Egyptian astronomical heavens. The kneeling figure at the top (13) is *Shu*, the son of Ra. In the great cosmic legend of ancient Egypt it was *Shu* who divided the heavens from the earth, and supported the celestial vault with his hands, and it is thus that he is represented. On the left of the head-dress of Isis will be noted the upper part of a tiny porcelain sceptre (14), in the form of a column surmounted by the favorite calyx capital. These charms when perfect reproduce the form of the hieroglyphic sign signifying growth, verdure, and the like. They are always green, and are found suspended round the necks of mummies in token of the second life which, like the spring-time, shall follow the winter of death. Next below this fragment is seen a small alabaster capital (reversed) which may have been the head of a staff (15). To the left of this object, just above the bronze Horus, stands a curious double kohl-pot (16) of alabaster, 2½ inches in height. Though found in a private house, this indispensable adjunct to an Egyptian lady's toilet service resembles a funerary object rather than a pot for actual use; and Mr. Petrie is disposed to think from the nature of some of the things found in the House of Statuettes that a mummy had been rifled here, a quantity of charred linen, some finger-bones, and a tooth (all at Boston) having been found in one of the rooms.

* Though abounding in gold, copper, and emerald mines, Egypt is apparently destitute of iron and silver. Iron is supposed, on the authority of Plutarch, to have been identified by the Egyptians with the substance of the bones of Set, or Typhon, the evil principle of the native Pantheon, and therefore to have been held in abhorrence. But it is nevertheless certain that it was highly prized as a rare and valuable metal. Thothmes III., returning from a campaign in Phœnicia, records that he brought thence, among his booty, iron vases with silver handles, and there are two sacrificial instruments of iron in the Louvre.

In the House of the Sculptor, besides minor objects connected with his craft, there was found the subject of our illustration on page 727—an unfinished limestone figure of a kneeling devotee holding a tray of offerings.* This was most likely intended for a votive portrait-statue. The "House of the Painter" contained paint-pots, colors, limestone tablets ruled in squares like our sectional copying paper, lump emery for erasing purposes, and the like. These two houses are of early Ptolemaic date, and they seem to have been deserted and ruined long before the time of the Bucolic Revolt. Not so the house of Bakakhin and the "House of the Greek Term," which were in occupation up to the moment of the outbreak.

Bakakhin and the owner of the "House of the Greek Term" were next-door neighbors, and they lived in two large mansions situate in the north gateway of the great temple enclosure. Both houses were plundered, and both perished in the general conflagration. It so happened, however, that when the floorings gave way in Bakakhin's rooms, the furniture was precipitated into the cellar, and so buried under the débris; whereas the other house, which probably did not take fire so soon, was not only more thoroughly sacked, but was apparently better worth sacking. Many hundreds of Bakakhin's possessions have consequently been found, while comparatively few of his neighbor's belongings were left for the explorer. Their household goods betray something of the ways and tastes of the owners. Bakakhin was a man of business, and perhaps a man of law. His neighbor was apparently a man of culture; possibly a Roman, and if so, a government official. Everything in Bakakhin's house, save a few small objects of Syrian art, was thoroughly Egyptian; but the other, being a virtuoso, possessed beautiful things which can only have been brought from Italy and Greece. Again, Bakakhin's cellar cupboard contained six waste-paper baskets full of business letters and business

* This figure is technically important for the additional light which it throws upon Egyptian methods, thus corroborating the argument of M. Émile Soldi, who first pointed out that the tool used by Egyptian sculptors for blocking out and shaping the figure in soft stone was none other than the ordinary stone-gouge of the present day. This is demonstrated by the channelling of the surface. Cf. *La Sculpture Egyptienne*, par É. Soldi., p. 112 *et seq.* Paris: 1876.

documents, written on papyrus in the demotic or current Egyptian script of the period; whereas in a similar basketful discovered in the adjoining mansion half the papyri were written in Greek, which it need scarcely be said was the scholarly and literary language of the time. Also, instead of being mere crumpled notes, accounts, inventories, and so forth, these documents were in large rolls, such as befitted a gentleman's library in the time of the Cæsars.*

Next to the papyri, which are always of paramount value, the most interesting object in Bakakhin's house was a portrait statuette of himself, bearing his name upon the front of the pedestal—"Bakakhin, son of his mother Ta-Ankh."† As the work of a provincial artist in an age of decadence, it may be indulgently criticised; at all events, it places the man before us "in his habit as he lived"—short, bald, debonair, with a placid kindly face which looks as if it might belong to a brother of the famous "Wooden Man" at Boulak.‡ His numerous belongings, his

* Though charred and broken, about half of these papyri are still legible. They have been laid between sheets of glass by the authorities of the MSS. Department at the British Museum, and are in course of translation.

† "Bakakhin" means "Servant of Light," and "Ta-Ankh," "The Life-given." The inscription is in demotic, thus translated by Professor Revillout.

‡ The statuette of Bakakhin, which occupies the principal place in our illustration on page 730, is twenty-one inches high, including the plinth. The stone is much browned by the action of smoke and fire, but is otherwise uninjured. Next in interest to the portrait of the master of the house is the fragment of bass-relief representing a female sphinx with curved wings and a turreted mural crown, seated, with one paw upraised, and resting against a pillar surmounted by a florid ornament. In this curious little work, strongly imbued as it is with the characteristics of Asiatic art, Mr. Petrie suggests that we may perhaps see a symbolic image of the genius of the city of Tanis. The four small deities are in blue glazed pottery, and the large one, representing Thoth (fourteen inches high), is in alabaster. The left foot of this fine image is broken off, and the beak, which was let in, and probably of silver, has been taken out. The small female figure with a large head-dress is a product of the Phœnician market, and represents the Syrian Venus, Astarte; the material is terra-cotta. The large jar ornamented with a grotesque face is of unbaked pottery, of the kind still made in large quantities at Ballas, in Upper Egypt. The face is supposed to represent that of Bes, the god of mirth and jollity. A few objects not found in the house of Bakakhin, but in a small chapel, or shrine, of the time of Ptolemy II., outside the great temple enclosure, are included in the group, notably a statuette of a king wearing the double crown and basilisk of royalty, uninscribed, and standing twenty-two inches in height. The

lamps, his inkstand, his drawing materials, his pots and pans, his cups, saucers, bowls, amphoræ, mortars, bronzes, amulets, and household gods, are all in one case at the British Museum.

Though fewer things were found in the adjoining house, those few were chiefly objects of value, the two most important being the Glass Zodiac and the Greek Term. The former, painted in gold and color on a sheet of thin greenish glass, is the only known specimen of ancient glass-painting, and is executed in the finest Pompeiian style of decorative design.* The latter, a charming Græco-Roman female head, on a terminal pillar, is executed in what looks like Carrara marble. It supported a limestone shelf, which lay beside it when found. This interesting work, the most perfect of its school and period discovered during the excavations of 1884, has found a home at Boston. The owner of these things, a man evidently of taste and wealth, must have possessed jewels, plate, money, yet a much-worn coin of Vespasian was all the treasure that his house contained. In Bakakhin's cellar, the only object found in the way of precious metal was a tiny silver spatula. It may be that the two neighbors escaped while there was yet time, taking their valuables with them; but the hand of the plunderer is nevertheless visible. The stored barley in Bakakhin's cellar was found poured out of the big jars and spilled about the floor in the search for hidden treasure. One of the waste-paper baskets had been pulled out from the cup-

style is provincial and the execution poor. It probably represents Ptolemy II. The small tablets sculptured with bass-reliefs of bulls crowned with the solar orb are votive tablets to Apis, the Memphite bull-god. These Ptolemaic objects date from about B.C. 300, and the objects belonging to Bakakhin date from A.D. 174, the time of the Bucolic Revolt.

* This square of glass is first surrounded by a border line of gilding, within which are a series of circles in gilding, the first circle containing heads emblematic of the twelve months of the year, the next containing the twelve signs of the zodiac, and the centre an ornamental device which is too much injured to be intelligible. The vacant spaces of ground-work are parsemé with gold stars. The whole thing has suffered terrible damage, being broken into about two hundred fragments, and much warped and twisted by the action of fire. Still, repaired as it is with much expenditure of care and skill by Mr. Petrie, the beauty of the design is fully appreciable, and many of the heads are perfect. Two or three are especially beautiful and spirited; one, a youth, with locks blown by the wind, is remarkably like the famous Pompeiian head of Achilles in the British Museum.

board, hurriedly examined, and left upon the stairs, and the beak of a fine alabaster Thoth, which was surely in silver, is wrenched off and gone.

Of the horrors of this Egyptian Jacquerie, of the rage, the terror, the flight, the pursuit, the slaughter, the sack of temples and dwellings, the desecration of graves, we know nothing. Roman history passes lightly over this incident of rebellion in a distant province, while to the brief record of the Bucolic Revolt and its suppression by Avidius Cassius (A.D. 172), Tanis contributes only the mute testimony of her ruins. The story of her fall, like the story of her foundation, must be sought at the edge of the spade. What we do know is that she died the death foretold by the prophet, and that it was death without resurrection. A few late Roman huts—the resort probably of herdsmen and fishers—are the only human habitations of subsequent date. The end of Pompeii was scarcely more sudden; the abandonment of Palmyra was not more complete. Thenceforth the trade of the district centred in Tennis, a new and thriving town situate between thirty and forty miles to the northeastward, near the mouth of the Tanitic Nile. Commanding the markets of the plain, and yet lying close to the sea, the position of Tennis was commercially superior to that of Tanis, and the place rose rapidly to importance. Like Tanis, it was built upon a sandy eminence in the midst of a pastoral flat. It is now an island in Lake Menzaleh. Local tradition long preserved the date of the catastrophe which not only wrought this transformation, but submerged the adjacent plain and part of the "field of Zoan." That tradition, carefully recorded by Mas'-oudy, a learned Arab traveller and historian of the tenth century, has thus been handed down in its integrity to the present day. Writing of "the lake of Tennis and Damietta" (i. e., Menzaleh), he says:

"The place occupied by the lake was formerly a district which had not its equal in Egypt for fine air, fertility, and wealth. Gardens, plantations of palms and other trees, vines, and cultivated fields met the eye in every direction. In short, there was not a province in Egypt, except the Fayoom, to be compared with it for beauty. This district was distant about one day's journey from the sea.... But in the year 251 of the era of Diocletian (A.D. 535) the waters of the sea flowed in and submerged that part of the plain which now is called the Lake of Tennis; and every year the inundation increased, so that at last it covered the whole province. All the towns which were in the lowest levels were destroyed, and only those which were built on rising grounds remained unharmed. The total submersion of this part took place one hundred years before the conquest of Egypt."

Thus the whole face of the country was changed, and the rich flats across which the Great Colossus had been visible from afar off in the palmy days of Tanis were again devoured by that same hungry sea.

POST-SCRIPTUM.—Since the foregoing pages were written, a new light has been cast upon one of the obscurest passages of ancient Egyptian history by the unbandaging of the mummy of King Sekenenra Ta-āken, on the 9th of last June, at the Boulak Museum. As we have seen, Sekenenra, the Theban hero of the legendary romance contained in the 1st Sallier Papyrus, placed himself at the head of the national rising against the Hyksôs tyranny, and began that famous War of Independence which ended some generations later in the total rout and expulsion of the foreign invaders. Till the other day we knew not that the popular leader fell on the field of battle. This, however, is evident from the condition of the mummy, which has no less than four wounds on the head and face: *i. e.*, a wide gash down the left cheek, which laid it open and clove the jaw; a circular hole in the right temple, probably from a lance or dagger point; a slanting cut over the left eye; and a terrific skull wound, evidently inflicted with a hatchet. Of

from which nature had reclaimed them, inch by inch, in ages long past. As time went on, the towns thus islanded in an unhealthy lagoon languished, were deserted, and became the haunts of myriads of wild-fowl. Meanwhile the vapors from this vast salt lake poisoned and blighted the vegetation of the surrounding country, which has been finally ruined by the canalization of the river, and the shutting off of the annual inundation. Now all is desolate—a province laid waste, a temple in ruins, a city in ashes; on the one hand, a wilderness of waters; on the other, a wilderness of desert. "The rest is silence."

these, Professor Maspero remarks in his report that "Ta-āken, first struck upon the jaw, fell stunned, whereupon his enemies precipitated themselves upon him, and despatched him where he lay." He also observes that "the Egyptians must have been victorious in the combat which took place over the body of their chief, since they succeeded in rescuing it and bearing it off the field." The battle, we may assume, took place somewhere in Lower Egypt; but the king's corpse, hastily embalmed the day after the battle, was conveyed to Thebes, and there received the rites of sepulture. The face of the mummy wears an expression of intense agony. The features are contorted, the mouth is drawn into a circle, the tongue projects, and is bitten partly through by the teeth. As it was in death, so it is now; and the embalmers, when they prepared it, made no effort to restore the stiffened features to a less painful expression, or to release the bitten tongue from the grip of the teeth.   A. B. E.

THE BRAHMAN'S SON.

BY RICHARD HENRY STODDARD.

THE Brahman's son was dead; the Brahman's heart
Stricken, as if a thunder-bolt had fallen
Out of a clear sky, emptied of all light,
And suddenly black with midnight. Nevermore
Would life be what it had been, for the hand
That, reaching from the darkness, plucked the flower,
Plucked up by the roots the stem that bore the flower,
And dashed it down to die the self-same death.
It seemed so, for the aged Brahman thrice
Fainted upon the bosom of his son,
And each time, longer coming back to life,
Sank deeper deathward. When he lay as dead
They took the body from his lifeless arms,

And having washed it in the sacred stream,
And wound it in the perfumed linen sheet,
Laid it upon a bier bestrown with flowers,
And bore it softly to the burial-place.
When, lying there, the unhappy father woke,
He knew that all was over, for the tears,
That had refused to flow, began to fall,
As after a long drought the summer rain.
Moreover, he saw the elders of his caste,
Graybeards, who had no children, rating him
Because he sorrowed for his dear dead child.
Stunned by their harsh reproofs, that smote his ear
With words of commination, he was mute.
Driven hither by his sorrow for his son,
And thither by his duty to the gods,
To whom all sorrow, save what they inflict
By priestly hands, for gifts withheld from them,
Is sin, the Brahman sought to overcome
The dark remembrance of his dreadful loss
By brooding over the Beneficence
Which fills the world with light, the night with stars;
By wisdom, which the wisest of his caste
Proclaimed the only happiness of man,
But sought in vain; for all day long he saw
The face, the form, the presence of his child.
Turn where he would, it was; in-doors and out;
It went before him, and it followed him;
Was at his scanty meals, and at his prayers;
Rose when he rose at morning from his sleep,
And in the troubled watches of the night
Was with him in his dreams—a beauteous shape.
Haunted by memories he could not escape,
And grief that would not heal, the Brahman sighed:
"I am not—cannot be—like other men;
For having their dead, as I have, they forget,
While I remember; and not being wise—
No more than I am—they contrive to find
(They say so) wisdom, which I cannot find.
I will seek Yama, therefore, King of Death,
And pray him to give back my dear dead son."
The Brahman straightway rose, and clothed himself
In the long vestments of his priestly caste,
And having performed the ceremonial rite,
And offered up the sacrificial flowers,
Went forth alone to seek the King of Death.
He questioned all he met where he might find
That lord of vanished kingdoms.—Where is Death?
Some stared at him, wide-eyed, but answered not,
Thinking him mad; some answered, mocking him;
And other some advised him to return,
Lest, sooner than he would, he should find Death.
Scarred soldiers, riding by in mail, cried out
That Death was in the rush of battle-storms,
Beneath the bursting of the arrow-clouds,
Amidst the lightning of the crossing swords,
Before the ranks of fighting elephants.
And swarthy sailors, swaggering in their cups,
Boisterous as stormy sea-winds, shouted, "Death
Is in the long waves roaring on the reefs,

And in the water-spouts of the mid-sea."
And dancing-girls, whose feet, like those of Spring,
Twinkled to music, and whose floating arms
Circled about their brows like flights of doves,
Sang, in the pauses of their amorous hymn:
"Not in the cold dark caverns of the sea
Seek Death, nor in the dreadful battle-field,
But rather in our arms and on our lips,
Strained to our hearts in kisses! So to die—
No life is half so sweet as such a death!"
The rippling laughter of the merry girls
Was like the chime of bells on temple eaves
When winds of summer lip their silver tongues.
He wandered by the banks of many streams,
And in the shade of many city walls,
Until he came to the great wilderness
Below the holy Mountains of the East.
Dangerous the way was, for in forest paths
Were hooded serpents, pendent from the boughs,
With flickering forkèd tongues; and, couchant near,
Leopards, the anger of whose cruel eyes
Flamed ominously through the jungle grass;
And, still more deadly, the enormous boa,
Whose tortuous passage through the furrowed weeds
Was like a boat's wake on the heaving sea.
Fearless he passed them: what had he to fear
From deaths like these, who sought the King of Death?
At length he reached the harmless hermitage
Where dwelt the oldest Brahmans—holy men,
Reverend in their white hairs and drifts of beard.
The shadows of the ancient rocks and trees
Lengthened and shortened with the slow-paced hours,
And circled with the circling of the sun;
All, save the shadow of the sacred trees
Wherein they sat and mused, which circled not,
Steadfast as earth was in the shifting light.
They sat in silence, staring at the sun,
Not blinded by it, and the birds of heaven,
Seeing they stirred not, nestled in their beards.
Awed by the stern composure of their looks,
The Brahman stopped, like one who in a dream
Fears to go on, yet feels he must go on.
Then, bowing lowly to these holy men,
He said: "O Brahmans! Fathers of the caste,
As Brahma is the Father of the Gods,
Supreme in wisdom as the Gods are, hear,
And, hearing, help a most unhappy man,
Who, worn with fruitless wanderings to and fro
In search of Yama, rajah of the dead,
Beseeches ye to tell him where he is:
Direct him, Fathers, to the King of Death."
He spake, and waiting for their answer, heard
The humming of innumerable bees,
The inarticulate whisper of the leaves,
The rivers chanting their eternal song,
And in the distant woods the roar of beasts.
But now the Brahmans heard, or seemed to hear,
Like those whom voices overtake in sleep,
And who, persuaded by the voices, wake,

"BOWING LOWLY TO THESE HOLY MEN."

Not knowing where they are or who they are,
Pausing until their souls come back to them.
"What man art thou?   And wherefore seekest thou
Yama, who comes unsought to every man?"
Few words sufficed to tell them what he was:
A Brahman (as they saw), but one to whom
The wisdom of his caste had not been given,
Though he had sought it long, with all his mind—

Sought it with fasts and prayers for threescore years.
Seeing (he said) that he was growing old,
And was not growing wise—a simple man,
Who never could be wiser than he was—
He took a wife, as was his duty then,
To bear him holy children. She bare one,
A son, who was the comfort of his age.
Him did he dedicate to holiness,
Instilling at all hours in his young life
The love of wisdom, teaching all he knew,
Till, no more teaching, he was taught himself,
Fathered in knowledge by his wiser child.
"But he was taken from me in his bloom,
Taken with the down of manhood on his lip,
Taken without warning, leaving me alone!
Wherefore I pray ye, Fathers, holy men,
Who, knowing all things, know where Yama dwells,
Tell me where I may find the King of Death,
That I may pray him to give back my son."
They answered him together, with one voice,
As when the sounds of many swollen streams
Become one sound: "There is no giving back;
Death takes his own, and keeps it; takes all things.
The stars die in their courses, like the dew
That shines and is not; the containing heavens
Wither like leaves in autumn; all the worlds,
And all the creatures that inhabit them,
Vanish like smoke of incense—which they are,
From the beginning offered up to Death.
Thou canst not visit Yama's dread abode,
For no man goes that way with mortal feet.
But if thy faith be sure, thy courage high,
Thou mayst do one thing. Many a league from here,
Hundreds of leagues toward the setting sun,
There is a valley; in the midst of it
There stands a City, wherein dwells no man,
But the Gods only, when their pleasure is
To clothe themselves in Shape, and live on earth.
There, when the eighth day of the month is come,
Comes Yama, from the dark realms of the dead,
To share the bright life of his brother Gods.
Go there, and there find Yama. Now depart.
We have heard and answered thy complaining words,
And earned the right to meditate again."
Thus they, and silence followed; as, when day
Dies in the purple west, the birds fly home,
Forgetful of the songs they sang at dawn;
The leaves are hushed, the winds are laid, and night
Shuts suddenly, darkly, in the starless sky.
Through sunlight, moonlight, starlight, like a cloud
Driven by the strong wings of a steady wind
Whose speed is in his steps, the Brahman went
Hundreds of leagues toward the setting sun.
At last he reached the end o' th' world, and saw
The valley whereof the Fathers had foretold,
Immeasurable, and in the midst of it
The great and glorious City of the Gods.
A City builded in the summer clouds
By masonry of winds, fantastic, strange;

Tier over tier, in mountain terraces,
Sheer from the hollows of that happy vale,
It rose, resplendent; leagues of palaces,
The sudden opening of whose doors disclosed
The light of thrones within; what temples seemed,
Interminable columns, crowned with domes;
Towers, wall-surrounded, high, mysterious;
Arches, wherethrough one saw the rise and fall
Of dazzling fountains in perpetual bloom:
Towers, temples, palaces—and over all
The great gate of the Palace of the Gods.
Beside the fiery pillars of this gate,
With folded wings, two watchful Spirits stood,
Guarding the entrance lest some evil thing
Should unperceived steal in; who, when they saw
The Brahman coming where his prayers had come
So long before him—for the prayers of men
Are ladders mounting from the earth to heaven—
They knew his life had been acceptable
To the high Gods; and though he was the first
Who, without dying, ever came that way,
They stayed him not, such fearlessness of death
Was in his eyes, such certainty of life.
As when at set of sun on summer eves
The heavens are opened, and a single cloud,
Rising above the threshold of the west,
Pauses a moment, then is lost in light,
So paused the Brahman, till the golden gate,
Unfolding slowly with melodious song—
If song it was, and not the spiritual touch
Of unseen hands on unknown instruments,
That welcomed him—admitted him beyond,
There, where the Gods were in divine repose.
Not as where sculptured in colossal forms,
With fourfold faces, and with sceptred hands,
They sit cross-legged among their worshippers,
In tall pagodas, or in temple-caves
Quarried in mountains, ancient as themselves;
But Presences, wherein the Power they were
Was felt, not seen. A sense of awfulness
Fell on the Brahman's soul, and closed his lips,
That would have uttered supplicating cries
To have his son restored, but dared not there.
From out the silence of that sacred Place—
But whether nigh at hand or far away,
From the great roof of brightness overhead,
Or from the cavernous darkness in whose depths
The firm foundation of that world was set
From the beginning, who may say?—there came,
Or seemed to come, a low, mysterious Voice:
"Thy prayers are answered. All the Gods can do
For man is done when they have heard his prayers
And answered them. The consequence of prayer,
Or good or evil, must be borne by man:
The Gods are powerless to undo their work.
Thy son is in the Garden of the East.
Go to him; I permit it." And he went,
Following he knew not how that heavenly Voice,
Sweeter than music on the sea at night,

But sadder than the moaning of the sea
When, pitying, it gives back the dead—too late!
Lovelier than all the gardens of the earth
It was—a region of eternal bloom;
Of flowers that, budding or full blown, were fresh
With lucent dews, whose bright leaves faded not;
Of fruits that, ripening on the laden boughs,
Dropped not, but hung all-golden in the sun—
If sun it was whose mellow light was there—
An everlasting day! Like one in dreams,
Who bears about with him in unknown worlds
Remembrance of the only world he knows,
The unhappy Brahman wandered up and down—
Through groves of summer boskage blithe with birds,
And meadow hollows murmurous with bees;
Past sheets of still, clear water islanded
With lily-pads—a Lotus Paradise—
And shafts of fountains flashing as they rose
In rainbow mists: past all, and saw them not—
Saw nothing but his poor, forsaken home
Beside the Ganges, and the mound of earth
That covered his dead boy—until at last
The film passed him, and he saw the boy,
More beauteous than on earth, though beauteous there,
Divinely fair—the same, but not the same.
Trembling, with outstretched hands, and a great cry,
He ran to him, and clasped him in his arms.
"O my sweet boy! O my beloved first-born!
Hast thou forgot me?—me, thy father?—me,
Whose loving heart was broken at thy death?"
"I know thee not," the soul of his dead child
Replied, escaping from his arms like mist.
"My son! my son! hast thou indeed forgot
Thy father, who loved thee more than his own life?
Who taught thy baby lips the words of prayer—
Deliverance from the power of Evil Ones,
And thanks for the protection of the Gods?
Hast thou forgot thy mother, who, like me,
Weeps, but alone, seeing that I am gone
From her on this long journey after thee?
O look at me! O come to me again,
And look at me, and thou wilt know me!" Still
The child came not, but said: "I know thee not:
Thou art a stranger to me. All I know
Is—that thou art a mortal, and not wise;
For wert thou wise, as we are, thou wouldst know
That 'father,' 'mother,' here are foolish names,
Belonging to conditions that are past.
Depart, unhappy one! I know thee not.
Thou art no more to me than to the moon
The wind that drives the clouds across her face,
The torch gone out at noonday. Get thee hence:
It profits not to bring thy sorrow here."
The child, the garden—all things—disappeared;
All, save the Brahman, and the tears he shed:
Not long; for, lifting up his eyes, he saw
Buddha before him, seated on his throne,
Godlike and human, merciful as wise,
With eyes that read the secrets of all hearts.

"O LOOK AT ME! O COME TO ME AGAIN!"

Pitying this father who had lost his child,
He stooped and laid his hand upon his breast,
And healing its long heart-ache, gave him peace.
"Brahman! thou hast been punished grievously
For understanding neither life nor death;
For knowing not the spirits of the dead
Receive new bodies after they are dead,
So that their late-left tenements of clay
Are no more to them than a way-side inn
To which as guests they never go again.
The ties of kindred—father, mother, child—
That seem to bind the world with bands of steel,
Are frailer when death comes than spiders' threads;
For death comes like a torrent from the hills,
Which, swollen with rains, sweeps away all love,
And all love clings to with its dying hold.
Thy first, last duty, Brahman, is to live;
True to thyself and others; swerving not
From what the voice within pronounces good.
Who lives well, dies well." So the Brahman found,
For he returned to earth, and wept no more;
But taking up the burden of his life,
He lived it out, and earned a quiet grave;
The thought of which, as he drew near to it,
Was a prophetic promise of his rest,
And of his bright Companion gone before,
Of whom his last words were, He knows me now!

DAN TUGWELL MEETS WITH AN IMPEDIMENT.—[SEE NEXT PAGE.]

SPRINGHAVEN.

BY R. D. BLACKMORE.

CHAPTER XXVII.

FAIR IN THEORY.

NE Saturday evening, when the dusk was just beginning to smoothe the break of billow and to blunt the edge of rock, young Dan Tugwell swung his axe upon his shoulder, with the flag basket hanging from it in which his food had been, and in a rather crusty state of mind set forth upon his long walk home to Springhaven. As Harry Shanks had said, and almost everybody knew, an ancient foot-path, little used, but never yet obstructed, cut off a large bend of the shore, and saved half a mile of plodding over rock and shingle. This path was very lonesome, and infested with dark places, as well as waylaid with a very piteous ghost, who never would keep to the spot where he was murdered, but might appear at any shady stretch or woody corner. Dan Tugwell knew three courageous men who had seen this ghost, and would take good care to avoid any further interview, and his own faith in ghosts was as stanch as in gold; yet such was his mood this evening that he determined to go that way and chance it, not for the saving of distance, but simply because he had been told in the yard that day that the foot-path was stopped by the land-owner. "We'll see about that," said Dan; and now he was going to see about it.

For the first field or two there was no impediment, except the usual stile or gate; but when he had crossed a little woodland hollow, where the fence of the castle grounds ran down to the brow of the cliff, he found entrance barred. Three stout oak rails had been nailed across from tree to tree, and on a board above them was roughly painted: "No thoroughfare. Tresspassers will be prosecuted." For a moment the young man hesitated, his dread of the law being virtuously deep, and his mind well assured that his father would not back him up against settled authorities. But the shame of turning back, and the quick sense of wrong, which had long been demanding some outlet, conquered his calmer judgment, and he cast the basket from his back. Then swinging his favourite axe, he rushed at the oaken bars, and with a few strokes sent them rolling down the steep bank-side.

"That for your stoppage of a right of way!" he cried; "and now perhaps you'll want to know who done it."

To gratify this natural curiosity he drew a piece of chalk from his pocket, and wrote on the notice-board in large round hand, "Daniel Tugwell, son of Zebedee Tugwell, of Springhaven." But suddenly his smile of satisfaction fled, and his face turned as white as the chalk in his hand. At the next turn of the path, a few yards before him, in the gray gloom cast by an ivy-mantled tree, stood a tall dark figure, with the right arm raised. The face was indistinct, but (as Dan's conscience told him) hostile and unforgiving; there was nothing to reflect a ray of light, and there seemed to be a rustle of some departure, like the spirit fleeing.

The ghost! What could it be but the ghost? Ghosts ought to be white; but terror scorns all prejudice. Probably this murdered one was buried in his breeches. Dan's heart beat quicker than his axe had struck; and his feet were off to beat the ground still quicker. But no Springhaven lad ever left his baggage. Dan leaped aside first to catch up his basket, and while he stooped for it, he heard a clear strong voice.

"Who are you, that have dared to come and cut my fence down?"

No ghost could speak like that, even if he could put a fence up. The inborn courage of the youth revived, and the shame of his fright made him hardier. He stepped forward again, catching breath as he spoke, and eager to meet any man in the flesh.

"I am Daniel Tugwell, of Springhaven. And no living man shall deny me of my rights. I have a right to pass here, and I mean to do it."

Caryl Carne, looking stately in his suit of black velvet, drew sword and stood behind the shattered barrier. "Are you ready to run against this?" he asked. "Poor peasant, go back; what are your rights worth?"

"I could smash that skewer at a blow," said Daniel, flourishing his axe as if to do it; "but my rights, as you say, are not worth the hazard. What has a poor man to do with rights? Would you stop a man of your own rank, Squire Carne?"

"Ah, that would be a different thing indeed! Justice wears a sword, because she is of gentle birth. Work-people with axes must not prate of rights, or a prison will be their next one. Your right is to be disdained, young man, because you were not born a gentleman; and your duty is to receive scorn with your hat off. You like it, probably, because your father did. But come in, Daniel; I will not deny you of the only right an English peasant has—the right of the foot to plod in his father's footsteps. The right of the hand, and the tongue, and the stomach—even the right of the eye is denied him; but by some freak of law he has some little right of foot, doubtless to enable him to go and serve his master."

Dan was amazed, and his better sense aroused. Why should this gentleman step out of the rank of his birth, to talk in this way? Now and then Dan himself had indulged in such ideas, but always with a doubt that they were wicked, and not long enough to make them seem good in his eyes. He knew that some fellows at "the Club" talked thus; but they were a lot of idle strangers, who came there chiefly to corrupt the natives, and work the fish trade out of their hands. These wholesome reflections made him doubt about accepting Squire Carne's invitation; and it would have been good for him if that doubt had prevailed, though he trudged a thousand miles for it.

"What! Break down a fence, and then be afraid to enter! That is the style of your race, friend Daniel. That is why you never get your rights, even when you dare to talk of them. I thought you were made of different stuff. Go home and boast that you shattered my fence, and then feared to come through it, when I asked you." Carne smiled at his antagonist, and waved his hand.

Dan leaped in a moment through the hanging splinters, and stood before the other, with a frown upon his face. "Then mind one thing, sir," he said, with a look of defiance, while touching his hat from force of habit, "I pass here, not with your permission, but of right."

"Very well. Let us not split words," said Carne, who had now quite recovered his native language. "I am glad to find a man that dares to claim his rights, in the present state of England. I am going towards Springhaven. Give me the pleasure of your company, and the benefit of your opinion upon politics. I have heard the highest praise of your abilities, my friend. Speak to me just as you would to one of your brother fishermen. By the accident of birth I am placed differently from you; and in this country that makes all the difference between a man and a dog, in our value. Though you may be, and probably are, the better man—more truthful, more courageous, more generous, more true-hearted, and certain to be the more humble of the two. I have been brought up where all men are equal, and the things I see here make a new world to me. Very likely these are right, and all the rest of the world quite wrong. Englishmen always are certain of that; and as I belong to the privileged classes, my great desire is to believe it. Only I want to know how the lower orders—the dregs, the scum, the dirt under our feet, the slaves that do all the work and get starved for it—how these trampled wretches regard the question. If they are happy, submissive, contented, delighted to lick the boots of their betters, my conscience will be clear to accept their homage, and their money for any stick of mine they look at. But you have amazed me by a most outrageous act. Because the lower orders have owned a path here for some centuries, you think it wrong that they should lose their right. Explain to me, Daniel, these extraordinary sentiments."

"If you please, sir," said Dan, who was following in the track, though invited to walk by the side, of Caryl Carne, "I can hardly tell you how the lower orders feel, because father and me don't belong to them. Our family have always owned their own boat, and worked for their own hand, this two hundred years, and, for all we know, ever since the Romans was here. We call them the lower orders, as come round to pick up jobs, and have no settlement in our village."

"A sound and very excellent distinction, Dan. But as against those who make the laws, and take good care to enforce them, even you (though of the upper rank here) must be counted of the lower order. For instance, can you look at a pheasant, or a hare, without being put into prison? Can you dine in the same room with Admiral Darling, or ask how his gout is, without being stared at?"

"No, sir. He would think it a great impertinence, even if I dared to do such a thing. But my father might do it, as a tenant and old neighbour. Though he never gets the gout, when he rides about so much."

"What a matter-of-fact youth it is! But to come to things every man has a right to. If you saved the life of one of the Admiral's daughters, and she fell in love with you, as young people will, would you dare even lift your eyes to her? Would you not be kicked out of the house and the parish, if you dared to indulge the right of every honest heart? Would you dare to look upon her as a human being, of the same order of creation as yourself, who might one day be your wife, if you were true and honest, and helped to break down the absurd distinctions built up by vile tyranny between you? In a word, are you a man—as every man is on the Continent—or only an English slave, of the lower classes?"

The hot flush of wrath, and the soft glow of shame, met and deepened each other on the fair cheeks of this "slave"; while his mind would not come to him to make a fit reply. That his passion for Dolly, his hopeless passion, should thus be discovered by a man of her own rank, but not scorned or ridiculed, only pitied, because of his want of manly spirit; that he should be called a "slave" because of honest modesty, and even encouraged in his wild hopes by a gentleman, who had seen all the world, and looked down from a lofty distance on it; that in his true estimate of things there should be nothing but prejudice, low and selfish prejudice, between— Well, he could not think it out; that would take him many hours; let this large-minded man begin again. It was so dark now, that if he turned round on him, unless he was a cat, he would be no wiser.

"You do well to take these things with some doubt," continued Carne, too sagacious to set up argument, which inures even young men in their own opinions;

"if I were in your place, I should do the same. Centuries of oppression have stamped out the plain light of truth in those who are not allowed it. To me, as an individual, it is better so. Chance has ordained that I should belong to the order of those who profit by it. It is against my interest to speak as I have done. Am I likely to desire that my fences should be broken, my property invaded, the distinction so pleasing to me set aside, simply because I consider it a false one? No, no, friend Daniel; it is not for me to move. The present state of things is entirely in my favour. And I never give expression to my sense of right and wrong, unless it is surprised from me by circumstances. Your bold and entirely just proceedings have forced me to explain why I feel no resentment, but rather admiration, at a thing which any other land-owner in England would not rest in his bed until he had avenged. He would drag you before a bench of magistrates and fine you. Your father, if I know him, would refuse to pay the fine; and to prison you would go, with the taint of it to lie upon your good name forever. The penalty would be wrong, outrageous, ruinous; no rich man would submit to it, but a poor man must. Is this the truth, Daniel, or is it what it ought to be—a scandalous misdescription of the laws of England?"

"No, sir; it is true enough, and too true, I am afraid. I never thought of consequences, when I used my axe. I only thought of what was right, and fair, and honest, as between a man who has a right, and one who takes it from him."

"That is the natural way to look at things, but never permitted in this country. You are fortunate in having to deal with one who has been brought up in a juster land, where all mankind are equal. But one thing I insist upon; and remember it is the condition of my forbearance. Not a single word to any one about your dashing exploit. No gentleman in the county would ever speak to me again, if I were known to have put up with it."

"I am sure, sir," said Daniel, in a truly contrite tone, "I never should have done such an impudent thing against you, if I had only known what a nice gentleman you are. I took you for nothing but a haughty land-owner, without a word to fling at a poor fisherman. And now you go ever so far beyond what the Club doth, in speaking of the right that every poor man hasn't. I could listen to you by the hour, sir, and learn the difference between us and abroad."

"Tugwell, I could tell you things that would make a real man of you. But why should I? You are better as you are; and so are we who get all the good out of you. And besides, I have no time for politics at present. All my time is occupied with stern business—collecting the ruins of my property."

"But, sir—but you come down here sometimes from the castle in the evening; and if I might cross, without claiming right of way, sometimes I might have the luck to meet you."

"Certainly you may pass, as often as you please, and so may anybody who sets value on his rights. And if I should meet you again, I shall be glad of it. You can open my eyes, doubtless, quite as much as I can yours. Good-night, my friend, and better fortunes to you!"

"It was worth my while to nail up those rails," Carne said to himself, as he went home to his ruins. "I have hooked that clod, as firm as ever he hooked a cod. But, thousand thunders! what does he mean, by going away without touching his hat to me?"

CHAPTER XXVIII.

FOUL IN PRACTICE.

"I HOPE, my dear, that your ride has done you good," said the Rector's wife to the Rector, as he came into the hall with a wonderfully red face, one fine afternoon in October. "If colour proves health, you have gained it."

"Maria, I have not been so upset for many years. Unwholesome indignation dyes my cheeks, and that is almost as bad as indigestion. I have had quite a turn—as you women always put it. I am never moved by little things, as you know well, and sometimes to your great disgust; but to-day my troubles have conspired to devour me. I am not so young as I was, Maria. And what will the parish come to, if I give in?"

"Exactly, dear; and therefore you must not give in." Mrs. Twemlow replied with great spirit, but her hands were trembling as she helped him to pull off his new rid-ing-coat. "Remember your own exhortations, Joshua—I am sure they were beautiful—last Sunday. But take something, dear, to restore your circulation. A reaction in the system is so dangerous."

"Not anything at present," Mr. Twemlow answered, firmly; "these mental cares are beyond the reach of bodily refreshments. Let me sit down, and be sure where I am, and then you may give me a glass of treble X. In the first place, the pony nearly kicked me off, when that idiot of a Stubbard began firing from his battery. What have I done, or my peaceful flock, that a noisy set of guns should be set up amidst us? However, I showed Juniper that he had a master, though I shall find it hard to come down-stairs to-morrow. Well, the next thing was that I saw James Cheeseman, Church-warden Cheeseman, Buttery Cheeseman, as the bad boys call him, in the lane, in front of me not more than thirty yards, as plainly as I now have the pleasure of seeing you, Maria; and while I said 'kuck' to the pony, he was gone! I particularly wished to speak to Cheeseman, to ask him some questions about things I have observed, and especially his sad neglect of public worship—a most shameful example on the part of a church-warden—and I was thinking how to put it, affectionately yet firmly, when, to my great surprise, there was no Cheeseman to receive it! I called at his house on my return, about three hours afterwards, having made up my mind to have it out with him, when they positively told me—or at least Polly Cheeseman did—that I must be mistaken about her 'dear papa,' because he was gone in the pony-shay all the way to Uckfield, and would not be back till night."

"The nasty little story-teller!" Mrs. Twemlow cried. "But I am not at all surprised at it, when I saw how she had got her hair done up, last Sunday."

"No; Polly believed it. I am quite sure of that. But what I want to tell you is much stranger and more important, though it cannot have anything at all to do with Cheeseman. You know, I told you I was going for a good long ride; but I did not tell you where, because I knew that you would try to stop me. But the fact was that I had made up my mind to see what Caryl Carne is at, among his owls and ivy. You remember the last time I went to the old place I knocked till I was tired, but could get no answer, and the window was stopped with some rusty old spiked railings, where we used to be able to get in at the side. All the others are out of reach, as you know well; and being of a yielding nature, I came sadly home. And at that time I still had some faith in your friend Mrs. Stubbard, who promised to find out all about him, by means of Widow Shanks and the Dimity-parlour. But nothing has come of that. Poor Mrs. Stubbard is almost as stupid as her husband; and as for Widow Shanks—I am quite sure, Maria, if your nephew were plotting the overthrow of King, Church, and Government, that deluded woman would not listen to a word against him."

"She calls him a model, and a blessed martyr"—Mrs. Twemlow was smiling at the thought of it; "and she says she is a woman of great penetration, and never will listen to anything. But it only shows what I have always said, that our family has a peculiar power, a sort of attraction, a superior gift of knowledge of their own minds, which makes them— But there, you are laughing at me, Joshua!"

"Not I; but smiling at my own good fortune, that ever I get my own way at all. But, Maria, you are right; your family has always been distinguished for having its own way—a masterful race, and a mistressful. And so much the more do the rest of mankind grow eager to know all about them. In an ordinary mind, such as mine, that feeling becomes at last irresistible; and finding no other way to gratify it, I resolved to take the bull by the horns, or rather by the tail, this morning. The poor old castle has been breaking up most grievously, even within the last twenty years, and you, who have played as a child among the ruins of the ramparts, would scarcely know them now. You cannot bear to go there, which is natural enough, after all the sad things that have happened; but if you did, you would be surprised, Maria; and I believe a great part has been knocked down on purpose. But you remember the little way in from the copse, where you and I, five-and-thirty years ago—"

"Of course I do, darling. It seems but yesterday; and I have a flower now which you gathered for me there. It grew at a very giddy height upon the wall, full of cracks and places where the evening-star came through; but up you went, like a rocket or a race-horse; and what a fright

I was in, until you came down safe! I think that must have made up my mind to have nobody except my Joshua."

"Well, my dear, you might have done much worse. But I happened to think of that way in, this morning, when you put up your elbow, as you made the tea, exactly as you used to do when I might come up there. And that set me thinking of a quantity of things, and among them this plan which I resolved to carry out. I took the trouble first to be sure that Caryl was down here for the day, under the roof of Widow Shanks; and then I set off by the road up the hill, for the stronghold of all the Carnes. Without further peril than the fight with the pony, and the strange apparition of Cheeseman about half a mile from the back entrance, I came to the copse where the violets used to be, and the sorrel, and the lords and ladies. There I tethered our friend Juniper in a quiet little nook, and crossed the soft ground, without making any noise, to the place we used to call our little postern. It looked so sad, compared with what it used to be, so desolate and brambled up and ruinous, that I scarcely should have known it, except for the gray pedestal of the prostrate dial we used to moralise about. And the ground inside it, that was nice turf once, with the rill running down it that perhaps supplied the moat—all stony now, and overgrown, and tangled, with ugly-looking elder-bushes sprawling through the ivy. To a painter it might have proved very attractive; but to me it seemed so dreary, and so sombre, and oppressive, that, although I am not sentimental, as you know, I actually turned away, to put my little visit off, until I should be in better spirits for it. And that, my dear Maria, would in all probability have been never.

"But before I had time to begin my retreat, a very extraordinary sound, which I cannot describe by any word I know, reached my ears. It was not a roar, nor a clank, nor a boom, nor a clap, nor a crash, nor a thud, but if you have ever heard a noise combining all those elements, with a small percentage of screech to enliven them, that comes as near it as I can contrive to tell. We know from Holy Scripture that there used to be such creatures as dragons, though we have never seen them; but I seemed to be hearing one as I stood there. It was just the sort of groan you might have expected from a dragon, who had swallowed something highly indigestible."

"My dear! And he might have swallowed you, if you had stopped. How could you help running away, my Joshua? I should have insisted immediately upon it. But you are so terribly intrepid!"

"Far from it, Maria. Quite the contrary, I assure you. In fact, I did make off, for a considerable distance; not rapidly as a youth might do, but with self-reproach at my tardiness. But the sound ceased coming; and then I remembered how wholly we are in the hand of the Lord. A sense of the power of right rose within me, backed up by a strong curiosity; and I said to myself that if I went home, with nothing more than that to tell you, I should not have at all an easy time of it. Therefore I resolved to face the question again, and ascertain, if possible, without self-sacrifice, what was going on among the ruins. You know every stick and stone, as they used to be, but not as they are at present; therefore I must tell you. The wall at the bottom of the little Dial-court, where there used to be a sweet-briar hedge to come through, is entirely gone, either tumbled down or knocked down—the latter I believe to be the true reason of it. Also, instead of sweet-briar, there is now a very flourishing crop of sting-nettles. But the wall at the side of the little court stands almost as sound as ever; and what surprised me most was to see, when I got further, proceeding of course very quietly, that the large court beyond (which used to be the servants' yard, and the drying-ground, and general lounging-place) had a timber floor laid down it, with a rope on either side, a long heavy rope on either side; and these ropes were still quivering, as if from a heavy strain just loosened. All this I could see, because the high door with the spikes, that used to part the Dial-court from this place of common business, was fallen forward from its upper hinge, and splayed out so that I could put my fist through.

"By this time I had quite recovered all my self-command, and was as calm as I am now, or even calmer, because I was under that reaction which ensues when a sensible man has made a fool of himself. I perceived, without thinking, that the sound which had so scared me proceeded from this gangway, or timberway, or staging, or whatever may be the right word

for it; and I made up my mind to stay where I was, only stooping a little with my body towards the wall, to get some idea of what might be going forward. And then I heard a sort of small hubbub of voices, such as foreigners make when they are ordered to keep quiet, and have to carry on a struggle with their noisy nature.

"This was enough to settle my decision not to budge an inch, until I knew what they were up to. I could not see round the corner, mind—though ladies seem capable of doing that, Maria—and so these fellows, who seemed to be in two lots, some at the top and some at the bottom of the plankway, were entirely out of my sight as yet, though I had a good view of their sliding-plane. But presently the ropes began to strain and creak, drawn taut—as our fishermen express it—either from the upper or the lower end, and I saw three barrels come sliding down—sliding, not rolling (you must understand), and not as a brewer delivers beer into a cellar. These passed by me; and after a little while there came again that strange sepulchral sound, which had made me feel so uneasy.

"Maria, you know that I can hold my own against almost anybody in the world but you; and although this place is far outside my parish boundaries, I felt that as the Uncle of the present owner—so far at least as the lawyers have not snapped him up—and the brother-in-law of the previous proprietor, I possessed an undeniable legal right — quo warranto, or whatever it is called — to look into all proceedings on these premises. Next to Holy Scripture, Horace is my guide and guardian; and I called to mind a well-known passage, which may roughly be rendered thus: 'If the crushed world tumble on him, the ruins shall strike him undismayed.' With this in my head, I went softly down the side-wall of the Dial-court (for there was no getting through the place where I had been peeping) to the bottom, where there used to be an old flint wall, and a hedge of sweet-briar in front of it. You remember the pretty conceit I made—quaint and wholesome as one of Herrick's—when you said something—but I verily believe we were better in those days than we ever have been since. Now don't interrupt me about that, my dear.

"Some of these briars still were there,

or perhaps some of their descendants, straggling weakly among the nettles, and mullein, and other wild stuff, but making all together a pretty good screen, through which I could get a safe side-view of the bottom of the timber gangway. So I took off my hat, for some ruffian fellows like foreign sailors were standing below, throwing out their arms, and making noises in their throats, because not allowed to scream as usual. It was plain enough at once to any one who knew the place, that a large hole had been cut in the solid castle wall, or rather, a loophole had been enlarged very freely on either side, and brought down almost to the level of the ground outside. On either side of this great opening stood three heavy muskets at full cock, and it made my blood run cold to think how likely some fatal discharge appeared. If I had been brought up to war, Maria, as all the young people are bound to be now, I might have been more at home with such matters, and able to reconnoitre calmly; but I thought of myself, and of you, and Eliza, and what a shocking thing it would be for all of us—but a merciful Providence was over me.

"Too late I regretted the desire for knowledge, which had led me into this predicament, for I durst not rush off from my very sad position, for my breath would soon fail me, and my lower limbs are thick from the exercise of hospitality. How I longed for the wings of a dove, or at any rate for the legs of Lieutenant Blyth Scudamore! And my dark apprehensions gained double force when a stone was dislodged by my foot (which may have trembled), and rolled with a sharp echo down into the ballium, or whatever it should be called, where these desperadoes stood. In an instant three of them had their long guns pointed at the very thicket which sheltered me, and if I had moved or attempted to make off, there would have been a vacancy in this preferment. But luckily a rabbit, who had been lying as close as I had, and as much afraid of me perhaps as I was of those ruffians, set off at full speed from the hop of the stone, and they saw him, and took him for the cause of it. This enabled me to draw my breath again, and consider the best way of making my escape, for I cared to see nothing more, except my own house-door.

"Happily the chance was not long in coming. At a shout from below—which seemed to me to be in English, and sounded uncommonly like 'now, then!'—all those fellows turned their backs to me, and began very carefully to lower, one by one, the barrels that had been let down the incline. And other things were standing there, besides barrels: packing-cases, crates, very bulky-looking boxes, and low massive wheels, such as you often see to artillery. You know what a vast extent there is of cellars and vaults below your old castle, most of them nearly as sound as ever, and occupied mainly by empty bottles, and the refuse of past hospitality. Well, they are going to fill these with something—French wines, smuggled brandy, contraband goods of every kind you can think of, so long as high profit can be made of them. That is how your nephew Caryl means to redeem his patrimony. No wonder that he has been so dark and distant! It never would have done to let us get the least suspicion of it, because of my position in the Church, and in the Diocese. By this light a thousand things are clear to me, which exceeded all the powers of the Sphinx till now."

"But how did you get away, my darling Joshua?" Mrs. Twemlow enquired, as behoved her. "So fearless, so devoted, so alive to every call of duty—how could you stand there, and let the wretches shoot at you?"

"By taking good care not to do it," the Rector answered, simply. "No sooner were all their backs towards me, than I said to myself that the human race happily is not spiderine. I girt up my loins, or rather fetched my tails up under my arms very closely, and glided away, with the silence of the serpent, and the craft of the enemy of our fallen race. Great care was needful, and I exercised it; and here you behold me, unshot and unshot-at, and free from all anxiety, except a pressing urgency for a bowl of your admirable soup, Maria, and a cut from the saddle I saw hanging in the cellar."

CHAPTER XXIX.
MATERNAL ELOQUENCE.

SUFFICIENT for the day is the evil thereof; and more than sufficient with most of us. Mr. Twemlow and his wife resolved discreetly, after a fireside council, to have nothing to say to Carne Castle, or about it, save what might be forced out of them. They perceived most clearly, and very deeply felt, how exceedingly wrong it is for anybody to transgress, or even go aside of, the laws of his country, as by Statute settled. Still, if his ruin had been chiefly legal; if he had been brought up under different laws, and in places where they made those things which he desired to deal in; if it was clear that those things were good, and their benefit might be extended to persons who otherwise could have no taste of them; above all, if it were the first and best desire of all who heard of it to have their own fingers in the pie—then let others stop it, who by duty and interest were so minded; the Rector was not in the Commission of the Peace—though he ought to have been there years ago—and the breach of the law, if it came to that, was outside of his parish boundary. The voice of the neighbourhood would be with him, for not turning against his own nephew, even if it ever should come to be known that he had reason for suspicions.

It is hard to see things in their proper light, if only one eye has a fly in it; but if both are in that sad condition, who shall be blamed for winking? Not only the pastor, but all his flock, were in need of wire spectacles now, to keep their vision clear and their foreheads calm. Thicker than flies around the milk-pail, rumours came flitting daily; and even the night— that fair time of thinking—was busy with buzzing multitude.

"Long time have I lived, and a sight have I seed," said Zebedee Tugwell to his wife, "of things as I couldn't make no head nor tail of; but nothing to my knowledge ever coom nigh the sort of way our folk has taken to go on. Parson Twemlow told us, when the war began again, that the Lord could turn us all into Frenchmen, if we sinned against Him more than He could bear. I were fool enough to laugh about it then, not intaking how it could be on this side of Kingdom Come, where no distinction is of persons. But now, there it is—a thing the Almighty hath in hand; and who shall say Him nay, when He layeth His hand to it?"

"I reckon, 'a hath begun with you too, Zeb," Mrs. Tugwell would answer, undesirably. "To be always going on so about trash trifles, as a woman hath a right to fly up at, but no man! Surely Dan hath

a right to his politics and his parables, as much as any lame old chap that sitteth on a bench. He works hard all day, and he airns his money; and any man hath a right to wag his tongue of night-time, when his arms and his legs have been wagging all day."

"Depends upon how he wags 'un." The glance of old Tugwell was stern, as he spoke, and his eyebrows knitted over it. "If for a yarn, to plaise children or maidens, or a bit of argyment about his business, or talk about his neighbours, or aught that consarns him—why, lads must be fools, and I can smoke my pipe and think that at his age I was like him. But when it comes to talking of his betters, and the Government, and the right of everybody to command the ship, and the soup—soup, what was it?"

"Superior position of the working classes, dignity of labour, undefeasible rights of mankind to the soil as they was born in, and soshallistick—something."

"So—shall—I—stick equality," Mr. Tugwell amended, triumphantly; "and so shall I stick him, by the holy poker, afore the end of the week is out. I've a-been fool enough to leave off ropesending of him now for a matter of two years, because 'a was good, and outgrowing of it like, and because you always coom between us. But mind you, mother, I'll have none of that, next time. Business I means, and good measure it shall be."

"Zeb Tugwell," said his wife, longing greatly to defy him, but frightened by the steadfast gaze she met, "you can never mean to say that you would lay your hand on Dan—a grown man, a'most as big as yourself, and a good half-head taller! Suppose he was to hit you back again!"

"If he did, I should just kill him," Zeb answered, calmly. "He would be but a jellyfish in my two hands. But there, I'll not talk about it, mother. No need to trouble you with it. 'Tis none of my seeking—the Lord in heaven knows—but a job as He hath dutified for me to do. I'll go out, and have my pipe, and dwell on it."

"And I may lay a deal of it on myself," Mrs. Tugwell began to moan, as soon as he was gone; "for I have cockered Dan up, and there's no denying it, afore Tim, or Tryphena, or Tabby, or Debby, or even little Solomon. Because he were the first, and so like his dear father, afore he got on in the world so. Oh, it all comes of that, all the troubles comes of that, and of laying up of money, apart from your wife, and forgetting almost of her Christian name! And the very same thing of it—money, money, and the getting on with breeches that requireth no mending, and the looking over Church-books at gay young ladies —all of it leadeth to the same bad end of his betters, and the Government, and the Soshallis-tick Quality.

"Why, with all these mercies," continued Mrs. Tugwell, though not in a continuous frame of mind, as Daniel came in, with a slow heavy step, and sat down by the fire in silence, "all these mercies, as are bought and paid for, from one and sixpence up to three half-crowns, and gives no more trouble beyond dusting once a week—how any one can lay his eyes on other people's property, without consideration of his own, as will be after his poor mother's time, is to me quite a puzzle and a pin-prick. Not as if they was owing for, or bought at auction, or so much as beaten down by sixpence, but all at full price and own judgment, paid for by airnings of labour and perils of the deep. And as Widow Shanks said, the last time she was here, by spoiling of the enemies of England, who makes us pay tremenjious for 'most everything we lives on. And I know who would understand them crackeries, and dust them when I be gone to dust, and see her own pretty face in them, whenever they has the back-varnish."

Dan knew that the future fair owner and duster designed by his mother was Miss Cheeseman, towards whom he had cherished tender yearnings in the sensible and wholesome days. And if Polly Cheeseman had hung herself on high— which she might have done without a bit of arrogance—perhaps she would still

MR. TWEMLOW GETS A SIDE VIEW.

have been to this young man the star of fate and glory, instead of a dip, thirty-two to the pound; the like whereof she sold for a farthing. Distance makes the difference.

"He that won't allow heed shall pay dear in his need;" the good mother grew warm, as the son began to whistle; "and to my mind, Master Dan, it won't be long afore you have homer things to think of than politics. 'Politics is fiddle-sticks' was what men of my age used to say; sensible men with a house and freehold, and a pig of their own, and experience. And such a man I might have had, and sensible children by him, children as never would have whistled at their mother, if it hadn't been for your poor father, Dan. Misguided he may be, and too much of his own way, and not well enough in his own mind to take in a woman's—but for all that he hath a right to be honoured by his children, and to lead their minds in matters touching of the King, and Church, and true religion. Why only last night, no, the night afore last, I met Mrs. Prater, and I said to her—"

"You told me all that, mother; and it must have been a week ago; for I have heard it every night this week. What is it you desire that I should do, or say, or think?"

"Holy mercy!" cried Mrs. Tugwell, "what a way to put things, Dan! All I desire is for your good only, and so leading on to the comfort of the rest. For the whole place goes wrong, and the cat sits in the corner, when you go on with politics as your dear father grunts at. No doubt it may all be very fine and just, and worth a man giving his life for, if he don't care about it, nor nobody else —but even if it was to keep the French out, and yourn goeth nearer to letting them in, what difference of a button would it make to us, Dan, compared to our sticking together, and feeding with a knowledge and a yielding to the fancies of each other?"

"I am sure it's no fault of mine," said Daniel, moved from his high ropes by this last appeal; "to me it never matters twopence what I have for dinner, and you saw me give Tim all the brown of the baked potatoes the very last time I had my dinner here. But what comes above all those little bothers is the necessity for insisting upon freedom of opinion. I don't pretend to be so old as my father, nor to know so much as he knows about the world in general. But I have read a great deal more than he has, of course, because he takes a long time to get a book with the right end to him; and I have thought, without knowing it, about what I have read, and I have heard very clever men (who could have no desire to go wrong, but quite the other way) carrying on about these high subjects, beyond me, but full of plain language. And I won't be forced out of a word of it by fear."

"But for love of your mother you might keep it under, and think it all inside you, without bringing of it out, in the presence of your elders. You know what your father is—a man as never yet laid his tongue to a thing without doing of it— right or wrong, right or wrong; and this time he hath right, and the law, and the Lord, and the King himself, to the side of him. And a rope's-end in his pocket, Dan, as I tried to steal away, but he were too wide-awake. Such a big hard one you never did see!"

"A rope's end for me, well turned twenty years of age!" cried Daniel, with a laugh, but not a merry one; "two can play at that game, mother. I'll not be ropes ended by nobody."

"Then you'll be rope-noosed;" the poor mother fell into the settle, away from the fire-light, and put both hands over her eyes, to shut out the spectacle of Dan dangling; "or else your father will be, for you. Ever since the Romans, Dan, there have been Tugwells, and respected ten times more than they was. Oh do 'e, do 'e think; and not bring us all to the grave, and then the gallows! Why I can mind the time, no more agone than last Sunday, when you used to lie here in the hollow of my arm, without a stitch of clothes on, and kind people was tempted to smack you in pleasure, because you did stick out so prettily. For a better-formed baby there never was seen, nor a finer-tempered one, when he had his way. And the many nights I walked the floor with you, Dan, when your first tooth was coming through, the size of a horse-radish, and your father most wonderful to put up with my coo to you, when he had not had a night in bed for nigh three weeks—oh, Dan, do 'e think of things as consarneth your homer life, and things as is above all reason; and let they blessed politics go home to them as trades in them."

Mrs. Tugwell's tender recollections had given her a pain in the part where Dan was nursed, and driven her out of true logical course; but she came back to it, before Dan had time to finish the interesting pictures of himself which she had suggested.

"Now can you deny a word of that, Dan? And if not, what is there more to say? You was smacked as a little babe, by many people kindly, when ever so much tenderer than you now can claim to be. And in those days you never could have deserved it yet, not having framed a word beyond 'Mam,' and 'Da,' and both of those made much of, because doubtful. There was nothing about the Constitooshun then, but the colour of the tongue and the condition of the bowels; and if any fool had asked you what politics was, you would have sucked your thumb, and offered them to suck it; for generous you always was, and just came after. And what cry have bigger folk, grown upright and wicked, to make about being smacked, when they deserve it, for meddling with matters outside of their business, by those in authority over them?"

"Well, mother, I daresay you are right, though I don't altogether see the lines of it. But one thing I will promise you—whatever father does to me, I will not lift a hand against him. But I must be off. I am late already."

"Where to, Dan? Where to? I always used to know, even if you was going courting. Go a-courting, Dan, as much

what that means, Dan. But I know what your father has got in his pocket for you. And he said the next time you went there, you should have it."

CHAPTER XXX.

PATERNAL DISCIPLINE.

"THE Fair, Free, and Frisky"—as they called themselves, were not of a violent or-

"OH, DAN, DO 'E THINK OF THINGS AS CONSARNETH YOUR HOMER LIFE."

as ever you like, only don't make no promises. But whatever you do, keep away from that bad, wicked, Free and Frisky Club, my dear."

"Mother, that's the very place I am just bound to. After all you have said, I would have stayed away to-night, except for being on the list, and pledged in honour to twenty-eight questions, all bearing upon the grand issues of the age."

"I don't know no more than the dead,

der at all, neither treasonable, nor even disloyal. Their Club, if it deserved the name, had not been of political, social, or even convivial intention, but had lapsed unawares into all three uses, and most of all that last mentioned. The harder the times are, the more confidential (and therefore convivial) do Englishmen become; and if Free-trade survives with us for another decade, it will be the death of total abstinence. But now they had bad times, without Free-trade—that Goddess being still in the goose-egg—and when two friends met, without a river between them, they were bound to drink one another's health, and did it, without the unstable and cold-blooded element. The sense of this duty was paramount among the "Free and Frisky," and without it their final cause would have vanished long ago, and therewith their formal one.

None of the old-established folk of the blue blood of Springhaven, such as the Tugwells, the Shankses, the Praters, the Bowleses, the Stickfasts, the Blocks, or the Kedgers, would have anything to do with this Association, which had formed itself among them, like an anti-corn-law league, for the destruction of their rights and properties. Its origin had been commercial, and its principles aggressive, no less an outrage being contemplated than the purchase of fish at low figures on the beach, and the speedy distribution of that slippery ware among the nearest villages and towns. But from time immemorial the trade had been in the hands of a few staunch factors, who paid a price governed by the seasons and the weather, and sent the commodity as far as it would go, with soundness, and the hope of freshness. Springhaven believed that it supplied all London, and was proud and blest in so believing. With these barrowmen, hucksters and pedlars of fish, it would have no manifest dealing; but if the factors who managed the trade chose to sell their refuse or surplus to them, that was their own business. In this way perhaps, and by bargains on the sly, these petty dealers managed to procure enough to carry on their weekly enterprise, and for a certain good reason took a room and court-yard handy to the *Darling Arms*, to discuss other people's business and their own. The good reason was that they were not allowed to leave the village, with their barrows or trucks or baskets, until the night had fallen, on penalty of being pelted with their own wares. Such was the dignity of this place, and its noble abhorrence of anything low.

The vision of lofty institutions, which one may not participate, inspires in the lower human nature more jealousy than admiration. These higglers may have been very honest fellows, in all but pecuniary questions, and possibly continued to be so in the bosom of their own families. But here in Springhaven, by the force of

circumstances they were almost compelled to be radicals; even as the sweetest cow's milk turns sour, when she can just reach red clover with her breath, but not her lips. But still they were not without manners, and reason, and good-will to people who had patience with them. This enabled them to argue lofty questions, without black eyes, or kicking, or even tweak of noses; and a very lofty question was now before them.

To get once into Admiral Darling's employment was to obtain a vested interest; so kind was his nature and so forgiving, especially when he had scolded anybody. Mr. Swipes, the head gardener for so many years, held an estate of freehold in the garden—although he had no head, and would never be a gardener, till the hanging gardens of Babylon should be hung on the top of the tower of Babel—with a vested remainder to his son, and a contingent one to all descendants. Yet this man, although his hands were generally in his pockets, had not enough sense of their linings to feel that continuance, usage, institution, orderly sequence, heredity, and such like, were the buttons of his coat and the texture of his breeches, and the warmth of his body inside them. Therefore he never could hold aloof from the Free and Frisky gatherings, and accepted the chair upon Bumper-nights, when it was a sinecure benefice.

This was a Bumper-night, and in the chair sat Mr. Swipes, discharging gracefully the arduous duties of the office, which consisted mainly in calling upon members for a speech, a sentiment, or a song, and in default of mental satisfaction, bodily amendment by a pint all round. But as soon as Dan Tugwell entered the room, the Free and Friskies with one accord returned to loftier business. Mr. Swipes, the gay Liber of the genial hour, retired from the chair, and his place was taken by a Liberal—though the name was not yet invented—estranged from his own godfather. This was a hard man, who made salt herrings, and longed to cure everything fresh in the world.

Dan, being still a very tender youth, and quite unaccustomed to public speaking, was abashed by these tokens of his own importance, and heartily wished that he had stopped at home. It never occurred to his simple mind that his value was not political, but commercial;

not "anthropological," but fishy, the main ambition of the Free and Frisky Club having long been the capture of his father. If once Zeb Tugwell could be brought to treat, a golden era would dawn upon them, and a boundless vision of free-trade, when a man might be paid for refusing to sell fish, as he now is for keeping to himself his screws. Dan knew not these things, and his heart misgave him, and he wished that he had never heard of the twenty-eight questions set down in his name for solution.

However, his disturbance of mind was needless, concerning those great issues. All the members, except the chairman, had forgotten all about them; and the only matter they cared about was to make a new member of Daniel. A little flourish went on about large things (which nobody knew, or cared to know), then the table was hammered with the heel of a pipe, and Dan was made a Free and Frisky. An honorary member, with nothing to pay, and the honour on their side, they told him; and every man rose, with his pot in one hand and his pipe in the other, yet able to stand, and to thump with his heels, being careful. Then the President made entry in a book, and bowed, and Dan was requested to sign it. In the fervour of good-will, and fine feeling, and the pride of popularity, the young man was not old enough to resist, but set his name down firmly. Then all shook hands with him, and the meeting was declared to be festive, in honour of a new and noble member.

It is altogether wrong to say—though many people said it—that young Dan Tugwell was even a quarter of a sheet in the wind, when he steered his way home. His head was as solid as that of his father; which, instead of growing light, increased in specific, generic, and differential gravity, under circumstances which tend otherwise, with an age like ours, that insists upon sobriety, without allowing practice. All Springhaven folk had long practice in the art of keeping sober, and if ever a man walked with his legs outside his influence, it was always from defect of proper average quite lately.

Be that as it may, the young man came home with an enlarged map of the future in his mind, a brisk and elastic rise in his walk, and his head much encouraged to go on with liberal and indescribable feelings. In accordance with these, he expected his mother to be ready to embrace him at the door, while a saucepan simmered on the good-night of the wood-ash, with just as much gentle breath of onion from the cover as a youth may taste dreamily from the lips of love. But oh, instead of this, he met his father, spread out and yet solid across the doorway, with very large arms bare and lumpy in the gleam of a fireplace uncrowned by any pot. Dan's large ideas vanished, like a blaze without a bottom.

"Rather late, Daniel," said the captain of Springhaven, with a nod of his great head, made gigantic on the ceiling. "All the rest are abed, the proper place for honest folk. I suppose you've been airning money, overtime?"

"Not I," said Dan; "I work hard enough all day. I just looked in at the Club, and had a little talk of politics."

"The Club, indeed! The stinking barrow-grinders! Did I tell you, or did I forget to tell you, never to go there no more?"

"You told me fast enough, father; no doubt about that. But I am not aboard your boat, when I happen on dry land, and I am old enough now to have opinions of my own."

"Oh, that's it, is it? And to upset all the State, the King, the House of Lords, and the Parliamentary House, and all as is descended from the Romans? Well, and what did their Wusships say to you? Did they anoint you king of slooshings?"

"Father, they did this—and you have a right to know it;" Dan spoke with a grave debative tone, though his voice became doubtful, as he saw that his father was quietly seeking for something; "almost before I knew what was coming, they had made me a member, and I signed the book. They have no desire to upset the kingdom; I heard no talk of that kind; only that every man should have his own opinions, and be free to show what can be said for them. And you know, father, that the world goes on by reason, and justice, and good-will, and fair play—"

"No, it don't," cried the captain, who had found what he wanted; "if it had to wait for they, it would never go on at all. It goes on by government, and management, and discipline, and the stopping of younkers from their blessed foolery, and by the ten commandments, and the proverbs of King Solomon. You to teach

"DON'T CARE IF I DON'T."

your father how the world goes on! Off with your coat, and I'll teach you."

"Father," said Dan, with his milder nature trembling at the stern resolution in his father's eyes, as the hearth-fire flashing up showed their stronger flash, "you will never do such a thing, at my age and size?"

"Won't I?" answered Zebedee, cracking in the air the three knotted tails of the stout hempen twist. "As for your age, why, it ought to know better; and as for your size, why, the more room for this!"

It never came into Daniel's head that he should either resist or run away. But into his heart came the deadly sense of disgrace at being flogged, even by his own father, at full age to have a wife and even children of his own.

"Father," he said, as he pulled off his coat and red striped shirt, and showed his broad white back, "if you do this thing, you will never set eyes on my face again—so help me God!"

"Don't care if I don't," the captain shouted. "You was never son of mine, to be a runagate, and traitor. How old be you, Master Free and Frisky, to larn me how the world goes on?"

"As if you didn't know, father! The fifteenth of last March I was twenty years of age."

"Then one for each year of your life, my lad, and another to make a man of thee. This little tickler hath three tails; seven threes is twenty-one —comes just right."

When his father had done with him, Dan went softly up the dark staircase of old ship timber, and entering his own little room, struck a light. He saw that his bed was turned down for him, by the loving hand of his mother, and that his favourite brother Solomon, the youngest of the Tugwell race, was sleeping sweetly in the opposite cot. Then he caught a side view of his own poor back in the little black-framed looking-glass, and was quite amazed; for he had not felt much pain, neither flinched, nor winced, nor spoken. In a moment self-pity did more than pain, indignation, outrage, or shame could do; it brought large tears into his softened eyes, and a long sob into his swelling throat.

He had borne himself like a man when flogged; but now he behaved in the manner of a boy. "He shall never hear the last of this job," he muttered, "as long as mother has a tongue in her head." To this end he filled a wet sponge with the red proofs of his scourging, laid it where it must be seen, and beside it a leaf torn from his wage-book, on which he had written with a trembling hand: "He says that I am no son of his, and this looks like it. Signed, Daniel Tugwell, or whatever my name ought to be."

Then he washed and dressed with neat's-foot oil all of his wounds that he could reach, and tied a band of linen over them, and, in spite of increasing smarts and pangs, dressed himself carefully in his Sunday clothes. From time to time he listened for his father's step, inasmuch as there was no bolt to his door, and to burn a light so late was against all law. But nobody came to disturb him; his mother at the end of the passage slept heavily, and his two child-sisters in the room close by, Tabby and Debby, were in the land of dreams, as far gone as little Solly was. Having turned out his tools from their flat flag basket, or at least all but three or four favourites, he filled it with other clothes likely to be needed, and buckled it over his hatchet-head. Then the beating of his heart was like a flail inside a barn, as he stole along silently for one terrible good-bye.

This was to his darling pet of all pets, Debby, who worshipped this brother a great deal more than she worshipped her heavenly Father; because, as she said to her mother, when rebuked—"I can see Dan, mother, but I can't see Him. Can I sit in His lap, mother, and look into His face, and be told pretty stories, and eat apples all the time?" Tabby was of different grain, and her deity was Tim; for she was of the Tomboy kind, and had no imagination. But Debby was enough to make a sound and seasoned heart to ache, as she lay in her little bed, with the flush of sleep deepening the delicate tint of her cheeks, shedding bright innocence fresh from heaven on the tranquil droop of eyelid and the smiling curve of lip. Her hair lay fluttered, as if by play with the angels that protected her; and if she could not see her heavenly Father, it was not because she was out of His sight.

A better tear than was ever shed by self-pity, or any other selfishness, ran down the cheek she had kissed so often, and fell upon her coaxing, nestling neck. Then Dan, with his candle behind the curtain, set a long light kiss upon the forehead of his darling, and with a heart so full, and yet so empty, took one more gaze at her, and then was gone. With the basket in his hand, he dropped softly from his window upon the pile of seaweed at the back of the house—collected to make the walls wholesome—and then, caring little what his course might be, was led perhaps by the force of habit down the foot-path towards the beach. So late at night, it was not likely that any one would disturb him there, and no one in the cottage which he had left would miss him before the morning. The end of October now was near, the nights were long, and he need not hurry. He might even lie down in his favourite boat, the best of her size in Springhaven, the one he had built among the rabbits. There he could say good-bye to all that he had known and loved so long, and be off before dawn, to some place where he might earn his crust and think his thoughts.

CHAPTER XXXI.
SORE TEMPTATION.

WHEN a man's spirit and heart are low, and the world seems turned against him, he had better stop both ears than hearken to the sound of the sad sea waves at night. Even if he can see their movement, with the moon behind them, drawing paths of rippled light, and boats (with white sails pluming shadow, or thin oars that dive for gems), and perhaps a merry crew with music, coming home not all sea-sick—well, even so, in the summer sparkle, the long low fall of the waves is sad. But how much more on a winter night, when the moon is away below the sea, and weary waters roll unseen from a vast profundity of gloom, fall unreckoned, and are no more than a wistful moan, as man is!

The tide was at quarter-ebb, and a dismal haze lay thick on shore and sea. It was not enough to be called a fog, or even a mist, but quite enough to deaden the gray light, always flowing along the boundary of sky and sea. But over the wet sand and the white frill of the gently gurgling waves more of faint light, or rather perhaps, less of heavy night, prevailed. But Dan had keen eyes, and was well accustomed to the tricks of darkness; and he came to take his leave forever of the fishing squadron, with a certainty of knowing all the five, as if by daylight—for now there were only five again.

As the tide withdrew, the fishing-smacks (which had scarcely earned their name of late) were compelled to make the best of the world until the tide came back again. To judge by creakings, strainings, groanings, and even grindings of timber millstones [if there yet lives in Ireland the good-will for a loan to us], all these little craft were making dreadful hardship of the abandonment which man and nature inflicted on them every thirteenth hour. But all things do make more noise at night, when they get the chance (perhaps in order to assert their own prerogative), and they seem to know that noise goes further, and assumes a higher character, when men have left off making it.

The poor young fisherman's back was getting very sore by this time, and he began to look about for the white side-streak which he had painted along the water-line of that new boat, to distract the meddlesome gaze of rivals from the peculiar curve below, which even Admiral Darling had not noticed, when he passed her on the beach ; but Nelson would have spied it out in half a second, and known all about it in the other half. Dan knew that he should find a very fair berth there, with a roll or two of stuff to lay his back on, and a piece of tarpauling to draw over his legs. In the faint light that hovered from the breaking of the wavelets he soon found his boat, and saw a tall man standing by her.

"Daniel," said the tall man, without moving, "my sight is very bad at night, but unless it is worse than usual, you are my admired friend Daniel. A young man in a thousand—one who dares to think."

"Yes, Squire Carne," the admired friend replied, with a touch of hat protesting against any claim to friendship : "Dan Tugwell, at your service. And I have thought too much, and been paid out for it."

"You see me in a melancholy attitude, and among melancholy surroundings."

THE POSTERN-GATE, CARNE CASTLE.

Caryl Carne offered his hand as he spoke, and Dan took it with great reverence. "The truth is, that anger at a gross injustice, which has just come to my knowledge, drove me from my books and sad family papers, in the room beneath the roof of our good Widow Shanks. And I needs must come down here, to think beside the sea, which seems to be the only free thing in England. But I little expected to see you."

"And I little expected to be here, Squire Carne. But if not making too bold to ask —was it anybody that was beaten?"

"Beaten is not the right word for it, Dan; cruelly flogged and lashed, a dear young friend of mine has been, as fine a young fellow as ever lived—and now he has not got a sound place on his back. And why? Because he was poor, and dared to lift his eyes to a rich young lady."

"But he was not flogged by his own father?" asked Dan, deeply interested in this romance, and rubbing his back, as the pain increased with sympathy.

"Not quite so bad as that," replied the other; "such a thing would be impossible, even in England. No; his father took his part, as any father in the world would do; even if the great man, the young lady's father, should happen to be his own landlord."

A very black suspicion crossed the mind of Dan, for Carne possessed the art of suggesting vile suspicions: might Admiral Darling have discovered something, and requested Dan's father to correct him? It was certain that the Admiral, so kind of heart, would never have desired such severity; but he might have told Captain Tugwell, with whom he had a talk almost every time they met, that his eldest son wanted a little discipline; and the Club might have served as a pretext for this, when the true crime must not be declared, by reason of its enormity. Dan closed his teeth, and English air grew bitter in his mouth, as this belief ran through him.

"Good-night, my young friend; I am beginning to recover," Carne continued, briskly, for he knew that a nail snaps in good oak, when the hammer falls too heavily. "What is a little bit of outrage, after all? When I have been in England a few years more, I shall laugh at myself for having loved fair play and self-respect, in this innocent young freshness. We must wag as the world does; and you

know the proverb, What makes the world wag, but the weight of the bag?"

"But if you were more in earnest, sir— or at least—I mean, if you were not bound here by property and business, and an ancient family, and things you could not get away from, and if you wanted only to be allowed fair play, and treated as a man by other men, and be able to keep your own money when you earned it, or at least to buy your own victuals with it—what would you try to do, or what part of the country would you think best to go to?"

"Dan, you must belong to a very clever family. It is useless to shake your head—you must; or you never could put such questions, so impossible to answer. In all this blessed island, there is no spot yet discovered, where such absurd visions can be realized. Nay, nay, my romantic friend; be content with more than the average blessings of this land. You are not starved, you are not imprisoned, you are not even beaten; and if you are not allowed to think, what harm of that? If you thought all day, you would never dare to act upon your thoughts, and so you are better without them. Tush! an Englishman was never born for freedom. Good-night."

"But, sir, Squire Carne," cried Dan, pursuing him, "there is one thing which you do not seem to know. I am driven away from this place to-night; and it would have been so kind of you to advise me where to go to."

"Driven away!" exclaimed Carne, with amazement. "The pride of the village driven out of it! You may be driving yourself away, Tugwell, through some scrape, or love affair; but when that blows over you will soon come back. What would Springhaven do without you? And your dear good father would never let you go."

"I am not the pride, but the shame, of the village." Dan forgot all his home-pride at last. "And my dear good father is the man who has done it. He has leathered me worse than the gentleman you spoke of, and without half so much to be said against him. For nothing but going to the Club to-night, where I am sure we drank King George's health, my father has lashed me so, that I am ashamed to tell it. And I am sure that I never meant to tell it, until your kindness, in a way of speaking, almost drove it out of me."

"Daniel Tugwell," Carne answered, with solemnity, "this is beyond belief, even in England. You must have fallen asleep, Dan, in the middle of large thoughts, and dreamed this great impossibility."

"My back knows whether it has been a dream, sir. I never heard of dreams as left one-and-twenty lines behind them. But whether it be one, or whether it be twenty, makes no odds of value. The disgrace it is that drives me out."

"Is there no way of healing this sad breach?" Carne asked, in a tone of deep compassion; "if your father could be brought to beg your pardon, or even to say that he was sorry—"

"He, sir! If such a thing was put before him, his answer would be just to do it again, if I were fool enough to go near him. You are too mild of nature, sir, to understand what father is."

"It is indeed horrible, too horrible to think of"—the voice of this kind gentleman betrayed that he was shuddering. "If a Frenchman did such a thing, he would be torn to pieces. But no French father would ever dream of such atrocity. He would rather flog himself within an inch of his own life."

"Are they so much better, then, and kinder, than us Englishmen?" In spite of all his pain and grief, Dan could not help smiling at the thought of his father ropesending himself. "So superior to us, sir, in every way?"

"In almost every way, I am sorry to confess. I fear, indeed, in every way, except bodily strength, and obstinate, ignorant endurance, miscalled 'courage,' and those rough qualities—whatever they may be—which seem needful for the making of a seaman. But in good manners, justice, the sense of what is due from one man to another, in dignity, equality, temperance, benevolence, largeness of feeling, and quickness of mind, and above all in love of freedom, they are very, very sadly far beyond us. And indeed I have been led to think from some of your finer perceptions, Dan, that you must have a share of French blood in your veins."

"Me, sir!" cried Dan, jumping back, in a style which showed the distance between faith and argument; "no, sir, thank God there was never none of that; but all English, with some of the Romans, who was pretty near equal to us, from what I hear. I suppose, Squire Carne, you thought that

low of me because I made a fuss about being larruped, the same as a Frenchman I pulled out of the water did about my doing of it, as if I could have helped it. No Englishman would have said much about that; but they seem to make more fuss than we do. And I dare say it was French-like of me, to go on about my hiding."

"Daniel," answered Caryl Carne, in alarm at this British sentiment; "as a man of self-respect, you have only one course left, if your father refuses to apologise. You must cast off his tyranny; you must prove yourself a man; you must begin life upon your own account. No more of this drudgery, and slavery for others, who allow you no rights in return. But a nobler employment among free people, with a chance of asserting your courage and manhood, and a certainty that no man will think you his bondslave because you were born upon his land, or in his house. My father behaved to me—well, it does not matter. He might have repented of it, if he had lived longer; and I feel ashamed to speak of it, after such a case as yours. But behold, how greatly it has been for my advantage! Without that, I might now have been a true and simple Englishman!"

Carne (who had taken most kindly to the fortune which made him an untrue Englishman) clapped his breast with both hands; not proudly, as a Frenchman does, nor yet with that abashment and contempt of demonstration which make a true Briton very clumsy in such doings; while Daniel Tugwell, being very solid, and by no means "emotional"—as people call it nowadays—was looking at him, to the utmost of his power (which would have been greater by daylight), with gratitude, and wonder, and consideration, and some hesitation about his foreign sentiments.

"Well, sir," said Dan, with the usual impulse of the British workman, "is there any sort of work as you could find for me, to earn my own living, and be able to think afterwards?"

"There is work of a noble kind, such as any man of high nature may be proud to share in, to which it is possible that I might get an entrance for you, if there should be a vacancy; work of high character, such as admits of no higgling and haggling, and splitting of halfpence, but an independent feeling, and a sense of advancing the liberty of mankind, without risking a penny, but putting many guineas into one's own pocket, and so becoming fitted for a loftier line of life."

"Is it smuggling, sir?" Daniel asked, with sore misgivings, for he had been brought up to be very shy of that. "Many folk consider that quite honest; but father calls it roguery—though I never shall hear any more of his opinions now."

"Sigh not, friend Daniel; sigh not so heavily at your own emancipation." Carne never could resist the chance of a little bit of sarcasm, though it often injured his own plots. "Smuggling is a very fine pursuit, no doubt, but petty in comparison with large affairs like ours. No, Dan Tugwell, I am not a smuggler, but a high politician, and a polisher of mankind. How soon do you think of leaving this outrageous hole?"

Despite the stupid outrage upon himself, Dan was too loyal and generous of nature to be pleased with this description of his native place. But Carne, too quick of temper for a really fine intriguer, cut short his expostulations.

"Call it what you please," he said; "only make your mind up quickly. If you wish to remain here, do so: a man of no spirit is useless to me. But if you resolve to push your fortunes among brave and lofty comrades, stirring scenes, and brisk adventures, meet me at six to-morrow evening, at the place where you chopped down my rails. All you want will be provided, and your course of promotion begins at once. But remember, all must be honour bright. No shilly-shallying, no lukewarmness, no indifference to a noble cause. Faint heart never won fair lady."

The waning moon had risen, and now shone upon Carne's face, lighting up all its gloomy beauty, and strange power of sadness. Dan seemed to lose his clear keen sight beneath the dark influence of the other's gaze; and his will, though not a weak one, dropped before a larger and stronger. "He knows all about me and Miss Dolly," said the poor young fisherman to himself; "I thought so before, and I am certain of it now. And, for some reason beyond my knowledge, he wishes to encourage it. Oh, perhaps because the Carnes have always been against the Darlings! I never thought of that before."

This was a bitter reflection to him, and might have inclined him the right way, if time had allowed him to work it out. But no such time was afforded; and in the confusion and gratitude of the moment, he answered, "Sir, I shall be always at your service, and do my very best in every way to please you." Caryl Carne smiled; and the church clock of Springhaven solemnly struck midnight.

A BAND OF BLUEBIRDS.

(IN AUTUMN.)

BY WILLIAM H. HAYNE.

OH, happy band of bluebirds,
　Brave prophets of the Spring,
Amid the tall and tufted cane,
　How blithesomely you sing!
What message haunts your music
　'Mid Autumn's dusky reign?
You tell us Nature stores her seed
　To give them back in grain!

Your throats are gleeful fountains,
　Through which a song-tide flows;
Your voices greet me in the woods,
　On every wind that blows!

I dream that Heaven invites you
　To bid the Earth "good-by";
For in your wings you seem to hold
　A portion of the sky!

＊　　＊　　＊　　＊

Oh, happy band of bluebirds,
　You could not long remain
To flit across the fading fields
　And glorify the grain....
You leave melodious memories,
　Whose sweetness thrills me through:
Ah, if my songs were such as yours,
　They'd almost touch the Blue!

"THE RIVER FLOWETH ON."

BY HELEN GRAY CONE.

ON a pleasant summer afternoon a young girl sat leaning against the trunk of an oak-tree. One slender hand held her forgotten sewing; the other, with the dented thimble yet on its second finger, was mechanically fretting the long grass beside her, which grew thickly, and flowed in the breeze with a silvery continuous murmur. At the foot of the bluff, whose crown was covered with this restless growth, flowed also, but almost in silence, a great river, like the stream of time proceeding in still power with all the change it bears, beside and beyond and despite the ephemeral murmurs of that flesh which is as the grass of the field.

Another sound was audible on the bluff-top—was even at times more insistent than this thin, protesting voice: the oak leaves laughed in a light, half-slumberous way, as though the trees had happy day-dreams there above the steadily moving water. The leaf shadows flickered on Millicent's pale, long-featured face, and on her soft, smoothly arranged chestnut hair. She was without her hat, and had chosen to wear a certain becoming white dress, which gave her, with its full skirt and short waist, quite a picturesque appearance. She had not, however, studied to attain the air of her own ancestress, and perhaps did not fully understand the effect of her costume. In her pale blue girdle she had placed a bunch of the daisies that grew abundantly in the surrounding field, springing up, it seemed, like Wordsworth's Lucy, with a maidenly beauty born of lonely listenings.

The path that Milly had followed, passing close beside a small broad-based pedestal of brown sandstone crowned with a laurelled urn, led northward to a slanting fence, unpainted, and gray with age; the gate had long stood open, sagging with a total abandonment of responsibility from its broken upper hinge. On the other side an old-fashioned, somewhat lax civilization began; there was a dilapidated garden with box borders, broad and sturdy, as though still stolidly defending the rights of flowers long dead, on which rights their own square, cobwebbed shoulders nevertheless inconsistently encroached. In one of the beds

yet bloomed a bush of pink roses, starry, and exquisitely fragrant with the fragrance of the wild rose. Beyond the garden stood the wide old white house in which Millicent Banks had dwelt during twelve of her young years. It was the home of her mother's father, Godfrey Pinkney, and had been built by another Pinkney nearly a century ago, in the much-rhymed-of times

> "When men lived in a grander way,
> With ampler hospitality."

A country house it was called in those days. Now the great city, stretching itself like a waking giant, had thrown an arm out even to the base of the hill—had, indeed, laid claim to the land south of the ruinous fence, which remained unused, though a park was projected. Meanwhile Millicent walked and read and sewed under the oaks; and sometimes a couple of horsemen drew rein there, having strayed in from the boulevard, which had its terminus not far below, and sometimes a family of Germans, bearing congenial viands in baskets, came toiling up the steep and dusty way from the huddled houses at the hill's foot, and supped in the face of the sunset in true Teutonic wise.

On this particular afternoon Milly had been quite undisturbed; but now, turning to look homeward across the straggling garden, she saw that a vehicle, of the unpretentious yet portentous kind generally used by physicians, had passed noiselessly over the grass-grown carriage road and stopped in front of the porch. Milly beheld it with mingled curiosity, trepidation, and satisfaction. It was her cousin's carriage. Henry Nixon's relationship to her dead father was remote, but his most distant kinsmen claimed the clever doctor with a knowing pride, as though in some untraceable way they had contributed to his successes. He had yesterday announced in a concise note that he would to-day bring with him the recently promised boarder, a patient who had just recovered from an illness caused by overwork. Dr. Nixon had himself arranged the matter for the convalescent clerk, whom he described as a nice young fellow, unfortunately without friends in the city. Mr. Campion having been obliged to resume his office duties, it was advisable that he should at least rest and sleep in ampler air. Here was good fortune, or the germ of good fortune, thrust upon the family, Milly thought, for her grandfather had given a reluctant consent to the doctor's proposition; and would not this precedent serve as the small end of a wedge, opening the half-empty house to that select company of summer boarders which Milly and her aunt had, for grave prudential reasons, long desired?

Yet as she rose from the grass it occurred to Milly that one boarder was perhaps a rather ghastly innovation, a narrowing of the relations of household and sojourner to an acute point, and she hoped that Aunt Maria could soon venture upon a modest advertisement, properly stiffened with the specification, "References exchanged." Her mind was busy with somewhat sordid considerations as she sauntered, needle-work in hand, through the gateway and up the path; yet she went, unconsciously, to put certain important stitches in the garment of her own life, with a silken thread not at all resembling the dull yarn of domestic economy.

Fate is forever mocking us with these incongruities. The laughter of the oak leaves increased after Milly had disappeared, as though the Hamadryads, by a fine instinct, divined the future.

"Stay to tea? Couldn't think of it, thank you," said Dr. Nixon, with one foot on the carriage step. "I hope you'll get along all right, Maria," he continued, gathering up the reins. "Mr. Pinkney's almost due, isn't he? Sorry not to have seen him." He nodded, and drove off. As his gleaming wheels went spinning along the white boulevard, an expression of sardonic amusement grew about his mouth under the black mustache that was beginning to be streaked with gray. "I'd like to see the old gentleman when he gets home!" he said to himself. The doctor was a perfectly practical person. He had obliged George Campion, and had at the same time done the household on the hill a substantial favor; it could not matter greatly that certain ridiculous notions of its eldest member were slightly rasped in the process.

"I don't know as your grandfather's going to like it," remarked Millicent's aunt Maria.

She had come out to rest a minute after hulling the strawberries, and seated herself beside Milly in the square porch with twin huge fluted pillars, which faced the water, lovely in the evening light. The river moved on stately toward the north in a broad gray-blue sweep, streaked with currents in lines and dashes of soft silver. Two azure points approached each other in the distance; they were known by the names of two rude forts which had been reared there in the Revolution. Looking southward along the top of the bluff, strange elevations and depressions were noticeable; they seemed artificial, but made Nature's again by years of enwrapping in her green mantle. It was a June landscape, full yet fresh; the great horse-chestnut that stood in the midst of the garden was covered with creamy, rose-tinged spires of bloom.

Godfrey Pinkney was always "your grandfather" with Aunt Maria; she looked to Milly for a clew to his probable conduct and opinions as to one really united to him by the mysterious ties of blood. She herself was an outsider—the sister of Webster Banks, the keen young travelling salesman from Connecticut, with whom his father-in-law's sympathy had never been full. He had gone to the war as a sergeant of volunteers, and died in Andersonville, and Milly's mother did not long survive him. His memory found a devout worshipper in the daughter that grew up in Godfrey Pinkney's house, cared for by the paternal aunt, whose presence was tolerated for her sake. While Milly was yet in her early teens, Miss Maria was accustomed to take counsel of her, as of one to whom she must soon surrender a provisional rule; and now, at twenty, the younger woman was virtually mistress of all situations. The present situation she did not consider deeply.

"Well, he can't help being an Englishman now," she said, generously, unconsciously implying that the case would have been otherwise had Mr. Campion been consulted at his birth.

"Oh, he ain't to blame," said Maria, as generously. "But Henry'd ought to have told your grandfather while he was about it, making arrangements. I don't know as it was considerate—do you? Maybe he won't find out right away," she suggested, faintly. Milly smiled incredulously: she thought George Campion the most obvious Briton she had ever beheld.

"It can't be helped now," she repeated; "and I don't believe grandfather'll mind it much—after the first plunge. If only there were other boarders here already! But it isn't our fault, any more than it is *his*. I think grandfather'll be reasonable." She felt that the new-comer was a person to be received without great strain on any one's amiability; he had impressed her rather agreeably. How difficult it is for fluent youth to realize the hardened limitations of age! Milly had her own passionate enthusiasms and condemnations, but her opinions had not yet petrified into a code that would admit no exceptions. She was accustomed to look upon Godfrey's life-long hatred of the kindred race which he had been early taught to regard as less than kind with such amusement as was consistent with affection. She was not stirred except to a secret indulgent mirth by the tirades of this dear but occasionally absurd grandfather, who had listened to thrilling tales of the Revolution on his father's knee; whose elder brother, the hero of his impressible boyhood, had been mortally wounded in one of the sea-fights of 1814; and whose surroundings were inevitable reminders, daily fuel to his low-burning but never extinguished indignation. Milly, whose pulse quickened at the least allusion to the civil war, felt that these faraway struggles with England were simply "history"; mention of them carried her thought back to a dull text-book with an ugly cover which she had used at school. *Before* us the deluge—a flood as of the waters of Lethe, blotting out the remembrance of wrestlings and wrongs!

George Campion, who had spent the few months since he came to America in the midst of a busy city with a population drawn from all quarters of the earth, had now chanced, by the Sophoclean irony of fate, upon a narrow corner wherein prejudice lingered, like snow in a shaded rift, while the sun of March shines broadly elsewhere. Unaware of this, and feeling a boyish enjoyment of the novelty of his environment, he was moving about the upper chamber which had been assigned to him, making some change in his dress before going down to tea. He was tired of his room in St. Mark's Place, which held feverish associations of his illness in

every crack of its plastering; he thought he should find these glinting river-glimpses, this delicious air, most grateful after his gas-lit days in the close office where he passed, with rapidly transferred intentness, from neat figure to figure. The oval mirror in its tarnished gilt frame gave back dimly, as he stood before it adjusting his scarf, a picture calculated to conciliate. George's was a frank Saxon face, and, though still a trifle pale, had the clean healthiness of look that was his rightful heritage. Poor old mirror! it had imaged in its day spirited maidens in tall combs, and curly-pated beaux in stiff stocks; it blurred outlines sadly now. George drew his straight brows together and half closed his eyes, in the manner of a near-sighted person. Some one had placed on the bureau a stout ginger jar, covered with "those little, lawless, azure-tinctured grotesques, that under the notion of men and women float about, uncircumscribed by any element, in a world before perspective," and out of it were crowding a gracious company of roses from the bush in the garden. Their perfume came over Campion's soul "like the sweet South"; it was an unwonted feminine touch, and made him, good fellow, think of his mother, and the three lavishly affectionate sisters, toward whom, to tell the truth, he had somewhat acted the tyrant all his life. As he settled his cuffs he wandered to the round-topped window; it looked into the branches of a mighty pine; the highest ones were goldenly embrowned by the late sunlight, but a dead limb quite stripped of bark gleamed baldly from the shadows lower down. But what was this gray bulk, in the tree and yet not of it? On closer examination it seemed the worn figure-head of a ship, made in the likeness of some vastly bewigged dignitary. The riddle of its presence in the pine George found himself incapable of solving. With a final glance around his new habitation, he shut his door, and betook himself down the broad curving stair.

It descended into a square hall with a dark-stained floor, whose stability quite shamed our later flimsinesses. At one side white pilasters, with delicately carved Corinthian capitals, upheld a graceful arch, behind which were visible the obliquely opening doors of two octagonal rooms. This hall contained only a small table and several heavily built old chairs, their mahogany darkened, their damask faded from its royal hue to a faint terra-cotta. Above the table hung a flat oil-painting of a youth with light brown side-curls and short whiskers; he wore a trim, many-buttoned blue coat with a high collar; the formalized features expressed none of the spirit that this young naval officer had doubtless possessed.

As Campion paused before this portrait he perceived that a powder-horn of primitive fashion was suspended beneath it by a cord. Rudely cut letters straggled across its yellowish-gray surface. Without thought George turned it in his hand to read the legend that passed around it.

"By your side a FRIEND I'll be
While you fight for LIBERTY,"

ran the roughly indicated words.

While Campion's hand yet lay upon this relic of the Revolution he became conscious of a presence behind him, and turning, faced a tall old man who had just entered from the porch, and who stood opposite him with a grimly questioning look. George was not imaginative, or he might have thought that his touch upon the horn had raised up the ghost of its original possessor to confront him, for the face of this old man, with its expression between simplicity and sternness, would have accorded well with the "ragged regimentals" of a Continental soldier. His gaunt figure was, however, wrapped in a loose, limp duster, which, falling backward, allowed it to be seen that his worn long-sleeved black coat was also too loose for him; a gigantic collar, moiled by travel, rose on each side of his leathern throat; he had not taken off a straw hat, under which appeared white hair, not bushy, but soft, and oddly like the curls of youth; a curly white whisker grew on his thin, brownish-mottled cheek. He fixed George with a pair of piercing gray eyes, surrounded by many wrinkles, and set under peaked brows; the lines of his firm mouth made the same upward angle.

Campion flushed to his fair hair with an inexplicable sense that he was accused. The strange old man said nothing at all, but gave a little dry, forced cough. So they stood, the young Englishman growing angry under his stiff exterior, when Milly entered from the dining-room as though impelled by a sudden fear. The tones of her voice dropped upon the strained situation like the gentle rain from heaven.

"Grandfather," she said, momentarily feeling that he was somehow larger and more massive than usual, "this is Mr. Campion—Cousin Henry's friend, you remember," she added, urgently, looking into his eyes.

The old man returned the look with a kind of injured majesty. "My mem'ry's very good, Milly," said he; "maybe it's better than some young folks' mem'ries." He brought his gaze again to bear on George. "Your servant, sir," he said, with magnificent ironical courtesy, and in a preternaturally deep voice. Campion was constrained to perform the peculiar conjunctive movement of knee and neck that constitutes the British bow.

Milly felt her grandfather's mood like a damp wind. "I thought Aunt Maria went down the road to meet you?" she questioned, softly. That lady had, indeed, undertaken to prepare Godfrey for the first encounter with Campion, but the immediate result of her endeavors had been so far from happy that she had shrunk from witnessing the sequel.

"Oh yes, your aunt Maria came to meet me," answered Godfrey, as he turned toward the staircase, carrying in one veinous hand his dark green, flowered carpet-bag. "Your aunt Maria's mighty thoughtful," he continued, in a low tone, as though to himself. They heard him repeat, "She's mighty thoughtful," with senile sarcasm, half-way up the stair.

George looked at Milly. "He is surprised to see you," she said, lightly and rapidly. "The doctor didn't set the day, when they were talking together, and when his note came yesterday, grandfather was away; he has been away a week. I suppose he is tired; he doesn't like to travel; and it must have startled him to find a stranger here."

"Oh, ah," said the young Englishman. This commentary was not full, but it somehow expressed good-will. Both smiled a little. George had a pleasant smile that showed the white teeth under his mustaches; it was his key. Usually undemonstrative, he might have been suspected of a poverty of feeling, but this sudden bright and confiding look, a legible promise to pay, gave one the impression of wealth behind it. He was, indeed, capable of strong sentiment, without self-consciousness.

In Milly's face the hazel eyes were the traitors, guilty of all betrayals, breaking the gravity of her pale countenance, with its saintly drooping lines, by flashes of mischief, hints of hidden mirth. Now that the impressive figure of her grandfather was removed from the scene, she was relieved, and able to taste the humor of the rigid salutations she had just witnessed. Hence there was a sparkle in these generally mild eyes as she raised them to Campion's, which were honest and intensely blue. The mutual look was a countersign, unknown to age. These two belonged to the prejudice-obliterating army of youth.

George lounged lonely in his room, his lamp yet unlighted, after a supper stately and sad as a stage banquet. His decreasing cheerfulness was not reënforced by the low, fervent croon of the old negress, once a slave, and for many years Godfrey Pinkney's devoted servant, who was rocking her body to and fro in accompaniment to a camp-meeting hymn at the kitchen door. This ancient African was a perpetual perplexity to Miss Maria, who had cherished reverent and singularly unpractical views of the race before encountering a specimen as a fixture in the home to which fate had brought her. For her part, Sally held in her guileful old heart some disapproval of the plain and melancholy New England lady; she had her standards, like another.

Meanwhile Mr. Campion's cause was being judiciously argued for him in the porch, whither Godfrey had betaken himself for his evening smoke—without his coat, as his royally careless custom was. He was, although not an uneducated man, as careless with the Queen's English as though he felt his right in the language as indisputable as that dignitary's. He had much difficulty this evening in getting his pipe to draw, and went through a great deal of nervous pressing and poking at the tobacco in the bowl with his lean finger, and crossed the hall two or three times to get another match, not asking Milly to go, though she sat at his feet regarding him earnestly, and sprang forward on perceiving his want. Once settled, he remained immovable, with one bony knee crossed above the other, and an intricately puckered brow.

"Grandfather," said Milly, faintly. He turned toward her with a disturbed and at the same time severe expression. "It's nobody's fault, grandfather," she pleaded; "that is, nobody here; and I'm sure Cousin Henry didn't know how you would feel. And I don't see what we can do about it *now*." Milly was telling herself that she would be glad if there were any natural and easy way of solving the difficulty; she wanted no more funereal meals —not she; but as the only ready solution was a rude cutting of the Gordian knot, why, she for one could make the best of things for the present. She had the young elasticity that promptly adapts itself rather than relinquish a plan. "It would seem too bad, wouldn't it, to do anything —to say anything—now that it's all arranged? It would be a sort of a—flying in the face of Providence," she continued, adopting an expression of her aunt's. "You know we do *need* boarders"—he nodded his head sardonically a number of times, as though impatient of the pressure of this point—"and now there's all the more reason for advertising. I don't believe you'd mind him at all if a few other people came—do you think you would? He's very quiet."

Godfrey smiled—a smile that puzzled his granddaughter sorely. At first she fancied it suspicious and offended; again she thought it grieved. Altogether it was a superior and removed expression, and reminded her for a minute that he had lived longer than she had, and possibly possessed recesses she had not fully explored.

"*I* ain't going to say anything, Milly," he announced.

The effect of this was as though he had suddenly released something for which Milly had been struggling. It was a most inglorious victory, and she was ashamed. She watched his face, hesitating, and felt relief when he began to speak again, although his words surprised her.

"You ain't over-fond of the Southerners yourself, Milly," he remarked, dryly. "Our own brothers too, as I may say. These things are born in us, a'most."

He had been thinking of an occasion when the child, taken by him to visit some relation of her mother's, had marched out of the room with erect head and flashing face, rather than remain to hear the pretty, florid Southern war-songs, "True-heart Southrons," and "Maryland, my Maryland," and "The Bonny Blue Flag that bears the Single Star." And he remembered another day when, having chanced to step into her play-room, he found the walls pasted over with startling battle-scenes cut from the illustrated papers, and roughly daubed here and there with Prussian blue from the paint-box he had given her; the Confederates in these works of art were depicted as phenomenally lean and tigerish. He had resisted the impulse to tell her, in the tone that reddens childish cheeks with unreasoning shame, that such things were "not pretty for little girls." Godfrey had been a Peace Democrat in those war times, the cautious chill of age having influenced the growth of his later opinions, though all the hot juices of his youth survived in the cellared vintage of his earlier ones. "What was near he saw as in the distance, and what had vanished was to him the only reality." He had failed to sympathize on this point with the little creature dearest to him in the world; but now these incidents returned upon his remembrance as a means of making the girl comprehend the bitterness he could hardly voice.

His few words touched her, though not deeply. She colored, and cried out impatiently, "Grandfather, I don't want him to stay—he mustn't stay." Both were silent a moment; then prudence reasserted itself in Milly's mind—a mind methodical and just. She felt the force of homely obligations which less often presented themselves to Godfrey. "Isn't it a pity, though?" she wavered. "There are those little debts to be paid; and when Aunt Maria's willing to take the trouble—"

Godfrey gave a short, hard laugh. "Your aunt Maria!" said he, in a manner that conveyed his sense of the futility of discussing her aunt Maria. He arose, and went earlier than was his habit into the house, sending back over his shoulder the scorn-tipped Parthian shaft, "Boarders! there ain't any of *our* family ever took boarders!"

Milly remained, reddening again, but this time with annoyance; he had estranged her just-awakened sympathy by this ignoble thrust. She was not at all sure now what she wished, and as Godfrey adhered to his unexpected determination not to do or say anything in regard to the matter, it went by default.

George viewed his visage many mornings in the oval mirror, and slept many nights in the high-post bedstead, and as for his dreams, who knows with what they dealt?

Not with Godfrey, I surmise, to whose perfect sanity George would not have sworn. At breakfast the first morning, the guest, who had taken an early walk along the bluff-top, innocently asked the cause of the irregularities in the ground. "Earthworks!" said the old man, with astounding energy, the set line of his mouth breaking into a dry smile over his coffee. He felt an advantage, and the exhilaration of a dramatic situation. George stared. He had not been thinking about the Revolutionary War, nor had it occurred to him as possible that the wolfish construction of prejudice could visit upon a person of lamb-like intentions the offences of his forefathers.

Miss Maria advertised, and seven or eight others eventually came to claim her attention and Milly's. An amiable but inactive lady, whose husband's business made it desirable that his family should go no further than the suburbs in summer, insatiably read novels in the porch. The husband himself appeared at the evening meal, and absently discussed politics with Godfrey. A hammock was swung near the house, and much occupied by a very young lady, whose very young fiancé visited her semi-weekly, whelmed in his quantity of cuff and hat-brim, and bearing as a votive offering a box where sweets compacted lay. Nimble children pervaded the place, frightening the little brown squirrel that never had troubled himself to run up his tree at Milly's approach, and the tall robins that had marched fearlessly about the walks— "those bouncing red-waistcoated thrushes, you know," George Campion called them. Old Sally, too, shook her bandanna furiously at the juvenile intruders. But Milly retained the sense that Campion was the really important innovation. She could not tell whether he remained as vividly present to her grandfather, who did not return to the subject when alone with her.

George was, as she had said, very quiet; Milly thought him "hahnsome an' brave an' not tu knowin'," as Hosea Biglow said of his boys. They were very unlike, these two; and their differences, which were, however, not antagonisms, became more apparent as their acquaintance advanced—slowly advanced, invariably taking, after two steps forward, one backward step. If they chanced to have a chat of unusual length, it was sure to be followed by several days of silence, broken only by cool good-mornings and good-evenings. It seemed to George that Milly was responsible for these retrogressions; this was not the least, nor the pleasantest, of the puzzles which she presented to him. He used to sulk a little at first: he had found this expedient useful with his sisters. But he soon abandoned his injured attitude, crestfallen at finding that Milly utterly failed to perceive it. Presently she asked him some trifling question in so innocent and friendly a tone that he colored with pleasure, and answered her with one of his bright smiles. He at last accepted with resignation this unexplained law of high and low tide in their intercourse, retiring at the silent periods to his room, where he sat gazing out of window into the pine, as it were in conference with the gray figurehead stolidly confronting him, which reminded him of Quilp's battered admiral. Milly had told him that this effigy, said to have belonged to an English ship, had been, at an uncertain date, washed ashore at the foot of the bluff, and he had himself discovered the features to be intended for those of King Charles the Second. The image would stare dully back at him in the starlight; it represented the Merry Monarch as a dense fellow enough, who could never have either said anything witty or done anything wise in his lifetime. But one wild windy moonlit evening the shaken shadow of a branch imparted to the wooden eyeballs the appearance of motion; it seemed grimacing at Campion in a manner that implied a mutual understanding —at which comicality George burst into loud laughter. But perhaps this many-seasoned exile, carved by English hand from English tree in the likeness of the buried majesty of England, had really an idea to express to the younger, flesh-and-blood Briton. "Aha! you've come at last, you've come at last, after all the years I've waited for a kinsman, sitting perched in the pine as my original sat in the oak after Worcester, looking down on fanatical prejudice. They were bitter against us here for a while, coz—too bitter. It couldn't last—nothing unnatural lasts; nature goes on—goes on—on—"

The creaking of the image as it rubbed against the tree-trunk was lost in a swell of the wind that made the great pine toss its branches up to heaven and moan. Between the dark arms glimmered the ever-moving river, its moonlit ripples pulsing as in the figures of a dance.

Milly was not in fact capricious. She looked upon Campion's society as forbidden fruit—a fruit which she enjoyed tasting, not so much because it was pleasant as because it was not indigenous, and she was curious. Her curiosity was forever bringing her to the tree, and her conscience was forever driving her away again. She knew that it must displease her grandfather to see her in conversation with George; but her grandfather was not always present to be displeased, and surely it was the part of wisdom to improve one's opportunities of conversing with a person who had walked quite as a matter of course all those London streets with the odd, familiar names—who, as a boy at school, had actually fagged! Milly was not widely read, but she had caught from her reading a little of the English flavor; and she received George as an agreeable enlargement of her experience.

In August, Campion had a vacation of ten days, during which he hung much about the house, throwing himself, in the intervals between his long rambles, on the warm grass with a book, oftenest some dog-eared volume of Dickens, half of whose novels he knew by heart. To Milly's astonishment, however, he regarded with the next degree of liking certain ultra-American works which pictured in huge outlines and violent colors the rough life of the West. It was all new and enticing to him; if it was unreal or exaggerated, he did not know that. It seemed as though some deep vein of romance, lying all encrusted with neat conventionalities, was touched in the young man by these tales of adventure; it was the same quality that was stirred in the breasts of the young Englishmen of the sixteenth century by stories of the wonderful West, narrated by some returned adventurer " with a blacke sonne-burned face," perhaps to dashing blades in the aisle of Paul's, perhaps to an open-eyed audience of smock-frocked rustics in the ale-house of his native village.

George expected Milly to like these books, even to be able to throw light on obscure passages. He was much surprised to find that she preferred some "awfully slow" English fictions, which sent him to sleep. Did she like that every-day sort of thing—really, now, really? She should see the place at Chalksley, in

Wiltshire, where his mother lived, in a little old dark red house with a mossy peaked roof, and a great black-green hedge around the garden as high as your head. In such a direction you could see the chalk wolds; this was woodland; down here the cottages; the inn; the church, more than half covered with ivy; and over there ran the Curl, the tiny, pretty river, where— At this point George began to babble of trout and grayling, of March browns, cock-a-bundies, and yellow Sallys. Stay—that matter of the church: there was something rather curious about that. He had seen from the bluff-top one so much like it down in the hollow; would she walk with him a little way along that path?

Milly had nothing else to do at that minute, and she strolled along at his side across the parched grass, to which he objected as they went. "At home·the fields keep green—such a green! Our weather's so much softer. You can hardly get such a green in the parks here, for all your pains." The sun had looked upon George himself as well as the field; the even bronze was becoming to his manly countenance; he was not exactly one to be always regarded merely as an impersonal extension of a young woman's experience.

"And all this, now"—he deprecated the yet flowerless stalks of the golden-rod— "these weeds—"

"Oh, wait till you see them in bloom!" cried Milly, with transient indignation.

"Ah! perhaps. There!"—turning, he swept his hand to the northeast—"that's not at all unlike the church at Chalksley, except that one misses the ivy, you know." He seemed to find the resemblance friendly and pleasing.

"That's the church where I go," said Milly. "I have a class in the Sunday-school there."

Oh, had she a class, really?—(of course he said clahss). His sister Fanny taught the cottage children; his sister Fanny was so fond of doing good. He became at once desirous of discovering more coincidences. Did Milly paint in water-colors? Not at all. His sister Emily painted quite sweetly in water-colors; if he had but brought some of her nice little bits, he could give Milly an idea of the country about Chalksley. Tennyson—did she admire Tennyson? Ah, indeed! So did his sister Bell; she doted on the Idyls. Milly was amused as well as interested; she did

not think she doted on anything. George's sisters would have been surprised at the frankness of fraternal affection developed in their idol by the interposition of so many liquid leagues.

By this time Milly and Campion, in the course of their homeward saunter, had come again to the sandstone cenotaph overlooking the river. They mechanically seated themselves on the wide ledge afforded by its base. George had long ago read the inscription, against which he was now resting his broad shoulders, and Milly knew it as we know rhymes conned in childhood:

"In Memory of Lieutenant DAVID PINKNEY, eldest Son of Mr. PETER PINKNEY, who died at Sea on the 17th of May, 1814, aged 20 yrs. & 3 mos., of Wounds received in the service of his Country during the disastrous Action between the U. S. frigate Ilex and his Britannic Majesty's ships Dian and Cupido. "NUNC ILLUM FLUCTUS HABET."

"It was two to one, child—two to one," Godfrey had told the little girl long ago. He had explained to her what the scrap of Latin meant: it was the only Latin he knew. The child had had her fancies about this lonely memorial; it used to seem to her that the crickets in summer echoed about it, in monotonous mourning cadence, those strange, significant words: "fluctus—habet! fluctus—habet! fluctus —habet!" They were repeating this burden now, but Milly did not hear it; her thoughts were not busied with that young great-uncle whom the far-off wave possessed.

"Ah! Miss Milly, there's no place like the home one remembers as a boy," resumed Campion, tritely and sincerely— "at least till a man has made a new home for himself." He sighed.

A sudden ripple passed through the oak leaves overhead. "The wind's rising," said Milly. "Isn't it refreshing after the hot day? But you didn't come here straight from home; you lived awhile in London, didn't you?" she asked.

"Oh, not very long," said he. "I heard of an opportunity here; it promised well, but it hasn't—ah—panned out." He involuntarily made a droll face as he uttered this Westernism. Milly laughed. "So that I may not remain; I sha'n't, if I can do better. I'd like the West immensely. I've a friend a sheep-farmer in Colorado."

"You'd like to get away from the beaten track," said the girl.

"That I would," he cried.

"'Oh, who would cast and balance at a desk,
    Perched like a crow upon a three-legg'd stool,'

if he could do anything else? But it's all
as uncertain as—where that moth's going." He made a futile lurch after the
winged wanderer with his hat. "I dare
say I shall end by going to clerk it in
New Orleans, for all my thinking about
the sheep farm. There may be an opening, as the fellow in Dickens used to say—
Herbert Pocket, wasn't it? My cousin
down there may help me to an opening."

"Oh, have you a cousin in New Orleans?" asked Milly. "But an Englishman, of course."

"I fancy," said the young man, "my
cousin Fleming thinks himself quite an
American by this time. He's my mother's cousin; he came over when he was
a mere lad. In point of fact, he fought
in your war—for the Lost Cause, as I believe you say; he's a colonel, or something."

"We must be going back," said Milly.
"The tea-bell will ring in a minute."
She rose at once, and began to walk quick-
ly along the path.

George did not divine the cause of her
apparent slight discomfiture. "I beg a
thousand pardons for plaguing you with
my plans," said he.

"Oh, I'm interested," said Milly, with
a somewhat penitent side glance. "But
it's so late."

The sky was in truth rosy with sunset,
and around the subtly desecrated cenotaph
the changeless refrain of the crickets was
increasing in volume as the night came
on. "Him the sea hath—him the sea
hath," rose the querulous chorus from
the ground, quite drowning the soft
wash of the river against its bank as it
flowed on under the sunset, under the
twilight, under the rising and the setting
of the stars. How many of these insect
lives it should outlast!

Milly sat with her aunt in the dining-
room that evening, occupied with her
fancy-work, when Godfrey entered, chuck-
ling, newspaper in hand. "Where's the
girl?" said he. "Milly, I want you to
listen. Here's the *best* article."

He seated himself opposite her, drew
the lamp near him, folded the paper to the
width of two columns for convenience,
and gave a cough of preparation. "You've

always thought," he remarked, as prologue, "that I was peculiar in my feelings about some things. Now you'll see
what a member of the House of Representatives of the United States"—he gave
the grand title its due emphasis—"what
a Congressman, Milly, with the interests
of our country in view, thinks fit to write
to the paper about them things."

The signature toward which he jour-
neyed with tremulous delight through an
epistle of unmerciful length was that of a
political Nestor of local fame, who was
drizzling a shower of rhetoric, hitherto suppressed by some unkindly circumstance,
upon the public through the press. He
assailed British morals and manners, in-
cidentally slaying an actress or two and
several noblemen; fulminated against the
fashionable Anglomania, scathing at one
fell swoop the latest lecturing lion and
the prevalent pernicious mutton-chop
whisker; and closed with such a liberal
display of national pyrotechnics as is now
seldom seen.

Milly was shocked. She now became
conscious, with a leap of the blood, that
somehow her vulnerability had been extended as well as her experience. Formerly assumptions of aboriginal war-
paint had only made her smile. She did
not smile at all as Godfrey, having concluded, leaned back exhausted by the five-
barred words he had taken at a bound,
but with triumph radiating through his
exhaustion. His own feeling, seen to be
shared by a member of the House of Representatives of the United States, assumed
new and heroic proportions—was raised,
as it were, upon the tragic buskin.

"Now ain't that *good?* Don't ye—
don't ye like it?" he asked, with eagerness.
Surely she, even she, who had till now remained neutral, must be convinced by
language of such might from an authority
of such magnitude.

"I don't think it's very fair," said Milly, rising with assumed indifference. She
had a little red spot on each cheek. To
Godfrey, looking darkly after her, it seemed the scarlet seal of all he hated most,
set by malicious fate upon the creature
that most he loved.

"That"—he hesitated for an epithet—
"that *Englishman*," he said, turning
upon the nervously anticipative Maria,
"sha'n't pass another day under this roof.
It's *mine!*" He lifted his shaking hand.

"Grandfather," Miss Banks besought

him, "don't you be rash. What reason could you give? And there's something about Milly that I guess you don't just see. She ain't caring now about this young man; but don't you let her feel that he's wrongly treated. I know her father's way, and she's Webster Banks right over again, if she *don't* look like him."

So the little whirligig of Time brought in its revenges. This speech of Maria's, uttered with complete unconsciousness, avenged with one exquisite stiletto-thrust the sneers of a decade past. She was not his—she never had been his; she was her dead father's; and none could say whose she might be to-morrow.

Milly had a weird dream just before dawn. She thought herself in the garden, which was filled with flowers she had never seen growing there, and George Campion was beside her, and they stopped to gather a rose from the bush she knew, which was all abloom and a-blush as if it were June—when out from behind the horse-chestnut stepped David Pinkney, dressed as in his portrait, and frowning, and with a drawn sword in his hand. Milly sprang forward and caught his arm. "But the waves have you—the waves have you!" she cried in terror. "The waves have *you!*" he answered her, "and they carry you whither they would." Then, in a heart-beat's time, the youth died out of his indignant face as a fire dies; it became her grandfather's, and she awoke.

That day was the last of George Campion's vacation, and in the afternoon he sauntered down and around the hill to the worm-eaten dock to try, with improvised tackle, his fortune at his favorite craft. He was as untroubled in mind as a piscator should be, for Godfrey had taken Maria's counsel and had said nothing. As for Milly, she had been invited to go out in a sail-boat by the very young lady of the hammock and her semi-weekly Mr. Slender. Godfrey thought it a favorable opportunity to visit Dr. Nixon's office in the city. He waited a long time in a room with a depressingly scientific atmosphere; he was so reduced in spirit by his surroundings that, when the doctor at last appeared, he made but a feeble protest and appeal. The man of science and action said but a few reasonable words before Godfrey felt that he had made a fool of himself pleading antique sentiment with that impartial audience of osseous facts. But his impotent rage returned

in the open air. As, nearing his home, he ascended the hill from the eastern side he struck at the lemon-and-orange toad-flax that bordered the way with his knotted stick. "Summer's going," he said to himself with an angry joy, feeling an autumn suggestion in the altered weather. The summer could not go too soon for him.

As he crossed the rustic bridge over the bed of the brook long dry he could catch a glimpse between two hillocks of the purple-gray river. How it had changed during the afternoon! He had left it smoky-blue and smooth, and enlivened with white sails. The day had become sad-colored and vaguely regretful.

He went in at the entrance in the rear—that being nearest—passed through the empty dining-room, and sat down to rest in one of the tall chairs in the square hall, leaning his elbow on the table under his brother's picture. The ponderous front door, as usual, stood open, and the sound of an excited voice in narration came to Godfrey's ears from the porch; he recognized it by its consequential tone as that of the shrill Al Slender.

"Of course, you see, *I* went for Hattie; it was my first impulse. Any man naturally feels—"

The sound grated upon Godfrey, who had a Spartan contempt for this modern youth. "When *I* was a Boy," he was wont to say, "I was a *Boy;* and when I got to be a *Man*, I *was* a Man." He had risen to leave the distasteful neighborhood, but was arrested by the foot-fall of Maria Banks as she came down the stair. There was an inexplicable something in the modulation of this foot-fall that touched the springs of memory; calamity was indescribably suggested. Godfrey threw back his head and scowled scrutinizingly at her.

"You've heard about it, grandfather? They told you?" she said, with quivering eagerness.

"What did they tell me?" asked Godfrey, gruffly. Then he noticed her paleness and her tear-filled eyes.

"She's all right now," she went on, as though in her agitation she had not been able to receive his words with understanding. "We had a time bringing her 'round. Under Providence, I can't think what we don't owe to that young man."

"What's happened? Where's Milly? What young man?" cried Godfrey, trembling. "Good Lord, *can't* ye tell me?"

"The boat— There, now, he's coming

down. Do say something to him—do, grandfather. Just think, he's saved our Milly's life!"

Miss Maria seized Godfrey's wrist in her anxiety that he should for once be gracious to George Campion, who, settling his neck in an exceedingly stiff fresh collar, and wearing the bored expression of an undemonstrative man who presages a scene, was now descending the stair.

Godfrey caught at the table with a groan; his face was terribly convulsed for a moment. The next, he mastered himself sufficiently to speak Campion's name. George approached; the two men stood on the spot where they had first met.

"If what I'm told—if what I'm told's the truth," Godfrey contrived to say, "I owe you, sir"—oh, what those three words cost him!—"more'n I can ever pay." He stretched out his hand and gave George's a fierce grip.

"I beg—I *beg* you won't say anything more about it," said Campion, shamefacedly; then found it convenient to merge his embarrassment in wrath. "The boat never would have capsized except for the carelessness of that crass idiot," said he, with a compression of the lips and blue glare of the eyes that have been English since the battle of Brunanburg.

Godfrey wrung his hand once more, and broke weakly away. He seemed choking; he leaned out of window, and the breeze played in his curly white hair. Was it the sight of these blowing curls that in some strange way made Maria Banks feel sorry as for a suffering child? In that instant the first cord of sympathy bridged the gulf between their souls.

Campion being of a race that flees with horror from thanks, it was inevitable that this event should be followed by a period of constraint; but the veil of formality grew thinner and thinner, and at last disappeared, never to be drawn again between him and Milly. No more sudden chillinesses, no more conversations broken sharply off, with a pang of remorse on Milly's part, at Godfrey's approaching step. George had his right now—a right well won; she would not deny him her friendship, since he evidently desired it. She gave up balancing her conduct between duty and inclination; she ceased, with a long sigh of relief, to keep watch upon herself. The fleet weeks flew; the summer sojourners departed. George Campion was the last to go. The mild

days of early autumn arrived; the blufftop was glorified with a spouting and swaying fulvous flood, the fountain-shaped sprays of the golden-rod intensifying with their rich contrasting color the pure ethereal blue of the hills beyond the river. The fawn-colored leaves of the oaks around the cenotaph of David Pinkney had a crispness as of light irony in their laughter when on the Sunday afternoon before Campion's departure he and Milly rested there, as they had done many times since their first walk together. On this particular day they had found a great deal to say to each other, and the tenor of what they had said may be gathered from George's first words, as, leaning back against the stone, he thoughtfully stirred an acorn in the dry grass with his foot.

"I wanted to speak to him first, you know," he said; "but, in fact, he didn't seem to wish to see me this morning. And really I couldn't wait."

"You mustn't speak to him," cried Milly, her happiness suddenly invaded. "You don't know him at all; it would be so much harder for him to hear it from you. It would be unbearable." George lifted his brows, with a mental note of the unimagined supersensitiveness of grandfathers. "I'll tell him," she went on; "but I must have a little time to think just how. I don't feel used to it yet myself."

"My darling," said he, smiling down at her as though he thought she would soon be used to it. "There's one thing we haven't spoken of," he began, after a silent interval. Milly looked at him with expectant eyes. They had been exchanging the thousand illuminated reminiscences and explanations of trivialities natural to the occasion, and she was hungry for one more. "Oh, it's nothing of any importance, you know," said George; "it's merely how we are to live."

Milly laughed. It seemed to her absurdly inconsequent. The dry oak leaves shook with amusement over her head. Was this the same young person who had passed under them in June prudently planning?

"You surely didn't suppose," said George, "that I would ask you to live on the pittance I've been getting?"

"I didn't think anything at all about it," said she. "And I don't know what you've been getting."

"Ah, true," said George, confused.

"It wasn't much, and I had to drudge for it in the busy season, I can tell you. But I've a fine chance now, and it's that that has—emboldened me, you know."

"Oh, is it that?" said Milly. He saw that she was laughing at him, and giving way, laughed at himself, blushing red. Both knew that he must in any event have spoken some telltale word that day.

"But seriously, now," he resumed, "something *has* turned up. I'm to go in January—Milly, you'd be willing to go a great way off with me? Say you would. Ah! I know you would." But none the less he scrutinized her face anxiously.

"Over the hills and far away," said Milly. "To the ends of the earth, George, if you must." Then, shaking off some embarrassment at the earnestness she thought too evident under her light words, "Do you want me to preside over a cattle ranch?" she asked, gayly, alluding to his passion for the untried West.

"Ah, not quite," said he, relieved. "It's a different kind of life that's offered me; less primitive, but more practical, if a man expects to marry." A shade of sadness crossed his face as he relinquished forever all thought of Colorado.

It passed through Milly's mind in a flash that he had been called back to England. She had just time to recognize that her startled feeling at this turn of affairs had a strange element of pleasure, before the idea was dispelled. George drew a letter from his breast pocket. "My cousin Fleming, you know, down there in New Orleans—" he began.

Milly sprang up. "Oh, George, anything but that! Don't ask me—you can't ask me—to live at the South!"

He regarded her with astonishment, setting his lips rather grimly. "I don't understand you," said he.

"No, you don't! Oh, you *can't!*" cried Milly, in despair. "How can I make you understand?"

"It's one of those chances," said George, with a quiet sternness, returning the letter to its envelop, "that come to a fellow only once in his lifetime." He left her, and paced back and forth along the bluff-top.

She stood alone by the monument, patting her hand nervously against the stone. Yes, he had spoken of this before; why had it not at once recurred to her? But I have said that her animosities had not yet petrified; and the force opposed to them was surprising to herself. In a few minutes she stole up behind him and slipped her hand into his arm. "George," she said. He turned a pale, disappointed countenance upon her. "Dear," she whispered, "don't look like that. I'll go—indeed I'll go. It was only that I didn't expect it." He put his arm around her and kissed her there under the oaks. There was a glow in her hazel eyes no one but himself had ever seen; it warmed his heart. He thought her face beautiful just then, but he did not fully read its expression. He could no more realize that she was at that minute assuming a heavy burden for his sake than she could appreciate the certainty of its diminution with the coming years.

They loitered longer in the golden field, and he brought her a spray of the splendid flower for her belt. "You had the most immense white daisies in your belt the first time I saw you," said he. "You wore a white gown."

"Oh, you remember that!" said Milly.

The breeze took the loose strands of her hair, and the sun transmuted them to gold beside the sweet curve of her fair cheek. She wound her long dark blue veil around her throat. "How it blows! and see, how wild the river is to-day!—all white-caps. Listen: you can hear its dash so plainly."

It was summer again. Workmen had begun to level those softly rounded rises that told of old-time war, clothed as they were with the high grass in fragrant gray-green flower. The monument of David Pinkney was protected by a new iron railing, bestowed upon it by the powers as an act of compensatory justice. The bluff-top was progressing, through a period of chaos, toward the trig, unindividual prettiness of a park, where the well-kept lawns should be forever of a truly English emerald. It saddened Godfrey to look southward; when he sat, as now, in the porch, his eyes habitually rested upon the river in its steady, peaceful flow.

They so rested this Sunday evening while he talked with Miss Maria and Dr. Nixon, and the physician noted the change; Godfrey had been wont to confront him with the direct, stern gaze of an eagle.

"I must say I was 'most afraid to have her try it," said Miss Maria; "I was afraid she wouldn't make friends down there. I don't know but what Milly was prejudiced; maybe I was myself. And I guess it *wasn't* all smooth sailing at first, though she never said a word in her letters. But she writes now, since *he* had that little sick turn, that she couldn't ask for more kindness—such a whole-hearted, generous set of folks!"

"Oh, well, prejudice wears off, you know," said the doctor. "No time for prejudice in this stage of the world. Did well enough in the Middle Ages. People have come to look at things practically. I always thought Milly was sensible."

"Yes, sir," said the old man, with his riverward look; "prejudice wears away. It wears away, I've found."

"Grandfather's wearing away himself," said Maria, softly, nodding after him as he shambled off to his garden seat under the horse-chestnut tree.

"Yes, he's failing," assented the doctor, gravely but easily.

"He's *suffered*," said Maria. "It was a blow to him, losing Milly." She looked at Dr. Nixon in a peculiar way; but he did not seem oppressed by any morbid sense of his own responsibility.

Whatever Godfrey had suffered, he was not all unhappy as he sat under his blossomed tree at sunset. His was the calm that comes, after struggle, of submission to the Will that utters the rivers like speech, and of which the steady stream of Time itself is but an agent and a minister.

THE REAPERS.

BY WILL WALLACE HARNEY.

WHEN the tired reapers, with fragrant sheaves,
  Come out of the corn, as the sun goes down,
And the sky is rich as the falling leaves
  In crimson and purple and golden brown,
I sit in the mellow and marvellous eves
And watch, as the loom of the sunset weaves
  Its cloth of gold over country and town.

And I think how the summers have come and gone
  Since we saw the shuttle across the blue
That wove the colors of dusk and dawn
  When the musk of the sleeping roses flew
On the wings of the south wind over the lawn,
And the evening shadows were longer drawn,
  And the sun was low, and the stars were few;

When Love was sweet in the lives we led
  As the leaven that lives in the latter spring
To grow in the flowers, the books we read,
  The romp and rush of the grape-vine swing,
In words and work, to be filled and fed
On brooks of honey and wasted bread,
  And sung in the songs that we used to sing.

And out of the shadows they come to me,
  As flowers of the spring come, year by year,
The lovers we had when to love was free,
  The stars were few and the skies were clear,
And we knew it was happiness just to be,
Through the sheaves of the cloud-land fair to see,
  While the weary reapers are drawing near.

Though the red and white roses have lost their leaves
  In the ashes of summers of long ago,
They come, through the mellow and marvellous eves,
  With the harvest of love that we used to sow,
As rich as the garlands the sunset weaves
When the tired reapers with fragrant sheaves
  Come out of the corn and the sun is low.

UNITED STATES NAVAL ARTILLERY.

BY REAR-ADMIRAL EDWARD SIMPSON, U.S.N.

FROM the time of the introduction of cast-iron cannon in 1558 until a comparatively late period, development in naval artillery proceeded at a very slow rate. The security that was attained by the adoption of cast-iron was so great, as compared with the danger attending the use of the more ancient artillery, that the new guns were regarded as fully supplying all the demands of a suitable battery. The guns were muzzle-loaders, making the manipulation simple, the previous rude attempts at breech-loading being abandoned. The number of calibres that were introduced was very numerous, partly to suit the weight of the batteries to the ships,

BRONZE BREECH-LOADING CANNON CAPTURED IN COREA, AGE UNKNOWN.

and partly to accommodate the fancy of the time for placing in different parts of the ships guns varying much in size and destructive effect. The general character of the batteries and the multiplication of calibres can best be illustrated by noting the armament of two typical ships of the seventeenth century.

The *Royal Prince*, a British ship built in 1610, carried 55 guns. Of these, two were *cannon-petronel*, or 24-pounders; six were *demi-cannon*, medium 32-pound-

ers; twelve were *culverins*, 18-pounders, which were nine feet long; eighteen were *demi-culverins*, 9-pounders; thirteen were *rakers*, 5-pounders, six feet long; and four were *port-pieces*, probably swivels. These guns were disposed as follows: on the lower gun-deck, two 24-pounders, six medium 32-pounders, and twelve 18-pounders; on the upper gun-deck the battery was entirely of 9-pounders; and the forecastle and quarter-deck were armed with 5-pounders, and the brood of smaller

BRONZE BREECH-LOADER USED BY CORTEZ IN MEXICO.

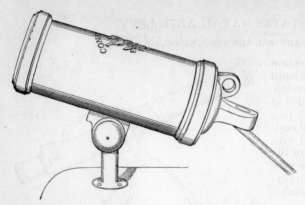

BREECH-LOADER CAPTURED IN THE WAR WITH MEXICO.

gagements between the English and Dutch ships, which were sometimes protracted through three days.

The brood of "murdering pieces" of small calibre and little energy was, after many years, dispersed by the introduction of carronades—a short cannon of large calibre, which was found to be a convenient substitute for the 8-pounders and 9-pounders on upper decks, and for the "lighter ordnance," which was ineffective; but this change was brought about slowly, as is seen by referring to the batteries of some ships which fought at Trafalgar.

pieces which swelled the nominal armament.

The *Sovereign of the Seas*, built in 1637, in the reign of Charles I., was unequalled by any ship afloat in her time. She mounted on three gun-decks 86 guns. On the lower deck were thirty long 24-pounders and medium 32-pounders; on her middle deck, thirty 12-pounders and 9-pounders; on the upper gun-deck,

The Spanish seventy-fours in that action had fifty-eight long 24-pounders on the gun-decks; on the spar-deck, ten iron 36-pounder carronades and four long 8-pounders; and on the poop, six iron 24-pounder carronades—total, 78 guns.

The *Victory*, the English flag-ship, mounted on her three gun-decks ninety

BRONZE 12-POUNDER, "EL NEPTUNO," 1781.

long 32-, 24-, and 12-pounders; and on the quarter-deck and forecastle, ten long 12-pounders and two 68-pounder carronades.

The *Santissima Trinidada* mounted on the lower gun-deck thirty long 36-pounders; on the second deck, thirty-two long 18-pounders; on the third deck, thirty-two long 12-pounders; and on the spar-deck, thirty-two 8-pounders. In the British accounts she is said to have had 140 guns, which number must have included swivels mounted for the occasion.

At the end of the eighteenth century the 18-pounder was the preferred gun for the main-deck batteries of frigates, guns of larger calibre being found only on the lower decks of line-of-battle ships. The 18-pounder was the maximum calibre that was employed on the ships of the United

"other lighter ordnance"; and on her quarter-deck and forecastle, "numbers of murdering pieces."

In the obstinately contested actions between Blake and Van Tromp in the Cromwellian time, the ships and batteries did not differ in any great degree from those contemporaneous in construction with the *Sovereign of the Seas*, and when we remember the inferior character of the powder used in those days, we can account for the duration of some of the en-

Colonies of North America in the war of the Revolution. The resources of the colonies did not admit of building ships to contend with vessels fit to take their place in line of battle, but such as were constructed were well adapted to resist the small British cruisers, and to capture transports and store-ships. The so-called frigates of that day were vessels varying from six hundred to a thousand tons, and, according to their capacity, carried 12-pounders or 18-pounders in the main-deck batteries. There was usually no spar-deck, but the forecastle and quarter-deck, which were connected by gangways with gratings over the intermediate space, were provided with an armament of light 6-, 9-, or 12-pounders. A few carronades came into use during this war.

At the conclusion of this war the Colonial fleet disappeared, and it was not until the time of the depredations on the growing commerce of the United States by the Algerine corsairs that the Congress felt justified in incurring the expense of establishing a national marine. The ships which were built under the law of 1794 were fully up to the most advanced ideas of the time, and some of these ships carried on their gun-decks a full battery of 24-pounders, thirty in number, while the others were armed with 18-pounders on the gun-deck, with spar-deck batteries of 9- and 12-pounders, the carronade not having been yet definitely adopted for spar-deck batteries.

It is not until the war of 1812 that we find the carronade fully established as the spar-deck armament of frigates. The *Constitution* and the *Guerrière* carried 32-pounder carronades of very similar

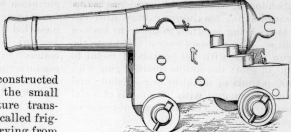

U. S. N. MEDIUM 32-POUNDER.

weight and power, in the place of the long guns of smaller calibre, on the spar-deck. The original name of this piece of ordnance was the "Smasher," the leading purpose of the inventor, General Melville, of the British artillery, being to fire 68-pounder shot with a low charge, thus effecting a greater destruction in a ship's timbers by the increased splintering which this practice was known to produce. Carronades of small calibre were subsequently cast, which were adopted for spar-deck batteries of frigates and line-of-battle ships; and, as they grew in favor, formed the entire battery of sloops of war and smaller vessels until about 1840, when the attention that had been given for some years to the subject of naval ordnance began to assume tangible shape, and the effort was made to proceed in this matter in accordance with an intelligent system.

The advantage of large calibre was firmly impressed upon those who occupied themselves with the ordnance matters of the navy. As the fleet was developed, the 24-pounder gave way to the 32-pounder, and for the lower-deck battery of line-of-battle ships the 42-pounder was introduced. Some 42-pounder carronades were also introduced as spar-deck batteries for these larger ships. With the disappearance of this class of ship, the 42-pounder was

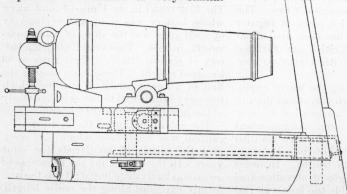

U. S. N. CARRONADE, SLIDE, AND CARRIAGE.

abandoned, and the 32-pounder was retained as the maximum calibre, different classes being assigned to different sizes of ships. These classes were divided into the gun proper, with 150 pounds of metal to one of shot; the double-fortified gun, with 200 pounds of metal to one of shot; and the medium gun, with 100 pounds of metal to one of shot. The carronade of the same calibre, mounted on a slide, had a proportional weight of 65 pounds of metal to one of shot.

In the interval between 1840 and 1845 the double-fortified 32-pounder was replaced by a gun of the same calibre of 57 hundred-weight, called the long 32-pounder, and to suit the capacity of the different classes of ships then in the service there were introduced the 32-pounders of 46 hundred-weight, 42 hundred-weight, and 27 hundred-weight, in addition to the regular medium gun of 32 hundred-weight. This period also marks the introduction of shell guns as part of the battery.

To this time no explosive projectiles had been used with cannon properly so called; their use had been limited to mortars and howitzers. The mortar was originally used for projecting huge balls of stone at high angles. The first practical use made of them for projecting bombs was in 1624, but the unwieldy weight of the mortar and its bomb, the latter sometimes exceeding 300 pounds, prevented their use in field operations. To provide for this, light mortars were cast, which, being mounted on wheels, were denominated howitzers. Frederick the Great of Prussia brought this form of artillery to its highest development for field and siege use, and the Continental powers of Europe adopted it to a large extent for projecting bombs at high angles of fire. The mortar has never had a place in regular naval armaments; it has been used afloat for bombardment of cities and fortified positions, but never with a view to contending with ships.

The success attending the use of explosive projectiles at high elevations did not lead at once to their application to horizontal firing from cannon. An important link in the progress of the idea resulted from the effort to avail of the advantage of ricochet firing with bombs. In order to effect this, the angle of elevation had to be reduced to enable the bomb to roll along the ground. The reduced angle of elevation was still greater than that used for cannon, but the success of the experiment led to the casting by the French of an VIII-inch siege howitzer, which, in connection with the development in the manufacture of fuses, made it practicable to apply the idea of firing shells, like shot, horizontally, and the chief object in view seems to have been to operate against ships.

The combining of the elements necessary for the achievement of this important step in naval artillery is by common consent credited to General Paixhans, of the French artillery, who, though not claiming the invention of any of the numerous details involved in the system, succeeded in so judiciously arranging the parts as to make the system practicable by which the whole character of naval armaments was revolutionized.

Following the progressive ideas of the age, shell guns were introduced in the United States navy. These were of VIII-inch calibre, and of weights of 63 hundred-weight and 55 hundred-weight. The guns were shaped in accordance with the form adopted by General Paixhans, and were easily distinguishable in the battery from the ordinary shot gun; from this circumstance they obtained the title of Paixhan-guns, though there was nothing special in the gun itself to merit an appellation. The whole system was Paixhans's; the gun was only a part of the system.

It required many years to bring the shell gun into such general application as to displace the solid-shot gun. They were assigned tentatively to ships in commission, and in 1853, by a navy regulation, the battery of a frigate was provided with only ten of these guns, which were collected in one division on the gun-deck. The first vessel in the United States navy whose battery was composed exclusively of shell guns was the sloop of war *Portsmouth*, in 1856. This vessel carried a battery of sixteen VIII-inch shell guns of 63 hundred-weight. These were among the first of a new pattern of gun for which the navy is indebted to the skill and study of the late Rear-Admiral Dahlgren.

The determination of the best form for cannon was a question which had occupied the minds of artillerists for some years. In the older guns the thickness of metal was badly distributed; it was too uniformly extended along the entire length, not arranged in such proportions as to

U. S. N. IX-INCH DAHLGREN (IX-INCH SMOOTH-BORE).

accord with the differing strains along the bore. Colonel Bumford, of the United States ordnance, had been among the first to consider this subject, and for many years the results of his experiments had guided construction to a great degree. General Paixhans made a farther step in advance by reducing very much the thickness of metal along the chase of his guns, but it remained for Rear-Admiral Dahlgren to produce the perfection of form in the gun so widely known bearing his name. In this gun the thickness of metal is proportioned to the effort of the gases in the bore, and all projections and angular changes of form are suppressed, giving to all parts a curved and rounded surface. The suppression of angular formations on the exterior of a casting has a remarkable effect on the arrangement of the crystals while cooling; these arrange themselves normal to the cooling waves, which, if entering from directions not radial with the cylindrical casting, produce confusion in their arrangement, establishing planes of weakness where the waves meet, which, in case of overstrain on the piece, assist rupture and determine the course of the fracture.

With the introduction of the Dahlgren shell gun, the transition of the artillery of the United States navy may be said to have been completed. The shell gun of IX-inch and XI-inch calibres followed the VIII-inch, and ships were armed with such as were appropriate to their capacity as rapidly as the new guns could be manufactured. When fully equipped, the armament of the United States navy was superior to that of any other navy in the world.

The substitution of shells for solid shot marks an important epoch in naval artillery. The probable effect of a shot could be predetermined and provided for; that of a shell was unknown. In order to produce serious injury with a shot, it was necessary to perforate the side of an enemy. This was not indispensable with a shell; with the latter, perforation might be dispensed with, as penetration to such a depth as would give efficacy to the explosion might prove more destructive to the hull than would absolute perforation. With the shot, damage was done to life and material in detail; with the shell, if successfully applied, destruction was threatened to the entire fabric, with all it contained. Naval artillery entered a new phase; the rough appliances of the past would no longer answer all demands. The founder could not alone equip the battery; the laboratory was called into use and pressed to provide from its devices. The "new arm" depended upon the successful working of the fuse of the shell, without which it was but a hollow substitute for a solid shot, and this detail demanded the utmost care in preparation. It was the perfecting of this device which, more than aught else, delayed the general adoption of the new artillery for so long a time after its advantages had been recognized.

The fuses that were used to explode the

ancient bombs were long wooden plugs bored cylindrically, and filled with powder condensed by tamping it to a hard consistency. The fuse case projected from the bomb, and to avoid being bent by the shock of discharge, was placed carefully in the axis of fire. Before the discharge of the mortar the fuse was lighted by a match. In applying the fuse to shell guns fired horizontally, the problem was so to arrange it as to ignite it by the flame of discharge, and so to support it in the wall of the shell as to prevent any dislocation of the fuse composition, the cracking of which would permit the penetration of the flame into the mass. This was successfully accomplished, and the United States navy fuse was justly famous, one feature of it being a simple but most effective device called a "water-cap," which guarded against the injurious introduction of sand or water when the shell was fired *en ricochet*. The introduction of a safety-plug in the bottom of the fuse case, which required the shock of discharge to displace it in order to open a way of communication between the fuse and the bursting charge in the shell, and the absence of all accidents in manipulation, inspired such confidence that the new arm advanced to favor, and both officers and men were proud to be identified with it.

Previous to the introduction of shells there had been in use incendiary projectiles, not explosive, but intended to set fire to an enemy's vessel. Hot shot were applied to this purpose, but the use of these was chiefly confined to shore batteries, where a suitable heating furnace could be conveniently provided. The projectile for this purpose chiefly used from ships was the carcass, which was a shot in which several radial cylindrical holes were formed, which were filled with powder tamped to a hard consistency; these columns of composition were ignited by the flame of discharge, and continued to burn until consumed. The flame issuing from these holes served to ignite consumable material in their vicinity. The chief danger from a carcass was from lodgement in the side of a ship; if it landed on deck, it could be removed and thrown overboard, as there was no danger from explosion; the addition of the bursting charge in the cavity of a shell produced a projectile which was far in advance both for generating a flame and for preventing interference with its mission.

The probable destructive effect of shells exploding in the sides or on the open decks of ships was thoroughly recognized, and experiments at targets sufficiently proved it; but circumstances on a proving ground and in action are so dissimilar that the experience of a naval engagement was looked forward to with much interest, in order to satisfy as to the effect of the new projectile in all the varying conditions of a sea-fight. Referring to the history of the past thirty years, which marks the period of the general introduction of shell guns, it is remarkable how few engagements between ships have taken place; but on every occasion of the use of shells, when unarmored vessels were engaged, the effect has been most decided and complete. Three instances only can be referred to of purely sea-fights, viz., the engagement between the Russian and Turkish fleets at Sinope in 1853, during the Crimean war, the engagement between the United States steamer *Hatteras* and the Confederate cruiser *Alabama* during the war of the rebellion, and the fight between the *Kearsarge* and the *Alabama* during the same war. In the affair at Sinope the Russian ships used shells; the Turkish had only solid shot. The result was the total destruction of the Turkish force. Not one ship escaped; all were burned or sunk. The fight between the *Alabama* and the *Hatteras* resulted in the sinking of the *Hatteras;* and the contest between the *Alabama* and the *Kearsarge* ended the career of the *Alabama*. And it may be noticed that but for the failure to explode of a shell that was imbedded in the stern-post of the *Kearsarge*, that vessel might have accompanied her antagonist to the bottom of the sea.

The gallant attempt of Rear-Admiral Lyons with the British wooden fleet before the forts of Sebastopol is an instance which proved the uselessness of subjecting unarmored vessels to the steady fire of fortified positions using shells from their batteries.

One other instance of a sea-fight can be cited in the engagement in 1879 between two Chilian armored vessels and the lightly armored Peruvian turreted vessel *Huascar*. The *Huascar* was terribly overmatched during this fight, but at its conclusion her boilers and engines were intact, and indentations on her sides showed that her light armor had deflected a number of projectiles; but the effect of the shells that had burst on board of her was apparent in the great destruction of life.

The necessity of providing a defence against shells was recognized both by England and France during the Crimean war, and a protection of armor was supplied to some floating batteries built at that time, which were intended to operate before fortified positions; and at the conclusion of the war the English built the *Warrior*, and the French

and the racking side of the question was so obstinately held that the British government imported in 1867 from the United States a xv-inch gun for the purpose of determining by their own experiments what foundation there was for the advantages that were claimed for it. The gun was bought of Charles Alger and Co., of Boston; it weighed 19 tons, and threw a cast-iron spherical solid shot of about 450 pounds. It was mounted at

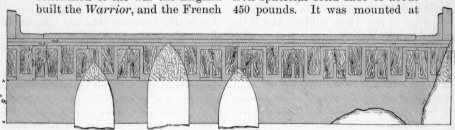

HORIZONTAL SECTION OF MILLWALL SHIELD.

built *La Gloire*. These were the first specimens of iron-clad ships of war. They were capable of resisting successfully the entrance of shells from guns of the period. It is thus seen that, almost coincident with the general adoption of horizontal shell firing, naval construction entered a new phase, and a new problem was submitted to the naval artillerist.

Against an iron-faced target the solid shot might be partially effective, but the impact of the spherical shell was harmless, and the explosive effect of the bursting charge enclosed in it would be superficial. This was amply demonstrated in actual practice during our war experience, notably at Mobile Bar in the engagement with the Confederate iron-clad *Tennessee*, the roughly constructed armor of which vessel resisted a storm of our heaviest shells.

The impotency of the spherical shell against armor being recognized by foreign governments, they proceeded to develop the rifled cannon, which with its elongated projectile offered the means of effecting the object of the time—to perforate armor with an explosive projectile. Our authorities, however, persevered in their faith in the smooth-bore, and held that the *racking* effect of a spherical projectile of sufficiently large calibre was superior to that produced by the perforation of a rifle projectile of inferior diameter. The xv-inch and xx-inch smooth-bore cannon were cast in accordance with this idea,

Shoeburyness, and was fired in competition with English rifled cannon of ix-inch and x-inch calibres. The result of the experiments went to show that, against a target with a power of resistance inferior to the energy of the projectile, the effect of the large sphere at short range is more disastrous than that of the elongated rifle projectile of the same weight; but that, against a target able to resist the total energy of both, the injury done by the rifle projectile is by far the greater. The comparative effect is well shown on a target called the "Millwall Shield," consisting of a plate nine inches in thickness, backed by Hughes's hollow stringers—an arrangement of target which, to the time of the experiment, had proved invincible. The xv-inch smooth-bore spherical shot rebounded from the target six feet, leaving a 3-inch indentation on the plate, while the ix-inch rifle projectile, weighing 250 pounds, made complete penetration of the plate, passing two or three inches into the backing, and the x-inch rifle projectile, weighing 400 pounds, penetrated to the rear of the backing itself.

During the years of inaction in the United States that have intervened since these experiments the smooth-bore partisans have had time to reflect and to learn lessons of practical usefulness from observing what has been transpiring abroad. Opportunities have been afforded to note the progress made in armor and artillery, and though the smooth-bore shell is still operative against unarmored vessels, the advantages of the rifled gun under all the circumstances of navy experiences have been admitted, and in the transition through which our naval artillery is now passing we are not embarrassed by the presentation of views antagonistic to the principles on which it has been determined our new artillery is to be constructed. The system at the basis of our present acts is founded on a comprehensive view of the whole subject, and is intended to provide our ships with a surplus of offensive power over what their capacity for defence might seem to call for.

Our navy will possess a certain number of armored vessels for coast defence, and possibly some armored sea cruisers may be included in the list, but the more numerous class will be unarmored, and the first problem to be solved is that of providing for these a suitable armament.

The work to be done by an unarmored cruiser must be done from a distance when risking an engagement with an armored enemy. The superiority of armament must compensate for deficiency in defensive power which precludes close quarters. To make these ships effective they must be armed with guns capable of doing an extraordinary amount of work, and yet the size of the vessels will not admit of their carrying guns of immense weight. In order to get this amount of work out of a comparatively light gun we must secure great initial velocity for the projectile; this can only be done by burning a large charge of powder, which involves a long bore in which to burn it, while care is necessary to secure a large margin of strength in the material of which the gun is constructed. These essential demands require a radical change in the form and material of our present armament; they also force a change in the method of construction.

The superior fitness for cannon of steel over cast-iron was recognized many years ago, but the difficulty of casting steel in large masses prevented the introduction of steel guns, and the generally acceptable treatment of cast-iron made it answer satisfactorily the demands for gun-metal not subjected to unusual strains. Mr. Frederick Krupp, of Essen, in Germany, was the first steel manufacturer who succeeded in casting steel in large masses, and he produced a number of steel guns cast from crucibles in solid ingots, which were bored, turned, and fashioned as in the case of cast-iron smooth-bore guns. These guns held a position in advance of other manufactures on the score of strength of material. But the introduction of the rifle system, the call for higher velocities, the increased charges of powder, with the consequent increase of strain, enhanced by the friction attending the passage of the projectile forced along the bore, had the effect of calling attention to the weakness that was inherent in the method of construction of cannon. It is well known that an explosive force operating in the interior of a hollow cylinder of any thickness is not felt equally throughout the wall of metal; the parts near the seat of explosion are called upon to do much more work in restraining the force generated than are the parts more remote. It has been determined that the strain brought upon the portions of the wall is in inverse proportion to the squares of their distances from the seat of effort. Thus, in a gun cast solid, if we take a point two inches from the bore, and another four inches from the bore, the strain felt at those points respectively will be inversely in the proportion of four to sixteen, or, in other words, the metal at two inches from the bore will be strained four times as much as that at the distance of four inches. From this it can be seen that the metal near the seat of effort may be strained beyond its tensile strength while that more distant is only in partial sympathy with it. Rupture thus originates at the interior portion, and the rest of the wall yields in detail. No additional strength of material can change this relationship between the parts, they result from a law, and show that this method of construction for a cannon is untrustworthy where the strains approach the tensile strength of the material.

The means of providing against this successive rupture of overstrained parts is found in the "built-up gun," in which an interior tube is surrounded by encircling hoops of metal, which are shrunk on at sufficient tension to compress the portions which they enclose. This is the principle of "initial tension," which is the basis of the modern construction of cannon. By adopting this method an ingot to form a tube to burn the required amount of powder can be cast of a light weight in comparison with what would be needed for a complete gun, and the

PUTTING THE JACKET ON A VI-INCH BREECH-LOADING RIFLE TUBE.

strength and number of reënforcing rings to be shrunk around it can be readily determined, proportioned to the known strain that will be brought upon the bore of the piece. The late developments in the manufacture of steel by the open-

BREECH-LOADING RIFLE TUBE READY FOR RECEIVING JACKET.

hearth process remove all difficulty to procuring the necessary metal in masses suitable for all parts of the heaviest guns.

The built-up steel gun is the one now adopted in Europe by the leading powers, and it is the gun with which the United States navy will be armed; but, before its final adoption, efforts were made to convert old smooth-bore cast-iron guns into rifles, and to construct new guns partially of steel and partly of wrought iron. As some of these methods of conversion offered an economical means of acquiring rifled cannon, our naval authorities were led into the error of countenancing the effort to a moderate degree.

The system that was adopted was that originally suggested by Mr. P. M. Parsons in England, which was afterward patented by Major Palliser, R.A., and bears his name. It consisted in enlarging the bore of a cast-iron gun, and inserting a tube of wrought iron formed of a bar arranged in the form of a coil when heated. The tube was expanded by firing charges of powder, and afterward rifled. The guns are muzzle-loaders, and are not increased in length beyond that of the cast-iron gun which forms the casing for the tube. The length is thus limited in order to preserve the preponderance of the piece, and because of the want of longitudinal

strength in the coil, which cannot be depended on beyond a few tons' strain; the arrangement of metal in a coil provides very well for circumferential or tangential strains, but in the Palliser conversion the longitudinal strength depends on the cast-iron casing. The idea of the coiled wrought-iron tube originated with Professor Treadwell, of Harvard University, in 1841. He utilized it by enclosing a tube of cast-iron or steel in the same manner as it is applied in the wrought-iron Armstrong and Woolwich guns.

The administration of our naval ordnance has abandoned conversions, and has concentrated its efforts on the production of an armament of built-up steel guns. The system of construction that has been adopted originated in England, but was for many years ignored by the government authorities. It involved the use of steel in all its parts, and this was charged as an objection, as confidence in this metal was not established in the minds of the English artillerists. That government committed itself entirely to the wrought-iron gun proposed by Mr. (now Sir William) Armstrong, whose system was a reproduction of that successfully experimented on by Professor Treadwell, and the entire force of the government works at Woolwich and of the Armstrong works at Elswick-on-the-Tyne was occupied with the production of this style of ordnance. The English steel gun invented by Captain Blakely and Mr. J. Vavasseur was ignored in England, but its merit could not be suppressed, and its superiority has forced a tardy recognition by that government.

This gun came prominently into notice for a short time at the breaking out of the war of the rebellion: some guns were imported for the service of the Southern States. At the exhibition in London in 1862 a Blakely 8.5-inch gun was one of the features of attraction in the department of ordnance. The principle of the construction was shown in this gun, consisting in shrinking a long jacket of steel around an enclosed steel tube, the jacket extending to the trunnions. Mr. Vavasseur was the manager of the London Ordnance Works, and was associated with Captain Blakely in the manufacture of

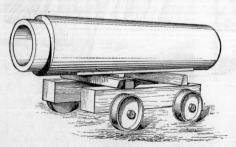

BREECH-LOADING RIFLE JACKET ROUGH BORED AND TURNED.

his earlier guns, but the entire business soon fell into the hands of Mr. Vavasseur, whose name alone is associated with the succeeding developments of the gun.

In 1862 the guns manufactured by Mr. Krupp were solid forgings. He advanced but slowly toward the construction of built-up cannon, and it was not until the failure of some of his solid-cast guns that he entered on the built-up system. His first steps were to strengthen the rear portion of new guns by shrinking on hoops, and to increase the strength of old guns he turned down the breech and shrunk on hoops. He confined this system of strengthening to the rear of the trunnions until he was reminded of the necessity of strength along the chase of the gun by the blowing off of the chase of some XI-inch guns of his manufacture. His system was then modified so as to involve reënforcing the tube of the larger calibred guns along its whole length with hoops, and his later and largest productions are provided with a long jacket reënforcing the entire breech portion of the tube—a virtual adoption of the great element of strength which has always formed the essential feature in the Vavasseur gun which is now adopted in the United States navy.

In the building up of the steel gun for the navy advantage is so taken of the elastic characteristic of the metal that all parts tend to mutual support. The gun proper consists of a steel tube and a steel jacket shrunk around it, reaching from the breech to and beyond the location of the trunnion band. Outside the jacket and along the chase of the gun there are shrunk on such hoops as the known strain on the tube may make necessary for its support. The tube is formed from a casting which is forged, rough-bored, and turned, and then tempered in oil, by which its elasticity and tensile strength are much increased. It is then turned on the exterior, and adjusted to the jacket, the proper difference being allowed for shrinkage. The jacket, previously turned and tempered, is then heated, and rapidly lowered to its place. The front hoops over the chase are then put on, and the gun is put into a lathe, and turned to receive the trunnion band, and rear and

front hoops. The gun is then fine-bored and rifled.

Each part, as successively placed in position, is expected to compress the parts enclosed through the initial tension due to contraction in cooling. This tension is the greater the farther the part is removed from the tube; thus the jacket is shrunk on at a less tension than are the encircling hoops. By this means full use is made of the elastic capacity of the tube which contributes the first resistance to the expanding influence of the charge. The tension of the jacket prevents the tube being forced up to its elastic limit, and it in turn experiences the effect of the tension of the other encircling parts which contribute to the general support; thus no part is strained beyond its elastic limit, and on the cessation of the pressure all resume their normal form and dimensions. A comparison of this method of common and mutual support of parts with that given by the wall of a gun cast solid

BREECH-LOADING RIFLE AFTER RECEIVING JACKET.

will serve to demonstrate the superior strength of the construction. In order to achieve this intimate working of all the parts it is necessary that the metal of which they are respectively composed must be possessed of the same essential characteristics; in a word, the gun must be homogeneous. It was the absence of this feature in the Armstrong gun which has caused its abolition. This gun was built up, and the parts were expected to contribute mutual support, but the want of homogeneity between the steel tube and the encircling hoops of wrought iron made it impossible for them to work in accord, in consequence of the different elastic properties of the two metals, which, after frequent discharges, resulted in a separation of surfaces between the tube and hoops, when the tube cracked from want of support.

In the construction of the guns for the United States navy, as in the new steel guns now being manufactured in England, the theory of the built-up system is practically conformed to; more so than by Krupp or the French artillerists, who use a thicker tube than is considered judicious at Woolwich or at the Washington Navy-yard. Any increase of thickness of the tube beyond what is necessary to receive the initial pressure of the charge is open to the objections made to the gun with a solid wall, the proportion of the strain communicated to the hoops is reduced, and rupture may ensue from overstraining the tube. The thicker the tube, the less appreciable must be the compression induced by the tension of the encircling hoops.

BREECH-LOADING RIFLE AFTER RECEIVING JACKET AND CHASE HOOPS.

The gun is a breech-loader. The system adopted for closing the breech is an American invention (see note, p. 794), but having been employed in France from the earliest experimental period, it is known as the French *fermeture*. A screw is cut in the rear end of the jacket to the rear of the tube, and a corresponding screw is cut

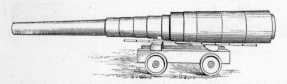

BREECH-LOADING RIFLE WITH JACKET, CHASE HOOPS, AND JACKET HOOPS IN PLACE.

upon a breech plug. The screw threads are stripped at three equi-distant places, the screw and plane surfaces alternating, thus forming what is called an "interrupted" or "slotted" screw. The screw portions of the breech plug enter freely along the plane longitudinal surfaces cut in the tube, and being then turned one-sixth of its circumference, the screw of the plug locks in that of the tube, and the breech is closed.

The success of this system of breech mechanism was not so pronounced on its introduction as it is to-day. The plug forms the base of the breech of the gun, and all the effort of the gases to blow out the breech is exerted at this point. The impact upon the end of the plug is very severe, and it is calculated to *upset* the metal, there-

by increasing the diameter of the plug, which would prevent its removal after the discharge of the piece. With quick-burning powder, as was generally in use for cannon at the inception of the breech-loading experiments, this result ensued if the charges of powder were carried above a certain limit, and the consequent restriction that was put upon velocities was a serious obstacle to the adoption of the system; but the progress that has been made of late years in the science of gun-powder manufacture has relieved the subject from this embarrassment, powder being now provided which communicates very high velocities while developing pressures so moderate and regular as to be entirely under the control of the artillerist.

The projectiles for the new armament are of two kinds; both, however, are shells. That for ordinary use against unarmored vessels is styled the common shell, and is of cast-iron. The length bears a uniform proportion to the gun, being in all cases three and a half calibres. The armor-piercing shell is made of forged steel, and is three calibres in length. The following table gives the particulars, approximately, of the common shell:

Gun.	Length.		Weight.	Bursting Charge.
	Inches.	Calibre.	Pounds.	Pounds.
v-in. breech-loading rifle	17.97	3.59	60	2
vi-in. breech-loading rifle	20.90	3.48	100	4
viii-in. breech-loading rifle	28.10	3.51	250	12
x-in. breech-loading rifle	35.00	3.50	500	22
xii-in. breech-loading rifle	42.00	3.50	850	38 (?)
xvi-in. breech-loading rifle	56.00	3.50	2000	90 (?)

U. S. N. VI-INCH BREECH-LOADING RIFLE.

The armor-piercing shell of the same weight is reduced in length, and its walls are thicker; the bursting charge is consequently much reduced. The following are the particulars, approximately determined:

Gun.	Length.		Weight.	Bursting Charge.
	Inches	Calibre.	Pounds.	Pounds.
v-in.breech-loading rifle	15.07	3.01	60	1
vi-in.breech-loading rifle	17.91	2.98	100	1.50
viii-in.breech-loading rifle	24.25	3.03	250	3.50
x-in.breech-loading rifle	30.00	3.00	500	7 (?)
xii-in.breech-loading rifle	36.00	3.00	850	14 (?)
xvi-in.breech-loading rifle	48.00	3.00	2000	30 (?)

The rifle motion is communicated by one rotating ring of copper, which is placed at the distance of 1.5 inch from the base of the projectile.

The uniform windage for all calibres is .04 inch; thus, taking the vi-inch gun as an example, the diameter of the bore across the lands is 6 inches, the diameter of the shell is 5.96 inches, the depth of the grooves is .05 inch; thus the diameter of the bore across the grooves is 6.10 inches. In order to permit the rotating ring to fill the grooves, it must have a diameter of 6.14 inches; this causes a *squeeze* of .05 inch between the lands and the rotating ring.

There is no subject in the development of the new naval artillery more important than the powder. That used with the old artillery is entirely unsuited to the new conditions that obtain in the modern high-power guns. A brown powder, introduced first in Germany, has exhibited decided advantages over all others, and the efforts to reproduce it have been thoroughly successful at the Du Pont Mills. It is generally known as "cocoa" powder. Its peculiarity exists in the method of preparing the charcoal; this affects the color, and results in a brown instead of a black powder. With this powder, experiments with the vi-inch gun give a muzzle velocity of over 2000 feet per second with a projectile of 100 pounds, using charges of 50 pounds, and this result is obtained with less than 15 tons pressure per square inch in the powder chamber. The grain is prismatic, with a central perforation, and as regards its rate of burning, is under complete control in the manufacture; the form pro-

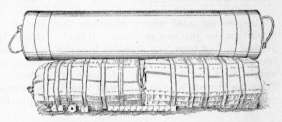

CARTRIDGE CASE AND GRAINS OF POWDER, U. S. N.

vides an increasing surface for the flame during the period of combustion, thus relieving the gun from abnormal pressures at the moment of ignition, but continuing the extreme pressure farther along the bore. The progressive nature of the combustion is very apparent when comparing an unburned grain with others partially consumed, blown out from the gun.

The gun-carriage, which is a separate study in itself, is carried to a high pitch

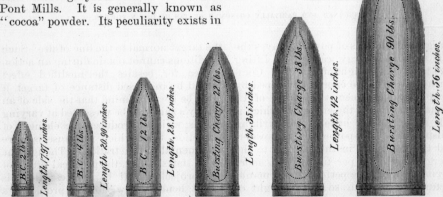

COMMON SHELLS, U. S. N.

of perfection, and presents many features being adopted abroad. The importance of a suitable carriage can be appreciated by inspecting the following table, which exhibits the *energy* that must be controlled by it:

weight of gun, which will enable our unarmored cruisers to hold their own with vessels moderately armored. The power of the battery is greater than is required to contend with unarmored ships, there is a great surplus of power of offence, and

Gun.	Weight of Charge.	Weight of Projectile.	Muzzle Velocity.	Muzzle Energy.	Penetration in Wrought Iron.	Muzzle Energy per Ton of Gun.	Weight of Gun.	Weight of Carriage.
	Pounds.	Pounds.	Feet.	Foot-Tons.	Inches.	Foot-Tons.	Pounds.	Pounds.
v-inch steel breech-loading rifle...	30	60	1915	1,525	10.7	552	6,187	4,200
vi-inch steel breech-loading rifle...	50	100	1915	2,542	13.2	521	11,000	6,400
viii-inch steel breech-loading rifle...	125	250	2050	7,285	18.2	560	28,000	14,000
x-inch steel breech-loading rifle...	250	500	2100	15,285	23.7	588	58,240	32,482
xii-inch steel breech-loading rifle...	425	850	2100	25,985	27.6	591	44 tons	....
xiv-inch steel breech-loading rifle...	675	1350	2100	41,270	32.2	550	75 tons	....
xvi-inch steel breech-loading rifle...	1000	2000	2100	61,114	36.8	571	107 tons	....

This *energy*, total energy, expresses the work that the gun can perform. It is expressed in foot-tons, and signifies that the energy developed is sufficient to raise the weight in tons to a height of one foot. Thus the projectile from the small v-inch gun, weighing 60 pounds, fired with a

the effort is very properly made to sustain this at the highest practicable point. The table shows that the v-inch gun can perforate 10.7 inches of wrought iron at the muzzle; but the results given in tables are predicated upon deliberate firing made on a practice ground, with the position of

UNBURNED AND PARTIALLY CONSUMED GRAINS OF U. S. N. POWDER.

charge of 30 pounds of powder, leaves the gun with an energy capable of lifting 1525 tons to the height of one foot! Comparing this with the energy developed by the 100-ton hammer at the forge of Le Creuzot in France, the energy of which is 1640 foot-tons, we have a most striking illustration of the power of gunpowder, and the testimony in the table as to the energy developed per ton of gun more forcibly exhibits the perfection of a manufacture which, with so little weight of gun, can develop such gigantic power.

It is this power, united with a moderate

the target normal to the line of fire. Such conditions cannot obtain during an action at sea, for, besides the modified effect caused by increased distance of target, it must be borne in mind that the side of an enemy's ship will be presented at varying angles, which introduces the element of deflection, than which no cause is more detrimental to penetration. Though the table states a fact, the practical effect of the projectile will be far less than is stated, hence the wisdom of providing a large surplus of power to compensate for the resistance to its operation.

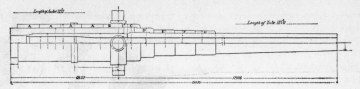

SECTION OF U. S. N. VI-INCH BUILT-UP STEEL BREECH-LOADING RIFLE.

It will readily be conceded that the artillerist has a very responsible duty to perform in so designing his gun that the parts shall lock and interlock to guard against chance of dislocation in the structure. A study of the illustration of the vi-inch built-up gun as constructed at the Washington Navy-yard will show the system there adopted.

In the list of guns, each calibre is represented by one gun. We have not, as of old, several guns of the same calibre differing in weight; multiplicity of classes will be avoided; but this will apply only to the main battery, for history is singularly repeating itself at this time in the restoration of the "murdering pieces" which have been cited as forming part of naval armaments in the seventeenth century. The needfulness of machine guns for operating against men on open decks, for effecting entrance through port-holes, for repelling attacks in boats, and for resisting the approach of torpedo-boats, is so widely recognized that no vessel of war is considered properly equipped without a secondary battery of these "murdering pieces." They are mounted on the rail, on platforms projecting from the sides, and in the tops. The types adopted in the United States navy are the Hotchkiss

revolving cannon and rapid-firing single-shot guns, and the smaller calibre machine guns of Gatling. The heavier pieces, throwing shells of 6 pounds weight, are very effective against vessels of ordinary scantling.

In contemplating the present condition of our new naval armament we have the consolation of knowing that, so far as concerns the study of the subject generally and in detail, the designs, and the initial manufacture, all has been done that could have been done with the resources available. What has been achieved has been without the facilities that are provided in modern gun factories; but notwithstanding all the drawbacks, it is probably safe to assert that no guns in the world to-day are superior to those that have been fabricated at the Washington Navy-yard of steel on the new adopted pattern. The work at this ordnance yard is carried on without ostentation; there is no flourish of trumpets accompanying its operations; it is not advertised, and the people do not yet know how much they owe to the ordnance officers of the navy for the initiation of this new industry, which enables us to assert our ability to advance in this manufacture through the incontrovertible proof of work accomplished. The results

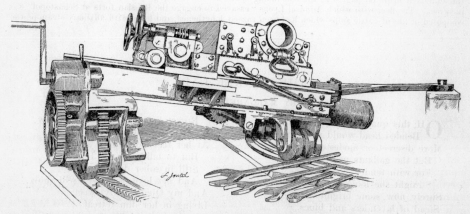

BROADSIDE CARRIAGE FOR VI-INCH BREECH-LOADING RIFLE.

RAPID-FIRING SINGLE-SHOT HOTCHKISS GUN.

are meagre in quantity, and at the present rate of manufacture it will require many years to equip our fleet with modern artillery; this should be remedied, as there is now no doubt as to the success of the productions of this establishment. The plant should be enlarged on a liberal and well-matured plan, and the work should be encouraged by generous appropriations.

It may not be generally known that the steel forgings required for the few VIII-inch and the two X-inch guns now in hand are imported from abroad, for the reason that they cannot be furnished of domestic manufacture, from the want of casting and forging facilities in the United States for work of such magnitude. This is a deficiency in our resources that requires prompt attention to secure us a position of independence in this important matter.

The method of achieving the object has been carefully studied out by a mixed board of army and navy officers, and presented in a document known as the "Gun Foundery Board Report," and the subject has had the attention of committees from both Houses of Congress; all of these reports virtually agree as to the method, but there is delay in concluding upon action; large expenditure of money is required, and there is a hesitancy in assuming the responsibility of recommending it. The object is one of national importance, and public opinion should demand its accomplishment. The ordnance officers of the navy have proved their ability to carry on the work successfully; they only need the opportunity, and they will establish the artillery of the United States navy in a position of which the country may again be proud.

Note.—The original guns, four in number, constructed with breech mechanism on the French *fermeture* principle for the British government during the Crimean war are now in the "Grave-yard" at Woolwich arsenal.

N.B.—In an article on the United States Navy published in the June number of *Harper's Magazine* the statement made on page 5 in the concluding sentence of the paragraph relating to the *Merrimac* is incorrect. The fleet with which Admiral Lyons "essayed to engage the Russian forts at Sebastopol" was composed of line-of-battle ships which had been razeed, lengthened, and fitted with auxiliary steam-power.

E. S.

THE QUAKER LADY.

BY MARGARET DELAND.

OH, this quaint and quiet Quaker!
    Bended head would never make her
More discreet or modester.
    But the gallants pass her by,
    For with tender steadfast eye
    Straight she looks up at the sky!
Surely, now, some brighter hues,
'Stead of lavenders and blues,
    Would delight some jolly fellow-

Russet bee, with bands of yellow;
Or a golden butterfly
At her feet would love and sigh'
    But to talk's no use, I know;
    Still in sober dress she'll go,
    And her love of heaven will show;
And my Quaker lady sweet,
Living in her dim retreat,
Sees no lover at her feet.

YOUNG Sardanapalus recently remarked that the only trouble with his life in college was that the societies and clubs, the boating and balling, and music and acting, and social occupations of many kinds, left him no time for study. He had the best disposition to treat the faculty fairly, and to devote a proper attention to various branches of learning, and he was sincerely sorry that his other college engagements made it quite impossible. Before coming to college he thought that it might be practicable to mingle a little Latin and Greek, and possibly a touch of history and mathematics, with the more pressing duties of college life, but unless you could put more hours into the day, or more days into the week, he really did not see how it could be done.

It was the life of Sardanapalus in college which was the text of some sober speeches at Commencement dinners during the summer, and of many excellent articles in the newspapers. They all expressed a feeling which has been growing very rapidly and becoming very strong among old graduates, that college is now a very different place from the college which they remembered, and that young men now spend in a college year what young men in college formerly thought would be a very handsome sum for them to spend annually when they were established in the world. If any reader should chance to recall a little book of reminiscences by Dr. Tomes, which was published a few years ago, he will have a vivid picture of the life of forty and more years ago at a small New England college; and the similar records of other colleges at that time show how it was possible for a poor clergyman starving upon a meagre salary to send son after son to college. The collegian lived in a plain room, and upon very plain fare; he had no "extras," and the decorative expense of Sardanapalus was unknown. In the vacations he taught school or worked upon the farm. He knew that his father had paid by his own hard work for every dollar that he spent, and the relaxation of the sense of the duty of economy which always accompanies great riches had not yet begun. Sixty years ago the number of Americans who did not feel that they must live by their own labor was so small that it was not a class. But there is now a class of rich men's sons.

The average rate of living at college differs. One of the newspapers, in discussing the question, said that in most of the New England colleges a steady and sturdy young man need not spend more than six hundred dollars during the four years. This is obviously too low an estimate. Another thinks that the average rate at Harvard is probably from six hundred to ten hundred a year. Another computes a fair liberal average in the smaller New England colleges to be from twenty-four to twen-

ty-six hundred dollars for the four years, and the last class at Williams is reported to have ranged from an average of six hundred and fifty dollars in the first year to seven hundred and twenty-eight dollars in the Senior. But the trouble lies in Sardanapalus. The mischief that he does is quite disproportioned to the number of him. In a class of one hundred the number of rich youth may be very small. But a college class is an American community in which every member is necessarily strongly affected by all social influences.

A few "fellows" living in princely extravagance in superbly furnished rooms, with every device of luxury, entertaining profusely, elected into all the desirable clubs and societies, conforming to another taste and another fashion than that of the college, form a class which is separate and exclusive, and which looks down on those who cannot enter the charmed circle. This is galling to the pride of the young man who cannot compete. The sense of the inequality is constantly refreshed. He may, indeed, attend closely to his studies. He may "scorn delights and live laborious days." He may hug his threadbare coat and gloat over his unrugged floor as the fitting circumstance of "plain living and high thinking." It is always open to character and intellect to perceive and to assert their essential superiority. Why should Socrates heed Sardanapalus? Why indeed? But the average young man at college is not an ascetic, nor a devotee, nor an absorbed student unmindful of cold and heat, and disdainful of elegance and ease and the nameless magic of social accomplishment and grace. He is a youth peculiarly susceptible to the very influence that Sardanapalus typifies, and the wise parent will hesitate before sending his son to Sybaris rather than to Sparta.

When the presence of Sardanapalus at Harvard was criticised as dangerous and lamentable, the President promptly denied that the youth abounded at the university, or that his influence was wide-spread. He was there undoubtedly, and he sometimes misused his riches. But he had not established a standard, and he had not affected the life of the university, whose moral character could be favorably compared with that of any college. But even if the case were worse, it is not evident that a remedy is at hand. As the President suggested, there are two kinds of rich youth at college. There are the sons of those who have been always accustomed to riches, and who are generally neither vulgar nor extravagant, neither ostentatious nor profuse; and the sons of the "new rich," who are like men drunk with new wine, and who act accordingly.

The "new rich" parent will naturally send his son to Harvard, because it is the oldest of our colleges, and of great renown, and because he supposes that through his college associations his son may pave a path with gold into "society." Harvard, on her part, opens her doors upon the same conditions to rich and poor, and gives her instruction equally, and requires only obedience to her rules of order and discipline. If Sardanapalus fails in his examination he will be dropped, and that he is Sardanapalus will not save him. If his revels disturb the college peace, he will be warned and dismissed. All that can be asked of the college is that it shall grant no grace to the golden youth in the hope of endowment from his father, and that it shall keep its own peace.

This last condition includes more than keeping technical order. To remove for cause in the civil service really means not only to remove for a penal offence, but for habits and methods that destroy discipline and efficiency. So to keep the peace in a college means to remove the necessary causes of disturbance and disorder. If young Sardanapalus, by his extravagance and riotous profusion and dissipation, constantly thwarts the essential purpose of the college, demoralizing the students and obstructing the peaceful course of its instruction, he ought to be dismissed. The college must judge the conditions under which its work may be most properly and efficiently accomplished, and to achieve its purpose it may justly limit the liberty of its students.

The solution of the difficulty lies more in the power of the students than of the college. If the young men who are the natural social leaders make simplicity the unwritten law of college social life, young Sardanapalus will spend his money and heap up luxury in vain. The simplicity and good sense of wealth will conquer its ostentation and reckless waste.

The late exciting election in England produced an extraordinary display of what may be called public manners. The manifestoes and letters and speeches and newspaper articles were far more acrimonious and ribald than any which this generation has seen, and the depth of bitter feeling can be perceived in the remark of the London *Saturday Review* upon the manifesto of Lord Randolph Churchill. The manifesto was a prolonged tirade of what in America we call blackguardism, and the *Saturday Review*, which was in sympathy with My Lord, smoothly referred to it as illustrating "Lord Randolph Churchill's not unusual fault of saying perfectly true things in a manner somewhat destitute of urbanity." Mr. Gladstone was publicly accused by his opponents of deliberate misstatements, that is, of lying; and Mr. Gladstone himself, in his Edinburgh speech, charged Lord Salisbury with lowering the standard of Parliamentary manners. Lord Randolph Churchill's speeches were whirlwinds of scurrility, and there was never a more personal or vituperative canvass than that which overthrew Mr. Gladstone.

It is generally thought that American public manners of this kind are worse than those of any other country. But in fact they are undoubtedly the best. Whenever the members of the President's cabinet or the more important leaders of a party speak during a canvass, the speeches are full of serious criticism and humorous chaff, but there is seldom in such speeches such blackguardism as appeared in the corresponding English speeches during the late campaign. It is, indeed, a distinctive part of an American canvass that the Blue newspapers should from time to time as the canvass advances publish astounding disclosures from "the record" of the Buff candidate, and the Buff organs do not fail to retort in due season. It is very seldom, however, that a person is nominated for a high office in this country whose character can be drawn justly into question, and when such is the fact the candidate is generally defeated. But if judgment were to be pronounced according to the reciprocal accusations of the Blue and the Buff, every candidate deserves the penitentiary, if not the gallows, and by the side of such offenders Benedict Arnold and Judas Iscariot are haloed saints.

But this is Pickwickian politics. It is the stage thunder of the party press, and its bolts are harmless. It is very different from the intense personal feeling of the tone of the late English speeches. All the newspapers in the land might roar bargain and corruption at Henry Clay, and he would not answer. But when John Randolph hissed out his sneer of the pact of the Puritan and the Blackleg, Mr. Clay challenged him. In the mouth of a party leader the sneer, unheeded in a thousand newspapers, became a sting. We are not saying that in the papers it is pointless, but only that it has come to be regarded as irresponsible insult—one of the expected properties of press combats in an election. If it be true, it will be perceived by the public, who will act accordingly. But the presumption is against it. The great press explosion of the Chinese letter against Garfield failed of its effect largely because of the habit of just such explosions at the critical moment, and the general public impression that they are movements of a sham-fight—mere powder without ball.

The mistake of vituperators like Lord Randolph Churchill is that they forget how much sharper is the clear edge of truth than truth dulled by rhetorical extravagance. It is not worth while to gild gold nor to paint the lily. True invective requires great imagination. But to cover a man with epithets is not to assail him with invective. When Wendell Phillips said of a famous advocate that thieves before stealing inquired of his health, the wit and the scorn pierced like a stiletto. But to assert that Mr. Gladstone's course is "insanity trafficking in treason, condoning crime, exalting disloyalty, abasing loyalty, and a monstrous mixture of imbecility, extravagance, and political hysterics," and to assert that "the united and concentrated genius of Bedlam and Coneyhatch would strive in vain to produce a more striking tissue of absurdities than those gravely recommended by senile vanity to a people renowned for common-sense," is not to sting, or wound, or deride ; it is merely to insult. It is only what Jeames Yellowplush might call, with admiration, "bad langwidge." It is the forcible-feeble ribaldry which does not even irritate its subject or its subject's friends.

The true doctrine of naturalism or realism is as applicable in political discussion as it is in literature. The simple truth is the most powerful weapon, and the moment its blade, wielded in debate, is hidden in rhetorical epithets, there is an instinctive conviction that there is a reason for concealment, and that the blade alone cannot be trusted. Goldwin Smith recently said that he did not believe that since Demosthenes there had been a dozen greater orators than John Bright. However this may be, John Bright's oratory has the essential Demosthenean quality of massive simplicity. The absence of that quality in polemical speech or writing is suspicious. The most effective oratory in Congress and on the stump is that which is most direct, and the most powerful newspaper writing is the least vituperative. " Calling names," personal flings and sarcasms, volleys of superlatives, elaborate sneers, and affected contempt are the lees of discussion. They show that the press is "runnin' emptins." They do not convince, nor confound, nor convert. They prove merely that serious argument is exhausted.

This truth is pointedly illustrated by an incident which sometimes occurs in Congressional debate. A clever and ready speaker will apparently carry his point by opening upon his opponent a confusing fusillade of chaff and ridicule and innuendo and biting sarcasm, or even of caustic vituperation, and by means which have nothing to do with the question he will seem to score an easy victory. But a few simple statements of fact in retort will leave the assailant utterly overthrown and hopelessly defeated. The indisputable assertion, for instance, that he has a personal interest in the cause that he advocates at once sweeps away all the bewildering rattle and smoke of his sarcasm and ridicule, and makes his moral victory impossible. In the late English canvass the manifesto of John Bright, simple, dignified, almost pathetic in its tone of sincere regret for difference of opinion, compared with the artificial fury of Lord Randolph Churchill's, was "a mighty amiral" contrasted with a tossing skiff, and during the extraordinary excitement by far the most effective speeches against Mr. Gladstone were those of Bright, Goschen, and Lord Hartington, which were also the most temperate, serious, and respectful in tone.

Young writers and speakers may well study this aspect of one of the most exciting and important of modern political controversies, and learn that fury is not force, and that ribald vituperation, the easiest and cheapest of rhetorical tricks, is not that powerful invective which is as rare as wit.

THERE is some impatience with the epoch of Queen Anne. We do not mean the Augustan age, as it used to be called—in which, however, it would not be easy to point out the Virgil or the Horace—but the era of the Queen Anne house, the epoch of decorative art in building and in furnishing. But, on the other hand, the epoch of Queen Anne is a delightful insurrection against the monotonous era of rectangular building and of the divorce of beauty and use. The distinction of the present or recent dispensation is that the two are blended, that neither the house nor anything in it need be clumsy or ugly. There is no longer an excuse for an unsightly table or chair or utensil or the least object of household convenience. There need be no more waste spaces in the house. The old entry, which had degenerated from a hall into a mere lobby or vacant passage, is now taken into the general "treatment" of the interior, and becomes a delightful part of it, as pleasant and home-like as any other. The staircase is no longer a railed ladder, but has risen into a chief ornament of the house, as the noble staircases in the new Capitol of New York are the most imposing of its details and decorations.

The same good genius which has changed the whole design of the house touches with its magic every little point and part of its arrangement, and the old formal, conventional distribution and adjustment, which made every house the painful mimic of every other, have disappeared. From the match-box upon the night-stand by the bed to the state dinner service in the dining-room, the good fairy of taste and grace and beauty extends her gentle sway, and invites the guest, who may be somewhat dilatory in marching with the spirit of the age, to look a little more closely to his own refinement, and to live up to his house, if not to his teapot.

It is a spirit which of course has its amusing excesses and extravagancies. If the man of the next century should ever see the amusing little opera of *Patience*, which has so pleased us who are his great-grandfathers and queer old ancestors, he will understand not only that this age was the renaissance of taste, and not only that it had its contemporaneous caricatures of its characteristic tendency, but that it was conscious of them and greatly enjoyed them. The droll "æstheticism" which produced a figure like Oscar Wilde and a kind of social cult evident enough to give point to the pictorial laugh of *Punch* was only a ravelling out of the solid and golden fabric of refined and elegant taste. The worship of the teapot is only an extravagance of the impulse which designs the beautiful house and fills it with beautiful things.

The moral of the new age of Queen Anne

is that a little care in every detail of life is
worth while, and is rewarded in ways that we
do not suspect. The age of pretty houses is
very recent, and decorative art in house-fur-
nishing, and village improvement societies to
secure a fit setting for pleasant homes, and a
village comely as a whole as its homes are
comely as individual parts of it, are all signs
of the same spirit and tendency. The impulses and moving causes of such progress—
or if progress be denied, then of such changes
in the old order—are latent and elusive. Why
the close of the century should be distinguished by this dispensation of taste, and the earlier parts of it should be of another character,
is not a question to be definitely answered.
But it is a fact that the rise of the profession of
architecture among us is coeval with this new
age of Anne. It is only about forty years
since young Americans began to devote themselves to that profession, and it is only since
they were versed in it and actively practising
it that the development which is now characteristic began. It is within the memory of
men not yet old that if a man wished to build
a beautiful and convenient house, he would be
at a loss to find a proper artist, and he must
either recur to the tradition of the colonial
mansion or intrust the realization of his hopes
and wishes to a "builder."

But with the appearance of the trained and
accomplished architect art has come to the
aid of the citizen who would build a house,
and invention and imagination and taste have
blent themselves with skill, and enabled him
to do what he desired, but knew not how to
effect. The decorative details followed. The
art which designed and executed the house
regarded it necessarily as a whole, and was
not satisfied that the graceful vase should be
filled with rubbish, nor the exquisite casket
with pebbles. The knowledge and taste and
obedient hand which built could be trusted,
as they instinctively desired, to furnish; and
when the house became a work of art, it was
incomplete and abortive if it was not harmonious. It was but natural and reasonable,
therefore, that the proprietor should distrust
his own ability to complete a work which
from want of training he could not undertake
or execute. He could no more wisely assume
that he knew how a house should be furnished
than how it should be designed. Of course
he knew his general wish and the limit of his
resources, but he could trust the taste of the
artist to furnish, as he could trust his ability
to design.

There is no more common error than the
supposition that every man and woman knows
what he or she wishes in a house. Undoubtedly the woman wishes "plenty of closets" and
"house-keeping conveniences." But she does
not know how to provide them, and still less
how to provide them most conveniently and
becomingly. Her interest and her knowledge
are in the art of house-keeping. But she summons the artist to provide the mechanical

means of keeping house conveniently and
agreeably, because his interest and knowledge
are in that art. He cannot teach her husband
how to make the money with which to build
a house, but he can supply him with suitable
and attractive plans, and superintend its erection. He cannot teach her how to make coffee, but he can design a graceful coffee-pot and
pretty cups into which to pour it.

Let not indignation demand whether the
Easy Chair means that men and women should
be mere puppets in their own houses. Gracious Heaven forefend! But are they puppets
in their own clothes and carriages, and are not
those conveniences of man constructed by special artists? Will indignation reply that at
least the individual selects them, and pleases
his own taste? But is that quite true? Does
a man select a high-collared coat when fashion requires a low collar? Does a woman
wear hoops when fashion imposes flowing
Grecian drapery, or a sweeping train when
fashion ordains short skirts? Mrs. Grundy
forbid! Yet what is fashion in dress but the
will and taste of others applied to garments,
to which we all willingly conform, not, indeed,
in excess, but in general? And why, if we
naturally and gladly conform to the behests
of special artists in clothes, should we hesitate to take the same course, for the same good
reason, in houses and in house furnishing and
decorating?

There are undoubtedly Jacobites in this
new age of Anne who drink significantly to
the king over the water. They ask whether
this new-fangled caprice of architectural gim-
crackery of houses all peaks and corners and
bulges and oddity, is better than the simple,
dignified, spacious old rectangular colonial
mansion of which we spoke? But, dear courtier of the Pretender, that is not the question.
The flowing silken coats flowered with gold
embroidery, the white silken hose and silver-
buckled shoes, and full-bottomed wigs or
dainty queues, of our ancestors may have been
a very stately and picturesque costume, but
our question is, What costume is most convenient and serviceable for the great body of
citizens to-day? The colonial Dons lived in
fine mansions, but the plain little frame houses
were the great mass of dwellings. It is the
praise of our new age of Anne that it does not
lose the excellencies of the older mansions,
while it gives a charm to the little houses
which they never knew before. Whether you
will pay five thousand or fifty thousand dollars for your house, the good Queen Anne
will have it a pretty and convenient house,
and if you choose she will furnish it prettily
and conveniently.

But if, loyal to the justly dethroned James,
you insist upon wearing clothes of your own
fashion and shoes of your own making, you
will doubtless also insist upon living in a
house of your own designing. Yet none the
less it is true that under the rule of the benign
Anne there is no excuse for acquiescing in ug-

liness of any kind, and the responsibility for every man's unhandsome and inconvenient surroundings must be upon his own head.

THE practice of celebrating centennial anniversaries, which began so happily with those of Revolutionary incidents, becomes more and more general, and, as we said last month, promises to furnish us with our pleasantest and most useful holidays. We say useful because such holidays are lessons in history among a people which cannot be assumed always to know the national annals or to comprehend the national traditions. Thus in the city of New York the earliest tradition is Dutch, but the Dutch character is now the least obvious and the Dutch influence the least powerful. New York, we believe, is the largest Irish city in the world, and a Dutch celebration of the foundation of the city would be exceedingly interesting, but it would not command the universal and instinctive sympathy of the community.

But they manage these things differently in Albany. The Dutch tradition is there supreme, and while there is the mingling of nationalities which is common in the population of every American city, the original element is more apparent and controlling, at least in sentiment, if not at the polls. It was to this sentiment that Mr. McElroy, in his admirable poem at the recent bicentennial commemoration, appealed. He called his poem "Peter Schuyler's Mandate," and he happily made the first Mayor the good genius of the ancient city, and demanded that the Dutch should have their due.

The poem was a very skilful and ingenious plea, in a half-playful tone, and it was most felicitously adapted to the occasion. The poet, commemorating the Dutch, and feeling that the solid and conservative but liberty-loving and liberty-protecting genius of Holland had been somewhat neglected by American history and tradition, which has exalted the Pilgrim and the Puritan, did not spare his good-natured jibes at the local Yankee and the Puritan sins. Old Peter Schuyler, in his habit as he lived, adjures the minstrel:

"Turn not on the Pilgrim with jeers:
    He thought he was serving his Maker
When he cut from the Baptist his ears
    And strangled the decorous Quaker;
His witchcraft you're not to unhood,
    Nor tell of the saints that he banished,
For we know his intentions were good,
    And his bigotry long ago vanished."

The minstrel hears and heeds, and in a generous and noble strain responds, alluding to Henry Hudson's vessel:

"Our souls shall magnify those days of yore;
    We'll not forget—we'll not give up the ship,
Nor love the *Mayflower* less, but love the *Half-Moon* more."

But whatever the defects of the Puritans, and however history may have credited the Pilgrims with the virtues that belong to Holland, surely St. Nicholas will own that if tradition has given to St. Jonathan any unwarranted precedence over the elder saint, the younger saint has atoned completely by giving to the Dutch Republic its great historian, and by providing that the tale of liberty in Holland should be most effectively told upon Plymouth Rock. It is one of the historic incidents which most please the imagination, that after more than two centuries and a half from the Pilgrim flight and the Dutch hospitality, the great Pilgrim debt should have been acknowledged and discharged in another country, under conditions wholly changed, and in the most impressive and enduring manner. If many pages of history glow with the great Puritan story, in which the essential substance of increasing liberty sloughs off undoubted weakness, inconsistency, and injustice, not less has a son of the Puritans written upon these pages in characters of light as luminous the heroic Dutch chapter of Liberty. And equally of both countries now, as of Albany and Plymouth, are the last words of the poem of the Albany poet true:

"And Schuyler, like some watchman by his bell
    Who from a lookout tower Time's passage cries,
Responds, in accents that of rapture tell,
Two by the century's clock, and all is well!"

The story of Albany is one of the most significant in American annals, and it was thoroughly told during the celebration, prolonged through a week. Governor Hill in the oration recalled the chief incidents and associations of the city, and the presence of the President, who became known to the country as an official resident of Albany, completed the interest of a memorable occasion. Its permanent memorial, however, will be the commemorative tablets which have been placed in various parts of the city to mark the most significant historical sites. This is a charm which our cities have hitherto lacked, and in the incessant change of building the precise spot of famous incidents or of association with famous persons is lost. It is an instinct of true public spirit to commemorate them, and the performance of the pious duty will foster and strengthen the same spirit.

Indeed, all such celebrations, conducted with the zeal and success which characterized that at Albany, show the awakening of a spirit which has not been conspicuous in New York. The imperial State has seemed to be careless of its own renown, as if its character would assert itself and needed no blazoning. This large indifference is in itself a certain sign of greatness. But, on the other hand, a just pride is a spur and a spring of greatness. The sons of heroic sires burn to be heroes. But without the tradition they do not know the ancestral heroism. *Noblesse oblige* is a truth and a law which the Easy Chair has often celebrated. It supplies not only romance to life, but the impulse of nobler and more generous living. This is the inspiration of a week like that which Albany devoted to proud and ennobling recollections. It was fitting that as she abolished, in obedience to the just demands of a changed situation, one of the oldest customs of the town—the market of country wagons in State Street—the ancient city should renew her loyalty to the sturdy spirit and the memorable deeds of an ancestry whose costume and customs she may properly renounce, but whose rectitude and courage and love of liberty she may well periodically and elaborately commemorate.

It is a fact which becomes more and more notable that eminent Senators and Representatives complain of the manners of the press and of current speech toward Congress. They declare that it has become a habit to defame the national Legislature, and to speak of public men in a tone which implies that they are to be considered rascals until they prove their honorable character. One Senator speaks of the current defamation of public men, and another stigmatizes certain misrepresentations as illustrations of the way in which the newspapers generally speak of members of Congress.

These are serious accusations. Mr. Stoddard, the poet, was recently charged with some jealous strictures upon other poets. But he replied, very truly, that no critic, however envious, could write down a good book, and that, in fact, nobody but the author could really injure the author. The Quarterly was very "savage and tartarly" upon John Keats. But "Hyperion" and the "Eve of St. Agnes" and the Odes survive. The reviewers laughed at Byron's "Hours of Idleness," but they deserved the laugh, and it stung the poet into real verses. This is true, but it is also true that bitter wrong may be done by an unjust or even a careless criticism. If the reader sees in his paper that a book is worthless, he will not hasten to buy it. The newspaper critic is the public taster of new books, and as he declares the draught to be thin and weak and sour, or rich and fruity and exquisite, the general impression will be produced. According as he says that the wine is a poor table claret or a true Tokay will the public respond, "No, thank you," or "If you please."

In the same general way the newspapers taste Congress for the public. It is not the voter in general, but the editor, who reads the Record, and knows in detail what Congress says and does. But the voter in general reads the newspaper, and receives from its comment his impression of Congress. There is, indeed, in the paper the very brief abstract, or rather mention, of Congressional proceedings. But it is utterly inadequate, often inaccurate, and even that abstract is less read than the editorial comment. The power of the press, therefore, in moulding the general public impression of a member of Congress is unquestionably great, and it is a power which should

be exercised with the deepest sense of responsibility. The charge of members of Congress is that it is mischievously and carelessly, if not maliciously, exercised, and that great injury is done to the national name by a habit of ridiculing or denouncing the chosen representatives of the nation.

But is the charge well founded? Is it true that any particular member of Congress or that Congress as a whole is seriously misrepresented? It will happen, of course, that in commenting immediately upon a long debate a newspaper may misapprehend an argument or mistake a fact, as Senators and Representatives do during the debate. There is also the ex officio tone of the party organ, which praises the speeches and votes of its own party friends, and sneers at those of the opposition. But this is always understood, and its effect is corrected by an instinctive good sense in the reader. The Whig caricatures of Democratic leaders, and the Democratic lampoons of the Whigs, did not seriously affect the public judgment. What Mr. Croswell might say of Henry Clay, or Mr. Weed of Martin Van Buren, was always involuntarily "discounted." Clay and Van Buren might have complained that they were calumniated by the press of the other party. But they would not have said that in any general sense there was a habit of speaking ill of public men—except the custom of the party press of maligning party opponents.

Is there any change in this situation, and if there be, is it the press or the public men who are to blame? If there be a change, it is rather to be sought in the greater independence of the press and the consequent actual criticism of public men, instead of the perfunctory praise and blame of partisanship to which they have been accustomed. A Senator, for instance, accepts as of course the abuse and misrepresentation of a newspaper of the other party. But if a paper which is not unfriendly to him as a partisan questions and censures his conduct, he naturally winces, and why? Because the paper points out to him that he is doing as a partisan Senator precisely what the partisan editor does. He despises such conduct in the opposition editor. But why should he wonder that an intelligent observer censures it in him? The defamation of which public men complain is not accusation of corruption so much as condemnation not of partisanship, because every member of Congress belongs to a party, but of unworthy partisanship. When a Senator votes for a measure that he does not approve; when, having shown that a bill ought not to pass, he then supports it because his party requires it, or because he fears the effect upon a class of voters, or because of any similar reason, he is an unworthy partisan. He lacks the independence which every good citizen has the right to require of a national legislator, and when this is severely stated, and he is strongly censured, he feels that he hears not the unmeaning voice of a professional opponent, but of that public intelligence and morality whose good opinion he naturally desires.

When low motives actuate public conduct, and when public men in public speeches commend and justify such conduct, the natural comment upon it will seem to them to be defamation. But we do not believe that any member of Congress who makes his honest view of the public welfare the guide of his speeches and votes will have reason to complain of calumny or misrepresentation. He need not plead that under our system party is essential to good government, because it is not denied. But will he plead that because party requires unmanly conduct he must therefore be unmanly, and that to call him unmanly is slander? And if he should say that the Easy Chair proposes an impossible course, and that any man who should pursue it would be regarded as a traitor and would never return to Congress, would his plea be, or would it not be, the confession that the tone of remark of which he complained is fully justified?

Editor's Study.

I.

THERE comes to us from Venice, in these summer months which will be autumn months before our words reach the reader, a book which the author hopes may become, so to speak, "the Bible of all lovers," and which we think may be at least praised to the race at large as a work of monumental industry and prodigious scholarship, not to speak of its artistic qualities. It is, in its way, one of those feats in which the Italians come to the front, apparently when they will, and claim in this sort or that their world-old primacy; or if the reader will not allow that, then it is one of those achievements of patient learning and of thorough intelligence in which they are now rivalling the Germans. It is called *Il Libro dell' Amore,* and it consists of versions into Italian of twenty-eight hundred poems in celebration of the well-known passion of love in every phase, from more than ninety languages, and seven hundred and fifty poets, not to speak of unknown and popular origins. The versions, save some eight or ten, were made by the compiler, Professor Marco Antonio Canini, and if we may judge by the translations from the English (to omit the other forty or fifty languages familiar to us), they are all not only "very choice Italian," but extremely spirited and faithful. In the case of poems from the Latin, ancient Greek, Neo-Hellenic, Greek vernacular, French, Spanish, old and modern Provençal, Romansch, Roumanian, Catalan, Portuguese, Gallegan, Creole, German, and English, he has translated from the original text, and in the others he has used such versions as he could find in other European tongues.

We cannot wonder, as he says in his most delightful introduction, that if he could have confronted the idea of the work such as it now is, before putting hand to it, he would have turned from it in despair. But Professor Canini is an old scholar inured to heroic toil in the compilation of his *Dizionario Etimologico di Vocaboli Italiani,* and in his *Solution de Cent Problèmes Étymologiques;* he is the author of a volume of amorous verse, fitly entitled *Amore e Dolore,* and he was therefore equipped for the work that grew upon him, by his science and his imaginable acquaintance with the subject—to which few of us, indeed, are altogether strange. Let us add, however irrelevantly here, that he is of that noble tradition of Italian authors who have suffered for their country, and let us remember, as we turn over the pages of his work, that he was banished after the fall of the Venetian republic of '48, and that his *Vingt Ans d'Exil* is an autobiographical contribution to the knowledge of

> "come sa di sale
> Lo pane altrui, e quanto è dura calle
> Lo scendere e il salir per l' altrui scale."

In his introduction, which is not only a formal exposition of his literary ideas and the scope of his work, but at times a charming and touching personal confidence, he tells us: "My labor was more difficult, because performed in Italy, than it would have been in Paris or London or Berlin or Vienna, on account of the difficulty of finding the necessary books, and above all because performed at Venice, rather than in some large city of Italy, for the same reason. My outlay to procure even a part of these books has been very great." He proclaims, with a pride which the sympathetic reader will find as amiable as it is just, that he is "the first to publish a collection so ample of lyrical love-poems, whether popular or written by educated poets, in the principal languages of the world, distributed under a certain number of heads, and translated, where foreign, by the collector himself. There will pass," he goes on to say, "under the reader's eye the love-poetry of all times, from the remotest antiquity to our own days, ...and as to distant epochs, so to various and far-off climes do the verses of this collection belong....Poets of all social conditions, the highest and the lowest, are united here. I have given the verses of famous princes, like Solomon King of Jerusalem, Soliman II. the Magnificent, Sultan of the Turks, and the Grand Mogul Shah Alam II., as well as those of obscure peasants and workmen, in Italy and elsewhere, even to the miserable blacks. And, to confess the truth, the songs of the Pauv' Zizi, the Louisiana slave, move me more than those of the two mighty Mussulman emperors."

It will be perceived that Professor Canini writes like a poet; but he works like a savant, and his subject is scientifically treated. This subject, he says, is the love of a man for a woman, or a woman for a man, and excludes the sensualized mysticism of many devotional poems, as well as all other forms of human love. To keep the book still more within bounds, he rejects romances and ballads as being primarily narrative and only secondarily lyrical, and he admits only a few passages from the Iliad and the great Sanscrit poems. The entire work is in two volumes, and as "all the world loves a lover," the reader will wish to know that the first is divided into eight chapters, namely, What is Love? Beauty and Woman; Need of Loving; First Love; Spring and Love; The Two Loves, Sensuous and Platonic; Expressions of Love in Sonnets; Expressions of Love in Various Metres; while the second volume treats in twelve parts of Love-Songs after the Oriental; The Kiss; Hope Fulfilled; Marriage; Disdain and Infidelity; Reconciliation and Love Renewed; Death of the Beloved; The Widow and the Widower; New Love; Love in Old Age; Memories.

Professor Canini confesses difficulties in the work of selection and rejection, arising chiefly from the delicacy of the theme and the indelicacy of the poets, into which we need not follow him; it is enough that he decided to restrict the expressions of sensuous love, and that, therefore, as he quaintly acknowledges, this division of his work is somewhat wanting. The *naïveté* with which he gives his reasons upon this and other points in his introduction is always charming. "Let no one marvel," he says, "that I have translated so few sonnets. Nothing is more difficult than to translate a German or an English sonnet into an Italian sonnet, because of the different nature of the tongues. For example, the English say with one syllable, *spring*, what we must say in four, *primavera*. To render the conceit of fourteen German or English verses into fourteen Italian verses you must lay them on a very bed of Procrustes." And, again, he says of his chapter on Love in Old Age: "Let no one be surprised that I have given this a special heading. I will not repeat the sophisms of the Gérontes of Molière, or those of Bajazet II., Sultan of the Turks—and poet, as were other sultans—to prove that a woman should prefer the love of an old man to any other. Not so; suffice it to affirm that an elderly man can inspire love in a young girl. Even an elderly woman can enamour a young man, but this case is rarer. It is enough to cite the instance of the son of Madame de Sévigné, who killed himself for Ninon de l'Enclos when she was already of mature age. Love in old age is not rare, especially in the poets, who are gifted with a livelier fancy than most other men."

These flavors of a Montaignesque simplici-

ty and frankness are to be tasted in many passages of Professor Canini's essay; and it is full of curious and striking observations. He notes that the popular poetry is always more sincere than that of the more lettered Muse, and he invites us to notice that in the premeditated art the poetesses are always fewer than the poets, while the contrary happens in popular poetry. Then he adds, with a generosity that ought to endear him to the sex which has not always received from criticism that overrunning measure of justice which it likes when the justice is in its favor: "Woman, according to my thinking, expresses love more naturally, more tenderly, and more vividly than man. I believe that some of the most ancient erotic poems which remain to us—Chinese, Egyptian, Hebrew—are the work of women"; and we, for our part, make bold to say that if any fair reader has conceived a rancor in her heart against Professor Canini for more than insinuating that an old woman is less capable of inspiring love than an old man, she ought straightway to unpack it in the handsomest words she can think of.

The remarks and judgments of Professor Canini on the qualities and relative excellence of the different poets and the different races in the business of making love-songs are all worth attention; and he believes rightly that his work will serve a useful end in the study of comparative literature, that latest of the sciences, which we are beginning to hear something of on many sides nowadays. "In this phase of the lyrism of each people there is a special character, but it all has a common ground: an Italian in love might often, to express his feelings, make use of forms invented by a Turk, and *vice versa*. Therefore the study of contrasted literatures, in what concerns the utterance of love, is a new proof of the unity of the human race, and ought to contribute to the fraternization of men."

He gives a third of his entire space to the Italian poets in pursuance of a design to present a history of love-poetry from the earliest traces of it among his compatriots to its latest achievements; but he frankly says that the German love-songs have been the best of our century, in the literary sort. "Nothing surpasses the *Lied*. Among us, Leopardi alone is not inferior to the Germans;" yet at the present moment he declares without hesitation that "the Hungarian and the Portuguese are the first literatures in the poetry of love. There is, in the Hungarian songs, passion, power, originality; they portray the national character, so vivacious, sometimes so violent.... I consider as the greatest living poet, not only in Portugal, but in all Europe, Giovanni de Deus." The cognate Brazilians are impassioned and full of fire; the Spaniards are not now at their best; the Spanish Americans are careless, but abound in fantasy and passion; the popular love-poetry of the modern Turks is good, but the lettered sort, on the other hand, is a "mixture of Turkish, Arabic, and Persian —a curious mosaic which records the successive dominations of the Turanian, Semitic, and Aryan races"; some of the poems of the Circassians and Georgians are among the most beautiful of all, in Professor Canini's opinion; "in the Sanscrit and Pracrit love-poetry there is not only the ardor of the senses, but lively sentiment and affection. . . . In the Hindu songs fancy prevails; in those of the old Aryan or Dravidic populations, tenderness." He finds few love-songs of merit in the Russian, except some that lament the death of the beloved, which curiously attests the universal sadness of Russian literature. The Malaysian lyrics "show a deep tenderness and a refined art;" the Chinese are passed without comment; the Japanese are slighted as rather poor stuff; those of the Patagonians and Araucanians are full of fancy and sentiment; but Professor Canini blames us Americans of both continents for having profited so little by "the poetic treasures of the nations who preceded" us here.

He recognizes the new life of Scandinavian poetry in Björnson, Tegnér, and Oehlenschläger, but regards the literary love-poetry of France, except the new Provençal, as mostly an intellectual toy. What he says of the Anglo-American is worth reproducing at length, as a means of judging his judgments of other literatures. "The Scotch love-songs," he says, "would be much more numerous in my book if I had not been obliged, as noted above, to exclude ballads. Of the English love-literature I have given various pieces from the sixteenth century onward. Readers acquainted with Shakespeare only as a dramatic poet may see that he was also an excellent love-poet in his sonnets and songs. Sufficiently numerous are the pieces which I have given from Burns and from Moore, whom I believe the best of the English love-poets. It grieves me to see how the fame of Moore has for some time declined in England. I have translated almost entire an exquisite lyric of Shelley's, written as it was for an Italian lady, Emiliana Viviani, of Pisa. I have not failed to give some of the best love-poems of Byron, and to offer examples of the more modern poets, as Tennyson, considered the first English poet living; Browning, profound and bizarre; Barrett - Browning, his predeceased wife, whose Sonnets from the Portuguese (really original English poems) are *chefs-d'œuvre ;* G. Dante Rossetti; and Swinburne. The last two have been praised to the skies by many critics, including Italians. To tell the truth, Rossetti seems to me too labored and sometimes too sibylline; I have attempted, not too successfully, I fear—others, including the able critic Nencioni, have judged the task impossible—to translate some of his sonnets. Perhaps the poems of Rossetti's first youth were less artificial and simpler. When he had risen in renown his friends urged him to publish them, but he said that the only copy in exist-

ence was enclosed in the casket which the woman he loved had begged in dying to have buried with her. The grave was opened, and it was found that the hair of the poor dead thing had grown so long and had twined itself around the box so closely that this could not be opened without cutting off the tresses. I will say also that Swinburne as a lyric poet does not please me overwell; as a dramatist this is not the place to speak of him. Certainly he has a rich fancy, and a style harmonious and correct; but I think that in his poems the images are heaped up too much, and the conceits rather too sixteenth-centuryish, just as they are in Victor Hugo, of whom Swinburne is a great admirer. For my part, I stick to the half-forgotten Moore—yes, and to Burns: I like the simple verse that gushes from the heart. I offer the reader some poems from the American poets who have written in English, which are lovely indeed. But Walt Whitman is not a love-poet; the love-songs of Longfellow are few ; and Russell Lowell, who is the first of their love-poets, has greater fame as a humorist."

II.

From the most if not the whole of this it will have been seen that Professor Canini knows what he is talking about, and if his knowledge of other literatures is as wide and as critical, he is authorized to speak with the decision he uses. We cheerfully let him speak for us, since we have not, as we must own, read above two thousand, if so many as that, out of the twenty-eight hundred love-poems in his collection. At the age of fifty, or thereabouts, there comes a distinct abatement, as some poets have themselves noted, in the appetite for love-poetry, however voracious it may once have been. We should say that two or three hundred love-songs are then quite enough at a sitting, and we should admire the digestion that could compass more, without wishing to rival it at the risk of a surfeit.

"As long as the sun shines upon our planet," says Professor Canini, at the close of that essay which we should so much rather read than the songs that follow it, "as long as plants and animals feel a new life in the spring-time, as long as the birds sing among the April leaves, the human heart will be wrought, now to rapture and now to anguish, by the need of loving. And as long as the world endures, man will strive to express, to utter in rhythmic phrase, the sentiment, mixed of earth and heaven, which gives him his keenest joys and his cruelest pangs, Love." Yet while confidently prophesying to this effect, our poet-savant does not conceal from himself that "the decadence of this as well as other kinds of poetry is a fact general in Europe ; . . . . in no place is it so evident as in Italy. . . . Will it always remain there, as it actually is, more or less, in all the other countries of Europe, hectic and infirm ? I do not think so: there have been other like periods of decadence, on which have followed epochs of fresh and glorious efflorescence."

This seems, indeed, to be the mood, trustful and amiable, of all the critics now vaticinating on the subject of poetry; and it is notably the mood of Mr. G. P. Lathrop, whose introduction to Miss Jeannette L. Gilder's collection of *Representative Poems of Living Poets* we have been reading with so much pleasure and respect. The volume is peculiarly interesting because the selections were all made, at Miss Gilder's invitation, by the poets themselves, and are accompanied by fac-similes of their autographs, the sole exception being that of Lord Tennyson, who would not choose, but who sent word by his son that the list chosen for him, and submitted to him, "would answer the purpose." We think, saving his lordship's respect, it answers the purpose very ill; and perhaps the most striking thing in this collection is how very unfit most of the poets seem to have been to make the choice asked of them. We are not saying that any universally satisfactory selection could have been made; we are merely saying that in many cases there could hardly have been a less satisfactory one. It is, of course, quite impossible that any man should know what is the most characteristic thing in his own work, and yet this is just what other people would like him and expect him to know. Nevertheless, in its way, this collection is one of unique value, and if no poet has given us only his best, each has given us some of his best, and none certainly has offered us his worst. We have that to be glad of; and if we could know upon what theory of himself or his powers each of the poets had acted, we should have still greater cause for gratitude. But this theory, naturally, the editor is not able to reveal.

Among those poets who have made acceptable, or more or less acceptable, selections may be mentioned Mr. Aldrich, who includes his weird little poem of "Identity," and sonnet on "Sleep"—one of the great sonnets of the language. Mrs. Akers Allen gives, with others, her beautiful poem "Among the Laurels," which subtly expresses one of the sweetest and truest moods known to rhyme. Mr. Bunner rests content with one piece, "The Way to Arcady," which, indeed, for a bewitching grace and movement is enough for half a dozen poets. Mr. Cranch puts in his "Bobolinks," which is also a happy representation of his quality. Mr. Dobson gives us "A Dead Letter" and "The Ballad of Prose and Rhyme," with four other poems of happy choice. From Dr. Holmes the choice of "The Chambered Nautilus," "The Last Leaf," "Old Ironsides," and "The Voiceless" is altogether good; and Mr. Lowell is quite as satisfactory with his extract from the "Commemoration Ode," "A Parable," "The Present Crisis," "What is so rare as a Day in June?" and "The Courtin'." Mr. Lathrop places first of his four poems

"The Singing Wire," an admirable piece, meriting remembrance for its imaginative modernness. Mrs. Piatt's choice is very characteristic of her, and Mr. Stoddard's, containing his noble ode on "Abraham Lincoln," and that exquisitely tender little sigh, "The Flight of Youth," is entirely acceptable. "Atalanta," "A Prelude," and "Wild Honey" suggest fairly well the range from elegant to sylvan of one of our most charming and original poets, Mr. Maurice Thompson. Mr. Trowbridge with "The Vagabonds," and Mr. Whittier with "My Playmate," place themselves perfectly before us in at least one phase of their best. The others go from tolerably good to bad and worse, with quite marvellous maladroitness in some instances.

The next most surprising thing after the inability of the poets is their very great number. We had not the least notion there were so many living English and American poets, of all ages and sexes, especially since our violent explosion against their tribe in the March or February number of this Study. It shows what a really poor article of dynamite we use in these outbursts. Judging from the vehemence of our feelings on that occasion, we should say that a few tattered scraps of laurel, and some splintered and blackened lyres, picked up in the adjoining counties, ought to be all that was left of the twanging and twittering crew; but even in this volume alone we count no less than seventy-eight poets and poetesses, most of them in the full vigor of youth, and all apparently in perfect repair. In view of a fact so bewildering, so discouraging, our sole consolation comes from the patriotic pride which will be flattered in every true American by the immense numerical superiority of our poets and poetesses. We have no less than sixty — a round sixty — to the paltry eighteen of the English.

III.

But this idle talk is keeping us from the essay of Mr. Lathrop, which, like most of his critical work, is mostly well felt and well thought. If it does not always impart to the reader the seriousness of the writer, that is the fault of the subject, about which it requires a deliberate and careful resolution to be serious. When it comes to asking whether we are going to have any more poetry, and if not, why, one must remember to be grave, or one is apt to smile. When it comes to specifics for its production, one must stuff one's handkerchief in one's mouth. The critics are all alike droll at that pass; and it is difficult to keep one's countenance even with a lady who, like Madame Bentzon, has written so much and so amicably of American literature, when she prescribes what we ought *not* to do if we wish to create poetry. At the close of her late review of Mr. Stedman's *American Poets* in the *Revue des Deux Mondes* she warns us not to be too American if we wish to be at all, and to beware of making Americanism a fanatic cult, as Walt Whitman does. Guard against the dangerous facility of assimilation, says she; and then guard against an abuse of dialect. Let your poetry, says she, become what it must in entire freedom. By observing these three simple rules we shall see what we shall see.

Mr. Lathrop is not so didactic with us. He seems to think, with Mr. Stedman, that a great deal can be done in poetry by thinking you can do a great deal, or that "the genesis of the greatest poetry involves, first of all, an unbounded, although silent and devout, confidence, in the mind of the artist, that he can rise to the loftiest heights of thought and feeling on wings of the most musical expression. He must believe implicitly that he will one day reach those upper spheres if left to his own manner of flight." Certainly the experiment is worth trying, though we suspect that the difficulty would always be in first getting your silent and devout confidence; plenty of the other sort we see all round us. However, we quite agree with Mr. Lathrop that "if we are constantly telling" the intending poet "that the state of the atmosphere is such as absolutely to prevent any one's rising above a certain plane, or that careful research has disclosed a fatal weakness in the wing-power of the present generation, or that the measurements of his throat demonstrate that he can never give more than a small volume of sound—if we are always doing this, we shall be doing what we can to destroy that native faculty of self-reliance and joyous inspiration that makes him a poet." We not only agree with Mr. Lathrop in this position, but we think that most of his positions are sound and good, and merit entirely serious assent. He invites us to observe that in all ages the poetic future has always been a dark one, just like the political future and the moral future, which are at this very moment simply Egyptian in their blackness. He speaks interestingly and usefully of the critical future, which he finds in even a worse way than the poetic, and he would have us begin its reform "by abolishing superstitions" such as "that we must make unreasoning reference of all new work to the standard of supposed flawless examples produced in the past," and here he stands on the solid ground taken by Mr. Posnett and Mr. Perry. "The rational development of poetry cannot be a climbing backward along the slope that leads to some peak far behind us," he says; and he says this after saying some things of the impeccable masters

which will strike many devout and venomous persons as little short of flat burglary, if not beyond it. "To speak frankly, I am not of those who in commending some beautiful example of modern song—eminent, it may be, for a single well-defined quality—feel constrained always to make the reservation that it is the best of its kind 'after Shakespeare.' .... Much of the popular indifference to poetry in our day comes indirectly, I think, from this servile attitude toward writers of the past.... There is scarcely a poet who does not pour us out a measure of dross with his gold. Even in Shakespeare—the very part of him which is generally admitted to be his true body—may be found an occasional mixture of triviality, doggerel or bombast, *which would not be tolerated in a modern poet of high standing.*"

IV.

It is we who have italicized those last terrible words.

Does Mr. Lathrop perhaps remember how a few years ago the British Isles were shaken to their foundations, and their literary dependency here quaked

"From one to the other sea,"

and all the dead conventionalities rose to a sitting posture in their graves with horror, because some one casually said that the "mannerism of Dickens and the confidential attitude of Thackeray would not now be tolerated," fiction having become "a finer art than it was in their day"? Has Mr. Lathrop forgotten that awful moment? Are we to have that day of wrath all over again? Mr. Lathrop is a poet, and at times a very charming one: does he realize that he has placed himself in a position to be asked whether he thinks he writes greater poetry than Shakespeare? Is he aware that to many worthy persons he will actually seem to have said so?

Its former occupant might well take pleasure in stepping out of the pillory of which Mr. Lathrop seems emulous, and in turning to heave the first half-brick at him. He is young, and has his best work before him, and brickbats will do him good, if he keeps on speaking the truth and saying things which, if said on any other subject, would seem the stalest truisms. The world moves—this terrestrial ball—that was settled by science, which knows; the æsthetic world does *not* move—that was settled by taste, which does not need to know.

Monthly Record of Current Events.

POLITICAL.

OUR Record is closed on the 18th of August. —The first session of the Forty-ninth Congress was finally adjourned August 5. The total number of bills and joint resolutions introduced was 13,202 (House 10,228, and Senate 2974). Of these, 987 were finally enacted, 746 originating in the House, and 241 in the Senate. The President vetoed 115 bills, of which 102 were private pensions and 6 for the erection of public buildings.

The total appropriations voted by Congress

at this session were $264,783,579, as follows: agricultural, $654,715; army, $23,753,057; consular and diplomatic, $1,364,065; District of Columbia, $3,721,051; Indian, $5,546,262; legislative, etc., $20,654,346; Military Academy, $297,805; navy, $12,989,907; pension, $76,075,-200; post-office, $54,365,863; river and harbor, $14,473,900; sundry civil, $2,657,510; deficiencies, $13,960,880; *Alabama* awards, $5,769,015; naval increase, $3,500,000; miscellaneous, $5,-000,000.

The following resolutions and bills were passed by Congress during the month: Morrison resolution, House, July 14, Senate, July 30, requiring any surplus in the Treasury above $100,000,000 to be used in the redemption of bonds whenever such excess amounts to $10,000,000, but allowing the Secretary of the Treasury, in his discretion, to hold a working balance over and above these sums not exceeding $20,000,000 (failed to get the President's signature); Fortifications Bill, House, July 19, Senate, July 28; River and Harbor Bill, conference report agreed upon August 3; taxing oleomargarine two cents per pound, Senate, July 20, House concurring July 23; New Ships Bill, House agreed to Senate amendments August 2; Reagan Inter-State Commerce Bill, House, July 30; increasing (twenty to twenty-five per cent.) pensions given to veteran soldiers wounded in the arm, hand, leg, or foot; Alien Landlord Bill, House, July 31.

Secretary of State Bayard, August 2, sent to Congress the department correspondence in the Cutting case. The Secretary said that he had made a demand for the release of Cutting, and was answered that Cutting was being tried for a violation of a Mexican federal statute which provides for the punishment of a foreigner who, in a foreign country, commits an offence against a Mexican citizen. To this Mr. Bayard replied that our government could not tolerate the application of such a law to American citizens, and renewed his demand for Cutting's release, which had not been complied with.

A. P. Williams was elected, August 3, United States Senator from California.

The Alabama State election, held August 2, resulted in the election of the entire Democratic ticket, including Seay for Governor.

Mr. Gladstone, July 21, received notification of the royal acceptance of his retirement from office. On the same day Lord Salisbury was summoned by the Queen. The new Ministry received their seals of office August 3. The following is the official list: Prime Minister and First Lord of the Treasury, Marquis of Salisbury; Foreign Secretary, Earl of Iddesleigh; Lord Chancellor, Lord Halsbury; Lord President of the Council, Viscount Cranbrook; Chancellor of the Exchequer and Leader of the Commons, Lord Randolph Churchill; Home Secretary, Mr. Henry Matthews, Q.C.; Colonial Secretary, Mr. Edward Stanhope; Secretary for War, Mr. William Henry Smith; Secretary for India, Sir R. Cross (with a peerage); First Lord of the Admiralty, Lord George Hamilton; Lord Chancellor of Ireland, Lord Ashbourne; Chief Secretary for Ireland, Sir M. Hicks-Beach; Chancellor of the Duchy of Lancaster, Lord John Manners; President of the Board of Trade, Sir F. Stanley (with a peerage).

Complete returns of the elections for the British House of Commons are as follows: Conservatives, 316; Union Liberals, 78; Gladstone Liberals, 191; Parnellites, 85—making a Unionist majority of 118.

Rioting was renewed in Belfast August 7, lasting three days. More than eleven people were killed and 130 wounded, and many houses were wrecked.

There was serious rioting in Amsterdam July 25 and 26, because of the prohibition of certain popular games on Sunday. The troops fired into the mob, killing twenty persons and wounding eighty.

The elections held in France, August 1, for the General Councils resulted in the choice of Republicans in 847 districts and Conservatives in 411. In 177 districts a second ballot would be required.

The Spanish Chamber of Deputies, July 28, unanimously passed a resolution that the government as soon as possible free the remaining 26,000 slaves in Cuba.

DISASTERS.

July 28.—The theatre at Tinnevelly, British India, burned, and one hundred lives lost.

July 30.—Schooner *Sarah Craig*, on a pleasure excursion from Philadelphia, capsized in a storm off Sandy Hook. Seven of the eleven passengers drowned.

August 13.—Thirty-six men killed by an explosion in the Woodend Colliery, Leigh, Lancashire, England.

OBITUARY.

July 16.—At Stamford, New York, Edward Z. C. Judson ("Ned Buntline"), aged sixty-four years.

July 21.—At Munich, Germany, Carl Von Piloty, painter, aged sixty years.

July 23.—In Berlin, Germany, Maximilian Wolfgang Duncker, historian, aged seventy-four years.

July 31.—At Baireuth, Abbé Liszt, in his seventy-fifth year.

August 4.—At Greystone, Yonkers, ex-Governor Samuel J. Tilden, aged seventy-two years.

August 7.—In Berlin, Germany, Professor William Scherer, historian and author, aged forty-five years.

August 9.—In London, England, Sir Samuel Ferguson, Q.C., LL.D., President Royal Irish Academy, aged seventy-six years.

August 10.—In Covington, Kentucky, ex-Governor John W. Stevenson, of Kentucky, aged seventy-three years.

August 11.—In New York city, Dr. Frank H. Hamilton, aged seventy-three years.

Editor's Drawer.

WANTED, a reading public. This is what the publishers say is needed—that is, serious readers, those who care enough about books to buy them, own them, and really possess themselves of their contents. This is what the writers say is needed—the writers who are becoming almost more numerous than the readers. Nearly everybody writes for publication; it is impossible to provide vehicles enough for their contributions, and the reading public to sustain periodicals does not increase in proportion. Everybody agrees that this is the most intelligent, active-minded age that ever was, and in its way the most prolific and productive age. Is there a glut and overproduction in the literary world as well as in other departments? Isn't it an odd outcome of diffused education and of cheap publications, the decline in the habit of continuous serious reading? We have heard a great deal, since Lord Brougham's time and the societies for the diffusion of knowledge, of the desirability of cheap literature for the masses. The Congressmen place cheapness above honesty in their sincere desire to raise the tone of the American people. There is no product that men use which is now so cheap as newspapers, periodicals, and books. For the price of a box of strawberries or a banana you can buy the immortal work of the greatest genius of all time in fiction, poetry, philosophy, or science. But we doubt if the class that were to be specially benefited by this reduction in price of intellectual food are much profited. Of course some avail themselves of things placed within their reach which they could not own formerly, but it remains true that people value and profit only by that which it costs some effort to obtain. We very much doubt if the mass of the people have as good habits of reading as they had when publications were dearer. Who is it who buy the five, ten, and twenty cent editions? Generally those who could afford to buy, and did buy, books at a fair price, to the remuneration of author and publisher. And their serious reading habit has gone down with the price. We have an increasing leisure class. When does it read? Not much in the winter, for the demands of society are too exigent then. For private reading there is no time, and a short-cut to information is sought by means of drawing-room lectures and clubs, which are supposed to give to social life, without interfering with it, a lacquer of culture. In summer it is impossible to read much; what is called the mind needs rest by that time, and the distractions of out-door life in the mountains and by the sea forbid anything but the most desultory skimming of the very lightest products of the press. To be sure, the angel of the Atlantic Ocean sees a row of pretty girls on the coast, seated on rocks or in the sand, all the way from Campo Bello to Cape May, with novels in their hands—one of the most pleasing imitations of intellectual life ever presented in the world. It is perfect when there is breeze enough to turn over the leaves. And the young men—those who are in business, or who are supposed to be getting a more or less "conditional" education—do they read as much as the young ladies? It is a curious comment on the decay of the reading habit in households, the blank literary condition of the young men who come up to the high-schools and colleges. Is it owing entirely to the modern specialization of knowledge that they usually have read little except their text-books?

Now we are not trying to defend the necessity of reading. They say that people got on in the Middle Ages very well without much of it, and that the women then were as agreeable, and the men as brave and forceful, as in this age. But it is certainly interesting to consider whether, by reason of cheap and chopped-up literary food, we are coming round practically to the Middle Ages relative to reading, that is, to reading anything except what is called news, or ingenious sorts of inventions and puzzles which can be talked about as odd incidents in daily life are talked about. Reading to any intellectual purpose requires patience and abstraction and continuity of thought. This habit of real reading is not acquired by the perusal of newspapers, nor by the swift dash which most people give to the cheap publications which are had for the picking up, and usually valued accordingly. It is an open question whether cheap literature is helping us any toward becoming a thoughtful and reading people.

AT what age is a sense of humor usually developed? It very rarely exists in children under twelve. The funny things that small children say are not funny to them; the odd and startling questions they ask have to them no element of the incongruous. It is usually only when they lose the faculty of making odd or deep observations that they begin to see any humor in them. Much of their apparent brightness comes from ignorance of the true relation of things. A couple of incidents illustrate this. A gentleman in Massachusetts who was born for a soldier, but had never the opportunity to indulge himself in this capacity, was made a member of the Governor's staff. He at once procured a uniform that for gold and gorgeousness surpassed anything ever seen in the militia. Arrayed in this dazzling costume, he called one evening at a house to accompany a young lady to a reception. The little girl of the family, who was above-stairs watching the progress of her sister's toilet, ran to the balustrade and peeped over when the bell rang, and saw this Resplendent Being enter the hall.

"Who is it, Joe?" cried the sister.

"I don' know," replied the appreciative child—"I don' know, but I think it is God."

The other incident may be called more subjective. A lady one day drove to the house of a clergyman who served a large parish, and of course was frequently sent for to attend funerals. While the carriage was waiting, the coachman took up one of the children of the family, a boy of three years, and drove round the square. When he was set down, the boy marched into the parlor, and, by way of acknowledgment, said to the lady, "Aunt Lu, *I've been ridin' in your funeral.*"

STRANGE HABITS.

THE late Professor Greene, author of *Greene's Analysis*, and the English Grammar with which so many have wrestled in their school-days, was one of the most genial and fatherly of men. During the later years of his life he was Professor of Mathematics and Astronomy in a New England college. There was in one of his classes a somewhat slow-witted though studious young man, whom we may call Jones. On a certain occasion, after Jones had repeated carefully the text-book statements about the effects of the motions of the earth, and was trying to remember what came next in the book, the Professor interposed with,

"Were you ever in the shadow of the earth, Mr. Jones?"

JONES (slowly). "No, sir."

PROFESSOR. "Where do you spend your nights, sir?"

Jones didn't want to tell.

NOT GHOSTS AS CUSS.

THE question to Lethe Sayles, when she was upon the witness stand, as to whether or not she believed in ghosts, in one of Miss Murfree's stories, reminds me of a dialogue I once heard between a lawyer and a witness in Independence, Jefferson County, Missouri. One of the "James gang," as the band of robbers were called who for a few years previous to that time (1881) had committed numerous crimes in that portion of the State, was on trial for participation in what was known as the "Glendale train robbery." Mrs. ——, a witness for the State, testified that on the night before the robbery occurred she saw the prisoner, and heard him talking to her husband about the proposed robbery. Upon her cross-examination the following dialogue took place:

Q. "Now, Mrs. ——, tell us again how you happened to see the prisoner upon the evening in question."

A. "He come to the house 'long in the fust part of the evenin', an' asked me where was my old man. I said out-doors someers, an' he went out to find him. Bime-by I 'lowed I'd better see if he'd found him; an' when I got out-doors I heerd voices in the corn patch, an' I went along kinder still like, an' looked through the fence. I was a couple o' fence corners from 'em. 'Twas light as day, 'most."

Q. "You saw them distinctly?"

A. "Yaas."

Q. "Well, Mrs. ——, I want to know if you believe in ghosts—in spooks."

A. "Waal, I don' know as it's any o' your business what I believe."

"You must answer the question," said the Judge.

A. "Waal, then, I do. I've seen 'em."

Q. "Your house is said to be haunted, isn't it?"

A. "Yaas."

Q. "And ghosts have been seen walking about outside by yourself and your family?"

A. "Yaas."

Q. "I thought so. Now can you swear that it wasn't ghosts that you saw and heard out in the cornfield that evening?"

A. "Yaas, I can."

Q. "Well, how do you know?"

A. "'Cause they war a-cussin. I've seen an' heerd ghosts, but never ghosts as cuss."

ELEANOR.

You can see her, if you look
    Behind that door.
'Tis a place, I know full well,
    She's been before,
For the sofa, small and neat,
With a cushion for her feet,
Makes a very charming seat
    For Eleanor.

I have sat with her ofttimes
    Behind the door,
For my love I told her there
    In days of yore.
And her eyes were black as jet,
While she murmured, "darling," "pet"—
But she is an arch coquette,
    This Eleanor.

You would better leave her there
    Behind the door,
Else your heart she'll surely make
    Extremely sore.
So now let us drink our wine,
While some other doth recline,
Undergoing feelings fine
    For Eleanor.
            PEARCE BAILEY.

THE OLDEST NAME IN THE WORLD.

"CURIOUS, isn't it, that we should all meet in this way, all three going to different places, and all three belonging to different countries?"

It *was* curious, undoubtedly. The three hungry guests who were doing full justice to the good cheer of the Black Lion were a Londoner on his summer holiday, a Scotchman from the mouth of the Clyde, and an American tourist from New England taking a hasty run to Europe and back. They had encountered one another in front of the snug little wayside inn, at a point where several roads met, and had agreed to dine together in honor of the coincidence.

The dinner lasted a good while, for all three had walked far that morning. But nothing can last forever, except a lawsuit or a serial which is paid by the sheet, and at length our heroes showed signs of having had enough.

"Well," said the American, casting a glance through the open window at the westering sun, "I don't know how *you* feel, gentlemen, but it seems to *me* that it's just about time to be starting again."

"And before we go," suggested the Englishman, "let's toss up for who shall pay for the dinner."

"Aweel," remarked the canny Scot, "I'm thinkin' the best way wad be for each man to pay his ain share."

"No; I'll tell you how we'll do it," interposed the Yankee. "We haven't told each other our names yet, so whichever of us has got the oldest name shall go free, and the other two shall halve the score between 'em."

"Done!" cried his two companions, with one voice; and the Englishman, thrusting his hand into his pocket, produced, with a confident smile, a card inscribed "Richard Eve."

"My name's as old as humanity itself, anyhow," said he.

"Ay; but before Eve there was *Adam*, ye ken," observed the gentleman from Clydesdale, with a dry chuckle, as he displayed the name of "Adam McTaggart." "Can ye beat *that*, freend?" added he, turning to the New-Englander.

"Seems to me I can," replied the unmoved Yankee, "for my name's the oldest in the world."

And so it was; for the card that he threw upon the table—at which the two others gazed with a stare of blank bewilderment that gradually broadened into a hearty laugh—bore the name of "*Mr. B. Ginning*."

DAVID KER.

A POWERFUL BOTTLE.

THE following story is told of the General Traffic Manager of a Southern railroad. Some time ago, as he was returning to New York from the South, the train on which he was riding stopped at Elizabeth, and among the passengers who boarded it was a richly dressed lady, who entered the car in which he sat, and anxiously glanced around for a seat. The train was crowded, and Mr. O—— immediately arose and gave the lady his—the outer half of the—seat, and stood in the aisle near by. When Newark was reached, the gentleman who occupied the other half got out and left the car. The lady at once arose, as if to give Mr. O—— his portion of the seat, shook out her skirts, seated herself again with her back to the aisle, and put her little hand-satchel on the other half of the seat. By this time many of the passengers had become interested in the

situation. When the train reached that portion of the meadows between Newark and Jersey City on which the phosphate works are situated, the terrible stench, so familiar to those who habitually travel on the Pennsylvania and Morris and Essex railroads, penetrated the cars. Quick as thought, the lady seized her satchel, got out a bottle of smelling-salts, and clapped it to her nose. Mr. O—— saw this, and leaning over, he said to a couple of gentlemen in the seat immediately behind her, "Gentlemen, what in the name of heaven has that woman got in that bottle?"

The lady instantly turned, and said, "*It is not this bottle, sir, which smells.*"

Amid the universal laughter he retired to another car, but not until he had shot back, "Madam, as long as I live I'll *never forget the smell from that bottle.*"

THE EASIEST WAY.

YOUR letter just came to me, Willy,
　And you find that you don't forget?
You've tried for these months (oh, you silly!),
　And are sure that you love me yet?
Ah! those days were sweet, I acknowledge,
　In that dear old town by the sea,
When the head of his class in college
　Took a fancy to me.

Don't say that I haven't a heart, Will:
　I think of the past with regret;
And though we've so long been apart, still
　I too find it hard to forget.
What nonsense I'm writing! Ned Carey
　Has broken with Lillian Lee,
And he and Ralph Sands—you know Mary—
　Are devoted to me.

Jack Whitney has come into money;
　And so has Nell Page; by-the-way,
She married old Dale—ain't it funny?
　He's seventy, if he's a day.
Her trousseau, of course, came from Paris;
　Her bridemaids were Maggie McKee,
The Weston girls, Beatrice Harris,
　Celia Carter, and me.

Another, they say, in September
　Will be the event of the year.
The groom is young Boyd—you remember
　Your trio: Boyd, Billiards, and Beer?
'Tis Grace wed to Gold, says Dame Grundy;
　That his gifts are a sight to see;
That she tries on her dress on Monday;
　That it's ordered by me;

That mine's the opinion that's asked for
　The flowers, the feast, and the wine;
That my poor little wits are tasked for
　The entire performance, in fine.
The happy girl isn't Grace Greeley,
　Nor even my cousin Marie;
They say—you know tongues run so freely—
　That the bride, too, is me.

RUTH HALL.

A NEW APOSTLE.

IN a Friends' meeting-house in Philadelphia there was once gathered a great assembly in the expectation that the spirit would move to speak a distinguished Friend from Baltimore, who was present. It did move him, and for nearly two hours he held forth in an excited strain that was contagious with his hearers. Toward the end of his discourse he depicted in gloomy and glowing colors the place of punishment of the wicked, and besought them to flee the wrath to come, "So that in the day of judgment they should not be found among the frightened herd, who would look in vain for some way of escape; yea, they would give then all their worldly possessions, they would be ready to cry, 'A horse! a horse! my kingdom for a horse!' as did the holy evangelist."

IT was in old days, on the Missouri River, that two squatters lived long together as bachelors, the one hunting, and the other providing the firing material and doing the cooking. Repeatedly had the elder one gone East with a view to matrimony, but as often returned wifeless. On the last visit for this purpose he succeeded, at least near enough to write back to his mate, "Clean up the cabin, and kill a hog, for I have got her this time, sure."

JOHNNY'S mother was the wife of a fisherman of Marblehead not many years ago, but is now, alas! his widow. She was not one of "the women of Marblehead" who tarred and feathered and carried in a cart the old hardhearted sea-captain Floyd; but she came of the same race, and Johnny often suffered dire bodily punishment at her hands when he had unfortunately aroused her anger. One day, to prevent a threatened and doubtless deserved chastisement, he took to his heels. His mother immediately gave chase; but as she was large and fat, she was left somewhat behind at the start. Johnny held his course down the narrow street, however, and the heavy wind in their rear proved so efficient an aid to his pursuer that Johnny's sprier feet and superior agility were hardly apt to serve him to escape. The strong press of wind against his mother's spreading and voluminous garments was carrying her down the street at such a rapid rate that to an unmoved observer it appeared very much as if the little fellow was destined to suffer to appease his parent's wrath, which, of course, was greatly increased by the excitement and exercise of the chase. One of Johnny's friends, who was standing on the corner, coolly and calmly—because he himself was not in any danger—observed the chase, and quickly calculated the chances. He immediately perceived Johnny's disadvantage, and putting his hands to his mouth trumpetwise, "Try her on the wind, Johnny—try her on the wind," he shouted, and together the two young friends doubled the corner, and soon left the old lady far in the rear, breathless and impotent with rage.

WOMEN'S RIGHTS.

MR. SMITH. "I must admit, Miss Constance, that women occasionally rival men in intellect and character; but I contend that their inferiority in strength and stature will prove an insuperable bar to their ever being placed on a footing of equality with the sterner sex."

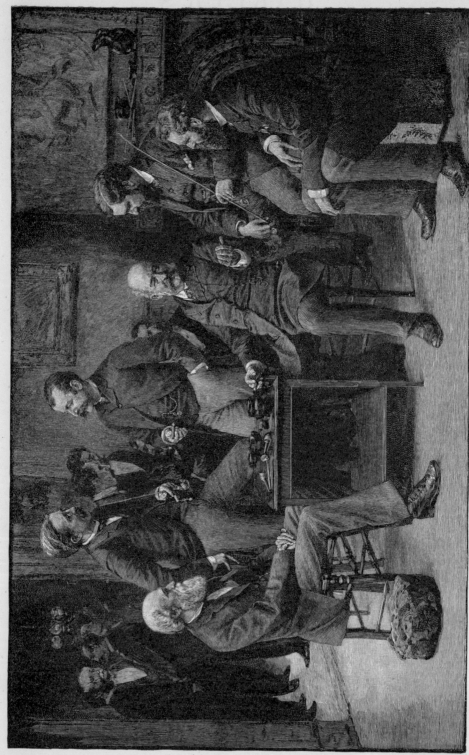

O. B. Bunce. G. C. Eggleston. Laurence Hatton. Noah Brooks. G. P. Lathrop. R. U. Johnson.

AT THE AUTHORS' CLUB, NEW YORK.—[See page 831.]

HARPER'S
NEW MONTHLY MAGAZINE.

Vol. LXXIII.   NOVEMBER, 1886.   No. CCCCXXXVIII.

THE LITERARY MOVEMENT IN NEW YORK.

BY GEORGE PARSONS LATHROP.

I.

AT the dinner of a famous Greek letter society in Cambridge, Massachusetts, a few years ago, the poet of the day, who had been chosen from the metropolis beside the Hudson, made a speech. He began by paying eloquent tribute on behalf of New York to the authors of Boston and Cambridge—a tribute received with rapturous enthusiasm. Going on, he expressed his belief that in New York a literature would grow up as lofty as that which Massachusetts has given to the world, but somewhat wider in its range, and of a more dramatic quality. This part of the speech was followed by a dead silence. The conscientious Massachusetts company refused to veil its skepticism by so much as a single thin round of applause. It did not believe that there could be a literature in New York, and the mere idea that one might be developed was hardly less than sinful in its sight.

A similar lack of faith prevails largely in New York itself. New-Yorkers are very apt to question whether New York has any definite characteristics, and they doubt whether, without them, it can produce or sustain a literature. The Rev. Mr. Burnaby, who visited the city about 1750, was likewise perplexed by the absence of salient local traits. "The inhabitants of New York," he wrote, "in their character very much resemble the Pennsylvanians. Being, however, of different nations, different languages, and different religions, it is impossible to give them any precise or definite character." It would be interesting to ascertain, if we could, how the New-Yorkers resembled the Pennsylvanians, and how at the same time that they were of various nationalities, they had no definite character of their own. But this is a problem that still baffles inquiry, and is likely to do so up to the end of time. New York's characteristics insist upon remaining as undefined as those of London; and perhaps it is better, on the whole, that they should. Were the fact otherwise, New York would be simply another kind of Boston.

It is certain, however, that New York has quietly gone on growing, that it harbors a large number of cultivated and interesting human beings, and that, however illogical the result may seem, it has paid a good deal of attention to art and literature, and has given rise to a good many authors.

From the latter part of the eighteenth century down to the epoch of Irving, Halleck, and Cooper a continuous though slender stream of literary example and tradition runs through the history of New York. Governor Hunter, who had been a warm friend of Addison, Steele, and Swift, and brought the influence of their taste to these shores; Governor William Burnet (son of Bishop Burnet, the historian), who brought from Philadelphia that multifarious writer Cadwallader Colden; William Livingston, who wrote the colony's one periodical, the *Independent Reflector*—these arrange themselves in the first group. They are followed by the flowered waistcoats and silken turbans that crowded the receptions of Mrs. Secretary Knox, where essays were read on politics, religion, diplomacy, and finance. Later, the Drone Club was formed, which embraced the first American novelist, Brockden Brown, Judge Kent, and William Dunlap, historian of early American art and of the early American stage. Finally, Paulding—essayist, rhymer, novelist, and Secretary of the Navy—joined Irving in the composition of *Salmagundi*. Then Irving came out with his *Knickerbocker's*

History and the *Sketch-Book*—a full-grown and speedily famous author. Joseph Rodman Drake and Fitz-Greene Halleck made a great stir with their "Croaker" verses, and Halleck lived to triumph in his celebrity as the author of "Marco Bozzaris," and as the Horace of New York. Fenimore Cooper published his novels of American frontier life, and came to the full noon of a world-wide fame. Edgar Poe also connected himself for some time with New York. The effort to establish literary periodicals was exemplified in the *Talisman*, the *Atlantic Magazine*, the *Literary Review*, the *New York Review;* afterward in the *Knickerbocker Monthly* and the *Democratic Review*. William Cullen Bryant edited the *New York Review*, and it was not long after he came to live in New York that he took his place among the foremost American poets. The first periodicals that lifted up their heads did not hold them up very long. *Putnam's Magazine*, however, under the editorship of George William Curtis, not only took high rank, but managed to keep alive for some years. Besides this, we have had the *Galaxy*—one of the most varied and entertaining monthlies ever issued in New York. *Harper's New Monthly Magazine* and the *Century Magazine* now have the field to themselves.

We may safely say, then, that New York has contrived to keep up its interest in literary matters down to the present. It may be that its first period of production was marked by a greater dependence upon foreign models, on the part of Halleck, Irving, and Cooper, than Hawthorne, Lowell, Emerson, and Whittier showed. But it is to the point to observe that Bryant and Cooper were recognized authors, and that Irving had returned from a seventeen years' absence abroad, to receive public ovation and acclaim from his fellow-townsmen, at a date when the members of the Boston school had barely emerged into public notice.

II.

When we review in catalogue some of the better known men of letters here, the showing is certainly not insignificant. Several among them are closely related still to the literary New York of thirty years ago, and their presence connects that past phase with the present one of gradual progressive growth. George William Curtis, for example, in *The Poti-*

phar Papers, continued—although with a distinct manner and touch that were his own—a strain of light and gentle satire on society, which has a certain kinship with the mood of Washington Irving in his earlier days. The note which he struck is appropriate, and is likely to be repeated, or at least responded to, by other voices in our metropolitan literature— voices of individual quality and various in range; for good-humored ridicule of the current shams and foibles is a constant factor in the lighter literature of great cities. The satirical power which the late Richard Grant White possessed was little known to the public, because he studiously avoided the presentation of his claims on that score. His *New Gospel of Peace*, published at a critical period during the war, was a pamphlet hardly to be classed as literature, but it was exceedingly clever and trenchant, it gained a wide popularity, and had a great effect on opinion. The author never acknowledged it, preferring to rest upon his well-earned reputation as a Shakespearian commentator and editor, and as a writer on the use of English. His book of observation on England, however, and his semi-satirical story concerning the experience of Mr. Washington Adams in that country, made him known in a new way both abroad and at home. By his scholarly attitude and work, as well as by his frequent anonymous contributions to press criticism of books, he rendered good service to the cause of American letters. He also maintained and helped to diffuse an active interest in the drama and in music as fine arts. Mr. White has gone, and Mr. Curtis has for some years given his energies chiefly to editorial composition and to political reforms. So, too, Parke Godwin, who formerly aided the intellectual march by works of biography, history, political philosophy, and by translations from the German, has ceased from active production, and has interested himself in journalism. It is pertinent here to recall—in view of Mr. Godwin's relationship to Bryant both by marriage and in business—the fact that the poet in like manner centred his career upon the *Evening Post*. There is an advantage, perhaps, in establishing points of connection between authorship on the one side and non-literary society on the other, or with public affairs, questions of state, of sociology, and the influence wielded by

EDMUND CLARENCE STEDMAN.
From a photograph by Mora, New York.

newspapers. The Hon. John Bigelow, formerly minister to France—a politician of the self-respecting, therefore not self-seeking, type—represents another of these points, in that he has latterly given much of his time to biographical studies.

But the faculty of producing pure literature—whether history, poetry, biography, fiction, drama, criticism, miscellaneous essays, or travels narrated in the distinctively artistic way—is a faculty so delicate that it may be dimmed or cor-roded by a breath of accident, and it finds a most destructive solvent in the distractions of society, public life, and journalism. Hence it happens that our writers who occupy these middle places between the world of art and the world of artifice, although they fulfil a very useful function, surrender to conventional demands more than they gain for literature. In Boston, with the exception of Dr. Holmes, the authors of most renown have held exclusively to literary pursuits; but there is

W. H. BISHOP.

something about the local conditions in New York which has led writers, at least since the time of Irving and Cooper, to divide their allegiance and attach themselves in part to some other occupation, often uncongenial. This, no doubt, in some cases, has been due to the pressure of particular circumstances. But literary life in New York has no well-defined position as compared with the other activities of the city. The cost of living is high; and on both these accounts authors find it well to fortify themselves with the support furnished by commercial and editorial connections.

The two poets who have done the most to preserve the fine traditions of their art, during the period that followed Bryant's comparative abandonment of creative work, long before he died, are Richard Henry Stoddard and Edmund C. Stedman. Both of them have been absorbed in great measure by employments not favorable to the highest phase of inspiration—Stedman in conducting the business of a banker and broker, without the advantages and ease of Samuel Rogers, and Stoddard in accomplishing routine duties as a custom-house official or as the literary editor of a daily paper. No college or university has enlisted them to lecture on

belles-lettres; few special honors or emoluments have been bestowed upon them; most of the positions offered them have been worthless. They are far enough from enjoying the studious leisure guaranteed by sufficient means to men like Tennyson, Browning, Swinburne, Longfellow, Lowell. It has never even been thought worth while to give them the security of permanent government posts, such as Matthew Arnold, Bryan Waller Procter, Lang, Dobson, and Gosse have benefited by in England. But these facts make it all the more remarkable that they should have done what they have done. Stoddard and Stedman have served the Muse not only with the spontaneous fervor of early manhood, but also with the steady faith and endurance that alone make action possible when all hope of due reward has been relentlessly denied. The credit must be awarded to them alone; to their unbroken fidelity in ministering to an ideal aim, and worshipping the beauty and wholeness of true art. The city with which their careers have been identified, which they unselfishly love and are proud of, deserves no credit at all.

Mr. Stedman made his first important public appearance more than twenty-five years ago, as the author of "The Diamond Wedding," which occupied several columns in the *Tribune.* Perhaps no *jeu d'esprit* of the kind could now produce the effect which that did then, but at the time of its publication "The Diamond Wedding"—celebrating in witty and satirical verse a match that was attracting much attention—set the whole town astir with laughter and excitement, and brought upon the young poet a challenge to mortal combat. Compared with the "Croaker" verses, or Halleck's once famous "Recorder," it was as wine to water; it had all the verve, the fun, the technical dexterity, of Thomas Hood, with a fresh tone and touch belonging to the author himself. He has not chosen to preserve it among his collected works. But the future biographer or careful historian will keep it in memory as a brilliant rhymed skit which has not been surpassed on this side of the water, notwithstanding the whilom popularity of "Nothing to Wear," by William Allen Butler, another New-

RICHARD HENRY STODDARD.
From a photograph by Pach, New York.

Yorker. I have dwelt upon this early piece in order to remind the reader of Stedman's versatility. We all know how he has since built up by patient and artistic workmanship an honorable and enviable reputation as a poet; forcible, refined, charging his lines with varied emotion, and at times with exquisite tenderness and reflectiveness. His masculine, warlike ballad, "How Old Brown Took Harper's Ferry," will live long after the prejudices of civil strife are dead ; his "Blameless Prince" is a beautifully wrought story, which, had it come from a foreign poet, would have won a greater fame than has been vouchsafed it. In "Alice of Monmouth" he took a native theme, related to the war for the Union, and placed the scene partly in New Jersey, giving to the common sights of daily American life a picturesqueness which they seem to be quite able to sustain. "Pan in Wall Street," again, is a charming fantasy that penetrates the most sordid of neighborhoods, the national money centre, with a playful and refreshing

EDGAR FAWCETT.

ing and relating the works of its past. Certainly, when we consider that his study and composition have been carried on wholly in the nights between fatiguing business days, or in brief vacations, the double achievement of Stedman in verse and prose becomes wonderful as well as admirable.

Mr. Stoddard has not concerned himself to touch the local note; but that is of slight moment in view of the exalted purpose which has controlled him. Pacing for many years the streets of our metropolis, he has not found his inspiration there, but in his own occult faculty of causing exotic flowers of fancy to spring up in a place where there was believed to be no seed or soil for these growths. Under most discouraging circumstances, in the face of sorrow and bitterness, he has kept pure his faith in the highest ideal of

breeze of poetic humor and sentiment. Stedman, therefore, may be said to have definitely expressed himself as an American poet dealing with American subjects, although, very properly, he has held himself free to treat whatever subject appealed to him, irrespective of locality. But, in addition to this, he enjoys the distinction of having written with infinite care, with sensitive appreciation and impartiality, the sole volume of standard criticism and review of the Victorian poets, and the only work on the poets of America that adequately comprehends the subject. This in itself would form a sufficient basis for a claim to permanent recognition. The two volumes are not only packed with information, the result of painstaking research; they are also remarkable for their breadth of view combined with delicacy of perception, and the matter is woven into a verbal style as rich, yet simple and explicit, as the design of an old tapestry. Mr. Stedman's criticism is philosophical as well as imaginative. Unlike that of the New England school, it leads the mind along on creative lines, searching for the law of progress, and assisting to build up the future of literature as well as analyz-

poetic art, giving to the world scores of exquisite lyrics, some of which have been wafted far and wide through the country, and have found shelter in many a sympathetic heart. The solemn, direct power and pathos of his short poem on Thackeray's death would be hard to match elsewhere; his Shakespeare ode needs no praise; and he has sung in noble cadences of "The Dead Master," Bryant. Many of his poems are imbued with sadness, but it is the melancholy of a virile although sensitive mind. On the other hand, what could be more brilliantly gay and picturesque than "A Wedding under the Directory"? The massive Horatian ode on Abraham Lincoln is cast in quite another mould, and renews the stern majesty of Andrew Marvell's memorial strain. Through all his Eastern songs one traces an aroma, evanescent and enchanting, which cannot be described, but blends, as if in a sensible perfume, the potency of love, fancy, sorrow, in their most recondite phases. As for his workmanship, it has the fine, firm chiselling, the airy grace and certainty of aim, characterizing the older English poets; but it is not imitative. There is an individuality about all that Stoddard writes which cannot be mistaken. This, however, is not the place in which to do him justice. I will add only that the simplicity of style, the beauty and completeness of effect, employed in his long poems, "The King's Bell" rapid survey of the later singers—Fawcett, Gilder, Bunner, De Kay, Mrs. Mary Mapes Dodge, Miss Hutchinson, and others. Edgar Fawcett, devoting himself wholly to literature, has been before the public for fifteen years, and during that

RICHARD WATSON GILDER.

and "Wratislaw," prove him to be a narrative poet of a very high order. I marvel at the perfection of the best that he has done. But I marvel still more that, in the great city where he has wrought so long, no public honor has been paid him, no formal tribute rendered by his fellow-craftsmen.

The room of a magazine article is small for even a brief mention of the poets. We must therefore content ourselves with a period he has been more prolific both of verse and prose than any of his fellows among local authors. His *Fantasy and Passion*, *Song and Story*, and *Romance and Revery* represent a part of his poetic productions ; several of his plays have been acted ; and one, *The False Friend*, which evidenced unusual strength and adroit technical handling, held the stage for an entire season. In addition, Mr. Fawcett has put forth seven or eight

JOHN BURROUGHS.
From a photograph by Vail Brothers, Poughkeepsie.

exception to his style and methods, in some respects, as one might also take exceptions in discussing the various other writers named in these pages; but it is not my present object to criticise. It will be much more useful simply to record what has been done that is worth reading and considering. Richard Watson Gilder, editor of the *Century Magazine*, is a worthy leader in the small band of genuine poets. His note is clear, pure, aspiring always, in his "New Day," "The Poet and His Master," and his collected *Poems and Lyrics*. He has, in many pieces, the irresistible singing quality—that motion of music which carries us along as naturally as the earth does in its rotary flight through space. Alive to all the beauty of sense, sound, color, physical pleasure, he adores no less the beauty of thought, the splendor of divinity; and all these things are taken up into the comprehensive spirituality of his mood, so that to read his verse is like receiving a new access of the glad, pure candor which belongs to youth. Charles De Kay, a brother-in-law of Richard Gilder, and a grandson of Joseph Rodman Drake, has undertaken in his *Vision of Nimrod* and his *Esther* a poetic work of much larger imaginative scope than is usually attempted in these days, least of all in the United States. By his choice of subject and of method he has restricted himself to a limited audience; but in these more ambitious works, as well as in his shorter collected *Poems*, he manifests an independent artistic conscience which will not be swayed from its settled course, and frequently guides him to commanding heights of descriptive beauty or delicate insight. Were it desirable to make a special plea on behalf of New York, we might securely instance De Kay and Gilder as examples to prove that the absolutely ideal tendency finds room for its development in this somewhat sordid but still more abused city.

Will Carleton, who lives in Brooklyn, but is essentially a New York author, follows a line entirely apart from those on which the poets travel whom we have already mentioned. He strives to inter-

novels, together with a book of character sketches under the title of *Social Silhouettes*, and is understood to be the author of an anonymous mock-tragedy, *The Buntling Ball*, the unstinted praise bestowed upon which was in curious contrast to the carping criticism with which New York reviewers have generally greeted his signed publications. The poetry of Edgar Fawcett, on the whole, differs decidedly from that of most of his American contemporaries by its greater intensity of instinctive romance and by its sensuous effects. He is liberal in his use of color where other American poets paint usually in black and white or subdued tones. The rhythm and music of his lines suggest what may be called the verbal orchestration of Swinburne rather than the purely melodic style of composition most in vogue here. Perhaps on this account he does better in imaginative than in reflective or purely lyrical poetry, representing thus the tendency to dramatic purpose which begins to characterize New York writers; but that fact does not prevent him from arriving at keen intellectual deductions and epigrammatic statement. Doubtless one might honestly take

EDWARD EGGLESTON.
From a photograph by Zimmerman, St. Paul.

pret the life of the people as it is to-day, in the country-side or in the city, on far-away farms and prairies, and in the crowded streets of the sea-board centres.* The enormous popularity of Mr. Carleton's *Farm Ballads* and *City Ballads* bears witness to the precision with which he has gauged the popular sympathy. There are fashions, conventions, formal traditions, in poetry as in other fields of

* A portrait of Will Carleton was published in *Harper's Magazine* for March, 1884, page 577.

human thought, and there are critics who are distressed by the idea that a simple and sincere exposition of every-day occurrences, or of common phases of emotion, in unaffected rhythmic and rhymed language, should be classed with other poetic literature of a more classical type. These same critics, however, recognize that when Tennyson writes a "May Queen," or dialect pieces like "The Northern Farmer," or "Grandmother's Apology," he conquers a realm of realistic interpretation which is quite as well worth ruling in as the more artificial one represented by poems cast in the formal and accepted mould.   If a significant national literature, or a local New York literature (as a part of it), is to be developed, there ought not to be much doubt that we must cordially give place to every frank expression of American life which finds its way into honest and workman-like utterance in verse or prose, whether or not it conforms to certain standards of finish arbitrarily fixed.

JULIAN HAWTHORNE.
From a photograph by Sarony, New York.

Among the more recent candidates for poetic honors is Henry Cuyler Bunner, the witty editor of the comic weekly *Puck*, whose *Airs from Arcady* has won him a crown of laurel, still in the bud, perhaps, but with vigorous leaves of perfect achievement sprouting out from the circle here and there.   Mr. Bunner is equally at home in *vers de société* and in poems of emotion.   His mingled chords of gayety and tenderness have already placed him among the most charming and delicately artistic of our singers. Maurice F. Egan and George Edgar Montgomery have also joined the choir; the former with a small volume of poems redolent of sympathy with the beautiful and of religion; the latter with scattered poems in which he strives to bring out the poetry of science. In another direction, David L. Proudfit, writing under the pseudonym of "Peleg Arkwright," has succeeded in giving to certain episodes of humble life a poetic coloring, as his "Love among the Gamins" may attest.

Nor should it be forgotten, in making this summary, that N. P. Willis — once a most popular poet — centred his life upon New York, that John G. Saxe, who formerly held sway as the most widely known of humorous verse-writers, lived in its neighborhood, or that Dr. J. G. Holland was for a time one of the active and important figures in its literary circles.   Bayard Taylor, who never wrote anything specifically illustrative of New York, had his home here, and here completed some of his most ambitious poetic works.   Fitz-James O'Brien was a New-Yorker, and put forth enough pieces in verse, sometimes roughly vigorous, sometimes tenderly sentimental, sometimes lightly sarcastic, to show that, had he lived, he would have taken no mean position as an effective rhymer.   More recently Joaquin Miller made New York his home for several years, before he removed to Washington.

E. P. ROE.

The women poets do not now stand out so prominently as in earlier times. Mrs. R. H. Stoddard, it must be said with regret, has apparently given up her activity both as novelist and poet; so has Mrs. Botta resigned her place among productive singers. Mrs. Mary Mapes Dodge continues, at rare intervals, to publish poems exceptional in their power of conveying, by exquisite modulations of word and sound, the finest sense of rare perceptions as well as of common experiences. Miss Ellen Hutchinson, too, has wrought into verse many delicate fantasies with a touch that denotes a subtle poetic gift.

But of all the people with poetic voices who have lived on this populous island, Walt Whitman alone has attempted to reproduce its elements in a shape suggesting their mass and variety, and with a spirit responding to and interpreting them; for, "Ah, what," he says, "can ever be more stately and admirable to me than mast-hemm'd Manhattan?" His method, to be sure, is crude, unfinished, often mistaken; and he alternates dull prose with gleams of splendid poetry. But perhaps by virtue of this mixture he is all the better fitted to express the actual New York. The largeness of his grasp,

BRANDER MATTHEWS.

Warner, it is true, are distinctively associated with Hartford, but they visit New York at short intervals, and are both members of its Authors Club. In general, also, one thinks of their work as showing more affinity with metropolitan tendencies than with the New England school. Charles Nordhoff, at his summer home on the Palisades, may be added to the list, as the author of *Cape Cod Stories* and a volume on California. At Newark, again, frequently coming into town, lives Noah Brooks, together with Thomas Dunn English, whose "Ben Bolt" has been sung around the world for nearly forty years. Julian Hawthorne, returning to this country after a long stay abroad, made his residence in New York at first, and is still in close relation with the city, so that he, as well as Edward Eggleston, must be included in its noticeable group of novelists, along with

and his purely native tone, will always serve to remind us of the radical course and the independent steps that must be taken before this part of the world can have an adequate portrayal in poetry.

In Boston the theoretical centre is somewhere about the Common ; Cambridge and Concord being, if one may say so, a kind of outside centres, or "eccentrics." Similarly we find, attached to New York and sometimes revolving on its axis, sundry writers who live in other places, but must be counted as belonging to its system ; for example, John Burroughs, at Esopus ; E. P. Roe, at Cornwall on the Hudson ; Julian Hawthorne, at Scotch Plains, New Jersey ; Edward Eggleston, at Lake George, formerly of Brooklyn ; and the Misses Warner, of whom only one survives. Samuel L. Clemens (Mark Twain) and Charles Dudley

BRONSON HOWARD.
From a photograph by Barraud, London.

Edgar Fawcett, W. H. Bishop, Professor H. H. Boyesen, Brander Matthews, H. C. Bunner, Mrs. Stoddard, Anna Katherine Greene, Mrs. L. W. Champney, Dr. William S. Mayo, Dr. William A. Hammond, Mr. O. B. Bunce, and Mr. George H. Picard.

sity of the city which is known, and will long be known, as "the *Cecil Dreeme* room." It was there that Winthrop worked; and had he lived to mature, he would have given us much to be proud of. Fitz-James O'Brien was a far more pol-

J. B. M^cMASTER.
From a photograph by Pach, New York.

If we leave out Cooper's works, it must be confessed that for a long time the novel did not flourish in New York; yet there is one striking exception to be made in the case of Theodore Winthrop, whose *Cecil Dreeme* and *John Brent*, although marred by an abrupt and *outré* style, were among the freshest and raciest of American stories. There is a small square apartment in one of the gray towers of the Univer-

ished artist, who, however, did not go beyond the limits of the short story; and his highly fanciful conceptions were not characteristic of the soil. Another fictionist of great promise was Albert F. Webster, who died ten years ago, after producing a long series of remarkable short stories, original, vivid, weird, and yet natural, which brought from across the water the warm praises of Charles Reade. But it

H. H. BOYESEN.
From a photograph by Pach, New York.

inventive and imaginative of our novelists, who commands a refreshingly clear and unaffected style. At the present writing Mr. Frank R. Stockton's reputation rests upon his humorous narrative—I had almost said extravaganza —*Rudder Grange*, and upon the marvellous and delectably quaint conceits that form the motive of his short stories in *The Lady and the Tiger*. Doubtless Mr. Stockton is, in one sense, the most original of American tale-writers; his fun is inimitable and underived; his art is flawless; but as yet the reflections of life which he presents resemble those amusing yet lawful distortions that we see in highly polished convex mirrors. Some of the best current fiction appears in the form of short stories —a form in which both Mrs. Constance Cary Harrison and Mrs. Champney have cast many excellent compositions. It has further been most advantageously used by Mr. T. A. Janvier, whose ingenious, picturesque *Color Studies* have their scene in New York, where the author passes half the year. The Norwegian tales of Professor Boyesen, which have attained to a wide celebrity, supply another instance in point.

Dr. Mayo's romance of African adventure, *Kaloolah*, long ago enjoyed a deserved popularity; but his last work, an American novel called *Never Again*, although it was hailed in England as a satisfactory reproduction of reality, did not meet with equal favor at home. Neither have Dr. Hammond's novels, *Lal* and its successors, been accorded a definite place as literature; yet they stand remarkably well as amateur productions, and show an unusual familiarity with both Western and Eastern scenes. Anna Katherine Greene's stories of mystery and detectives are thoroughly well carried out as to plot, and equally meritorious in their succinct, appropriate verbal style. Quite recently the Hon. W. W. Astor has made his ap-

was reserved for others to make careful pictures of New York life in the later realistic manner. This is what Mr. Bishop has done in his *House of a Merchant Prince*, and Professor Boyesen in his *Daughter of the Philistines*. But Mr. Edgar Fawcett has carried the work further than any one else. *A Gentleman of Leisure, A Hopeless Case*, and *An Ambitious Woman*, all from his pen, present the evidences of a thorough study of some social aspects; and the *Ambitious Woman* renders very strongly certain effects and situations proper to the locality. Messrs. Bunner and Brander Matthews have handled the short story in collaboration with brilliant artistic success; and Mr. Matthews's novelette, *The Last Meeting*, contains some clever sketching from the semi-Bohemian sort of authors' and artists' society. Mr. Julian Hawthorne's glances at the life and character of the place in *Beatrix Randolph* and *Love, or a Name?* comprehend the less agreeable side; but we have in him one of the most

pearance as the author of a historical novel, *Valentino*, which, however, leaves the question open as to whether he is to be reckoned permanently one of the novelists. Two other writers who have lately ventured upon the perilous path, but show decided creative ability and a good promise of art in fiction, are Henry Harland ("Sidney Luska"), the author of *As It was Written*, and George H. Picard, the author of *A Matter of Taste* and *A Mission Flower*. Mr. Picard resolutely sets himself to deal with American themes in a modestly independent way, and Mr. Harland shows a liking for the exceptionally strange romantic. But he is sincere about it, and in spite of recent edicts that have been issued in one quarter, condemning all romanticism, romance still remains a reality and interests readers.

It is one of the significant circumstances of our transitional period that our men and women of letters often turn their hands to several different kinds of writing, not so much with a desire to illustrate the national "shiftiness," adaptability, or versatility, as from necessity. Thus we find Mr. O. B. Bunce at one point in his career producing stage plays, at another time essays under the disguise of "Bachelor Bluff," and at still another time novels. Formerly Henry T. Tuckerman figured as an art critic, poet, and literary essayist, and Professor Boyesen to-day has added to his claims as a poet, story-writer, novelist, and to scholarly achievement in his volume on Goethe and Schiller, a fairly successful acting play.

The native drama does not advance rapidly. But New York has at least produced one playwright distinguished not only for practical ability in fitting the mechanism of the theatre, but also for genuine literary workmanship. Bronson Howard has steadily made his way, in the face of the most virulent and repressive criticism, to

CHARLES NORDHOFF.
From a photograph by Kurtz, New York.

JOHN HABBERTON.
From a photograph by Rockwood, New York.

a place at the head of the small band of New York playwrights. Edgar Fawcett appears again in this band, with Henry Guy Carleton, who has made a good beginning, and David D. Lloyd, the author of *For Congress*. Joaquin Miller has written copiously for the stage, but with no marked success since *The Danites*. George Fawcett Rowe is another of the dramatic authors who, although English by birth, is settled in New York. The plays of Bartley Campbell and Fred Marsden, unlike in scope and material, must be classed together as representing the outcome of dramatic artisanship rather than artistry, and to this side of the stage David Belasco likewise belongs. On the other hand, Brander Matthews has written charmingly about the stage and about actors, and has produced a notably fine biography of Sheridan, but has not yet had the good fortune to keep any one of his comedies long on the boards. The difference between the playwright and the literary playwriter has often been remarked, and it is obvious that a union of the two is essential to any supremely good and enduring achievement on the stage.

But the balance just now is in favor of the artisan, and probably not until New York has a standard theatre, supported for the purpose of cultivating the best drama in all kinds, will dramatic literature attain to an excellence worthy of our ambitions.

Finally, without professing to make an exhaustive enumeration, we may run over the names of a number of literary men—magazinists, critics, and general authors—who have at one time or another made long sojourns in New York, or who now have their abode here. Among the former were Charles G. Leland and Bret Harte; T. B. Aldrich also began his career and gained his first successes in this "Empire City." So did J. T. Trowbridge. Charles Astor Bristed, in his day, assisted in the creation of a literary "atmosphere." Donald G. Mitchell (Ik Marvel) a short time ago devoted several years to active editorial life within the bounds of Manhattan. John Hay remained for a considerable time identified with New York, and Clarence King still remains so, but—unfortunately for authorship—has relinquished his gift of writing in favor of scientific investigation. John Habberton, the author of *Helen's Babies*, is now on the editorial staff of the *Herald*. The *Popular Science Monthly*, however, under the editorship of Professor E. L. Youmans, continues to maintain, as the distinguished editor himself has so long done, a powerful bond between natural science and the graver sorts of philosophical and sociological literature. In the department of historical studies we find Sydney Howard Gay and Eugene Lawrence still indefatigably occupied. Mr. J. B. McMaster's *History of the People of the United States* (of which two volumes have appeared) is a remarkable example of novel methods and novel effects in this field of research. The late Dr. George Ripley, the chief editor of the *American Cyclopædia*, gave his wealth of knowledge during a long term to criticism of current books in *Harper's Magazine* and the *Tribune*. Laurence Hutton, man of leisure as well as man of letters, and a New Yorker to the core, has filled an important gap by writing a comprehensive *History of the American Stage*, and has accomplished another very useful and attractive work in his *Literary Landmarks of London*. One of the most gifted of dramatic critics, as well as a graceful poet, is William Winter, who, apart from his untiring labors as a member of the *Tribune* staff, has found time to make notable additions to dramatic biography. Clarence Cook has fulfilled an equally important function as an art critic. Paul Du Chaillu makes his head-quarters in New York, together with Colonel Thomas W. Knox, whose numerous volumes of travels for boys are well known, and Edward Greey, the author of several entertaining works on Japan. Moncure D. Conway, liberal theologian, magazinist, and correspondent, has come back from a period of congenial exile in London to dwell in Brooklyn. That suburban municipality also has the credit of attracting George Cary Eggleston, author of *A Rebel's Recollections* and various boys' books of history, as well as of giving domicile to William Hamilton Gibson, who is not only a pictorial artist of rare delicacy, but also has the power of describing in language of singular charm what he has seen in landscape, in the procession of the seasons, and the play of plant life and bird life.

My space is too short to admit of doing more than to mention Mary L. Booth and Martha J. Lamb, the historians of New York—a dual triumph for women, by-the-way, in an exacting field; the magazinists Junius Henri Brown and Ernest Ingersoll; Rossiter Johnson; the Hon. S. G. W. Benjamin, ex-Minister to Persia, and author of several books, no less than of many contributions to periodicals; and Frank D. Millet, a successfully transplanted Bostonian, best known by his pictures, but distinguished also as a war correspondent, a writer for the magazines, and the author of good short stories. I ought, however, to have spoken before this of Mary Hallock Foote, whose extraordinary talent in illustration by black and white drawings has been nearly matched by her well-wrought short stories and novelettes.

From what has been said in the preceding paragraphs, I think it is evident that—however famished the authors themselves may be—New York does not suffer from a famine of authors. It may be conceded freely that the metropolis exercises no positive and dominating literary influence. There is no generally recognized "New York school." We have a number of excellent writers; their sway, nevertheless, does not extend itself to other localities. The leaders of style and the discoverers of new fields seem to come from various parts of the country remote from New York. There is consolation to be had, notwithstanding. One swallow, it is generally agreed, does not make a summer; but neither does the absence of several first-class swallows bring about the blankness and desolation of winter. New York does not pretend to dictate centralization in the republic of letters. An author, wherever he may be, reaches the best of all literary centres when he "hits the bull's-eye." And New York, which usually is not slow to acknowledge hits of this kind, can afford to wait, knowing that the true focus of appreciation will ultimately be found in the largest aggregation of intelligence and wealth. For what other reason than the fostering of ideal aims should intelligence and wealth exist, or be collected more abundantly in one place than another?

III.

In New York, association between authors and people having other occupations is somewhat more general than elsewhere in the country, partly because the authors and the other people are more numerous than elsewhere. But it is also, in part, for another reason, which is that, while authorship is not so distinctly honored here as in Boston, authors on that very account are allowed to ramble harmlessly through the various circles of society, being regarded not as lions, but as mere tributary lambs. One is also quite likely to meet at clubs, parties, dinners, in this city, various men who have written a book or two without cackling or being cackled about—men who do not dream of becoming professional authors. Clubs, by-the-way, play an important part in promoting the alliance of the better social forces with those of art and literature. The Century Club has done more for New York in this direction than any other association.

In the modest but unique and agreeably arranged interior of the Century's house on Fifteenth Street, writers, painters, editors, publishers, lawyers, merchants, and doctors meet under the most favorable auspices. The Saturday night gatherings are full of quiet charm and pleasant converse, bringing together as they do a host of distinguished and cultivated men, including guests from all parts of the world. Once a month the artist members give an exhibition of their latest works in the club library. The St. Botolph Club was founded on the model of the Century a few years ago, in Boston, where, until that time, no similar organization had existed; and when Thackeray was in this country he used to declare that in no place did he feel so much at home as in the Century Club.

But, as I have said, the Century does not fully represent the number of men who sympathize with its tastes. The Lotos Club, which occupies a spacious mansion opposite the Union Club on Fifth Avenue, was begun some fifteen years ago, under the presidency of Whitelaw Reid, who is still at its head. In its membership it includes authors, journalists, and actors; it has strong affiliations with the stage, and is always foremost in giving banquets and receptions to representatives of the English theatre. The Union Club, with its thousand members, is an exponent of wealth and social influence, which is supposed to exercise a powerful control over various matters in which society is interested. Its bias is not in the least literary, yet you will find on its roll not only amateurs of letters, but also men who write professionally, editors, and publishers. In fact, there are few clubs of importance in the city that do not contain some spokesmen of the humanities. The latest house club, the Calumet, though inclined to elegance and patrician exclusiveness, has admitted several authors, artists, and architects, and makes an annual display of paintings. The University Club, on Madison Square, closed to all but college graduates, rejoices in a mildly bookish atmosphere, and forms one more among the collectively favorable influences. In Twenty-sixth Street, near Sixth Avenue, stands a roomy house with a pleasant interior, where quite another sort of association, consisting of wearers of the sock and buskin, assembles, under the playful title of The Lambs. There of an evening, after the theatre, may always be found an agreeable group of night owls; and there

the actors, on four Sunday evenings every winter, give a dinner, to which authors, journalists, and artists are always invited. These dinners are the scene of a joyous and pastoral revelry:

"And while the young Lambs bound,
　As to the tabor's sound,"

no thought of grief comes near them, but they rather give Intimations of Immortality not contemplated by Wordsworth in his ode. Lester Wallack presides as Shepherd, wearing a collar of the Golden Fleece, and the dinner is followed by a rare entertainment of songs and recitations, given by some of the most skilful men on the stage.

A new brotherhood was formed a year or two since, with a branch in New York and another in London, called The Kinsmen. Its nature is indicated by the title, and by the fact that of the twenty members there are counted among the English kin William Black, Austin Dobson, Edmund Gosse, Henry Irving, and Andrew Lang; among the American, Lawrence Barrett, Edwin Booth, Joseph Jefferson, Charles Dudley Warner, W. D. Howells, E. A. Abbey, S. L. Clemens, H. C. Bunner, and others. I think I shall not betray the confidence of my fellow-Kinsmen in saying that Mr. Irving, on his first visit to this country, gave to each member a "bone," or cabalistic ivory, admitting each Kinsman and his friends, for life, to the Lyceum Theatre, whereupon some one unearthed from *Romeo and Juliet* the quotation,

"with some great Kinsman's bone,
　As with a club"—

suggesting the irresistible force with which the club and the bone would make their way into the Lyceum. But The Kinsmen remain still in the germinal stage, meeting only at long intervals and in various places on both sides of the Atlantic.

The Authors Club, inaugurated at the close of 1882, is the first organization in New York solely designed to consolidate authors and those engaged in distinctively literary work. The number is limited to one hundred and fifty, and George William Curtis, Parke Godwin, Edward Eggleston, Julian Hawthorne, E. C. Stedman, R. H. Stoddard, Messrs. Bunner and Matthews, with Professor Boyesen, Professor Beers, and Bronson Howard, are among the members. John Greenleaf Whittier,

James Russell Lowell, and Matthew Arnold have accepted honorary membership; and as the club was not intended to be simply local, such names as George H. Boker, John Hay, and Henry James have found places on its roster. For some time the Authors assembled at the houses of resident members; afterward it was hospitably accommodated in the studio of the Tile Club; but it now meets fortnightly in its own rooms, which have been pleasantly fitted up in a simple style of decoration, with good pictures, old engravings, and casts of Greek sculpture on the walls. The meetings, every other Thursday, are largely attended, and as each member may bring one guest, the company and the conversation are always varied. Three years ago the club gave Matthew Arnold a public reception, and winter before last Mr. Edmund Gosse was received at the club rooms.

Thus a casual survey brings out the fact that there are now many agencies at work, knitting together in a web of closer texture the interests of authorship and those of cultivated society.

IV.

Moreover, the ambition to introduce an intellectual element into social diversions has made increasing headway. About 1870, and for two or three years afterward, there flourished a semi-literary society of ladies and gentlemen called The Fraternity, in which Octavius B. Frothingham, George Haven Putnam, and Mr. J. Herbert Morse (now known as an occasional critic and writer of verse) were leaders. But this was only an early forerunner of similar amateur associations that have multiplied within the last five years, such as the Review Club and the Thursday Club, the latter of which regales itself with music and natural science as well as with belles-lettres; the Emerson Club, and the Drawing-Room Club. But the Nineteenth Century Club stands quite at the head in this genre. Founded by Mr. Courtlandt Palmer, it has made a custom of meeting once a fortnight during the season — in his drawing-rooms at the beginning, and since then in the rooms of the American Art Association— there to listen to a paper on fiction, the drama, religion, philosophy, art, or reform, as the case may be. These papers are nearly always prepared by some competent thinker, and are followed by a discussion so planned as to set forth opposing views, and lead toward a better understanding. The assembly consists of men and women in about equal proportions. Clergymen, scientific men, literary men, artists, are constantly to be met with there, as well as people who represent merely the dressing and dining order; and the seed of thought is thus often lodged in unexpected places. In a word, the Nineteenth Century Club has decidedly and usefully added to the ways and means of a common intellectual life.

Whatever may be thought of the desirability of salons in New York, they are not forth-coming, and I question whether they are what we need. The late Mrs. Henry M. Field used to gather about her on Sunday evenings a collection of guests who had somewhat the air of constituting a salon, and the Drawing-room Club of to-day, meeting in the house of a Russian lady of noble blood, might perhaps be put in that category. But the true salon requires time for its building, and more leisure than society in the present age can command. Besides, the conditions in New York are too uncertain and changeable to supply a secure basis. Instead of such institutions, therefore, we have a number of houses in which agreeable companies, skilfully blended of various elements, are brought together without pretension. There are plenty of afternoon teas, at which the aroma of art and literature mingles faintly with that of the Oolong and the Souchong. There are also receptions at Mrs. Botta's, as well as in the unique and pretty house of Mr. and Mrs. Gilder, and on Saturday nights at Miss Booth's.

Notwithstanding all this, the constituent parts of literary society are still somewhat scattered. They are obliged to house themselves transiently in the most incongruous spots, with little, if any, "atmosphere" about them. They suffer from the want of those cheap, healthful, and at the same time convenient suburbs, and those quiet corners within the municipality, which make it possible for their kindred in Paris or London to lead lives so far free from sordid care that a sense of lettered ease may be enjoyed, and time be gained for the leisurely evolution of masterpieces. The loud grinding of the huge metropolitan machine, while it stimulates the faculties to alertness, tends to unsettle that contemplative point of view which is essential to creative work.

In the older middle portion of the town there is an irregular region — around Washington Square, extending to the eastward below Union Square, and stretching up to Stuyvesant Square on the north— which by an exercise of fancy may be regarded as the "Latin Quarter." In this irregular section there are many studios; there are second-hand book-stores and print-shops; it is within easy reach of two or three libraries, reading-rooms, and publishing houses. The gray old University of the City on Washington Square has sheltered many a struggling poet or aspiring artist within its Norman doorways and gloomy corridors and lonesome chambers. And on the mid-channel of Broadway, a quarter of a mile distant, is the spot where for a brief period—from 1856 to 1859—the only Bohemian group that ever made a name for itself in New York used to hold its reunions. One winter's night three contributors to the journals of the time met at the corner of Fourth Street, and began to talk over plans for a new weekly paper. Snow began to fall, and they hastily took refuge in a dingy resort below the level of the sidewalk, where beer was sold in a room screened off from the domestic department by a calico curtain. This was Pfaff's; and thus arose the "Pfaff group," which assisted in the publication of the *Saturday Press*, and included in its circle Walt Whitman, Fitz-James O'Brien, T. B. Aldrich, and William Winter, with the painters George H. Boughton, Homer Martin, Winslow Homer, and some whose names are less widely known.

But "the Latin Quarter," after all, is a somewhat shadowy thing. It is hemmed in on all sides and partly divided by the highways of trade; it has no very distinctive marks, and its continued existence is doubtful. The addition to Columbia College of a superb library building, not surpassed by any similar edifice in the country—a library open on all but two days in the year until ten o'clock at night, and easily accessible by means of reading cards given out to literary men—promises to form in the neighborhood of Fiftieth Street and Madison Avenue a kind of "university quarter" of the town; for Columbia is in fact, though not in name, a university. But scholars and literary men are not likely to congregate in great numbers close by the dwellings of millionaires, and New York is still without a distinctively literary quarter.

The great publishing establishments of the city, however, through their popular magazines, reviews, and weekly periodicals, in union with the great dailies, which afford many opportunities for literary work, exercise a centripetal force which brings writers of all sorts crowding hither. They find plenty of routine employment. The city's attractive power is further exemplified in the removal hither from Boston of the venerable *North American Review*, and the youthful *Outing*, a periodical devoted to sports and travel, but preserving a literary tone in its treatment of these topics. Of late years, also, New York has sustained in *The Critic* the first purely critical weekly which has secured a permanent footing here. But we are still compelled to admit, year after year, that no literary development has taken place commensurate with the enormous material growth which we have witnessed. To what shall we attribute this?

In the first place, New York remains, as it always was, fickle and indifferent, a conglomerate of incongruous masses, caring nothing for the honor of developing a worthy literature. What it has had in this line has come rather by accident than by encouragement.

In the next place, the national neglect to give foreign authors a copyright in this country deprives the native author of a fair field for the disposal of his work. Publishers swarm; authors are decimated. We are "a nation of readers," reading foreign books, and receiving from crude dogmatists the assurance that it is a great blessing to remain provincially dependent on the brains of other countries. A true national literature is the only sure bulwark of national health, pride, and honor. The result of our doing nothing to encourage one is seen on the one hand in the diffusion of an absurd Anglomania, and on the other in an ill-considered and dangerous communism—both of them diseases engendered by a diet of imported ideas. If it were not for the magazines, the greater part of American literary production would cease instantly, for to all but one or two individuals they offer the sole hope of substantial reward.

That there is no single New York type, any more than there is a type for London or Paris, may be admitted. But there are *types*, and of the widest variety. It must ensue that if we have writers at all, a characteristic accent will in time be heard, like that which Emerson found in Carlyle's utterance : "I thought as I read this piece that your strange genius was the instant fruit of London. It is the aroma of Babylon." The want of a popular intellectual enthusiasm, and the prevalence of a mercenary spirit, are obstacles which have presented themselves elsewhere as well as here. But we are told that New York is a camp, a caravansary, a sort of human quicksand. Moreover, it is said not to be an ideal American community. A true democracy we have not and never had in New York; nor has it shown, like old Boston, a highly finished republicanism, granting room for an aristocracy. New York has remained simply a crowd. The crowd, nevertheless, offers a curious and entertaining spectacle. When all is said, it illustrates in full force the tendencies that are to be embodied in our future, and it tolerates the greatest latitude of opinion and character. If American authors should ever be allowed by international copyright the chance which all other persons are given of maintaining themselves modestly without becoming jacks-of-all-trades—lec-

turing, teaching, editing, farming, doing business, and creeping into clerkships to eke out a living—then we might expect that they would use the great opportunities of New York, and make it the matrix for many a noble and inspiring creation of genius.

It will at once be seen, on reading over the names of authors who have been referred to in this article, that New York writers are not actuated by any impulse in common ; that they are not united in striving toward one particular goal, and that they do not concern themselves about making a special New York literature. Why should they do so ? Why should they try to narrow the scope of an art which ought to be broad enough to fit all places and all times ? That we cannot find in the writing that has been done here any special drift or any indelible traces of localism argues nothing adverse. Wherever it is possible for creative minds to concentrate themselves upon a single spot, thriving on its resources, and yet to remain—according to their bent—of the place or not of it, there we are sure to get in the end the richest fruitage of literature.

THE TRAGIC STORY OF BINNS.

BY HARRIET PRESCOTT SPOFFORD.

THERE is no use in making any pretences about it. It was no dark and splendid young pirate fascinated by the rosy rustic maiden. It was no foreign prince in disguise attracted by the grace of an unfettered shape while balancing water pails at the spring, and ready to override all the conventions of society and make the girl his wife. It was Binns, the butcher-boy.

A scrap of a fellow, he was; so short, so slight, so pale, so insignificant, that it seemed as if, should he take off his long blue blouse, there would really be nothing left of him—but his freckles. And Roxy, she was half again his height, and buxom and blooming, not to say blowsy, deep-colored, and altogether with a great deal of her.

If Roxy were not Roxy, the cook, talking at the kitchen storm-door with Binns, whose scraggy horse dropped his head so low with the dropping of the reins that he looked as if he would drop in the street

altogether if the authorities did not interfere—if Roxy were not Roxy, but were Gladys tossing a rose over the drawing-room balcony to the gallant young cavalry officer on his prancing Abdallah that had carried him through the terrific ambushes and skirmishes of an Indian campaign, then I will admit that more entertainment and much finer company might be had out of the affair. The dinners which we might attend together in the course of our acquaintance would be very different from the surreptitious turnovers and custards with which Roxy regaled Binns; the music we might hear would have far other charms than those strains which Roxy, in her hours of leisure, called out from a bit of comb wound with a bit of paper; the dresses, too, would be far more satisfactory to the soul and the soul's eye than Roxy's dirt-colored calicoes, bought to wash and hide the dirt as long previously as might be; and we will say nothing of the diamonds, the pictures, the operas, and all the rest that we might arrive at in our experiences; for Roxy had no diamonds but her tears, and very few of them in the beginning; no pictures but cuttings from the comic weeklies, which she pinned up about the kitchen; and as for the dinners, again, I doubt if we should bring better appetites to our sumptuous banquet, with terrapin and canvas-back and champagne *frappé*, than Binns had when grinning over his apple turnover, wiping his mouth on his blue sleeve after it, and giving Roxy a resounding smack, to receive in return as resounding a slap. "She's a clipper, I say," Binns would chuckle, as if it were a love-pat after his own heart. Meanwhile not an opera of all the list is to be heard with more satisfaction than that wont to be evinced by Binns as he sat, during his evenings "on," while Roxy, after her voluntary upon the comb and paper, which she kept in the drawer of the kitchen table with the nutmegs and allspice, sang in her loud and clear if somewhat nasal voice the simple ballad of "Whoa, Emma!" or

> "I don't know why I love him,
> He does not care for me,
> But my poor heart will wander
> Wherever he may be.
> If I had minded mother
> I'd not been here to-day,
> But I was young and foolish,
> And easy led astray;"

or reverted to older tunes, "Oh, where have you been, Lord Ronald, my son," and "Drownded, drownded, in the middle of the sea," with other like tearful selections. To be sure, Binns's delight was chiefly manifested by a frequent use of his coat sleeve in the manner of lachrymose individuals without a handkerchief, in a very luxury of woe; for if the comb and paper tickled the cockles of his heart, as some mellow flute or honied violin might do, the enjoyment was just as ecstatic which made the tears pour forth over the sad fate of the lovers "'Way down in Salem town," while he thought nothing of an unprotected outright boohoo, with his face twisted into all sorts of a coil, over the last words of the wretched person who implores,

> "Oh, make my grave quick, brother, make my grave deep;
> The sooner I lay there the sooner I'll sleep;
> For why should I wait from th. s sad world to part,
> When the girl that I love so has broken my heart?"

Nevertheless, it was not of love, at any rate not of love of Roxy, that Binns would ever die. Roxy's turnovers and gingersnaps and five-fingered doughnuts, her liberal bowls of coffee and secret draughts of mineral water, were very agreeable variations in his daily fare. When Roxy asked him to come in and spend an evening with some friends of hers and have a game of forty-five, he saw visions of the same run of dainties, and was much pleased by the rosy apples and tingling cider and roasted chestnuts of the regale. Come again? Of course he would come again: one did not need to be asked twice to things of that sort. He came again, and this time the nuts were butternuts, and there were cookies as nearly poundcake as it is the nature of cookies to approach, and Binns munched and cracked and picked and sipped, and thought that Roxy was a mighty cute body to be able to have the kitchen to herself at this hour, and to have whatever she chose in it, moreover. And so he came again.

Was it Roxy's cakes and ale alone, then, that allured Binns? Was not the face reflected in the pewter platter she scoured, as she sang her doleful ditties, as fair to him as the face of Gladys thrown up from a golden salver would have been to the cavalry officer? Sooth, I know not. I only know that a cosy kitchen, with a hot stove and bright tins, is a pleasant place, and a capacious rocking-chair with long rockers, in which you are allowed to travel all about the kitchen, is a comfortable thing, and that hands never look more kindly than when pressing toothsome dainties upon you, and that if one has nothing better to do one is rather inclined to repeat such experiences than not. If then it is suggested, very palpably suggested, to one, in return, that the old butcher's nag should be hitched into the pung, with the horse-blanket for a robe, and a sleigh ride should be given the generous purveyor of doughnuts and peanuts, could one do less? And as for scaring Roxy from any repetition of the suggestion by tipping her over into a crusty snow-drift, one's mind would have to move a great deal more quickly than what answered Binns for a mind was able to do in order to be up to such an opportunity.

"I'll tell you what," said Roxy. "The next time, Binns, I'll take the big red comforter off my bed for an extra robe, and a couple of hot flat-irons—or bricks would be better, wouldn't they?—wrapped in news-papers, and we'll be as warm as toast. Say Friday. There'll be a first-rate moon. And we'll have a real egg and cider flip with the hot stove-lifter in it when we get back."

"If—if—he'll let me have the horse," said Binns, doubtfully, and not with ra-diating pleasure.

"Oh, of course he will. Now you put the blanket on him, and come in, and we'll have some hot hash—I've got some left over all ready to warm up—and a lit-tle taste of sangaree."

If I should say that Roxy's sangaree was made of vinegar and hot water, and brown sugar, and nutmeg, and other like substances, you would not believe how Binns smacked his lips over it; so what is the use of saying anything of the sort? But it is true that Binns went away re-peating to himself, "Well, for getting sun-thin outer northing, she's a beater!" And so I am sure—in view of Binns—she was.

When—hardly knowing how to help it, Roxy having taken it so for granted, feeling that he was driven by an inexora-ble fate when Roxy said that on Monday the moon would be good, as if the moon wasn't always good—Binns asked for the horse the third time, his master slapped him on the back with a force that sent him half across the shop. "Well, Binns," said he, "so you've got a girl, you sly dog! I never thought you'd muster face enough for that. Have the old horse and welcome; there's no danger of fast driving when two folks are in love." During this kindly if not altogether delicate ad-dress, Binns was pink and purple, yel-low, green, blue, and white, by turns, with fright, with shame, with gratified vanity, with a sense of manly power, but, above everything else, with a prevailing awe and terror of it all, anyway, as the full meaning of his master's words overcame him, and the gulfs of the future yawned before him. To eat Roxy's turnovers was one thing, to marry her was quite another. The possibility had not occurred to him before—only a vague conscious-ness of the impossibility of anything else was beginning to oppress him, all the more vaguely, perhaps, because of his ex-treme unwillingness to utter anything of the sort even to himself.

If Binns had not had to stop at the house for the dinner order, it is doubt-ful if he would have seen Roxy that day.

But "there was no going back on the shop," he said to himself, and looking like a lamb, he went prepared to take the order for beef.

"Roxy!" the old gardener called, open-ing the door, for Binns, on the idea of get-ting it over with, was a little earlier than common, and Roxy was not upon the out-posts as usual, "here's your young man!"

"Roxy!" cried the mischievous and vulgar Kitty, "here's your feller!"

"You go along!" said Roxy, making her appearance, and wiping her hands on her pink print apron. And there stood Binns, as pink as the apron; and he stam-mered something about to-night at half past seven sharp, and hurried off, forget-ting all about the order. He had to come back, of course, and he found Roxy sit-ting on the edge of a water pail inside the storm-door, with her pink apron thrown over her pink face, sobbing fit to break her heart.

"Why—why—Roxy—why, what's the matter, Roxy?" he exclaimed. But Roxy only sobbed, the sob none the less affecting to a tender-hearted hearer because broken by a hiccough. "Why, Roxy — why, what on earth—has anybody been a-hurt-ing of you? Why don't you tell me?"

But Roxy's sobs still preserved the secret.

Mr. Binns really began to feel badly himself. What man unmoved can see lovely woman shed tears? "Come now, Roxy, don't you be a-fretting," he urged. "You just wipe your eyes and tell me all about it."

"Oh! No! I—I can't."

"Oh, come now, Roxy."

"It's—it's—that hateful—that—oh, I can't—that spiteful Kitty—a-calling you my feller."

"Well," said Binns, "ain't I?"

Wretched Binns! To have taken pains not to call Roxy *dear*, to tell her to wipe her eyes, not her bright eyes, and to be caught in this unguarded way by three chance words! It was all over now; he was in for it, he saw plainly; he might as well give up handsomely. And yet—he couldn't. All that he could do was to take to his heels and clip down the steps and into the pung and drive away as if the Wild Ladies—or something else—were after him. It was Roxy's voice that was after him, shrill as a view-halloo. "Oh, Binns! A tenderloin roast! First cut! Don't forget—ten pounds—"

But Binns had to face the music that night, or else Mr. McMasters would have to get another butcher-boy, as otherwise he would not dare face Roxy to-morrow, and there had been too much trouble from people needing employment in those over-crowded days for him to give up his place for a trifle. Well, he would go. And he would say, "Roxy, now let's be friends, two friends, two fellers together, two folks bound to have a good sleigh ride, with no sparking about it, no nonsense, no—you know—no spooning. You're a first-rate girl, and I don't know such a hand at turnovers in all the kitchens I see; but that's no reason we should be a couple of fools with nothing to be fools on. If I was in the marrying way, there's nobody I wouldn't marry quicker'n you," and here he knew his conscience would twinge him, but he would say it. "But I ain't, and you ain't, and so we'll just continue the services as we were going on before."

And did he say it? Did Binns say it? Not a word of it! Roxy was at the gate, all alert, peering out, with the bright red comforter over her arm, and running back for the hot bricks, she had whisked into that pung, and tucked the comforter about them, and chirruped to the old nag, all in a moment, and Binns found himself slipping along the road without a word, but—I am ashamed to tell it—with a shrewd suspicion that somehow he had better not lean back, for that was Roxy's arm behind him.

"I declare!" said Roxy. "Splendid sleighing, splendid moonlight, warm as toast, and your—your—you know who—beside you, a-driving as if he could turn round on the point of a pin—I don't know as any one needs to be any happier."

Perhaps the compliment on his driving was soothing to Binns's perturbed soul; but he was naturally reticent, and at that moment he did not commit himself. One thing was safe—music; and presently he had piped up a warlike song:

"Ne'er shall oppressors brave us,
    Or foreign power enslave us;
    Our stripes and stars shall wave us
    To freedom or glory's tomb!
    Hark! 'tis the war-trump sounding!"

followed by another effort indicative of the leadings of his fancy, whose refrain rang:

"Pride of the pirate's heart!"

This failure of Binns to improve his opportunity evidently struck no chill to Roxy's ardor. They were approaching Trimble's Hollow, where a bridge crossed the frozen mill-stream, and Binns leaned forward for the whip in order to accelerate their motion—one could not say speed—when suddenly Roxy flung herself a little on one side, crying out, "No, no, now, you mustn't begin that!"

"Mustn't begin what?" said Binns, gruffly.

"Kissing me at every bridge we come to, just as all the other boys do. It's something I never did approve of."

"Nor I nuther," said Binns. But what if you don't approve of a thing—when a rosy cup of wine is held to your lips, and the fire tingles there, and the color sparkles, and the aroma is that of a garden of flowers under your nose, do you always have the strength of mind to set that cup down instantly? Instantly; for the man as well as the woman who hesitates is lost. And Binns, with those sparkling eyes sparkling into his, that rosy cheek close beside his own, those wholesome rosy lips—I am sure that neither you nor I would have done the like—but Binns was only Binns. And what you have done once it is so easy to do again. Before they reached home, that wicked Binns —the poor innocent little fellow—felt himself quite on the way to become what, in his ignorance of the existence of Don Giovanni, stood for the same thing. But as for Roxy, she felt very well satisfied with herself and her excursion. Binns was hers; he himself had said it that morning, and on the sleigh ride that evening he had conducted very much as in her imagination and belief all lovers should conduct. The horse was blanketed at the hitching-post, and Binns was brought in whether he would or no, and some sequestered turkey bones were grilled, and a flip was made, and there had been daring possession taken of a mince-pie, the goodly share of which transformed into a part of Binns might have caused a procession of the ghosts of all his grandmothers since the flood to walk across his counterpane that night. And Binns ate and drank, and actually made several little jokes, and apropos of the pastry he sang:

"When Washington was but a boy
    As big as you or I, .
    He climbed his mother's cupboard
    And he stole her apple-pie,"

appearing to Roxy as he sang as delightful a personage as an end man; and when he went away Roxy bent and put her arms about his neck, and gave him a good fair kiss on his mouth, as any girl should kiss her sweetheart.

It was not in these days that Binns gave Roxy the hearty smack, and received the no less hearty slap in return; that was when smacks and slaps meant nothing, and in the innocence of his heart Binns was treating Roxy as he did most of the other kitchen girls upon his rounds. Later on, when the nature of Roxy's attentions, and of her intentions too, became more pointed, these little occurrences were susceptible of misconstruction; and Binns was even embarrassed as to the return he should make for her tarts and jellies, without, however, being able to forego the dainties offered by the assiduous charmer. But now —well, if one must be kissed, Roxy's was a sweet and wholesome mouth, and that whip of frothy cream with plum preserve at the bottom of it was sweet and wholesome too.

It was generally understood in the household now that Roxy and Binns were "keeping company," and nobody was surprised to see Roxy always, in the afternoon hours, with a piece of white cloth in her hand, sometimes a part of what appeared to be an elaborate trousseau made chiefly of tucks and insertings and edgings, sometimes a table-cloth she was hemming, or towels she was fringing, with a pride of possession that needed no bashful concealment. She had a sewing-machine of her own in her attic chamber, and who would have had the heart to stop its low melodious thunder, long after every soul in the house was in bed? If it were Gladys, softly stitching folds of lace on sheer lawn, and you saw the light in her lattice, she would indeed have been a subject of romantic interest.

It was not exactly a pleasant thing, all this unreserve of Roxy's; and it was really a relief to know that it had its side of maidenly delicacy and diffidence. This was exhibited in some faint degree when one afternoon Binns, who had been belated, stopped at the door, with a cargo of up-country calves, to take the order for next day's provision, and suddenly there was a hurrying and scurrying, and Roxy was hiding something white and bunchy under her apron, and then throwing it under the table, very red in the face herself,

half giggling, half crying, and Kitty, making a dive, was drawing the article from its temporary refuge, and holding it up in the face of all creation.

"What's that?" said Binns.

"Oh my, Kitty! Oh, don't! How can you, Kitty? Ain't you 'shamed?" cried Roxy. And up went the apron across the hair, making a muss of all the crimps that had cost her an hour over kerosene lamp and slate-pencil when the kitchen work was done.

"Why, what's all the fuss about that?" said Binns, good-naturedly, with Kitty's contagious laugh.

"As if you didn't know!" said Kitty.

"I don't see anything particular in a cotton bag," said Binns.

"It's house-keeping goods, you stupid!" cried Kitty. "Isn't it, Roxy?"

"Well, what if it is?"

"Oh, Binns!" cried Roxy, pulling down the apron and showing a face where the mismated eyes were full of liquid brightness, and the ruddy cheeks were redder still with blushes. "It's—it's ours!"

"Ours!"

"And I've got a dozen of them!"

"A dozen—"

"I've a dozen of everything," cried Roxy, exultantly, all barriers burned away, "except towels, and I've six dozen of them. I sent up to the great sale where Rivers is running linen goods against Black's running of gloves, and got 'em for ninepence apiece. Think of that!"

A long whistle escaped from Binns's pursed-up lips, round as which his eyes had opened, and then, without another syllable, the astonished bridegroom and prospective householder darted down the back steps and into his cart, and galloped away, looking as nearly like one of the calves inside the rack as a human being could.

It must have been a rather tremendous moment for Binns. Up to that interview with one of the dozen of them he had been comparatively a free man, with nothing definitely pledged, with everything that was really decisive so far away that he could look at it without shutting his eyes, and with all the contingencies of time and space between. But now—house-keeping goods! Bought and paid for. Every article of them was like a winding-sheet that bound him hand and foot. He felt himself fettered, with all the world for witness; and even if he could have escaped otherwise, here in some mysterious manner, a complication of moral force, were the great firm of Rivers and the great firm of Black, in the great metropolis, brought in as restraining influences. Something like this must have wrought on Binns's inner consciousness as nothing ever did before, for he wound himself up to the pitch of coming that very evening for a voluntary and unappointed call upon Roxy, who, sitting on the back steps, for it was late in the spring, had just put the last thread that she could see into her hemstitching.

"Roxy," said Binns, after a preliminary skirmish, "you're a great seamstress. But don't you think, say—that—that this is a little previous?"

"I'm so glad you feel so, Binns," said Roxy, demurely, taking only the latest usage of the word. And then, looking up with her happiest smile, she added, "I think it's a little previous myself."

"Then what in the world are you doing it for?" blurted out Binns.

"Doing it for?" said Roxy, in amazement. "Why, for our house—for us."

"Don't you think we're a couple of fools, Roxy?" he said, in a tremulous voice, looking in the direction of Europe or Africa, or anything but Roxy.

"A—couple—of—fools?"

"Not to let well enough alone," he contrived to add before his voice failed and went out.

"I don't know what you mean, Binns," said Roxy.

"Well," said Binns, moistening his lips in order to articulate, "I mean—you're very well off as you be, and so'm I at home. And how are we going—to live—with nothing—to live on? and where? And what's the use of all your house-keeping goods?"

"Binns!" cried Roxy. And there was ominous silence for a moment before the floodgates of her eloquence were opened. "When we only want three rooms!" she cried. "And can hire them in your own mother's house. And I've money enough put by for a carpet and a cooking-stove and a rocking-chair. And I've got a chamber set of my own, and a sewing-machine, and a dozen napkins, and six table-cloths, and a dozen sheets, and a dozen pillow-cases, and six dozen towels, and four blankets, and a comforter I made myself, and patchwork quilts enough to make a circus tent, and two worked motters, and

no end of braided mats—for I've always, always been getting ready! And there's all the wedding presents to come, and clothes enough to last me a couple of years and more, and I'll never come upon you for any. And you with six dollars a week and some hens, and I able to run a kitchen-garden myself while you're at the shop, and raise all the vegetables we'll use, and the ladies of the house here going to give me their clear-starching to do, any way, and you to have your clothes mended and your washing done with no expense, and no board to pay—"

"I don't pay board now," stammered Binns, his words a straw upon the flood.

"And after a little we could take a couple of boarders, you know, or I would have shoes to bind from the shop, or we could do both, and have the cheerfulest kind of evenings, and you could get your butcher's-meat first cost, of course."

"How many turnovers, and whips, and jellies, and sangarees, and hearts and rounds, and doughnuts do you think we could get on six dollars a week?" asked Binns, with courageous sarcasm.

"Well, I guess we sha'n't go without doughnuts," answered Roxy, scornfully. "And as for turnovers, there's apple-trees right in your mother's yard."

"But they're mother's."

"What if they are?"

"I guess you'd find out if you went to picking mother's apples for your sauce."

"Well, then, we can set some out ourselves. And as for sangarees, I rather think I know how to make them as cheaply as the next. And maybe we can keep a cow after a little. *I'll* milk her, Binns. And I'm sure I mean to have a couple of little black pigs. And by-and-by, if we can manage to raise turkeys, it will be money in our pockets. Yes, Binns, there isn't any doubt about it, it will be money in our pockets to go to house-keeping right away, and I make no doubt I will have silver spoons given me here, and money, and everything. And then, Binns, you're nothing now but McMasters's butcher-boy—but then you'll be a married man—McMasters's man; and they won't be calling you by your given name, and ordering you round. You'll be somebody, and receive consideration; and I think the sooner we set the day the better, on account of getting the garden started. What do you say to this day fortnight? That 'll give me time for the cake."

"I—I'll see," cried the agonized Binns, who may have felt as if an anaconda had swallowed him. And he stood up and listened to a lad whistling as he went up the road unseen behind the high garden wall, his hands in his pockets, a free spirit, while he—

He turned and looked at Roxy. She was not attractive-looking, she was only good-natured; her teeth were uneven, although her mouth was wholesome, her skin was rough and red, her hair was frowzy, her snapping eyes were not a pair. He sat down upon the steps again, and hid his face in his hands, and groaned aloud. "I—I don't see how I can leave my mother," he said.

Poor Binns. He was no beauty himself, with his red head and his freckles, his pale eyes and lips, and his dwarfish stature, and it is doubtful if another girl in town would have thought of him as lover and husband. But what did he care for that? He had not thought of another girl. Nor of this one either. And how it had all come about he was sure he did not know. It seemed to him as if he were in a dreadful dream, where one thing happens and another follows without any relation, till it all becomes a nightmare.

The next day no Binns arrived to take the dinner order. And on the following day a tall, thin fellow, who looked like Binns pulled out and flattened, appeared at the storm-door in his place; and on the third day we learned that Binns was sick in bed at home.

Anything like Roxy's importance and bustle now was seldom seen in the house. At first her reddish hue waned, and then she went about her work with one tear trickling after another down her nose and glittering suspended on its tip. At last, however, nature gave way, and Roxy sat down in a corner of the kitchen and gave way too.

"Well, if ever!" said Kitty. "If you ain't as big a baby as Binns is!"

"I guess you'd cry," whimpered Roxy, "if—if—your—"

"Well? My—"

"Your—sweetheart was—suffering—at home—and he might as well be in Egypt, with that mother of his—and you didn't know—"

"As if 'twas worse for Binns than for the rest of us to have a toothache or his head hurt him! What on earth are you worrying about it for, anyway?"

"Because it's my duty to," said Roxy, severely. And it being her afternoon out, she put on her things and stalked up the road to Binns's home, where she made herself and her errand known, and remained till after nightfall, to everybody's surprise Binns himself returning with her.

Binns and Roxy, however, did not occupy the whole attention of the family, and after the first glance it was not observed whether they came into the kitchen or went strolling down the vegetable garden together. But some time after the house should have been closed and Roxy should have been reposing by Kitty's side, it was found that she had not come in, and the hat and feather with which she exaggerated her height were seen conspicuously touched by the ray of the late-rising moon outside the high street fence. Needless to say that Binns was not seen at all.

But Binns was present all the same, as in the active conversation going on out there, in answer to Roxy's shrill expostulations, a gruff little growl seemed to rise from the bowels of the earth, the voice of Binns.

"But I'm all ready, Binns. I've got everything except the carpet and the cooking-stove, and I haven't asked you to get a thing, and I've spent all the money, except enough for them, that I've laid up since I've been having my wages myself."

"You needn't," said the unseen owner of the growl. "Nobody asked you to."

"I didn't wait for anybody to ask me. It isn't my way. I like to be generous. I meant to surprise you, and please you, and show you that I came to you pretty forehanded." And there Roxy's voice was apparently drowned in tears.

"I can't help it," muttered Binns, in the pause. "Mother says it's ridiculous; she says side by side we look like a clothespin and a clothes-pole, and we'll have everybody laughing at us."

"I'll have everybody laughing at me," sobbed Roxy, her voice rising to the surface again. "They'll say—I don't know what they won't say. And that spiteful Kitty! And oh, Binns, when I'd counted on such a happy home!"

"Mother says there never was such a tall woman in the family," growled the bass tones again.

"As if tallth made any difference in hearts!" cried Roxy, very reasonably.

"And I ain't old enough to go and be married. And I don't want to be, either. I never said yes, hi, or no about it. And when I don't want to be, I don't see—"

"Binns," said Roxy, solemnly, "I could sue you for breach of promise to-morrow" —as she paused an inarticulate rumble spoke for Binns's shudder—"if I was so mean as some folks," she added.

"Then you ain't going to," he said. "And besides, what good 'd it do you? I 'ain't got nothing."

"Your mother has," answered Roxy, with repeated solemnity, as became the implied and dreadful threat, which again gave Binns pause. "But I'd scorn it," said Roxy, after letting the idea work a moment. "I don't hold my affections so slight that any money— Oh, Binns! If you feel too young to settle yet, and want to have your fling out, I'll wait—"

"There's no use in waiting," ejaculated Binns.

"That's just what I say," cried Roxy, in a sudden flush of hope and misinterpretation. But the dead silence told her mistake. "Do you mean to say it's all off?" she cried, in a despair.

"It's all off," growled Binns, in the boldness of desperation. "My mother says—"

"Oh, bother your mother!" exclaimed Roxy.

Perhaps Binns looked aghast at such a proposition, for she added at once, "I mean—I don't mean—any disrespect to her. But I never knew that mothers could—"

"Mine can," said Binns, comprehending the hiatus, and still under the impulse of his last access of courage. "My mother stood by me when I couldn't stand alone. And now I'm going to stand by her."

"I never asked you not to!" cried out Roxy. "I'd be as good a daughter to her as any she's got. I know she'd like my short-cake. And oh, Binns, it would have been so nice and cosy for you when you came home, and I had onions all smothering in the spider, and there's nobody can fry the rind any crisper than I can." And at this juncture a rush, a stumble, a quick patter of footsteps, might have been heard, and Binns had resorted to his last refuge, as usual, and was running away up the street and out of sight as fast as his little legs could carry him. And Roxy came into the house, and sat down by the kitchen window in the moonlight, and cried as if she were doing the weeping for all the disconsolate damsels in the world, and got up and found herself some tarts, and ate them with a relish, feeling in every mouthful that Binns would never have those tarts to-morrow, and went to bed and to sleep.

The next day an air of expectation kept Roxy all alert, and her hope that possibly Binns had run home to ask his mother, after all, alternated with her despairing certainty that she should never see him again. Occasionally she burst forth in song that showed the drift of her thoughts:

"Go ask your mother for fifty cents
    To see Bill Barnum jump the fence,"

the quickly following tears obscuring the rest of the words that had once come home with her from a circus. But the despairing certainty became a fixed one when a week passed, and the long, thin young man still came to take the orders. She made no attempt at pride or concealment; she tried to do her work, and she failed; and she went away at last, saying her heart was broken, and she could live no longer in a place full of cruel associations.

A year afterward, Roxy having been heard of as established in another home, and paying her attentions to another object, it was presumed that the old wound was healed; and her former mistress, happening to meet her one day in the street-car, was pleased with the smiling face that towered over her under its tall hat and scarlet feather. This lady had what she called a warm interest in humanity, but what her husband was daring enough to call an intense curiosity, and the unexpected meeting with Roxy inspired her with a keen desire to know something further of the tragic story of Binns. But she could not bring herself to the fateful point, and was spared the trouble by Roxy herself asking her if Binns came for the dinner orders nowadays, and closing the brief conversation that ensued by turning a melancholy eye upon her former mistress, and sighing, as she left the car,

"Oh, it hurts there still!"

And so one year passed, and another, and the world rolled over on its sunny side, and rolled over again on its dark one; and the clouds of sorrow broke in their sad deluge, and the sun burst forth again, filling the horizon with transformation, and new points in every landscape rose in brilliancy or sank into shadow, and Roxy was one of the points that sank into shadow — the shadow of forgetfulness.

It is a singular liability we have, after losing sight of any in whom we have had interest, to feel as if they remained exactly where we left them, heedless of the way in which the forces of the universe are building up and tearing down, and of the fact that fate and fortune never let any remain at rest. If any of the old household thought of Roxy, it was still as somebody's kitchen-girl laying her sieges and approaches to some unwilling heart. Is not Gladys, in our memory, still at her lattice looking after the cavalry officer? But fate and fortune, despite our indifference, were conscious of Roxy as an integral atom of the great cosmos, and in the interval of forgetfulness were as busy with her as with any other of the lovers whose loves give the *raison d'être* to the universe.

It was one late summer afternoon, a few years after that eventful night when Binns's footsteps had been heard pattering up the street, that Roxy's former mistress, having been taken by her liege lord on a little tour of their native county, passed slowly along a rural lane, some dozen miles away from home, and held the reins while her husband paused to throw back the top of the phaeton, looking about the soft afternoon landscape meanwhile. On one side a thick woodland shut off the view and the easterly winds, but on the other was a rolling hill-country broken by farms and orchards, and just at hand was a tiny cottage, with open windows and blowing curtains that allowed sight of the interior and its various mottoes framed upon the walls. A cow grazed in the grass-plot beyond; there were symptoms of a pig-sty, and a decided hennery in the rear; and there were lines of cabbages like great green roses, and potatoes, and onions, and beans, and blushing beet-tops, and a honeysuckle and a rose bush, and a bed of sweet-peas, and a beehive, and a gigantic elm-tree overtopping everything. What a picture of content and comfort it was! "What a country this is," said the lady in the phaeton, "where the poorest can have such a peaceful home as this, where some happy young farmer has brought home his timid little wife, and their cares

are few, and they have nothing to regret, and little left to wish for!"

Somebody was bustling about inside the pretty nest, a white cloth was spread upon the table, there was a clatter of dishes, and then there stole forth an odor—an odor of nectar and ambrosia to the hungry travellers a dozen miles from home—an odor of onions smothering in the spider. Suddenly a figure appeared at the side window beckoning some one, a tall, an immensely tall and gaunt young woman, and on her face, her reddish face, with its snapping, unpaired brown eyes, surmounted by a wilderness of slate-pencil crimps, a smile that could only be the habitual smile of perfect satisfaction. "Stop a moment," said the lady in the phaeton— "one moment. Surely—that must be— it is—" Just then the young woman sat down by the window, and began to beguile the tedium of her waiting with music, nasal, to be sure, but still a familiar tune. "Hark!" said the gentleman. "Did I hear a bagpipe?"

"A comb and paper," said the lady. "I wonder if she keeps it still in the drawer with the nutmegs?"

I don't know why neither of that guilty couple cared at that crisis to leave the phaeton. It would seem natural to have delayed a little, to have asked some questions, to have tasted, perchance, the contents of that redolent dish, to have learned if there are any in the world to whom their very wishes give them not their wish, to have learned if cruel fate were as cruel to any in the fact as in the fear. But the lady shrank into her corner, and the gentleman laid an urgent hand upon the reins, and they went on and up the winding road. Who is it cares to see the struggle of the fly in the web? For at the moment that they started up, as if for the capping race at Coulterlee, there appeared, coming slowly round the row of pole-beans, the person who had been beckoned —a little scrap of a fellow, stout and stocky in his long blue blouse, pale-eyed, red-headed, freckled, holding in his arms a teething baby, which he soothed with a monotonous melody as he sang, half under his breath,

"If I had minded mother
I'd not been here to-day;
But I was young and foolish,
And easy led astray."

Unmistakably it was Binns.

HALLOWEEN: A THREEFOLD CHRONICLE.

BY WILLIAM SHARP.

OLD superstitions die hard, and it will certainly be long before the festival of Halloween becomes as much a thing of the past as has practically become the Guy Fawkes celebration on the 5th of November. Long before the Christian faith made way among the untutored peoples of ancient Britain, the Druids had performed special rites on what is now known as Hallowmas Eve: fires were lit deep in remote forests, upon outlying spurs of hills, even upon the great plains that stretched between dense forests and partially cleared woodlands; mystic rites were performed, the help of the true God was implored, the machinations of evil powers were protested against. The earliest records bear witness to a universal belief that on this night the powers of darkness muster in great force, that all supernatural beings hold revel within the sphere of humanity, and that therefore it behooved all persons to be careful on this night of all nights, for any sin committed rendered the perpetrator liable to be brought under the influence of some evil spirit throughout a whole year thereafter. To this day any child born in Scotland on the eve of the 31st of October is supposed to be in possession of certain mysterious faculties, to hold—if not consciously, at least unconsciously in the midnight hours when the senses are obscured by sleep— communion with the supernatural world, and to be at all times a person whose actions, however eccentric, must be regarded charitably. Those who have read Sir Walter Scott's *Monastery* will remember that he has made use of this circumstance. "She's as flytie as a Halloween wean" is a phrase that may even yet be occasionally heard north of the Tweed, and in most of the popular accounts of wizards and all uncanny folk the date of their births is generally set down as on the last day of October. When, later on, All-hallow Eve became a Christian observance, the old customs pertinent to its celebration did not pass into disuse; on the contrary, they became more and more deeply established, every here and there accumulating some new superstition, or annexing some old belief that had long lingered without direct association with any special day, season, or locality. Bonfires are still lit

on Hallowmas Eve, though perhaps only one or two here and there among the members of the innumerable village communities who thus celebrate the great event know that the practice is a remnant of paganism; indeed, it is surprising, in the use of this as of many other popular customs, to find how few know anything whatever of the significance of their celebrations. "We do as our fathers did before us," is sufficient to account for everything. In Protestant countries the vigil of All-souls is no longer a religious observance, or, at any rate, is not so in Scotland, England, or 'Germany. It may be said that Halloween, as we understand it, is only celebrated by the Teutonic and Celtic races; with the Latins it is merely a religious vigil, round its observance clinging few if any of those wild legends or superstitions that are so plentiful in Scandinavia, Scotland, and Ireland. The nearest approach to the Northern solemnity, and even weirdness, is the Venetian *notte delle morti*, or night of all the dead; but the religious ceremonies attendant thereon take place not on the 31st of October, but on the eve of All-souls Day, that is, the day following. It is in Scotland and Ireland that Halloween is kept in its entirety; in the former, curiously enough, more in the east, mid-country, and Lowlands than in the remoter Highland districts; in other words, more among the Scots proper than among the pure Celts. The best chronicle of Hallowmas Eve that exists is the well-known poem of Burns, containing as it does some record of the most generally practised customs in connection with this really ancient vigil, but, considering the popularity of the subject, there is a wonderfully limited "Halloween" literature. The succeeding threefold chronicle may possibly, then, contain something novel as well as of interest to many readers. It may be that the time is not far distant when All-hallows Eve will lose its hold upon rural as completely as it has upon urban populations, when bonfires will be lit only by a few youngsters, when apples will cease to be ducked for, and when nuts will no longer be set ablaze amid the red-hot coals; but the writer, for one, believes that such a time is not yet at hand, and disbelieves that Halloween will disappear altogether as a festival.

It is not only that there would be a revolution in the child-world if such sacrilegious disuse were to become the fashion, but that there are too many older children interested in the famous eve to allow its celebration to drop altogether yet awhile. At sea, in Canada, the States, Australia, even in India, wherever a true Scottish or Irish family is located, there is sure to be at least one voice raised in favor of the genial old custom. Its superstitious observances must undoubtedly pass away—have, indeed, to a great extent already become obsolete—but the good-fellowship, the laughter, the nut-roasting, the apple-ducking, the candle-singeing, ought long to be specially associated with the 31st of October.

Of some of these weirder observances, and of some strange stories connected with them, the writer will now give a short account, in great part a record of what he has himself witnessed.

I.—HALLOWEEN IN IRELAND.

One wild, blustering afternoon—the afternoon of the last day of October—I made my way as best I could across a stretch of hilly moorland, vainly hoping that I might meet with some one able to direct me to my destination. I was on a visit to an old college friend, the vicar of a place I shall call Derree, in the western county of Clare, and at his hospitable table had met with a Mr. Connolly, who, hearing that my friend had to go south to Limerick on the last day of the month on important business, pressed me so hard to join his family circle on Hallowmas Eve that I could not with courtesy have refused his genial invitation, even had I wished to do so. As a matter of fact, I was only too glad to agree to his kind proposals, and listened attentively to his instructions as to the route I was to take. I was to go along the Derree road till I came to the base of the high hill called Creachan Knoc, which I was to skirt to the left, and then to cross the moor as if making for the central height of the Caisteall Abhaill, or Peaks of the Castles, and when I came to the stream I was to look for the ford, and having crossed this, to branch off abruptly to the left, and walk onward for about a mile, till I should see the farm-house nestling at the base of the strangely shaped, apparently insecurely

poised hill locally known as Drunken Tim. These were Mr. Connolly's directions, in the event of the 31st proving a fine day, and of my continuing in my determination to reach his farm on foot; otherwise I was to drive along the Derree road for some ten miles to the village of Clac-mha-reagh, and thence northward by the Castle road. The forenoon turned out to be bright and fine, to my great satisfaction, and I started in good hope, not only of enjoying the walk, but also of reaching the farm of my new acquaintance early in the afternoon. But by the time I had skirted the Creachan Knoc a white autumnal mist had shrouded the Caisteall Abhaill from view, so I had only to make a guess as to the right direction. Plunging suddenly into the edge of a bog made me realize that I had diverged from the route I was told to keep. The wind was rising with boisterous gusts, and I was beginning to wish that I had taken Mr. Connolly's advice and started by the more circuitous but safer way *via* Clac-mha-reagh, when I heard a loud hail far away to the right. Looking round, I perceived a man waving his arm to me, and as I approached him I noticed that he was a piper—a fact of which he soon informed me himself, adding that he was on the way to Mr. Connolly's farm to provide the music for the dancing that was sure to follow the regular Halloween festivities. It was well he descried me on the moor, for if I had proceeded further in the direction I had been following I would have probably found myself floundering in the huge and treacherous bog called in the neighborhood Red Mike's Rest. On the way Larry O'Hara—for so I learned was the piper's name—gave me much curious information about the customs of Hallowmas Eve in that part of Ireland, and as his account of how the great bog from which I had narrowly escaped got its name is germane to my subject, I will give it here.

"Rèd Mike, your honor, was the only son of Widow O'Flaherty. He was a queer one from his birth, an' no wonder, for he first saw the light atween dusk an' dark o' a Hallowmas Eve. Hereabouts the people say that if a babby be born on this night, it rins a moighty good chance o' bein' possessed by some sproite or other; it may or may not be true, oi'm sure it's beyont the likes o' me to say whether soch things are possible or not, but oi *will* say that Mike O'Flaherty was different to other men from the first. He wor always up to some game, he wor, an' nivver for good—leastways I nivver heard o' anny good he iver did. He lied and broke his troth to man an' woman, an' got into bad odor with priest an' magistrate, for nigh upon twelve years arter he came to manhood, until the judgment o' God came upon him. One Hallow Eve he was at the house o' the Flannigans, up by Glen Creachan. He was courtin' Mary Flannigan, though ivery one on us knew she didn't care two straws for Red Mike, but was all aglow wi' love for Larry O'Rourke, the Limerick carrier. It's the custom in these parts for the childer to run into the cabbage yard afore the evenin' fun begins, an' to pick out a number o' cabbage stalks, an' name them arter any seven o' the folk they have annything to do with; then, having finished wi' this choosin', they dance round the place, shouting out,

'One, two, three, an' up to seven;
If all are white, all go to heaven;
If one is black as Murtagh's evil,
He'll soon be screechin' wi' the devil.'

No, your honor," responded O'Hara to my question, "I don't know what's the maning of Murtagh's evil, nor, for that matter, which Murtagh is meant; no one in our time, annyway—for I sang the same loines meself whan I wor a spalpeen. Well, as I wor about to tell ye, Flannigan's childer, havin' finished their song, ran into the house an' asked all the folk to come out an' *see their sowls*. Ould Flannigan pulled *his* cabbage stalk, an' Mrs. Flannigan hers, an' young Tim Flannigan his, an' Mrs. Tim hers, an' purty Mary Flannigan hers, an' Larry O'Rourke his, until it came to Mike O'Flaherty's turn. The stalks of all the others had been quite clean an' white, but when Red Mike pulled up his, it was all black and foul wi' worms an' slugs, an' wi' a real bad smell ahint it. Larry O'Rourke laughed, an' Mary Flannigan giggled, an' the others all looked moighty consarned. Mike glared about him for a moment, more like a mad bull or a haythin Turk nor a Christian. Then he up an' says: 'Ye may laugh, Larry O'Rourke, but ye'll no be laughin' long; ay, ye may snigger, Mary, but ye'll be cryin' for manny a day, whan yer lover's below the sod, as he will be before the year's out. As for you, ould Flannigan, you an'

your son an' all that belong to ye will have cause to curse the day when ye mocked Red Mike, as ye call me. Ye forget I was born on Hallow Eve! I've the gift o' the sight, I have, and on this day my curse can blast whatever I choose.' What more Red Mike would have said I don't know, but at that moment Father O'Connor came up to where all were stan'-in'. 'Curses come home to roost,' says he to O'Flaherty, in a starn voice, 'an' it's you that 'll suffer, Mike O'Flaherty, an' no one here. Get ye gone at once, or I'll put the word on ye.'* 'I'll go whan I choose, Father O'Connor,' says Red Mike, surlily. The next moment the priest drew a crucifix from his breast, saying to O'Flaherty that even if he wor in league wi' the devil, he could not withstand *that*. Mike gave a howl jist loike a wild baste, an' thin turned an' ran down the glen as fast as he could. Ould Thady King, the piper (now dead, God rest his sowl!), wor crossing this moor that night, an' who should he see but Red Mike dancin' an' shoutin' like mad, an' screamin' in mortal fear. 'Mike! Mike!' ould Thady cried; but O'Flaherty paid no attintion to him, but kept on screamin', an' sometimes shoutin' out, 'My time is up! my time is up!' Suddenly he bent forrard an' ran like the wind, took one great leap, an' disappeared in the ground as if he had jumped into the sea. Nothin' more wor ever seen o' Red Mike, *leastwise as a man*. An' that's why the great bog yonder is called Red Mike's Rest."

O'Hara's narrative made me feel all the more thankful that I had not been left to blunder on as best I could, especially with a stormy night fast closing round. Even the fact that I was *not* born on All-hallows Eve would have stood me in little stead if I had once floundered into the actual quagmire of Red Mike's Rest. I thought the piper's "leastwise as a man" a finely suggestive way of hinting at something weirdly supernatural, but before I could draw anything further out of him we came in sight of The Three Larches, as Mr. Connolly's farm was called. As we arrived at the low doorway of the large, old-fashioned house there was quite a noisy chorus of hospitable greetings, mainly, of course, addressed to my evidently eagerly anticipated companion.

"*Cead-mille-a-faltha*—a hundred

* An expression often heard in some parts of western Ireland, to denote a priestly anathema.

thousand welcomes," cried my host him-self, and erelong I found myself at a ta-ble literally covered with good things, but none so pleasant to look upon as the fresh faces of a troop of children and some

been held, Mr. Connolly was going to have omitted, but a smiling assurance from his wife caused him to change his mind. This was the "livelong" ceremony. "Live-long" is the local name of certain green

W. SMALL

"NOTHIN' MORE WOR EVER SEEN O' RED MIKE."

eight or ten young men and girls around its sides. The dinner was a great success; and if hunger is the best sauce, every one present seemed amply supplied with that condiment.

After the dinner was over, and after each one had taken at least a sip of the fragrant punch that had been brought in in a great bowl, there was a general break up. One ceremony that had always

plants that are hung up in a loft or barn or disused room as early as midsummer; in fact, they must be hung up on Midsum-mer Eve; and if on Halloween they are still green, all will be well throughout the year with the children who had hung them up. If one should be sickly or dead, so will it be with the child. One of the little Connolly girls was a delicate child, and her father feared that if perchance were visible in the "livelong" hung up, it would have a bad effect on her susceptible nature. Mrs. Connolly, however, had privately paid a visit to the tool shed where they had been hung, and seeing that all the plants were undecayed, she thought the observance of the old custom would do the children more good than harm. What a shout of joy there was when all the "livelongs" were seen to be in good preservation! and this, the first ceremony of the evening, being so successful, was taken as a good augury for all to follow.

When we entered the house again, and passed into the great kitchen, wherein the shadows and the fire-light gleams held revel in a fashion that would have delighted Rembrandt himself, we caught a glimpse of some half-dozen dairy-maids and farm servants sitting dumbly in one corner of the room, and apparently engaged in moulding something with their hands.

"They're going through the dumb-cake ceremony," whispered Mrs. Connolly, "which consists in their kneading with their *left* thumbs a piece of cake without uttering a single word. If one of them intentionally or accidentally should breathe a single syllable, the charm would be broken, and not one of them would have her burning hopes of seeing her future husband in her dreams fulfilled."

The sturdy damsels certainly seemed in dead earnest, clinching their lips so that not a sound should escape them, one stout dairy-maid actually panting in her excitement or under the unwonted restraint. Meanwhile the children had fairly started the game of "snap-apple." Neither the dipping for apples nor the degenerate fork-dropping had any fascination for these young "spalpeens o' Clare" in comparison with this older and much more exciting form of the game. High up among the dusky rafters — wherefrom hung flitches of bacon, ox tongues, onions, and other articles of strange hue and shape—one of the boys had fastened a piece of strong cord; suspended at the lower end of this, within a few feet from the ground, was a short skewer gripped about midway by the knot of the string, and at either end of the skewer was respectively a tempting ruddy apple and a lighted tallow candle. As soon as the cord was set in motion, the game began. Little Harry Connolly was the first to es-

say for the luscious prize; but in his eager spring he missed both apple and candle, springing past the novel pendulum, and landing with a loud whack on the feet of gouty old Peter McMullen, the chemist and village doctor from Clac-mha-reagh, whose agonized "Oh, mother of Moses!" caused a roar of laughter from every one. Young Jack Hennessy, a cousin of the first youngster, and as fiery-haired a young Celt as ever revelled in mischief, tried next. Carefully watching his opportunity as the cord swung back from right to left, he sprang like an arrow, but was just a moment too soon, for he hit the candle with his face, and sent it spinning to the floor. His red locks were well singed, and a goodly splotch of tallow lay on his perky nose; but he laughed as heartily as the others, and seemed in no wise put out at his discomfiture. With varying adventures the different children all had their chances, no one, however, to the general merriment, proving successful —till at last young Hennessy's turn came round again. This time his sharp white teeth grabbed the coveted prize, and he retired from the game, another equally tempting apple being put in the last one's place. Much amusement was caused by little Johnnie Stevens, a pale-faced, apathetic-looking youngster. When his turn came he quietly slid under the swinging cord, waited for its backward motion from left to right, and then, meeting the apple full face, secured it with ease. "He's a cautious yin, he is," chuckled old Macfarlane, Lord Donaghadee's Scotch bailiff; "an' it's weel seen he comes o' guid Scottish bluid: he war determeened that if he didna grab the aipple, he wud at enny rate mak sicker o' no bein' singed wi' the cawnle."

Leaving the children still enjoying this their favorite sport, we passed by the servant-maids again. Their dumb-cake ceremony was long over, and they were now busily engaged in finding out the state of life to which their respective future lovers belonged. To gain this interesting information it was necessary that molten lead should be poured into cold spring-water. According to the fanciful shapes the lead took as each small quantity was poured out, so each girl framed her fancy: now something like a horse would cause the jubilant maiden to call out, "A dragoon!" now some dim resemblance to a helmet would suggest a handsome member of the

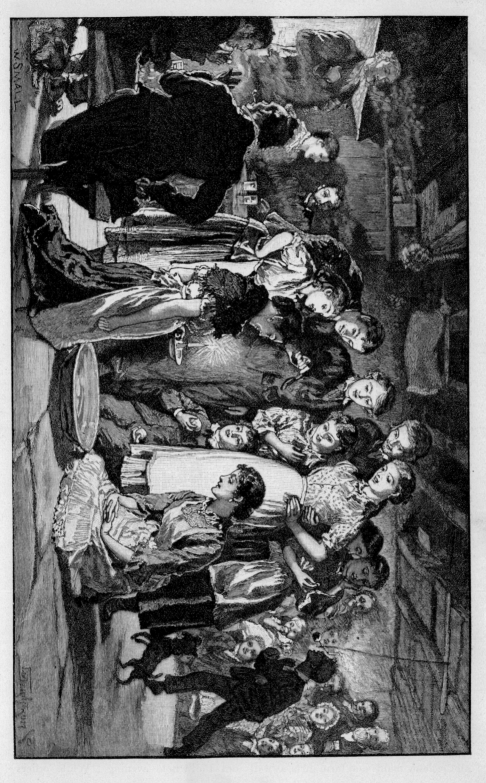

HALLOWEEN IN IRELAND.

W. SMALL.

mounted police; or a round object with a spike would seem a ship, and this of course meant a sailor; or a cow would suggest a cattle dealer, or a plough a farmer, and so forth. Anyhow, great amusement seemed to be got from the rite, and in one or two cases, to judge by the laughter and blushing denials, the guesses seemed to be based on something more substantial than mere fancy.

At last came the crowning delight of the evening, the Halloween jig. This was a reel in which every one joined, and there was nothing short of ecstasy in the tumult of stamping feet, snapping fingers, happy laughter, mingling with the wild music of Larry O'Hara's pipes, and the frantic screams—for they were nothing else— from the fiddle of the great musician, One-eyed Murtagh.

It was late that night before even the youngest went to bed, and certainly enough noise was made to scare away any evil spirits that might be hoping to gain some advantage on this night of all nights. The music came to an end at last, and the latest words that One-eyed Murtagh sighed out to his friend O'Hara, before both succumbed under their last glass of whiskey punch, were, "Larry, me boy, in hiven 'twill always be Halloween."

II.—IN SCOTLAND.

In the last week of a certain October I got an invitation from a connection in whose genial household I had spent many a happy Halloween. An answer in the affirmative was at once sent to The Shaws, as my friend Campbell's place was called. Linlithgow was little more than an hour's railway drive from Glasgow, but though I reached the old town shortly after four o'clock, it was quite dark, partly owing to the dense mass of dull gray snow-clouds that obscured the sky. When, after a drive of half an hour, the dog-cart stopped before the old manor-house, the first of the winter's storms had fairly set in, and the great flakes of snow were whirling wildly under the branches of the beeches, oaks, and elms that lined the avenue, seeming, indeed, as if they had straggled out of the adjacent forest of Polmont for that very purpose.

After dinner we went forth in a party— a small one, and well protected with wraps, owing to the steady snow-storm outside— to witness the pulling of the kale stalks. Some of the house servants, and of course all the dairy-maids and farm girls, as well

as all the young men in the neighborhood, had come together in the great kitchen of the home-farm; some of them, and the older and younger folk, were busy with preparations for all the customary festivities. No engaged and of course no married persons can participate in the "kaling." The right way is for two young people (in some parts of the country it must be two of one sex, in others each pair must consist of youth and lass) to go hand in hand, blindfolded, out into the kale or cabbage yard, and there pull the first stalks they meet with, returning at once to the fireside, when they are unbandaged, and left to read their matrimonial fortunes as foretold in the kale stalks. In the notes to his poem, Burns has explained the method of prediction. According as the stalk is big or little, straight or crooked, so shall the future wife or husband be of the party by whom it is pulled; the quantity of *yird*, or earth, sticking to the root denotes the amount of *tocher* (*i. e.*, fortune, or dowry); and the taste of the pith, or *custoc*, indicates the temper. Finally, the stalks, or *runts*, are placed, one after another, over the door, and the Christian names of the persons who chance thereafter to enter the house are held in the same succession to indicate those of the individuals whom the parties are to marry.

With much amusement all watched the fortune-seekers of the night. A huge carter named Jock Meiklejohn, a man about six feet two, stolidly allowed himself to be coupled with a bouncing partner, and without the slightest apparent interest, pulled the first cabbage stalk he came across; great laughter, however, came from every one at the rueful expression which stole over his honest face when he saw what augury of the future had been vouchsafed to him—a dumpy, crooked little kale stalk, devoid of a particle of *yird*. "Taste the *custoc*, Jock," "Taste the pith, mon," came from many of his tormentors; but while he mournfully shook his head, a pretty girl undertook the experiment on his behalf, and when her wry face showed what the real or pretended taste of the *custoc* was, every one laughed louder than before, and Jock's cup of misery was full. "D'ye think I'm a gowk tae believe a' this tamfoolery?" I heard him muttering to a sympathetic friend, though I noticed that the gloom of his predicted fate oppressed him throughout the whole evening. While others

TASTING THE CUSTOC.

were trying their fortune I spoke to Mr. Macdonald, the bailiff, asking him if the superstition had any real hold upon the people in the neighborhood.

"Weel, sir, it's dying oot. Schoolin' an' railways an' a' the rest o't's bad for auld customs like these. In some airts the pu'in' o' the kale stalks is no' to be seen at a'; in ithers it's lingerin' on amang the farm folk; but every here and there it's believed in as firmly as it was in the day o' oor grandfaithers."

Meanwhile two washing-tubs had been placed in the centre of the great kitchen, and round them was gathered an eager company intensely enjoying the fun of the apple-dipping. In the cold water bobbed about a few rosy-cheeked apples, so round and red and tempting, and yet so slippery, so apparently aggravatingly coy, that the excitement of the participators in the "dipping" grew almost into frenzy. Now and again some youngster grew desperate, and thrusting head and neck below the icy water, pursued an apple till he had pinned it against the bottom, and then grabbed it with his teeth. One young fellow, whose carroty locks had been plentifully bear's-greased in honor of the festivity, and perhaps of some fair farm girl, caused great laughter. With utmost caution he advanced his protruding lips toward a large pippin as it bobbed toward him, and it seemed as if the next moment his teeth would be firmly fixed in it; a slight wobble, however, sent it bumping against his nose, and then away it swam, with quite a coquettish little hitch, just as if it knew what was going on, and relished the fun as much as any one. Red-hair finally grew desperate, as the same thing occurred again and again. Reckless of all consequences to his carefully brushed and richly greased locks, he plunged his head deep into the water, and grubbed about frantically for the aggravating pippin. A roar of laughter came from all around as the latter was seen to bob up close behind Red-hair's head, the latter all unconscious of the fact, and with closed eyes still struggling with adverse fate.

Further away, around the huge fireplace, sat and stood a number of laughing lads and lasses, finding their existent or expected courtship imaged forth for them in the way the nuts on the red-hot bars or among the coals blazed or sputtered. No better description could be given than Burns's well-known lines:

"The auld guidwife's weel-hoardet nits
  Are round an' round divided,
An' monie lads' an' lasses' fates
  Are there that night decided:
Some kindle, couthie, side by side,
  An' burn thegither trimly;
Some start awa wi' saucie pride,
  An' jump out owre the chimlie
      Fu' high that night.

"Jean slips in twa, wi' tentie e'e;
  Wha 'twas she wadna tell;
But this is Jock and this is me,
  She says in to hersel'.
He bleez'd owre her, an' she owre him,
  As they wad never mair part;
Till, fuff! he started up the lum,
  An' Jean had e'en a sair heart
      To see't that night....

"Nell had the fause-house in her min',
  She pits hersel' an' Rob in:
In loving bleeze they sweetly join,
  Till white in ase* they're sobbin'.
Nell's heart was dancin' at the view;
  She whisper'd Rob to leuk for't;
Rob, stowlins, prie'd her bonnie mou',
  Fu' cozie in the neuk for't,
      Unseen that night."

The still lingering superstitious practices of the sark sleeve, the stalks o' corn, the kiln pot, the sowing of hemp-seed, the Halloween winnowing, the bean stack, the three dishes, and the looking-glass are to all intents customs of a by-gone day. The writer has only personally met with the "hemp-seed" and "the three luggies." All deal with the same matter of interest, namely, the state of one's future husband or wife. In the winnowing ceremony it is necessary for the experimentalist to go alone to the barn, and to be unperceived by any one; he should then, if he can manage it, unhinge the doors, for, as Burns says, there is danger that the *being* who is about to appear may shut the doors and work his summoner some mischief. The next thing is to take the flail, or *wecht*, "and go through all the attitudes of letting down corn against the wind." The action must be thrice repeated, "and the third time an apparition will pass through the barn, in at the windy door and out at the other," having the features and figure and marks of the station in life of the seer's future partner. The "sark sleeve" is another weird ceremony. The eager prier into futurity must go out after dark to a south-running streamlet where "three lairds' lands meet," and in the flowing water thereof dip his left shirt sleeve. On returning to the house he must go to bed in sight of a fire, hav-

* Ash.

BURNING NUTS.

ing first hung his shirt before it to dry. About midnight an apparition, exactly resembling the future partner in life, will glide up to the shirt, and turn the wet sleeve as if to dry the other side of it. Needless to say, there are many stories extant of sark-sleeve apparitions, mostly accounted for in each case by the fact that the swain did not go to bed without freely screwing up his courage with strong "barley brie." In "sowing the hempseed" the same imaginary performance must be gone through as in the case of the "winnowing the corn"; that is, "one must steal out unperceived, and sow a handful of hemp-seed," harrowing it with anything that can conveniently be drawn after one. On repeating now and then, "Hemp-seed, I sow thee; hemp-seed, I sow thee; and him [or her] that is to be my true love, come after me and pou thee," and on looking over the left shoulder, the apparition of the person invoked will be seen in the attitude of pulling hemp. The "kiln trial" is perhaps even more eerie. Burns again is responsible for the following explanation: Steal out all alone to the kiln, and, darkling, throw into the pot a clew of blue yarn; wind it in a new clew off the old one; and toward the latter end something will hold the thread. Demand, "Wha hauds?" (*i. e.*, who holds?) An answer will be returned from the kiln pot, naming the Christian and surname of your future spouse.

The "bean stack" ceremony is calculated to try the nerves of an excitable person more than any other Halloween rite, except perhaps the "looking-glass" spell. The first stipulation characterizes each of these rites, viz., the necessity of proceeding alone and unnoticed. One must then go to a bean stack, fathom it round three times, and, just as this is accomplished, "you will catch in your arms the apparition of your future conjugal yoke-fellow."

A much more social and less dubious experiment is that of the "three luggies," or dishes. On the hearth-stone the three chosen vessels are placed, one of them containing clean water, another turbid, and the last being empty. Blindfolded, the person about to essay his or her fortune is led up to where the dishes stand. If she (supposing the questioner to be a woman) chances to dip her hand—which, by-the-bye, must be the left one—into the clean water, then her future spouse will come to the marriage altar a bachelor; if in the turbid water, then he will be a widower; and if by ill luck she dips her finger into the *toom* or empty dish, then it is a sure sign that she will never be married at all. It is *vice versa*, of course, in the case of a man being the inquirer; in either case, however, the ceremony must be gone through three times, and correctly each time, otherwise the predictions have no value. Many may remember the humorous stanza in Burns's poem:

> " In order, on the clean hearth-stane,
>   The luggies three are ranged,
> And ev'ry time great care is ta'en
>   To see them duly changed :
> Auld Uncle John, wha wedlock's joys
>   Sin' Mar's year did desire,
> Because he gat the toom dish thrice,
>   He heav'd them on the fire
>   In wrath that night."

A strange story connected with the looking-glass rite came under my notice thousands of miles away from Scotland, which, as it is short, I shall be able to narrate in the space at my command. But first I must say that still another quotation from Burns's poem should be made in connection with that delightful evening at The

Shaws, now, alas! gone out of the possession of the family who had owned it for ten generations. "Fu' blythe that night" we were indeed, and of all there it might verily be said:

> " Wi' merry sangs, an' friendly cracks,
>   I wat they didna weary ;
> Wi' unco tales, an' funnie jokes,
>   Their sports were cheap an' cheery."

III.—AT SEA.

For three days we had been driving along before a fierce westerly gale. The *Glenlyon*, as our stout ship was called, had left the west of Scotland more than two months before, and now we were rather more than half-way between the Cape of Good Hope and that Cape Otway which would be the first glimpse of Australia we would have. The captain had informed us at breakfast that toward the late afternoon we should probably sight St. Paul's, that loneliest and most desolate of islands in the track of any great trade route; but our pleasure was a little damped by the additional information that unless the wind fell rapidly he might not only have to give the barren isle a wide berth, but also that our projected Halloween sports would not be feasible. For we were as Scotch all round as could well be the case: the *Glenlyon* had been built on the Clyde, and belonged to a famous Glasgow shipping company; the officers all hailed from the land o' cakes, as did the crew, with the exception of the English steward and a couple of Swedish seamen; and of the thirty cabin and second-cabin passengers there was only one who had the misfortune (as he was often jokingly reminded) to belong to another nationality. Thus it was quite natural that we should wish to keep Halloween as best we could under the circumstances; but the only custom it was in our power to observe was that of dipping for apples; this, however, would prove impossible unless the sea greatly moderated, for it was all the steadiest of us could do to keep our feet at all.

About half an hour after noon, however, the wind died away completely—or rather it seemed to do so, for, as a matter of fact, there was still enough pressure to prevent the main-sail from idly flapping to and fro. Nevertheless, so threatening was the aspect of the sea that none of us expected there would be any material change before night, if then. The writer

"YET THEY MANAGED TO FALL IN LOVE WITH EACH OTHER."—[SEE PAGE 854.]

has sailed on many seas, but not even off the iron coast of Tierra del Fuego has he seen such enormous billows as those that followed the *Glenlyon* that 31st of October far down in the Southern Ocean. Huge masses of lustrous emerald, with an enormous crown of white foam on their summits, they rolled their vast volume of water after and alongside our vessel much in the way that a herd of wild horses might career round a flying pony, which any moment they might overwhelm and crush to death. Nor has he ever seen any turbulent sea subside with such extraordinary rapidity. In the early morning, with the gale passed away but the wind still fresh, these gigantic billows had been so terrible that if they had not been avoided by the most skilful steering it would have gone badly with our vessel, A1 1400-

tonner though she was; by noon they were still phenomenally large and magnificent, but by four o'clock there was a marked subsidence, and two hours later the sea was, comparatively speaking, quite moderate.

Twilight arrived without our catching any glimpse of St. Paul's—much to our disappointment, as for two months we had sighted no land whatever—but this was partly owing to a slight mist that hung away to starboard, for we were really in close proximity to the island.

In tin wash cans, potato tins, and other vessels were soon bobbing about a number of apples, turned out by the steward in liberal quantity by the command of Captain Bennett. Every now and again a sudden lurch of the ship would send one or more of these flying over, and great was the agility displayed in the efforts to escape wetting, and loud the laughter that greeted every mishap. The passengers of both cabins and most of the crew indulged in the amusement as heartily as if they had all been school-boys, and of course the few children were in a perfect frenzy of delight. At length the last apple was disposed of, and nearly every one turned his or her attention to the music and dancing that immediately began. On the foredeck some of the sailors had dressed themselves in fantastic costumes, and as they sprung to and fro to the shrill sounds of the cook's fiddle, while the red gleam of the galley fire or the foremast lantern flashed across them, the scene was at once wild and picturesque. Life, movement, loud laughter, brilliant light, and shifting shadow within these planks; without, the dark, shoreless sea, the long waves heavily rising and falling; and above, the vague whiteness of the sails stretching cloud-like up toward the mysterious depths of heaven.

A little later, leaning over the taffrail on the poop, I was joined by a fellow-passenger. After some conversation anent our varied experiences of Halloween, he confided to me a strange story of an event which had happened in his own family, of which the following is a condensed account. As I have already hinted, this story deals with the looking-glass superstition.

Some ten or twelve years ago a family named Falconer had an estate in western Perthshire, the family consisting, besides husband and wife, of three daughters. A short distance away lived some neighbors of the name of Morgan. The only son of John Morgan—Ralph—was only seventeen years old, and Madge, the youngest daughter of the Falconers, only fourteen, yet they managed to fall in love with each other. Of course their boy-and-girl passion was not as deep as that of lovers of maturer age, but at the same time it was ardent and sincere enough to exercise a strong influence on their lives. At last came news of young Ralph's appointment to a good position on a coffee plantation in Ceylon, and before leaving home he determined to speak to Mr. Falconer concerning his love for Madge; but though, after the confession was duly made, the young girl's father did not absolutely prohibit her entertaining the idea of ultimate marriage with Ralph Morgan, he insisted that there should be no engagement, explicit or tacit, until she was of age, and in a better position to be sure of her sentiments. So the matter had to remain. Years passed, not without occasional correspondence, but slowly the love of the girl for her absent lover faded, though it did not quite pass away. A November was almost at hand—a November wherein Madge's twenty-first birthday would arrive; but before this family festival came round there was the still greater annual one of Halloween. In the midst of the fun of the evening a sudden fancy seized the youngest Miss Falconer. She had often heard of and laughed at the superstition of the Halloween mirror, as a looking-glass in a moonlit room on this night is called. As soon as she reached her bedroom she saw that one circumstance, at any rate, was favorable— a long moonbeam streamed in at a side window, and fell so near the looking-glass that in a minute or two it would shine right into it. Madge had brought the apple with her to munch before the glass, but she forgot all about this part of the ceremony as her thoughts brought back to her the memory of Ralph Morgan. She remembered, too, that her twenty-first birthday was almost at hand, and a sudden emotion of tenderness came over her as she thought of her absent lover and his long patience. She felt certain that he still hoped she would be his wife, but as for herself, she doubted much if she any longer loved him in return. As a matter of fact, a certain tender affection was all she experienced toward Ralph, the girlish passion having completely died away.

A burst of laughter from down-stairs brought Madge out of her reverie. She felt inclined to laugh at her own foolishness, and was just about to rejoin her friends without looking into the glass, when she suddenly yielded to an irresistible influence and passed rapidly toward it.

She looked eagerly into it, but saw nothing save her own pale face and startled eyes. Suddenly she grew chill with horror as she distinctly saw another face close to her own—a face that she did not know, and of a type altogether different from that of Ralph Morgan; even in her sickening dread she noticed a peculiar scar over the right eyebrow, such as she had never seen in any one she had ever met. The next moment she fainted, and a little later her alarmed friends found her lying insensible on the floor. When she came round again she managed to pass the whole thing off as a stupid fright she had given herself when in an overexcited state, and in a short time every one except herself forgot all about the incident.

A few days after her birthday Madge received two letters from India— one from Ralph Morgan, who was now a partner in the Bombay branch of the firm, and one from an aunt, a Mrs. Martin, who resided in the same city. The former letter she fancied strangely cold, and she could not help feeling that Ralph was writing more out of duty than from affectionate impulse: the latter was an invitation to Madge to go and live with Mrs. Martin and her hus-

"A SUDDEN FANCY SEIZED THE YOUNGEST MISS FALCONER."

band for a year, or for as long as she felt inclined. To make my friend's narrative as short as possible, I may briefly state that after much consideration Madge Falconer decided to accept her aunt's invitation, while she explained to Ralph Morgan that nothing could be decided until after they had met again. In due time she reached Bombay, but at the very first interview the two former lovers perceived that some radical change had taken place in each other. Before a month had elapsed Madge frankly told the young man that she could not marry him, and it was with real pleasure she learned that to Ralph also their mutual agreement was welcome. A few months later the latter married—Madge shrewdly suspecting that the young lady had been the main factor in Ralph's readiness to break off his long engagement.

But, before this marriage took place, Madge met at the house of her aunt a certain Major Colville. On their first meeting his face puzzled her greatly. She knew she had seen it before, but could not recollect where. Suddenly a memory flashed through her mind. On only one face had she ever seen such a scar as that over the right eyebrow of Major Colville— a scar which in the latter's case had been caused by a bullet in one of the battles during the Sikh war. It was with a strange and uncomfortable sense of something eerie that she remembered the face in the looking-glass last Hallowmas Eve: *that* face and the face of Major Colville were absolutely identical. Perhaps this strange fact predisposed the girl in the young major's favor. In any case, the result was that, not long after Ralph Morgan's marriage, Madge Falconer became Mrs. Colville.

This was the strange story told me by my friend; the names are altered, but the personages signified are all living. Madge was the narrator's own sister, and he informed me that even yet Mrs. Colville felt troubled at times at the mysterious event of that memorable Halloween.

HOW I FORMED MY SALON.

BY MADAME EDMOND ADAM (JULIETTE LAMBER).

I HAD come to Paris from my provincial home; I had written my first book *Idées anti-Proudhonniennes;* and after the publication of that book, in which I had defended the Comtesse d'Agoult (Daniel Stern) and Georges Sand against the insults and coarse attacks of P. J. Proudhon, I had received a note from each of these two greatest women of our epoch. Madame Sand's note ran thus: "I send to you my friend Captain D'Arpentigny, so that he may tell me who you are, and offer to you my affection if you desire it." The letter of Daniel Stern was as follows: "Monsieur, it is extraordinary that we women should assume the name of a man when we write, but it seems to me still more extraordinary that a man in the same case should take the name of a woman." Captain D'Arpentigny was very much pleased with me. He asked permission to read my fortune in the palms of my hands, predicted that I should have the most brilliant future, and invited me to come to see Madame Sand. My reply to Daniel Stern was this: "You believe that I am a man, madame. Come and see."

I visited Madame D'Agoult first, because the day mentioned by her in a second note was nearer than the day appointed by Captain D'Arpentigny for visiting Madame Sand. At first sight Madame D'Agoult conceived a tender affection for me, invited me to her Friday receptions, and when, in reply to her questions, I told her how Madame Sand had sent Captain D'Arpentigny to negotiate with me, she said: "If you wish to become intimate with me, do not see Madame Sand; we have quarrelled, and one or the other of us might be led to have words in your presence, and to do each other ill turns. You admire Georges Sand; I shall not deprive you of that admiration; and I hope that you will learn to love me. Thus all will be for the best." I wrote to Madame Sand and told her frankly what Daniel Stern had said, and the author of *Horace* (it is in this volume that she paints the portrait of Madame D'Agoult) replied, "It is all well, my child: you will come back to me."

The first time that I entered a political salon was, therefore, at the house of the Comtesse d'Agoult, author of *La Révolution*

MADAME ADAM.

de 1848. She had passed in review before her all the men of our party, and had kept as friends those whom she had treated with favor. Daniel Stern was the mother of two daughters by Liszt, the one, Blandine, married to M. Emile Ollivier, the other, Cosima, by her first marriage, Baroness Hans von Bülow, and afterward Madame Wagner. Although she was the mother-in-law of Emile Ollivier, the salon of Madame D'Agoult was rather a salon of abstentionists. Abstention had been the only form of protest of the vanquished Republicans against the Empire, a silent protest more dignified than clever, as was afterward said by those who took the oath of allegiance with mental reserves.

From 1852 to 1857 not a single voice had dared to make itself heard against the *coup d'état*. The elections had been purely official elections, discussed and arranged beforehand in the prefectures and in the cabinets of the ministers. The candidates were chosen amongst those who had given most proofs of devotion to the Empire, and when once accepted by the Emperor, they were nominated. Crushed by events, the men of 1848 had not been able to recover their moral elasticity. Horribly calumniated by the imperialist organs, cursed by the insurgents of June, the utmost they had tried to do had been to reconquer their honor. What could one do except defend one's self personally? It was impossible to organize a public meeting, for in doing so one was liable to the most severe penalties, and as for private meetings of a purely political character, people had no taste for them, inasmuch as they could meet merely to lament the past. Abstention was thus the only negative force of which we could dispose, and so a necessity had been transformed into a doctrine.

In the salon of Madame D'Agoult the assiduous attendants at the Friday receptions were the abstentionists Grévy, Carnot, Neftzer (editor of *Le Temps*), Littré, Edmond Adam, and then Emile de Girardin and Emile Ollivier, who believed a liberal empire possible. In 1858 Carnot and Goudchaux, in the name of the abstentionist doctrine, had refused to take the oath of allegiance to the Empire. This declaration, and, on the other hand, the nomination of the five deputies who had accepted their mandate with the obligations of the oath, constituted the first awakening of opinion under the Empire;

the five were, Emile Ollivier, Darimon, Hénon, Jules Favre, Ernest Picard. How often have I listened to fine discussions in which the moral element predominated! Carnot, Littré, Grévy, and Adam would admit no compromise, declaring that politics could never exact from a man that he should cease to honor his word, while Emile de Girardin and Emile Ollivier would repeat: "There are cases of overwhelming necessity: when you are caught in a wood by a gang of bandits, you promise not to denounce them, and the first police station you come to you do denounce them." It was with the abstentionist that I used to side; I already feared that compromises were dangerous for the morality of my party, and sincere and ardent Republican as I was, having faith in the greatness of Republican principles, I felt that I was the secret enemy of those whose resolutions did not rest upon a basis of strict honor. My republic was already the republic which cannot last unless it is founded upon virtue.

The attempt of Orsini had thrown the Parisians into a state of feverish excitement. Paris nominated as its deputy Jules Favre, the barrister who had defended Orsini. By the death of Cavaignac the moderate party lost its chief, and the young Republicans dreamed of creating a new political life for the country. Many signs announced the awakening. In the salon of Madame D'Agoult, where I was being educated as a hostess and *maîtresse de maison*, I saw from time to time the "little Olliviers," as they were called—Floquet, Adalbert, Phillis. We heard, too, the unknown names of those new men who were grouping themselves around an ambitious chief—Jules Ferry, Gambetta, Spuller, Ranc. All accepted the compromises of the oath of allegiance, and held in political matters theories as lax as those of the men of 1848—the "vieilles barbes," as they began to call them —had been severe. Laurent-Pichat had opened his salon to these young men, and we were curious—Madame D'Agoult and myself—to make the acquaintance of this new element of our party; but those who came did not please us. Their want of respect for the men of 1848, for those whom they called the "naïfs" and the dupes of Napoleon III., shocked me. They went further than Girardin and Ollivier as regards the oath of allegiance, saying that it ought to be a pleasure to violate

THE SALON OF MADAME D'AGOULT.

an oath made to a man who had violated his own oath.

These discussions gave great animation to Madame D'Agoult's salon. I used to observe and reflect upon what I saw, and soon I came to the conclusion that a political salon can only be founded with very multiple elements. A common principle must dominate, and all those who meet in the salon must belong to the same party, but not to the same sect; they must feel the need of joining forces in order to combat a common enemy; both the past and the future must be kept in view; young men and old must be brought together, and tradition must be defended against the attacks of the new-comers. In these conditions the discussion will be generalized, and not get belated amidst questions of persons. The pronoun "we" must be constantly used, and thoughts will then become more elevated and projects more broad. You feel that on the day of the battle which is being prepared union will not be wanting, and that the violent will be useful, while the prudent will warm into enthusiasm. A political salon cannot continue to exist unless those who compose it belong to an opposition. It is formed in view of a battle; the ranks are filled up, and the soldiers exercised and drilled for action; but as soon as the victory has been won, the ranks break, each one looks after his lodging and accoutrements, each soldier knows the post that he is to occupy, and which he no longer has to conquer, but only to keep; each personality in the staff of the party finds his field of action, acts in his individual sphere, and thinks that he has no longer any need of a common understanding.

Both the abstentionists and those who had taken the oath of allegiance had a common hatred of the Empire, and applied themselves with equal zeal to forming a solid group and gaining new recruits. The Italian war interrupted this movement, and gave the Empire new forces. Up to 1863 the elections were favorable to the Empire, but after that date, even in the provinces, the opposition gained ground and strength. The Mexican war then came, and brought us valuable assistance, and soon afterward those who were partisans of an immediate struggle, hand to hand, against the Empire, began the combat at the Palais Bourbon. After my return from the South I used to

go to the sittings of the Chambers, with a view to becoming thoroughly acquainted with the men of my party, knowing as I did that to see men in the intimacy of a salon is not sufficient to enable one to judge them, but that one must follow them in the acts of their public life, and surprise the spontaneous movements of their nature under the shock of their adversaries.

Thiers, Berryer, Jules Simon, Glais-Bizoin, Eugène Pelletan, represented our opinions in the Corps Législatif. Among the partisans of the Empire there was neither a famous name in literature and in art nor a single great figure, except perhaps Sainte-Beuve, who was very incompletely enlisted. The first salon of Madame D'Agoult had been gradually modified. The veterans of 1848, the "vieilles barbes," had almost deserted it; the young men who could not make up their minds to follow Emile Ollivier in his evolutions had withdrawn and left the field free for Prince Napoleon. I myself held aloof, having no taste for the new elements of liberal imperialism. And so finally I left the salon where I had received my training, for Daniel Stern initiated me in her manners and in those traditions of the eighteenth century which she had acquired by her education in her aristocratic family, and she had taught me also the rôle of a *maîtresse de maison* by asking me to receive in her place when she was herself occupied with some particularly distinguished guest. "You are just the woman to have a salon," she used often to say to me; "you have the faculty of interesting yourself in twenty people at the same time; you like general conversations; you can keep them up by adding something of your own; whereas I prefer above everything to exchange thoughts with a single person."

This idea of a salon recurred to me constantly after I had left that of Madame D'Agoult, but the circumstances of my life did not permit me to carry into execution the wishes I had formed on the subject. The formation of a political salon was not possible while I was alone. I was too young to attract and to retain around me the men of the moderate parties of 1848. People said that my opinions were too advanced, and they were so in reality. My friends, the friends who truly represented my views, were above all the exiles.

GAMBETTA'S FIRST APPEARANCE AT MADAME ADAM'S SALON.

I became a widow, and then married Edmond Adam, who belonged to the group of the men of 1848. He had been secretary to M. Thiers in an election campaign, and, like M. Thiers, he belonged to the editorial staff of the *National* newspaper. In 1848 he had taken the place of Armand Marrast at the "mairie" of Paris. Apropos of the *National*, I will relate here an anecdote. Adam, who never even saluted Emile de Girardin at Madame D'Agoult's, and who had never pardoned him for having caused the death of Armand Carrel in a fatal duel, said to me a few weeks after our marriage, one day that I met Emile de Girardin in the street and gave him a smile of recognition: "I beg of you never to salute Girardin when you are on my arm; it pains me." One day I met Girardin in the street when I was alone; I stopped him and repeated Adam's words. He expressed his regret in terms which touched me, and replied simply, "I am not astonished, *que voulez-vous ?*" When I lost Adam, in June, 1877, I received the following little note from Girardin: "He detested me while he was alive: will you permit me to love him now that he is dead ?"

It was in 1868. Those who had been vanquished by the *coup d'état* had recovered from their defeat. They spoke aloud, and were heard. Ernest Picard had dared to say in the Corps Législatif to M. Rouher, who was glorifying the *coup d'état*, "The 2d of December is a crime!" One day M. Thiers, as he was coming out of the Palais Bourbon, took Adam by the arm and asked him to accompany him on foot to the Rue Saint-Georges. They had a long conversation, and M. Thiers, as usual, blamed Adam and his abstentionist principles, adding, in conclusion, "My dear friend, we must work with all our forces against the Empire, for the Republic alone is possible henceforward."

Adam, astonished at these words, repeated them to me with emotion. They had a great influence upon his mind, and it was certainly these words of M. Thiers which decided the formation of our salon.

"Here certainly," I said to Adam, "is the greatest proof of the possibility of the Republic; but our friends are separated: we must find or create a centre around which to group the scattered elements. The editorial rooms of newspapers, cafés, the lobbies of the Chamber of Deputies, are not adequate meeting-places for a great party. In order to centralize our forces and to find an exercising ground, a salon is necessary."

"The salon of M. Thiers groups the veterans, and Laurent-Pichat's evening receptions bring the young men together."

"The young and the old must be united."

"It is impossible."

I did not insist, for I knew that with Adam it was best to prepare things slowly. In spite of the words of M. Thiers, Adam could not cure from one day to the other the moral wound he had received at the *coup d'état*. He did not dare to believe in the future. He often said to me that the crime of the 2d of December had wounded him doubly, both as a Republican and as a writer on the *National*. But I felt that the day when he did recover hope, with his stalwart nature, he would dream of nothing but action in all its forms. His loyal character, calm and bold at the same time, and highly esteemed by all the Republican groups, marked him out to play an enviable rôle by his moral influence.

Little by little we began to gather around us at dinner on Fridays some friends of Adam and of my own. They seemed to get on together very well, and then we extended our invitations. The opinions of the people we brought together varied from Orleanism to irreconcilable republicanism. The enemy to be combated was so powerful that his enemies, with all their forces, had none to spare. The books and writings of the time were everywhere favorable to the opposition, and the mind of the public was full of them. The greatest successes were the *Voyage d'un Transporté*, by Jules Vallès, the *Légende de Martin Bidauré*, Madame Guinet's *Légende d'Exil*, and Rochefort's *Lanterne*. The exiles of December were beginning to raise their voices, and their words came sounding over the frontiers. In the long silence that had been imposed upon them the voices of these exiles seemed to have grown stronger and more vibrating. Audacious once more, our friends outside France uttered the cry of vengeance, and then we, the exiles inside, began to be astonished at our patience, and felt within us the violence of those sentiments over which we had brooded so long. From week to week our Friday meetings grew more numerous. Our indignation found freer vent; our enthusiasm increased with our courage. Around the person of Napoleon III. some alarm began to be felt at these new rumors, which reached even the court. Why was this storm beginning to rumble, when the ruler was simply continuing his past *régime*, without any additions?—on the contrary, had not a little liberalism penetrated through the imperial coat of mail? But the guardians of the throne had grown old. The most illustrious combatants of the early days were dead. Security had brought lukewarmness, and the imperial servitors were no longer ready at any moment for resistance. Napoleon III., who read everything, and knew how to get information, was astounded to see this rising tide. He asked his courtiers; but he was surrounded by none but ambitious men, and it was not public opinion that they accused, it was this and that personality, which enjoyed the Emperor's protection. The favorites, past, present, and future, were firing upon their own troops. Confusion was everywhere.

The newspapers said very little about these internal struggles at the Tuileries, but we nevertheless heard all about them. An open salon attracted everybody on certain days; we told each other of the contradictory orders, and we used to say, "They are confused; they have lost their heads and lost their cause."

The Legitimists and the Orleanists had not accepted the Empire any more than the Republicans; they had submitted to it out of respect for public order, terrified by the insurrection of June; but they had now got over their fear, and applauded everything which helped to break up the Empire.

As we were in the habit of passing some of the winter months in the south of France, we used to receive before our departure, and our salon was the first to open. We ceased our receptions just at the moment when everybody is overwhelmed with invitations, and running from salon to salon without having time to stop in any one; and then, on our return, we reopened our salon just when other people were closing theirs. Adam had often spoken to me of Laurent-Pichat's evenings, at which he was a regular attendant. He talked to me especially about a young man whose name began to be mentioned a good deal in our circle, Gambetta, who told the men of 1848 what he

thought of them, without mincing his words, saying again and again that their traditions must be broken, that it was no good troubling about the dogmas of the party, which hampered its action, like swaddling clothes kept too long around the body of a child, and that this naïve policy must be replaced by a march, step for step, in the path traced by the enemy.

"To try to conquer with projectiles flung from too great a height is mere silliness," said M. Léon Gambetta; "we are under the Empire, let us combat the Empire with the methods of the Empire. It is useless to put on dancing shoes in order to walk in a sewer; let us put on sewermen's boots. M. Louis Blanc, if he returned, would vote again, from principle, for the return of Prince Napoleon. Facts never touch principles, however much they may give them the lie. Very good; let us wipe out the principle, and let us take account of the fact only. If we shut ourselves up in our doctrines, we shall never triumph. We must drive Napoleon III. back upon his own men, and overthrow Rouher with the enemies of Rouher. Principles! We have had enough of principles!"

Adam admired all this completely. I made reserves.

"A good doctrine for combat," I said, "but very demoralizing the day of the victory. For what will be the prize and object of the victory? Mere victory? That is not enough."

"The proof that we were wrong, and that this young man is right," replied Adam, "and that the ideal doctrine is false, is that not only have we been crushed, but we have been stupid. This Gambetta says dozens of things that I thought in 1848, and which I have not dared to formulate since. He is right. None of those who have been directing us ever took advantage of events. If we had only had a man with the character of Cavaignac, the eloquence of Lamartine, the democratic passion of Ledru-Rollin, then we should have triumphed. Will you believe it?—M. Léon Gambetta makes me think of this trinity united in one single man."

"Ah! if that be the case, I want to know him. You must bring him to see me."

"The fact is that his ways are very— how shall I say?—very Latin Quarter student-like. He is as free and careless in his language as he is in his dress. He speaks with a terrible accent; he discusses with insolence; and I should be sorry for you to hear the way he treats me because I am one of the 1848 set."

"But is he extraordinary, or is he not ?"

"He is extraordinary, but a thorough Bohemian; vulgar, living as nobody else lives, brutal, audacious. He is a man for the populace, a kind of Danton, only more shrewd. He speaks with great authority."

"I want to know him," I replied.

At that time, November, 1868, some manifestations had taken place at the tomb of Godefroy Cavaignac and of Baudin. In the *Avenir National*—a journal founded by Adam and his friends—a subscription had been opened for the purpose of raising a monument to Baudin. This question had been debated at length at one of our Friday meetings. My wishes were realized ; our salon was indeed a political salon, where all shades of republican opinion were blended. The circle, very restricted at first, had become larger. The Buadin subscription was a great event. The lists gave us the opportunity of counting our numbers, and the coalition against the Empire dates from then. Our friends found at our house wise and bold council in Adam, and enthusiasm in his wife. The moderate men could come to see him; the more advanced to see me.

Adam was summoned by M. Thiers, who wished to prevent the Baudin manifestation, and who had heard of the resolutions taken at our house. He was irritated with Adam, and told him that the affair was foolish. "It is simple faction," he said. "Such enterprises lead only to riots, and not to revolutions." M. Thiers was mistaken, and he confessed his mistake afterward. Berryer subscribed. The movement was taken up by the schools and by the working-men. It was fairly launched. In the government M. Rouher, attacked on all sides, began to lose his presence of mind. The Emperor wished to make some examples, and to apply the laws for assuring public safety. M. Rouher resisted, saying that such measures would only serve to secure a triumph for the organizers of the manifestation.

Adam, who now began to smell gunpowder, had been active amongst the organizers of the subscription. The *Avenir National*, whose ardor he had excited, was prosecuted, together with the *Réveil* and the *Tribune*, but the other opposition newspapers having declared their intention of bearing their share of the responsibility and of the dangers, the whole liberal press then opened its columns to the subscription; and so it was against all the journals of the opposition that the government brought its suit.

On November 14, Gambetta, who in the morning was only known to a small circle of friends, became famous in the evening, thanks to his defence of Delescluze, the editor of *Le Réveil*. His pleading flew like a signal all over France.

The great force of Gambetta lay in his faculty of translating currents of opinion into words, which had no real value in themselves, or, at any rate, a value which they soon lost, but which at the moment calmed each one's spirit of inquiry, and were the exact expression of the opinions of all. This speech in defence of Delescluze, which caused so much emotion, and rendered so admirably and so completely the explosion of the general conscience of France, seems nothing exceptional if we read it over now, but you can feel in it the vibration of a soul which others made to vibrate. Between Gambetta and public opinion, so far as he abandoned himself to opinion and did not try to oppress it, there was an extraordinary sympathetic communication. He gave back one hundredfold what he received from it, satisfying it just in the degree to which it wished to be satisfied. He was the model of a democratic orator. Often have I seen him, at the time when we were intimate, hesitate in his reflections, question, grow excited in order to provoke contradiction, exercise his oratory in our little circle as if he were trying to feel the pulse of opinion, just as formerly he used to exercise himself in the midst of his comrades so that he might judge the resources of his eloquence. But in presence of a crowd or of an assembly, whatever his preconceived idea might be, his mind would catch with marvellous facility the general tendency of the mind of his audience, and there would take place within his mind, as it were, a chemical process, the formation of a sublimated mixture of diverse elements. How could he fail to force the attention of those to whom he returned their own thoughts strengthened, broadened, and adorned with superb flights of eloquence?

Before our departure for the south I sent a note to Gambetta inviting him to dinner. He imagined, as he afterward told me, that he was coming to the table of a literary woman, a blue-stocking, and so he arrived dressed in one of those costumes that one wears in the morning for want of something better. His coat was neither a frock-coat nor a jacket, but something between a pilot-coat and an overcoat. As he was subject to bronchitis, he wore a check flannel shirt, on which he had pinned a white collar and cuffs, but the flannel was visible in certain places, and he pushed back the recalcitrant folds with an ease that betrayed long habit.

Adam and our friends were all in evening dress, and I in a decollete gala costume. Gambetta looked at us with amazement. Eugène Pelletan, who knew him, introduced the new-comer to me. Adam was chatting in another room. Gambetta apologized for not having a dress-coat. "I never wear one," he said; "and if I had known—"

"You would not have come, monsieur. That is very unamiable on your part," I replied, laughing.

Pelletan, with his usual kindness, then added: "Madame Adam prefers that her friends should not come to her house in evening dress."

However, the appearance of the room demonstrated the contrary. In such cases as this everybody is embarrassed. My old friend Jules de Lasteyrie, a "Lafayette" in manners, and generally so kind, said to me in a whisper, "A frock-coat I can admit—yes; but I cannot go so far as —that."

It was Lasteyrie's arm which I should have taken to go in to dinner, and I replied: "And yet, my dear friend, the only way to rehabilitate that at my table is to give it the best place. It is you whom I deprive, but you will approve me."

He put on his air of a grand gentleman, and answered: "You are quite right; that is what must be done. We shall be better able to judge the man thus, and we shall see if he understands, and if he has anything of the 'grand' nature in him."

I took Gambetta's arm, to his profound astonishment, and I placed him at table on my right hand, while Jules de Lasteyrie sat at my left.

Hardly had we taken our seats when Gambetta leaned toward me and whispered, "Madame, I shall never forget a lesson given in this manner."

He had something of the "grand" nature in him.

This place on my right hand Gambetta was destined to keep in my house.

Ten years later, one day that he entered my salon in a dress-coat, with a spotless white cravat, straw-colored kid gloves, and a gardenia in his button-hole, I said to him, laughingly, "My dear friend, the flannel shirt was not dressy enough for the situation; all this is too dressy."

When Berryer died, Gambetta put himself up as candidate for Marseilles, and our friends were enthusiastic partisans of his election. From our home at Golfe Juan we followed all the details of his very clever campaign, which ended in victory. At these same general elections in May and June, 1869, Carnot was replaced in the first circumscription of the Department of the Seine by Gambetta, but the latter chose to represent Marseilles, which city would never have pardoned him had he deserted, and it was Rochefort who took his place at Paris.

At these elections the opportunist party grew largely. Those who made concessions to the Empire were already repudiated. Bancel took the place of Ollivier, who was accused of weakness. The victims of the *coup d'état* and of the imperial persecutions were successful everywhere; 116 opposition deputies, most of them our friends, were elected; M. Thiers, reëlected, became the chief of the young Republicans, and followed with interest the development of their ideas. Adam had attempted to become a candidate in the Department of the Eure, but when the moment came for signing the oath of loyalty to Napoleon III., his scrupulous nature got once more the upper hand, and he threw down the pen. I liked him better so. For that matter, our salon would have had less influence at this time if the master of the house had belonged to such or such a group and voted with it. He would have inevitably dissatisfied one or the other, and would not have attracted them all.

One after the other, in rapid succession, we discussed essays of liberal empire and the restitution of parliamentary preroga-

"THE IMPERIAL POLICE CHASING WITH DRAWN SWORDS THE PEOPLE ON THE BOULEVARD."

tives. Sometimes a sinister accompaniment came from the street outside; it was the imperial police chasing with drawn swords the people on the boulevard who ventured to assume an attitude of independence. It seemed that the government must succumb under the weight of its abuses. Emile Ollivier had essayed the transformation of liberal empire which had been prepared in Madame D'Agoult's salon. Gambetta, who had often returned to see us, had greatly struck our friends by the sureness of his tactics, and by what Adam called "his ponderated superabundance, his reasonable passions." He talked a little too much about Ollivier, whom he often saw, and whose ruin he watched with some interest, for he believed that by means of a liberal empire a useful transition could be provoked. This association of the idea of liberal reforms with an authoritative government was already the subject of discussions which were destined later on to separate me from my friends. Ernest Picard and Jules Ferry were the very men to work at this task of transforming the Empire, and if it had not been for the war, Emile Ollivier would certainly have associated them with a policy which

they would have usefully served. These two and many others in our party might have been liberal imperialists, but they were never to become liberal republicans. Liberal empire or authoritative republic, the difference between the two is very slight; the institutions are the same; there is only one detail of the machinery that is different, namely, the emperor.

After the proclamation of the Republic, during the war, when the exiles returned, most of them joined the vanguard of the combatants in our salon. The meetings were curious. Throughout the siege of Paris we kept up our Fridays in the salon of the Boulevard Poissonnière, and it was certainly not the least interesting epoch in the history of that salon. Gambetta himself did not abandon us, for he made me promise to write to him every week, and keep him informed of the opinion that reigned in my salon, for he knew that this would be the opinion of Paris.

After the siege the new political men from the provinces flocked to our house, and formed themselves there to the ways and manners of Parisian public life, while those who had suffered under the Empire or during the siege returned, always happy to meet again. Adam, deputy for Paris, brought his colleagues from the Versailles Chamber. The first few times that Gambetta came to see us, after his famous stay at Saint-Sébastien, he did not make a great figure. Adam and myself and a few rare friends alone supported him; the others blamed his last decrees, his ambiguous conduct during the Commune, whereas we saw in him the man of the National Defence, the man who had saved the only thing that could then be saved, the honor of France.

Little by little, however, Gambetta recovered a better and finally a preponderating position. Our house, our influence, our relations, helped him, for there he met, besides the parliamentary people, artists whom he charmed, and men of the world and financiers in whom he inspired confidence.

One day in 1874, at one of my Friday dinners, at which Gambetta was present, we received the following telegram:

"Escaped. Send twenty-five thousand francs, Sydney. HENRI."

"It is Rochefort. He has escaped. Bravo!" was the cry. "What a humiliation for the Duc de Broglie!"

"Do not believe a word of it," said some one. "The telegram is from some sharper who wishes to get hold of twenty-five thousand francs."

We discussed the matter, and each one gave his opinion for or against the supposition.

"If it were a sharper," I said, "he would have signed 'Rochefort,' and not 'Henri.'"

"She is right," said Adam and Gambetta together. "The money must be sent."

The reaction, just like the opposition under the Empire, again gave our salon its true character after May 24, 1873, when M. Thiers resigned, and Marshal McMahon was elected President of the Republic, with the Duc de Broglie as his guide and counsellor. It became exclusively a political rendezvous, where the elements of the struggle were centralized, and the grand manœuvres thought out and arranged. The gravest resolutions were taken there, and remained always secret. In the lobbies at Versailles appointments were made to meet at the Boulevard Poissonnière to decide upon the course to be taken and the combinations to be planned. The influence of our salon went on increasing until May 16, 1877. Alas! Adam was soon to be taken from us.

NOTE.—After having achieved extraordinary celebrity both by her books and her famous political salon, Madame Adam is now occupied in writing the memoirs of her life from childhood onward, and the preceding pages, although written expressly for *Harper's Magazine*, will ultimately be incorporated in the autobiography of the author. Since the death of Gambetta, Madame Adam's salon has ceased to exist as a marked political influence in France, or even as a rendezvous for statesmen and politicians. The French republic has not taken that Athenian turn which is the ideal of Juliette Lamber, and so the receptions which that amiable hostess now holds are purely social and literary. The account of the formation of her salon which Madame Adam has here given us may be considered complete, although she breaks off her narrative in 1877. At that date her receptions had reached the height of their *éclat* and influence.—TH. C.

A PLEA FOR THE GRASSY ROAD.

BY WILLIAM HAMILTON GIBSON.

"You may go round the world
By the old Marlborough road."

I WOULD say a few earnest words in intercession for a patient, venerable neighbor of ours and yours, who has few champions, who suffers in silence, who is fast becoming discouraged at the treatment of his thankless posterity, and who thus, year by year, is yielding up his hold among us. Country people everywhere among the hills, let me introduce to you the "old grassy road," the "mountain turnpike," the old "wood road," the "lane"—thus to bespeak the aid of the local vocabulary in fixing the identity I would bring to your mind—for there is an "old Marlborough road" in every town; if not, then more's the pity.

These ancient highways spread like a net over our New England hills, a net whose meshes are fast being lost among the growth which has sprung up around them. These old roads are all akin—essentially the same everywhere. Possessing in spirit a common origin, the history of one is repeated in all. It is the track of the pioneer who opened up the privileges we now enjoy; it is the scar of a hard-fought battle; the mark of courage, fortitude, and heroic self-sacrifice, the road our forefathers trod, and now in many instances the last eloquent visible link between the unworthy present and noble ancestral memories which should be kept green. I would turn the eyes of the errant into this forgotten path, and if possible keep it worn by reverent footsteps, and guarded against the impending invasion—that "improving" hand of "progress."

For it is manifest on every hand that the acquisition of prosperity among our country towns is fast crowding out our rural lanes and ancient roads, tearing up their venerable landmarks, obliterating their footprints, smoothing away their mounds, and ploughing up their ashes. This seems little less than sacrilege—the deplorable fruit of that rage for "rural improvement" which is now a terror in the air, following in the train of wealth and prosperity and a certain era in the history of every growing town. Not but that in its proper place, where it pertains and ministers to individual home comforts, it may be highly proper and desirable; but when it sweeps the country, not unlike a scourge of locusts, and at length drives the would-be "country" pilgrim or native inhabitant to the limits of the township to find a bit of nature "unadorned," is it not time to cry halt?

Even the great metropolis hath suburbs —a verdant rim which may be reached by horse-cars.

In truth I wonder at the apathy with which these ancient weed-grown footprints are viewed by the average village mind. Even though blind to natural beauty, is there no other awakening touch to which such might respond amid surroundings where every visible feature is eloquent with that spirit which makes the whole world kin?

In this old road dwells a presence not known to the highway, nor to the wilder or more recent paths of nature. A quickening pathos lurks in the air, and the saunterer wends his way in a kind of quiet rapture of contemplation not known to other haunts; a mood which is the sympathetic, inseparable concomitant of this, and the gift of no other foot-path, by which I almost fancy one might know its touch though blind.

Look where you may, then, how touching are the testimonies beneath the mere beauty of Nature's adornment, and none of her haunts seem more tenderly cared for than this. There are no such blooming borders, I often think, no such exquisite festoons of draping vines, no such bird-voices as you will find here, where Nature seems to garland the memory of her long-departed, and ever whisper their pathetic elegy.

These wandering walls, "frost flung and broken," these overhanging ancient orchards, lichened and craggly, with their wealth of blossom, but thankless fruit, do they not speak to us? These weedy clumps, picturing the site of some rural treasure-house long reduced to mould; the silent vacant village pound—now but a harbor for pensive thoughts—brimming over with its crop of weeds, all mementos of its old-time lowing fugitives; and here the touching relic which more than all the rest invites our lingering—a void in which our eye may dwell, and turn away bedimmed—the ruined cellar with the silent chimney and the cold empty hearth. Its crumbling walls are filled with trees and banked with weeds, its borders browed with lilacs still fragrant with memories of kind hands "that laid their infant roots in earth." What a reflective silence the hollow of this sleeping well! How pathetic are these faces of the old-time flowers that meet you here on every hand!

I have listened long and often at the brink of these old cellars. I recall the message of the whippoorwill, echoing from the shadows, itself unseen, the soulful hymn of the hermit in the neighboring pines. I recall, too, the flight of hovering spirits against the twilight sky. Some said they were only chimney swallows, but no eye could ever find their nest.

It has been my fortune recently to have become possessed of an ideal grassy road, or rather, I should say, more properly, of a companionable charge which it carries tenderly and inseparably in its bosom.

"I saw the new moon late yestreen,
    Wi' th' auld moon in her arm."

This is my farm. It is 'way up there, the old road circling along its edge and winding away somewhere into the clouds. I have never yet found its end, and never shall. Ere this I had known a certain

INVITATION TO THE GRASSY ROAD.

restlessness, but now I am content "to breathe my native air in my own ground." I shall live out my appointed days ere I exhaust this single path; what need then of guide-books to Europe—to see the world, the Continent, the Orient? I could sit within this realm and fill my portfolio with them all. Here is my cross and crescent. What is the roar of Niagara compared to this still small voice—the Alpen peaks, the Matterhorn? Indeed, my grassy road has carried me much higher than these.

The features of these old roads, as I have said, are alike in all. How naturally are the feet of the saunterer drawn thither! and even when he would take his leave to seek some distant hunting ground, or familiar wood or brook, how irresistibly is he induced to procrastinate!

This free, unrestrained meandering course of the grassy road possesses a continuous irresistible charm—the ever-recurring vista with the invariable tantalizing curve beyond. How does that elusive beckoning curve coquet with your fancy! What possibilities does it not suggest? What will be the prospect?—hill or valley, shimmering pond, rippling river, or billowing field, dusky wood, or hazy tremulous distance of blue hills? There is all the mystery of a to-morrow haunt-

catch her in yonder closed covert among the junipers; there is no escape; but lo! she has sped a hundred feet beyond, where in the guise of jutting fence beam be-

A QUIET VISTA.

ing that elusive curve. Yes, a witching presence hovers there; it is the spirit of the path luring you on and on with ever-enticing promises, never disappointing you, never satisfying you. Now we shall

neath the beckoning aspens she points you still onward; and what is that! a well-known voice, now strangely modulated to my fancy, cries plainly now, if never before, "Come, more yet." Yes, "more yet,"

RETURNING SPIRITS.

this is the very watchword of the grassy road. There is a segment of eternity in that beautiful curve beyond.

There are all sorts of lessons as we turn the leaves, loitering by the way. Sitting here under my favorite tree, as is my wont, like Hamlet at the feet of his mistress, eager and expectant, though be it admitted with spirit not precisely akin to his, I await my entertainment. The play begins immediately. A bell note from the woods rings the curtain up; a tanager flits by as though to fire the foot-lights; and ere we are fairly seated a mysterious presence steals upon the stage and rivets our attention—a more ominous prologue than I could wish. Note the sombre garb, the stealthy approach. I recognize him, and his is an unwelcome shadow among these bushes. But the intruder has observed us, and is off again as fast as his black wings can take him. This is the

MEADOW-RUE.

bird whose flocks we observed scampering around the nose of the cow pasturing in the field near by. It is said that they seek the insects aroused into activity by her cropping, but I half suspect it is as much the sweetness of that scented breath that attracts them.

Look across this open vista with its sunny

mist of bloomy grasses, and their gleaming daisies, and all walled beyond with the luxuriant bank of foliage—of hazels, with their prickly filberts; of crimson-fruited sumachs, their foreshortened

A SUSPICIOUS RETREAT.

branches silvery-edged with their "staghorn" velvet; of drooping boughs of wild apple-trees and turquoise-beaded ju-nipers, and all draped with clambering vines of ground-nut, woodbine, and shrubby bitter-sweet. We need go no further than this one verdant gallery to fill one short day with enjoyment. How beautiful that tall bouquet of the graceful meadow-rue, with its fluent tapering stem, its airy crest of creamy tufted tassels and sensitive foliage answering to the faintest zephyr—the fairest of our weeds. And there by its side, what a revel of the bracted bind-

A BREEZY UPLAND.

weed! (*Convolvulus sepium*)—claiming the sole right of way, involving all, almost obscuring the identity of the generous milk-weed which first gave it a start in the world, reaching out on right and left, snatching this leaf, that neighboring stem, finally winding off in spiry eager tips from every accomplished goal, and endeavoring to propitiate all with its plenteous show of pink-white blossoms. What is that rustle among the leaves? "*Fidgety, fidgety, fidgety, fidgety*," a sharp voice now rings out from the bushes near by, and a tiny feathered form skims over the grass and alights among our bind-weed, pausing just long enough to say, "I have a yellow breast and a black cheek, and am in a great hurry," and is lost amid the tangle, from whence again he sends up his restless call. His voice has fairly ceased when a pursuing shadow flits over the leaves, and there reappears close at hand the same wily presence which we observed a short time since—a bird of ill omen, her black plumage glistening in the sun as she prowls around among the thicket, within which she too now disappears, and where I also would pursue her were it not for the barrier of brambles. How closely does she follow in the wake of that piloting voice, and how certain as doom will she trace it to the source of its inspiration! Who ever heard of a cow-blackbird that did not manage somehow to find its feathered nest? For this is none other than that scourge and parasite of our smaller birds, the American counterpart of the European cuckoo, and fully its equal, it would seem, in the successful pursuit of its hideous calling.

In some of my youthful nest hunts I remember that it would seem as though hardly a single nest in certain localities had escaped the curse of this bird's visit, evinced either by the presence of the brown spotted egg, or the fat, overgrown fledgling, the "Black Douglas" of the bird home, crushing the emaciated little starvelings, the rightful brood, against the side of the nest, or crowding them over its edge. I have several times come to the rescue of such a household. My long string of cow-birds' eggs was the proudest trophy among my ornithological specimens.

The sparrows and the warblers are especially the sufferers. This little warbler which has just taken refuge among the bind-weeds, and which is now about to be added to the list of victims, is a favorite with the cow-bird. It is the Maryland yellow-throat; he is marked, and seems to afford in that black cheek a target on which the eager eye of his pursuer is focussed as she threads the underwood.

It is pleasant to sit and watch the play of sunshine and shadow among this bright mosaic: the image of leaf on leaf, the luminous hollow of the translucent blossom-tube where the buzzing fly creeps and seems loath to leave as it sips the nectar far within.

What is that tiny hovering gem, almost like a shooting spark, that flashes circling in the sun above the vines? See, there's another; it falls upon the foliage, leaving a glittering streak in its track, and immediately glides beneath the leaf. Come closer. We have struck a gold mine among this bind-weed. Ah, how your eyes brighten! More of nature's "harm-

dents who have known of this suggestive presence among the bind-weed. Yes, this sort of genuine winged gold is 'way below par. It is not quoted on the market, and hence the world knows it not. A nugget in the clod, and how quickly had they discovered it!

Catch the sprightly atom quick, for he is as elusive as fortune; hold him by his tiny feet, and tell me truly was ever such a burnish seen on gold of man's. You may see your face in it. How small we look! but the heavens are there too, if we focus our eye right for them. Yes, even now a strange azure film seems to cloud the gold, and in a moment more it gleams

AFTERNOON SHADOWS.

less gold," for gold more brilliant and dazzling never shone from trinket or dollar. Yes, it is more than gold—gold, pearl, and coral in wondrous alchemy. Look here beneath this leaf, that burnished drop. This is the cassida—the golden-tortoise beetle—the one most richly endowed atom, I venture to say, which the insect world can show. How the eager eyes of the visionary alchemist of old would have responded to this dance of the glittering midge! And yet I have never seen three people outside of special stu-

with the iridescence of marvellous nacre, now in deeper glow suggests an opal, anon has become a bead of pure red coral, and so remains until the air of freedom is once more permitted beneath the pellicle.

There is an obvious reason to me why this little insect should have chosen the bind-weed out of all creation as his haunt; but perhaps this was a private confidence. In any event his is a history well worth studying, for whether in his winged or more primitive estate his life among these leaves is full of interest, I assure you.

MOUNTAIN-LAUREL.

What endless pictures come to us from among those well-remembered curves! Of sidelong-shadowed aisles overhung with drooping branches, canopied with luminous fox-grape, hemmed in on either side with sumachs and blooming elders; of hazel thickets and green alders screened beneath clambering clematis and false-buckwheat, twined and intermeshed across the pathway in playful taunt, with "no thoroughfare" laughing in every strand and tendril; of morning gossamers and evening skies; of pink-domed piles of cloud rising to the zenith beyond the "sundown tinted hill," with shadowed glen and purling brook beneath. There are massive banks of chestnut foliage fraying out in yellow tassels, and wild-apples in crimson drift rows circling the sloping stone-piles. There is a silent ruined mill I well remember, and a long stretch across a breezy upland where the road has taken its wild freedom among the terraced pastures, thick with mulleins and fragrant with memories of scented blue-curls (*Trichostema*) and noisy rattle-boxes (*Crotalaria*), and dotted with scrubby tufts of thorny dwarf wild apple—those welcome pavilions to the nesting birds.

Yonder, at the sky-line of the hill, a dense bank of trees invites my footsteps, and I discover that the truant road and myself are now of one mind again, as it approaches my side, and speeds ahead until lost beneath the shadowy recess of the woods.

Here we enter the sanctum of the laurels—a labyrinth of tortuous branches, with glistening leaves and literal banks of pink bouquets of bloom alternating as far as the eye can penetrate—a charmed spot where we are tempted as always to linger.

Here in the twilight you may hear the hum of the sphinx-moth hovering humming-bird-like above these honeyed cups, and note the answering salute of the blossoms with their tiny puffs of smoke. Here the small nocturnal feathered moths are showered with a dust softer than their own, as they creep with eager, trembling wings among the tempting chalices, dislodging the expectant anthers from their twelve snug pockets, and filling the adjacent air with mimic pyrotechnics of sulphurous pollen dust. Look at these knobby, distorted roots, the stubborn harvest of the craftsman of rustic goods, the maker of flower baskets, stands, and "ornamental" gnarled seats; how fantastic are some of these globular shapes as they crop out here and there, even among the rocks at the edge of this precipice upon whose rim we have suddenly approached! Note this fresh-oxidized fissure in the rock. We have all seen the marvel of the soft toadstool, like a tiny red-faced Atlas, sustaining and still lifting its huge stone above its head. Here in this fracture in the rock we may note an analogous instance of persuasive power in the misshapen root which has served as Time's servant—a factor in the disintegration of this rocky precipice. See how it has wedged and insinuated itself within the crevice, opening the way for the frost, and at last, in one supreme effort, has wrenched asunder the huge piece of granite, which has thundered down the ledge and ploughed its way through the trees below.

This precipice is a sort of jumping-off place of our grassy road, it would seem, terminating at the brow of a sheer cliff four hundred feet in height, with the babbling river, flecked with floating foam and cleaved with wedge-shaped ripples, far down beneath us.

There below an eagle screams and spreads his sails upon his vantage-tree, and launches out, soaring above the giddy height until out of sight among the distant hills. The bell note of the blue-jay comes up from some mysterious haunt, and now the celestial voice of the hermit-thrush. And what is this? There is a flutter of wings back among the laurels, and instantly a small bird darts past us, and, seemingly intent on suicide, plunges headlong over the precipice. Down, down, down it falls—but look! What a thrilling spectacle! In its own good time it finds both wings and voice, descending, as it were, upon invisible spiral stairs of air, and sending up its rapturous voice tuned to the beating of its wings. And now it drops into the outstretched arms of the hemlocks far below, and its mouth is stopped—I can almost fancy how—while if we listen carefully we may catch a faint plashing of a bubbling mountain brook, for this winged voice is one of its choice spirits.

What a lesson of trusting faith and exalted devotion! Hark! How truly has the poet caught the tenor of that ringing message which now comes up from the shadowy hemlocks below, "Teacher, *teacher*, TEACHER, TEACHER, *TEACHER!*"

Thus, on one memorable evening long ago, did I sit in the deep twilight musing on this cliff, and was twice permitted to witness this inspiring episode, which, with its irresistible spiritual correspondencies, has left a cherished impress which years nor cares nor misfortunes can ever estrange. I am thy humble pupil, bird of trust and hope and praise; may I prove worthy of thy confidence!

The song of the oven-bird, or golden-crowned thrush, for such was the mundane title of my bird, is, as Burroughs further says, "one of the rarest bits of bird-melody to be heard." And although on this occasion the bird was but a nameless spirit to me, I have since learned to know him well, and I think I have on one or two occasions identified that same rhapsody from a hovering speck aloft in the realm of the skylark.

But the old road does not stop here. It is only a resting-place by the way, where it stops to take a look and covet a little, perhaps, or get a whiff of valley air. From among these laurels it takes an abrupt turn and leads out into the mountain wilds, where for a time it seems to be getting forgetful in its old age, losing its identity among the numerous distracting old wood roads by which it is continually waylaid. But it manages to get its wits together again upon the receding brow of the mountain beyond, where it winds off and is lost to sight among the sloping woods and pastures, and would indeed lead us into nightfall were we to follow.

Before returning homeward it is worth our while to penetrate the jungle of laurels for another outlook a little further down the ledge. It is a close squeeze while it lasts, but here we shall discover a rare nook, whose presence, though only a few rods from our former position, would never be imagined, so artfully has nature concealed it by the conformation of the cliff—a depression or niche in its face reached by a short descent over the crags, but where once secure we might defy the dogs of war, or even our creditors. The craziest anchorite could scarce wish a more inviting isolation. A smooth floor of rock leading to a cave-like fissure at the back, walled in on either side with towering granite crags—a prospect sweeping the country to its horizon, and a dizzy brink which leans out as though about to fall into the abyss. It would appear a simple matter to toss a pebble into the rushing torrent below.

Close at the verge you may observe a suggestive nest-like hollow, in which your fancy may play forever—a smooth basin worn in the solid granite, with a pair of smaller hollows by its side. How quickly the figure of the old squaw is spirited thither, and assumes her wonted place kneeling at the old samp mortar! How the mountain wilds again echo with the red man's whoop and yell! For we stand upon the empty throne of the Indian..

In the freshly planted field stretching out like a map upon the plain below us you may follow the brown furrows and pick up your handfuls of arrow-heads and tomahawks—the smallest fragments of stone seem to possess mysterious nicks and shapes—arrow-heads of granite, felspar, and hornblende, lances of quartz and flint, some of minerals not else known in these

parts, or within hundreds of miles, *all* trackless forests when these found their bed, sped thither by no eager wings of arrow—rather the token of friendly barter and pipes of peace. What a sermon in this stone! What a heart-stirring poem we hold in our hand in one of these mute sculptured flints! They are interesting trophies to the geologist and antiquarian, but how much more profoundly so to the *man* as the emblems of a strange extinct race—a race of brethren formed like him in the image of their Maker!

Strolling through a wild upland wood in New Hampshire, I once met a mountaineer who urged me to accompany him up the mountain road to a certain cliff, where he would show me the "old samp mortar," with its round stone pestle still resting within it, and which with the hollow in which it stands was kept smooth and free from lichens by the ghosts of the defunct tribes, who still kept vigil there. Every year, he said, a small clump of "genuine wild tobacco" flourished near this spot, but was always cut down the first night after it flowered. He had often found a stone hatchet near the place at such a time—all of which only goes to show, my credulous woodsman, that some keen old hermit of a simpler dwells thereabouts somewhere, and she is evidently fond of her pipe.

This "genuine wild tobacco" is but one of the blossoming host which serve to link our present walk with that of the past. This is a rare road for the botanist. In addition to the numerous familiar as well as strange faces which he is certain to find here, there is a delightful page of sentimental botany to which this old road affords the only access. It has a flora peculiarly its own—the loyal gardens of colonial days, with their old-fashioned flowers, which still perpetuate their Puritan memories.

How many of our common "naturalized" plants can trace their lineage to this old road! The "Bouncing-Bet," the eglantine, the barberry, live-for-ever, Jerusalem artichoke, toad-flax, May-weed, tansy, feverfew, feather-geranium, so familiar to our pastures and highway borders.

This mossy tufted bed of cypress-spurge which we are now passing, how certainly does it prophesy the proximity of one of those crumbling cellars which are the ever-recurring, and withal the most touching, attribute of these by-gone foot-paths! Yes, here it is. Well may you ask, "Where?" Yonder dense screen of lilacs, apple-trees, and wild grape, which obscure its ruined chimney, and are still true to their trust, and cover its retreat. From this one source have sprung a beneficence of interceding blossoms all along the path— the spotted orange-lilies which we just observed peeping above the lichened wall, that tall clump of pink-blossomed phlox, this tangle of blue-blossomed gill. And look! a rare find this—the yellow "whin" of the British downs. What pictures of the

"Green strath and flowery brae,"

through eyes bedimmed, has this bright flower awakened! The dear old roses too, they must not be forgotten. See how they smile among the ruins—red roses, white roses, pink roses, or even yellow roses— *genuine* roses all, true to their foster-memories, their artificial draperies of the floriculturist renounced, now mostly single flowers and fruitful. There is a long list of interesting flowers to be met among these old homestead sites. Of the others which I have found in various localities I might mention the celandine (*Chelidonium*), bladder-campion (*Silene inflata*), motherwort (*Lysimachia*), larkspur, stonecrop (*Sedum acre*), meadowsweet (European), double buttercup (now almost single again), and lastly, the scouring rush (*Equisetum*), with its significant reminders of toil in the shape of the ancient scrubbing-brush, for which these hollow, gritty tubes were in demand by the colonial housewives and maidens.

And then there are our own endless childish memories of this path—how they rise and float across my page as I intercede for the grassy road!—of years when all the weeks seemed playing holidays; of strolls and picnics, hunts and bouts and games; of fragrance of sweet orchards and wild-grape blossoms, of aromatic fern and evening-primrose, of wild ripe strawberries and clover, wafted thither. Here the shrubby bitter-sweet climbed highest; here the brightest sky-blue eggs were found, and here flew the loveliest butterflies; here the shagbarks showered down their twinkling nuts among the brown October leaves, and the prickly chestnut burrs were ready to open, while patient hazels, like their companion harvests of every season, awaited our coming, and dropped their brown clusters into our eager hands. Ah, yes, how well now, as then, we know

"Where the whitest lilies blow,
Where the freshest berries grow,"

where to turn for the happiest harvest of our thought! Is there any music to be compared to the sounds which echo down the years from this old grassy road?—the bright young voices, the

"Pasture bars that clattered as they fell,"

the lowing cows, the tinkling bell among the sundown shadows, the answering twilight voice and clinking pail, the bird-like whistle of a lightsome heart, and merry, merry laugh—ah, why should such a merry laugh as that moisten the eye and bow the head?

Hundreds of pretty vignettes conspire to disturb our reverie as we pursue our way: A vesper song from a mullein-top; a chipmunk rustling the dried leaves, planting a bunch of hickories for posterity; a reiterated bit of weather-wisdom from the rain-crow somewhere near, or a soft plaint from a mourning dove amid the chestnut-trees; a black-veined butterfly listless and lulled at the generous milkweed's breast; a flashing water-fall; a sweet, low warble from the junipers.

But what violent discord is this—this rude commotion in the bushes—a bull, a bear, a tiger? No; worse than these—a Hottentot.

"Rascal! what are you doing here?"

"I'm here be ordthers, sor."

"No such thing. I know your guild too well. Your place is on the road with the 'selectmen.' Keep to the highways, where you belong. Gouge the banks, hack and girdle the trees, mutilate the road-sides with all conceivable diabolical ingenuity, if you will, but spare this quiet, unused path. No one wants you to touch a *leaf* upon it."

"Faith 'n' wasn't it Misther Goth himself, o' the Village Improvement Society, wuz afther showin' me me day's wurrk beyant, 'n' tellin' me t' *clane it up?* Is it the dirthy wades 'n' bushes ye want, I don' know? Quit, is it? No, 'n' I won't quit. I'm wurrkin be the ordthers uv the town, 'n', faith, I'll shtay !"

And now a new impetus seems to possess his brush-hook. A beautiful Virginia creeper, which for a decade has draped the neighboring apple-tree to its summit in its alternating verdant and scarlet festoons, is severed at its root in a single stroke, and now the canopy of blossoming clematis is torn from its long airy rest above the overhanging bushes by the wall, as he pries his way among them with eager blade. I cannot stand and see this butchery. I— 'Sh! never mind. Let us leave him. He will be punished. Blessed is the Vandal who is innocent of botany! to whom the poison-sumac gives no timely warning! I would not raise my hand to restrain him; for, after all, is he not engaged in honest toil? and will he not get his reward? Meanwhile let us haste to intercede with Mr. Goth, for our grassy road is indeed in peril.

Yes, the grassy road is a prize indeed. But, alas! even a grassy road, like all dear possessions, brings its proportionate anxieties. How earnestly shall I pray for that subtle grace skilfully to propitiate the kindly, generous, philanthropic village-improvement-society man who owns the opposite bank!

In a certain nameless town in Massachusetts, where Nature has been cut and scraped to the bone, her very vertebræ of granite laid bare in unsightly barren fields, I knew of a hotel proprietor who had owned a large contiguous tract of forest land, the only piece of wood then left in the immediate vicinity, a beautiful oasis in the desert, which had kept its

memory green for years in the hearts of a host of its summer pilgrims. But it was sold to the Goths and Vandals for a song, because, as our worldling said, he "couldn't afford to throw away six hundred dollars *for mere sentiment*." Thus the last remnant of the temple of the groves was sacrificed—went up in smoke from the pipes of the charcoal fiend.

A blind speculation this. The pocket was heavier that year, but I fancy, and certainly hope, that it has been deservedly lighter since than ever before.

Therefore, whether from considerations of sentiment or worldly motives, I pray you, "Woodman, spare that tree." Cherish the old grassy road, my village! my Judea! Guard it as the apple of thine eye, the jewel of thy coronet. Bar up this "living way" as consecrated ground. Shut out every foot-fall which shall approach it without reverence, and set this warning at its threshold:

No Thoroughfare!
Goths and Vandals beware!
Let no "beautifying" hand enter here!

And so adieu, my grassy road. When next I return to thee, may these cobweb barriers which the evening zephyrs are now floating across thy doorway be still unbroken!

THE AMERICAN COW-BOY.

BY JOSEPH NIMMO, JUN.

DURING the last fifteen years the American cow-boy has occupied a place sufficiently important to entitle him to a considerable share of public attention. His occupation is unique. In the exercise of his function he is always a man on horseback. His duty as a worker in the cattle business is at times to ride over the range in order to see that straying cattle do not rove too far from the assigned limits of the herd of which he has charge; at times to drive the herd from one locality to another; and at times to "round up" the dispersed cattle, by which is meant to collect them together for the purpose of branding calves, or of selecting beef cattle, which latter are driven to railroad stations for shipment to market. The chief qualifications of efficiency in this calling are courage, physical alertness, ability to endure exposure and fatigue, horse-

manship, and skill in the use of the lariat.

The original cow-boy of this country was essentially a creature of circumstance, and mainly a product of western and southwestern Texas. Armed to the teeth, booted and spurred, long-haired, and covered with the broad-brimmed sombrero— the distinctive badge of his calling—his personal appearance proclaimed the sort of man he was.

The Texas cow-boys were frontiersmen, accustomed from their earliest childhood to the alarms and the struggles incident to forays of Indians of the most ferocious and warlike nature. The section of the State in which they lived was also for many years exposed to incursions of bandits from Mexico, who came with predatory intent upon the herds and the homes of the people of Texas. The carrying of fire-arms and other deadly weapons was consequently a prevalent custom among them. And being scattered over vast areas, and beyond the efficient protection and restraints of civil law, they of necessity became a law unto themselves.

It is not a strange thing that such an occupation and such environment should have developed a class of men whom persons accustomed to the usages of cultivated society would characterize as ruffians of the most pronounced type. But among the better disposed of the Texas cow-boys, who constitute, it is believed, much more than a majority of them, there were true and trusty men, in whom the dangers and fortunes of their lives developed generous and heroic traits of character. The same experiences, however, led the viciously inclined to give free vent to the worst passions. Upon slight provocation they would shoot down a fellow-man with almost as little compunction as they fired upon the wild beasts.

But the peculiar characteristics of the Texas cow-boys qualified them for an important public service. By virtue of their courage and recklessness of danger, their excellent horsemanship, and skill in the use of fire-arms, and by virtue also of the influence which they have exerted upon their gentler brethren of the northern ranges, they have been an efficient instrumentality in preventing Indian outbreaks, and in protecting the frontier settlements of the entire range and ranch cattle area against predatory incursions and massacres by Indians. This has been a natural result of the fact that the cowboys constitute throughout that region a corps of mounted scouts, armed and equipped, twenty thousand strong. They traverse vast ranges, ford rivers, and search for cattle amid mountain fastnesses and in lurking-places of the river bottoms. No hostile movement could for a day escape their notice. It is certain that they have done much toward subduing a vast area to the arts of peace, and that an unarmed man may now travel alone throughout Wyoming, Dakota, Montana, and Idaho, and even in Texas, as safely as in the New England or the Middle States. As a pioneer of civilization the American cow-boy has therefore performed a public service which as fully entitles him to recognition as do the commercial results of his labors.

It is only twenty years since the discovery was made that between the line of settlement in Dakota, Nebraska, and Kansas at the east, and the Sierra Nevada and Coast ranges at the west, there was an area as large as the portion of the United States which is situated east of the Mississippi River, throughout which cattle could be raised and fattened on the open range, seeking their own food, water, and shelter without any aid from man, from the time they were dropped until they were in condition to be driven to a railroad station for shipment to market. This discovery, greater in its importance than the discovery of gold in California, or silver in Nevada, or petroleum in Pennsylvania, happened, according to the most reliable accounts, in this wise. Early in December, 1864, a government trader, with a wagon train of supplies drawn by oxen, was on his way west to Camp Douglas, in the Territory of Utah, but being overtaken on the Laramie Plains by an unusually severe snowstorm, he was compelled at once to go into winter-quarters. He turned his cattle adrift, expecting, as a matter of course, they would soon perish from exposure and starvation, but they remained about the camp, and as the snow was blown off the highlands the dried grass afforded them an abundance of forage. When the spring opened they were found to be in even better condition than when turned out to die four months previously. This at once led to the experiment of herding cattle on the northern ranges. But it was for years a slow and hazardous business. At that time it was the custom to allow the Indians upon the reservations to wander off during the summer months throughout the present range and ranch cattle area, in order that they might hunt buffaloes and other large game, and thus sustain themselves in their accustomed way until the approach of winter, when they returned to their reservations to be again provided for by the government. Permission to depart on these expeditions was always given upon the promise made to the military and civil officers of the United States that while absent they would be "good Indians." But as cattle were more easily caught than buffaloes, they found it greatly to their advantage to swoop down upon the herds, stampede them, and slaughter at their leisure as many as their needs required. Oftentimes, by way of amusement, they lifted the scalp of a stray cowboy. In many instances they massacred whole camps of settlers, whose chief occupation was cattle herding. Occasionally these "wards of the nation" so far forgot themselves as to put on war-paint and set the United States at defiance. The massacre of General Custer and his detachment, on the 25th of June, 1876, at Little Big Horn, Dakota, near the present location of Fort Custer, led, however, to the adoption of a more stringent policy on the part of the United States government with respect to requiring the Indians to remain upon their reservations. During the five years following that tragic event our valiant little army, widely scattered over a vast area, had many bloody encounters with the savages. At last the spirit of resistance was broken, and Montana, Idaho, and Dakota became comparatively safe for the introduction of the range cattle business, which had already become known in Colorado and Wyoming as a highly attractive enterprise and a speedy avenue to wealth. As the work of the army drew nigh to completion the cow-boy galloped in, and became the mounted policeman of a vast area, always on patrol.

But even after the red man had retired to his reservation the lot of the cattlemen was not entirely serene. From time immemorial the horse-thief and the cattle-thief seem to have been a sort of parasitic growth upon frontier life, apparently begotten of its conditions. So it was on the range. For several years the entire region from Kansas and Colorado at the south to Montana and Dakota at the north was infested by cattle-thieves. The country afforded apparently illimitable scope for this nefarious traffic. It seemed at one time somewhat a matter of doubt as to which should prosper most, the herdsmen or the cattle-thieves. As the cattle of many proprietors intermingled freely on vast ranges, it was comparatively easy and safe for a few marauders to pounce down upon detached groups of cattle here and there separated from the main body of the herds, and drive them off over some mountain range to a distant valley or range where grazing was abundant, and there brand the calves with a chosen hieroglyphic representative of a separate ownership, and change the marks of cattle already branded, by one or more

dashes with a red-hot iron. It was clearly seen that in order to stamp out this new and threatening evil recourse must be had to a drastic remedy. Accordingly the various cattle associations organized a detective service, composed mainly of brave and trusty cow-boys, who were charged with the duty of reconnoitring the whole country in order to discover the miscreants in their lairs, also to watch for altered and surreptitious brands at the railroad shipping stations. In this way a large number of stolen cattle was recovered, and many cattle-thieves were apprehended. When the latter were arrested within the limits of the efficient administration of the law, they were handed over to the civil authorities. But when caught beyond the limits of organized counties, administrative justice was extemporized. The cattle-men and the cow-boys themselves supplied judges, jurymen, witnesses, attorneys, constables, and executioners. Sometimes a level-headed cow-boy was placed upon the judicial bench. The cattle-men assert that the extreme and only penalty was never inflicted except upon the clearest evidence of guilt.

When the verdict of guilty was pronounced, a short shrift, and a stout rope, and a grave without a coffin or a winding-sheet, ended the proceedings.

But a great change has taken place. On the northern ranges cattle stealing has become almost entirely a thing of the past. States and Territories have enacted laws requiring that all cattle shall be branded, and that the brands shall be recorded in the office of the clerk of the county in which the owner of each herd resides. The brands are also published. Thus the light of publicity is thrown upon the whole range cattle business, and at the same time it has acquired all those securities which characterize organized and well-ordered commercial enterprises.

At first the raising of cattle on the northern ranges was confined mainly to settlers possessed of small means. But soon men of enterprise and capital saw that the placing of great herds on the ranges of the north, as had been done for years in Texas and in Mexico, would, under adequate protection, be attended with great profit, for already railroads traversing or extending out into the Territories afforded the facilities for transporting cattle to the three great primary cattle markets of the United States, viz., Chicago,

St. Louis, and Kansas City—Chicago being by far the largest—and thence to the markets of the world.

It was an enterprise which required both capital and courage. The State of Texas had for years been a prolific breeding ground for cattle. At that time cattle were worth on the ranges of that State but little more than their hides and tallow. Two-year-old steers could be purchased in almost unlimited numbers for from $3 50 to $4 50 a head. Besides, Texas had an army of cow-boys, who were acquainted with the Indian in all his ways, and who rather courted than refused a passage at arms with the savage. Here were therefore three material elements of success in a great undertaking—capital, cattle, and cow-boys. Intelligent enterprise came in and formed the combination, and not long afterward it became a matter of personal interest with the Indian to remain on his reservation all the year round. Speedily the Texas steer superseded the buffalo, and the cowboy became the dominant power throughout New Mexico, Colorado, Wyoming, Montana, and the western portions of Dakota, Nebraska, and Kansas. Within the brief period of fifteen years the cordon of cattle interests was drawn so close around the Indian reservations that the monarch of the plains became "ye gentle savage."

As a general rule the ranch cattle business has, under good management, been wonderfully successful. Hundreds of men who a few years ago went into the business with exceedingly limited means have become "cattle kings," and now count their assets by hundreds of thousands and even by millions. In certain instances also women have embarked in the enterprise, and among the number are those who now rejoice in the sobriquet of "cattle queens."

The market value of the surplus product of the entire range and ranch cattle area during the year 1884 was about $40,000,000, aside from the consumption within that area. Besides, the increased value of herds during the year is estimated at quite as much more. Throughout that area the cattle business is the chief commercial enterprise; but as trade makes trade, it has been instrumental in creating important collateral and related trade interests. One of the most important results of this has been that the several transcontinental railroads have built up a large and profitable local traffic. The original conception of transcontinental traffic was that it would be confined almost entirely to "through business," but the local tonnage of the Northern Pacific Railroad during the year 1884 constituted ninety-five per cent. of its total tonnage, and the local tonnage of the Union Pacific Railroad constituted forty-three per cent. of its total tonnage.

The cow-boy of to-day, especially on the northern ranges, is of entirely different type from the original cow-boy of Texas. New conditions have produced the change. The range cattle business of Kansas, Nebraska, Colorado, Wyoming, Montana, and Dakota is, as already stated, a new business. Those engaged in it as proprietors are chiefly from the States situated east of the Missouri River and north of the Indian Territory. Among them are also many Englishmen, Scotchmen, Frenchmen, and Germans of large means, embracing titled men who have embarked in the business quite extensively. Many of these came to America originally as tourists or for the purpose of hunting buffaloes, but the attractiveness of the cattle business arrested them, and they have become virtually, if not through the act of naturalization, American herdsmen. Some of this class have, from the force of romantic temperament and the exhilaration of range life, themselves participated actively in the duties of the cowboy.

Organization, discipline, and order characterize the new undertakings on the northern ranges. In a word, the cattle business of that section is now and has from the beginning been carried on upon strictly business principles. Under such proprietorships, and guided by such methods, a new class of cow-boys has been introduced and developed. Some have come from Texas, and have brought with them a knowledge of the arts of their calling, but the number from the other States and the Territories constitutes a large majority of the whole. Some are graduates of American colleges, and others of collegiate institutions in Europe. Many have resorted to the occupation of cowboy temporarily and for the purpose of learning the range cattle business, with the view of eventually engaging in it on their own account, or in the interest of friends desirous of investing money in the enterprise.

The life of the cow-boy is always one of excitement and of romantic interest. His waking hours when "riding on trail" are spent in the saddle, and at night he makes his bed upon the lap of mother earth.

The great herds which are yearly driven out of Texas to the northern ranges usually embrace from 2500 to 4000 young cattle each, and the movement has since its beginning, about eighteen years ago, amounted to about 4,000,000 head, worth nearly $50,000,000. Each herd is placed in charge of a boss, with from eight to ten cow-boys, a provision wagon, and a cook. Four horses are supplied to each cow-boy, for the duty is an arduous one. The range cattle when away from their accustomed haunts are suspicious and excitable, and need to be managed with the greatest care to keep them from stampeding. When "on trail" they are "close herded" at nightfall, and all lie down within a space of about two acres. The cow-boys then by watches ride around them all night long. The sensible presence of man appears to give the animals a feeling of security.

The journey from southern Texas to Montana requires from four to six months. Herds are also driven from Oregon and Washington Territory to Wyoming and eastern Montana. It is impossible for one who has not had actual experience in "riding on trail" to imagine the difficulties involved in driving a large herd of wild cattle over mountain ranges, across desert lands where in some cases food and water are not found for many miles, and where streams must be crossed which are liable to dangerous freshets.

A large part of the northern ranges is embraced in the area which Silas Bent, an accomplished meteorologist, terms "the birthplace of the tornado." Thunder and lightning are here frequent, and they are especially terrifying to range cattle. The most thrilling incident in the life of the cow-boy occurs on the occasion of a thunder-storm at night. Such an occurrence is thus described from personal observation by Mr. William A. Baillie Grohman, an English writer:

"On the approach of one of these violent outbursts the whole force is ordered on duty; the spare horses—of which each man has always three, and often as many as eight or ten—are carefully fed and tethered, and the herd is 'rounded up,' that is, collected into as small a space as possible, while the men continue to ride around the densely massed herd. Like horses, cattle derive courage from the close proximity of man. The thunder peals, and the vivid lightning flashes with amazing brilliancy, as with lowered heads the herd eagerly watch the slow, steady pace of the cow-ponies, and no doubt derive from it a comforting sense of protection. Sometimes, however, a wild steer will be unable to control his terror, and will make a dash through a convenient opening. The crisis is at hand, for the example will surely be followed, and in two minutes the whole herd of 4000 head will have broken through the line of horsemen and be away, one surging, bellowing mass of terrified beasts. Fancy a pitch-dark night, a pouring torrent of rain, the ground not only entirely strange to the men, but very broken, and full of dangerously steep water-courses and hollows, and you will have a picture of cow-boy duty on such a night. They must head off the leaders. Once fairly off, they will stampede twenty, thirty, and even forty miles at a stretch, and many branches will stray from the main herd. Not alone the reckless rider, rushing headlong at breakneck pace over dangerous ground in dense darkness, but also the horses, small, insignificant beasts, but matchless for hardy endurance and willingness, are perfectly aware how much depends upon their speed that night, if it kills them. Unused till the last moment remains the heavy cowhide 'yuirt,' or whip, and the powerful spurs with rowels the size of five-shilling pieces. Urged on by a shout, the horses speed alongside the terrified steers until they manage to reach the leaders, when, swinging around, and fearless of horns, they press back the bellowing brutes till they turn them. All the men pursuing this manœuvre, the headlong rush is at last checked, and the leaders, panting and lashing their sides with their tails, are brought to a stand, and the whole herd is again 'rounded up.'"

Throughout the northern ranges sobriety, self-restraint, decent behavior, and faithfulness to duty are enjoined upon the cow-boys. A great improvement is also observable in the cow-boys of Texas. Deeds of violence among them are now few. The *morale* of the entire range and ranch cattle business of the United States now compares favorably with that of other large enterprises.

SPRINGHAVEN.

BY R. D. BLACKMORE.

CHAPTER XXXII.

THE TRIALS OF FAITH.

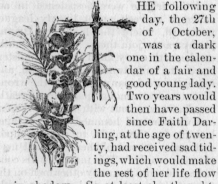

HE following day, the 27th of October, was a dark one in the calendar of a fair and good young lady. Two years would then have passed since Faith Darling, at the age of twenty, had received sad tidings, which would make the rest of her life flow on in shadow. So at least she thought, forgetful (or rather perhaps unconscious, for she had not yet learned the facts of life) that time and the tide of years submerge the loftiest youthful sorrow. To a warm and stedfast heart like hers, and a nature strong but self-controlled, no casual change, or light diversion, or sudden interest in other matters, could take the place of the motive lost. Therefore, being of a deep true faith, and staunch in the belief of a great God, good to all who seek His goodness, she never went away from what she meant, that faith and hope should feed each other.

This saved her from being a trouble to any one, or damping anybody's cheerfulness, or diminishing the gaiety around her. She took a lively interest in the affairs of other people, which a "blighted being" declines to do; and their pleasures ministered to her own good cheer without, or at any rate beyond, her knowledge. Therefore she was liked by everybody, and beloved by all who had any heart for a brave and pitiful story. Thus a sweet flower, half closed by the storm, continues to breathe forth its sweetness.

However, there were times when even Faith was lost in sad remembrance, and her bright young spirit became depressed by the hope deferred that maketh sick the heart. As time grew longer, hope grew less; and even the cheerful Admiral, well versed in perils of the deep, and acquainted with many a wandering story, had made up his mind that Erle Twemlow was dead, and would never more be heard of. The rector also, the young man's father, could hold out no longer against that conclusion; and even the mother, disdaining the mention, yet understood the meaning, of despair. And so among those to whom the subject was the most interesting in the world, it was now the strict rule to avoid it with the lips, though the eyes were often filled with it.

Faith Darling at first scorned this hard law. "It does seem so unkind," she used to say, "that even his name should be interdicted, as if he had disgraced himself. If he is dead, he has died with honour. None who ever saw him can doubt that. But he is not dead. He will come back to us, perhaps next week, perhaps to-morrow, perhaps even while we are afraid to speak of him. If it is for my sake that you behave thus, I am not quite so weak as to require it."

The peculiar circumstances of the case had not only baffled enquiry, but from the very beginning precluded it. The man with the keenest eyes, sharpest nose, biggest ears, and longest head, of all the many sneaks who now conduct what they call "special enquiries," could have done nothing with a case like this, because there was no beginning it. Even now, in fair peace, and with large knowledge added, the matter would not have been easy; but in war universal, and blank ignorance, there was nothing to be done but to sit down and think. And the story invited a good deal of thinking, because of its disappointing turn.

During the negotiations for peace in 1801, and before any articles were signed, orders were sent to the Cape of Good Hope for the return of a regiment of the line, which had not been more than three months there. But the Cape was likely to be restored to Holland, and two empty transports returning from India were to call under convoy, and bring home these troops. One of the officers was Captain Erle Twemlow, then about twenty-five years of age, and under probation, by the Admiral's decree, for the hand of the maiden whose heart had been his from a time to itself immemorial. After tiresome days of impatience, the transports arrived under conduct of a frigate; and after another week, the soldiers embarked with fine readiness for their native land.

But before they had cleared the Bay, they met a brig-of-war direct from Portsmouth, carrying despatches for the officer in command of the troops, as well as for the captain of the frigate. Some barbarous tribes on the coast of Guinea, the part that is called the Ivory Coast, had plundered and burnt a British trading station within a few miles of Cape Palmas, and had killed and devoured the traders. These natives must be punished, and a stern example made, and a negro monarch of the name of Hunko Jum must have his palace burned, if he possessed one; while his rival, the king of the Crumbo tribe, whose name was Bandeliah, who had striven to protect the traders, must be rewarded, and have a treaty made with him, if he could be brought to understand it. Both sailors and soldiers were ready enough to undertake this little spree, as they called it, expecting to have a pleasant run ashore, a fine bit of sport with the negroes, and perhaps a few noserings of gold to take home to their wives and sweethearts.

But, alas! the reality was not so fine. The negroes who had done all the mischief made off, carrying most of their houses with them; and the palace of Hunko Jum, if he possessed one, was always a little way further on. The Colonel was a stubborn man, and so was the sea-captain—good Tories both, and not desirous to skulk out of scrapes, and leave better men to pick up their clumsy breakages. Blue and red vied with one another to scour the country, and punish the natives —if only they could catch them—and to vindicate, with much strong language, the dignity of Great Britain, and to make an eternal example.

But white bones are what the white man makes, under that slimy sunshine and putrefying moon. Weary, slack-jointed, low-hearted as they were, the deadly coast-fever fell upon them, and they shivered, and burned, and groaned, and raved, and leaped into holes, or rolled into camp fires. The Colonel died early, and the Naval Captain followed him; none stood upon the order of their going; but man followed man, as in a funeral, to the grave, until there was no grave to go to. The hand of the Lord was stretched out against them; and never would one have come back to England, out of

more than five hundred who landed, except for the manhood and vigour of a seaman, Captain Southcombe, of the transport *Gwalior*.

This brave and sensible man had been left with his ship lying off to be signalled for, in case of mishap, while his consort and the frigate were despatched in advance to a creek, about twenty leagues westward, where the land-force triumphant was to join them. Captain Southcombe, with every hand he could muster, traced the unfortunate party inland, and found them led many leagues in the wrong direction, lost among quagmires breathing death, worn out with vermin, venom, and despair, and hemmed in by savages lurking for the night, to rush in upon and make an end of them. What need of many words? This man, and his comrades, did more than any other men on the face of this earth could have done without British blood in them. They buried the many who had died without hope of the decent concealment which our life has had, and therefore our death longs for; they took on their shoulders, or on cane wattles, the many who had made up their minds to die, and were in much doubt about having done it, and they roused up and worked up by the scruff of their loose places the few who could get along on their own legs. And so, with great spirit, and still greater patience, they managed to save quite as many as deserved it.

Because, when they came within signal of the *Gwalior*, Captain Southcombe, marching slowly with his long limp burdens, found ready on the sand the little barrel, about as big as a kilderkin, of true and unsullied Stockholm pitch, which he had taken, as his brother took Madeira, for ripeness and for betterance, by right of change of climate. With a little of this given choicely and carefully at the back of every sick man's tongue, and a little more spread across the hollow of his stomach, he found them so enabled in the afternoon that they were glad to sit up in the bottom of a boat, and resign themselves to an All-wise Providence.

Many survived, and blessed Captain Southcombe, not at first cordially—for the man yet remains to be discovered who is grateful to his doctor—but gradually more and more, and with that healthy action of the human bosom which is called expectoration, whenever grateful memories were rekindled by the smell of tar. But this is a trifle; many useful lives were saved, and the Nation should have thanked Captain Southcombe, but did not.

After these sad incidents, when sorrow for old friends was tempered by the friendly warmth afforded by their shoes, a muster was held by the Major in command, and there was only one officer who could neither assert himself alive, nor be certified as dead. That one was Erle Twemlow, and the regiment would rather have lost any other two officers. Urgent as it was, for the safety of the rest, to fly with every feather from this pestilential coast, sails were handed, boats despatched, and dealings tried with Hunko Jum, who had reappeared with promptitude, the moment he was not wanted. From this noble monarch, and his chiefs, and all his nation, it was hard to get any clear intelligence, because their own was absorbed in absorbing. They had found upon the sands a cask of Admiralty rum, as well as a stout residue of unadulterated pitch. Noses, and tongues, and historical romance—for a cask had been washed ashore five generations since, and set up for a god, when the last drop was licked—induced this brave nation to begin upon the rum; and fashion (as powerful with them as with us) compelled them to drink the tar likewise, because they had seen the white men doing it. This would have made it hard to understand them, even if they had been English scholars, which their ignorance of rum proved them not to be; and our sailors very nearly went their way, after sadly ascertaining nothing, except that the cask was empty.

But luckily, just as they were pushing off, a very large, black head appeared from behind a vegetable-ivory tree, less than a quarter of a mile away, and they knew that this belonged to Bandeliah, the revered king of the Crumbos, who had evidently smelled rum far inland. With him they were enabled to hold discourse, partly by signs, and partly by means of an old and highly polished negro, who had been the rat-catcher at the factory now consumed; and the conclusion, or perhaps the confusion, arrived at from signs, grunts, grins, nods, waggings of fingers and twistings of toes, translated grandiloquently into broken English, was not far from being to the following effect:

To wit, that two great kings reigned inland, either of them able to eat up Hunko Jum and Bandeliah at a mouthful, but both of them too proud to set foot upon land that was flat, or in water that was salt. They ruled over two great nations called the Houlas, and the Quackwas, going out of sight among great rivers and lands with clear water standing over them. And if the white men could not understand this, it was because they drank salt-water.

Moreover, they said that of these two kings, the king of the Houlas was a woman, the most beautiful ever seen in all the world, and able to jump over any man's head. But the king of the Quackwas was a man, and although he had more than two thousand wives, and was taller by a joint of a bamboo than Bandeliah—whose stature was at least six feet four—yet nothing would be of any use to him, unless he could come to an agreement with Mabonga, the queen of the Houlas, to split a durra straw with him. But Mabonga was coy, and understanding men, as well as jumping over them, would grant them no other favour than the acceptance of their presents. However, the other great king was determined to have her for his wife, if he abolished all the rest, and for this reason he had caught and kept the lost Englishman as a medicine-man; and it was not likely that he would kill him, until he failed or succeeded.

To further enquiries Bandeliah answered that to rescue the prisoner was impossible. If it had been his own newest wife, he would not push out a toe for her. The great king Golo lived up in high places that overlooked the ground, as he would these white men, and his armies went like wind and spread like fire. None of his warriors ate white man's flesh; they were afraid it would make them cowardly.

A brave heart is generally tender in the middle, to make up for being so firm outside, even as the Durian fruit is. Captain Southcombe had walked the poop-deck of the *Gwalior* many a time, in the cool of the night, with Erle Twemlow for his companion, and had taken a very warm liking to him. So that when the survivors of the regiment were landed at Portsmouth, this brave sailor travelled at his own cost to Springhaven, and told the Rector the whole sad story, making it clear to him beyond all doubt, that nothing whatever could be done to rescue the poor young man from those savages, or even to ascertain his fate. For the Quackwas were an inland tribe, inhabiting vast regions wholly unknown to any European, and believed to extend to some mighty rivers, and lakes resembling inland seas.

Therefore Mr. Twemlow, in a deep quiet voice, asked Captain Southcombe one question only—whether he might keep any hope of ever having, by the mercy of the Lord, his only son restored to him. And the sailor said—yes; the mistake would be ever to abandon such a hope, for at the moment he least expected it, his son might stand before him. He pretended to no experience of the western coast of Africa, and niggers he knew were a very queer lot, acting according to their own lights, which differed according to their natures. But he was free to say, that in such a condition he never would think of despairing, though it might become very hard not to do so, as time went on without bringing any news. He himself had been in sad peril more than once, and once it appeared quite hopeless; but he thought of his wife and his children at home, and the Lord had been pleased to deliver him.

The parson was rebuked by this brave man's faith, who made no pretence whatever to piety; and when they said Goodbye, their eyes were bright with the goodwill and pity of the human race, who know trouble not inflicted as yet upon monkeys. Mr. Twemlow's heart fell when the sailor was gone, quite as if he had lost his own mainstay; but he braced himself up to the heavy duty of imparting sad news to his wife and daughter, and worst of all to Faith Darling. But the latter surprised him by the way in which she bore it; for while she made no pretence to hide her tears, she was speaking as if they were needless. And the strangest thing of all, in Mr. Twemlow's opinion, was her curious persistence about Queen Mabonga. Could any black woman—and she supposed she must be that—be considered by white people to be beautiful? Had Captain Southcombe ever even seen her; and if not, how could he be in such raptures about her attractions? She did not like to say a word, because he had been so kind and so faithful to those poor soldiers, whom it was his duty to bring home safe; but if it had not been for that, she might have thought that with so many children and a wife at Limehouse, he

should not have allowed his mind to dwell so fondly on the personal appearance of a negress!

The Rector was astonished at this injustice, and began to revise his opinion about Faith as the fairest and sweetest girl in all the world; but Mrs. Twemlow smiled, when she had left off crying, and said that she liked the dear child all the better for concluding that Ponga—or whatever her name was—must of necessity and at the first glance fall desperately in love with her own Erle. Then the Rector cried, "Oh, to be sure, that explained it! But he never could have thought of that, without his wife's assistance."

Two years now, two years of quiet patience, of busy cheerfulness now and then, and of kindness to others always, had made of Faith Darling a lady to be loved for a hundred years, and for ever. The sense of her sorrow was never far from her, yet never brought near to any other by herself; and her smile was as warm, and her eyes as bright, as if there had never been a shadow on her youth. To be greeted by her, and to receive her hand, and one sweet glance of her large goodwill, was enough to make an old man feel that he must have been good at some time, and a young man hope that he should be so by-and-by; though the tendency was generally contented with the hope.

CHAPTER XXXIII.

FAREWELL, DANIEL.

THOUGHTFUL for others as she always was, this lovely and loveable young woman went alone, on the morning of the day that was so sorrowful for her, to bear a little share of an elder lady's sorrow, and comfort her with hopes, or at any rate with kindness. They had shed tears together when the bad news arrived, and again when a twelvemonth had weakened feeble hope; and now that another year had well-nigh killed it in old hearts too conversant with the cruelties of the world, a little talk, a tender look, a gentle repetition of things that had been said at least a hundred times before, might enter by some subtle passage to the cells of comfort. Who knows how the welted vine leaf, when we give it shade and moisture, crisps its curves again, and breathes new bloom upon its veinage? And who can tell how the flagging heart, beneath the cool mantle of time, revives, shapes itself into keen sympathies again, and spreads itself congenially to the altered light?

Without thinking about it, but only desiring to do a little good, if possible, Faith took the private way through her father's grounds leading to the rectory, eastward of the village. It was scarcely two o'clock, and the sun was shining, and the air clear and happy, as it can be in October. She was walking rather fast, for fear of dropping into the brooding vein, when in the little fir plantation a man came forth on her path, and stood within a few yards in front of her. She was startled for an instant, because the place was lonely, and Captain Stubbard's battery crew had established their power to repulse the French by pounding their fellow-countrymen. But presently she saw that it was Dan Tugwell, looking as unlike himself as any man can do (without the aid of an artist), and with some surprise she went on to meet him.

Instead of looking bright, and bold, and fearless, with the freedom of the sea in his open face, and that of the sun in his clustering curls, young Daniel appeared careworn and battered, not only unlike his proper self, but afraid of and ashamed of it. He stood not firmly on the ground, nor lightly poised like a gallant sailor, but loosely and clumsily like a ploughman who leaves off at the end of his furrow to ease the cramp. His hat looked as if he had slept in it, and his eyes as if he had not slept with them.

Miss Darling had always been fond of Dan, from the days when they played on the beach together, in childhood's contempt of social law. Her old nurse used to shut her eyes, after looking round to make sure that there was "nobody coming to tell on them," while as pretty a pair of children as the benevolent sea ever prattled with were making mirth and music and romance along its margin. And though in ripe boyhood the unfaithful Daniel transferred the hot part of his homage to the more coquettish Dolly, Faith had not made any grievance of that, but rather thought all the more of him, especially when he saved her sister's life in a very rash boating adventure.

So now she went up to him with a friendly mind, and asked him softly and pitifully what trouble had fallen upon him. At the sweet sound of her voice,

and the bright encouragement of her eyes, he felt as if he was getting better.

"If you please, miss," he said, with a meek salutation, which proved his panisic ideas to be not properly wrought into his system as yet—"if you please, miss, things are very hard upon me."

"Is it money?" she asked, with the true British instinct that all common woes have their origin there; "if it is, I shall be so glad that I happen to have a good bit put by just now."

But Dan shook his head with such dignified sadness that Faith was quite afraid of having hurt his feelings. "Oh, I might have known," she said, "that it was nothing of that kind. You are always so industrious and steady. But what can it be? Is it anything about Captain Stubbard and his men, because I know you do not like them, and none of the old Springhaven people seem to do so? Have you been obliged to fight with any of them, Daniel?"

"No, miss, no. I would not soil my hand by laying it on any of such chaps as those. Unless they should go for to insult me, I mean, or any one belonging to me. No, miss, no. It is ten times worse than money, or assault and battery."

"Well, Daniel, I would not on any account," said Faith, with her desire of knowledge growing hotter by delay, as a kettle boils by waiting—"on no account would I desire to know anything that you do not seem to think my advice might help you to get out of. I am not in a hurry, but still my time is getting rather late for what I have to do. By the time I come back from the rectory, perhaps you will have made up your mind about it. Till then, good-bye to you, Daniel."

He stepped out of the path, that she might go by, and only said, "Then good-bye, miss; I shall be far away when you come back."

This was more than the best-regulated, or largest—which generally is the worst-regulated—feminine mind could put up with. Miss Darling came back, with her mind made up to learn all, or to know the reason why.

"Dan, this is unworthy of you," she said, with her sweet voice full of sorrow. "Have I ever been hard or unkind to you, Dan, that you should be so afraid of me?"

"No, miss, never. But too much the

other way. That makes it so bad for me to say good-bye. I am going away, miss. I must be off this evening. I never shall see Springhaven no more, nor you, miss —nor nobody else."

"It is quite impossible, Dan. You must be dreaming. You don't look at all like yourself to-day. You have been doing too much over-time. I have heard all about it, and how very hard you work. I have been quite sorry for you on Sundays, to see you in the gallery, without a bit of rest, still obliged to give the time with your elbow. I have often been astonished that your mother could allow it. Why, Dan, if you go away, you will break her heart, and I don't know how many more in Springhaven."

"No, miss, no. They very soon mends them. It is the one as goes away that gets a deal the worst of it. I am sure I don't know whatever I shall do, without the old work to attend to. But it will get on just as well without me."

"No, it won't," replied Faith, looking at him very sadly, and shaking her head at such cynical views; "nothing will be the same, when you are gone, Daniel; and you ought to have more consideration."

"I am going with a good man, at any rate," he answered, "the freest-minded gentleman that ever came to these parts. Squire Carne, of Carne Castle, if you please, miss."

"Mr. Caryl Carne!" cried Faith, in a tone which made Daniel look at her with some surprise. "Is he going away? Oh, I am so glad!"

"No, miss; not Squire Carne himself. Only to provide for me work far away, and not to be beholden any more to my own people. And work where a man may earn and keep his own money, and hold up his head while adoing of it."

"Oh, Dan, you know more of such things than I do. And every man has a right to be independent, and ought to be so, and I should despise him otherwise. But don't be driven by it into the opposite extreme of disliking the people in a different rank—"

"No, miss, there is no fear of that— the only fear is liking some of them too much."

"And then," continued Faith, who was now upon one of her favourite subjects past interruption, "you must try to remember that if you work hard, so do we, or nearly all of us. From the time my father gets up in the morning, to the time when he goes to bed at night, he has not got five minutes—as he tells us every day —for attending to anything but business. Even at dinner, when you get a good hour, and won't be disturbed—now will you?"

"No, miss; not if all the work was tumbling down. No workman as respects himself would take fifty-nine minutes for sixty."

"Exactly so; and you are right. You stand up for your rights. Your dinner you have earned, and you will have it. And the same with your breakfast, and your supper too, and a good long night to get over it. Do you jump up in bed, before you have shut both eyes, hearing or fancying you have heard the bell, that calls you out into the cold, and the dark, and a wet saddle, from a warm pillow? And putting that by, as a trouble of the war, and the chance of being shot at by dark tall men"—here Faith shuddered at her own presentment, as the image of Caryl Carne passed before her—"have you to consider, at every turn, that whatever you do—though you mean it for the best—will be twisted, and made into wickedness that you never dreamed of, by envious people, whose grudge against you is that they fancy you look down on them? Though I am sure of one thing, and that is that my father, instead of looking down upon any honest man because he is poor, looks up to him; and so do I; and so does every gentleman or lady. And any one who goes about to persuade the working-people—as they are called, because they have to use their hands more—that people like my father look down upon them, and treat them like dogs, and all those wicked stories—all I can say is, any man who does it deserves to be put in the stocks, or the pillory, or even to be transported as an enemy to his country."

Dan looked at the lady with great surprise. He had always known her to be kind and gentle, and what the old people called "mannersome," to every living body that came near her. But to hear her put, better than he could put them, his own budding sentiments (which he thought to be new, with the timeworn illusion of young Liberals), and to know from her bright cheeks, and brighter eyes, that her heart was in every word of it, and to feel himself rebuked for the evil he had thought, and the mischief he had given ear to—all this was enough to make him angry with himself, and uncertain how to answer.

"I am certain that you never thought of such things," Miss Darling continued, with her gentle smile returning; "you are much too industrious and sensible for that. But I hear that some persons are now in our parish who make it their business, for some reason of their own, to spread ill-will and jealousy and hatred everywhere, to make us all strangers and foes to one another, and foreigners to our own country. We have enemies enough, by the will of the Lord (as Mr. Twemlow says), for a sharp trial to us, and a lesson to our pride, and a deep source of gratitude, and charity, and good-will—though I scarcely understand how they come in —and, above all, a warning to us to stick together, and not exactly hate, but still abhor, everybody who has a word to say against his own country at a time like this. And ten thousand times as much, if he is afraid to say it, but crawls with crafty poison into simple English bosoms."

"There is nothing of that, miss, to my knowledge, here," the young fisherman answered, simply; "Springhaven would never stand none of that; and the club drinks the health of King George every night of their meeting, and stamps on the floor for him. But I never shall help to do that any more. I must be going, miss —and thank you."

"Then you will not tell me why you go? You speak of it as if it was against your will, and yet refuse to say what drives you. Have you been poaching, Dan? Ah, that is it! But I can beg you off immediately. My father is very good even to strangers, and as for his doing anything to you—have no fear, Dan; you shall not be charged with it, even if you have been in Brown Bushes."

Brown Bushes, a copse about a mile inland, was the Admiral's most sacred spot, when peace allowed him to go shooting, because it was beloved by woodcocks, his favourite birds both for trigger and for fork. But Daniel only shook his head; he had not been near Brown Bushes. Few things perhaps will endure more wear than feminine curiosity. But when a trap has been set too long, it gets tongue-bound, and grows content without contents.

"Daniel Tugwell," said Miss Darling,

severely, "if you have not been fighting, or conspiring against society, or even poaching, I can well understand that you may have reasons for not desiring my assistance or advice. And I only wonder that under such circumstances you took the trouble to wait for me here, as you appear to have done. Good-bye."

"Oh, don't be cross, miss! please not to be cross," cried Daniel, running after her; "I would tell you all about it this very instant moment, if it were behoving to me. You will hear all about it when you get to Parson Twemlow's, for I saw mother going there, afore she had her breakfast, though I was not concernable to let her see me. If the Squire had been home, she would have gone up to Hall first. No, miss, no. I done nothing to be ashamed of; and if you turn back on me, you'll be sorry afterwards."

Faith was more apt to think that she had been too sharp than to be so in behaviour to any one. She began at once, with a blush for her bad ideas, to beg Dan's pardon, and he saw his way to say what he was come to say.

"You always were too good, Miss Faith, too good to be hard upon any one, and I am sure you have not been hard upon me; for I know that I look disrespectable. But I couldn't find words to say what I wanted, until you spoke so soft and kind. And perhaps, when I say it, you'll be angry with me, and think that I trespass upon you."

"No, I won't, Dan; I will promise you that. You may tell me, as if I were Mr. Swipes, who says that he never lost his temper in his life, because he is always right, and other people wrong."

"Well, miss, I'm afraid that I am not like that, and that makes me feel so uncomfortable with the difference between us. Because it is all about Miss Dolly, and I might seem so impudent. But you know that I would go through fire and water to serve Miss Dolly, and I durstn't go away forever without one message to her. If I was in her own rank of life, God Almighty alone should part us, whether I was rich or whether I was poor, and I'd like to see any one come near her! But being only an ignorant fellow without any birth or book-learning, I am not such a fool as to forget that the breadth of the world lies between us. Only I may wish her well, all the same— I may wish her well and happy, miss?"

"Certainly you may." Faith blushed at the passion of his words, and sighed at their despair. "You have saved her life. She respects and likes you, the same as my father and I do. You may trust me with your message, Dan."

"I suppose it would not be the proper thing for me to see her once before I go; just for one minute, with you standing by her, that I might—that she might—"

"No," answered Faith, though it grieved her to say it; "we must not think of that, Dan. It could do you no good, and it might do her harm. But if you have any message, to be useful to her—"

"The useful part of it must be through you, miss, and not sent to her at all, I think, or it would be very impertinent. The kind part is to give her my good-bye, and say that I would die to help her. And the useful part is for yourself. For God's sake, miss, do keep Miss Dolly out of the way of Squire Carne! He hath a tongue equal to any woman, with the mind of a man beneath it. He hath gotten me body and soul; because I care not the skin of a dab what befalls me. But oh, miss, he never must get Miss Dolly. He may be a very good man in some ways, and he is wonderful free-minded; but any young lady as marries him had better have leaped into the Culver Hole. Farewell, miss, now that I have told you." He was gone before Faith could even offer him her hand, but he took off his hat and put one finger to his curls, as he looked back from the clearing; and her eyes filled with tears, as she waved her hand and answered, "Farewell, Daniel!"

CHAPTER XXXIV.

CAULIFLOWERS.

"THEY cocks and hens," Mr. Swipes used to say in the earlier days of his empire—"bless you, my lord, they cocks and hens knows a good bit of gardening as well as I do. They calls one another, and they comes to see it, and they puts their heads to one side and talks about it, and they say to one another, 'Must be something good there, or he wouldn't have made it so bootiful'; and then up go their combs, and they tear away into it, like a passel of Scotchmen at a scratching-match. If your lordship won't put a lock on the door, you will never taste a bit of good vegetable."

Admiral Darling was at length persuaded to allow Mr. Swipes the privilege of locking himself in the kitchen-garden; and then, for the purpose of getting at him, a bell was put in the gable of the tool-house, with a long handle hanging outside the door in the courtyard towards the kitchen. Thus he was able to rest from his labours, without incurring unjust reproach; and gradually as he declined, with increasing decision, to answer the bell when it rang, according to the highest laws of nature it left off ringing altogether. So Mr. Swipes in the walled kitchen-garden sought peace and ensued it.

One quiet November afternoon, when the disappearance of Dan Tugwell had been talked out and done with, a sad mishap befell this gardener, during the performance, or, to speak more correctly, the contemplation of his work. A yawn of such length and breadth and height and profundity took possession of him that the space it had so well occupied still retained the tender memory. In plainer words, he had ricked his jaw, not from general want of usage, but from the momentary excess.

"Sarves me right," he muttered, "for carrying on so, without nothing inside of 'un. Must go to doctor, quick step, and no mistake."

In this strait he set off for John Prater's (for it was a matter of luck to get ale at the Hall, and in such emergency he must not trust to fortune), and passing hastily through the door, left it unlocked behind him. Going down the hill he remembered this, and had a great mind to go back again, but the unanimous demand of his system for beer impelled him downwards. He never could get up that hill again without hydraulic pressure.

All might have gone well, and all would have gone well, except for the grievous mistake of Nature in furnishing women with eyes whose keenness is only exceeded by that of their tongues. The cook at the Hall, a superior person—though lightly esteemed by Mrs. Cloam—had long been ambitious to have a voice in the selection of her raw material. If anything was good, who got the credit? Mr. Swipes, immediately. But if everything was bad, as more often happened, who received the blame? Mary Knuckle-

"FOR GOD'S SAKE, MISS, DO KEEP MISS DOLLY OUT OF THE WAY OF SQUIRE CARNE!"

down. Her lawful name was "Knuckle-up," but early misfortunes had reduced her to such mildness that her name became converted—as she expressed it—in harmony with her nature. Facts having generally been adverse to her, she found some comfort in warm affection for their natural enemies and ever-victorious rivals —words. Any words coming with a brave rush are able to scatter to the winds the strongest facts; but big words—as all our great orators know—knock them at once on the head and cremate them. But the cook was a kind-hearted woman, and liked both little and big words, without thinking of them.

She had put down her joint, a good aitch-bone, for roasting—than which, if well treated, are few better treats—to revolve in the distant salute of the fire (until it should ripen for the close embrace, where the tints of gold and chestnut vie), when it came into her provident mind with a flash that neither horse-radish nor cauliflower had yet been delivered by Mr. Swipes. She must run out and pull the long handle in the yard, and remind him gently of her needs, for she stood in some awe of his character, as a great annalist of little people's lives.

Leaving the small dog *Dandolo* with stern orders to keep the jack steadily going, with a stick on the dresser to intimidate one eye, and a sop in the dripping-pan to encourage the other, Mrs. Knuckledown ran into the court-yard, just in time to see the last swing of the skirt of that noble gardener's coat, as he turned the wall corner on his march towards the tap. She longed to call him back, but remembered just in time how fearfully cross that had made him once before, and she was yielding with a sigh to her usual bad luck, when an eager and triumphant cluck made her look about. The monarch and patriarch of cocks, a magnificent old Dorking, not idly endowed with five claws for the scratch, had discovered something great, and was calling all his wives, and even his sons, as many as yet crowed not against him, to share this special luck of fortune, or kind mood of Providence. In a minute or two he had levied an army, some half-hundred strong, and all spurring the land, to practise their liberal claws betimes for the gorgeous joy of scattering it. Then the grand old cock, whose name was "Bill," made them all fall in behind him, and strutting till he almost tumbled on his head, led the march of destruction to the garden door.

But, alas, he had waited for his followers too long, eager as they were for rapine. When he came to his portal of delight, there stood, stout as Britannia herself, and sweeping a long knife for her trident, the valiant cook, to protect her cauliflowers. "You be off, Bill," she cried. "I don't want to hurt you, because you have been a good bird in your time, but now you be growing outrageous." Bill made a rush for it, but losing a slice of his top-heavy comb, retired.

"Now's my opportunity," said Mary to herself, "for to cut my own cabbage for once in my life, and to see what that old beast does in here. Oh my! The old villain, and robber that he is! Bamboozlement is the language for it." Embezzlement she should have said, and to one who knew as she did how badly the table of the master was supplied, the suspicion was almost unavoidable. For here she saw in plenteous show, and appetising excellence, a many many of the very things she had vainly craved from Mr. Swipes. And if it was so now in November, what must

it have been two months ago? Why, poor Miss Faith—Mary Knuckledown's idol, because of her kindness and sad disappointment—had asked a little while ago for a bit of salsify, not for herself—she never thought of herself—but for a guest who was fond of it; also the Admiral himself had called out for a good dish of skirrets. But no; Mr. Swipes said the weather and the black blight had destroyed them. Yet here they were; Mary could swear to them both, with their necks above-ground, as if waiting for the washing! Cauliflowers also (as the cooks call broccoli of every kind), here they were in abundance, ten long rows all across the middle square, very beautiful to behold. Some were just curling in their crinkled coronets, to conceal the young heart that was forming, as Miss in her teens draws her tresses around the first peep of her own palpitation; others were showing their broad candid bosoms, with bold sprigs of nature's green lace crisping round; while others had their ripe breasts shielded from the air by the breakage of their own broad fringe upon them.

Mary knew that this was done by Mr. Swipes himself, because he had brought her some in that condition; but the unsuspicious master had accepted his assurance that "they was only fit for pigs as soon as the break-stalk blight come on 'em"; and then the next day he had bought the very same, perhaps at ninepence apiece, from Mr. Cheeseman's window, trimmed and shorn close, like the head of a monk. "I'll see every bit of 'un, now that I be here." Mrs. Knuckledown spoke aloud, to keep up her courage. "Too bad for that old beast to keep us locked out from the very place us ought to have for pommylarding, because he saith all the fruit would go into our pockets. And what goes into his'en, I should like to know? Suppose I lock him out, as he hath locked us out. He won't be back yet for half an hour, anyway. Wish I could write—what a list I would make, if it was only of the things he denieth he hath got!"

Strong in her own honesty and loyalty to her master, the cook turned the key in the lock, and left Swipes to ring himself into his own garden, as he always called it. That is to say, if he should return, which was not very likely, before she had time for a good look round. But she saw such a sight of things she had longed for, to redeem her repute in the vegetable way, as well as such herbs for dainty stuffing, of which she knew more than cooks generally do, that her cap nearly came off her home unexpected, and failing to find him at work, had turned the key against him, while himself inside. If so, his situation would be in sad peril, and many acres of

"THE GRAND OLD COCK, WHOSE NAME WAS 'BILL,' LED THE MARCH."

head with amazement, and time flew by unheeded. Until she was startled and terrified sadly by the loud, angry clang of the bell in the gable. Not only was Mr. Swipes come back, but he was in a furious rage outside, though his fury was chilled with some shivers of fear. At first, when he found the door locked against him, he thought that the Admiral must have come lies would be required to redeem it. For trusting in his master's long times of absence, and full times of public duty when at home, Mr. Swipes had grown more private stock, as he called it, and denied the kitchen more, than he had ever done before, in special preparation for some public dinners about to be given at the *Darling Arms*, by military officers to naval, and in turn by the latter to the former; for those were hospitable days, when all true Britons stuck their country's enemy with knife and fork, as well as sword.

But learning, as he soon did at the stables, that the Admiral was still away, and both the young ladies were gone for a ride with Miss Twemlow, the gardener came back in a rage, and rang the bell. "Oh, whatever shall I do?" the trembling Mary asked herself. "Best take the upper hand if I can. He's a thief, and a rogue, and he ought to be frighted. Does he know I can't write? No, for certain he dothn't. One of his big lies about me was a letter I wrote to poor Jonadab."

With her courage renewed by the sense of that wrong, she opened the door, and stood facing Mr. Swipes, with a piece of paper in her hand, which a woman's quick wit bade her fetch from her pocket.

"Halloa, madam!" the gardener exclaimed, with a sweep of his hat and a low salute, which he meant to be vastly satirical; "so your ladyship have come to take the air in my poor garden, instead of tending the spit. And what do your ladyship think of it, so please you? Sorry as I had any dung about, but hadn't no warning of this royal honour."

"Sir," said Mrs. Knuckledown, pretending to be frightened a great deal more than she was—"oh, sir, forgive me! I am sure I meant no harm. But the fowls was running in, and I ran up to stop them."

"Oh, that was how your ladyship condescended; and to keep out the fowls, you locked out me! Allow me the royal and unapparelled honour of showing your ladyship to her carriage; and if I ever catch her in here again, I'll pitch you down the court-yard pretty quick. Be off, you dirty baggage, or I won't answer for it now!"

"Oh, you are too kind, Mr. Swipes; I am sure you are too gentle, to forgive me, like of that! And the little list I made of the flowers in your garden, I shall put it in a teapot till the Quality wants something."

Mr. Swipes gave a start, and his overwatered eyes could not meet those of Mary, which were mildly set upon them. "List!" he muttered—"little list! What do you please to mean, Miss?"

"Well, the 'dirty baggage' means nothing unparalleled, sir, but just the same as anybody else might do. Some people calls it a Inventionary, and some an Emmarandum, and some a Catalogue. It don't interfere with you, Mr. Swipes; only the next time as Miss Dolly asks, the same as she was doing the other day—"

"Oh, she was, was she? The little ——!" Mr. Swipes used a word concerning that young lady which would have insured his immediate discharge, together with one from the Admiral's best toe. "And pray, what was her observations, ma'am?"

"It was Charles told me, for he was waiting at dinner. Seems that the turnip was not to her liking, though I picked out the very best of what few you sent in, so she looks up from her plate, and she says: 'Well, I cannot understand it! To me it is the greatest mistress in the world,' she says, 'that we never can get a bit of vegetable fit for eating. We've got,' she says, 'a kitchen-garden close upon two acres, and a man who calls himself head gardener, by the name of Swipes'—my pardoning to you, Mr. Swipes, for the young lady's way of saying it—'and his two sons, and his nephew, and I dare say soon his grandsons. Well, and what comes of it?' says she. 'Why, that we never has a bit of any kind of vegetable, much less of fruit, fit to lay a fork to!' Charles was a-pricking up his ears at this, because of his own grumbles, and the master saw it, and he says, 'Hush, Dolly!' But she up and answers spiritly: 'No, I won't hush, papa, because it is too bad. Only you leave it to me,' she says, 'and if I don't keep the key from that old thief'—excoose me, Mr. Swipes, for her shocking language—'and find out what he locks up in there, my name's not Horatia Dorothy Darling.' Oh, don't let it dwell so on your mind, Mr. Swipes! You know what young ladies be. They says things random, and then goes away and never thinks no more about it. Oh, don't be upset so—or I shall have to call Charles!"

Mr. Swipes took his hat off to ease his poor mind, which had lost its way altogether in other people's wickedness. "May I never set eyes on that young man no more!" he exclaimed, with more pathetic force than reasoning power. "Either him or me quits this establishment to-morrow. Ah, I know well why he left his last place, and somebody else shall know to-morrow!"

"What harm have poor Charles done?" the cook asked, sharply; "it wasn't him

"SO YOUR LADYSHIP HAVE COME TO TAKE THE AIR IN MY POOR GARDEN."

that said it; it was Miss Dolly. Charley only told me conferentially."

"Oh, I know what 'conferentially' means, when anything once gets among the womenkind! But I know a thing or two about Miss Dolly, as will give her enough to do at home, I'll warrant, without coming spying after me and my affairs. Don't you be surprised, cook, whatever you may hear, as soon as ever the Admiral returneth. He's a soft man enough in a number of ways, but he won't put up with everything. The nasty little vixen, if she don't smart for this!"

"Oh, don't 'e, now don't 'e, Mr. Swipes, that's a dear!" cried the soft-hearted Mrs.

Knuckledown; "don't 'e tell on her, the poor young thing. If her hath been carrying on a bit with some of them young hofficers, why, it's only natteral, and her such a young booty. Don't 'e be Dick-tell-tale, with a name to it, or without. And perhaps her never said half the things that Charles hath contributed to her." The truth was that poor Dolly had said scarcely one of them.

"Bain't no young hofficer," Mr. Swipes replied, contemptuously; "ten times wuss than that, and madder for the Admiral. Give me that paper, Miss, and then, perhaps, I'll tell 'e. Be no good to you, and might be useful to me."

Mary could not give up the paper, because it was a letter from one of her adorers, which, with the aid of Jenny Shanks, she had interpreted. "No, no," she said, with a coaxing look; "by-and-by, Mr. Swipes, when you have told me who it is, and when you have promised not to tell on poor Miss Dolly. But nobody sha'n't see it, without your permission. We'll have another talk about that to-morrow. But, oh my! look at the time you have kept me, with all the good things to make a hangel's mouth water! Bring me two cauliflowers in two seconds. My beef will want basting long ago; and if Dandy hathn't left his job, he'll be pretty well roasted hisself by now."

Mr. Swipes went muttering up the walk, and was forced to cut two of the finest cauliflowers intended for Cheeseman's adornment to-morrow. This turned his heart very sour again, and he shook his head, growling in self-commune: "You see if I don't do it, my young lady. You speaks again me, behind my back, and I writes again you, before your face; though, in course, I need not put my name to it."

CHAPTER XXXV.

LOYAL, AYE LOYAL.

ONE of the dinners at the *Darling Arms*, and perhaps the most brilliant and exciting of the whole, because even the waiters understood the subject, was the entertainment given in the month of December, A.D. 1803, not only by the officers of two regiments quartered for the time near Stonnington, but also by all the leading people round about those parts, in celebration of the great work done by His Majesty's 38-gun frigate *Leda*. Several smaller dinners had been consumed already, by way of practice, both for the cooks and the waiters and the chairman, and Mr. John Prater, who always stood behind him, with a napkin in one hand and a corkscrew in the other, and his heart in the middle, ready either to assuage or stimulate. As for the guests, it was always found that no practice had been required.

"But now, but now"—as Mr. Prater said, when his wife pretended to make nothing of it, for no other purpose than to aggravate him, because she thought that he was making too much money, in proportion to what he was giving her—

"now we shall see what Springhaven can do for the good of the Country and the glory of herself. Two bottles and a half a head is the lowest that can be charged for, with the treble X outside, and the punch to follow after. His lordship is the gentleman to keep the bottle going."

For the Lord-Lieutenant of the county, the popular Marquis of Southdown, had promised to preside at this grand dinner; and everybody knew what that meant. "Short tongue and long throat," was his lordship's motto in the discharge of all public business, and "Bottle to the gentleman on my left!" was the practical form of his eulogies. In a small space like this, there would be no chance for a sober-minded guest to escape his searching eye, and Blyth Scudamore (appointed to represent the officers of the *Leda*, and therefore the hero of the evening) felt as happy as a dog being led to be drowned, in view of this liquid ordeal. For Blyth was a temperate and moderate young man, neither such a savage as to turn his wine to poison, nor yet so Anti-Christian as to turn it into water.

Many finer places had been offered for the feast, and foremost amongst them the Admiral's house; but the committee with sound judgment had declined them all. The great point was to have a place within easy reach of boats, and where gallant naval officers could be recalled at once, if the French should do anything outrageous, which they are apt to do at the most outrageous time. But when a partition had been knocked down, and the breach tacked over with festoons of laurel, Mr. Prater was quite justified in rubbing his red hands and declaring it as snug a box as could be for the business. There was even a dark elbow where the staircase jutted out, below the big bressemer of the partition, and made a little gallery for ladies to hear speeches, and behold the festive heroes while still fit to be beholden. And Admiral Darling, as vice-chairman, entering into facts masculine and feminine, had promised his daughters and Miss Twemlow, under charge of the rector's wife and Mrs. Stubbard, a peep at this heroic scene, before it should become too convivial. The rescuers also of the *Blonde*, the flesh and bone, without which the master brain must still have lain stranded, were to have a grand supper in the covered skittle-alley, as the joints came away from their betters, this lower deck being in command of Captain Tugwell, who could rouse up his crew as fast as his lordship roused his officers.

Admiral Darling had been engaged of late in the service of his Country so continually, and kept up and down the great roads so much, or in and out of any little port where sailors grew, that his own door had nearly forgotten his shadow, and his dining-room table the reflection of his face. For, in those days, to keep a good table implied that the table must be good, as well as what was put upon it; and calico spread upon turpentine was not yet considered the proper footing for the hospitable and social glass.

"When shall Twemlow and I have a hobnob again?" the Admiral asked himself many a time. "How the dear old fellow loves to see the image of his glass upon the table, and the ruby of his port reflected! Heigho! I am getting very stiff in the back, and never a decent bit of dinner for'ard. And as for a glass of good wine—oh Lord! my timbers will be broken up, before it comes to mend them. And when I come home for even half an hour, there is all this small rubbish to attend to. I must have Frank home, to take this stuff off my hands, or else keep what I abominate, a private secretary."

Among the pile of letters that had lain unopened was one which he left to the last, because he disliked both the look and the smell of it. A dirty, ugly scrawl it was, bulged out with clumsy folding, and dabbed with wax in the creases. With some dislike he tore it open; and the dislike became loathing, as he read:

"Hon^d Sir. These foo lines comes from a umble but arty frend to command. Rekwesting of your pardon sir, i have kep a hi same been father of good dawters on the goings on of your fammeley. Miss Faith she is a hangel sir but Miss Dolly I fere no better than she ort to be, and wonderful fond of been noticed. I see her keeping company and carryin on dreadful with a tall dark young man as meens no good and lives to Widow Shankses. Too nites running when the days was short she been up to the cornder of your grounds to meat he there ever so long. Only you hask her if you dont believe me and wash her fase same time sir. Too other peple besides me nose it. Excoose hon^d sir this trubble from your obejiant servant

"FAX AND NO MISSTAKE."

The Admiral's healthy face turned blue with rage and contempt, and he stamped with his heel, as if he had the writer under it. To write a stabbing letter, and to dare to deal the stab, and yet fear to show the hand that deals it, was at that time considered a low thing to do. Even now there are people who so regard it, though a still better tool for a blackguard—the anonymous post-card—is now superseding it.

All the old man's pleasure, and cheer, and comfort, and joy in having one day at home at last, were dashed and shattered and turned into wretched anxiety by this vile scrawl. He meant to have gone down, light of heart, with a smiling daughter upon either arm, to the gallant little festival where everybody knew him, and every one admired and loved him. His two pretty daughters would sit upstairs, watching from a bow-window (though themselves unseen) all the dashing arrivals and the grand apparel. Then when the Marquis made his speech, and the King and Queen and Royal Family rode upon the clouds, and the grandeur of Great Britain was above the stars of heaven, the ladies in the gallery would venture just to show themselves, not for one moment with a dream of being looked at, but from romantic loyalty, and the fervour of great sentiments. People pretending not to know would ask, "Who are those very lovely ladies?" And he would make believe to know nothing at all about it, but his heart would know whether he knew it or not.

On the very eve of all this well-earned bliss, when it would have refreshed his fagged body and soul—which were now not so young as they used to be—to hear from some scoundrel without a name, that his pet child, the life of his life, was no better than she ought to be, which being said of a woman means that she is as bad as she can be! This fine old gentleman had never received such a cowardly back-handed blow till now, and for a moment he bent under it.

Then, greatly ashamed of himself, he arose, and with one strong word, which even Mr. Twemlow might have used under such provocation, he trod the vile stuff under foot, and pitched it with the fire-tongs into the fire. After this he felt better, and resolving most stoutly that he never would let it cross his mind again, made a light and cheerful answer to the

"THE ADMIRAL, WITH OFFICERS CROWDING AROUND, READ AS FOLLOWS."—[SEE PAGE 904.]

profligate one—his young girl who came seeking him.

"Oh, father, and you ought to be dressed!" she cried. "Shall we keep His Majesty the Lord-Lieutenant waiting? Don't let us go at all. Let us stop at home, papa. We never see you now, more than once in a month; and we don't want to see you from a staircase hole, where we mustn't even blow a kiss to you. I have got such a lot of things to tell you, dear father; and I could make you laugh much more than they will."

"But, my darling—all these grand things?" said the father, gently fingering but half afraid to look at her, because of what had been in his own mind; "the sweetest Navy blue, and the brightest Army red, and little bits of silver lace so quiet in between them! I am sure I don't know what to call a quarter of it; but the finest ship ever seen under full sail, with the sun coming through her from her royals to her courses—"

"Now, papa, don't be so ridiculous. You know that I am not a fine ship at all, but only a small frigate, about eighteen guns at the outside, I should say—though

she would be a sloop of war, wouldn't she?—and come here at any rate for you to command her, if you are not far too lofty an Admiral."

"Do you love your old father, my dear?" said he, being carried beyond his usual state by the joy in her eyes as she touched him.

"What a shame to ask me such a question? Oh, papa, I ought to say, 'Do you love me?' when you go away weeks and months almost together! Take that, papa; and be quite ashamed of yourself."

She swept all her breast-knots away anyhow—that had taken an hour to arbitrate—and flung back her hair that would never be coiled, and with a flash of tears leaping into laughing eyes, threw both arms round her father's neck, and pressed her cool sweet lips to his, which were not at all in the same condition.

"There, see what you've done for me now!" she cried. "It will take three-quarters of an hour, papa, to make me look fit to be looked at again. The fashions are growing so ridiculous now—it is a happy thing for us that we are a hundred years behind them, as Eliza Twemlow had the impudence to say; and really, for the daughter of a clergyman—"

"I don't care that for Eliza Twemlow," the Admiral exclaimed, with a snap of his thumb. "Let her show herself as much as there is demand for. Or rather, what I mean to say is, let Miss Twemlow be as beautiful as nature has made her, my dear; and no doubt that is very considerable. But I like you to be different; and you are. I like you to be simple, and shy, and retiring, and not to care twopence what any one thinks of you, so long as your father is contented."

Dolly looked at her father, as if there were no other man in the world for the moment. Then her conscience made her bright eyes fall, as she whispered: "To be sure, papa. I only put these things on to please you; and if you don't like them, away they go. Perhaps I should look nicer in my great-aunt's shawl. And my feet would be warmer, oh ever so much! I know where it is, and if you prefer the look of it—"

"No, no!" cried the simple old father, as the girl tripped away in hot haste to seek for it; "I forbid you to make such a guy of yourself. You must not take my little banter, darling, in such a matter-of-fact way, or I must hold my tongue."

"Thank God," he continued to himself, as Miss Dolly ran away, to repair her damages; "the simple little soul thinks of nobody but me! How could I be such a fool as to imagine harm of her? Why, she is quite a child, a bigger child than I am. I shall enjoy my evening all the more for this."

And truly there seemed to be no reason why all the guests at that great festival, save those who had speeches to make, should not enjoy their evening thoroughly. Great preparations had been made, and goodly presents contributed; plenty of serving-men would be there, and John Prater (now growing white-headed and portly) was becoming so skilful a caterer that if anything was suggested to him, he had always thought of it long ago. The only grief was that the hour should be so late—five o'clock, an unchristian time, as they said, for who could have manners after starving so long?

There was some sense in this; but the unreasonable lateness of the hour could not be helped, because the Lord-Lieutenant had to wait upon the King at eight o'clock that morning. That he could do

so, and yet be in Springhaven by five, seemed almost impossible; for only ten years ago the journey took two days. But the war seemed to make everything go quicker, and it was no use to wonder at anything. Only if everything else went quicker, why should dinner (the most important of them all) come slower? And as yet there was nobody to answer this; though perhaps there is no one to ask it now.

All things began very beautifully. The young ladies slipped in unobserved, and the elder blessings of mankind came after, escorting themselves with dignity. Then the heroes who had fought, and the gallants who had not had the luck yet, but were eager for it, came pleasantly clanking in, well girt to demolish ox and sheep, like Ajax, in lack of loftier carnage. The rector said grace, and the Marquis amen, and in less than two minutes every elbow was up, and every mouth at business. There was very little talking for the first half hour. In those days emptiness was not allowed to make the process of filling a misery.

While these fine fellows were still in the prime of their feeding, bent over and upon it, two men with empty stomachs, and a long way between them and their victuals, stood afar regarding them. That is to say, just far enough to be quite out of sight from the windows, in the gloom of the December evening; but at the same time near enough, to their own unhappiness, to see and even smell the choice affairs across the road.

"For what, then, hast thou brought me here?" the shorter man sharply asked the tall one, both being in an uncomfortable place in a hedge, and with briars that scratched them. "Is it to see other people eat, when to eat myself is impossible? You have promised to show me a very fine thing, and leagues have I traversed to please you. Fie, then, what is it? To see eat, eat, eat, and drink, drink, drink, and have nothing for myself!"

"My friend," said the tall man, "I have not brought you here with any desire to improve your appetite, which is always abundant, and cannot be gratified for several hours, and with poor stuff then, compared to what you are beholding. Those men are feeding well. You can see how they enjoy it. There is not a morsel in their mouths that has not a very choice flavour of its own distinguished relish.

See, there is the venison just waiting to be carved, and a pheasant between every two of them. If only the wind was a little more that way, and the covers taken off the sauce-boats, and the gravy—ah, do I perceive a fine fragrance, or is it a desirous imagination?"

"Bah! you are of the cold-blood, the wicked self-command. For me it is either to rush in, or rush away. No longer can I hold my nose and mouth. And behold they have wine—grand wine—the wine of Sillery, of Medoc, of Barsac, and of Burgundy! By the bottles I can tell them, and by all the Saints—"

"Be not so excited, for you cannot smack the lips. It is too late now to envy them their solids, because they have made such speed with them. But listen, my dear friend"—and here the tall man whispered into the ear of his brisk companion, who danced with delight in the ungenial hedge, till his face was scarred with brambles.

"It is magnificent, it is droll, it is what you call in England one grand spree, though of that you understand not the signification. But, my faith, it is at the same time barbarous, and almost too malignant."

"Too benevolent Charron," said the tall stern man, "that shall rest upon my conscience, not on yours. The object is not to spoil their noisy revel, but to gain instruction of importance. To obtain a clear idea of the measures they adopt—ah, you see, you are as quick as lightning. This urgent message is upon official paper, which I have taken from the desk of that very stupid Stubbard. Take the horse Jerry holds at the corner, and the officer's hat and cape provided are ample disguise for so dark a night. Take the lane behind the hills, and gallop two miles eastward, till you come to the shore again, then turn back towards the village by way of the beach, and you will meet the Coast-guard on duty, a stupid fellow called Vickers. Your horse by that time will be piping and roaring: he can go like the wind, but his own is broken. The moment you see Vickers, begin to swear at your horse. I have practised you in d—ns, for an emergency."

"Ten thousand thunders, I can say d—n now to equal and surpass the purest born of all Britons."

"Not so loud, my friend, until by-and-by. The Coast-guard will come to you, and you pull up with your horse hanging down his head, as if dead-beaten. Using your accomplishment again, you say: 'Here, take this on to Admiral Darling. My nag is quite done, and I must get to Stonnington to call Colonel James. For your life, run, run. You'll get a guinea, if you look sharp.' Before he can think of it, turn your horse, and make back to the lane, as if for Stonnington. But instead of that, gallop back to our ruins; and we'll go up the hill, and see what comes of it."

"It is very good, it is magnificent. But will not the sentinel perceive my voice and accent?"

"Not he; he is a very honest and therefore stupid fellow. Give him no time, answer no questions. Be all in a rush, as you so generally are. I would do it myself, but I am too well known. Say, will you undertake it? It will be a fine joke for you."

About half an hour after this, the Lord-Lieutenant having hammered on the table with an empty bottle, stood up to propose the chief toast of the evening—the gallant crew of the *Leda*, and the bold sailors of Springhaven. His lordship had scarcely had a bottle and a half, and was now in the prime of his intellect. A very large man, with a long brocaded coat of ruby-coloured cloth, and white satin breeches, a waistcoat of primrose plush emblazoned with the Union-jack (then the popular device) in gorgeous silks with a margin of bright gold, and a neckcloth pointed and plaited in with the rarest lace, worth all the rest put together—what a pity it seemed that such a man should get drunk, or at any rate try so hard to do it. There was not a pimple on his face, his cheeks were rosy and glistening, but not flushed; and his eyes were as bright and clear and deep as a couple of large sapphires.

This nobleman said a few words, without any excitement, or desire to create it, every word to the point, and the best that could be chosen not to go beyond the point. There was no attempt at eloquence, and yet the speech was eloquent, because it suggested so much more than was said. More excitable natures, overcome by half a bottle, resolved to have the other half, in honour of that toast.

Then the Marquis did a very kind and thoughtful thing, for which he deserved a bottle of the Royal Tokay, such as even Napoleon could not obtain. When the cheering was done, and every eye was fixed upon the blushing Scudamore—who felt himself, under that fixture, like an insect under a lens which the sun is turning into a burning-glass—the Chairman perceived his sad plight, and to give him more time and more spirit, rose again.

"Gentlemen," he said, "or I would rather call you brother Englishmen at this moment, I have forgotten one thing. Before our young hero replies to his health, let us give him that spirited song 'Billy Blue,' which is well known to every man here, I'll be bound. Tell the drummer down there to be ready for chorus." Billy Blue, though almost forgotten now (because the enemy would not fight him), the blockader of Brest, the hardy, skilful, and ever watchful Admiral Cornwallis, would be known to us nearly as well as Nelson, if fame were not a lottery.

As the Lord-Lieutenant waved his hand, the company rose with one accord, and followed the lead of his strong clear voice in the popular song, called

"BILLY BLUE."

1.

"'Tis a terrible time for Englishmen;
  All tyrants do abhor them;
Every one of them hath to fight with ten,
  And the Lord alone is for them.
But the Lord hath given the strong right hand,
  And the courage to face the thunder;
If a Frenchman treads this English land,
  He shall find his grave thereunder.

CHORUS.

Britannia is the Ocean-Queen, and she standeth
  staunch and true,
With Nelson for her faulchion keen, and her
  buckler Billy Blue.

2.

"They are mustering on yon Gallic coasts,
  You can see them from this high land,
The biggest of all the outlandish hosts
  That ever devoured an island.
There are steeds that have scoured the Continent,
  Ere ever one might say, 'Whoa, there!'
And ships that would fill the Thames and Trent,
  If we would let them go there.

CHORUS.

But England is the Ocean-Queen, and it shall be
  hard to do;
Not a Frenchman shall skulk in between herself
  and her Billy Blue.

3.

"From the smiling bays of Devonshire
  To the frowning cliffs of Filey,
Leaps forth every son of an English sire,
  To fight for his native isley.

He hath drawn the sword of his father now
  From the rusty sheath it rattled in;
And Dobbin, who dragged the peaceful plough,
  Is neighing for the battle-din.

CHORUS.

For Albion still is Ocean-Queen, and though her
  sons be few,
They challenge the world with a dauntless mien,
  and the flag of Billy Blue.

4.

"Then pledge me your English palm, my lad;
  Keep the knuckles for Sir Frenchman;
No slave can you be till you change your dad,
  And no son of yours a henchman.
The fight is to come; and we will not brag,
  Nor expect whatever we sigh for,
But stand as the rock that bears the flag
  Our duty is to die for.

CHORUS.

For Englishmen confront serene whatever them
  betideth;
And England shall be Ocean's Queen as long as
  the world abideth."

What with the drum and the fifes of one of the regiments now at Stonnington, and the mighty bass of some sea-captains vehement in chorus, these rough and rolling lines were enough to frighten a thousand Frenchmen, while proving the vigour of British nerve, and fortitude both of heart and ear. When people have done a thing well, they know it, and applaud one another to include themselves; and even the ladies, who were meant to be unseen, forgot that and waved their handkerchiefs. Then up and spoke Blyth Scudamore, in the spirit of the moment; and all that he said was good and true, well-balanced and well-condensed, like himself. His quiet melodious voice went further than the Lord-Lieutenant's, because it was new to the air of noise, and that fickle element loves novelty. All was silence while he spoke, and when he ceased—great uproar.

"That lad will do," said the Marquis to his supporter on the right hand; "I was just like him at that age myself. Let me draw this cork—it is the bottle of the evening. None but my own fellows understand a cork, and they seem to have got away somewhere. What the doose are they about—why, halloa, Darling! What's the meaning of all this, at such a time?"

"Well, my lord, you must judge for yourself," said the Admiral, who had made his way quietly from the bottom of the table. "We know that false alarms are plentiful. But this looks like business, from the paper it is written on; and I know that old Dudgeon is as solid as myself. Vickers the Coast-guard brought it in, from an officer whose horse was blown, who had orders to get somehow to Stonnington."

"Is Vickers a knave, or a fool who is likely to be made the victim of a very low joke? There are hundreds of jealous scoundrels eager to spoil every patriotic gathering. Ah, this looks rather serious, though, if you can vouch for the paper."

"I can vouch for the paper, my lord, and for Vickers; but not for Dudgeon's signature. Of that I have no knowledge —though it looks right enough, so far as I know. Shall I read it aloud, and let officers who are not under my command judge for themselves, as I shall judge for those I have the honour to command?"

The Lord-Lieutenant, with his cork just squeaking in the neck of the bottle, nodded; and the Admiral, with officers crowding round, read aloud as follows, part being in type, and part in manuscript:

"Commander of Coast-defence at Hythe, to Vice-Admiral Darling, Springhaven.

"French fleet standing in, must have slipped Cornwallis. Do all you can. Not a moment to lose.
(Signed) "BELLAMY DUDGEON."

"Well, it may be true, or it may be a lie," said the Marquis, pouring carefully; "my opinion is the latter; but I have nothing to do with it officially, according to the new arrangements. Every gentleman must judge for himself. And I mean to abide by my own judgment, which strongly recommends me to finish this bottle."

"Probably you are right enough; and in your place perhaps I should do the same," the Admiral answered, quietly; "but be the alarm either true or false, I am bound to act otherwise. All Naval Officers present will be good enough to follow me, and prepare to rejoin if ordered. We shall very soon know from the signal-point, unless fog has set in suddenly, whether we are bound to beat a general alarm."

All the sons of the sea arose quietly, and were despatched with brief orders to the right and left, to communicate with their signal stations, while Stubbard hurried back to his battery.

"What cold blood they do display!" whispered the Frenchman, who had returned with the author of the plot to watch the issue from a point of vantage. "My faith, they march slowly for their native land! Not less than six bottles of great French wine did I anticipate to steal through the window, while they fell out precipitous. But there sits a man big enough to leave me nothing—not even a remainder of my own body. Soul of St. Denis, can it be that they question the word of a gentleman?"

"Not they!" replied Carne, who was vexed, however; "they are taking things easily, according to the custom of the nation. But two good things we have done, friend Charron; we have learned their proceedings, and we have spoiled their feasting."

"But not at all; they are all coming back to enjoy it all the more!" cried the Frenchman. "Oh that I were an Englishman, to get such a dinner, and to be so loyal to it!"

NOTE.—"Springhaven" will be omitted from the December number, owing to the pressure of Christmas articles in that number, but a double instalment (Parts IX. and X.) will appear in the January number.

THE TRAGEDY OF THE MOUFFETICH.

AN EPISODE OF KHEDIVE ISMAÏL'S REIGN.

BY EDWIN DE LEON.

THE unchangeable character of the Eastern man and of Oriental government, even under the varnish of an apparent adoption of Western usages and civilization, has found its most striking exemplifications in the inner history of the Khedive's Egypt of yesterday. To those travellers who during the late reign visited Egypt and marvelled at its apparent progress, who witnessed a new Rue de Rivoli replacing the narrow streets and shady gardens of Cairo, or enjoyed the hospitalities of the Khedive, at his balls, his opera-house, or dinner parties, the transformation of Egypt and the Egyptian court from the Eastern to the Western model would have seemed complete.

Yet the famous axiom of Napoleon, in

regard to the Russian, applies even more forcibly and truly to his Turkish brother, as well as to his Egyptian. If on "scratching the Russian" you "find the Tartar" beneath the epidermis, most assuredly also do you discover, by experiment, that the civilization of the Oriental, monarch or subject, is but skin-deep, and as easily displaced, and that, under new forms and external shows, the rule both of Turkey and of Egypt is on the same old plan, and full of dramatic surprises, often comic, yet still more frequently intensely tragic. One of the most strange and startling of these dramatic episodes, toward the close of Ismaïl Pasha's reign in Egypt — of which the truth is indeed stranger than fiction — was the story of "the Mouffetich," Ismaïl Sadyk Pasha, the Khedive's foster-brother. This man was the Wolsey or Strafford of that reign, and his rise was more sudden and his fall far more terrible than that of those Western statesmen, whose fate has long been used to point the moral of the pains and penalties of ambition. Unlike those historic characters, this Eastern statesman, who rose, blazed, and was extinguished like a baleful meteor flashing over the Eastern sky, was born and reared to manhood in a mud hut in a small village on the Nile, and to the hour of his death knew nothing of foreign languages or foreign countries or institutions. Uneducated, untrained, and ignorant of all knowledge save "how to squeeze the fellahs" (that is, how to wring the largest sums out of his fellow-peasants by fair means or foul) for his grasping and prodigal master's use, he yet contrived to perplex and mystify the European Commissioners sent to control the revenues of Egypt for the benefit of her creditors, for five successive years, with an ingenuity that seemed inexhaustible.

Ismaïl Sadyk was the foster-brother of the Khedive Ismaïl, whose mother, like most Eastern Sultanas, preferred performing her maternal duties by proxy, and who summoned a poor fellah woman of the lowest class to supply her place with the future ruler of Egypt. This duty done, the woman was sent back to her mud hut and native village, where she afterward lived and died on the pittance assigned her, and brought up her son (of the same name as the Khedive) amidst the ignorance, squalor, and poverty of such surroundings; for no one

who has not visited and closely inspected one of those Nile villages, which look so picturesque and pleasant to the Nile voyager as he glides past them in his dahabeeyah, smoking his chibouque of fragrant latakia under the awning on deck, can imagine what they really are, or how wretched the lives of their inmates. With distance lending enchantment to the view, the Nile village—shaded by its feathery-topped palms, with its dome-topped mosque and needle-like minarets, and its clustering huts, crowned with pigeon-houses, over which the birds are constantly circling on snowy wings, with naked children gambolling around the village fountain, too distant for the repulsive attributes of dirt and poverty to be visible—presents a picture on which the eye of the artist loves to linger. But step ashore, and picking your way around the great mound of filth and refuse which ever rises in front of these villages, on which savage wild dogs without a master prowl in search of garbage, their only food; pass into the crooked lanes which separate the mud huts, more like ant-hills than the habitations of man, without windows or chimney, wherein blear-eyed hags and filthy children squat in the midst of smoke, dirt, and unsavory smells, and goats and dogs dispute your narrow passageway—and you will soon retreat from the inspection or vicinity of what seemed so charming when viewed remotely. And the lives of the poor wretches are as dreary and devoid of charm as their habitations and surroundings. For them life has but one meaning, daily drudgery; but one object, the hoarding up and hiding away the few coins they can secure from the merciless exactions of the tax-gatherer or local sheik, who represents the government, i.e., the Khedive; for on the shoulders of the poor fellah falls the double weight of contributing to the great horse-leech at Cairo, and of satisfying also the lesser leeches, his instruments.

For the wealth and luxury of Egyptian rulers come from this lowly source. All comes out of the land; and these apparently poverty-stricken wretches constitute the peasant proprietors of Egypt, each with his little holding, out of whom $40,000,000 or $50,000,000 per annum were ground between the upper and nether millstones of Khedive and foreign creditors.

Of this class, and reared in such company, was Ismaïl Sadyk; and his earlier years were spent in acting as a kind of overseer or bailiff on the upper Nile for some smaller estates of his foster-brother the Khedive, who was a keen man of business before he became Viceroy. In this school he learned the lesson in which he was said to excel any native employé, viz., "how to squeeze the fellah," whose arts and artifices for the concealment of his piastres were vain against him, and soon obtained the reputation of being more exacting, unscrupulous, and merciless than any of his competitors. On such merits he rose rapidly in the esteem and confidence of his foster-brother, and as years passed he was promoted to the fulfilment of larger duties and higher trusts, until Ismaïl became Viceroy and Khedive, and beginning to feel the want of more and more money to gratify his ambition and his greed, leaned more and more on this servant, who never failed him, but "squeezed" gold out of the squalid tenants of the mud huts, by cunning devices or fearful cruelty, which made his name a synonym for oppression throughout the valley of the upper Nile.

Coming into collision with the foreign creditor, who had "squeezed" him as his agents had the peasantry, the Khedive summoned Sadyk to Cairo, made him his Minister of Finance and head of the Treasury, and constituted him his sole confidant and secret adviser, using him as a buffer against the foreign creditors and their accredited representatives from England and France, Messrs. Goschen and Joubert. The Mouffetich proved equal to the emergency. Backed by his master, and by the aid of the Coptic clerks—the most astute accountants in the world—with whom ciphering is a science, he confronted the clamorous creditors and their chosen representatives, selected from the ablest financiers of England and France.

Aided by those cunning scribes and his knowledge of the country, for six years did the Mouffetich baffle and keep at bay the hungry pack of his master's foreign creditors, raising millions of pounds in ways mysterious still to every one but that master, and keeping up the shadow of Egyptian credit at home and abroad, after the bankruptcy of its exchequer had been clearly demonstrated by facts and figures. During these years of close intimacy with his patron, the character and habits of the man underwent a change as great as his altered fortunes.

It was then the writer first knew him, and formed the opinion of his intellect and character, which was never changed, namely, that he was a bold, bad man of great natural energy, of no culture, no scruples, and narrow views, yet with a thorough knowledge of the resources of Egypt and of its people. Of a nature as ruthless as that of a hyena, and a bad Mussulman in the practice of religious obligations, he was inspired by a truly orthodox hatred of "the infidel" and all his ways. Yet he had acquired a taste for foreign vices, as well as for show, luxury, and animal enjoyment, contrasting strangely not only with his early training, but with his personal aspect and bearing as well.

To the last, while revelling like a Sardanapalus in private orgies (in which the Khedive was said to participate), dwelling in a palace, or cluster of palaces, covering twenty acres of ground, and furnished in a style and at an expense even more regal than the Khedive's, with a thousand persons congregated under his roof, and more female slaves than Solomon, the man's personal appearance and address were still those of an Arab fellah—mean, sordid, and repulsive. Although he wore the semi-European Stambouli costume, and in addition, to give dignity to his appearance, a huge pair of gold-mounted spectacles, his face and figure never could gain the stamp of a Turkish gentleman, and his manner, either arrogant or cringing, always inspired his interlocutor with repulsion or distrust.

The temporary shifts and extraordinary contrivances by which the Mouffetich, as Finance Minister, contrived to postpone the evil day of Egyptian insolvency piled up still higher the mountain of debt accumulated by the Khedive's wasteful and reckless expenditure, and the European bondholders became clamorous, and put pressure on the Khedive, through their governments, for the dismissal of Sadyk, and the substitution of a foreign Board of Control.

Against this Sadyk stood like a wolf at bay, fighting not only for place, but for life and property as well; since no one knew better than he what his removal from office and the confidence of the Khedive would entail. Banishment and confiscation of his estates and property, he well knew, would swiftly follow his disgrace, even if liberty and life were spared him by a master whose secrets were known to him, and to him only.

Witnessing the waning courage of the Khedive, and fearing his abandonment to the hands of enemies who would not spare him, the Mouffetich, forgetting his usual cunning and caution, attempted to force the Khedive to support him through fear of the consequences which might otherwise ensue. It is said he even hinted at the compromising papers in his possession which would prove the master's complicity in some of the most dishonest transactions, of which the servant alone bore the blame.

In taking this step he sealed his fate, for he forgot that, although himself a dangerous wolf, he yet rested under the paw of a royal tiger, whose terrible talons had not yet been pared by European captors, but who still possessed the power of life or death, and could exact absolute blind obedience from his native subjects.

But the alarmed and offended Khedive, with the dissimulation of which he was so great a master, betrayed no feeling to his victim, nor allowed him to suspect his intention of disposing of him and his revelations by the short and easy method so much practised in the East by pashas toward inconvenient servants. On the contrary, he persuaded Sadyk that he felt they were in the same critical position, and must confer together, as well as coöperate in the deliverance of Egypt from foreign influences, and then adroitly arranged a trap for his destruction, to be worked by his own hands.

The scheme was this: Sadyk was to raise a native Mohammedan party in Egypt for the expulsion of the Christian infidels, which would give the Khedive the excuse of summarily getting rid of these troublesome intermeddlers, but was to do this without committing his master, who would be held blameless by foreign powers for acting under compulsion of his fanatical people. The Ulemas, or heads of the religion, were to be confidentially consulted in the first place, and their exhortations would suffice to rouse the people to the proper pitch for such a movement.

To the brain of the Mouffetich, bewildered partly by his peril, partly by his excesses, which had of late passed all reasonable bounds, this suggestion seemed full of promise. He fell into the trap so skilfully prepared for him, and at once went to the Ulemas and urged his plot, darkly intimating that he did so by authority of the Khedive. But the Ulemas, who may be considered the Jesuits of Islam in sagacity and skill, although hating the infidel with a holy horror, and anxious to get rid of him at any price, placed no confidence either in the Mouffetich or his master—like himself a most unorthodox Mussulman, and reproach to the Church and faith.

They sent a deputation of their order to the Khedive to demand the truth of the Mouffetich's hints, and to protest against a plot so fraught with danger to the whole community that it would bring them into collision with the whole Christian world, which would unite to crush them. Thus the trap was sprung, and the wolf safely in the toils prepared for him. Yet the Khedive still dissembled. He assured the Ulemas that the whole affair was the coinage of the Mouffetich's brain, which he hinted was disordered, and demanded that they should put in writing their allegations and charges against the minister who was thus plotting against his master, and trying to disturb the peace of the country. At the same time he bound the priests to secrecy.

Yet adroit as he was, the suspicions of Sadyk were aroused; and, maddened probably by strong drink or cerebral excitement, he again threatened his master with revelations, intimating that he had kept the compromising documents safely locked up in his private palace, and might produce them if provoked or abandoned.

With the exquisite courtesy and self-control which characterizes the Eastern ruler, the Khedive only smiled at these wild words, gave him "renewed assurances of his high consideration" in choice Arabic, and invited him to take a drive next morning alone with him in his brougham, that the whole population might see that he still honored the Mouffetich with his confidence.

With pride and joy Sadyk accepted the flattering invitation, and the next morning repaired to the palace for that purpose. Leaning on his arm in the most friendly manner, the Khedive descended the steps and entered his carriage, and the joyful Sadyk followed and took the seat opposite, according to etiquette. Escorted as usual by mounted guards in uniform, the carriage rolled rapidly through the thoroughfares of Cairo, the people marvelling to see the Khedive's apparent familiarity with a minister supposed to be in disgrace previously. After this public exhibition of familiarity the Khedive ordered the carriage driven to his palace of Gezireh, on the Nile, about two miles distant from Cairo.

Arriving at the door, at a sign from the Khedive, the attendants crowded around him as he descended from the carriage, separating him from his companion, who saw him disappear through the doorway, but who, on attempting to follow, was seized by one of the Khedive's officers, surrounded by a file of soldiers, and made a prisoner.

Of the scene that then ensued, and of those which followed in quick succession, a thousand and one stories were circulated throughout Cairo within the next twenty-four hours; but which version was the true one no man yet knows, save the actors, and they were silenced, or have since been silent.

The young officer charged with the arrest and subsequent fate of the Mouffetich, who had been educated in Europe, and was therefore not of as tough fibre as his home-staying comrades, was so affected by what he had to do and witness that he went mad, and was for some time kept under restraint. Several other pashas who were cognizant of the facts died very suddenly and in quick succession, some immediately after partaking of the Khedive's hospitalities; and in a book recently published at London by Blanchard Jerrold (*Egypt under Ismaïl Pasha*), the accusation of several successive murders is made against the Khedive consequent on the indubitable one of the Mouffetich. For, from the hour of his arrest as above described, Ismaïl Sadyk disappeared as suddenly and as mysteriously from the sight of men as does the bubble on the ocean or the mirage on the desert; and to this day the place where his bones are laid is equally unknown, although circumstantial and official accounts were tardily given in the government papers on these subjects, which, however, nobody credited.

It is believed that he was not allowed to survive his capture more than a few hours, but was strangled or poisoned by the attendants, on the old principle of "dead men telling no tales." The public announcements, a few days later, of his having been tried and found guilty of treason by the Privy Council for attempting to incite an insurrection against the Khedive and the Christians, for which he was condemned to transportation to Upper Egypt and confiscation of his estates, as well as of his being conveyed to Dongola in a closed dahabeeyah, were considered as blinds only. That such statements were made in the official *Moniteur Egyptien*, and that a dahabeeyah, said to convey the state prisoner up the Nile, was despatched, with its blinds carefully closed, and did ascend the Nile, are undisputed facts. But the public impression then and since undoubtedly was and is that the execution of the sentence preceded the supposed trial, and that the mortal remains of Ismaïl Sadyk rest at the bottom of the Nile near the palace of his foster-brother.

The immense property of which he died possessed was all confiscated, and appropriated to the Khedive's uses. His palaces, lands, slaves, the jewelry of his women, all were sold, and a commission appointed to cash the proceeds. The jewelry alone was estimated at three and a quarter millions of dollars. His real estate amounted to thirty thousand acres of arable lands. Bonds and shares amounting to a million more were found among his papers. The value of his palaces and furniture must have reached several millions more. His annual expenditure amounted to a million and a half, according to his accounts, and his indebtedness to about a million, which was paid out of the proceeds of the sale of his effects, which was public, and largely attended by the European and native population of Egypt. At that sale his only son, who had been married to a stepdaughter of the Khedive (promptly divorced from him after his father's death), might have been seen tranquilly sitting on a divan dispensing pipes and coffee to his friends in apparently the most tranquil frame of mind. His palaces, three connected with each other, surrounded by beautiful gardens, were most sumptuously decorated and furnished in French style. Some idea of their extent may be formed from the fact of its having taken a party four hours to stroll through the apartments, without stopping in any of them.

OUR COAST-GUARD.

A BRIEF HISTORY OF THE UNITED STATES REVENUE MARINE SERVICE.

BY LIEUTENANT WORTH G. ROSS, U.S.R.M.

REVENUE ENSIGN AND PENNANT.

THE establishment of the Revenue Marine, or what is more familiarly known as the Revenue-cutter Service, antedates that of the present navy. The former was organized in 1790, and consequently has nearly reached the centennial anniversary of its existence. While it is known that such a corps is a part of the government machinery, there is little understanding by the public generally regarding its scope and character and the magnitude of its varied duties.

That matchless organizer and master of details, Alexander Hamilton, first Secretary of the Treasury, as early as 1789, recommended the employment of "boats for the security of the revenue against contraband," and in a bill which he afterward presented to Congress submitted a proposition for ten boats to be distributed along the seaboard as follows: two for the coast of Massachusetts and New Hampshire, one for Long Island Sound, one for New York, one for the Bay of Delaware, two for the Chesapeake and neighboring waters, and one each for North Carolina, South Carolina, and Georgia. They were to measure from thirty-six to forty feet in length of keel, at an estimated cost of $1000 each, manned by two officers and six marines, and armed with swivels. Congress appropriated $23,327 50 to support ten equipped cutters, with 10 masters, 30 mates, 40 mariners, and 20 boys. This was the original plant—an unpretending fleet of small, sharp-built, single-

masted, light-draught sailing vessels; in fact they were not much larger than yawls of the present day. The officers and crews, besides receiving regular pay, were entitled to a proportion of the amounts derived from fines, penalties, and forfeitures that were collected in case of seizures, and for violations of the navigation and customs laws. This prize-money, as it was termed, was in later years abolished, and an increased compensation voted the officers. By degrees, and as occasion arose, the service was augmented in strength and armament, frequently acting in concert with the naval branch. The comparatively meagre commercial relations of the country, with a thinly populated and unsettled sea-coast, did not require at that time a large force for the protection of the revenue; but with the rapid growth of foreign trade, and a shipping interest that was constantly developing at home, the necessity for a cordon of capable and swift cruisers became manifest. An act of Congress of 1799 gave authority to the

U. S. REVENUE CADET.

U. S. REVENUE-CUTTER "ALBERT GALLATIN."

President to maintain as many revenue-cutters as should be necessary to provide for the proper collection of import and tonnage duties, the expenses whereof should be paid out of such sum as should be annually appropriated therefor. Thus the corps gradually grew in size and importance; its vessels became larger and better. In addition to the usual duties, they suppressed piracy, that had become common on account of the many adventurers attracted to American waters. A distinctive revenue ensign and pennant were also provided by law, the former consisting of sixteen vertical alternate red and white stripes, and a union containing a blue eagle on a white ground surmounted by thirteen blue stars.

Revenue-cutters have participated in all wars of the United States except the Algerine war. While action of the service in the nation's defence has not been separately chronicled in history, its work has always been timely and efficient, and its record honorable. In 1797 its vessels, owing to the belligerent attitude of France, were placed on a strict war footing, and during the troublous times that followed that year were unceasing and effective agents in coöperation with the navy in maintaining the dignity and position of the government. On the cessation of hostilities the cutters resumed their functions under the Treasury Department. In 1798 a number were employed cruising in the waters of the West Indies. The embargo act of 1807, intended to countervail Napoleon's decrees, brought the service into special requisition in guarding the seaboard and arresting the departure of unauthorized merchant ships. In the war of 1812 its force was actively employed in repelling foreign invasion: vessels were despatched on hazardous missions, and charged with perilous and difficult duty, and were frequently in the thick of action. To the cutter *Jefferson*, William Ham, master, is due the credit of the first marine capture of the conflict, that of the British schooner *Patriot*, with a valuable cargo of sugars, while on her way from Guadeloupe to Halifax, June 25, 1812, just seven days after the proclamation of war. Many deeds of daring and bravery were displayed by officers and crews.

In 1813 the revenue-cutter *Vigilant*, Captain Cahoone, captured the British privateer *Dart*, off Newport, after a decisive struggle, in which a number of the assailants were wounded, and several privateersmen, including the first officer, were killed. The cutters *Madison* and *Gallatin* also made important prizes of three brigs on the Southern coast, laden with ammunition and supplies, and carried them into Charleston and Savannah. During the nullification troubles of 1832–3 several revenue-cutters were stationed off Charleston, prepared to enforce the execution of the tariff laws. At the time of the Seminole war they transported troops

pursuing blockade-runners, doing guard and *reconnoissance* duty, watching Confederate batteries, and sharing in numerous engagements, a number of which resulted in the loss of officers and men.

The Revenue Marine at the present time has a complement of 40 vessels, 14 of which are sloops, steam-launches, and harbor boats, 1 a sailing bark, and the remaining 25 steamers ranging from 130 to 500 tons burden. The *Bear*, noted for the part taken in the Greely relief expedition, which was recently transferred to this service, is slightly in excess of the tonnage mentioned. In 1843 steamers were first introduced, and by gradual

U. S. REVENUE-CUTTER "THOMAS CORWIN," CAUGHT IN DRIFT ICE.

and munitions, and afforded protection to settlers along the coast. In the war with Mexico eight vessels were ordered to proceed to the theatre of operations, where they participated at the naval attacks on Alvarado and Tabasco, and worked in unison with the naval squadron. The revenue steamer *McLane* and the schooner *Forward*, manning six guns each, were a part of the expedition under Commodore M. C. Perry, against the latter port and Frontera, October, 1846. During the war of the rebellion the cutters were actively concerned conveying despatches,

steps were substituted for the old top-sail schooner type of craft then in use (a relic of the days of privateering), until now but one sailing cutter is left. The first screw-propellers were the *Legaré* and *Spencer;* these proved failures, and soon went out of use. The side-wheel steamer *Harriet Lane*, christened after the accomplished niece of President Buchanan, was among those first built. Her career was a notable one. She took part in the naval expedition to Paraguay, and in the late war was several times under fire. Most of the fleet are stanch, fast, thor-

U. S. REVENUE-CUTTER "LEVI WOODBURY."

ough sea-going vessels, of good manage-able qualities in rough weather, and equipped for almost any emergency like-ly to arise. The greater number of them have been constructed under the imme-diate supervision of officers of the corps, and have been devised with special refer-ence to the wants of the several stations, and many are considered admirable mod-els of their size and type. They are usu-ally armed with from two to four breech-loading rifled cannon, and provided with necessary small-arms for the use of crews. The *Commodore Perry*, one of the hand-somest and swiftest cutters in the service, cruising on Lake Erie, made an average speed of nineteen miles an hour on her trial trip. It is believed that this result has not been exceeded by any govern-ment vessel. It has been the practice in late years to name the vessels after for-mer Secretaries and Assistant Secretaries of the Treasury. Thus four of the cut-ters shown in our illustrations are named respectively after Albert Gallatin (Sec-retary of the Treasury 1801–09) ; Levi Woodbury (1834–41) ; George M. Bibb

(1844) ; and Thomas Corwin (1850–53) ; while another is named after James C. Dobbin (Secretary of the Navy 1853–57). But such appellations as *Andrew John-son, William H. Seward, Schuyler Col-fax*, and *U. S. Grant* appear on the list. The last of these, a bark-rigged steam-propeller of splendid construction, sta-tioned at New York, is the only ship belonging to the United States that bears the name of the great soldier.

The steamers of the Revenue Marine are, as a general rule, ready at a mo-ment's call to proceed upon prolonged and important missions; as has been stated, they have been among the first armed force to repel a foreign enemy, or aid in the prevention or settlement of in-ternational complications. In less than ten days after the ratification of the treaty (1867) for the purchase of Alaska, the revenue steamer *Lincoln*, under com-mand of Captain John W. White, was despatched to that region, and much in-formation was obtained regarding the geography, resources, productions, cli-mate, etc., of the country. This cruise has been followed yearly by the cruising of revenue vessels in the waters of Alaska, and up to the present time no vessel of the service has met with disaster while engaged in such arduous work. As this article is being prepared, word comes from the Pacific coast that the whaling bark *Amethyst* is supposed to have been cast away in Behring Sea. In the short space of five days from the reception of the first tidings, the revenue-cutter *Richard Rush*, by order of the Secretary of the Treasury,

Francisco May 4, 1881, destined for Alaska and the northwest polar sea. The object of the cruise was, in addition to revenue duty, to ascertain the fate of two missing whalers (*Mount Wollaston* and *Vigilant*), and to communicate, if possible, with the exploring steamer *Jeannette*. During the previous year five ineffectual attempts were made by the *Corwin* to reach Herald Island. On this trip a landing was made, after a hazardous run through the drift ice, and Wrangel Land

U. S. REVENUE-CUTTER "GEORGE M. BIBB."

started from San Francisco, in the midst of winter, on a 4000-mile voyage to the polar ocean, in search of the crew of the missing ship.

A vessel that has gained a distinctive public reputation for her various expeditions to the arctic is the steam-cutter *Thomas Corwin*. She sailed from San

was at the same time sighted to the westward. To convey a partial idea of the perilous nature of navigating the waters (or rather the ice) of the arctic, the following incident, taken from the report of Captain Hooper, affords a graphic illustration: "The wind had increased to a moderate gale, and the snow fell so thick

THE OLD U. S. REVENUE-CUTTER "J. C. DOBBIN" (LAST TYPE OF THE TOPSAIL-SCHOONER CLASS).

that observation beyond the length of the vessel was impossible. Shortly after midnight we found ourselves entirely surrounded by heavy ice, and were compelled to use the engine to work out of it; in doing so the rudder was broken and unshipped, every pintle being carried away. The situation was anything but pleasant, caught in the end of a rapidly closing lead, 120 miles from open water, in a howling gale and driving snow-storm, and without a rudder. It at first appeared as if the destruction of the vessel was inevitable. However, after several hours of hard work, steering as best we could by means of the sails, and giving the vessel a great many hard bumps and nips, we succeeded in getting into the open lead again, and by six o'clock we had prepared a jury-rudder."

One of the most eventful features of the cruise was the first landing on Wrangel Land (north latitude 71° 04'), August 12. After much difficulty in pushing the *Corwin* through the floating and grounded masses of ice, an open space was reached a short distance from the island,

where the vessel was anchored, and a party succeeded in getting on shore in a small boat. Lieutenant W. E. Reynolds, of the party (which included Captain Hooper, Dr. I. C. Rosse, Assistant Engineer F. E. Owen, Mr. John Muir, Mr. E. W. Nelson, of the Signal Service, and the boat's crew), planted the United States flag on a cliff, where were secured a copy of the *New York Herald* and a record of the *Corwin*'s cruise, and possession was formally taken of the newly acquired ice-clad territory amid enthusiastic cheers and a salute from the guns of the cutter. In an extract from the Bulletin of the American Geographical Society (No. 3, 1883), Dr. Rosse says, regarding "the first landing on Wrangel Island": "It may be remarked with pardonable pride that the acquisition of this remote island, though of no political or commercial value, will serve the higher and nobler purpose of a perpetual reminder of American enterprise, courage, and maritime skill."

During the cruises of the *Corwin* in 1880, '81, which covered 12,000 miles, valuable surveys and soundings and interesting meteorological observations were made, and much data collected relative to the currents and natural features of the country, while special attention was given to the physical characteristics of the natives and the diseases prevalent among them. Important coal deposits were discovered and located; information was gathered concerning the lost whalers, and the fate of one determined; regular duty was performed in preventing unlawful incursions upon the sealing interests, and a number of predatory vessels were seized engaged in illicit traffic.

A brief mention of four succeeding cruises (1882, '3, '4, '5) of the *Corwin* to Alaska, in command of Captain M. A. Healy, will prove of interest, the first being made to St. Lawrence Bay, Siberia, to bring away the people of the burned naval relief steamer *Rodgers*, which went north in the spring of 1881 in search of the *Jeannette*. The *Corwin* made a second cruise the same year to protect the seal fisheries. Various explorations were also made into the interior of Alaska, and a serious outbreak of the natives on the main-land quelled. During the last two cruises of the *Corwin* much valuable assistance was rendered to shipwrecked sailors and destitute miners, fifty-nine persons, without means of transportation, being brought away at one time. Under the vigilant cruising of revenue vessels in Alaskan waters the unscrupulous selling to the natives of fire-arms and spirits, by masters and owners of lawless trading crafts, has greatly diminished. Owing to the fact that the *Corwin* is too limited in coal-carrying capacity, and is, in other essential details, unadapted to the rigors of arctic cruising, she will in future be replaced by the revenue steamer *Bear*, of larger dimensions and stronger build.

The Revenue Marine, while being a part of the Treasury organization, has always been regarded as belonging to the military force of the government. While aiding the civil establishment in the enforcement of certain laws, it can, at the pleasure of the President, be accounted as part of the navy. Congress has conferred naval rank and authority upon the officers, who are appointed by the President by and with

U. S. REVENUE SCHOOL-SHIP "SALMON P. CHASE."

the advice and consent of the Senate, and hold their commissions during good behavior. The Secretary of the Treasury is intrusted with the immediate control and management of the service, as well as the stationing of vessels and officers; he determines the number of petty officers and seamen, and designates the Collector of Customs under whose supervision each vessel is placed. Subordinate to him are the Chief and Assistant Chief of the Revenue Marine Division, occupied respectively by Mr. Peter Bonnett and Mr. W. S. Eaton. In 1883 a proposition was made to transfer the administration of this arm to the Navy Department, and make of it a special naval corps. A bill incorporating such a scheme was introduced in Congress, and was strongly recommended and advocated by the Secretary of the Navy, and as strenuously opposed by officers of the Treasury, but the measure never left the committee-room where it was referred. Among most European powers similar services are in charge of officers detailed from the navy, who coöperate with the custom-house officials in the discharge of their duties.

The *personnel* of the Revenue Marine consists of five grades of the line and three grades of engineers, namely, 36 captains, 36 first lieutenants, 36 second lieutenants, 36 third lieutenants and cadets; and 25 chief engineers, 20 first assistant engineers, 27 second assistant engineers; and, in addition, about 800 men. Officers are required to be proficient in the knowledge of gunnery and military drills, and to instruct and exercise the crews in the use of great guns, rifles, carbines, pistols, cutlasses, etc. The discipline maintained on revenue-cutters is that usually prevailing on a man-of-war. A knowledge of the multifarious questions contained in the customs and navigation laws, and other statutory provisions bearing upon the duties committed to the service, as well as a familiarity with the regulations affecting the maritime interests of the country, is essential to a skilled revenue officer. A long period of application and experience is necessary to acquire this knowledge. He must, besides, give considerate attention and study to many other professional matters. His tour of duty on a particular station is regulated by the exigencies of the service, but is usually limited to a term of three years. Promotions are governed by written competitive examinations, from

three to five of the senior officers of a lower grade being designated to compete for a vacancy that occurs, by resignation or casualty, in a higher grade. The engineer staff was organized about 1844, soon after the introduction of steam into revenue vessels as a propelling power. Second assistant engineers are appointed from civil life after undergoing a searching technical examination; the method of subsequent advancement is similar to that employed for deck officers.

The jurisdiction of the customs authority is confined within a limit extending four leagues from the coast. Vessels arriving in United States waters are boarded and examined, their papers certified to, and proper fastenings, if deemed necessary, affixed to the hatches communicating with the holds. This work is often accompanied with much difficulty and danger, as any mishap in lowering a boat in a heavy sea, or a want of skilful management in going alongside of a ship under way, might occasion disaster and loss of life. Whenever a vessel liable to seizure or examination does not *bring to* when required to do so, the commander of a cutter, after the discharge of a cautionary gun, can fire into such vessel, and all persons acting under his orders are indemnified from any penalties or actions for damages.

Formerly candidates were admitted to the grade of third lieutenant after undergoing an examination which was required to give competent proof of proficiency and skill in navigation and seamanship. By this plan a great many capable persons entered the lists from the merchant marine and volunteer navy. The names of two officers are borne on the register (Captain Louis N. Stodder and Lieutenant Samuel Howard) who were a part of the force on the *Monitor* during its notable fight with the *Merrimac* in Hampton Roads. The former was also on board of the *Monitor* when she sank off Cape Hatteras, and was among the few saved. In July, 1876, Congress adopted a measure to appoint cadets to fill vacancies which occurred in the line. The text of the law is as follows: "That hereafter, upon the occurring of a vacancy in the grade of third lieutenant in the Revenue Marine Service, the Secretary of the Treasury may appoint a cadet, not less than eighteen nor more than twenty-five years of age, with rank next below that of third lieutenant, whose pay shall be three-fourths that of a third lieutenant, and he shall not be appointed to a higher grade till he shall have served a satisfactory probationary term of two years, and passed the examination required by the regulations of said service; and upon the promotion of such cadet another may be appointed in his stead, but the whole number of third lieutenants and cadets shall at no time exceed the number of third lieutenants now authorized by law." The object of this bill is to educate young men for officers. Any individual of the above qualifications who can furnish satisfactory evidence of good moral character, correct habits, and who meets the requirements of the regulations as to physical soundness and conditions, can compete in the examinations that take place annually at the Treasury Department to fill vacancies. Appointments are not influenced by political considerations or favoritism, but are made strictly on the score of merit. It is now in contemplation to require applicants to have a further qualification of eighteen months' practical sea service. The subjects embraced in the initial examination include the whole of arithmetic; algebra to equations of the second degree; English grammar; the history of the United States; geography, reading, writing, spelling, and composition. The minimum standard of eligibility is fixed at 75 out of a possible 100. In orthography a separate standard is fixed: thirty words are usually given, and a failure to spell twenty of them correctly is considered a bar to appointment. The qualifications are more exacting than for admission to the Naval Academy, and a class is formed from those evincing the highest degree of aptitude. This is then instructed to report on board the revenue bark *Salmon P. Chase*, stationed at New Bedford, Massachusetts, where the members are allowed a few days to prepare themselves for sea and get accustomed to ship's routine.

The cadet school-ship is a bark about 154 tons burden, with a length between perpendiculars of 106 feet, and a breadth of beam of 25 feet. She was built in Philadelphia in 1878 expressly for this service, and is designed and equipped for the training and accommodation of cadets. She carries a battery of four broadside guns. The steerage, or apartment in which the cadets live, contains six state-rooms, with two berths each, wash-stand,

and lockers sufficient for clothing. At present there are two classes under instruction, designated as senior and junior, and since the organization of the system seven classes have been graduated, consisting of a total membership of thirty-one, and commissioned as third lieutenants. The classes vary in number from year to year, in accordance with existing vacancies, the largest thus far containing eleven members, and the smallest three.

The port routine is made up of daily application and recitation in the academical branches; physical exercises, which include simple athletics, rowing, and going aloft; and professional studies and drills in navigation, seamanship, gunnery, signalling, etc., either practical or theoretical, as the temper of the weather permits. Certain hours are provided by the internal regulations of the ship for recreation, and only on Wednesday and Saturday afternoons, and on Sunday after "muster and inspection," are the cadets granted liberty on shore, except by special approval of the commanding officer. They mess among themselves, and elect their own caterer, and while under instruction are required to wear a prescribed uniform. The use of tobacco and intoxicating beverages, in any form, is prohibited. A list of demerit marks is in force for breaches of discipline or violations of the rules, and careful records are kept of the standing of each cadet in his studies and deportment, and submitted to the department, which, with his examination averages, determine his relative rank in his class after the graduating ceremonies at Washington at the end of the course. The last-named consists of two years (subject to an additional year), and is divided into four terms, each year embracing two terms, as follows: from June to January, which includes the practice cruise at sea of the three summer months, and a week's vacation during the Christmas holidays; and from January to June. In the latter parts of December and May occur the semiannual and annual examinations respectively, which contain a sum-

SIGNAL LETTERS.

mary of questions and exercises covering the subjects that have previously been pursued.

The academic course is under the charge of Mr. Edwin Emery, a graduate of Bowdoin College, and for a long time a teacher and principal in public schools. It takes up arithmetic, algebra, geometry, astronomy, and trigonometry (plain and spherical); the history of the origin and growth of the English language; composition, rhetoric, and correspondence, in which the cadets are required to write upon abstract, imaginary, descriptive, and professional subjects, and to construct official letters, reports, and forms; philosophy and steam-engineering, the latter being treated both practically and theoretically, and supplemented by lectures of Consulting Engineer Charles E. Emery, Ph.D., of New York; history of the world in general, and of the United States in particular; that part of international law which deals with the rights of nations in peace and war, rights of jurisdiction over the sea, and of commerce; embargoes, law of contraband, blockade, right of search, offences against the law of nations, piracy, etc. In constitutional law the history of the Constitution is taught, and the legislative, executive, and judicial departments, and powers of Congress, are discussed, while the revenue law comprehends all that relates to the duties of an officer of the customs, such as the regulations of commerce and navigation, collection districts, and ships' papers.

About the 1st of June the *Chase* puts to sea, with four officers, a surgeon, two classes of cadets, and a crew of thirty men. She is provisioned, stored, and fitted for a three months' cruise. Here is where the test of a young man's endurance, pluck, and energy commences, as he is subjected to many of the inconveniences and discomforts incident to a sea-voyage, at the same time having to perform all the duties belonging to the vocation of a sailor. He has a taste of the sternest and most trying obligations at the threshold of his undertaking, which results in a pretty thorough test of his metal, and if any one is actually unfit for the sea, physically or otherwise, the fact is at once brought to the surface, and gives him an opportunity to turn back at the beginning of a career in which he would not be likely to succeed.

The cadets are arranged into watches,

and in this capacity they are under the instruction of the officer of the deck, and are required to write up the remarks in the rough log, to observe carefully the making and taking in of all sail, to study the various evolutions of the vessel, transmitting and giving commands when directed, and, after reaching a certain degree of proficiency, they are exercised in charge of the deck, and in working ship in the important operations of tacking and wearing. The object is to impress them with the duties and responsibilities of deck officers, and the strictest obedience to every detail is enforced. Knotting, splicing, making mats, and learning the nomenclature of the different parts of the hull and spars, and the names and uses of ropes and sails, are among the first lessons in seamanship, and during periods of calm weather the rigging is reset and rattled down. The cadets are given constant practice in raising shears, stepping masts, reefing, furling, and shifting sails, and in sending up and down yards. Each takes his "trick" at the wheel, and acquaints himself with the mysteries of the compass and the steering gear. The marline-spike, slush and tar pots, are the insignia of a thorough-going salt, and the young man who has never immersed his hands in the resinous substance finds ample opportunity on a practice cruise.

In navigation the cadets are exercised in taking altitudes with the sextant, of the sun, moon, planets, and stars. They are required to determine daily the latitude and longitude of the vessel, and establish the ship's position by dead-reckoning and by the different sailing problems. The variation, deviation, and error of the compass is ascertained; in port, artificial horizon sights are used to discover the error of chronometer. The classes are educated in the international and general service signal codes, the latter usually being practised on shore, the cadets receiving and transmitting messages by a system of flag movements. The use of small-arms and broadswords is comprised in the port routine, the cadets being drilled in military marches and tactics, target-shooting, etc. The gunnery exercises consist in the distribution of officers and men at general quarters. The cadets are trained in the working of all classes of broadside and pivot guns, and are familiarized with the duties and stations of officers of divisions; they are taught the construction of

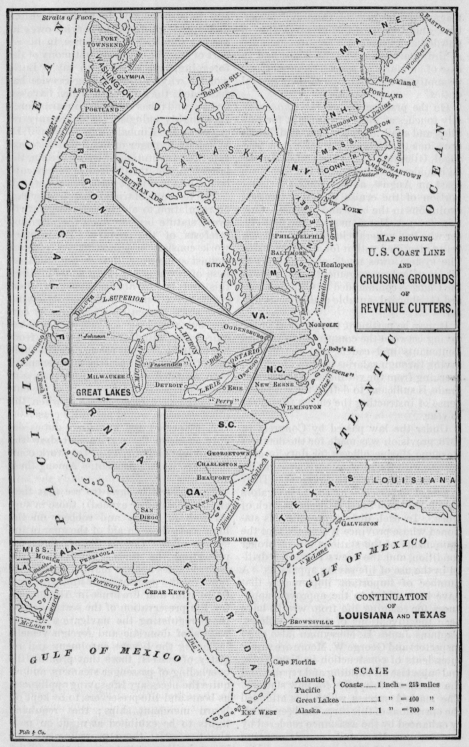

MAP SHOWING
U. S. COAST LINE
AND
CRUISING GROUNDS
OF
REVENUE CUTTERS.

CONTINUATION
OF
LOUISIANA AND TEXAS

SCALE
Atlantic } Coasts...... 1 inch = 213 miles
Pacific
Great Lakes .... 1 " = 400 "
Alaska..................... 1 " = 700 "

NOTE.—Besides those mentioned there are fourteen vessels engaged in harbor duty, or upon inland waters, a sailing bark, and two steamers out of commission.

magazines, the uses of fuses and projectiles, and the nature and properties of powder and combustibles; are stationed at fire quarters and at the boats, and in case of an alarm at sea are required to act promptly in the discharge of their several duties.

On the practice cruises the *Chase* usually touches at some foreign port for supplies and mail, having been on different occasions to England, France, Spain, Portugal, Gibraltar, the Azores and Bermuda islands. She returns to the American coast in August, and devotes the latter portion of the cruise to active nautical evolutions in the bays and harbors. Captain John A. Henriques was the first officer who had general charge of the school, being identified with it for about six years. The system owes much of its success to his excellent management. At present the *Chase* is commanded by Captain Leonard G. Shepard, an able and efficient officer.

It may be pertinent to remark that the saving between the compensation of third lieutenants and cadets, and the annual saving through salaries held in abeyance, accruing from the vacancies in the former grade, is sufficient to defray the entire expense of instructing the cadets from year to year.

Under the law passed by Congress in 1878, provision was made for the detail of Revenue Marine officers for duty in connection with the Life-saving Service, as inspectors and assistant inspectors. Their extended experience as coast navigators ably fitted them for this special branch of work. In each district an officer is stationed whose province it is to see that the equipments of the stations are in proper condition, and the crews regularly drilled in the use of life-saving apparatus. A number of important implements that have been added to the approved appliances for rescuing life from wrecks have been the inventions of revenue officers. Captains James H. Merryman (also chief inspector) and George W. Moore are superintendents of construction in New York, and supervise all building and repairs, and the purchase of supplies for new stations. The marked success which has attended the operations of this corps has been greatly enhanced by the assistance rendered by the Revenue Marine, its vessels cruising an average of 15,000 miles yearly on life-saving duty. Mr. S. I. Kimball, the General Superintendent, to whose persistent and untiring efforts the service owes its present standard of excellence, in his report of 1882, in flattering testimony of the foregoing, had occasion to say, "Little wonder why the Life-saving Service has succeeded; the souls of such men have entered it, and it has become an incarnation." In a highly eulogistic letter recently received by Mr. Kimball from Admiral J. R. Ward, ex-Manager of the Royal National Life-boat Institution of Great Britain, the latter concedes the United States service to be the best and most perfect in the world.

The Revenue Marine is required by law or regulation to aid in enforcing nearly every statute bearing upon the maritime interests of the country. Its primary work consists in protecting the revenue against smuggling, though the effectiveness of revenue vessels in accomplishing this end is not always apparent, their strict surveillance of the coast having long since broken up smuggling by cargo; but whenever an exigency has required the withdrawal of a vessel from her cruising grounds for any considerable time, the unlawful practice has generally been resumed, with prosperous results to those engaged, until the return of the cutter to the field of depredation, when the illicit vocation would naturally cease.

A glance at the numerous duties devolving upon the service will show the magnitude and variety of the work committed to its enforcement. Among these are:

The neutrality laws (to see that they are not violated or evaded); those in suppression of piracy and robbery on the high seas; those in aid of the quarantine system of the various States; those for protecting the timber reserves of the United States against marauding parties; those for the prevention of unlawful traffic in rum and fire-arms in Alaska, and for the preservation of the seal fisheries; those regulating the navigation in our waters of domestic and foreign vessels, including the license, enrolment, and registry of vessels; those that prohibit the overlading of passenger steamers, and require the necessary life-saving appliances, as boats and life-preservers, to be kept on board merchant ships; that requiring lights to be exhibited at night on merchant vessels; those providing for the name, hailing port, tonnage, and official numbers to be properly affixed; the regulations requiring steamers to carry the necessary evidence of inspection to hulls and machinery, and that the officers are fitly licensed. The revenue forces suppress mutinies upon vessels of the merchant marine, and form an efficient means in harbors to save shipping from conflagration; they are, under the law, an important part of the Life-saving Corps; they report upon the absence of buoys and lights upon the sea-coast, and they carry out the humane enactments of Congress by actively cruising in the winter season in aid of distressed mariners. Besides these regular duties there are numerous others to which they are detailed from time to time, such as aiding the Light-house Establishment, the Coast Survey, the Fish Commissioner, the ocean telegraph lines, as well as all scientific enterprises coming within the scope of their operations.

For several years the Revenue Marine has been a useful factor in coöperating with the Marine Hospital Service and the civil authorities in confining and alleviating the yellow-fever, cholera, and small-pox epidemics that have at different times made their appearance on our shores. This service has been accomplished by carrying physicians, nurses, medicines, and supplies to those afflicted, and by assisting in the maintenance of a rigid national quarantine at various points.

From December to April of each year, during the dangerous and inclement season, the President directs the cutters (under the law of 1837) to cruise vigorously on their stations to afford aid to vessels in distress. Those detailed for this duty are provided with supplies, including extra provisions for the shipwrecked, and are instructed to extend to all requiring relief such assistance as may be adapted to their condition and necessities. By the terms of their orders they are not to put into port unless compelled to do so by stress of weather or other unavoidable circumstances. The revenue-cutters stationed on the Great Lakes are, during the period of open navigation, particularly charged with similar important work. The performance of this duty entails untiring vigilance and activity, subjecting the cutters and crews to the keenest exposure, and oftentimes to the utmost danger.

Relief is given to hundreds of imperilled vessels each season, in one way or another, either by towing helpless and disabled craft to harbors of safety, hauling others off reefs and shoals, keeping channels clear of ice and removing obstructions, or by giving succor and aid to shipwrecked mariners. No more fitting illustration can be given of the great good that has been effected in this respect than the timely and incalculable services of the revenue steamer *Dexter*, rendered in connection with one of the most awful marine catastrophes of modern times. The details, even at this late day, are fresh in the minds of many people. Few events have ever occurred that excited so much profound and wide-spread horror, public interest, and sympathy. On Thursday afternoon, January 17, 1884, the 2000-ton steamer *City of Columbus*, of the Boston and Savannah line, left Boston for the port of Savannah, with 81 passengers and a ship's company of 45 persons. She was a stanch, iron-built vessel, thoroughly equipped for sea, commanded by Captain S. E. Wright, an old and experienced seaman, and up to this voyage a successful commander. Many of the passengers were invalids seeking to restore lost health in Southern climes. The wind had increased to a fitful hurricane in the night, a heavy and irregular sea was running, and the weather was crisp and cold. The steamer was standing on her usual course through Vineyard Sound, and had passed nearly all the dangerous points which lie thick in those waters, and in a few moments would have reached the open ocean. Unfortunately, at a critical time, the captain left his post of duty and went below, giving directions to the helmsman how to steer. Three-quarters of an hour afterward, between three and four o'clock of the morning of the 18th, the *City of Columbus* struck hard and fast upon Devil's Bridge, a rugged reef that juts out five-eighths of a mile from Gay Head promontory, and which is plainly marked on all charts. No tongue can depict the awful terror of the situation: darkness prevailed, the wind howled and the sea roared, and a hundred human beings were swept into the icy waves and perished. Those who could, took refuge in the rigging, and many who were exhausted and benumbed by the cold dropped into the lashing waters. The boats that were cleared away were either dashed to pieces or swamped. Soon after daylight the revenue-cutter *Dexter*, cruising in the vicinity, arrived on the scene. Captain Eric Gabrielson, her commander, at once sent out two boats in charge of Lieutenants Rhodes and Kennedy; thirteen men were rescued, all of whom were forced to jump from the rigging into the sea, and were picked up as they rose to the surface. The trips to the wreck in the small boats, on the top of a boisterous sea, were a most hazardous undertaking, and required unflinching courage. An equal number of survivors, as well as many lifeless bodies, were transferred to the decks of the *Dexter* through the praiseworthy and intrepid efforts of the Gay Head Indians, who manned the first life-boat that went to the scene of disaster. One hundred and two souls were lost in this dreadful calamity.

ed certificates for "humane efforts," etc., while each of the crew received a money reward. Joint resolutions were presented in Congress giving the thanks of that body to the officers and crew of the *Dexter*. The Secretary of the Treasury made the matter the subject of a congratulatory circular, bestowing warm praise on those concerned, and urging emulation on the part of others, which was read in the presence of officers and men throughout the service, and the President directed that Lieutenant Rhodes be advanced twenty-one files in the line of promotion.

The following table exhibits, as well as such figures can, the work of the Revenue Marine, and the expense of maintaining it, for the past five years:

Year ended.	Aggregate number of miles cruised.	Vessels boarded and examined.	Vessels seized or reported for violation of law.	Number of persons picked out of the water and saved from drowning.	Number of vessels assisted in distress.	Value of vessels and their cargoes, imperilled by the sea, to which assistance was rendered.	Annual cost of maintaining the service.
June 30, 1881.....	282,027	29,101	3,163	141	148	$2,766,882 00	$846,791 99
June 30, 1882.....	303,562	24,008	1,042	111	147	2,254,716 00	846,423 34
June 30, 1883.....	300,880	25,587	2,240	60	224	4,885,175 00	853,553 83
June 30, 1884.....	317,843	26,282	2,270	63	246	7,015,572 00	851,311 86
June 30, 1885.....	312,569	24,481	1,425	60	274	5,568,043 00	819,897 89
Average per year	303,376	25,892	2,028	87	208	$4,498,078 00	$843,595 78

The fines and penalties incurred by vessels violating the law average per year, in round numbers, about $645,000, or more than three-fourths of the entire cost of conducting the service.

The average number of persons on board vessels assisted each year, irrespective of those actually saved from drowning, was 2783.

It was during these hours of life-saving work that Lieutenant John U. Rhodes performed an act of unrivalled heroism which made him famous. Two men hung in the rigging, unable to move on account of exhaustion, and were the only persons remaining on the ill-fated vessel. The latter could not be boarded without great peril, and Rhodes tried to swim through the freezing surf to the steamer. In his first endeavor he was struck by a piece of floating timber, and had to abandon the attempt. Although bruised, he insisted on making another trial, and succeeded in removing the helpless, half-frozen creatures, both of whom died after reaching a place of safety. The Legislature of Connecticut, his native State, unanimously passed a resolution thanking him for his "gallant conduct," and he received the gold medal of the Massachusetts Humane Society "for heroic exertions, at the imminent peril of his own life, in rescuing two persons from the steamer *City of Columbus*," besides many other medals and testimonials from various sources. Captain Gabrielson also received the Society's medal, and the officers in general were award-

From the foregoing it will be seen that the estimated value of property assisted, in the brief period of five years, reaches the aggregate of $22,490,388. In a single year the value of assistance was over eight times the annual public outlay.

The business of revenue-cutters brings them principally into the waters along the coast, thus subjecting them always to dangers of navigation far greater than are encountered in mid-ocean. By such exceptional experience their officers become trained and skilled in coastwise cruising. Within the past ten years the vessels of the service have sailed an aggregate of two million and a half miles, combating every condition of wind and weather, and during that period no accident of moment has happened to any of them. The Revenue Marine holds a well-earned popularity among those engaged in conducting the floating commerce of the country, and among the public generally, and is recognized as increasing the receipt of the Treasury, and saving to the shipping interests of the nation each year many times the cost of its maintenance.

COÖPERATION AMONG ENGLISH WORKING-MEN.

BY A. H. D. ACKLAND.

THE changes toward a further democratic government which have gradually been taking place in England must lead Englishmen to consider seriously what is the manner of life which obtains among the working-men of England, what is the capability of this class for self-government, how far is it educated, provident, and constant. Even the most sanguine of forward politicians recognize the necessity of avoiding revolutionary changes. In the great towns of England we have the grand safeguard of possessing a solid backbone of working-men, developed through associative work and the practice of self-government among themselves. For this we have largely to thank three movements —trades-unionism, friendly societies, and coöperation. It is thus that in considering the last of these three, the importance to be attached to it is so much greater than that of the mere figures which represent its vast business. A coöperative society is not to be regarded simply as a store managed on profit-sharing principles. It is a great means of educating the working classes both in town and country through independent association among themselves, and of fitting them for the work of local self-government which must shortly be intrusted to their hands.

The coöperative movement began about forty years ago. In 1844 the twenty-eight Rochdale pioneers started a little store on the principle of dividing profits according to the amount of purchases. Their business capital was no more than £28, which had been most carefully collected and hoarded. From these humble beginnings the movement has spread among a vast number of the working classes throughout England and Scotland. In its present condition it is no doubt open to some criticisms, but not even Robert Owen and the Christian Socialists, including F. D. Maurice, C. Kingsley, T. Hughes Ludlow, and E. Vansittart Neil, who urged the importance of the matter, could possibly have hoped at the time that coöperation would ever reach its present development. A few figures will perhaps be useful as showing the extent to which the work has spread. In 1862 the amount of sales by coöperative societies in the United Kingdom was less than 2½ millions

sterling. In 1883 (the last returns made out) the sales amounted to more than 28 millions, the number of societies which made returns of their business to the central board was 1157, and the total profits amounted to 2½ millions, and the money applied to education amounted to nearly £16,000. In the twenty years 1862–82 the total sales amounted to 275¼ millions, and the profits to nearly 22 millions. All this, it must be remembered, is working-men's money, and the whole of this business is managed by working-men themselves, or through representatives whom they have elected from their own numbers. To show more clearly what an immense hold coöperation has over certain districts, the fact may be mentioned that in the county of Durham the members of coöperative societies amount to more than 30 per cent. of the total population; in Yorkshire, to 27 per cent.; in Lancashire, to 27 per cent.; in Cumberland, to 24 per cent.; and in Northumberland, to 22½ per cent. Thus in some of the great centres of English industry a large proportion of the working classes are attached to the movement. At present the societies are larger and more numerous in the north than in the south.

It will be well to consider how an ordinary distributive store is started from the beginning, and how a working-man becomes a member of a society and profits by its business. The usual way in which a store is started in a town or village is that some working-man*.who is a leading spirit among his fellows hears what is being done by working-men coöperators in England or Scotland. He talks the matter over with his friends, obtains and circulates tracts bearing upon the subject, and finally he and his friends make up their minds to see if they can start a society. A small provisional committee is then appointed, which enters into communication with other working-men in the place. The next step is very often to hold a public meeting, to which the Central Board of the Coöperative Union is always willing to send two or more speak-

---

* In describing the elementary growth I have not hesitated to borrow part of the matter from a little work written by my friend Mr. B. Jones and myself, called *Working-men Coöperators*.

ers free of charge, and at the close of such a meeting a very slight amount of urging will probably induce a good many people to give their names as members of the proposed society. This done, a certain amount of money must be collected before a start can be made. The whole system is based upon ready-money dealing, and each store must have ready money to pay for its outfit before it makes a beginning. Some of the committee act as collectors, and push the matter as well as they can. If a shop is to be opened all day, there should be at least £130 of capital, 100 members, and a fair prospect of doing a trade of from £40 to £50 a week. Nothing less will insure payment of expenses and a fair dividend.

In an ordinary case, to become a member of such a store it is only necessary to deposit 1s. 3d. That done, the store is open to any one of any class who may wish to belong to it. The member, whether man or woman, or one of the family, goes to the store, which may be a building worth £40,000 or one rented at £5 a year; in either case the methods are exactly the same. He buys goods at the ordinary market price of the town or village, for which he pays ready money over the counter, and on no pretext whatever is credit allowed. When the purchase is done, the shopman gives him tin or paper tokens, stamped or marked so as to show how much he has spent, whether it be sixpence or several pounds. These tokens are kept till the end of the quarter, for it is upon the amount he has spent at the store that his dividend or share of profits depends. Such a member is not allowed to withdraw the whole of his first dividend. He is bound to leave a sum equal to 3d. per week until he is a shareholder to the amount of at least a £1 share, in order that the society may have some working capital of its own to fall back upon. After he has got this £1 share he may withdraw all future dividends if he chooses. If he is wise, he will let it accumulate at the store, which will thus become his savings-bank, and will pay him 5 per cent. After a time he may find himself in possession of £50 or £100 in the store, as is the case with hundreds of working people, the savings being the result of no other effort on their part than that of paying ready money for their daily supplies. From the very beginning a member may attend the month-

ly and quarterly meetings, where important matters are discussed, and there he finds that his vote counts for just as much as that of the member who may have £200 of share capital. The constitution of these societies is entirely democratic: all are equal here: each has one vote, and none has more than one vote.

A coöperative society has ordinarily one great advantage over a savings-bank in encouraging thrift. It almost invariably gives 5 per cent. on all share capital—a fact which is a great inducement to its members to increase their number of shares, and which has been a great source of strength to the movement at large. At the same time, when a business has been extended to its utmost limits, the society often finds it difficult or impossible to obtain 5 per cent. without risk. Owing to this consideration, and sometimes, too, because the members who have little capital in the store are jealous of the 5 per cent. being given to the members who have much, most of the societies have limited the amount of capital which one member may hold in a store to a sum far below the legal limit of £200. Of the grave disadvantages of such a policy I shall have occasion to speak a little later on.

If, as sometimes happens, sufficient capital cannot at once be collected to open the store for the whole day, then a shop is frequently opened for the evening only, in the house or cottage of one of the members, a member of the committee, or possibly a member's wife, acting as shopkeeper for the time being. But if things go on well, the store will not long remain in a private house. The committee will begin to look about for suitable premises, and, when they have found them, lay the matter before a general meeting of members. In doing this, particular care must be taken not to get into the hands of a landlord who may have pressure put on him to act contrary to the advantage of the store; indeed, if a shop is built, it is almost essential that the land on which it is built should be freehold or long leasehold. The next step is to engage a manager; if possible, one who is a genuine believer in the coöperative principle, who has been trained in coöperative methods, and acquainted with the routine of the wholesale societies. When the shop is opened, the prices charged must be the ordinary shopkeepers' prices of the district, whether the average be high or low. The shopkeepers may, of course, by lowering prices, compel the store to follow, and in some cases the store may lead the way, but it is the aim of coöperators to charge the average retail price of the district, and not to sink below the level without good reason. The saving effected by the dividend must be emphasized as one of the most important parts of the system, and members must be attracted to the store by that, and not by any strained effort to undersell the local shopkeepers. Coöperation proper thus differs from the civil service system, the attraction of which to a great proportion of those who deal at its stores lies in the fact that its prices are lower than the average of retail traders.

The question will very naturally be asked, How do the private shops fare in competition with the coöperative system? There is a feeling which is very common, and by no means to be wondered at, considering all the circumstances, that coöperation poaches improperly upon the preserves of retail trade. As a matter of fact, the single management of a first-rate man of business will always hold its own in many ways against stores which are managed by committees. It is the little private shops founded by a working-man, his wife or his widow, that are destroyed by the stores; for the people that keep them have no contact with the wholesale market, their goods are bad, and they are themselves often enough in debt to the traveller or to the wholesale man he represents; they are likely to overcharge and to adulterate, and they prey upon their fellow-working-men in a disastrous way. To such shops coöperative stores often bring an extinction which cannot be considered undesirable. The coöperators' goods are the best, their system is attractive, and their existence a real benefit to the mass of the people. But, as I have already said, it is no part of the coöperative principle to enter into a ruinous competition with neighboring shopkeepers, or to beat down prices with the object of ruining a private dealer.

The new coöperative store almost invariably begins its business with groceries and provisions. As that succeeds, a department of hardware, crockery, brushes, and the like, can easily be attached to the grocery department. The next step is usually a bakery, which has been found one of the most successful branches in those parts where members expect shop bread, and do not bake at home. As this succeeds, the store will proceed to hire or build a bakehouse of its own, and many stores have bakehouses of the best kind, fitted with excellent machinery, patent ovens and gas-engines, and do an immense business. A bakery necessitates a cart, and where bakeries exist, delivery is universal. A successful store might then go on to start a department in boots and shoes, and then perhaps another in coals. When societies which are not near collieries grow large, they order truck-loads or ship-loads, and many own trucks, barges, or ships of their own. Tailoring is a not uncommon department, and some societies keep or employ their own tailors. Many stores do an excellent business in milk, dairy, and farm produce, and if some of the village societies could see their way to feeding their own cows and renting a piece of land near their village, they would probably do well. Two departments which have caused considerable trouble to many coöperative committees are drapery and butchery. In the case of drapery, it may be that if the committees were a little more ready to take the lady members of the society into their confidence, the difficulty might be avoided. Perhaps, too, when the societies reach the point of cultivating small farms of their own, the difficulties connected with butchery will also be obviated.

Such, in outline, is the way in which a distributive store may gradually develop its business from the smallest beginnings. Formerly the difficulties were greater, but many of the obstacles which beset the earlier coöperators have been overcome by the existence of wholesale societies in England and Scotland. At one time it not unfrequently happened that the private shopkeepers boycotted a coöperative society by threatening to take away their trade from any wholesale firms which also supplied the store.

The smaller stores had further to contend with many difficulties. The men who managed them had rarely been trained in business. They were ignorant of the qualities of goods, the variations in prices, and the complexities of wholesale markets. Now, on the other hand, the smallest and most inexperienced society has from its outset the immense advantage of ad-

vice and help from the wholesale societies. These wholesale societies are the
work of a federation of coöperative stores,
and they are open to all who wish to join.
They are the chief security which a small
store can have from a business point of
view. Further, they form a link between
the various societies which make up the
great body of coöperators; for while the
individual societies are entirely self-gov-
erning, while they are responsible for
their own failure or their own success, yet
in their dealings with the wholesale, in
the advice and assistance they derive from
it, and in the part control which they or
their delegates exercise over it, the members of each are led to feel that they are
part of a wider movement. If the wholesale society be well managed, and if the
individual society likewise be well managed, the control of the one working
smoothly with the control of the other,
then there is no reason why this federated
system should not be more and more successful. For this end two things are needful. The whole body of members in each
society must take a genuine interest in the
affairs of their own society; they must attend the monthly and quarterly meetings
in the most regular manner; they must
be careful about the selection of their
own officers and committee, and criticise
the management of the business in a reasonable spirit with constant watchfulness.
In the second place, each society must feel
its responsibility in choosing delegates to
manage the wholesale society, and do its
utmost honestly to choose the most competent. It must grasp the vital and essential importance to coöperation of the
wholesale societies, and endeavor to work
with them in all possible business.

If we take two definite examples, one
of a great town coöperative society, and
another of a village society, we may perhaps be able to grasp the importance of
these businesses conducted with working-
men's money, and entirely under working-men's management. The largest of
the town distributive societies is at Leeds.
At the end of 1884 it numbered over 22,000
members, its share capital amounted to
£222,000, and its loan capital to over
£17,000, while it had a reserve fund of
nearly £8000. The value of its land, buildings, and fixed stock was £165,000; the
money received over the counter during
the year amounted to nearly £500,000, and
the total net profits to £58,000.

The educational value to the working-
men concerned of having an immense
business like this under their own entire
control can hardly be estimated too highly. In the intercourse which it promotes,
the discussions which arise as to the appropriation of its funds, the opportunities
at the monthly and quarterly meetings
for every member to raise his voice, if he
choose, upon the affairs of his society, the
education of the citizen for democratic
government is daily advanced. The interests of the society are not confined to its
business. Several of them make a considerable grant yearly for educational
purposes, part of which is now being
spent on lectures by university men.
There are various social and recreative
gatherings promoted by them which help
to unite the members by a stronger tie
than a mere business connection. If a
trades-union may do excellent work in
combining the members of one industry, a
really great coöperative society may encourage the broader spirit which comes of
the intercourse of many who are variously employed.

The second example is of a village coöperative society. It is obvious that any
movement which like coöperation encourages a spirit of self-reliance is, if anything, of greater importance in the country districts than in the large towns. So
far, from a social and educational point of
view, the agricultural laborer is at a great
disadvantage compared with the skilled
artisan. Except where the Agricultural
Laborers' Union has worked, he is isolated, and almost entirely dependent upon
his employer. The one thing needful to
improve his general condition is to afford
him an opportunity to educate himself.
The independent association of a coöperative society, the entire management of its
own business by itself and for itself, without the interference of any inspired authority, is one of the best possible means
of achieving this end. At Harbury, a
village in Warwickshire, such a society
has long existed, to the great benefit of
the country population. At present it
contains 710 members, over 500 of whom
are agricultural laborers, the remainder
being quarrymen. The amount of money
received over the counter per annum is
about £18,000; the property in land and
cottages (nearly all freehold) is worth
£3700, including 23 cottages let to various members of the society, £400 invested

in the wholesale society, and £400 in an association farm in the neighborhood. This society is managed with great success, mainly by agricultural laborers, and the education arising out of the discussions at the monthly and quarterly meetings—such discussions, for instance, as whether this £400 should or should not be invested in the association farm—are most valuable. To show the amount of savings which are accumulated in this society, and the uses to which they are put, I may mention the fact that not long ago five members withdrew a certain portion of their savings (amounting to not less than £300) and invested it in a farm, which they rent as joint tenants, employing a bailiff to manage it. All this was saved without conscious effort out of laborers' wages, which, as a rule, are from 13s. to 14s. a week in the district. At Harbury the store also does the work of a building society for its own members, with infinitely greater security than the ordinary societies, which are too often traps laid for the unwary by designing persons. It has built or acquired 23 cottages, which it lets to its own members at reasonable rents. The Harbury coöperative store has indirectly been most invaluable in extending the allotment system. In the first place, it provides the savings which a laboring-man can profitably put into the soil, then it enables the allotment holder to keep an additional pig, with the certainty of finding a market for the bacon. In another way, less obvious at first sight, it assists the same movement. The presence of a store inevitably lessens the competition for land, inasmuch as where good food can be obtained cheaply the inducement for ordinary people to obtain land and produce for themselves is largely removed.

A similar society to this one at Harbury might exist in every country district in the kingdom, if the laborers were only awake to the immense advantages of the system. There is only one condition—not always to be found—which is essential; that is, that it should be possible to obtain a piece of freehold or long leasehold land on which to build the store. If this condition is wanting, the dread of possible confiscation by a landlord or landlord's agent will paralyze the action of the society. Yet though the obstacles are few and the benefits many, it must be said that this great means of self-improvement is not availed of by the ordinary run of agricultural laborers. Too often neither the politicians proper, nor the clergy, nor the squires, concern themselves to enlighten the men on these things. In these, as in most other matters, they must either remain ignorant, or learn hap-hazard by indirect means.

There is a wide range of work which might be done by a coöperative society if managed with energy and enterprise. As at Harbury, it may also be a building society; it may be, and frequently is, a bank, accepting deposits of money as shares, which have been saved in other ways, and not only by dividend in the stores. Another very important outgrowth of the coöperative movement is association farming, which, if soundly worked on a proper basis, might be of immense assistance in solving the problem how to place the agricultural laborer in a more or less independent position, with a direct interest in the proper cultivation of the land. Coöperative societies could, if they chose, surround themselves with all the healthier influences of working-men's clubs; discussions, debates, and musical gatherings might be promoted in connection with them: they might, in a word, become centres of society for the working classes.

I have already alluded to the educational work which is being done by some of the societies.* Since the coöperative movement began upon its present lines, forty years ago, there never has been a time when education has not been considered by a great many coöperators a most important part of their work. There are at present a large number of societies which do something in this direction through libraries, news-rooms, lectures, and the like, spending altogether over £18,000 in this work. But it must be confessed that a large number of them do almost nothing, and that far the largest part of this sum comes from a few big societies in Lancashire and Yorkshire. But it is also true that many of the best societies which do nothing for education are waking up to the fact that even from a business point of view it is desirable to have an educational fund. It has been shown with considerable force that in many districts the societies which give money for education are doing a better business and paying a better dividend than the socie-

* The Coöperative Wholesale Society's Annual, 1885, p. 423.

ties which do nothing. It is becoming gradually recognized that the business capacity, the energy, and the tact requisite for the coöperative leaders of the future will not come without a very solid addition to the education which finishes with the sixth standard in the national school, or at the age of fifteen or sixteen in one of the secondary schools.

Many coöperators will regard the matter from a still higher point of view. Just as in many a village or town, by doing away with debt and encouraging thrift, the coöperative society has raised the physical and moral condition of hundreds of people, so it may still do a vast deal more for its neighborhood at a trifling cost to each individual member. It might provide a general education in topics which are either of social interest or in the broadest sense political. Apart from teaching on subjects of a more abstract interest, coöperative societies might reasonably make it their aim to educate citizens and voters to a higher level of intelligence, to a greater sense of responsibility, and a more searching examination of their political faith. Readings, lectures, pamphlets, discussions, dealing with the government under which we live, its form, its recent history, and the like, would be most valuable. The health of the citizen; his education; the way in which his life in his house or cottage and his town may be affected for the worse or for the better by government action; what the community must aim at for the general welfare—all these things might be discussed and illustrated. Simple outlines of the present state and government of other nations, simple statements of some of the more recognized beliefs about labor and capital, wages, free-trade, and the like, could be considered and discussed without causing any party rancor or divisions. In this work trained teachers, lecturers, guides of discussions, both university men and others, might be of great use. The work is already being done to a small extent. It might be immensely developed if it were warmly taken up by the working-men's organizations. Let any one who doubts the need or value of such educational work watch closely the municipal elections in many of our towns, and try to ascertain the motives which actuate many of the voters in making their choice. If they will only become alive to this need, trades-unions and coöperative bodies may both

alike do excellent work in making the people more capable and less selfish in their position as citizens.

The vast majority of coöperative societies now in existence are federated into the Coöperative Union, which must be entirely distinguished from the Wholesale Society, which exists solely for business purposes. The Union has a regular constitutional government. Each society has entire home rule with regard to its own affairs, but there is also a federal government, consisting of the Central Board, which is divided into six sections for various parts of the country, Midland, Northern, Northwestern, and so on. Each section elects its own members, each of the societies comprising that section being allowed a voice in the election. Beyond these sectional boards there is one United Board, which is composed of representatives from each of the sectional boards, and holds three regular meetings a year. Subject to the resolutions of the annual Congress, the United Board is the governing body of the Coöperative Union. The Congress has met annually since 1869, and consists of delegates from all the societies which compose the Union. For each annual subscription of 1000d. to the Congress each society is allowed to send one delegate. The meetings take place at Whitsuntide, and the place of meeting is changed yearly. It is the practice to invite some eminent man to preside on the first day and deliver an inaugural address. Among the most interesting of recent Congresses was that held at Oxford in 1882, under the presidency of Lord Reay. The delegates were entertained with right good will by the university men, both junior and senior, for several days. The week opened with a special service in the cathedral, at which Canon Scott Holland preached. The delegates were all entertained at luncheon in Christ-church Hall; they held their business meetings in the Town-hall, but invited the head of a college to give an address. Parties of the delegates were guided round the colleges and university buildings, and one day ended with teas or suppers in various undergraduates' rooms, where much friendliness was shown on both sides, which has not yet been forgotten by either.

It used to be said by the late Professor Smith that the ordinary undergraduate's knowledge of English working-men was a hasty generalization from his scout,* and on the other hand, a coöperative friend of mine, when he introduced me as coming from Oxford, used invariably to explain that that was "the place where they turned out the parsons in bandboxes." A good many of these preconceptions on both sides were considerably modified by the Congress of 1882. Some of us may be allowed to hope that a few days spent at Oxford in the perfect time of the May term did something to stimulate the coöperators in their own educational work.

The organization for propaganda work, the general interests of the union, and such political matters as affect the principle of coöperation are intrusted to the Central Board. Party politics are avoided by coöperators in their dealings as coöperators, although on occasions political action has been forced upon them by the hostility of private traders.

Another work intrusted to the Union, or Central Board, is the literary department, and by it a vast deal of literary matter dealing with coöperation is annually published. This includes the Congress Report (a volume of 120 pages), which contains a full record of the transactions at Congress, together with detailed statistics of coöperation. Then there are business publications, manuals on book-keeping, auditing, and such forth, intended to aid coöperators in the management of their associations. Besides these there are books, tracts, and pamphlets bearing on the principles and objects of coöperation, a large number of which are given away with a view to rousing an interest in the subject. The Wholesale Society likewise does its work in the literary propaganda. It publishes a yearly annual containing a fund of information on subjects connected with coöperation, and also papers on various subjects by well-known men. Lastly, there is the journal of the movement, the *Coöperative News*, which is conducted by a special news society, with a weekly circulation of nearly 30,000. It is remarkable as being almost the only true working-men's paper in England. Its cost is only 1*d*., and it is about the size of the *Spectator* or *Saturday Review*, and is a mine of information on working-men's subjects.

Such is, in the main, an outline of the distributive side of the coöperative movement. On this side it has been, when

* A college servant.

worked with watchfulness upon business-like principles, an entire success, while admitting still of infinite extension. The same cannot be said of the productive side, the comparative failure of which is now the chief difficulty of coöperators. It has already been shown that one of the grand objects of the distributive societies is to encourage saving, and that with this end in view 5 per cent. is given upon dividends which are not withdrawn, and upon other money which is allowed to accumulate in the store; but sooner or later most of the societies reach that point where they have more money than can be used in the extension of their own business. The problem then confronts them, where can they find an investment which will safely bring them in 5 per cent., and save them from loss in paying their members this comparatively high rate of interest? The consequence is that a vast number of societies refuse to allow their members to leave more than £100 in the store, and some even draw the line at £30 or £50. Yet to refuse capital, when the further objects of coöperation as a means of giving employment to working-men with working-men's own capital are considered, is obviously suicidal. Possibly it would be better to lower the rate of interest paid upon savings than to be driven to such an alternative. However that may be, if all the money which working-men might have left with societies had been profitably invested from the beginning, and none refused which members offered, there would now be many millions more of working-men's money in hand, which has passed from them into the pockets of great capitalists. The hopes which have long been cherished by earnest coöperators, and which have so far been in the main unfulfilled, are that this money may be employed in coöperative production. Though thousands of pounds are available for the purpose, little has yet been done in this direction, and to-day many coöperative societies have far more money on their hands than they know what to do with. However, these hopes are not abandoned by coöperators, and that the same hopes are cherished by others, who have not been directly connected with the coöperative movement, may be seen from the fact that many of the leading trades-unions, bodies which also have large sums invested in the ordinary enterprises promoted by big capitalists, are looking to the employment of these funds in coöperative industry. The productive side of coöperation then has two main ends in view, neither of which has yet been adequately fulfilled. One is to employ profitably the large sums of money which are accumulating in the distributive stores; the other—which is the higher and ultimate end—to make working-men their own capitalists, and promote self-employment by groups of workers.

Unquestionably one of the greatest causes of disappointment has arisen from the English Wholesale Society. Here there is a society doing a business of nearly £5,000,000 a year, and still purchasing many articles which coöperators had hoped they would have had the genius and capacity to manufacture for themselves. Yet, with the exception of some boot manufactories at Leicester, and one or two other insignificant works elsewhere, they do nothing in the way of manufacturing, and have taken no really important new departure in the course of the last ten years. Working-men have constantly argued that many of the great industrial geniuses who have contributed to the making of large profits in the industries of England during the last quarter of a century are men who have passed out of the ranks of the working class. How is it that many such men have not found their way on to the management of the Wholesale Society?—men of unique financial and industrial genius, men who might have commanded the confidence of their fellows, and being real "masters of industry," have succeeded in employing profitably in manufacturing the immense sums of money which the Wholesale Society might have had at its disposal. The hopes thus expressed by many have only been realized to a very small degree indeed, and the Wholesale Society, as well as many of the larger societies, have not unfrequently large sums lying idle at their bankers' which they do not know how to employ. It remains to be seen whether the views of Professor Walker—one of the ablest economists of our day—are likely to prove permanently true. After speaking of the failure of certain coöperative industries, Professor Walker goes on to say: "I see nothing which indicates that, within any near future, industry is to become less despotic than it now is. The power of the master in production, 'the captain of industry,' has steadily increased

throughout the present century with the increasing complexity of commercial relations, with the greater concentration of capital, with improvements in apparatus and machinery, with the multiplication of styles and fashions, with the localization and specialization of manufactures."

There are undoubtedly, but not on a large scale, coöperative productive enterprises in existence which are an exception to the general statement of Mr. Walker. Among these are the shoe-works of the Wholesale Society at Leicester, already mentioned, the Coöperative Printing Society at Manchester, the Fustian Manufacturing Society at Hebden Bridge, in Yorkshire, and some others. At the Leicester works the coöperative principle is not perfectly applied. The workers have no share of the profits, as they have in the two other industries. Yet when these have been mentioned, it still remains true, on the whole, that there is no sign of any very great change at present in the direction of coöperative production, although, as I have shown, the working-men have plenty of money for the purpose of making experiments. It is not for want of discussion that progress is prevented. The subject is being perpetually discussed, but no advance results. There is a Coöperative Aid Association in the south, and another called the Labor Association, which aims at specially developing the productive work. Small beginnings are being made, to which all reasonable people will wish success.

I am not here dealing with schemes of industrial partnership, or of profit-sharing. They form another though a kindred subject, and doubtless many of the same remarks apply, with certain modifications, to them also. The present article deals with working-men's money and coöperative effort by working-men for working-men. And what is the strength of this kind of association is also in certain points its weakness. It is thoroughly democratic in its government; it is self-supporting, self-reliant, and the power of a vote belongs to all its members. But it has also the weakness of a democracy. Where it is necessary to choose men of special business capacity and mechanical genius, as, for instance, to conduct the business of the Wholesale Society, a wide popular suffrage is not in all cases calculated to make the desirable choice. The best men are often unknown, or withdraw themselves with unnecessary modesty from the public service of the society, while inferior candidates for honor are numerous, and, when once elected, are too likely to be elected over and over again.

Thus to those who would reverse Plato's method, and look to see the state writ small in some association or combined enterprise, there will be much that is striking in the study of this coöperative movement. They may gather from it in anticipation some of the evils and many of the bright points in the completer democracy to which we are unquestionably moving. Its importance in preparing the people for such political changes can hardly be overestimated.

In a country which till the last two generations was governed on a method which was practically feudal, it is, above all things, to independent association among working-men that we must look to foster the spirit of self-reliance which alone can avoid the evils and choose the good of popular government. The coöperative movement is open to criticism in many ways, but its supporters may fairly claim for it that it has encouraged thrift, that it has promoted a feeling of sympathy with public aims, and a desire for the well-being of the community generally, and also that it has developed a knowledge of business which has a high social and political value. The distributive stores have in many places rescued from a position of disadvantage those who can least of all afford to be in such a position. Where they have been successfully established in the country they have placed the best possible goods before the country people at ordinary prices, and

have given them the opportunity of saving out of the scantiest wages. What has been done in one village might be done in many others, and one of the pressing needs of the future is to enable the agricultural laborer to learn what an immense disadvantage he is at compared with his brothers in the town, and to teach him the methods by which he may lessen some of the difficulties which surround him.

Only those who know what the condition of the English working classes some fifty years ago really was can properly appreciate the changes which have been wrought largely by independent associative work in trades-unions, coöperative societies, and friendly societies. The three movements have gone on hand in hand, and some day I trust the link between unionists and coöperators will be tightened. Mr. Burt, whose opinion is so widely respected by his fellow-unionists and all who care for English working-men, has told us that he too looks forward in hope that coöperative industry may do great things for the future of the industrial class. The wastefulness of our present method of supply through unnecessary middle-men, and the constant strain of relations between employers and employed, are two of the problems of to-day which need the thoughtful consideration of all earnest men. The coöperative movement has attempted to deal with them, and in so doing may fairly claim the widest sympathy. If it has not altogether succeeded, yet the work it has accomplished in forty years has surpassed the hopes of those who were most sanguine at its beginning.

LOVE'S DESERTED PALACE.

BY PHILIP BOURKE MARSTON.

REGARD it well, 'tis yet a lordly place,
  Palace of Love, once warmed with sacred fires,
Sounding from end to end with joy of lyres,
Fragrant with incense, with great lights ablaze.
The fires are dead now; dead the festal rays;
  No more the music marries keen desires,
  No more the incense of the shrine aspires,
And of Love's godhead there is now no trace.

Yet if one walked at night through those dim halls,
  Might it not chance that ghostly shapes would rise,
And ghostly lights glide glimmering down the walls,
  That there might be a stir, a sound of sighs,
And gentle voices answering gentle calls,
  And gentle, wandering wraiths of melodies?

HARVEST NOON.

BY CHARLES W. COLEMAN, JUN.

A BEE through clover droning;
A butterfly apause upon a rose;
A long low stretch of meadow, daisies blooming;
A reaper singing as he fieldward goes;
A wafted breath of woodbine rich perfuming;
Adown the dusty road a dol'rous dove
    Low moaning;
O'er all the world around, below, above,
The golden heat-haze hanging in the harvest noon's repose.

The crimson poppies sleeping
Amid the wheat's ripe tassels' treasure bent;
The cattle knee-deep in the sweet marsh sedges,
Slow chewing cuds of indolent content;
A reaper whisp'ring low his passion pledges,
A brown girl gleaner answ'ring looks of love,
    Tryst keeping;
O'er all the world, around, below, above,
The golden heat-haze hanging, and the harvest noon is spent.

IN THE GARDEN.

BY FRANCES L. MACE.

WAS it thou, Mignonette?
    For while the South Wind stills his low complaints
To bear the censer of thy rich perfume,
I read, upon a terrace warm with bloom,
Flower-stories of the Virgin and the Saints.
I read that Mary, passing through a field,
Her heart oppressed with that mysterious gloom
Which ever falls on those whom Heaven has sealed
For glory's crown—and doom,
Stooped often, in her meditative walk,
To pluck some favored blossom from its stalk,
Some happy flower, which bowed its beauteous head
And Summer's odorous benediction shed.
But one poor fragile weed,
Nor beautiful nor sweet,
Which she would never heed
But that it clung so close about her feet,
With tender touch she gathered; to her breast
And to her lips the slighted floweret pressed,
Because so frail, so hopeless, loved the best!

Oh, then the pâle weed strove
To whisper forth its rapture and its love;
And while it mutely trembled and adored,
Like praise of spirit risen
From long and woful prison,
A tide of fragrance from its heart was poured!
Nor once in all the ages has it sighed
For beauty's coronal of brilliant hue,
Red of the rose, or violet's winsome blue,
By that one kiss of pity glorified.
The garden's lowly, well-beloved flower,
A miracle of sweetness from that hour—
Mignonette, was it thou?

THEIR PILGRIMAGE.

BY CHARLES DUDLEY WARNER.

CHAPTER XVI.

THE occupation of being a red man, a merchant of baskets and bead-work, is taken up by so many traders with a brogue and a twang at our watering-places that it is difficult for the traveller to keep alive any sentiment about this race. But at a station beyond Lewiston our tourists were reminded of it, and of its capacity for adopting our civilization in its most efflorescent development. The train was invaded by a band of Indians, or, to speak correctly, by an Indian band. There is nothing in the world like a brass band in a country town; it probably gives more pleasure to the performers than any other sort of labor. Yet the delight it imparts to the listeners is apt to be tem-

pered by a certain sense of incongruity between the peaceful citizens who compose it and the bellicose din they produce. There is a note of barbarism in the brassy jar and clamor of the instruments, enhanced by the bewildering ambition of each player to force through his piece the most noise and jangle, which is not always covered and subdued into a harmonious whole by the whang of the bass drum.

There was nothing of this incongruity between this band of Tuscaroras and their occupation. Unaccustomed to associate the North American Indian with music, the traveller at once sees the natural relation of the Indians and the brass band. These Tuscaroras were stalwart fellows, broad-faced, big-limbed, serious, and they carried themselves with a clumsy but impressive dignity. There was no uniformity in their apparel, yet each one wore some portion of a martial and resplendent dress—an ornamented kepi, or a scarlet sash, or big golden epaulets, or a military coat braided with yellow. The leader, who was a giant, and carried the smallest instrument, outshone all the others in his incongruous splendor. No soon-

er had they found seats at one end of
the car than they unlimbered, and began
through their various reluctant instruments to deploy a tune. Although the
tune did not get well into line, the effect
was marvellous. The car was instantly
filled to bursting. Miss Lamont, who
was reading at the other end of the car,
gave a nervous start, and looked up in
alarm. King and Forbes promptly opened windows, but this gave little relief.
The trombone pumped and growled, the
trumpet blared, the big brass instrument
with a calyx like the monstrous tropical
water-lily quivered and howled, and the
drum, banging into the discord, smashed
every tympanum in the car. The Indians
looked pleased. No sooner had they broken one tune into fragments than they
took up another, and the car roared and
rattled and jarred all the way to the lonely station where the band debarked, and
was last seen convoying a straggling Odd-
Fellows' picnic down a country road.

The incident, trivial in itself, gave rise
to serious reflections touching the capacity
and use of the red man in modern life.
Here is a peaceful outlet for all his wild
instincts. Let the government turn all
the hostiles on the frontier into brass
bands, and we shall hear no more of the
Indian question.

The railway along the shore of Lake
Ontario is for the most part monotonous.
After leaving the picturesque highlands
about Lewiston, the country is flat, and
although the view over the lovely sheet
of blue water is always pleasing, there is
something bleak even in summer in this
vast level expanse from which the timber
has been cut away. It may have been
mere fancy, but to the tourists the air
seemed thin, and the scene, artistically
speaking, was cold and colorless. With
every desire to do justice to the pretty
town of Oswego, which lies on a gentle
slope by the lake, it had to them an out-
of-doors, unprotected, remote aspect. Seen
from the station, it did not appear what it
is, the handsomest city on Lake Ontario,
with the largest starch factory in the
world.

It was toward evening when the train
reached Cape Vincent, where the steamer
waited to transport passengers down the
St. Lawrence. The weather had turned
cool; the broad river, the low shores, the
long islands which here divide its lake-
like expanse, wanted atmospheric warmth,

and the tourists could not escape the feeling of lonesomeness, as if they were on
the other side of civilization, rather than
in one of the great streams of summer
frolic and gayety. It was therefore a
very agreeable surprise to them when a
travelling party alighted from one of the
cars, which had come from Rome, among
whom they recognized Mrs. Farquhar.

"I knew my education never could be
complete," said that lady as she shook
hands, "and you never would consider
me perfectly in the Union, until I had
seen the Thousand Islands; and here I
am, after many Yankee tribulations."

"And why didn't you come by Niagara?" asked Miss Lamont.

"My dear, perhaps your uncle could
tell you that I saw enough of Niagara
when I was a young lady, during the
war. The cruelest thing you Yankees
did was to force us, who couldn't fight, to
go over there for sympathy. The only
bearable thing about the fall of Richmond was that it relieved me from that
Fall. But where," she added, turning to
King, "are the rest of your party?"

"If you mean the Bensons," said he,
with a rather rueful countenance, "I believe they have gone to the White Mountains."

"Oh, not lost, but gone before. You
believe? If you knew the nights I have
lain awake thinking about you two, or
you three! I fear you have not been wide-
awake enough yourself."

"I knew I could depend on you, Mrs.
Farquhar, for that."

The steamer was moving off, taking a
wide sweep to follow the channel. The
passengers were all engaged in ascertaining the names of the islands and of the
owners of the cottages and club-houses.
"It is a kind of information I have learned to dispense with," said Mrs. Farquhar.
And the tourists, except three or four resolutely inquisitive, soon tired of it. The
islands multiplied; the boat wound in and
out among them in narrow straits. To
sail thus amid rocky islets, hirsute with
firs, promised to be an unfailing pleasure.
It might have been, if darkness had not
speedily fallen. But it is notable how
soon passengers on a steamer become indifferent and listless in any sort of scenery. Where the scenery is monotonous
and repeats itself mile after mile and hour
after hour, an intolerable weariness falls
upon the company. The enterprising

ILLUMINATING.

group who have taken all the best seats in the bow, with the intention of gormandizing the views, exhibit little staying power; either the monotony or the wind drives them into the cabin. And passengers in the cabin occupying chairs and sofas, surrounded by their baggage, always look bored and melancholy.

"I always think," said Mrs. Farquhar, "that I am going to enjoy a ride on a steamer, but I never do. It is impossible to get out of a draught, and the progress is so slow that variety enough is not presented to the eye to keep one from *ennui.*" Nevertheless Mrs. Farquhar and King remained on deck, in such shelter as they could find, during the three hours' sail, braced up by the consciousness that they were doing their duty in regard to the enterprise that has transformed this lovely stream into a highway of display and enjoyment. Miss Lamont and the artist went below, frankly confessing that they could see all that interested them from the cabin windows. And they had their

reward; for in this little cabin, where supper was served, a drama was going on between the cook and the two waiting-maids and the cabin boy, a drama of love and coquetry and jealousy and hope deferred, quite as important to those concerned as any of the watering-place comedies, and played with entire unconsciousness of the spectators.

The evening was dark, and the navigation in the tortuous channels sometimes difficult, and might have been dangerous but for the light-houses. The steamer crept along in the shadows of the low islands, making frequent landings, and never long out of sight of the illuminations of hotels and cottages. Possibly by reason of these illuminations this passage has more variety by night than by day. There was certainly a fascination about this alternating brilliancy and gloom. On nearly every island there was at least a cottage, and on the larger islands were great hotels, camp-meeting establishments, and houses and tents for the entertain-

ALEXANDRIA BAY.

ment of thousands of people. Late as it was in the season, most of the temporary villages and solitary lodges were illuminated; colored lamps were set about the grounds, Chinese lanterns hung in the evergreens, and on half a dozen lines radiating from the belfry of the hotel to the ground, while all the windows blazed and scintillated. Occasionally as the steamer passed these places of irrepressible gayety rockets were let off, Bengal-lights were burned, and once a cannon attempted to speak the joy of the sojourners. It was like a continued Fourth of July, and King's heart burned within him with national pride. Even Mrs. Farquhar had to admit that it was a fairy spectacle. During the months of July and August this broad river, with its fantastic islands, is at night simply a highway of glory. The worldlings and the camp-meeting gatherings vie with each other in the display of colored lights and fire-works. And such places as the Thousand Islands Park, Wellesley and Wesley parks, and so on, twinkling with lamps and rosy with pyrotechnics, like sections of the sky dropped upon the earth, create in the mind of the

steamer pilgrim an indescribable earthly and heavenly excitement. He does not look upon these displays as advertisements of rival resorts, but as generous contributions to the hilarity of the world.

It is, indeed, a marvellous spectacle, this view for thirty or forty miles, and the simple traveller begins to realize what American enterprise is when it lays itself out for pleasure. These miles and miles of cottages, hotels, parks, and camp-meetings are the creation of only a few years, and probably can scarcely be paralleled elsewhere in the world for rapidity of growth. But the strongest impression the traveller has is of the public spirit of these summer sojourners, speculators, and religious enthusiasts. No man lives to himself alone, or builds his cottage for his selfish gratification. He makes fantastic carpentry, and paints and decorates and illuminates and shows fire-works, for the genuine sake of display. One marvels that a person should come here for rest and pleasure in a spirit of such devotion to the public weal, and devote himself night after night for months to illuminating his house and lighting up his island, and tearing open the sky with rockets and shaking the air with powder explosions, in order that the river may be continually *en fête.*

At half past eight the steamer rounded into view of the hotels and cottages at Alexandria Bay, and the enchanting scene

If Alexandria Bay was less enchanting as a spectacle by daylight, it was still exceedingly lovely and picturesque; islands and bays and winding waterways could not be better combined for beauty, and the structures that taste or ambition has raised on the islands and rocky points are

"A SORT OF LINEN-DUSTER CONGREGATION."

drew all the passengers to the deck. The Thousand Islands Hotel, and the Crossman House, where our party found excellent accommodations, were blazing and sparkling like the spectacular palaces in an opera scene. Rows of colored lamps were set thickly along the shore, and disposed everywhere among the rocks on which the Crossman House stands; lights glistened from all the islands, from a thousand row-boats, and in all the windows. It was very like Venice, seen from the lagoon, when the Italians make a gala-night.

well enough in keeping with the general holiday aspect. One of the prettiest of these cottages is the Bonnicastle of the late Dr. Holland, whose spirit more or less pervades this region. It is charmingly situated on a projecting point of gray rocks veined with color, enlivened by touches of scarlet bushes and brilliant flowers planted in little spots of soil contrasting with the evergreen shrubs. It commands a varied and delicious prospect, and has an air of repose and peace.

I am sorry to say that while Forbes and

Miss Lamont floated, so to speak, in all this beauty, like the light-hearted revellers they were, King was scarcely in a mood to enjoy it. It seemed to him fictitious and a little forced. There was no message for him at the Crossman House. His restlessness and absent-mindedness could not escape the observation of Mrs. Farquhar, and as the poor fellow sadly needed a confidante, she was soon in possession of his story.

"I hate slang," she said, when he had painted the situation black enough to suit Mrs. Bartlett-Glow even, "and I will not give my sex away, but I know something of feminine doubtings and subterfuges, and I give you my judgment that Irene is just fretting herself to death, and praying that you may have the spirit to ride rough-shod over her scruples. Yes, it is just as true in this prosaic time as it ever was, that women like to be carried off by violence. In their secret hearts, whatever they may say, they like to see a knight batter down the tower and put all the garrison except themselves to the sword. I know that I ought to be on Mrs. Glow's side. It is the sensible side, the prudent side; but I do admire recklessness in love. Probably you'll be uncomfortable, perhaps unhappy—you are certain to be if you marry to please society and not yourself—but better a thousand times one wild rush of real passion, of self-forgetting love, than an age of stupid, conventional affection approved by your aunt. Oh, these calculating young people!" Mrs. Farquhar's voice trembled and her eyes flashed. "I tell you, my friend, life is not worth living in a conventional stagnation. You see in society how nature revenges itself when its instincts are repressed."

Mrs. Farquhar turned away, and King saw that her eyes were full of tears. She stood a moment looking away over the sparkling water to the soft islands on the hazy horizon. Was she thinking of her own marriage? Death had years ago dissolved it, and were these tears not those of mourning, but for the great experience possible in life, so seldom realized, missed forever? Before King could frame, in the tumult of his own thoughts, any reply, she turned toward him again, with her usual smile, half of badinage and half of tenderness, and said,

"Come, this is enough of tragedy for one day; let us go on the *Island Wander-er*, with the other excursionists, among the isles of the blest."

The little steamer had already its load, and presently was under way, puffing and coughing, on its usual afternoon trip among the islands. The passengers were silent, and appeared to take the matter seriously—a sort of linen-duster congregation, of the class who figure in the homely dialect poems of the Northern bards, Mrs. Farquhar said. They were chiefly interested in knowing the names of the successful people who had built these fantastic dwellings, and who lived on illuminations. Their curiosity was easily gratified, for in most cases the owners had painted their names, and sometimes their places of residence, in staring white letters on conspicuous rocks. There was also exhibited, for the benefit of invalids, by means of the same white paint, here and there the name of a medicine that is a household word in this patent-right generation. So the little steamer sailed, comforted by these remedies, through the strait of Safe Nervine, round the bluff of Safe Tonic, into the open bay of Safe Liver Cure. It was a healing voyage, and one in which enterprise was so allied with beauty that no utilitarian philosopher could raise a question as to the market value of the latter.

The voyage continued as far as Gananoque, in Canada, where the passengers went ashore, and wandered about in a disconsolate way to see nothing. King said, however, that he was more interested in the place than in any other he had seen, because there was nothing interesting in it; it was absolutely without character, or a single peculiarity either of Canada or of the United States. Indeed, this north shore seemed to all the party rather bleak even in summer-time, and the quality of the sunshine thin.

It was, of course, a delightful sail, abounding in charming views, up "lost channels," through vistas of gleaming water overdrooped by tender foliage, and now and then great stretches of sea, and always islands, islands.

"Too many islands too much alike," at length exclaimed Mrs. Farquhar, "and too many tasteless cottages and temporary camping structures."

The performance is, indeed, better than the prospectus. For there are not merely the poetical Thousand Islands; by actual count there are sixteen hundred and ninety-two. The artist and Miss Lamont were trying to sing a fine song they discovered in the Traveller's Guide, inspired perhaps by that sentimental ditty, "The Isles of Greece, the Isles of Greece," beginning,

"O Thousand Isles! O Thousand Isles!"

It seemed to King that a poem might be constructed more in accordance with the facts and with the scientific spirit of the age. Something like this:

"O Sixteen Hundred Ninety-two Isles!
    O Islands 1692!
Where the fisher spreads his wiles,
    And the muskallonge goes through!
Forever the cottager gilds the same
    With nightly pyrotechnic flame;
And it's O the Isles!
    The 1692!"

Aside from the pyrotechnics, the chief occupations of this place are boating and fishing. Boats abound — row-boats, sail-boats, and steam-launches for excursion parties. The river consequently presents an animated appearance in the season, and the prettiest effects are produced by the white sails dipping about among the green islands. The favorite boat is a canoe with a small sail stepped forward, which is steered without centre-board or rudder, merely by a change of position in the boat of the man who holds the sheet. While the fishermen are here, it would seem that the long, snaky pickerel is the chief game pursued and caught. But this is not the case when the fishermen return here, for then it appears that they have been dealing mainly with muskallonge, and with bass by the way. No other part of the country originates so many excellent fish stories as the Sixteen Hundred and Ninety-two Islands, and King had heard so many of them that he suspected there must be fish in these waters. That afternoon, when they returned from Gananoque, he accosted an old fisherman who sat in his boat at the wharf awaiting a customer.

"I suppose there is fishing here in the season?"

The man glanced up, but deigned no reply to such impertinence.

"Could you take us where we would be likely to get any muskallonge?"

A FISHERMAN.

"Likely?" asked the man. "What do you suppose I am here for?"

"I beg your pardon. I'm a stranger here. I'd like to try my hand at a muskallonge. About how do they run here as to size?"

"Well," said the fisherman, relenting a little, "that depends upon who takes you out. If you want a little sport, I can take you to it. They are running pretty well this season, or were a week ago."

"It is too late?"

"Well, they are scarcer than they were, unless you know where to go. I call forty pounds light for a muskallonge; fifty to seventy is about my figure. If you ain't used to this kind of fishing, and go with me, you'd better tie yourself in the boat. They are a powerful fish. You see that little island yonder? A muskallonge dragged me in this boat four times round that island one day, and just as I thought I was tiring him out he jumped clean over the island, and I had to cut the line."

King thought he had heard something like this before, and he engaged the man for the next day. That evening was the last of the grand illuminations for the season, and our party went out in the common steam-launch to see it. Although some of the cottages were vacated, and the display was not so extensive as in August, it was still marvellously beautiful, and the night voyage around the illuminated islands was something long to be remembered. There were endless devices of colored lamps and lanterns, figures of crosses, crowns, the Seal of Solomon, and the most strange effects produced on foliage and in the water by red and green and purple fires. It was a night of enchantment, and the hotel and its grounds on the dark background of the night were like the stately pleasure-house in "Kubla Khan."

But the season was drawing to an end. The hotels, which could not find room for the throngs on Saturday night, say, were nearly empty on Monday, so easy are pleasure-seekers frightened away by a touch of cold, forgetting that in such a resort the most enjoyable part of the year comes with the mellow autumn days. That night at ten o'clock the band was scraping away in the deserted parlor, without not another person in attendance, without a single listener. Miss Lamont happened to peep through the window-blinds from the piazza and discover this residuum of gayety. The band itself was half asleep, but by sheer force of habit it kept on, the fiddlers drawing the perfunctory bows, and the melancholy clarionet men breathing their expressive sighs. It was a dismal sight. The next morning the band had vanished.

The morning was lowering, and a steady rain soon set in for the day. No fishing, no boating; nothing but drop, drop, and the reminiscence of past pleasure. Mist enveloped the islands and shut out the view. Even the spirits of Mrs. Farquhar were not proof against this, and she tried to amuse herself by reconstructing the season out of the specimens of guests who remained, who were for the most part young ladies who had duty written on their faces, and were addicted to spectacles.

"It could not have been," she thought, "ultra-fashionable or madly gay. I think

the good people come here; those who are willing to illuminate."

"Oh, there is a fast enough life at some of the hotels in the summer," said the artist.

"Very likely. Still, if I were recruiting for school-marms, I should come here. I like it thoroughly, and mean to be here earlier next year. The scenery is enchanting, and I quite enjoy being with Proverbial Philosophy people."

Late in the gloomy afternoon King went down to the office, and the clerk handed him a letter. He took it eagerly, but his countenance fell when he saw that it bore a New York post-mark, and had been forwarded from Richfield. It was not from Irene. He put it in his pocket and went moodily to his room. He was in no mood to read a homily from his uncle.

Ten minutes after, he burst into Forbes's room with the open letter in his hand.

"See here, old fellow, I'm off to the Profile House. Can you get ready?"

"Get ready? Why, you can't go anywhere to-night."

"Yes, I can. The proprietor says he will send us across to Redwood to catch the night train for Ogdensburg."

"But how about the Lachine Rapids? You have been talking about those rapids for two months. I thought that was what we came here for."

"Do you want to run right into the small-pox at Montreal?"

"Oh, I don't mind. I never take anything of that sort."

"But don't you see that it isn't safe for the Lamonts and Mrs. Farquhar to go there?"

"I suppose not; I never thought of that. I never cared anything about the rapids. You have dragged me all over the continent, and I didn't suppose there was any way of escaping the rapids. But what is the row now? Has Irene telegraphed you that she has got over her chill?"

"Read that letter."

Forbes took the sheet and read:

"NEW YORK, *September* 2, 1885.

"MY DEAR STANHOPE,—We came back to town yesterday, and I find a considerable arrears of business demanding my attention. A suit has been brought against the Lavalle Iron Company, of which I have been the attorney for some years,

THE OBSERVATION CAR.

for the possession of an important part of its territory, and I must send somebody to Georgia before the end of this month to look up witnesses and get ready for the defence. If you are through your junketing by that time, it will be an admirable opportunity for you to learn the practical details of the business. . . . Perhaps it may quicken your ardor in the matter if I communicate to you another fact. Penelope wrote me from Richfield, in a sort of panic, that she feared you had compromised your whole future by a rash engagement with a young lady from Cyrusville, Ohio—a Miss Benson—and she asked me to use my influence with you. I replied to her that I thought that, in the language of the street, you had compromised your future, if that were true, for about a hundred cents on the dollar. I have had business relations with Mr. Ben-

son for twenty years. He is the principal owner in the Lavalle Iron Mine, and he is one of the most sensible, sound, and upright men of my acquaintance. He comes of a good old New England stock, and if his daughter has the qualities of her father—and I hear that she has been exceedingly well educated besides—she is not a bad match even for a Knickerbocker.

"Hoping that you will be able to report at the office before the end of the month,

"I am affectionately yours,

"SCHUYLER BREVOORT."

"Well, that's all right," said the artist, after a pause. "I suppose the world might get on if you spend another night in this hotel. But if you must go, I'll bring on the women and the baggage when navigation opens in the morning."

A HALT FOR THE VIEW.

CHAPTER XVII.

THE White Mountains are as high as ever, as fine in sharp outline against the sky, as savage, as tawny; no other mountains in the world of their height so well keep, on acquaintance, the respect of mankind. There is a quality of refinement in their granite robustness; their desolate, bare heights and sky-scraping ridges are rosy in the dawn and violet at sunset, and their profound green gulfs are still mysterious. Powerful as man is, and pushing, he cannot wholly vulgarize them. He can reduce the valleys and the show "freaks" of nature to his own moral level, but the vast bulks and the summits remain for the most part haughty and pure.

Yet undeniably something of the romance of adventure in a visit to the White Hills is wanting, now that the rail-

ways penetrate every valley, and all the physical obstacles of the journey are removed. One can never again feel the thrill that he experienced when, after a weary all-day jolting in the stage-coach, or plodding hour after hour on foot, he suddenly came in view of a majestic granite peak. Never again by the new rail can he have the sensation that he enjoyed in the ascent of Mount Washington by the old bridle-path from Crawford's, when, climbing out of the woods and advancing upon that marvellous backbone of rock, the whole world opened upon his awed vision, and the pyramid of the summit stood up in majesty against the sky. Nothing, indeed, is valuable that is easily obtained. This modern experiment of putting us through the world—the world of literature, experience, and travel—at excursion rates is of doubtful expediency.

I cannot but think that the White Mountains are cheapened a little by the facilities of travel and the multiplication of excellent places of entertainment. If scenery were a sentient thing, it might feel indignant at being vulgarly stared at, overrun and trampled on, by a horde of tourists who chiefly value luxurious hotels and easy conveyance. It would be mortified to hear the talk of the excursionists, which is more about the quality of the tables and the beds, and the rapidity with which the "whole thing can be done," than about the beauty and the sublimity of nature. The mountain, however, was made for man, and not man for the mountain; and if the majority of travellers only get out of these hills what they are capable of receiving, it may be some satisfaction to the hills that they still reserve their glories for the eyes that can appreciate them. Perhaps nature is not sensitive about being run after for its freaks and eccentricities. If it were, we could account for the catastrophe, a few years ago, in the Franconia Notch flume. Everybody went there to see a bowlder which hung suspended over the stream in the narrow cañon. This curiosity attracted annually thousands of people, who apparently cared more for this toy than for anything else in the region. And one day, as if tired of this misdirected adoration, nature organized a dam on the side of Mount Lafayette, filled it with water, and then suddenly let loose a flood which tore open the cañon, carried the bowlder away, and spread ruin far and wide. It said as plainly as possible, You must look at me, and not at my trivial accidents. But man is an ingenious creature, and nature is no match for him. He now goes, in increasing number, to see where the bowlder once hung, and spends his time in hunting for it in the acres of wreck and débris. And in order to satisfy reasonable human curiosity, the proprietors of the flume have been obliged to select a bowlder and label it as the one that was formerly the shrine of pilgrimage.

In his college days King had more than once tramped all over this region, knapsack on back, lodging at chance farmhouses and second-class hotels, living on viands that would kill any but a robust climber, and enjoying the life with a keen zest only felt by those who are abroad at all hours, and enabled to surprise Nature in all her varied moods. It is the chance encounters that are most satisfactory; Na-

ture is apt to be whimsical to him who approaches her of set purpose at fixed hours. He remembered also the jolting stage-coaches, the scramble for places, the exhilaration of the drive, the excitement of the arrival at the hotels, the sociability engendered by this juxtaposition and jostle of travel. It was therefore with a sense of personal injury that, when he reached Bethlehem Junction, he found a

AN EPISTLE FROM THE SUMMIT.

railway to the Profile House, and another to Bethlehem. In the interval of waiting for his train he visited Bethlehem Street, with its mile of caravansaries, big boarding-houses, shops, and city veneer, and although he was delighted, as an American, with the "improvements" and with the air of refinement, he felt that if he wanted retirement and rural life, he might as well be with the hordes in the depths of the Adirondack wilderness. But in his impatience to reach his destination he was not sorry to avail himself of the railway to the Profile House. And he admired the ingenuity which had carried this road through nine miles of shabby firs and balsams, in a way absolutely devoid of interest, in order to heighten the effect of the surprise at the end in the sudden arrival at the Franconia Notch. From

THE CLOUDS BREAKING.

couples promenaded up and down; and from the distant parlor, through the long passage, came the sound of the band. It was easy to see at a glance that the place had a distinct character, freedom from conventionality, and an air of reposeful enjoyment. A large proportion of the assembly being residents for the summer, there was so much of the family content that the transient tourists could little disturb it by the introduction of their element of worry and haste.

King found here many acquaintances, for fashion follows a certain routine, and there is a hidden law by which the White Mountains break the transition from the sea-coast to Lenox. He was therefore not surprised to be greeted by Mrs. Cortlandt, who had arrived the day before with her usual train.

"At the end of the season," she said, "and alone?"

"I expect to meet friends here."

whichever way this vast white hotel establishment is approached, it is always a surprise. Midway between Echo Lake and Profile Lake, standing in the very jaws of the Notch, overhung on the one side by Cannon Mountain and on the other by a bold spur of Lafayette, it makes a contrast between the elegance and order of civilization and the untouched ruggedness and sublimity of nature scarcely anywhere else to be seen.

The hotel was still full, and when King entered the great lobby and office in the evening a very animated scene met his eye. A big fire of logs was blazing in the ample chimney-place; groups were seated about at ease, chatting, reading, smoking;

"So did I; but they have gone, or some of them have."

"But mine are coming to-morrow. Who has gone?"

"Mrs. Pendragon and the Bensons. But I didn't suppose I could tell you any news about the Bensons."

"I have been out of the way of the newspapers lately. Did you happen to hear where they have gone?"

"Somewhere around the mountains. You need not look so indifferent; they are coming back here again. They are doing what I must do; and I wish you would tell me what to see. I have studied the guide-books till my mind is a blank. Where shall I go?"

FISHING LODGE, LONESOME LAKE.

"That depends. If you simply want to enjoy yourselves, stay at this hotel—there is no better place—sit on the piazza, look at the mountains, and watch the world as it comes round. If you want the best panoramic view of the mountains, the Washington and Lafayette ranges together, go up to the Waumbec House. If you are after the best single limited view in the mountains, drive up to the top of Mount Willard, near the Crawford House—a delightful place to stay in a region full of associations, Willey House, avalanche, and all that. If you would like to take a walk you will remember forever, go by the carriage road from the top of Mount Washington to the Glen House, and look into the great gulfs, and study the tawny sides of the mountains. I don't know anything more impressive hereabouts than that. Close to, those granite ranges have the color of the hide of the rhinoceros; when you look up to them from the Glen House, shouldering up into the sky, and rising to the cloud-capped summit of Washington, it is like a purple highway into the infinite heaven. No, you must not miss either Crawford's or the Glen House; and as to Mount Washington, that is a duty."

"You might personally conduct us and expound by the way."

King said he would like nothing better. Inquiry failed to give him any more information of the whereabouts of the Bensons; but the clerk said they were certain to return to the Profile House. The next day the party which had been left behind at Alexandria Bay appeared, in high spirits, and ready for any adventure. Mrs. Farquhar declared at once that she had no scruples about going up Washington, commonplace as the trip was, for her sympathies were now all with the common people. Of course Mount Washington was of no special importance, now that the Black Mountains were in the Union, but she hadn't a bit of prejudice.

King praised her courage and her patriotism. But perhaps she did not know how much she risked. He had been talking with some *habitués* of the Profile, who had been coming here for years, and had just now for the first time been up Washington, and they said that while the trip was pleasant enough, it did not pay for the exertion. Perhaps Mrs. Farquhar did not know that mountain-climbing was disapproved of here as sea-bathing was at Newport. It was hardly the thing one would like to do, except, of course, as a mere lark, and, don't you know, with a party.

Mrs. Farquhar said that was just the reason she wanted to go. She was willing to make any sacrifice; she considered herself just a missionary of provincialism up North, where people had become so cosmopolitan that they dared not enjoy anything. She was an enemy of the Boston philosophy. What is the Boston philosophy? Why, it is not to care about anything you do care about.

The party that was arranged for this trip included Mrs. Cortlandt and her bevy of beauty and audacity, Miss Lamont and her uncle, Mrs. Farquhar, the artist, and the desperate pilgrim of love. Mrs. Farquhar vowed to Forbes that she had dragged King along at the request of the proprietor of the hotel, who did not like to send a guest away, but he couldn't have all the trees at Profile Lake disfigured with his cutting and carving. People were running to him all the while to know what it meant with "I. B.," "I. B.," "I. B.," everywhere, like a grove of Baal.

From the Junction to Fabyan's they rode in an observation car, all open, and furnished with movable chairs, where they sat as in a balcony. It was a picturesque load of passengers. There were the young ladies in trim travelling suits, in what is called compact fighting trim; ladies in mourning; ladies in winter wraps; ladies in Scotch wraps; young men with shawl-straps and opera-glasses, standing, legs astride, consulting maps and imparting information; the usual sweet pale girl with a bundle of cat-tails and a decorative intention; and the *nonchalant* young man in a striped English boating cap, who nevertheless spoke American when he said anything.

As they were swinging slowly along the engine suddenly fell into a panic, puffing and sending up shrill shrieks of fear in rapid succession. There was a sedate cow on the track. The engine was agitated, it shrieked more shrilly, and began backing in visible terror. Everybody jumped and stood up, and the women clung to the men, all frightened. It was a beautiful exhibition of the sweet dependence of the sex in the hour of danger. The cow was more terrible than a lion on the track. The passengers all trembled like the engine. In fact, the only calm being was the cow, which, after satisfying her curiosity, walked slowly off, wondering what it was all about.

The cog-wheel railway is able to transport a large number of excursionists to the top of the mountain in the course of the morning. The tourists usually arrive there about the time the mist has crept up from the valleys and enveloped everything. Our party had the common experience. The Summit House, the Signal Station, the old Tip-top House, which is lashed down with cables, and rises ten feet higher than the highest crag, were all in the clouds. Nothing was to be seen except the dim outline of these buildings.

"I wonder," said Mrs. Farquhar, as they stumbled along over the slippery stones, "what people come here for?"

"Just what we came for," answered Forbes—"to say they have been on top of the mountain."

They took refuge in the hotel, but that also was invaded by the damp chill atmosphere, wrapped in and pervaded by the clouds. From the windows nothing more was to be seen than is visible in a Russian steam bath. But the tourists did not mind. They addressed themselves to the business in hand. This was registering their names. A daily newspaper called *Among the Clouds* is published here, and every person who gets his name on the register in time can see it in print before the train goes. When the train descends, every passenger has one of these two-cent certificates of his exploit. When our party entered, there was a great run on the register, especially by women, who have a repugnance, as is well known, to seeing their names in print. In the room was a hot stove, which was more attractive than the cold clouds, but unable to compete in interest with the register. The artist, who seemed to be in a sardonic mood, and could get no chance to enter his name, watched the scene, while his

"THE LINES WERE INEXTRICABLY TANGLED."

friends enjoyed the view of the stove. After registering, the visitors all bought note-paper with a chromo heading, "Among the Clouds," and a natural wild flower stuck on the corner, and then rushed to the writing-room in order to indite an epistle "from the summit." This is indispensable.

After that they were ready for the Signal Station. This is a great attraction. The sergeant in charge looked bored to death, and in the mood to predict the worst kind of weather. He is all day beset with a crowd craning their necks to look at him, and bothered with ten thousand questions. He told King that the tourists made his life miserable; they were a great deal worse than the blizzards in the winter. And the government, he said, does not take this into account in his salary.

Occasionally there was an alarm that the mist was getting thin, that the clouds were about to break, and a rush was made out-of-doors, and the tourists dispersed about on the rocks. They were all on the *qui vive* to see the hotel or the boarding-house they had left in the early morning. Excursionists continually swarmed in by rail or by carriage road. The artist, who had one of his moods for wanting to see nature, said there were too many women; he wanted to know why there were always so many women on excursions. "You can see nothing but excursionists; whichever way you look, you see their backs." These backs, looming out of the mist, or discovered in a rift, seemed to enrage him.

At length something actually happened. The curtain of cloud slowly lifted, exactly as in a theatre; for a moment there was a magnificent view of peaks, forests, valleys, a burst of sunshine on the lost world, and then the curtain dropped, amid a storm of "Ohs!" and "Ahs!" and intense excitement. Three or four times, as if in response to the call of the spectators, this was repeated, the curtain lifting every time on a different scene, and then it was all over, and the heavy mist shut down on the registered and the unregistered alike. But everybody declared that they preferred it this way; it was so much better to have these wonderful glimpses than a full view. They would go down and brag over their good fortune.

The excursionists by-and-by went away out of the clouds, gliding breathlessly down the rails. When snow covers this track, descent is sometimes made on a toboggan, but it is such a dangerous venture that all except the operatives are now forbidden to try it. The velocity attained of three and a half miles in three minutes may seem nothing to a locomotive engineer who is making up time; it might seem slow to a lover whose sweetheart was at the foot of the slide; to ordinary mortals a mile a minute is quite enough on such an incline.

Our party, who would have been much surprised if any one had called them an excursion, went away on foot down the carriage road to the Glen House. A descent of a few rods took them into the world of light and sun, and they were soon beyond the little piles of stones which mark the spots where tourists have sunk down bewildered in the mist and died of exhaustion and cold. These little mounds help to give Mount Washington its savage and implacable character. It is not subdued by all the roads and rails and scientific forces. For days it may lie basking and smiling in the sun, but at any hour it is liable to become inhospitable and pitiless, and for a good part of the year the summit is the area of elemental passion.

How delightful it was to saunter down the winding road into a region of peace and calm; to see from the safe highway the great giants in all their majesty; to come to vegetation, to the company of familiar trees, and the haunts of men! As they reached the Glen House all the line of rugged mountain peaks was violet in the reflected rays. There were people on the porch who were looking at this spectacle. Among them the eager eyes of King recognized Irene.

"Yes, there she is," cried Mrs. Farquhar; "and there—oh, what a treacherous North! —is Mr. Meigs also."

It was true. There was Mr. Meigs apparently domiciled with the Benson family. There might have been a scene, but fortunately the porch was full of loungers looking at the sunset, and other pedestrians in couples and groups were returning from afternoon strolls. It might be the crisis of two lives, but to the spectator nothing more was seen than the everyday meeting of friends and acquaintances. A couple say good-night at the door of a drawing-room. Nothing has happened— nothing except a look, nothing except the want of pressure of the hand. The man lounges off to the smoking-room, cool and indifferent; the woman, in her chamber, falls into a passion of tears, and at the end of a wakeful night comes into a new world, hard and cold and uninteresting. Or the reverse happens. It is the girl who tosses the thing off with a smile, perhaps with a sigh, as the incident of a season, while the man, wounded and bitter, loses a degree of respect for woman, and pitches his life henceforth on a lower plane.

In the space of ten steps King passed through an age of emotions, but the strongest one steadied him. There was a general movement, exclamations, greetings, introductions. King was detained a moment by Mr. and Mrs. Benson; he even shook hands with Mr. Meigs, who had the tact to turn immediately from the group and talk with somebody else; while Mrs. Farquhar and Miss Lamont and Mrs. Cortlandt precipitated themselves upon Irene in a little tempest of cries and caresses and delightful feminine fluttering. Truth to say, Irene was so overcome by these greetings that she had not the strength to take a step forward when King at length approached her. She stood with one hand grasping the back of her chair. She knew that that moment would decide her life. Nothing is more admirable in woman, nothing so shows her strength, as her ability to face in public such a moment. It was the critical moment for King—how critical the instant was, luckily, he did not then know. If there had been in his eyes any doubt, any wavering, any timidity, his cause would have been lost. But there was not. There was infinite love and tenderness, but there was also resolution, confidence, possession, mastery. There was that that would neither be denied nor turned aside, nor accept any subterfuge. If King had ridden up on a fiery steed, felled Meigs with his "mailed hand," and borne away the fainting girl on his saddle pommel, there could have been no more doubt of his resolute intention. In that look all the mists of doubt that her judgment had raised in Irene's mind to obscure love vanished. Her heart within her gave a great leap of exultation that her lover was a man strong enough to compel, strong enough to defend. At that instant she knew that she could trust him against the world. In that moment, while he still held her hand, she experienced the greatest joy that woman ever knows—the bliss of absolute surrender.

"I have come," he said, "in answer to your letter. And this is my answer."

She had it in his presence, she read it in his eyes. With the delicious sense thrilling her that she was no longer her own master there came a new timidity. She had imagined that if even she should meet Mr. King again, she should defend her course, and perhaps appear in his eyes in a very heroic attitude. Now she only said, falteringly, and looking down, "I— I hoped you would come."

That evening there was a little dinner given in a private parlor by Mr. Benson in honor of the engagement of his daughter. It was great larks for the young ladies whom Mrs. Cortlandt was chaperoning, who behaved with an elaboration of restraint and propriety that kept Irene in a flutter of uneasiness. Mr. Benson, in mentioning the reason for the "little spread," told the story of Abraham Lincoln's sole response to Lord Lyons, the bachelor Minister of her Majesty, when he came officially to announce the marriage of the Prince of Wales—"Lord Lyons, go thou and do likewise;" and he looked at Forbes when he told it, which made Miss Lamont blush, and appear what the artist had described her to King—the sweetest thing in life. Mrs. Benson beamed with motherly content, and was quite as tearful as ungrammatical, but her mind was practical and forecasting. "There'll have to be," she confided to Miss Lamont, "more curtains in the parlor, and I don't know but new paper." Mr. Meigs was not present. Mrs. Farquhar noticed this, and Mrs. Benson remembered that he had said something about going down to North Conway, which gave King an opportunity to say to Mrs. Farquhar that she ought not to despair, for Mr. Meigs evidently moved in a circle, and was certain to cross her path again. "I trust so," she replied. "I've been his only friend through all this miserable business." The dinner was not a great success. There was too much self-consciousness all round, and nobody was witty and brilliant.

The next morning King took Irene to the Crystal Cascade. When he used to frequent this pretty spot as a college boy, it had seemed to him the ideal place for a love scene—much better than the steps of a hotel. He said as much when they were seated at the foot of the fall. It is a charming cascade fed by the water that comes down Tuckerman's Ravine. But more beautiful than the fall is the stream itself, foaming down through the bowlders, or lying in deep limpid pools which reflect the sky and the forest. The water is as cold as ice and as clear as cut glass; few mountain streams in the world, probably, are so absolutely without color. "I followed it up once," King was saying, by way of filling in the pauses with personal revelations, "to the source. The woods on the side are dense and impenetrable, and the only way was to keep in the stream and climb over the bowlders. There are innumerable slides and cascades and pretty falls, and a thousand beauties and surprises. I finally came to a marsh, a thicket of alders, and around this the mountain closed in an amphitheatre of naked perpendicular rock a thousand feet high. I made my way along the stream through the thicket till I came to a great bank and arch of snow—it was the last of July—from under which the stream flowed. Water dripped in many little rivulets down the face of the precipices—after a rain there are said to be a thousand cascades there. I determined to climb to the summit, and go back by the Tip-top House. It does not look so from a little distance, but there is a rough zigzag sort of path on one side of the amphitheatre, and I found this, and scrambled up. When I reached the top the sun was shining, and although there was nothing around me but piles of granite rocks, without any sign of a path, I knew that I had my bearings so that I could either reach the house or a path leading to it. I stretched myself out to rest a few moments, and suddenly the scene was completely shut in by a fog. [Irene put out her hand and touched King's.] I couldn't tell where the sun was, or in what direction the hut lay, and the danger was that I would wander off on a spur, as the lost usually do. But I knew where the ravine was, for I was still on the edge of it."

"Why," asked Irene, trembling at the thought of that danger so long ago—"why didn't you go back down the ravine?"

"Because," and King took up the willing little hand and pressed it to his lips, and looked steadily in her eyes—"because that is not my way. It was nothing. I made what I thought was a very safe calculation, starting from the ravine as a base, to strike the Crawford bridle-path at

least a quarter of a mile west of the house. I hit it—but it shows how little one can tell of his course in a fog—I struck it within a rod of the house! It was lucky for me that I did not go two rods further east."

Ah me! how real and still present the peril seemed to the girl! "You will solemnly promise me, solemnly, will you not, Stanhope, never to go there again—never—without me?"

The promise was given. "I have a note," said King, after the promise was recorded and sealed, "to show you. It came this morning. It is from Mrs. Bartlett-Glow."

"Perhaps I'd rather not see it," said Irene, a little stiffly.

"Oh, there is a message to you. I'll read it."

It was dated at Newport.

"MY DEAR STANHOPE,—The weather has changed. I hope it is more congenial where you are. It is horrid here. I am in a bad humor, chiefly about the cook. Don't think I'm going to inflict a letter on you. You don't deserve it besides. But I should like to know Miss Benson's address. We shall be at home in October, late, and I want her to come and make me a little visit. If you happen to see her, give her my love, and believe me your affectionate cousin,　PENELOPE."

The next day they explored the wonders of the Notch, and the next were back in the serene atmosphere of the Profile House. How lovely it all was; how idyllic; what a bloom there was on the hills; how amiable everybody seemed; how easy it was to be kind and considerate! King wished he could meet a beggar at every turn. I know he made a great impression on some elderly maiden ladies at the hotel, who thought him the most gentlemanly and good young man they had ever seen. Ah! if one could always be in love and always young!

They went one day by invitation, Irene and Marion and King and the artist—as if it made any difference where they went—to Lonesome Lake, a private pond and fishing lodge on the mountain-top, under the ledge of Cannon. There, set in a rim of forest and crags, lies a charming little lake—which the mountain holds like a mirror for the sky and the clouds and the sailing hawks—full of speckled trout, which have had to be educated by skilful sportsmen to take the fly. From this lake one sees the whole upper range of Lafayette, gray and purple against the sky. On the bank is a log cabin touched with color, with great chimneys, and as luxuriously comfortable as it is picturesque.

While dinner was preparing the whole party were on the lake in boats, equipped with fishing apparatus, and if the trout had been in half as willing humor as the fisher, it would have been a bad day for them. But perhaps they apprehended that it was merely a bridal party, and they were leaping all over the lake, flipping their tails in the sun, and scorning all the visible wiles. Fish, they seemed to say, are not so easily caught as men.

There appeared to be a good deal of excitement in the boat that carried the artist and Miss Lamont. It was fly-fishing under extreme difficulties. The artist, who kept his flies a good deal of the time out of the boat, frankly confessed that he would prefer an honest worm and hook, or a net, or even a grappling-iron. Miss Lamont, with a great deal of energy, kept her line whirling about, and at length on a successful cast landed the artist's hat among the water-lilies. There was nothing discouraging in this, and they both resumed operations with cheerfulness and enthusiasm. But the result of every other cast was entanglement of each other's lines, and King noticed that they spent most of their time together in the middle of the boat, getting out of snarls. And at last, drifting away down to the outlet, they seemed to have given up fishing for the more interesting occupation. The clouds drifted on; the fish leaped; the butcher-bird called from the shore; the sun was purpling Lafayette. There were kinks in the leader that would not come out, the lines were inextricably tangled. The cook made the signals for dinner and sent his voice echoing over the lake time and again before these devoted anglers heard or heeded. At last they turned the prow to the landing, Forbes rowing, and Marion dragging her hand in the water, and looking as if she had never cast a line. King was ready to pull the boat on to the float, and Irene stood by the landing expectant. In the bottom of the boat lay one poor little trout, his tail curled up and his spots faded.

"Whose trout is that?" asked Irene.

"It belongs to both of us," said Forbes, who seemed to have some difficulty in adjusting his oars.

"But who caught it?"

"Both of us," said Marion, stepping out of the boat; "we really did." There was a heightened color in her face and a little excitement in her manner as she put her arm round Irene's waist and they walked up to the cabin. "Yes, it is true, but you are not to say anything about it yet, dear, for Mr. Forbes has to make his way, you know."

When they walked down the mountain, the sun was setting. Half-way down, at a sharp turn in the path, the trees are cut away just enough to make a frame, in which Lafayette appears like an idealized picture of a mountain. The sun was still on the heights, which were calm, strong, peaceful. They stood gazing at this heavenly vision till the rose had deepened into violet, and then with slow steps descended through the fragrant woods.

In October no region in the North has a monopoly of beauty, but there is a certain refinement, or it may be a repose, in the Berkshire Hills which is in a manner typical of a distinct phase of American fashion. There is here a note of country life, of retirement, suggestive of the old-fashioned "country-seat." It is differentiated from the caravansary or the cottage life in the great watering-places. Perhaps it expresses in a sincerer way an innate love of rural existence. Perhaps it is only a whim of fashion. Whatever it may be, there is here a moment of pause, a pensive air of the closing scene. The estates are ample, farms in fact, with a sort of villa and park character, woods, pastures, meadows. When the leaves turn crimson and brown and yellow, and the frequent lakes reflect the tender sky and the glory of the autumn foliage, there is much driving over the hills from country place to country place; there are lawn-tennis parties on the high lawns, whence the players in the pauses of the game can look over vast areas of lovely country; there are open-air fêtes, chance meetings at the club-house, chats on the highway, walking excursions, leisurely dinners. In this atmosphere one is on the lookout for an engagement, and a wedding here has a certain éclat. When one speaks of Great Barrington or Stockbridge or Lenox in the autumn, a certain idea of social position is conveyed.

I do not say that Irene's letters to Mr. King were entirely taken up with descriptions of the beauty of Lenox. That young gentleman had gone on business to Georgia. Mr. and Mrs. Benson were in Cyrusville. Irene was staying with Mrs. Farquhar at the house of a friend. These letters had a great deal of Lovers' Latin in them—enough to have admitted the writer into Yale College if this were a qualification. The letters she received were equally learned, and the fragments Mrs. Farquhar was permitted to hear were so interrupted by these cabalistic expressions that she finally begged to be excused. She said she did not doubt that to be in love was a liberal education, but pedantry was uninteresting. Latin might be

convenient at this stage; but later on, for little tiffs and reconciliations, French would be much more useful.

One of these letters southward described a wedding. The principals in it were unknown to King, but in the minute detail of the letter there was a personal flavor which charmed him. He would have been still more charmed could he have seen the girl's radiant face as she dashed it off. Mrs. Farquhar watched her with a pensive interest awhile, went behind her chair, and leaning over, kissed her forehead, and then with slow step and sad eyes passed out to the piazza, and stood with her face to the valley and the purple hills. But it was a faded landscape she saw.

HINTS ON SPEECH-MAKING.

BY THOMAS WENTWORTH HIGGINSON.

THE number of graduates who go forth each year from our American colleges must be nearly five thousand, since the number of undergraduates is about twenty thousand. If we add those who are graduates of academies—those who have, as Mr. Poore generously puts it in his *Congressional Record*, "received an academical education"—the number will be greatly swelled. The majority of all these graduates will be called upon, at some time or other during their lives, to make a speech, as will also thousands of young Americans who have never seen the inside of college or academy. Per-

haps a few hints on speech-making may not be unavailing, when addressed to this large class by a man much older—one who has made so many speeches that the process has almost ceased to have terror to him, whatever dismay it may sometimes cause to his hearers. Certainly there are a few suggestions to be made which are not to be found in the elocutionary manuals, and which would have saved the present writer much trouble and some anguish had any one thought of offering them to him when he left college.

The first requisite of speech-making is, of course, to have something to say. But this does not merely mean something that may be said; it means something that must be said—that presses on the mind uncomfortably until it is said. Kinglake, in his *History of the Crimean War*, declares it to be essential to a general that he should have some taste for fighting; for, he says, there are almost always as many good reasons for postponing an engagement as for risking it, and unless the general has sufficient love of fight to turn the scale, no battle will ever take place. Whether this would be an intolerable calamity is another question, though Kinglake clearly thinks that it would. Be this as it may, there are always so many good reasons for not making a speech that, unless a speaker has a real desire to make it, the thing never will be done; and nothing so creates and intensifies this desire as an earnest purpose. Some people speak from loquacity or from habit; I knew men in the Massachusetts Legislature who could not go by a bill to regulate the breadth of wagon wheels without being inspired with a "little amendment"; but, after all, the crotchet of the little amendment was what propelled the speech, so that even these men talked under the pressure of something that they wished very much to say. As a general rule it may be assumed that most of the speeches on a given question—in a town meeting, for instance—are by those who speak because they "have a message to deliver," as Carlyle would say. And that is the oratory most effective. The words which almost always command most attention in any legislative body are those coming from men who have never before opened their lips in State-house, but who have some matter that thoroughly possesses them—usually a local question, or a question of their particular trade or business—and on this they speak with a force such as the members who pass for "orators" can rarely bring to bear. It is almost invariable that such a man, being modest, goes first to some more conspicuous member, and tries to get him to make the speech, and he is almost always told that it will be tenfold more effective if he makes it himself. Pole, in his new rules for whist-playing, says that only two things can excuse a man from following his partner's lead of trumps—sudden illness, or the fact that he has not a single trump in his hand. So the only thing that can really excuse a man for trans-

ferring to anybody else the task of making a speech on a subject that he has mastered is either sudden illness, or the fact that he has changed his opinion, and has no speech to make. If neither of these misfortunes has happened, his own stammering statement will be worth all the flowery eloquence of the habitual debater. The first rule for public speaking therefore is, *Have something that you desire very much to say.*

The second rule is, *Always speak in a natural key, and in a conversational way.* The days of pompous and stilted eloquence are gone by, and it was perhaps Wendell Phillips more than anybody else who put an end to it, and substituted the conversational manner. I remember a striking instance of this change of manner at a Harvard Commencement dinner. The late George S. Hillard, of Boston, a man of much local fame, now rapidly fading, was in my youth considered almost the model orator for such an occasion—acute, well trained, skilful, and in his way even persuasive. For many years, however, he absented himself, partly through political antagonism, from the college gatherings. At last, some ten years ago, he reappeared, and gave one of his old, cultured, highly elaborated speeches. After he had sat down, amid courteous but not ardent applause, my classmate the late Dr. Edward H. Clarke, who sat by me, said, in a whisper: "Is the change in Hillard or in me? I remember the time when that speech would have seemed to me the perfection of oratory. Now it utterly fails to move me." Curiously enough, I had been myself making the same reflection; and Dr. Clarke himself, being afterward called upon, made a plain, telling, straightforward statement about the condition and needs of the medical school, which took a hearty hold of those present, although the "classic orator" had failed to reach them. There is no question that within thirty years our American public speaking has been pitched upon a far more natural key.

But how to reach that natural key is the serious question. Many a man has risen with the best intention to speak naturally, and has been swept away into a false or constrained manner before he has fairly said "Mr. President and gentlemen." It is hard, therefore, to answer the question how to reach this desired attitude. The best way, of course, is to be natural without effort, if one only could. In that delightful book about children by Mrs. Diaz, called *William Henry's Letters*, the simple-hearted boy cannot quite comprehend the necessity of being sent to dancing-school" in order to know how to enter a room," as his fastidious aunts have advised. "I told her I didn't see anything so very hard about entering a room. I told 'em, 'Walk right in!'" But the dancing-school is meant to reassure boys less frank than William Henry, and so all suggestions as to beginning a speech are for those to whom it is not easy to walk right in.

Tennyson says of manners:

"Kind nature is the best: those manners next
  That fit us like a nature second-hand,
  Which are indeed the manners of the great."

If people are shy and awkward and conscious about their speeches, how shall they gain an easy and natural manner? That is, how shall they begin their speeches in that way—for after the beginning it is easy enough to go on.

There is one very simple method—as simple as to swallow a mouthful of water slowly to cure one's hiccough—and yet one which I have seldom known to fail. Suppose the occasion to be a public dinner. You have somebody by your side to whom you have been talking. To him your manner was undoubtedly natural, and if you can only carry along into your public speech that conversational style of your private talk, the battle is gained. How, then, to achieve that result? In this simple way: Contrive to say over to your neighbor conversationally the thought, whatever it is, with which you mean to begin your public speech. Then, when you rise to speak, say merely what will be perfectly true, "I was just saying to the gentleman who sits beside me that" —and then you repeat your remark over again. You thus make the last words of your private talk the first words of your public address, and the conversational manner is secured. This suggestion originated, I believe, with a man of inexhaustible fertility in public speech, Rev. E. E. Hale. I have often availed myself of it, and have often been thanked by others for suggesting it to them.

In the third place, *Never carry a scrap of paper before an audience.* If you read your address altogether, that is very different; and some orators, especially the French, produce remarkable effects by speaking from manuscript. It is the combination that injures. So long as a man is absolutely without notes, he is not only thrown on his own resources, but his hearers see and know that he is; their sympathy goes along with him; they wish him to go triumphantly through. But if they once see that he is partly relying on the stilts and leading-strings of his notes, their sympathy languishes. It is like the difference between a man who walks a tight rope boldly, trusting wholly to his balance pole, and the man who is looking about every moment for something by which to steady himself. What is the aim of your notes? You fear that without them you may lose your thread, or your logical connection, or some valuable facts or illustration. But you may be sure that neither thread nor logic nor fact nor argument is so important to the audience as that they should be kept in entire sympathy with yourself, that the magnetic contact, or whatever we call it, should be unbroken. The chances are that nobody will miss what you leave out, if you forget anything; but you will lose much if you forego the continuous and confiding attention given to a speaker who is absolutely at his ease.

The late Judge B. R. Curtis once lost a case in court of which he had felt very sure—one in which John P. Hale, of New Hampshire, a man not to be compared with him as a lawyer, was his successful antagonist. When asked the reason, he said: "It was very curious: I had all the law and all the evidence, but that fellow Hale somehow got so intimate with the jury that he won the case." To be intimate with your audience is half the battle, and nothing so restricts and impedes that intimacy as the presence of a scrap of paper.

Then comes the question, How shall you retain your speech in your head? Shall you write it and commit it to memory, or merely note down the points? Some of the most agreeable public speakers known to me, as, for instance, Hon. John D. Long, of Massachusetts, habitually write their speeches, and yet deliver them with such ease that you would think them embarked without previous preparation on an untried sea, which they ride with buoyant safety. Wendell Phillips rarely made special preparation; his accumulated store of points and illustrations was so inexhaustible that he did not need to do anything more than simply draw upon it when the time came. Yet I remember that after hearing his Phi Beta Kappa oration, in which he had so carried away a conservative and critical audience that they found themselves applauding tyrannicide before they knew it, I said to him, "This could not have been written out beforehand," and he said, "It is already in type at the *Advertiser* office." I could not have believed it.

Nevertheless, in the long-run, it is essential that one who speaks much, or even who speaks little, should acquire command enough of himself to speak what has not been written out. In this case the fourth rule must be, *Plan out a series of a few points, as simple and orderly as possible.* They should be simple, both for the convenience of the audience and for your own, since otherwise you may lose yourself in subtleties and metaphysics. They should be orderly, if only that you may remember them by the method of natural succession, each one suggesting the next, and thus putting as little tax as possible on the memory. Where the points are wholly detached, you can substitute an artificial order, perhaps fixing each point in your mind by some leading word that will suggest it, and then arranging these alphabetically; the object being always to tax your memory as lightly as possible, that it may do its work the better. You have now the points of your speech planned and provided—so many stepping-stones to carry you safely across the stream.

But points alone are not enough. You must hold your audience, and this must be done, not by lowering yourself in any way, but by giving that audience variety of food, and reaching their minds by facts, fancy, and wit, as well as by logic. Therefore the fifth rule is, *Plan beforehand for one good fact and one good illustration under each head of your speech.* One is enough, for the chance is that the impulse of the occasion will give you more. The fact may be from your own experience or from a book; but it must be brief, clear, and telling. The illustration may be grave or gay, from poetry or from the newspaper corner, Shakespeare or Artemus Ward: no matter, so that it hit the mark. Most people have a sense of humor, high or low; all people have more or less imagination,

however concealed by the stolid habits of daily life. George Herbert says,

" A verse may find him who a sermon flies,"

and if he had written "jest" in place of "verse," it would have been quite as true. But my present aim is to help the inexperienced speaker, and it is therefore well to repeat the rule, to fortify one's self beforehand with at least one good fact and one good illustration or anecdote for each main point of the discourse. You will thus make sure of distributing your reasoning and your relief all through the speech, and will not put all the dough in one pan and all the yeast in another.

And by way of closing admonition I should give this sixth and final rule: *Do not torment yourself up to the last moment about your speech, but give your mind a rest before it.* To combine simple preparation with a state of freshness —that is the problem. Who does not know how fresh the mind is when we wake in the morning, how we solve problems and think out perplexing questions while bathing and dressing before breakfast, although the previous night the mind was inert and dead? That is what is meant by mental freshness; and what we need is to bring this precise quality— this oxygen of the mind—into our speeches. The students at Oxford and Cambridge in England, after preparing for the severe examinations for honors—far severer than any of ours, though the ordinary "pass" examinations for the mere academical degree are not so hard as ours —make it a rule not to work at all on the day before the ordeal, but to spend that day, if possible, out-of-doors and away from books. They thus refresh their minds and get rid of that terrible feeling of expectancy. I have been told by clergymen who enjoyed the actual process of preaching that no one could describe the mental depression they felt on Saturday evening, and even on the morning hours of Sunday, in looking forward to that exercise, not knowing whether they should succeed or fail. There is a rather apocryphal story of Carlyle that he was once driven to despair by the noise of some neighboring peacocks. "But," said the neighbor, "they do not scream more than twice in twenty-four hours." "Perhaps not," said Carlyle, "but consider the agonies that I undergo in waiting for that scream!" It is not the public speaking that wears upon a man; it is the waiting for it. Look at the faces of the after-dinner speakers at a public dinner: how woe-begone till their time comes! how cheerful after it! To make your speeches successful, therefore, learn the art of completing your preparation beforehand, and then indulging in entire rest—newspapers, Mark Twain, sleep, anything you please—until the important moment comes.

These are all very simple rules—almost too simple, it may seem, to put on paper. Compared with the elaborate counsels of the books on rhetoric, how trivial they are! Yet I am sure, from observation and experience, that there is a great deal of help in them, and while they may not secure for any man the power to make a great speech, they will at least aid him to avail himself of his own gifts, such as they are, and bring him up to a good average of successful execution. The power of public speaking is probably the most transitory of all kinds of intellectual influence, for it dies with the death of its individual auditors, whereas a good book keeps on. But it is, on the other hand, the most concentrated and telling of all forms of mental action, the most stimulating to those who hear it, and, by reflex action, to the speakers themselves. No writer has any echo so intoxicating as the applause of a visible audience; no writer can elicit from himself sparks so brilliant as those which seem to be struck out between your eyes and the answering eyes of your hearers. The best things in any speech are almost always the sudden flashes and the thoughts not dreamed of before. Indeed, the best hope that any orator can have is to rise at favored moments to some height of enthusiasm that shall make all his previous structure of preparation superfluous, as the ship in launching glides from the ways and scatters cradle-timbers and wedges as superfluous chips upon the waters that are henceforth to be her home.

Editor's Easy Chair.

THE recent defalcations by men of the highest social standing have not only greatly shocked the public mind, but they have aroused a great deal of reflection upon the probable causes of such conduct in such men. Many crimes of the worst kind are at least intelligible. Eugene Aram murders Clarke for money, like the hero of Dostoïevsky's *Le Crime et le Châtiment*, of whom we were lately told in the Editor's Study. Old Mr. White, in Salem, was murdered by men who would gain by his death. There are also crimes of passion, of anger, of jealousy, of revenge, which are all comprehensible in a certain sense. Then there are crimes which are no crimes, as when a starving boy steals a leg of mutton, in which case the moral guilt disappears.

But when a man is not only of comfortable pecuniary condition, but is rich; when he is lapped in luxury and ease; carefully educated and trained in the most refined and exemplary society, in which the mere suspicion of dishonesty is fatal; when neither circumstance nor health nor temperament solicits him to dishonor, and he is perfectly conscious of the unspeakable consequences of his conduct to those whom he loves tenderly; when there is no conceivable temptation or reason or excuse, within or without, no apparent weakness of the moral sense, no hereditary tendency, and the man suddenly proves to be a thief and a swindler, and is so overwhelmed with the discovery of his dishonesty that he kills himself—what is the explanation?

It should seem that a man of this kind, whose suicide shows that he perfectly comprehends the situation, would certainly avoid it. A dull, ignorant, destitute, desperate bully, or a man mad with passion, neither sees nor regards the consequences of crime. But the man that we suppose not only understands and foresees it, but he knows also the certainty of disclosure; he knows that the kind of crime which is open to him cannot be long concealed; and he knows also that although when it is revealed he can shoot himself, yet that he dooms those who are dearest to him not only to a sorrow common to all mortals, but to a terrible moral shock, to the destruction of their confidence in human nature. He is not a bad man. He loves deeply and strongly. He can calmly measure and weigh the whole situation, and then commits the crime.

It is a mystery, and all the profounder because of the meanness of the obvious motive. When the starving boy steals food, we say the moral guilt vanishes, although the English law used to hang him for it, but had no penalty for Colonel Charteris, or for the Duke of Queensbury, who was a hereditary law-maker. In the case we are considering, however, the only motive is inexpressibly contemptible. It is the wish to paint the lily, to gild the gold. The man who has one yacht would have two yachts. His dinner service is of Sèvres, but he would have another of Dresden. His horse is the fleetest of horses, but he would have a pair. He has fresh figs daily from his greenhouse, but he would have fresh pomegranates also. His house is costly and beautiful, but he would rival the Alhambra. His wife's diamond tiara dazzles every beholder, but she must add to it a necklace of black pearls. These are his aims, and for these he dishonors his name, blows out his brains, and wounds irremediably the hearts that fondly love him.

His crime is the result of an undue exaltation of wealth, and such exaltation is the bane and peril of American society. To penetrate the charmed pale of "society" is the instinct of wealth, and in a country where there is no social hierarchy, wealth can have and does have its way. It is one advantage of a society of class that wealth cannot buy its way beyond its caste. H.R.H., indeed, may condescend to eat your exquisite dinners and admire your precious collection, but you are not therefore admitted *ad eundem.* The blue blood, whatever that sacred fluid may be, flows in the veins of yonder beldam, shrivelled in body and in purse, and she instinctively takes haughty precedence of the gem-crusted beauty who flashes with new splendor upon the court. But the beauty knows and the husband knows, and they both know that everybody else knows, that all the gems of Golconda cannot be transmuted into one drop of that mystic blood.

But in a country where you can break into the sacred pale with a bar of gold, everybody knows that the pit out of which social distinction is digged is a gold mine. To scale society is only to climb a golden stair. The more gold, the more distinction. Not rank for public service, a coronet or Westminster Abbey, not the noble tradition of a long line of ancestors whispering sternly *noblesse oblige,* but mere profuse and splendid expenditure, will open the awful gates and seat you at the highest table. And it is the plain moral of all the recent betrayal of trust, the *mene, mene,* flashing upon the wall of the banqueting chamber, that while we accept money as the credential and passport, instead of actual service, actual accomplishment and distinction, we put a premium upon dishonesty and robbery.

This tendency is encouraged by nothing more than by the reports in the newspapers of the trivial details of the lives of rich people. The dinners and the drives of Midas are of as much intrinsic public interest when he earns ten dollars a week as when his income is ten thousand dollars a day. The only reason that they are daily recorded in the latter event is that his income is immense. This casts a prodigious glamour upon the mere fact of wealth, and greatly strengthens the temptation to obtain it at any cost. The daily announcement that Mr. and Mrs. Bonanza yesterday entertained Mr. and Mrs.

Gulch at dinner is not merely a ludicrous imitation of the foreign gazette of a recognized social hierarchy, but it is a stimulant to get within the circle the incidents of whose social intercourse are recorded like those of royalty or of an aristocracy. The key to that circle is a key of gold, and the stimulant incites the legion who crave that kind of notoriety more than any other prize to get the gold key—honestly if they can, but quickly at all events. "I love my wife dearly," said the husband, "but she has been ill very long, and I wish she would get well—or suthin'."

Such events as those which have amazed and pained Boston show Jenkins in a very serious light. The airy Count Fosco, in Collins's story, who warbled gayly at the piano, and chattered and frisked, was, after all, a cunning villain. Jenkins is not. He is neither cunning nor a villain. He does with perfectly innocent intent what he is hired to do. But he is hired to do what is not only essentially mean, but what—to Jenkins's honest amazement if he could understand it—is very mischievous, and leads on to crime and cruel suffering.

THE Reverend Edward Everett Hale, whose public services are of many kinds, and whose diocese of delighted followers extends far beyond the domain of his religious denomination, recently read a paper upon Washington, which has excited some amusing discussion. Mr. Hale feels, as many other sensible Americans have felt, that there is some danger in allowing Washington to become a mere mythological figure compact of all the unrelieved virtues, and he therefore proposed to depict him as a fellow man and mortal. That did not mean an intent to unveil vices hitherto unsuspected, and to dispose of Washington as the good wolf of Romulus and Remus, and Robin Hood and William Tell and other legends, have been disposed of, but to describe a good man and a great man as he actually appeared in daily intercourse; to remind us not only that he prayed at Valley Forge, if we may trust Weems, but that he "used language" at Monmouth, and that he fell in love and deported himself in that condition very much like men who are invested with no mythologic halo.

This is a very good and a very desirable thing to do. How many men since the discovery of the photograph have not wished that it might have been discovered in time to show us Shakespeare and Milton and Washington himself, and all the great gods of history, in their habits as they lived! Mr. Hale proposed to show us a photograph of Washington, and even more, for his touch could not be colorless. It should be a faithful portrait, not, indeed, the Washington of the camp or of the Chief Magistracy, not Washington in parade uniform and in state, but in domestic retirement, in the hours of relaxation and ease, or again in the stress of conflict, whether in the field or the cabinet. But the critics lamented the probable disenchantment, if not degradation, of a noble character. Fudge! said Mr. Burchell, when the doubtful Miss Skeggs asked Lady Blarney of the same complexion where virtue was to be found.

Lord Chatham came to the House of Lords to make his speeches elaborately arrayed. Cuvier sat down in full dress to his work in his library. And what painter did the same upon entering his studio to paint a portrait? That was the trouble. Too much of the full dress was apt to get into the discourse or the picture. Did Raphael paint the man Julius or the Pope? Even if Cromwell wished all the wens to be represented, not every painter cares to paint them. But he need not fear. Greatness is not a wen, and it is not a wen that we see in seeing Cromwell. The biographer of Colonel Ingham may be trusted to see something else in Washington than a love-sick swain or a swearing trooper. Washington would not tell a lie, but he did cut down the cherry-tree—if that wretched Weems, determined that his hero should not be degraded, has not fooled us all. Mr. Hale perceives the stricken cherry-tree, and he sees the human nature in that blow of the boy no less than in the heroic truth-telling.

The apprehension that truth-telling would belittle Washington springs from the feeling which declares that no man is a hero to his valet. That is to say that greatness will not bear close inspection. It is a suit of clothes which the valet daily sees taken off. Thackeray drew a droll vignette for one of his essays, representing Louis the Fourteenth without his royal robes and full-bottomed wig, and a puny little manikin he is. The artist's instinct was just. The greatness of Louis was a greatness that could be taken off. It was made up of wig and velvet and ermine. He had greatness thrust upon him by his valet every day. It is the clothes, not the wearer of them, that the valet respects. It is the king with the visible crown, not the saint with the invisible aura, whom the valet soul reveres. So there are valet writers and valet readers, but Colonel Ingham's biographer is not among them.

We recall no well-authenticated story of Washington that really degrades him, or which is inconsonant with the feeling that his country cherishes for him. He had a hot temper, but he had also immense self-command. He was not a scholar, nor a man of large and liberal education. He did not spell correctly, and he is known to have taken refuge upon occasion in some solacing oaths. But they served only to emphasize his usual moderation and restraint, and they were as innocent as the profanity of gentle little Miss Bremer, who, in speaking of this very subject, said, "Yes; but when I am insensate I must swear."

The rule of historic and biographic representation is a rule of good sense. Good sense is an essential part of the equipment of the biographer or the historian. So is a sense of proportion. No sensible man, even if he could, would describe every incident in the life of his hero, as no artist paints every hair that he suggests in the portrait. The newspaper is a daily mirror of the world and of local life, but it would be an intolerable nuisance if it showed everything, and it would be summarily suppressed. Sympathetic fidelity to the fact, not distortion of it by undue light or shade, is the virtue of the biographer. And we have no doubt that it was Mr. Hale's apprehension of the consequences of a growing infidelity to the truth which has led him to depict the Washington that we might have known, and certainly should have loved and revered.

Mr. Felix Oldboy has been writing in the *Evening Post* some charming chapters of reminiscence of older New York. The Easy Chair is hardly able to say old New York, because Mr. Oldboy's New York is one which those who still consider themselves young boys well remember. The horizon flies before us. There is nothing pleasanter than to mark how the line of old age recedes as we advance. The ancient poet who declared the years of man's life to be threescore years and ten took no account of the young octogenarians. There are our Jefferson and Adams sweetening as they ripened into the eighties, and our Josiah Quincy, their worthy successor, still young in heart and mind when he had crossed the line; and here is our Bancroft at eighty-six still in the saddle by the sea, with mind and eye alert, our Whittier still singing as he nears the eighties, and our Holmes at seventy-six the bright particular star of the glittering London season.

It is not an old, but it was a smaller, New York which the men of threescore remember. It was also more distinctively American, although New York was from the first more cosmopolitan than any other of our cities. Even when the commerce of Newport was greater than that of New York, New York had yet a kind of metropolitan dominance, which it has never lost, and which, while other cities deride and deny, they do yet practically concede. When a city counts more than a million of inhabitants, and is linked by a stately highway hung in air to a city only smaller than itself, and is the great gate of continental commerce and communication with the rest of the world, and the seat of vast capital and boundless enterprise, its position as chief city cannot be disputed, however beautiful and prosperous and rich, and whatever marvels of swift growth, other cities may be. There is Chicago, indeed— But even the Queen of Sheba paid homage to the splendor of Solomon.

The rise of modern New York, as of the United States altogether, is a fairy tale. Contrasted with other cities, it has risen like Aladdin's palace. The difference between the present city of the Great Bridge, of the Central Park, of the Metropolitan Opera-house, of Murray Hill and beyond, and the recent New York of the Park Theatre, the City Hotel, old Tammany Hall, the Bloom-ingdale Road, and the Reverend Doctors Brownlee and De Witt proceeding to their pulpits on Sunday morning in bands and wide-flying silken gowns, is the difference between a little domestic town where every-body knows everybody and all interests are common, and a magnificent peopled wilder-ness in which no man knows his neighbor. The very suggestion of Contoit's Garden and of the old Niblo's, with the Ravels, makes all the Felix Oldboys smile as at a freshened pic-ture of domestic little Nuremberg or Dresden.

Yet these changes are within the easy re-membrance of men still living, and still very comfortably upon the hither side of that hori-zon line beyond which, according to the dis-mally foreboding old poet, lies a limbo of labor and sorrow. To record them is an ex-cellent service, because it supplies the ro-mance and delicate coloring of historic an-nals. The deepest interest in a city is not founded in the statistics of its prosperity, nor is it sustained by them. It springs from its human associations, and the details of its so-cial habits and their changes. Here Jonathan Edwards walked and meditated. Here Wash-ington Irving was born. Here the Sons of Liberty assembled nightly. Here Washington took leave of his officers. Here he took the oath as President of the United States. This is Golden Hill, where, *pace* State Street, the first forcible resistance was made to British aggression. Here Summerfield preached, and here Dr. Channing. Here Malibran sang, and there Beethoven was first played in America. These things and the details of the daily life in which they were set give the local and dis-tinctive charm to the story of the city.

Mrs. Lamb's history is a notable contribu-tion to this story, but its materials must be constantly gathered and treasured, and it is this service which Mr. Felix Oldboy renders. Such sketches as his are *mémoires pour servir* in the best sense. The general pleasure in them is shown by the popularity of Mr. Mac-Master's *History of the People of the United States*, in which, however, they seem to us to occupy a disproportioned place. As Judge Mellen Chamberlain has well pointed out, the chief interest of the American people lay not out of politics, as elsewhere, but in politics. Their great work, the work and engagement of all the people, lay in establishing and de-veloping their government; and really, there-fore, to understand the people, we must at-tend chiefly to their politics. But to compose a fascinating and truthful picture, the details of life, the characteristic circumstance, must be skilfully touched in, and the Felix Oldboys set the palette for that purpose.

Mr. Oldboy mentions that somebody pro-posed that a Professorship of New York should

be founded in some of our colleges, and of course Columbia is the college. The proposi-tion, as intimating that we should be taught a great deal more of the life of our own neigh-borhood than has been the custom, is capital and timely. The examination of most inter-est in a district school that we remember was one in which the pupils were questioned about the general history and the flora and fauna and habits and customs of their own neigh-borhood. That "exercise" gave them an in-terest in the similar details of other and dis-tant and ancient communities which nothing else could have done, and tended to impress them with the essential kinship of all people, and to stimulate the truest interest in the his-tory of the world.

Mr. Oldboy may be very sure that "small service is true service while it lasts," and that the old soldier who shows at the fireside how fields were won stimulates new victories.

THE prolonged railway strikes, the sudden prominence of the Knights of Labor, the boy-cotts, the bloody riots in Chicago and Mil-waukee, and the verdict of death against seven of the anarchists in Chicago, have been the chief events in our American year, and are full of interest and suggestion. A man by the name of Most, an immigrant from Germany or Bohemia, has been in the country for three or four years, living upon the proceeds of lectures in beer saloons and elsewhere, in which he sets forth the tyranny of society, and preaches murder and anarchy as the remedy. Most es-tablished a paper to disseminate his cheerful doctrines, but his talk was so wild, and seem-ed to be so clearly the shift of a lazy vagabond to live without labor, that it was wholly dis-regarded until the Chicago massacre. It was then seen to be important, and upon a charge of inciting to riot and crime the man was caught hiding under his paramour's bed, and after due trial was sentenced to prison.

While Most has preached anarchy in tours about the country, there has been in Chicago an organization of anarchists. The popula-tion of Chicago is largely foreign, and recent events have disclosed the fact that Poles, Bo-hemians, and the people of countries from which the emigration to this country was not supposed to be large, supply some of the worst elements of our population. From time to time it has been reported that societies of these foreigners were drilling with arms, and were constantly taught the use of destructives, and were ready at a moment's notice to reduce to practice the doctrines which were constant-ly set forth in their papers. But those doc-trines to the American mind were so absurd, and the methods of European conspirators are so foreign to Americans, and there is so just an indisposition to interfere with any freedom until it actually attacks the general welfare, that the stories were assumed to be exagger-ated, and serious trouble was not appre-hended.

But the great railroad strikes had excited the public mind, and the conduct of some authorities in the State of Illinois and in the city of Chicago was not such as to intimidate criminal designs, and during an outbreak, which the police of that city were trying to suppress, dynamite bombs were thrown, and there was a massacre of policemen, who displayed a cool intrepidity and undaunted heroism which could not be surpassed. The whole country rose in a cry of consternation and indignation at the crime of European anarchists upon American soil. It was a crime at once monstrous and causeless. It struck at liberty and justice and order. It was perpetrated by the most worthless of men, who are pests everywhere, and whose presence in this country American generosity had tolerated. In this country and under our institutions the crime of the anarchists was unpardonable, and nothing could more clearly vindicate the spirit of Americans and the worth of those institutions than the fact of the conviction of the ringleaders after a prolonged trial, in which every ruling of the judge was passionless and merciful to the prisoners.

The strikes and the anarchist massacres taken together show that there is not only great discontent, but also the will and the skill to organize discontent into revolution. The discontent is not the political discontent from which revolution has usually proceeded. But it is similar in kind. Political discontent is a protest against the political organization known as government when it has oppressed the great body of the people, who have had no voice in the government. But the discontent here is a protest against the huge industrial organizations known as corporations, which, in the judgment of the protestants, like unjust governments, abridge the rights of their employés. The instinctive American reply to this protest is that the majority of the people live by their daily labor, and, if injustice is done, the majority can secure justice through the law, and there is no plea whatever for disorder. But the rejoinder to this reply is this, that however true such a statement may be in our normal condition, yet it is a fact that the oppressive corporations illicitly control the government by bribing the law-makers and the judges, as the old barons overawed the king. It is therefore, says the rejoinder, mere mockery to refer the discontented to the ballot-box.

But this rejoinder is fatally defective, because it is not true that the legislature and the judiciary are generally corrupt. Venal legislators and corrupt judges there may be, but they are few. Moreover, there is a general American love of fair play and an instinctive sympathy for the oppressed. Any strike upon a railroad or in a shop which states plainly and promptly its reason is immediately supported by the press if the reason be obviously fair. If, however, the strikers complaining of oppression instantly proceed to oppress, and claiming the right to decide upon what terms they will labor, deny that right to others, the same instinctive love of fair play intervenes, and again befriends the oppressed as against the oppressor. A corporation of labor can be quite as unjust as a corporation of capital, and the striker who hurls his rightful complaint against the company must take great care that his conduct does not make the complaint a boomerang which will suddenly turn about and smite him in the forehead.

Every striker, however he may be stung by what he feels to be brutal tyranny, ought to see that while public sympathy will support his lawful action, it will not sustain courses which threaten public calamity. If it is proposed to settle differences between employers and employés not by appeal to the law, but to lawlessness and disorder, the issue proposed is anarchy against society, and the American verdict upon that appeal will certainly repeat the Chicago verdict against the anarchists.

It may not be true that the greatest poets "die with all their music in them," and the wise man may have been justified in saying that he doubted his young friend's genius when he said that he did not seek an audience. But Browning's artist who says,

"I could have painted pictures like that youth
　Ye praise so,"

but did not paint them, and was content to paint pictures without praise and in total obscurity and poverty, told the old truth that virtue is its own exceeding great reward. He told the truth, but he did not feel it fully, or his tone would not have been one of profound pathos. Virtue does not truly reward her votary if she leaves him sad and half doubting whether it would not have been better to serve vice.

The world is a great deal richer than the number of its noted men would imply, and if everybody would tell the truth it would appear that it is the unnoted, the rank and file of the world, who make up its chief charm. The few conspicuous officers with the three and four stars upon their shoulders, with the guards saluting and the drums rolling whenever they pass by, are fine fellows, the heroes of famous fields, to whom no one grudges all the honors. Blenheim to Marlborough, the coronet to Nelson, the Prime Ministership to Canning, the university doctorates and all the blue ribbons in every land to whom they are justly due. They are rewards well won, and as they are received we all shout and applaud.

But in such cases, evidently, virtue is not its own reward. The bread of life is not only buttered, but it is covered with honey. If the old saying be true, its verification must be found elsewhere, and it is found elsewhere. It is verified by the private soldiers who are not mentioned in the reports, and who receive no stars or orders or ribbons.

> " Into the jaws of death,
> Into the mouth of hell,
> Rode the six hundred."

But who they were nobody knows, nor ever will know, although the poet assures us,

> " Ne'er shall their glory fade."

How many who, as it were, die without a sign, whose names are not blazoned, and of whom Wordsworth's maid beside the springs of Dove is the type, make other lives happy, and enrich the world!

But there is no consciousness upon the part of these benefactors that virtue is its own reward. They are content to do their work cheerfully. They are blithe and busy, unvexed by ambition, by the desire of praise or display, full of delightful accomplishment and cultivation, equally admiring Orpheus, whose verses fill the world with music, and amused by Mrs. Halibut, who traces her descent through Haddocks and Flounders up to the original Whale. Orpheus cannot sing a new song, nor Mrs. Halibut buy a new bonnet, but the news "is blown about the world." These votaries of virtue write verses and buy bonnets of which no reporter ever whispers a hint. But they are happier than the poet or the fine lady of newspaper notoriety, for virtue is its own reward, although they do not know it.

In their case, virtue is not a special gift or distinction; it is merely contentment. There are loud grasshoppers in the field, says Burke, but pray do not imagine that those who make the noise are the only inhabitants of the field.

There are the truly famous and the conspicuous, and those who are trying to be seen or heard, but the multitude are of another kind. They see the pictures of the youth at which everybody is looking, and which all the connoisseurs are praising. They could have painted such pictures if their consciences had permitted. But they take greater comfort in a good conscience than in a salute of praise without the smile of conscience. They paint in the solitary studio, and if neither fashion nor fortune knocks at the door, they are content to paint as they think they ought to paint, that is, to do as they ought to do. And virtue is not justified of her children if they repine.

It is, as the sagacious reader perceives, a little sermon of content. It is natural for the poet, musing in the country church-yard at twilight, to murmur that some unknown Hampden or mute Milton may sleep there. But the good farmer, while he lived and loved and did his daily work, and taught his children to do theirs, did all that Hampden and Milton did in using to the utmost his gifts and his opportunities. If the Hampden were latent in him, and the hour had struck, the man would have answered. His was another place, another day, another duty. "In the cool wind that sings out of these Northern mountains, behold Charles the Fifth's day, behold Hampden's day . . . . another, yet the same."

If the youth thinks that he is a Raphael or a Milton, let him prove it. The world is always eager for genius, and knows it at sight. But if the proof fails and the crown lingers, is it the world that is to blame?

Editor's Study.

I.

IN *The Mayor of Casterbridge* Mr. Hardy seems to have started with an intention of merely adventurous fiction, and to have found himself in possession of something so much more important that we could fancy him almost regretting the appeal first made to the reader's wonder. Henchard's sale of his wife is not without possibility, or even precedent; Mr. Hardy sufficiently establishes that; and yet when the grave, every-day problems resulting from that wild act began to grow under his hand, so fine an artist might well have wished them derived from some fact more commonly within the range of experience. After you have said this, however, you can have very little else to say against the story; and we are not strenuous that this is much against it. We suppose it is a condition of a novelist's acceptance by the criticism of a country now so notably behind the rest of Europe in fiction as England that he must seize the attention in an old-fashioned way; and we willingly concede to Mr. Hardy the use of the wife-sale for this purpose, though we are not sure that the non-professional readers of his book, even in England, would have exacted so much of him. The tangled web woven from Henchard's error is of the true modern design and honesty of material; and one forgets that he sold his wife in following all the consequences to his innocent and beneficent after-life, and to the good and guiltless lives of others. The wrong he has done cannot be repaired, because it cannot, to his mistaken thinking, be owned; and in the tragedy of its expiation your pity is more for him than for all the others. That wrong pursues him, it hunts him to death, with what natural reliefs and pauses the reader knows. Mr. Hardy has never achieved anything more skilful or valuable in its way than the recognition and development of these in his last story; we are not sure that he has not placed himself abreast of Tolstoï and the greatest of the Continental realists in their management.

Then the book is full of his proper and peculiar charm, which is for us always very great. It is a quality which, if he had no other great quality, would give him a claim upon his generation hardly less than that of any other contemporary novelist. It seems to exist apart from any beauty of style or felicity of phrase, and is like the grace of his women, which remains in your thought when you have ceased to think of their different pretty faces and variously alluring figures. It would be as hard to say what it is as to say what that grace is, and we can only suggest that it is a very frank and simple way of dealing with every kind of life, and of approaching men and women as directly as if they had never been written about before. In fact, thanks no doubt to his early training in another profession (Mr. Hardy was an architect), his first sense of people is apparently not a literary sense, but something very much more natural. He studies their exterior graphically, and deals with their souls as we do with those of our neighbors, only perhaps a little more mercifully. This absence of literosity, if we may coin a word as offensive as the thing, accounts for an occasional bluntness of phrase, which we have sometimes felt in Mr. Hardy's work, and for here and there an uncouthness of diction—or call it awkwardness; but we gain infinitely more than we lose by it. His natural method gives us in this story country folks as veritable as those in *Far from the Madding Crowd*, or *Under the Greenwood Tree*, never ironically or sentimentally handled, but left to make their own impression, among scenes and in surroundings portrayed as sympathetically and unconventionally as themselves. In fact, his landscapes are no more composed than his figures, and share evenly with them the charm of his treatment; no one except Tourguénief gives a fact or trait of nature with a more living freshness.

We should say that *The Mayor of Casterbridge* was not inferior to any other story of Mr. Hardy's in its grasp of character; and his humanity is so very pervasive that each of the leading personages has almost to the same degree that charm of his which we have not been very successful in defining. Henchard is brutal only in our first moments of him; his life, after these, is a willingness, if not an effort, to repair his wrong to his wife; and the heart aches with him through all his necessary ruin to the pitiable end of the old, broken, friendless man. Then that young Scot, Farfrae, gay, thrifty, and good, who supplants his benefactor in business, in love, and in public honors, without intending harm to Henchard, is one of the freshest and most clean-cut figures in recent fiction; if you have known any bright young Scotchman, this one will make you think of him. Henchard's wife

is one of those women, single-minded, unknowing, upright, which Mr. Hardy has the secret of divining and presenting to us in all their probability; there is not much of her, but every word of that little seems true. There is not very much of Lucetta either, but she too is every word true; she is perhaps only too captivating in that combination of shrewdness and blind imprudence, of fickleness and tender-heartedness, of fascinating grace and helplessness. She is of the order of women whom Mr. Hardy is rather fond of drawing, like Bathsheba in *Far from the Madding Crowd*, like Fancy in *Under the Greenwood Tree*, like Elfride in *A Pair of Blue Eyes*, and some delicious young person in nearly every one of his books; the sort who guiltlessly compromise themselves by some love impulse, and then more or less amusingly, more or less distressingly, pay for it, but remain in the reader's mind an appealing, a distracting presence. Nothing is better in the book than Lucetta's dropping Henchard, and her conquest of the young Scotchman, whom she wins away from Henchard's putative daughter, Elizabeth Jane, such being the fond and foolish heart of man in the thriftiest and best of us. But Elizabeth Jane, with her unswerving right-mindedness and her never-failing self-discipline, is a very beautiful and noble figure; and Mr. Hardy has made her supremely interesting merely by letting us see into her pure soul. Hers is the final triumph, unmixed with remorse, because nothing but goodness like hers could come unscathed out of all that sorrow and trouble. The author who can discover such a type, on whom the reader's liking may wholesomely rest, has done his public a real favor. It is a very great thing to show goodness and justice and mercy like hers in their actual relation to other lives, and lovable; and it is all the more useful to know Elizabeth Jane because her limitations are more than suggested, and she is not made St. Elizabeth Jane.

II.

In turning from a book like this, in which the allegiance to the lessons of life is so deeply felt, to a story like *Pepita Ximenez*, one is aware of the need of applying more purely literary criterions to Señor Don Juan Valera's brilliant work, if one would judge it fairly. Yet we doubt very much whether any one will be able to regard it simply as a work of art, though the author frankly declares himself "an advocate of art for art's sake." We heartily agree with him that it is "in very bad taste, always impertinent and often pedantic, to attempt to prove theses by writing stories," and yet we fancy that no reader whom Señor Valera would care to please can read his *Pepita Ximenez* without finding himself in possession of a great deal of serious thinking on a very serious subject, which is none the less serious because it is couched in terms of such delicate irony. If it is true that "the object of a novel should be to charm through a faithful representation of human actions and human passions, and to create by this fidelity to nature a beautiful work," and if "the creation of the beautiful" is solely "the object of art," it never was and never can be solely its effect as long as men are men and women are women. If ever the race is resolved into abstract qualities, perhaps this may happen; but till then the finest effect of the "beautiful" will be ethical, and not æsthetic merely. Morality penetrates all things, it is the soul of all things. Beauty may clothe it on, whether it is false morality and an evil soul, or whether it is true and a good soul. In the one case the beauty will corrupt, and in the other it will edify, and in either case it will infallibly and inevitably have an ethical effect, now light, now grave, according as the thing is light or grave. We cannot escape from this; we are shut up to it by the very conditions of our being. What is it that delights us in this very *Pepita Ximenez*, this exquisite masterpiece of Señor Valera's? Not merely that a certain Luis de Vargas, dedicated to the priesthood, finds a certain Pepita Ximenez lovelier than the priesthood, and abandons all his sacerdotal hopes and ambitions, all his poetic dreams of renunciation and devotion, to marry her. That is very pretty and very true, and it pleases; but what chiefly appeals to the heart is the assertion, however delicately and adroitly implied, that their right to each other through their love was far above his vocation. In spite of himself, without trying, and therefore without impertinence and without pedantry, Señor Valera has proved a thesis in his story. They of the Church will acquiesce with the reservation of Don Luis's uncle the Dean that his marriage was better than his vocation, because his vocation was a sentimental and fancied one; we of the Church-in-error will accept the result without any reservation whatever; and we think we shall have the greater enjoyment of the delicate irony, the fine humor, the amusing and unfailing subtlety, with which the argument is enforced. In recognizing these, however, in praising the story for the graphic skill with which Southern characters and passions are portrayed in the gay light of an Andalusian sky, for the charm with which a fresh and unhackneyed life is presented, and the unaffected fidelity with which novel conditions are sketched, we must not fail to add that the book is one for those who have come to the knowledge of good and evil, and to confess our regret that it is so. It would be very unfair to it, however, not to say that though it is of the elder tradition of fiction in this, it is not conscienceless, or forgetful of what so many good old British classics, for instance, which we are so much advised to go back to, trampled under their satyr-hoofs; even "art for art's sake" cannot be that in these days, and the "beautiful work" created by "fidelity to nature" must pay its devoir to what is above nature.

In the preface to the American edition, which is also a new translation of the novel, Señor Valera addresses himself to our public with a friendly directness which cannot fail of sympathetic response, and with a humor of attitude and wit of phrase which will pleasantly recall the prefatory moods of Cervantes. After the fashion of that master, he gives us the genesis of his romance, and he lets us see that if it is not his favorite, it is at least very near to his heart. Yet we feel that this novel, so full of joyous charm, so brilliant in color, so vivid in characterization, is far from representing its author fully, and we hope his publishers will not be slow to follow it up with his *Doña Luz*, which is in some sort a pendant of *Pepita Ximenez*, with a heroine who is the counterpart of that impassioned little personality. The fascination of Doña Luz and her history is that of a most tender and tragic beauty; it is again the story of a priest's love, but Doña Luz and her lover meet long after his vocation has been decided, and there is nothing for him but to die with his secret. We know hardly any figure in fiction more lovely and affecting than Doña Luz, a beautiful girl growing old in a small country place, and marrying in her second youth a wretch infamously unworthy of her love, and suffering patiently and helplessly on. All her traits are studied with a minute and respectful compassion which leaves the reader a fast friend of the author, and, as it were, her intimate acquaintance. It is a character which makes that of Pepita seem slight and narrow, by comparison with a certain noble depth of feeling in it, and all the tones of the picture are graver. Like the story of Pepita, it presents a small group of persons, but each of these is strongly realized, and is made the exponent of local conditions in which the reader seems to live. It is all very fine and masterly work, scarcely to be matched in the contemporary fiction of our language, if that is not putting the case too faintly.

Señor Valera, who, as the reader may know, has been the Minister of Spain in this country for several years past, and has now left us for a diplomatic post in Europe, is one of those many-sided publicists of southern Europe beside whom our own politicians do not seem so gigantic as we like to think them when the other party is not running them for office. He has passed his life, we believe, in the public service, yet he has not only found time to write the two novels we have mentioned, but four or five others, as well as a treatise on the Poetry and Art of the Arabs in Spain and Sicily, a volume of Critical Studies, a volume of Literary Judgments and Dissertations, another of Poems, another of Dramas. We cannot attempt to ascertain his standing as an author in Spain; that is a thing for the Spaniards to do; but no reader of his books, even at second hand and in translation, can fail to perceive in them a very great talent. Whatever his theories of literary art may be, about the creation of the beautiful and all that, he works primarily, as all the great talents work now, in the interest of what is true, and with a poetic fidelity to facts and conditions. In this way the fiction of our time, such of it as is worth reading, is constituting itself, as never before, the interpreter of history; so that hereafter public events can be accurately read in its light, and whoever would know what this or that people were, at the time they made such and such laws and wars and treaties, may learn their intimate life from the report of their novels.

III.

We are glad to see announced a translation of *Marta y Maria*, the excellent story of Don Armando Palacio Valdés, which we praised some months ago; and we wish we could praise in equal terms two other stories of Señor Valdés which have since come to our hands. One of these is certainly charming as a picture of Spanish life, and would be utterly so but for the leprous taint of illicit intrigue which seems to infect all Latin work. It is called *Riverita*, after the hero, whose career is portrayed from his childhood to his marriage with delightful sympathy and humor, and with a fidelity to circumstance which does not allow itself to be doubted. The Spanish boy, it seems, is very like the American boy, and there are familiar episodes of this book in which he takes a lively part. The scene of the story is in Madrid, and there are immensely amusing sketches in it of Madrid journalism and journalists, of amateur bull-fighting, and of domestic and social life. It is all very modern, but enough of the inalienable Spanish flavor—the tang of the wine-skin—remains to make the reader feel that he is with old friends.

The other book is *José*, a study of people in a little fishing village on the Spanish coast, and the story of two humble lovers there. All the figures are struck out with refreshing vigor, to which one forgives an occasional unsparing truth of line and color. But the author helps himself out with a romantic and superfluous bit of self-sacrifice, and spoils the pleasure of the judicious in his work by the final behavior of an otherwise admirably studied hidalgo, the decayed gentleman of the place. Still, the story is worth reading if one has the Spanish for it.

If one has the Italian for it, the study of people in a little fishing village on the Italian coast, by Verga, is better worth reading. It is called *I Malavoglia*, and is not so new a book as *José*. It is simply the history of a poor family struggling to pay off an unjust debt, and patiently suffering and even perishing in the long struggle. Some passages are of harrowing pathos, and others of a noble sublimity. The father lost at sea; two of the brothers conscripted, and one killed in battle and the other growing desperately up to vice and crime; the devoted mother dying of chol-

era; the eldest daughter giving up her lover to become the stay of the tottering home; the youngest driven to shame; and the old grandfather submissively, heroically toiling on till the hospital receives him, and he dies away from the *tetto natio*, which the youngest of the Malavoglia retrieves at last, are the incidents of this simple and beautiful story of those common people whom vulgar people call commonplace. It has an incomparable grasp of Italian actualities, as they present themselves on such a small stage—social, political, domestic, and religious—and there is, so far as we remember, " no offence in it." The book is eminently worthy of translation.

A curious contribution to international fiction is the little volume of *Misfits and Remnants*, in which Messrs. L. D. Ventura and S. Shovitch, an Italian and a Russian naturalized among us, have embodied eight or ten interesting sketches of life in New York. These studies are chiefly of poor and friendless foreigners, and have a prevailing charm, in spite of their slightness, and of something like amateurishness at times. The prettiest and best of them is Peppino, a little Italian bootblack, in whom the graceful fidelity of a race whose very vices are engaging is affectionately recognized. There is heart-breaking truth in the history of Bobbo and Rita, the small slaves of a brutal padrone, into whose hands the child-exiles have fallen in the strange, great city; and the Herr Baron is a picturesque nobleman who has lost his fortune at play, and has come over to recover it as waiter and then owner in a New York restaurant. It would be invidious to distinguish between the authors of this pleasant and amiable book, but we may say that Mr. Shovitch seems to ply the laboring oar in sentiment, and that Mr. Ventura has the lighter touch for national character, with which he deals honestly as well as tenderly.

Whilst we are about speaking of novels and novelists of the living sort, let us commend to the reader M. Ernest Dupuy's volume of essays on *Les Grands Maîtres de la Littérature Russe*, of which an American version has appeared, and *La Roman Russe*, sketches and criticism by M. Eugène-Melchior de Vogüé, which has not yet been translated. M. Dupuy speaks of Gogol, Tourguénief, and Tolstoï; M. de Vogüé takes rather a wider range and includes Dostoïevsky. Together, the books form a most valuable commentary upon authors and works of unrivalled mastery, and Mr. Dole, who translates the essays of M. Dupuy, adds to the interest of the volume by collecting into an appendix many facts relating to the writers discussed. These are chiefly from Russian sources, but in the case of Tourguénief he turns to French witnesses of that author's long Parisian exile, and in one place he quotes from M. Viardot words which have a bearing upon matters often discussed in this Study. " Plots, Tourguénief thought, spoiled novels, which were *peintures de mœurs*, and he was glad to see that the taste for them was dying out. . . . The plot was necessary for a drama, but in the way of a novelist, who should above everything else keep the truth in view. . . . Tourguénief was of opinion that a splendidly picturesque country was a bad soil for literary or artistic production. Strong emotions or sensations tended to dethrone the faculty of exact observation, upon which we are dependent for æsthetic enjoyments in flat districts. . . . 'My first acquaintance with the skylark was precisely in looking about for compensation for the ugliness of a flat near Berlin. I shall never forget the broadening out of the æsthetic faculty on this occasion. . . . I then remarked the beauty of the sky and of many other things which I should not otherwise have noticed.'"

Here is consolation—if they merit consolation—for the feeble-hearted who complain that there is no inspiration in our level social and moral landscape.

IV.

The prospect is not wanting, indeed, in elements of tremendous drama, which in the apparently fortuitous combinations of life sometimes assume the proportions and majesty of the noblest tragedy for those who have the eyes to see. Life, after all, is the greatest of masters, and now and then one of its facts has shape so perfect that it makes all imitation of life seem clumsy prentice-work, and all comment upon the imitation idle chatter. Such a fact comes to us in the biography of Judge Richard Reid, of Kentucky, by his wife, Elizabeth Jameson Reid, who gives the cruel story with a richness and minuteness of detail intensified in its effect by the artlessness of the work. It is a book that burns and thrills in every leaf with an inextinguishable sense of wrong, with a most impassioned tenderness and devout reverence for the martyr whose suffering it commemorates. This we cannot give again, either directly or at second-hand, for it is so pervasive and so wrought into the very texture of the narrative that it must remain there for the reader; and we wish, for the sake of civilization, of religion, that the book might have as wide a currency as our praise of it.

Very probably our readers have forgotten the name of Richard Reid, but they cannot have forgotten his tragedy, and we need only remind them that he was the Kentucky justice who two years ago was attacked and beaten by a brother lawyer in the little country town where they lived together in civic amity and church fellowship. This lawyer, whom, when she does not name him, Mrs. Reid always speaks of as "the murderer," believed himself injured in fortune and repute by a decision of the court; and although Judge Reid was not sitting in the case, he attributed the decision to him. He decoyed him into his office, and while the judge sat

looking over the papers that the lawyer had submitted to him, the latter began to beat him on the head with a heavy cane. The stunned and stupefied man staggered to his feet and blindly struggled into the street, the lawyer following with a cowhide, that he might add the shame of a public chastisement to the injury he had already inflicted. There would then have naturally remained but one thing for the victim of an assault like that, in a community like that, to do. It was wonderful that he had not been killed; having survived, he must kill his assailant.

Judge Reid seems to have been a man of the local civilization, gentle, indeed, of blameless life, and refined by a love of letters and a Christian conscience as regards most affairs of life, but not different probably from many of his neighbors, and probably not better. He himself owned that the natural and established thing for him to do was to take his gun and shoot his enemy on sight. He had always abhorred violence, but it does not appear that he had strongly felt the enormity of a system of violence like slavery, and when the rebellion broke out he was prevented from taking part in the war to perpetuate slavery only by physical disability. He was, as we have said, a man of his time and place; and yet he found it impossible to kill his deadly enemy, as was so natural and customary. He perceived that as a judge he must not break the law, he saw that as a Christian he must not shed blood. He obeyed his revelation; he submitted. He did not submit or take up his cross willingly, and he took it up far from triumphally; but he took it up, and he bore it before the people.

The election for judge was coming on, and he was a candidate. He determined to make his canvass practically upon the principle which forbade him to repay wrong for wrong, or to take vengeance upon his enemy in a community where, whatever was the reasoned approval of his course, there must have been an instinctive contempt for it at the bottom of men's souls, and, worse yet, of women's souls. The heads were all right, and hundreds of letters manifest the abhorrence in which the outrage was held in every part of Kentucky; but the victim believed that there was a slight for his righteousness in these hearts inured to private war, to feuds fought out in village streets and country lanes, to shame washed out in blood. This belief preyed upon his bruised and tortured brain, but still he held out. He had not only to forbear from vengeance, but he had to stay the hands of others, willing and eager to avenge him. The hour came when, in sight of his political triumph, he could bear the stress no longer, and the atrociously injured man took his own life. This is what publicly appeared, though there is a possibility that he did not lift his stainless hand against himself, but perished by some unknown assassin. To such a possibility the author of this most moving book clings with all the faith of a love that suffered unto death with the victim. In either case, Richard Reid fell the prey of implacable hate, and an offering in the cause of civilization and religion. His enemy was tardily expelled from the church where they had communed together; being tried in the court for his crime, he received a sentence of three years' imprisonment, from which he appealed to a higher court, and is still unpunished. This, again, though an unspeakable wrong, is a matter of comparative indifference. The great matter is that magnanimity like that of Richard Reid should be recognized as less than none in human history, and honored as a supreme public benefaction. In this age many things are denied and many are doubted, but more and more one truth shines inextinguishable: that whatever the public interest in a wrong may be, there can be no end to it but forgiveness between him who suffers and him who injures. That is not only religion, but that is also reason; and the martyrdom of Richard Reid dedicates it anew to the human mind and conscience. As for the people of the section in which he lived and died, and which has been so often stained with the blood of private vengeance, they could not do better than leave all commemoration of civic and military greatness among them, and join in raising some imperishable monument to his righteousness.

V.

An interesting study of their character and conditions is unconsciously made in the autobiography of Cassius M. Clay, of Kentucky, the first volume of which has appeared. It is this volume which will chiefly interest the reader; the writings and speeches of which the second is to be made up may be unenviously left to posterity. They had their use in their day, but what Cassius M. Clay was is much more important at present than what he said. His autobiography has the merits of the best in that kind, and is frank and bold even in its reticence, of which there is very little. Mr. Clay has not found it necessary to withhold himself on many points, and he is as explicit concerning his *domestici affanni* and his quarrel with his wife as he is about the difficulties which he has at different times conducted to a more successful issue with the bowie-knife and shot-gun and revolver. He is now mainly a historical figure, and in spite of his foibles he is a striking figure in our history. It was a great and a noble thing for him, a slave-holder, and bred to all the social traditions of his section, to renounce slavery, its principles and prejudices, forty years ago, and join himself with the despised abolitionists of the North in the crusade against it. He was not content with freeing his slaves and bearing a silent witness against their wrongs. He remained in Kentucky, where he was born and reared, to fight

slavery and slave-holders in the opinions and persons of his old friends, his kinsmen, and his neighbors; and he fought them not only with the tongue and pen, but literally with fire and sword. He renounced slavery, but he did not renounce the slave-holder's code of honor; he was prompt with knife and pistol; he was ready for rencontre and duel; he carved up his adversaries in the flesh as well as the spirit; he did not fly from any danger; and further to establish his thrice-approved courage to their sense, this soldier of freedom became a soldier of slavery, and did valiant service in the war with Mexico, begun and carried on that new lands might be brought under its blight and ban. In the later war for freedom he bore a comparatively slight part, and he can hardly be said to have shone above his fellow-statesmen in the diplomatic service of his country. The last fact that brought him prominently before the country was his shooting a negro whom he believed guilty of poisoning one of his family. His later political life, however sincere, has been eccentric and uncertain, and he is not a figure of contemporary importance.

In some aspects he is not a contemporary at all, but purely mediæval, like the society from which he sprang; as mediæval as Uguccione or Castruccio, as feudal as a Donati or an Uberti. But in his way he is always heroic; he has his magnificently generous side, which suffers nothing in his robust and positive representation. This or that chance might have been better for his fame than what actually happened, but nothing that has since happened can obscure the lustre of the fact that when he saw the right he dared all for it, and was willing either to live or to die for it. He came out from the South politically, but geographically he has never ceased to be a Southerner, and socially he is one of the most distinct Southern types.

His book is thoroughly interesting, and has a unique value as a contribution to the history of American civilization. It is not possible always to agree with Mr. Clay about himself, but he is a man, and it is no harm that he should know it. One need not care that he is not aware of his limitations, that he speaks with equal confidence on all points, and that his bold ideas of art and literature are somewhat grotesque. When others, who knew art and literature so very much better, were cowering before that hideous idol of slavery, he rose and dealt it a deadly blow in its sanctuary, among worshippers whose hands were instantly lifted against his life. About a book or a statue we can let him be mistaken, since he was right about humanity.

He was not altogether right, and his heroism was on a lower level than that of Richard Reid. We must not forget that. We cannot pay him that reverence which must be forever the due of such a martyr, and yet we can fitly recognize in him the moral sense, which, if sometimes too strongly qualified by virile force, was yet an extraordinary moral sense.

We commend both of these books to the reader in spite of literary disabilities and æsthetic lapses which it would be easy to point out. We can readily forgive Mrs. Reid her adoration of her husband, since she does not exaggerate his suffering and the value of his example, and we do not object to Mr. Clay's appreciation of himself which sometimes seems inordinate, for he has lived some great things. At the end of the ends, and with all their faults, the books are of the kind which uncommon lives can alone add to literature.

Monthly Record of Current Events.

POLITICAL.

OUR Record is closed on the 15th of September.—State elections resulted as follows: Arkansas, September 6, Democratic majority, 20,000; Vermont, September 7, Republican majority, 18,000; Maine, September 13, Republican plurality, 13,000.

The contest between the Boston sloop *Mayflower* and the British cutter *Galatea* for the *America's* cup resulted in a victory for the former. The first race was sailed September 7, and the second September 11, with an uncompleted run in fog and rain September 9.

Eight of the Chicago anarchists were found guilty of murder August 20, seven to be hanged, and one imprisoned for life.

The hostile Apaches, including Geronimo, surrendered to General Miles September 4, on Skeleton Canyon, about sixty-five miles southeast of Fort Bowie, Arizona.

Seven hundred Chinese Christians were massacred and forty villages burned in the province of Manhoa.

Mr. Parnell's Land Bill was read for the first time in the House of Commons September 10. It proposes to admit leaseholders to the benefits of the act of 1881, to allow the Irish Land Commission to revise rents generally, and to suspend evictions when the tenant offers one-half the rent, if the court is satisfied that he cannot pay more.

Prince Alexander of Bulgaria was forced by conspirators, August 21, to abdicate his throne and leave the country. Afterward, on the overthrow of the provisional government, he returned to the capital, and was recrowned by the officers of the army. The Czar disapproving of his return, Alexander again abdicated, September 4.

Prussia and the Vatican have signed a convention terminating the religious controversy between them so far as it related to all secondary matters, and regulating the presentation of benefices and appointments to ecclesiastical seminaries within the kingdom of Prussia.

Cutting was released from prison August 23, the Supreme Court of Mexico holding that as Medina, whom he libelled, refused to prosecute him civilly, his imprisonment before the trial had been punishment enough. Mexico did not, however, withdraw its claim to the right to try an American citizen in that country for a crime committed in the United States.

DISASTERS.

August 20.—Hurricane on the Texas coast and for two hundred miles inland. Thirty-eight persons killed.

August 21.—Two hundred lives lost by the burning of the passenger steamer *Vera*, near Saratov, on the river Volga, in Russia.

August 23.—The city of Mandalay flooded by the bursting of one of the banks of the Irrawaddy River. Twenty-five lives lost.

August 28.—Earthquake in Greece. Six hundred people killed on the islands, and several towns destroyed.

August 29.—Steamer *Daniel Drew*, of the Albany Line, burned to the water's edge, at her moorings at Kingston Point, New York.

August 30.—Five men killed by an explosion in the Fairlawn Colliery, Scranton, Pennsylvania.—Seven persons killed in a railway collision at Mödling, near Vienna.

August 31.—Earthquake at about ten o'clock at night in a large part of the United States east of the Mississippi River. Especially severe in the South. In Charleston, South Carolina, several buildings were demolished and many badly damaged. Sixty-one persons killed.

September 12.—Fifteen persons crushed to death during a panic in the Pilgrimage Church, in Radna, Transylvania.

September 14.—Collision on New York, Chicago, and St. Louis Railroad, thirty miles west of Buffalo, New York. Twenty-three persons killed.

OBITUARY.

August 16.—In Mexico, Dolores Fosta, widow of General Santa Anna.

August 19.—At Flushing, Long Island, John Dougall, founder and editor of the New York *Daily Witness*, aged seventy-eight years.

August 20.—In Newport, Rhode Island, Mrs. Ann S. Stephens, novelist, aged seventy-three years.

August 30.—At Framingham, Massachusetts, Brevet Major-General George H. Gordon, aged sixty-one years.

September 4.—At Bristol, Rhode Island, General Lloyd Aspinwall, of this city, in his fifty-second year.—In Nashville, Tennessee, General B. F. Cheatham, aged sixty-four years.—In London, England, Samuel Morley, philanthropist, aged seventy-seven years.

Editor's Drawer.

IT is getting to the time of year now when we begin to think about eating again, society having been occupied all the summer enjoying the beauties of nature, improving its mind in summer schools, making love or pretending to make love, and holding in suspense for a time what is called house-keeping and the serious pleasures of the table. Of course "dinners" have been given and eaten by the fortunate who never campaign anywhere, any more than did Alexander the Great, without a complete establishment, and of course, also, there has been chronic grumbling everywhere about hotel fare and farm-house fare; indeed, the "table" always furnishes, if it offers little else, a good share of watering-place conversation. But all this has been incidental. Feeding people who are engaged in recreation is one thing, and eating as a fine art is another. And the Drawer, whose sympathies are openly with country life, is obliged to confess that cooking is much better understood in the large cities than it is in the country. It is true that bad cooking probably predominates in the cities, so much of it is left to unskilled hands, but the science of gastronomy—that is, the preparation and order of viands with reference to their adaptation to the human organism—is scarcely considered in the country at all; and even some of the simplest processes, such as the making of edible, thoroughly baked bread, cannot be considered in America a country accomplishment at all. Now and then will be found a woman who is born a cook, just as a poet is born, and she always has a wide neighborhood reputation, and if her husband keep a tavern, visitors will go long distances to taste the product of her genius; and occasionally bread can be found that would be good if it were properly baked. But geniuses are too rare in any department of life to be very important in our economy; and with reference to cooking, the spread of scientific knowledge is indispensable to the national comfort and health. The Drawer offers no apology for again making this topic prominent, for the happiness of the family, the beauty of woman, the ability of man, the cheerfulness of life, depend largely upon adequate nutrition, and that, again, upon the proper preparation of food. Indeed, it is believed that if really wholesome cooking prevailed, there would be much less discontent, more amenity in social intercourse, better poetry, less pessimistic writing, more amiable criticism of authors, and less need of prohibiting people from supplying the place of proper nutriment with violent stimulants. Bad food, with its common supplement of bad liquor, is probably at the bottom of anarchy and of most strikes.

With perhaps a want of seriousness, but with a sincere desire to add to the occupations of women, the Drawer suggested some months ago (in June) that women going into the country for the season might find employment in spreading a knowledge of the art of cooking; this was, however, merely incidental to the great truth that if women in all ranks of life would seriously consider the preparation of food, there would be much less complaint of want of employment for women. This overture of the Drawer has had several responses. Some of them are sarcastic. The following is selected on account of its brightness and spirit of humility:

June 4, 1886.

EDITOR'S DRAWER,—I embrace this first opportunity, after due consideration, to ask that a "missionary," understanding what good cooking is, be sent to this "rural district." We want, as a matter of course, a lady of "dainty taste" that can show us how to prepare "dainty" dishes like "deviled kidneys" and "angel food" for our "dainty" farmer men and boys.

We are not, in the "rural districts," as a general thing, conceited, if we are ignorant; we are anxious to learn, and want the missionary bad. We had supposed that cooking is a high science and a delicate art, supposed that cooks are *born*, not *made*, that they are the result of innate genius as well as acquired knowledge; in other words, that cooking in its best development must be done with brains and heart and soul and purpose, as well as with neatness and manual skill; but if you have "dainty" ladies that can learn how, in the short space of time that your article seems to suggest, to teach us proverbially poor cooks to do the thing better, we have hopes that, with our eagerness to do things "city fashion," we may all acquire the "dainty" art.

A few years since a lady of "dainty" taste came to this "rural district" to spend a few months—quite a literary lady, wife of a physician in New York city, one that knew all the advantages of the city and disadvantages of the country. Although numbers of *Harper's Monthly*, *The Century*, *Atlantic Monthly*, *Arthur's Home Magazine*, *Youth's Companion*, a Chicago weekly, New York weeklies, and several local papers graced the table where she was staying, she was in a perpetual ferment for "something to read"; she must have the Doctor send her "something to read," which "the Doctor" did—sent the Sunday *Sun*, several publications from the American News Company—enough, so that she *had* the "something to *read*." But then no gentleman or lady would ever commit a like error about cooking. And now that the Drawer has manifested so much interest for the "rural districts" as to suggest that "missionaries" from the city come to teach us to cook, we would be worse than the heathen not to be grateful, not only for the good that we will derive from it ourselves, but also as a means of employment for other women enjoying a higher civilization than we of the "rural districts" do or can.

We want the best "missionary" there is; we think we know "pusley" when we see it, and shall be a little particular perhaps.

Pardon me for occupying so much of your time; but there is so little for women to do that if "missionaries" and cooking is the work, we want to help it all along. We have tried poultry raising until many of us are discouraged. Then we thought silk-worms was the straw that was to save us, but that has proved a bubble that has burst; but we must have something. Bless you for suggesting cooking! and send us the "missionary." Yours fervently,

P.S.—Let us know when the "missionary" is ready, and we will send directions where and how to come.

It seems that the field is white for the harvest, and that the missionaries are few. We expressed some apprehension about this, namely, that women in city homes do not know how to cook; and if this is true, as our correspondent insinuates, it is useless to send one of them into Pennsylvania. And yet it is probable that that State needs cooking schools. In fact, our grateful correspondent admits as much in the expression of her idea of "dainty" food, that it is "deviled kidneys" and "angel food" and the like, and in the notion that farmer men and boys do not need as dainty food as men and boys in cities. The farmer and the farmer's boy (who is by-and-by to be President) need as good food as any city man. It is a part of his civilization that his potato, and his summer squash, and his roast, and his corned beef and cabbage, should be "daintily" cooked and served. It is greatly to his disadvantage that the women who cater for him and for themselves do not take the trouble to learn the best way of preparing the most wholesome, simple food, but feed his vitiated stomach with cake and pie and angel food, and dream of "deviled" things as the topmost achievement of civilized cooking.

It is in sorrow, therefore, that the Drawer passes this letter along for the perusal of those who, living in the centres of civilization, apparently neglect one of the most important means of extending and preserving it.

A CURIOUS HARVARD WILL.

WALDOBOROUGH, MAINE.

THERE was long in the possession of the writer's grandfather, the late John Bulfinch, Esq. (Harvard, 1812), the following humorous farewell to college life at Cambridge. The lines were written by William Biglow, of Natick, a member of the class of 1794, and probably have never been published. As their age, wit, and lively description of life at Harvard almost one hundred years ago will interest many, I send them to the Drawer for publication.   Yours,   JOHN H. LOWELL.

A WILL.

Being the last words of Charles Chatterbox, Esq., worthy and much lamented member of the Laughing Club of Harvard College, who departed college life June 4, 1794.

I, Charley Chatter, sound of mind,
To making fun am much inclined,
So, having cause to apprehend
My college life is near an end,
All future quarrels to prevent,
I make this will and testament.
My soul and body, while together,
I send the storms of life to weather,
To steer as safely as they can,
To honor God and profit man.

Imprimis, then, my bed and bedding,
My only chattels worth the sledding—
Consisting of a maple stead,
A counterpane and coverlet,
Two cases with the pillows in,
A blanket, cord, a winch and pin,
Two sheets, a feather-bed and hay-tick—
I order sledded up to Natick,

And that with care the sledder save them
For those kind parents first who gave them.
Item.—The Laughing Club so blest,
Who think life what it is—a jest—
Collect its flowers from every spray,
And laugh its nigged thorns away,
From whom to-morrow I dissever,
Take one sweet grin, and leave forever,
My chest and all that in it is
I give and bequeath them, viz.:
Westminster grammar, old and poor;
Another compiled by Moore;
A bunch of pamphlets *pro* and *con*
The doctrine of....salvation;
The college laws I'm free from minding;
A Hebrew Psalter stript from binding;
A Hebrew Bible too lies nigh it,
Unsold because no one would buy it;
My manuscripts in prose and verse
They take for better and for worse—
Their minds enlighten with the best,
Their pipes and candles with the rest—
Provided that from them they cull
My college exercises dull,
On threadbare themes with minds unwilling,
Strain'd out through fear t' avoid a shilling,
To teachers paid t' avert an evil,
Like Indian worship to the devil—
The above-named manuscripts, I say,
To club aforesaid I convey,
Provided that said themes so given,
Full proof that genius won't be driven,
To our physician be presented
As the best opiates yet invented.
Item.—The government of college,
Those liberal helluos of knowledge,
Who e'en in these degen'rate days
Deserve the world's unceasing praise—
Who. friends of science and of men,
Stand forth Gomorrah's righteous ten—
On them I nought but thanks bestow;
For, like my cash, my credit's low,
So I can give nor clothes nor wines,
But bid them welcome to my fines.
Item.—My study desk of pine,
That work-bench sacred to the nine,
Which oft hath groan'd beneath my metre,
I leave to pay debts to Peter.
Item.—Two penknives with white handles,
A bunch of quills, a pound of candles,
A lexicon compiled by Cole,
A hammer, and two homespun towels,
For which I yearn with tender bowels,
Since I no longer can control them,
I leave to those....sly rogues who stole them.
A gown much greased in commons,
A hat between a man's and woman's,
A tattered coat of college blue,
A fustian waistcoat torn in two,
With all my rust through college carried,
I give to classmate O——, who's married.
Item.—C—— P—— has my knife
During his nat'ral college life,
That knife that ugliness inherits,
And due to his superior merits;
And when from Harvard he shall steer,
I order him to leave it here,
That 't may from class to class descend,
Till time and ugliness shall end.
The said C—— P——, humor's son,
Who long shall stay when I am gone,
The muse's most successful suitor,
I constitute my executor;
And for his trouble to requite him,
Member of Laughing Club I write him.
Myself on life's broad sea I throw,
Sail with its joys or stem its woe;
No other friend to take my part
But careless head and honest heart.

My purse is drained ; my debts are paid ;
My glass is run ; my will is made.
To beauteous Cam I bid adieu,
And with the world begin anew.

Finis.

WILLIAM BIGLOW, L. S., of Natick.

NOTE.—Olds was married while member of college to a Miss Taft, of Uxbridge. The blank C—— P—— may be filled up Charles Prentiss.   J. B.

"THE CHILDREN'S HOUR."

CHILD-LORE.

ALL the world, it is said, loves a lover, but it is no less true that all the world loves children ; and while we may tire of tales of love, however ardent and sentimental they and we may be, we are always ready to smile over stories of the vagaries of childhood. There are glimpses of the awakening of the powers of the mind in these anecdotes of children, of which every parent has more or less to tell, and we perhaps pardon the weakness of vanity more readily in this direction than in any other.

The whimsically distorted shapes into which the thoughts and theories of older people are transformed in passing through a child's brain are often suggestive as well as entertaining.

"The mind," a little fellow says, "is something that turns round and round in your head and makes up stories."

And, upon the whole, one is inclined to comment that metaphysicians do not come much nearer to any clear definition of the intellectual faculties. The drollness of children's remarks oftenest consists in their looking at things ideal or intellectual from a strictly material basis. They measure probabilities by their experience, and have not yet learned to construct a world of theory beyond that apparent to the senses.

"The clouds," observed a little four-year-old girl, "must be solid, or the angels would tumble through."

"Oh, they can fly like the birds !" her brother, two years older, assured her.

"Oh no !" she replied, calling to mind the fact that she had seen the tail feathers of the hens clipped to keep them from flying, "of course they can't, for they haven't any tails."

On another occasion this same child observed to her mother, in the most matter-of-fact tone : "I wish I was as high as the moon and the stars, and then I'd take a great ladder and go up and look on God's mantel-piece, and see if I could find any peppermints there."

Children amuse and bewilder alike by their logic and their want of it.

"Dear Aunt Susan," little Bob says, in the fulness of his admiration for his aunt, "when I grow up I hope I shall be just such a woman as you are."

And yet on another occasion he inquired if some cheese which was on the table came from heaven, and it was only careful inquiry that brought to light the fact that the question was the result of profound reasoning from the statement he had heard a playfellow make that the moon was made of green cheese.

Sometimes the definitions of children are most amusing. A little fellow of three years called a kaleidoscope "a bucket with pictures in it" ; another spoke of a hearse as "a dead-hack, where people lie down when they ride" ; while still a third replaced the expression "sets my teeth on edge" by the more original and striking phrase, "It makes my teeth itch."

Dr. Burt G. Wilder, the well-known naturalist, relates that his parents being Grahamites, his earliest years were passed in ignorance of the fact that people used flesh for food. By some change of opinion, however, they came to more ordinary customs, and one day a roasted chicken was served for dinner. The six-year-old lad gazed in bewilderment at this mysterious dish for some moments, the light of a great discovery dawning upon him, and at length he burst out in conviction and astonishment, "I bet that's a dead hen !"—a conclusion there was no gainsaying.

The most triumphant moment of a boy's life, everything being taken into account, is when he first discards petticoats for trousers. It is to be supposed that the feminine mind is deprived of the ecstatic thrill of this delicious moment, for the first trained dress does not come until long after the child is old enough to know that bitter is mingled with the sweet of every cup, so that it is impossible to give herself up to enjoyment with the same abandonment of the wee man who gets his first genuinely masculine garments. A little fellow of five, to whom had come this supreme period of his existence, drew himself up proudly before his sister of three, and proceeded to impress upon her his true greatness.

"Kittie," he observed, "you can't never wear pants." A pause, in which he observed the effect of his words. "Kittie, you can't never have a mustache." A second rhetorical pause, during which the little sister looked up with pleading eyes ; and then the climax, delivered in a tone of the most commiserating contempt, "Kittie, you can't never be a man nohow."

The accumulation of woe was too much for poor Kittie, who burst into a piteous howl at the perspective negation of her abased state, while her brother gazed proudly upon her distress with the air of a conqueror.

Small Robin showed himself under similar circumstances more of a gentleman. Arrayed in his new suit, he was at first speechless with sheer delight. Then at length his joy found tongue, and he burst out : "Oh, mamma, pants make me feel so grand ! Didn't it make you feel grand when—"

But an awful consciousness came over him that this bliss had never been shared by his mother, and he laid his wee chubby hand pityingly against her cheek, saying, pathetically, "Poor mamma ! poor mamma !"

ARLO BATES.

The sound of her voice was sweet to hear,
And was wafted o'er many a wave,
Till at last it fell, like a siren spell,
On the heart of a merman brave.

He listened awhile, then smiled a smile
As he looked at himself in the glass,
Then dressed with speed in an ulster of weed
And trousers of tangle and grass.

He went to the place where the lady sang,
And he heard what she'd got to say;

THE LAY OF THE LOBSTER.

ILLUSTRATED BY EDWIN A. ABBEY.

Go button your boots with a tiger's tail,
Comb down your golden hair,
And live for a week upon bubble and squeak
On the steps of a winding stair.

And whenever you feel like a conger-eel,
Or as hard as an old split pea,
Unfasten the lid as the hedgehog did,
Then come and listen to me.

It happened when the sun was high,
And the wind blew fresh and free,
When the bottle-nosed whale was lunching on shale,
And washing it down with the sea.

It was close by the side of a lonely stream
That foamed on a desolate strand;
A lady fair was sitting there,
And a box was in her hand.

She raised the box, and she gave it a shake,
And she smiled when she found it was full;
Then she played on a fife with the edge of a knife,
Keeping time with a three-foot rule.

And this was the song that the lady sang:
"Just open this box for me;
I love sardines when they're boiled with beans,
And mixed with the sands of the sea."

She told him the dish was sardine fish,
But he bolted clean away.

For his brother-in-law was of kin to a skate;
The skate was of high degree,
And every one knew it was perfectly true
Sardines were the cousins of he.

With a terrible frown he dived straight down
To the depths of the ocean green;
His trousers he tore and his ulster, and swore
They would never again be seen.

But the lady sang as she sang before:
"Just open this box for me,

"HE HEARD WHAT SHE'D GOT TO SAY."

For I love sardines when they're boiled with beans,
And mixed with the sands of the sea."

She sang this same, but as nobody came,
She thought it as well to try,
So down on the rocks she hammered the box,
And then she began to cry:

"Oh, I love sardines when they're boiled with beans,
And mixed with the sands of the sea.
I am dying for some. Will nobody come
And open this box for me?"

Now all alone, close under a stone,
A lobster was lying asleep;
At the sound of her cries he rubbed his eyes,
And picked himself up for a peep.

He could open the box without any knocks,
So he went and he offered his claw.
At the sight of the beast her misery ceased,
And she asked for a shake of his paw.

"HE BOLTED CLEAN AWAY."

He gave her his claw on the desolate strand,
But he never would let her go.
"My lady," says he, "you'll come with me
To the regions down below."

He took the lady straight away
To the depths of the ocean blue,
And whatever became of that beautiful dame
There is nobody ever knew.

There are some folks say on the 1st of May
She is seen with a glass in her hand,
And that she was sold to the merman bold
Who came to the desolate strand.

But every night when the moon shines bright
The ghost of the lady is seen,
All dressed at her need in an ulster of weed,
And her hair is a bright sea-green.

And the ghost of a great big sardine box
Comes stalking along the shore,
And the ghost of a little sardine fish
Goes rollicking on before.

And the fishermen hear the sound of knocks,
And, "Open this box for me,
'Cause I love sardines when they're boiled with beans,
And mixed with the sands of the sea."

MORAL.

Now, ladies all, both short and tall,
Who love to eat sardines,
If you ever take any, don't let it be many,
And never with sand and beans.

W. D. SCOTT-MONCRIEFF.

A KISS—BY MISTAKE.

UPON the railway train we met—
She had the softest, bluest eyes,
A face you never could forget—
"Sixteen," with all that that implies.
I knew her once, a little girl,
And meeting now a mutual friend,
Our thoughts and hearts got in a whirl;
We talked for miles without much end.

I threw my arm around the seat
Where, just in front, she sideways sat,
Her melting eyes and face to meet
(And no one wondered much at that).
For soon the station where she left
Would on the sorrowing vision rise,
And I at least should feel bereft;
I thought a tear stood in her eyes.

She was but kith, not kin, of mine—
Ten years had passed since last we met;
And when, in going, she did incline
Her face, 'twas natural to forget.
It seemed so like the child I knew,
I met her half-way for that sake;
And, coming near those eyes of blue,
She gently kissed me—*by mistake!*

She saw her error, and straightway ran
With flaming blushes, rosy red;
I should not be one-half a man
If thought of wrong came in my head;
In fact, I'd take that very train
And travel daily for her sake,
If she would only come again
And gently kiss me—*by mistake!*

JOEL BENTON.

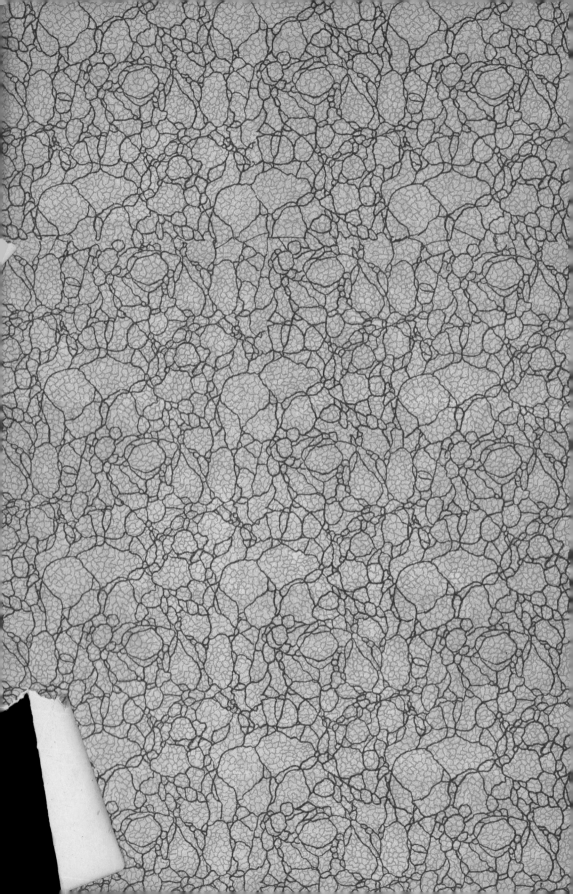